Recent Advances in Simulated Evolution and Learning

ADVANCES IN NATURAL COMPUTATION

Series Editor: **Xin Yao** (University of Birmingham, UK)

Assoc. Editors: **Hans-Paul Schwefel** (University of Dortmund, Germany)
Byoung-Tak Zhang (Seoul National University, South Korea)
Martyn Amos (University of Liverpool, UK)

Vol. 1: Applications of Multi-Objective Evolutionary Algorithms
edited by Carlos A. Coello Coello (CINVESTAV-IPN, Mexico) and Gary B. Lamont (Air Force Institute of Technology, USA)

Advances In Natural Computation – Vol. 2

Recent Advances in Simulated Evolution and Learning

editors

Kay Chen Tan
National University of Singapore, Singapore

Meng Hiot Lim
Nanyang Technological University, Singapore

Xin Yao
University of Birmingham, UK

Lipo Wang
Nanyang Technological University, Singapore

World Scientific

NEW JERSEY • LONDON • SINGAPORE • BEIJING • SHANGHAI • HONG KONG • TAIPEI • CHENNAI

Published by

World Scientific Publishing Co. Pte. Ltd.

5 Toh Tuck Link, Singapore 596224

USA office: Suite 202, 1060 Main Street, River Edge, NJ 07661

UK office: 57 Shelton Street, Covent Garden, London WC2H 9HE

British Library Cataloguing-in-Publication Data
A catalogue record for this book is available from the British Library.

RECENT ADVANCES IN SIMULATED EVOLUTION AND LEARNING
Advances in Natural Computation — Vol. 2

ISBN 981-238-952-0

Printed in Singapore by World Scientific Printers (S) Pte Ltd

PREFACE

Inspired by the Darwinian framework of evolution through natural selection and adaptation, the field of evolutionary computation has been growing very rapidly, and is involved today in many diverse application areas. Evolutionary computation encompasses a wide range of adaptive and computational algorithms, methods and techniques that are inspired by natural evolution: e.g., genetic algorithms, evolutionary programming, evolution strategies, genetic programming and related artificial life strategies. Such simulated evolution and learning techniques offer advantages of simplicity, ease of interfacing with existing techniques, and extensibility in finding good solutions efficiently to complex practical problems.

This volume contains substantially extended and revised papers selected from the 4th Asia-Pacific Conference on Simulated Evolution and Learning (SEAL'2002), 18-22 November 2002, Singapore. SEAL'2002 received a total of 230 submissions with 5 special sessions featuring various applications of evolutionary computation. After extensive reviews by the technical committee, 139 papers were accepted for oral presentation and 25 for poster presentation. Among the accepted papers, 43 papers were invited to be extended and revised for inclusion in this volume. The double review processes have ensured a volume of the highest quality. We hope the readers will enjoy it.

The papers included in this volume cover the latest advances in the theories, algorithms, and applications of simulated evolution and learning techniques. It also highlights future research directions in the field. The volume is organized into two broad categories, e.g., evolutionary computation theory and evolutionary computation applications. The first category, comprising Chapters 1 through 18, provides insights to different evolutionary computation techniques. The second category, Chapters 19 through 43, presents many practical applications of evolutionary computation techniques, such as scheduling, control and power systems, robotics, signal processing, data mining, and bioinformatics.

This volume will be of significant interest and value to all postgraduates, research scientists and practitioners dealing with evolutionary computation or complex real-world problems. We hope that this volume will motivate researchers and practitioners to extend the presented results of evolutionary computation and to broaden their implementations in practice.

The editors thank authors of all the chapters for their excellent contributions to this volume. Without their valuable work, this volume would not have been possible.

EDITORS
Kay Chen Tan, Meng Hiot Lim, Xin Yao and Lipo Wang

TABLE OF CONTENTS

PART 1
EVOLUTIONARY THEORY

CHAPTER 1

CO-EVOLUTIONARY LEARNING IN STRATEGIC ENVIRONMENTS

Akira Namatame, Naoto Sato and Kazuyuki Murakami

Dept. of Computer Science
National Defense Academy, Yokosuka, JAPAN
E-mail: nama@nda.ac.jp

An interesting problem is under what circumstances will a collection of interacting agents realize efficient collective actions. This question will depend crucially on how self-interested agents interact and how they learn from each other. We model strategic interactions as dilemma games, coordination games or hawk-dove games. It is well known that the replicator dynamics based on natural selection converge to an inefficient equilibrium. In this chapter, we focus on the effect of co-evolutionary learning. Each agent is modeled to learn interaction rules defined as the function of own strategy and the strategy of the neighbor. We show that a collection of interacting agents converges into equilibrium in which the conditions of efficiency and equity are satisfied. We investigate interaction rules acquired by all agents and show that they share several rules with the common features to sustain equitable social efficiency. This chapter also presents a comparative study of two evolving populations, one in a spatial environment, and the other in a small-world environment. The effect of the environment on the emergence of social efficiency is studied. The small-world environment is shown to encourage the emergence of social efficiency further than the spatial structure.

1. Introduction

In many applications it is of interest to know which strategies can survive in the long run. While the concept and techniques of game theory have been used extensively in many diverse contexts, they have been unsuccessful in explaining how agents realize if a game has many equilibria[8]. Introspective or educative theories that attempt to explain equilibrium selection problem directly at the individual decision-making level impose very strong informational assumptions. The game theory is also not able to address issues on how agents know which equilibrium should be realized when games have multiple equally plausible equilibria[3]. The game theory is also not able to provide answer in explaining how agents should behave in order to overcome an inefficient equilibrium situation[7].

One of the variations involves the finitely iterated games. The standard interpretation of game theory is that the game is played exactly once between fully rational individuals who know all details of the game, including each other's preferences over outcomes. Evolutionary game theory, instead, assumes that the game is repeated many times by individuals who are randomly drawn from large populations[15,18]. An evolutionary selection process operates over time on the population distribution of behaviors. It is also of interest to know which strategies can survive in the long run. According to the fundamental theorem principle of natural selection, the fitter behavior is selected.

The evolutionary dynamic model with the assumption of uniform matching can be analyzed using replicator dynamics[4]. The criterion of evolutionary equilibrium highlights the role of mutations. The replicator dynamics, highlight the role of selection. Evolutionary game theory assumes that the game is repeated by individuals who are randomly drawn from large populations[6]. However, the growing literatures on evolutionary models have not considered learning at individual levels[9]. They treat agents as automata, merely responding to changing environments without deliberating about individuals' decisions. Within the scope of our model, we treat models in which agents make deliberate decisions by applying rational reasoning about what to do and also how to decide[13,14]. Two features of this approach distinguish it from the introspective approach. First, agents are not assumed to be so rational or knowledgeable as to correctly guess or anticipate the other agent's strategies. Second, an explicit dynamic process is specified describing how agents adapt their strategies as they repeat the games.

An interesting problem is under what circumstances agents with individual learning may converge to some particular equilibrium[1,2]. We endow our agents with some simple way of learning and describe the evolutionary dynamics that magnifies tendencies toward better situation. By incorporating a consideration of how agents interact into models we not only make them more realistic but we also enrich the types of aggregate behavior that can emerge[10,11,12]. It is an important question to answer the following question: how the society groups its way towards an efficient equilibrium in an imperfect world when self-interested agents learn from each other.

The term evolutionary dynamics often refers to systems that exhibit a time evolution in which the character of the dynamics may change due to internal mechanisms. In this chapter, we focus on evolutionary dynamics that may change in time according to certain local rules. Evolutionary models can be characterized both by the level at which the mechanisms are working and the dimensionality of the system. We use the evolutionary models based on microscopic individuals who interact locally[16]. The search for evolutionary foundations of game-theoretic solution concepts leads from the notion of an evolutionarily stable strategy to alternative notions of evolutionary stability to dynamic models of evolutionary processes. The commonly used technique of modeling the evolutionary process as a system of a deterministic difference or differential equations may tell us little about equilibrium concepts other than that strict Nash equilibrium are good. We can attempt to probe deeper into these issues by modeling the choices made by agents with their learning models.

We focus on collaborative learning in strategic environments. Non-cooperative games are classified into dilemma games coordination games, and hawk-dove games. It is well known that natural selection does leads to inefficient equilibria in these games. In this chapter each agent learns interaction rules by repeating games. We provide a general class of adaptation models and relate their asymptotic behavior to equilibrium concepts. We assume agents behave myopically, and they evolve their interaction rule over generation. They learn from the most successful strategy of their neighbor. Hence their success depends in large part on how well they do in their interactions with their neighbors.

If the neighbor is doing well, the rule of the neighbor can be imitated, and in this way successful rule can spread throughout a population, from neighbor to neighbor.

We consider two fundamental models of interaction, local interaction with the lattice model and small-world model[17]. We show that all agents mutually learn acquire the common-rule, which lead to social efficiency. We also investigate acquisition by rules, and show that those rules of agents are categorized into a few rules with some commonality.

2. Interaction with Lattice Model and Small-World Networks

It is important to consider with whom an agent interacts and how each agent decides his action depending on others' actions. In order to describe the interactions among agents, we may have two fundamental models, random matching and local matching[9]. The approach of random (or uniform) matching is modeled as follows: In each time period, every agent is assumed to match (interact) with one agent drawn at random from a population.

An important assumption of the random matching is that they receive knowledge of the current strategy distribution. Each agent makes his rational decision strategy based on a sample of information about what other agents have done in the previous time period. Agents are able to calculate best replies and learn the strategy distribution of play in society. Agents may adapt based on the aggregate information representing the current status of the whole system (global adaptation). In this case, each agent chooses an optimal decision based on aggregate information about how all other agents behaved in the past. An agent calculates her reward and plays her best response strategy. An important assumption of global adaptation is that they receive knowledge of the aggregate.

In many situations, however, agents are not knowledgeable so as to correctly guess or anticipate other agents' actions, or they are less sophisticated and that they do not know how to calculate best replies[8]. We assume that a spatial environment is a more realistic representation since interactions in real life rarely happen on such a macro scale; Spatial interaction is generally achieved through the use of a 2D grid as shown in Fig. 1(a), with each agent inhabiting a cell on the grid. Interaction between agents is restricted to neighboring cells. This may allow for individuals, which may have been eliminated if assessed against all players, to survive in a niche.

The recognition of the importance of spatial interactions has led to many exploring and extending aspects of it. Nowak and May focused upon evolutionary niching and the pattern of emergence of cooperation in the spatial environment[13]. With local adaptation each agent is modeled to adapt to his neighbors. The hypothesis of local adaptation also reflects limited ability of agents' parts to receive, decide, and act based upon information they receive in the course of interaction. Agents observe the current performance of their neighbors, and learn from the most successful agent. Agents are less sophisticated in that they do not know how to calculate best replies and are using other agent's successful strategies as guides for their own choices. Each agent interacts with the agents on all eight adjacent squares and imitates the strategy of any better performing one. In each generation, each agent attains a success score measured by its average performance with its eight neighbors. Then if an agent has one or more neighbors who are more successful, the agent converts to the rule of the most successful neighbor.

Complex networks describe a wide range of systems in nature and technology. They can be modeled as a network of nodes where the interactions between nodes are represented as edges. Recent advances in understanding these networks revealed that many of the systems show a small-world structure. Watts and Storogatz introduced a small-world network which transforms from a nearest neighbor coupled system to a random coupled network by rewiring the links between the nodes[17]. Two parameters are used to describe the transition. The mean path length L, which specifies the global property of the network, is given as the mean of the shortest path between all pairs of vertices. In contrast, the clustering coefficient C characterizes the local property of the system and can be calculated as the fraction of the connections between the neighbors of a node divided by the number of edges of a globally coupled neighborhood, averaged over all vertices.

Consider one lattice model in which each node is coupled with its nearest neighbors as shown in Fig. 1(b). It has a large mean path length and a high clustering coefficient. If one rewires the links between the node with a small probability the local structure of the network remains almost conserved keeping the clustering coefficient contrast. In contrast, due to the introduction of short cuts by the rewiring procedure the mean path length becomes strongly reduced. Networks with these properties are small-world networks. Further increase of the rewiring probability results in a random coupled network with a short mean path length and a low clustering coefficient.

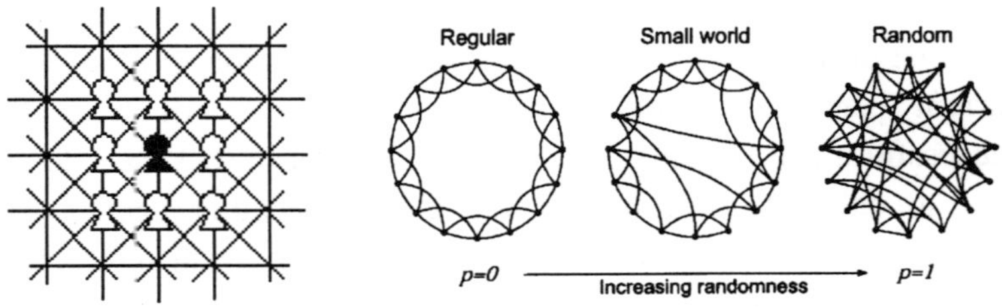

(a) Local interaction with a lattice model (b) Interaction with a small-world network (Illustration of one-lattice model)

Fig. 1. The topology of interaction

3. Learning Models

Game theory is typically based upon the assumption of a rational choice[8]. In our view, the reason for the dominance of the rational-choice approach is not that scholars think it to be realistic. Nor is game theory used solely because it offers good advice to a decision maker, because its unrealistic assumptions undermine much of its value as a basis for advice. The real advantage of the rational-choice assumption is that it often allows deduction.

The main alternative to the assumption of rational choice is some form of adaptive behavior. The adaptation may be at the individual level through learning, or it may be at the population level through differential survival and reproduction of the more successful individuals. Either way, the consequences of adaptive processes are often very hard to deduce when there are many interacting agents following rules that have nonlinear effects. Among many adaptive mechanisms that have been discussed in the literature on learning are classified as follows:

(1) Best response learning

In most game theoretic models, agents have perfect knowledge of the consequences of their decision. An important assumption of best-response learning is that they receive knowledge of the current strategy distribution. Agents can calculate their best strategy based on information about what other agents have done in the past. Then agents gradually learn the strategy distribution in the society. Agents adopt actions that optimize their expected payoff given what they expect others to do. In this learning model, agents choose the best replies to the empirical frequencies distribution of the previous actions of the others.

(2) Reinforcement learning

Agents tend to adopt actions that yielded a higher payoff in the past, and to avoid actions that yielded a low payoff. Payoff describes choice behavior, but it is one's own past payoffs that matter, not the payoffs of the others. The basic premise is that the probability of taking an action in the present increases with the payoff that resulted from taking that action in the past.

(3) Evolutionary learning

Agents with higher payoff are at a productive advantage compared to agents who use low-payoff strategies, hence the latter decrease in frequency in the population over time (natural selection). In the standard model of this situation agents are viewed as being genetically coded with a strategy and selection pressure favors agents that are fitter, i.e., whose strategy yields a higher payoff against the population. The idea of using a genetic algorithm (GA) to create strategies has been developed further by Lindgren[9]. He showed that strategies could be made more robust by seeding the initial population with expert, hand-coded strategies.

(4) Social learning

Agents learn from each other with social learning. For instance, agents may copy the behavior of others, especially behavior that is popular to yield high payoffs (imitation). In contrast to natural selection, the payoffs describe how agents make choices, and agents' payoff must be observable by others for the model to make sense. The crossover is a kind of social learning.

4. Evolutionary Dynamics with Individual Learning

We make a distinction between evolutionary systems and adaptive systems. The equations of motion in an evolutionary system reflect the basic mechanisms of biological evolution, i.e., inheritance, mutation, and selection. In an adaptive system, other mechanisms are allowed as well, e.g., modifications of strategies based on individual forecasts on the future state of the system. But, increasing the possibilities for individualistic rational behavior does not necessarily improve the outcome for the species to which the individual belongs in the long run.

The introduction of spatial dimensions, so that individuals only interact with those in their neighborhood, may affect the dynamics of the system in various ways. The possibility of space-temporal structures may allow for global stability where the mean-field model (random matching) would be unstable. The presence of these various forms of space-temporal phenomena may, therefore, also alter the evolutionary path compared with the mean-field model and we may see other strategies evolve.

Different aspects of the evolutionary behavior have been investigated by many researchers: (i) by varying the payoff matrix of the game, (ii) by introducing spatial dimensions, and (iii) by introducing co-evolution. An important aspect of evolution is the learning strategy adapted by individuals[3]. Evolution in the hawk-dove game, for instance, drives the population to an equilibrium polymorphism state. But this symmetrical mixed equilibrium of hawk-dove is so inefficient that it is far from optimal.

The term evolutionary dynamics often refers to systems that exhibit a time evolution in which the character of the dynamics may change due to internal mechanisms. In this chapter, we focus on evolutionary dynamics that may change in time according to certain local rules of individuals. Evolutionary models can be characterized both by the level at which the mechanisms are working and the dimensionality of the system. Therefore we describe the evolutionary dynamics specifying microscopic behavior with individuals learning.

The search for evolutionary foundations of game-theoretic solution concepts leads from the notion of an evolutionarily stable strategy to alternative notions of evolutionary stability to dynamic models of evolutionary processes. The commonly used technique of modeling the evolutionary process as a system of a deterministic difference or differential equations may tell us little about equilibrium concepts other than that strict Nash equilibrium is good. We can attempt to probe deeper into these issues by modeling the choices made by the agents with their own internal models. We also focus on dynamical systems described by equations of motion that may change in time according to certain rules, which can be interpreted as crossover operations. Each agent learns to acquire the rule of interaction in the long-run. Non-cooperation games can be categorized into, dilemma games coordination games, Hawk-Dove games and minority games. It is known that natural selection does not lead to social efficiency in these games. We show that all agents mutually learn to cooperate which result in social efficiency.

5. Learning Coupling Rules

In most game theoretic models, agents calculate their best strategy based on information about what other agents have done in the past. Then agents may gradually learn the equilibrium strategy. A number of evolutionary models based on the iterated general non-cooperation games have been proposed. Many dynamical systems and evolutionary models have been constructed with the PD[1]. Yao applied a genetic algorithm (GA) to the iterated Prisoner's Dilemma and used a bit-string representation of finite memory strategies[21].

We use the different approach. In the models that we discuss here, the equations of motion for the different individuals are usually coupled, which means that we have co-evolutionary systems. The success or failure for a certain type of individual depends on which other individuals are present. In this case, there is not a fixed fitness landscape in which the co-evolutionary dynamics climbs toward increasing to fitness. This ever-changing character of the world determining the evolutionary path allows for evolutionary phenomena.

Co-evolutionary dynamics differ, in this sense, from the common use of the genetic algorithm, in which a fixed goal is used in the fitness function and where there is no coupling between individuals. In the genetic algorithm, the focus is on the final result what is the best or a good solution. In models of co-evolutionary systems, one is usually interested in the transient phenomenon of evolution.

Each strategy in the repeated game is represented as a binary string so that the genetic operators can be applied. In order to accomplish this we treat each strategy as deterministic bit strings. We use a memory of one or two, which means that the outcomes of the previous one or two moves are used to make the current choice. We assume that 0 = S_1 and 1 = S_2 then as Fig. 2(a) shows, there are four possible outcomes between two agents for each move S_1S_1(0,0), S_1S_2(0,1), S_2S_1(1,0), S_2S_2(1,1). We can fully describe a deterministic strategy by recording what the strategy will do in each of the 4 different situations that can arise in the iterated game. Since no memory exists at the start, an extra 2 for 4 bits are needed to specify a hypothetical history. Each rule can be defined by a 6 bit string as shown in Fig. 2(b).

bit	previous strategy		next strategy
	Own	Opp	
4	0	0	#
5	0	1	#
6	1	0	#
7	1	1	#

(a) Coupling Rule

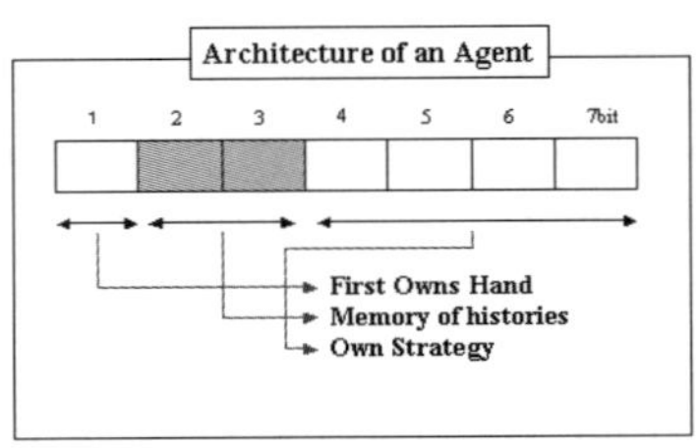

(b) Rule Representation

Fig. 2. An interaction rule of memory one

At each generation, agents repeatedly play the game for T iterations. Agent i, $i \in$ [1…N] uses a binary string i to choose his strategy at iteration t ,$t \in$.[1…T]. Each position of a binary string in Fig. 2(b) as follows: The first position, p_1 encodes the action that agent takes at iteration $t = 1$. A position p_j ,$j \in [2,3]$ encodes the memories that agent i takes at iteration $t - 1$ and his opponent. A position p_j, $j \in [4...7]$, encodes the action that agent i takes at iteration $t > 1$, corresponding to the position p_j, $j \in [2,3]$. An agent i compares the position p_j, $j \in [2,3]$, decides the next action.

Each agent mimics the rule of the most successful neighbor. We arrange agents for an area of 20×20 (N = 400 agents) with the lattice model as shown in Fig. 1(a) with no gap, and four corners and end of an area connect it with an opposite side. At each time period t, each agent plays with his 8 neighbors. At the next time period, each agent mimic the interaction rule of the most successful neighbor who obtain the highest payoff.

6. Simulation Results

Non-cooperation games can be categorized into dilemma games coordination games, hawk-dove games. It is known that equilibrium situations led by natural selection is far from social efficiency. A genetic algorithm is used to evolve strategies. A generation involves each player playing with 8 neighbors with the spatial model or some proportion of partners to interact are chosen from all other members in the population with the model of small-world networks. The iterated game is played fifty times between each agent. The fitness of an agent is the average payoff it achieved over repeating games. Mutation of random alleles may occur with a probability of 0.01 for all cases.

6.1. Dilemma Game

Many works on evolution of cooperation have been focused on dilemma games, which is formulated as follows: Each agent faces the problem of selecting one of two decisions, cooperate (S_1) or defect (S_2). The payoff for each decision depends on the decisions of the other agent. Table 1 shows the payoffs for all the possible combinations of decisions. The most startling effect of the iterated Prisoner's Dilemma simulation, as observed by Axelrod[1], is the fact that a group of purely egotistical individuals, working towards nothing but improving themselves can lead to a population which is actually highly cooperative.

Each pair of agents interacts 50 times at one generation. Fig. 3(a) shows the ratio of agents who chose the cooperative strategy S_1 with the lattice model. After few generations the ratio of the cooperative becomes to be 0.85. Initially the ratio of defective strategy increases, however, it is quickly wiped out and more cooperative opponents obtain higher payoffs, and the population exhibits reciprocal cooperation. Fig.3(b) shows the same experiment in a small-world network model. There are a couple of important differences in this graph and the graph obtained using the spatial environment (Fig.3(a)). Fig.3(b) shows that it is actually *easier* for cooperation to evolve in a small-world network environment. As a result the cooperative strategy could be realized with the dilemma game after a few generation. The cooperation is clearly more stable in the small-network environment.

At beginning, each agent has a different interaction rule specified by the 4 bits information. All rules learnt by 400 agents, which were aggregated into only one type as shown in Table 3.

Table 1. The payoff matrix of a dilemma game

The Other's Strategy / The Own's Strategy	S_1	S_2
S_1	3 3	5 0
S_2	0 5	1 1

Table 2. Learnt Rules by 400 agents in small-world environment

Initial strategy	Array Location				Number of Agents
	4	5	6	7	
0	0	1	1	1	400

Table 3. Learnt Interaction rule

bit	previous strategy		strategy at t
	Own	Opp	
4	0	0	0
5	0	1	1
6	1	0	1
7	1	1	1

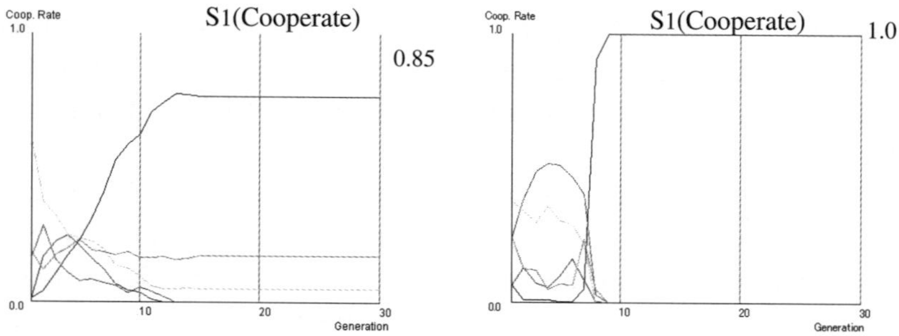

(a) Local interaction with a lattice model (b) Interaction with a small-world network

Fig. 3 The ratio of cooperation in iterated dilemma games

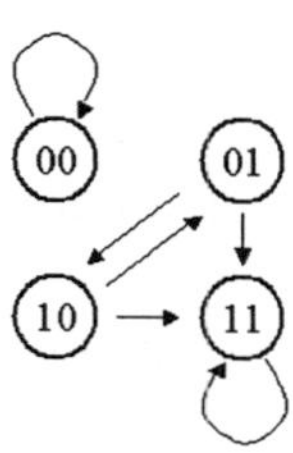

Fig. 4 The state transitions specified by the rule in Table 3

The acquired rule specified as "0111" in Table 3 can be interpreted as follows: If agents behave as "cooperate", then both agents behave "cooperate", however one of them "defect", then both agents behave "defect". The state transition of this learnt rule is illustrated in Fig. 4 as the state transition diagram. There are two absorption points "00" and "11". Since each agent also acquires the rule to behave "cooperate" at the first play of each generation as shown in Table 2, they remain at the absorption points "00".

6.2. Coordination Games

The coordination game with the payoff matrix in Table 4 has two equilibria with the pairs of the pure strategies (S_1 , S_1), (S_2 , S_2), and one equilibrium of the mixed strategy. The most preferable equilibrium, Pareto-dominance is (S_1 , S_1), which dominates the other equilibrium. There is another equilibrium concept, the risk-dominance, and (S_2 , S_2) risk-dominates (S_1 , S_1). How do agents choose their strategy when the equilibria of Pareto-dominance and the risk-dominance are different? With such indigenous selection of strategy, the question is whether the society of agents may select the socially efficient Pareto-optimal strategy.

Fig. 5(a) shows the ratio of agents to choose the Pareto-optimal strategy S_1 with the lattice model. After few generations the ratio of the Pareto-optimal strategy becomes to be 0.85. Fig.5(b) shows the same experiment using a small-world network framework. There are a couple of important differences in this graph and the graph obtained using the spatial environment (Fig.5(a)). Fig.5(b) shows that it is easier for the Pareto-optimal strategy to evolve in a small-world network environment. As a result Pareto optimal strategy could be spread out after a few generation.

At beginning, each agent has a different interaction rule specified by the 4 bits information. In Table 5, we show the rules learnt by 400 agents, which are aggregated into only one type. After 10 generations, all rules of agents were converged into one rule as shown in Table 5. The acquired rule specified as "0111" in Table 5 can be interpreted as follows: If both agents choose the Pareto-optimal strategy, then they choose the same one, however if one of them chooses the risk-dominant strategy, then both agents choose the risk-dominant strategy. The state transition of the learning rule is illustrated in Fig.6 as the state transition diagram. There are two absorption points "00" and "11". Since each agent also acquires the rule to choose "Pareto-optimal strategy" at the first play of each generation as shown in Fig.6, they remain at the absorption points "00".

Table 4. Payoff matrix of a coordination game

The Own's Strategy \ The Other's Strategy	S1	S2
S1	1 / 1	0 / −9
S2	−9 / 0	0 / 0

Table 5. Learnt Rules by 400 agents in Interaction with a small-world network

Initial strategy	Array Location 4	5	6	7	Number of Agents
0	0	1	1	1	400

Table 6. Interaction rule

bit	previous strategy Own	Opp	strategy at t
4	0	0	0
5	0	1	1
6	1	0	1
7	1	1	1

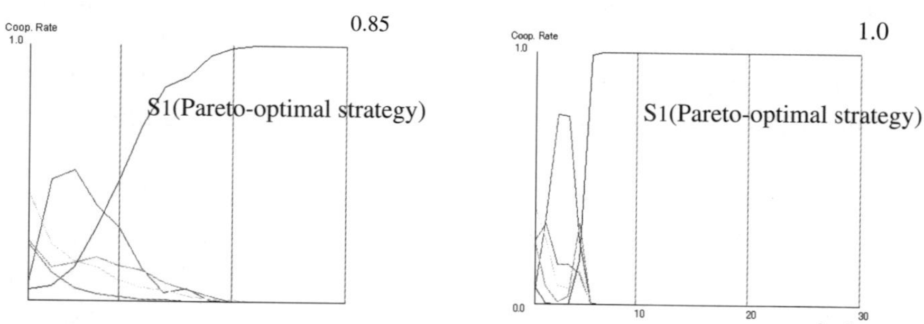

(a) Local interaction with a lattice model (b) Interaction with a small-world network

Fig. 5. The ratio of Pareto-optimal strategy (S1) in iterated coordination games

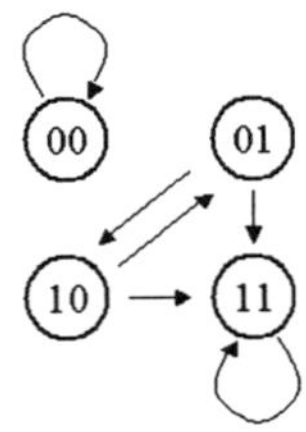

Fig. 6. The state transitions specified by rules in Table 6

6.3. Hawk-Dove Game

The hawk-dove game is formulated with the payoff matrix in Table 7. In this game, we suppose there are two possible behavioral types; one escalates the conflict until injury or sticks to display and retreats if the opponent escalates. These two types of behavior are described as "hawk" and "dove". There is the unique symmetric Nash equilibrium in mixed strategies, both agents use the strategy S_1 ('hawk') with probability $p=V/C$ and the strategy $S2$ ('dove') with the probability $1\text{-}p =1\text{-}(V/C)$ [2]. Therefore if the cost of injury C is very large, the hawk frequency (V/C) will be small. At equilibrium of the mixed strategy, the expected fitness is given at the level of $(V/2)\{1\text{-}(V/C)\}$. If each agent chooses the strategy $S2$ ('dove'), (however, the situation that both behave as doves are not equilibrium) he receives $V/2$. This implies that the mixed-strategy results in inefficient equilibrium. And evolutionary game can realize Pareto optimal equilibrium but it is possible that an inferior equilibrium is chosen.

Fig.7(a) shows the ratio of agents to choose the strategy of Dove (S_2) with the lattice model. We set to V=10, C=12 in Table 7. After few generations the ratio of the strategy of Dove becomes 0.95. Fig.7(b) shows the same experiment using a small-world network framework.

In Table 8, we show the rules learnt by 400 agents, which are aggregated into only one type. After 10 generation, all rules of agents were converged into one rule as shown in Table 8. The acquired rule specified as "C001" in Table 8 can be interpreted as follows: If both agents choose the Dove strategy, then they choose the same one, however one of them chooses the Hawk strategy, then both agents choose the Hawk strategy. The state transition of the learnt rule is illustrated in Fig. 8 as the state transition diagram. There are two absorption points "00" and "11". Since each agent also acquires the rule to choose " the Dove strategy" at the first play of each generation as shown in Table 8, they remain at the absorption points "11".

Table 7. The payoff matrix of the Hawk-dove game

Own's Strategy \ The Other's Strategy	S_1 (Hawk)	S_2 (Dove)
S_1 (Hawk)	(V-C)/2 (V-C)/2	0 V
S_2 (Dove)	V 0	V/2 V/2

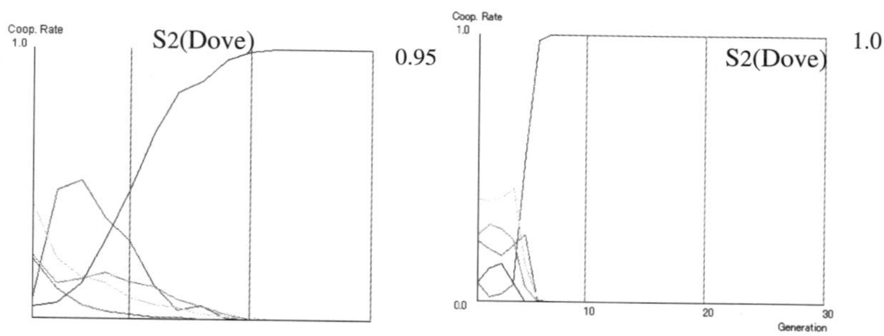

(a) Local interaction with a lattice model (b) Interaction with a small-world network
Fig.7. The ratio of Dove (S2) in iterated dilemma games

Table 8. Learnt Rules by 400 agents with a small-world network

Initial strategy	Array Location				Number of Agents
	4	5	6	7	
1	0	0	0	1	400

Table 9. Interaction rule

bit	previous strategy		strategy at t
	Own	Opp	
4	0	0	0
5	0	1	0
6	1	0	0
7	1	1	1

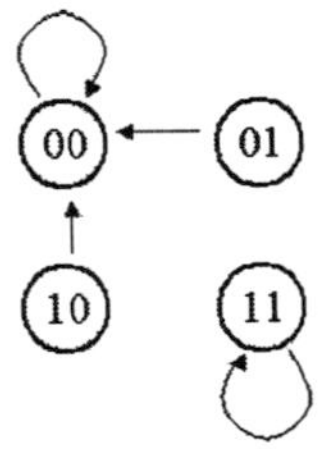

Fig. 8. The state transitions specified by rules in Table 8

7. Conclusion

We focused on co-evolutionary dynamical systems described by equations of motion that may change in time according to rules. In the models that we discuss here, the equations of motion for the different individuals are usually coupled, which means that we have co-evolutionary systems. The success or failure for a certain type of individual depends on which other individuals are present. In this case, there is not a fixed fitness landscape in which the evolutionary dynamics climbs toward increasing elevation, but a position that at one time is a peak may turn into a valley. This ever-changing character of the world determining the evolutionary path allows for complex dynamic phenomena. Co-evolutionary dynamics differ, in this sense, from the common use of the genetic algorithm, in which a fixed goal is used in the fitness function and where there is no interaction between individuals. In the genetic algorithm, the focus is on the final result what is the best or a good solution. In models of co-evolutionary systems, we consider the case of open-ended evolution.

We discussed the role of individual learning in realizing social efficiency. The hypotheses we employed here reflect the limited ability of interaction with the individual learning capability. The learning strategy employed here is a kind of meta-learning. One of the variations involves the finitely iterated game that has Nash equilibria of inferior strategies. It is illustrated that when the interaction architecture of the small-world network is added, evolution usually avoids this inferior state.

Our comparison of individuals playing the social games evolved in a spatial and small-world network environment has yielded some interesting results. It has been demonstrated in this chapter that interaction on a small-world network framework encourages and promotes efficiency to a greater extent, and in a more stable way, than when interaction is performed on a spatial model. This suggests that efficiency will be easier to attain when exchanges are restricted to those in an open society rather than a closed society.

References

1. R. Axelrod, *The Complexity of Cooperation* (Princeton Univ. Press, 1997).
2. W. B. Arthur, *American Economic Review*, Vol.84, 406 (1994).
3. D. Challet and C. Zhang, *Physica,* **A246** (1997).
4. D. Fudenberg and D. Levine, *The Theory of Learning in Games* (The MIT Pres, 1998).
5. P. Hammerstein and R. Selten, in *Handbook of Game Theory with Economic Applications*, Vol.2, Eds. Auman, R., Hart, S, (Elsevier Science, 1994), p. 931.
6. J. Hansaryi and R. Selten, *A Game Theory of Equibrium Selection in Games* (MIT Press, 1988).
7. J. Hofbauer and K. Sigmund, *Ecolutionary Games and Population Dynamics* (Cambridge Univ. Press, 1998).
8. M. Kandori and G. Mailath, *Econometrica*, Vol.61 (1993) p29.
9. Y. Kaniovski, A. Kryazhimskii and H. Young, *Games and Economics Behavior*, Vol 31, (2000) p50.
10. K. Lindgren, *The Economy as an Evolving Complex System II*, (1997) p337.
11. Y. Murakami, H. Sato and A. Namatame, *in International Conference on Computational Intelligence and Multimedia Applications,* (2001) p241.
12. Y. Murakami, H. Sato, and A. Namatame, *in The 5th Australia-Japan Joint Workshop on Intelligent & Evolutionary Systems,* (2001) p19.
13. M. A. Nowak et al., *The Arithmetics of Mutual Help* (Scientific American, June, (1995).
14. M. A. Nowak and R. M. May, *Evolutionary Games and spatial Chaos*, (Nature, 359, 1992) p826.
15. M. Sipper, *Evolution of Parallel Cellular Machines* (Springer, 1996).
16. J. M. Smith, *Evolution and the Theory of Games* (Cambridge University Press, 1982).
17. K. Uno, and A. Namatame, *in GECCO'99 Workshop on Artificial life,* (1999).
18. D. J. Watts, *Small Worlds* (Princeton University Press, 1999).
19. J. Weibull, *Evolutionary Game Theory* (The MIT press, 1996).
20. X. Yao, and P. Darwen, *Informatica*, Vol.18 (1994) p435.

CHAPTER 2

USING EVOLUTION TO LEARN USER PREFERENCES

Supiya Ujjin and Peter J. Bentley

Department of Computer Science
University College London, Gower Street, London WC1E 6BT
S.Ujjin@cs.ucl.ac.uk, P.Bentley@cs.ucl.ac.uk

Recommender systems are new types of internet-based software tools, designed to help users find their way through today's complex on-line shops and entertainment websites. This chapter describes a new recommender system, which employs a genetic algorithm to learn personal preferences of users and provide tailored suggestions.

1. Introduction

The rapid expansion of the Internet has brought about a new market for trading. Electronic commerce or e-commerce has enabled businesses to open up their products and services to a massive client base that was once available only to the largest multinational companies. As the competition between businesses becomes increasingly fierce, consumers are faced with a myriad of choices. Although this might seem to be nothing but beneficial to the consumer, the sheer wealth of information relating to the various choices can be overwhelming. One would normally rely on the opinions and advice of friends or family members but unfortunately even they have limited knowledge.

Recommender systems provide one way of circumventing this problem. As the name suggests, their task is to recommend or suggest items or products to the customer based on his/her preferences. These systems are often used by E-commerce websites as marketing tools to increase revenue by presenting products that the customer is likely to buy. An internet site using a recommender system can exploit knowledge of customers' likes and dislikes to build an understanding of their individual needs and thereby increase customer loyalty[1, 2].

This chapter focuses on the use of evolutionary search to fine-tune a profile-matching algorithm within a recommender system, tailoring it to the preferences of individual users. This enables the recommender system to make more accurate predictions of users' likes and dislikes, and hence better recommendations to users.

The chapter is organised as follows: section 2 outlines related work, and section 3 describes the recommender system and genetic algorithm. Section 4 provides experimental results and analysis. Finally section 5 concludes.

2. Background

From the literature, it seems that the definition of the term "recommender system" varies depending on the author. Some researchers use the concepts: "recommender system", "collaborative filtering" and "social filtering" interchangeably[3,4]. Conversely, others regard "recommender system" as a generic descriptor that represents various recommendation/prediction techniques including collaborative, social, and content based filtering, Bayesian networks and association rules[5,6]. In this chapter, we adopt the latter definition when referring to recommender systems.

MovieLens (http://www.movielens.umn.edu), a well-known research movie recommendation website, makes use of collaborative filtering technology to make its suggestions. This technology captures user preferences to build a profile by asking the user to rate movies. It searches for similar profiles (i.e., users that share the same or similar taste) and uses them to generate new suggestions. One shortcoming that most websites using collaborative filtering suffer from is that they do not have any facility to provide explanations of how recommendations are derived. This is addressed in the paper[7] which proposes explanation facilities for recommender systems in order to increase users' faith in the suggestions.

By contrast, LIBRA (http://www.cs.utexas.edu/users/ libra) combines a content-based approach with machine learning to make book recommendations. The content-based approach differs from collaborative filtering in that it analyses the contents of the items being recommended. Furthermore, each user is treated individually - there is no sense of "community" which forms the basis of collaborative filtering.

Dooyoo (http://www.dooyoo.co.uk) operates in a slightly different way. It too is a useful resource that provides recommendations to those seeking advice, but it focuses mainly on gathering qualitative opinions from its users, and then making them available to others. Visitors will often submit reviews on items or services ranging from health spas to mobile phones. These items are categorised in a similar fashion to the layout on a structured search engine, such as Yahoo!

Researchers at the University of the West Of England have also been working on a movie Recommender System[9]. Their idea is to use the immune system to tackle the problem of preference matching and recommendation. User preferences are treated as a pool of antibodies and the active user is the antigen. The difference in their approach and the other existing methods is that they are not interested in finding the one best match but a diverse set of antibodies that are a close match.

3. System Overview

The system described in this chapter is based around a collaborative filtering approach, building up profiles of users and then using an algorithm to find profiles similar to the current user. (In this chapter, we refer to the current user as the *active user*, *A*). Selected data from those profiles are then used to build recommendations. Because profiles contain many attributes, many of which have sparse or incomplete data[7], the task of finding appropriate similarities is often difficult. To overcome these problems, current systems (such as MovieLens) use stochastic and heuristic-based models to speed up and improve the quality of profile matching. This work takes such ideas one step further, by applying an evolutionary algorithm to the problem of profile matching.

3.1. *MovieLens Dataset*

The dataset collected through the MovieLens website (http://www.movielens.umn.edu) has been made available for research purposes and used in this research. The database contains details of 943 users, each with many parameters or *features*: demographic information such as age, gender and occupation is collected when a new user registers on the system. The evolutionary recommender system uses 22 features from this data set: movie rating, age, gender, occupation and 18 movie genre frequencies: action, adventure, animation, children, comedy, crime, documentary, drama, fantasy, film-noir, horror, musical, mystery, romance, sci-fi, thriller, war, western. Table 1 and Fig. 1 show the relationships and dependencies between the various elements in the database.

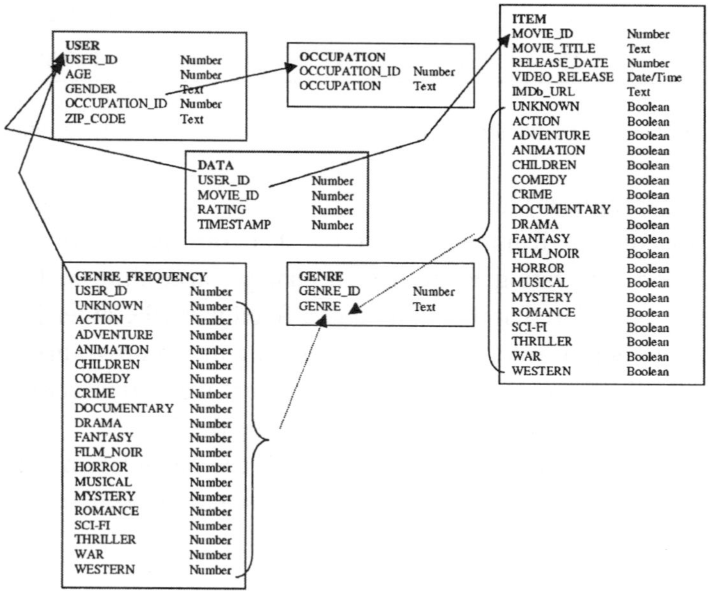

Fig. 1. Relationships and dependencies between the various elements in the database

Table 1. Table Descriptions

DATA	100,000 ratings by 943 users on 1682 items. Each user has rated at least 20 movies.
USER	Demographic information about the users.
ITEM	Information about the items (movies). The last 19 fields represent the genres, a boolean value, 0 or 1 indicates whether the movie belongs to the specific genre; a movie can be in several genres.
OCCUPATION	A list of the occupations.
GENRE	A list of the genres.
GENRE_FREQUENCY	The frequencies of the genres for all the items the user has rated. This has been added to the database as it is thought to represent how much the user prefers each genre.

3.2. *Profile Generator*

Before recommendations can be made, the movie data must first be processed into separate profiles, one for each person, defining that person's movie preferences.

1 Rating	2 Age	3 Gender	4 Occupation	..22 18 Genre frequencies
5	23	0	45	000000100010000000

Fig. 2. *profile(j,i)* - profile for user *j* with rating on movie item *i*, if *i* has a rating of 5

A profile for user *j*, denoted *profile(j)* is represented as an array of 22 values for the 22 features considered. The profile has two parts: a variable part (the rating value, which changes according to the movie item being considered at the time), and a fixed part (the other 21 values, which are only retrieved once at the beginning of the program). Because user *j* may have rated many different movies, we define *profile(j,i)* to mean the profile for user *j* on movie item *i*, see fig. 2.

Once profiles are built, the process of recommendation can begin. Given an active user *A*, a set of profiles similar to *profile(A)* must be found.

3.3. *Neighbourhood Selection*

The success of a collaborative filtering system is highly dependent upon the effectiveness of the algorithm in finding the set or neighbourhood of profiles that are most similar to that of the active user. It is vital that, for a particular neighbourhood method, only the best or closest profiles are chosen and used to generate new recommendations for the user. There is little tolerance for inaccurate or irrelevant predictions.

The neighbourhood selection algorithm consists of three main tasks:

(i) profile selection
(ii) profile matching
(iii) best profile collection.

3.3.1 Profile Selection

In an ideal world, the entire database of profiles would be used to select the best possible profiles. However this is not always a feasible option, especially when the dataset is very large or if resources are not available. As a result, most systems opt for random sampling and this process is the responsibility of the profile selection part of the algorithm.

This work investigates two methods of profile selection:

(i) Fixed: the first n users from the database are always used in every experiment
(ii) Random: n users are picked randomly from the database,

where $n = 10$ or 50 in our experiments.

3.3.2 Profile Matching

After profile selection, the profile matching process then computes the distance or similarity between the selected profiles and the active user's profile using a distance function. This research focuses on this profile matching task, i.e., the evolutionary algorithm is used to fine-tune profile matching for each active user.

From the analysis of Breese et al.[3], it seems that most current recommender systems use standard algorithms that consider only "voting information" as the feature on which the comparison between two profiles is made. However in real life, the way in which two people are said to be similar is not based solely on whether they have complimentary opinions on a specific subject, e.g., movie ratings, but also on other factors, such as their background and personal details. If we apply this to the profile matcher, issues such as demographic and lifestyle information which include user's age, gender and preferences of movie genres must also be taken into account. Every user places a different importance or priority on each feature. These priorities can be quantified or enumerated. Here we refer to these as *feature weights*. For example, if a male user prefers to be given recommendations based on the opinions of other men, then his feature weight for gender would be higher than other features. In order to implement a truly personalised recommender system, these weights need to be captured and fine-tuned to reflect each user's preference. Our approach shows how such weights can be evolved by a genetic algorithm.

A potential solution to the problem of evolving feature weights, $w(A)$, for the active user, A is represented as a set of weights as shown below in Fig. 3 where w_f is the weight associated with feature f whose genotype is a string of binary values.

w_1	w_2	w_3	...	w_{22}

Fig. 3. Phenotype of an individual in the population

Each individual contains 22 genes, which are evolved by an elitist genetic algorithm (described in section 3.4). The comparison between two profiles can now be conducted using a modified Euclidean distance function, which takes into account multiple features. *Euclidean(A,j)* is the similarity between active user A and user j:

$$euclidean(A,j) = \frac{1}{z}\sum_{i=1}^{z}\sqrt{\sum_{f=1}^{22} w_f * diff_{i,f}(A,j)^2}$$

where: A is the active user

j is a user provided by the profile selection process, where $j \neq A$

z is the number of common movies that users A and j have rated.

w_f, is the active user's weight for feature f

i is a common movie item, where *profile(A,i)* and *profile(j,i)* exists.
$diff_{i,f}(A,j)$ is the difference in profile value for feature f between users A and j on movie item i.

Note that before this calculation is made, the profile values are normalised to ensure they lie between 0 and 1. When the weight for any feature is zero, that feature is ignored. This way we enable feature selection to be adaptive to each user's preferences. The difference in profile values for occupation is either 0, if the two users have the same occupation, or 1 otherwise.

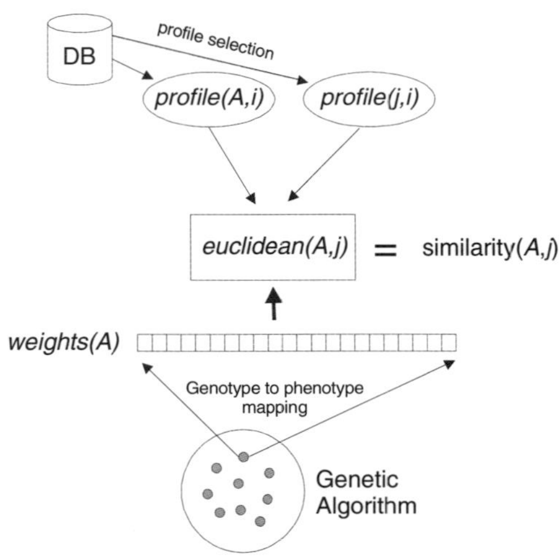

Fig. 4. Calculating the similarity between A and j

3.3.3 Best Profile Collection

Once the Euclidean distances, *euclidean*(A,j), have been found between *profile(A)* and *profile(j)* for all values of j picked by the profile selection process, the "best profile collection" algorithm is called, see Fig. 4. This ranks every *profile(j)* according to its similarity to *profile(A).* The system then simply selects the users whose Euclidean distance is above a certain threshold value (considered most similar to the active user) as the neighbourhood of *A*. This value is a system constant that can be changed.

3.4. *Making a Recommendation*

To make a recommendation, given an active user *A* and a neighbourhood set of similar profiles to *A*, it is necessary to find movie items seen (and liked) by the users in the neighbourhood set that the active user has not seen. These are then presented to the active user through a user interface. Because the neighbourhood set contains those users who are most similar to *A* (using in our case the specific preferences of *A* through evolved weighting values), movies that these users like have a reasonable probability of being liked by *A*.

3.5. *Genetic Algorithm*

As described earlier, a genetic algorithm is used to evolve feature weights for the active user, and hence help tailor the matching function to the user's specific personality and tastes.

An elitist genetic algorithm was chosen for this task, where a quarter of the best individuals in the population are kept for the next generation. When creating a new generation, individuals are selected randomly out of the top 40% of the whole population to be parents. Two offspring are produced from every pair of parents, using single-point crossover with probability 1.0. Mutation is applied to each locus in genotype with probability 0.01. A simple unsigned binary genetic encoding is used in the implementation, using 8 bits for each of the 22 genes. The GA begins with random genotypes.

A genotype is mapped to a phenotype (a set of feature weights) by converting the alleles of the binary genes to decimal. The feature weights can then be calculated from these real values. First, the importance of the 18 genre frequencies are reduced by a given factor, the *weight reduction size*. This is done because the 18 genres can be considered different categories of a single larger feature, Genre. Reducing the effect of these weights is therefore intended to give the other unrelated features (movie rating, age, gender, occupation) a more equal chance of being used. Second, the total value of phenotype is then calculated by summing the real values for all 22 features. Finally, the weighting value for each feature can be found by dividing the real value by the total value. The sum of all the weights will then add up to unity.

3.5.1 Fitness Function

Calculating the fitness for this application is not trivial. Every set of weights in the GA population must be employed by the profile matching processes within the recommender system. So the recommender system must be re-run on the MovieLens dataset for each new set of weights, in order to calculate its fitness.

But running a recommender system only produces recommendations (or predictions), not fitnesses. A poor set of weights might result in a poor neighbourhood set of profiles for the active user, and hence poor recommendations. A good set of weights should result in a good neighbourhood set, and good recommendations. So a method of calculating the quality of the recommendations is required, in order that a fitness score can be assigned to the corresponding weights.

One solution would be to employ the active user as a fitness function. This would involve obtaining feedback from the user by asking him to judge the quality of recommendations[8]. His input could be used to help derive fitness scores for the current set of feature weights. This fitness score would give a highly accurate view of the user's preferences. However, it is unlikely that every user will be willing to participate in every recommendation – the time needed would be too great.

Instead, it was decided to reformulate the problem as a supervised learning task. As described previously, given the active user *A* and a set of neighbouring profiles, recommendations for *A* can be made. In addition to these recommendations, it is possible to predict what *A* might think of them. For example, if a certain movie is suggested because similar users saw it, but those users only thought the movie was "average", then it is likely that the active user might also think the movie was "average". Hence, for the MovieLens dataset, it was possible for the system to both recommend new movies and to predict how the active user would rate each movie, should he go and see it.

The predicted vote computation used in this chapter has been taken from the paper[3] and modified such that the Euclidean distance function (section 3.2.2) now replaces the weight in the original equation. The predicted vote, *predict_vote(A,i)*, for *A* on item *i*, can be defined as:

$$predict\_vote(A,i) = mean_A + k\sum_{j=1}^{n} euclidean(A,j)(vote(j,i) - mean_j)$$

where: $mean_j$ is the mean vote for user *j*

k is a normalising factor such that the sum of the euclidean distances is equal to 1.

vote(j,i) is the actual vote that user *j* has given on item *i*

n is the size of the neighbourhood.

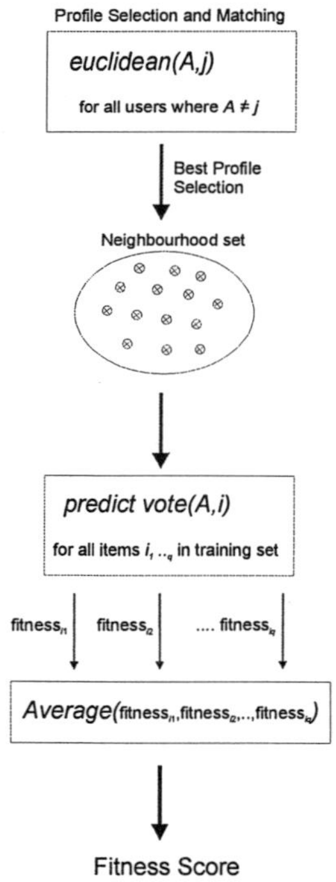

Fig. 5. Finding the fitness score of an individual (the active user's feature weights)

All the movie items that the active user has seen are randomly partitioned into two datasets: a training set (1/3) and a test set (2/3). To calculate a fitness measure for an evolved set of weights, the recommender system finds a set of neighbourhood profiles for the active user, as described in section 3.3. The ratings of the users in the neighbourhood set are then employed to compute the predicted rating for the active user on each movie item in the training set. Because the active user has already rated the movie items, it is possible to compare the actual rating with the predicted rating. So, the average of the differences between the actual and predicted votes of all items in the training set are used as fitness score to guide future generations of weight evolution, see Fig. 5.

4. Experiments

Four sets of experiments were designed to observe the difference in performance between the evolutionary recommender system and a standard, non-adaptive recommender system based on the Pearson algorithm[3]. In each set of experiments, the predicted votes of all the movie items in the test set (the items that the active user has rated but were not used in weights evolution) were computed using the final feature weights for that run. These votes were then compared against those produced from the simple Pearson algorithm.

The Pearson algorithm used in the experiments is based on the k Nearest Neighbour algorithm. A correlation coefficient, shown below, is used as the matching function for selecting the k users that are most similar to the active user to give predictions. This replaces the *Euclidean* function described earlier; all other details remain the same.

$$correlation(A,j) = \frac{\sum_{i=1}^{z}(vote(A,i) - mean_A)(vote(j,i) - mean_j)}{\sqrt{\sum_{i=1}^{z}(vote(A,i) - mean_A)^2 (vote(j,i) - mean_j)^2}}$$

The four experiments also evaluated two system variables to assess their effect on system performance: the *profile selection* task (the way in which profiles were selected from the database), and the size of the neighbourhood. Table 2 lists parameter values used in all four experiments.

Table 2. Parameter values used in the experiments

Parameter Name	Parameter Value	Description
population size	75	The number of individuals in the population at each generation.
termination threshold	0.06	When the fitness score of the best individual (set of feature weights) is below the threshold, a good solution is found and this set of weights is used as the final result for the current run.
maximum generations (per run)	300	If the number of generations reaches this value and the solution has not been found, the best individual for that generation is used as the final result.
weight reduction size	4	The scaling factor for the 18 genre frequencies.
number of runs	30	The number of times the system was run for each active user.
k users (Pearson algorithm)	5 or 25	½ of the number of users in each experiment

The four sets of experiments were as follows:

Experiment 1: Each of the first 10 users was picked as the active user in turn, and the first 10 users (fixed) were used to provide recommendations.

Experiment 2: Each of the first 50 users was picked as the active user in turn, and the first 50 users (fixed) were used to provide recommendations.

Experiment 3: Each of the first 10 users was picked as the active user in turn, and 10 users were picked randomly and used to provide recommendations (the same 10 used per run).

Experiment 4: Each of the first 50 users was picked as the active user in turn, and 50 users were picked randomly and used to provide recommendations (the same 50 used per run).

4.1. *Results*

Figs. 6 to 9 show the results for experiments 1 to 4, respectively. Each graph shows the percentage of the number of ratings that the system predicted correctly out of the total number of available ratings by the current active user. Whilst the predictions computed with the Pearson algorithm always remain the same given the same parameter values, those obtained from the GA vary according to the feature weights of that run. Out of the 30 runs for each active user in each experiment, the run with the best feature weights (that gave the highest percentage of right predictions) was chosen and plotted against the result from the Pearson algorithm.[1]

Fig. 6 shows that in the first experiment, the GA recommender performed equally well (or better) compared to the Pearson algorithm on 8 active users out of 10.

Fig. 7 shows that in the second experiment, out of the 50 users the accuracy for the GA recommender fell below that of the Pearson algorithm for 14 active users. On the rest of the active users, the accuracy for the GA recommender was found to be better – in some cases the difference was as great as 31%.

The random sampling for experiment 3 showed great improvement on the prediction accuracy for the GA recommender, see Fig. 8. All 10 active users performed better than the Pearson algorithm.

The results for the last experiment show that the accuracy for the GA recommender was significantly better for all but 4 active users, see Fig. 9.

---

[1] The best rather than average was plotted since this is closest to the real world scenario where this system could be run off-line and the current best set of feature weights would be set as the initial preference of the active user. Following this, the evolved weights could be stored on the user's local machine. A local copy of the system would then be responsible for fine-tuning the weights to suit that user's preferences further. This way the processing load on the server would be reduced and parallelism can be achieved.

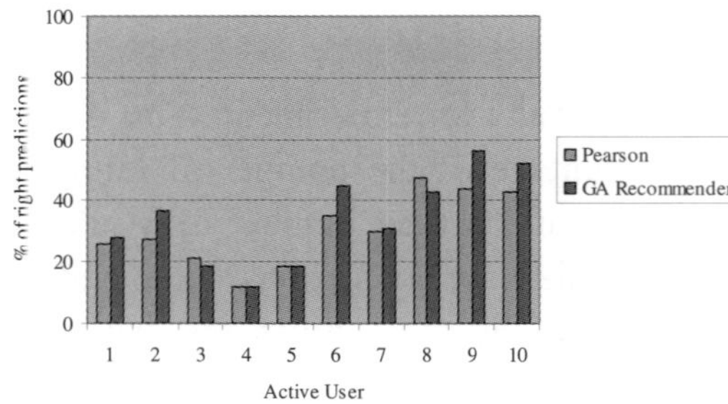

Fig. 6. Results for experiment 1

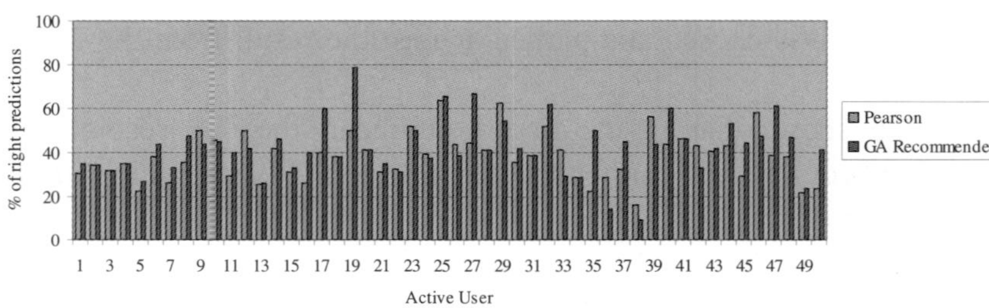

Fig. 7. Results for experiment 2

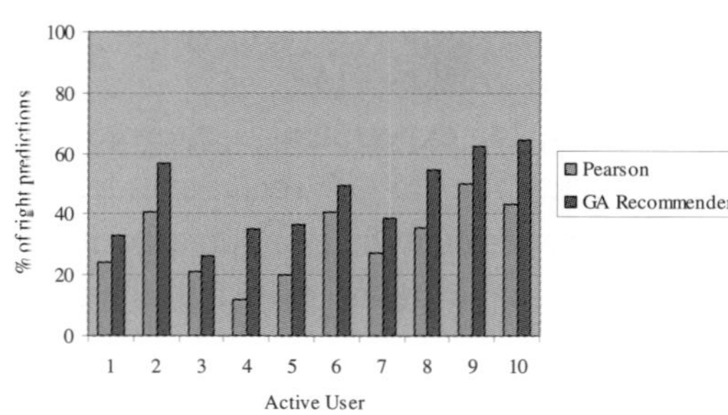

Fig. 8. Results for experiment 3

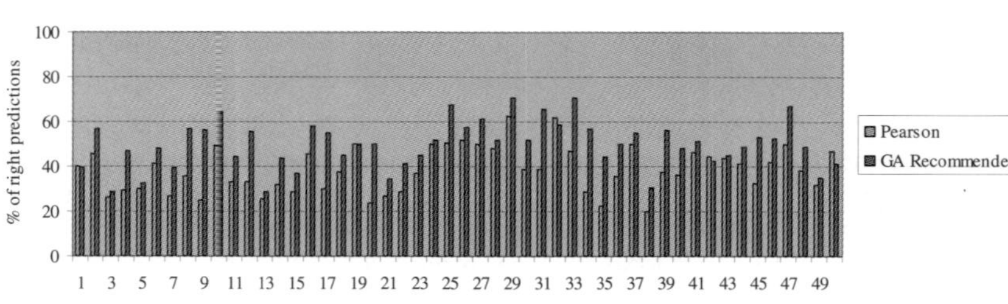

Fig. 9. Results for experiment 4

4.2. *Analysis of Results*

Fig. 6 indicates that the prediction accuracy for the active user 3 and 8 on the GA recommender was worse than that obtained from using the Pearson algorithm. But when the number of users was increased to 50 in experiment 2, the accuracy for the two mentioned active users rose and outperformed the other algorithm. This was expected – as the number of users goes up, the probability of finding a better matched profile should be higher and hence, the accuracy of the predictions should increase as well.

The patterns in both experiments 3 and 4 for the active users 1 to 10 look very similar. Both show an improved accuracy compared to the Pearson algorithm but in experiment 4 there seems to be a greater improvement. Again, this is likely to be because of the increase in the number of users. The results suggest that random sampling is a good choice for the *profile selection* task of retrieving profiles from the database. Random sampling was expected to be better than fixing which users to select because it allowed the search to consider a greater variety of profiles (potentially 10*30 runs = 300 users in experiment 3 and 50 * 30 = 1500 users in experiment 4) and hence find a better set of well matched profiles.

As mentioned earlier, only the run(s) with the best feature weights for each active user were considered for this analysis. We now look into these runs in more detail to see how the feature weights obtained and users selected for the neighbourhood in these runs played a part in determining user preference.

Looking at experiment 1, when more than 1 run for an active user achieved the same best performance (highest number of votes being predicted correctly) results indicate that the same set of users had been selected for the neighbourhood to give recommendations. Moreover, for other runs that did not perform as well as the best run(s), different users that gave the best performance had been selected. For example, for active user 2 in experiment 1, all the runs that got the same percentage as the best, chose user 4 to be in the neighbourhood. The other active users did not select any users to give recommendations, instead the mean vote was used. Data gathered during experiment 2 corroborates this view. In addition, as the number of users was increased, the users that were originally selected for the neighbourhood in experiment 1 were still being chosen in experiment 2 as a subset of a larger neighbourhood. For example, as mentioned above, in experiment 1 user 2 picked user 4 to be in the neighbourhood, in experiment 2 this user picked users 4,13,18,22,42,43,49. This, however, only applies to the active users that performed better than the Pearson algorithm in experiment 1. The accuracy for active user 8 was worse in experiment 1, in which users 4, 5, 7 and 10 were selected. In experiment 2 when users 4 and 10 were not included in the neighbourhood, the accuracy improved tremendously as seen in Fig. 7.

The trend described could not be observed when random sampling was used in experiments 3 and 4, as it was more difficult for the system to select the same users to examine at each run.

Looking at the final feature weights obtained for each active user, many interesting observations have been found. Here we focus on the first two experiments as they have 10 common active users. Firstly, in experiment 2 when more than 1 run came up with the best performance, the feature weights seem to show very similar trends. For example, Fig. 10 shows the weight emphasis on the first 2 features: rating and age. It is also clear that this user does not show any interest in the 3rd feature which is gender. So as long as the people that are giving him recommendations have similar opinions and are in the same age group as him, he does not care whether they are male or female.

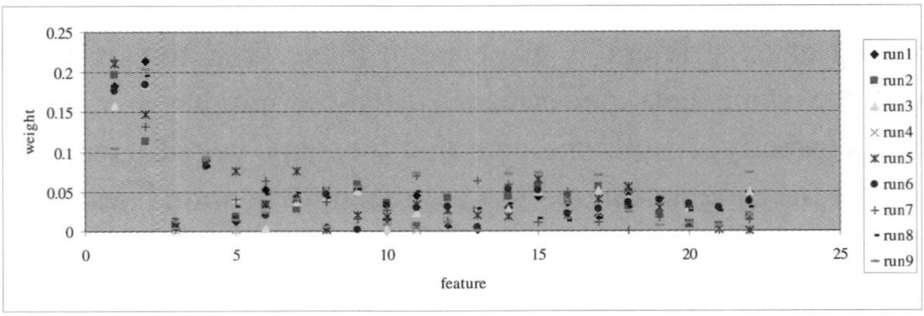

Fig. 10. Feature weights for active user 2 (weights 5 to 22 are lower because of the scaling factor)

The feature weights obtained for active user 8 were also interesting. They show that for this user, age and gender (features 2 and 3) are more significant. By looking further at the movie genres (features 5-22), we found that people who have similar opinions as this user on action (feature 5), adventure (feature 6), horror (feature 15), romantic (feature 18) and war (feature 21) movies are likely to be picked for the neighbourhood set. As these genres are stereotypically related to gender and age, for example, men prefer action movies and war movies, the weights showed consistent description of the user's preference.

Another example is active user 7 whose weights show strong feelings for documentary, mystery, sci-fi and thriller genres and emphasis on age. This user is a 57-year old male who may explain reduced significance of children and romance genres. Also, we discover that children and animation genre features usually have similar weights – this could be because these two genres are usually related i.e. most animation films are children's films like Disney cartoons.

From the observations above, we can see that age is often as or more important as rating. This shows that the theory behind the original collaborative filtering does not always hold. This is hardly surprising as everyday experience suggests that most people listen to the recommendations made by their friends who are most likely to be in the same age group as them.

In experiment 1, all active users seem to have similar feature weights as the ones obtained in experiment 2 apart from users 3, 8, 9 and 10. We divide our analysis of this into 2 parts. Firstly, users 3 and 8 performed worse than the Pearson algorithm in experiment 1. This was because the weights obtained did not describe the users realistically. As the number of users was increased in experiment 2, the weights could be captured better and hence produce better performance. Secondly, the weights for active users 9 and 10 did not display any useful information in experiment 2. This resulted in reduced performance for them compared to the original algorithm. But in experiment 1, the weights for these 2 users show a consistent trend resulting in increased accuracy compared to the Pearson algorithm in this experiment.

This approach has been shown to work well, but there are problems. As fitness scores are computed by getting the differences between the actual and predicted votes, this is only achievable if the user has already actively voted on movies, otherwise the intersection between recommended items and those already voted for by the active user would return very few titles or even none. In this case, this approach will fail, as a fitness score cannot be determined.

Table 3. Recommended movies for active user 1

Film	Action
Braveheart	Yes
Apollo 13	Yes
Blade Runner	No
Aladdin	No
Independence Day (ID4)	Yes
Die Hard	Yes
Top Gun	Yes
Empire Strikes Back, The	Yes
Return of the Jedi	Yes
GoodFellas	No
Blues Brothers, The	Yes
Sting, The	No
Dead Poets Society	No
Star Trek: First Contact	Yes
Raising Arizona	No
Men in Black	Yes

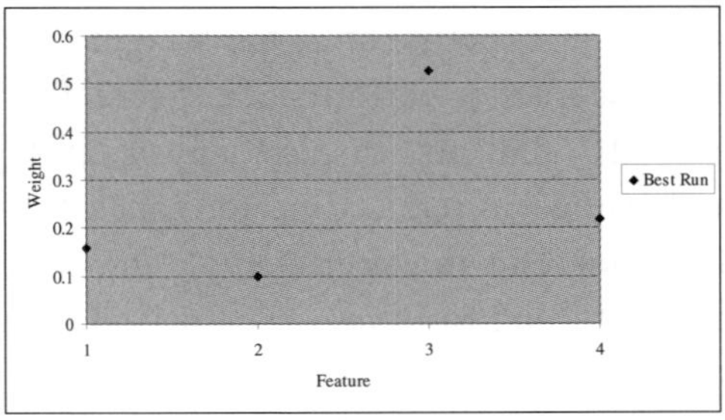

Fig. 11. Feature weights for active user 1 in 4-feature experiment

In an earlier experiment with only 4 features: Rating, Age, Gender and Occupation, it was noticed that many solutions were found for items which are sometimes associated with gender (inferred by gender). For example, when the active user's feature weights showed that the user preferred to be recommended by people of the same gender (3rd feature), solutions were often found for items that belonged to the Action genre. Fig. 11 and Table 3 illustrate this. 10 out of 16 items (with a predicted vote of 4 or above) that were being recommended to the active user using this set of weights are action movies. Because of this, it would be interesting to see if results can be improved if we make use of association rules.

5. Conclusions

This work has shown how evolutionary search can be employed to fine-tune a profile-matching algorithm within a recommender system, tailoring it to the preferences of individual users. This was achieved by reformulating the problem of making recommendations into a supervised learning task, enabling fitness scores to be computed by comparing predicted votes with actual votes. Experiments demonstrated that, compared to a non-adaptive approach, the evolutionary recommender system was able to successfully fine-tune the profile matching algorithm. This enabled the recommender system to make more accurate predictions, and hence better recommendations to users.

References

1. J. B. Schafer, J. A. Konstan and J. Riedl. E-Commerce Recommendation Applications. *Journal of Data Mining and Knowledge Discovery* (2001).
2. J. B. Schafer, J. Konstan and J. Riedl. Recommender Systems in E-Commerce. *Proceedings of the ACM 1999 Conference on Electronic Commerce* (1999).
3. J. S. Breese, D. Heckerman and C. Kadie. Empirical analysis of predictive algorithms for collaborative filtering. *Proceedings of the 14th Conference on Uncertainty in Artificial Intelligence*, pp. 43-52 (1998).
4. K. Goldberg, T. Roeder, D. Gupta and C. Perkins. Eigentaste: A Constant Time Collaborative Filtering Algorithm. *UCB ERL Technical Report M00/41* (2000).

5. L. Terveen and W. Hill. Beyond Recommender Systems: Helping People Help Each Other In *HCI In The New Millenium*, J. Carroll ed. Addison-Wesley (2001).
6. J. A. Delgado. Agent-Based Information Filtering and Recommender Systems on the Internet. PhD thesis, Nagoya Institute of Technology (2000).
7. J. L. Herlocker, J. A. Konstan and J. Riedl. Explaining Collaborative Filtering Recommendations. *Proceedings of the ACM 2000 Conference on Computer Supported Cooperative Work* (2000).
8. P. J. Bentley and D. W. Corne. *Creative Evolutionary Systems*. (Morgan Kaufman Pub, 2001).
9. S. Cayzer and U. Aickelin. A Recommender System based on the Immune Network. *Proceedings of 2002 World Congress on Computational Intelligence*, pp 807-813 (2002)

CHAPTER 3

A PARALLEL GENETIC ALGORITHM FOR CLUSTERING

Juha Kivijärvi, Joonas Lehtinen and Olli S. Nevalainen
Turku Centre for Computer Science (TUCS)
Department of Information Technology
University of Turku, 20014 Turku, Finland
E-mail: juha.kivijarvi@utu.fi

Parallelization of genetic algorithms (GAs) has received considerable attention in recent years. Reasons for this are the availability of suitable computational resources and the need for solving harder problems in reasonable time. We describe a new parallel self-adaptive GA for solving the data clustering problem. The algorithm utilizes island parallelization using a genebank model, in which GA processes communicate with each other through the genebank process. This model allows one to implement different migration topologies in an easy manner. Experiments show that significant speedup is reached by parallelization. The effect of migration parameters is also studied and the development of population diversity is examined by several measures, some of which are new.

1. Introduction

The objective in clustering is to divide a given set of data objects into a number of groups called *clusters* in such a way that similar objects belong to the same cluster whereas dissimilar objects are in different ones[1,2]. The problem appears as many variations in numerous fields of science such as data compression, pattern recognition, image analysis, medical data analysis, data mining, social sciences, bioinformatics, etc. The problem instances are commonly large in several respects: the dimensionality of data objects may be high, their number may be thousands or millions, and the number of clusters may be several hundreds. Thus the amount of computation needed for finding satisfactory solutions is often high, even if the hope of finding a true global optimum is abandoned.

In the present study we consider the case of *Euclidean* clustering. In particular, we assume that the data objects can be considered as points in a Euclidean space and calculation of artificial cluster centers is meaningful. Furthermore, the number of clusters is expected to be known. This situation is met for example in vector quantization[3].

There exists a great number of algorithms for clustering[4,5]. These can be classified as *partitional* and *hierarchical*. Partitional algorithms aim to divide the given data into a number of clusters whereas hierarchical methods generate a hierarchy of clusterings of different sizes. Partitional algorithms are commonly *iterative*, i.e. they start with an initial solution and iteratively improve it. *Hierarchical* methods can be divided into *divisive* and *agglomerative* methods. They apply split and merge operations, respectively, until a clustering with the desired number of clusters has been reached[6].

General heuristic search techniques[7] have gained popularity in solving hard combinatorial optimization problems and clustering is not an exception. High quality results have been reported for e.g. *simulated annealing*, *tabu search*[8] and especially *genetic algorithms* (GAs)[9,10]. In the present study we concentrate on GAs since they are very effective while still conceptually simple and have been shown to achieve excellent results in clustering problems[11].

GAs perform *stochastic optimization* by applying stochastic evolution inspired operators to a set of candidate solutions. These operations include *mutation*, *crossover* and *selection*. There are several properties which have increased the popularity of GAs as a general framework for solving hard optimization problems. The quality of solutions found by GAs is in many cases excellent. The method is also easy to understand and an exact mathematical formulation is not needed; it suffices to determine a suitable representation for the individuals and a pertinent crossover operator.

All the above benefits, however, are not earned for free: GAs often suffer from very long running times so that a common complaint on their usefulness deals with the practicality of the approach. This drawback is underlined in many practical applications of GAs which include complicated objective functions or time constraints for problem solving. In addition, there are many design alternatives to choose from, and the final efficiency often strongly depends on details of the design and parameter values.

To overcome the latter difficulty, adaptive GAs have been developed[12,13]. A *self-adaptive genetic algorithm for clustering* (*SAGA*) is described in Ref. 14. In this algorithm, each individual contains several parameter values in addition to the actual solution. SAGA was demonstrated to be very robust and to achieve excellent results. The main drawback of the method is the long running time. Fortunately, GAs are known to be easily parallelizable. Thus, using several interconnected processors one would expect to be able to reduce the actual running time considerably. Our primary goal is to speed up SAGA, but it is also interesting to see whether parallelization leads to algorithmic benefits as occasionally suggested. For a discussion of different models of parallelizing GAs and a literary survey, see Ref. 15. In Ref. 16 one can find in-depth mathematical analysis on different aspects of parallel GAs.

2. Clustering Problem

The clustering problem is defined as follows. Given a set of N data objects x_i, partition the data set into M clusters in such a way that similar objects are grouped together and dissimilar objects belong to different groups. Each object x_i has K *features* $x_i^{(k)}$. The features are assumed to be numerical and of the same scale. Mapping P defines a clustering by giving for each data object x_i the index p_i of the cluster it is assigned to. Furthermore, each cluster j has a *cluster representative* c_j.

We measure the *dissimilarity* (*distance*) between objects x_i and x_j by the *Euclidean distance*

$$d(x_i, x_j) = \sqrt{\sum_{k=1}^{K} (x_i^{(k)} - x_j^{(k)})^2}. \tag{1}$$

Our representation of a solution to the clustering problem includes both mapping and cluster representatives, i.e. a solution is of the form $\omega = (P, C)$ where $P = (p_1, \ldots, p_N)$ and $C = (c_1, \ldots, c_M)$. The objective is to find a solution with minimal *mean square error* (MSE), which is calculated as

$$e(\omega) = \frac{1}{NK} \sum_{i=1}^{N} d(x_i, c_{p_i})^2. \tag{2}$$

Given a mapping P, the optimal cluster representatives are the cluster *centroids*

$$c_j = \frac{\sum_{P_i=j} x_i}{\sum_{P_i=j} 1}, 1 \le j \le M, 1 \le i \le N. \tag{3}$$

The optimality of centroids leads to a simple and widely used clustering method, the *k-means* algorithm[17]. It improves an initial solution by repeatedly recalculating the cluster representatives using Eq. 3 and refining the mapping by assigning each object with the cluster which has the nearest representative. Even though the results of the k-means are usually modest, it is highly useful as a hill-climbing method in more complicated algorithms.

3. Self-Adaptive Genetic Algorithm for Clustering

The self-adaptive genetic algorithm (SAGA) applied here[14] uses *individual level self-adaptation*[12,13], where each individual consists of a candidate solution to the problem and a set of *strategy parameters*. An individual ι is of the form $\iota = (\omega_\iota, \gamma_\iota, \psi_\iota, \mu_\iota)$, where $\omega_\iota = (P_{\omega_\iota}, C_{\omega_\iota})$ is a solution. The inclusion of both mapping and representatives allows us to make several speed optimizations. The strategy parameters included in ι are *crossover method* γ_ι, *mutation probability* ψ_ι and *noise range* μ_ι.

The general structure of SAGA is show in Alg. 1. Six crossover methods are available: random multipoint, centroid distance, largest partitions, multipoint pairwise, one-point pairwise and pairwise nearest neighbor crossover. All these methods exploit some problem-specific knowledge instead of considering the solutions as plain bit strings. A detailed description and discussion of the algorithm can be found in Ref. 14.

(1) Generate S random individuals to form the initial generation.
(2) Iterate the following T times.
   (a) Select S_B surviving individuals for the new generation.
   (b) Select $S - S_B$ pairs of individuals as the set of parents.
   (c) For each pair of parents (ι_a, ι_b) do the following:
      i. Determine the strategy parameter values $(\gamma_{\iota_n}, \psi_{\iota_n}, \nu_{\iota_n})$ for the offspring ι_n by inheriting each of them randomly from ι_a or ι_b.
      ii. Mutate the strategy parameter values of ι_n with the probability Ψ (a predefined constant).
      iii. Create the solution ω_{ι_n} by crossing the solutions of the parents. The crossing method is determined by γ_{ι_n}.
      iv. Mutate the solution of the offspring with the probability ψ_{ι_n}.
      v. Add noise to ω_{ι_n}. The maximal noise is ν_{ι_n}.
      vi. Apply k-means iterations to ω_{ι_n}.
      vii. Add ι_n to the new generation.
   (d) Replace the current generation by the new generation.
(3) Output the best solution of the final generation.

Algorithm 1: Self-adaptive genetic algorithm for clustering (SAGA).

4. Parallel Self-Adaptive GA for Clustering

Our parallel GA (*ParSAGA*) uses the ***island parallelization*** model[18], where Q GAs run independently and communicate with each other. The processes are seen as islands which occasionally send individuals ("emigrants") to other islands. We have implemented island parallelization using a *genebank model.* In the genebank model, instead of sending emigrants directly to other islands, islands communicate only with the *genebank process.* The genebank process maintains a *genebank*, a population of the best B individuals received from islands. For the communication purposes, three steps need to be added to SAGA, see Alg. 2. The genebank process, see Alg. 3, requires very little processor time and thus if e.g. Q processors are available, it could be run in side of one of the island processes.

(2) (e) Send an individual to the genebank.
  (f) Receive an individual from the genebank and add it to the current population.
  (g) Remove an individual from the current population.

Algorithm 2: Steps added to SAGA for island processes.

(1) Select coordinates κ_q for each island q.
(2) Repeat the following steps until a stopping condition is fulfilled.
  (a) Sleep until an island process r makes a communication request.
  (b) Receive an individual ι_r from r.
  (c) Select an individual ι_s from the genebank.
  (d) Send ι_s to island r.
  (e) Add ι_r to the genebank.
  (f) If the genebank contains $B + 1$ individuals, remove the worst individual from the genebank.
(3) Return the solution of the best individual in the genebank.

Algorithm 3: Genebank process.

Each island process is assigned a two-dimensional coordinate $\kappa_i = (x_i, y_i)$, where $0 \leq x_i, y_i \leq 1$, corresponding to the "location of the island

i". The cost of traveling from location κ_i to κ_j is defined as:

$$d_t(\kappa_i, \kappa_j) = \sqrt{\begin{array}{l} \min(|y_i - y_j|, 1 - |y_i - y_j|)^2 + \\ \max \begin{pmatrix} \min(\frac{x_i - x_j}{w}, 1 - x_i + x_j), \\ \min(x_j - x_i, \frac{1 + x_i - x_j}{w}) \end{pmatrix}^2 \end{array}}. \quad (4)$$

The *direction control parameter* $w \in [0, 1]$ controls how much traveling from left to right is favored. The smaller the value of w, the stronger the imbalance in directions. Setting $w = 1$ gives no emphasis on the direction and $w = 0$ (which should be interpreted so that $\min(\frac{a}{0}, b) = b$) completely forbids traveling from right to left.

Note that if all the individuals in the genebank originate from the island making the communication request, the genebank process informs the island about this and sends no individual. As a result of this, the island process skips the steps 2(f) and 2(g).

The default, resulting in *island topology*, is to choose the coordinates κ_i randomly, let $w = 1$ and use *roulette wheel selection* with weights $\frac{1}{d_t(\kappa_s, \kappa_r)}$ for selecting an individual ι_s to be sent to island r from the genebank. Here κ_s is the location of the island ι_s originates from. The individuals originating from island r are not considered in selection.

This model is sufficiently general to allow us to employ several alternative network topologies. For example, the traditional *ring topology* is achieved by setting $\kappa_i = (\frac{i-1}{Q-1}, 0)$ for $i = 1, \ldots, Q$. The direction control parameter w controls whether the ring model is unidirectional ($w = 0$) or bidirectional ($w = 1$). Furthermore, island i is allowed to receive an individual from island j only if $d_t(\kappa_i, \kappa_j) \leq \sqrt{\frac{1}{Q-1}}$ (the distance between neighboring islands). *Torus topology*, where each processor is connected to four neighboring processors, can be realized by a similar setting in two dimensions.

Regarding the classification of parallel island GAs given by S.-C. Lin *et al.*[19], our parallel SAGA is an *asynchronous heterogeneous island GA with a static connection scheme*. The following settings for the migration parameters are applied:

- migration rate: one individual migrates
- migration frequency: migration occurs once in each generation
- migration topology: adjustable
- migration policy: several policies have been implemented, see Sec. 6.

Our model somewhat resembles the island model GA with a master processor used by F. J. Marin *et al.*[20]. However, they differ in three important aspects. First, our model allows emulating several different topologies by adjusting the activities of the control process. It also applies asynchronous emigration, which simplifies the management of the island processes and adds to efficiency. Finally, the GAs on the islands are self-adaptive. The adaptive parallel GA by S. Tongchim and P. Chongstitvatana[21] is also quite different. Their algorithm utilizes population level adaptation whereas ParSAGA adapts on individual level. Furthermore, ParSAGA applies a very flexible neighborhood topology.

Even though the method scales up well, one could consider a case with a very large number of objects, fast processors and a slow communications network. Then, problems may be caused by the transmission of the object-to-cluster mapping of size $\Theta(N)$ which happens in each communication. Fortunately, one can speed up the communication simply by discarding the mapping from the sent individual and recalculating it each time an island receives an individual.

5. Statistical Measures for the Island Model

The operation of a parallel GA can be evaluated by *genotypic measures* or *phenotypic measures*. Genotypic measures consider the data representation of objects whereas phenotypic measures consider properties of solutions, in practice usually the fitness. M. Capcarrère *et al.*[22] have considered the case of cellular parallel GAs and defined several measures for describing the advancement of an evolutionary algorithm. The genotypic measures, including frequency of transitions, entropy of population and diversity indices, are related to the number of duplicate solutions. The phenotypic measures include performance (i.e. average error of solutions), diversity and ruggedness, which measures the dependency of individual's fitness from its neighbor's fitness.

The genotypic measures seem not to be applicable to an island model with very few duplicates, and we therefore give new measures for the island model. On the other hand, the phenotypic measures are applicable also for the coarse-grained case and we recall them shortly.

We assume that there are Q islands, and island q has a population of size s_q. The individuals on island q are $I_q = \{\iota_{q,i} | i = 1, \ldots, s_q\}$.

5.1. *Genotypic measures*

Genotypic measures deal with the representation of individuals. They are therefore specific to the particular problem in question and to the coding of individuals. In order to define our genotypic measures we first need to define the dissimilarity of two individuals ι_1 and ι_2. We ignore the strategy parameter values and concentrate on calculating the difference between solutions ω_{ι_1} and ω_{ι_2}. By defining a bijective *assignment* $a_{1\leftrightarrow 2}(\omega_{\iota_1}, \omega_{\iota_2}) = \langle i, \alpha_{1\leftrightarrow 2}(i)\rangle (i = 1, \ldots, M)$ for the clusters in the solutions, we can calculate the dissimilarity of individuals ι_1 and ι_2 simply by summing up the distances between the representatives of the associated clusters:

$$\delta_b(\iota_1, \iota_2) = \sum_{i=1}^{M} d(c_{\omega_{\iota_1},i}, c_{\omega_{\iota_2},\alpha_{1\leftrightarrow 2}(i)}) \tag{5}$$

where $c_{\omega_{\iota_1},i}$ is the representative of the ith cluster in the solution of ι_1. The problem in using Eq. 5 is the proper selection of the assignment. The natural choice would be the assignment resulting to the smallest dissimilarity. Unfortunately, the problem of finding the optimal assignment is difficult. One could settle for a heuristically selected suboptimal assignment, but this would make the dissimilarity measure depend on the selection of the heuristic.

This problem can be solved by abandoning the demand for bijectivity. We define assignment $a_{1\to 2}$ so that each cluster of ω_{ι_1} is assigned with the nearest cluster in ω_{ι_2} measured by the distance between cluster representatives. Assignment $a_{2\to 1}$ is defined correspondingly. Now we can define the dissimilarity between ι_1 and ι_2 as the average of the distances calculated using these two assignments:

$$\delta_i(\iota_1, \iota_2) = \frac{1}{2}\left[\sum_{i=1}^{M} d(c_{\omega_{\iota_1},i}, c_{\omega_{\iota_2},\alpha_{1\to 2}(i)}) + \sum_{i=1}^{M} d(c_{\omega_{\iota_2},i}, c_{\omega_{\iota_1},\alpha_{2\to 1}(i)})\right]. \tag{6}$$

This is a computationally feasible definition since the two assignments can be determined in $\mathcal{O}(M^2K)$ time.

A completely different approach to defining dissimilarity is to concentrate on mappings instead of cluster representatives. A straightforward way to define dissimilarity using mappings is to define an $N \times N$ binary matrix $\mathbf{B}^{(\iota)}$ for mapping P_{ω_ι} so that $\mathbf{B}^{(\iota)}_{i,j} = 1$ iff $p_{\omega_\iota,i} = p_{\omega_\iota,j}$, i.e. objects i and j are mapped to the same cluster in solution ω_ι. The mapping dissimilarity of two individuals is the number of differing elements in the corresponding matrices:

$$\delta_m(\iota_1, \iota_2) = \sum_{i=1}^{N} \sum_{j=1}^{N} |\mathbf{B}_{i,j}^{(\iota_1)} - \mathbf{B}_{i,j}^{(\iota_2)}|. \tag{7}$$

Due to the size of the matrices the calculation of this dissimilarity measure takes $\mathcal{O}(N^2)$ time.

Now we can define the *average dissimilarity* $A^{(\delta)}(q)$ of island q as

$$A^{(\delta)}(q) = \sum_{i=1}^{s_q} \sum_{j=1}^{i-1} \frac{2\delta(\iota_{q,i}, \iota_{q,j})}{s_q(s_q - 1)} \tag{8}$$

and the *average dissimilarity of the island model* as

$$A^{(\delta)} = \frac{\sum_{q=1}^{Q} s_q(s_q - 1)A^{(\delta)}(q)}{\sum_{q=1}^{Q} s_q(s_q - 1)}. \tag{9}$$

Here any suitable dissimilarity measure δ can be applied resulting to e.g. *average assignment dissimilarity* $A^{(\delta_i)}$ and *average mapping dissimilarity* $A^{(\delta_m)}$. The average dissimilarity measures the diversity of the individuals. Obviously, it tends to zero as the population converges to several copies of a single individual. By observing the development of $A^{(\delta)}$ we can get an understanding on the speed of convergence.

5.2. *Phenotypic measures*

Since Eq. 2 is the optimization criterion of the solution, we can evaluate the population of an island by calculating the *average distortion on island* q

$$A^{(e)}(q) = \frac{1}{s_q} \sum_{i=1}^{s_q} e(\omega_{\iota_{q,i}}) \tag{10}$$

and the *standard deviation of distortion on island* q:

$$\sigma^{(e)}(q) = \sqrt{\frac{1}{s_q} \sum_{i=1}^{s_q} \left(A^{(e)}(q) - e(\omega_{\iota_{q,i}})\right)^2}. \tag{11}$$

Furthermore, we can define the *average distortion of the island model*

$$A^{(e)} = \frac{\sum_{q=1}^{Q} s_q A^{(e)}(q)}{\sum_{q=1}^{Q} s_q} \tag{12}$$

and the *standard deviation of distortion of the island model*

$$\sigma^{(e)} = \sqrt{\frac{\sum_{q=1}^{Q} s_q \left[(\sigma^{(e)}(q))^2 + \left(A^{(e)}(q) - A^{(e)}\right)^2\right]}{\sum_{q=1}^{Q} s_q}}. \tag{13}$$

The average distortion gives information on the progress of the algorithm and it can be compared to the distortion of the best solution for a rough view on diversity. The standard deviation of diversity measures phenotypic diversity more accurately.

6. Results

6.1. *Test setting*

We have used four different test problems, see Table 1. Three of them originate from the field of vector quantization and one from a biological application of clustering. *Bridge* consists of 4×4 pixel blocks sampled from a gray-scale image with image depth of 8 bits per pixel. *Bridge2* has the blocks of *Bridge* after a BTC-like quantization into two values according to the average pixel value of a block. The cluster representatives for *Bridge2* are rounded to binary vectors. *Lates mariae* contains data from pelagic fishes of Lake Tanganyika. The data originates from a research, in which the occurrence of 52 different DNA fragments was tested for each fish sample using RAPD analysis and a binary decision was obtained whether the fragment was present or absent. The cluster representatives are real vectors. *Miss America* has been obtained by subtracting two subsequent image frames of a video image sequence and constructing 4×4 pixel blocks from the residuals.

Table 1. Dimensions of the test problems

data set	attributes	objects	clusters
Bridge	16	4096	256
Bridge2	16	4096	256
Lates mariae	52	215	8
Miss America	16	6480	256

The parameters for SAGA are the default parameters from Ref. 14: parameter mutation probability $\Psi = 5\%$, number of k-means iterations $G = 2$, population size $S = 45$ and the roulette wheel selection method.

The tests were run on a single two-processor (400 MHz each) computer using 10 island processes thus emulating the situation of 10 interconnected computers. The communication costs are very low compared to the computational costs, so the results should be well comparable to the situation with an actual computer network. The amount of processor time consumed by each process was considered instead of the real time.

The statistical significance of differences has been verified by Student's t-test, $p < 0.05$.

6.2. *Test results*

ParSAGA was compared to seven other clustering algorithms, see Table 2. The results of k-means[17,23] and *stochastic relaxation* (SR)[24] are averages of 100 runs with random initializations. Divisive and agglomerative hierarchical methods are respectively represented by *splitting method with local repartitioning* (SLR)[25] and *Ward's method*[26]. These results were not repeated since the methods are deterministic. The results of *randomised local search* (RLS-2)[27], genetic algorithm (GA)[11], self-adaptive genetic algorithm (SAGA)[14] and ParSAGA are averages of 20 independent runs. GA and SAGA were run 1000 generations with a population of 45 individuals. ParSAGA was run 100 generations with 10 islands of 45 individuals. The result of a single ParSAGA run is the MSE of the best solution in the genebank after all islands have completed their run.

We observe that ParSAGA achieves results similar to SAGA, i.e. results of excellent quality whereas simpler methods give considerably weaker results. An exception here is *Lates mariae* for which, in addition to the GAs, RLS-2 arrives each time at the same result. While there is no significant difference between the results of ParSAGA and SAGA, the difference between ParSAGA and GA is significant on other sets than *Lates mariae* ($p = 4.6 * 10^{-10}$, $7.3 * 10^{-10}$, $3.0 * 10^{-9}$ for *Bridge*, *Bridge2* and *Miss America*, respectively). When comparing to other methods, the significance of difference is obvious. However, Ward's method reached almost as good a result for the easy problem *Lates mariae*. For the other problems Ward's method was less successful.

The rest of the results are for *Bridge* only and they are averages of 20 runs of 100 generations and 10 islands of 45 individuals as above. See Sec. 4 for the default migration topology parameters. Table 3 compares different migration policies. Best results are achieved by sending the best individuals and replacing the worst, as one would expect. Sending the best gives constantly better results than sending random individuals ($p = 8.3 * 10^{-8}$, 0.036, $6.5 * 10^{-5}$ for replacing worst, sent and random, respectively).

Also, replacing the sent individual seems to be a bad policy when the best is sent ($p = 0.0077$).

Table 4 compares three different migration topologies. The topology doesn't seem to have a great effect on results, at least with this small a number of islands, since the differences are not statistically significant.

The effect of the direction control parameter can be seen in Table 5. It turns out that restricting the direction of emigration ($w = 0$) is disadvantageous ($p = 0.040, 0.043$ for island and ring topology, respectively, for $w = 1$

Table 2. Comparison of clustering methods. The best result and the results not statistically significantly worse ($p < 0.05$) are boldfaced

	Bridge		*Bridge2*	
	av. MSE	st. dev	av. MSE	st. dev
k-means	180.073	1.442	1.489	0.015
SLR	170.221	0.000	1.362	0.000
Ward's method	169.253	0.000	1.429	0.000
SR	162.607	0.275	1.469	0.014
RLS-2	164.220	0.251	1.264	0.004
GA	161.403	0.089	1.263	0.004
SAGA	**161.183**	0.102	**1.252**	0.003
ParSAGA	**161.153**	0.100	**1.254**	0.003
	Lates mariae		*Miss America*	
	av. MSE	st. dev	av. MSE	st. dev
k-means	0.0703	0.0054	5.963	0.056
SLR	0.0662	0.0000	5.398	0.000
Ward's method	0.0627	0.0000	5.507	0.000
SR	0.0683	0.0045	5.265	0.013
RLS-2	**0.0626**	0.0000	5.262	0.019
GA	**0.0626**	0.0000	5.108	0.004
SAGA	**0.0626**	0.0000	**5.100**	0.003
ParSAGA	**0.0626**	0.0000	**5.099**	0.002

Table 3. Comparison of different migration policies

send	replace	av. MSE	st.dev.
best	worst	161.153	0.100
best	sent	161.262	0.140
best	random	161.195	0.098
random	worst	161.357	0.095
random	sent	161.347	0.105
random	random	161.344	0.111

versus $w = 0$).

Table 4. Comparison of different migration topologies

	av. MSE	st.dev.
island	161.153	0.100
ring	161.170	0.133
torus (2x5)	161.204	0.096

Table 5. Effect of the direction control parameter

	island topology		ring topology	
w	av. MSE	st.dev.	av. MSE	st. dev.
1	161.153	0.100	161.170	0.133
0.5	161.210	0.107	161.192	0.119
0	161.236	0.144	161.249	0.103

Increasing the genebank size from the default 20 to 100 did not give significant improvement. However, the difference between this result (161.117 with standard deviation of 0.098) and the result of SAGA (see Table 2) is significant ($p = 0.044$).

Figure 1 shows the speedup of ParSAGA in comparison to SAGA at various moments of time in two cases: 1000 generations of SAGA with a population of 45 individuals and 100 generations of SAGA with a population of 450 individuals. Speedup is calculated as a function of time so that speedup

$$s(t) = \frac{t}{T_{ParSAGA}(R_{SAGA}(t))} \tag{14}$$

where $R_{SAGA}(t)$ is the MSE of the best result found by SAGA after running t seconds (averaged over 20 runs) and $T_{ParSAGA}(R)$ is the time ParSAGA needs to find such a solution ω that $e(\omega) \leq R$ (also averaged over 20 runs). This approach has been selected because the methods are able to keep on finding better results and thus a single point of time for speedup observations can not be chosen justifiably. Since ParSAGA is run with 10 islands, speedup of 10 would be linear.

We observe that ParSAGA is very fast in comparison to SAGA with a large population even though this SAGA setting resembles more closely the setting of ParSAGA. This is because SAGA would need many more generations to successfully handle this large a population with the roulette-wheel selection. After 100 generations the average result is only 161.963 with standard deviation of 0.188. In ParSAGA, the large population is essentially divided into smaller intercommunicating populations thus resulting to excellent speedup. On the other hand, since ParSAGA in practice applies a considerably larger population than SAGA with a population of 45 individuals, it can preserve genetic variation longer and thus is still able to achieve regular progress when SAGA can only find better solutions occasionally. This is illustrated by the almost linear final portion of the 1000*45 curve.

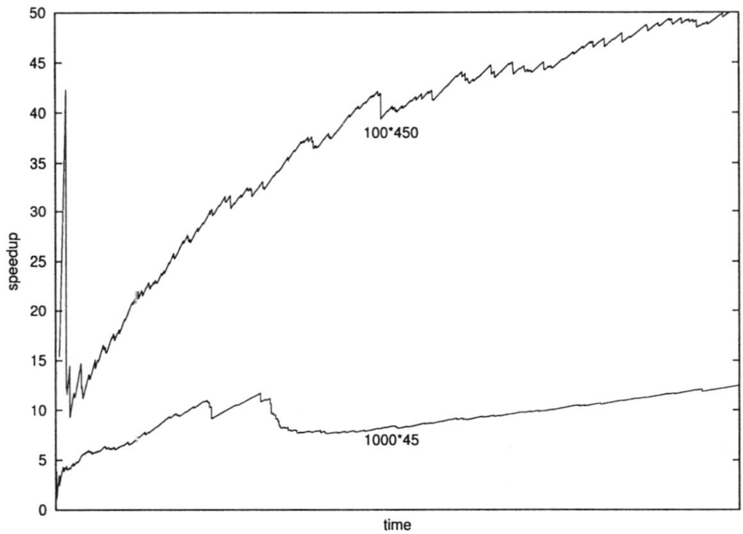

Fig. 1. Speedup of ParSAGA over 1000 generations of SAGA with a population of 45 individuals and 100 generations of SAGA with a population of 450 individuals as a function of time spent by SAGA

Figures 2 – 4 show the development of several statistical measures in three different cases. In Fig. 2 the default parameters are used, in Fig. 3 migration is performed only once every 10 generations (instead of every generation) and in Fig. 4 20 k-means iterations are applied to each solution instead of default 2. The diversity measures clearly show that reducing the migration frequency slows down the decline of diversity. This is probably most apparent in the graph of average assignment dissimilarity ($A^{(\delta_i)}$), but also the difference between average distortion ($A^{(e)}$) and best distortion as well as the standard deviation of distortion ($\sigma^{(e)}$) portray the same behavior. Increasing the number of k-means iterations leads to rapid decline of diversity in the beginning, as one would expect. However, after a while the diversity sets on roughly the same level as with the default parameters. It should be noted that due to the smart k-means implementation[23], 20 k-means iterations per solution is only slightly slower than the default 2. The increase of k-means iteration count does not change the quality of results significantly (161.122 with standard deviation of 0.104).

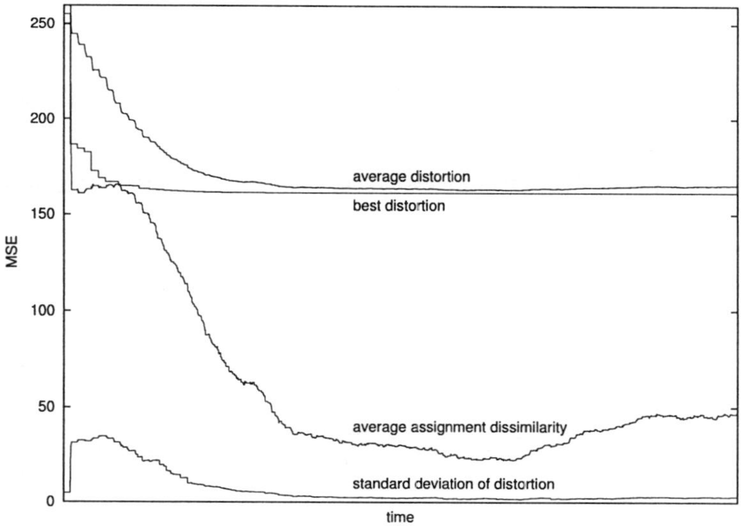

Fig. 2. Development of several measures for default parameters

The development of the average mapping dissimilarity ($A^{(\delta_m)}$) is shown in Fig. 5. Here, all the previous cases have been plotted in a single figure. Same observations as above can also be made from this figure.

One further thing to notice about the measures is the fact that even though the phenotypic diversity declines steadily, genotypic diversity can still occasionally increase noticeably. This might suggest that the search has found new promising areas of problem space to study closer.

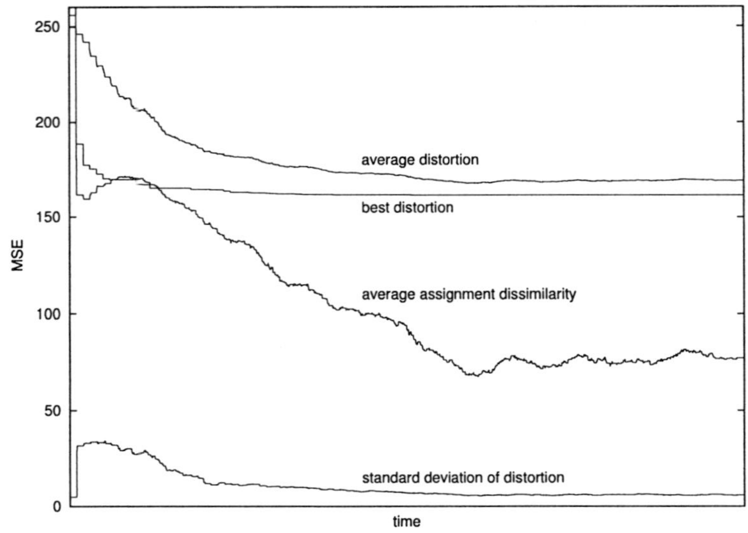

Fig. 3. Development of several measures for migration frequency once in 10 generations

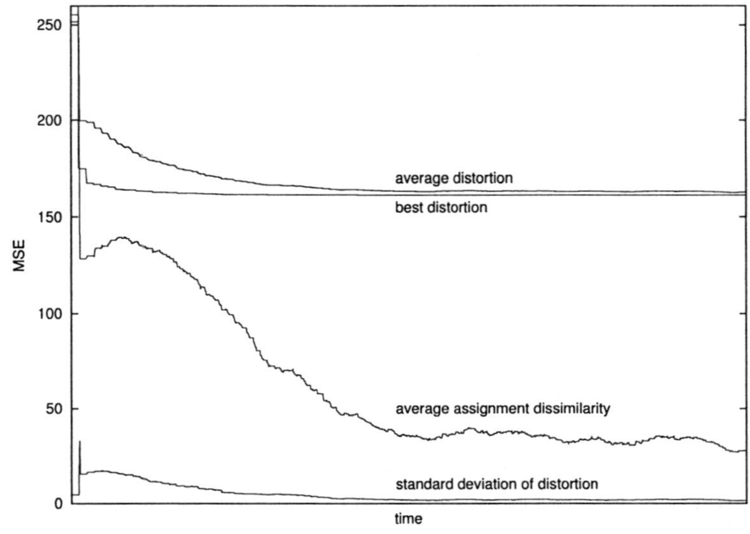

Fig. 4. Development of several measures for 20 k-means iterations per solution

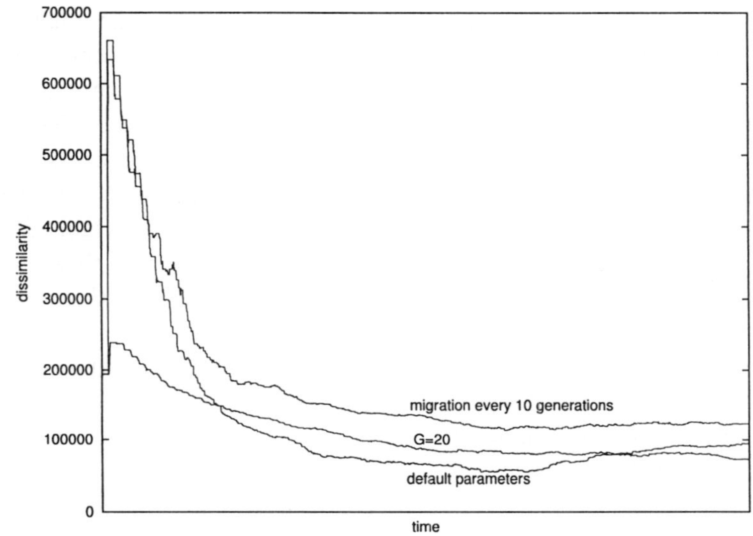

Fig. 5. Development of the average mapping dissimilarity for default parameters, for migration frequency once in 10 generations and for 20 k-means iterations per solution

7. Conclusions

Parallelization of a self-adaptive genetic algorithm for clustering was studied. Our parallel algorithm applied the genebank model for organizing the emigration. In the model, all the communication between SAGA processes is directed through the genebank process, which maintains a collection of the best individuals received. This general model has the advantage of allowing one to implement different topologies flexibly by simple parameter adjustments.

The parallel SAGA achieved results of the same quality as the sequential SAGA but in considerably shorter time. SAGA and ParSAGA outperform the other tested methods in all the cases except for the easy problem *Lates mariae* where several algorithms consistently reached the same solution (Table 2).

Speedup of ParSAGA was studied against two different SAGA setups (Fig. 1). When ParSAGA is compared to SAGA with a population of corresponding size, i.e. the number of islands times the population size of an island, ParSAGA is remarkably efficient. Superlinear speedup could be claimed here, even though it is obviously due to different functioning of the algorithms. This efficiency is explained by SAGA's inability to handle such a large population reasonably fast. On the other hand, when the population size of SAGA is set to the population size of a single island and the difference in the amount of work is compensated by increasing the number of generations, the speedup is close to linear. However, in this case the larger effective population size of ParSAGA allows it to retain more diversity and thus keep on finding better solutions more efficiently in the later stages of the search process. Thus, slight superlinearity could also be claimed here when the speedup is observed near the end of the search time chosen.

Comparison of different migration policies (Table 3) showed that sending the best and replacing the worst individuals is the most effective migration policy. This policy causes the highest selection pressure among the methods studied. Restricting the direction of migration turned out to be disadvantageous (Table 5) even though the selection of actual topology was found insignificant (Table 4).

We gave two new genotypic diversity measures for the parallel GA. Average assignment dissimilarity measures the average distances between matching cluster centroids of two individuals and average mapping dissimilarity compares two mappings.

Several things can be learned by observing the development of the statistical measures (Figs. 2 – 5). First, the measures clearly demonstrate that by reducing the frequency of migration, the decline of genetic variation can be effectively slowed down. Furthermore, the presented genotypic measures show that even though there are no considerable changes in diversity measured by phenotypic measures, genotypic diversity may still increase noticeably. This may be due to finding new promising areas to search.

Figure 4 demonstrates another interesting phenomenon. When the number of k-means iterations per solutions is increased to 20, diversity drops very fast in the beginning, as expected. However, even though phenotypic measures suggest that genetic variation stays very low, genotypic measures reveal that the diversity of solutions is actually similar to the default case. This also explains why this setting does not lead to inferior results even though the genetic variation seems to decrease rapidly when examined by ordinary phenotypic measures.

Finally, the usefulness of the statistical measures is not limited to learning important things about the behavior of the algorithm and the effect of different parameter settings. They could also be used in guiding the algorithm. Parameters controlling the operation could be adjusted according to the values of these measures. However, this would be more appropriate with other adaptation schemes, see Ref. 12. Since the calculation of measures is rather slow, one might consider calculating an approximation from a randomly selected sample instead of applying full measures.

References

1. B. S. Everitt, *Cluster Analysis (3rd ed.)* (Edward Arnold / Halsted Press, London, 1993).
2. L. Kaufman and P. J. Rousseeuw, *Finding Groups in Data: An Introduction to Cluster Analysis* (John Wiley & Sons, New York, 1990).
3. A. Gersho and R. M. Gray, *Vector Quantization and Signal Compression* (Kluwer, Dordrecht, 1992).
4. A. K. Jain and R. Dubes, *Algorithms for Clustering Data* (Prentice Hall, Englewood Cliffs, 1988).
5. A. K. Jain, M. N. Murty and P. J. Flynn, *ACM Comp. Surv.* **31**, 264 (1999).
6. T. Kaukoranta, *Iterative and Hierarchical Methods for Codebook Generation in Vector Quantization* (Turku Centre for Computer Science, Turku, 1999).
7. C. R. Reeves, Ed., *Modern Heuristic Techniques for Combinatorial Problems* (Blackwell, Oxford, 1993).
8. P. Fränti, J. Kivijärvi and O. Nevalainen, *Patt. Rec.* **31**, 1139 (1998).
9. J. H. Holland, *Adaptation in Natural and Artificial Systems* (University of Michigan Press, Ann Arbor, 1975).
10. D. E. Goldberg, *Genetic Algorithms in Search, Optimization and Machine Learning* (Addison-Wesley, Reading, 1989).
11. P. Fränti, J. Kivijärvi, T. Kaukoranta and O. Nevalainen, *Comp. J.* **40**, 547 (1997).
12. R. Hinterding, Z. Michalewicz and A. E. Eiben, in *Proc. 1997 IEEE International Conference on Evolutionary Computation* (IEEE, New York, 1997), p. 65.
13. G. Magyar, M. Johnsson and O. Nevalainen, *IEEE Trans. Evol. Comp.* **4**, 135 (2000).
14. J. Kivijärvi, P. Fränti and O. Nevalainen, *J. Heur.* **9**, 113 (2003).
15. J. Kivijärvi, J. Lehtinen and O. Nevalainen, TUCS Technical Report 469 (Turku Centre for Computer Science, Turku, 2002).
16. E. Cantú-Paz, *Efficient and Accurate Parallel Genetic Algorithms* (Kluwer, Boston, 2000).
17. J. B. McQueen, in *Proc. 5th Berkeley Symposium on Mathematical Statistics and Probability*, Eds. L. M. Le Cam and J. Neyman (University of California Press, Berkeley, 1967), p. 281.
18. M. Tomassini, in *Evolutionary Algorithms in Engineering and Computer Science*, Eds. K. Miettinen, M. M. Mäkelä, P. Neittaanmäki and J. Periaux (John Wiley & Sons, Chichester, 1999), p. 113.
19. S.-C. Lin, W. F. Punch and E. D. Goodman, in *Proc. 6th IEEE Symposium on Parallel and Distributed Processing* (IEEE, New York, 1994), p. 28.
20. F. J. Marin, O. Trelles-Salazar and F. Sandoval, in *Parallel Problem Solving from Nature - PPSN III, International Conference on Evolutionary Com-*

putation, Eds. Y. Davidor, H.-P. Schwefel and R. Männer (Springer-Verlag, New York, 1994), p. 534.
21. S. Tongchim and P. Chongstitvatana, in *Proc. 1st International Conference on Intelligent Technologies*, Eds. V. Kreinovich and J. Daengdej (Assumption University, Bangkok, 2000), p. 94.
22. M. Capcarrère, A. Tettamanzi, M. Tomassini and M. Sipper, *Evol. Comp.* **7**, 255 (1999).
23. T. Kaukoranta, P. Fränti and O. Nevalainen, *IEEE Trans. Image Proc.* **9**, 1337 (2000).
24. K. Zeger and A. Gersho, *Electronics Lett.* **25**, 896 (1989).
25. P. Fränti, T. Kaukoranta and O. Nevalainen, *Optical Engineering* **36**, 3043 (1997).
26. J. H. Ward, *J. American Stat. Ass.* **58**, 236 (1963).
27. P. Fränti and J. Kivijärvi, *Pattern Analysis & Appl.* **3**, 358 (2000).

CHAPTER 4

USING SIMD GENETIC PROGRAMMING FOR FAULT-TOLERANT TRADING STRATEGIES

Nils Svangård, Peter Nordin and Stefan Lloyd

Complex Systems Group, Chalmers University of Technology
SE-41296 Gothenburg, Sweden
E-mail: nils@svangard.org, peter.nordin@mc2.chalmers.se

In this chapter we study the effects of representing a traditional portfolio optimization problem as a classification task in order to reduce the computational cost, and finding more reliable solutions. We use N-Version Genetic Programming to represent the market as a binary classification problem, and evolve two trading strategies that independently look for either buy, or sell, opportunities in parallel. The system is made more fault-tolerant using majority voting for the investment decisions. As inputs to our system we use a large number of instruments from technical analysis, which allows us to increase the execution speed over 100 times using a Sub-Machine-Code Genetic Programming system that evaluates 128 fitness cases in parallel. We see that the strategies generalize well and outperform the buy-and-hold strategy on simulated out-of-sample trading, so there is a clear connection between good classification results and returns on trading. We also see that the n-version voting system can successfully be used to reduce risk. Finally we see that some of the technical analysis instruments appear more frequently than others in the most successful strategies, which could be an indication on actual correlations to the future share price.

1. Introduction

When trying to build an automatic trading system based on soft computation techniques it has been quite popular to use various forms of

Technical Analysis (TA) as inputs. Common techniques for TA include strategies based on relative strength, moving averages, as well as support and resistance. The majority of researchers that have tested technical trading systems have found that prices adjust rapidly to stock market information and that technical analysis techniques are not likely to provide any advantage to investors who use them. In fact, the vast majority of studies of technical theories have found the strategies to be of little use in predicting securities prices[1,2].

Despite the vast amount of research rejecting technical analysis as a trading strategy, there are still market practitioners who use it extensively, and who also claim to be successful[3,4]. Even though many empirical tests have rejected technical analysis using the established methods, recent research in adaptive systems, and Genetic Programming in particular, have proved to be harder to reject. Tests using GP to evolve trading strategies, as a form of technical analysis, have proven successful[5-9], and compared to neural networks genetic programming have the advantage that they produce solutions that are easier to interpret by the user. This is especially useful, and interesting, when it comes to analyzing trading systems.

Most applications of genetic programming on financial problems either treat it as a time series prediction problem, or as a portfolio optimization problem. We argue that it could just as well be seen as a traditional classification problem where you try to determine whether it is a good opportunity to buy, or sell, stocks at a particular time, and that this allows us to breed strategies faster (in terms of computational time) and also produce more reliable solutions using fault-tolerant voting systems.

One popular approach to software fault tolerance employs multiple versions of the same software to mask the effect of faults when a minority of versions fails[17]. Design diversity, *i.e.*, several diverse development efforts, has been proposed as a technique for generating these redundant versions. The difference in the programs, which is generated by the different design methods, is called software diversity. The hope is that the diversity in the programs will make them exhibit different failure behavior; they should not fail for the same input and, if they do, they should not fail in the same manner.

There are two main drawbacks with the approach of design diversity: (1) it is not obvious if and how we can guarantee that the programs fail independently and (2) the life cycle cost of the software will likely increase. The original idea of N-version programming (NVP) opted for the specification of the software to be given to different development teams[17]. The teams should independently develop a solution, and this independence between the teams should manifest itself in independent failure behavior. Since there are many ways to control the evolution of the GP solutions they do not suffer from the problems or cost the human software development personnel have. On the contrary it is very easy to control the diversity of the evolution and you can even incorporate solutions from different methods into one large solution. In our case we ensure software diversity by breeding strategies that either look for sell, or buy, opportunities in parallel, and use a majority voting system to decide which action to take at any point in time.

When working with binary classification problems like this it is tempting to make all inputs discrete binary signals since this allows us to execute many fitness cases in parallel on a regular workstation using a Sub-Machine-Code GP (SMCGP)[10,11]. Sub-machine-code GP systems treat every bit of the variables as an individual register, and this allows us to speed up GP over 100 times by exploiting the internal parallelism of sequential CPU's.

We believe this is the first work that applies genetic programming on the financial market as a classification problem and think that the discrete representation will produce more generalized solutions compared to traditional systems.

2. Background

This section intends to give a brief introduction to N-Version Genetic Programming and Sub-Machine-Code Genetic Programming.

2.1. *N-Version Genetic Programming*

In the software and engineering industry there have been several attempts to safeguard the systems from unpredictable scenarios and errors by increasing the fault tolerance in various ways. One popular approach to software fault tolerance employs multiple versions of the same software to mask the effect of faults when a minority of versions fails[17]. Design diversity, *i.e.*, several diverse development efforts, has been proposed as a technique for generating these redundant versions. The difference in the programs, which is generated by the different design methods, is called software diversity. The hope is that the diversity in the programs will make them exhibit different failure behavior; they should not fail for the same input and, if they do, they should not fail in the same manner.

There are two main drawbacks with the approach of design diversity: (1) it is not obvious if and how we can guarantee that the programs fail independently and (2) the life cycle cost of the software will likely increase. The original idea of N-version programming (NVP) opted for the specification of the software to be given to different development teams. The teams should independently develop a solution, and this independence between the teams should manifest itself in independent failure behavior.

Some researches have with success tried to use genetic programming to generate the different software versions for NVP-problems[18,19]. Since there are many ways to control the evolution of the GP solutions they do not suffer from the problems or cost the human software development personnel have. On the contrary it is very easy to control the diversity of the evolution and you can even incorporate solutions from different soft-computation methods into one large solution.

Instead of using only one solution as traditional GP-systems does, our Fault-Tolerant Genetic Programming system tries to embrace the N-version programming philosophy by taking the best solutions from many independent evaluations of the problem and combining them as the final solution using majority voting. We argue that every single solution is likely to have found some important parts of the optimal problem solution but is unlikely to have found all. Thus, when combining many such partial solutions we should get a better, more reliable and accurate solution to the problem.

2.2. *Sub-Machine-Code Genetic Programming*

Since financial problems usually require the same strategy to be executed a large number of times on long time series, these experiments can benefit greatly from being executed in parallel. This is especially the cased when applied on intra-day data[12].

We implemented a sub-machine-code system using linear genomes on a PowerMac G4 system. The G4 CPU is very interesting for sub-machine-code as well as other parallel GP-systems since they are equipped with a number of "vector units". These units handle SIMD (Single Instruction Multiple Data) operations on vectors of 128-bit data through a very intuitive C API[13]. We believe this is the first experiment that explicitly uses Apple's AltiVec technology for a GP-system.

In this implementation we treated every bit of the vectors as a register, and thus we were able to evaluate 128 fitness cases in parallel at the cost of only one clock cycle per GP-instruction. This required that we limited the instruction set to the standard binary operations (and, or, xor, not) and avoided conditional jumps or feedback variables which we argue is a small drawback for such a dramatic increase in computational power.

3. Method

For these experiments we built a register based Genetic Programming system working with linear genomes. In order to speed up the evaluation of genomes we automatically removed introns before execution by processing the genome backwards and removing all but the instructions accessing registers previously written to. We also generated the "human-readable" expressions seen in the results in a similar way. We used tournament based evolution and the standard genetic operators.

3.1. *Input Data*

As the inputs to our system we used focused on a single stock (PHA) from the Swedish stock market. The data had been sampled on a daily basis from 1998-01-02 to 2002-04-12, and we used the bid price, and the traded volume of a share, to calculate a number of measures from technical analysis for every sample. These were:

(i) Moving average of the price and volume (MA)
(ii) Linear trend of the price and volume (by linear regression)
(iii) Linear trends of all moving averages (by linear regression)
(iv) Rate of change (ROC)
(v) Momentum of the price

These values were all calculated for the past 3, 5, 10, 20 and 50 days. The ROC and momentum were also calculated for a single day.

This summed up to a total of 70 binary indicators and 973 samples (including the out-of-sample data, but with the first 100 samples discarded since they were used to calculate the initial moving averages).

These values were then converted into binary signals. The trends, ROC and momentum took a value of 1 if they are less than or equal to zero, otherwise 0. The moving averages were compared to the current price, and if it was greater than or equal to the current prize it took a value of 1, otherwise 0.

3.2. *Classification Signals*

We use this system to classify two different signals in parallel. The first signal is 1 when we can sell a share of stock in n days at a higher price than today, and otherwise 0. The other signal is 1 if we can buy a share at a lower price than it has today in n days, and otherwise 0. For a value of n greater than 1 these signals are not mutually exclusive. From now on we will call these signals "Buy" and "Sell" respectively.

One of the goals of this chapter is to study how various values of n affect the performance of the system, which we will discuss in further detail in Section 4.

3.3. *Fitness Function*

One problem with classification with genetic programming on data where there are more cases of either true or false signals, is that solutions that always return true (or false) can get an advantage over more general solutions and thus affect the evolution negatively. We tried to avoid this problem by calculating the percentage of correct classifications of both true (C1), and false (C0), classification cases independently, *i.e.*, the average precision of the classifier.

The final fitness is then one minus the average of these two values as can be seen in Equation 1. Thus a fitness value of 0 means perfect classification with all cases correct. A fitness value of 0.5 is approximately the result we will get if we flip a coin for each case and a fitness value of 1 means we did not classify any case correctly.

$$f(x) = 1 - \frac{C1(x) + C0(x)}{2} \tag{1}$$

3.4. *Parallel Evolution*

In order to ensure software diversity for the N-Version Programming system we evolve the buy and sell classifiers in parallel, but independently of each other. After a fixed number of runs we calculate the performance of the most successful individuals from both classification problem, and apply them on the out-of-sample data set.

We also determine the strategies actual performance as portfolio managers in a simulated trading system. Both strategies are executed simultaneously on every sequential sample (of the out-of-sample data) and signal whether it's time to buy or sell. Then the trading logic (a simple majority voting system) determines whether we should actually buy or sell our holdings at that particular time. See Fig. 1 for a diagram of the system architecture.

In our implementation we test two different voting systems:

(i) We listen to either strategy (*i.e.*, we buy when buy-strategy returns a true value, and sell when the sell-strategy returns a true value)

(ii) We listen to both the buy and sell strategy and only act if they agree (*i.e.*, we buy if the buy-strategy returns a true value, and the sell-strategy returns a false value)

At the end of this simulation we calculate the performance of these different portfolios and compare it with the simple "buy and hold" strategy.

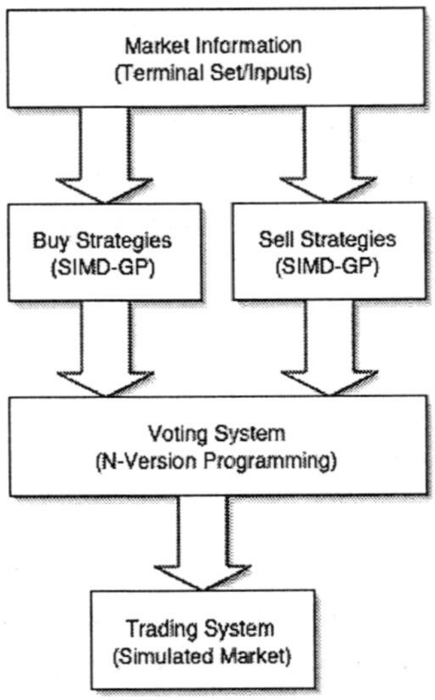

Fig. 1. A diagram illustrating the system architecture and the flow of information

4. Experiments

Short of just studying whether this method is applicable on evolving trading signals we carry out a number of experiments that study how various setups of the original system affect it's performance:

(i) Classification signals. We study how the choice of the time frame for capitalization on investments, used for determining the buy and sell signals, affect the systems performance. The time intervals we test are 1, 3, 5 and 10 days.

(ii) Use of input signals. For the most successful strategies we study which inputs they use, and calculate the frequencies of their appearance.

(iii) Voting systems. We study the effects on using a voting system where both the buy and sell strategy have to agree, compared to if they may act individually.

5. Results

For these experiments we used a population size of 2500 individuals and evolved it for 1000 generations. All experiments are repeated 10 times independently of each other and the results are averaged.

The training fitness values are the value of the best strategy in the last generation, while the best validation fitness is the best validation fitness of the strategy with the best training fitness ever seen during evolution. The best strategies are then applied on the out-of-sample data to generate the trading results and "applied" fitness values.

The training data set is composed of the first 768 samples, the validation set the following 128 days, and finally the out-of-sample (applied) data set is the remaining 77 samples.

5.1. *Classification Results*

Table 1-8 contains the mean fitness values and the standard deviation for all experiments, averaged over the ten independent runs.

One interesting observation is that based on the training fitness it seems like the sell-classification task is harder than buy-classification. In a similar way we can also see that it's harder to find strategies for the short classifications (*i.e.,* 1- & 3-day classification) rather than 5- & 10-day classifications.

Table 1. Average fitness values for 1-day "buy" classifications

Data set	Mean	Best	Worst	σ
Training	0.397	0.357	0.424	0.024
Validation	0.481	0.458	0.509	0.019
Applied	0.456	0.312	0.729	0.128

Table 2. Average fitness values for 1-day "sell" classifications

Data set	Mean	Best	Worst	σ
Training	0.416	0.406	0.430	0.006
Validation	0.460	0.415	0.477	0.016
Applied	0.739	0.395	0.875	0.159

Table 3. Average fitness values for 3-day "buy" classifications

Data set	Mean	Best	Worst	σ
Training	0.407	0.357	0.419	0.022
Validation	0.506	0.439	0.525	0.027
Applied	0.337	0.267	0.6	0.103

Table 4. Average fitness values for 3-day "sell" classifications

Data set	Mean	Best	Worst	σ
Training	0.396	0.382	0.415	0.011
Validation	0.431	0.405	0.460	0.014
Applied	0.562	0.345	0.828	0.150

Table 5. Average fitness values for 5-day "buy" classifications

Data set	Mean	Best	Worst	σ
Training	0.369	0.261	0.412	0.043
Validation	0.491	0.431	0.551	0.031
Applied	0.534	0.273	0.773	0.208

Table 6. Average fitness values for 5-day "sell" classifications

Data set	Mean	Best	Worst	σ
Training	0.397	0.368	0.415	0.013
Validation	0.416	0.393	0.457	0.018
Applied	0.499	0.429	0.667	0.091

Table 7. Average fitness values for 10-day "buy" classifications

Data set	Mean	Best	Worst	σ
Training	0.307	0.220	0.384	0.054
Validation	0.437	0.416	0.468	0.019
Applied	0.586	0.2	0.8	0.208

Table 8. Average fitness values for 10-day "sell" classifications

Data set	Mean	Best	Worst	σ
Training	0.351	0.291	0.375	0.025
Validation	0.429	0.404	0.509	0.032
Applied	0.461	0.444	0.50	0.025

5.2 *Trading*

Table 9-12 contains the return of the best trading strategies when allowed to trade on the out-of-sample data. Below each table we list the best buy and sell strategy for each experiment. Table 13 contains a legend of the inputs used by the best strategies, and finally Fig. 2 shows an example of how the 1-day trading strategy behaves on the out-of-sample data.

All but one of the runs makes positive return on the out-of-sample data, which is very encouraging results. Also, all but one other strategy performs better than the Buy-and-hold strategy, thus beating the trend with active trading. It is also interesting to see that even though the precision of the classifier can be slightly worse than the baseline, the trading results can be quite good. The 5-day classifier is a good example of this behavior. The reason for this is probably that trends in the market are (at least) a couple of days long, so the classifier doesn't have to find the extreme points of the trend but can buy in the middle of a trend and still make a good profit.

Another interesting observation is that the system appears to be exploiting some kind of cyclic, or rebound-, market behavior. A slightly simplified example of this behavior is the 1-day strategies that in essence will buy if the 5-day trend is negative, and sell if the 5-day trend is positive. This could possibly be explained by that investors are prone to play it safe and divest their holdings after a few days positive market to claim their profit.

Table 9. Returns on trading for 1-day classification strategies

Strategy	Mean	Best	Worst	σ
Buy and hold	1.036	-	-	-
Buy or Sell	1.130	1.197	1.043	0.044
Buy and not Sell	1.150	1.190	1.027	0.049
Buy strategy	(v[6] OR ((v[19] OR v[44]) AND v[25]))			
Sell strategy	(NOT (v[5] AND (NOT (v[30] AND v[49]))))			

Table 10. Returns on trading for 3-day classification strategies

Strategy	Mean	Best	Worst	σ
Buy and hold	1.036	-	-	-
Buy or Sell	0.989	1.101	0.941	0.060

Buy and not Sell	1.042	1.142	0.977	0.049
Buy strategy	(EITHER v[5] OR (v[43] AND v[26]))			
Sell strategy	(NOT ((v[8] OR v[51]) AND v[5]))			

Table 11. Returns on trading for 5-day classification strategies

Strategy	Mean	Best	Worst	σ
Buy and hold	1.036	-	-	-
Buy or Sell	1.068	1.183	0.925	0.089
Buy and not Sell	1.038	1.183	0.940	0.078
Buy strategy	(v[6] OR (v[2] AND v[40]))			
Sell strategy	(NOT (v[3] OR (EITHER v[39] OR v[9])))			

Table 12. Returns on trading for 10-day classification strategies

Strategy	Mean	Best	Worst	σ
Buy and hold	1.036	-	-	-
Buy or Sell	1.092	1.154	0.929	0.068
Buy and not Sell	1.025	1.122	0.950	0.045
Buy strategy	(v[25] OR v[6])			
Sell strategy	(NOT (v[33] OR v[4]))			

Table 13. Legend to the inputs used by the trading strategies

Input	Signal
2	Current price is greater than 10-day mean
3	Current price is greater than 20-day mean
4	Current price is greater than 50-day mean
5	3-day trend is negative
6	5-day trend is negative
8	20-day trend is negative
9	50-day trend is negative
19	50-day trend of volume is negative
25	5-day trend of 3-day mean is negative
26	5-day trend of 5-day mean is negative
30	10-day trend of 3-day mean is negative
33	10-day trend of 50-day mean is negative
39	20-day trend of 50-day mean is negative
40	50-day trend of 3-day mean is negative
43	50-day trend of 20-day mean is negative
44	50-day trend of 50-day mean is negative
49	3-day trend of 50-day mean volume is negative
51	5-day trend of 5-day mean volume is negative

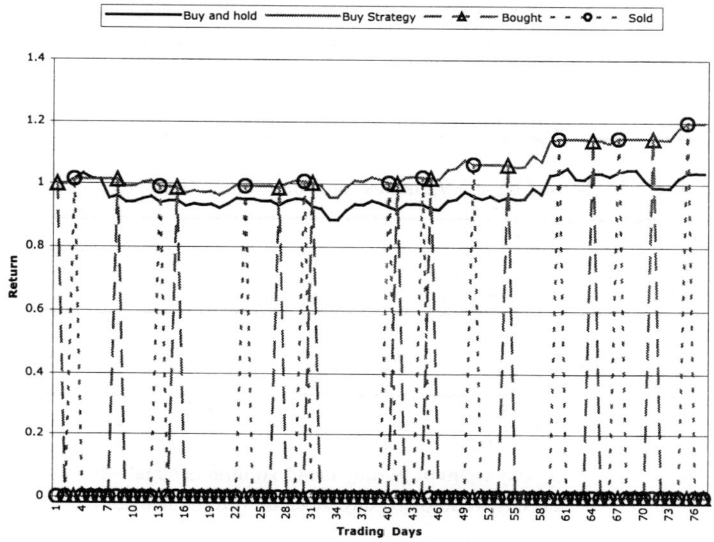

Fig. 2. The return of the 1-day trading strategy (the grey line) compared to return on the passive buy and hold strategy (the black line) on out-of-sample test data. The dashed line with triangle marks indicates at what point in time the trading strategy bought shares and respectively the dotted line with circle marks indicates where the shares were sold

5.3. *Use of Input Signals*

Table 14-21 list the most frequent variables used by the best strategies on validation data, the frequency is averaged over the best strategies from each of the 10 independent runs.

One interesting observation is the heavy use of the 5-day trend, and also that the short-term strategies focus on short instruments, while the long-term (or rather, longer-term) strategies more heavily uses the long-term instruments.

Table 14. Most frequent variables for 1-day "buy" strategies

Frequency	Signal
100%	5-day trend is negative
90%	5-day trend of 3-day average is negative

Table 15. Most frequent variables for 1-day "sell" strategies

Frequency	Signal
90%	5-day trend is negative
70%	5-day trend of 3-day average is negative

Table 16. Most frequent variables for 3-day "buy" strategies

Frequency	Signal
90%	3-day trend is negative
70%	5-day trend of 20-day mean is negative

Table 17. Most frequent variables for 5-day "buy" strategies

Frequency	Signal
80%	5-day trend is negative
50%	50 day trend of 50-day mean volume is negative
40%	20-day trend of 10-day mean of volume is negative
40%	5 day trend of 20-day mean is negative
30%	3 day trend is negative

Table 18. Most frequent variables for 5-day "sell" strategies

Frequency	Signal
60%	Price is higher than 50-day mean

Table 19. Most frequent variables for 10-day "buy" strategies

Frequency	Signal
80%	5-day trend is negative
50%	50-day trend of 50-day mean volume is negative
40%	5-day trend of 3-day mean is negative
40%	50-day trend of 50-day mean is negative
40%	20-day trend of 10-day mean volume is negative

Table 20. Most frequent variables for 10-day "sell" strategies

Frequency	Signal
60%	Price is higher than 50-day mean
60%	10-day trend of 20-day mean is negative
40%	20-day trend of 3-day mean volume is negative

6. Discussion

It appears like the short-term classification problem (1- and 3-day capitalization window) is a much harder than the other cases. We base this observation on that the training fitness is worse for these experiments than the others. However, when applied on the out-of-sample data the 1-day strategy yield a far superior return on an average compared to the other experiments, and we believe this is the result of a more aggressive trading behavior than seen in the other experiments. It is also interesting to see that almost all strategies outperform the buy-and-hold strategy on an average and that they do this even when their classification precision is slightly lower than the baseline.

Individual strategies appear to yield a higher return on average, than when both buy and sell strategies have to agree. This is not unexpected since the combined trading strategy will generate fewer signals than the individual strategy. However, the return of the combined strategy appears to be more stable (less standard deviation), and will be a less risky strategy to use. When the classification results for the individual strategies are bad, the combined strategy performs better than the individual strategies on trading since they will filter away some of the noisy and incorrect signals when they do not agree.

It is also interesting to see that there seem to be some common inputs used among the successful strategies. In particular the 3- and 5-day strategies focus on the 3- and 5-day trend respectively, while the 10-day strategies focus on long trends and means.

7. Future Research

Even though the system is quite fast as it is, its performance could be significantly improved if it directly evolved machine code instead of interpreted code. Using AIMGP this could probably improve the performance up to 30 times[14-16].

One problem with time series based on daily quotes is that the close price is not always correctly calculated, nor does it fully reflect the market dynamics of that day's trades. This suggests using intra-day data might be more efficient, and worth investigating further.

8. Conclusion

We found that treating the financial problem as a classification problem work very well, and on an average the strategies outperform the buy and hold strategy on average when trading on unseen data. In other words there seem to be a clear correlation between good classification results and positive trading results. The strategies also generalize quite well, and appear to find correlations between the technical analysis instruments and the future price of the stock.

Finally we concluded that making investment decisions based on multiple strategies in a voting systems yields almost as high return as individual strategies, but it reduces risk and the number of bad investments, which is a good thing.

We believe evolving trading strategies based on the classification problem shows great promise and should be investigated further.

References

1. E.F Fama, Random Walks in Stock Market Prices, *Financial Analysts Journal*, September/October 1965
2. F. Allen, and R. Karjalainen, Using genetic algorithms to find technical trading rules, *Working paper at Rodney L*, White centre for Financial Research, 1995
3. M. Taylor and H. Allen, The use of technical analysis in the foreign exchange market, *Journal of International Money and Finance*, 11, 1992, pp. 304-314
4. F.K. Reilly, *Investment Analysis and Portfolio Management*, 4th ed, published by Dryden Press, 1994
5. E.P.K. Tsang and J. Li, Improving technical analysis predictions: An application of Genetic Programming, in *Proceedings of 12th annual Florida Artificial Intelligence International Research Conference* (FLAIRS 99), May 1999
6. E.P.K. Tsang and J. Li, Investment decision making using FGP - A case study, 2000
7. C. Fyfe, J.P Marney and H. Tarbert, Technical trading versus market efficiency - A Genetic Programming, *Applied Financial Economics*, 1999
8. C. Fyfe, J.P Marney, H. Tarbert and D. Miller, Technical analysis versus market efficiency: the quest continues, Barcelona: *Computing in economics and finance*, 2000
9. H. Iba and T. Sasaki, Financial data prediction by means of Genetic Programming, 2000
10. P. Riccardo and W. B. Langdon, Submachine-code Genetic Programming, Technical Report CSRP-98-18, University of Birmingham, School of Computer Science, August 1998

11. P. Riccardo, Sub-Machine-Code GP: New results and Extensions
12. N. Svangård, S. Lloyd, P. Nordin and C. Wihlborg, Evolving short-term trading strategies using Genetic Programming, *Congress on Evolutionary Computation*, 2002
13. Apple's AltiVec Home Page, http://developer.apple.com/hardware/ve/
14. P. Nordin, A compiling genetic programming system that directly manipulates the machine code, In Kenneth E. Kinnear, Jr. editor, *Advances in Genetic Programming*, chapter 14, pages 311-331, MIT Press, 1994
15. P. Nordin, Evolutionary Program Induction of Binary Machine Code and its Applications, PhD thesis, der Universitat Dortmund am Fachereich Informatik, 1997
16. P. Nordin, AIMGP: A formal description, In John R. Koza, editor, *Late breaking Papers at the Genetic Programming 1998 Conference*, University of Wisconsin, Madison, Wisconsin, USA, 22-25 July 1998, Standford
17. Avizienis and L. Chen, On the implementation of N-version programming for software fault-tolerance during program execution, *Proc. of COMPSAC-77*, 1977, pp. 149-155
18. K. Imamura and J. A. Foster, Fault-Tolerant Computing with N-Version Genetic Programming, In *Proceedings of the Genetic and Evolutionary Computation Conference* (GECCO-2001), 2001
19. R. Feldt, Generating multiple diverse software versions using genetic programming, *Euromicro Conference 1998*, August 1998, Västerås, Sweden

CHAPTER 5

AN EFFICIENT COEVOLUTIONARY ALGORITHM BASED ON MERGING AND SPLITTING OF SPECIES

Myung Won Kim, Soungjin Park and Joung Woo Ryu

School of Computing, Soongsil University
1-1, Sangdo 5-Dong, Dongjag-Gu, Seoul, Korea
E-mail: mkim@comp.ssu.ac.kr, comark@ilkr.com, ryu0914@orgio.net

A coevolutionary algorithm is an extension of the conventional genetic algorithm that incorporates the strategy of divide and conquer in developing a complex solution in the form of interacting co-adapted subcomponents. It takes advantage of the reduced search space by evolving species associated with subsets of variables independently but cooperatively. In this chapter we propose an efficient coevolutionary algorithm combining species splitting and merging together. Our algorithm conducts efficient local search in the reduced search space by splitting species for independent variables while it conducts global search by merging species for interdependent variables. We have experimented the proposed algorithm with several benchmarking function optimization problems and the inventory control problem, and have shown that the algorithm outperforms existing coevolutionary algorithms.

1. Introduction

Evolutionary algorithm is a general and efficient optimization method and it is successfully applied to various problems including resource management, scheduling, and pattern recognition. However, one of the common problems of the algorithm is that search time grows exponentially as the dimension of search space expands.

Recently, attempts have been made to improve the search speed of the evolutionary algorithm. Potter and De Jong have proposed the cooperative coevolutionary algorithm which improves the search speed significantly[1]. In the algorithm a complete solution is divided into a set of subcomponents corresponding to a single variable called species each of which evolves independently but cooperatively. Each species evolves independently using its own evolution strategy and it corresponds to the search of the 1-dimensional space of a single variable and consequently it allows efficient search. In the algorithm, however, each species cooperates with other species in such a way that an individual of the species is evaluated by evaluating a complete chromosome that is assembled from itself and the best individuals of other species. In this way species evolves independently but cooperatively. And it shows especially good results when it is applied to the problems of concept learning[2] and the task assignment problem between agents[3]. But the method can be even less efficient than ordinary algorithms in particular cases that there are lots of Nash equilibrium points and that variables are strongly interdependent. In order to overcome this problem, K. Weicker and N. Weicker proposed adaptive cooperative coevolution algorithm with which they solved the problem by combining species representing variables if there is variable interdependency[4]. But when most variables are interdependent with one another and after combining all species representing the variables, evolutionary speed sharply decreases as it does in ordinary algorithms due to the rapid expansion of the search space.

In this chapter we propose a new coevolutionary algorithm as an improvement of Weickers' algorithm. In our algorithm species are not only merged but also split into subcomponent species if necessary. Merging species allows more global but slow evolutionary search while splitting species allows local but fast evolutionary search. Efficiency can be achieved by combining species merging and splitting appropriately. We use variable interdependency as a decision criterion for dynamically controlling species merging and species splitting. In our algorithm species are split when variables are independent while species are merged when variables are interdependent.

The chapter is organized as follows. In Section 2 we describe existing evolution algorithms and compare them with our algorithm. In

Section 3 we describe our algorithm based on merging and splitting of species in detail. Section 4 describes the experimental results of our algorithm on the benchmarking function optimization problems, and the inventory control problem. Finally, we draw a conclusion of the chapter.

2. Existing Coevolutionary Algorithms

2.1. *Cooperative Coevolution*

Conventional genetic algorithm, proposed by John Holland is a general and global search method based on the natural selection and evolution mechanism. Genetic algorithm initializes and maintains a population of chromosomes that encode potential solutions to a given problem. Each chromosome is generally a fixed length sequence of bits put in order. The algorithm is depicted in Fig. 1 and the brief explanation of the procedure is described in the following.

```
procedure SimpleGA
  begin
    t=0
    initialize( p_t )
    evaluation( p_t )
    while not termination-criteria do
    begin
      t=t+1
      p_t = reproduction( p_{t-1} )
      p_t = crossover( p_t )
      p_t = mutation( p_t )
    end
  end
```

Fig. 1. Convertional Genetic Algorithm

First, the initial population of chromosomes are generated usually at random. Then each chromosome of the population is evaluated resulting in the fitness score. Genetic operators such as crossover and mutation are applied to generate a new population of chromosomes. Crossover generates two offspring chromosomes from their parent chromosomes by exchanging parts of the parent chromosomes. In crossover, parent chromosomes are selected in such a way that more fit chromosomes are more likely selected. Mutation randomly changes small segments of a chromosome in order to introduce a diversity of chromosomes. This process of generating a new population and evaluation is repeated until the termination criteria are met. When the algorithm terminates, the best fit chromosome will be taken as a solution to the given problem.

Potter and DeJong proposed the cooperative coevolutionary genetic algorithm (CCGA) improving the conventional genetic algorithm, which suffers from slow evolution when the search space is large. In CCGA each chromosome is divided into its subcomponents each of which corresponds to partial solutions associated with one or more variables involved in the objective function to be optimized. We call a collection of such a specified subcomponent a species. In the algorithm each species evolves independently but cooperatively in such a way that each chromosome of a species is evaluated by assembling it together with representative chromosomes of the other species. In this way each species evolves independently while it collaborates with the other species for evaluation. In CCGA each species is associated with a single variable and by allowing each species evolve independently the algorithm reduces the search space significantly.

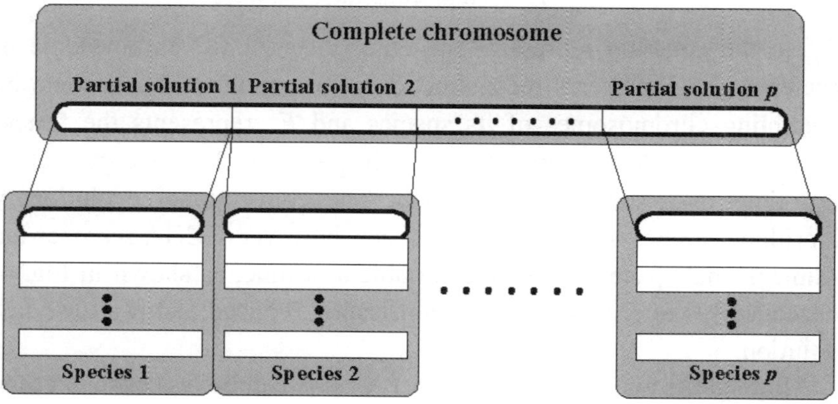

Fig. 2. Species structure of CCGA

```
procedure CCGA1
  begin
    t=0
    for each species S do
    begin
      initialize( p_t^S )
      evaluation( p_t^S )
    end
    while not termination-criteria do
    begin
      t=t+1
      for each species S do
      begin
        p_t^S = reproduction( p_{t-1}^S )
        p_t^S = crossover( p_t^S )
        p_t^S = mutation( p_t^S )
      end
    end
  end
```

Fig. 3. CCGA algorithm

If we let p be the number of species, the fitness of $c_i^{S_k}$ the i-th chromosome of species S_k , is determined as in Eq. 1.

$$F^{CCGA}(c_i^{S_k}) = F(\langle c_{elite}^{S_1}, c_{elite}^{S_2}, \ldots, c_i^{S_k}, \ldots, c_{elite}^{S_p} \rangle) \tag{1}$$

$c_{elite}^{S_k}$ in the equation represents the elite (the best fit) chromosome of species S_k, $\langle\ \rangle$ represents reconstruction of a complete chromosome by assembling chromosomes of its species and F represents the fitness function of complete chromosomes. Each species evolves one generation at a time in a round robin fashion. The conventional evolutionary algorithm searches the whole search space, however, CCGA searches the 1-dimensional space for a single variable at a time, as shown in Fig. 4, consequently the search space is significantly reduced and it allows fast evolution.

Although its evolution speed is fast, CCGA can be less efficient than the ordinary algorithm for problems in which there are strong variable interdependency such that there are lots of Nash equilibrium points[5]. Potter and DeJong also proposed a variant (CCGA2) of the original

CCGA (CCGA1) to alleviate the local optimum problem of the original CCGA, particularly when there is strong variable interdependency. The evolution method of CCGA2 is similar to that of CCGA1 but it differs from CCGA1 in that it uses the different evaluation method. The fitness of $c_i^{S_k}$ of the i -th chromosome of species S_k is shown in Eq. 2.

$$F^{CCGA\ 2}\left(c_i^{S_k}\right) = \max \left\{ \begin{array}{l} F(\langle c_{elite}^{S_1}, c_{elite}^{S_2}, \ldots, c_i^{S_k}, \ldots, c_{elite}^{S_p} \rangle), \\ F(\langle c_{rand}^{S_1}, c_{rand}^{S_2}, \ldots, c_i^{S_k}, \ldots, c_{rand}^{S_p} \rangle) \end{array} \right\} \quad (2)$$

Here, $c_{elite}^{S_k}$ represents the elite chromosome of species S_k and $c_{rand}^{S_k}$ represents a randomly chosen chromosome from species S_k. In order to evaluate a species chromosome two complete chromosomes are assembled by selecting the best fit species chromosomes and selecting species chromosomes randomly. Each of them is evaluated and the maximum is chosen to the fitness score of the species chromosome. In this way CCGA2 allows to escape Nash equilibrium points

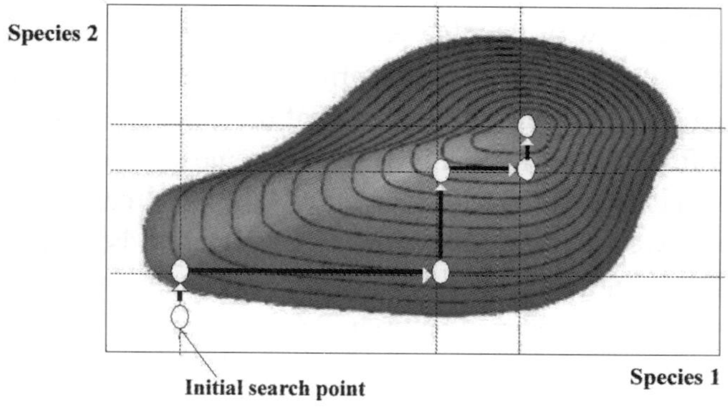

Fig.4. Evolution Search in CCGA

2.2. *ACC (Adaptive Cooperative Coevolution)*

The Adaptive Cooperative Coevolution Algorithm (ACC) was proposed by K. Weicker and N. Weicker to improve CCGA by allowing global search for those strongly interacting variables[4]. It is similar to CCGA except that species can be merged in ACC. During evolution in ACC, variable interdependency is computed and represented by a dependency matrix, and it is used to control species merging. Two species are merged if variable interdependency between their associated variables (or variable sets) exceeds a given threshold. In the following we describe how variable interdependency is computed. Let Γ be the set of all variables to be considered to optimize the given objective function and the number of species at generation t be $s(t)$. And let $S_{V_k}(t)$ represent the species associated with a set of variables V_k $(\bigcup_{k=1}^{s(t)} V_k = \Gamma, V_k \cap V_j = \phi\,(k \neq j))$ at generation t. Then, the fitness of the i-th chromosome $c_i^{S_{V_k}(t)}$ of species $S_{V_k}(t)$ is determined as

$$F^{ACC}\left(c_i^{S_{V_k}(t)}\right) = \max\begin{pmatrix} F\left(\langle c_{elite}^{S_{V_1}(t)}, c_{elite}^{S_{V_2}(t)}, \ldots, c_i^{S_{V_k}(t)}, \ldots, c_{elite}^{S_{V_{s(t)}}(t)} \rangle\right) \\ F\left(\langle c_{elite}^{S_{V_1}(t)}, \ldots, c_{rand}^{S_{V_j}(t)}, \ldots, c_i^{S_{V_k}(t)}, \ldots, c_{elite}^{S_{V_{s(t)}}(t)} \rangle\right) \end{pmatrix} \quad (3)$$

where $c_{elite}^{S_{V_k}(t)}$ represents the elite chromosome of species $S_{V_k}(t)$ and $c_{rand}^{S_{V_j}(t)}$ represents a randomly chosen chromosome from $S_{V_j}(t)$. The first term of the right hand side of Eq. 3 evaluates the chromosome $c_i^{S_{V_k}(t)}$ collaborating with the elite chromosomes of the other species as CCGA1 does while the second term evaluates the chromosome collaborating with the elite chromosomes of the other species except the j-th species for which a randomly chosen chromosome is used. In this evaluation, when the second term of max of Eq. 3 is chosen to be the fitness score, we increase the value of dependency between species $S_{V_j}(t)$ and $S_{V_k}(t)$ in the dependency matrix. And we merge both species when the value of dependency between them exceeds a given threshold. If there is no interdependency among variables, the first term of max will always be chosen as the fitness score and the evolution will be progressing as CCGA1 does. If more than two variables are interdependent, variables corresponding to the merged species will evolve at the same time and it possibly allows to escape a local optimum. The process of merging species in ACC is done as follows. Suppose we merge two species $S_{V_j}(t)$ and $S_{V_k}(t)$ associated with variable sets V_j and V_k, respectively. The merged species $S_V(t)$ is determined as follows.

$$\text{merge}\left(S_{V_j}(t), S_{V_k}(t)\right) = S_V(t) \tag{4}$$

$$\begin{aligned} S_{V_j}(t) &= (c_1^{S_{V_j}(t)}, \ldots, c_n^{S_{V_j}(t)}) \\ S_{V_k}(t) &= (c_1^{S_{V_k}(t)}, \ldots, c_n^{S_{V_k}(t)}) \\ &\rightarrow \\ S_V(t) &= (c_1^{S_V(t)}, \ldots, c_n^{S_V(t)}) \end{aligned} \tag{5}$$

where $V = V_j \cup V_k$. $c_i^{S_V(t)}$, the i-th chromosome of the merged species $S_V(t)$, is given as

$$c_i^{S_V(t)} = \begin{cases} c_{elite}^{S_{V_j}(t)} \circ c_{elite}^{S_{V_k}(t)} : if\ i = 1, \\ c_{elite}^{S_{V_j}(t)} \circ c_{rand}^{S_{V_k}(t)} : if\ 2 \le i \le \left\lceil \frac{n}{2} \right\rceil, \\ c_{rand}^{S_{V_j}(t)} \circ c_{elite}^{S_{V_k}(t)} : otherwise \end{cases} \tag{6}$$

where $\circ$ represents a concatenation of two species chromosomes. In other words, for i=1, the elite chromosomes of two species are merged. For about one half of the population we merge the elite chromosome of species $S_{V_j}(t)$ and a randomly chosen chromosome from species $S_{V_k}(t)$. Similarly for the other half of the population we merge a randomly chosen chromosome from species $S_{V_j}(t)$ and the elite chromosome of species $S_{V_k}(t)$.

3. SMCA: Splitting and Merging Coevolutionary Algorithm

When it is applied to problems in which variables are strongly interdependent, ACC is no longer efficient because species are merged into a large species as evolution progresses and the evolution speed gets slow down since the search space expands rapidly. To solve this problem of ACC, we propose a new coevolution algorithm called SMCA in which species are not only merged but also split if necessary.

In SMCA, species are merged in a similar way in ACC. SMCA starts with the set of base species each of which is associated with a single variable. During evolution process, interdependencies between species are maintained by a dependency matrix. Two species are merged when their associated interdependency value exceeds a given threshold. A merged species is split into a set of base species if it fails to improve its elite chromosome within a certain period of time. Split species can be merged again based on interdependency between species. Merged species allow more global search, however, they slow down the search speed while split species speed up the search but it may suffer from local search. SMCA combines local but fast search and global but slow search by combining merging and splitting of species appropriately.

3.1. *Species Merging*

In SMCA its merging method is similar to that of ACC. In case species $S_V(t)$ is a merged species that created from species $S_{V_j}(t)$ and $S_{V_k}(t)$ when $V = V_j \cup V_k$, the population of the new species $S_V(t)$ is determined as in Eq. 7. $c_i^{S_V(t)}$ the i-th chromosome of the new population $S_V(t)$ is determined as follows.

$$c_i^{S_V(t)} = \begin{cases} c_{elite}^{S_{V_j}}(t) \circ c_{elite}^{S_{V_k}}(t) : if\ i = 1, \\ c_{elite}^{S_{V_j}}(t) \circ c_{rand}^{S_{V_k}}(t) : if\ 2 \le i \le \left\lceil \frac{n}{3} \right\rceil, \\ c_{rand}^{S_{V_j}}(t) \circ c_{elite}^{S_{V_k}}(t) : if \left\lceil \frac{n}{3} \right\rceil < i \le \left\lceil \frac{2n}{3} \right\rceil, \\ c_{rand}^{S_{V_j}}(t) \circ c_{rand}^{S_{V_k}}(t) : otherwise \end{cases} \tag{7}$$

As the result, the merged species $S_V(t)$ consists of four different kinds of chromosomes created by merging species chromosomes in four different ways; (1) the elite chromosomes of both species, (2) the elite chromosome of species $S_{V_j}(t)$ and randomly chosen chromosomes of species $S_{V_k}(t)$, (3) randomly chosen chromosomes of species $S_{V_j}(t)$ and the elite chromosome of species $S_{V_k}(t)$, and (4) randomly chosen chromosomes of both species. Here, we set the size of population of each kind of chromosomes except (1) to be one third of the population of the merged species. As in ACC, a species is merged when the value of species interdependency in the dependency matrix exceeds a given threshold.

3.2. *Species Splitting*

Species splitting is to speed up evolution by reducing the search space. If a merged species does not improve the fitness of its elite chromosome within a certain period of time, we consider that the search point places where search is slow and we try to split species for speeding up evolution by chance. Let $\mathrm{proj}(c_i^{S_{V_k}(t)}, V)$ represent a function of extracting genes that encode variables in set V from the i-th chromosome $c_i^{S_{V_k}(t)}$ of species $S_{V_k}(t)$, corresponding to variable set $V_k(t)$, when there exists species $S_{V_k}(t)$, and $V\square V_k$. In this case, if $P=\{U_1,U_2,\ldots,U_m\}\left(\bigcup_{i=1}^{m} U_i = V_k, U_i \cap U_j = \phi\ (i \neq j)\right)$ is a partition of variable set V_k, $S_{U_i}(t)$, the i-th species split from species $S_{V_k}(t)$, and $c_j^{U_i(t)}$, the j-th chromosome of species $S_{U_i}(t)$, are determined as follows.

$$\mathrm{split}(S_{V_k}(t),P)=\{S_{U_1}(t),S_{U_2}(t),\ldots,S_{U_m}(t)\}$$
$$S_{U_i}(t)=(c_1^{S_{U_i}(t)},c_2^{S_{U_i}(t)},\ldots,c_n^{S_{U_i}(t)}) \tag{8}$$

$$c_j^{S_{U_i}(t)}=\mathrm{proj}(c_j^{S_{V_k}(t)},U_i):1\le i\le n, 1\le j\le m \tag{9}$$

In other words, the original species is split into a set of different species each of which corresponds to a set of variables. Apparently many different ways of splitting are possible depending on how the set of variables associated with the species to split is partitioned. In this chapter, to make our algorithm simple, we split a species into a set of single variable species.

4. Experiments

4.1. *Function Optimization*

We experimented with our algorithm on some of the benchmark function optimization problems including the Ackley function, the Rosenbrock function, and the Schwefel function. For comparison purposes, we used each function in its original form and in its coordinate rotated form to introduce variable interdependency[6]. Parameters and methods used in our function optimization experiments are shown in Table 1.

Table 1. Experiment Parameter Values

parameters	value
population size	100
bits/variable	16
crossover rate	0.6
mutation rate	1/(chromosome length)
selection method	fitness proportionate
crossover method	2 point crossover

We compare the average performance over 10 runs of our algorithm and others as shown in Figs. 5, 6, and 7.

The original form of the Ackley function is defined as

$$F(\vec{x}) = -20\exp(-0.2\sqrt{\frac{1}{n}\sum_{i=1}^{n}x_i^2}) - \exp(\frac{1}{n}\sum_{i=1}^{n}\cos(2\pi x_i)) + 20 + e, -20 \le x_i \le 20 \qquad (10)$$

The global optimum of the function is $F(\vec{x}) = 0$ at $\vec{x} = (0, 0, \ldots, 0)$. The Ackley function does not have variable interdependency in its original form but its rotated form has variable interdependency. In our experiment n (dimension) is fixed to 30.

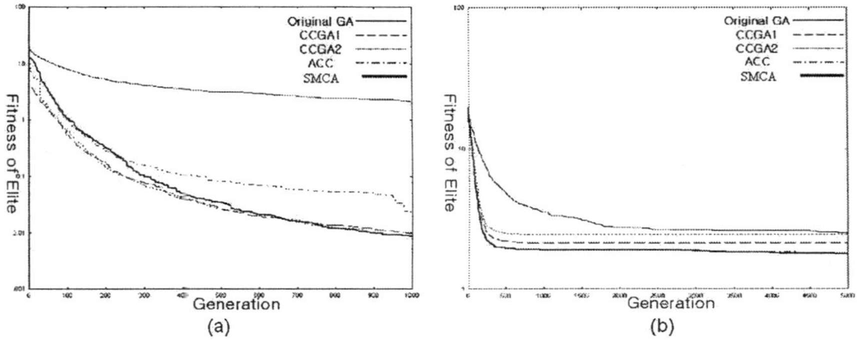

Fig. 5. (a) Ackley and (b) Rotated Ackley

The Rosenbrock function is given as in Eq. 11 and it has a weak variable interdependency in its original form.

$$F(\vec{x}) = \sum_{i=1}^{n/2}[100(x_{2i} - x_{2i-1}^2)^2 + (1 - x_{2i-1}^2)^2], -2.048 \leq x_i \leq 2.048 \qquad (11)$$

The Rosenbrock function has its global minimum at the point $\vec{x} = (1, 1, \ldots, 1)$. An interesting characteristic of this function is that variable interdependency exists only between variables x_{2i} and x_{2i-1} when $0 < i \leq n/2$.

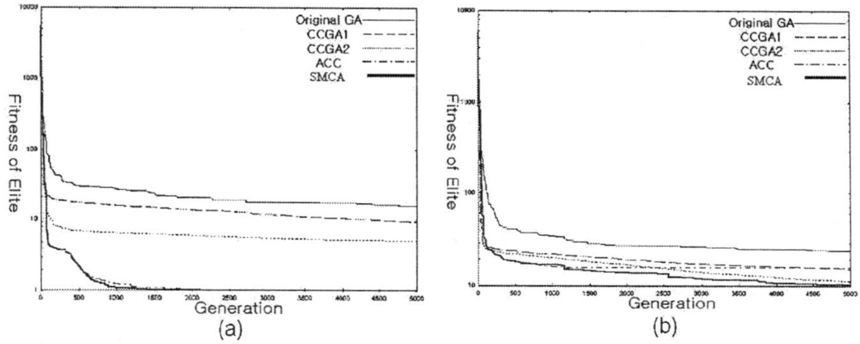

Fig. 6. (a) Rosenbrock and (b) Rotated Rosenbrock

The Schwefel function has a term that contains the sine function and oscillation is getting larger as it moves outward from the center $\vec{x} = (0, 0, \ldots, 0)$. The original form of the function is defined as

$$F(\vec{x}) = \sum_{i=1}^{n}[-x_i \cdot \sin(\sqrt{|x_i|})], -500 \leq x_i \leq 500 \qquad (12)$$

The global optimum of this function is $F(\vec{x}) = -n \cdot 418.9829$ at the point $\vec{x} = (420.9687, 420.9687, \ldots, 420.9687)$.

In summary, CCGAs are efficient when no variable interdependency exists, however, otherwise they are not efficient. ACC is efficient even when variable interdependency exists, however, it quickly saturates when strong variable interdependency exists. The experiment results clearly show that SMCA is all-time efficient no matter how much variable interdependency exists.

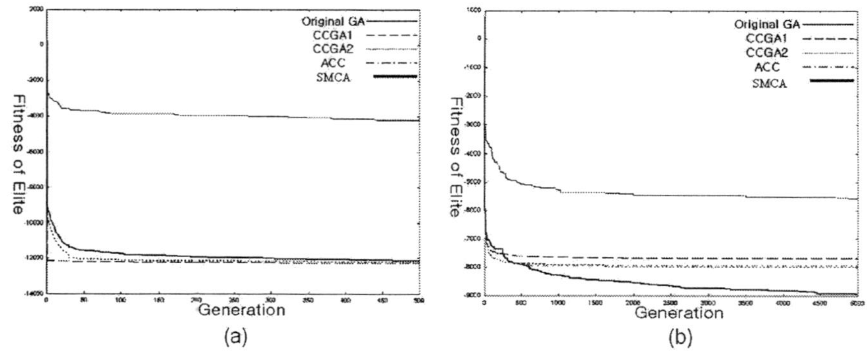

Fig. 7. (a) Schwefel and (b) Rotated Schwefel

4.2. *ICP* (*Inventory Control Problem*)

ICP is one of common practical optimization problems[7]. Traditionally, ICP is reduced to the problem of deciding when (order point) to place replenishment order and how many units of individual items (order quantity) to order to minimize the total cost, which is composed of various types of costs such as lost sales cost, transportation cost, order cost, and storage space cost. In our experiment we simulated ICP using randomly generated sales data. The sales data set consists of sales transactions, each of which includes time, product items, and the quantities sold. We took 10 product items and the sales quantity of an item was randomly chosen within a certain range. We need to determine the order point and the order quantity for each item to minimize the total cost. Thus we had 20 variables in total to optimize. Because we allowed orders for multiple items satisfying a certain condition to be transported at a time to reduce the transportation cost, such variables are interdependent each other. In this experiment we represent the order point by the number of the item units left in storage. We ran the simulation 10 times and averaged the performance. Fig. 8 compares the performances of different algorithms and it is clear that SMCA outperforms other existing algorithms.

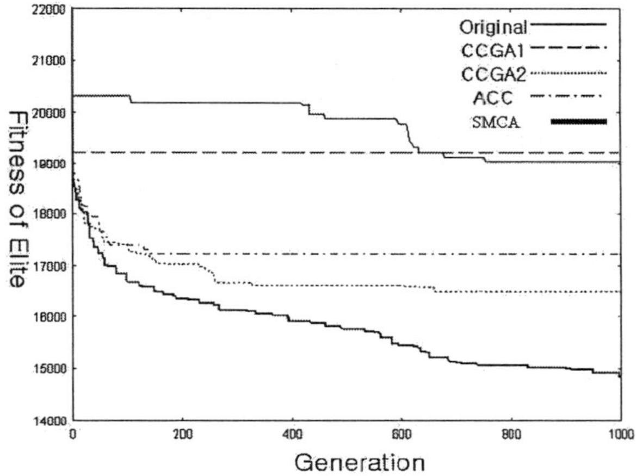

Fig. 8. Performance Comparison for ICP

5. Conclusion

In this chapter we described a new coevolutionary algorithm that improves the existing coevolutionary algorithms. In CCGA species corresponding to a single variable evolve independently by cooperatively, which significantly reduces the search space and consequently results in fast evolution. However, CCGA suffers from the problem of local optimum when variable interdependency exists. To overcome this problem ACC was proposed and it merges species associated with interdependent variables. Merging species allows more global search than splitting species. However, ACC also suffers from slow evolution when variables are strongly interdependent. In this case species are quickly merged into a larger species, causing the expanded search space. SMCA, however, combines species merging and splitting appropriately in order to take advantage both of fast evolution of CCGA and of global search of ACC. Our experiment results have shown that SMCA outperforms existing evolutionary algorithms.

References

1. M. A. Potter and K. A. DeJong, "A cooperative coevolutionary approach to function optimization," *Proc. of the Third Conference on Parallel Problem Solving from Nature*, Springer-Verlag, pp.249-257 (1994).
2. M.A. Potter and K.A DeJong, "Cooperative Coevolution: An Architecture for Evolving Coadapted Subcomponents," *Evolutionary Computation* 8(1), MIT press, pp.1-29 (2000).
3. M. Mundhe and S. Sen, "Evolving agent societies that avoid social dilemmas," *Proc. Of GECCO-2000*, Las Vegas, Nevada, pp.809-816 (2000).
4. K. Weicker and N. Weicker, "On the improvement of coevolutionary optimizers by learning variable interdependencies," *Congress on Evolutionary Computation (CEC99)*, pp.1627-1632 (1999).
5. J. Nash, "Non-cooperative games", *Annals of Mathematics* 5(2), pp. 286-295 (1951).
6. R. Salomon, "Reevaluating genetic algorithm performance under coordinate rotation of benchmark functions," *BioSystems* 39, pp.210-229 (1996).
7. R. Eriksson and B. Olsson, "Cooperative Coevolution in Inventory Control Optimisation," *Proc. of 3rd International Conference on Artificial Neural Networks and Genetic Algorithms (ICANNGA97)*, Norwich, UK (1997).

CHAPTER 6

SCHEMA ANALYSIS OF GENETIC ALGORITHMS ON MULTIPLICATIVE LANDSCAPE

Hiroshi Furutani

Department of Information Science
Kyoto University of Education
Fushimi-ku, Kyoto, 612-8522 Japan

A method has been developed to derive an evolution equation of schemata under the action of genetic operators. The method makes use of the fact that schema frequencies can be given by Walsh transformation of genotype frequencies. It is applied to genetic algorithms (GAs) on the multiplicative landscape. On this landscape, an exact evolution equation for the first order schemata can be derived within the framework of an infinite population model, and this makes it possible to carry out an analytical investigation of genetic operators. The theoretical results are compared with numerical experiments. The analysis of the experiments focuses on the interplay of mutation and crossover, and investigates the effect of linkage due to finite population size.

1. Introduction

The schema theorem proposed by Holland is one of a few theories on the foundation of genetic algorithms (GAs)[1], which many researchers consider very useful for studying the evolution. However, it is also true that there are many criticisms on its effectiveness. For example, it states trivial tautologies, and gives only a lower bound on the schema frequency. It is also pointed out that it only takes into account the destructive effect of mutation and crossover on schemata without considering their constructive roles.

There have been several attempts to derive more quantitative theories. Altenberg developed a method to derive a schema evolution equation by using Price's theorem [2]. Stephens and Waelbroeck obtained exact schema evolution equations for mutation and crossover [3,4].

Another approach to derive a quantitative schema theorem makes use of the Walsh transformation of genotype frequencies [5,6,7]. The evolution equations for mutation and crossover can be expressed in very simple forms by Walsh transformation [6,8]. Therefore, it is not difficult to obtain the schema evolution equations for mutation and crossover [7].

Selection is one of the most important operators in GAs, and plays the role of driving solutions to the optimum. However, the schema evolution for selection is in general very complicated, and is difficult to obtain a meaningful result from it. In this chapter, we consider the evolution of a population on the multiplicative landscape. Previously, we have shown that the evolution equation for that population can be solved exactly [9]. We apply the schema theorem to this problem, and study the roles of genetic operators microscopically. We derive an exact evolution equation of schemata evolving under the action of selection, mutation. The effect of crossover is considered in the relation to linkage. This article is based on previous works [10,11].

2. Mathematical Model

2.1. *Model*

In this chapter, we study selection, mutation and crossover in GAs. We use the fitness proportionate selection and uniform crossover. A population is assumed to evolve in discrete and non-overlapping generations, and the process is described by a set of difference equations. We consider a theory of GAs with infinite population size, and neglect random sampling. The effects of random sampling are studied in the analysis of numerical calculations with finite population size.

An individual is represented by a binary string of length ℓ, and there are $n = 2^\ell$ possible strings, which we call genotypes. The binary representation of an integer i is

$$i =< i(\ell), \cdots, i(1) > \quad (0 \le i \le n-1),$$

where $i(k)$ is a binary value of i at position k $(1 \le k \le \ell)$. The ith genotype B_i is identified with the integer i. We use the notation $|i|$ for the number of ones in i

$$|i| = \sum_{k=1}^{\ell} i(k). \tag{1}$$

We use the relative frequency $x_i(t)$ of the genotype B_i at generation t for the analysis. The relative frequencies satisfy the normalization condition

$$\sum_{i=0}^{n-1} x_i(t) = 1. \tag{2}$$

2.2. Walsh Transformation

The Walsh function W_{ij}, $0 \leq i, j \leq n-1$, is defined as

$$W_{ij} \equiv \prod_{k=1}^{\ell} (-1)^{i(k) \cdot j(k)}, \tag{3}$$

with $i =< i(\ell), \ldots, i(1) >$ and $j =< j(\ell), \ldots, j(1) >$. In this study, the evolution of GA system is described by the Walsh transform of $x_i(t)$

$$\tilde{x}_i(t) \equiv \sum_{j=0}^{n-1} W_{ij} x_j(t). \tag{4}$$

We call $\tilde{x}_i$ as the ith Walsh coefficient. When it is necessary to show the number of ones and their positions in i

$$k = |i|, \quad 1 \leq b_1 < \ldots < b_k \leq \ell,$$

we use the notation

$$\tilde{x}_i(t) = \tilde{x}^{(k)}[b_1, \ldots, b_k](t), \tag{5}$$

where k is the degree of Walsh coefficient.

Substituting $W_{0j} = 1$ into equation (4), and using the normalization condition (2), we have the zeroth order Walsh coefficient $\tilde{x}_0$

$$\tilde{x}_0(t) = \sum_{j=0}^{n-1} x_j(t) = 1. \tag{6}$$

The following relation will be used later

$$\tilde{x}^{(k)}[b_1, b_2 \ldots b_k] = \sum_{j=0}^{n-1} \prod_{m=1}^{k} (-1)^{j(b_m)} x_j, \tag{7}$$

where $j(b_1), \ldots, j(b_k)$ stand for the binary values of j at the positions of ones $\{b_1, \ldots, b_k\}$.

2.3. Evolution Equation

We derive here the evolution equations for selection, mutation and crossover. In proportionate selection, the frequency of genotype B_i at generation $t+1$ is given in terms of genotype frequencies at generation t

$$x_i(t+1) = \frac{f_i}{\bar{f}(t)} x_i(t) \quad (i = 0, \ldots, n-1), \tag{8}$$

where f_i is a fitness of B_i, and $\bar{f}(t)$ the average fitness of the population

$$\bar{f}(t) \equiv \sum_{i=0}^{n-1} f_i \, x_i(t). \tag{9}$$

To show explicitly that the evolution equation (8) is for the selection process, we use the notation

$$x_i(t+1) \to \widehat{S} x_i(t),$$

where $\widehat{S} x_i$ stands for the frequency of B_i after selection.

The Walsh transform of the evolution equation (8) becomes

$$\widehat{S} \tilde{x}_i(t) = \frac{1}{n \bar{f}(t)} \sum_{j=0}^{n-1} \tilde{f}_j \, \tilde{x}_{i \oplus j}(t), \tag{10}$$

where $\oplus$ is the bitwise exclusive-or operator,

$$i \oplus j \; = < i(\ell) \oplus j(\ell), \ldots , i(1) \oplus j(1) > .$$

The fitness $\tilde{f}_i$ is the Walsh transform of f_i

$$\tilde{f}_i = \sum_{j=0}^{n-1} W_{ij} f_j. \tag{11}$$

The average fitness is given by

$$\bar{f}(t) = \frac{1}{n} \sum_{j=0}^{n-1} \tilde{f}_j \, \tilde{x}_j(t). \tag{12}$$

There is an important relation between the average fitness $\bar{f}(t)$ and the variance of the fitness $V[f](t)$ [12]

$$V[f](t) \equiv \sum_{i=0}^{n-1} f_i^2 \, x_i(t) - \bar{f}(t)^2. \tag{13}$$

By using equations (8) and (13), we can obtain the change in the average fitness, $\Delta \bar{f}(t) = \bar{f}(t+1) - \bar{f}(t)$,

$$\Delta \bar{f}(t) \; = \; V[f](t) / \bar{f}(t). \tag{14}$$

This is a variation of Fisher's " Fundamental Theorem of Natural Selection" [12].

The change in the frequency under mutation is

$$x_i(t+1) = \sum_{j=0}^{n-1} M_{ij} x_j(t), \tag{15}$$

where the mutation matrix M_{ij} stands for the probability of mutation from B_j to B_i over one generation. An (i,j)th element of M is a function of the Hamming distance $d(i,j)$ between strings i and j.

$$M_{ij} = (1-p)^{\ell - d(i,j)} p^{d(i,j)}, \tag{16}$$

where p denotes the mutation rate at one bit position over one generation.

The matrix M_{ij} can be diagonalized by Walsh functions

$$\sum_{i'=0}^{n-1} \sum_{j'=0}^{n-1} W_{ii'} \, M_{i'j'} \, W_{j'j} = n\,(1-2p)^{|i|}\, \delta_{i,j}.$$

Thus the Walsh transform of the evolution equation under mutation (15) is

$$\widehat{M}\, \tilde{x}_i(t) \; = \; (1-2p)^{|i|}\, \tilde{x}_i(t), \tag{17}$$

where $\widehat{M}$ symbolically shows the effect of mutation.

The evolution equation under crossover can be given in terms of crossover tensor C

$$x_k(t+1) \; = \; \widehat{C}\, \tilde{x}_k(t) \; = \; \sum_{i=0}^{n-1} \sum_{j=0}^{n-1} C(k|i,j)\, x_i(t)\, x_j(t), \tag{18}$$

where $\widehat{C}$ denotes the effect of crossover. Using the Walsh transformation, we obtain a very simple expression [6,8]

$$\widehat{C}\, \tilde{x}_k(t) \; = \; \sum_{i=0}^{n-1} c_{i,i\oplus k}\, \tilde{x}_i(t)\, \tilde{x}_{i\ominus k}(t), \tag{19}$$

The coefficient c_{ij} contains all information on the action of crossover.

For uniform crossover, we have an analytical expression

$$c_{ij} = (1-\chi)\frac{\delta[i]+\delta[j]}{2} + \chi \prod_{m=1}^{\ell} \frac{\delta[i(m)]+\delta[j(m)]}{2}, \tag{20}$$

where χ is a crossover rate. Here, the δ function is defined by

$$\delta[i] \equiv \begin{cases} 1 \ (i=0) \\ 0 \ (i \neq 0), \end{cases}$$

and when i is a binary string of length ℓ, $i = < i(\ell), \ldots, i(1) >$

$$\delta[i] = \prod_{m=1}^{\ell} \delta[i(m)].$$

3. Schema Theorem

3.1. *Holland's Schema Theorem*

A schema $\mathcal{H}$ is the set of all strings with certain defining values at fixed positions. It is represented by three types symbols, 0,1 and $*$. The bits 0 and 1 are defining bits, and $*$ is a wild card that allows both 0 and 1. The order of schema $\mathcal{O}(\mathcal{H})$ is the number of defining bits, and the defining length $\mathcal{L}(\mathcal{H})$ is the distance between the outermost defining bits.

For example, the schema theorem with one-point crossover was given by Holland [1]

$$h(\mathcal{H},t+1) \geq h(\mathcal{H},t)\frac{f(\mathcal{H})}{\bar{f}(t)}\{1-\chi\frac{\mathcal{L}(\mathcal{H})}{\ell-1}-p\,\mathcal{O}(\mathcal{H})\}, \qquad (21)$$

where $h(\mathcal{H},t)$ is the relative frequency of the schema $\mathcal{H}$ at generation t, and $f(\mathcal{H})$ is the average fitness of genotypes included in $\mathcal{H}$.

We also use the notation showing explicitly the order of schema, the positions of defining bits, and their binary values,

$$\mathcal{H} = \mathcal{H}^{(k)}[i(b_1), i(b_2), \dots, i(b_k)],$$

Here, $k = \mathcal{O}(\mathcal{H})$, and $1 \leq b_1 < b_2 < \dots < b_k \leq \ell$ are positions of defining bits. In the similar manner, we use the notation for the relative frequency $h(\mathcal{H})$,

$$h(\mathcal{H}) = h^{(k)}[i(b_1), i(b_2), \dots, i(b_k)].$$

3.2. *New Schema Theorem*

In this subsection, we derive the new schema theorem by using the Walsh transformation. For binary values $i(k)$ and $j(k)$, the condition of $i(k) = j(k)$ is given by

$$\delta[i(k)-j(k)] = \frac{1}{2}\{1+(-1)^{i(k)}(-1)^{j(k)}\}.$$

From this, we can obtain an expression for the frequency $h(\mathcal{H})$ of the first order schema $\mathcal{H}^{(1)}[i(b_1)]$. Using the normalization condition (2) and definition (7), we have

$$
\begin{aligned}
h^{(1)}[i(b_1)] &= \sum_{j=0}^{n-1} \delta[i(b_1) - j(b_1)]x_j \\
&= \sum_{j=0}^{n-1} \frac{1}{2}\{x_j + (-1)^{i(b_1)}(-1)^{j(b_1)}x_j\} \\
&= \frac{1}{2}\{1 + (-1)^{i(b_1)}\tilde{x}^{(1)}[b_1]\}.
\end{aligned}
$$

Thus we have the Walsh representation of the first order schemata

$$
\begin{aligned}
h^{(1)}[i(b_1) = 0] &= (1 + \tilde{x}^{(1)}[b_1])/2, \\
h^{(1)}[i(b_1) = 1] &= (1 - \tilde{x}^{(1)}[b_1])/2.
\end{aligned} \tag{22}
$$

For the Lth order schema, noting

$$
h^{(L)}[i(b_1), i(b_2), \ldots, i(b_L)] = \sum_{j=0}^{n-1} \prod_{m=1}^{L} \delta[i(b_m) - j(b_m)]x_j,
$$

and expanding the products of the delta functions, we have a new expression for the schema frequency in terms of the Walsh coefficients. Giving the positions of all defining bits $S = \{b_1, \ldots, b_L\}$, and its subset $S' = \{b_1^{'}, \ldots, b_k^{'}\}$, we have

$$
h^{(L)}[i(b_1), \ldots, i(b_L)] = \frac{1}{2^L} \sum_{S'} (-1)^{i(b_1^{'}) + \cdots + i(b_k^{'})} \tilde{x}^{(k)}[b_1^{'}, \ldots, b_k^{'}]. \tag{23}
$$

Here the summation is taken over all subsets S' of S. Using equation(23), we have the second order term

$$
\begin{aligned}
h^{(2)}[i(b_1), i(b_2)] = \frac{1}{4}\{&1 + (-1)^{i(b_1)}\tilde{x}^{(1)}[b_1] + (-1)^{i(b_2)}\tilde{x}^{(1)}[b_2] \\
&+ (-1)^{i(b_1)+i(b_2)}\tilde{x}^{(2)}[b_1, b_2]\}.
\end{aligned}
$$

The inverse transformation is given by

$$
(-1)^{i(b_1)+\cdots+i(b_L)}\, \tilde{x}^{(L)}[b_1, \ldots, b_L] = \sum_{S'} (-1)^{L-k}\, 2^k\, h^{(k)}[i(b_1^{'}), \ldots, i(b_k^{'})], \tag{24}
$$

where the summation is taken over all subsets of S.

It becomes possible to derive the schema evolution equation for genetic operators. From the evolution equation of the Walsh coefficient under mutation (17), we obtain

$$
\widehat{M}\, h^{(L)}[i(b_1), \ldots, i(b_L)] = \sum_{S'} (1 - 2p)^k\, p^{L-k}\, h^{(k)}[i(b_1^{'}), \ldots, i(b_k^{'})]. \tag{25}
$$

The summation is taken over all subsets of S.

For the first order Walsh coefficients, we have

$$\widehat{M}\,h^{(1)}[i(b)] = (1-2p)\,h^{(1)}[i(b)] + p. \tag{26}$$

There is another form of the schema equation for mutation. Noting

$$h^{(1)}[i(b)] + h^{(1)}[\overline{i(b)}] \;=\; 1,$$

where $\overline{i(b)}$ is the one's complement of $i(b)$. Then we have

$$\widehat{M}\,h^{(1)}[i(b)] = (1-p)\,h^{(1)}[i(b)] + p\,h^{(1)}[\overline{i(b)}], \tag{27}$$

where we use the relation $p = ph^{(1)}[i(b)] + ph^{(1)}[\overline{i(b)}]$ in equation (26).

For crossover, we give here the final results of the schema theorem under uniform crossover. The process of derivation is described in the previous paper [7]. We use an integer $i(\mathcal{H})$ as another representation of the schema $\mathcal{H}$

$$\{0,1\} \to 1, \quad \{*\} \to 0 \tag{28}$$

For example, the new representation of $\mathcal{H} = *10*$ is $i(\mathcal{H}) =< 0,1,1,0 >$. Though this representation does not distinguish between 0 and 1, it may not bring any confusion in the case of crossover process.

The schema theorem for crossover can be given by

$$\widehat{C}\,h(k) \;=\; \sum_{i=0}^{n-1} c_{i,i\oplus k}\; h(i)\,h(i\oplus k), \tag{29}$$

The integers i and k in $h(k)$ and $h(i)$ are the binary expression of schema (28). The coefficient $c_{i,i\oplus k}$ is zero when i and $i\oplus k$ both take the value of one at the same bit position.

If we use uniform crossover, it has no effect on the first order schema

$$\widehat{C}\,h^{(1)}[i(b)] \;=\; h^{(1)}[i(b)].$$

For the second order schema, we have

$$\widehat{C}\,h^{(2)}[i(b),i(b')] \;=\; (1-\frac{\chi}{2})h^{(2)}[i(b),i(b')] + \frac{\chi}{2}h^{(1)}[i(b)]h^{(1)}[i(b')].$$

3.3. *Linkage Equilibrium*

We will use a shorthand notation

$$h^{(1)}[i(k)=1] \to h[1_k], \quad h^{(1)}[i(k)=0] \to h[0_k].$$

In this analysis, the notion of linkage [13] is very important, and the second order linkage disequilibrium coefficient D is defined as

$$D[k,m] = h^{(2)}[i(k)=1, i(m)=1] - h[1_k]h[1_m]. \tag{30}$$

When each gene evolves independently, a population is in linkage equilibrium, while if there are any correlations among genes at different loci, it is in linkage disequilibrium. When the population is in linkage equilibrium, all D coefficients are zero, $D[k,m] = 0$. In this state, the frequency of genotypes B_i is given in terms of the first order schema frequencies

$$x_i = \prod_{k=1}^{\ell} h[i(k)]. \tag{31}$$

4. Multiplicative Landscape

This section gives some mathematical results for GAs on the multiplicative landscape obtained by the schema theorem.

4.1. *Selection*

The fitness function of multiplicative form is defined as

$$f_i = (1-s)^{|i|} = \prod_{k=1}^{\ell} (1-s)^{i(k)}, \quad (0 \le s < 1), \tag{32}$$

where s is a parameter for the strength of selection. In the previous work[9], we have shown that the evolution equation of genotypes can be solved exactly for GAs under the action of selection and mutation with the multiplicative fitness. Therefore it is natural to consider that we can obtain an exact schema theorem.

Then, we assume that the population is in linkage equilibrium state at generation t, and it will later become clear that this is an essential assumption for the analysis. Thus we use equation (31), and show that the average fitness is also given in the product form

$$\bar{f}(t) = \prod_{k=1}^{\ell} \{h[0_k] + (1-s)h[1_k]\} = \prod_{k=1}^{\ell} (1 - s\,h[1_k]). \tag{33}$$

Then we may define the fitness function at each bit as

$$g_k = 1 - s\,h[1_k],$$

and its variance

$$v_k = h[0_k] + (1-s)^2 h[1_k] - {g_k}^2 = s^2 h[1_k]\,(1-h[1_k]).$$

To show the assumption of linkage equilibrium explicitly, we will use the notation

$$\bar{f}^{(\mathrm{eq})} = \prod_{k=1}^{\ell} g_k.$$

The variance of the fitness in linkage equilibrium can be obtained

$$V[f]^{(\mathrm{eq})} = \prod_{k=1}^{\ell} \{1-(2s-s^2)h[1_k]\} - \prod_{k=1}^{\ell} (1-sh[1_k])^2.$$

For small s, $V[f]^{(\mathrm{eq})}$ can be given approximately

$$V[f]^{(\mathrm{eq})} \approx s^2 \sum_{k=1}^{\ell} h[1_k]\,(1-h[1_k]) = \sum_{k=1}^{\ell} v_k. \tag{34}$$

The Walsh transform of the fitness function is obtained as

$$\tilde{f}_i = \prod_{k=1}^{\ell} \{1+(-1)^{i(k)}\,(1-s)\} \tag{35}$$

Under the assumption of linkage equilibrium, we can obtain the schema equation of the first order schemata for selection. Substituting equation (35) into evolution equation for selection (10), we have

$$\widehat{S}\tilde{x}_i(t) = \prod_{k=1}^{\ell} \frac{\beta[i(k)](t)}{\beta[0_k](t)}. \tag{36}$$

Here, the function $\beta[i(k)]$ is defined as

$$\beta[0_k] = h[0_k] + (1-s)h[1_k],$$
$$\beta[1_k] = h[0_k] - (1-s)h[1_k].$$

If $|i| = 1$ in equation (36), the equation takes the form

$$\widehat{S}\tilde{x}^{(1)}[k](t) = \beta[1_k](t)/\beta[0_k](t).$$

The evolution equation of the first order schema $h[i(k)]$ can be derived by using equation(22). The results are

$$\widehat{S}\,h[0_k](t) = \frac{h[0_k](t)}{h[0_k](t) + (1-s)h[1_k](t)}, \tag{37}$$

and

$$\widehat{S}\, h[1_k](t) \;=\; \frac{(1-s)\, h[1_k](t)}{h[0_k](t) + (1-s)h[1_k](t)}. \tag{38}$$

With the initial values $h[0_k](0)$ and $h[1_k](0) = 1 - h[0_k](0)$ at $t = 0$, we have

$$h[i(k)](t) \;=\; \frac{a[i(k)]^t\, h[i(k)](0)}{h[0_k](0) + (1-s)^t h[1_k](0)}, \tag{39}$$

where $a[0_k] = 1$ and $a[1_k] = 1 - s$.

Then we can derive the schema equation of the Lth order schemata $h^{(L)}[i(b_1), \dots, i(b_L)]$. With the set of defining bits $S = \{b_1, \dots, b_L\}$, we have

$$\widehat{S}\, h^{(L)}[i(b_1), \dots, i(b_L)](t) = \prod_{k \in S} \frac{a[i(k)]\, h[i(k)](t)}{h[0_k](t) - (1-s)h[1_k](t)}. \tag{40}$$

The solution of this equation is

$$h^{(L)}[i(b_1), \dots, i(b_L)](t) = \prod_{k \in S} \frac{a[i(k)]^t\, h[i(k)](0)}{h[0_k](0) + (1-s)^t h[1_k](0)}. \tag{41}$$

It is important to note that the schemata after selection also satisfy the condition of linkage equilibrium. From equations (25) and (29), we can also verify that the schemata after mutation and crossover satisfy the condition of equilibrium. Thus, if the population is in linkage equilibrium at $t = 0$, then it always satisfies the condition of equilibrium.

The change in the fitness function g_k under the action of selection is

$$\Delta g_k(t) \equiv \widehat{S} g_k(t) - g_k(t).$$

and we have

$$\Delta g_k(t) = \frac{v_k(t)}{g_k(t)}. \tag{42}$$

We can consider this equation as a schema form of Fisher's theorem in equation (14). The theoretical prediction of $g_k(t)$ is given by

$$g_k(t) = \frac{h[0_k](0) + (1-s)^{t+1} h[1_k](0)}{h[0_k](0) + (1-s)^t h[1_k](0)}. \tag{43}$$

4.2. *Effects of Mutation and Crossover*

Mutation has a direct effect on the first order schemata, which is given by equation (27). The effect of selection and mutation (mutation after selection) is given by

$$\widehat{M}\,\widehat{S}h[0_k] = (1-p)\,\widehat{S}h[0_k] + p\,\widehat{S}h[1_k],$$
$$\widehat{M}\,\widehat{S}h[1_k] = p\,\widehat{S}h[0_k] + (1-p)\,\widehat{S}h[1_k].$$

The effect of selection is given by using equations (37) and (38), and we have a linear system

$$\begin{aligned} h[0_k](t+1) &= \frac{(1-p)\,h[0_k](t) + p\,(1-s)\,h[1_k](t)}{h[0_k](t) + (1-s)\,h[1_k](t)}, \\ h[1_k](t+1) &= \frac{p\,h[0_k](t) + (1-p)\,(1-s)\,h[1_k](t)}{h[0_k](t) + (1-s)\,h[1_k](t)}, \end{aligned} \tag{44}$$

where we use the notation $h[i(k)](t+1)$ for $\widehat{M}\widehat{S}h[i(k)](t)$. To solve this system, we consider an auxiliary system

$$\begin{aligned} y_0(t+1) &= (1-p)y_0(t) + p(1-s)y_1(t), \\ y_1(t+1) &= py_0(t) + (1-p)(1-s)y_1(t), \end{aligned} \tag{45}$$

with the initial values $y_0(0) = h[0_k](0)$ and $y_1(0) = h[1_k](0)$. Noting

$$y_0(t+1) + y_1(t+1) \;=\; y_0(t) + (1-s)\,y_1(t),$$

and $y_0(0) + y_1(0) = 1$, it is easy to show

$$\begin{aligned} h[0_k](t) &= \frac{y_0(t)}{y_0(t) + y_1(t)}, \\ h[1_k](t) &= \frac{y_1(t)}{y_0(t) + y_1(t)}. \end{aligned} \tag{46}$$

We introduce a matrix A

$$A \;=\; \begin{bmatrix} (1-p) & p\,(1-s) \\ p & (1-p)\,(1-s) \end{bmatrix},$$

and write the auxiliary system (45) in the form of

$$\boldsymbol{y}(t+1) \;=\; A\,\boldsymbol{y}(t),$$

where $\boldsymbol{y}(t) = (y_0(t), y_1(t))^T$.

The solution of the auxiliary system is

$$\boldsymbol{y}(t) \;=\; A^t\,\boldsymbol{y}(0).$$

Two eigenvalues of the matrix A are

$$\lambda_{0,1} = \frac{1}{2}\left\{(1-p)(2-s) \pm \sqrt{(1-2p)s^2 + p^2(2-s)^2}\right\}, \tag{47}$$

where λ_0 corresponds to the $+$ sign in the equation, and λ_1 to the $-$ sign, respectively. The eigenvectors $\boldsymbol{v}_0$ and $\boldsymbol{v}_1$ are

$$\boldsymbol{v}_0 = \begin{bmatrix} 1-s \\ \gamma \end{bmatrix}, \quad \boldsymbol{v}_1 = \begin{bmatrix} \gamma \\ -1 \end{bmatrix}, \tag{48}$$

where

$$\gamma = \frac{1}{2p}\left\{-(1-p)s + \sqrt{(1-2p)s^2 + p^2(2-s)^2}\right\}. \tag{49}$$

At $t = 0$, we write $\boldsymbol{y}(0)$ by using $\boldsymbol{v}_0$ and $\boldsymbol{v}_1$

$$\boldsymbol{y}(0) = \alpha_0\, \boldsymbol{v}_0 + \alpha_1\, \boldsymbol{v}_1.$$

Two constants are given by

$$\alpha_0 = \frac{y_0(0) + \gamma y_1(0)}{1 - s + \gamma^2},$$
$$\alpha_1 = \frac{\gamma y_0(0) - (1-s) y_1(0)}{1 - s + \gamma^2}.$$

Then we have

$$\begin{aligned} \boldsymbol{y}(t) = A^t\, \boldsymbol{y}(0) &= A^t\, (\alpha_0 \boldsymbol{v}_0 + \alpha_1 \boldsymbol{v}_1) \\ &= \lambda_0^t \alpha_0 \boldsymbol{v}_0 + \lambda_1^t \alpha_1 \boldsymbol{v}_1. \end{aligned}$$

The explicit form of the solution is

$$\begin{aligned} y_0(t) &= \frac{\{(1-s)\lambda_0^t + \gamma^2 \lambda_1^t\} y_0(0) + (1-s)\gamma\{\lambda_0^t - \lambda_1^t\} y_1(0)}{1-s+\gamma^2}, \\ y_1(t) &= \frac{\gamma\{\lambda_0^t - \lambda_1^t\} y_0(0) + \{\gamma^2 \lambda_0^t + (1-s)\lambda_1^t\} y_1(0)}{1-s+\gamma^2}. \end{aligned} \tag{50}$$

The solutions for the first order schemata $h[0_k]$ and $h[1_k]$ are given by using equation (46) with the initial values $y_0(0) = h[0_k](0)$ and $y_1(0) = 1 - y_0(0)$.

We can write the unified effect of selection and mutation on the fitness function g_k by using equation (26)

$$\widehat{M}\, \widehat{S} h[1_k] = (1-2p)\widehat{S} h[1_k] + p.$$

Then we have

$$\widehat{M}\, \widehat{S} g_k = 1 - s\, \widehat{M}\, \widehat{S} h[1_k] = \widehat{S} g_k + 2ps\left(\widehat{S} h[1_k] - \frac{1}{2}\right). \tag{51}$$

The change in the fitness $\Delta g_k = \widehat{M}\widehat{S}g_k - g_k$ is given by

$$\Delta g_k = \frac{v_k(t)}{g_k(t)} + 2ps\left\{\frac{(1-s)h[1_k]}{1-sh[1_k]} - \frac{1}{2}\right\}. \tag{52}$$

When $h[1_k] > 1/(2-s) > 1/2$, the second term is positive, and mutation has the effect of increasing the fitness function g_k. However in the course of practical calculation, when $t \to \infty$, $h[1_k](t)$ goes to 0. Therefore after some generations in the calculation, $h[1_k]$ becomes less than $1/(2-s)$, and g_k decreases by the action of mutation.

If we set the crossover rate $\chi = 1$, the effect of crossover is given by the new schema theorem [8]. For uniform crossover,

$$\widehat{C}D[k,m] = \frac{1}{2}D[k,m], \tag{53}$$

we can see that crossover reduces the magnitude of D coefficients. The effect of mutation on D coefficient is

$$\widehat{M}D[k,m] = (1-2p)^2\, D[k,m]. \tag{54}$$

Mutation also reduces the magnitude of D coefficients.

4.3. *Effect of Linkage*

Here we consider the effect caused by linkage disequilibrium. The population becomes linkage disequilibrium when the population size N is small. In previous paper[14], we showed that the variance of Hamming distance V_H from the optimum solution can be given by

$$V_H = V_a + V_e, \tag{55}$$

where

$$V_a = \sum_{k=1}^{\ell} h[1_k]\,(1 - h[1_k]),$$

and

$$V_e = 2\sum_{k<k'} D[k,k'].$$

We note from equation (34) that $V[f]^{(\mathrm{eq})} = s^2 V_a$ for small s. In general, we can derive the relation for small s

$$V[f] \approx s^2\, V_H. \tag{56}$$

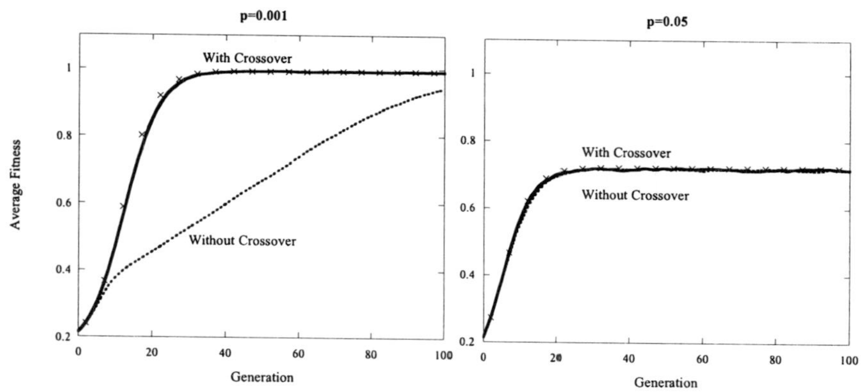

Fig. 1. Evolution of the average fitness $\bar{f}(t)$. The leftmost graph shows the results with weak mutation ($p = 0.001$). The GA calculations with $\chi = 1$ (solid line) and $\chi = 0$ (dotted line) are compared with the theoretical prediction ($\times$). The rightmost graph shows the same results with strong mutation ($p = 0.05$).

From equations (53) and (54), we show the effect of crossover on V_e

$$\widehat{C}V_e = \frac{1}{2}V_e, \tag{57}$$

and that of mutation

$$\widehat{M}V_e = (1 - 2p)^2 V_e. \tag{58}$$

5. Results

We carried out GA calculations on the multiplicative landscape with uniform crossover, and their results were compared with the theory given in the previous section. The number of individuals was 200, and bit length was $\ell = 8$. The selection parameter was $s = 0.2$. We used the mutation rates p of 0.001 and 0.05. The effect of crossover was studied by comparing the experiments with the crossover rates $\chi = 0$ and 1. At $t = 0$, we used the initial value of $h[1_k] = 7/8$. The calculations were performed repeatedly with the same parameters, and their results were averaged over 100 runs.

Figure 1 demonstrates the average fitness $\bar{f}(t)$ by four types of calculations and theoretical prediction ($\times$). Solid lines show the results with crossover $\chi = 1$, and dotted lines without crossover $\chi = 0$. To study the role of mutation, we compared the results with $p = 0.001$ and $p = 0.05$.

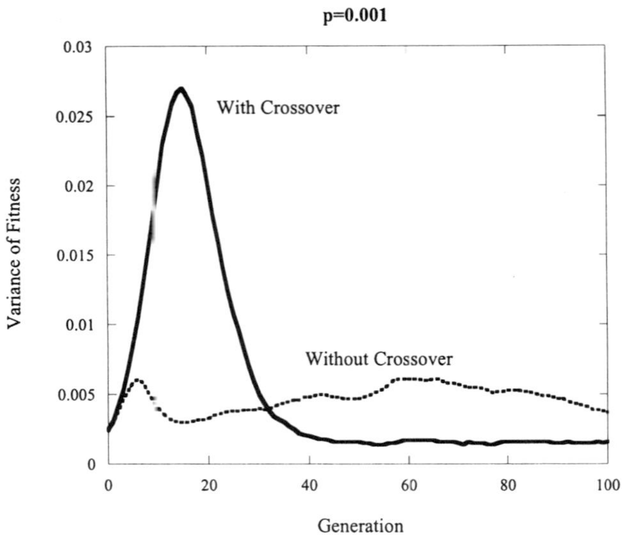

Fig. 2. Variance of fitness $V[f]$ with weak mutation ($p = 0.001$). The solid line stands for the result with crossover ($\chi = 1$), and the dotted line for the result without crossover ($\chi = 0$).

The best performance is observed in the experiment with $p = 0.001$ with crossover. This result is almost identical to the theoretical prediction $\bar{f}^{(eq)}$. When mutation is strong ($p = 0.05$), the effect of crossover is not observed and two calculations, with and without crossover, show the same performance. The worst case is the calculation of weak mutation ($p = 0.001$) without crossover. Therefore crossover is very important when mutation is weak.

These results suggest that the effect of crossover strongly depends on how mutation works in the evolution process. Figure 2 gives the results with weak mutation. This figure shows two variances of fitness $V[f]$ defined in equation (13). If crossover is absent, the variance $V[f]$ is small in the region of $t < 30$. On the other hand, if crossover is active, $V[f]$ is larger than the variance obtained without crossover in this region. Fisher's theorem states that the large variance of fitness can perform well[14].

In Fig. 3, two graphs show the effects of crossover and mutation on V_e. If mutation is weak and without crossover, V_e takes negative large values. Thus this term has a negative contribution to the variance of fitness and reduces the magnitude of $V[f]$. However, if crossover is active, this operator

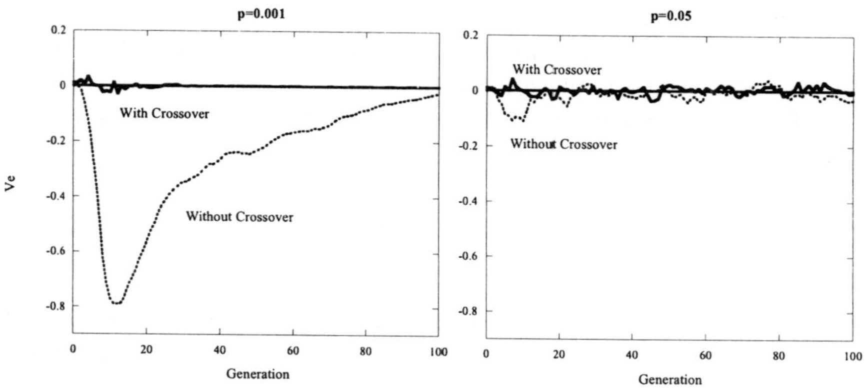

Fig. 3. Variance V_e with ($\chi = 1$) and without ($\chi = 0$) crossover. The leftmost graph shows the results with weak mutation ($p = 0.001$), and the rightmost graph with strong mutation ($p = 0.05$). The solid lines stand for V_e with crossover ($\chi = 1$), and the dotted lines for V_e without crossover ($\chi = 0$).

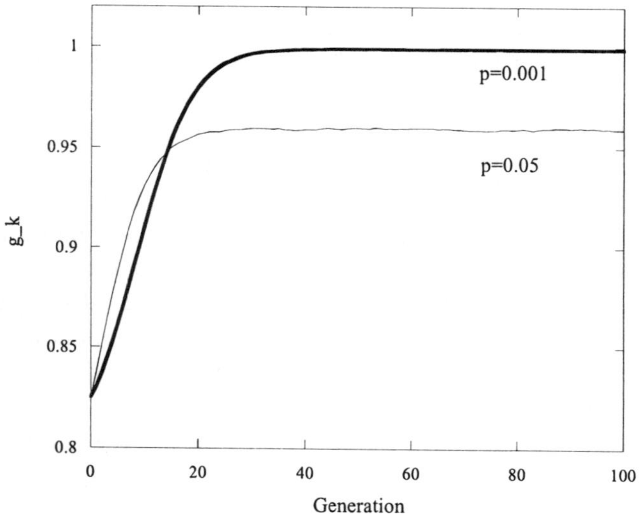

Fig. 4. The rate of approaching the stationary state for $\bar{g}_k$ under crossover. The thick solid line for weak mutation with $p = 0.001$, and the thin solid line for strong mutation with $p = 0.05$.

reduces the magnitude of V_e, and recovers the $V[f]$. In the case of strong mutation (rightmost graph), mutation reduces the magnitude of V_e, and thus crossover has no place to work.

Figure 4 shows the time dependence of the fitness function $g_k(t)$. To estimate g_k, we defined $\bar{g}_k$ as

$$\bar{g}_k = \bar{f}^{1/\ell}.$$

The fitness $\bar{g}_k$ with $p = 0.001$ is compared with $\bar{g}_k$ with $p = 0.05$. At the stationary region, the schema frequency $h[1_k]$ and g_k can be estimated by using equation (52). Setting $\Delta g_k = 0$, we find that $h[1_k] = 0.2$ and $g_k = 0.96$ for $p = 0.05$. This value of g_k agrees quite well with the numerical result at large t. For $p = 0.001$, the fixed point is $h[1_k] = 0.005$ and $g_k = 0.999$.

6. Summary

In this chapter, we studied the evolution of GAs on the multiplicative landscape by applying a new schema theorem. If we use the infinite population model, and ignore random sampling, the assumption of linkage equilibrium holds at all generations when the initial state is in linkage equilibrium. Therefore, the system is completely determined by the first order schema frequencies $h[1_k]$. We showed that the exact schema theorem for $h[1_k]$ can be derived for the GA with the fitness function of multiplicative form.

The theorem for $h[1_k]$ includes the effects of selection and mutation. The process of crossover is not considered because crossover has no effect on a population in linkage equilibrium. However, in practical calculations, there appear effects of random sampling, which make the population in linkage disequilibrium. Therefore we have to take the action of crossover into account in the analysis of GA calculations.

Crossover works as a beneficial operator in this problem. It reduces the magnitude of D coefficients, and makes the linkage of population equilibrium. As a result, crossover accelerates the speed of evolution by increasing the variance of fitness $V[f]$.

As shown in equations (52) and (54), mutation has both positive and negative effects on GA evolution. The effects of mutation in equation (54) are essentially the same as crossover's in equation (53). It is important to note that mutation and crossover are not independent operators, and we have to consider these effects simultaneously in the analysis of GA evolution.

References

1. J.H. Holland, *Adaptation in Natural and Artificial Systems*, (MIT Press, Cambridge, 1992).
2. L. Altenberg, in *Foundations of Genetic Algorithms* 3, (Morgan Kaufmann, San Francisco,1995), p.23.
3. C. R. Stephens and H. Waelbroeck, *Physical Review*, **E57**, 3251 (1998).
4. C. R. Stephens and H. Waelbroeck, *Evolutionary Computation*, **7**, 109 (1999).
5. A. H. Wright, Technical report, University of Montana, Missoula, **MT59812** (1999).
6. M.D. Vose, *The Simple Genetic Algorithms*, (MIT Press, Cambridge, 1999).
7. H. Furutani, in *Foundations of Genetic Algorithms* 7, (Morgan Kaufmann, San Francisco, 2003), p.9.
8. H. Furutani, *IPSJ Journal*, **42**, 2270 (2001).
9. H. Furutani, *Proceedings of the Simulated Evolution and Learning Conference, SEAL'00*, 2696 (2000) .
10. H. Furutani, *Proceedings of the Simulated Evolution and Learning Conference, SEAL'02*, 230 (2002).
11. H. Furutani, *Proceedings of the Genetic and Evolutionary Computation Conference, GECCO-2003*, Lecture Notes in Computer Science, **2723**, 934 (Springer, Berlin, 2003).
12. R.A. Fisher, *The Genetical Theory of Natural Selection*, 2nd edition, (Dover, New York, 1958).
13. J. Maynard Smith, *Evolutionary Genetics*, 2nd edition, (Oxford University Press, Oxford, 1998).
14. H. Furutani, *Proceedings of the Genetic and Evolutionary Computation Conference, GECCO-2001*, 320 (Morgan Kaufmann, San Francisco, 2001).

CHAPTER 7

EVOLUTIONARY LEARNING STRATEGIES FOR ARTIFICIAL LIFE CHARACTERS

Marcio Lobo Netto, Henrique Schützer Del Nero, Cláudio Ranieri

Department of Electronic Systems Engineering, São Paulo University
05508-900 São Paulo, Brazil
E-mail:{lobonett, hdelnero, cranieri}@lsi.usp.br

This chapter describes the incorporation of an adaptive learning model to the framework we have designed to implement artificial life characters. This model is based on language structures representing actions and strategies developed by these artificial characters to solve their problems. A set of problems related to how characters evolve and learn may be studied here, ranging from basic survival in their environment to the emergence of knowledge exchange supported by the usage of language to communicate ideas. Furthermore, it presents also a virtual reality application that has been implemented at the USP Digital CAVE. It is an aquarium inhabited by artificial fishes that are able to evolve in this environment using their learning ability. These fishes have their own cognition, which control their actions – mainly swimming and eating. Through contact and communication with other fishes they learn how to behave in the aquarium, trying to remain alive. The simulation has been implemented in JAVA 3D. A main server and five clients compose the distributed VR version. The server comprehends the simulation of the aquarium and contained fishes, while the clients are responsible for the different views of this aquarium (from inside) projected at each of the five CAVE walls.

1. Introduction

Artificial life is a very promising research area[1]. Although its first concepts were developed for fifty years by eminent scientists as Turing and Von Neumann, involved with the foundations of the computation theory, only recently computers achieved the required power levels to allow interesting experiments. As virtual reality became feasible and computers achieved a very high performance, scientists began to use them as virtual laboratories, where they can coexist with their experiment, and analyze it in new and unprecedented ways.

Artificial Life characters have been employed in a large diversity of situations. In many of them analytical models as cellular automata[2-4] or logic coupled maps[5] are well applied, but other requires a closer representation of true characters[6-9]. This last case comprehends many computer animation purposes, where movie directors just want to coordinate sequences of actions played by virtual actors. While in the first case analytic functions can be used to represent each element and its relationship (dependence) with other elements in the virtual environment, in the second case structured and hierarchical models need to be used. Here morphological and functional aspects should be considered.

As researchers interested in artificial life and cognitive sciences, while also involved for a long time with high performance and distributed computer graphics, we have proposed the development of an Artificial Life Framework, conceived to be open and flexible to accept the addition of new features as time goes by. Object oriented paradigm has been used as a reference to its development. So, different artificial beings can be designed combining the framework features, which includes modules to emulate some of the most important aspects of live beings, as perception, cognition, reasoning, communication, and acting. We have not yet focused on physical body properties, but on the mental models that control the behavior of these artificial creatures.

We have been working on some of the many aspects related to artificial life, and therefore the conceived framework describes the parts that compose the multi functional structure of interesting virtual characters. This framework allows us to add new features to those modules already conceived, or even to add new modules. This chapter describes this architecture, focusing particularly on those assigned to provide character-learning skills, including the actor perception (visual) and cognition, with a stronger emphasis given to the second aspect. This framework has been conceived to provide an interface between the actor and its environment based on sensors, simulating human senses. We have focused our implementation firstly in the vision system, including an image capturing process and its consecutive analysis and classification. This process is conducted by pre-designed perceptual systems, using neural networks, or by other functionally equivalent modules. The perception is passed to a cognitive module, responsible for the decision taking, leading to commands given to actuators and communicators.

The following sections present the related work (2), the character framework (3), a proposed language model (4) and the character-learning skills (5). Finally, we present the virtual reality implementation with the achieved results (6) and conclude with further work (7).

2. Related Work

Many authors are currently working with artificial life, a rich research field. In this chapter we focus our attention on those authors that have been applying cognitive skills to control the behavior of virtual characters, providing these actors with some kind of personality.

2.1. *Work from other Groups*

Some researchers have been involved with this field looking for models that would describe how real life began and evolved. In fact they were looking for a universal life concept, which should be independent of the media on which they exist[2]. Other scientists were looking for physical models to give natural appearance to their characters[6-7], with interesting results. Although very different in nature, these work have been related to evolution and natural selection concepts. In some of them, evolutionary computing schemes such as genetic algorithms have been an important tool to assist the conduction of transformations in the genotype of virtual creatures, allowing them to change from one generation to another. Mutation and combination (by reproduction) provide efficient ways to modify characteristics of a creature, as in real life. Selection plays a role, choosing those that, by some criteria, are the best suited, and therefore allowed to survive and reproduce themselves.

Terzopoulos[6] presented papers showing how to develop artificial beings supporting strategies to simulate natural behavior and cognition. Furthermore he showed the possibility to train these characters to perform certain classes of actions, or even to let them learn how to perform sophisticated actions. Sims[8] proposed an evolutionary model to evolve creatures, where both morphology and behavior adaptation is considered. The results are impressive. Performing some adjustments on initial models, leads to characters well adapted to their environment.

2.2. *Our Previous Work*

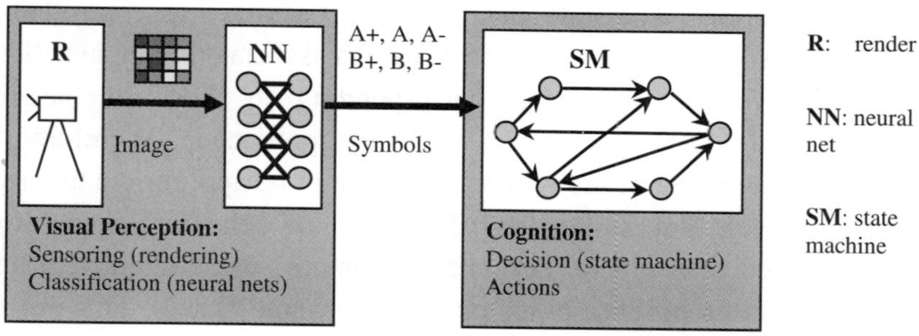

Fig. 1. WOXBOT Character Framework

A general and flexible framework has been proposed in our first project, WOXBOT[9], allowing us to establish an open and extensible model to support different types of implementation. This model consisted of three main classes of modules [Fig. 1]. Each character has a set of sensors, responsible for gathering environmental information and translating it into an internal representation. This information passes through different processing stages, intended to classify it. For instance, the visual module transforms a pictorial representation of an image, gathered through a visual process simulating photography, into a set of logical symbols, which are given to the cognitive module. This module is able to conduct decision processes based on this input and on its own internal state. Neither knowledge acquirement nor handling is considered here. No learning skill is present, and the actors (robots) perform their actions instinctively, following always the same rules, corresponding to their particular state machine. This machine is genetically coded as a bit string, and can evolve through generations. The decisions taken are given to actuators, which implement the command.

In this project the input and output modules were designed to perform their tasks, and no adjustment has been carried out after any creature has become alive. A virtual camera followed by a neural network, trained in advance to correctly classify the scene elements, providing information about it to the cognitive module, implemented the vision system.

The cognitive module has been conceived as a state machine, represented as a bit string that as such could evolve through generations. Therefore the state machine can be adaptively adjusted to perform more convenient actions. The state change in the machine was controlled by the inputs passed by the sensors. Each state is associated with an action.

The initial state machines, corresponding to those of the first generation of characters, were randomly produced. Therefore the behavior of these characters was not expected to be appropriate to ensure a long survival. But a statistical dispersion of behaviors made some better adjusted than others. Periodically some of these characters have been selected to reproduce based on their measured fitness. This process of reproduction (combining crossover and mutation) allowed an improvement in collective behavior after some generations [Fig. 2]. But no learning ability was present in these virtual beings. In this chapter we discuss the introduction of this skill.

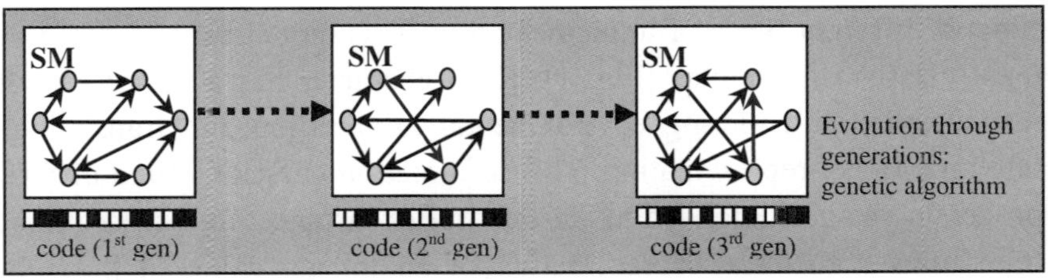

Fig. 2. WOXBOT Evolutionary Model

An overview of the WOXBOT simulation process, showing the environment and some results, is presented below [Fig. 3]. It presents the robot in the arena, and shows also its own view of the scene, allowing it to take the decisions. Different genotypes have been produced after some generations, showing a diversity of strategies considered to be well adjusted to the survival proposal.

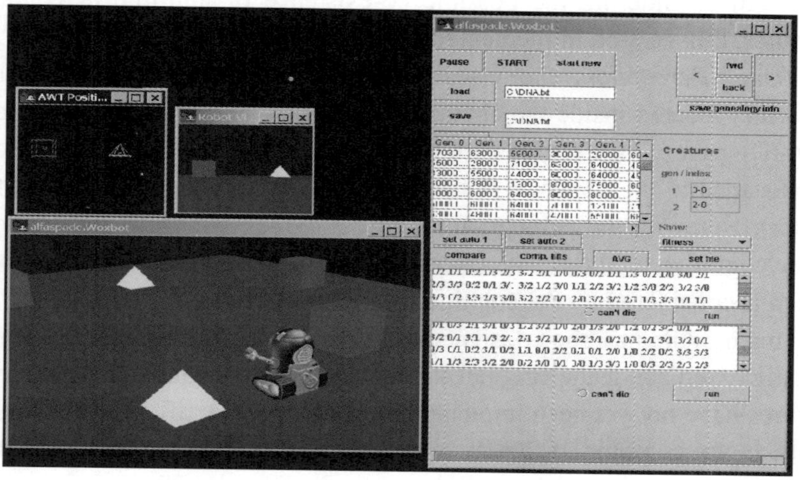

Fig. 3. WOXBOT Simulation

3. Character Framework

The ALGA project presents a new family of characters, represented by fishes[10-11]. It has different perception and cognition modules and a new communication module. The perception is subdivided into a sensor and a classifier, while the cognition comprehends an analyzer and a communication interface [Fig. 4].

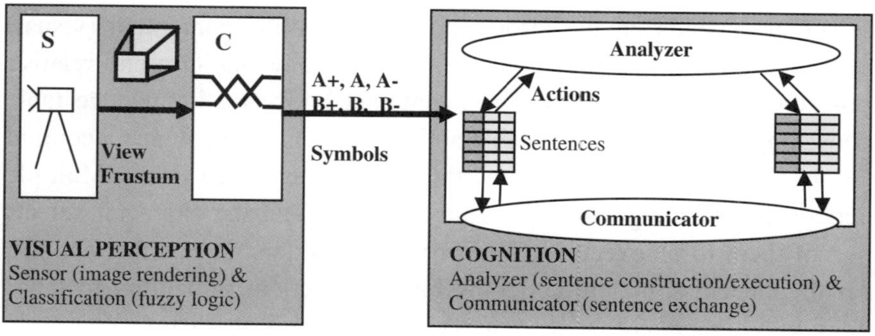

Fig. 4. FISH Character Framework

3.1. *Perception*

Although considering the possible co-existence of multiple perceptual modules, this version implemented just the visual one.

Visual Perception: the visual perception identifies objects in the aquarium located inside the character view frustum, a pyramidal section in a 3D space. Some regions are distinguished in this volume, based on the distance to the observer (far / close) and relative angle (left / right / center). Herewith the perception module provides symbolic information to the cognitive module. This information describes a particular situation, which is considered by the cognition for taking actions.

This module has been designed as an adaptively adjusted fuzzy logic classifier, replacing the original neural network. Currently the adaptive features have not yet been implemented. One of the Artificial Life Group goals is to combine different approaches of evolution and learning strategies. So we intend to study how an adaptive classifier can improve the characters ability to classify scene objects, and how effective it can be to provide refined information to the cognitive module.

3.2. *Cognition*

A simple language interpreter, replacing the previous state machine, represents the cognitive model.

Cognition: each character has a simple language interpreter, which periodically selects one sentence from one book for execution. The selection depends on the information given by the perceptual (visual) system, which provides symbols describing the recognition and relative position of scene elements. The mentioned book is a knowledge table consisting of a set of performable actions at each circumstance, acquired by one fish through contact with other more experienced fishes. Multiple actions can be assigned to the same situation, and the character selects one of them to be executed. This process considers all possible actions, for the current situation, assigning higher selection probability to those ones with higher success score in the history of this character.

Therefore this module can be described as composed by two components: a sentence analyzer and a sentence constructor. Two approaches have been considered here. The first one is to combine single words into sentences looking forward to build behavior strategies. The second one considers a vanishing memory concept, assigning rewards to each decision in a backwards form. Every time a character achieves its goal (catching a peace of food for instance) it is rewarded. This reward is progressively assigned backwards, to the previous actions. So each action that contributes to a successful result in the near future receives part of the rewards acquired by the final action. As a consequence all actions in a sequence that leads to the achievement of a goal are rewarded, and therefore receive an increase in their scores.

In each case the level of success or failure associated to the execution of each sentence (single or multiple action) is kept internally, and represents the characters own knowledge. This information is used to assist the selection process for the execution or construction of new sentences. The current implementation used just the second strategy (Markov chain). In accordance with our goal, we intend to combine both, exploiting the large diversity of strategies that should arise.

Analyzer: the analyzer coordinates the selection of statements (words representing single actions, or sentences expressing more elaborated strategies). This selection is carried out based on the character's own experience, expressed by the level of certainty assigned to each statement, as well as to the expected level of success. The first term (certainty or experience) represents the number of times that the character has been in that situation, when it decided by one of the possible statements. The second term (success) is associated to each of these statements, and is a measure of success assigned to this particular choice.

A first implementation considers statements just as words (single actions). We implemented a vanishing memory concept based on Markov chains, in order to be able to evaluate latter the effectiveness of the present actions, since they do not necessarily, and normally not, can be evaluated immediately. For instance, the decision to follow a piece of food falling in the water is necessary to let the fish approximate itself from this piece, being then able to catch it. Therefore a memory mechanism is used to allow the association of a success value with each decision, even if they do not lead immediately to a reward. In fact, currently the only reward comes from eating, since it leads to an increase of the actual energy level of each creature.

We intend to extend this concept, allowing the construction of sentences from basic words. These sentences would then be associated to strategies. In this approach, sentences are a set of actions and should be evaluated as a unity, to which we can assign a level of success at the end of the execution. This would allow us to analyze closed strategies, those that remain fixed until they have been completed.

The vanishing memory approach is more flexible, allowing a real time correction of any emerging strategy, since a new decision is taken at every simulation step. Furthermore it presented nice results, showing the emergence of a common sense among all fishes. This could be observed comparing the books (actions repertoire) from all fishes and the certainty values assigned to each word on their books.

Communicator: A communicator is present in this framework, giving the characters the possibility to exchange their knowledge, and so allowing some characters to teach others. The language model, described ahead, gives more details of this structure and functionality.

The implementation is based on the message passing concept between different characters running as independent threads. When one fish fill the proximity of another one in its neighborhood, it sends him a message, basically giving a tip, which may be or not accepted by its interlocutor.

The following sub-sections provide more details about the procedures used to construct and execute sentences (or statements).

3.2.1. Sentences Constructor

The sentences constructor is responsible for analyzing the repertoire of sentences in order to propose the construction of new ones, using its vocabulary. One part of the vocabulary is instinctive (the character is born with a small set of words) and another one may be extended during its existence. In order to construct new sentences the constructor combines existing sentences, considering their level of success.

Every character is born with a small vocabulary, corresponding to all known sentences at the beginning of its life. New vocabularies and sentences may be acquired when talking to other characters.

New sentences may be acquired in two forms: a) listening to speeches (tips) from colleagues and considering their suggestions (reflecting how appropriate they are), or b) by an internal inspection conducted by the constructor, which in some cases proposes new sentences, combining other already existent. This concept emulates a type of reasoning or self-reflection by the character. Currently only the first approach has been implemented.

3.2.2. Sentences Executor

The sentences executor is periodically required to take one sentence and to execute it, leading to a character action. Currently, the implementation assigns up to four actions for each situation. The executor makes some measurements on internal character variables (states) in order to observe how they change, and, based on them, modifies the history of success or failure associated to that sentence in conjunction with the circumstance where it happened. A typical internal variable is the stored energy of the character. A sentence can pertain to one of three classes, listed bellow:

Action Sentences: these sentences lead to an action as gathering, touching, bringing, etc... When executing bad actions (inside a context) the character is punished, while good actions rewards it. For instance a valid sentence here could be:

Context: if ball is close Sentence: then catch the ball

Movement Sentences: movement sentences control the character motor system with actions as: step ahead, step back, turn right, turn left or stay, and are a particular sub-class of action sentences.

Speech Sentences: speech sentences determine the transmission of some information (normally just a sentence accompanied by its context).

Context: if interlocutor is younger Sentence: then give him a tip

Where the tip itself is another sentence with its context.

3.3. *Communicator*

The communication module is responsible for message exchange between characters. Considering their relative proximity, two characters may exchange information (sentences from their internal knowledge).

Verbal Communicator: the communication module represents a speech mechanism, being responsible for the knowledge exchange between fishes. Therefore it is a core component in the new learning ability associated to the cognition.

3.4. *Learning Ability*

A learning ability has been added to the cognition, and is strongly related to the communication ability. The learning process is composed by two phases. First, inexperienced fishes receive tips from more experienced colleagues, adding these tips as new statements to their own knowledge book. Second, they classify these statements using an importance approach, considering the accumulative experience on that situation and the success rate of each statement to incrementally increase their certainty on the selection of the most appropriate statement for each situation. Its implementation is better described above (cognition).

4. Language Model

Here we describe the language components (tables) and procedures (rules) to handle them, in order to build and execute sentences.

4.1. *Language Components*

Two tables are used to keep the known vocabulary and repertoire of sentences of each character.

4.1.1. Dictionary / Vocabulary

Every character has a small vocabulary, which basically consists of actions that it can perform. This vocabulary is a subset of the universal vocabulary comprehending all words known by all individuals.

A character is born with a fixed small set of words, representing those actions that can be associated with an instinctive procedure. During its life it can learn new words, based on its own personal experience. An example of a vocabulary is presented below [Table 1]. Two possible situations are considered here: learning by doing and learning by talking, which are better described ahead. Every word has two indices: one showing how frequently it appears in sentences, and another saying how important they are. The importance is calculated analyzing the effectiveness of the correspondent action.

Table 1. Vocabulary / Subset of the Universal Dictionary

Word	Frequency of use	Importance
A	10%	High
B	30%	Low
C	40%	Medium
C	20%	Medium
D	50%	High
Instinctive vocabulary (genetically coded) – basic actions		
Vocabulary acquired by experience (not genetically coded)		

4.1.2. Sentences Book

Each character has also a table where it keeps its acquired knowledge, expressed in simple language structures, composed by a set of few words. One example could be: *step ahead – turn right – catch something*, where each of these 3 actions corresponds to one word of its vocabulary. The sentences book [Table 2] keeps all sentences from one character (single to multiple word sentences). Although one sentence relates to just one situation (input), the same situation can be associated with multiple sentences. In this case a Monte Carlo method selects the sentence, based on their probability of occurrence (confidence) and importance (fitness).

Table 2. Sentences Book

Sentences	Inputs	Confidence	Fitness
A	x	40%	High
B	y	40%	Medium
C	z	20%	High
AB	x	40%	High
BCA	y	60%	Low
ADC	x	20%	Medium
DDB	z	80%	Low
Instinctive sentences (genetically coded) – basic actions			
Sentences acquired by experience, on self-reflexive analysis (a type of reasoning) or on talks (not genetically coded)			

When a new generation of characters is computed, the genetically coded part of these tables are combined, producing a new one. Herewith we allow the perpetuation of basic (instinctive) skills through generations. The non-genetically coded lines remain empty, and will be filled by experience, acquired during life process.

4.2. *Language Analysis and Composition*

The process of analysis and composition is responsible for continuously evaluating the history of all valid sentences, in order to classify them according to its convenience of being selected at each circumstance. Furthermore, the composition is responsible for the proposition of new sentences, based on expected results, which can be foreseen considering the history of other known sentences.

These processes consider the local vocabulary and sentences book. The usage of the vocabulary allows trials with those words that have not yet been inserted into sentences. But the analysis of existing sentences, and their combination into new ones allows the exploitation of more complex sequences of actions. The system acts in response to its own experimentations. Therefore if a new sentence seems to be inappropriate, it will probably receive a low importance score, and may be either rarely used, or even excluded from the sentences book. By another side good sentences tend to receive high importance scores, and therefore will probably be selected more frequently than other with lower scores.

4.3. *Execution of Language Statements*

The execution of language statements, or sentences, is performed by a process that considers the importance conferred to them in different situations, as well as their probability of occurrence (confidence), based on their history. Therefore both aspects are relevant to the decision. Those sentences associated to higher frequency of occurrence represent a more conservative character behavior, while those with higher importance may represent more dared character behavior.

The framework permits the usage of a variable to describe the predominant behavior, or the character personality.

4.4. *Evolving Strategies from Combination of Sentences*

Our goal is to implement a system, formed by an analyzer and a composer, able to propose sentences where strategies are present. Since we have implemented this system as an open framework, more sophisticated models based on artificial intelligence may be added to it. We believe that AI may provide fruitful results for the achievement of intelligent strategies, but we are also considering the usage of simple schemas based on genetic algorithms to evolve these sentences.

5. Learning Skills

The learning skills of these characters are two fold: information may be acquired by communication or by self-analysis abilities.

5.1. *Communicating Knowledge (Social Learning)*

The first learning skill results from the possibility of information exchange between characters, which have been implemented with an inter-character communication mechanism. This allows the exchange of symbols accompanied by statistics associated to it. Herewith we allow a character, wanting to cooperate with another one, to tell some sentences to this other one, which are from its point of view, convenient at certain circumstance. As a consequence we can identify learning by talking skill.

Learning by Talking: the proximity of two characters may induce their conversation, which in fact is the transfer of a single word or sentence involved by its semantics, from one to the other. For instance if both recognize that something is good for them, one can teach the other one what to do in that case, based on its own previous experience. Two situations are foreseen here. The character may want to cooperate, teaching the right action (word or sentence), or it can defect, telling the other wrong words or sentences. This pre-disposition to tell the truth always, sometimes or never may be represented in some intern personality feature of the character, and may be part of those coded genetically or not.

5.2. *Self-Analysis (Adaptive Learning)*

The cognitive module has been conceived as a set of tables containing language information (words, sentences and the history of success / failure associated to them) and an analyzer, which selects one sentence to be executed. For this selection all sentences related to the current input are considered, but weighted by their importance, which in turn is obtained from its history and rate of success. As presented in section 4, new sentences may be proposed, or removed from the sentences book. Here we can identify the learning by reasoning skill.

Learning by Reasoning: in this case some actions may lead to a situation where the repertoire of the character is increased, or the relative importance of its elements change, by the assumption that a new word or sentence has a special meaning at that circumstance.

6. Aquarium and Fishes Implementation

The simulation environment, the aquarium, corresponds to the space inhabited by a population of fishes, all implemented in JAVA 3D as independent running threads. Multiple view cameras can be used, allowing the user to select one of them in a single monitor version, or to watch simultaneously 5 cameras in the CAVE version. These cameras may be fixed outside or inside the aquarium, or even be attached to one of the fishes, giving the users the possibility to follow the movement of this particular fish [Fig. 5]. Furthermore interesting information is provided about the vocabulary of the fishes (cognition), as well as about accumulated energy histories (statistics), their instantaneous vision and corresponding action. The main results are: a 3D virtual environment for the simulation of artificial beings; its virtual reality implementation, running on a CAVE; and the extension of a general purpose artificial life character framework, through the incorporation of learning abilities.

6.1. *Desktop Implementation*

The desktop version is useful particularly to study the evolution of cognitive skills. The simulator API provides different tabs.

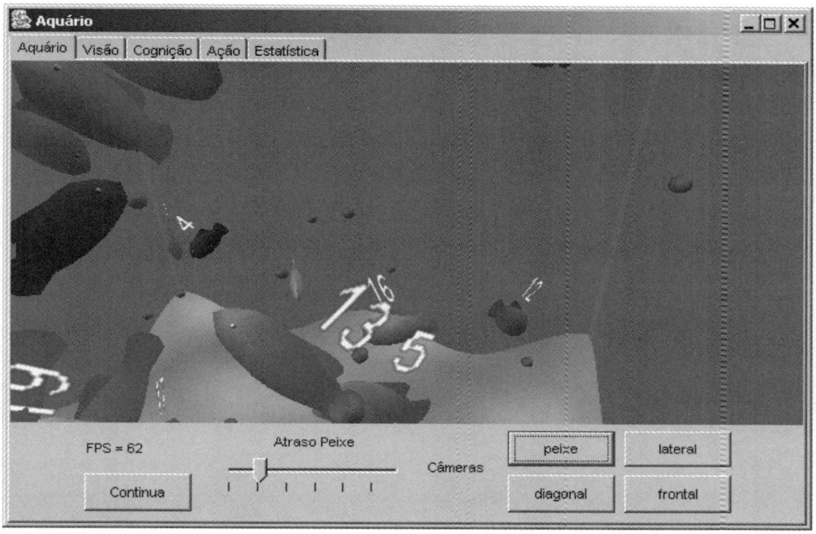

Fig. 5. Fish Perspective View from the Aquarium

Aquarium: a 3D view from the environment and fishes. Fishes are represented by different colors depending on their knowledge, which evolves during the time. They are born yellow and then turn to orange and red, as their knowledge grows [Fig. 6].

Vision: symbolic information about the vision of each fish (what is seem by each fish).

Cognition: the knowledge book of each fish, with the actual set of words of this table.

Statistics: measurements about actual energy (food) levels, the accumulated value of it (history of everything eaten), and the actual percentage of acquired knowledge.

This simulator is available as an applet (2D and 3D versions[a]) in the Project–Prototype part of the ALGA project website[12-13], and therefore runs in web browsers.

[a] The 3D applet version requires the installation of JAVA3D.

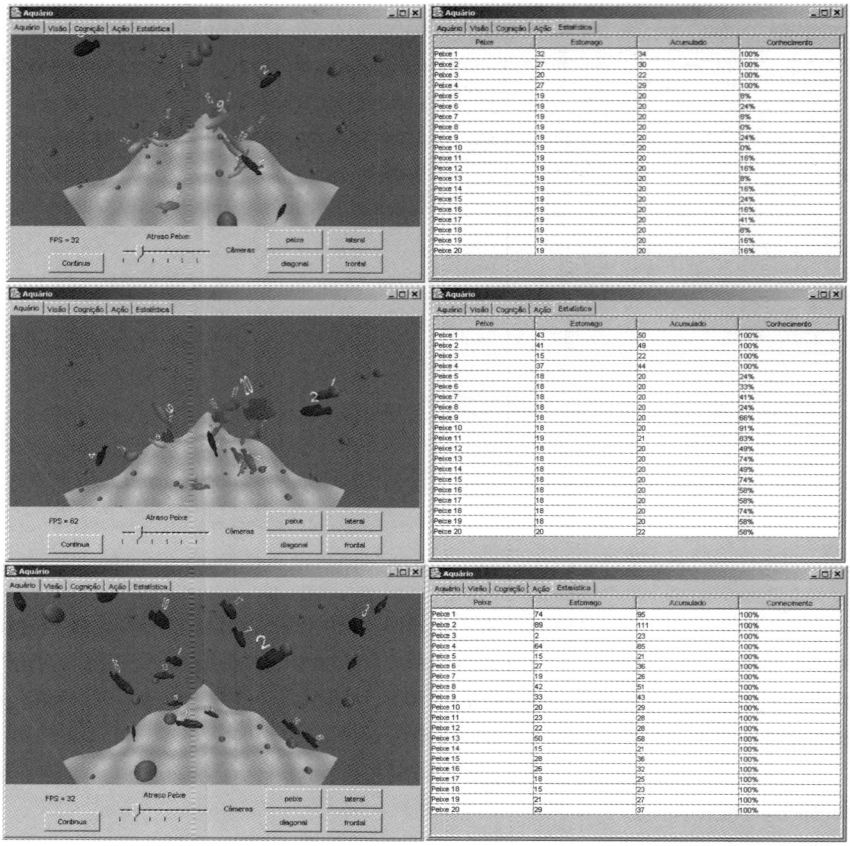

Fig. 6. AQUARIUM Life Cycle View (left) and Statistics (right)
Initial (top), Intermediary (middle) and Final (bottom)

6.2. *Distributed Virtual Reality (CAVE) Implementation*

The CAVE distributed implementation runs on a PC cluster. The model used is composed by a main server, responsible for the core simulation of the fish's behavior (multi-threaded approach) and by 5 clients, for rendering the images from virtual cameras, projected on the CAVE sides (4 walls and the floor). In this implementation we use a replication of the entire scene description in all cluster PCs, but while the main simulation runs in one of them, the other five are the sole responsible for the real time rendering of each of the 5 views. All clients request the server for updated information concerning the scene elements, mainly the position and orientation of each fish and other objects as food particles. The synchronization is carried out automatically, during the update request, keeping all clients with consistent scene information. The JAVA Remote Method Invocation (RMI) is used to establish the communication and correspondent synchronization between the server and all 5 clients. Furthermore the JAVA 3D stereo mode is enabled, allowing a really immersive experience in the CAVE using appropriate stereo glasses. This simple structure was enough to ensure a real-time frame rate (around 40 frames per second) without any perceptual slide between the animations presented at each of the 5 CAVE sides. The users have an immersive experience [Fig. 7], felling as they were inside the aquarium. In the near future we intend to exploit the distribution of the server among different PCs in a cluster, implementing then a truly distributed VR application. The use of multi-threading, implementing each fish as a separate character, will help in the distribution of this simulator. The current number of fishes in the simulation, 20, did not impose any requirements for this distribution, but this will certainly be necessary for a larger aquarium inhabited by hundreds or thousands of fishes.

We present here images taken in the CAVE environment, showing the results of the distributed version running on the PC cluster. The first image is an internal CAVE view running the virtual aquarium simulation, and the second one shows a user having this 3D immersive experience.

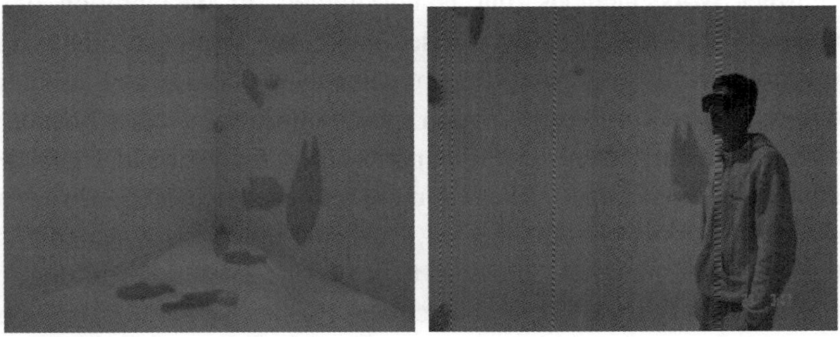

Fig. 7. AQUARIUM a) Distributed VR Implementation; b) User immersion

7. Conclusion and Further Work

This chapter presents how a learning approach has been incorporated to our artificial life framework. This new approach added an inter-character communication feature, expressed through the use of a simple language, also used to express the reasoning of these artificial life creatures.

We have conceived and implemented this new framework, using our previous experience with the WOXBOT model. Through this learning skill the ALGA characters are able to compose new sentences and to verify how appropriate they are to conduct more frequently the most appropriate actions (increasing some character scores, as energy for instance). Furthermore we have proposed a communication structure that allows characters to exchange part of their own knowledge (words or sentences associated with the character perception and its importance in certain circumstances). The scenario used for the current project is an aquarium, inhabited by fishes of different species.

This chapter presented some implementation results. One of them, the desktop tool, has shown to be very useful in the analysis of the artificial life beings, mainly their learning and decision taking skills. Different information is provided at run-time, allowing us to understand how the cognition of these creatures evolves, based on their learning capabilities. The other implementation, on a virtual reality CAVE environment, shows the possibility to involved humans in an immersive experience in this virtual aquarium. Finally another important issue is that this distributed implementation runs on a PC cluster.

Further work includes, but is not limited, to the addition of an adaptively adjusted classifier (based on fuzzy logic) to the visual perception module, and other types of perceptual modules, as a simulated audition. This new visual perception should improve the classification of distinct situations, based on the experience of the artificial characters. Also, the mentioned approaches for more refined statement constructions and analysis should be implemented. Particular interest is assigned to the extension of all modules, allowing their genetic evolution, through the use of genetically coded general machines. Finally, we intend also to use this model to simulate diverse social behaviors, expecting to be able to identify both - competition between different species and cooperation between characters. We intend to analyze a large set of experiments in a scene populated by these characters. Members of the Artificial Life and Cognitive Sciences Groups (Artlife & Cognitio) are interested to use this framework to study global economical and sociological phenomena.

Acknowledgments

Our thanks to Brazilian National Research Council (CNPq) for the under-graduation scholarship (PBIC), granted to this project.

References

1. M. L. Netto and J. E. Kogler Jr. Eds. Artificial life: Towards New Generation of Computer Animation. *Computers & Graphics.* 25.6, Holland, Elsevier (2001)
2. C. Adami, *Introduction to Artificial Life*, Springer Verlag (1998)
3. E. W. Bonabeau and G. Therulaz, Why do we need artificial life? *Artificial Life an Overview*, C. G. Langton Eds., MIT Press (1995)
4. D. B. Fogel, *Evolutionary Computation, Toward new Philosophy of Machine Intelligence*, IEEE Press (1995)
5. K. Kaneko, The Coupled Map Lattice: Introduction, Phenomenology, Lyapunov Analysis, Thermo- dynamics. *Theory and Applications*, John Wiley Sons (1993)
6. D. Terzopoulos (org.), Artificial Life for Graphics in Animation, Multimedia and Virtual Reality, in *ACM/SIGGRAPH 98* Course Notes 22, (1998)
7. C. Phillips and N. I. Badler, Jack: A toolkit for manipulating articulated figures. *ACM/SIGGRAPH Symposium on User Interface Software*, Banff, Canada, (1988)
8. K. Sims, Evolving 3D Morphology and Behavior by Competition. *Artificial Life* (1994)
9. F. R. Miranda et al An Artificial Life Approach for the Animation of Cognitive Characters. *Computers & Graphics*. 25.6, Holland, Elsevier (2001)
10. M. L. Netto et al An Evolutionary Learning Strategy for Multi Agents *SEAL2002 - 4th Asia-Pacific Conference on Simulated Evolution and Learning*, Singapore (November 2002)
11. M. L. Netto and C. Ranieri Artificial Life Simulation on Distributed Virtual Reality Environments. *SRV2003 - VI Symposium on Virtual Reality*, Brazil (October 2003)
12. ALGA Project WebSite http://www.lsi.usp.br/~alga
13. ARTLIFE Group WebSite http://www.lsi.usp.br/~artlife

CHAPTER 8

ADAPTIVE STRATEGY FOR GA INSPIRED BY BIOLOGICAL EVOLUTION

Hidefumi Sawai and Susumu Adachi

Communications Research Laboratory
588-2, Iwaoka, Nishi-ku, Kobe 651-2492 Japan
E-mail: {sawai, sadachi}@crl.go.jp

Gene duplication theory was first proposed by a Japanese biologist, Ohno, in the 1970s. Inspired by the theory, we developed a gene-duplicating genetic algorithm (GDGA) with several variants. Individuals with various gene lengths are evolved based on a parameter-free genetic algorithm (i.e., a new GA without genetic parameters set in advance) and then genes with different lengths are concatenated by migrating among sub-populations (i.e., a population was divided in advance into several sub-populations according to each gene-duplication type). To verify the algorithm's performance, we previously performed a comparative study and found a relationship between the features of the test functions and the adequate types of gene-duplication. In this study, we further describe how we have extended the scheme by automatically adapting its search strategy to various test functions without *a priori* knowledge of them, and verify the performance of the adaptive strategy compared to that of an adequate type of gene-duplication.

1. Introduction

The genetic algorithm (GA) [2] is an evolutionary computational paradigm inspired by biological evolution [1]. GAs have been successfully used for many practical applications such as functional optimization, combinatorial optimization, and optimizing the design of parameters for machines [3]. However, the design of an optimal evolutionary strategy in a GA [14,15] is difficult because the evolutionary algorithm must be run many times for the trial-and-error process to work. To avoid this problem with the setting of adaptive parameters, we have developed a parameter-free GA (PfGA) [27] for which specific initial values need not be set as control parameters for genetic operations. This algorithm uses simple random values or probabilities to set almost all genetic parameters. The PfGA has also been implemented as a parallel distributed process on a parallel computer [28,29].

For the case when a strong epistasis [7] between genes exists, several approaches to linkage learning [11] have been investigated. These includes the messy GA [6,8], linkage learning by estimating distributions [9,10], BOAs (Bayesian optimization algorithms) [13], linkage identification by nonlinearity or non-monotonicity checks [12], and so on.

Gene duplication is a rather different approach to solving such problems. The principle was first advocated by a Japanese biologist, Ohno, in the 1970's [16]. Biological organisms, including viruses, plants, and animals, duplicate their own genes during the process of evolution. Inspired by the theory of gene duplication, we have developed gene-duplicating GAs (GDGAs) with several variants [30]. These variants include a gene-concatenating GA, gene-prolonging GA, gene-coupling GA, and extended gene-coupling GA.

We discussed the feasibility of basing a gene-duplicating GA on the PfGA, on the basis of results from test functions, at the first ICEO held in 1996 [30]. We then continued our discussion of the performance of the GDGA, in terms of more general test functions [26,5]. When we solve a multidimensional (e.g., n-dimensional) optimization problem, each variable x_i in each sub-dimension, $(i = 1, 2, \ldots, n)$, is first coded as a gene. Next, a fitness function, e.g., $f(x_1, x_2, \ldots, x_i)$ is defined for each sub-dimension, e.g., $j = 1, 2, \ldots, i$, and the GA then produces a quasi-optimal solution, e.g., $(x_1^*, x_2^*, \ldots, x_i^*)$. Individuals with genes corresponding to quasi-optimal solutions are evolved by concatenating the genes, which allows the optimization to be solved in a higher dimension k $(i \leq k \leq n)$. We have ascertained the best strategy, including the best type of duplication, good migration rates, and the best basic GA, depending on the features of the test functions used [31].

On the other hand, if the features of a given test function are unknown, how should we determine the appropriate strategy to obtain good performance? In this study, we describe an adaptive strategy of evolution for any function without *a priori* knowledge. To evaluate the performance of the adaptive GDGAs, we use a set of general test functions. We verify whether the strategy (i.e., the gene-duplication type) selected automatically through the adaptive process is identical with the best strategy. We also determine what level of performance can be obtained without *a priori* knowledge by comparing our results to results obtained with *a priori* knowledge of the test function.

2. Review of GAs Inspired by Biological Evolution

2.1. *Disparity Theory of Evolution*

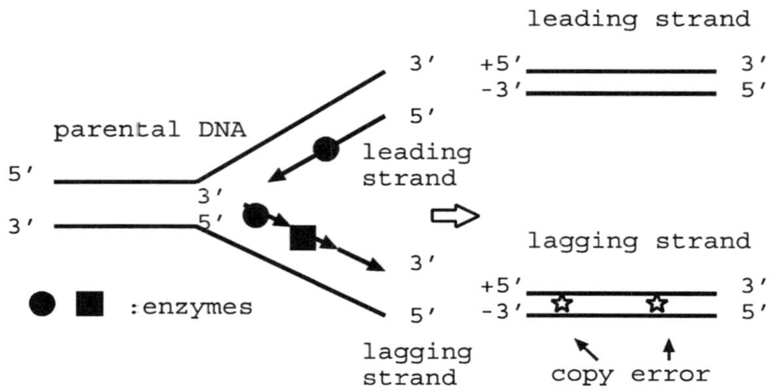

Fig. 1. A hypothesis in the *disparity theory of evolution*

As Charles Darwin claimed in the "Origin of Species" in 1859[1], a major factor contributing to evolution is mutation, which can be caused by spontaneous misreading of bases during DNA synthesis. Semiconservative replication of double-stranded DNA is an asymmetric process where there is a leading and a lagging strand. Furusawa et al. proposed a "disparity theory of evolution"[17] based on a difference in frequency of strand-specific base misreading between the leading and lagging DNA strands (i.e., *disparity model*). Fig.1 shows a hypothesis in the disparity theory of evolution. In the figure, the leading strand is copied smoothly, whereas in the lagging strand a copy error can occur because plural enzymes are necessary to produce its copy. This disparity or asymmetry in producing each strand occurs because of the different mutation rates in the leading and lagging strands. This maintains "diversity" of DNAs in population as generations proceed. The disparity model guarantees that the mutation rate of some leading strands is zero or very small. When circumstances change, though the original *wild type* can not survive, selected mutants might adapt under the new circumstances as a *new wild type*. In their study, the disparity model was compared with a parity model in which there was no statistical difference in the frequency of base misreading between strands as in the generally accepted model.

The disparity model outperformed the parity model in a knapsack optimization problem. They clearly showed that the advantageous situation for the disparity model happened in the cases of small population, strong pressure, high mutation rate, sexual reproduction with diploidy, and strong competition. On the other hand, survival conditions for the parity model are large population, weak selection pressure, low mutation rate, asexual reproduction with haploidy, and weak competition.[18]

2.2. *Parameter-free GA*

We have developed a parameter-free genetic algorithm (PfGA)[28] in which no control parameters for genetic operations need to be set as constants in advance. It merely uses random values or probabilities for setting almost all genetic parameters. The PfGA is inspired by the *disparity theory of evolution* mentioned above. The idea is based on the disparity of copy error rates in the *leading* and *lagging* strands of DNA when each strand makes its copy. This leads to *diversity* in a biological ecosystem. The search strategy in the PfGA is based on a dynamic change of sub-population size extracted from the population. This strategy enables an adaptive search to achieve a delicate balance between global and local search methods.

In this section, the PfGA is described in detail. Its basic procedure and the selection scheme with a local elitist-preserving strategy will be explained. First of all, the population of the PfGA is considered as a whole set **S** of individuals which corresponds to all possible solutions. From this whole set **S**, a subset **S'** is introduced. All genetic operations such as selection, crossover, and mutation are conducted for **S'**, thus evolving the subpopulation **S'**. From the subpopulation **S'**, we introduce a *family* which contains two parents and two children generated from the two parents. Fig.2 shows the population **S**, subpopulation **S'**, *family* **S"** (left) and selection rule (right) in the PfGA.

The PfGA procedure is as follows:

Step 1. Select one individual randomly from the whole population **S**, and add this individual to the subpopulation **S'**.

Step 2. Select one individual randomly from the whole population **S**, and again add this individual to the subpopulation **S'**.

Step 3. Select two individuals randomly from the subpopulation **S'** and perform crossover between these individuals as parent 1 (P_1) and parent 2 (P_2).

Step 4. For one randomly chosen child of the two children generated from the crossover, perform mutation at random.

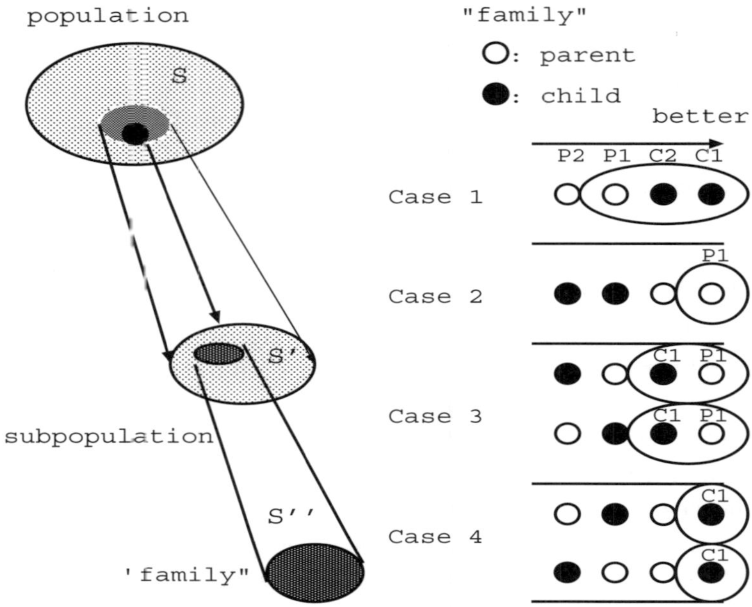

Fig. 2. Population, subpopulation and family (left), and selection rules (right) in Parameter-free GA

Step 5. Among the parents (P_1 and P_2) and the two generated children (C_1 and C_2) select one to three individuals depending on the following cases (i.e., Case 1 to 4), and feed them back to the subpopulation **S'**.

Step 6. If the number in subpopulation **S'** is greater than one, go to Step 3; otherwise, go to Step 2.

For the crossover operation of PfGA, we use multiple-point crossover in which randomly changeable crossover points and locations between two parents' chromosomes is adopted every time when the crossover is operated. For the mutation operation, one child is randomly chosen from the two offspring. Then a randomly chosen portion of the child's chromosome is randomly inverted (i.e., bit-flipped). For the selection operation, we compare the fitness values of all individuals (C_1, C_2, P_1, P_2) in the family. Selection rules shown in Figure 2 are used for four different cases depending on the fitness values of the parents and children.

Case 1: If the fitness values of the two children are better than those of the parents, then C_1, C_2 and $arg\ max_{P_i}(f(P_1), f(P_2))$ are left in **S'**, thus increasing the size of **S'** by one. Since in this case the two parents produced better children, these children should be preserved and only the better parent with possibly good schemata is preserved to avoid increasing the number of individuals in **S'**.

Case 2: If the fitness values of C_1 and C_2 are worse than those of P_1 and P_2, then only $arg\ max_{P_i}(f(P_1), f(P_2))$ is left in **S'**, thus decreasing the size of **S'** by one. In this case no better children were produced from the two parents. Because no optimal solutions would be guaranteed if all individuals were removed from **S'**, only the better parent should be preserved to maintain the stability of the system.

Case 3: If the fitness value of either P_1 or P_2 is better than that of the children, $arg\ max_{C_i}(f(C_1), f(C_2))$ and $arg\ max_{P_i}(f(P_1), f(P_2))$ are left in **S'**, thus maintaining the size of **S'**. In this case one of the children is worse than the better parent, but better than the worse parent. At least the better parent should be preserved to maintain the stability of the system. Since at least one child better than the worse parent was produced, that child should replace the worse parent and remain in **S'**.

Case 4: In all other situations, $arg\ max_{C_i}(f(C_1), f(C_2))$ is preserved and then one individual randomly chosen from **S** is added to **S'**, thus maintaining the size of **S'**. In this case one of the children is better than the better parent. At least one better child should be preserved in **S'**. Moreover, to guarantee the flexibility of the system, the subpopulation **S'** should not be prematurely converged. A new individual should be added to the subpopulation **S'** from the population **S**.

2.3. *Parallel Distributed Processing of PfGA*

Generally speaking, parallel processing aims at accelerating the speed of processing. In the case of GA, it aims at reaching better solutions faster than sequential processing by extending the search space. Parallel and distributed processing of GA has been extensively studied, [19–23] where the *granularity* is ranging from fine- to coarse-grained, and the mode of processing is covering both synchronous and asynchronous processing. The granularity concerns the size of a process assigned to a processor. In the case of a fine-grained parallel GA model, the (overlapping) neighborhoods of the individuals constitute the units of processing. On the other hand, coarse-grained parallel GA assigns a subpopulation as a unit of processing, and some few individuals are migrated among subpopulations at an appropriate rate. The latter model is called an "island model," and one island (subpopulation) constitutes one "deme" which is a minimum recombinational unit of biological species.

We have developed a uniformly distributed architecture and a hierarchical master-slave architecture for parallel processing of the PfGA. Effects of hierarchical migration methods are verified where the methods effectively decrease the number of evaluations to converge with the success rates held or improved by increasing the number of subpopulations [29].

2.4. *GAs Inspired by Gene Duplication*

Inspired by the gene-duplication theory, we have developed a gene-duplicating GA (GDGA). Several variants for this algorithm are considered. Individuals with various gene lengths are evolved based on the PfGA and then genes with different lengths are concatenated through migration among sub-populations. We use four types of gene-duplicating GAs as possible variants: a gene-concatenating GA, a gene-prolonging GA, a gene-coupling GA, and an extended gene-coupling GA. The sub-solutions, e.g., $\{(x_1^*, x_2^*, \ldots, x_i^*)\}$, within each sub-population concatenate with each other in different manners ranging from type A to type D. Each type of gene-duplication is described in detail as follows:

(1) **Gene-concatenating GA (Type A):**
As shown in Fig. 3, the sub-solutions, $\{x_i^*\}$, $(i = 1, 2, \ldots, n)$ in each sub-population, S_i' $(i = 1, 2, \ldots, n)$ evolve in parallel by using the PfGA. These sub-solutions are concatenated at the same time within the sub-population S' after a few generations. This concatenation of sub-solutions is realized when an offspring better than its parents emerges in each sub-population S_i' $(i = 1, 2, \ldots, n)$. The fitness function for each individual is defined as $f(a_1, a_2, \ldots, a_{i-1}, x_i, a_{i+1}, \ldots, a_n)$, where a_i is a constant value. Each constant value a_i should be set based on the features of a test function. However, if there is separability among the dimensions of the test function, the constant value can be set to zero. Even if there is no separability among different dimensions, some combinations or concatenations of the sub-solutions might be applicable, to some extent, to obtaining the final solution in sub-population S'.

(2) **Gene-prolonging GA (Type B):**
As shown in Fig. 4, the first sub-solution x_1^* in the corresponding first sub-population S_1' evolves after a few generations when an offspring better than its parents emerges, and then the sub-solution is copied and concatenated with itself (i.e., x_1^*), generating a double-sized sub-solution, (x_1^*, x_1^*), that migrates to the second sub-population S_2'. This process will continue until the final solution with size n, i.e., $(x_1^*, \ldots,$

x_n^*) is obtained. Each individual $(x_1, \ldots, x_i)$ with a gene of length $i \times l$ (l is the gene-length in each dimension i) evolves in each S_i' according to the fitness function $f(x_1, x_2, \ldots, x_i, a_{i+1}, \ldots, a_n)$, where a_i is a constant value. For a reason similar to that with type A, the constant value a_i can be set to zero for simplicity. The sub-solution in a lower dimension is copied and concatenated with itself, which preserves the characteristics of the lower dimension in successive higher dimensions.

(3) **Gene-coupling GA (Type C):**
As shown in Fig. 5, sub-solutions of different sizes (e.g., x_1^* and (x_1^*, x_2^*, x_3^*)) evolve in parallel in the corresponding sub-populations (e.g., S_1' and S_3'), and then these sub-solutions are coupled with each other (e.g., forming $(x_1^*, x_1^*, x_2^*, x_3^*)$) for migration to sub-populations of corresponding sizes (e.g., S_4'). Each individual in each sub-population S_i' evolves according to the PfGA and judgments based on the fitness function $f(x_1, x_2, \ldots, x_i, a_{i+1}, \ldots, a_n)$, where a_i is a constant value. The constant value can again be set to zero for simplicity; however, this definition allows different contributions for each gene depending on the gene coupling order.

(4) **Extended Gene-coupling GA (Type D):**
As shown in Fig. 6, unlike type C, which does not distinguish the loci of genes, the sub-solutions (e.g., (x_1^*, x_2^*) and x_3^*) in each sub-population (e.g., S_6' and S_3') are coupled with each other by distinguishing each gene locus. The sub-solutions (e.g., (x_1^*, x_2^*, x_3^*)) then migrate to the corresponding sub-populations (e.g., S_{10}'). The fitness function of individuals with two adjacent genes, for example, is defined as $f(a_1, \ldots, a_{i-1}, x_i, x_{i+1}, a_{i+2}, \ldots, a_n)$, where a_i is a constant value. The constant value can once again be set to zero for simplicity, but unlike type C, the gene-coupling that distinguishes the loci of genes allows the specific contribution of the intermediate size of genes in each sub-population.

In the adaptive type S, these four types of gene-duplication can be integrated into one system, which is the same as type D with all migration types from A to D included as subsets. In the next section, an adaptive strategy for GDGAs will be described.

3. Adaptive Strategy for GDGAs

Until now, we have determined the best strategy for a given test function by performing a comparative study on different types of gene-duplication

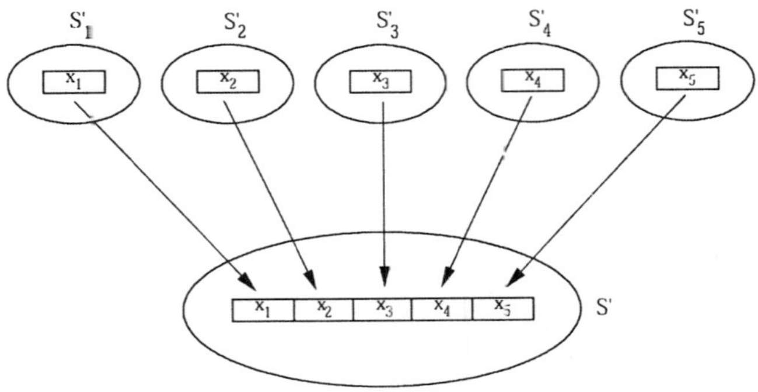

Fig. 3. Gene-concatenating type A for dimension $n = 5$. Sub-solutions $\{x_i^*\}$ $(i = 1, 2, \ldots, n)$ are concatenated at the same time to form the final solution $(x_1^*, x_2^*, \ldots, x_n^*)$ within the sub-population S'

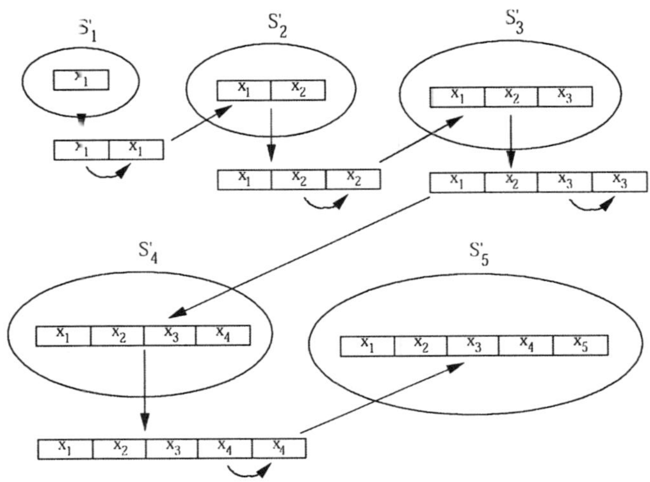

Fig. 4. Gene-prolonging type B for dimension $n = 5$. Sub-solution $(x_1^*, x_2^*, \ldots, x_i^*)$ is prolonged to $(x_1^*, x_2^*, \ldots, x_i^*, x_{i+1}^*)$ by copying the last part x_i^* $(i = 1, 2, \ldots, n-1)$. The final solution $(x_1^*, x_2^*, \ldots, x_n^*)$ is obtained in the sub-population S'_n

using the PfGA and SSGA [31]. As a whole, the PfGA is better than the SSGA for evolving sub-populations in a GDGA. However, if we don't have *a priori* knowledge of the features of the test function, we must develop an adaptive strategy for automatically evolving genes for a given function. In this section, we extend the gene-duplicating GA to an adaptive algorithm as follows:

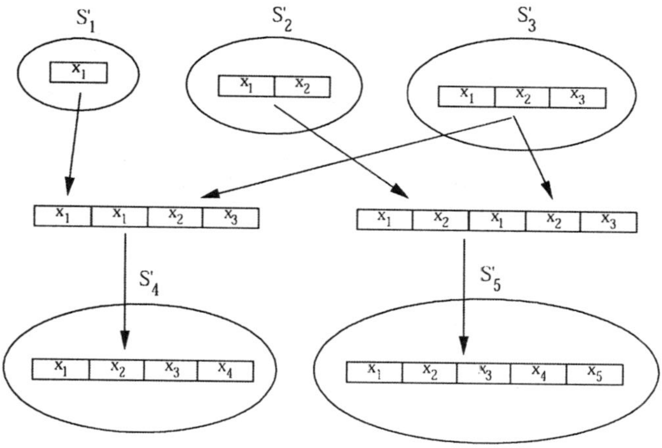

Fig. 5. Gene-coupling type C for dimension $n = 5$. Sub-solutions are coupled with other sub-solutions to form new sub-solutions. For example, the sub-solutions, x_1^* and (x_1^*, x_2^*, x_3^*), in the sub-populations, S_1' and S_3', are coupled with each other to form a solution $(x_1^*, x_1^*, x_2^*, x_3^*)$ which will migrate to the sub-population S_4'. This kind of process continues until the final solution $(x_1^* x_2^*, \ldots, x_n^*)$ is obtained in the sub-population S_n'

(1) **Initialization:** As an initial strategy, the adaptive gene-duplicating GA is performed with the same probability (i.e., 0.25) for each gene-duplication type (A-D).
(2) **Determination of adaptive strategy:** A promising strategy is determined based on "an evaluation criterion." (The evaluation criterion is discussed later.)
(3) **Application of adaptive strategy:** Based on procedure 2, the adaptive strategy (i.e., the adaptive gene-duplication type) is applied.
(4) **Termination criterion:** If a termination criterion (e.g., exceeding a constant number of evaluations) is satisfied, the algorithm terminates. When the termination criterion is not satisfied, the algorithm returns to procedure 2.

How should we determine the evaluation criterion for a promising strategy? In this study, we count the instances of each gene-duplication type as being the "best strategy" during a constant number of generations (e.g., 100 generations), where the best strategy is defined in terms of the type as follows: If an immigrant to a sub-population (i.e., S' in type A, S_n' in types B and C, and $S_{n(n+1)/2}'$ in type D) with gene-length $n \times l$ is better than the worst individual in the sub-population, the immigration succeeds. If this happens with duplication type i ($i = A, B, C, D$), the

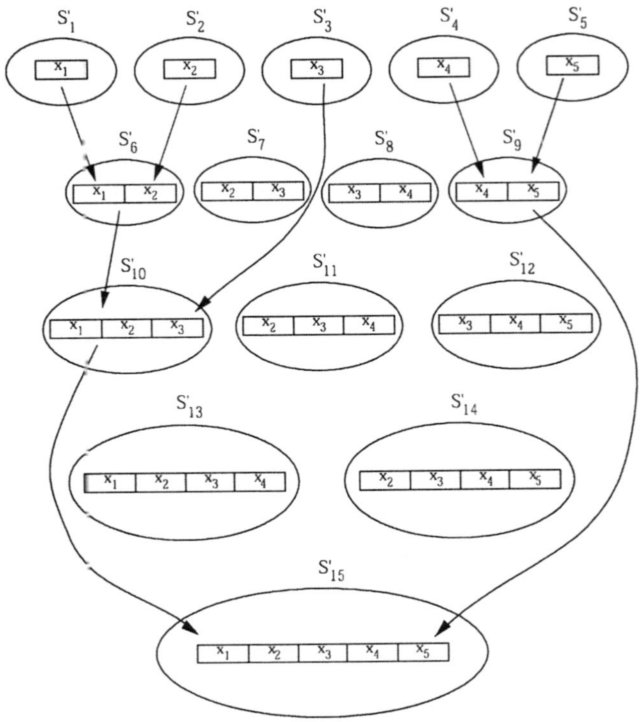

Fig. 6. Extended gene-coupling type D for dimension $n = 5$. Sub-solutions are coupled with each other by distinguishing each sub-solution's gene locus. For example, the sub-solutions, (x_1^*, x_2^*) and x_3^*, in the sub-population, S_6' and S_3', are coupled with each other to form the new sub-solution $(x_1^* x_2^*, x_3^*)$, which will migrate to the sub-population S_{10}'. This kind of process continues until the final solution $(x_1^* x_2^*, \ldots, x_n^*)$ is obtained in the sub-population $S'_{n(n+1)/2}$

count $n(i)$ is incremented by one. If no type allows successful immigration, the false count $n(F)$ is incremented by one. For subsequent generations (after the initial constant number of generations used to determine the "best strategy"), the selection probability $P_{sel}(i)$ for each adaptive strategy (type) can be set in proportion to the normalized count of each; i.e., $P_{sel}(i) = n(i)/(n(A) + n(B) + n(C) + n(D))$. If all $n(i)$ are equal to zero, the probabilities for all types from A to D are set to 0.25.

4. Experiment

The four types of gene-duplication algorithms were applied to nine optimization (minimization) problems. The functions included frequently used

Table 1. Test functions used to evaluate the adaptive strategy for GA inspired by gene-duplication. The functions include five benchmark functions used in the first ICEO and four other test functions, all of which are categorized into eight classes according to whether they are unimodal or multimodal, symmetrical or asymmetrical, and separable or inseparable, in terms of the variable x_i. The VTR is defined according to the function. r_j, a_{ij}, and c_i are random values

(1)Sphere model (Sp): unimodal, symmetric, separable

$$f(x) = \sum_{i=1}^{n}(x_i - 1)^2,$$
$$-5 \leq x_i \leq 5 \ (24bit),\ VTR = 10^{-6}$$

(2)Schwefel's Double Sum (Ds): unimodal, symmetric, inseparable

$$f(x) = \sum_{i=1}^{n}(\sum_{j=1}^{i} x_j)^2$$
$$-65.536 \leq x_i \leq 65.536 \ (27bit),\ VTR = 10^{-4}$$

(3)Random Sphere model (Rs): unimodal, asymmetric, separable

$$f(x) = \sum_{i=1}^{n}(x_i - r_i)^2,$$
$$-5 \leq x_i \leq 5 \ (24bit),\ VTR = 10^{-6}$$

(4)Random Double Sum (Rd): unimodal, asymmetric, inseparable

$$f(x) = \sum_{i=1}^{n}(\sum_{j=1}^{i}(x_j - r_j))^2$$
$$-65.536 \leq x_i \leq 65.536 \ (27bit),\ VTR = 10^{-4}$$

(5)Generalized Rastringin's function(Ra): multimodal, symmetric, separable

$$f(x) = 10n + \sum_{i=1}^{n}(x_i^2 - 10cos(2\pi x_i))$$
$$-5.12 \leq x_i \leq 5.12 \ (24bit),\ VTR = 10^{-6}$$

(6)Griewank's Function (Gr): multimodal, symmetric, inseparable

$$f(x) = \frac{1}{d}\sum_{i=1}^{n}(x_i - 100)^2 - \prod_{i=1}^{n}\cos(\frac{x_i - 100}{\sqrt{i}}) + 1,$$
$$d = 4000,\ -600 \leq x_i \leq 600 \ (31bit),\ VTR = 10^{-4}$$

(7)Michalewicz' Function (Mi): multimodal, asymmetric, separable

$$f(x) = -\sum_{i=1}^{n}\sin(x_i)\sin^{2m}(\frac{ix_i^2}{\pi}),$$
$$m = 10,\ 0 \leq x_i \leq \pi \ (22bit),\ VTR = -4.687$$

(8)Shekel's foxholes (Sh): multimodal, asymmetric, inseparable

$$f(x) = -\sum_{i=1}^{m}\frac{1}{\sum_{j=1}^{n}(x_j - a_{ij})^2 + c_i},$$
$$m = 30,\ 0 \leq x_i \leq 10 \ (24bit),\ VTR = -9$$

(9)Generalized Langerman's Function (La): multimodal, asymmetric, inseparable

$$f(x) = -\sum_{i=1}^{m} c_i \exp\left[-\frac{1}{\pi}\sum_{j=1}^{n}(x_j - a_{ij})^2\right]\cos\left[\pi\sum_{j=1}^{n}(x_j - a_{ij})^2\right],$$
$$m = 5,\ 0 \leq x_i \leq 10 \ (24bit),\ VTR = -1.5$$

benchmark functions and random transformations in terms of the variable x_i by using a uniformly distributed random number r_i $(0 \leq r_i \leq 1)$. Coordinates x_i^* $(i = 1, 2, \ldots, n)$ that take a global minimum move within a range from a lower bound to an upper bound of x_i through this random transformation. For example, these coordinates x_i^* can take values ranging from -65.536 to 65.536 for the random double sum (Rd), which makes it very difficult to search for its global minimum. The functions were in the general form of functions that can be categorized into eight classes according to whether they are unimodal or multimodal, symmetrical or asymmetrical, and separable or inseparable, in terms of the variable x_i. Table 1 shows nine such functions. Five of the functions – the sphere model (Sp), Griewank's function (Gr), Michalewicz' function (Mi), Shekel's foxholes (Sh), and the generalized form of Langerman's function (La) – were used at the first ICEO [24]. Genes were duplicated according to each type (type A to D) with a probability of duplication R, which was set to 1.0. Migration may occur with every generation. The incidences of the "best strategy" as defined in the previous section were counted for every generation. During every group of one hundred evaluations, the number of best-strategy occurrences was accumulated for each type of gene-duplication. For the following one hundred evaluations, the strategy i weighted according to the histogram, $P_{sel}(i)$, was applied to the adaptive algorithm. The dimension n was five or ten. (Due to limitation of space, we only show results for the case of five dimensions). Each value x_i was encoded as a Gray code in $l = 22$ to 31 bits, depending on the current function. One hundred independent trials with different random seeds (a trial was defined as 10,000 evaluations with five dimensions and 100,000 evaluations with ten dimensions) were performed for each sub-population $S'i$. The criteria [24] for evaluating the performance of each algorithm were the rates of success R_s, the rate of reaching the VTR (value to reach) or remaining below it, the ENES (expected number of evaluations), the BV (best value), and the RT (relative time) for all trials. The VTR was defined according to the function. The RT is defined as RT=(CT-ET)/ET where CT is the total CPU time required to perform the given algorithm and ET is the CPU time required to calculate fitness. All sub-populations could evolve in parallel. The computational load was roughly proportional to the gene length and heaviest for sub-populations with genes of length $n \times l$.

5. Results

5.1. *Comparison among PfGA, GDGAs and Other EAs*

As shown in Table 2, both the PfGA and the gene-duplicating GA (GDGA) are superior to the other algorithms, with one or two exceptions [31], presented at the first ICEO [24]. The PfGA-based GDGA is, as a whole, superior to the SSGA-based GDGA [31].

Table 3 shows the comparative results among the specific types A, B,

Table 2. Results at the 1st ICEO for PfGA and GDGAs. The results show only the top three places among the eight algorithms that participated in the ICEO. Each set of three lines shows the ENES, BV, and RT, from top to bottom. Performance was judged at the ICEO on the basis of the smallest ENES over 20 runs. If the PfGA had participated in the ICEO, it would have placed second. It is compact, has a low RT, and in general performs well. Although the RT is higher for the GDGA version, the ENES is significantly lower for the PfGA-based GDGA. As a whole, the PfGA-based GDGA would have taken second place and the SSGA-based GDGA would have taken third place. In addition, the algorithm which would retain first place, Bi-Pi, is a method called an *Inductive Search* that uses hill-climbing for the local search and the the Brent method for the global search, so it is slightly similar to type B

ENES BV RT	Sphe model (Sp)	Grie func (Gr)	Shek foxh (Sh)	Micha func (Mi)	Lange func (La)
Bi- Pi	20 3.88e-15 2	41 7.99e-6 2	74 -10.33 2	120 -4.688 2	176 -1.499 2
Li	243 0.0 12.7	21,141 1.69e-5 3.1	6,318 -10.40 0.25	6,804 -4.687 1.28	4,131 -1.499 1.62
Sto- Pri	736 - 4.67	5,765 - 1.79	76,210 - 0.80	1,877 - 1.11	5,308 - 1.35
PfGA	4,067 0.0 0.91	6,785 4.66e-7 0.90	1,619 -10.40 0.33	5,131 -4.688 0.90	5,274 -1.499 0.43
GD- PfGA	173 0.0 2.39	1,367 3.65e-10 2.35	456 -10.40 2.40	240 -4.688 3.54	2,330 -1.499 2.12
GD- SSGA	723 0.0 71.26	2,537 3.65e-10 70.76	3,632 -10.40 41.47	786 -4.688 79.24	3,460 -1.499 52.83

C, and D, and the adaptive strategy S. The performance is compared in terms of the average ENES. For the symmetric functions, such as the sphere model (Sp), Schwefel's double sum (Ds), Rastringin's function (Ra), and Griewank's function (Gr), the best gene-duplication type was B. For the asymmetric functions, such as the random sphere model (Rs), Random double sum (Rd), and Michalewicz' function (Mi), the best gene-duplication type was D. For the multimodal, asymmetric, and inseparable functions, such as Shekel's foxholes (Sh) and Langerman's function (La), the best

Table 3. Comparative results for GDGAs with different gene-duplication types. Nine functions are categorized into eight classes according to whether they are unimodal (uni:Yes) or multimodal (uni:No), symmetric (sym:Yes) or asymmetric (sym:No), and separable (sep:Yes) or inseparable (sep:No), in terms of value x_i. Here, $Rs(\%)$ is the rate of success. ENES.av. and BV.av are, respectively, the average values of ENES and the best value (BV), and ENES.dv and BV.min are, respectively, the standard deviation of ENES and the minimum value of BV, over 100 different trials

function (type)	feature uni sym sepa	R_s (%)	ENES .av	ENES .dv	BV .av	BV .min
(A)		100	283.5	77.2	0	0
(B)		**100**	**98.2**	38.2	0	0
Sp (C)	Yes Yes Yes	100	265.5	57.5	0	0
(D)		100	186.4	43.7	0	0
(S)		**100**	**110.9**	40.0	0	0
(A)		100	347.7	107.5	4.80e-12	7.15e-13
(B)		**100**	**135.2**	56.1	7.16e-13	7.15e-13
Ds (C)	Yes Yes No	100	671.4	233.6	8.20e-13	7.15e-13
(D)		100	266.3	62.2	7.16e-13	7.15e-13
(S)		**100**	**143.4**	45.9	7.16e-13	7.15e-13
(A)		100	277.9	83.2	2.25e-13	2.25e-13
(B)		100	2782.4	1190.0	1.82e-11	2.25e-13
Rs (C)	Yes No Yes	100	2569.5	668.1	2.41e-12	2.25e-13
(D)		**100**	**269.9**	76.1	2.25e-13	2.25e-13
(S)		**100**	**274.7**	77.6	2.25e-13	2.25e-13
(A)		0	-	0	6.46e-2	1.17e-4
(B)		0	-	0	8.43e-2	1.76e-4
Rd (C)	Yes No No	1	9725.0	0	9.71e-2	7.03e-5
(D)		**4**	**8461.0**	1375.3	2.40e-2	9.60e-6
(S)		**7**	**8474.6**	1310.8	2.58e-2	6.06e-7
(A)		100	314.7	137.5	9.24e-11	9.24e-11
(B)		**100**	**80.0**	49.2	9.24e-11	9.24e-11
Ra (C)	No Yes Yes	100	283.3	95.6	9.24e-11	9.24e-11
(D)		99	213.9	63.0	9.15e-11	0
(S)		**100**	**86.9**	38.2	9.24e-11	9.24e-11
(A)		0	-	0	5.90e-4	1.03e-2
(B)		**100**	**417.2**	255.9	8.92e-14	8.92e-14
Gr (C)	No Yes No	76	3336.9	2558.9	3.68e-3	8.92e-14
(D)		81	3203.6	2168.4	2.69e-3	8.92e-14
(S)		**100**	**529.1**	902.4	1.68e-09	8.92e-14
(A)		100	450.1	460.2	-4.69	-4.69
(B)		65	2979.6	2163.8	-4.66	-4.69
Mi (C)	No No Yes	66	2861.6	2282.2	-4.64	-4.69
(D)		**100**	**332.0**	258.0	-4.69	-4.69
(S)		**100**	**363.7**	265.2	-4.69	-4.69
(A)		3	4486.0	2171.7	-2.55	-10.40
(B)		9	4098.3	2196.4	-3.01	-10.40
Sh **(C)**	No No No	**6**	**3075.3**	3385.8	-3.04	-10.40
(D)		3	3155.3	3258.1	-2.57	-10.40
(S)		**3**	**3873.7**	3269.9	-2.53	-10.40
(A)		20	4276.2	3117.7	-0.919	-1.5
(B)		21	4332.6	2855.6	-0.946	-1.5
La **(C)**	No No No	**33**	**4015.1**	2750.7	-1.017	-1.5
(D)		30	4265.4	3196.6	-1.006	-1.5
(S)		**33**	**3524.2**	2618.3	-1.037	-1.5

gene-duplication type was C. The adaptive gene-duplication type (S) was as good as the best specific type for each function.

5.2. *Behavior of the Adaptive Strategy*

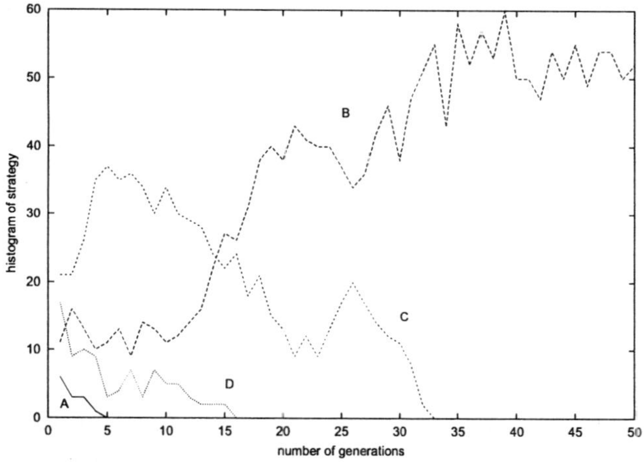

Fig. 7. Evolution of the adaptive strategy for Griewank's function (Gr). The horizontal axis unit is 100 generations. The vertical axis represents a histogram of each strategy (type) for every one-hundred generations. The "best strategy" is type C in the early stage of less than 1,500 generations, however, type B becomes the dominant strategy afterwards

The evolution of the adaptive strategy is shown in Figs. 7 and 8 for the functions Gr and Mi. (The horizontal axis represents the number of generations in units of one-hundred generations. The vertical axis represents a histogram of the adaptive strategy $P_{sel}(i)$ (%) for every one-hundred generations.) For the symmetric functions, such as Sp, Ds (Schwefel's double sum), Ra (Rastringin's function), and Gr (Fig. 7), type B was competitive with type D during the early stage of generations. Ultimately, however, the best type became type B in most cases of evolution. For the multimodal, symmetric, and inseparable functions such as Gr, type C was competitive with type B during the early and intermediate stages. For the asymmetric functions, such as Rs (random sphere model), Rd (random double sum), and Mi (Fig. 8), the best type was D. Type B, however, was competitive with type D for Rd because it is a unimodal function, so that the gene-prolonging strategy with type B is effective just as it is with Sp, Ds, etc.

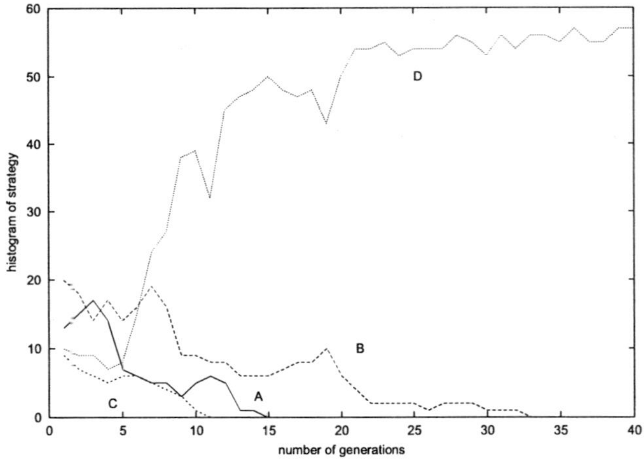

Fig. 8. Evolution of the adaptive strategy for Michalewicz' function (Mi). The horizontal axis unit is 100 generations. The vertical axis represents a histogram of each strategy (type) for every one-hundred generations. Type D becomes the dominant strategy after 600 generations

For the multimodal, asymmetric, and inseparable functions such as Sh and La, the best type was C in terms of the average ENES according to the results shown in Table 3. However, this type rarely appeared during the evolution of the adaptive types. Instead, type B or D or a mixture of them often appeared for both Shekel's foxholes and Langerman's function.

6. Discussion

The sub-solutions in lower dimensions are copied or concatenated with other sub-solutions, which preserve the characteristics of the lower dimensions and allow them to migrate to the successively higher dimensions. This procedure allows different contributions from each gene, depending on the order of gene coupling. Even if there is no separability among the different dimensions of a test function, some diverse combinations or concatenations of sub-solutions using the fitness function with zero-bias could be effectively applicable, to some extent, to obtain a globally optimal solution. Furthermore, the results in Table 3 confirm that the adaptive strategy can robustly perform as well as the best selected-GA type, without requiring significantly more function evaluations. For the random double sum (Rd) and Shekel's foxholes (Sh) which are asymmetric and inseparable functions, the success rates did not reach 10%. These functions are difficult to search for their global minima because the coordinates x_i^* $(i = 1, 2, \ldots, n)$ taking their global minima are completely different from each other because of the random transformation by r_j and a_{ij} in Table 1. Therefore, their epistasis is very strong because of such function features.

This kind of approach is completely different from the approaches of the messy GA [6] based on the building-block hypothesis, linkage learning [11,12] based on the correlation between gene loci, or estimating distributions [9,10,13]. The GDGA approach makes use of various combinations of schemata with various sizes in various sub-populations depending on the duplication types from A to D. This dynamic recombination in the adaptive strategy for the GDGAs, which is beyond conventional GAs based on static building-block hypothesis, further strengthens the strategy's search ability and robustness even for inseparable functions such as Griewank's and Langerman's functions.

7. Conclusion

We have described an adaptive strategy for a gene-duplicating genetic algorithm (GDGA) with four variants: gene-concatenating, gene-prolonging, gene-coupling, and extended gene-coupling. Our scheme divides a given problem into sub-dimensions and couples the sub-dimensions using the PfGA-based GDGAs. Each individual concatenates previously obtained sub-dimensional solutions and causes them to migrate among sub-populations by using different gene-duplication schemes. The probability for each type of gene-duplication is calculated by counting the occurrences of each type over some number of generations. To evaluate the adaptive strategy, we have used a set of general test functions including recent benchmark problems. From our results, we have confirmed that the adaptive strategy can robustly perform as well as the best selected gene-duplicating type, without requiring significantly more function evaluations. In future work, the adaptive strategy can be applied to combinatorial problems, deceptive problems, and problems in dynamic environments.

References

1. Charles Darwin, *On the Origin of Species by Means of Natural Selection or the Preservation of Favoured Races in the Struggle for Life*, London, John Murray, 1859.
2. J.H.Holland, *Adaptation in Natural and Artificial Systems*, The University of Michigan Press, 1975.

3. D.E. Goldberg, *Genetic Algorithms in Search, Optimization, and Machine Learning*, Addison Wesley, 1989.
4. G.Syswerda, A Study of Reproduction in Generational and Steady-State Genetic Algorithms, *Foundation of Genetic Algorithms*, Morgan Kaufmann, pp.94-101, 1991.
5. T. Baeck, D. Fogel and Z. Michalewicz (Eds.), *Handbook of evolutionary computation*, New York: Oxford University Press, 1997.
6. D.E. Goldberg, B. Korb and K. Deb, Messy Genetic Algorithms: Motivation, Analysis, and First Results, *Complex Systems*, Vol.3., No.5, pp.493-530, 1989.
7. Y.Davidor, Epistasis Variance: A Viewpoint on GA-Hardness, *Foundation of Genetic Algorithms*, pp.23-35, 1991.
8. D.E. Goldberg, K. Deb, H. Kargupta and G. Harik, Accurate Optimization of Difficult Problems Using Fast Messy Genetic Algorithms, *Proceedings of the Fifth Int. Conf. on Genetic Algorithms*, pp.56-64, 1993.
9. H.Muehlenbein and G. Paaβ, From Recombination of Genes of the Estimation of Distributions I. Binary Parameters, *Parallel Problem Solving from Nature-PPSN IV*, pp.178-187, 1996.
10. H. Muehlenbein, J. Bendisch and H.M.Voigt, From Recombination of Genes of the Estimation of Distributions II. Continuous Parameters, *Parallel Problem Solving from Nature-PPSN IV*, pp.188-197, 1996.
11. G.R. Harik and D.E.Goldberg, Learning Linkage, *Foundation of Genetic Algorithms 4*, pp.247-262, 1996.
12. M.Munetomo and D.E. Goldberg, Identifying Linkage Groups by Nonlinearity/Non-monotonicity Detection, *Proc. of the Genetic and Evolutionary Computation Conference (GECCO)'99*, pp.433-440, 1999.
13. M.Pelikan, D.E.Goldberg and E.C-Paz, BOA: The Bayesian Optimization Algorithm, *Proc. of the Genetic and Evolutionary Computation Conference*, Vol.1, pp.525-532, 1999.
14. R.Hinterding, Z.Michalewicz and Á.E.Eiben, Adaptation in Evolutionary Computation: A Survey, *Proc. of the 1997 IEEE Int. Conf. on Evolutionary Computation*, pp.65-69, 1997.
15. Á.E. Eiben, R. Hinterding and Z.Michalewicz, Parameter Control in Evolutionary Algorithms, *IEEE Trans. in Evolutionary Computation*, Vol.3, No.2, July 1999.
16. S.Ohno, *Evolution by Gene Duplication*, Springer-Verlag, 1970.
17. M. Furusawa and H. Doi, Promotion of Evolution: Disparity in the Frequency of Strand-specific Misreading between the Lagging and Leading DNA Strands Enhances Disproportionate Accumulation of Mutations, *J. Theor. Biol.*, vol. 157, pp.127-133, 1992.
18. K. Wada, H. Doi, S. Tanaka, Y. Wada, and M. Furusawa, A Neo-Darwinian Algorithm: Asymmetrical Mutations due to Semiconservative DNA-type replication Promote Evolution, *Proc. Natl. Acad. Sci., USA*, vol. 90, pp.11934-11938, Dec. 1993.
19. T.C.Belding, The Distributed Genetic Algorithm Revisited, *Proceedings of the Sixth International Conference on Genetic Algorithms*, pp114-121, Mor-

gan Kaufmann, 1995.

20. S.W.Mahfoud, A Comparison of Parallel and Sequential Niching Methods, *Proceedings of the Sixth International Conference on Genetic Algorithms*, pp136-143, Morgan Kaufmann, 1995.
21. E.C-Paz and D.E.Goldberg, Predicting Speedups of Idealized Bounding Cases of Parallel Genetic Algorithms, *Proceedings of the Seventh International Conference on Genetic Algorithms*, pp113-126, Morgan Kaufmann, 1997.
22. I.K.Evans, Embracing Premature Convergence: The Hypergamous Parallel Genetic Algorithm, *Proceedings of the 1998 International Conference on Evolutionary Computation (ICEC'98)*, pp621-626, 1998.
23. T.Maruyama, T.Hirose and A.Konagaya, A Fine-Grained Parallel Genetic Algorithm for Distributed Parallel System, *Proceedings of the Fifth International Conference on Genetic Algorithms*, pp184-190, Morgan Kaufmann, 1993.
24. The Organizing Committee: H.Bersini, M.Doringo, S.Langerman, G.Seront, L.Gambardella, Results of the First International Contest on Evolutionary Optimization (1st ICEO), *1996 IEEE Int. Conf. on Evolutionary Computation (ICEC'96)*, pp.611-615, 1996.
25. G. Bilchev and I. Parmee, Inductive Search, *IEEE Int. Conf. on Evolutionary Computation*, pp.832-836, 1996.
26. D.Whitley, K.Mathias, S.Rana and J.Dzubera, Building Better Test Functions, *Proc. of the Sixth Int. Conf. on Genetic Algorithms*, pp.239-246, Morgan Kaufmann, 1995.
27. H.Sawai and S.Kizu, Parameter-free Genetic Algorithm Inspired by Disparity Theory of Evolution, *Proc. of the 1998 Int. Conf. on Parallel Problem Solving from Nature-PPSN V*, pp.702-711, Sep. 1998.
28. H.Sawai and S.Adachi, Parallel Distributed Processing of a Parameter-free GA by Using Hierarchical Migration Methods, *Proceedings of the Genetic and Evolutionary Computation Conference (GECCO)'99*, vol.1, pp579-586, July 1999.
29. H.Sawai and S.Adachi, Effects of Hierarchical Migration in a Parallel Distributed Parameter-free GA, *Proceedings of the Congress on Evolutionary Computation (CEC)2000*, vol.2, pp1117-1124, July 2000.
30. H.Sawai and S.Adachi, Genetic Algorithm Inspired by Gene Duplication, *Proceedings of the Congress on Evolutionary Computation (CEC)'99*, vol.1, pp480-487, July 1999.
31. H.Sawai and S.Adachi, A Comparative Study of Gene-Duplicated GAs Based on PfGA and SSGA, *Proceedings of the Genetic and Evolutionary Computation Conference (GECCO)2000*, vol.1, pp74-81, July 2000.

CHAPTER 9

THE INFLUENCE OF STOCHASTIC QUALITY FUNCTIONS ON EVOLUTIONARY SEARCH

Bernhard Sendhoff[1], Hans-Georg Beyer[2] and Markus Olhofer[1]

[1]*Honda Research Institute Europe GmbH, Carl-Legien-Str. 30, 63073 Offenbach, Germany*

[2]*Dept. of Computer Science XI, University of Dortmund, 44221 Dortmund, Germany*

In this chapter, we will analyse the influence of noise on the search behaviour of evolutionary algorithms. We will introduce different classes of functions which go beyond the simple additive noise model. The first function demonstrates a trade-off between an expectation and a variance based measure for the evaluation of the quality in the context of stochastic optimisation problems. Thereafter, we concentrate on functions whose topology is changed when the expectation value is taken as the quality criterion. In particular, for functions with noise induced multi-modality (FNIM), the process can be regarded as a bifurcation. The behaviour of two types of evolution strategies is analysed for FNIMs.

1. Introduction

Optimisation in the presence of noise has been studied as early as 1970 in the area of stochastic programming[7]. In stochastic programming the objective function and possibly the constraints are subject to stochastic perturbations. The standard approach for these cases is to work on the expectation value of the objective functions and therefore, to render the optimisation problem deterministic. The remaining problem is that the evaluation of the expectation value might involve a prohibitively large number of function evaluations. Therefore, one is left to estimate the expectation value with a residual error. Since evolutionary algorithms are believed to be particularly robust optimisation techniques, their application to noisy objective functions seems particularly suitable. Fitzpatrick and Grefenstette[9] and later Aizawa and Wah[1] analysed genetic algorithms in a noisy environment. The influence of noise on the performance of evolution strategies was first discussed by Beyer[5]. Tsutsui and Gosh[13] claimed that it is not necessary to explicitly calculate the expectation value for each solution but instead that it is sufficient to evaluate the solution once and that the population inherently ascertains that the expectation value of the objective function is the target of the optimisation. Although their analysis relies on the schema theorem and is therefore restricted to proportional selection, empirical results show that indeed evaluating each individual solution only once instead of estimating the expectation value of the objective function can be most efficient.

In almost all cases of practical relevance, it is impossible to evaluate the expectation value analytically, therefore, it has to be estimated. Whether we estimate it explicitly by using a sample of size K or implicitly by exploiting the population, the optimisation method has to cope with statistical fluctuations. Therefore, although theoretically possible, practically, the stochastic problem can never be reduced to a deterministic one.

A stochastic problem is one where the quality landscape that the optimisation algorithms "sees" differs non-deterministically between two evaluations. The character of this difference depends on three main aspects:

The type of noise. Most analytical results on noisy evolutionary optimisation were obtained for the simple additive noise model, i.e., the noise term (usually normally or uniformly distributed) is added to the objective function value[2]. This case is depicted in Figure 1(a). Although interesting analytical results for the algorithm, e.g. on the role of the population, have been discovered, the character of the quality landscape is not changed. This differs for systematic noise models, where the noise term is not restricted to be additive but can occur anywhere inside the quality function. Robustness constraints on the optimisation, see e.g. Wiesmann *et al.*[14] and Branke[8], constitute a special case of the systematic noise models, where the noise term is added to the parameter set, which is depicted in Figure 1(b). In this chapter, we will concentrate on the systematic noise model.

The quality function. Every optimisation problem is unique depending on the quality function. However, in order to be able to apply empirical or analytical results to a class of problems, test functions are devised which are simple enough to be susceptible for analysis while capturing the specificity of the problem class. Examples are the sphere, the ridge function or the Ackley function for multi-modal search landscapes. In this chapter, we will propose and analyse a class of test functions which has been called functions with *noise-induced multi-modality (NIMM)* by Sendhoff *et al.*[12].

The evaluation criterion. For deterministic single-criteria optimisation problems the evaluation criterion is usually the minimisation or the maximisation of the quality function possibly according to some constraints. For noisy optimisation problems the expectation value is frequently used as the evaluation criterion although other choices are possible. Beyer *et al.*[6] proposed a differentiation between statistical momentum based criteria and threshold criteria, where (for maximisation problems) the probability that the quality value is below a certain threshold is minimised. It should be noted that the choice of the evaluation criterion can fundamentally alter the characteristics of the search landscape. In the next sections, we will apply the expectation value as a evaluation criterion mostly because the analysis involved in the threshold criterion is slightly trickier. However, we will also use the variance as an additional measure in Section 2.

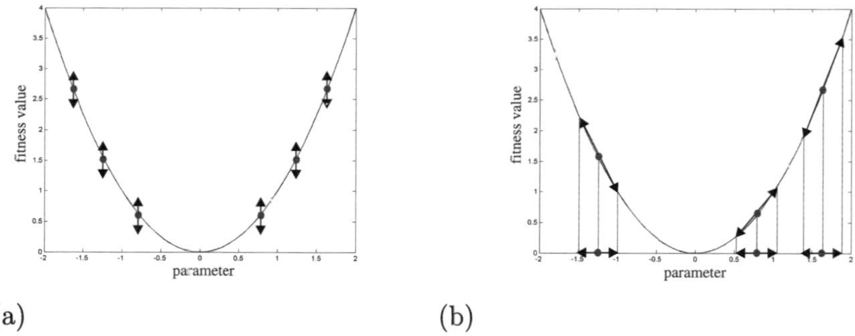

Fig. 1. (a) Variations due to additive noise on the quality function. The dots represent the fitnesses of individual solutions and the arrows the direction of variation, the underlying curve defines a one-dimensional fitness landscape. (b) Variations due to noise on the parameters resulting in variations along the fitness curve.

Stochastic problems are always (at least practically) dynamic optimisation problems[8]. However, in this chapter we will call problems *stochastic* if the time-scale of their change is fast compared to the change of the individual solutions and *dynamic* if this time-scale is slow compared to the change of the individual solutions. The latter problem is not the subject of this work. After the introduction of different noise models in the next section, we will analyse the behaviour of two types of evolution strategies for the new noise model, the NIM functions. In Section 4, we will extend the FNIM to higher dimensions. In Section 5, we will summarise this chapter.

2. Classes of Noisy Optimization Problems

As we pointed out in the introduction, the character of a noisy optimisation problem[a] is mainly determined by three factors. The type of noise, the quality function and the evaluation criterion. In this section, we will introduce three qualitatively different cases of noisy optimisation problems, which display a particular characteristic property. The first extension of additive noise models is the sphere function with a noise term added to the objective parameters $F(\mathbf{x}) = (\mathbf{x}+\mathbf{z})^2$, $\mathbf{z} \sim \mathcal{N}(\mathbf{0}, \varepsilon^2\mathbf{1})$. Here $\mathcal{N}(\mathbf{0}, \varepsilon^2\mathbf{1})$ denotes a vector of random numbers, where each component is normally distributed with zero mean and variance ε^2. Beyer *et al.*[6] have shown that for this function the minimum of the original sphere model ($\mathbf{x} = \mathbf{0}$) coincides with the minimum of the expectation value and of the variance of the quality function with systematic noise. Although further analysis nevertheless reveals some interesting properties in particular for the threshold measure, we will not discuss this case any further.

2.1. *Expectation Value – Variance Trade-Off*

Although usually only the expectation value is used for noisy optimisation problems, in particular for robust solutions it is often the minimisation of the variance which is needed for practical applications. As we noted above for the sphere model with systematic noise, minimisation of the expectation value also leads to minimisation of the variance. However, the following function shows that this does not hold in general:

$$F_1(\mathbf{x}) = (\mathbf{x}^2 - 1)\, z + \mathbf{x}^2, \quad z \sim \mathcal{N}(0, \varepsilon^2), \mathbf{x} \in I\!R^N. \tag{1}$$

Here $\mathcal{N}(0, \varepsilon^2)$ denotes a Gaussian distributed random number with zero mean and variance ε^2. The calculation of the expectation value and the variance gives:

$$\mathrm{E}[F_1(\mathbf{x})|\mathbf{x}] = \mathbf{x}^2, \tag{2}$$

$$\mathrm{Var}[F_1(\mathbf{x})|\mathbf{x}] = \varepsilon^2\, (\mathbf{x}^2 - 1)^2. \tag{3}$$

[a] Note, that in this chapter we will generally deal with minimisation problems unless otherwise stated.

Therefore, the minima of the expectation value and the variance are given by $\mathbf{x} = \mathbf{0}$ and $\mathbf{x}^2 = 1$. The minimum of the expectation value corresponds to a local maximum of the variance, as shown in Figs. 2(a) and (b). For functions like F_1 the expectation value and the variance cannot be minimised at the same time and the problem basically constitutes a multi-objective optimisation problem, see Jin and Sendhoff [11]. We note, that the characteristic of function F_1 is that the noise term z is multiplied both to the parameter values $\mathbf{x}$ as well as to a constant term (in this example "1"). If we replace the constant term by an external parameter, say a, this means that stochastic variations of the parameter values and of an external parameter, e.g. the cruising speed for an aerodynamic optimisation problem, share the same source which is not unlikely to occur in certain applications.

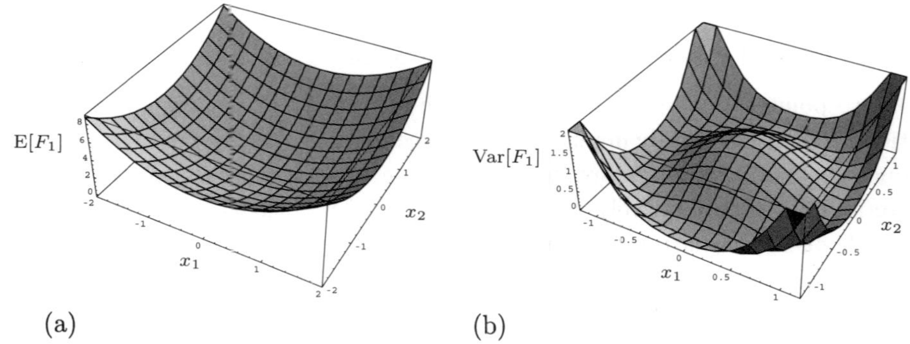

Fig. 2. The expectation value (a) and the variance (b) of function F_1 for $\varepsilon^2 = 1$, $N = 2$.

2.2. *Topological Changes of the Quality Landscape*

If the number of optima of the expectation value of functions is different from the noise-free case, we call these changes *topological*. These functions do not have to be very complex, like previously proposed in the literature[8,14], all that is needed is a noise induced variation between two minima. As one can easily imagine averaging over such functions will (in some cases) result in merging minima and thereby absorbing and erasing the maxima in between the minima:

$$F_2(\mathbf{x}) = \left((\mathbf{x}+\mathbf{z})^2 - a\right)^2, \quad \mathbf{z} \sim \mathcal{N}(\mathbf{0}, \varepsilon^2\mathbf{1}), \mathbf{x} \in I\!R^N. \tag{4}$$

Here $\mathcal{N}(\mathbf{0}, \varepsilon^2\mathbf{1})$ denotes a vector of random numbers, where each component is normally distributed with zero mean and variance ε^2. Using $\mathrm{E}[z^2] = \varepsilon^2$,

$\mathrm{E}[z^3] = 0$ and $\mathrm{E}[z^4] = 3\varepsilon^4$, for $z \sim \mathcal{N}(0, \varepsilon^2)$, the calculation of the expectation value gives:

$$\mathrm{E}[F_2(\mathbf{x})|\mathbf{x}] = (\mathbf{x}^2)^2 + 2\mathbf{x}^2 \left((N+2)\varepsilon^2 - a\right) \\ +\varepsilon^2 \left(N(N+2)\varepsilon^2 - 2aN\right) + a^2. \tag{5}$$

In Figure 3 function F_2 without noise ($\mathbf{z} = 0$) is shown together with the expectation value $\mathrm{E}[F_2|\mathbf{x}]$. The minima are merged into one global minimum at $(0, 0)$ replacing the local maximum. A closer look at Eq. (5) reveals

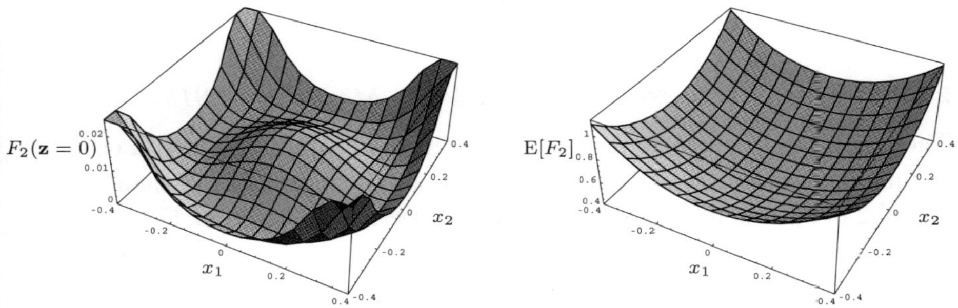

(a) (b)

Fig. 3. Figure (a): function F_2 without noise for $N = 2$ and $a = 0$ 1; figure (b): expectation value of F_2 for $N = 2$ and $a = 0.1$.

that this transition depends on the variance of the noise ε^2 and on the distance between the two minima of the noise free function controlled by the parameter a. The transition occurs if

$$\varepsilon > \left(\frac{a}{N+2}\right)^{\frac{1}{2}}. \tag{6}$$

The dependence on a is shown in Figure 4. Figure 3(a) also shows that function F_2 without noise does not have one optimum but infinitely many optima. If we compare this subspace of optimal solutions to the Pareto space in multi-objective optimisation where we also encounter a possibly continuous set of solutions of identical quality, it is reasonable to say that the identification of the whole space should be the target of the optimisation. We will come back to this point in Section 5. Here we only note that the optimal manifold of function F_2 without noise is given by the hyper-sphere

$$\mathbf{x}^2 = a. \tag{7}$$

For $N = 2$ the manifold is a circle with diameter a as shown in Figure 3(a).

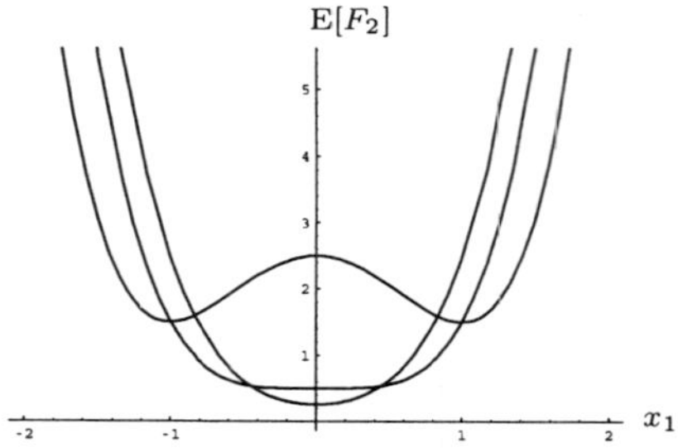

Fig. 4. The expectation value of function F_2 for $\varepsilon^2 = 0.25$, $x_2 = 0$, $N = 2$ and $a = 0.4, 1.0, 2.0$ (from top to bottom). As predicted by equation (6), the transition occurs below the critical value of $a = 1$.

2.3. *Functions with Noise Induced Multi-Modality (FNIM)*

The transition from single-modal to multi-modal characteristics in a class of functions under the influence of noise is less straightforward than the merging of optima demonstrated in the last section for function F_2.

The introduction of the FNIM in this section is motivated by the qualitative behaviour of evolution strategies for the design optimisation of gas-turbine blades. The behaviour suggests that the local fitness space might look similar to the fitness function shown in Figure 5. Since the dimensionality of the parameter space of the design optimisation problem is much higher, the model can only be regarded as one possible interpretation. In

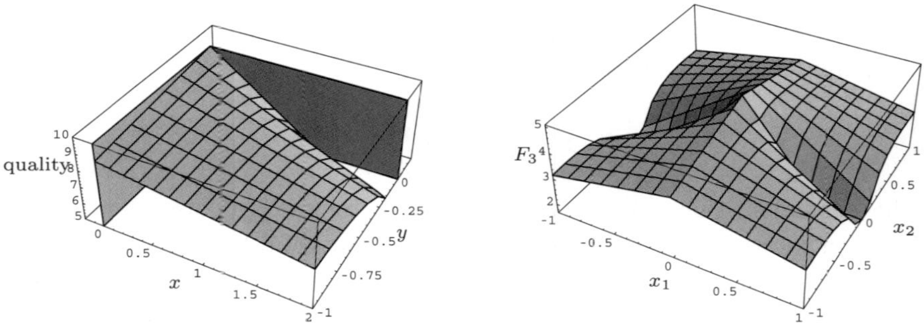

Fig. 5. Left: Qualitative model for the local fitness landscape motivated by the behaviour of evolution strategies for the design optimisation of gas-turbine blades. Right: Function F_3 with $n = 2, z = 0, a = 5$ and $b = 0.2$.

the direction of the y-axis (assuming $x = 0$) the fitness increases nearly linear along a ridge. The downwards slope from the ridge in the positive x-direction significantly increases with increasing fitness value. The fitness space is bounded by two regions of infeasible solutions (shown by the filled rectangles) for example due to geometric constraints or unstable results of the fluid-dynamics flow solver. Needless to say that the position of the infeasible region does not exactly coincide with the ridge, but can lie somewhere on the negative x-axis. Noise is introduced in this fitness model by demanding robustness of the parameter representing the x-direction perpendicular to the ridge. Thus, the resulting design should display stable performance under variations of the x-parameter. The optimum of the $x-$averaged fitness landscape will not remain at the $(y = 0)-$boundary to the infeasible region but move along the ridge to smaller y-values assuming that the increase of the downwards slope in the x-direction is sufficient.

Function F_3, Eq. (8), displays the linear increase along the ridge and the sharp decrease in the x_{N-1}-coordinate in the vicinity of the optimum at $(0,0)$.

$$\begin{aligned} F_3(\mathbf{x}) &= a - \frac{|x_{N-1}+z| + \sum_{i=1}^{N-2} x_i^2}{|x_N| + b} - |x_N| \\ & z \sim \mathcal{N}(0,\varepsilon^2),\ b > 0,\ \mathbf{x} \in I\!R^N. \end{aligned} \tag{8}$$

In order to be able to neglect the infeasible regions in the analysis, function F_3 has been designed in such a way that a clear optimum exists when no robustness is taken into account. Thus, without noise $(z = 0)$ F_3 is a uni-modal function, as shown in Figure 5 for $N = 2$. Next, we derive $\mathrm{E}[F_3|\mathbf{x}]$:

$$\mathrm{E}[F_3|\mathbf{x}] = a - \frac{E[|x_{N-1}+z|] + \sum_{i=1}^{N-2} x_i^2}{|x_N| + b} - |x_N|. \tag{9}$$

For $z \sim \mathcal{N}(0,\varepsilon^2)$, $\mathrm{E}[|x+z|]$ is given as follows:

$$\mathrm{E}[|x+z|] = \mathrm{E}[x+z]_{z>-x} + \mathrm{E}[-(x+z)]_{z<-x} \tag{10}$$

$$= \frac{1}{\sqrt{2\pi\varepsilon^2}} \left(x \int_{-x}^{x} e^{(\frac{-z^2}{2\varepsilon^2})} dz + 2 \int_{x}^{\infty} z\, e^{(\frac{-z^2}{2\varepsilon^2})} dz \right) := \xi(x) \tag{11}$$

Using (11), we get

$$\mathrm{E}[F_3|\mathbf{x}] = a - \frac{\xi(x_{N-1}) + \sum_{i=1}^{N-2} x_i^2}{|x_N| + b} - |x_N|. \tag{12}$$

$\mathrm{E}[F_3|\mathbf{x}]$ is shown in Figure 6 for fixed values of b and ε. In particular when we observe the 2D cross section shown in Figure 6, it is evident that the uni-modal function has changed into a bi-modal function due to averaging over the variations in one of the design parameters.

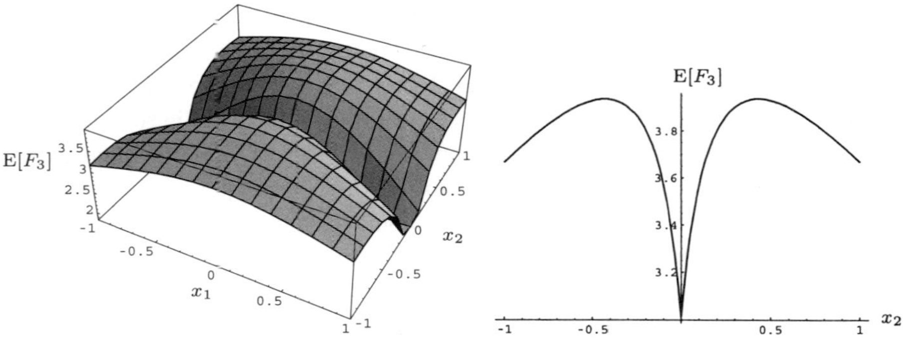

Fig. 6. Left: E[$F_3|\mathbf{x}$] with $N = 2$, $a = 5, b = 0.2$ and $\varepsilon^2 = 0.25$. Right: Two-dimensional cross section ($x_1 = 0$).

Qualitatively this process of changing a uni-modal fitness function into a multi-modal function (or in our example into a bi-modal function) by averaging over the variations of one parameter is similar to a *bifurcation* process. The global maximum becomes a local minimum and two new local maxima (of the same height) occur. The bifurcation depends on the parameter b and on the noise strength, the variance ε^2. Numerically, this dependence is shown in Figure 7. We note that for large b values and for small variances no bifurcation occurs. Both dependencies are easily understood. The parameter b governs the steepness of the slope near the optimum $(0, 0)$; the smaller b, the steeper the slope. The noise strength determines the fluctuation along the coordinate x_{N-1}. Together they both determine whether the single optimum will persist or whether it will bifurcate.

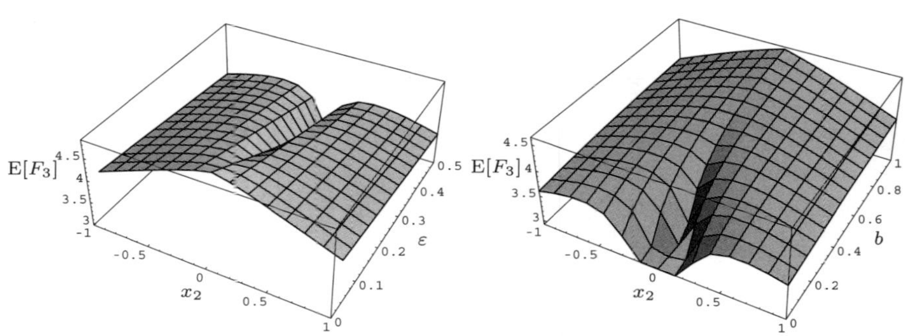

Fig. 7. The dependence of the bifurcation from a uni-modal to a bi-modal function on the standard deviation ε (left figure) and on the parameter b (right figure).

In order to analytically investigate the bifurcation behaviour further, Eq. (11) is too complex. Therefore, we smooth out the ridge and the slope in Eq. (8) and arrive at the following function F_4 which qualitatively shows a similar behaviour as F_3, as shown in Figure 8 for different levels of noise.

$$F_4(\mathbf{x}) = a - \frac{(x_{N-1}+z)^2 + \sum_{i=1}^{N-2} x_i^2}{x_N^2 + b} - x_N^2,$$
$$z \sim \mathcal{N}(0, \varepsilon^2),\ b > 0,\ \mathbf{x} \in I\!R^N. \tag{13}$$

Calculating the conditional expectation of F_4 is an easy task. Using $\mathrm{E}[(x_{N-1}+z)^2] = x_{N-1}^2 + \varepsilon^2$, we get:

$$\mathrm{E}[F_4|\mathbf{x}] = a - \frac{\varepsilon^2 + \sum_{i=1}^{N-1} x_i^2}{x_N^2 + b} - x_N^2. \tag{14}$$

Furthermore, it is straightforward to generalise F_4 and $\mathrm{E}[F_4|\mathbf{x}]$ to the multimodal case:

$$F_5(\mathbf{x}) = a - \frac{\sum_{i=1}^{N_1}(x_i+z_i)^2 + \sum_{i=N_2+1}^{N} x_i^2}{b + \sum_{N_1+1}^{N_2} x_i^2} - \sum_{N_1+1}^{N_2} x_i^2, \tag{15}$$

$$z_i \sim \mathcal{N}(0, \varepsilon^2),\ b > 0,\ \mathbf{x} \in I\!R^N,\ N_1 < N_2 \le N. \tag{16}$$

Function F_4 is a special case of F_5 with $N_1 = 1, N_2 = 2$ (note that the indices are changed). We will come back to function F_5 in Section 5.

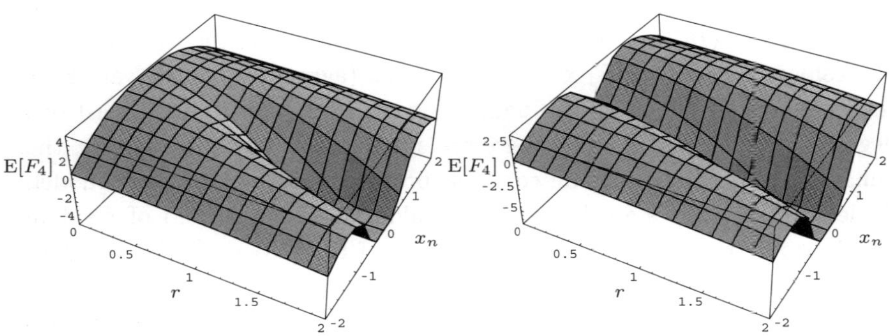

Fig. 8. Expected value landscapes of F_4 given by Eq. (14) for $\varepsilon = 0.25$ (left) and $\varepsilon = 1.0$ (right) - ($a = 5, b = 0.2$).

Writing $\sqrt{\sum_{i=1}^{N-1} x_i^2} := r$, we can further shorten $\mathrm{E}[F_4|\mathbf{x}]$:

$$\mathrm{E}[F_4|\mathbf{x}] = a - \frac{r^2 + \varepsilon^2}{x_N^2 + b} - x_N^2. \tag{17}$$

The conditional variance is given by

$$\mathrm{Var}[F_4|\mathbf{x}] = \frac{4\varepsilon^2}{(x_N^2+b)^2}(x_{N-1}^2+\varepsilon^2/2). \tag{18}$$

Now we are in a position to determine the extrema of function F_4 by taking the partial derivative of (17) with respect to x_N and setting it to zero

$$\frac{\partial \mathrm{E}[F_4|\mathbf{x}]}{\partial x_N} = \frac{2x_N(r^2+\varepsilon^2)}{(x_N^2+b)^2} - 2x_N \stackrel{!}{=} 0. \tag{19}$$

Solving for x_N one gets the $\hat{x}_N$ points of the local optima. Besides the trivial solution $\hat{x}_N = 0$ there exist also nontrivial ones:

$$\hat{x}_N = \pm\sqrt{\sqrt{r^2+\varepsilon^2}-b} \quad \text{for} \quad r > \sqrt{b^2-\varepsilon^2}. \tag{20}$$

A closer examination of $\mathrm{E}[F_4|\mathbf{x}]$ reveals that there is a single maximum as long as the square root on the left-hand side in Eq. (20) is imaginary, i.e., for $\sqrt{r^2+\varepsilon^2}-b < 0$. In this case the maximum is located at $(r, x_N) = (0,0)$ and the maximality condition for $\hat{x}_N = 0$ becomes $\varepsilon < b$. That is, there is a single maximum provided that $\varepsilon < b$. For $\varepsilon > b$ the single maximum *bifurcates* into two maxima symmetrically located with respect to the r-axis. This happens, according to (20), for $r > \sqrt{b^2-\varepsilon^2}$.

3. The Dynamics of Evolution Strategies for FNIMs

Due to the complicated functional structure of $\mathrm{E}[F_4|\mathbf{x}]$, Eq. (14), and $\mathrm{Var}[F_4|\mathbf{x}]$, Eq. (18), one cannot apply the sphere model theory[6] in a simple fashion. Actually, $\mathrm{E}[F_4|\mathbf{x}]$ depends on two (aggregated) state variables, therefore, the dynamics and an underlying theory must contain at least two degrees of freedom. However, there are some clues that, qualitatively, the behaviour should share some common properties with the sphere model. At least the steady-state behaviour should exhibit some kind of residual localisation error for the optimiser: Because of Eq. (18) $\mathrm{Var}[F_4|\mathbf{x}] > 0$ does always hold (provided that $\varepsilon > 0$), even for the case $(r, x_N) = (0,0)$.

In order to get a certain feeling how the ES evolves on function F_4, ES runs have been performed. They are displayed in Figs. 9 – 11. The value of the parental vector $\mathbf{x}$ was randomly initialised on a hyper-sphere with radius $R^{(0)}$. Considering the shape of F_4 for vanishing noise (cf. Fig. 8, $\varepsilon = 0$), it becomes clear that under such random conditions the quadratic x_N part in (14) dominates resulting in large negative F_4-values. The ES increases these F_4-values very fast as can be seen in Fig. 9 (the average $\langle F_4 \rangle$ of the μ parent fitnesses is displayed). The fast F_4 increase stops when

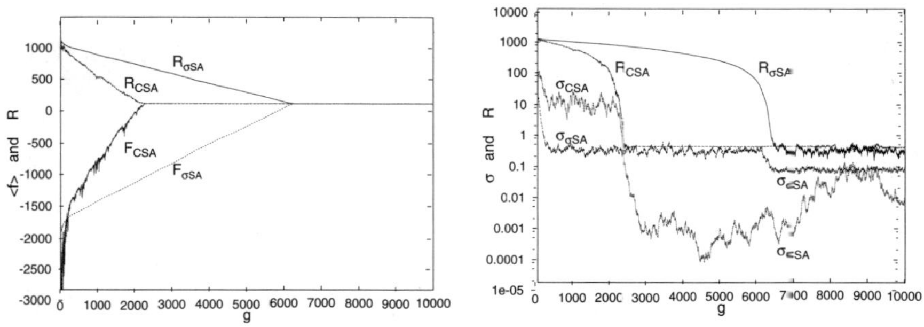

Fig. 9. The R- and σ-dynamics of a $(30/30_I, 60)$-ES on F_4 with $N = 20$, $a = 5$, $b = 0.5$, and $\varepsilon = 0.5$ using CSA and σSA, respectively. In the left figure, a linear vertical scale has been used while a logarithmic one in the right figure. The initial values are $R^{(0)} = 1000$ ($\mathbf{x}$-vector randomly initialised with $\|\mathbf{x}\| = R^{(0)}$) and $\sigma^{(0)} = 10$.

the "ridge"-like region has been reached. Then the dynamics changes into a linear one, the parental distance to the optimum $R^{(g)} = \|\mathbf{x}^{(g)}\|$ decreases obeying an almost perfect linear time law. The CSA-ES evolves faster to the steady-state than the σSA-ES. The steady-state is again characterised by a non-vanishing localisation error.

Figure 10, left-hand side, shows the approach to the steady-state considering the evolution of the x_N coordinate. Apart from the burst between

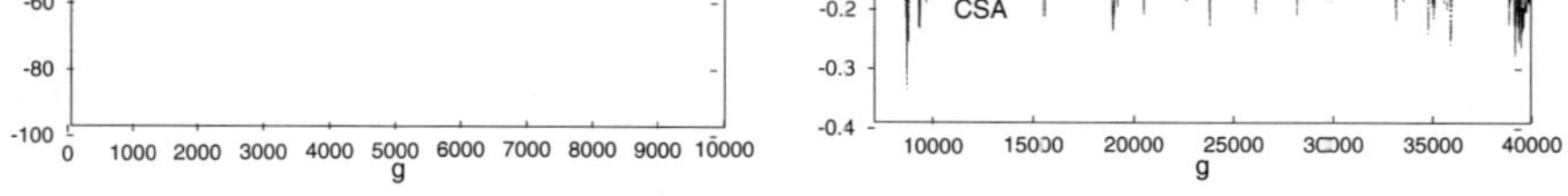

Fig. 10. Dynamics of the x_N-coordinate of the $(30/30_I, 60)$-ES run from Fig. 9 on F_4 using CSA and σSA, respectively. Left figure: transient phase; right figure: steady-state phase.

generation $g = 1700$ to 2200, there is nothing special with that coordinate. In the steady-state (right-hand side) it fluctuates around the zero line. However, consider Fig. 11, the difference to the ES run considered in Figs. 9 and 10 is the increased noise strength $\varepsilon = 0.75$. For this noise parameter, the

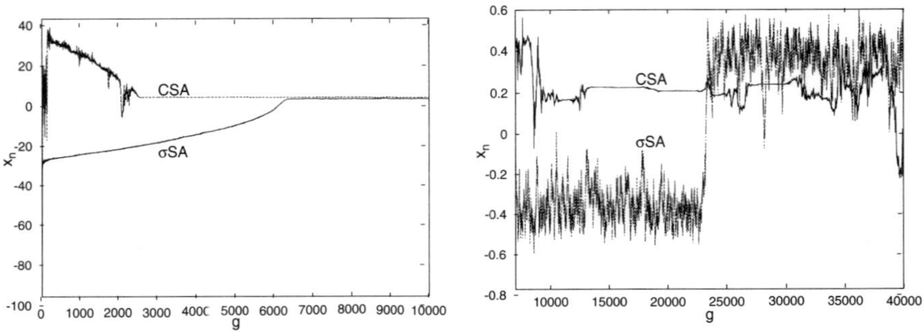

Fig. 11. The same conditions as in Fig. 10, but $\varepsilon = 0.75$ has been chosen.

σSA-ES exhibits a (random) periodic behaviour jumping back and forth between two attractors. Using a slightly smaller noise strength $\varepsilon = 0.7$, the time period gets smaller, Conversely, using larger noise strengths, e.g. $\varepsilon = 1.0$, the σSA-ES stays in one of the attracting regions forever (see the right-hand side in Fig. 12). While the σSA-ES exhibits periodic behaviour

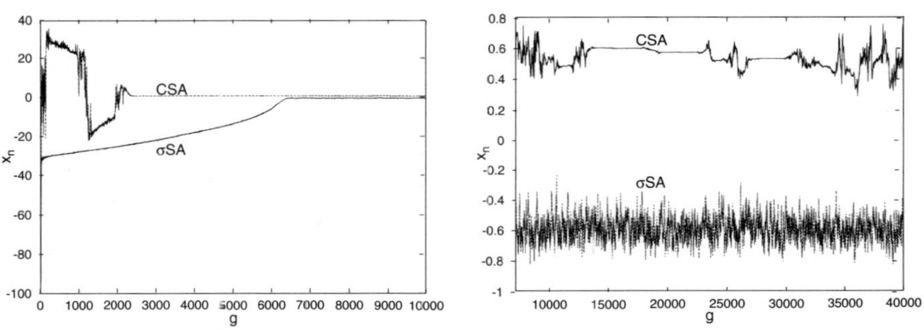

Fig. 12. The same conditions as in Fig. 10, but $\varepsilon = 1.0$ has been chosen.

for a certain noise level interval, the behaviour of the CSA-ES is more conservative. The reason for that lies in the small mutations strengths σ the CSA-ES randomly evolves when reaching the (almost selection neutral) steady-state. That is, unlike the σSA-ES, there is not enough mutation strength to push the ES system from one attractor to the other.

4. Steady State Behaviour of the Evolution Strategy on Function F_4

In order to estimate a lower bound on the residual localisation error we apply findings from the "standard" fitness noise model for evolution strategies, see the work by Arnold and Beyer[3,4] and Beyer *et al.*[6]. In the standard model the noise term in the fitness function is additive and normally distributed $\delta \sim N(0, \sigma_\delta^2)$. In order to apply the stability condition to ensure local convergence in the mean, which is given by (see Arnold and Beyer[4])

$$\sigma_\delta < \frac{R^2\,|\beta|}{N}\,\mu\, c_{\mu/\mu,\lambda}, \tag{21}$$

($R = R^{(g)}$ denotes the parental distance to the optimum, $c_{\mu/\mu,\lambda}$ the progress coefficient and β the factor of the sphere function) we first have to introduce appropriate sphere model approximations. Therefore, we have to neglect the influence of x_N in the denominator of Eq. (13). This step yields an ellipsoidal model. In a next *ad hoc* step, we assume that the eccentricity of the ellipsoid can be neglected. This leads to the desired sphere approximation (dropping the constant term a)

$$Q_{\text{sp}}(\mathbf{x}) = -\|\mathbf{x}\|^2/b = -R^2/b. \tag{22}$$

In the variance expression (18) we neglect x_{N-1} and x_N totally, as a result

$$\sigma_\delta = \sqrt{\text{Var}[f_2]} = \sqrt{2}\varepsilon^2/b. \tag{23}$$

Now, the evolution criterion (21) together with (23) and $\beta = -1/b$ is applied

$$\frac{\sqrt{2}\varepsilon^2}{b}\frac{Nb}{2R^2} < 2\mu c_{\mu/\mu,\lambda} \tag{24}$$

and finally solving for R, one obtains

$$R > R_\infty = \frac{\varepsilon}{2}\sqrt{\frac{\sqrt{2}N}{\mu c_{\mu/\mu,\lambda}}}. \tag{25}$$

Figure 13 shows the predictive quality of this formula. Even though the predictions seem to be relatively good, one should keep in mind that this result was obtained for a "moderate" b-value. One can easily violate the sphere condition by choosing more extreme b-values. Furthermore, considering larger ε-values, it appears that the asymptotic behaviour of (25) seems not to be correct.

Figure 13 (bottom) shows the behaviour of the mean value of the x_N coordinate in the steady-state. It reflects the behaviour observed in Figs. 10 – 12: Up to a certain ε the mean value is zero. After specific ε, the absolute mean values grow monotonously with the noise strength.

5. Extending F_4 to a More General Function Class

Considering broader and different classes of FNIM, respectively, is useful for at least two reasons. First, it broadens the view concerning the behaviour of EA in noisy settings, thus providing deeper insight in certain aspects of robust optimisation. Second, finding a special FNIM class which is especially suited for an analytical investigation of the ES behaviour on this functions. We discuss the properties of Function F_5 introduced in Section 2, Eq. (15) in this section in more detail. Using a slightly different notation, function F_5 can be re-written as:

$$F_5(\mathbf{x}) := a - \frac{r_1^2 + \sum_{i=N_1}^{N_2-1}(x_i + z_i)^2}{b + r_3^2} - r_3^2, \qquad b > 0, \tag{26}$$

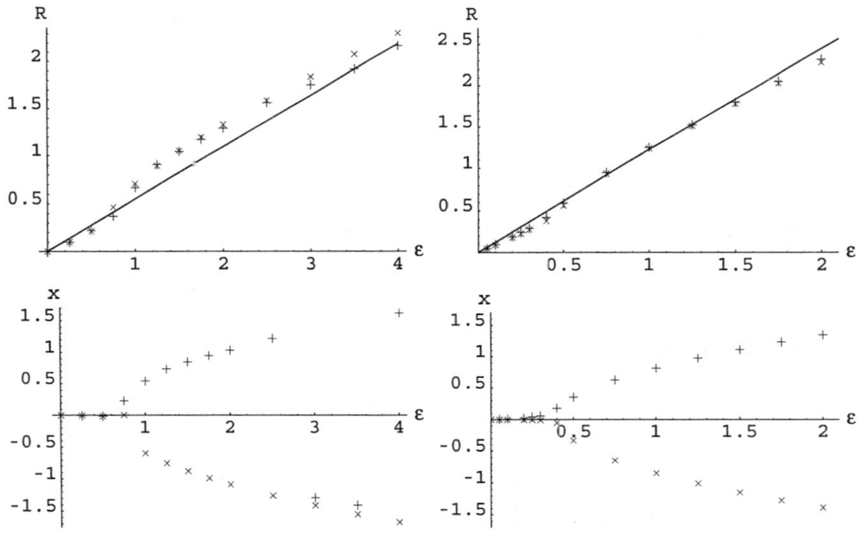

Fig. 13. Dependence of the mean value of the steady-state R (top figures) and of the steady-state x_N (bottom figures) on the noise strength ε. For the simulations a $(30/30_I, 60)$-ES has been used. Parameters of f_2 are $a = 5, b = 0.5$. The left figure was obtained for dimensionality $N = 20$ ($\varepsilon = 0, 0.25, 0.5, 0.75, 1, 1.25, 1.5, 1.75, 2, 2.5, 3, 3.5, 4$) and the right figure for $N = 100$ ($\varepsilon = 0, 0.05, 0.1, 0.2, 0.3, 0.4, 0.5, 0.75, 1, 1.25, 1.5, 1.75, 2$). The data points from the CSA-ES, displayed by "+"-symbols, are the average over generations $g = 3000$ (7000 for $N = 100$) to 40000 those of the σSA-ES, displayed by "×", are the average over generations $g = 8000$ (10000 for $N = 100$) to 40000. The linear curves represent Eq. (25).

where

$$r_1 := \sum_{i=1}^{N_1-1} x_i^2, \qquad r_3 := \sum_{i=N_2}^{N} x_i^2, \qquad 1 \leq N_1 < N_2 \leq N, \tag{27}$$

with

$$z_i \sim \mathcal{N}(0, \varepsilon^2). \tag{28}$$

We will discuss F_5 with respect to the mean value robustness. Since for each parameter space component with $i = N_1, \ldots, N_2 - 1$ the result of Eq. (14) holds similarly, we obtain for the expected value

$$\mathrm{E}[F_5|\mathbf{x}] = a - \frac{r_2^2 + (N_2 - N_1)\epsilon^2}{b + r_3^2} - r_3^2 \tag{29}$$

with r_2 defined by

$$r_2 := \sum_{i=1}^{N_2-1} x_i^2. \tag{30}$$

Comparing this expression with (17) we see the great similarity of both expressions. This also transfers to the optimal object parameter settings: $\mathrm{E}[F_5|\mathbf{x}]$ is locally optimised for $r_2 = 0$, that is, the first $N_2 - 1$ x_i coordinates must be zero. Applying the stationarity condition $\partial \mathrm{E}[F_5|\mathbf{x}]/\partial r_3 = 0$ for the coordinate aggregation r_3 yields

$$\tilde{r}_3 = 0, \qquad \text{for} \quad r_2 \leq \sqrt{b^2 - (N_2 - N_1)\varepsilon^2}, \tag{31}$$

$$\tilde{r}_3 = \sqrt{\sqrt{r_2^2 + (N_2 - N_1)\varepsilon^2} - b}, \quad \text{for} \quad r_2 > \sqrt{b^2 - (N_2 - N_1)\varepsilon^2}. \tag{32}$$

Thus, we see that the global optimiser (use $r_2 = 0$ in (31)) depends on ε according to

$$\hat{\mathbf{x}} = \mathbf{0}, \qquad \text{for} \quad \varepsilon \leq b/\sqrt{N_2 - N_1}, \tag{33}$$

$$\hat{\mathbf{x}} = (0, \ldots, 0, \hat{x}_{N_2}, \ldots, \hat{x}_N)^{\mathrm{T}}, \qquad \text{for} \quad \varepsilon > b/\sqrt{N_2 - N_1}, \tag{34}$$

where the $\hat{x}_{N_2}, \ldots, \hat{x}_N$ must conform the condition $\hat{r}_3 = \sqrt{\sqrt{N_2 - N_1}\varepsilon - b}$

$$\sum_{i=N_2}^{N} \hat{x}_i^2 = \sqrt{N_2 - N_1}\, \varepsilon - b. \tag{35}$$

This is an interesting result: For $N_2 < N$ there are no two global optimal solutions, but a $(N - N_2)$-dimensional manifold of solutions located on a (hyper-sphere) of radius $\sqrt{\sqrt{N_2 - N_1}\, \varepsilon - b}$ and origin at $(0, \ldots, 0)$ in the $\mathbb{R}^{N-N_2+1}$ subspace of the coordinates $x_{N_2}, \ldots, x_N$. This may be regarded as an extreme form of multi-modality or as some kind of indifference. One can easily calculate the maximal expected fitness by inserting (33) and (35) into (29) with the result

$$\hat{\overline{F}}_5 = a - (N_2 - N_1)\, \varepsilon^2/b, \qquad \text{for} \quad \varepsilon \le b/\sqrt{N_2 - N_1}, \tag{36}$$

$$\hat{\overline{F}}_5 = a + b - 2\sqrt{N_2 - N_1}\, \varepsilon, \quad \text{for} \quad \varepsilon > b/\sqrt{N_2 - N_1}. \tag{37}$$

Summing up, test function (26) allows for two types of noise-induced multi-modality:

(1) bimodality for $N_2 = N$ and
(2) infinite multi-modality for $N_2 < N$.

While the existence of the first case has already been confirmed by real ES runs in the last section, the second case is presented here. Figures 14 and 15 shows steady state values of ES runs on F_5 with $a = 5$, $b = 1$, $N = 40$, $N_1 = 23$, $N_2 = 39$. That is, r_3 is the aggregation of x_{N-1} and x_N. As one

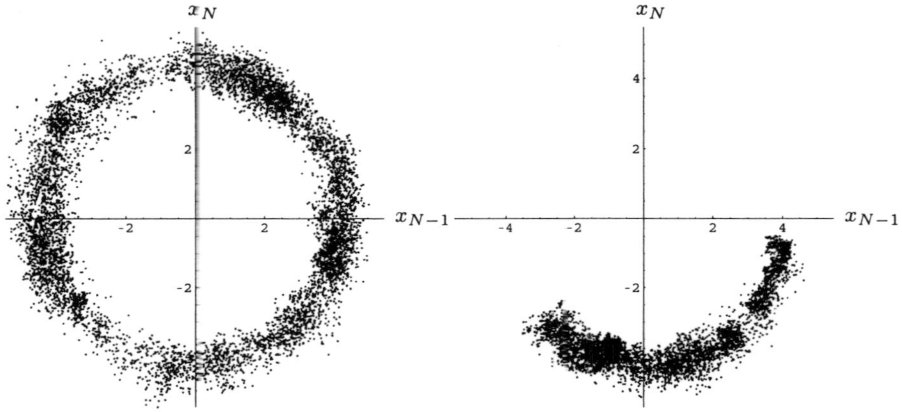

Fig. 14. On the distribution of the optimiser states of function F_5 ($a = 5$, $b = 1$, $N_1 = 23$, $N_2 = 39$, $N = 40$) in the vicinity of the steady state (8000 data points used) for $\varepsilon = 3$. The left figure was obtained using the $(5/5_I, 10)$-σSA-ES, the right figure using the $(5/5_I, 10)$-CSA-ES.

can see, if ε is sufficiently large, the behaviour predicted by (34) is observed. For small ε, x_{N-1} and x_N as well as the other x coordinates fluctuate around the zero state. This is in accordance with (33). The fluctuation around the optimiser state is the typical behaviour evolutionary algorithms do exhibit when evolving in a noisy environment. Note, while (35) describes

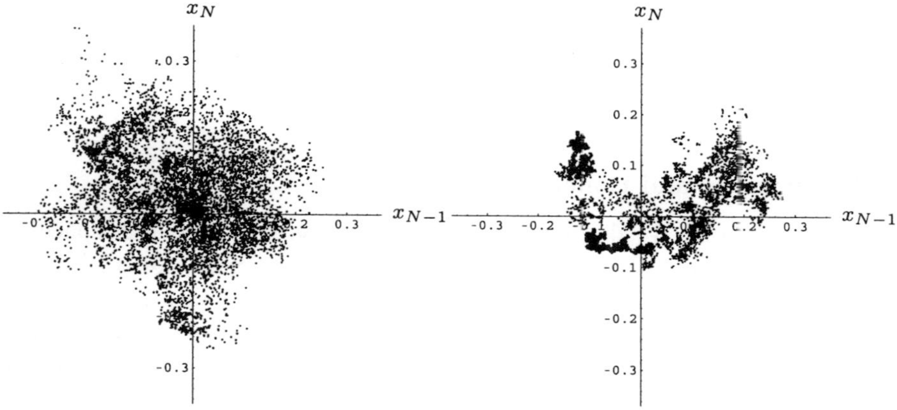

Fig. 15. On the distribution of the optimiser states of function F_5 ($a = 5$, $b = 1$, $N_1 = 23$, $N_2 = 39$, $N = 40$) in the vicinity of the steady state (8000 data points used) for $\varepsilon = 0.1$. The left figure was obtained using the $(5/5_I, 10)$-σSA-ES, the right figure using the $(5/5_I, 10)$-CSA-ES.

the optimum distance to the origin the x coordinates should realize, the actually observed mean value of the steady state r_3 deviates from this optimum. In the experiments conducted for Figs. 14 and 15 one measures $r_3 \approx 4.3$ for the $(5/5_I, 10)$-σSA-ES and $r_3 \approx 4.1$ for the CSA-ES ($\varepsilon = 3$). The optimum value, however, is $\hat{r}_3 = \sqrt{11} \approx 3.32$. The actually observed mean value is a result of the evolutionary algorithms and depends on the strategy parameters. Its calculation is still a pending problem.

It is interesting to notice the different behaviours the σSA-ES and the CSA-ES exhibit for the case $\hat{r}_3 > 0$. As one can see in Fig. 14, the CSA-ES (right figure) does not occupy the whole circle (notice, this is a plot of a single ES run). Depending on the initial values chosen, it is likely to observe this typical pattern. The reason for this observation can be traced back to the evolution of the mutation strength in CSA-ES under the influence of heavy noise also observed in the evolution dynamics of F_4 and other test functions (see Sendhoff *et al.*[12]). Under heavy noise, the CSA-ES first reduces the mutation strength σ and then it more or less performs a random walk in the σ values, but keeping these values small. However, small σ values result in small changes of the object parameters. (This can also be observed in the right picture of Fig. 15.) In other words, the CSA-ES becomes less explorative. Under such conditions, the CSA-ES is not able to explore the whole $r_3 = \mathit{const.}$ subspace efficiently. This is in contrast to the σSA-ES which does not reduce the mutation strength in such situations. Which one of the two behaviours is more desirable, however, is application dependent. Therefore, we cannot give a definitive answer as to the question which of the two σ-adaptation rules should be preferred.

6. Summary and Conclusion

In this chapter, we discussed the effect of noise on the search space in evolutionary algorithms. We introduced three main characteristics which go beyond the simple additive noise model. The *expectation-variance trade-off*, the *topology changing* functions and the *functions with noise induced multi-modality (FNIM)*. The last two function classes have the remarkable property of qualitatively changing the topology under the influence of noise. For the FNIM's the change from uni-modal to bi-modal or multi-modal fitness landscapes which we termed a bifurcation process using the analogue from nonlinear dynamics, occurs when a measure for the robustness or stability of the solution is used for the fitness.

We derived the conditions for bifurcation and empirically analysed the influence of the topological change of the fitness landscape on the behaviour of two types of evolution strategies, the cumulative step-size adaptation method and the "standard", mutative self-adaptation method. Whereas the later one exhibits periodic behaviour for a certain noise level interval, the CSA method tends to converge to one of the two optima. Although the proposed class of test functions is rather different from the sphere model, we were able to transfer some results from sphere model analysis at least qualitatively. In order to extend this analysis to a more quantitative one, which could help to give some insight into appropriate ranges of parameters like population size and selection pressure, requires a substantial step in the theory of evolutionary algorithms. However, at the same time, it can serve as an interesting test problem in this domain, because of its "natural" transition from uni-modal to bi-modal characteristics.

The extension of FNIMs $F_{3,4}$ to a more general class of functions F_5 in the last section demonstrated an additional important aspect for comparing CSA-ES and σSA-ES. The fact that for function F_5 the bifurcation leads to a manifold of optimal solutions (instead of to two isolated optima) highlighted the different behaviour of the two types of evolution strategies for exploring selectively neutral parts in search space. However, as we have seen already for function F_2 the fact that optima are not necessarily unique is by no means restricted to noisy optimisation tasks. Whether we should demand from an optimiser to identify one single solution as fast as possible

(CSA-ES) or the identification of the whole set of optimal solutions (σSA-ES) has to be answered for each specific application separately. At the same time, looking at the area of multi-objective optimisation where the notion of a space of optimal solutions, i.e. the Pareto space, occurs naturally, the identification of all solutions might be desirable.

Acknowledgements

B. Sendhoff and M. Olhofer thank E. Körner for his support. H.-G. Beyer acknowledges support from the Collaborative Research Center SFB 531 sponsored by the Deutsche Forschungsgemeinschaft (DFG).

Appendix A. Description of the Evolution Strategies

The σ self-adaptation technique is based on the coupled inheritance of object and strategy parameters. Using the notation

$$\langle \mathbf{a} \rangle^{(g)} := \frac{1}{\mu} \sum_{m=1}^{\mu} \mathbf{a}_{m;\lambda}^{(g)} \tag{A.1}$$

for intermediate recombination (centroid calculation, i.e., averaging over the **a** parameters of the μ best offspring individuals), the $(\mu/\mu_I, \lambda)$-σSA-ES can be expressed in "offspring notation"

$$\forall l = 1, \ldots, \lambda : \begin{cases} \sigma_l^{(g+1)} := \langle \sigma \rangle^{(g)} \mathrm{e}^{\tau \mathcal{N}_l(0,1)} \\ \mathbf{y}_l^{(g+1)} := \langle \mathbf{y} \rangle^{(g)} + \sigma_l^{(g+1)} \boldsymbol{\mathcal{N}}_l(\mathbf{0}, \mathbf{1}). \end{cases} \tag{A.2}$$

As learning parameter $\tau = 1/\sqrt{N}$ has been chosen in the simulations.

While in evolutionary self-adaptive ES each individual get its own set of endogenous strategy parameters, cumulative step-size adaptation uses a single mutation strength parameter σ per generation to produce all the offspring. This σ is updated by a deterministic rule which is controlled by certain statistics gathered over the course of generations. The statistics used is the so-called (normalised) cumulative path-length $\mathbf{s}$. If $\|\mathbf{s}\|$ is greater than the expected length of a random path, σ is increased. In the opposite situation, σ is decreased. The update rule reads

$$\begin{aligned} &\forall l = 1, \ldots, \lambda : \mathbf{y}_l^{(g+1)} := \langle \mathbf{y} \rangle^{(g)} + \sigma^{(g)} \boldsymbol{\mathcal{N}}_l(\mathbf{0}, \mathbf{1}) \\ &\mathbf{s}^{(g+1)} := (1-c)\mathbf{s}^{(g)} + \sqrt{(2-c)c}\frac{\sqrt{\mu}}{\sigma^{(g)}} \left(\langle \mathbf{y} \rangle^{(g+1)} - \langle \mathbf{y} \rangle^{(g)} \right) \\ &\sigma^{(g+1)} := \sigma^{(g)} \exp\left(\frac{\|\mathbf{s}^{(g+1)}\| - \overline{\chi}_N}{D\overline{\chi}_N} \right) \end{aligned} \tag{A.3}$$

where $\mathbf{s}^{(0)} = \mathbf{0}$ is chosen initally. The recommended standard settings for the cumulation parameter c and the damping constant D are used, i.e., $c = 1/\sqrt{N}$ and $D = \sqrt{N}$, see also Hansen and Ostermeier[10].

References

1. A.N. Aizawa and B.W. Wah. Scheduling of genetic algorithms in a noisy environment. *Evolutionary Computation*, 2(2):97–122, 1994.
2. D. Arnold. *Noisy Optimization with Evolution Strategies.* Kluwer Academic Publishers, 2002.
3. D. V. Arnold and H.-G. Beyer. Local performace of the $(\mu/\mu_I, \lambda)$-ES in a noisy environment. In W. Martin and W. Spears, editors, *Foundations of Genetic Algorithms, 6*, pages 127–141. Morgan Kaufmann, 2001.
4. D. V. Arnold and H.-G. Beyer. Performance analysis of evolution strategies with multi-recombination in high-dimensional $\mathbb{R}^N$-search spaces disturbed by noise. *Theoretical Computer Science*, 289:629–647, 2002.
5. H.-G. Beyer. Toward a theory of evolution strategies: Some asymptotical results from the $(1,^+ \lambda)$-theory. *Evolutionary Computation*, 1(2):165–188, 1993.
6. H.-G. Beyer, M. Olhofer, and B. Sendhoff. On the behavior of $(\mu/\mu_I, \lambda)$-ES optimizing functions disturbed by generalized noise. In K. A. De Jong, R. Poli, and J. E. Rowe, editors, *Foundations of Genetic Algorithms VII*, pages 307–328, 2002.
7. J.R. Birge and F. Louveaux. *Introduction to Stochastic Programming.* Springer Series in Operations Research. Springer Verlag, 1997.
8. J. Branke. *Evolutionary Optimization in Dynamic Environments.* Kluwer Academic Publishers, 2001.
9. J.M. Fitzpatrick and J.J. Grefenstette. Genetic algorithms in noisy environments. In P. Langley, editor, *Machine Learning: Special Issue on Genetic Algorithms*, volume 3, pages 101–120. Kluwer Academic Publishers, 1988.
10. N. Hansen and A. Ostermeier. Completely derandomized self-adaptation in evolution strategies. *Evolutionary Computation*, 9(2):159–196, 2001.
11. Y. Jin and B. Sendhoff. Trade-off between optimality and robustness: An evolutionary multiobjective approach. In C. M. Fonseca, P. J. Fleming, E. Zitzler, K. Deb, and L. Thiele, editors, *Evolutionary Multi-Criterion Optimization*, pages 237–251. Springer Verlag, 2003.
12. B. Sendhoff, H.-G. Beyer, and M. Olhofer. On noise induced multi-modality in evolutionary algorithms. In L. Wang, K.C. Tan, T. Furuhashi, J.-H. Kim, and X. Yao, editors, *Proceedings of the 4th Asia-Pacific Conference on Simulated Evolution And Learning - SEAL*, volume 1, pages 219–224, 2002.
13. S. Tsutsui and A. Gosh. Genetic algorithms with a robust solution searching scheme. *IEEE Trans. on Evolutionary Computation*, 1(3):201–208, 1997.
14. D. Wiesmann, U. Hammel, and T. Bäck. Robust design of multilayer optical coatings by means of evolutionary algorithms. *IEEE Trans. on Evolutionary Computation*, 2(4):162–167, 1998.

CHAPTER 10

THEORETICAL ANALYSIS OF THE GA PERFORMANCE WITH A MULTIPLICATIVE ROYAL ROAD FUNCTION

Hideaki Suzuki

ATR, Human Information Science Laboratories
2-2-2 Hikaridai, Seika-cho, Soraku-gun, Kyoto 619-0288 Japan
E-mail: hsuzuki@atr.jp

Hidefumi Sawai

Communications Research Laboratory
588-2, Iwaoka, Iwaoka-cho, Nishi-ku,Kobe, 651-2492 Japan
E-mail: sawai@crl.go.jp

The performance of genetic algorithms (GAs) is theoretically estimated with multiplicative royal-road functions (mRR-functions). Using a *macro-schema* analysis, the effects of selection, mutation, and crossover are quantitatively estimated, which enables formulation of the innovation time and takeover time of component schemata as a function of genetic parameters. Theoretical estimation is compared to the experimental results of a simple GA, and it is shown that the theoretical results are in good agreement with experimental ones specifically when the innovation time is much larger than the takeover time.

1. Introduction

Since their proposal [7], royal-road functions (RR-functions) have been widely used to study the searching mechanisms of genetic algorithms (GAs) [7,8,5,20,21,10,11,12]. The basic concept behind the design of a RR-function is the building block hypothesis and implicit parallelism asserting that GAs can swiftly find an optimal solution because a longer, more advantageous schema is created by the combination of shorter component schemata that might spread in parallel. The RR-function was designed so that a population might evolve this way using explicitly defined advantageous schemata (blocks). From some careful experiments [7,8,9], however, the RR-function did not ensure that GAs evolve a population in the expected way, but rather cast doubt on the GAs' basic hypotheses. A shorter component schema is easily made extinct by a longer, more advantageous schema by hitchhiking. It takes a long time for a population to recreate the lost component schema, which makes the GA performance worse than that of a random mutation hill-climbing method [8,9].

The analytic estimation of the performance of RR-GAs was first given by Nimwegen *et al.* [10]. They used a statistical method to analyze a population expressed as a fitness distribution, and succeeded in estimating the rate of evolution. Their analyses [10,11,12], however, included only selection and mutation, and the GA's most characteristic operation, crossover, was not incorporated. Theoretical analysis on crossover in RR-GAs, on the other hand, was first given by Suzuki and Iwasa [13,14,15]. They assumed a one-block RR-function (which they called a Babel-like fitness function) and calculated the acceleration rate by crossover under a variety of genetic parameter sets. The present chapter extends their method and estimates the performance of multi-block RR-GAs with a quantitative analysis on crossover. Applying a *macro-schema* analysis introduced by [16,17], we formulate the innovation time and takeover time of schemata as a function of the genetic parameters, such as the population size, fitness coefficient, and mutation/crossover rates. This enables us to theoretically estimate the waiting time until the domination of the longest schema. We also conduct a simple GA simulation and compare its results with the theoretical estimation. It is shown that the theory and the experiments are in good agreement with each other under specific conditions.

In the following, after explaining the multiplicative royal-road (mRR) function studied in this chapter in Section 2, the mathematical formulation is presented in Section 3. A comparison between theory and the simple GA simulation is presented in Section 4, and several arguments are given in Section 5. Section 6 presents concluding remarks.

2. Multiplicative RR-Function

We consider a population of binary strings with length I. A RR-function is a fitness function defined with a set of explicitly defined elementary blocks. We assume that the final target schema (denoted by H) consists of E advantageous elementary blocks (denoted by Bs) with the same order (o_B). Through this chapter, non-coding regions in/between the blocks are not incorporated; hence, the order of H is equal to $I = E \times o_B$. The fitness of a string is determined by the number of the blocks the string has. Let the fitness of a string with B be $(1 + s_B)$-times as large as that of strings without B, where s_B is the fitness coefficient that represents the fitness's difference between strings with B and without B. Though the conventional RR-functions are defined using an *additive* fitness scheme [7,8], i.e. the fitness value of a string is ls'_B (where l is the number of blocks the string has), we here assume a *multiplicative* fitness scheme [2] in which the fitness value of a string is given by $(1+s_B)^l$. This type of fitness function is transformed with log-scaling into the additive fitness function as $\log(1+s_B)^l = l \cdot \log(1+s_B) = ls'_B$, where $s'_B = \log(1+s_B)$ was substituted. Under the multiplicative fitness scheme, the fitness advantage of a string having a new created block is always $(1 + s_B)$-times as large as one not having the block, which enables us to formulate the occurrence and spreading of a block with a unified formula.

3. Analytic Estimation

Following Goldberg *et al.* [4,18], we refer to the waiting time for the creation of a new block (the waiting time until a schema starts spreading in the population) as the *innovation time* (T_i), and the time taken for a block to spread through the population as the *takeover time* (T_t). If the crossover rate is so high that a new block can be created by all the individuals while the previously created block is spreading as well, the waiting time until the final (longest) schema H dominates the population (T_d) is represented by the sum of the innovation time of E blocks and the takeover time of the last created block:

$$T_d = \sum_{l=1}^{E} T_i^{(l)} + T_t, \tag{1}$$

where $T_i^{(l)}$ is the innovation time for the lth-created block. The $\sum_l$ is summed just for l satisfying $2^{l \cdot o_B} > N$ (N is the population size), because when N is larger than $2^{l \cdot o_B}$, the block is already included in an initial population (we assume a random population as an initial state) and the innovation time is practically zero.

In the following, we first explain a macro-schema analysis [16,17] and formulate $T_i^{(l)}$, principally considering the randomization effect by mutation and crossover. After that, T_t is formulated, considering the selective advantage of an elementary block and neglecting the effects by mutation and crossover during the spreading process. Such an approximate analysis is valid when the order and the selective advantage of an elementary block is sufficiently large and a population evolves in a punctuated way with a long period of neutral evolution and a short period of adaptive evolution taking place alternately.

3.1. *Macro-schema Analysis*

To analyze the evolution of the target schema H, we separate the whole bit field (I binary loci) into E *subfields* ($F_1, \cdots, F_E$) in accordance with the locations of the elementary blocks Bs. A macro-schema $G_{\boldsymbol{i}} = G_{(i_1,\cdots,i_E)}$ is defined as the union of a set of schemata (subspaces) which have i_1 anti-bits in F_1, i_2 anti-bits in F_2, and so on (where an 'anti-bit' is a defining bit different from Hs). For example, if $H = [0000]$ and $B = [00**]$ or $[**00]$, macro-schema $G_{(2,1)}$ is

$$G_{(2,1)} = [1110] \vee [1101].$$

For a given mRR-function, the number of different macro-schemata is $(o_{\mathrm{B}} + 1)^E$.

The macro-schema set defines a partition of the genotype space, and based upon this partition, we can describe the state of a population using a $(o_{\mathrm{B}} + 1)^E$-dimensional frequency vector $\boldsymbol{x} \equiv \{x_{\boldsymbol{i}}\} = \{x(\boldsymbol{i})\}$ whose $\boldsymbol{i}$th element $x_{\boldsymbol{i}}$ is the frequency of $G_{\boldsymbol{i}}$, namely, the probability of a string in the population being a '$G_{\boldsymbol{i}}$ string'. (A '$G_{\boldsymbol{i}}$ string' is a string in the $G_{\boldsymbol{i}}$ subspace.) Then, the evolutionary dynamics of an *infinite* population under a simple GA are represented by a set of $\boldsymbol{x}$'s recursion formulas for selection, mutation, and crossover.

Here, we define Δm_{B} as the expected increases in the block frequency m_{B} from zero. Using the macro-schema recursion formulas for mutation and crossover, we can formulate Δm_{B} as

$$\Delta m_{\mathrm{B}} = \frac{1}{2^{o_{\mathrm{B}}}} \left(p_{\mathrm{m}} o_{\mathrm{B}} + p_{\mathrm{c}} \frac{o_{\mathrm{B}} - 3}{I - 1} \right), \tag{2}$$

where p_{m} is the mutation rate per bit per generation and p_{c} is the occurrence rate of one-point crossover per crossover pair per generation. See Appendix A for the detailed derivation. Equation (2) is also regarded as the creation probability of E in a string because an individual of the next generation is chosen between having B and not having B using m_{B} (a Wright-Fisher model of the *finite* population [19,3,1]). The term $p_{\mathrm{c}}(o_{\mathrm{B}} - 3)/(I - 1)$ in Eq. (2) reflects the crossover's function to help create a new elementary block.

3.2. *Formulation of* $T_i^{(l)}$

The innovation time is calculated from the creation probability of an elementary block by mutation and crossover formulated as Eq. (2), and the extinction probability z, of a newly created block formulated as follows.

Let μ be the expected frequency ratio of a newly created block. Considering the effects of selection, mutation, and crossover, μ is written as

$$\mu \equiv (1 + s_B)(1 - p_m o_B)\left(1 - p_c \frac{o_B - 1}{I - 1}\right). \tag{3}$$

If we assume that the number of the offspring having the block obeys a Poisson distribution with the mean value μ, z satisfies the relation

$$z = \sum_{k=0}^{\infty}\left(\frac{\mu^k}{k!}e^{-\mu}\right)\cdot z^k = \exp(\mu(z-1)). \tag{4}$$

The average number of occurrences of the block until its spreading is then given by $\sum_{k=1}^{\infty} k \cdot z^{k-1}(1-z) = 1/(1-z)$ (see [15] Section 3.4). If s_B is so small and/or p_m and p_c are so large that μ is smaller than one, z's solution of Eq. (4) is $z = 1$ or $1/(1-z) = \infty$, which means that even if an elementary block is created, it is always destroyed and cannot spread.

As was mentioned earlier, Δm_B is the creation probability of a block in a string; hence, if we assume that all N individuals in the population always participate in the creation of a block, the block creation probability in a population is given by $N\Delta m_B$. This enables us to formulate the innovation time T_i, that is, the waiting time until a block is created in a population, as

$$T_i^{(l)} = \sum_{t=1}^{\infty}(1 - N\Delta m_B)^{t-1}\cdot N\Delta m_B \cdot t = \frac{1}{N\Delta m_B}.$$

The above formula does not incorporate the extinction probability z, but when μ is not much larger than one, we cannot neglect z, and T_i must be modified by multiplying the average number of blocks that should be created before one block begins spreading as

$$\begin{aligned} T_i^{(l)} &= \frac{1}{N\Delta m_B}\cdot\frac{1}{1-z} \\ &= \frac{2^{o_B}}{N}\left(p_m o_B + p_c\frac{o_B - 3}{I - 1}\right)^{-1}\cdot\frac{1}{1-z}. \end{aligned} \tag{5}$$

3.3. *Formulation of* T_t

After a newly created block escapes from the initial risk of destruction, its frequency m_B increases approximately obeying

$$m_B(0) = 1/N \tag{6}$$

$$\frac{dm_B}{dt} = \frac{(1+s_B)m_B}{1+s_Bm_B} - m_B = \frac{s_Bm_B(1-m_B)}{1+s_Bm_B}, \tag{7}$$

where we neglected the influence of mutation and crossover on the spreading process assuming that s_B is sufficiently large. Then, the takeover time T_t until m_B exceeds the threshold frequency γ, above which a block is judged to dominate the population, is formulated as

$$T_t = \int_{(m=1/N)}^{(m=\gamma)} dt = \int_{1/N}^{\gamma} \frac{1+s_Bm}{s_Bm(1-m)} dm$$
$$\simeq \frac{\log\gamma - (1+s_B)\log(1-\gamma) + \log N}{s_B}. \tag{8}$$

For theoretical estimation, we use $\gamma = 0.9$ in this chapter. Strictly speaking, mutation makes the maximum value of the schema frequency smaller than one (see Eq. (10)); and yet, we surmise that Eq. (8) substituted with $\gamma = 0.9$ can be a good approximation because mutation causes the reduction of the growth rate of m_B as well.

3.4. *Several Parameter Conditions*

In order for the previous argument to be valid, several parameter conditions have to be satisfied:

$$N \cdot p_m \geq 0.5, \tag{9}$$

$$m_H(\infty) = 1 - \frac{1+s_B}{s_B} \cdot p_m \cdot o_B \geq \gamma. \tag{10}$$

Inequality (9) is the condition that a population can maintain sufficient diversity to make crossover effective [6,15]. The right side value 0.5 was determined from empirical data. Inequality (10) is the condition that the saturated frequency of the final longest schema H exceeds γ, so it can dominate the population. γ is related to the stopping condition of a GA simulation.

4. Experiments

To experimentarily study the evolution in mRR-GAs, we conduct numerical experiments of the simple GA with one-point crossover. Starting from a random population prepared in a memory, the simple GA operations are applied to the population. The condition parameters are the block order o_B, the block number E, the population size N, the fitness coefficient s_B, the mutation rate p_m, and the crossover rate p_c. We repeat the generation cycle until m_H exceeds $\gamma = 0.9 \times m_H(\infty)$, by which the domination time T_d is evaluated. The evaluation to calculate the average is conducted fifty times for the parameter conditions in Table 1 or twenty times for other parameter conditions using different random number sequences.

Table 1. Theoretical and experimental results for mRR-functions with various parameter values. Experimental results for T_d are averages over fifty trial runs, except that the result of the column (m) is taken from the paper by Mitchell *et al.*, which used a RR function with the additive fitness scheme.

		(a)	(b)	(c)	(d)	(e)	(f)	(g)	(m)
String length, l		24	16	16	8	24	24	16	64
Block order, o_B		12	8	8	4	8	8	4	8
Block number, E		2	2	2	2	3	3	4	8
Population size, N		5000	5000	500	5000	5000	500	10000	128
Fitness coeff., s_B		1	1	1	1	1	1	0.5	0.5
Mutation rate, p_m		0.0001	0.0001	0.004	0.0001	0.0001	0.004	0.002	0.005
Crossover rate, p_c		0.25	0.25	1	0.25	0.25	1	0.25	0.7
Theory	T_i	12	0.85	22	0.12	1.2	4.4	0.12	47
	T_t	13	13	11	13	13	11	25	16
	T_d	25	14	33	13	15	20	25	389
Experiment	T_d	174	15.5	23	9.26	18.4	23	20.9	556

Table 1 shows several examples of the experimental results together with the theoretical results. All parameter conditions satisfy Inequality (9). (Inequality (10) is always satisfied because $\gamma = 0.9 \times m_H(\infty)$.) With a few exceptions, agreement between theory and experiments is at a satisfactory level. Table 2 shows the contrast between good and bad agreement more clearly . For the parameter condition (i), the theoretical values of T_d agree well with the experimental ones, but for the condition (m)", the theory underestimates T_d by a factor of about three times compared to the experiment. Including these examples, we conducted GA experiments for about forty different parameter sets, whose results are shown in Fig. 1 According to this figure, we can generally say that our analytical method correctly estimates T_d when the value of T_d is large, whereas the method underestimes T_d for smaller values of T_d.

Table 2. Theoretical and experimental results for mRR-functions with various parameter values. Experimental results for T_d are averages over twenty trial runs.

(i) $I = E \times o_B = 4 \times 16 = 64$, $s_B = 1.5$, $p_m = 0.017$, $p_c = 0.71$							
N		128	256	512	1024	2048	4096
Theory	T_i	2070	1035	516	259	129	64.6
	T_t	7.0	7.5	7.9	8.4	8.9	9.3
	T_d	8286	4147	2078	1043	526	268
Exper.	T_d	8282	5640	2474	1342	701	392

(m)" $I = E \times o_B = 8 \times 8 = 64$, $s_B = 1.5$, $p_m = 0.043$, $p_c = 0.73$							
N		128	256	512	1024	2048	4096
Theory	T_i	8.5	4.2	2.1	1.1	0.53	0.26
	T_t	7.0	7.5	7.9	8.4	8.9	9.3
	T_d	74.8	37.1	22.8	15.8	12.6	11.1
Exper.	T_d	248	100	60.5	45.9	32.2	29.1

5. Discussion

5.1. *Effectiveness and Limitation of the Analyses*

The analyses in Section 3 used the following basic assumptions.

- Assuming a large crossover rate, hitchhiking, that is, the competition between two or more blocks spreading in parallel, was neglected.
- Assuming the large selective advantage of a block, the effects of mutation and crossover during the spreading process were neglected.
- The creation/fixation of elementary blocks was assumed to be ordered, and the innovation time (Eq. (5)) was formulated focusing only on the creation of a particular block B.

Among them, the first assumption is the most fundamental. When crossover is moderately operated on a population, the disruption of linkage between loci is not perfect and there remains interference between the spreading processes of blocks. For example, if the block B_2 is created in a string without B_1 while B_1 is spreading in a population, B_1 and B_2 begin spreading at the same time, but one of the two is forced to be extinct unless crossover combines B_1 and B_2 into a single string to create a longer schema. Hitchhiking that diminishes the evolutionary rate in this way happens very often when $T_i < T_t$; hence, the theory neglecting the hitchhiking underestimates T_d in Table 2(m)". When $T_i > T_t$, on the other hand, a population

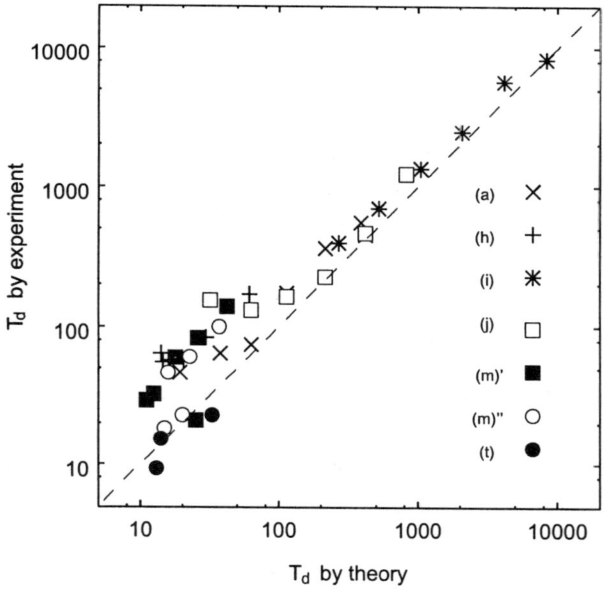

Fig. 1. Experimental values vs. theoretical values of T_d. Parameter conditions are (a): $I = E \times o_B = 2 \times 12 = 24$, $s_B = 1.0$, $p_m = 0.021$, $p_c = 0.18$; (h): $I = E \times o_B = 4 \times 8 = 32$, $s_B = 1.0$, $p_m = 0.037$, $p_c = 0.071$; (i): $I = E \times o_B = 4 \times 16 = 64$, $s_B = 1.5$, $p_m = 0.017$, $p_c = 0.71$; (j): $I = E \times o_B = 4 \times 12 = 48$, $s_B = 1.0$, $p_m = 0.021$, $p_c = 0.36$; (m)': $I = E \times o_B = 8 \times 8 = 64$, $s_B = 1.3$, $p_m = 0.041$, $p_c = 0.51$; (m)": $I = E \times o_B = 8 \times 8 = 64$, $s_B = 1.5$, $p_m = 0.043$, $p_c = 0.73$; (t): the same as in Table 1. Experimental values are averages over fifty trial runs for (t) and twenty trial runs for the others. N was taken to be 128, 256, 512, 1024, 2048, or 4096 for (a) to (m)". The values of I, E, and o_B for (a), (m)', and (m)" are the same as those for (a) and (m) in Table 1.

under the RR-GAs evolves in a discontinuous way. A long stasis of neutral evolution (whose length is T_i) is intermittently punctuated by the short adaptive evolutionary phases (whose length is T_t), and the evolutionary rate is principally determined by T_i (Table 2(i)). Because the evolutionary speed is generally low under such circumstances, our analytic method can correctly estimate the performance of GA for larger T_d (Fig. 1).

5.2. *Crossover's Roles in GAs*

Crossover in GAs has two different functions: the creation of a new elementary schema in an individual and the combination of spreading schemata into one individual to make a longer, more advantageous schema. The present analyses precisely incorporated the former effect by crossover (see the p_c's term in Eq. (2)), but the latter effect was only crudely considered assuming that hitchhiking is eliminated by crossover. However, we consider that the former effect is as important as, or sometimes more important than the latter effect. This was also pointed out in a study by Nimwegen *et al.* [10] who analyzed the epochal dynamics of RR-GAs. From the observation of the crossover's acceleration in experiments, they conjectured "The effect of crossover on the GA's dynamics is that it increases the mixing rate – the rate at which new blocks can be aligned. Since crossover works as a mutational operator specifically on the unaligned blocks – and aligned blocks are not disrupted by crossover – it speeds up the search for new aligned blocks." Though the crossover's creation effect is of no use when the mutation rate is sufficiently high, when a population has already found and stored a number of blocks, the mutation rate must be adjusted to a very low value to maintain the blocks. The crossover's function as a mutational operator is useful for such a population [13]. It facilitates the creation of new blocks and accelerates evolution when the order of a block is fairly large, or in other words, evolution is truly 'difficult'. The conventional building block hypothesis asserting that a larger schema is created by the combination of the smaller component schemata by crossover reflects just one side of the crossover's functions. We have to consider both of the crossover's functions in detail to correctly assess the effectiveness of crossover.

6. Conclusion

We considered royal-road functions with a mutiplicative fitness scheme (mRR-functions) and established a theoretical method to estimate the evolutionary speed in mRR-GAs. The method elaborately formulates a crossover's function to create a new elementary schema by within-schema recombination and also roughly incorporates a crossover's function to combine spreading schemata into a single individual assuming that the crossover rate is high enough to eliminate hitchhiking. The estimation results were compared with the experimental ones for a number of sets of genetic parameters, and it was shown that the theoretical analysis can correctly evaluate the evolutionary rate in RR-GAs especially when the order of the elementary blocks is fairly large and evolution proceeds in a discontinuous way.

Acknowledgement

A part of this study was begun during the first author's stay at the lab. of Prof. Whitley, Colorado State University, in the summer of 2000. Dr. K. Shimohara of ATR labs actively encouraged the study. The first author's work for this research was supported in part by the Telecommunications Advancement Organization of Japan and by Doshisha University's Research Promotion Funds.

Appendix A. Derivation of Eq. (2)

The evolutionary dynamics of an infinite population under a simple GA with one-point crossover are represented by a set of macro-schema recursion formulas for selection, mutation, and crossover as

$$x_{\boldsymbol{i}} \xrightarrow{\text{sel.}} \frac{f(G_{\boldsymbol{i}})}{\overline{f}} x_{\boldsymbol{i}}, \tag{A.1}$$

$$x_{\boldsymbol{i}} \xrightarrow{\text{mut.}} \sum_{\boldsymbol{j}} x_{\boldsymbol{j}} M_{\boldsymbol{j}\boldsymbol{i}}, \tag{A.2}$$

$$\begin{aligned} x_{\boldsymbol{i}} \xrightarrow{\text{cross.}} & (1-p_c)x_{\boldsymbol{i}} + p_c \sum_{r=1}^{I-1} \frac{1}{I-1} \\ & \times \sum_{j_{e_2}} \cdots \sum_{j_E} x(i_1, \cdots, i_{e_2-1}, j_{e_2}, \cdots, j_E) \\ & \times \sum_{k_1} \cdots \sum_{k_{e_1}} x(k_1, \cdots, k_{e_1}, i_{e_1+1}, \cdots, i_E) \\ & \times \left[C'(r', j_{e_1}, k_{e_1}, i_{e_1})\right]^{\delta_{e_1 e_2}}, \end{aligned} \tag{A.3}$$

where $f(G_{\boldsymbol{i}})$ is the average fitness of strings belonging to macro-schema $G_{\boldsymbol{i}}$; $\overline{f}$ is the average population fitness; $\sum_{\boldsymbol{j}}$ in Eq. (A.2) is a reduced expression for $\sum_{j_1=0}^{o_B} \cdots \sum_{j_E=0}^{o_B}$; p_c is the probability of a one-point crossover occurring per string pair; e_1/e_2 is the subfield number to which the rth/r+1th defining locus belongs (the defining loci are numbered $1, 2, \cdots, I$); the rth defining locus is the r'th defining locus in the subfield; and $\delta_{e_1 e_2}$ is the Kronecker's delta. $M_{\boldsymbol{j}\boldsymbol{i}}$ is an element of the mutation matrix defined as the probability of a $G_{\boldsymbol{j}}$ string being transformed to a $G_{\boldsymbol{i}}$ string by mutation and is written as

$$\begin{aligned} M_{\boldsymbol{ji}} &= \prod_{e=1}^{E} M_{j_e i_e} \\ &= \prod_{e=1}^{E} \sum_{k_e=\max(0,i_e+j_e-o_{\mathrm{B}})}^{\min(i_e,j_e)} \binom{j_e}{k_e}\binom{o_{\mathrm{B}}-j_e}{i_e-k_e} \\ &\quad \times (1-p_{\mathrm{m}})^{o_{\mathrm{B}}-i_e-j_e+2k_e} \cdot p_{\mathrm{m}}^{i_e+j_e-2k_e}. \end{aligned} \tag{A.4}$$

$C'(r', j_{e_1}, k_{e_1}, i_{e_1})$ is an element of the reduced crossover tensor and is written for a diversified population as

$$C'(r', j_{e_1}, k_{e_1}, i_{e_1}) = \frac{\sum_s \binom{r'}{s}\binom{o_{\mathrm{B}}-r'}{j_{e_1}-s}\binom{r'}{k_{e_1}-i_{e_1}+s}\binom{o_{\mathrm{B}}-r'}{i_{e_1}-s}}{\binom{o_{\mathrm{B}}}{j_{e_1}}\binom{o_{\mathrm{B}}}{k_{e_1}}}, \tag{A.5}$$

where r' is the ordinal number of the rth defining locus in a subfield and the summation for s in Eq. (A.5) is taken from $\max\{i_{e_1}+r'-o_{\mathrm{B}}, j_{e_1}+r'-o_{\mathrm{B}}, i_{e_1}-k_{e_1}, 0\}$ to $\min\{i_{e_1}, j_{e_1}, i_{e_1}-k_{e_1}+r', r'\}$. See [17] for the derivation of Eqs. (A.4) and (A.5).

The creation probability is represented by an increase in the block frequency $m_{\mathrm{B}} = m(B)$ from zero by the transitions by mutation and crossover, which means that Eq. (2) is derived by substituting the right-hand sides of Eqs. (A.2) and (A.3) with a random distribution with no block and adding them up. In the following, we conduct these substitutions in turn using the formula for $x_{\boldsymbol{i}}^{(0)}$, a frequency vector for the population such that the l blocks are completely fixed and the remaining $E-l$ blocks are absent. If we define X and A as the subset of the fixed and absent blocks (or their subfields) respectively, $x_{\boldsymbol{i}}^{(0)}$ is written as

$$x_{\boldsymbol{i}}^{(0)} = K \cdot \prod_{e\in X} \delta_{i_e 0} \cdot \prod_{e\in A} \binom{o_{\mathrm{B}}}{i_e}(1-\delta_{i_e 0})$$

or using a reduced expression $\delta_\alpha \equiv \delta_{\alpha 0}$ and omitting e,

$$x_{\boldsymbol{i}}^{(0)} = K \cdot \prod_{X} \delta_i \cdot \prod_{A} \binom{o_{\mathrm{B}}}{i}(1-\delta_i), \tag{A.6}$$

where

$$K = \left\{\prod_{A}(2^{o_{\mathrm{B}}}-1)\right\}^{-1} = (2^{o_{\mathrm{B}}}-1)^{l-E}. \tag{A.7}$$

is a normalization factor determined so that $\sum_{\boldsymbol{i}} x_{\boldsymbol{i}}^{(0)} = 1$ might be satisfied.

To formulate the creation probability of the next block, we assume that the creation of the RR-blocks is ordered and describe the block to be created next (or its subfield) by n. The n's creation probability by mutation is given by the increase in the n's frequency from $x_{\boldsymbol{i}}^{(0)}$ by Eq. (A.2),

$$\Delta m_{\mathrm{B}}^{(\mathrm{mut.})} = \sum_{\boldsymbol{i}}{}' \sum_{\boldsymbol{j}} x_{\boldsymbol{j}}^{(0)} M_{\boldsymbol{ji}}, \tag{A.8}$$

where $\sum_{\boldsymbol{i}}'$ is the summation for $\boldsymbol{i}$ such that macro-schemata $x_{\boldsymbol{i}}$ include blocks in $X+n$ and do not include blocks in $A-n$ and is written as

$$\sum_{\boldsymbol{i}}{}' = \sum_{\boldsymbol{i}} \prod_{X+n} \delta_i \cdot \prod_{A-n} (1-\delta_i). \tag{A.9}$$

Substituting Eqs. (A.9), (A.6), and (A.4) for Eq. (A.8),

$$\begin{aligned}
\Delta m_{\mathrm{B}}^{(\mathrm{mut.})} &= \sum_{\boldsymbol{i}} \prod_{X+n} \delta_i \cdot \prod_{A-n} (1-\delta_i) \sum_{\boldsymbol{j}} K \cdot \prod_{X} \delta_j \cdot \prod_{A} \binom{o_{\mathrm{B}}}{j} (1-\delta_j) \prod_{X+A} M_{ji} \\
&= \prod_{X+n} \sum_{i} \delta_i \cdot \prod_{A-n} \sum_{i} (1-\delta_i) \cdot K \cdot \prod_{X} \sum_{j} \delta_j \cdot \prod_{A} \sum_{j} \binom{o_{\mathrm{B}}}{j} (1-\delta_j) \\
&\quad \cdot \prod_{X} M_{ji} \cdot M_{j_n i_n} \cdot \prod_{A-n} M_{ji} \\
&= \prod_{A-n} \sum_{i} (1-\delta_i) \cdot K \cdot \prod_{A} \sum_{j} \binom{o_{\mathrm{B}}}{j} (1-\delta_j) \\
&\quad \cdot \prod_{X} M_{00} \cdot M_{j_n 0} \cdot \prod_{A-n} M_{ji} \\
&= K \cdot (M_{00})^{l} \cdot \sum_{j_n} \binom{o_{\mathrm{B}}}{j_n} (1-\delta_{j_n}) M_{j_n 0} \\
&\quad \cdot \prod_{A-n} \sum_{i} (1-\delta_i) \sum_{j} \binom{o_{\mathrm{B}}}{j} (1-\delta_j) M_{ji}.
\end{aligned} \tag{A.10}$$

Because from Eq. (A.4)

$$M_{00} = (1-p_{\mathrm{m}})^{o_{\mathrm{B}}}, \tag{A.11}$$

$$\sum_{j_n} \binom{o_{\mathrm{B}}}{j_n} (1-\delta_{j_n}) M_{j_n 0} = 1 - (1-p_{\mathrm{m}})^{o_{\mathrm{B}}}, \tag{A.12}$$

$$\sum_{i} (1-\delta_i) \sum_{j} \binom{o_{\mathrm{B}}}{j} (1-\delta_j) M_{ji} = 2^{o_{\mathrm{B}}} - 2 + (1-p_{\mathrm{m}})^{o_{\mathrm{B}}}, \tag{A.13}$$

Eq.(A.10) is transformed as

$$\begin{aligned} \Delta m_{\mathrm{B}}^{(\mathrm{mut.})} &= (1-p_{\mathrm{m}})^{l \cdot o_{\mathrm{B}}} \cdot \{1-(1-p_{\mathrm{m}})^{o_{\mathrm{B}}}\} \cdot \frac{\{2^{o_{\mathrm{B}}}-2+(1-p_{\mathrm{m}})^{o_{\mathrm{B}}}\}^{E-l-1}}{(2^{o_{\mathrm{B}}}-1)^{E-l}} \\ &\simeq \frac{p_{\mathrm{m}} \cdot o_{\mathrm{B}}}{2^{o_{\mathrm{B}}}}. \end{aligned} \tag{A.14}$$

Quite similarly, the block n's creation probability by crossover is given by the partial sum ($\sum'_{\boldsymbol{i}}$) of the right-hand side of Eq.(A.3) substituted with $x_{\boldsymbol{i}}^{(0)}$ as

$$\begin{aligned} \Delta m_{\mathrm{B}}^{(\mathrm{cross.})} = (1-p_{\mathrm{c}}) {\sum_{\boldsymbol{i}}}' x_{\boldsymbol{i}}^{(0)} + p_{\mathrm{c}} \sum_{r=1}^{I-1} \frac{1}{I-1} \\ \cdot {\sum_{\boldsymbol{i}}}' \sum_{j_{e_2}} \cdots \sum_{j_E} x^{(0)}(i_1, \cdots, i_{e_2-1}, j_{e_2}, \cdots, j_E) \\ \cdot \sum_{k_1} \cdots \sum_{k_{e_1}} x^{(0)}(k_1, \cdots, k_{e_1}, i_{e_1+1}, \cdots, i_E) \\ \cdot [C'(r', j_{e_1}, k_{e_1}, i_{e_1})]^{\delta_{e_1 e_2}}, \end{aligned} \tag{A.15}$$

Because $\delta_{i_n}(1-\delta_{i_n}) = 0$, both the first term and the second term for $e_1 \neq e_2$ in Eq. (A.15) are always zero. If we define L and R as the subset of blocks (subfields) on the left and the right side of the $e_1 = e_2$th block (subfield) respectively, the principal part of the second term is transformed as

$$
\begin{aligned}
&\sum_{i}^{\prime}\sum_{j_{e_1}}\cdots\sum_{j_E} x^{(0)}(i_1,\cdots,i_{e_1-1},j_{e_1},\cdots,j_E)\\
&\cdot\sum_{k_1}\cdots\sum_{k_{e_1}} x^{(0)}(k_1,\cdots,k_{e_1},i_{e_1+1},\cdots,i_E)\cdot C'(r',j_{e_1},k_{e_1},i_{e_1})\\
&=\sum_{i}\prod_{X}\delta_i\cdot\delta_{i_n}\cdot\prod_{A-n}(1-\delta_i)\\
&\quad\times\sum_{j_{e_1}}\sum_{j_{X\wedge R}}\sum_{j_{A\wedge R}} K\cdot\prod_{X\wedge L}\delta_i\cdot\prod_{X\wedge e_1}\delta_j\cdot\prod_{X\wedge R}\delta_j\\
&\qquad\cdot\prod_{A\wedge L}\binom{o_B}{i}(1-\delta_i)\cdot\prod_{A\wedge e_1}\binom{o_B}{j}(1-\delta_j)\cdot\prod_{A\wedge R}\binom{o_B}{j}(1-\delta_j)\\
&\quad\times\sum_{k_{X\wedge L}}\sum_{k_{A\wedge L}}\sum_{k_{e_1}} K\cdot\prod_{X\wedge L}\delta_k\cdot\prod_{X\wedge e_1}\delta_k\cdot\prod_{X\wedge R}\delta_i\\
&\qquad\cdot\prod_{A\wedge L}\binom{o_B}{k}(1-\delta_k)\cdot\prod_{A\wedge e_1}\binom{o_B}{k}(1-\delta_k)\cdot\prod_{A\wedge R}\binom{o_B}{i}(1-\delta_i)\\
&\quad\times C'(r',j_{e_1},k_{e_1},i_{e_1})\\
&=\sum_{i}\prod_{X}\delta_i\cdot\delta_{i_n}\cdot\prod_{A-n}(1-\delta_i)\cdot\prod_{A\wedge L}\binom{o_B}{i}(1-\delta_i)\cdot\prod_{A\wedge R}\binom{o_B}{i}(1-\delta_i)\\
&\quad\times K\cdot\prod_{X\wedge e_1}\sum_{j}\delta_j\cdot\prod_{A\wedge e_1}\sum_{j}\binom{o_B}{j}(1-\delta_j)\cdot\prod_{A\wedge R}\sum_{j}\binom{o_B}{j}(1-\delta_j)\\
&\quad\times K\cdot\prod_{X\wedge e_1}\sum_{k}\delta_k\cdot\prod_{A\wedge L}\sum_{k}\binom{o_B}{k}(1-\delta_k)\cdot\prod_{A\wedge e_1}\sum_{k}\binom{o_B}{k}(1-\delta_k)\\
&\quad\times C'(r',j_{e_1},k_{e_1},i_{e_1}).
\end{aligned}
\tag{A.16}
$$

If $n\in A\wedge L$ or $n\in A\wedge R$, Eq. (A.16) is zero on account of $\delta_{i_n}\cdot\prod_{A\wedge L}\binom{o_B}{i}(1-\delta_i)\cdot\prod_{A\wedge R}\binom{o_B}{i}(1-\delta_i)$. Accordingly, we consider $e_1=n\in A$ and $X\wedge e_1=\phi$, with which Eq. (A.16) becomes

$$\begin{aligned}
&\sum_{i_n} \delta_{i_n} \cdot \prod_{A-n} \sum_{i} \binom{o_\mathrm{B}}{i} (1-\delta_i) \\
&\times K \cdot \sum_{j_n} \binom{o_\mathrm{B}}{j_n} (1-\delta_{j_n}) \cdot \prod_{A \wedge R} \sum_{j} \binom{o_\mathrm{B}}{j} (1-\delta_j) \\
&\times K \cdot \prod_{A \wedge L} \sum_{k} \binom{o_\mathrm{B}}{k} (1-\delta_k) \cdot \sum_{k_n} \binom{o_\mathrm{B}}{k_n} (1-\delta_{k_n}) \times C'(r', j_n, k_n, i_n) \\
&= K^2 \cdot \left\{ \prod_{A-n} \sum_{i} \binom{o_\mathrm{B}}{i} (1-\delta_i) \right\}^2 \\
&\quad \times \sum_{j_n} \binom{o_\mathrm{B}}{j_n} (1-\delta_{j_n}) \cdot \sum_{k_n} \binom{o_\mathrm{B}}{k_n} (1-\delta_{k_n}) \cdot C'(r', j_n, k_n, 0) \\
&= (2^{o_\mathrm{B}} - 1)^{2l-2E} \cdot (2^{o_\mathrm{B}} - 1)^{2E-2l-2} \\
&\quad \times \sum_{j_n} \sum_{k_n} (1-\delta_{j_n})(1-\delta_{k_n}) \cdot \binom{o_\mathrm{B} - r'}{j_n} \binom{r'}{k_n} \\
&= (2^{o_\mathrm{B}} - 1)^{-2} \cdot (2^{o_\mathrm{B}} - 2^{o_\mathrm{B} - r'} - 2^{r'} + 1). \qquad \text{(A.17)}
\end{aligned}$$

Then, $\Delta m_\mathrm{B}^{(\mathrm{cross.})}$ is given by applying $p_\mathrm{c} \sum_r \frac{1}{I-1}$ to Eq. (A.17);

$$\begin{aligned}
\Delta m_\mathrm{B}^{(\mathrm{cross.})} &= \frac{p_\mathrm{c}}{I-1} (2^{o_\mathrm{B}} - 1)^{-2} \cdot \sum_{r'=1}^{o_\mathrm{B}-1} (2^{o_\mathrm{B}} - 2^{o_\mathrm{B} - r'} - 2^{r'} + 1) \\
&= \frac{p_\mathrm{c}}{I-1} \frac{(o_\mathrm{B} - 3) 2^{o_\mathrm{B}} + o_\mathrm{B} + 3}{(2^{o_\mathrm{B}} - 1)^2} \\
&\simeq \frac{p_\mathrm{c}}{I-1} \cdot \frac{(o_\mathrm{B} - 3)}{2^{o_\mathrm{B}}}. \qquad \text{(A.18)}
\end{aligned}$$

The final formula for Δm_B is given by the sum of Eqs. (A.14) and (A.18).

References

1. W.J. Ewens: *Mathematical Population Genetics*. Springer-Verlag, New York (1979)
2. J. Felsenstein The evolutionary advantage of recombination. *Genetics* **78** 737-756 (1974)
3. R.A. Fisher: *The Genetical Theory of Natural Selection*. Dover Publications, New York (1930, 2nd Ed. 1958)
4. D.E. Goldberg, K. Deb: A comparative analysis of selection schemes used in genetic algorithms. In: Rawlins, G.J.E. (ed.): *Foundations of Genetic Algorithms (FOGA-1)*, Morgan Kaufmann Publishers, San Mateo, CA 69–93 (1991)

5. T. Jones: A Description of Holland's Royal Road Function. *Evolutionary Computation* **2**(4) 409-415 (1995)
6. M. Kimura: *The Neutral Theory of Molecular Evolution.* Cambridge Univ. Press, Cambridge (1983)
7. M. Mitchell, S. Forrest, J.H. Holland: The royal road for genetic algorithms: Fitness landscapes and GA performance. In: Varela, F.J., Bourgine, P. (eds.): *Toward a Practice of Autonomous Systems: Proceedings of the First European Conference on Artificial Life.* MIT Press, Cambridge, MA 245-254 (1992)
8. M. Mitchell, J.H. Holland, S. Forrest: When will a genetic algorithm outperform hill climbing? In: Cowan, J.D., Tesauro, G., Alspector, J. (eds.): *Advances in Neural Information Processing Systems (NIPS) 6.* Morgan Kaufmann 51-58 (1994)
9. M. Mitchell: *An Introduction to Genetic Algorithms.* MIT Press, Boston (1996)
10. E.v. Nimwegen, J.P. Crutchfield, M. Mitchell: Statistical Dynamics of the Royal Road Genetic Algorithm. *Theoretical Computer Science* **229** (1999) 41-102, or Santa Fe Institute Working Paper 97-04-035 (1997)
11. E.v. Nimwegen, J.P. Crutchfield: Optimizing Epochal Evolutionary Search: Population-Size Independent Theory. *Computer Methods in Applied Mechanics and Engineering*, Special Issue on Evolutionary and Genetic Algorithms in Computational Mechanics and Engineering. Goldberg, D. (ed.) **186**(2-4) (9 June 2000) Or Santa Fe Institute Working Paper 98-06-046 (1998)
12. E.v. Nimwegen, J.P. Crutchfield: Optimizing Epochal Evolutionary Search: Population-Size Dependent Theory. *Machine Learning Journal* **45** 77-114 (1999) Or Santa Fe Institute Working Paper 98-10-090 (1998)
13. H. Suzuki: The optimum recombination rate that realizes the fastest evolution of a novel functional combination of many genes. *Theoretical Population Biology* **51** 185–200 (1997)
14. H. Suzuki, Y. Iwasa: GA Performance in a Babel-like Fitness Landscape. In: *Proceedings of the Ninth IEEE International Conference on Tools with Artificial Intelligence*, IEEE Computer Society Press, Los Alamitos 357–366 (1997)
15. H. Suzuki, Y. Iwasa: Crossover Accelerates Evolution in GAs with a Babel-like Fitness Landscape: Mathematical Analyses. *Evolutionary Computation* **7**(3) 275-310; Errata: **8**(1) 121-122 (1999-2000)
16. H. Suzuki, H. Sawai: Schema Evolution Equation Using Quasi-schema Representation. In: Spector, L. et al. (eds.): *Proceedings of the Genetic and Evolutionary Computation Conference, GECCO-2001.* Morgan Kaufmann Publishers, San Francisco, CA 784 (2001)
17. H. Suzuki, H. Sawai: Crossover Accelerates Evolution in GAs with a Royal Road Function. *2001 Genetic and Evolutionary Computation Conference Late-breaking Papers.* 405-412 (2001)
18. D. Thierens: Scalability problems of simple genetic algorithms. *Evolutionary Computation* **7**(4) 331-352 (1999)
19. S. Wright: Evolution in Mendelian populations. *Genetics* **16** 97-159 (1931)
20. A.S. Wu, R.K. Lindsay: Empirical Studies of the Genetic Algorithm with

Noncoding Segments. *Evolutionary Computation* **3**(2) 121-147 (1995)
21. A.S. Wu, R.K. Lindsay: A Comparison of the Fixed and Floating Building Block Representation in the Genetic Algorithm. *Evolutionary Computation* **4**(2) 169-193 (1997)

CHAPTER 11

A REAL-CODED CELLULAR GENETIC ALGORITHM INSPIRED BY PREDATOR-PREY INTERACTIONS

Xiaodong Li and Stuart Sutherland

School of Computer Science and Information Technology, RMIT University
GPO Box 2476v, Melbourne, VIC 3001, Australia
E-mail: xiaodong@cs.rmit.edu.au

This chapter presents a real-coded cellular GA model using a new selection method inspired by predator-prey interactions. The model relies on the dynamics generated by spatial predator-prey interactions to maintain an appropriate selection pressure and diversity in the prey population. In this model, prey, which represent potential solutions, move around on a two-dimensional lattice and breed with other prey individuals. The selection pressure is exerted by predators, which also roam around to keep the prey in check by removing the weakest prey in their vicinity. This kind of selection pressure efficiently drives the prey population to greater fitness over successive generations. Our preliminary study has shown that the predator-prey interaction dynamics play an important role in maintaining an appropriate selection pressure in the prey population, thereby helping to generate suitably fit prey solutions. Our experimental results are comparable or better in performance than those of a standard serial and distributed real-coded GA.

1. Introduction

Genetic algorithms are efficient algorithms for searching complex fitness landscapes by employing methods inspired by biological evolution. GAs have been successfully applied to many difficult optimization problems.[1] However, one common problem experienced when using GAs is premature convergence, where as a result of rapid loss of diversity in a GA population, search is trapped to sub-optimal solutions. Many algorithms have been proposed to help maintain a more diverse population so as to prevent premature convergence. Among them, most popular are those based on the idea of spatial separation.[2,3,4] In particular cellular GAs (CGA), or fine-grained Parallel Gas, have been shown to be very effective in maintaining population diversity.[5,6,7] In a cellular GA, individuals are commonly mapped onto a 2-dimensional lattice, with each cell corresponding to an individual. Selection and interaction (e.g., crossover) are restricted within the local neighbourhood of each individual. This "isolation-by-distance" feature allows a slow diffusion of good genes across the lattice, thereby maintaining a more diverse population than a serial GA with no such spatial structure. Most current work on CGAs use a static spatial structure that remains unchanged throughout a GA run. This contrasts with the fact that in nature we often observe dynamically changing spatial relationships among individuals.

Representation is another critical issue because GAs directly work on the coded representation of a problem. However, GA representations of solutions have been dominated by the use of fixed length and binary coded strings, largely due to the fact that in the early stage of GA research there was a specific emphasis on the use of binary representation.[8,9] The binary representation is often considered to be inappropriate in dealing with continuous search domains with large dimensions or when a higher numerical precision is required.[9] On the other hand, directly using a real-coded representation seems to be naturally suitable when dealing with problems using variables in a continuous domain. In this case, an individual is a vector of floating point numbers. This type of real-coded GAs has proven to be very successful.[10,11,12]

In this research we aim to tackle the above issues of diversity and representation by extending a cellular GA in two ways. Firstly a selection method making use of the dynamics generated by predator-prey interactions is introduced to the GA population. We use prey individuals to represent solutions to the problem being optimized. These prey are allowed to wander around on a two-dimensional lattice and breed with their immediate neighbouring prey. There are also predators roaming around on the lattice that kill off the weakest prey, thereby encouraging fitter prey solutions to survive and breed. In contrast with the static spatial structure of a cellular GA, in this instance prey and predators are mobile, mimicking the dynamically changing spatial relationships of predator-prey interactions observed in nature. The essential aspect to the predator-prey interactions is that the predators keep the number of prey in check (i.e., to avoid prey population explosions) whilst not completely eliminating the prey population. One important feature that sets this model apart from other CGAs is that selection pressure is maintained only through the predators killing off prey, rather than relying on a direct replacement of the least fit individuals in the neighbourhood by the fitter offspring, which is what often occurs in a conventional CGA. Our work also differs from previous work on competitive co-evolution such as those by Angeline and Pollack[15], and Rosin and Belew[16], where the model does not take into account the spatial properties of a GA population.

The second part of this work is to use real-coded GAs with suitable crossover and mutation operators. In conjunction with the use of dynamics of predator-prey interaction, we hope this extended model can outperform existing models.

The chapter is organised as follows. Section 2 describes the proposed predator-prey CGA model, including the basic algorithm, a mechanism for balancing the predator and prey populations, and the selection and migration schemes. This is followed by section 3 describing the real-coded crossover and mutation operators. Section 4 describes the test functions used, the basic configuration for experiments and performance measurement criteria. Section 5 provides the experimental results as well as analysis. Finally, section 6 concludes with a summary of our findings and future research directions.

2. The Predator-Prey CGA Model

The model consists of a two-dimensional lattice where the predator and prey populations reside. The lattice has its boundaries wrapped around to the opposite edge, therefore eliminating any boundary conditions. Each individual, whether predator or prey, is only allowed to occupy one cell at one time. At the beginning of a GA run, prey are randomly generated and distributed across the lattice. The predators, which keep the prey in check (i.e., their task is to kill the least fit prey), are also distributed randomly across the lattice. As illustrated in Fig. 1, we normally start with a large number of prey and relatively small number of predators.

Fig. 1. Predators and prey are randomly distributed across the 2d lattice at the beginning of a run.

After the above initialisation, the predator-prey CGA model proceeds in the following steps:

1) Each prey is given the chance to move into one of the neighbouring cells according to a pre-specified parameter *randomMoveProbability* (which is normally set to 0.5, so that half the prey would attempt to move one step on the lattice whereas the other half would remain where they were). If the prey were allowed to move, they could chose a random direction, i.e., one of the eight cells in a 8-cell Moore neighbourhood

(north, south, east, west, and plus four diagonal neighbours), to move into. They then attempt to move. If the cells they are attempting to move into are occupied by other prey or predators, then they try again. This occurs 10 times. If the prey is still unable to find a place to move, it remains where it is.

2) After the prey have moved they are then allowed to breed. Each prey selects from its neighbours the fittest prey (excluding itself). If the prey has no neighbours it is not allowed to breed. Otherwise the prey and its fittest neighbour create an offspring using crossover and mutation operators (see section 3 for details). The creation of a new child is essentially one function evaluation. There are two methods for placing the child prey on the lattice. The first method randomly places the child on the lattice a maximum of two cells away from the parent prey. 10 attempts are tried to place the child, but if no free spot was found, the child is not generated. The second method simply places the child randomly anywhere on the lattice. Again 10 attempts are made to place it on the lattice. If all the attempted cells are occupied, the child is not generated.
3) The predators are then allowed their turn. The predators first look around their neighbourhood to see if there are any prey. If so, the predator selects the least-fit prey and kills it. The predator then moves onto the cell held by that prey. If a predator has no neighbouring prey, it moves in exactly the same way as prey (see above step 1). However it is possible to allow the predators to move more than once per prey time step (see section 2.1).
4) Go back to step 1), if the number of required evaluations is not reached.

2.1. *Balancing the Predator and Prey Populations*

One of the problems often encountered in predator-prey models is the difficulty of keeping a proper balance between the predator and prey populations. In order to prevent predators from completely wiping out the entire prey population, the following formula is adopted, where *iterations* is the number of moves the predators may take before the prey can make their moves:

$$iterations = \left\lfloor \frac{numPreys_{Actual} - numPreys_{Preferred}}{num_{Predators}} \right\rfloor \quad (1)$$

A predator can kill at most one prey per iteration, so Equation (1) is basically used to keep the actual number of prey ($numPrey_{Actual}$) to a number similar to the preferred number of prey ($numPrey_{Preferred}$). The predators are encouraged to minimise the difference between these two values. The floor operator ensures that the predators do not wipe out the prey population entirely. For example, if there are 450 prey, the preferred number of prey is 120, and the number of predators is 80, then the predators would iterate 4 times before the prey have a chance to move and breed again. Another merit of using equation (1) is that as the minimum number of prey (the floor value) is reached, more new-born prey would have a better chance to survive than otherwise. As a result, the number of prey individuals would start to increase, rather than to continue its decline. This trend would continue until it gets to a point, where the effect of applying equation (1) is once again tipped to be in favour of predators. Using equation (1) in a way provides a mechanism of varying the prey population size dynamically.

2.2. *Selection and Migration Methods*

The elitist selection method is adopted in this model. Each prey is allowed to select the fittest prey from its eight neighbours (8 Moore neighbourhood) to breed with. A prey and its fittest neighbour create a child prey using real-coded crossover and mutation operators (as described in section 3).

After a child prey is created, we use two methods for placing the child on the lattice. These two methods are analogous to the migration schemes often used in an island model.[3] In the first method, 'nearby', the child prey is placed randomly up to two cells away from the parent prey. 10 attempts are tried to place the child, but if no free spot is found, then the child is not generated. The second method, 'lattice', simply places the child randomly anywhere on the lattice. Again 10 attempts are made to place it on the lattice, but if no cells are free, then the child is not generated. The first method seems to mimic what occurs in nature, where prey tend to cluster together for protection, however the children prey tend only to find spaces at the edges of these clusters (see Fig. 2 a).

Note that in this model we do not use any replacement scheme as in a typical CGA model, where often the offspring is used to replace the parent or the least-fit individual in its neighbourhood. The killing and removal of the least fit prey are only carried out by the roaming predators. Through this kind of predator-prey interaction, we hope an appropriate selection pressure may be maintained over the prey population.

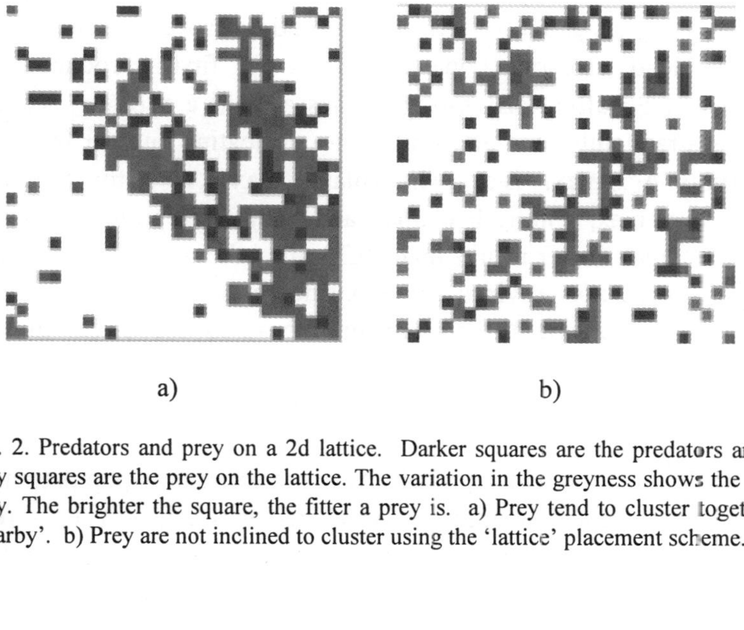

Fig. 2. Predators and prey on a 2d lattice. Darker squares are the predators and lighter grey squares are the prey on the lattice. The variation in the greyness shows the fitness of prey. The brighter the square, the fitter a prey is. a) Prey tend to cluster together using 'nearby'. b) Prey are not inclined to cluster using the 'lattice' placement scheme.

3. Crossover and Mutation Operators

We adopt a real-coded GA for the predator-prey model and test it over a number of benchmark test functions defined over a continuous domain. In our real-coded predator-prey CGA model, each prey individual represents a chromosome that is a vector of genes, where each gene is a floating point number.[10] For example, a parameter vector corresponding to a GA individual can be represented as $x = (x_1, x_2, \ldots, x_n)$, where $x_i \in [a_i, b_i] \subset \Re$, $i = 1 \ldots n$. The GA works in exactly the same way as the binary GA counterpart except that the crossover and mutation operations are slightly different.

The real-coded crossover is a mixed crossover involving two operations. The first operation is a real crossover operator, which behaves similar to standard crossover. The difference is that instead of swapping binary values, the values in the slots of a floating-point array, i.e., a chromosome consisting of genes each representing a real-number variable, are swapped. For example, if we have two parents, $\mathbf{x} = (x_1, x_2, \ldots, x_n)$ and $\mathbf{y} = (y_1, y_2, \ldots, y_n)$, and the crossover point is between x_i and x_{i+1}, then one child corresponds to $\mathbf{c1} = (x_1, x_2, \ldots, x_i, y_{i+1}, \ldots y_n)$ and the other $\mathbf{c2} = (y_1, y_2, \ldots, y_i, x_{i+1}, \ldots x_n)$. The second crossover operator is the so called blend crossover operator (BLX-α), first introduced by Eshelman and Schaffer.[13] BLX-α generates a child $\mathbf{c} = (c_1, c_2, \ldots, c_n)$ where c_i is a randomly (and uniformly) chosen floating number from the interval $[\min_i - \Delta\cdot\alpha, \max_i + \Delta\cdot\alpha,]$, where $\max_i = \max\{x_i, y_i\}$, $\min_i = \min\{x_i, y_i\}$, and $\Delta = \max_i - \min_i$. Eshelman and Schaffer reported BLX-0.5 (with α=0.5) gives better results than BLX with other α values. It seems that with α=0.5, BLX provides a nice balance between exploration and exploitation (convergence), therefore we choose to use α=0.5 in this model. We apply 50% real crossover, i.e., to select a gene value from one parent or the other, and 50% BLX-0.5 to obtain the remaining gene values for an offspring.

We apply mutation with a probability to the entire prey population. It is a very simple mutation operator, which replaces a gene (i.e., a real parameter value) in a chromosome with another floating-point number randomly chosen within the bounds of the parameter values.

4. Experimental Design

To evaluate the performance of the predator-prey model, four benchmark test functions are used, all of which have a global minimum of 0.[14] The dimension n of these functions has been chosen to be 25 The four functions are given as follows:

Sphere:

$$f(\vec{x}) = \sum_{i=1}^{n} x_i \text{, where } -5.12 \le x_i \le 5.12;$$

Griewangk:

$$f(\vec{x}) = 1 + \sum_{i=1}^{n} \frac{x_i^2}{4000} - \prod_{i=1}^{n} \cos\left(\frac{x_i}{\sqrt{i}}\right) \text{, where } -600 \le x_i \le 600;$$

Generalized Rastrigin:

$$f(\vec{x}) = 10n + \sum_{i=1}^{n} x_i^2 - 10 \cdot \cos(2\pi x_i) \text{, where } -5.12 \le x_i \le 5.12;$$

Generalized Rosenbrock:

$$f(\vec{x}) = \sum_{i=1}^{n-1} (100 \cdot (x_{i+1} - x_i^2)^2 + (x_i - 1)^2) \text{, where } -2.048 \le x_i \le 2.048.$$

For each test function, we run the model 30 times (each time with a different random number seed), each run with 100,000 evaluations. We measure the mean value of the best-fit individual (on logarithmic scale) over the 30 runs (see Figs. 3 - 6). We also measure the performance of the model based on the following criteria: ***A*** - the average of the best fitness found at the end of each run; ***SD*** - standard deviation at the end of each run; ***B*** - best of the fitness values found over the 30 runs. Two configurations have been tried, 'nearby', one with new born prey randomly distributed only within a distance of 2 cells from the parent, and 'lattice', which allows such random distribution over the entire lattice. Table 1 gives the model parameter configuration used for our experiments.

Table 1. Predator-prey model configuration.

Predator-prey CGA model parameters	
Representation	Floating point numbers
Two dimensional lattice size	30 by 30
Crossover operators	50% real-coded crossover and 50% BLX-α (α=0.5) crossover
Mutation probability	0.01
Selection method	Elitist from a local neighbourhood
RandomMoveProbability	0.5
Neighbourhood	8 Moore neighbourhood

We also measure the predator-prey model's ability of maintaining population diversity and the dynamic changes of the prey population size over generations. The results and analysis are given in the following section.

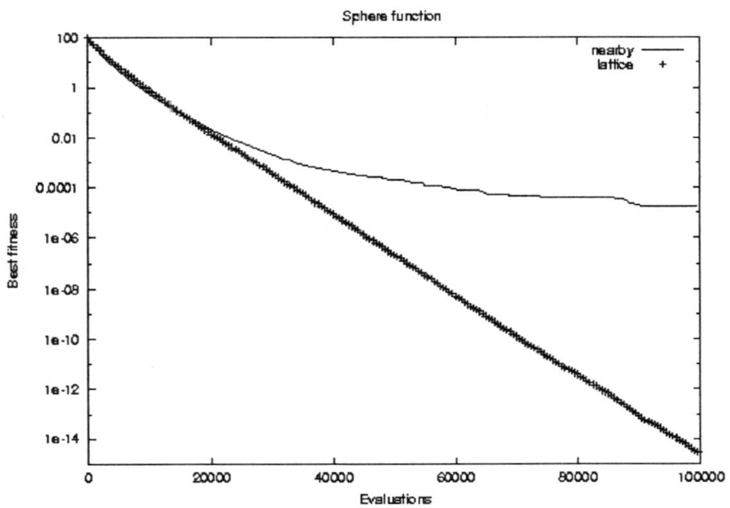

Fig. 3. Mean best fitness over 100,000 evaluations for the Sphere function.

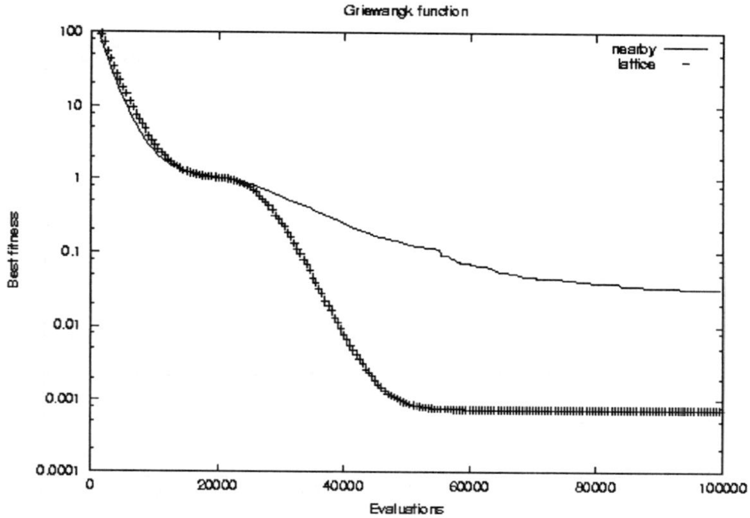

Fig. 4. Mean best fitness over 100,000 evaluations for the Griewangk function.

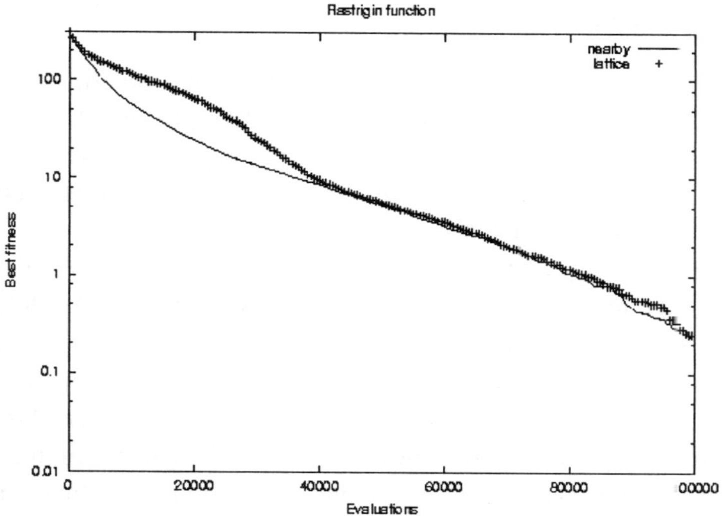

Fig. 5. Mean best fitness over 100,000 evaluations for the Rastrigin function.

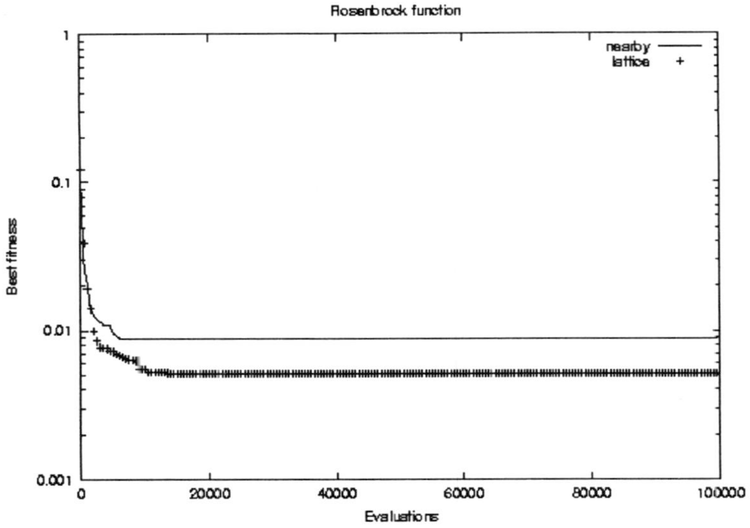

Fig. 6. Mean best fitness over 100,000 evaluations for the Rosenbrock function.

5. Results and Analysis

Figs. 3 - 6 show the mean best fitness for the four test functions over 30 runs, each run with 100,000 evaluations. We study the effect of the two different methods of placing the new born preys – 'nearby', which randomly places the new born within 2 cells from the parent; 'lattice', which places the prey randomly over the entire lattice.

The predator-prey model using the 2nd method of placement gives better results in three of all the four test functions used. Only for Rastrigin function, the model gives almost the identical result as that of the 1st method. The results on Sphere and Griewangk functions are particularly good. The model is not only able to converge very fast, but also continue to get even lower towards 0.0 (i.e., the global minimum). It does not become stagnant for two out of the four test functions in 100,000 evaluations. The only results showing signs of early stagnancy are that of the Rosenbrock function, which is notoriously difficult, as it has a flat valley on its fitness landscape.

Table 2. Summary of the results on the four test functions.

Config.	*Sphere*			*Griewangk*		
	A	***SD***	***B***	***A***	***SD***	***B***
nearby	1.70E-05	3.26E-05	2.24E-07	3.19E-02	2.21E-02	1.39E-03
lattice	2.79E-15	2.50E-15	3.63E-16	7.40E-04	2.26E-03	1.56E-13
R-BLX	9E-07	6E-07	2E-07	6E-01	1E-01	4E-01
D-BLX	1E-14	7E-15	3E00	2E-02	2E-02	4E-12
	Rastrigin			*Rosenbrock*		
nearby	2.30E-01	3.53E-01	5.53E-04	8.79E-03	1.21E-02	7.85E-07
lattice	2.53E-01	5.03E-01	2.51E-09	5.09E-03	9.91E-03	2.49E-07
R-BLX	4E01	9E00	2E01	3E01	3E01	2E01
D-BLX	1E01	3E00	7E00	2E01	1E01	2E01

Table 2 summarise the results of ***A***, ***SD***, and ***B*** using 'nearby' and 'lattice'. For comparison, we also include the results of a sequential GA using BLX-0.5 crossover operator (R-BLX) and a distributed GA using BLX-0.5 (D-BLX), as provide by Herrera and Lozana [14] (Table VI on p.53). These results, especially the results of the 'lattice' configuration compare favourably to those of R-BLX and D-BLX. Note that we tried to use the same performance measurement, and the dimension for the test functions (n=25) as those of Herrera and Lozana,[14] in order to compare our results with theirs fairly. However, their results on the R-BLX and D-BLX were obtained after 500,000 evaluations.

5.1. *Maintaining Population Diversity*

Fig. 7 shows a typical single run of the predator-prey model on the Griewangk function with the 'lattice' option. Note that the x-axis shows the number of generations instead of evaluations, as at each generation, there are multiple new-born prey/evaluations. An evaluation is only carried out when a child prey is successfully produced. Although the average fitness of the prey population gets stagnant after generation 100, the best fitness continues to improve with no sign of slowing down. This is not surprising because of two reasons. Firstly the predators only kill prey within their vicinity (i.e., restricted killing), and secondly there is a constant influx of new-born prey into the prey population throughout the run. The new-born are not necessarily always the best-fit ones, therefore the average fitness value of the population remains relatively high (assuming minimization). This indicates that the overall diversity of the prey population is still rather high even when the model approaches the end of a run.

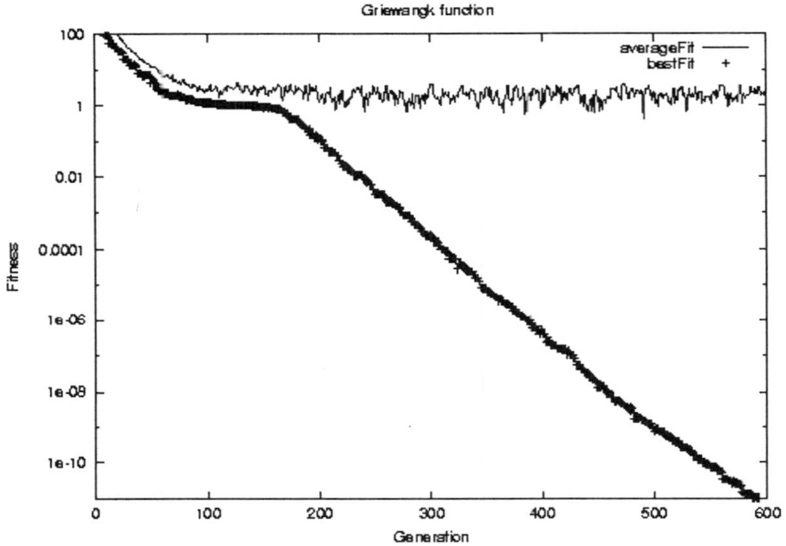

Fig. 7. Average and best fitness of the prey population over a single run.

5.2. *Prey and Predator Population Sizes*

Fig. 8 shows the fluctuation of the prey population sizes in two settings, the 'lattice' and 'nearby', and the invariant number of predators in a single run. The use of 'nearby' migration scheme shows that the clustering of prey (see Fig. 2 a), to some extent, has an effect of preventing predators from killing off more prey in the population, as compared with the 'lattice' setting (see Fig. 2 b). Equation (1) seems to provide a very effective way in maintaining a variable but balanced prey population.

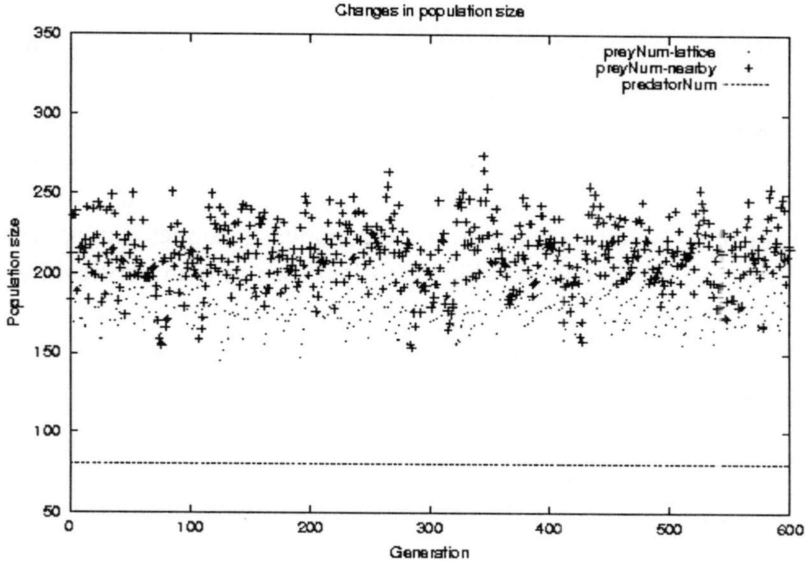

Fig. 8. Variable prey population sizes and an invariant predator population size.

6. Conclusion

In this chapter we have proposed the use of predator-prey interactions as an effective selection method in the context of a real-coded cellular GA model. Selection pressure is dynamically imposed upon the prey population through the killing carried out by the roaming predators on a two-dimensional artificial world. Our experimental results have shown that this type of selection method using the dynamics produced by predator-prey interactions is effective in maintaining an appropriate selection pressure and diversity in the prey population, thereby leading to a substantial improvement in performance. Compared with standard real-coded serial and distributed GAs, it has been shown empirically that the performance of the predator-prey CGA on all the four test functions are comparable or better than the existing models found in literature.

Future works will investigate the optimal predator-prey ratio and the effect of using different lattice sizes, or similarly the population density of the prey and predators. We could also introduce additional biologically and ecologically inspired features such as an energy level and lifespan of an individual prey and predator, or food source as an environmental variable. Extensions such as these would allow the predator-prey model to generate more complex dynamics analogous to those observed from nature, which are often seen as being critical to the survival or demise of the prey and predator populations.

References

1. D. Goldberg, *Genetic Algorithms in Search, Optimisation and Machine Learning*, Addison-Wesley, Massachusetts (1990).
2. R. Tanese Distributed Genetic Algorithms. In *Proceeding of the Third International Conference on Genetic Algorithms*, Schaffer, J.D. (Ed.), Morgan Kaufmann Publishers, San Mateo, p.434-439 (1989).
3. E. Cantu-Paz, A Survey of Parallel Genetic Algorithms. Technical Report IlliGAL 97003, University of Illinois at Urbana-Champaign (1997).
4. M. Tomassini, Parallel and distributed evolutionary algorithms: a review, in *Evolutionary Algorithms in Engineering and Computer Science*, edited by Miettinen, K. et al., New York: John Wiley & Sons ltd, p.113-133 (1999).
5. B. Manderick and P. Spiessens, Fine-grained parallel genetic algorithms. In *Proceedings of the Third International Conference on Genetic Algorithms*, Morgan Kaufmann, p. 428-433. (1989).
6. J. Sarma, and K. De Jong, An analysis of the effects of neighborhood size and shape on local selection algorithms. In *Proc 4th PPSN*, LNCS **1141**, Springer Verlag, p.236-244 (1996).
7. X. Li and M. Kirley, "The Effects of Varying Population Density in a Fine-grained Parallel Genetic Algorithm", in *Proceeding of 2002 Congress on Evolutionary Computation (CEC'02)*, vol: **2**, p.1709 -1714 (2002).
8. D.E. Goldberg, Real-Coded Genetic Algorithms, Virtual Alphabets, and Blocking. *Complex Systems* **5**, p.139 - 167 (1991).
9. F. Herrera, M. Lozano, J.L. Verdegay, Tackling Real-Coded Genetic Algorithms: Operators and tools for the Behaviour Analysis. *Artificial Intelligence Review* **12**, p.265-319, (1998).
10. A. Wright, Genetic Algorithms for Real Parameter Optimization. *Foundations of Genetic Algorithms* **1**, G.J.E. Rawlin (Ed.), (Morgan Kaufmann, San Mateo), p.205 - 218 (1991).
11. L. Davis, *Handbook of Genetic Algorithms*. Van Nostrand Reihold, New York (1991).

12. H. Muhlenbein and D. Schlierkamp-Voosen, Predictive Models for the Breeder Genetic Algorithm I: Continuous Parameter Optimization. *Evolutionary Computation* **1**, p.25-49 (1993).
13. L.J. Eshelman and J. Schaffer, Real-coded genetic algorithms and interval-schemata. *Foundation of Genetic Algorithms*, p.187-202 (1991).
14. F. Herrera and M. Lozano, Gradual Distributed Real-Coded Genetic Algorithms. *IEEE Transactions on Evolutionary Computation* **4**:1, p.43-63 (2000).
15. P. J. Angeline and J. B. Pollack, Competitive environments evolve better solutions for complex tasks. In: *Proceedings of the Fifth International Conference on Genetic Algorithms*, p.264--270. Morgan Kaufmann, San Mateo, USA (1993).
16. C. Rosin and R. Belew, New methods for competitive co-evolution. *Evolutionary Computation*, vol. **5**(1):1--29. MIT Press, Cambridge, USA (1997).

CHAPTER 12

OBSERVED DYNAMICS OF LARGE SCALE PARALLEL EVOLUTIONARY ALGORITHMS WITH IMPLICATIONS FOR PROTEIN ENGINEERING

Martin Oates[1], David Corne [2] and Douglas Kell [3]

[1] *Evosolve Ltd, Stowmarket, UK*
E-mail: moates@btinternet.com
[2] *Department of Computer Science, University of Reading, UK*
E-mail: d.w.corne@reading.ac.uk
[3] *Institute of Biological Sciences, University of Aberystwyth, UK*
E-mail: dbk@aber.ac.uk

The 'bi' and 'higher modal features' are aspects of Evolutionary Algorithm (EA) behaviors that are revealed, for a wide range of conditions, when extensive parametric studies are done to explore convergence time over a wide range of mutation rates. The bimodal feature indicates optimal mutation rates in terms of convergence time, which often correspond to optimal mutation rates in terms of final solution quality. The significance of the bimodal feature lies in parameter setting issues, and it is of interest to see how it varies with parameters and EA designs. Previous work shows that it appears in a wide range of conditions, but attenuates (the local optimum in convergence time becomes less apparent) with larger population sizes and low selection pressure. This chapter extends exploration of the bimodal feature into EAs with much larger population sizes, and shows that under sufficiently high selection pressure it 'returns'. It is interesting to note that these observations apply directly in the emerging field of 'Directed Evolution' for novel bio-molecules, in which large parallel populations undergo evolutionary search, with solution quality and number of generations being vital to optimise. This has potentially highly significant consequences for setting of mutation rates in Directed Evolution and high selection pressure large-scale parallel EAs in general.

1. Introduction

Much experimental and theoretical work has been done examining optimum parameter settings for Evolutionary Algorithms when applied to a very wide range of problems such as combinatorial and function optimisation, for example [4, 5, 10, 12, 15, 32, 18, 26]. These parameters have included, amongst others, population size, selection pressure, mutation rate, crossover rate and crossover operator. Previous work by the authors has focussed on optimising the search process for an industrial application (such as automated web load balancing [20, 21, 27]) with an emphasis on the repeatability, speed and accuracy of the search). In general this application was facilitated by the use of small, embedded controllers where sequential processing has been the norm and thus the inherent parallelisation of EAs to allow concurrent fitness evaluation has not been readily exploitable. This has provided results indicating that small populations running with steady state algorithms with Tournament [6] style selection pressure and traditionally high mutation rates tend to produce good results in a minimum number of evaluations. However, in direct contrast to this, biological studies in 'Directed Evolution' [1, 29], where bacteriological samples are bred to improve a desired characteristic such as toxin immunity etc, are interested in getting reliable results in a minimum number of generations, and where the use of large populations with parallel evaluation is commonplace [2, 7, 36]. Much work has also been done by others on parallel EAs, where fitness evaluation is carried out across a cluster of processors, utilised by a central (or sometimes distributed) Evolutionary Algorithm controller. These configurations lend themselves more naturally (though not exclusively) to Generational style EAs using a form of Elitist 'Breeder' [17] style selection strategy.

In support of a biological study utilising 'Directed Evolution' targeted at rapid, novel enzyme development the authors are part of a team now examining [8, 9, 27] the performance characteristics of some of these large population, minimum generation EAs to attempt to optimise the bacteriological and virological studies being carried out by the biologists. In these biological studies it is possible to have populations of several thousand members, derived from a considerably smaller elitist breeding pool, with parallel evaluation. Each generational evaluation cycle may take hours or days to complete regardless of the population size. To give an example of where Directed Evolution may be applied, consider the early development of an epidemic of a new strain of bacteriological or virological threat. Here infection rates typically rise exponentially, and thus it is crucial to cut the number of such evaluation cycles to a minimum in the search for an effective vaccine. Therefore it is critical to find control parameters which deliver good results in a minimum number of generations, with far less regard to the actual number of evaluations carried out. Perhaps not surprisingly, existing work in bacterial strain improvement traditionally uses mutation rates focussed around the reciprocal of the chromosome length ($1 / L$), based on work commonly attributed to Baltz [7]. This mutation rate is typically induced by exposure to radiation or specific chemicals, the latter of which can also be used for 'targetted mutation' at particular loci and/or alleles. However emerging evidence from more recent studies suggests considerably higher mutation rates can prove more effective [3, 36].

This chapter presents some of the initial results from this new study showing that with very large population sizes and very high selection pressure, higher than traditional mutation rates deliver improved results on a range of standard test problems. The chapter begins with a background summary of relevant previous work leading to the experiments carried out to date. A discussion of these new results is provided together with initial conclusions and plans for future work.

2. Background

Fig. 1 shows the mean performance profile (averaged over 50 runs) for a steady state, 3 way single tournament EA using uniform crossover [30] and 'New Random Allele' mutation at a specified rate per gene on Watson's H-IFF problem (described later). The algorithm has a population size of 20 and each run is allowed 1,000,000 evaluations. The graph shows cyclical and phasic behaviour in the number of evaluations used to first find the best solution found, the standard deviation in this value and the fitness of the best solution found. This has been explained in [26], where it was shown that the performance of the algorithm over the range of mutation rates examined passes through 3 distinct phases, which repeat at least 3 times. In the first cycle of the first phase, the algorithm is starting to exploit the low level of mutation available to it, predominantly occurring as single point mutations. As mutation rates rise, these mutations occur with increasing frequency allowing the algorithm to utilise an increasing number of evaluations, until a point is reached where the usefulness of single point mutations is exhausted. As mutation rates increase, this point is reached earlier in the run, and hence the number of evaluation used falls. This is the second 'phase' of the performance profile and is further characterised by the flattening of the best found fitness plot and the reduction in the standard deviation of the number of evaluations used. At this point, mutation rates are still too low for the occurrence of 2 point mutations within the same chromosome to have any significant affect. However, as mutation rates increase, a point is reached where the likely occurrence of 2 point mutation becomes significant and this occasionally allows the algorithm to break though the 'fitness barrier' [14] surrounding the local optimum it has become stuck in. Hence the number of evaluations used becomes erratic (shown by a sudden, marked increase in its standard deviation. This is now the third 'phase' of performance behaviour. As mutation rates continue to increase, 2 point mutations become commonplace and the algorithm reverts back to its original phase behaviour exploiting increasing occurrences of these and the 3 phase cycle repeats until the usefulness of 2 point mutations is exhausted. The cycle is shown to repeat at least one further time, before excessive mutation rates cause the algorithm to deteriorate into random search. This explanation is described and analysed in far more detail in [26] and is shown to exist in a range of multi-modal problems in [24, 25]. In mono-modal problems, only a single cycle of these 3 phases is usually observed as would be expected by such a hypothesis, as no 'fitness barriers' exist which require specific types of mutation to breach.

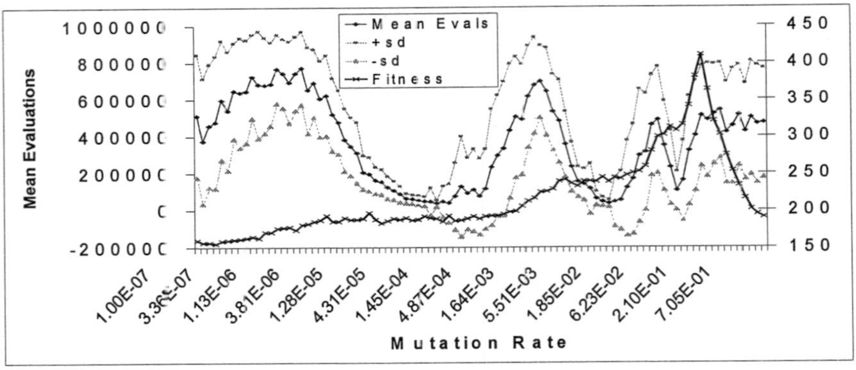

Fig. 1. H-IFF 64 Performance Profile at 1 Million evaluations

Fig. 2 shows the performance of a steady state Evolutionary algorithm on an instance of the Royal Staircase problem (length 50, block size 1), showing the co-incidence in troughs of minimum error, minimum evaluations used and minimum coefficient of variation (standard deviation divided by the mean ie a minimum in the normalised process variability). The results are again the average of 50 runs of the algorithm, each time with a population size of 100, uniform crossover at a probability of 1.0 and New Random Allele replacement mutation at the indicated rate per gene. Each run was allowed 20,000 evaluations, reporting the first evaluation number at which the best result in the run was first seen. The algorithm employed 3 way, single Tournament selection. As can be seen, in the trough of optimum performance (at mutation rate of around 2.5%), the algorithm requires around 5,000 evaluations to find the global optimum.

The experiment was then repeated with the selection pressure increased to a single 8 way Tournament, where 8 members of the population are chosen at random and ranked. The first and second best are used as parents to produce a child which replaces the 8th ranked member of the Tournament back in the original population. This increased selection pressure can be seen in Fig. 3 to have 3 predominant effects on the performance profile. Firstly, the number of evaluations used in the trough of optimum performance was seen to fall from around 5,000 evaluations (3 way Tournament) to below 3,000 evaluations (8 way Tournament). Secondly, the average error of 'best solutions found' at low mutation rates was seen to deteriorate with higher selection pressure, and finally the average number of evaluations used at these mutation rates was seen to fall. Neither of these last two effects are surprising as the increased selection pressure is clearly causing earlier premature convergence from which the algorithm cannot escape due to lack of mutation. These results are a subset of previously published results in [22, 23] wherein these effects are shown over a wider range of population sizes, problem instances and algorithm designs.

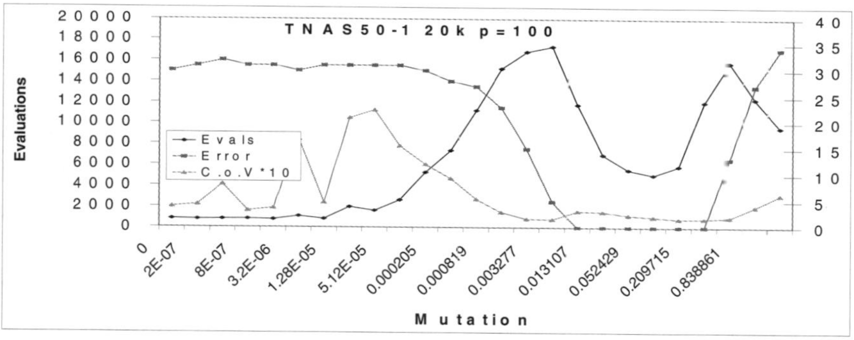

Fig. 2. Royal Stair 50-1 Performance Profile with 3 way Tournament selection

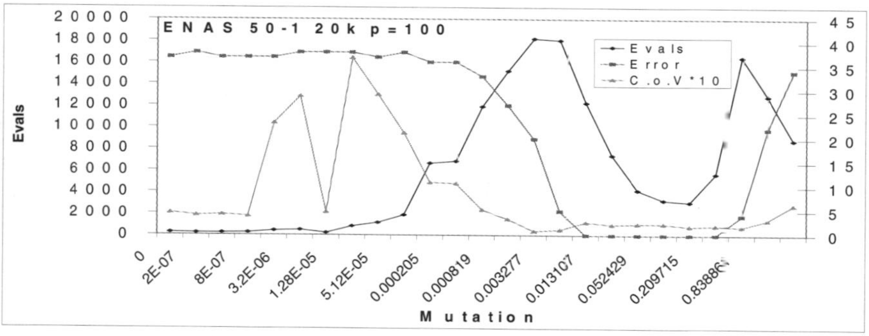

Fig. 3. Royal Stair 50-1 Performance Profile with 8 way Tournament selection

These results show the aforementioned effects on a steady state algorithm, whilst Figs. 4-7 show similar effects on Generational Breeder style algorithms incorporating 50% at 10% elitism respectively. Here the algorithm ranks the entire population and then discards the lower performing half (or 90%). The surviving members of the population are then randomly selected in pairs as parents (using uniform crossover at probability 1.0 followed by per gene mutation) to restore the population to original size.

Population sizes from 10 through to 500 (in steps of 10) have been trialled with mutation rates ranging from 1 E^{-7} to 0.83 per gene. In all cases the results are the average of 50 runs each of which is allowed 20,000 evaluations. What can clearly be seen from a baseline in Fig. 4 is that whilst the bimodal performance profile is clearly apparent at low population sizes, it is attenuated by increased population size.

Fig. 5 shows that at low population sizes, only a specific sub-range of mutation rates can deliver good performance (zero error from the optimum fitness value), whilst as population size increases, performance at these lower mutation rates improves, until by a population size of 500, adequate performance is just beginning to be delivered. Fig. 6 shows the contrast where selection pressure is increased by only allowing the top 10% of each generation to breed. Here, as in the case of the steady state algorithm, the 3 effects of increased selection pressure can clearly be seen : reduced evaluations needed at optimum mutation rates; more rapid premature convergence at low mutation rates; with this convergence on poorer solutions. What is also important however, is the clear continuation of the bimodal performance profile into higher population sizes. Whilst at low population sizes the affect is attenuated with respect to the lower selection pressure case, the effect is still clear in the population size 500 case, which was not true for the low selection pressure example.

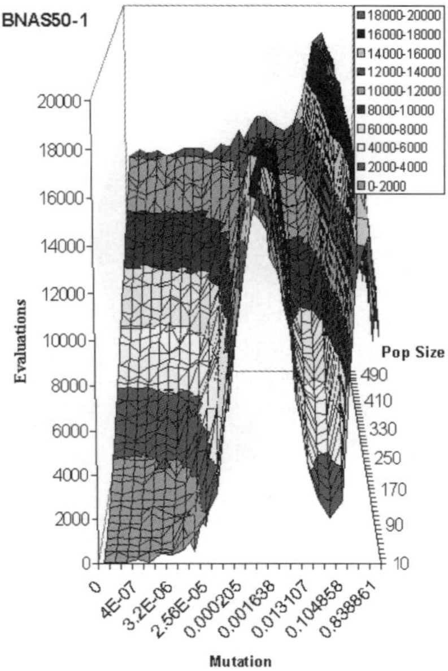

Fig. 4. Evals used, RS50-1,50% Elitism

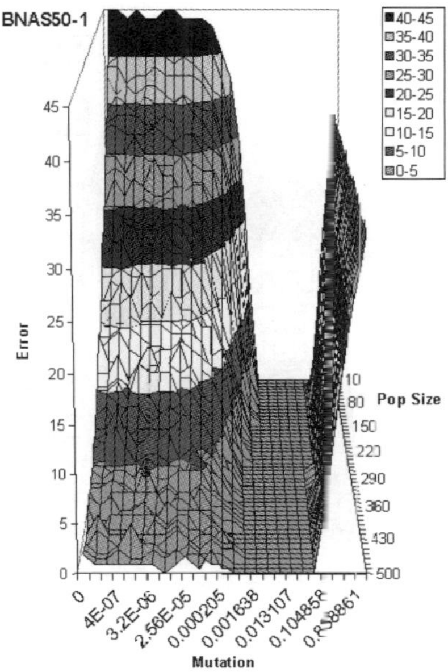

Fig. 5. Errors, RS50-1, 50% Elitism

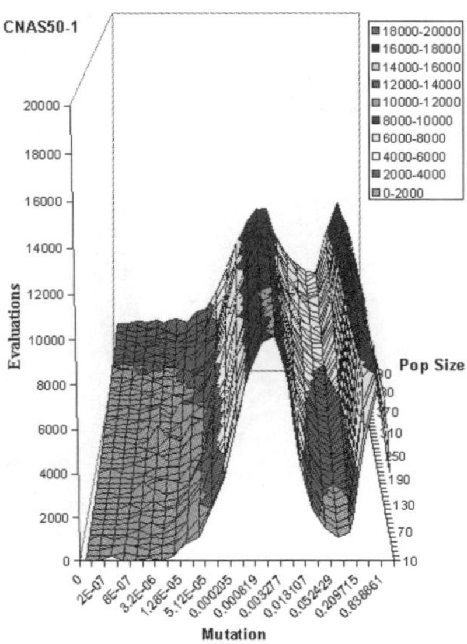

Fig. 6. Evals used, RS50-1, 10% Elitism

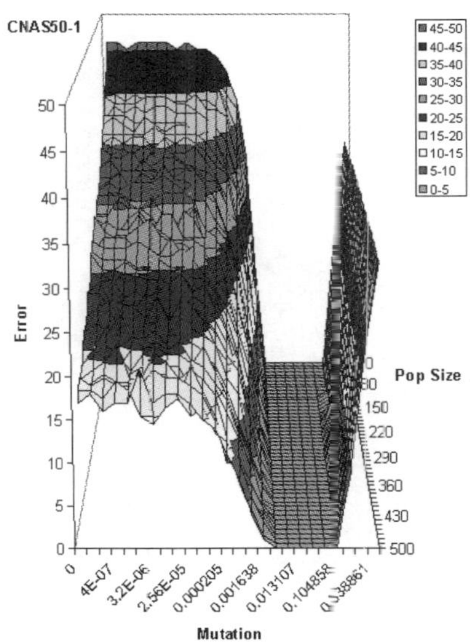

Fig. 7. Errors, RS50-1, 10% Elitism

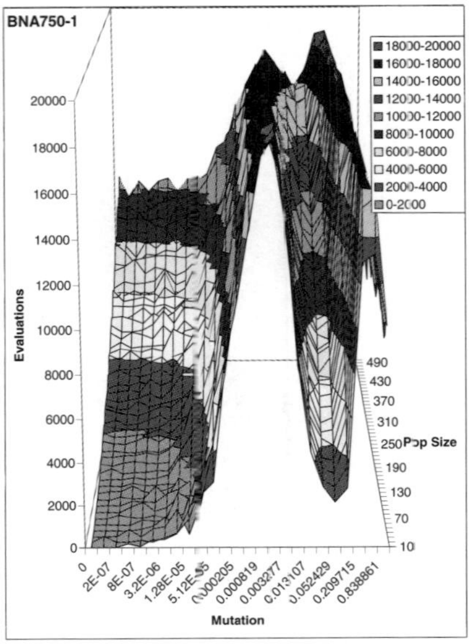

Fig. 8. Evals used, RS50-1, 75% x-over

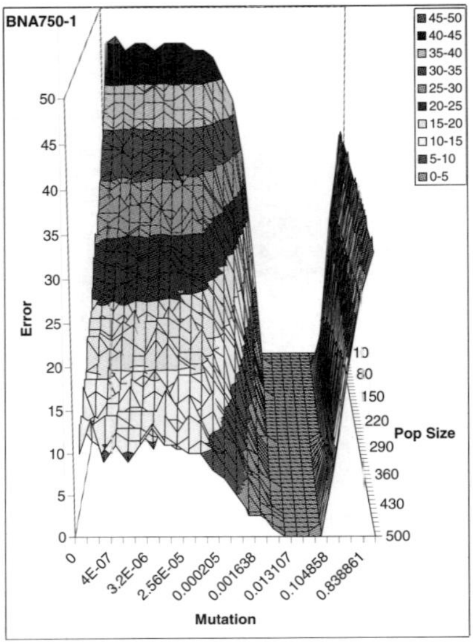

Fig. 9. Errors, RS50-1, 75% x-over

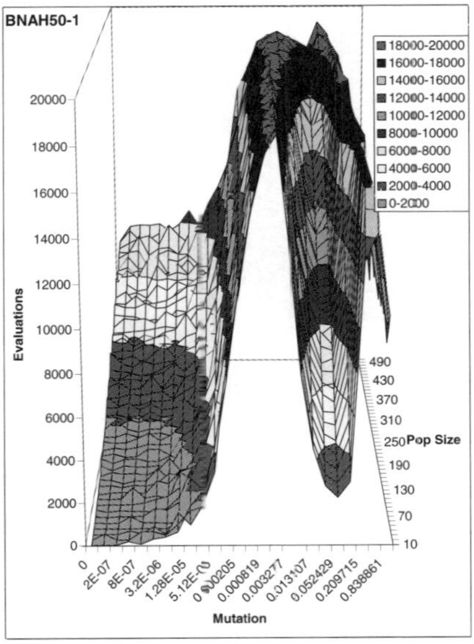

Fig. 10. Evals used, RS50-1, 50% x-over

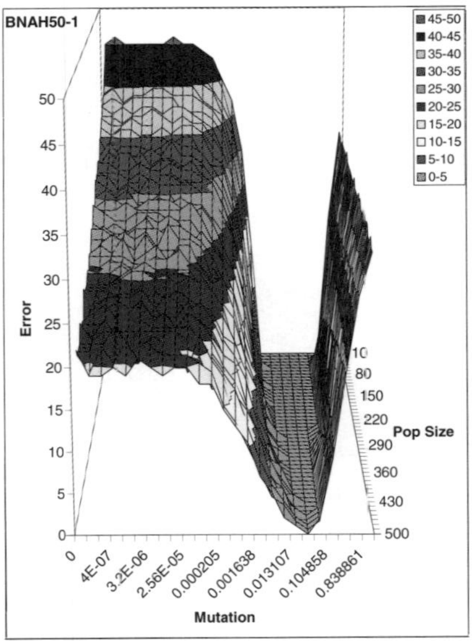

Fig. 11. Errors, RS50-1, 50% x-over

Fig. 8 and Fig. 9 contrast with Fig. 4 and Fig. 5, showing results where selection pressure remains at 50%, however the probability of performing crossover is reduced to 0.75 (in the case of no crossover, a single parent is used with mutation only). Whereas in Fig. 4 the first ridge of high evaluations is seen to be attenuated by increased population size, in Fig. 8 this ridge remains high, but the trough of optimum performance is seen to rise. At a population size of 500 the bimodal profile is still just observable. Further experiments with the probability of crossover reduced to only 50% and 10% continue these trends and the 50% crossover results for 'evaluations used' and 'errors' are shown in Fig. 10 and Fig. 11 respectively.. These results on the Royal Staircase problem are in direct support of earlier results in [21, 23] on the One Max problem

Thus it has been clearly shown that there exist ranges of optimal mutation rates capable of delivering highly robust performance in a minimum of evaluations with a high degree of accuracy.

These studies have shown that the bimodal effect, normally most prevalent at low population sizes, can be extended to affect algorithm performance at higher population sizes where high levels of selection pressure and reduced crossover are utilised. Further it can be seen that whilst this is generally at the expense of a greater number of evaluations required, it can also lead to a significant reduction in the number of generations required.

3. Experimental Method

A natural extension of the above experiments is to investigate the performance of an algorithm with a very large population, derived via a highly elitist selection strategy, over a range a traditionally high mutation rates. This models the situation when Directed Evolution is applied. In this section we present results from a range of initial experiments using such an algorithm utilising a population size of 10,000 members (initially randomly generated), where the next generation is entirely derived from the single fittest member of the population subjected to 'per gene' mutation at a specified rate. 'New Random Allele' rates of mutation from 1.024 E^{-4} to 0.838 have been trialled on an exponential scale where the mutation rate doubles between each experiment in the 14 case set. In each case, the algorithm is allowed 50 generations (ie 500,000 evaluations), reporting the fitness of the best solution found, and the generation number this was first found at. Each experiment is then repeated 50 times and results plotted show the mean results of these 50 runs, and the standard deviation of the number of generations used across the 50 runs.

Experiments have been carried out on a range of standard test problems (Max Ones, Royal Staircase [19], Kauffman NK [15], H-IFF [33] etc) with only a representative sample given here for space reasons. The tunable Royal Staircase problem in this instance is a mono-modal problem with significant regions of neutral fitness plateaux. Fitness is derived by counting the number of consecutive blocks of all 1s in the chromosome starting from the left-hand side and has been extensively researched by Crutchfield and Van Nimwegen [19].

With this problem, with a block size set at 5, a string of 12 1's followed by any (non zero) number of 0's followed by any combination of 1's and 0's delivers a fitness of 2 out a possible global optimum of 10. A string containing 49 1's preceded by a single 0 delivers a fitness of 0. A chromosome length of 50 was used in these experiments with block sizes set to 1, 2, 5 and 10.

The tunable Kauffman NK [15] problem allows varying levels of epistatic and positional linkage to be explored. In this implementation with a chromosome length of 50 and maximum block size of 6, a randomly generated look up table is generated containing 50 rows by 64 columns. For a given block size of 1, fitness is simply derived by taking each gene individually and summing either the first or second column entry, determined by allele, over the 50 genes in the chromosome (whose locus determines the row). This is in effect a form of 'max ones' mono-modal function. However for larger block sizes, consecutive sequences of genes are used as a binary word to derive a column index into the table. Thus for a block size of 3, each gene takes part in 3 table retrievals over the 50 needed to derive overall fitness of a chromosome. Therefore any single point mutation will affect multiple aspects of the overall fitness calculation. This creates an ever ruggedised search space deteriorating to a random field as block sizes approach the length of the chromosome. Block sizes of 1, through 6 have currently been investigated.

Watson's Hierarchical If and only If problem (H-IFF) [33] has been widely investigated by the author and others, and although first derived to explore the effects of crossover and schemata development, was critically instrumental in helping demonstrate the emergence and explanation of multi-modal algorithmic performance when subjected to varying rates of mutation. The fitness of a potential solution to this problem is the sum of weighted, aligned, decomposable blocks of either contiguous 1's or 0's. This produces a search landscape in which 2 global optima exist. one as a string of all 1's, the other of all 0's. However a single mutation away form either of these positions produces a much lower fitness. Secondary optima exist at strings of 32 contiguous 0's followed by 32 contiguous 1's (for a chromosome length of 64) and vice versa. Not surprisingly, Watson showed that hill-climbing performs extremely badly on this problem [34].

Together, these test problems provide an informative and diverse set to explore many aspects of algorithm performance on combinatorial optimisation problems with low allelic range.

4. Results

Fig. 12 shows the performance of the highly elite algorithm on the Royal Staircase problem with a chromosome length of 50 and block size of 1. Here it can clearly be seen that once sufficient mutation is available to the algorithm, the global optimum can be achieved 50 times out of 50 in less than 30 generations. As mutation rates increase, this number of generations required is seen to fall to a minimum of 9 at a per gene mutation rate of around 10%. Above this rate of mutation algorithm performance starts to deteriorate with a marked increase in error, number of generations needed and process unrepeatability. As the block size is increased to 2 (25 blocks thereof), this range of good mutation rates is seen to narrow (Fig. 13), with the lower end rates no longer delivering adequate performance. By the time the block size is increased to 5, the algorithm is failing to consistently find the global optimum solution and the number of generations used is seen to be high. A slight dip is observable at the now optimum mutation rate of 20% (Fig. 14).

The results for the Max Ones problem with a chromosome length of 50 are presented in Fig. 15 and can be seen to be very similar to the block size 1 Royal Staircase results. The Max Ones problem is also representative of the Kauffman NK problem with a block size of only 1. Fig. 16 shows results for the Kauffman NK problem with a block size of 2, now a multi-modal problem. Again we see the inability of low mutation rates to deliver good solutions, and an optimum performance at a mutation rate of around 10%. A dip is also seen in the number of evaluations used at a mutation rate of around 1.3%, but not accompanied by a similar dip in the fitness error. This is likely to be an effect similar to that seen at the beginning of this chapter on the highly structured multi-modal H-IFF problem. Here we see the effect of predominant one point mutation finding certain local optima, but with insufficient 2 point mutations available, the algorithm gets trapped in these solutions. As 2 point mutations become more prevalent, at higher mutation rates, so the fitness wells surrounding these local optima can be breached and the algorithm can exploit more evaluations.

Fig. 17 shows results for the NK problem with a block size of 3. Again an optimum mutation rate is seen in terms of fitness error, with a local minimum in the number of generations used. The preceding multi-phasic behaviour is not apparent, but this is probably due to the small number of mutation rates sampled. Fig. 18 shows similar results with a block size of 4, whilst Fig. 19 shows results with a block size of 5. By this time, the algorithm is showing clear signs of insufficient generations being allowed.

The multi-modal profile is severely attenuated, however there is still a clear minimum in the fitness error plot. The fact that the number of generations required is now relatively high is typical of results published for serial algorithms using both steady state and generational techniques, where the number of evaluations required is severely limited [21].

Fig. 20 shows the results for the highly structured multi-modal H-IFF problem with a chromosome length of 64. Here we again see a dip in the fitness error, but accompanied by increasing numbers of generations used. This is an extension of the effect described immediately above.

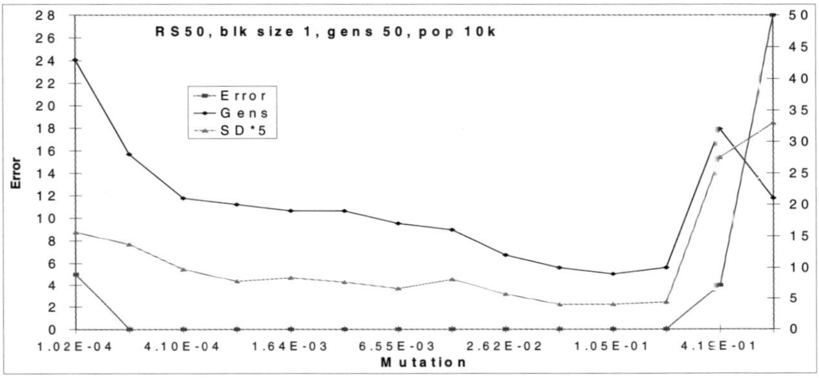

Fig. 12. Performance Profile for highly Elite algorithm on RS problem, block size 1

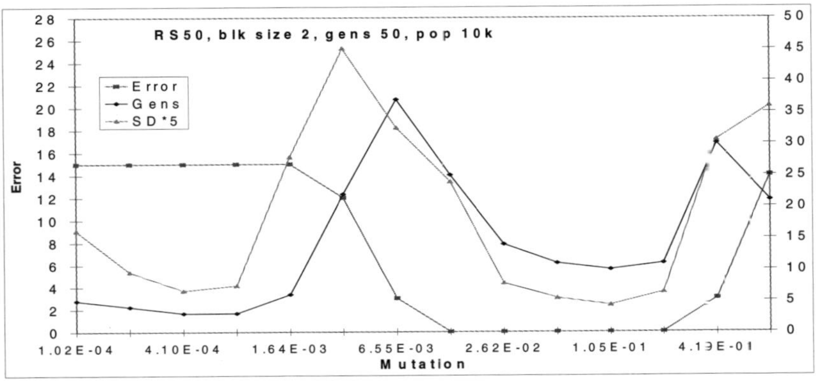

Fig. 13. Performance Profile for highly Elite algorithm on RS problem, block size 2

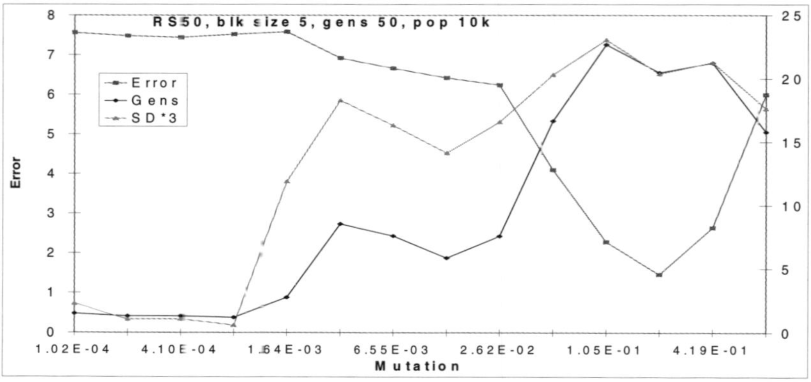

Fig. 14. Performance Profile for highly Elite algorithm on RS problem, block size 5

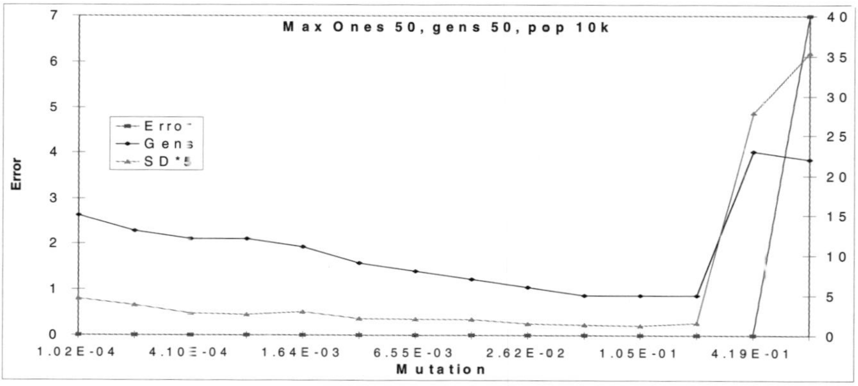

Fig. 15. Performance Profile for highly Elite algorithm on Max Ones length 50

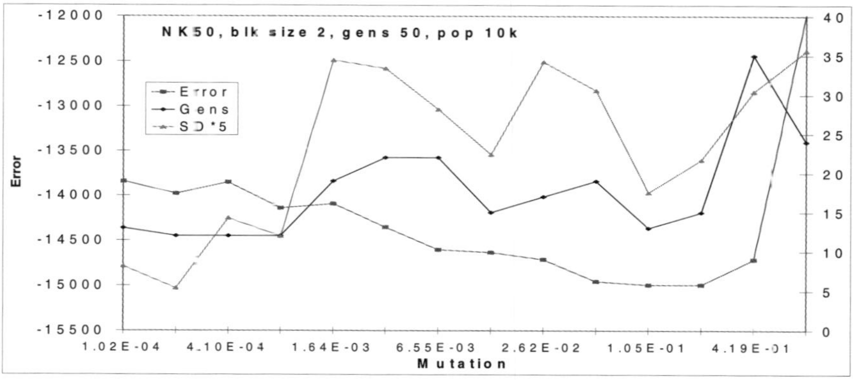

Fig. 16. Performance Profile for highly Elite algorithm on NK50, block size 2

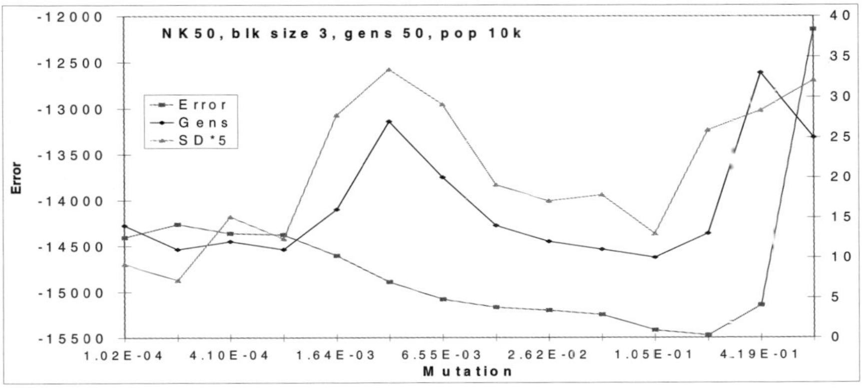

Fig. 17. Performance Profile for highly Elite algorithm on NK50, block size 3

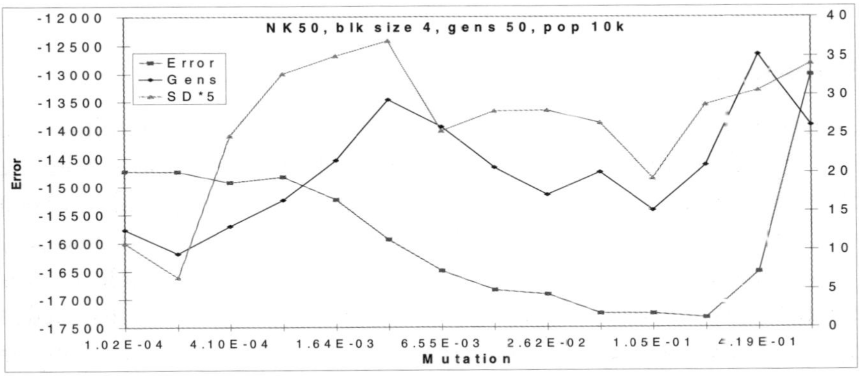

Fig. 18. Performance Profile for highly Elite algorithm on NK50, block size 4

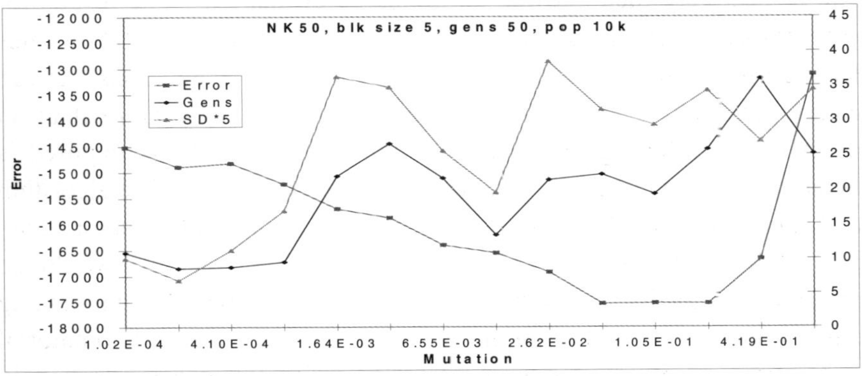

Fig. 19. Performance Profile for highly Elite algorithm on NK50, block size 5

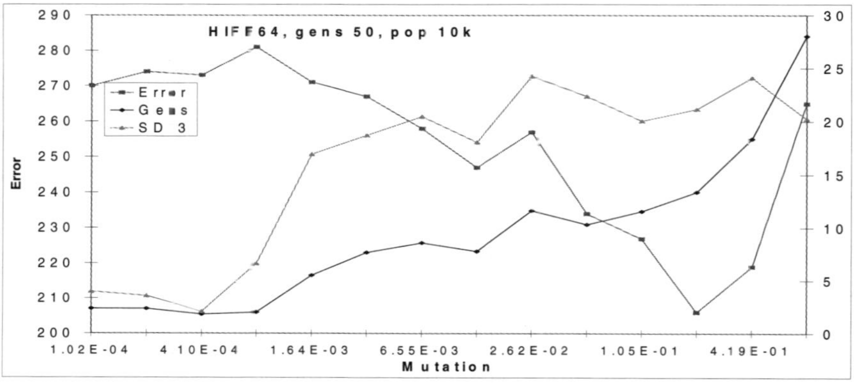

Fig. 20. Performance Profile for highly Elite algorithm on H-IFF 64 problem

5. Discussion

Contrasting the behaviour of these somewhat extreme algorithms to results with more conventional parameters shows that these results are obtained at a price. Whilst the number of generations required has been seen to be small, the number of evaluations required is considerably higher than that of an algorithm tuned for sequential use. Table 1 gives comparisons between the number of evaluations and generations needed by the highly elitist algorithm described in this chapter with experiments with a 50% elitist Breeder algorithm using population sizes of 100 and 500 respectively each allowed up to 20,000 evaluations. The results for each algorithm are the average over 50 runs at optimum mutation rates targeted for optimum fitness followed by minimum evaluations. As can clearly be seen, the number of evaluations is typically more than an order of magnitude greater, but the number of generations required is much reduced (typically by a factor of 3 or 4 between the Elite algorithm and the Population Size 500 algorithm, and by a similar factor again against the Population size 100 algorithm). This trade-off would be difficult to justify in terms of the massively parallel processing environment it would require for a typical EA combinatorial optimisation problem, but is a relatively insignificant price to pay in biological assay evaluations. It is also worth noting that on the NK 50-2, 50-3, 50-5 and 50-6 problems, the average fitness of best found solutions was better for the Elite algorithm than for either of the 50% Breeder algorithms. For the RS 50-1, RS 25-2 and Max 1s problems, the global optimum was consistently found by all 3 algorithms and for the RS 10-5, and NK 50-3 problems the elite algorithm average best found fitness was marginally worse. For the highly structured H-IFF problem, as would be expected with no population crossover, the elite algorithm consistently under-performed, in terms of best found fitness, relative to the other two algorithms.

Table 1. Relative reduction in number of Generations required with increased Pop Size

	50%	BDR	P 100	50%	BDR	P 500	Mono	Elite	P 10k
	Evals	Gens	SD	Evals	Gens	SD	Evals	Gens	SD
RS50-1	5050	99	23.6	14500	57	5.7	90K	9	0.80
RS25-2	6300	125	37.8	14000	55	7.1	100K	10	0.85
RS10-5	14200	283	80.7	17000	67	8.6	200K	20	6.8
MAX 1s	1750	34	4.9	4750	18	1.7	50K	5	0.24
NK50-2	6300	125	79.4	8750	34	6.4	130K	13	3.5
NK50-3	8350	166	87.3	13750	54	12.7	130K	13	5.2
NK50-4	9050	180	87.2	12250	48	10.4	210K	21	5.7
NK50-5	10600	211	103.9	17250	68	7.8	190K	19	5.9
NK50-6	11700	233	82.7	18000	71	7.2	240K	24	6.0
H-IFF64	5150	102	54.1	14000	55	10.1	130K	13	7.1

The extremely high level of selection pressure utilised by this algorithm (only the single fittest being used to produce all of the next generation) draws parallels with developments along the lines of Hill Climbers and other such, non-population based techniques. However such techniques tend to look only at single point mutations and as such contain no mechanism for escaping local or deceptive optima. The advantage of a high 'per gene' mutation rate is that over the 10,000 derivatives of the elite parent, a wide variety of differing mutation schedules is produced. Some variants will suffer only single point mutation, others 2 point, whilst potentially some could have all genes replaced by random alleles (no mutations is also a distinct, but wasted possibility). The higher the 'per gene' mutation rate, the more that multi-point mutations will dominate this distribution. During different stages of the optimisation, different types of mutation are likely to be of most use. Given the random generation of the first 10,000 evaluations, a relatively wide coverage of the search space is examined and thus low rates of mutation will allow local exploration to find a local optimum in the next generation. However, once found, in a multi-modal or deceptive search space, a considerably more disruptive mutation rate will be required to allow the search to break free of this optimum in the search for ever better optima.

6. Conclusions

The mutation rates seen to be effective under these circumstances on these problems appear well in excess of those traditionally used within the EA community, even higher than the now generally accepted optimal rates ($1/L$ and k/L) demonstrated by Mühlenbe in the paper [18]. However the absence of crossover and the extreme selection pressure used effectively invalidate such comparisons. This algorithm is indeed far closer to a traditional Evolutionary Strategy as developed by Rechenberg [28] than a standard Genetic Algorithm as developed by Holland [13] and Goldberg [11], but once again, mutation rates and offspring sizes are larger than would be typically used in even these algorithms. Initial population generation is also significantly different. Further work is clearly required with problems of wider allelic range and other population sizes, to see at what point the trade-off becomes marginalised. Relaxation of selection pressure also requires investigation allowing the possibility of reintroduction of crossover.

On the assumption that directed evolution fitness landscapes [1] (in contrast to those of natural evolution [36]) share similar properties to those problems investigated here, the reduction in number of generations required to obtain useful results becomes a highly significant advantage. This could lead, for example, to potential anti-toxins and vaccines being developed far earlier in the course of an epidemic leading to considerable reduction in suffering and potential reduction in loss of life.

References

1. F. Arnold, Directed evolution, *Nature Biotech.*, 16:617–618 (1998).
2. F. Arnold, Combinatorial and computational challenges for biocatalyst design. *Nature*, 409: 253–7 (2001).
3. F. Arnold, Evolutionary Protein Design (Academic Press, San Diego, 2001).
4. T. Bäck, Optimal Mutation Rates in Genetic Search, *Proc. 5th ICGA*, pp 2-9 (1993).
5. T Bäck, Selective pressure in evolutionary algorithms: a characterization of selection mechanisms, *Proc. 1st IEEE Conf. On Evolutionary Computation*, pp 57–62 (1994) .
6. T. Bäck, *Evolutionary Algorithms in Theory and Practice* (Oxford University Press, 1996).
7. R.H. Baltz, Mutation in Streptomyces, in Day, L, Queener S, (eds). The Bacteria, Vol 9, *Antibiotic-producing Streptomyces*, pp 61–94 (Academic Press, New York, 1986).
8. D. Corne, D.B. Kell and M. Oates, On Fitness Distributions and Expected Fitness Gain of Mutation Rates in Parallel Evolutionary Algorithms, in J.J. Merelo et al. (eds.) *Proc. PPSN VII* (Springer Verlag, Berlin, 2002).
9. D.W. Corne, M.J. Oates, and D.B.Kell, Fitness Gains and Mutation Patterns: Deriving Mutation Rates by Exploiting Landscape Information, in *Foundations of Genetic Algorithms 7*, pp 347-364 (Morgan Kaufmann).
10. K. Deb, S. Agrawal, Understanding Interactions among Genetic Algorithm Parameters, in *Foundations of Genetic Algorithms* (Morgan Kaufmann Publisher, 1998).
11. D. Goldberg, *Genetic Algorithms in Search Optimisation and Machine Learning* (Addison Wesley, 1989).
12. D. Goldberg, K. Deb and J.H. Clark, Genetic Algorithms, noise, and the sizing of populations, *Complex Systems* 6:333–362 (1992).
13. J. Holland, *Adaptation in Natural and Artificial Systems* (MIT press, Cambridge, MA, 1975).
14. T. Jones, Evolutionary Algorithms, Fitness Landscapes and Search, *PhD Dissertation*, UNM (1995).
15. S.A. Kauffman, *The Origins of Order: Self-Organization and Selection in Evolution* (OUP, 1993).
16. Z. Michalewicz, *Genetic Algorithms + Data Structures = Evolution Programs* (Springer, 1996).
17. H. Mühlenbein and D. Schlierkamp-Voosen, The Science of Breeding and its application to the Breeder Genetic Algorithm, *Evolutionary Computation* 1:335–360 (1994).
18. H. Mühlenbein, How genetic algorithms really work: I. Mutation and Hillclimbing, in Manner, Manderick (eds) *Proc. PPSN II*, pp 15–25 (Elsevier, 1993).
19. E. Van Nimwegen and J. Crutchfield, Optmizing Epochal Evolutionary Search: Population-Size Independent Theory, in D. Goldberg and K. Deb (eds) *Comp.*

Meth, in Applied Mechanics and Engineering, special issue on Evolutionary and Genetic Algorithms (1998).

20. M. Oates and D. Corne, Investigating Evolutionary Approaches to Adaptive Database Management against various Quality of Service Metrics, *Proc. of PPSN-V*, pp. 775-784 (1998).
21. M. Oates, D. Corne and R. Loader, Investigation of a Characteristic Bimodal Convergence-time/Mutation-rate Feature in Evolutionary Search, in *Proc. ICEC 99*, vol 3, pp 2175-2182 (1999).
22. M. Oates, D. Corne and B. Turton, The Effects of Selection Pressure on Parameter Choice in Evolutionary Search, in *Late Breaking Papers at GECCO 99*, pp.193–203 (1999).
23. M. Oates J. Smedley, D. Corne and R. Loader, Bimodal Performance Profile of Evolutionary Search and the Effects of Crossover, in Kallel, Naudts and Rogers (eds) *Theoretical Aspects of Evolutionary Computing* (Springer Verlag, 2000).
24. M. Oates, D. Corne and R. Loader, A Tri-Phase Multimodal Evolutionary Search Performance Profile on the 'Hierarchical If and Only If' Problem, in *Proc. of GECCO 2000* (2000).
25. M. Oates, D. Corne and R. Loader, Tri-Phase Performance Profile of Evolutionary Search on Uni- and Multi- Modal Search Spaces, in *Proc of Congress on Evolutionary Computation* (2000).
26. M. Oates and D. Corne, Overcoming Fitness Barriers in Multi-Modal Search Spaces, in *Foundations of Genetic Algorithms* 6 (Morgan Kaufmann Publisher, 2000).
27. M. Oates, Global Web Server Load Balancing using Evolutionary Computational Techniques, *Soft Computing* (2001).
28. M. Oates, D. Corne and D. Kell, The Bimodal Feature at Large Population Sizes and High Selection Pressure: Implications for Directed Evolution, in Wang et al. (Eds) *Proc. of 4th Asia-Pacific Conf on Simulated Evolution and Learning (SEAL 02)*, Vol 1, ISBN 981-04-7522-5 , pp81-85 (2002).
29. Rechenberg, *Evolutions strategie: Optimierung technischer Systeme nach Prinzipien der biologischen Evolution* (Frommann-Holzboog, Stuttgart, 1973).
30. G. Syswerda, Uniform Crossover in Genetic Algorithms, in Schaffer J. (ed) *Proc. of 3rd ICGA*, pp. 2-9 (Morgan Kaufmann, 1989).
31. C.A. Voigt, S. Kauffman and Z.G. Wang, Rational evolutionary design: The theory of in vitro protein evolution, in F. Arnold (ed) *Advances in Protein Chemistry*, Vol 55, pp 79-160 (2001).
32. M. Vose, *The Simple Genetic Algorithm: Foundations and Theory* (MIT Press, 1999).
33. R.A. Watson, G.S. Hornby and J.B. Pollack, Modelling Building-Block Interdependency, in *Proc. PPSN-V*, pp 97-106 (1998).
34. R.A. Watson, J.B. Pollack, Hierarchically Consistent Test Problems for Genetic Algorithms, in *Proc of Congress on Evolutionary Computation*, vol 2, pp 1406–1413 (1999).

35. S Wright, The roles of mutation, inbreeding, crossbreeding and selection in evolution, in D F Jones (ed) *Procs of 6th Intl Conf on Genetics*, vol 1, pp. 356-366 (Ithaca, NY, 1932).
36. M. Zaccolo and E. Gherardi, The effect of high-frequency random mutagenesis on in vitro protein evolution: A study on TEM-1 β-lactamase, *J. Mol. Biol.* 285:775-783 (1999).

CHAPTER 13

USING EDGE HISTOGRAM MODELS TO SOLVE FLOW SHOP SCHEDULING PROBLEMS WITH PROBABILISTIC MODEL-BUILDING GENETIC ALGORITHMS

Shigeyoshi Tsutsui† and Mitsunori Miki‡

†Department of Management and Information Science, Hannan University
5-4-33 Amamihigashi, Matsubara, Osaka 580-5802, Japan
E-mail: tsutsui@hannan-u.ac.jp
‡Department of Knowledge Engineering and Computer Sciences, Doshisha University, 1-3 Tatara, Miyakodani, Kyo-tanabe, Kyoto, 610-0321, Japan
mmiki@mail.doshisha.ac.jp

In evolutionary algorithms based on probabilistic modeling, the offspring population is generated according to the estimated probability density model of the parent instead of using recombination and mutation operators. In this chapter, we have proposed a probabilistic model-building genetic algorithms (PMBGAs) for solving flow shop scheduling problems using edge histogram based sampling algorithms (EHBSAs). The effectiveness of introducing the *tag node (TN)* in a string representation is also discussed.

1. Introduction

Genetic Algorithms (GAs)[7] are widely used as robust searching schemes in various real world applications, including function optimization, optimum scheduling, and many combinatorial optimization problems. Traditional GAs start with a randomly generated population of candidate solutions (individuals). From a current population, better individuals are selected by the selection operators. The selected solutions produce new candidate solutions by applying recombination and mutation operators.

Recently, there has been a growing interest in developing evolutionary algorithms based on probabilistic models.[13,19] In this scheme, the offspring population is generated according to the estimated probabilistic model of the parent population instead of using traditional recombination and mutation operators. The model is expected to reflect the problem structure, and as a result it is expected that this approach provides a more effective mixing capability than recombination operators in traditional GAs. These algorithms are called probabilistic model-building genetic algorithms (PMBGAs) or estimation of distribution algorithms (EDAs). In a PMBGA, better individuals are selected from an initially randomly generated population like in standard GAs. Then, the probability distribution of the selected set of individuals is estimated and new individuals are generated according to this estimate, forming candidate solutions for the next generation. The process is repeated until the termination conditions are satisfied.

Many studies on PMBGAs have been performed in discrete (mainly binary) domain and there are several attempts to apply PMBGAs in continuous domain. However, a few studies on PMBGAs in permutation representation domain are found.

In previous studies,[21,22] we have proposed an approach to PMBGAs in permutation representation domains, focusing on solving the Traveling Salesman Problem (TSP). In this approach, we developed a symmetrical *edge histogram matrix (EHM)* from the current population, where an edge is a link between two nodes in a string. We then sample nodes of a new string according to the edge histogram matrix. We called this method the *edge histogram based sampling algorithm (EHBSA)*. We proposed two types of EHBSAs, an *edge histogram based sampling algorithm without template (EHBSA/WO)* and an *edge histogram based sampling algorithm with template (EHBSA/WT)*. EHBSA/WO uses only the learned edge histogram matrix to generate new candidate solutions, whereas EHBSA/WT uses a template selected from the population of promising candidate solutions as a starting point and modifies the template to generate a new solution.

EHBSA/WO and EHBSA/WT were applied to several benchmark instances of the TSP with and without the use of local search. The results showed that the EHBSA/WT has performed significantly better than

EHBSA/WO and other PMBGAs proposed in the past for solving this type of problems. EHBSA had also proven to provide significantly better results than some other popular two-parent recombination techniques for permutations. Experimental results indicated that another advantage of EHBSA is the use of significantly smaller population sizes than those that are necessary with most other evolutionary algorithms for permutation problems.

In this chapter, we extend the EHBSAs to solving a flow shop scheduling problem, a typical, well known problem in the area of scheduling. In a flow shop scheduling problem, each string represents a sequence of jobs to be processed. For example, string s = {1, 2 3, 0} means that job 1 is first processed, then jobs 2, 3, and 0 follow in this sequence. In this case, there are four edges, i.e., 1–>2, 2–>3, 3–>0, and 0–>1. Thus, in the flow shop scheduling problem, each edge is directional and the edge histogram matrix becomes asymmetrical. This is a big difference from previous study.[21,22] In Section 2 of this chapter, a brief review of PMBGAs is given. In Section 3, the EHBSAs for flow shop scheduling problems are described. The empirical analysis is given in Section 4. In Section 5, introducing the tag node in a string representation aiming to improve the performance of EHBSAs is discussed. Section 6 concludes the chapter.

2. A Brief Review of PMBGAs

According to Pelikan, et al.,[13] these PMBGAs in binary string representation can be classified into three classes depending on the complexity of models they use; (1) no interactions, (2) pairwise interactions, and (3) multivariate interactions. In models with no interactions, interactions among variables are treated independently. Algorithms in this class work well on problems which have no interactions among variables. These algorithms include the population based incremental learning (PBIL) by Baluja,[1] compact GA (cGA) by Harik, et al.[8] and univariate marginal distribution algorithm (UMDA) by Muehlenbein & Paass[11]. In pairwise interactions, some pairwise interactions among variables are considered. These algorithms include the mutual-information-maximization input clustering (MIMIC) algorithm by De Bonet, et al.,[6] the algorithm using dependency trees by Baluja & Davies.[2] In models with multivariate interactions, algorithms use models that can cover multivariate interactions. Although the algorithms require increased computational time, they work well on problems which have complex interactions among variables. These algorithms include extended cGA (ECGA) by Harik[9] and Bayesian optimization algorithm (BOA) by Pelikan, et al.[12,14]

Studies to apply PMBGAs in continuous domains have also been done. These include continuous PBIL with Gaussian distribution by Sebag & Ducoulombier [15] and a real-coded variant of PBIL with iterative interval updating by Servet, et al.[16] The UMDA and MIMIC were introduced in continuous domain. None of the above algorithms cover interactions among the variables. In EGNA by Larranaga, et al.,[10] a Gaussian network learns to estimate a multivariate Gaussian distribution of the parent population. Two density estimation models, i.e., the normal distribution, and the histogram distribution, are discussed by Bosman & Thierens.[3] These models are intended to cover multivariate interaction among variables. It is reported that the normal distribution models have shown good performance by Bosman & Thierens.[4] A normal mixture model combined with a clustering technique is introduced to deal with non-linear interactions by Bosman & Thierens.[5] An evolutionary algorithm using marginal histogram models in continuous domain was proposed by Tsutsui, et al.[20]

A study on PMBGAs in permutation domains is found in Ref. 18. In it, PMBGAs are applied to solving TSP using two approaches. PMBGAs are also applied to solve job shop scheduling problems and graph matching problems.[19] Tsutsui, et al. proposed EHBSAs, several variants of PMBGAs based on learning and sampling an edge histogram matrix for solving permutation problems.[21,22]

3. Edge Histogram Based Sampling Algorithm for Flow Shop Scheduling

This section describes how the edge histogram based sampling algorithm (EHBSA) can be used to (1) model promising solutions and (2) generate new solutions by simulating the learned model.

3.1. *The Basic Description of the Algorithm*

An edge is a link or connection between two nodes and has important information about the permutation string. Some crossover operators, such as Edge Recombination (ER)[26] and enhanced ER (eER)[17] which are used in traditional two-parent recombination, use the edge distribution only in the two parents strings. The basic idea of the edge histogram based sampling algorithm (EHBSA) is to use the edge histogram of the whole population in generating new strings.

The algorithm starts by generating a random permutation string for each individual population of candidate solutions. Promising solutions are then selected using any popular selection scheme. An edge histogram matrix (EHM) for the selected solutions (population) is constructed and new solutions are generated by sampling based on the edge histogram model. New solutions replace some of the old ones and the process is repeated until the termination criteria are met.

3.2. *Developing Edge Histogram Matrix for Flow Shop Scheduling*

Previous study[21] proposed a symmetrical edge histogram matrix. In this chapter, we represent it as $EHM_{(S)}$. In a scheduling problem, an edge in a string is directional. Thus, we must consider an asymmetrical edge histogram matrix $EHM_{(A)}$.

Let string of kth individual in population $P(t)$ at generation t be represented as $s^t_k=(\pi^t_k(0), \pi^t_k(1), ..., \pi^t_k(L-1))$. ($\pi^t_k(0), \pi^t_k(1), ...,$ and $\pi^t_k(L-1)$) are the permutation of $(0, 1, ..., L-1)$ representing a possible job sequence, where L is the length of the permutation.

An asymmetric edge histogram matrix $EHM_{(A)}{}^t$ (e^t_{ij}) $(i, j=0,1, .., L-1)$ of population $P(t)$ consists of L^2 elements as follows:

$$e^t{}_{i,j} = \begin{cases} \sum_{\mathrm{k=1}}^{\mathrm{N}} \delta_{i,j}(s^t_k) + \varepsilon & \text{if } i \neq j \\ 0 & \text{if } i = j \end{cases} \tag{1}$$

where N is the population size, $\delta_{ij}(s^t_k)$ is a delta function defined as

$$\delta_{i,j}(s^t_k) = \begin{cases} 1 & \text{if } \exists h\,[h \in \{0,1,\cdots L-1\} \\ & \quad \wedge \pi^t_k(h) = i \wedge \pi^t_k((h+1) \bmod L) = j] \\ 0 & \text{othersise} \end{cases} \tag{2}$$

and ε ($\varepsilon > 0$) is a bias to control *pressure* in sampling nodes just like those used for adjusting the selection pressure in the proportional selection in GAs. The average number of edges of element e^t_{ij} (ij) in $EHM_{(A)}{}^t$ is $LN/(L^2-L) = N/(L-1)$. So, ε is determined by a bias ratio B_{ratio} ($B_{ratio}>0$) of this average number of edges as

$$\varepsilon = \frac{N}{L-1} B_{\text{ratio}} \tag{3}$$

A smaller value of B_{ratio} reflects the real distribution of edges in sampling of nodes and a bigger value of B_{ratio} will give a kind of perturbation in the sampling. An example of $EHM_{(A)}{}^t$ is shown in Fig. 1.

$$\begin{array}{l} s^t{}_1 = (\,0,\ 1,\ 2,\ 3,\ 4\,) \\ s^t{}_2 = (\,1,\ 3,\ 4,\ 2,\ 0\,) \\ s^t{}_3 = (\,3,\ 4,\ 2,\ 1,\ 0\,) \\ s^t{}_4 = (\,4,\ 0,\ 3,\ 1,\ 2\,) \\ s^t{}_5 = (\,2,\ 1,\ 3,\ 4,\ 0\,) \end{array} \qquad \begin{pmatrix} 0 & 2.05 & 1.05 & 2.05 & 0.05 \\ 1.05 & 0 & 2.05 & 2.05 & 0.05 \\ 1.05 & 2.05 & 0 & 1.05 & 1.05 \\ 0.05 & 1.05 & 0.05 & 0 & 4.05 \\ 3.05 & 0.05 & 2.05 & 0.05 & 0 \end{pmatrix}$$

$P(t)$ $\qquad$ $EHM_{(A)}{}^t$

Fig. 1. Examples of symmetrical and asymmetric edge histogram matrices for $N = 5$

3.3. *Sampling Methods*

In this subsection, we describe how to sample a new string from the edge histogram matrix $EHM_{(A)}{}^t$. As for $EHM_{(A)}{}^t$ in Ref. 21, there are two types of sampling methods; one is an edge-histogram based sampling algorithm without template (EHBSA/WO), and the other an edge-histogram based sampling algorithm with template (EHBSA/WT).

3.3.1. *EHBSA/WO*

In a symmetrical EHM such as used in the symmetrical TSP, the absolute positions (loci) of a string have no meaning. For example, string $s_1 = (0, 1, 2, 3, 4)$ and string $s_2 = (4, 0, 1, 2, 3)$ represent the same tour. However, in a asymmetrical EHM such as for scheduling problems, these two strings represent two completely different solutions. Thus, we must consider how to determine the initial position and what node we assign to the position. Here, we propose two types of EHBSA/WO, EHBSA/WO/T and EHBSA/WO/R.[23]

EHBSA/WO/T:

Let us represent a new individual permutation by $c[]$. In EHBSA/WO/T, the initial sampling position is always the first position, i.e. $c[0]$. The value for $c[0]$ is taken from a *pseudo template individual* $PT[]$ which is taken from the current population $P(t)$ randomly, and a new individual permutation $c[]$ is generated straightforwardly as follows:

1. Set the position counter $p \leftarrow 0$
2. Choose a pseudo template $PT[]$ from $P(t)$
3. Obtain the first node as $c[0] \leftarrow PT[0]$
4. Construct a roulette wheel vector $rw[]$ from $EHM_{(A)}{}^t$ as $rw[j] = e^t{}_{c[p],j}$ (j=0, 1, .., L–1)
5. Set to 0 previously sampled nodes in rw ($rw[\ c[i]\ ] = 0$ for i =0, 1, .., p)
6. Sample the next node $c[p+1]$ with probability $rw[x]\big/\sum_{j=0}^{L-1} rw[j]$ using roulette wheel $rw[]$
7. Update the position counter $p \leftarrow p+1$
8. If $p<L-1$, go to Step 4
9. Obtain a new individual string $c[]$

EHBSA/WO/R:

In EHBSA/WO/T, the initial sampling position is fixed to 0. On the other hand, in EHBSA/WO/R, the initial sampling position is chosen from [0, L–1] randomly as follows:

1. Obtain random initial sampling position p_{initial} from [0, L–1]
2. Choose a pseudo template $PT[]$ from $P(t)$
3. Obtain the first node as $c[p_{\text{initial}}] \leftarrow PT[p_{\text{initial}}]$
4. Set the position counter $p \leftarrow p_{\text{initial}}$
5. Construct a roulette wheel vector $rw[]$ from $EHM_{(A)}{}^t$ as $rw[j] = e^t{}_{c[p],j}$ (j=0, 1, .., L–1)
6. Set to 0 previously sampled nodes in rw ($rw[\ c[i]\ ] = 0$ for $i = p_{\text{initial}}$, $(p_{\text{initial}} + 1) \bmod L$, ..., p)

7. Sample the next node $c[(p+1) \bmod L]$ with probability $rw[x]/\sum_{j=0}^{L-1} rw[j]$ using roulette wheel $rw[]$
8. Update the position counter $p \leftarrow (p+1) \bmod L$
9. If $(p+1) \bmod L \neq p_{\text{initial}}$, go to Step 5
10. Obtain a new individual string $c[]$

Here, note both EHBSA/WO/T and WO/R are the same for problems which have a symmetrical EHM.

3.3.2. *EHBSA/WT*

$EHM_{(A)}{}^t$ described in Section 2.2 is in a marginal edge histogram. It has no graphical structure. EHBSA/WT is intended to make up for this disadvantage by using a template in sampling a new string, and is the same as EHBSA/WT proposed for $EHM_{(S)}{}^t$ in Ref. 21. In generating each new individual, a *template individual* is chosen from $P(t)$ (normally, randomly). The n (n>1) cut points are applied to the template randomly. When n cut points are obtained for the template, the template should be divided into n segments. Then, we choose one segment randomly and sample nodes for the segment. Nodes in other n–1 segments remain unchanged. We denote this sampling method by EHBSA/WT/n. Since average length of one segment is L/n, EHBSA/WT/n generates new strings that are different L/n nodes on average from their templates. Fig. 2 shows an example of EHBSA/WT/3. In this example, nodes of new string from after cut[2] and before cut[1] are the same as the nodes of the template. New nodes are sampled from cut[1] up to, but not including, cut[2] based on the $EHM_{(A)}{}^t$.

The sampling method for EHBSA/WT/n is as follows:

1. Choose a template $T[]$ from $P(t)$.
2. Obtain sorted cut point array cut[0], cut[1], .., cut[n–1] randomly.
3. Choose a cut point cut[l] by generating random number $l \in [0, n-1]$.
4. Copy nodes in $T[]$ to $c[]$ from after cut[(l+1) mod n] and before cut[l].
5. Set the position counter $p \leftarrow$ cut[l]–1.

6. Construct a roulette wheel vector $rw[]$ from $EHM_{(A)}{}^t$ as $rw[j] = e^t_{c[p],j}$ (j=0, 1, .., L−1).
7. Set to 0 copied and previously sampled nodes in $rw[]$ ($rw[\ c[i]\ ] = 0$ for i =cut[(l+1) mod n], .., p) .
8. Sample next node $c[(p+1) \bmod L]$ with probability $rw[x] / \sum_{j=0}^{L-1} rw[j]$ using roulette wheel $rw[]$.
9. Update the position counter $p \leftarrow (p+1) \bmod L$.
10. If $(p+1)$ *mod* L = cut[(l+1) mod n], go to Step 6.
11. Obtain a new individual string $c[]$.

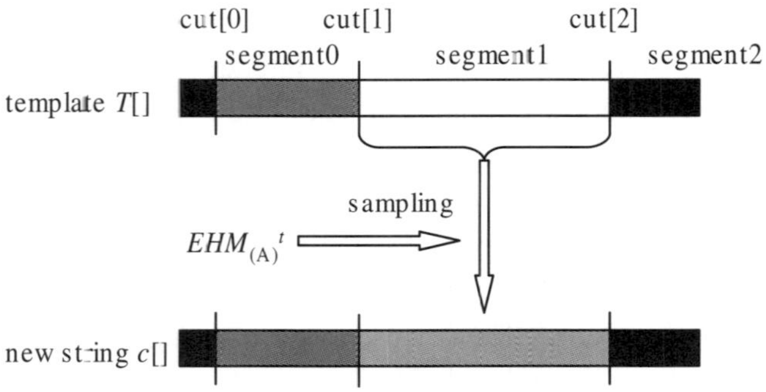

Fig. 2. An example of EHBSA/WT/3

Let $f(x)$ be the probability density function of the length of a segment to be sampled in EHBSA/WT/n. Then, $f(x)$ is obtained as[22]

$$f(x) = \frac{(n-1)}{L}\left(1-\frac{x}{L}\right)^{n-2}. \tag{4}$$

Fig. 3 shows the probability density function $f(x)$. For n = 2, $f(x)$ is uniformly distributed on [0, L]. Thus, the length of a segment to be sampled in EHBSA/WT/2 is uniformly distributed on [0, L]. When the length of the segment is small, the EHBSA/WT/2 samples a small number of nodes, performing a kind of local search improvement over the template individual. On the other hand, when the length is large, the EHBSA/WT/2 samples a large number of nodes, performing a kind of global search improvement over the template individual or produces a new string. Thus, we can expect the EHBSA/WT/2 to work by balancing global and local improvements. For $n > 2$, short segments are more likely to occur.

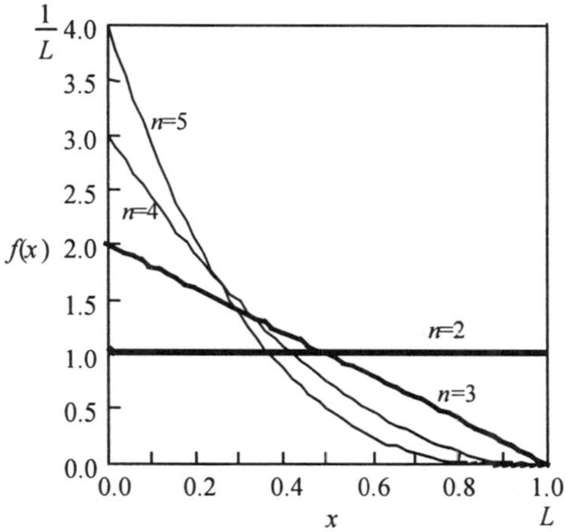

Fig. 3. Probability density function $f(x)$

4. Empirical Study

This section applies EHBSA/WO and EHBSA/WT to the flow shop scheduling problem, which is one of the most popular scheduling problems.

4.1. *Experimental Methodology*

4.1.1. *Evolutionary Models*

The evolutionary model is the same as the model used for symmetrical $EHM_{(S)}{}^t$ in Ref. 21 as follows:

The Evolutionary Model for EHBSA/WT:

Let the population size be N, and let it, at time t, be represented by $P(t)$. The population $P(t+1)$ is produced as follows (Fig. 4):

1. Edge distribution matrix $EHM_{(A)}{}^{t}$ described in Subsection 3.2 is developed from $P(t)$.
2. A template individual $T[]$ is selected from $P(t)$ randomly.
3. EHBSA/WT described in Subsection 2.3.2 is performed using $EHM_{(A)}{}^{t}$ and $T[]$, and generate a new individual $c[]$.
4. The new $c[]$ individual is evaluated.
5. If $c[]$ is better than $T[]$, then $T[]$ is replaced with $c[]$, otherwise $T[]$ remains, forming $P(t+1)$.

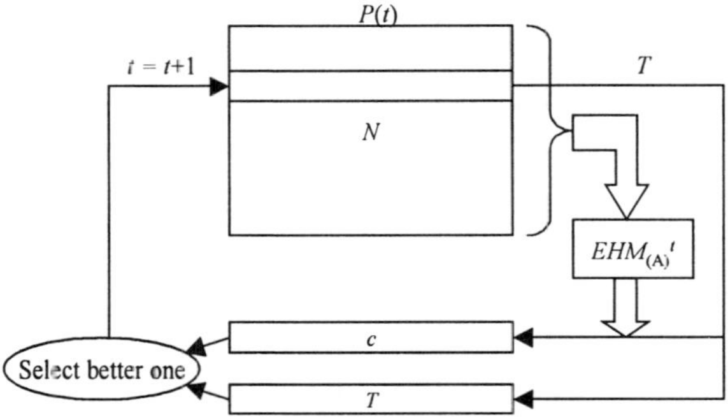

Fig. 4. Evolutionary model for EHBSA/WT

The Evolutionary Model for EHBSA/WO/T and EHBSA/WO/R:

The evolutionary model for EHBSA/WO is basically the same as the model for EHBSA/WT except EHBSA/WO uses a pseudo template $PT[]$.

The Evolutionary Model for Two-parent Recombination Operators:

To compare the performance of proposed methods with the performance of traditional two-parent recombination operators, we designed an evolutionary model for two-parent recombination operators. For fair comparison, we design it as similar as possible to that of the EHBSA. We generate only one child from two parents. Using one child from two parents is already proposed for designing the GENITOR algorithm by Whitley et al.[25] In our generational model, two parents are selected from $P(t)$ randomly. No bias is used in this selection. Then we apply a recombination operator to produce one child. This child is compared with its parents. If the child is better than the worst parent, then the parent is replaced with the child.

4.1.2. *Flow Shop Scheduling Problems and Performance Measures*

General assumptions of flow shop scheduling problems can be described as follows: Jobs are to be processed on multiple machines sequentially. There is one machine at each stage. Machines are available continuously. A job is processed on one machine at a time without preemption, and a machine processes no more than one job at a time. In this chapter, we assume that L jobs are processed in the same order on m machines. This means that our flow shop scheduling problem is the L-job and m-machine sequence problem. The purpose of this problem is to determine the sequence of L jobs. This sequence is denoted by a permutation string of $\{0, 1, ..., L-1\}$. The problem is to find a permutation which minimizes the *makespan* (i.e., the completion time of all jobs).

As test problems, we generated two flow shop scheduling problems, 20-job and 10-machine, and 30-job and 10-machine problems. In designing each problem, we specified the processing time of each job at each machine as a random integer in the interval [1, 99].

We compared EHBSA with popular order-based two-parent recombination operators, namely, the original order crossover OX,[24] the enhanced edge recombination operator eER,[17] and the partially mapped crossover.[7] 20 runs were performed. Each run continued until the population has converged, or evaluations reached E_{max}. Values of Emax were 300,000. The performance is measured by the minimum makespan (*best*), mean of the minimum makespan (*mean*) in 20 runs and standard deviation of the minimum makespan (*std*). Population sizes of 50, 100, 200 were used for EHBSA, and 50, 100, 200, 400, 800, and 1600 for other operators, respectively. As to the bias ratio B_{ratio} in Eq. 3, a B_{ratio} value of 0.02 was used.

4.1.3. *Blind Search*

In solving scheduling problems using GAs, mutation operators play an important role. Several types of mutation operators were proposed. Also, it is well known that combining GAs with local optimization methods or heuristics greatly improve the performance of the algorithms. However, in this experiment, we use no mutation and no heuristic in order to see the pure effect of applying the proposed algorithms. Thus, the algorithm is a *blind search*.

4.2. *Empirical Analysis of Results*

Results on the 20-job and 10-machine problem are shown in Table 1. EHBSA/WO/T and EHBSA/WO/R showed obviously poorer performance compared with EHBSA/WT and other two-parent recombination operators. Comparing EHBSA/WO/T and EHBSA/WO/R, we can see that the EHBSA/WO/R is better than EHBSA/WO/T. As was found in Refs 21 and 22 with TSP, EHBSA/WT shows much better performance than EHBSA/WO. In EHBSA/WT/2 with $N = 50$, the *mean* scored 1521.4, the best value in the experiment. In the other operators, PMX showed good performance. The *mean* of PMX with $N = 1600$ was 1522.5. OX also showed relatively good performance showing *mean* = 1523.4 with $N = 1600$. eER which showed good performance in TSP[21] showed poor performance in this problem. Comparing the performance of EHBSA/WT with other operators, EHBSA/WT is almost the same as PMX and OX. One big difference between EHBSA/WT and PMX/OX is that EHBSA/WT requires a smaller population size to work than PMX/OX.

Results on the 30-job and 10-machine problem are shown in Table 2. Again, the performance of EHBSA/WT is much better than EHBSA/WO. Comparing the performance of EHBSA/WT with other operators, EHBSA/WT is almost the same as PMX and OX, again showing that EHBSA/WT requires a smaller population size to work than PMX/OX.

From the results described above, we can see that EHBSA/WT works fairly well in flow shop scheduling problems used in this chapter. It has almost the same performance with popular traditional two-parent recombination operators, OX and PMX, and has much better performance than eER. One interesting feature of EHBSA/WT is that it requires smaller population size than traditional two parent recombination operators. This may be an important property of

EHBSA/WT. In our experiments, we used a blind search. When we combine EHBSA/WT/*n* with some heuristics, it would work well with a smaller population size.

Table 1. Results on 20-job and 10-machine problem

EHBSA	Performance Mesure	Population Size					
		50	100	200	400	800	1600
EHBSA/WO/T	best	1540	1538	1550			
	mean	**1563.4**	**1563.3**	**1571.0**			
	std	11.8	14.2	11.2			
EHBSA/WO/R	best	1523	1519	1539			
	mean	**1538.8**	**1536.1**	**1552.1**			
	std	6.6	8.1	8.3			
EHBSA/WT/2	best	1519	1519	1522			
	mean	**1521.4**	**1523.7**	**1530.6**			
	std	2.5	5.3	3.8			
EHBSA/WT/3	best	1519	1520	1524			
	mean	**1524.4**	**1524.3**	**1528.6**			
	std	2.8	4.4	2.6			
EHBSA/WT/4	best	1520	1920	1520			
	mean	**1525.7**	**1526.0**	**1529.8**			
	std	3.7	5.1	5.6			
OX	best	1533	1523	1520	1520	1518	1517
	mean	**1566.1**	**1549.5**	**1537.1**	**1529.1**	**1524.6**	**1523.4**
	std	16.2	12.9	9.6	7.0	3.8	3.6
eER	best	1567	1550	1576	1553	1584	1595
	mean	**1593.9**	**1584.2**	**1588.8**	**1598.0**	**1606.3**	**1613.1**
	std	11.6	15.6	7.9	13.1	11.6	9.0
PMX	best	1542	1523	1523	1521	1519	1518
	mean	**1562.8**	**1546.6**	**1534.9**	**1529.0**	**1525.7**	**1522.5**
	std	12.9	8.6	7.3	5.1	4.3	2.0

5. The Effect of Applying the Tag Node

In this section, we explore the effect of introducing the *tag node (TN)* in a string representation aiming to improve the performance of EHBSAs. In a scheduling problem where a solution is represented by a permutation string, the performance of each string is tightly linked not only to the relative sequence of nodes (jobs) but also to the absolute position of nodes in the string. Since EHM, described in Section 2, has no explicit information on the absolute positions of nodes in each string, it may be useful to introduce additional information on the absolute position of each node in a string.

The tag node (TN) proposed in this section is an approach to introduce information on the absolute position of each node in a string. In addition to normal nodes, we add a TN to each permutation string. We

Table 2. Results on 30-job and 10-machine problem

EHBSA	Performance Mesure	Population Size					
		50	100	200	400	800	1600
EHBSA/WO/T	best	2161	2173	2177			
	mean	**2193.8**	**2204.1**	**2211.7**			
	std	20.2	10.7	17.5			
EHBSA/WO/R	best	2116	2158	2193			
	mean	**2157.1**	**2182.3**	**2206.0**			
	std	21.8	13.1	9.2			
EHBSA/WT/2	best	2086	2100	2106			
	mean	**2105.4**	**2112.2**	**2120.3**			
	std	8.4	5.7	7.8			
EHBSA/WT/3	best	2087	2098	2107			
	mean	**2106.8**	**2111.0**	**2117.9**			
	std	8.9	5.4	3.9			
EHBSA/WT/4	best	2097	2099	2092			
	mean	**2107.8**	**2110.5**	**2116.3**			
	std	6.8	7.2	7.5			
OX	best	2133	2117	2107	2100	2087	2132
	mean	**2154.5**	**2137.0**	**2124.3**	**2115.4**	**2107.2**	**2141.5**
	std	13.2	11.1	10.0	6.4	10.0	6.1
eER	best	2191	2172	2208	2219	2214	2229
	mean	**2220.1**	**2211.1**	**2226.0**	**2231.9**	**2244.0**	**2253.0**
	std	19.2	19.4	13.2	9.2	12.3	13.9
PMX	best	2117	2100	2087	2087	2087	2096
	mean	**2137.3**	**2122.8**	**2111.1**	**2105.3**	**2094.7**	**2114.3**
	std	14.3	10.2	9.1	10.9	10.3	6.5

call a string with a TN a *virtual string* (VS). String length of a VS is $L_{VS} = L+1$, where L is the length of real string (RS; string without TN). The TN in VS works as a tag in a permutation string to indicate the first node (job), i.e., the next node following the TN is assumed to be the first node (job) in the solution. The TN is a *virtual node* because it does not correspond to any real nodes, or jobs.

Fig. 5 shows how to obtain RS from VS. In this case, $L = 6$. We can use any symbol to represent the TN in a VS. However, for implementation convenience, we use an integer number to represent it in a VS. Let us consider the string in Fig. 5, for example. In this example, string length $L = 6$ and the length of VS $L_{VS} = 7$. Nodes 0, 1, ..., 5 represent real nodes. Then, we assign number 6 to the TN (see Fig. 6). Thus, a VS of length $L+1$ is represented as a permutation $\{0, 1, \ldots, L-1, L\}$ corresponding the numbers 0, 1, ..., $L-1$ to real nodes and number L to the TN. With this representation, we do not need any special modification in basic EHBSAs.

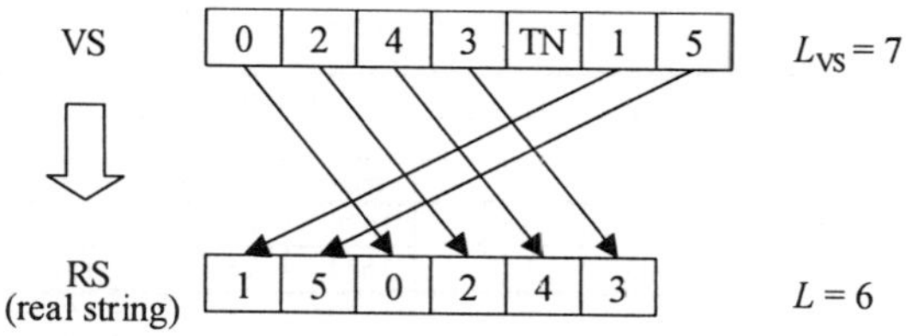

Fig. 5. An example of a VS

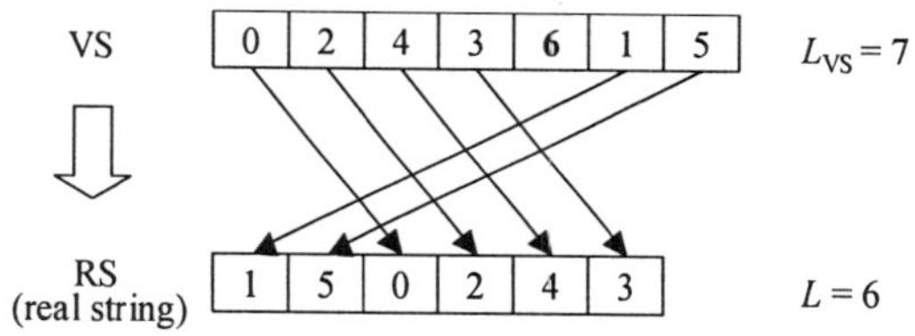

Fig. 6. Representation of the TN in a VS

The effect of applying the TN was tested using the 20-job and 10-machine problem in Section 3. The experimental settings are the same as those in Section 3. Table 3 shows results without and with the TN at evaluations = 200,000. The important observation is that in all experiments with EHBSA/WT, except for EHBSA/WT/2 with population size = 50, values of the *mean* with TN were better than those without TN, although the difference is not so remarkable. On average, the value of the *mean* with TN is smaller than those without TN by 0.21%. To see the statistical difference of mean values between the models with and without the TN, t values are presented in the table. Since we did 20 runs for each experiment, the value of $df = 39$. When we use the t-test with the value of 0.05 for the level of significance, t values over 1.6849 satisfy the test.

Tables 3 shows only results at evaluations = 200,000. Fig. 7 shows the convergence process of EHBSA/WT/3 with population size = 50 between evaluations = [0, 300,000]. From this figure, we can see that values of mean with TN converge faster than those without TN, taking significantly smaller values.

Table 3. The effect of applying the TN

EHBSA	TN	Population Size								
		50			100			200		
		mean	std	*t*	mean	std	*t*	mean	std	*t*
EHBSA/WT/2	without	1523.2	3.3	-0.3591	1526.8	3.7	4.4776	1534.0	2.8	7.3937
	with	1523.6	3.6		1522.0	2.8		1526.5	3.4	
EHBSA/WT/3	without	1526.5	3.6	4.6501	1526.9	3.9	2.9068	1531.6	3.5	4.1187
	with	1521.8	2.6		1523.9	2.4		1527.1	3.3	
EHBSA/WT/4	without	1528.5	3.7	3.7890	1528.4	4.9	0.3764	1532.7	5.6	1.7704
	with	1523.8	3.9		1527.9	4.0		1529.9	4.2	

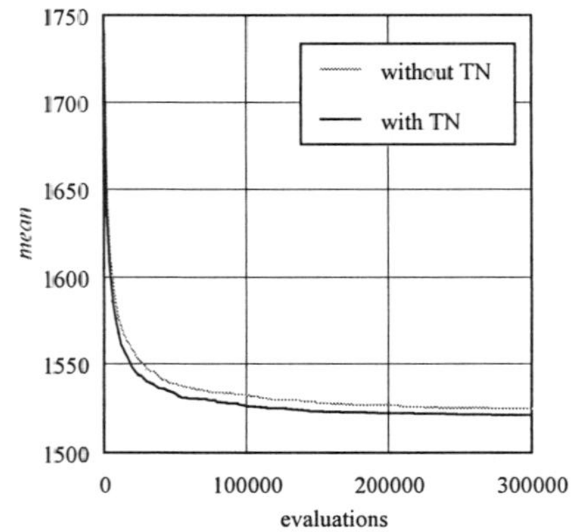

Fig. 7. Convergence process of EHBSA/WT/3 with and without TN

Since EHM has no explicit information on the absolute position of each node, the TN in EHBSA works as a tag that indicates the initial position in a string. Thus, as we intended, it improves the performance of a problem where in addition to the relative position of each node, the absolute position of each node effects the performance.

Here, we must note that without using the TN, EHBSA can somehow maintain information about absolute position of each node in a string of the population. That is because, for example in EHBSA/WT, nodes in a new string that are not sampled inherit the same absolute positions from its template string. Introducing the TN helps the managing of information on absolute position more and increases the performance.

Finally, since the TN is treated as just a normal node in algorithms, there is no special processing necessary in introducing the TN. The difference of computational complexity with and without TN is influenced only by the string length; without TN the length is L, and with TN the length is $L+1$.

6. Conclusions

In this chapter, we extended the EHBSAs to solving a flow shop scheduling problem, a typical, well known problem in the area of scheduling. In the flow shop scheduling problem, the edge histogram matrix becomes asymmetrical. This is a big difference from previous studies on EHBSAs. The results showed that EHBSA/WT also worked well on the flow shop scheduling problems and performed significantly better than EHBSA/WO. Comparing the performance of EHBSA/WT with some other popular two-parent recombination operators for permutations, EHBSA/WT is almost the same as PMX and OX. One big advantage of EHBSA is the use of significantly smaller population sizes than those that are necessary with PMX and OX as was observed in the previous studies. Although we used a blind search in this study, if we combine EHBSA/WT with some heuristics, it would work well with a smaller population size. Thus, we can confirm that the EHBSA also works well on flow shop scheduling problems. We also confirmed that applying the tag node (TN) in a string representation enhances the performance of the EHBSAs.

Despite the promising results, the chapter should be understood as one of the first steps toward scalable solution of scheduling problems with PMBGAs, because there are many opportunities for further research related to the proposed algorithms. The effect of parameter values of B_{ratio}, number of cut points of the template n, and size of population N, on the performance of the algorithm must be further investigated. We experimented with EHBSAs using a blind search to test the pure mixing capability of the proposed algorithms. But we must still test the algorithms with appropriate heuristics in problems with large numbers of nodes.

Acknowledgments

The authors gratefully acknowledge Prof. Martin Pelikan for his valuable comments on this work. This research is partially supported by the Ministry of Education, Culture, Sports, Science and Technology of Japan under Grant-in-Aid for Scientific Research number 13680469, and a grant to RCAST at Doshisha University from the Ministry of Education, Culture, Sports, Science and Technology of Japan.

References

1. S. Baluja, Population-based incremental learning, A method for interacting genetic search based function optimization and coemptive learning, *Tech. Rep. No. CMU-CS-94-163*, Carnegie Mellon University (1994).
2. S. Baluja and Davies, Using optimum dependency-trees for combinatorial optimization, learning the structure of the search space, *Tech. Rep. No. CMU-CS-97-107*, Carnegie Mellon University (1997)
3. P. Bosman and D. Thierens, An algorithmic framework for density estimation based evolutionary algorithms, *Tech. Rep. No. UU-CS-1999-46*, Utrecht University (1999).
4. P. Bosman and D. Thierens, Continuous iterated density estimation evolutionary algorithms within the IDEA framework, *Proc. of the Optimization by Building and Using Probabilistic Models OBUPM Workshop at the Genetic and Evolutionary Computation Conference GECCO-2000*, pp.197-200 (2000).
5. P. Bosman and D. Thierens, Mixed IDEAs, Tech. *Rep. No. UU-CS-2000-45*, Utrecht University (2000).
6. J. S. De Bonet, C. L. Isbell and P. Viola, MIMIC: Finding optima by estimating probability densities, In M. C. Mozer, M. I. Jordan and T. Petsche (Eds), *Advances in neural information processing systems*, Vol. 9, pp. 424-431 (1997).
7. D. E. Goldberg, *Genetic algorithms in search, optimization and machine learning*, Addison-Wesley publishing company (1989).
8. G. Harik, F. G. Lobo, and D. E. Goldberg, The compact genetic algorithm, *Proc. of the Int. Conf. Evolutionary Computation 1998 (ICEC 98)*, pp. 523-528 (1998).
9. G. Harik, Linkage learning via probabilistic modeling in the ECGA, *Tech. Rep. IlliGAL Report 99010*, University of Illinois at Urbana-Champaign (1999).
10. P. Larranaga, R. Etxeberria, J.A. Lozano and J.M. Pena, Optimization by learning and simulation of Bayesian and gaussian networks, *Tech. Rep. EHU-KZAAIK-4/99*, University of the Basque Country (1999).
11. H. Muehlenbein and G. Paass, From recombination of genes to the estimation of distribution I. Binary parameters, *Proc. of the Parallel Problem Solving from Nature (PPSN IV)*, pp. 178-187 (1996).
12. M. Pelikan, D. E. Goldberg and E. Cantu-Paz, BOA: The Bayesian optimization algorithm, *Proc. of the Genetic and Evolutionary Computation Conference 1999 (GECCO-99)*, Morgan Kaufmann, San Francisco, CA (1999).

13. M. Pelikan, D. E. Goldberg and F. G. Lobo, A survey of optimization by building and using probabilistic models, *Tech. Rep. IlliGAL Report 99018*, University of Illinois at Urbana-Champaign (1999).
14. M. Pelikan, D.E. Goldberg and E. Cantu-Paz, Linkage problems, distribution estimate, and Bayesian network, *Evolutionary Computation*, Vol. 8, No. 3, pp. 311-340 (2000).
15. M. Sebag and A. Ducoulombier, Extending population-based incremental learning to continuous search spaces, *Proc. of the Parallel Problem Solving from Nature (PPSN V)*, pp. 418-427 (1998).
16. I. L. Servet, L. Trave-Massuyes and D. Stern, Telephone network traffic overloading diagnosis and evolutionary computation techniques, *Proc. of the 3rd European Conf. on Artificial Evolution (AE 97)*, pp. 137-144 (1997).
17. T. Starkweather, S. McDaniel, K. Mathias, D. Whitley and C. Whitley, A comparison of genetic sequence operators, *Proc. of the 4th Int. Conf. on Genetic Algorithms*, Morgan Kaufmann, pp. 69-76 (1991).
18. V. Robles, P. D. Miguel and P. Larranaga, Solving the traveling salesman problem with EDAs, *Estimation of Distribution Algorithms*, P. Larranaga and J. A. Lozano (eds), Kluwer Academic Publishers, Chapter 10, pp. 211-229 (2002).
19. P. Larranaga and J. A. Lozano (eds), *Estimation of distribution algorithms*, Kluwer Academic Publishers (2002).
20. S. Tsutsui, M. Pelikan and D. E. Goldberg, Evolutionary Algorithm using Marginal Histogram Models in Continuous Domain. *Workshop Proc. of the 2001 Genetic and Evolutionary Computation Conf.*, pp. 230-233 (2001).
21. S. Tsutsui, Probabilistic Model-Building Genetic Algorithms in Permutation Representation Domain Using Edge Histogram, *Proc. of the 7th Int. Conf. on Parallel Problem Solving from Nature (PPSN VII)*, pp. 224-233, Springer-Velag, Granada (2002).
22. S. Tsutsui, M. Pelikan and D. E Goldberg, Using Edge Histogram Models to Solve Permutation Problems with Probabilistic Model-Building Genetic Algorithms, *Tech. Rep. IlliGAL Report No. 2003022*, University of Illinois (2003).
23. S. Tsutsui and M. Miki, Solving Flow Shop Scheduling Problems with Probabilistic Model-Building Genetic Algorithms using Edge Histograms, *Proc. of the 4th Asia-Pacific Conf. on Simulated Evolution And Learning (SEAL02)*, Singapore (2002).
24. I. Oliver, D. Smith and J. Holland, A study of permutation crossover operators on the travel salesman problem, *Proc. of the 2nd Int. Conf. on Genetic Algorithms*, pp. 224-230 (1987).
25. D. Whitley, The GENITOR algorithm and selective pressure, Why rank-based allocation of reproductive trials is best, *Proc. of the 3rd Int. Conf. on Genetic Algorithms*, Morgan Kaufmann, pp. 116-121 (1989).
26. D. Whitley, T. Starkweather and D. Fuquay, Scheduling problems and traveling salesman problem, The genetic edge recombination operator. *Proc. of the 3rd Int. Conf. on Genetic Algorithms*, Morgan Kaufmann.

CHAPTER 14

COLLECTIVE MOVEMENTS OF MOBILE ROBOTS WITH BEHAVIOR MODELS OF A FISH

Tatsuro Shinchi, Tetsuro Kitazoe, Masayoshi Tabuse, Hisao Ide
and Takahiro Horita

Division of Information Science and Multimedia,
Center for Educational Research and Practice
Faculty of Education and Culture, Miyazaki University
Gakuen Kibanadai Nishi 1-1, Miyazaki-city, 889–2192
E-mail: shin@edc.miyazaki-u.ac.jp

This chapter presents a simulation model of multiple autonomous mobile robots with behavior models of a fish school. Although a school of fish does not need a special individual to lead it, an autonomous movement emerges from interactions among neighboring bodies. This study aims to realize autonomous collective movements of mobile robots through interactions among robots like a fish school.We used Khepera robots to simulate mobile cars running on a freeway. Autonomous behavior is assumed for the robots to run freely by sensing neighboring robots or the guard rails by means of infrared rays. An evaluation function was applied to free style running robots to run forward efficiently without colliding with other robots or guard rails. Genetic algorithms(GA) were applied to optimize the behavior models of a robot. As a result, we have obtained a nice collective movement of multirobots, with high techniques, such as speeding up, slowing down, and overtaking a slow robot ahead.

1. Introduction

Many experiments with driverless robots have been carried out in attempts to develop safe and effective transportation. It will be our dream of having a truly autonomous robot which has its own way of driving and can choose its own speed. In researches about intelligent transportation systems (ITS), some have succeeded in realizing a collective movement of vehicles. However, those movements are very rigid; vehicles run by keeping a set distance from the robot ahead, or by following markers embedded on the road. Individuals simply run in a file. [1,2,3,4]

In this chapter, we use a fish school algorithm to get the basic movement style for an autonomous robot. [5] Fish display beautifully smooth movements in a school without making any collision at all. It is well known that each fish determines its motion by getting information from neighboring fish only, without knowledge of the whole school. Since the fish school algorithm is well known[6,7], we adapt behavior models of a fish to the specifications of Khepera. We introduce GA to train the robots to achieve smooth movements without any accidents. We used Khepera robots simulations [8], where a robot emits infrared rays and receives reflected signals from other neighboring robots or guard rails at sides of a road. As a result of the optimization of behavior models through GA, we eventually obtained a beautiful collective movement of robots along a road with no accidents, even when the road was narrow or it had curves. We often observed a robot that had good driving skills, overtaking another robot by adjusting its velocity and direction.

2. Fish School Algorithm

2.1. *Fish School*

It is well known that a lot of creatures show a collective movement in nature, such as flocks of pigeons, herds of cattle, and schools of fish. What has to be noticed is that functions of an individual in the group are not always perfect to survive, but the whole consisting of many individuals often shows a highly intelligent movement.

A fish school is one of the most familiar collective movements and fascinates us with its beauty. There are well over 22000 living species of fishes, including nearly all those of importance in commercial fisheries and aquaculture. It is estimated that 10000 species collect in schools. In a fish school, hundreds of fish glide in union like more a single organism than a collection of individuals. It is said that a fish school offers considerable advantages to survive in its sever environment. While a school is easily found by predators or fishermen, it contributes to the adaptability to the changes of its surroundings. For instance, a school reduces the risk that an individual is eaten once the school has been detected. A fish school behaves as if it has something gifted intelligent, though an intellectual level of an individual is not so high. Synchronized speed and response of individuals in a school are not controlled by a special system. Actually, a fish school does not need the special fish to lead the whole, but a fish school movement emerges solely from interactions among neighboring fish. [9,10,11,12,13]

2.2. *Behavior Models of a Fish*

Fish behavior has been observed to understand the features of a school, such as self-organization, emergence of autonomy. It has been cleared that a fish perceives surroundings with both its eyes and its lateral lines. A visual angle of eyes is often larger than 300° and lateral lines detect water currents, vibrations, and pressure changes. Operation of both eyes and lateral lines can be a clue to determine the character of a fish school, because mechanisms inherent in a school govern interactions with its social and physical environment.

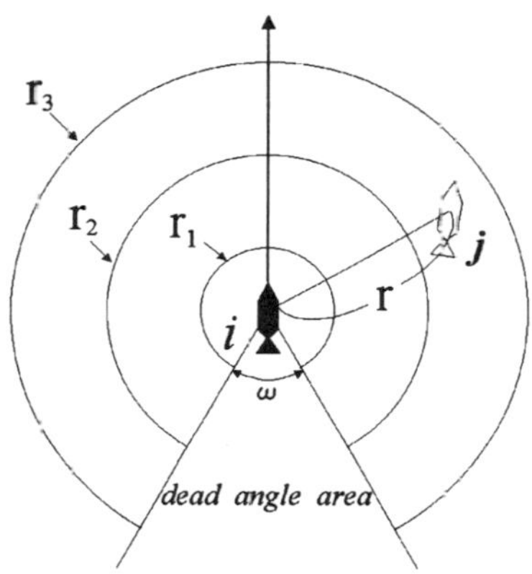

Fig. 1. Ranges of the basic behavior patterns. An action of the black fish(i) at next simulation step is determined by the distance r between the black fish (i) and the white fish(j) as follows, $r < r_1$:*repulsion*, $r_1 \leq r < r_2$:*parallel orientation*, $r_2 \leq r < r_3$:*attraction*, $r \geq r_3$ or dead angle area:*searching*.

Herein we consider a fish school as the decentralized system, which does not need the special fish to lead the whole but only interactions among neighboring fish. Behavior models on the basis of mutual relation between fish have been proposed[7,14,15,16]. I.Aoki suggested the behavior models for a fish, which produce an autonomous school movement [6,7]. Figure 1 shows the geometrical drawing to illustrate parameters specifying interactions in Aoki's models. There are four styles of behavior, *repulsion, parallel orientation, attraction* and *searching*, according to the distance to the area where the perceived neighboring fish is positioned. Each behavior determines the direction of a fish at every simulation step. An action of the fish(i) at next simulation step is determined by the distance r between the fish (i) and the perceived fish(j) as follows,

i) $r < r_1$ (*repulsion*):
If the perceived neighbor fish(j) is too close, the fish(i) tries to avoid a collision.

ii) $r_1 \leq r < r_2$ (*parallel orientation*):
If the perceived neighbor fish(j) is in a certain parallel orientation area, the fish(i) swims in the same direction as fish(j).

iii) $r_2 \leq r < r_3$ (*attraction*):
If the perceived neighbor fish(j) is too far away, the fish(i) approaches to the fish(i).

iv) $r \geq r_3$ or dead angle area(*searching*):
If the perceived fish (i) cannot perceive any neighbor, it begins to search for other fish by turning around by chance.

2.3. *Fish School Simulations*

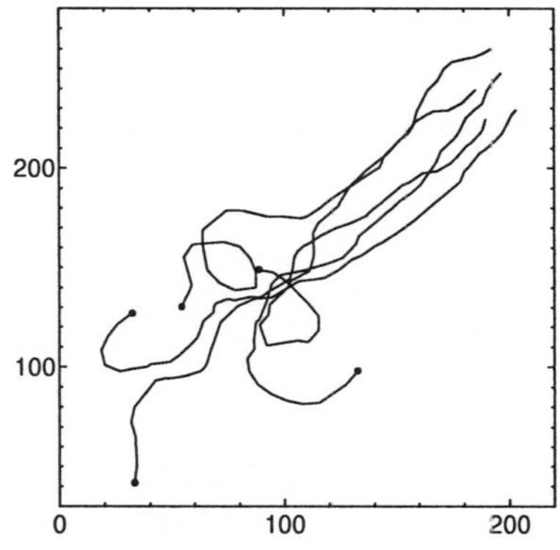

Fig. 2. Self-organization and polarization of a fish school(N=5), $t = 0 \sim 50$. Even if positions and orientations of fish are set randomly at the initial time in simulations, they are gradually self-organized into a fish school.

The simulated fish school movements by Aoki's models emerged through interactions. The fish(i) takes the new direction $\alpha_i(t+\Delta t)$ from $\alpha_i(t)$ with turning angle $\beta_i(t)$ as follows,

$$\alpha_i(t + \Delta t) = \alpha_i(t) + \gamma_{ij}\beta_i(t) + \sqrt{2}\beta_0, \tag{1}$$

where $\beta_i(t)$ is the turning angles suitable for the action i) $\sim$ vi), the term of $\sqrt{2}\beta_0$ is a fluctuation in determining a new direction, β_0 follows a Gamma distribution N(0,1). γ_{ij} is the constant which adjusts the degree of interactions. Figure 2 shows the initial 50 simulation steps of five individuals. Where $r_1, r_2, r_3, \gamma_{ij}, \beta_0$ are $0.5BL$, $2.0BL, 5.0BL$(BL: Body Length of a fish), 0.3, 0.0, respectively. In Figure 2, even if positions and orientations of fish are set randomly at the initial time in simulations, they are gradually self-organized into a fish school.

2.4. *Comparison Between Real School Movement and Simulated School Movements*

In this chapter, we apply the behavior models of a fish to the autonomous behavior of robots. Then, it is important to examine the validity of the behavior models of a fish. We have compared the complexity of movements between a real school and a simulated school. The real fish school movements were obtained as the video-recorded pictures of sardines school as shown Figure 3. The video-recorded pictures were taken at National Research Institute of Aquaculture in Mie prefecture, Japan in October, 1990. The water tank is 5.0[m] long, 6.0[m] width, where the school is composed of about 100 *sardines*. The water tank was set 0.75[m] deep to examine fish behaviors in the two dimensional space. Mean body length of *sardines* is 19.4[cm].

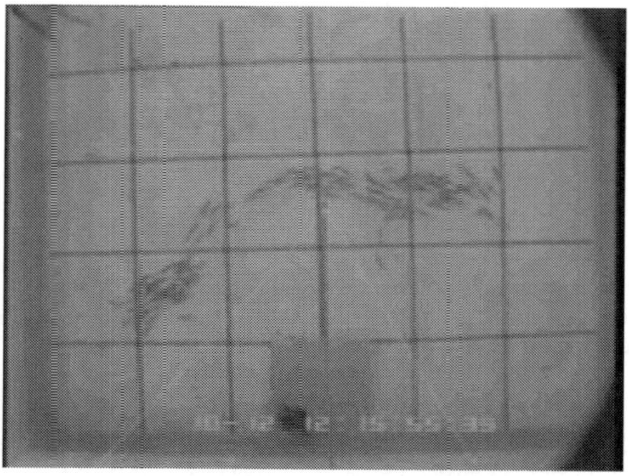

Fig. 3. One shot of *sardines* school movements captured from the video-recorded pictures. Straight lines are marked every each 1m for length and breadth of a floor of the tank. About 100 sardines are found in the middle of the tank.

Fractal analyses allow us to compare the character between the real fish school movement and the simulated movement with Aoki's models. We apply fractal geometry to understand features of complex behavior. It is needed to measure the length $< L(k) >$ of the trail pattern of a fish. When we compute $< L(k) >$ with time-series of position coordinates, a time-series $P(k)$ is defined as

$$P(k); P(m), P(m+k), P(m+2k), \ldots, P(m+[\frac{N-m}{k}]\cdot k)$$
$$(\text{m}=0,1,2,\ \ldots\ ,k\text{-}1),$$

where m indicates an initial time and k indicates an interval time. [ ] denotes the Gauss's notation. An initial time m is set as all integers in the range of $0 \sim k-1$ to obtain reliable $< L(k) >$, and we get k sets of time-series $P(k)$ with each different starting point in computing[18].

$< L(k) >$ is defined as

$$< L(k) > = \frac{1}{k}[\sum_{t=1}^{T-k}\sqrt{(x_{t+k}-x_t)^2+(y_{t+k}-y_t)^2} \cdot \frac{T}{(T-k)k}], \tag{2}$$

where x_t and y_t are elements of the position coordinate $P(t)$. The whole is multiplied by $1/k$, because $< L(k) >$ is found from k sets of time-series $P(k)$. T is whole time of the fish school simulation. And the term of $T/((T-k)k)$ normalizes the different number of subset. We call k and $< L(k) >$, the coarsening time and the coarsened length, respectively.

If measured length $< L(k) >$ is related to the *coarsening level of* k, as

$$< L(k) > \propto k^{-D}, \tag{3}$$

the system is called to have the fractal dimension D [20,21]. Generally, an assigned fractal dimension is non-integer, and shows how much complexity is being repeated at each scale (k).

The result of fractal analyses of the simulated fish school movements and the real fish school movements are shown as Figure 4 and Figure 5, respectively. In the both Figure 4 and Figure 5, the two straight lines were needed for fitting plots the *coarsened length* $< L(k) >$ against the *coarsening level* k. Each of lines in both Figure 4 and Figure 5 gives the two fractal dimension D_1 and D_2, which are obtained as the inclination of lines[22]. As a result of the fractal analyses for both simulated movement and the real movement, the *sardine* school movements give the similar fractal dimension with that of the simulated movement. Namely, it had been cleared that fish school simulations have a nice coincidence with the real fish school movements[19]. These mixture of different fractal in animal movements may help account for the idea that fractal excels in error tolerance[23]. It's speculated that the fractal school movements can be changed smoothly to the instantaneous target movement for a special purpose, such as a bait search action, an escape action, and a reproduction action etc.

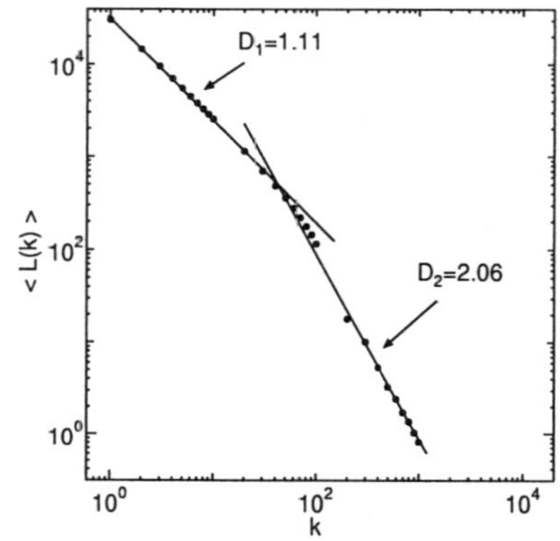

Fig. 4. The fractal analyses for the simulated fish school movement(N=100).

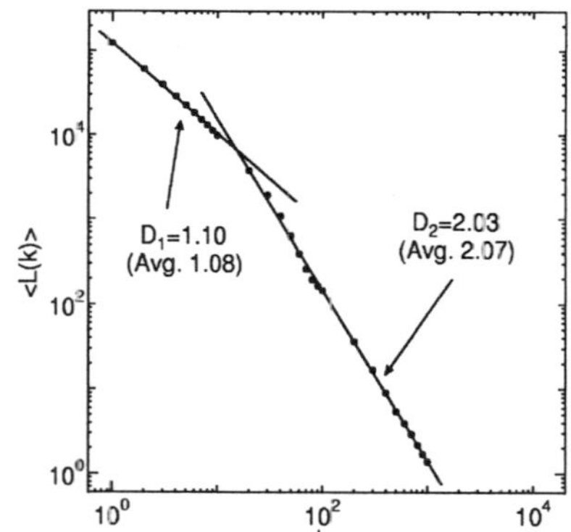

Fig. 5. The fractal analyses for the real fish(*sardine*) school movements (N≒100).

3. Experimental Environment

3.1. *Mobile Robot and Simulator*

In our experiments, we used the miniature mobile robot Khepera shown in Figure 6.[24] eight sensors(♯0 ∼ ♯7) detected obstacles and returned values in integer between 0 and 1023. The value returned from a sensor corresponds to the distance between the Khepera and the detected obstacle. A low-value means that there are no obstacles near the sensor, while a high value means that an obstacle is close to the sensor. Khepera communicates with a computer through a serial line, so the computer obtains the sensor values from the Khepera and regulates the wheel speed of the Khepera.

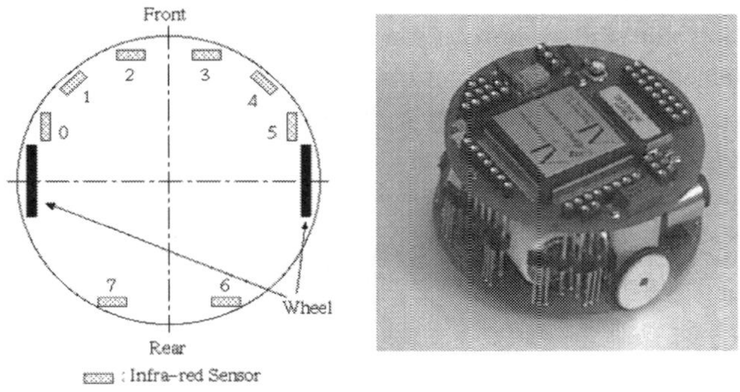

Fig. 6. Mobile Robot Khepera. Khepera has eight sensors(♯0 ∼ ♯7) used to detected obstacles. Its behavior is controlled by the wheel speed.

We simulated robot movements on the computer model to verify the rules of behavior. A difficult problem in the computer simulations is how to simulate the real world, including a proper treatment of noise. *Khepera Simulator ver. 2.0*, written by Olivier Michel, is an excellent software which takes into account the uncertainness which is supposed to exist in the real world. In this chapter, we investigated movements in computer simulations by using *Khepera Simulator ver. 2.0.* In this software, each motor can take a speed value ranging between -10 and $+10$. The simulator generates robot behavior under appropriate noise environment, simulating a real world. The added random noise of the returned value from sensors, the motor speed, and the direction are within $\pm 10\%, \pm 10\%$ *and* $\pm 5\%$ of each amplitude, respectively.

3.2. Conditions in the Simulator

We set up various types of road in our simulations. The example in Figure 7 shows the straight road and curved road. Two roads in Figure 7 are linked to each other. The upper terminal of the straight road (**a)** in Figure 7) is linked to the lower terminal of the carved road (**b)** in Figure 7). The upper terminal of the carved road(**b)**) is linked to the straight road (**a)**) at the lower terminal. And the robots run repeatedly round the looped with both **a)** and **b)**. The number of the robots running on the road is set as $N = 10$. The maximum motor speed of five robots is set as 4(faster), and that of other five robots is set as 3(slow). In this condition, each robot has frequent changes its behavior to find the other robots and interacts mutually based on the information from the sensors equipped on a robot. Generally, robots positioned densely cause traffic accidents and congestion. On the other hand, the emergence of autonomous collective movements requires the appropriate interaction between a robot and other robots or guard rails. The rule of a robot behavior needs to be optimized for the smooth movements of multirobots.

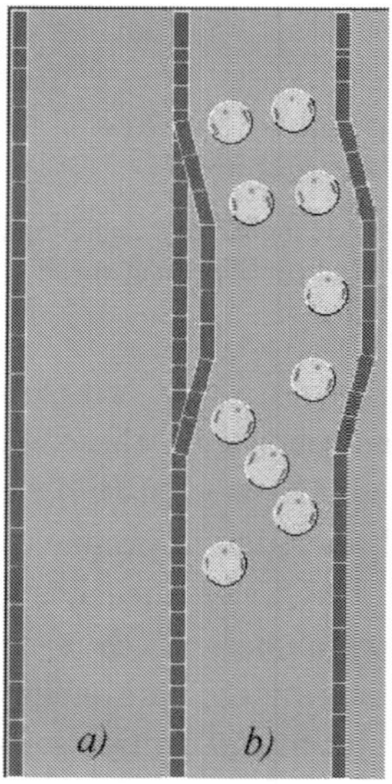

Fig. 7. One of road types in simulations, where ten robots are moving. Two roads **a)** and **b)** are linked each other. Robots run on **a)** $\rightarrow$ **b)** $\rightarrow$ **a)** $\rightarrow$ **b)** $\cdots$.

4. Behavior Models of a Mobile Robot

We apply the behavior models of a fish to the interactive rules between robots to realize an autonomous multirobots movement. Sensors equipped on Khepera can be used like as the sense organs of a fish, such as eyes or lateral lines. Since a fish has the dead angle as shown Figure 1, we do not use the values returned from sensor ♯6 and ♯7 to determine the interactive rules. As the distance r between fish determines the behavior type in the behavior models of a fish, the values s_x returned from sensor ♯x determines the behavior of a robot likewise. In the behavior models of a robot, eyes of fish correspond to the sensor ♯2 and ♯3 and lateral lines of a fish correspond to ♯0 & ♯1 and ♯4 & ♯5. Consequently, two pairs of values from s_0,s_1 and s_4,s_5 are coupled as $s_{0,1} = 0.5 \cdot (s_0 + s_1)$ and $s_{4,5} = 0.5 \cdot (s_4 + s_5)$, respectively.

The area for each behavior type of a robot is set concentric circles with boundary sensor values S_1, S_2, S_3 as shown in Figure 8. We define separately the front area and the lateral area of a robot. The front area ($a_1 \sim a_3$ in Figure 8)detected by sensor ♯2 or sensor ♯3 is defined with S_{a1}, S_{a2}, S_{a3}. The lateral area ($b_1 \sim b_3$ in Figure 8) detected by sensor ♯0 & ♯1 or sensor ♯4 & ♯5 is defined by S_{b1}, S_{b2}, S_{b3}.

Table 1 gives the behavior type of a robot based on the Aoki model[6], where the distance to an obstacle is measured with the returned value s. Table 2 gives the robot behavior which is translated from a fish school. Since a robot is required to avoid collisions, the largest value among the sensor values returned ($s_{0,1}, s_2, s_3, s_{4,5}$) is chosen to determine the robot behavior at the next simulation step.

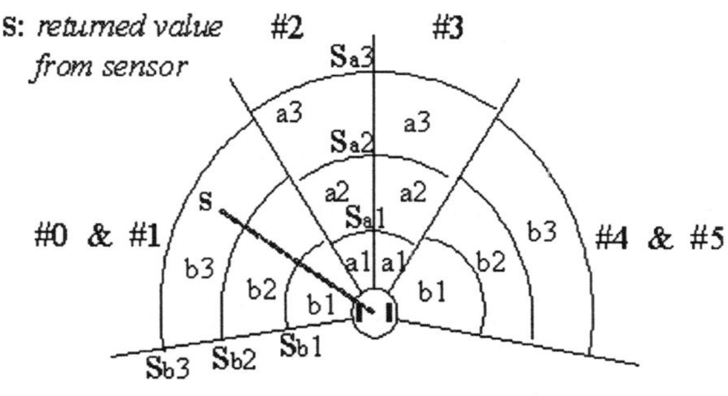

Fig. 8. Discernible Rages of Khepera Sensors. The region which determines the behavior type of a robot is divided concentrically with sensor values (S_1,S_2,S_3). Sensor of ♯2 *or* ♯3 detects objects in the area denoted as a with radius S_{a1}, S_{a2}, S_{a3}. Sensors of ♯0 & ♯1 and ♯4 & ♯5 detect in the lateral area denoted as b with S_{b1}, S_{b2}, S_{b3}, respectively. The distance to an obstacle is measured with the returned senor value s.

Table 1. The types of a robot behavior corresponding to the area where the obstacle is detected. "avoidance" means avoiding collisions against other robots or guard rails. " parallel " means advancing parallel with side robots or with guard rails. " approach " means approach to robots or guard rails. Though a fish school model has the same behavior types for both the forward obstacles and lateral obstacles, the behavior type of a robot is set individually in the area of in the area of $S_1 > s \geq S_2$. The distance to an obstacle is measured with the returned value s.

area	*a)* ♯2, ♯3	*b)* ♯0 & ♯1, ♯4 & ♯5
$s > S_1$	avoidance	avoidance
$S_1 \geq s > S_2$	avoidance	parallel
$S_2 \geq s > S_3$	approach	approach
$S_3 \geq s$	go straight	go straight

Table 2. The robot behaviors transferred from a fish school model in Table 1. The robot behaves corresponding to the area of sensor value where the detected obstacle is. When a robot behaves with " quick turn ", each wheel of both sides rotates opposite direction each other. When a robot behaves with " slight turn ", the speed of the one-side wheel increases until it reaches to the maximum speed, keeping another wheel at the present speed. " accelerate " or " decelerate " means for both wheels to speed up to the maximum speed or to slow down to zero speed, respectively.

area	*a)* ♯2 , ♯3	*b)* ♯0 & ♯1, ♯4 & ♯5
$s > S_1$	quick turn	quick turn
$S_1 \geq s > S_2$	decelerate	accelerate
$S_2 \geq s > S_3$	accelerate	slight turn
$S_3 \geq s$	accelerate	accelerate

5. Collective Movements of Multirobots

5.1. *Optimization of the Regions Which a Robot Can Discern with GA*

We introduce GA to optimize $S_{a1} \sim S_{a3}$ and $S_{b1} \sim S_{b3}$. A string of one gene is composed of $x_{a1} \sim x_{a3}$ and $x_{b1} \sim x_{b3}$, which determines $S_{a1} \sim S_{a3}$ and $S_{b1} \sim S_{b3}$ as follows,

$$\begin{aligned} S_{a1} &= 1024 \cdot x_{a1}, \quad S_{b1} = 1024 \cdot x_{b1}, \\ S_{a2} &= S_{a1} \cdot x_{a2}, \quad S_{b2} = S_{b1} \cdot x_{b2}, \\ S_{a3} &= S_{a2} \cdot x_{a3}, \quad S_{b3} = S_{b2} \cdot x_{b3}. \end{aligned} \tag{4}$$

$x_{a1} \sim x_{a3}$ *and* $x_{b1} \sim x_{b3}$ take real values between 0.0 and 1.0. The obtained gene will be applied equally to all 10 robots. We introduce twenty-five genes in one generation. Namely, twenty-five behavior types of multirobots are evaluated in one generation.

The evolutionary algorithm to obtain the best genes is given below.

1. In the first generation, twenty-five genes are randomly generated. Then let multirobots run on the road for 5000 simulation steps.
2. After an evaluation of the twenty-five behavior types of multirobots in one generation, the best five genes which took the high score of evaluation function are selected as the offspring at the next generation. Other twenty offspring are generated with both crossover operations and mutation operations. In the crossover operations, 10 pairs of genes are selected by the roulette method among the all twenty-five genes. The point of exchanging the strings of two genes is determined randomly. Namely, rate of crossover is 80.0%(20/25). Moreover, in the mutation operations(5.0%), chromosomes of twenty genes generated with crossover operation will be changed randomly in the value between 0.0 and 1.0. Let these offspring run for the same period.
3. Evolutionary computation then repeats processes 1. and 2. for 100 generations.

The function to evaluate each run for 5000 simulation steps is given as

$$g = \frac{Distance_y}{Collision_{robot} + Collision_{guardrail} + 1} \tag{5}$$

where $Distance_y$ measures how long the robots run forward (upward in Figure 7) in a trail. $Collision_{robot}$ and $Collision_{guardrail}$ mean the number of collisions with other robots and with guard rails, respectively.

Table 3. $S_{a1} \sim S_{b3}$ of the best 5 robots after 100 generations of GA.

	S_{a1}	S_{a2}	S_{a3}	S_{b1}	S_{b2}	S_{b3}	g
1	600	271	20	624	110	19	25.515
2	537	425	16	668	163	93	24.755
3	537	491	18	707	173	123	24.653
4	941	720	599	668	492	312	23.847
5	941	720	156	697	624	528	23.744

After applying the genetic algorithm as above, we obtained the best five genes shown in Table 3, robots ran together along a road very well. However, a robot sometimes cannot avoid collisions. The number of accidents are shown in Figure 9 against trial times. Figure 10 is one of the moments, where robots collided with other robots. Although the movement with optimized $S_{a1} \sim S_{b3}$ brings the collective and smooth movement, the ultimately autonomous movements without any accidents require more effective methods.

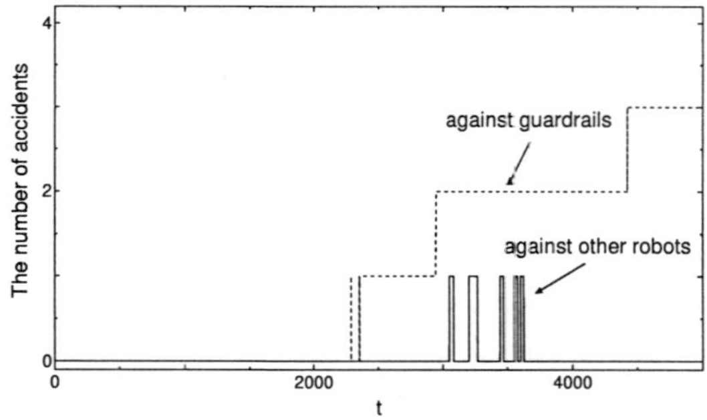

Fig. 9. The frequency of collision with other robots and guard rails against simulation steps.

Fig. 10. The collision of robots, where they overlap each other.

5.2. *Optimization of Robot Driving Types*

Besides the optimization of discernible regions defined by $S_{a1} \sim S_{b3}$, we optimize driving types of a robot. Driving types are defined by the speed of each wheel. While wheel speeds for a each behavior are fixed in the determination of $S_{a1} \sim S_{b3}$, driving types allow each speed of wheel to be set diversely[25]. Namely, we can aim to realize the more autonomous collective movements. Since it takes much time to decide the parameters for the discernible regions and the driving types at the same time, driving types are optimized based on the discernible regions in the previous subsection. Therefore, best $S_{a1} \sim S_{b3}$ in Table 3 are used in GA to optimize driving types.

The wheel speed is defined on the basis of $V_{max}/4$, where V_{max} means the maximum speed set in the simulations. A fast robot takes wheel speed among 0, $V_{max}/4$, $2V_{max}/4$, $3V_{max}/4$, V_{max}, while a slow robot takes wheel speed among 0, $V_{max}/4$, $2V_{max}/4$, $3V_{max}/4$. The driving type denoted as (**3**,**2**), for example, means that left wheel has the speed of $\mathbf{3}V_{max}/4$ and right wheel has the speed of $\mathbf{2}V_{max}/4$, respectively. i and j in driving type (i, j) are used as genes in GA operation. Since sensors on Khepera are equipped symmetrically, the driving types in the area for sensors of ♯3, ♯4 & ♯5 are taken just opposite to ♯2, ♯0 & ♯1, respectively. If the driving type in a_3 at ♯2 is (i, j), then the corresponding driving type in a_3 at ♯3 is taken as (j, i). When both s_2 and s_3 are lower than S_{a3} or both $s_{0,1}$ and $s_{4,5}$ are lower than S_{b3}, the robot is considered enough away from obstacles. Then the robot takes the driving type to go straight with maximum speed, which are denoted as $(3, 3)$ for a slow robot and as $(4, 4)$ for a fast robot.

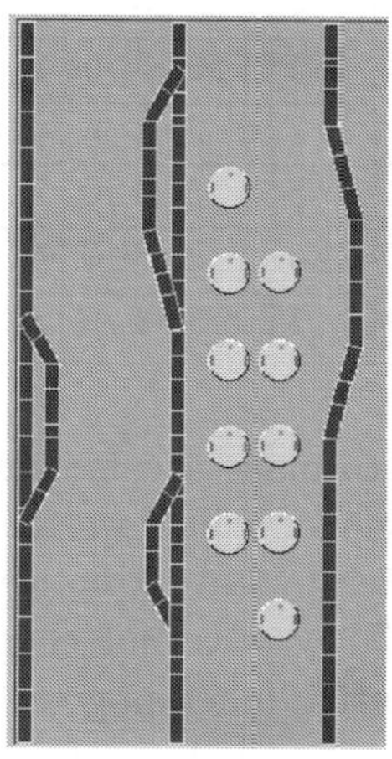

Fig. 11. Initial positions of robots which are randomly placed at each trial.

The road shown in Figure 11 was used to simulate a curved road or a block with a car left by an engine trouble, for instance. The ordering of fast robots and slow robots are placed randomly at each trial in the right side road as shown in Figure 11. At one generation of GA, twenty-five types of robots-runs with 2500 simulation steps are evaluated. The manner of GA to the optimize driving types is also basically same as those given in 5.1. However, the number of the selected best genes is ten. The other fifteen genes are generated through crossover operation. Namely, the crossover rate is 60.0%(15/25). The mutation rate is 5.0%. As a result of optimization, we obtained driving types shown in Table 4.

Table 4. Driving types(V_{left}, V_{right}) obtained by GA. $a_1 \sim a_3$ and $b_1 \sim b_3$ denote the area detected by sensor ♯2 and sensor ♯0 & ♯1,respectively. Driving types for the area detected by sensor ♯3 and sensor ♯4 & ♯5 are just opposite to those for ♯2 and ♯0 & ♯1, respectively. "♯ of no accident" means the period while multirobots has survived continuously without any accidents as a member of offspring, as generation proceeds.

best	robot	a_1	a_2	a_3	b_1	b_2	b_3	#of no accident
①	fast	0,0	2,3	2,4	3,0	4,3	4,3	28
	slow	1,0	1,3	1,3	3,0	3,3	3,3	
②	fast	0,0	2,3	0,2	3,0	4,4	4,3	25
	slow	1,1	1,3	1,3	3,0	3,3	3,3	
③	fast	0,0	1,3	0,2	3,0	4,4	4,3	23
	slow	0,0	2,3	1,3	3,0	3,3	3,3	
④	fast	0,0	2,4	1,2	3,0	4,4	4,3	20
	slow	0,0	0,3	0,3	3,0	3,3	3,3	

At this stage, we come to make a comment about situations in these distributed multirobot systems in which we meet something different from the ordinary examples applied by GA. A notice must be paid to select the best 4 robots in Table 4. They were not chosen only by the evaluation function. Exactly, the evaluation function gives high value after almost 100 generations if robots take the best 5 driving types for each generation. We, however, hardly determine them as the best 5 types because the best 5 types in GA often change. It would be due to change of the initial conditions and the added noise as generation proceeds. An important thing is not to choose driving types with high evaluation value but to take them having no accident as far as possible under a reasonable evaluation value. Therefore, we examined the driving types with the best offspring which made robots survive for a long period(100 to 700 generations) in GA. Though the movements were improved by GA, the accidents such as collision between robots were sometimes found. The behavior types shown in Table 4 brings the excellent movements. For example, collective robots with the behavior types of ① shown in, have moved with no accident for 28 generations continuously.

We notice, in Table 4, a similar tendency of behaviors in driving types ① ~ ④. They have the same driving mode to avoid collisions in the area of b_1. In the area of b_2, b_3, they show parallel movement along guard rails or slight avoidance from another neighboring robot. In the area of a_1, they all show a strong braking to avoid collision. In the area of a_2, a_3, they make a slow down, yet somehow approaching to an obstacle. The latter tendency will be obtained by following another robot ahead in order to go forward efficiently.

Test runs with obtained the driving types were performed for 30 trials for 2500 simulation steps. Most difficulties arise at the lower region of the left road in Figure 12, where many robots come together and go alternately through the narrow space. Robots with the driving types of ① had no accident for all 30 trials. They have a tendency to go together in a line after passing through a narrow space as shown in Figure 12a).

Robots with the driving types ② and ③ had accidents or stacked several times. Robots with the driving type of ④, on the other hand, also had no accident for all 30 trails and their movement looked like autonomous. They moved somehow distributed, not making a file and it happened that a fast robot sometimes overtook another slow robot as shown in Figure 12 b).

6. Conclusions

We studied the free-style movements of multirobots on a Khepera robot simulator. A fish school algorithm has been used to manipulate multirobots. Step-wise applications of GA were performed to get an optimization, because simulations take too much time on a computer to process these many distributed robot systems. Therefore, the first application of the GA was to optimize driving regions, while the driving-type for each area was fixed using a fish school model. The second step was to decide driving-type for each area, while using the parameters for the discernible region which were determined in the first step.

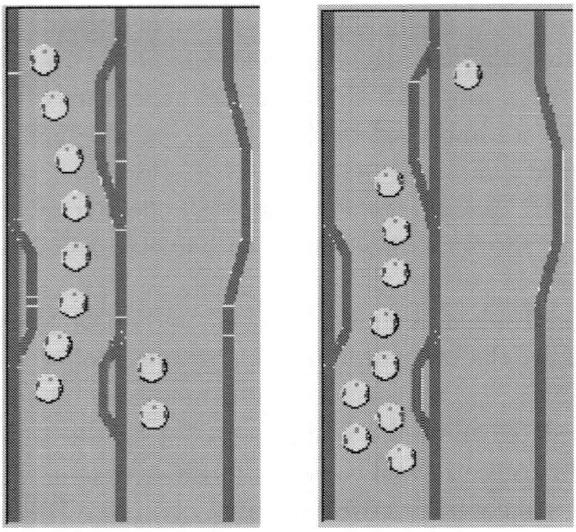

a) t=800 b) t=400

Fig. 12. The typical collective robot movements. a): Movements with driving type ① in Table 3 at t=800, b): Movements with driving type ④ at t=400.

Contrary to ordinary GA application, the evaluation function, in the present study, does not always fill the sufficient role to select the best offspring. A point is not to take a group of robots with high evaluation values but to select a group of robots which survives continuously as long as possible without any accidents, even if it will take somehow lower evaluation value. It is considered that this situation is caused by characteristics of multi-bodies systems in which the systems sometimes fall down to an accident due to a change of the initial starting setup of robots or a slight disturbance.

Consequently, by choosing robots which survive for a long period, autonomous collective movement has been observed successfully, where robots run very well without colliding against guard rails or other robots. Moreover, when there is enough space ahead, a fast robot will overtake a slow robot by adjusting its speed. In this study, it was not necessary to have a special system to control all the robots in order to realize autonomous multi robot movements. The safe, smooth running was realized solely due to the repetitions of single interactions among neighboring robots, showing the realization of the distributed robot control system.

References

1. Kwang Soo Chang, J Karl Hedrick, Wei-Bin Zhang, Pravin Varaiya, Masayoshi Tomizuka, and Steven E. Shladover, *IVHS Journal*, vol.1, no.1,63(1993)
2. Rillings, J., *NAHSC System Concept Workshop, October 18*(1995)
3. Reinhold Behringer, Markus Maurer, *Proc. 1996 IEEE Intelligent Vehicles Symposium*, 415-420(1996)
4. S.Tsugawa, S.Kato, K. Tomita, *Proc. 4th ITS World Congress(CD-ROM)*(1997)
5. T.Shinchi, M.Tabuse, A.Todaka, T.Kitazoe, *Proc. of the 4th Asia-Pacific Conference on Simulated Evolution and Learning*, vol.1, 365(2002)
6. Ichiro Aoki, *Bulletin of the Japanese Society of Scientific Fisheries*, 48(8), 1081(1982)
7. A.Huth and C.Wissel, *J.theor.Biol.*, 156, 365(1992)
8. T.Shinchi, M.Tabuse, A.Todaka and T.Kitazoe, *Proc. 10th IEEE International Workshop on Robot and Human Communication Bordeaux-Paris*, 280(2001)
9. Ichiro Aoki, *Bull.Ocean Res.Inst.Univ.Tokyo*, 12, 1(1980)
10. E.Shaw, *Scientific American*, vol.206, 128(1962)
11. E.Shaw, *In:L.Arson(ed) Development and Evolution of Behaviour*, 452(1970)
12. Braian L.Partridge, *Scientific American*,vol.246, 90(1982)
13. Ed. by Tony J.Pitcher, *The Johns Hopkins Univ. Press*(1986)
14. A.Huth and C.Wissel, *Ecological Modeling*, 75/76, 135(1994)
15. H.S.Niwa, *Computers Math. Applic.*, vol.32, no.11, 79(1996)
16. H.S.Niwa, *J.theor.Biol.*, 181, 47(1996)
17. I.Aoki, *Bulletin of the Japanese Society of Scientific Fisheries*, 50(5), 751(1984)
18. Tomoyuki Higuchi, *Pysica,* ***D31***, 277(1988)
19. T.Shinchi, T.Kitazoe, H.Nishimura, M.Tabuse, N.Azuma and I.Aoki, *The Journal of Artificial Life and Robotics*, Springer-Verlag, Vol.6, 35(2002)
20. B.B.Mandelbrot, *The Fractal Geometry of Nature*, Freeman San Francisco(1982)
21. Gary William Flake, *The Computational Beauty of Nature; Computer Explorations of Fractals, Chaos, Complex Systems, and Adaptation*, The MIT Press(1998)
22. T.Shinchi, H.Nishimura, and T.Kitazoe, *Information Processing Society of Japan Transactions*, vol.42, no.6, 1592(2001) (in Japanese)
23. West BJ : *Fractal Physiology and Chaos in Medicine*, World Scientific, Singapore(1990)
24. K-Team SA, *Khepera USER MANUAL Version 4.06*(1995)
25. T.Shinchi, M.Tabuse, T.Kitazoe, A.Todaka, *The Journal of Artificial Life and Robotics*, Vol.7, Springer-Verlag (in press)

CHAPTER 15

AUTOMATIC MODULARIZATION WITH SPECIATED NEURAL NETWORK ENSEMBLE

Vineet R. Khare and Xin Yao

School of Computer Science, The University of Birmingham
Birmingham B15 2TT, United Kingdom
E-mail: {V.R.Khare,X.Yao}@cs.bham.ac.uk

Decomposing a complex computational problem into sub-problems, which are computationally simpler to solve individually and which can be combined to produce a complete solution, can efficiently lead to compact and general solutions. Neural network ensemble is one such modular system that uses this divide-and-conquer strategy. Diverse set of networks improves ensemble's performance over its constituent networks. Artificial speciation is used here to produce this diverse set of networks that solve different parts of a data classification task and complement each other in solving the complete problem. Fitness sharing is used in evolving the group of neural networks to achieve the required speciation. Sharing is performed at phenotypic level using modified Kullback-Leibler entropy as the distance measure. The group as a unit solves the classification problem and outputs of all the networks are used in finding the final output. For the combination of neural network outputs 3 different methods - Voting, averaging and recursive least square are used. The evolved system is tested on two data classification problems (Heart Disease Dataset and Breast Cancer Dataset) taken from UCI machine learning benchmark repository.

1. Introduction

Ideally for a good decomposition, these sub-problems will be much easier than the corresponding monolithic problem. Designing a modular system, which can break the problem at hand into pieces and solve it, is difficult because it relies heavily on human experts and prior knowledge about the problem. Neural Network Ensembles (NNEs) combine a set of Artificial Neural Networks (ANNs) that learn to divide a problem and, therefore, are good candidates for an automatically modular system. For a good division of labour we want these ANNs to be diverse so that each of the sub-problems can be tackled by a different ANN or module (subset of all ANNs).

Diversity in a NNE can be achieved through statistical methods like negative correlation learning[1,2] and/or evolutionary computation techniques like artificial speciation.[3] In this chapter we will be focussing on the latter. In an attempt to achieve this modularization without any human intervention, speciation in an Evolutionary Algorithm is used here. Different evolved individuals (ANNs) in the population solve a part of a complex problem and compliment each other in solving the big complex problem. There is major emphasis on following two points - (1) *Automatic Modularization using Fitness-Sharing* - Here multiple speciated neural networks are evolved using fitness sharing which helps in automatic modularization. (2) *Making Use of Population Information in Evolving Neural Networks* - A population of ANNs contains more information than any single ANN in the population.[4] Such information can be used to improve the performance and reliability of the system. While evolving ANNs, instead of choosing the best ANN in the last generation, the final result is obtained by combining the outputs of individuals in the last generation. This will help us in utilizing all the information contained in the whole population. Three combination methods (voting, averaging and recursive least square) were used to combine the outputs of the individuals in the evolved population.

The rest of the chapter is organized as follows. Section 2 gives some background on the topic. Section 3 describes, in detail, how ANNs are evolved and the combination methods used to combine their outputs. Section 4 gives details on experimentation and the results obtained for the two benchmark problems (Heart Disease and Breast Cancer) taken from UCI datasets. Section 5 compares these results with the known results for the two problems and illustrates the effect of using full population instead of the best individual in the population. Finally Sec. 6 concludes with some suggested improvements and future work directions.

2. Background

There are various techniques available in literature that use NNEs for modularization. Various boosting[5,6] and bagging[7] methods, Mixture of Experts[8,9](MoE) and Hierarchical Mixture of Experts[10](HME) are a few examples of such techniques. But in all these techniques the number of individuals in the ensemble and their architecture is often predefined and fixed according to the prior knowledge of the problem to be solved.

Using speciation, the number of modules can be made an emergent property of the system. Previous work has been done on automatic modularization using speciation. Darwen and Yao[11] used automatic modularization in co-evolutionary game learning. A speciated population, as a complete modular system, was used to learn playing Iterated Prisoners Dilemma. More recently Ahn and Cho[12] developed a system of speciated neural networks that were evolved using fitness sharing. Final population was analysed using single linkage clustering method to choose representatives of each species. The outputs of these representative individuals were then combined to produce the ensemble output.

In this work, matrix encoding scheme (Sec. 3.2) is used to represent an ANN which doesn't require us to fix the number of hidden layers apriori and the number of modules (species) also emerge as the result of speciation. Though some priori knowledge is needed in the form of the maximum number of hidden nodes and the sharing radius used for fitness sharing.

3. Evolving Speciated Artificial Neural Networks

The task at hand here is to evolve (architecture and weights) a NNE that decomposes the data classification problem (Sec. 3.1) automatically such that each sub-problem may be tackled by a different individual NN (or a sub-set of NNs) in the ensemble. This is achieved by introducing speciation (Sec. 3.5) in the ANN population and it is expected that members of one species would work better than others in classifying a particular sub-set of data. Figure 1 shows the overview of the methodology, starting from population initialization to the combination of multiple ANNs evolved. NNs used here are all Feed Forward Neural Networks. Sections 3.2 - 3.7 give various steps involved in evolving the NNE.

3.1. *Benchmark Problems*

Two data classification problems from UCI benchmark database[13] have been used to judge the performance of evolved NNE. Both of these datasets have some attributes; based on these attributes, any given pattern has to be classified into one of two given classes. The two databases are - (1) Wisconsin Breast Cancer Database - which contains 699 instances, 2 classes (malignant and benign) and 9 integer-valued attributes. (2) Heart Disease Database which contains 270 instances, 2 classes (presence and absence) and 13 attributes (chosen out of 75) are all continuously valued. The whole dataset is to be divided into - Training Data ($\frac{1}{2}$ of full dataset), Validation

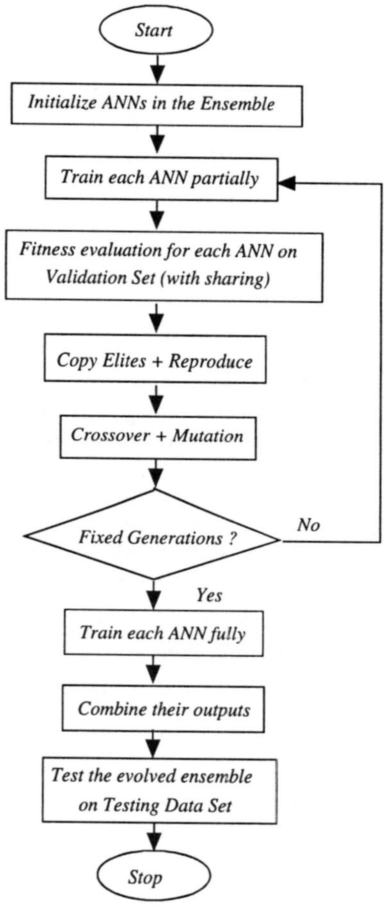

Fig. 1. An overview of the speciated EANN system.

Data ($\frac{1}{4}$th of full dataset) and Testing Data (remaining $\frac{1}{4}$th).

3.2. *Encoding of Neural Networks*

To evolve an ANN, it needs to be expressed in proper form. There are some methods to encode an ANN, e.g. binary representation, tree, linked list, and matrix. Representation used here to encode an ANN is matrix encoding.[12] If N is the total number of nodes in an ANN including input, hidden, and output nodes, the matrix is NXN, and its entries consist of connection links and corresponding weights.

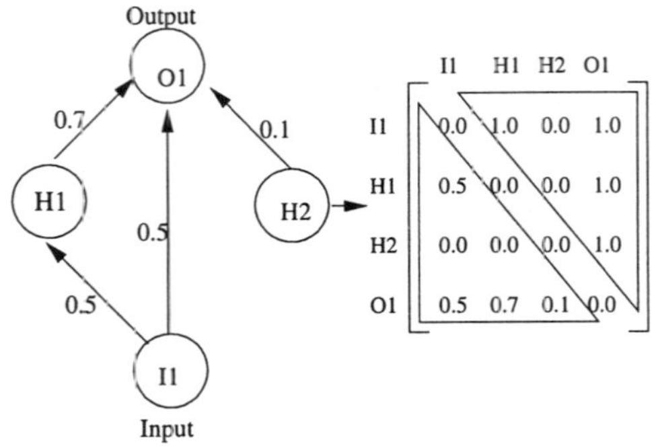

Fig. 2. Encoding of ANNs. Example of encoding of an ANN that has one input node, two hidden nodes, and one output node. In the figure, I1 describes one input node, H1 and H2 describes hidden nodes, O1 describes the output node.

In the matrix, upper right triangle (Fig. 2) has connection link information, which describes 1 when there exists connection link and 0 when there is no connection link. Lower left triangle describes the weight value corresponding connection link information. Important thing to note here is that there isn't any notion of hidden layers. Any hidden or output node can be connected to any other node that has a higher index (only *feed forward* connections).

3.3. *Ensemble Initialization*

Each ANN in the ensemble is generated with random initial weights and full-connection. Initial weights and biases are assigned randomly between $[-1, 1]$ and $[0, 1]$ respectively. 20 such ANNs are generated as initial population with 9 and 13 input nodes for breast cancer and heart disease datasets respectively. Number of hidden nodes are taken to be 5 and 6 respectively. In each case there is 1 output unit, which has a binary output.

3.4. *Partial Training - Lamarckian Evolution*

Each ANN is trained partially (200 epochs) with *training data*, at each generation, to help the evolution search the optimal architecture of ANN and is tested on validation data to compute the fitness. Partial training can be viewed as lifetime learning of an individual in the evolutionary process. The adjustment of the genotype (weight updates in Backpropagation) to the locally optimised offspring makes it *Lamarckian Evolution*.

3.5. *Fitness Evaluation and Speciation*

The fitness of ANN is the accuracy of classification of ***validation data*** and is computed using speciation. Raw fitness of an individual p, $f_{raw,p}$, is the inverse of *Mean Square Error* (MSE) calculated per pattern, per output unit. Hence raw fitness

$$f_{raw,p} = \frac{1}{MSE_p} \tag{1}$$

A constant can be added to the denominator to prevent fitness value going to infinity when an individual classifies all patterns correctly. For the purpose of speciation fitness sharing technique[14] is used here. Fitness sharing is done at the ***phenotypic*** rather than ***genotypic*** level, i.e. distance between two individuals is judged on the basis of their behaviour (phenotypes), not on the basis of their architecture or weights (genotypes).

To measure the distance between two individuals on the basis of their behaviour the output values produced by these individuals for the validation set data points have been used. The ***modified Kullback-Leibler entropy***[15] is used to measure the difference of two ANNs. As discussed in Ref. 12, the outputs of ANNs are not just likelihood or binary logical values near zero or one, instead, they are estimates of Bayesian a posteriori probabilities of a classifier. Using this property, the difference between two ANNs is measured with modified Kullback-Leilbler entropy, which is called relative entropy or cross-entropy.

Symmetric relative entropy is used as the distance measure. If p and q are the output probability distributions of two ANNs that consist of 1 output node and are trained with n data points, then, the similarity of the two ANNs can be calculated by

$$D(p,q) = \frac{1}{2}\sum_{j=1}^{n}(p_j \log \frac{p_j}{q_j} + q_j \log \frac{q_j}{p_j}) \tag{2}$$

where p_j means the output value of the ANN with respect to the jth training data. Lower values of this entropy imply similar behaviour in the two networks.

This distance measure is used to share the fitness of individuals in the population. Different values (0.5, 1, 2) for sharing radius (σ_s) were tried, but most of the experimentation was done with $\sigma_s = 1$, which was found to be the best one among the three values. Two individuals share the fitness, according to the standard fitness sharing technique,[14] only if the distance between them is less than σ_s.

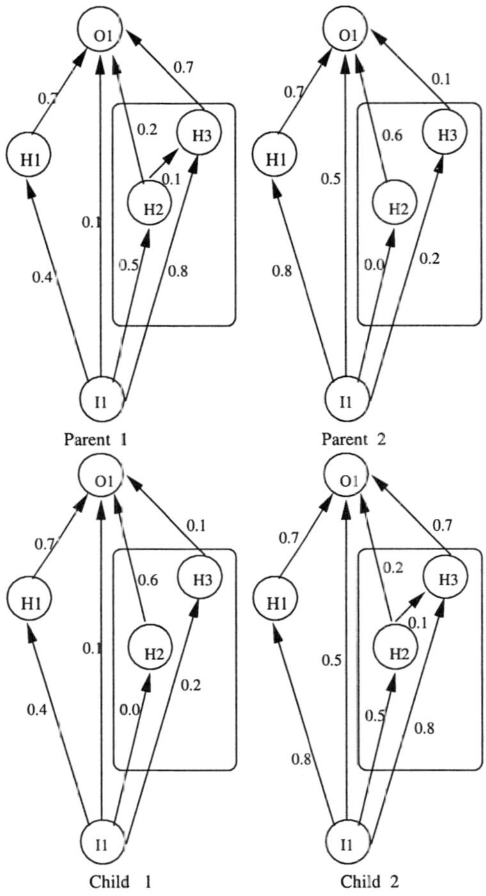

Fig. 3. Crossover - Exchanging sub-graphs. First a node is chosen randomly, say H1, and is added to the empty sub-graph. In parent 1, H1 is connected with I1, H3 and O1 and in parent 2 it is connected with I1 and O1. Hence H3 is added to the sub-graph. Now the sub-graphs (containing H2 and H3) have similar connections in both the parents and are exchanged.

3.6. *Evolutionary Process*

Generational GA with *elitism* is used here. Elitism performs two actions - (1) It makes a copy of the individual with best raw fitness in the old pool and places it in the new pool, thus ensuring the most fit chromosome survives. (2) Similarly one individual with the best shared fitness is copied to the new pool. To create the mating pool, on which the genetic operators will be applied, *roulette wheel selection* is used. Members of the mating pool are selected according to their shared fitness.

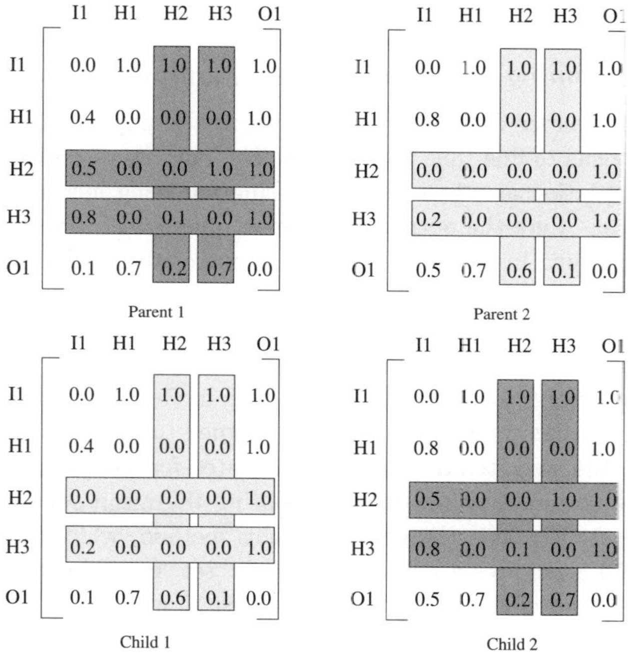

Fig. 4. Crossover - Changing row and column entries corresponding to nodes H2 and H3 of parent 1 and parent 2.

Both crossover and mutation operators are used. The crossover operator used here searches for similar sub-graphs in the two parents and swaps the two smaller sub-graphs to create two children (see Fig. 3). In the population of ANNs, crossover operator selects two distinct ANNs randomly and chooses one hidden node from each selected ANN. These two nodes should be in the same entry of each ANN matrix encoding of the ANN to exchange the architectures. If the selected nodes have similar connections, the two ANNs exchange the connection links (starting and ending at that node) and corresponding weights information of the node, else smallest similar sub-graph (containing the chosen node) in the two ANNs is searched and swapped. This can be done by recursively adding nodes to the node that was chosen first. Offspring can be obtained by swapping row and column entries (Fig. 4) corresponding to the nodes present in the subgraphs of the two parents.

Mutation operator either deletes an existing connection between two randomly chosen nodes in the ANN or creates a new connection between two isolated nodes with random weight.

3.7. *Full Training and Combination of Outputs*

After fixed number of generations, ANNs in the population are trained for 1000 epochs to fine-tune the weights. The outputs of evolved and fully trained population are then combined using following methods - (1) *Majority Voting* - Here the output of the most number of ANNs will be the combined output. In case of a tie, the output of the ANN (among those in the tie) with the lowest error rate on the validation set is selected as combined output. (2) *Averaging* - the combined output is the average of the outputs of all individuals present in the final population. (3) *Recursive Least Square (RLS)* - This method was used in Ref. 4 to find the ensemble output. In this method weights are assigned to different ANNs in the population and weighted average was calculated for the population. These weights are obtained by recursively updating the mean square error and minimizing it. We omit the details for this method, which can be found in Ref. 4. RLS requires a parameter α to be set. In our experimentation, we tried 3 values of α (0.1, 0.2 and 0.3). Best results, on an average were obtained for $\alpha = 0.3$.

4. Experimentation and Results

Data sets for each benchmark problem were divided into 3 parts - Training, validation and testing set (as discussed in Sec. 3.1). Various parameter settings for the experiments are given in Table 1.

Tables 2 and 3 list the training, validation and testing error rates obtained by the NNE evolved, for the breast cancer and heart disease problems respectively. These results are averaged over 30 runs for breast cancer problem and 24 runs for the heart disease problem. One run of the programme takes approximately 3 hours for heart disease problem (350 generations) and 2 hours 30 minutes for breast cancer problem (200 generations) on a 500 MHz Sun machine. Distance calculations in fitness sharing and partial training in each generation make the algorithm computationally expensive.

Table 1. Parameter settings for experiments.

Parameter	Breast Cancer	Heart Disease
Learning Rate	0.1	0.1
Crossover Probability	0.3	0.3
Mutation Probability	0.1	0.1
Sharing Radius	1	1
No. of Generations	200	350
No. of runs	30	24

Table 2. Error Rates (averaged over 30 runs) for Breast Cancer Problem

	Voting		
	Training	Validation	Testing
Mean	0.0378	0.0189	0.0231
SD	0.0100	0.0153	0.0176
Min	0.0074	0.0000	0.0000
Max	0.0544	0.0514	0.0514
	Averaging		
	Training	Validation	Testing
Mean	0.0374	0.0235	0.0229
SD	0.0102	0.0151	0.0137
Min	0.0078	0.0114	0.0000
Max	0.0544	0.0571	0.0514
	RLS		
	Training + Validation		Testing
Mean	0.0237		0.0167
SD	0.0152		0.0122
Min	0.0016		0.0000
Max	0.0267		0.0343

In tables 2 and 3, Mean, SD, Min, and Max indicate the Mean Value, Standard Deviation, Minimum and Maximum values respectively. Results are given for all three combination methods used - Voting, RLS and Averaging. For RLS training and validation sets both were used to find optimal weights for the linear combination of outputs of neural networks, hence combined error for both training and validation sets is given.

5. Discussion

In the following subsection (Sec. 5.1) we have compared our results with those available in literature for the two problems. Section 5.2 illustrates the effect of using the full population instead of the best individual by comparing the performance of best individual in the population with var-

Table 3. Error Rates (averaged over 24 runs) for Heart Disease Problem

	Voting		
	Training	Validation	Testing
Mean	0.1960	0.1623	0.1642
SD	0.0282	0.0265	0.0404
Min	0.1333	0.1194	0.1176
Max	0.2667	0.2388	0.2794
	Averaging		
	Training	Validation	Testing
Mean	0.1733	0.1828	0.1612
SD	0.0231	0.0293	0.0323
Min	0.1333	0.1194	0.1029
Max	0.2370	0.2388	0.2353
	RLS		
	Training + Validation		Testing
Mean	0.1462		0.1612
SD	0.0243		0.0337
Min	0.1188		0.1176
Max	0.2129		0.2500

ious combination methods. Best results were obtained using RLS method for combining the outputs on an average. Though RLS always produced best results on training data, there were runs in which voting or averaging method produced better results in terms of testing errors. In general we have achieved lesser error rates on validation sets than on training set, this is because our EA is trying to optimise the fitness which was calculated over the validation set.

Also better results were achieved when all the networks in the initial population were fully connected, in comparison to the case where there were random initial connections. Another point worth mentioning here is the relative degree of difficulty of classification in the two datasets. In heart disease, even after 350 generations, error rates are pretty big in comparison to the breast cancer problem. So heart disease dataset proves to be much harder to classify.

5.1. *Comparison With Known Results*

For the Breast Cancer problem, Ahn and Cho[12] obtained 1.71% test error rate as their best result using single linkage clustering with voting and averaging combination methods. For the same problem, Yao and Liu[16] obtained 1.38% test error rate using EPNet. In our evolved system, on an average over 30 runs, RLS combination method produced 1.67% error rate on test set, which is better than Ahn and Cho's result. But voting and averaging methods produced 2.31 and 2.29% error rates respectively, which are higher.

Yao and Liu[4] obtained 5.8% and 15.1% error rates, for training and testing datasets, as their best results for the heart disease problem. The best results achieved here are 14.62% and 16.12% respectively for the two sets. Though the testing error rate is comparable the training error rate is much higher.

5.2. *Comparing Best Individual Performance With Combination Methods*

To see how useful these combination methods are in comparison to the best individual present in the population, their performances (on training set) are plotted with the performance of best individual present in the population for the two problems. Figure 5 gives error rates versus the number of generations for the best individual and for all 3 combination methods used here (for a particular run).

For the Breast cancer problem (Fig. 5(a)) all combination methods except the RLS prove to be worse than the best individual present in the population. Few observations can be made from this plot - (1) It took around 125 generations for voting and averaging to reach the performance comparable to RLS or of the best individual. This is because, for voting and averaging, the performance is measured on training set while the fitness evaluation is done on the validation set. On the other hand error rates for the RLS method is based on both training and validation sets. (2) The best individual is almost as good as the best combination method (RLS). Good performance of the best individual was also observed in Ref. 12, this can be attributed to the classification problem being easy. These methods aren't exploited to their full extent in this problem. We will see in a moment that for a much harder problem these methods turn out to be useful and perform much *better than the best individual.*

For the Heart Disease problem (Fig. 5(b)) combination methods perform much better than the best individual present in the population. Few observations can be made from this plot - (1) RLS again gives the best performance, though averaging also performs quite well. Voting on the other hand performs no better than the best individual. (2) In this problem the difference between using the best individual and using the full population is visible. (3) This difference becomes more prominent when we look at the

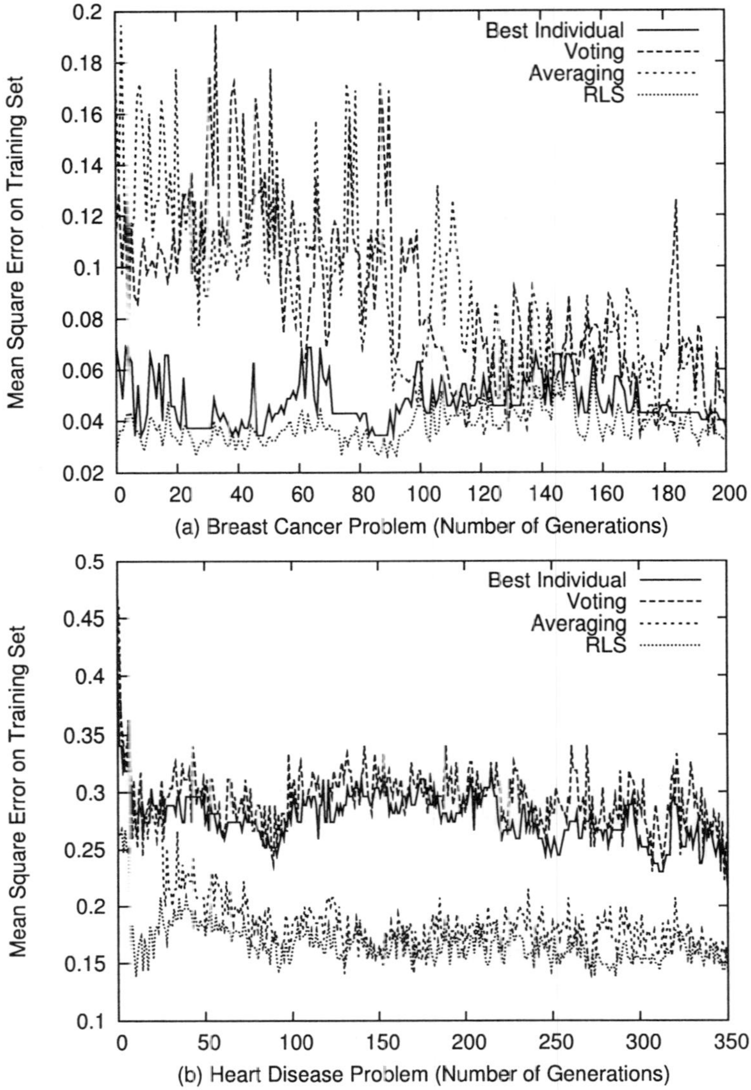

Fig. 5. Comparison between the best performing individual and various combination methods for the two problems.

performance on test set. For the same run (for which the plot has been provided) the best individual produced 17 wrong classifications out of 68 patterns in test set, i.e. 25% error rate while voting, averaging and RLS produced - 17.65%, 19.12% and 17.65% error rates.

6. Conclusion

Speciated EANN system was evolved using fitness sharing. Sharing was performed at phenotypic level using modified Kullback-Leibler entropy as the distance measure. To make use of population information present in the final generation of EA, the final result was obtained by combining the output of all the individuals present in the final population using various combination techniques - voting, averaging and RLS. The developed system was tested on two benchmark datasets from UCI benchmark datasets, namely Wisconsin Breast Cancer Dataset and Heart Disease Dataset. It was observed that the breast cancer dataset was much easier to classify than the heart disease dataset.

Significantly better results were achieved by using a validation set. Out of the three combination methods RLS produced the best results. Combination of outputs produced much better results than the best individual in the harder problem (heart disease problem). Results achieved for Breast Cancer problem were better than known results available. Comparable results were also achieved in Heart Disease problem.

Though the evolved system performed quite well on the two benchmark problems taken, still there are some criticisms too. First one obviously is that it is too expensive and should not be applied to relatively easier problems like the breast cancer problem, where it cannot be exploited to its full extent. Also, fitness sharing, as described in Ref. 17, is expensive because of distance calculations. Another drawback of the system is the choice of sharing radius, which was chosen empirically. Standard fitness sharing used here, makes two assumptions - (1) The first is the number of peaks in the space. (2) The second is that those peaks are uniformly distributed throughout the space. However, we don't usually know about the problem beforehand. Hence setting a suitable value for sharing radius is difficult. In the earlier stages of experimentation only three values were tried and the best one was chosen for the rest of experiments. More experimentation couldn't be performed, as running the code was quite expensive. More experiments with different values of sharing radius might have produced better results. Requirement of priori knowledge about the fitness landscape (in our case the sharing radius) is one of the limitations of standard fitness sharing technique. We will also face problems when the peaks have basins of different sizes. Thus an obvious modification to the system can be - the use of another niching or speciation technique, which doesn't require empirically setting the sharing radius and/or doesn't involve expensive distance calculations.

There are some niching techniques available in literature that require lesser amount of prior knowledge about the fitness landscape. Multinational EA[18] and DNC with fuzzy variable niching[19] can be two possible candidates here. Both of these schemes use hill-valley fitness topology function which allows the local analysis of the fitness landscape and thus help them in making more informed decisions, based on this analysis, about merging and splitting or merging and migrating two species in the two schemes respectively. On the other hand there are techniques like Simple Subpopulation Scheme[20] that can be used to make the system less expensive. Simple Subpopulation Scheme replaces the concept of distance between individuals with tag bits that identify the subpopulation to which an individual belongs. It also does not make the equal spacing assumption. One interesting extension to this work would be, to incorporate some of these niching techniques in the system.

Acknowledgments

This work was partially supported by The European Commission through its grant A51/B7-301/97/0126-08.

References

1. Y. Liu and X. Yao, Ensemble learning via negative correlation, *Neural Networks*, **12**(10), pp. 1399-1404, 1999.
2. Y. Liu and X. Yao, Simultaneous training of negatively correlated neural networks in an ensemble. *IEEE Transactions on Systems, Man, and Cybernetics, Part B: Cybernetics*, **29**(6), pp. 716-725. 1999
3. P. Darwen and X. Yao, Every niching method has its niche: fitness sharing and implicit sharing compared, In H. M. Voigt, W. Ebeling, I. Rechenberg, and H. P. Schewefel, editors, *Parallel Problem Solving from Nature (PPSN)* IV, vol. 1141 of *Lecture Notes in Computer Science*, Springer-Verlag, Berlin, pp. 398-407, 1996.
4. X. Yao and Y. Liu, Making Use of Population Information in Evolutionary Artificial Neural Networks, *IEEE Transactions on Systems, Man and Cybernetics, Part B: Cybernetics*, **28**(3), pp. 417-425, 1998.
5. R. E. Schapire. The Strength of Weak Learnability. *Machine Learning*, **5**, pp. 197-227, 1990.
6. Y. Freund and R. E. Schapire, Experiments with a new boosting algorithm, In *Proceedings of the 13th International Conference on Machine Learning*, Morgan Kaufmann, 1996.

7. L. Breiman, Bagging Predictors, *Machine Learning*, **24**(2), pp. 123-140, 1996.
8. R. A. Jacobs, M. I. Jordan, and A. G. Barto. Task Decomposition Through Competition in a Modular Connectionist Architecture: The What and Where Vision Tasks. *Cognitive Science*, **15**, pp. 219-250, 1991.
9. R. A. Jacobs, M. I. Jordan, S. J. Nowlan, and G. E. Hinton. Adaptive Mixtures of Local Experts. *Neural Computation*, **3**(1), pp. 79-87, 1991.
10. M. I. Jordan and R. A. Jacobs. Hierarchical Mixtures of Experts and the EM Algorithm. *Neural Computation*, **6**, pp. 181-214, 1994.
11. P. Darwen and X. Yao, Automatic Modularization by Speciation, *Proc. of the 1996 IEEE International Conference on Evolutionary Computation (ICEC '96)*, IEEE Computer Society Press, Nagoya, Japan, pp. 88-93, 1996.
12. J. H. Ahn and S. B. Cho, Speciated Neural Networks Evolved with Fitness Sharing Technique, *Proc. of the 2001 Congress on Evolutionary Computation*, Seoul, Korea, pp. 390-396, 2001.
13. C. L. Blake and C. J. Merz, UCI Repository of machine learning databases [http://www.ics.uci.edu/ mlearn/MLRepository.html]. Irvine, CA: University of California, Department of Information and Computer Science, 1998.
14. D. Goldberg, *Genetic Algorithms in Search, Optimization and Machine Learning*, Addison-Wesley, Reading Massachusetts, 1989.
15. S. Kullback and R. A. Leibler, On Information and Sufficiency, *Ann. Math. Stat.*, **22**, pp. 79-86, 1951.
16. X. Yao and Y. Liu, A New Evolutionary System for Evolving Artificial Neural Networks, *IEEE Trans. Neural Networks*, **8**(3), pp. 694-713, 1998.
17. D. Goldberg and J. Richardson, Genetic Algorithms with Sharing for Multimodal Function Optimization, *Proc. of the 2nd Inter. Conf. on Genetic Algorithms*, Cambridge, MA, pp. 41-49, 1987.
18. R. Ursem, Multinational Evolutionary Algorithms, *Proc. of the 1999 Congress on Evolutionary Computation CEC1999*, Washington D.C., USA, **3**, pp. 1633-1640, 1999.
19. J. Gan and K. Warwick, Dynamic Niche Clustering: A Fuzzy Variable Radius Niching Technique for Multimodal Optimisation in GAs, *Proc. of the 2001 Congress on Evolutionary Computation CEC2001*, Seoul, Korea, pp. 215-222, 2001.
20. W. M. Spears, Simple Subpopulation Schemes, *Proc. of 3rd Annual conf. on Evolutionary Programming*, World Scientific, pp. 297-307, 1994.

CHAPTER 16

SEARCH ENGINE DEVELOPMENT USING EVOLUTIONARY COMPUTATION METHODOLOGIES

Reginald L. Walker
Tapicu, Inc., P.O. Box 88492
Los Angeles, California 90009
rwalker@tapicu.com

Early search engines had their origin in information retrieval systems. These systems were typically developed by human editors to index a document set that was static over long periods of time. The information retrieval systems provided a stable user environment that was eventually optimized over time and facilitative of incremental growth in the document collection. Early search engines used this tried and tested information retrieval model, but encountered usability limitations when the document growth rate accelerated. The limitations of the model became magnified as the need for automated indexing mechanisms grew, and information retrieval systems began to be used with dynamic document datasets. These limitations are still apparent in current search engines which incorporate aspects of these early information retrieval systems. This chapter presents the Tocorime Apicu approach for replacing the information retrieval model with an information sharing model that adapts to changing conditions within the Internet using the stochastic optimization methodologies of evolutionary computation. Experimental results are presented.

1. Introduction

The purpose of the Tocorime Apicu [a] information sharing indexing (ISI) approach to indexing/ranking and clustering Web pages is to show the feasibility of implementing unique aspects of the search strategies of honeybees to address two major limitations of current search engines: 1) their inabil-

[a] The word *Tocorime*, meaning "spirit" [1], comes from an ancient Amazon Indian language. *Apicu* comes from the Latin *apis cultura*, meaning "honeybee culture" or "the study of honeybees." The phrase *Tocorime Apicu* is used as "in the spirit of bee culture."

ity to find and incorporate new information in a timely manner and 2) the general Web page classification system used in their IR systems.

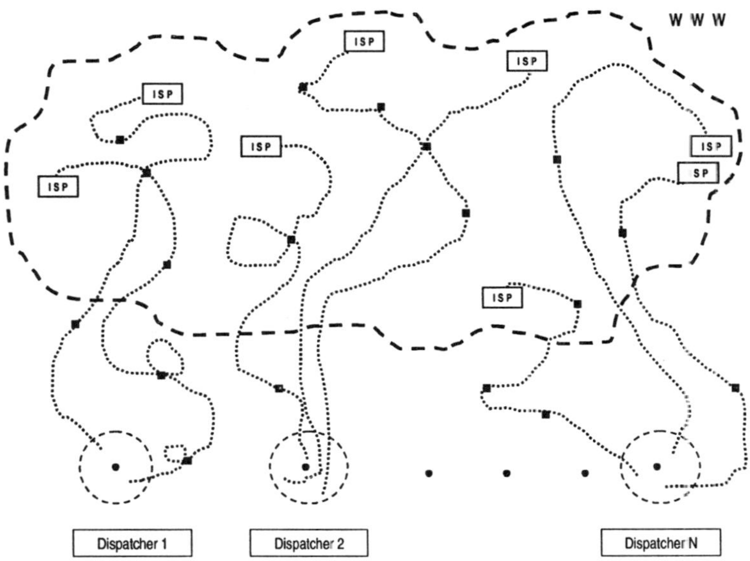

Fig. 1. The WWW viewed as an information ecosystem.

The Tocorime Apicu information sharing (IS) model is partitioned into four distinct components that use a hierarchical communication topology to access a system of stored information (referred to as an information ecosystem)—the Internet as shown in Figure 1. The information model consists of the following components: 1) a HTML resource discovery (HRD) model, 2) an information sharing indexing (ISI) model, 3) a browser reporting interface (BRI) model, and 4) a distributed file system model. The information ecosystem [2,3] maps the Internet to a composite set of self-contained ecosystems (Internet service providers). Figure 2 presents the honeybee-inspired design of the search engine. Information availability of each self-contained ecosystem reflects stochastic fluctuations that can occur within randomly selected areas of the Internet. As with each localized view of a honeybee colony's ecosystem, each self-contained information ecosys-

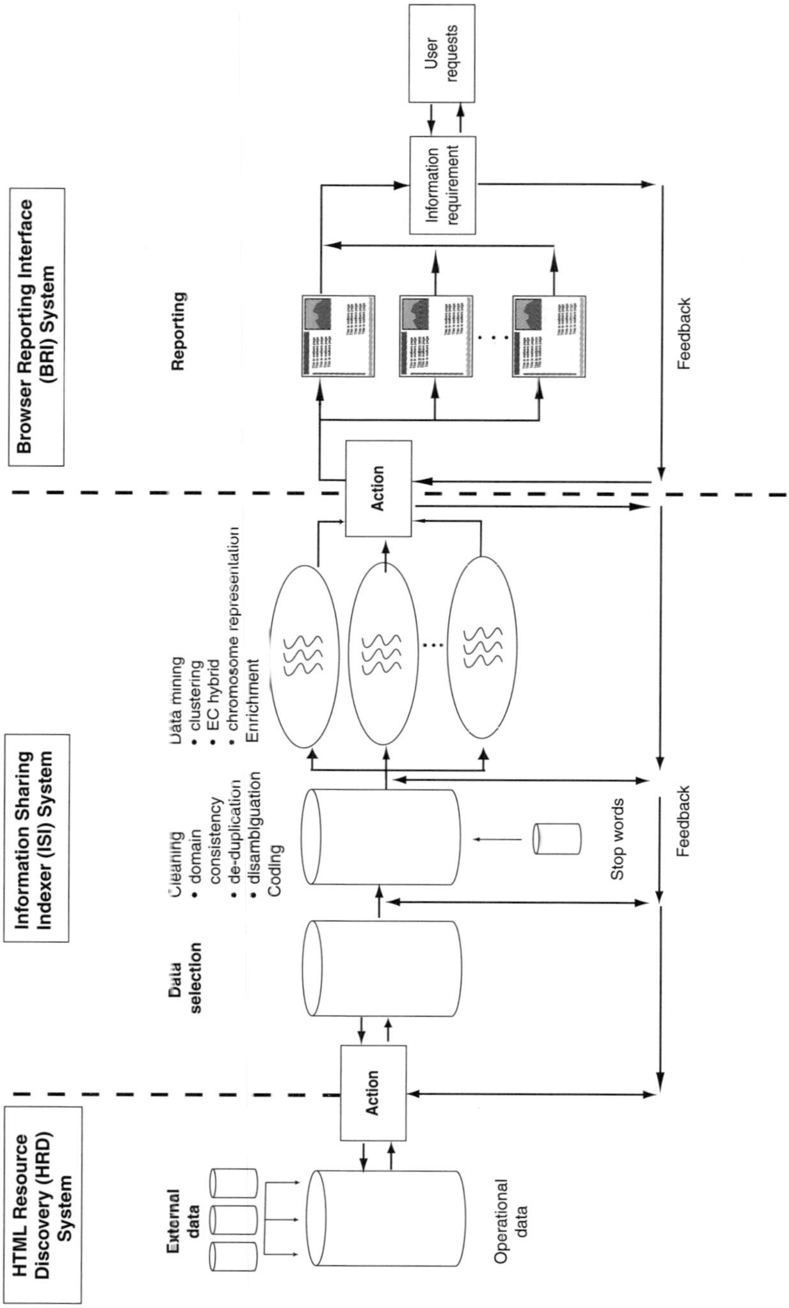

Fig. 2. The architecture of the integrated search engine.

tem responds differently depending on: 1) the time of day, 2) the time zone, 3) various holiday and/or vacation patterns, and 4) ever-occurring major newsworthy events. An extensive discussion of the information sharing model was presented in the author's Ph.D. dissertation [4].

The indexing mechanisms of search engines were developed as an extension of information retrieval (IR) systems [5,6] designed to index bibliographic data-bases. A common restriction of most IR systems was that they indexed only document titles or abstracts, as opposed to the text of a document—although some IR systems did full-text search. These early systems were known as document text retrieval systems, and they encompassed the following two components of current engines: 1) indexing—the retrieval mechanism needed to match expressions of the user's information need (query) with the items in selected files (documents and/or Web pages), and 2) searching—the mechanism that matches search query items with files.

Honeybees provide a good model for information optimization through evolution. The methodologies of evolutionary computation can serve as optimization methodologies by which the Tocorime Apicu information sharing (IS) system adapts to the changing Web conditions. This chapter presents the Tocorime Apicu approach for replacing the information retrieval model with an information sharing model that adapts to changing conditions within the Internet using stochastic optimization methodologies of evolutionary computation. The chapter is organized as follows. Section 2 describes related work. Section 3 presents an overview of improvements for current search engine models. Section 4 presents the honeybee and Tocorime Apicu information sharing models. Section 5 presents the application of the stochastic optimization methodologies of evolutionary computation. Section 6 presents experimental results. Finally, in Section 7, we draw some conclusions and outline directions of future research.

2. Related Work

Internet discovery agents [7] incorporated methodologies for auto-discovery of the inter-dependencies among services provided by Internet service providers (ISPs). These agents were used to implement a management system for hosts that support application servers associated with file transfer protocol (FTP), telnet, e-mail, news, domain name service (DNS), network file system (NFS), hypertext transfer protocol (HTTP), etc. The automated methodologies reduce the amount of human intervention needed to customize the system when new ISPs are located.

The exploration behavior of Internet agents [8,9] for the multiple access problem (MAP) considered the search strategy of n agents accessing m servers. The retrieval of information from the various shared servers was maximized through cooperating agents. Each agents sends a moderate number of queries. This prevents the deterioration of the server's performance which leads to exponential delay as the number of queries increases.

Avoidance of traps such as genetic (random) drift [10,11], which can result in convergence to local minima, is not accomplished by adjusting the recombination operator, but rather by applying a mutation operator. Additionally, the mutation operator aids an evolutionary computation (EC) application in a dynamically changing environment. Genetic drift is caused by a limited random search that is due to the stochastic nature of the selection operator and a relatively small population size.

The use of a single population leads to panmictic selection [12,13] where the individuals selected to participate in a genetic operation can be from anywhere in the population. The use of subpopulations (evolution of species) is an additional method for avoiding local optima associated with panmictic selection.

Classification methods can be enhanced by using communicating agents that perform genetic and cultural transmissions simultaneously by using *cultural co-evolution* [14]. This approach relies on the evolution of a set of diverse learning agents (genes) and the evolution of their data representations (culture). One of the most notable benefits of applying the operators associated with the methodologies of EC is their ability to generate successive iterations that possess the provision of "partial" classification whose continuous sums may ultimately lead to a suboptimal/optima classification. The goal of this approach is to develop a methodology that uses the strengths of EC to explore the disparate regions of the search space by partitioning its components among the agents.

Benefits associated with extensive use of the mutation operator [15] include removal of time limitations on genetic programming (GP) applications which were prone to converge to local minima. The use of the mutation operator is more extensive in evolutionary strategies (ES) and evolutionary programming (EP) than in genetic algorithms (GA) or GP.

3. Improvements Needed by Current Search Engines

The indexers for the early and current search engines used existing state-of-the-art techniques [16] to retrieve and rank relevant documents. However, the treatment of relevance rankings was not consistent because it depended on human and computer constraints. Reasons for improving IR systems include: 1) overhauling the precision and recall mechanisms of current IR systems [5,17,18,19] which handle millions of documents that may be centrally or distributedly located throughout the Internet [20], to reduce transmission delays and server efficiency; also 2) a reduction in the required knowledge about a given indexer to minimize useless searches over the Internet for keywords that produce no new results.

Most search engines present users with pre-indexed information whose transmission rate [23] is limited by the network traffic and user bandwidth. The form filing page associated with current search engines uses one entry box for the user's query. However, this form page contains advertising as well as other references to services that may be provided by the chosen engine. Due to the nature of search engines and the amount of information returned for a query, the nonessential information found within a page has been reduced. Some form of animation may be displayed in the form of product advertising, which in turn reduces the throughput of the query result page. Repeated searches also allow the user to view the query results based on various ordering schemes.

One of the major shortcomings of current engines is their inability to find and incorporate new information in a timely manner. The World Wide Web (WWW) is estimated to have a growth rate of approximately seven million new pages per day [18,21,22]. This results in weeks or even months passing before new pages are indexed. Faster indexing is available in some search engines using *paid-inclusion* or *pay-for-submission* services[b] such as GoTo.com [24,25] which is the Internet's leading pay-for-performance search engine. This service gives its subscribers an advertising network used by major search engines to supplement their database with the results produced by GoTo.com (producer of pre-indexed Web pages). The advertising network allows companies to target specific audiences to promote their sites and/or products. A second shortcoming of current engines is associated with the general Web page classification system used in their IR systems. Overcoming these two shortcomings is the major focus of this work.

---

[b]Inktomi was the first engine to use the pay-for-submission model [25].

The classification aspects of IR systems are based on viewing document retrieval as a dynamic process involving learning in response to training examples and feedback. The basic components of an IR system—files (documents or Web pages), index terms (search strings), and user requests (queries)—reflect that: 1) the indexing mechanism has the ability to classify/reclassify files which are placed in pre-indexed stores of information, and 2) the searching mechanism functions as a parser with the ability to distinguish between matching and non-matching components within files. The coupling of these two mechanisms results in an IR system incorporating the following tasks:

(1) Extraction—Identifying pre-specified types of information within a file.
(2) Categorization—Grouping files based on selected topics, or on a database topic structure/category that has been deemed important to potential users of the system.
(3) Summarizing—Abstracting the most important components of the file's content.
(4) Filtering or routing—Transmitting responses to users.

An operational IR system was the result of extending the basic model just discussed with Boolean query language, thereby supplying users with the ability to link terms with basic logical operators: the AND operator that linked different facets of a multifaceted subject, the OR operator that linked synonyms or alternative choices, and the NOT operator that eliminated documents indexed by terms known to be irrelevant. When used correctly, Boolean searches [16] can provide users with accurate results and reduce the number of refinements of the initial query.

4. Replacing the Information Retrieval Model with an Information Sharing Model

4.1. *The Basis of the Information Sharing Model*

The social structure associated with honeybee behavior [26] provides a simple solution to the problem of multiway rendezvous [27]. The organizing principle of a honeybee society [28] is information sharing (IS)—the ability to send and receive messages, and to encode and decode information that may be transmitted through chemical, tactile, auditory, and/or visual messages for the purpose of finding and communicating the location [29] of adequate food sources, including water.

Adaptation of the honeybee IS model establishes order in the inherent interactions between the search engine's indexer, Web foraging, and browser mechanisms by including the social (hierarchical) structure and simulated behavior of this complex system [3]. The simulation of behavior will engender mechanisms that are controlled and coordinated in their various levels of complexity. The benefits of incorporating and using the social behavior of honeybees include:

- Honeybees face fundamentally the same problems as Web IR, but nature has refined their solutions over millions of years.
- Honeybees provide a good model for information resource discovery since their foraging methodology can be successfully adapted to information searching.
- Honeybees provide a good model for information optimization through evolution since we can use the methodologies of evolutionary computation as optimization methodologies to adjust the Tocorime Apicu information sharing (IS) system to the changing Web conditions.
- Honeybees provide a good model for parallel computation, with the hierarchy of honeybee roles and their protocols serving as a model infrastructure for managing multiprocessor Web IR systems.

4.2. *The Tocorime Apicu Information Sharing Model*

The Tocorime Apicu IS model uses a Web foraging model [2] which focuses on locating ISPs hosting HTML services by using a wide area search-for-service strategy. These foragers—referred to as Web probes, scouts, and foragers—form a crucial component of the Tocorime Apicu search engine. Implementation of this search-for-service strategy—via its Web probes, scouts, and foragers—requires that quality-of-service (QoS) and quality of information-sharing be maintained for each ISP hosting HTML services in order to efficiently retrieve Web documents. Each forager set has a finite scope, limiting its activity to those ISPs inscribed within an area whose radius is given by a value V (its visibility). Web forager sets interact using information sharing mechanisms that encompass Internet congestion detection and congestion avoidance mechanisms.

The ISI model [30] uses a stochastic regulatory mechanism within a Web page indexing model. Applied continuously, the regulatory mechanism results in localized information fluctuations—its goal is improving the subclustering of Web pages in this distributive application. It maintains disjoint nodes for chosen sets of search queries known as probe sets. The optimization methodologies form the basis of a regulatory mechanism for sharing information—migration of Web pages between computers within the local area network (LAN). The regulatory mechanism uses probe sets (which may be determined statically or dynamically), a set of retrieval algorithms, and stochastic selection methodologies based on methods of evolutionary computation. The formulation of nearest neighbor clusters (NNCs) occurs by applying the regulatory mechanism, resulting in either random nearest neighbors (NN), multiple disjoint clusters, and/or overlapping clusters using neighborhood seeds (centroids) and drifters. Additionally, the regulatory mechanism permits the information sharing system to escape from local optima in its attempts to gather related Web pages at a node by analyzing page content (using a canonical representation of each Web page) and creating information fluctuations among the indexing nodes.

Supersedure emulation [33] was introduced in the Tocorime ISI system. It occurs when two or more seeds are nearest neighbors and form overlapping neighborhoods. Supersedure in honeybees [26] occurs when an existing or new queen is overtaken by a newly hatched queen during a fight which may result in the death of one or both queen(s). Two simulated breeding groups were formed—neighborhood seeds (queens) and drifters (drones). The occurrence of overlapping seed neighborhoods leads to selection, where a single seed breaks the impasse of indeterminacy, thus emulating the supersedure aspect of the social behavior of honeybees. This results in tournament selection, as it is known in evolutionary computation (EC). This impasse leads to the formulation of random clusters which may result in K-nearest-neighbors (Knn), with K being the number of drifters. This further results in a possible superstep [34] with the restriction that randomly chosen drifters are actual NN of the seed.

5. Optimization of Honeybee Search Strategies for a Better Web IS System

5.1. *The Stochastic Optimization Methodologies of Evolutionary Computation*

The stochastic optimization methodologies of evolutionary computation (EC) [35,36] contain mechanisms which enable the representation of certain unique aspects of honeybee behavior. The field of evolutionary computation encompasses stochastic optimization techniques, such as randomized search strategies, in the form of evolutionary strategies (ES), evolutionary programming (EP), genetic algorithms (GA), classifier systems, evolvable hardware (EHW), and genetic programming (GP). The chief differences

Table 1. EC methodologies that form the basis of the stochastic search strategies of the Tocorime Apicu HRD system.

EC method	Usage	Variation operator	Selection mechanism
Classifier systems	Web page parsers operate as general -purpose Turing complete algorithms comprised of production rules (HTML) as push -down automata.	Rules resulting from the application of a genetic algorithm build the next potentially modified classifier system.	The first-pass parser validates the structure of each retrieved Web page by a Web forager. The second strips unneeded information from each page provided by a Web forager.
EHW	Web mechanisms used a reconfigurable hardware methodology (active networks) to facilitate a network probe (signaling) facility to query networks for HTML resource discovery, diagnostics, network monitoring, etc.	Stochastic measures result from foraging selected areas of the Internet to detect and avoid network congestion.	Computational measures are used to access network bandwidth and CPU requirements.

among the various types of EC stem from: 1) the representation and/or usage of solutions (known as individuals in EC), 2) the design of the variation operators (mutation and/or recombination—also known as crossover), and 3) selection mechanisms. A common strength of these optimization approaches lies in the use of hybrid algorithms which are derived by combining one or more of the evolutionary search methodologies. These methodologies can be related to meaningful representation and effective matching of user needs with relevant documents. An individual in this research effort is considered a node/computer.

5.2. *Mapping the Optimization Methodologies to the Tocorime Apicu Architecture*

Tables 1 and 2 present the mapping of the optimization methodologies to the components of the Tocorime Apicu architecture. The HTML Resource Discovery (HRD) system [37] avoiding network congestion [7,8,9] by using the methodologies of EHW and active networks (AN) in its network probing facility to establish customized routes for the retrieval of remotely located Web pages. Certain aspects of EHW are also components of AN. The HRD system Web probe, scout, and forager dispatchers are responsible for retrieving external data using honeybee foraging strategies.

Table 2. EC methodologies that form the basis of the stochastic search strategies of the Tocorime Apicu ISI system.

EC method	Usage	Variation operator	Selection mechanism
ES	Supersedure emulation extends the representation of individuals to include strategy parameters for adaptive mutation and recombination rate(s).	Random speciation seed provides the selection features in the form of a probe set.	Tournament selection and proportional fitness selection are used.
EP	Supersedure emulation acts as a finite state machine (FSM) or automaton.	Recombination and mutation operators are used to change states of the FSM.	Employs fitness-based recombination selection of multiple individuals and mutation
GA	Web page indexing system uses chromosomes of fixed length as a page data structure.	Heavy use is made of recombination and mutation.	Fitness-proportional and random selection of individuals are used.
GP	Web page indexing system uses chromosomes of fixed length as a page data structure with syntax wrappers.	Heavy use is made of recombination and mutation.	Fitness-proportional and random selection of individuals are used.

Production rules are used to verify the format of raw pages retrieved by the HRD system during a first pass, and when the information sharing indexing (ISI) system Web document parser [30] performs a second pass. GA and GP have been combined to provide the basis of the ISI indexing strategy. Individual representations in the ISI system are hash table data structures of fixed length with syntax wrappers. Recombination and mutation are applied frequently. Workload redistribution/load balancing is controlled via stochastic optimization methodologies that incorporate GA, ES, EP, and GP. The selection operator uses fitness-proportional and random mechanisms to implement the nearest neighbors (NN) strategy [30]. The Web page dispatcher uses a stochastic regulatory mechanism to adaptively form clusters of indexer nodes—sets of nearest neighbors—that facilitate the migration of Web pages using the honeybee information sharing model. The ISI system uses probe sets (which may be determined statically or dynamically), a set of retrieval algorithms, and selection methodologies of evolutionary computation.

5.3. *Reductions in the Computational Effort*

The fitness of a species can be improved by the non-genetic transmission of cultural information [14,31,32] that uses a *meme* as the transmission mechanism rather than the genetically based *gene*. The difference between the two includes the fact that genetic transmissions (stochastic selection process) evolve over a period of generations, whereas cultural transmissions result from an educational process. The transmission of cultural information can be facilitated by preserving in memory the fitness evaluations associated with a previous generation using an *indexed memory* scheme. The advantage of such a preservation of cultural information is that it creates a reduction in the corresponding computational effort. It represents a non-genetic means for computing fitness evaluations. The term non-genetic implies that this mechanism can be used to enhance a population without the use of selection operators. The disadvantage to this approach is that the amount of data passed from one generation to the next increases without adapting the transmission (information sharing) mechanism.

6. Experimental Results

6.1. *HRD Results*

6.1.1. *Execution Environment*

The goal of this study was to test the run-time environment associated with Web dispatchers and determine the limitations in executing the HRD network probing software for extended periods of time. The HRD system was tested using HP Pavilions with four 733MHz (20 Gigabytes of memory) Intel Celeron processors, 128 MB SDRAM, and Intel Pro/100+ Server Adapter Ethernet cards, connected via two D-Link DSH-16 10/100 dual-speed hubs with switches through a 144 Kbps router. The dispatcher tests were run using Red Hat Linux release 7.0 (Guiness).

6.1.2. *Searching the Internet for ISPs Hosting Web Services*

The HRD system searched the Internet for those ISPs hosting Web services for a total of fifteen weeks, including three holidays celebrated in the United States—Thanksgiving, Christmas, and New Year's. The start date was 15 October 2001 and the terminating date was 28 January 2002 as shown in Table 3. Table 4 presents one-week data collection periods that span from Monday to Monday. The table summarizes the status of each probe dispatcher over seven-day collection periods. The target ratio was computed

Table 3. Cumulative access log summaries for Web probe dispatchers.

Item	Web probe dispatchers
Start date	15 Oct 2001
Stop date	28 Jan 2002
Duration in days	105 days
Duration in weeks	15 weeks
Simultaneous probe transmissions	128
Total requests	48193332.0
Avg requests per day	458984.1
HTML servers located	75367
DNS name resolutions	28727

using

$$Target\ ratio = \frac{\sum_{i=0}^{3} probes/week}{4\ \ million\ probes/week} \tag{1}$$

As evident from Table 4, the results reveal a steady increase in the total number of HTML servers associated with each node—which is not consistent with expected results. The results from four dispatchers are examined in this test of the HRD system. The weekly breakdown of the results reveals that there are detectable decreases in the bandwidth associated with each dispatcher. This reduction in bandwidth, which was reflected across all of the computers that are part of the discovery system, is probably due to the fact that the computers shared the same router and ISP host. The choice of Internet addresses that were probed was also a random variable in these studies.

All the nodes achieved their best combined performance during the first week of each distinct study. The subsequent weeks reflect the use of the same node hosting the probe dispatcher that also hosts its accompanying scout and forager dispatchers. This reduction in node efficiency reflects the sharing of computer resources among the dispatchers. The Web scout and forager dispatcher results presented reflect offline ISP discovery and page retrieval [38] where the requirements imposed by the real-time processing delays result in each unique Web group (i.e., probe, scout, and forager dispatchers) generating its best performance. The weekly ratios reflect subtle changes in the number of released probes, responding ISPs, DNS resolutions, and retrieved pages. These subtle changes can be seen in the weeks before Halloween, Thanksgiving, Christmas, New Year's, and Superbowl weekend.

Table 4. Cumulative access log summary for all Web probe dispatchers per week, starting on 15 Oct 2001 and terminating 28 Jan 2002.

Duration — Start — Stop	Web probe dispatchers Node 0	Node 1	Node 2	Node 3	Totals	Target ratio
15 Oct - 22 Oct	856898	866100	937825	860185	3521008	88.03%
22 Oct - 29 Oct	1554957	1590259	1650506	1579525	6375247	79.69%
29 Oct - 05 Nov	2316420	2353539	2411958	2360721	9442638	78.69%
05 Nov - 12 Nov	3154581	3156620	3214533	3176032	12701766	79.39%
12 Nov - 19 Nov	3938617	4008097	4025989	3976145	15948848	79.74%
19 Nov - 26 Nov	4709028	4810252	4814126	4772524	19105930	79.61%
26 Nov - 03 Dec	5490017	5576071	5595341	5560066	22221495	79.36%
03 Dec - 10 Dec	6308515	6405952	6377555	6369867	25461889	79.57%
10 Dec - 17 Dec	7272063	7384383	7350495	7342786	29349727	81.53%
17 Dec - 24 Dec	8036262	8122376	8112440	8101316	32372394	80.93%
24 Dec - 31 Dec	8850633	8915370	8872494	8848908	35487405	80.65%
31 Dec - 07 Jan	9660610	9694866	9647053	9608487	38611016	80.44%
07 Jan - 14 Jan	10480336	10497039	10473789	10445281	41896445	80.57%
14 Jan - 21 Jan	11318071	11298831	11289679	11253161	45159742	80.64%
21 Jan - 28 Jan	12072667	12042237	12049207	12029221	48193332	80.32%

Halloween and Superbowl weekend are not occasions associated with vacation time in the United States. The weeks of Thanksgiving, Christmas, and New Year's reflect Internet user activity consisting of home computers as opposed to the use of office computers. This results in unrestricted, extended periods of possible uninterrupted Internet access. The next subtle change in user patterns is expected to occur during the weeks following Super Bowl weekend but prior to Valentine's Day, unless one or more national/international events occur such as the effect of global Internet viruses (October 2002) and the war in Iraq (March 2003) [3] .

6.1.3. *Computational Results*

During the initial week, 15 Oct to 22 Oct, the dispatchers met approximately 88% of their target goal of releasing a composite of 4 million probes. Week 2 showed throughput fluctuations compared to the previous week and the week of Halloween. When viewing the first three weeks of this study, it appears that the HRD system was suffering from performance degradation because of memory leaks [2]—as there was approximately an overall decrease of 21% from the target ratio. This demonstrates that the Internet user activities increased during the week of Halloween (Week 3).

The next event considered was Thanksgiving with system coverage beginning the week of Halloween. Weeks 4 and 5 show increases in system throughput, reflecting possible reductions in user activity owing to the holiday seasons affecting Internet traffic. Week 6 shows a decrease in throughput from Week 5 but an increase compared to Week 4. The end of this collection period showed an approximate 20.4% difference between the results and the target ratio. The presence of traffic congestion is depicted in the charts by consistent throughput measurements of the number of released probes.

The next major holiday period considered was Christmas/New Year's with a collection period beginning Week 7 and terminating Week 12. The starting period reflects a reduction in user traffic following Thanksgiving. The optimal throughput for this period occurred during Week 9, which represents the middle of the collection period. The optimal throughput for the collection period containing Thanksgiving occurred near the middle of the period. The final week of this collection period showed a 19.56% difference from the target ratio.

The final event of this composite collection period was the Super Bowl weekend, a major event in the United States. The time period between Christmas and New Year's is short, and this is reflected in the data collection period associated with this system. The collection period started in Week 12 and terminated with Week 15. The optimal throughput occurred near the median point of this collection period which reflected patterns seen in the previous periods. The final week of this period showed a 19.68% deviation from the target ratio.

All of the collection periods contain localized optima that gradually decrease, followed by a gradual increase in user activity until the occurrence of the next event is initially acknowledged by Internet users. Offline results for the scout and forager dispatchers—tightly coupled—are presented for a two-week period, Weeks 16 and 17, using four nodes dedicated to these tasks (see Table 5).

6.2. *ISI Results*

6.2.1. *Execution Environment*

Earlier studies of the ISI system [16,30] were limited to 1024 Web pages and presented the benefits of incorporating honeybee search strategies. These results focus on the second pass of the two-pass ISI parser which has been expanded and tested using HP Pavilions with three 866 MHz (30 Giga-

Table 5. Selected Web documents retrieved by the HTML resource discovery (HRD) system.

Retrieval period	ISP response results	Web forager dispatcher				
		Node 0	**Node 1**	**Node 2**	**Node 3**	**Totals**
15 Oct 2001	HTML pages	1422	1127	1003	1112	4664
— 28 Jan 2002	Access forbidden pages					
	—Firewall pages	96	37	72	48	253
	—Web mail pages	324	288	345	328	1285
	—403 forbidden	7	4	5	5	21
	—404 not found	1	1	2	3	7
	Useful raw HTML pages	994	797	579	728	3098
28 Jan 2002	HTML pages	3526	2302	2819	2448	11095
— 13 May 2002	Access forbidden pages					
	—Firewall pages	220	61	55	43	379
	—Web mail pages	190	573	104	226	1093
	—403 forbidden	23	19	22	11	75
	—404 not found	8	6	4	4	22
	Useful raw HTML pages	3085	1643	2634	2164	9526
16 Sep 2002	HTML pages	1923	1558	1716	1459	6656
— 04 Mar 2003	Access forbidden pages					
	—Firewall pages	110	75	71	69	325
	—Web mail pages	486	514	534	540	2074
	—403 forbidden	37	13	53	17	120
	—404 not found	12	6	3	7	28
	Useful raw HTML pages	1278	950	1055	826	4109
Totals	HTML pages	6871	4987	5538	5019	22415
	Access forbidden pages					
	—Firewall pages	426	173	198	160	957
	—Web mail pages	1000	1375	983	1094	4452
	—403 forbidden	67	36	80	33	216
	—404 not found	21	13	9	14	57
	Useful raw HTML pages	5357	3390	4268	3718	16733

bytes hard drive) and one 800 MHz (30 Gigabytes of memory) Pentium III processors, 128 MB SDRAM, and Intel Pro/100+ Server Adapter Ethernet cards, connected via two D-Link DSH-16 10/100 dual-speed hubs with switches through a 144 Kbps router. The indexer tests use Red Hat Linux

Table 6. The ISI system input parameters.

Parameter	Version A	Version B	Version C	Version D	Version E
Dataset size + Yahoo pages	1024	1024	1024	1024	4664 + 1771
Max number of iterations	200	200	≤ 200	≤ 200	1024
Probe set size	16 Static words	16 Static words	16 Dynamic words	16 Dynamic words	47 Static words

release 7.0 (Guiness). The dataset tested consists of 1771 Yahoo Business Headline documents [39] supplemented by 4664 HRD raw (parsed for the correct format) data files supplied by the HRD system [2]. Table 6 shows the input parameters for the different versions of the ISI system.

This study relied on a set of 47 strings stored in a static probe set—the approach used by operational IR systems—in order to compute the associated stochastic measures for each Web page. A static probe set, which does not have adequate *a priori* knowledge about randomly chosen Web documents that supplement the dataset, must be developed by a human editor. The 47 search strings used in this study were derived from random phrases chosen from a disparate collection of Wall Street Journal articles [40] which are independent from the randomly chosen dataset of Web pages.

6.2.2. *Indexing a Random Dataset of Web Pages*

The initial dataset used in a search engine case study was 512 Web pages [16] followed by Versions A, B, C, and D of the ISI system [30] which were limited to 1024. Both of these studies used subsets of the 1771 Yahoo pages. The hash table used to store the dataset for indexing purposes was limited to 1024 elements. These five studies present feasibility results reflective of the effectiveness of honeybee search strategies as a clustering and indexing mechanism. Table 5 presents additional Web pages that have been retrieved and will be used to expand the results of Version E as future work.

The experimental results in this chapter for Version E were derived from a study aiming to assess the impact of Web page scalability on the ISI system. The HRD Web scouts located a total of 28727 raw data files that contained various forms of HTML documents written in a host of languages.

The HRD Web foragers were responsible for filtering the raw data files for the indexers by executing the first pass of the two-pass HTML parser. The foragers eliminated 6312 raw data files due to incorrect formats, corrupted files, and/or non-English files. The resulting file types are presented in Table 5. The resulting 22415 files were further partitioned into firewall pages, Web mail access pages, 403 (access) forbidden pages, 404 (file) not found pages, and useful raw HTML pages. The percentages of the files that comprised the dataset are 4.2%, 19.9%, 1.0%, 0.2%, and 74.7%, respectively.

Versions E and F of the ISI system (which differ from each other in the structure of the probe set) still need to be tested. These versions will differ from their predecessors in two distinct ways: the dataset size will be 22415 (+ 1771 Yahoo pages) which is a 22-fold increase in the dataset size, and the hash table will have at most 32768 elements.

Before the parallel version of Versions E and F are tested, the sequential version is being used with a pseudo-node that initially contains the 1771 Yahoo pages at the beginning of the simulation. The pseudo-node is used as a means of emulating a two-node indexer cluster coupled with the stochastic regulatory mechanism for information sharing between the two nodes. The UNIX function */usr/bin/time* was used to capture the runtime resource usage for the four distinct nodes executing the sequential version of Version E.

The hash table size was increased by powers of 2, starting from a hash structure size of 1024. The study was terminated with a hash size of 32768. The output generated by the UNIX command provides run-time information related to the way the application software utilizes major system resources—CPU and memory. Each of the nodes utilizes system resources differently based on internal fluctuations in each node's hardware. The UNIX *time* function is not useful when using MPI for the parallel versions.

6.2.3. *Computational Results*

As the table size was increased, the performance of Version E with various hash table sizes showed improvement in all areas of resource usage (see Table 7). These improvements occurred on a computer-by-computer basis as each machine responded uniquely to the table size variations. The elapsed CPU times for all the nodes showed decreases that ranged from approximately 5 hours for node 0 to approximately 16 hours for node 3. Node 2 had a decrease of approximately 9 hours. Each node experienced a resource usage increase for the hash table sizes of 8192 and 32768. These increases reflect the distribution of the pages within the hash table which, in turn, reflects collisions within each element. Additionally, the elapsed time for nodes 0 and 1 showed an approximate one-hour increase for a table size of 2048—where node 2 experienced a 3-hour decrease. However, node 3 experienced a 10-hour decrease for the same table size.

The user CPU times did not reflect the timing trends shown in the elapsed times. The CPU time measurements for elapsed time was hours:minutes:seconds, and seconds for the user and system times. The user CPU timings for each node decreased by approximately 2000.0 seconds (5 hours) with the increase in hash table size. The approximate difference between nodes was approximately 8000.0 seconds, with the table size varying from 1024 to 32768. The system CPU times showed timing fluctuations consistent with the elapsed CPU times. Nodes 0 and 3 showed decreases in system times consistent with elapsed times. As the elapsed time decreased, the system time decreased also. Nodes 1 and 2 did not follow any noticeable trend and fluctuate in what appears to be an inconsistent manner.

The most interesting components of this study were the variations in the percentage of CPU utilization—ranging from 1% to 8%. Node 0 started with 4% and reached a low of 1%. Node 1 had a similar percentage range of 7% which decreased down to 4%. Both of these nodes decreased by approximately 3%. Nodes 2 and 3 decreased by approximately 2%. All of the nodes exhibited a decrease until the table size was increased to 32768. The percentages of CPU utilization do not appear to reflect any single resource measurement but rather to result from a combination of measurements.

CPU utilization percentages also reflect the efficient use of memory which encompasses major and minor page faults and page swaps—all of which fluctuate with the increased hash table size. The ratio of the hash table size to the dataset size (4664 pages) was 0.22, 0.44, 0.88, 1.76, 3.51, and 7.03, respectively. The factor that appears to affect memory utilization as well as CPU utilization is the distribution of pages throughout the hash table. A reduction in the number of collisions within each table element results in a decrease in all memory and CPU measurement. As the dataset grows, limitations are imposed on the size of the hash table. The underlying goal of a good hash function is to distribute the elements of the dataset as equally as possible.

7. Summary

Stochastic optimization methodologies have been used extensively in the design of Tocorime Apicu. These optimization methodologies provide the foundation for improving IS system performance by working to reduce the imbalance in workloads, overlap among task workload assignments, saturation of file servers within a network (LAN, LAN+WAN, and WAN), and sensitivity to irregularities associated with Internet traffic.

This chapter has related the underlying mechanisms of the Tocorime IS system with the EC model. This mapping is extended by aspects of finding hidden knowledge in a collection of documents—related and/or unrelated. Canonical Web pages were generated to reduce the workload and storage requirements of the ISI system, resulting in a set of condensed documents forming the data warehouse. The ISI system continuously repartitions the document space among a set of distributed nodes using a stochastic regulatory system whose goal is to form subclusters of nodes which would redistribute the workload.

The Tocorime Apicu IS system has incorporated suggested approaches for improving the IR systems of current search engines supplemented with the search strategies of honeybees. Earlier studies of this model demonstrated the benefits of unsupervised clustering of Web pages using adaptive probe sets. The experimental results showed that the model will scale as additional Web pages are added to the dataset. Also, the data structure used to facilitate the unsupervised clustering of Web pages has a large impact on the efficiency of this adaptive implementation.

The CPU utilization percentages showed steady decreases which, at first glance, appears to indicate an inefficient application program. The measurement that is most noticeable in parallel applications is the reduction in elapsed CPU time, as opposed to the percentage of CPU utilization across all nodes in a parallel application. The speedups reflected in the sequential versions should transfer to the parallel version of this application.

Acknowledgments

The author wishes to express his gratitude to the reviewers whose detailed and useful comments helped tremendously to improve the quality of this chapter. This work was supported by Honeybee Technologies and Tapicu, Inc.

Table 7. Execution results for a pseudo-node with 1771 pages and a node with 4664 pages.

Hash table size	OS Usage	Node 0	Node 1	Node 2	Node 3
1024	CPU timing (elapsed)	86:56:06	76:42:33	89:34:06	91:44:48
	CPU timing (user)	95494.90	102740.60	95582.33	108248.18
	CPU timing (system)	3151.72	3419.16	8358.86	4611.25
	CPU utilization	4%	7%	5%	8%
	page faults (major)	20217567	21219010	23348805	22271294
	page faults (minor	18063326	18227509	18422797	18473458
	page swaps	891266	992168	1106580	1135227
2048	CPU timing (elapsed)	88:16:57	77:17:10	86:38:36	81:42:51
	CPU timing (user)	94494.37	101677.49	93302.16	107019.31
	CPU timing (system)	2989.58	3396.43	7722.58	4240.17
	CPU utilization	3%	6%	4%	8%
	page faults (major)	19699071	22141370	19809162	21803346
	page faults (minor)	17783977	18532508	17798479	18690136
	page swaps	714667	1138898	720854	1240631
4096	CPU timing (elapsed)	84:27:22	74:35:15	83:34:03	79:23:29
	CPU timing (user)	92226.53	99259.45	91692.19	105041.97
	CPU timing (system)	2855.57	3249.32	7870.62	4296.15
	CPU utilization	3%	6%	4%	8%
	page faults (major)	22210976	21335491	22199305	22540909
	page faults (minor)	18308356	18065741	18352411	18211708
	page swaps	980466	851953	1006141	893464
8192	CPU timing (elapsed)	88:36:29	76:50:48	86:09:27	81:53:56
	CPU timing (user)	90262.82	97639.74	89977.98	103455.31
	CPU timing (system)	2827.84	3391.01	7874.10	4639.60
	CPU utilization	2%	5%	3%	7%
	page faults (major)	24346468	24240287	23128138	25611445
	page faults (minor)	18814675	18473646	18757880	18469424
	page swaps	1408180	1189773	1366295	1181784
16384	CPU timing (elapsed)	81:23:12	71:49:00	80:15:21	75:14:24
	CPU timing (user)	88549.63	95136.15	87770.73	100379.20
	CPU timing (system)	2622.25	2935.13	7293.53	3833.38
	CPU utilization	1%	4%	3%	6%
	page faults (major)	20429131	20144997	20584363	19423002
	page faults (minor)	17940436	17724845	17957506	17687554
	page swaps	859842	728641	872209	682569
32768	CPU timing (elapsed)	84:23:08	74:58:50	83:52:38	76:51:55
	CPU timing (user)	91939.85	98812.46	91174.06	103942.82
	CPU timing (system)	2644.12	3037.01	7486.09	3875.40
	CPU utilization	2%	5%	4%	7%
	page faults (major)	21064694	22040748	22070392	19517012
	page faults (minor)	18638159	18401523	18588344	18302823
	page swaps	1189082	1019620	1149957	940127

References

1. P. Fritsch, *Wall Street Journal (Western Edition)* **CXLI**, 35 p. Sect A:1 (Col. 4) 2000).
2. R.L. Walker, *Journal of Network and Computer Applications*, To appear, (2004).
3. R.L. Walker, in *Proc. KIMAS 2003*, Ed. H. Hexmoor (IEEE Press, Piscataway, NJ, 2003), p. 497.
4. R.L. Walker, Tocorime Apicu: Design of an Experimental Search Engine using an Information Sharing Model, Ph.D. Dissertation, Univ. of California, Los Angeles (2003).
5. K.S. Jones and P. Willett, in *Readings in Information Retrieval*, (Morgan Kaufmann Publishers, Inc. (San Francisco), Chapter 1. 1997).
6. D.R. Swanson, *J. Amer. Society for Info. Sci.* **39**, 92 (1988).
7. S. Ramanathan, D. Caswell, and S. Neal, *J. Network and Systems Management* **8(4)**, 457 (2000).
8. J.C. Oh, in *Proc. IEEE Congress on Evol. Comp.*, (IEEE Press, Piscataway, NJ, 2000), p. 864.
9. J.C. Oh, in *Proc. IEEE Congress on Evol. Comp.*, (IEEE Press, Piscataway, NJ, 2001), p. 1261.
10. J. Branke, M. Cutaia, and H. Dold, in *Proc. GECCO-99*, Eds. W. Banshaf, J. Daidai, A.E. Eiben, M.H. Garzon, V. Honavar, M. Jakiela, and R.E. Smith, (Morgan Kaufman Publishers, Inc., 1999), p. 68.
11. F. Oppacher and M. Wineberg, in *Proc. GECCO-99*, Eds. W. Banshaf, J. Daidai, A.E. Eiben, M.H. Garzon, V. Honavar, M. Jakiela, and R.E. Smith, (Morgan Kaufman Publishers, Inc., 1999), p. 504.
12. E. Cantú-Paz, in *Proc. GECCO 2000*, (Morgan Kaufman Publishers, Inc., 2000), p. 910.
13. J.R. Koza and D. Andre, Stanford University Tech. Rep. No. STAN-CS-TR-95-1542 (1995).
14. M.Z. Abramson and L. Hunter, in *Proc. First Annual Genetic Prog. Conf.*, (MIT Press, 1996). p. 249.
15. W. Banzhaf, F.D. Francone, and P. Nordin, in *Proc. 5th Conf. Par. Problem Solving from Nature*, (Springer-Verlag, 1996), p. 300.
16. R.L. Walker, *Parallel Computing* **27 (1/2)**, 71 (2001).
17. M.W. Berry and M. Browne, *Understanding Search Engines: Mathematical Modeling and Text Retrieval*, (SIAM Press, Philadelphia, PA, 1999).
18. W. Fan, M.D. Gordon, and P. Pathak, in *Proc. Conf. Info. Sys.*, (2000) p. 20.
19. M.F. Porter, *Program* **14**, 130s (1980).
20. T. Ballardi, P. Francis, and J. Crowcroft, *ACM Trans. Comp. Sys.* **85**, (1993).
21. *Clever* Project Members, *Scientific Amer.*, **54** (1999).
22. A. Glossbrenner and E. Glossbrenner, *Search Engines for the World Wide Web* (Peachpit Press, Berkeley, 2001).
23. E. McMilin, in *Genetic Algorithms and Genetic Programming at Stanford*

2000, Ed. J.R. Koza, (Stanford University, 2000), p. 279.
24. GoTo, *GoTo.com Home Page*, GoTo.com, Inc., Pasadena, CA (2001).
25. F. Marckini, *Search Engine Positioning* (Wordware Publishing, Inc., Plano, TX, 2001).
26. J.B. Free, *The Social Organization of Honeybees. (Studies in Biology no. 81)*, (The Camelot Press Ltd, Southamptonm, 1970).
27. R. Bagrodia, *IEEE Trans. Software Engineering* **15(9)**, 1053 (1989).
28. J.L. Gould and C.G. Gould, *The Honey Bee* (Scientific American Library, New York, 1988).
29. G.E. Mobus, *J. Computing Anticipatory Systems* (2000).
30. R.L. Walker, in *Proc. Parallel and Distributed Processing Techniques and Applications*, Ed. H.R. Arabnia, (CSREA Press, 2002), p. 157.
31. L. Spector and S. Luke, in *Proc. First Annual Genetic Programming Conf.*, (MIT Press, 1996), p. 209.
32. M.C. Sinclair and S.H. Shami, in *Proc. Conf. on Genetic Algorithms in Engineering Systems: Innovations and Applications*, (IEE Press, 1997), p. 421.
33. R.L. Walker, in *Proc. IEEE Congress on Evol. Comp.*, (IEEE Press, Piscataway, NJ, 2001), p. 831.
34. D.C. Dracopoulos and S. Kent, *Neural Computing & Applications* **6(4)**, 214 (1997).
35. T. Bäck, U. Hammel, and H. Schwefel, *IEEE Trans. Evol. Comp.* **1(1)**, 3 (1997).
36. D.B. Fogel, in *Evolutionary Computation: The Fossil Record* (IEEE Press, Piscataway, NJ, Chapter 14, 1998).
37. R.L. Walker, in *Proc. Computational Methods and Experimental Measurements*, Eds. Y.V. Esteve, G.M. Carlomagno, and C.A. Brebbia, (WIT Press, 2001). p. 937.
38. T. Lizambri, F. Duran, and S. Wakid, *J. Network and Systems Management* **8 (4)**, 449 (2000).
39. Yahoo, Yahoo Web Page. Yahoo Inc., Santa Clara, CA (1998).
40. Wall Street Journal (Western Edition), Dow Jones and Company, 200 Liberty St., New York (2000-2003).

CHAPTER 17

EVALUATING EVOLUTIONARY MULTI-OBJECTIVE OPTIMIZATION ALGORITHMS USING RUNNING PERFORMANCE METRICS

Kalyanmoy Deb and Sachin Jain

Kanpur Genetic Algorithms Laboratory (KanGAL)
Indian Institute of Technology Kanpur
Kanpur, PIN 208016, India
E-mail: {deb,jsachin}@iitk.ac.in

With the popularity of evolutionary multi-objective optimization (EMO) methods among researchers and practitioners, an increasing interest has grown in developing new and computationally efficient algorithms and in comparing them with existing methods. Unlike in single-objective optimization in which often the goal is to find a single optimal solution, an EMO method attempts to find a set of well-converged and well-distributed set of trade-off solutions. In comparing two or more EMO methods, it is intuitive that more than one performance metrics are necessary. Although there exist a number of performance metrics in the EMO literature, they are usually applied to the final non-dominated set obtained by an EMO algorithm to evaluate its performance. In this chapter, we emphasize the need of *running* performance metrics, which will provide the *dynamics* of the working of an EMO algorithm. Either using a known Pareto-optimal front or an agglomeration of generation-wise populations, two suggested metrics reveal important insights and interesting dynamics of the working of an EMO and help provide a comparative evaluation of two or more EMO methods.

1. Introduction

Over the last decade, the field of multi-objective optimization has experienced a new and innovative turn by the introduction of evolutionary algorithms in finding multiple Pareto-optimal solutions in a single simulation run. In the so-called evolutionary multi-objective optimization (EMO) methods, a two-step *ideal multi-objective optimization procedure*[6] is followed: (i) Step 1 finds a set of well-converged and well-distributed set of Pareto-optimal solutions and (ii) Step 2 uses *higher-level* problem information to choose one solution. It is argued and amply demonstrated that the presence of multiple trade-off solutions helps a decision-maker in making a better decision rather than having to decide for a relative preference of each objective followed in the preference-based multi-objective optimization tasks[19,12].

Following the principle of ideal multi-objective optimization procedure, there exists a number of EMO algorithms, such as elitist non-dominated sorting GA or NSGA-II[7], modified strength Pareto EA or SPEA2[21], Pareto-archived evolution strategy or PESA[3], and others[6,2]. With the availability of many such efficient algorithms, users have been interested in comparing them on different test problems[7,15] and application-oriented problems[6,2]. Since the outcome of an EMO algorithm is a set of solutions (each having a vector of decision variables and a corresponding objective vector), the comparison of two such sets of solutions is by no means an easy task. Because of the multi-dimensionality of the objective vectors, a reliable comparison demands the need of using more than one performance metrics. A recent study[22] has argued that for an M-objective optimization problem, at least M performance metrics must be used. Due to the complicacies involved in comparing two sets of solutions (instead of two solutions to be compared in case of single-objective optimization tasks), researchers, in the past, have evaluated their EMO methods based on a single set of non-dominated solutions obtained in the final generation. However, from the beginning of single-objective EA studies, the history of population-best fitness and population-average fitness as they vary with generation counter were investigated. Such plots had shown a plethora of useful generation-wise information about the rate of convergence towards the final solution, evidence of any intermediate attractor, diversity of population etc., which have motivated researchers to look for ways to mitigate the difficulties demonstrated by the algorithm. In the context of EMO algorithms, there exists only a handful of studies in which such an attempt has been made[1,13] and the importance of such studies was recognized by the authors elsewhere[9]. It is not surprising that if appropriate performance measures of EMO populations are also recorded generation-wise and analyzed, salient information about their working principles would also be imminent. In this chapter, we consolidate the ideas put forward in the previous study[9] by suggesting and comparing more running metrics and by showing their advantages and usefulness in applying the technique to more test problems.

In the remainder of this chapter, we briefly review the existing performance metrics. Thereafter, we suggest a metric each for evaluating two functionalities described above. Finally, the need of using running metrics in EMO methods is amply demonstrated by applying them on a number of two and three-objective problems. By no means, the metrics used in this chapter are the most efficient ones. The main purpose of this study is to emphasize and motivate the readers to the need of using running metrics more and more in EMO studies. More such studies should result in more efficient running performance metrics for evolutionary multi-objective optimization.

2. Performance Metrics for Multi-Objective Optimization

A recent study[22] has argued and given a formal proof stating that for an M-objective problem, at least M performance metrics are needed to compare two or more set of M-dimensional solutions. Intuitively this makes sense, as otherwise this would suggest an inaccurate judgment made with a reduction in dimensionality. However, we mention here that although mathematically incorrect, it may be possible to compare two or more multi-dimensional sets *functionally* using only a few metrics, as is often followed in understanding behaviors of complex systems. In multi-objective optimization, there are two primary functionalities that an EMO must achieve: (i) approaching the Pareto-optimal front as close as possible and (ii) maintenance of as a diverse set of solutions as possible.

Figure 1 illustrates these two functionalities in a two-objective minimization problem. Although illustrated for two objectives only, the same principle can be extended to problems having more than two objectives, with the second functionality defining an appropriate diversity measure of the trade-off solutions. Thus, for a comparison based on the attainment of each of the two functionalities of multi-objective optimization, it may be possible to define at least *two* performance metrics, one for measuring each functionality exclusively, even for $M > 2$ objectives.

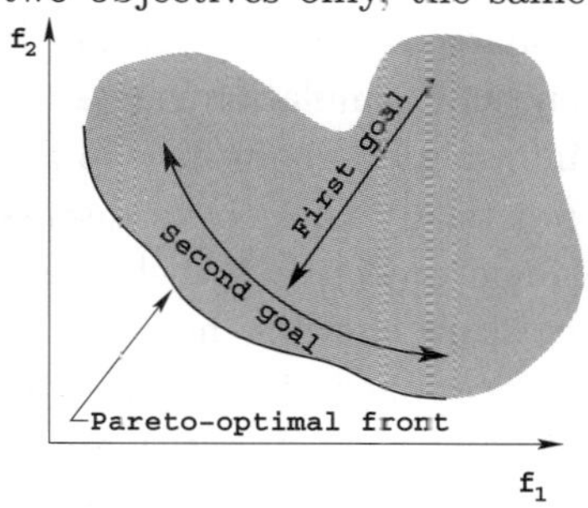

Fig. 1: Two functionalities of an EMO.

Veldhuizen[20], in his dissertation, reported a number of performance metrics for multi-objective optimization. Later, the first author, in his book[6], classified existing performance metrics into three classes: (i) metrics for convergence, (ii) metrics for diversity estimation, and (iii) metrics for both convergence and diversity. Although advantages and disadvantages of each metric were qualitatively mentioned, A study[16] analyzed most of these metrics on the basis of extent of outperformance relations between two sets of non-dominated solutions. This study suggested the use of any of the three performance metrics of Hansen and Jaszkiewicz[14].

For measuring diversity and convergence of obtained solutions, Zitzler's hyper-volume metric (also known as the $\mathcal{S}$-metric) can also be used. The metric computes the hyper-volume of the objective space dominated by an approximation set. Although a set with a good diversity of solutions would mean a larger hyper-volume metric value (hence better), the $\mathcal{S}$-metric value depends on the chosen reference point used for the hyper-volume calculation and demands normalization of the objectives before computing the metric. Moreover, a recent study[10] has indicated that the hyper-volume metric has a bias towards the extreme (individual optimum) solutions.

All these authors seem to have made one point clear: the comparison of two non-dominated set of solutions is not a straightforward matter, because of the dimensionality involved in the sets. However, based on our argument for using two functional metrics even in many-objective problems, we courageously suggest the use of running metrics in EMO studies.

2.1. *Need for Using Running Metrics*

In most EMO studies, including those involving performance metrics, two or more EMO methods have been usually compared mainly on the basis of what have been obtained at the *end* of a simulation run. Either a carefully updated archive (SPEA2 or PESA) or an EA population (NSGA-II) at the end of a simulation run is evaluated for this purpose. However, important information about how an EMO method arrives at the final population has practically never been discussed in an EMO study. On the contrary, most single objective EA studies analyze such a generation-wise performance measure showing how the average or best fitness or some other performance metric is varying with generation. Such a generation-wise history of population statistics must provide a lot of insights to the working of an EMO algorithm and helps decide which problems are difficult or easy for an EMO method. Such information will not only enable a reliable comparison of two or more EMO methods, they will also enable a researcher to develop a better and more efficient EMO method. As mentioned earlier, the main reason for the absence of such studies in the EMO literature is probably the cardinality of the necessary performance metrics to properly evaluate an EMO method and the complexities involved in computing them.

However, some recent studies[1,13,18] have just begun to show generation-wise dynamics of performance metrics. In this chapter, we demonstrate the use of two such running performance metrics for EMO methods by applying them on a number of test problems and discuss some interesting outcomes.

3. Suggested Running Metrics

In order to design running performance metrics for multi-objective optimization, the following properties are worth considering:

(1) The metric should take a value between zero and one in an absolute sense. Since the metric is to be compared generation-wise, an absolute scaling of a running metric between zero and one will allow to assess the change of the metric value from one generation to another.
(2) The target (or desired) metric value (calculated for an ideally converged and diversified set of points) must be known.
(3) The metric should provide a monotonic increase or decrease in its value, as the population gets improved or deteriorated slightly. This will also help in evaluating the extent of superiority of one approximation set with another.
(4) The metric should be scalable to any number of objectives. Although this is not an absolutely necessary property, but if followed, it will certainly be convenient for evaluating scalability issues of EMO methods in terms of number of objectives.
(5) The metric may be computationally inexpensive, although this may not be a stringent condition to be followed.

Since two independent metrics are to be chosen, one each for measuring two functionalities of multi-objective optimization, as discussed in the previous section, each metric may preferably evaluate the corresponding functionality only, ignoring the other functionality. On this account, some suggested metrics, such as the $D1_R$ metric (average distance of reference points from the approximation set) suggested by Czyzak and Jaszkiewicz[4] for convergence measure or the $\mathcal{S}$-measure (used in[23]) for diversity measure cannot be adequately used. Because of computational expenses involved in computing the R-metrics, they may not be suitable candidates to be used as running metrics. In the following two subsections, we propose two different metrics for evaluating EMO methods by keeping in mind the above-mentioned properties.

3.1. *Metric for Convergence*

We use a simple metric for evaluating convergence towards a reference set. A target set of points P^* (or reference set) can be either a set of Pareto-optimal points (if known) or the non-dominated set of points in a combined pool of all generation-wise populations obtained from an EMO run. Thereafter, for a population $P^{(t)}$ at each generation, we compute the convergence metric in the following manner:

Step 1 Identify the non-dominated set $\mathcal{F}^{(t)}$ of $P^{(t)}$.

Step 2 From each point i in $\mathcal{F}^{(t)}$, calculate the smallest normalized Euclidean distance to P^* as follows:

$$d_i = \min_{j=1}^{|P^*|} \sqrt{\sum_{k=1}^{M} \left(\frac{f_k(i) - f_k(j)}{f_k^{\max} - f_k^{\min}} \right)^2}. \tag{1}$$

Here, $f_k^{\max}$ and $f_k^{\min}$ are the maximum and the minimum function values of k-th objective function in P^*.

Step 3 Calculate the convergence metric by averaging the normalized distance for all points in $\mathcal{F}^{(t)}$:

$$C(P^{(t)}) = \frac{\sum_{i=1}^{|\mathcal{F}^{(t)}|} d_i}{|\mathcal{F}^{(t)}|}. \tag{2}$$

In order to keep the convergence metric within $[0, 1]$, once the above metric values are calculated for all generations, we normalize the $C(P^{(t)})$ values by its maximum value (usually occurring in the initial population, or $C(P^{(0)})$): $\overline{C}(P^{(t)}) = C(P^{(t)})/C(P^{(0)})$. Figure 2 shows the shortest Euclidean distance of each obtained solution from the chosen set P^*. The figure also demonstrates how the above metric can be useful in convex, non-convex, or disconnected Pareto-optimal fronts.

3.2. *Metric for Diversity*

A simple way to measure diversity would be to do the reverse of what is done in the above convergence metric. Instead of computing the average of shortest Euclidean distances of all obtained solutions from the reference set, the average of shortest Euclidean distances of reference solutions can be computed from the obtained set. This scenario is illustrated in Figure 3. However, here the reference set may be chosen in way so that the number of solutions in the set is the same as in the obtained solution set and that they all are as uniformly distributed over the entire Pareto-optimal

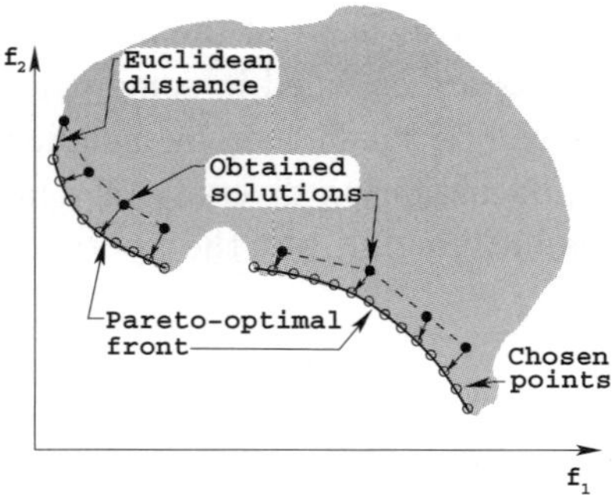

Fig. 2. The convergence metric computation.

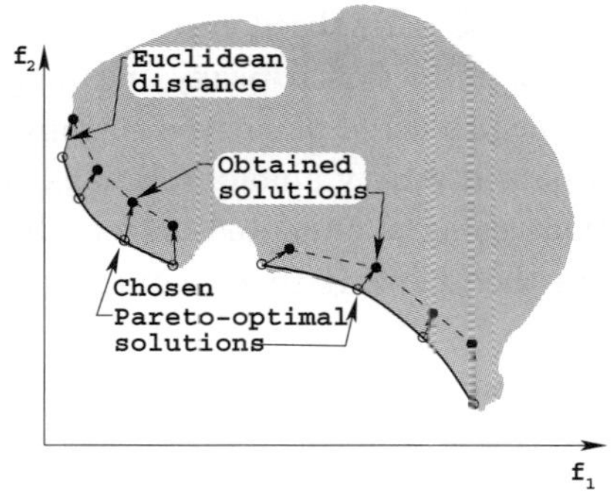

Fig. 3. A diversity metric computation.

region as possible. For test problems, creation of such a reference set is not a problem. For problems with unknown Pareto-optimal front, the agglomeration technique can be used and a k-mean clustering algorithm can be used to choose the desired number of well-distributed solutions from the set. Since the Euclidean distance measure is used, this metric may have the difficulty of measuring a mixed estimate of convergence and diversity of solutions. To only compute the diversity measure, the obtained solutions can be projected on the Pareto-optimal front (or on a hyper-surface generated using the agglomerated solutions) and the distance along the front can be measured for each reference solution. However, such a computation will be time-consuming. In the following, we suggest a computationally simple procedure.

In terms of measuring the diversity of solutions, a recent study[13] suggested an entropy-based technique. Each obtained solution is projected on a suitable hyper-plane[a]. Thereafter, a $(M-1)$-dimensional normally distributed entropy function is assigned with its mean being on each projected point and with a user-defined standard deviation. All such entropy functions for all projected points are added together and a normalized entropy function is calculated. If the projected points are well distributed on the hyper-plane and a suitable standard deviation of the entropy function is chosen, the resulting normalized entropy function will be a flat function, thereby causing a large value of the Shannon's entropy measure calculated

[a]A plane with a direction vector equal to the unit vector of the line joining the ideal point and the point with the worst individual objective values of the reference set is suggested in the original study.

using the normalized entropy function. On the other hand, if the resulting entropy function is peaky, meaning that points are crowded in some parts of the projected plane, the entropy measure will be small, thereby meaning a poor diversity among solutions. The idea of measuring diversity of solutions using a simulated entropy function is meaningful, but the approach has the following shortcomings:

(1) The entropy measure largely depends on the chosen standard deviation, as the resulting distribution being peaky or flat depends largely on the variance of the normal entropy function used.
(2) Since a continuous normal entropy function is used, if a problem involves disconnected Pareto-optimal fronts, this method may be erroneous.
(3) For problems where the Pareto-optimal front is a degenerated lesser-dimensional curve (such as DTLZ5[11]), a sub-optimal front may produce a higher entropy measure than a set of Pareto-optimal points, thereby allocating a large entropy value to an inferior set.
(4) A performance metric measuring the diversity of solutions cannot adequately measure the converging ability of an EMO method, and vice versa.

The diversity metric suggested next is similar in concept to the above metric, except that it attempts to alleviate most of the above difficulties. Moreover, this and the convergence metric suggested earlier together can be used to systematically evaluate EMO methods for both convergence and diversity properties. The suggested metric is also computationally fast.

The essential idea is that the obtained non-dominated points at each generation is projected on a suitable hyper-plane, thereby losing a dimension of the points. The plane is divided into a number of small grids (or $(M-1)$ dimensional boxes). Depending on whether each grid contains an obtained non-dominated point or not, a diversity metric is defined. If all grids are represented with at least one point, the best possible (with respect to the chosen number of grids) diversity measure is achieved. If some grids are not represented by a non-dominated point, the diversity is poor. The parameters required from the user are the direction cosine of the reference plane, the number of grids (G_i) in each of $(M-1)$ dimension, and the *target* (or reference) set of points P^*. Here is the procedure:

Step 1 From $P^{(t)}$, determine the set $\mathcal{F}^{(t)}$ which are non-dominated to P^*.

Step 2 For each grid indexed by $(i, j, \ldots)$, calculate following two arrays:

$$H(i,j,\ldots) = \begin{cases} 1, & \text{if the grid has a representative point in } P^*; \\ 0, & \text{otherwise.} \end{cases} \tag{3}$$

$$h(i,j,\ldots) = \begin{cases} 1, & \text{if } H(i,j,\ldots) = 1 \text{ and the grid has a representative point in } \mathcal{F}^{(t)}; \\ 0, & \text{otherwise.} \end{cases} \tag{4}$$

Step 3 Assign a value $m(h(i,j,\ldots))$ to each grid depending on its and its neighbor's $h()$. Similarly, calculate $m(H(i,j,\ldots))$ using $H()$ for reference points.

Step 4 Calculate the diversity metric by averaging the individual $m()$ values for $h()$ with respect to that for $H()$:

$$D(P^{(t)}) = \frac{\sum_{\substack{i,j,\ldots \\ H(i,j,\ldots)\neq 0}} m(h(i,j,\ldots))}{\sum_{\substack{i,j,\ldots \\ H(i,j,\ldots)\neq 0}} m(H(i,j,\ldots))}. \tag{5}$$

In the simple case, the *value function* $m()$ for a grid can be computed by using its $h()$ and two neighboring $h()$ dimension-wise. With a set of three consecutive binary $h()$ values, there are a total of 8 possibilities. Any value function may be assigned by keeping in mind the following:

- A 111 is the best distribution and a 000 is the worst.
- A 010 or a 101 means a periodic pattern with a good spread and may be valued more than a 110 or a 011. For example, the above valuation will make an approximation set with 50% coverage of grids but having a wider spread (such as 1010101010) better than another set having the same coverage but with a smaller spread (such as 1111100000).
- A 110 or a 011 may be valued more than a 001 or a 100, because of more covered grids.

Based on above observations, the following $h()$: $m()$ values are used in this study:

000: 0.00	001: 0.50	010: 0.75	011: 0.67
100: 0.50	101: 0.75	110: 0.67	111: 1.00

Identical value are used for $H()$. In the current study, two or more dimensional hyper-planes are handled by calculating the above metric dimension-wise, whereas a higher-dimensional version of the above value function can also be carefully designed by considering a moving set of hyper-boxes. One such consideration for a two-dimensional set of 9 boxes is shown below:

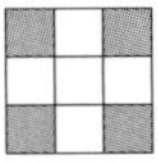 is better than 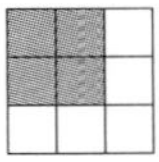

Obviously, with more number of objectives, the value function will be difficult to define. It remains as an interesting future study to find if such higher-dimensional hyper-boxes are really necessary compared to the dimension-wise calculation of the proposed one-dimensional metric.

As an illustration to the above calculation procedure, Figure 4 shows a set of target points (marked as filled circles) and a set of population points (marked as shaded and open boxes) for a two-objective minimization problem. The points marked with shaded boxes are the non-dominated points with respect to the target points and are used for the diversity calculation (this is Step 1 of the procedure). The $f_2 = 0$ plane is used as the reference plane here and the complete range of f_1 values are divided into $G_1 = 10$ grids. In the next step, for each grid both $h()$ and $H()$ values are calculated. For the boundary grids (extreme grids and grids $(\ldots, j, \ldots)$ with $H(\ldots, j-1, \ldots) = 0$ or $H(\ldots, j+1, \ldots) = 0$), an imaginary neighboring grid with a $h()$ or $H()$ value of one is always assumed. In the figure, these grids are shown in dashed boxes. The $h()$ values are one in the first two grids, fifth, seventh and eighth grids. Notice that although more than one point may exist in a grid, the $H()$ or $h()$ value is still one for that grid. Based on a moving window containing three consecutive grids, the $m()$ values are computed in the figure and the diversity metric is calculated. To avoid the boundary effects (the effect of using the imaginary grids), we normalize the above metric as follows:

$$\overline{D}(P^{(t)}) = \frac{\sum_{\substack{i,j,\ldots \\ H(i,j,\ldots)\neq 0}} m(h(i,j,\ldots)) - \sum_{\substack{i,j,\ldots \\ H(i,j,\ldots)\neq 0}} m(\mathbf{0})}{\sum_{\substack{i,j,\ldots \\ H(i,j,\ldots)\neq 0}} m(H(i,j,\ldots)) - \sum_{\substack{i,j,\ldots \\ H(i,j,\ldots)\neq 0}} m(\mathbf{0})},$$

where $\mathbf{0}$ is a zero-valued array. A careful thought will reveal that the $H(i,j,\ldots) \neq 0$ consideration in computing the $\overline{D}(P^{(t)})$ term and the boundary grid adjustment suggested above allow a generic way to handle problems with disconnected Pareto-optimal fronts. The metric does not include the value function for a grid on which there exists no reference solution. We have included one such test problem (ZDT3) in our simulation studies.

If the Pareto-optimal front is not known (particularly to real-world problems), the target set may be determined in the following way. First, an EMO method is run for T generations and the generation-wise populations ($P^{(t)}$, $t = 0, 1, \ldots, T$) are stored. Thereafter, the non-dominated members $\mathcal{F}^{(t)}$ of each population are combined together and the target set is defined as the non-dominated set of the combined population: $P^* = \text{Non-dominated}(\cup_{t=0}^{T} \mathcal{F}^{(t)})$.

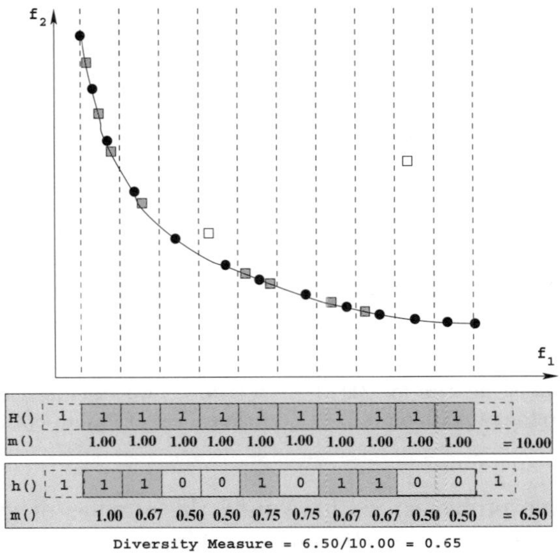

Fig. 4. The diversity metric computation is illustrated.

4. Simulation Results

In this section, we apply the above metrics on solutions obtained using NSGA-II[7] on a number of two and three-objective test problems suggested in the literature and on a real-world two-objective gearbox design problem. In each case, the metrics are applied on a typical run of NSGA-II. However, it is advised to apply the metrics on multiple runs of an EMO method and to report average metric values. In all cases with NSGA-II, we have used the SBX recombination operator[6] with $p_c = 1.0$ and $\eta_c = 10$, and the polynomial mutation operator[6] with $p_m = 1/n$ and $\eta_m = 20$.

First four test problems are two-objective ZDT test problems chosen from[23]. Since they are test problems and the exact location of the Pareto-optimal front is known in each case, we apply the suggested metrics using a set of 200 uniformly distributed points on the Pareto-optimal front (in the objective space).

Figure 5 shows the two metrics on simulation results obtained using NSGA-II using $N = 100$ population size running till 100 generations. In this and other problems of this study, we set number of grids in each dimension as $G_i = N^{1/(M-1)}$, where M is the number of objectives. Thus,

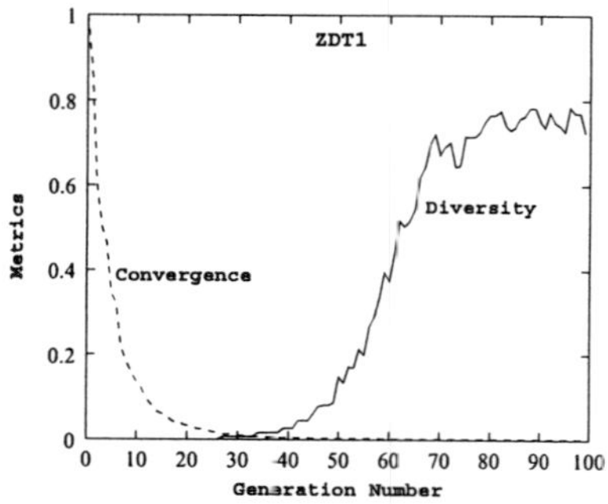

Fig. 5. Two running metrics for ZDT1 using a set of Pareto-optimal points.

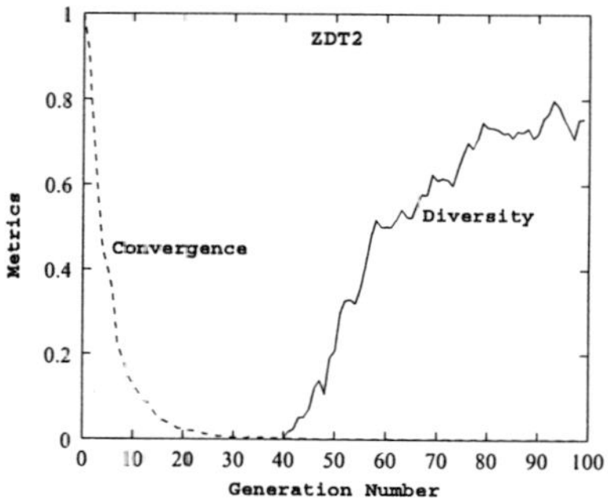

Fig. 6. Two running metrics for ZDT2 using a set of Pareto-optimal points.

for two-objective problems, we have used the number of grids equal to the population size, as if exactly one population member is expected on each grid. We also use $f_2 = 0$ plane to project the points, unless otherwise stated. The figure shows that the convergence metric quickly moves to zero, thereby implying that NSGA-II solutions starting from a random set of solutions quickly approach the Pareto-optimal front. A value of zero of the convergence metric implies that all non-dominated solutions match the chosen Pareto-optimal points. After about 30 generations, the NSGA-II population comes very close to the Pareto-optimal front. Similarly, the diversity metric shows that till about the first 26 generations, no solution non-dominated to the Pareto-optimal set was found. But from this generation onwards, NSGA-II finds more and more points non-dominated with the chosen Pareto-optimal points. The choice of points are such that the diversity metric increases exponentially till about 70 generations, after which the diversity remains more or less the same. Although the obtained points are very close the chosen Pareto-optimal points, diversity metric oscillates near a stable value, a matter which is inherent to NSGA-II and other EMO methods and has been nicely illustrated for NSGA-II and SPEA2 in a recent study[17].

Next, we choose the test problem ZDT2. This problem has a non-convex Pareto-optimal front. Figure 6 shows the two running metrics with the same GA parameters as before. The convergence metric shows in about 30 generations, NSGA-II population moves very close to the Pareto-optimal front. It is also interesting to note that NSGA-II takes about 14 more generations to find a solution non-dominated with the reference set in ZDT2 than that re-

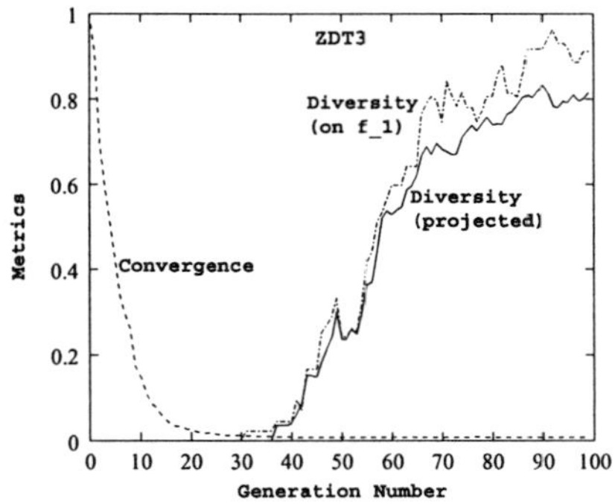

Fig. 7. Two running metrics for ZDT3 using a set of Pareto-optimal points calculated using f_1 axis and projected on an inclined plane.

quired in ZDT1. Once some solutions very close to the Pareto-optimal front are found, more and more points near the front are discovered and the diversity among solutions increases rapidly, indicating that NSGA-II finds solutions close to the Pareto-optimal front with a good diversity among them. It is interesting to note that the patterns of change of convergence metric in both ZDT1 and ZDT2 problems are quite similar, except that the non-convexity of the Pareto-optimal front causes NSGA-II to make a slow build-up of Pareto-optimal solutions.

The test problem ZDT3 has a disjointed set of Pareto-optimal fronts. NSGA-II with identical parameter setting are applied to this problem for 100 generations and the corresponding running metrics are shown in Figure 7. The figure shows a similar behavior as that in ZDT1. In this problem, we have also computed the diversity metric by projecting the points on an inclined line, as suggested in the footnote in section 3.2. The corresponding diversity metric is plotted with a solid line. The figure shows that although there is some difference in magnitude of the two diversity metric computations (projected on $f_2 = 0$ plane and projected on the inclined line), their behaviors are very similar. Once again, the convergence patterns of the above test problems are similar due to an identical 29-variable $g()$ function[5] used in all three problems. The $g()$ function is responsible for the convergence to the Pareto-optimal front. Although the growth of the diversity measure depends on the shape of the underlying front in the three ZDT problems, these results support the idea behind independent construction of function properties suggested in ZDT problems[5].

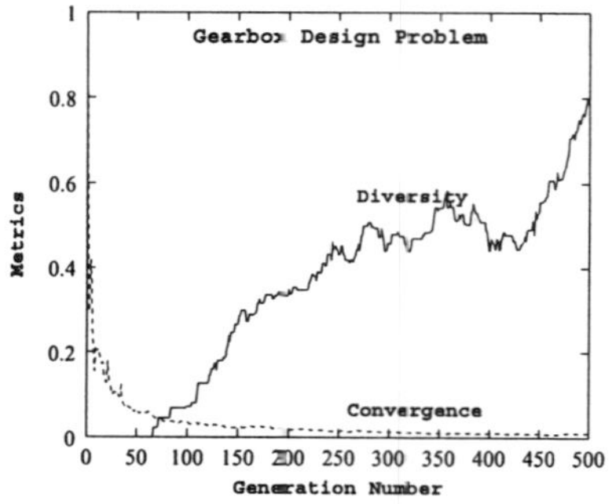

Fig. 8. Two running metrics showing the convergence and diversity in solutions of NSGA-II for the gearbox design problem.

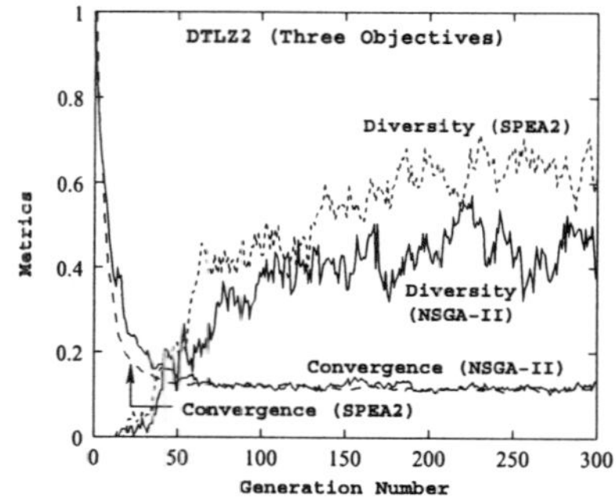

Fig. 9. Two running metrics for DTLZ2 using a set of Pareto-optimal points for NSGA-II and SPEA2.

Next, we use the population-agglomeration technique to evaluate the performance of NSGA-II to a two-objective gearbox design problem discussed elsewhere[8]. In this problem, the Pareto-optimal front is not known. With 100 grid points on f_1, the metrics are plotted in Figure 8 for NSGA-II run using 100 population members. The figure shows that the convergence near the obtained non-dominated front is fast and the first point near this front was found after about 65 generations. It is interesting to note that at the final generation the diversity metric value is less than one. This means that NSGA-II does not contain all 100 solutions used as a reference set at the end of the simulation run. Some better distributed solutions are lost during the run.

The final two test problems are three-objective test problems borrowed from[11]. The problem DTLZ2 has a spherical Pareto-optimal surface. Here, we use 100 population members and NSGA-II and SPEA2 are run for 300 generations. For computing the metrics, we have chosen 10×10 or 100 grids in the interval $[0, 1]$ of f_1 and f_2 axes. The $f_3 = 0$ plane is chosen to project the points. Figure 9 shows the corresponding metrics, as they vary with the generation number. The convergence metric values for both EMO methods suggest that not all non-dominated points even at the final generation have reached close to the chosen Pareto-optimal points. The diversity metric values show that both NSGA-II and SPEA2 have found a solution non-dominated to the chosen Pareto-optimal points at around 20th generation. Thereafter, more and more points with increasing diversity among them have been found. Thereafter, like in ZDT problems, the population

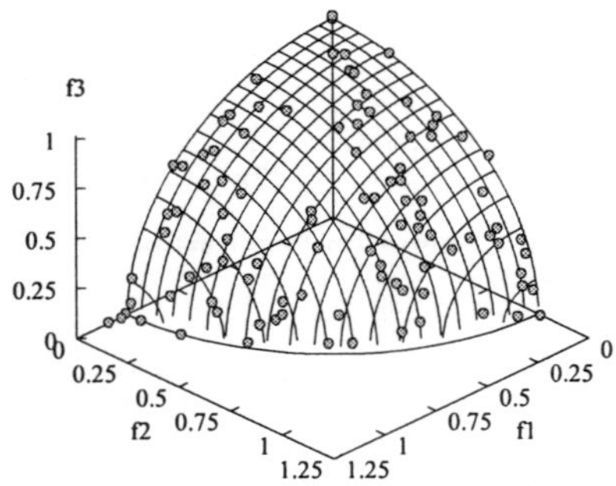

Fig. 10. Non-dominated points obtained using NSGA-II.

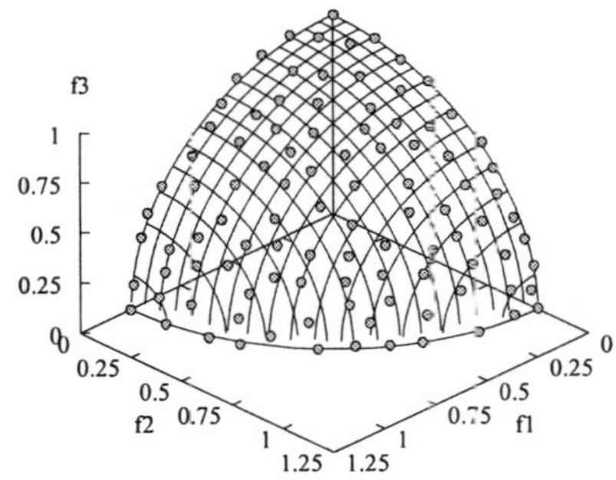

Fig. 11. Non-dominated points obtained using SPEA2.

maintains a particular level of diversity with some variations. However, the diversity of solutions obtained by SPEA2 is much better than that of NSGA-II in this problem. In order to investigate the diversity obtained in each case, we have plotted the final obtained non-dominated solutions in Figures 10 and 11 for NSGA-II and SPEA2, respectively. It is clear from these two plots that SPEA2 has obtained a better spread than NSGA-II. This study shows how the two suggested metrics can bring out the differences in the working of two EMO methods quantitatively over the entire run of the algorithms.

5. Discussions and Future Studies

The need of developing good running metrics and their use in EMO studies is now clear from the above computer simulations. Although two metrics are used in this study, more metrics measuring further detailed properties of an approximation set can also be used and are a matter of immediate research interests.

Although the suggested template-based diversity metric is a way to measure the extent of diversity in an approximation set, there are at least a couple of difficulties with this metric: (i) the metric value depends on the chosen template (the value function $m()$) and (ii) as mentioned earlier it is difficult to assign a value function for higher dimensions, although a dimension-wise application has reasonably worked well in this chapter. However, the overall strategy of projecting an approximation set to a suitable grid-ed hyper-plane and then applying a diversity metric remains a good approach for finding the diversity of an approximation set. Instead

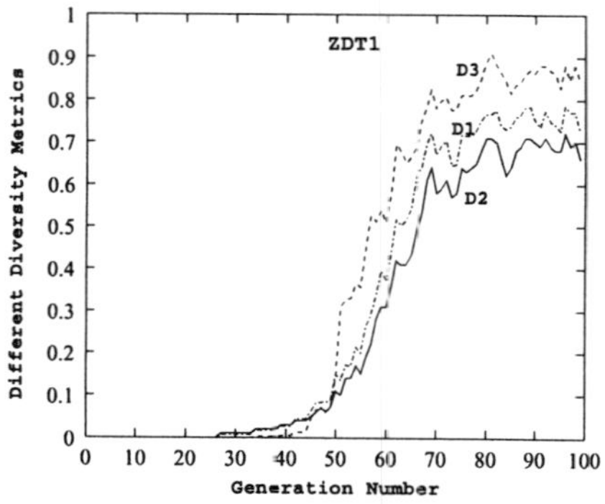

Fig. 12. Three diversity running metrics on ZDT1 are shown. D1 is the metric defined in section 3.2, D2 is the grid-count metric and D3 is the variance-metric V.

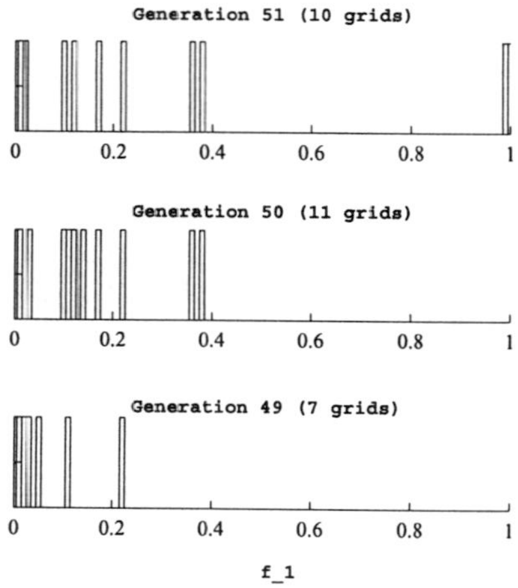

Fig. 13. The grids occupied by NSGA-II at generations 49, 50, and 51 are shown for ZDT1.

of the suggested template-based diversity metric, the following metrics can also be used:

(1) A *grid-count* diversity metric counting the number of occupied grids in the projected plane can simply be used. To normalize the metric, the count can be divided by the total number of occupied grids obtained using the reference set. Although this metric does not tell the sparseness of occupied grids, the sheer number of them may be an important factor for comparing two or more EMO methods. Figure 12 plots this normalized grid-count metric (shown as D2) on the populations obtained using NSGA-II in problem ZDT1. The plot shows that NSGA-II solutions share about 70% grids with the reference set at the end of the run.

(2) A variance in inter-member distances can be another measure of diversity of solutions on a projected plane. The calculation procedure is as follows. For a population $P^{(t)}$, first the non-dominated solutions $\mathcal{F}^{(t)}$ (with respect to P^*) are found and are projected to a chosen hyper-plane. Each occupied grid on the hyper-plane is represented by its center point $\vec{x}^{(i)}$. First, the centroid $\vec{g}$ of all occupied grids is calculated. Thereafter, the vector $\vec{v}^{(i)}$ from the grid $\vec{x}^{(i)}$ to the centroid $\vec{g}$ is computed. Then, a diversity

metric V is calculated as follows:

$$V(P^{(t)}) = \sum_{j=1}^{M-1} \sqrt{\sum_{i=1}^{|\mathcal{F}^{(t)}|} \left(v_j^{(i)}\right)^2}. \quad (6)$$

For each dimension j, the term inside the square-root is the sum of the square of the projections of all solutions from the centroid along the j-th dimension. Thus, if the solutions are sparsely placed, the above metric will produce a large value. Since the projections are squared and added, the positive and negative projections do not cancel each other.

In order to normalize the metric, the above value can be divided by the metric value of the reference set: $\overline{V} = V(P^{(t)})/V(P^*)$. Figure 12 also shows a plot of this metric (shown as D3) on ZDT1. The comparison of these three plots shows the similarity in their variations with generations. For ZDT1, it is clear that the undulations in the diversity metrics D1 or D3 are in tune with the undulations in the number of occupied grids (D2). An interesting difference among these three metrics is clear during the transition of the population from generation 49 through 51:

Generation number	Number of occupied grids	Diversity Metrics		
		D1	D2	D3
49	7	8.754/100	7/100	0.192/2.887
50	11	14.899/100	11/100	0.405/2.887
51	10	13.468/100	10/100	0.891/2.887

Figure 13 also shows the occupied grids at generations 49, 50, and 51. A total of 100 grids are assumed for $f_1 \in [0, 1]$. The grid-count (D2) metric for these generations does not reveal the fact that a better diversity of solutions is obtained in generation 51, although the grid-count is less in generation 51 compared to that in generation 50. Because of the use of the three-grid template in D1, the difference in diversity obtained from generation 50 to 51 is not apparent by this metric either. But the D3 metric shows a big jump in this metric value during this transition, meaning that a set with a much better diversity among them is obtained. However, the real difference among these metrics may be apparent in solving higher-dimensional or more complex problems and the choice of one metric over the other may also depend on the computational complexity associated with each metric.

(3) The entropy-based metric suggested elsewhere[13] can be modified to handle disconnected Pareto-optimal sets. The *holes* or discontinuities in the projected plane can be eliminated and all individual regions of Pareto-optimal sets can be placed next to each other, so that in the modified plane, there is no hole or discontinuity. Although the choice of the standard devi-

ation of the normal distribution still remains as an important factor, other distributions may also be tried.

(4) A few other measures can also be of importance to an user:

Number of distinct solutions in the best non-dominated front: Although the sheer number of non-dominated solutions does not provide any idea of their distribution, this measure may indicate the ability of an EMO algorithm in finding more and more non-dominated solutions after the algorithm has reached close to the true Pareto-optimal front.

Number of non-dominated fronts: In most problems, this measure should start with a large number and then decrease with generation number. However, the rate of decrease would remain as an important matter.

Front number for χ-percentile solution: For example, the median ($\chi = 50$) population member according to its non-domination rank would indicate the number of required fronts to rank top-half of the population.

Relative distance between fronts: In addition to the proximity of the best non-dominated front to the true Pareto-optimal front, the average shortest Euclidean distance between solutions of the best and the next-best front could be an interesting measure. This will indicate the effectiveness of creating the best non-dominated solutions by an EMO.

A detail study applying some of these metrics to the chosen test problems and comparing them with existing metrics such as the R-metrics or the $\mathcal{S}$-metric also remains an important future task.

6. Conclusions

To investigate the generation-wise dynamics of an EMO method, two running metrics are suggested in this chapter. The first metric is a distance measure of a population from a reference set and is used to measure the convergence ability of an EMO method. The second metric uses a local template based evaluation technique to estimate the diversity of one set compared to a reference set. Both metrics are normalized so as to have their values bounded between zero and one. On a number of two and three-objective test problems and one real-world engineering design problem, the application of these two metrics have shown interesting properties of NSGA-II and SPEA2. For problems with unknown Pareto-optimal front, this study has also suggested a way to construct a reference set based on an agglomeration of generation-wise non-dominated populations. Such a technique can also be used to compute other performance metrics requiring a reference set.

It is also important to highlight that the computational complexity of EMO methods is another important matter and must be taken into consideration while comparing two or more EMO methods. Nevertheless, the results of this study has shown the importance of using running metrics for multi-objective evolutionary computation and recommend more such studies using a number of other suggested metrics in the near future.

Acknowledgments

The first author completed this study while visiting the University of Karlsruhe in Germany on a Bessel research award from Alexander von Humboldt Foundation.

References

1. H. A. Abbass. The self-adaptive pareto differential evolution algorithm. In *Proceedings of the World Congress on Computational Intelligence*, pages 831–836, 2002.
2. C. A. C. Coello, D. A. VanVeldhuizen, and G. Lamont. *Evolutionary Algorithms for Solving Multi-Objective Problems.* Boston, MA: Kluwer Academic Publishers, 2002.
3. D. Corne, J. Knowles, and M. Oates. The Pareto envelope-based selection algorithm for multiobjective optimization. In *Proceedings of the Sixth International Conference on Parallel Problem Solving from Nature VI (PPSN-VI)*, pages 839–848, 2000.
4. P. Czyzak and A. Jaszkiewicz. Pareto simulated annealing – A metaheuristic for multiobjective combinatorial optimization. *Multi-Criteria Decision Analysis*, 7:34–47, 1998.
5. K. Deb. Multi-objective genetic algorithms: Problem difficulties and construction of test problems. *Evolutionary Computation Journal*, 7(3):205–230, 1999.
6. K. Deb. *Multi-objective optimization using evolutionary algorithms.* Chichester, UK: Wiley, 2001.
7. K. Deb, S. Agrawal, A. Pratap, and T. Meyarivan. A fast and elitist multi-objective genetic algorithm: NSGA-II. *IEEE Transactions on Evolutionary Computation*, 6(2):182–197, 2002.
8. K. Deb and S. Jain. Multi-speed gearbox design using multi-objective evolutionary algorithms. Technical Report KanGAL Report No. 2002001, Kanpur, India: Department of Mechanical Engineering, Indian Institute of Technology Kanpur, 2002.
9. K. Deb and S. Jain. Running performance metrics for evolutionary multi-

objective optimization. In *Simulated Evolution and Learning (SEAL-02)*, pages 13–20, 2002.

10. K. Deb, M. Mohan, and S. Mishra. Towards a quick computation of well-spread pareto-optimal solutions. In *Proceedings of the Second Evolutionary Multi-Criterion Optimization (EMO-03) Conference (LNCS 2632)*, pages 222–236, 2003.
11. K. Deb, L. Thiele, M. Laumanns, and E. Zitzler. Scalable multi-objective optimization test problems. In *Proceedings of the Congress on Evolutionary Computation (CEC-2002)*, pages 825–830, 2002.
12. M. Ehrgott. *Multicriteria Optimization*. Berlin: Springer, 2000.
13. A. Farhang-Mehr and S. Azarm. Diversity assessment of pareto-optimal solution sets: An entropy approach. In *Proceedings of the World Congress on Computational Intelligence*, pages 723–728, 2002.
14. M. P. Hansen and A. Jaskiewicz. Evaluating the quality of approximations to the non-dominated set. Technical Report IMM-REP-1998-7, Lyngby: Institute of Mathematical Modelling, Technical University of Denmark, 1998.
15. V. Khare, X. Yao, and K. Deb. Performance scaling of multi-objective evolutionary algorithms. In *Proceedings of the Second Evolutionary Multi-Criterion Optimization (EMO-03) Conference (LNCS 2632)*, pages 376–390, 2003.
16. J. Knowles and D. Corne. On metrics for computing non-dominated sets. In *Proceedings of the World Congress on Computational Intelligence*, pages 711–716, 2002.
17. M. Laumanns, L. Thiele, K. Deb, and Eckart Zitzler. Combining convergence and diversity in evolutionary multi-objective optimization. *Evolutionary Computation*, 10(3):263–282, 2002.
18. H. Lu and G. Yen. Rank-density based multiobjective genetic search. In *Proceedings of the World Congress on Computational Intelligence*, pages 944–949, 2002.
19. K. Miettinen. *Nonlinear Multiobjective Optimization*. Kluwer, Boston, 1999.
20. D. Van Veldhuizen. *Multiobjective Evolutionary Algorithms: Classifications, Analyses, and New Innovations*. PhD thesis, Dayton, OH: Air Force Institute of Technology, 1999. Technical Report No. AFIT/DS/ENG/99-01.
21. E. Zitzler, M. Laumanns, and L. Thiele. SPEA2: Improving the strength pareto evolutionary algorithm for multiobjective optimization. In *Evolutionary Methods for Design Optimization and Control with Applications to Industrial Problems (EUROGEN-2001)*, pages 95–100, 2001.
22. E. Zitzler, M. Laumanns, L. Thiele, C. Fonseca, and V. G. Fonseca. Why quality assessment of multiobjective optimizers is difficult? In *Proceedings of the Genetic and Evolutionary Computation Conference (GECCO-2002)*, pages 666–674, 2002.
23. Eckart Zitzler, Kalyanmoy Deb, and Lothar Thiele. Comparison of multiobjective evolutionary algorithms: Empirical results. *Evolutionary Computation Journal*, 8(2):125–148, 2000.

CHAPTER 18

VISUALIZATION TECHNIQUE FOR ANALYZING NON-DOMINANT PARETO OPTIMALITY

Kiam Heong Ang, Gregory Chong and Yun Li

Intelligent Systems Group
Department of Electronics and Electrical Engineering, University of Glasgow
Rankine Building, Glasgow, G12 8LT, U.K.
E-mail: {khang,g.chong,y.li}@elec.gla.ac.uk

One advantage of evolutionary computation over conventional optimization and search techniques is its ability to deal with multiple objectives. Multi-objective evolutionary algorithms (MOEAs) have proved very useful in many real-world applications and the number of publications in this area has exceeded 1000. However, no one offers a simple-to-use or widely accepted method for evaluating the performance of MOEAs. This is largely due to difficulties in visualizing non-dominated solutions in a multi-objective space when the number of objectives exceeds three. In this chapter, we propose a new visualization technique that should provide better understanding of high order multi-dimensional objectives, so as to assist the design and refinement of MOEAs.

1. Introduction

Real world problems often challenge simultaneous optimization of multiple, possibly conflicting, objectives. Typically, such problems do not admit a single optimal solution, but a set of so-called "Pareto-optimal", or "non-dominated", solutions. A non-dominated set of solutions describes the trade-offs in the problem, and helps user to understand the options available, therefore enabling the selection of a final solution.

Evolutionary algorithms are stochastic search and optimization methods inspired by the process of natural selection. They offer greater flexibility in the handling of multiple objectives than conventional optimization method. The growing interest devoted by the scientific community to evolutionary algorithms for multi-objective optimization has led to an increasing number of MOEA approaches reported in the literature.[5] Detailed discussions on the state-of-the-art in MOEA can be found in the papers referenced here.[6,8,13,18,20] Unfortunately, there is a serious lack of simple-to-use or widely accepted method to assess the performance of MOEAs.

This chapter proposes a new visualization technique to analyze optimized non-dominant set of solutions. The purpose is to gain insight rather than quantitative analysis. It is expected that users are likely to tolerate loss of information in the initial process of evaluating solutions data. Then, through dimensionality reduction and use of other visuals to represent data, they can numerically support the knowledge that they have extracted through performance metrics. Section 2 lays out background information and highlights why such a visualization technique would be useful and essential. The proposed technique will be detailed in Section 3. Sections 4 and 5 discuss experimental results and observations, followed by conclusions drawn in Section 6.

2. Background

At present, ways of comparing non-dominated set of solutions are through visual comparison in the objective space. This method is simple and straightforward. The criterion is to have solutions close to the true Pareto front and must be well distributed over the Pareto frontier. However, visualization is limited to a maximum of three objectives. There are also some other visualization techniques for viewing higher order objectives, e.g., scatter-plot matrix, value path, bar chart, star coordinate, etc.[8] However, these are not commonly used in MOEA studies, as they are only suitable for displaying a set of non-dominated solutions. Since a MOEA is a stochastic method, multiple runs are required in order to have any statistical significance. Hence, it can be very difficult to view all the runs together in a single plot using those techniques.

Hence, various quantitative and qualitative metrics have been proposed recently. They are developed to measure MOEA performance more accurately than just visual comparison. Some of them were designed upon basic criteria of a good MOEA, namely, closeness to the optimal solutions in objective space and coverage of a wide range of diverse solutions. Some of the metrics proposed were diversity[7], attainment surface[11], attainment surface sampling[14], generational distance[21], spacing[21], error ratio[21], maximum Pareto front error[21], overall non-dominated vector generation and ratio[21], size of the dominated space[23], coverage of two sets[23], coverage difference of two sets[23] etc. Detailed summaries of the metrics were discussed in the papers cited here.[2,8,15,17,24]

Conversely, all the proposed metrics have their limitations. The main problem is the lack of decision maker preferences in the comparison, thereby causing difficulty in some cases of comparison. Hansen and Jaszkiewicz[12] have proposed a formal framework for evaluating the quality of a non-dominated set. However, the proposed metrics only cover the distance between competing non-dominated sets or distance between a competing non-dominated set and a reference set. Moreover, there were a few settings that users need to determine, e.g., the choice of the set of utility function, the choice of probability distribution of the utility functions and utility function scaling. Hence, it is neither easy nor straightforward to use.

Recently, Zitzler et al.[24] classified the available metrics into unary and binary type. They have shown that all unary metrics failed to provide reliable performance indication based on dominance relations. However, Bosman and Thierens[4] have stated that most of the latest MOEAs results would most probably be classified as incomparable using dominance relations of Zitzler et al.[24] In addition, when two sets of non-dominated solutions are incomparable, one of the sets must be more preferable. Thus, unary metrics are still very useful. Farhang-Mehr and Azarm[9] proposed a conceptual framework based on excellence relations, which attempt to address all the desired aspects of a quality non-dominated solution set. However, to find or design a suitable metric for their framework is not a trivial task.

A common way of proving the creditability of a new proposed metric is always limited to two- or three-objective problems. A common and intuitive practice of proofing is to display those competing non-dominated solutions in objective space and show the metric reported results. However, it is difficult to provide any convincing evidence that a particular metric works for a two-objective problem is also effective for problems with more than three objectives.

All the problems, difficulties and complexities in comparing non-dominated solution sets boil down to one obvious problem, that is, visualization. In the following section, a new visualization technique will be presented to assist in the comparison process.

3. Distance and Distribution Chart Method

The motivation of this work is to find an easy way to visualize multi-dimensional objective data, in order to provide an insight into the design of MOEAs. This will be more effective when visualization is used together with available metrics, so as to further validate the results indicated by the metrics. Instead of plotting the non-dominated solutions in the objective space (which is only limited to three objectives), we propose to plot the non-dominated solutions against their performance indicated by unary metrics.

To begin, we start with the most basic technique, that is, plotting the non-dominated solutions against their distance to the approximate Pareto front[1] and their distance between each other, which we term the "Distance and Distribution" (DD) chart. The DD chart consists of three elements, namely, the approximate Pareto front, distance metric and distribution metric.

Approximate Pareto front, P^*, can be easily generated using either of the two methods. First method is to have an archive to store all the best-found non-dominated solutions for a particular problem. Second method is to use all the non-dominated solutions found by the competing algorithms and use it as an approximate Pareto front.

Distance metric is simply the normalized Euclidean distance of each solution to the nearest approximate Pareto front solution. This metric is similar to the generational distance metric[21] except that it is used for measuring the individual distance rather than the overall average distance. A zero value indicates that the solution is Pareto-optimal and any values above zero indicate that the solution deviates from the approximate Pareto front. This is denoted as:

$$d_i = \min_{k=1}^{|P^*|} \sqrt{\sum_{m=1}^{M} \left(\frac{f_m^{(i)} - f_m^{(k)}}{f_m^{\max} - f_m^{\min}} \right)^2} \tag{1}$$

where i is the i-th solution of the non-dominated solution set, $f_m^{(k)}$ is the m-th objective function value of the k-th member of the approximate Pareto front and $f_m^{\max}$ and $f_m^{\min}$ are the maximum and minimum m-th objective function value of the approximate Pareto front respectively.

Distribution metric is simply the normalized Euclidean distance between each solution and taking into consideration the distance between the boundary solutions and the approximate Pareto front. This metric is similar to the diversity metric[7] except that it is used for measuring the individual gap distance rather than the overall average gap distance. Thus, a low performance metric characterizes an algorithm with a good distribution capacity. This is denoted as:

$$g_i = \sqrt{\sum_{m=1}^{M} \left(\frac{f_m^{(i)} - f_m^{(j)}}{f_m^{\max} - f_m^{\min}} \right)^2} \tag{2}$$

where i and j are the solutions of the non-dominated solution set.

The computation for distance metric is straightforward. As for the distribution metric, it will get complicated when the number of objectives is more than two. In this case, Deb[8] proposed to use the non-dominated solutions to construct a higher-dimensional surface by employing the so-called triangularization method. As several distance metrics can be associated with such a triangularized surface, the average distance of all edges can be used as the gap distance. Note that this method is extremely computationally expensive.

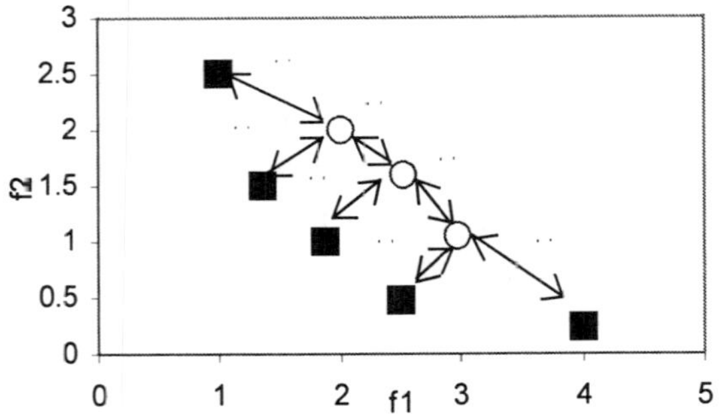

Fig. 1. An example plot

Hence, we proposed another method to compute distribution metric that is applicable to any number of objectives. This method is not as accurate, but it can served as a useful estimation for the distribution metric. First, the non-dominated solutions found must be sorted. It is recommended to sort, based on the first objective, e.g., if the first objective is to minimize then the solutions should be sorted in ascending order, based on the first objective value. Now, regardless of how many objectives, the two-boundary gap distance calculation is simply the normalized Euclidean distance between the first and last non-dominated solution and the first and last solution of the approximate Pareto front respectively. For example, the two-boundary gap distances (*g1* and *g4*) can be calculated based on the distance between the first solution found and the first solution of the approximate Pareto front as shown in Fig. 1, where f1 and f2 are the two objectives, the circles represent non-dominated solutions found, squares represent an approximate Pareto front, *d1* to *d3* represent the distance metrics and *g1* to *g4* represent the distribution metrics.

The number of non-dominated solutions required for the DD chart is about 10 to 100. Although, the amount of the competing non-dominated solutions does not need to be the same, they should not be different by more than 50%. Otherwise, it will be difficult to analyze and to deduce any conclusive results graphically.

Our proposal is to view the distance and distribution metric of each non-dominated solution found by an algorithm. Using one simple line chart to plot the non-dominated solutions against its distance metrics and another line chart to plot the non-dominated solutions against its distribution metrics. The distance chart will not only provide information on the overall distance of the solutions to the approximate front but also reveal the maximum Pareto front error. As for the distribution chart, it can reveal the coverage of the non-dominated solutions in the objective space.

4. Illustrated Examples

In the literature, visual comparison techniques have been the main tool to view objective space, but are limited to a maximum of three objectives. Here we will illustrate the visualization technique for the distance and distribution metrics.

The two algorithms used are the multi-objective evolutionary algorithm toolbox (MOEA_NUS)[19] and (1+1)-Pareto Archived Evolution Strategy (PAES)[14]. Though, MOEA_NUS and PAES are of different nature as MOEA_NUS is population-based and PAES is not. This might not be a fair comparison, but the focus of this experiment is to demonstrate the new visualization technique rather than comparison.

For MOEA_NUS, the population size is set to 100 and generation size to 250, with tournament selection, one-point crossover with a rate of 0.9 and classical mutation with a rate of $1/l$ (where l is the string length for binary-coded chromosome). As for PAES, the iteration is set to 25000, depth to 4 and archive size to 100. We use 30 bits to represent each decision variable.

4.1. *Test Case 1: Two-Objective Problem with a Connected Pareto Front*

A two-objective minimization problem is tested here for $-4.0 \le x_i \le 4.0$, $n = 1,2,3$, as an example to illustrate the development of proposed visualization technique[10]:

$$f_1(x) = 1 - \exp(-\textstyle\sum_{i=1}^{n}(x_i - 1/\sqrt{n})^2) \quad (3a)$$

$$f_2(x) = 1 - \exp(-\textstyle\sum_{i=1}^{n}(x_i + 1/\sqrt{n})^2) \quad (3b)$$

4.1.1. Single Run Test

This is to illustrate the result of a single run though it does not have any statistical significance. The result plotted in the objective space is shown in Fig. 2. Figures 3 and 4 show the distance and distribution charts respectively.

Based on Fig. 2, it is clear that solutions found by PAES are Pareto-optimal but not well distributed. As for the solutions found by MOEA_NUS, it is better distributed but not all the solutions are Pareto-optimal as compared with PAES. In Fig. 3, we can confirm that all PAES solutions are indeed Pareto-optimal. As for MOEA_NUS, the center portion of the solutions are Pareto-optimal and the boundary solutions deviate from the approximate Pareto front. In Fig. 4, there are two very high ‘spike’ in the distribution metric for PAES solutions. The first ‘spike’ on the left shows that the solutions are ‘far away’ from the left boundary of the approximate Pareto front. The second ‘spike’ simply indicates that there is a break in the continuity of the solutions. Note that the second ‘spike’ is common if the true Pareto front is disconnected.

4.1.2. Multiple Runs Test

In order to have statistical significance, multiple runs of each algorithm are performed. Here, each algorithm executes 10 times on the test problem. Figures 5 and 7 show the DD chart of MOEA_NUS and Figs. 6 and 8 show the DD chart of PAES.

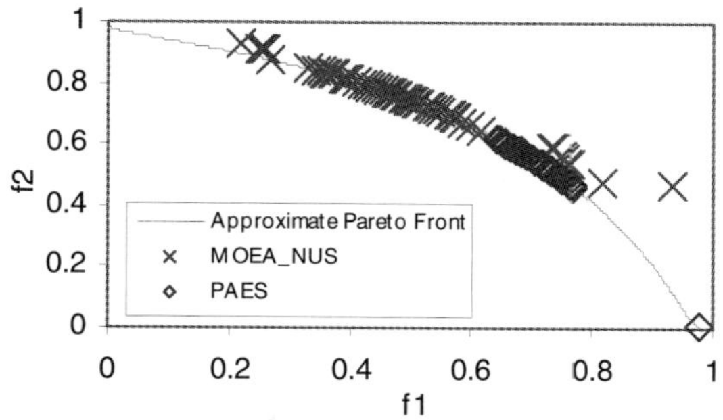

Fig. 2. Result of a single run – Test Case 1

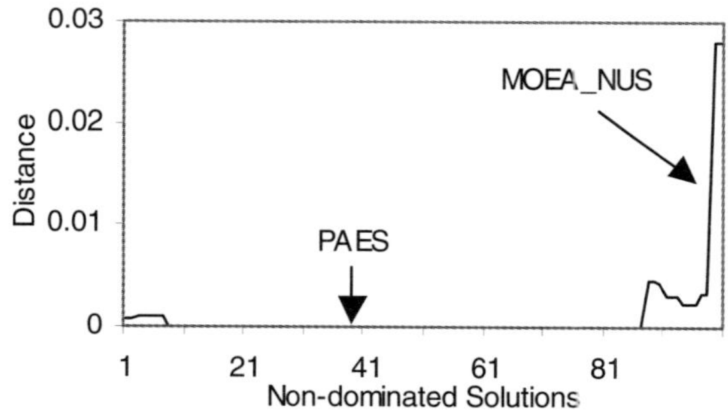

Fig. 3. Distance chart of a single run – Test Case 1

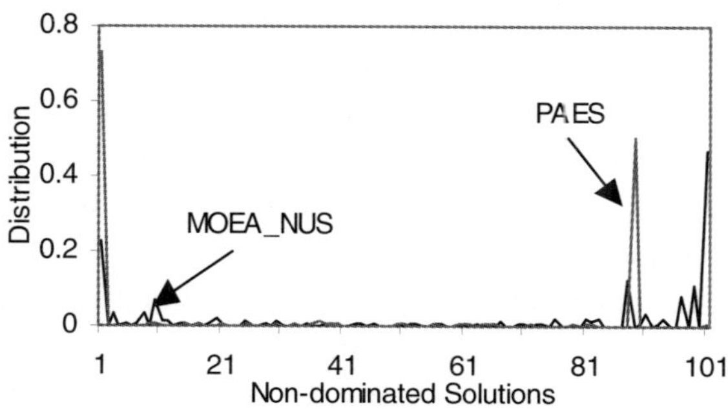

Fig. 4. Distribution chart of a single run – Test Case 1

Figure 5 again shows that the center portion of the solutions found by MOEA_NUS is close to Pareto-optimal. Figure 7 shows that the extent

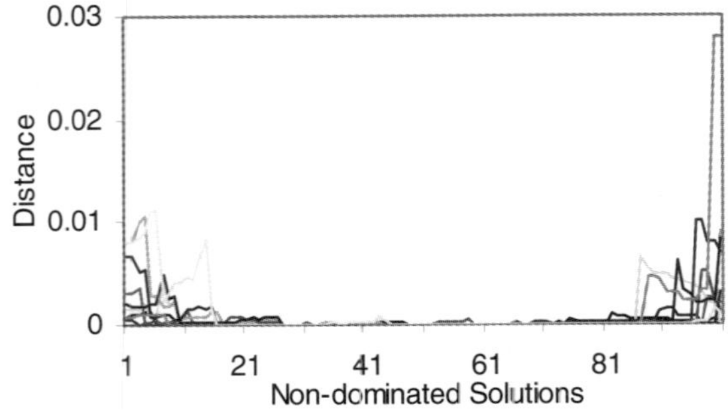

Fig. 5. Distance chart of MOEA_NUS (10 runs) – Test Case 1

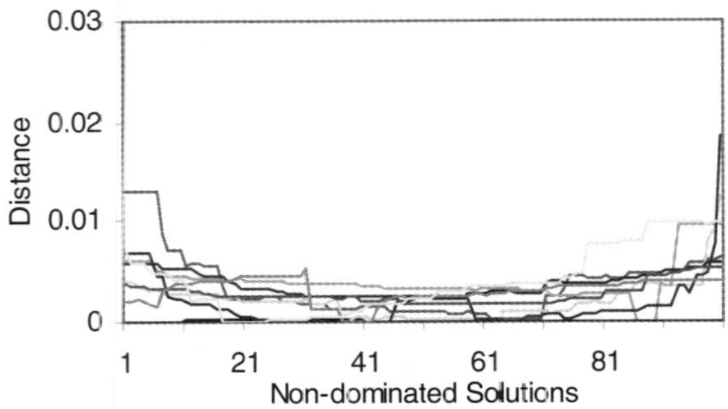

Fig. 6. Distance chart of PAES (10 runs) – Test Case 1

of the solutions does not span widely enough. In general, MOEA_NUS performance is considered quite consistent based on the results on single and multiple runs. Thus, DD chart can also be used to detect any performance inconsistency.

Figure 6 shows that on average, solutions found by MOEA_NUS are closer to the approximate Pareto front than PAES. Figure 8 indicates that there is a break in continuity among the solutions. However, this might be true for the case of a disconnected true Pareto front, but based on Fig. 7 it can be shown that the true Pareto front is not disconnected.

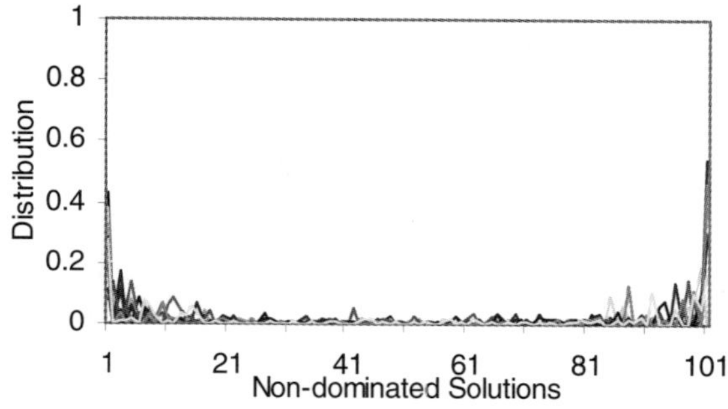

Fig. 7. Distribution chart of MOEA_NUS (10 runs) – Test Case 1

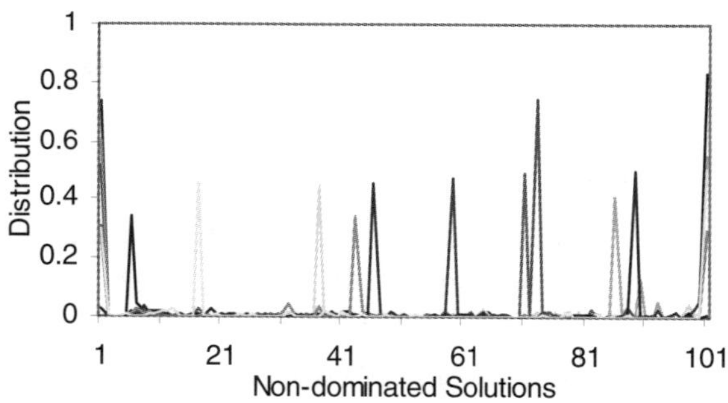

Fig. 8. Distribution chart of PAES (10 runs) – Test Case 1

4.2. *Test Case 2: Two-Objective Problem with a Disconnected Pareto Front*

The two-objective minimization problem illustrated here is[16]:

$$f_1(x) = \sum_{i=1}^{n-1} \left(-10\exp\left(-0.2\sqrt{x_i^2 + x_{i+1}^2}\right)\right) \tag{4a}$$

$$f_2(x) = \sum_{i=1}^{n} \left(|x_i|^{0.8} + 5\sin x_i^3\right) \tag{4b}$$

where $-5.0 \leq x_i \leq 5.0$, $n = 1,2,3$.

4.2.1. Single Run Test

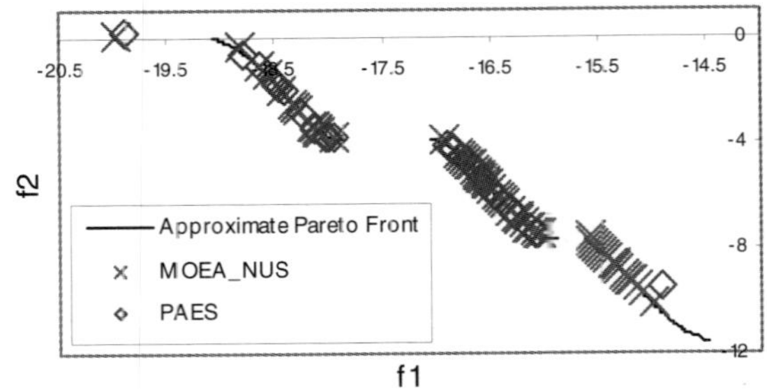

Fig. 9. Result of a single run – Test Case 2

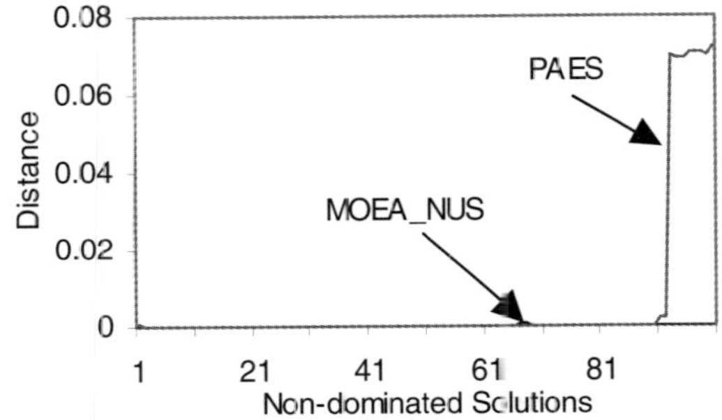

Fig. 10. Distance chart of a single run – Test Case 2

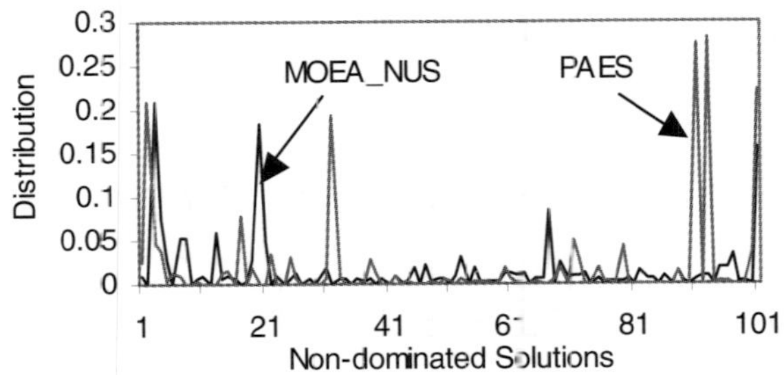

Fig. 11. Distribution chart of a single run – Test Case 2

The resultant objective space is plotted in Fig. 9. Figures 10 and 11 show the DD chart respectively. This is to verify if the DD chart is accurate in a single run.

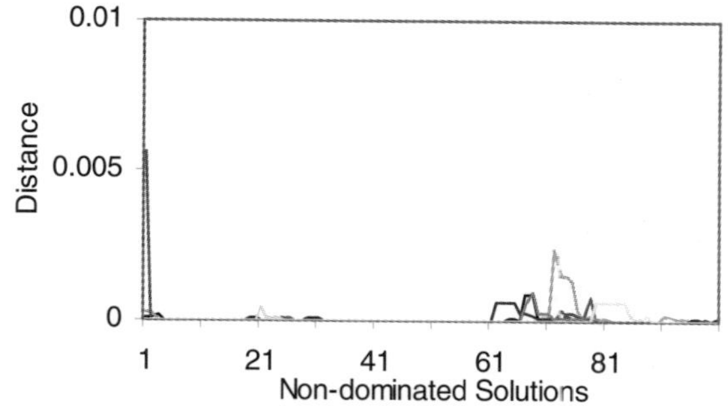

Fig. 12. Distance chart of MOEA_NUS (10 runs) – Test Case 2

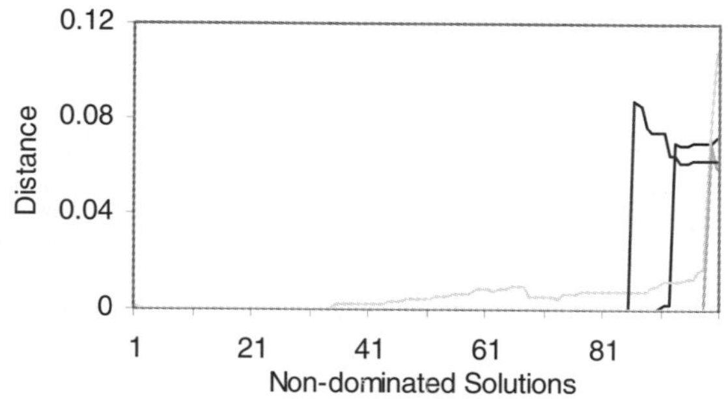

Fig. 13. Distance chart of PAES (10 runs) – Test Case 2

4.2.2. Multiple Runs Test

Here, each algorithm has been executed 10 times on the test problem. Figures 12 and 14 show the DD chart of MOEA_NUS and Figs. 13 and 15 show the DD chart of PAES.

The distance chart shows that PAES has some problems in achieving good convergence to the Pareto front for the last portion of their non-dominated solution set as compared with MOEA_NUS.

For the distribution chart, it is very confusing as compared with the single run. In order to alleviate the problem, the distribution chart of the approximate Pareto solutions is shown in Fig. 16. Simple pattern matching on the distribution charts between approximate Pareto front

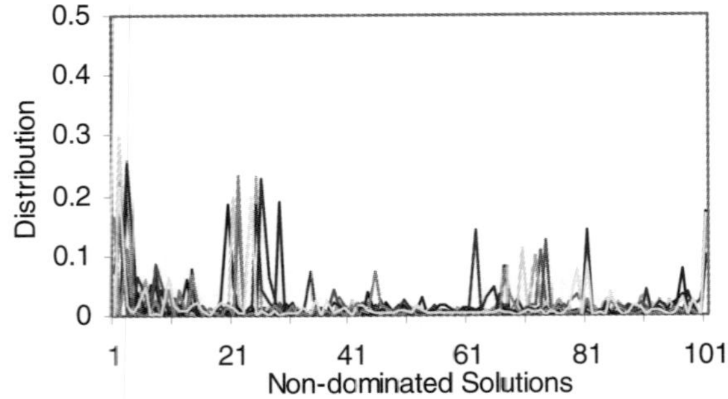

Fig. 14. Distribution chart of MOEA_NUS (10 runs) – Test Case 2

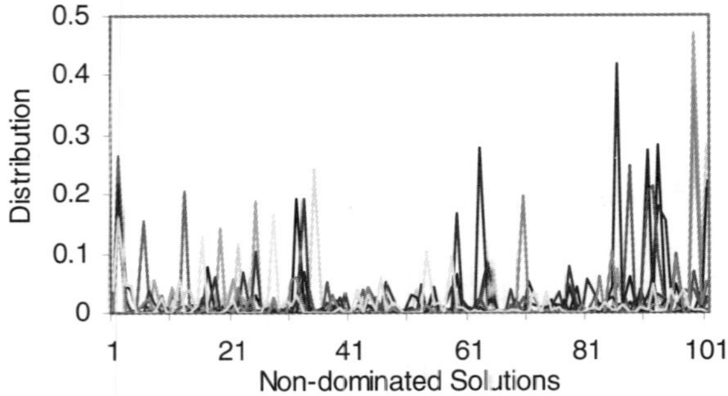

Fig. 15. Distribution chart of PAES (10 runs) – Test Case 2

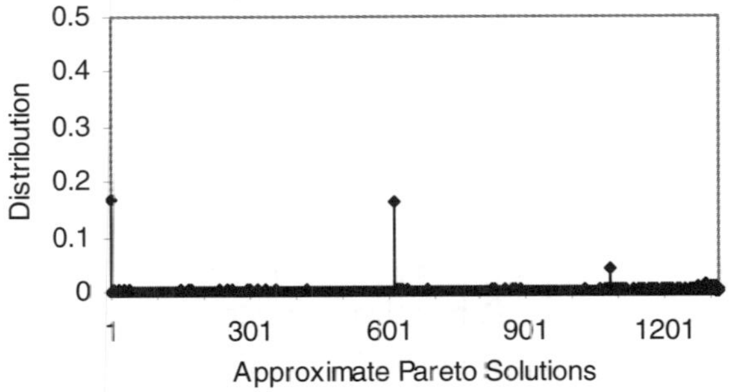

Fig. 16. Distribution chart of approximate Pareto Front solutions – Test Case 2

and the two algorithms show that MOEA_NUS has better distribution than PAES.

4.3. *Test Case 3: A Three-Objective Problem*

Currently, there exists no widely accepted or simple-to-use distribution-like metrics for problems with three objectives or more. Hence, the method presented in Section 3 will be used for the distribution metric. The three-objective minimization problem illustrated here is[22]:

$$f_1(x) = 0.5\left(x_1^2 + x_2^2\right) + \sin\left(x_1^2 + x_2^2\right) \tag{5a}$$

$$f_2(x) = \frac{\left(3x_1 - 2x_2 + 4\right)^2}{8} + \frac{\left(x_1 - x_2 + 1\right)^2}{27} + 15 \tag{5b}$$

$$f_3(x) = \frac{1}{\left(x_1^2 + x_2^2 + 1\right)} - 1.1e^{\left(-x_1^2 - x_2^2\right)} \tag{5c}$$

where $-3.0 \le x_1, x_2 \le 3.0$.

4.3.1. Multiple Runs Test

Here, each algorithm is executed 10 times on the test problem. Figures 17 and 19 show the DD chart of MOEA_NUS and Figs. 18 and 20 show the DD chart of PAES.

The distance chart shows that solutions found by MOEA_NUS are closer to approximate Pareto front and performance is quite consistent as compared with PAES. This observation might not be obvious if the solutions were to be plotted in objective space.

In order to overcome the inaccuracy of the distribution metric computation, the distribution chart of approximate Pareto solutions is also shown in Fig. 21. Here, the user can check if the resulting distribution chart has the similar pattern as compared with the approximate Pareto solutions. It does verify that distribution chart of MOEA_NUS has a similar pattern with the approximate Pareto solutions. The consistency of MOEA_NUS performance is again shown in the distribution chart.

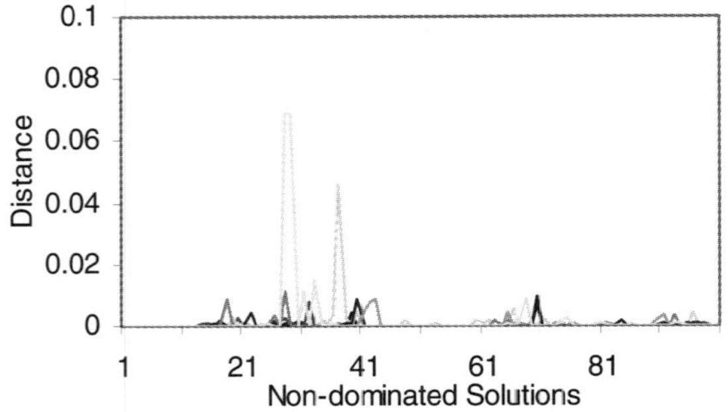

Fig. 17. Distance chart of MOEA_NUS (10 runs) – Test Case 3

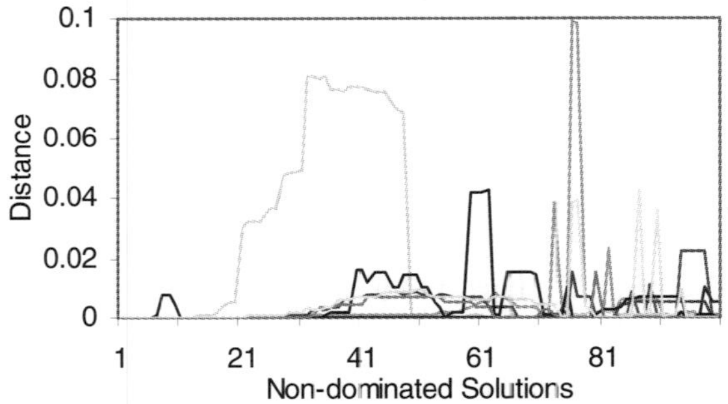

Fig. 18. Distance chart of PAES (10 runs) – Test Case 3

5. Observations

In the previous section, single and multiple runs have been simulated to illustrate the capability of DD chart. The distance chart is straightforward and easy to analyze but the distribution chart is less so. Care must be taken when analyzing the distribution chart as the true Pareto front might be disconnected and not well distributed. One of the possible solutions is to plot the distribution chart for the approximate Pareto front. Then, users may infer what should the best result look like. However, the number of approximate Pareto solutions does not need to be reduced to the same size as the competing non-dominated solutions. The objective is to give the user an idea of what could the ideal distribution look like.

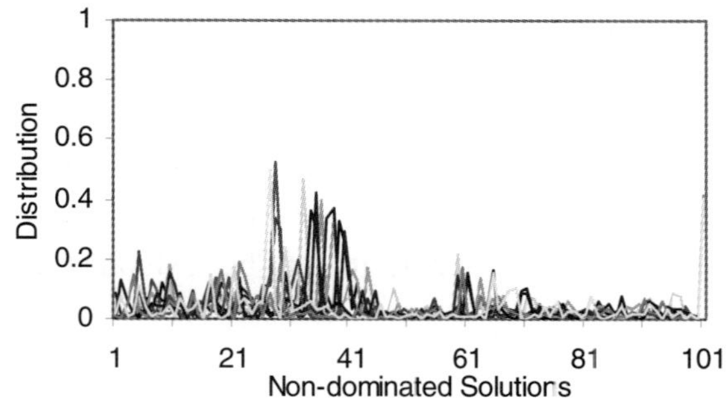

Fig. 19. Distribution chart of MOEA_NUS (10 runs) – Test Case 3

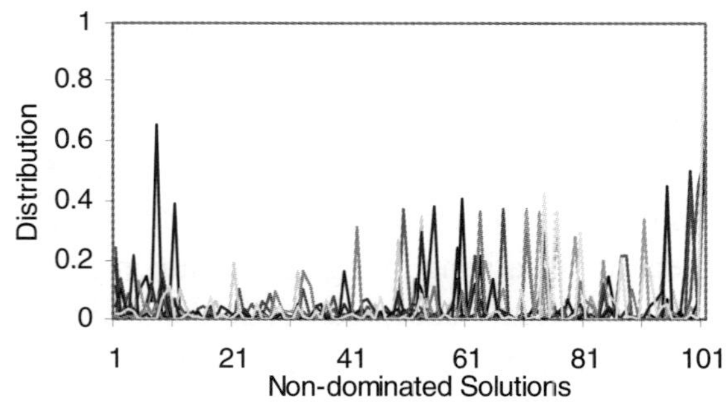

Fig. 20. Distribution chart of PAES (10 runs) – Test Case 3

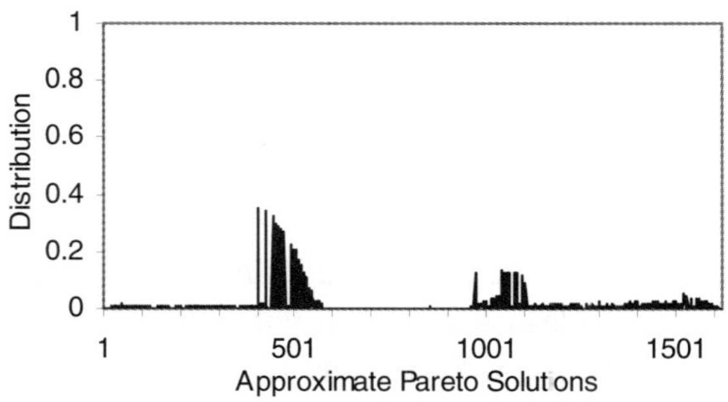

Fig. 21. Distribution chart of approximate Pareto Front solutions – Test Case 3

Another noticeable problem is the resulting range of the distance and distribution metrics.[3] Without any knowledge of the range, it is almost impossible to determine if the results can be considered similar. For example, if two result values are 20 and 80, we can determine that the differences between these two results are significant if the range is from 0 to 100. However, if the range is from zero to infinity, then the differences between these two results can be considered as unnoticeable.

This visualization technique is not limited to only distance and distribution metrics and in fact, it can be extended to any suitable metrics.

6. Conclusions

In this chapter, a novel and simple-to-use visualization has been presented. It does not meant to provide conclusive results in MOEAs comparison, instead it is design for guiding user to select the final preferable algorithm in the event where the results are incomparable. This technique simply used all the existing information that are generated during MOEAs comparison and present it in a different way in order to solve the problem of visualizing in high order dimensions.

Since, there is no widely accepted, reliable and simple-to-use metric available, so by supplementing this visualization technique together with any chosen existing metrics can enhance individual evaluation capability in high order dimensions. As this technique can easily reveal the coverage of non-dominated solutions in an objective space, validate results reported by any metrics and show if the performance of an algorithm is consistent, with no limitations on the number of objectives.

Acknowledgments

The first two authors would like to thank Universities UK and University of Glasgow for the sponsorship of their PhDs. The authors are grateful to Dr. J.D. Knowles, Dr. R.A. Sarker and Dr. K.C. Tan for all the fruitful discussions.

References

1. K.H. Ang, Y. Li and K.C. Tan, "Multi-Objective Benchmark Functions and Benchmark Studies for Evolutionary Computation", *Proceedings of the 2001 International Conference on Computational Intelligence for Modelling, Control & Automation (CIMCA 2001)*, pp. 132-139, Las Vegas, U.S.A., Jul. 2001.
2. K.H. Ang and Y. Li, "An Overview of Benchmarking Techniques for Multi-Objective Evolutionary Algorithms", *Soft Computing and Industry: Recent Applications*, R. Roy et al. (Eds), pp. 337-348, Springer, 2002.
3. K.H. Ang, G. Chong and Y. Li, "Preliminary Statement on the Current Progress of Multi-Objective Evolutionary Algorithm Performance Measurement", *Proceedings of the 2002 Congress on Evolutionary Computation (CEC'02)*, pp. 1139-1144, Hawaii, U.S.A., May 2002.
4. P.A.N. Bosman and D. Thierens, "The Balance Between Proximity and Diversity in Multiobjective Evolutionary Algorithms", *IEEE Transactions on Evolutionary Computation*, 7(2):174-188, Apr. 2003.
5. C.A.C. Coello, List of References on Evolutionary Multiobjective Optimization, http://www.lania.max/~ccoello/EMOO/EMOObib.html, Aug. 2003.
6. C.A.C. Coello, "A Comprehensive Survey of Evolutionary-Based Multiobjective Optimization Techniques", *Knowledge and Information Systems, An International Journal*, 1(3):269-308, Aug. 1999.
7. K. Deb, A. Pratap, S. Agarwal and T. Meyarivan, "A Fast and Elitist Multi-Objective Genetic Algorithm: NSGA-II", *KanGAL report 200001*, Indian Institute of Technology, Kanpur, India, 2000.
8. K. Deb, *Multi-Objective Optimization using Evolutionary Algorithms*, John Wiley & Sons, Chichester, U.K., 2001.
9. A. Farhang-Mehr and S. Azarm, "Minimal Sets of Quality Metrics", *Proceedings of the 2nd International Conference on Evolutionary Multi-Criterion Optimization (EMO 2003)*, pp. 405-417, Faro, Portugal, Apr. 2003.
10. C.M. Fonseca and P.J. Fleming, "Multiobjective Optimization and Multiple Constraint Handling with Evolutionary Algorithms I: A Unified Formulation", *Technical Report 564*, University of Sheffield, Sheffield, U.K., Jan. 1995.
11. C.M. Fonseca and P.J. Fleming, "On the Performance Assessment and Comparison of Stochastic Multiobjective Optimizers", *Parallel Problem Solving from Nature - PPSN IV*, Berlin, Germany, pp. 584-593, Springer-Verlag Lecture Notes on Computer Science no. 1141, 1996.
12. M.P. Hansen and A. Jaszkiewicz, "Evaluating the Quality of Approximations to the Non-dominated Set", *Technical Report IMM-REP-1998-7*, Institute of Mathematical Modelling, Technical University of Denmark, 1998.

13. D.F. Jones, S.K. Mirrazavi and M. Tamiz, "Multi-objective meta-heuristics: An overview of the current state-of-the-art", *European Journal of Operational Research*, 137(1):1-9, Feb. 2002.
14. J.D. Knowles and D.W. Corne, "Approximating the nondominated front using the Pareto Archived Evolution Strategy", *Evolutionary Computation*, 8(2):149-172, 2000.
15. J.D. Knowles and D.W. Corne, "On Metrics for Comparing Non-Dominated Sets", *Proceedings of the 2002 Congress on Evolutionary Computation (CEC'02)*, pp. 711-716, Hawaii, U.S.A., May 2002.
16. F. Kursawe, "A Variant of Evolution Strategies for Vector Optimization", *PPSN I*, H.-P. Schwefel and R. Manner Eds, Berlin, Germany: Springer, pp.193-197, 1990.
17. R. Sarker and C.A.C. Coello, "Assessment Methodologies for Multiobjective Evolutionary Algorithms", in [18], pp. 177-195.
18. R. Sarker, M. Mohammadian and X. Yao (eds), *Evolutionary Optimization*, Kluwer Academic Publishers, New York, 2002.
19. K.C. Tan, T.H. Lee, D. Khoo, E.F. Khor and R. Sathikannan, "MOEA Toolbox for Computer-Aided Multi-Objective Optimization", *Proceedings of the 2000 Congress on Evolutionary Computation (CEC'00)*, pp. 38-45, San Diego, U.S.A., Jul. 2000.
20. D.A. Van Veldhuizen and G.B. Lamont, "Multiobjective Evolutionary Algorithm Research: A History and Analysis", *Technical Report TR-98-03*, Dept. of Electrical and Computer Engineering, Graduate School of Engineering, Air Force Institute of Technology, Wright-Patterson AFB, Ohio, 1998.
21. D.A. Van Veldhuizen, "Multiobjective Evolutionary Algorithms: Classifications, Analyses, and New Innovations", PhD Thesis, Dept. of Electrical and Computer Engineering, Graduate School of Engineering, Air Force Institute of Technology, Wright-Patterson AFB, Ohio, May 1999.
22. R. Viennet, C. Fontiex and I. Marc, "Multicriteria Optimization Using a Genetic Algorithm for Determining a Pareto Set", *International Journal of Systems Science*, 27(2):255-260, 1996.
23. E. Zitzler, "Evolutionary Algorithms for Multiobjective Optimization: Methods and Applications", PhD Thesis, Swiss Federal Institute of Technology (ETH), Zurich, Switzerland, Nov. 1999.
24. E. Zitzler, L. Thiele, M. Laumanns, C.M. Fonseca and V.G. da Fonseca, "Performance Assessment of Multiobjective Optimizers: An Analysis and Review", *IEEE Transactions on Evolutionary Computation*, 7(2):117-132, Apr. 2003.

PART 2

EVOLUTIONARY APPLICATIONS

CHAPTER 19

IMAGE CLASSIFICATION USING PARTICLE SWARM OPTIMIZATION

Mahamed G. Omran[1], Andries P. Engelbrecht[1], and Ayed Salman[2]

[1] *Department of Computer Science, University of Pretoria*
Pretoria, South Africa
E-mail: mjomran@engineer.com, engel@driesie.cs.up.ac.za
[2] *Department of Computer Engineering, Kuwait University*
Kuwait, Kuwait
E-mail: ayed@eng.kuniv.edu.kw

In this chapter, a new unsupervised image clustering approach which is based on the particle swarm optimization (PSO) algorithm is presented. The algorithm finds the centroids of a user specified number of clusters, where each cluster groups together similar pixels. The new image clustering algorithm has been applied successfully to three types of images to illustrate its wide applicability. These images include synthetic, MRI and Satellite images. A comparison between the new approach and the well-known K-means clustering algorithm is provided to show the efficiency of PSO in the area of image clustering.

1. Introduction

Image clustering is the process of identifying groups of similar image primitives[1]. These image primitives can be pixels, regions, line elements and so on, depending on the problem encountered. Many basic image processing techniques such as quantization, segmentation and coarsening can be viewed as different instances of the clustering problem.[1]

There are two main approaches to image classification: supervised and unsupervised. In the supervised approach, the number and the numerical characteristics (e.g. mean and variance) of the classes in the image are known in advance (by the analyst) and used in the training step which is followed by the classification step. There are several popular supervised algorithms such as the minimum-distance-to-mean, parallelepiped and the Gaussian maximum likelihood classifiers.[2] In the unsupervised approach the classes are unknown and the approach starts by partitioning the image data into groups (or clusters), according to a similarity measure, which can be compared with reference to data by an analyst.[2] Therefore, unsupervised classification is also referred to as a clustering problem. In general, the unsupervised approach has several advantages over the supervised approach,[3] namely

- For unsupervised approaches, there is no need for an analyst to specify in advance all the classes in the image data set. The clustering algorithm automatically finds distinct classes, which dramatically reduces the work of the analyst.
- The characteristics of the objects being classified can vary with time; the unsupervised approach is an excellent way to monitor these changes.
- Some characteristics of objects may not be known in advance. The unsupervised approach automatically flags these characteristics.

The focus of this chapter is on the unsupervised approach. There are several algorithms that belong to this approach. These algorithms can be categorized into two groups: hierarchical and partitional.[4,5] In hierarchical clustering, the output is "a tree showing a sequence of clustering with each clustering being a partition of the data set".[5] This type of algorithms have the following advantages:

- The number of classes need not be specified *a priori*, and
- They are independent of the initial condition.

However, hierarchical clustering suffers from the following drawbacks:

- They are static, i.e. pixels assigned to a cluster can not move to another cluster.
- They may fail to separate overlapping clusters due to lack of information about the global shape or size of the clusters.[4]

On the other hand, partitional clustering algorithms partition the data set into a specified number of clusters. These algorithms try to minimize certain criteria (e.g. a square error function); therefore, they can be treated as an optimization problem. The advantages of the hierarchical algorithms are the disadvantages of the partitional algorithms and *vice versa*.

The most widely used partitional algorithm is the iterative K-means approach. The K-means algorithm starts with K cluster centers or *centroids*. Cluster centroids can be initialized to random values or can be derived from *a priori* information. Each pixel in the image is then assigned to the closest cluster (i.e. closest centroid). Finally, the centriods are recalculated according to the associated pixels. This process is repeated until convergence.[6] The K-means algorithm suffers from the following drawbacks:

- the algorithm is data-dependent;
- it is a greedy algorithm that depends on the initial condition, which may cause the algorithm to converge to suboptimal solutions; and
- the user needs to specify the number of classes in advance.[3]

ISODATA is an enhancement proposed by Ball and Hall[7] that operates on the same concept as the K-means algorithm with the addition of the possibility of merging classes and splitting elongated classes.

Another category of unsupervised partitional algorithms is the class of non-iterative algorithms. The most widely used non-iterative algorithm is MacQueen's K-means algorithm.[8] This algorithm works in two phases as follows: one phase to find the centroids of the classes and the second to classify the image pixels. Competitive Learning (CL), updates the centroids sequentially by moving the closest centroid toward the pixel being classified.[9] Non-iterative algorithms suffer the drawback of being dependent on the order in which the data points are presented. To overcome this problem, the choice of data points can be randomized.[3] Lillesand and Kiefer presented a non-iterative approach to unsupervised clustering with a strong dependence on the image texture.[2] A window (e.g. 3×3 window) is moved over the image and the variance of the pixels within this window is calculated. If the variance is less than a pre-specified threshold then the mean of the pixels within this window is considered as a new centroid. This process is repeated until a pre-specified maximum number of classes is reached. The closest centroids are then merged until the entire image is analyzed. The final centroids resulting from this algorithm are used to classify the image.[2] In general, iterative algorithms are more effective than the non-iterative algorithms, since iterative algorithms are less dependent on the order in which data points are presented.

The authors of this chapter introduced[10] a new PSO-based image clustering algorithm. This chapter explores this algorithm in more detail, and presents an improved fitness function proposed by Omran *et al.*[11] A comparison between K-means and the PSO-image clustering algorithm is given which shows that the PSO-based image clustering approach performs better than the K-means approach.

2. Particle Swarm Optimization

Particle swarm optimizers (PSO) are population-based optimization algorithms modeled after the simulation of social behavior of bird flocks.[12,13] The PSO is generally considered as an evolutionary computation (EC) paradigm. Other EC paradigms include: genetic algorithms, genetic programming (GP), evolutionary strategies (ES), and evolutionary programming (EP).[14] These approaches simulate biological evolution and are population-based. In a PSO system, a swarm of individuals (called *particles*) fly through the search space. Each particle represents a candidate solution to the optimization problem. The position of a particle is influenced by the best position visited by itself (i.e. its own experience) and the position of the best particle in the particle's neighborhood (i.e. the experience of neighboring particles). When the neighborhood of a particle is the entire swarm, the best position in the neighborhood is referred to as the global best particle, and the resulting algorithm is referred to as the *gbest* PSO. When smaller neighborhoods are used, the algorithm is generally referred to as the *lbest* PSO.[15] The performance of each particle (i.e. how close the particle is from the global optimum) is measured using a fitness function that depends on the optimization problem.

Each particle in the swarm is represented by the following characteristics:

- $\mathbf{x}_i$: The *current position* of the particle;
- $\mathbf{v}_i$: The *current velocity* of the particle;
- $\mathbf{y}_i$: The *personal best position* of the particle.

The personal best position of particle i is the best position (i.e. one resulting in the best fitness value) visited by particle i so far. Let f denote the objective function. Then the personal best of a particle at time step t is updated as

$$y_i(t+1) = \begin{cases} y_i(t) & \text{if } f(x_i(t+1)) \geq f(y_i(t)) \\ x_i(t+1) & \text{if } f(x_i(t+1)) < f(y_i(t)) \end{cases} \quad (1)$$

Two main approaches to PSO exists, namely *lbest* and *gbest*, where the difference is in the neighborhood topology used to exchange experience among particles. For the *gbest* model, the best particle is determined from the entire swarm. If the position of the global best particle is denoted by the vector $\hat{y}$, then

$$\hat{y}(t) \in \{y_0, y_1, \ldots, y_s\} = \min\{f(y_0(t)), f(y_1(t)), \ldots, f(y_s(t))\} \quad (2)$$

where s denotes the size of the swarm. For the *lbest* model, a swarm is divided into overlapping neighborhoods of particles. For each neighborhood N_j, a best particle is determined with position $\hat{y}_j$. This particle is referred to as the *neighborhood best* particle, defined as

$$N_j = \{y_{i-l}(t), y_{i-l+1}(t), \ldots, y_{i-1}(t), y_i(t), y_{i+1}(t), \ldots, y_{i+l-1}(t), y_{i+l}(t)\} \quad (3)$$

$$\hat{y}_j(t+1) \in \{N_j \mid f(\hat{y}_j(t+1)) = \min\{f(y_i(t))\}, \forall y_i \in N_j\} \quad (4)$$

Neighborhoods are usually determined using particles indices,[16] however, topological neighborhoods can also be used.[16] It is clear that *gbest* is a special case of *lbest* with $l = s$; that is, the neighborhood is the entire swarm. While the *lbest* PSO has larger diversity than the *gbest* PSO, it is slower than *gbest* PSO. The rest of the chapter concentrates on the faster *gbest* PSO.

For each iteration of a *gbest* PSO algorithm, the velocity $\mathbf{v}_i$ and position $\mathbf{x}_i$ are updated as follows:

$$\boldsymbol{v}_i(t+1) = w\boldsymbol{v}_i(t) + c_1\boldsymbol{r}_1(t)(\boldsymbol{y}_i(t) - \boldsymbol{x}_i(t)) + c_2\boldsymbol{r}_2(t)(\hat{\boldsymbol{y}}(t) - \boldsymbol{x}_i(t)) \quad (5)$$

$$\boldsymbol{x}_i(t+1) = \boldsymbol{x}_i(t) + \boldsymbol{v}_i(t+1) \quad (6)$$

where w is the inertia weight,[17] c_1 and c_2 are the acceleration constants and $\boldsymbol{r}_1(t), \boldsymbol{r}_2(t) \sim U(0,1)$. Equation 5 consists of three components, namely:

- The *inertia term*, which serves as a memory of previous velocities. The inertia weight controls the impact of the previous velocity: a large inertia weight favors exploration, while a small inertia weight favors exploitation.[15]
- The cognitive component, $\boldsymbol{y}_i(t) - \boldsymbol{x}_i$, which represents the particle's own experience as to where the best solution is.
- The social component, $\hat{\boldsymbol{y}}(t) - \boldsymbol{x}_i(t)$, which represents the belief of the entire swarm as to where the best solution is. Different social structures have been investigated,[18,19] with the star topology being used most.

The reader is referred to Van den Bergh[14] and Van den Bergh *et al*[20] for a study of the relationship between the inertia weight and the acceleration constants in order to select values which will ensure convergent behavior. Velocity updates can also be clamped using a user defined maximum velocity, $V_{\max}$, to prevent them from exploding, thereby causing premature convergence.[14]

The PSO algorithm performs repeated applications of the update equations above until a specified number of iterations have been exceeded, or until velocity updates are close to zero. The quality of particles is measured using a fitness function which reflects the optimality of the corresponding solution.

3. Image Clustering

This section defines the terminology used throughout the rest of the chapter. A measure is given to quantify the quality of image clustering algorithms, after which an overview of a K-means clustering algorithm is presented. The PSO-based image clustering algorithm is then introduced.

Define the following symbols:

- N_b denotes the number of spectral bands of the image set
- N_p denotes the number of image pixels
- N_c denotes the number of spectral classes (as provided by the user)
- $\mathbf{z}_p$ denotes the N_b components of pixel p
- $\mathbf{m}_j$ denotes the centroid (mean) of cluster j

Measure of Quality

Different measures can be used to express the quality of image clustering algorithms.[21] The most general measure of performance is the quantization error, defined as

$$J_e = \frac{\sum_{j=1}^{N_c}\left[\sum_{\forall \mathbf{z}_p \in C_j} d(\mathbf{z}_p, \mathbf{m}_j)\right] \Big/ |C_j|}{N_c} \tag{7}$$

where

$$d(\mathbf{z}_p, \mathbf{m}_j) = \sqrt{\sum_{k=1}^{N_b} (z_{pk} - m_{jk})^2} \tag{8}$$

C_j is the j-th cluster

$|C_j|$ is the cardinality of the j-th cluster
z_{pk} is the k-th component of $\boldsymbol{z}_p$
m_{jk} is the k-th component of $\boldsymbol{m}_j$

K-Means Image Clustering

The objective of K-means is to group a number of data vectors into a predefined number of clusters. The centroid vector of each of these clusters is initialized to arbitrary vectors. Each centroid vector represents the mean of the data vectors associated with the corresponding cluster. For image clustering, a data vector represents a pixel of the image. Each pixel is then assigned to the closest mean, or cluster centroid. After all pixels have been clustered, the mean of each cluster is recalculated based on the pixels associated with that cluster. This process is repeated until no significant changes result for each cluster mean.

The K-means clustering algorithm can then be summarized as
1. Randomly initialize the N_c cluster means
2. Repeat
   (a) for each pixel in the image set, assign the pixel to the cluster with the closest mean, using Euclidean distance
   (b) recalculate the N_c cluster means, using

$$\boldsymbol{m}_j = \frac{1}{n_j} \sum_{\forall \boldsymbol{z}_p \in C_j} \boldsymbol{z}_p \tag{9}$$

   where n_j is the number of pixels that belongs to cluster j, and C_j is the subset of pixel vectors that form cluster j

   until a stopping criterion is satisfied.

For the purpose of this study, a fixed number of iterations, $t_{\max}$, is used as the stopping criterion to allow fair comparison of the K-means and PSO algorithms. An alternative is to stop the clustering process when there are no significant changes in the mean vectors.

The iterative nature of K-means algorithms makes them computationally expensive. In addition, due to the greedy nature of K-means, these algorithms are susceptible to local minima.

PSO-Based Image Clustering

In the context of image clustering, a single particle represents the N_c cluster means. That is, each particle $\mathbf{x}_i$ is constructed as $\mathbf{x}_i = (\mathbf{m}_{i1},\ldots,\mathbf{m}_{ij},\ldots,\mathbf{m}_{iN_c})$ where $\mathbf{m}_{ij}$ refers to the j-th cluster centroid vector of the i-th particle. Therefore, a swarm represents a number of candidate image clusterings.

Omran *et al* introduced[10] a *gbest* PSO image clustering algorithm, where the quality of each particle is measured using

$$f(\boldsymbol{x}_i,\boldsymbol{Z}_i) = w_1\bar{d}_{\max}(\boldsymbol{Z}_i,\boldsymbol{x}_i) + w_2(z_{\max} - d_{\min}(\boldsymbol{x}_i)) \tag{10}$$

where $z_{\max}$ is the maximum pixel value in the image set (i.e. $z_{\max} = 2^s - 1$ for an s-bit image); $\boldsymbol{Z}_i$ is a matrix representing the assignment of pixels to the clusters of particle i. Each element z_{ijp} indicates if pixel $\mathbf{z}_p$ belongs to cluster j of particle i. The constants w_1 and w_2 are user defined constants used to weigh the contribution of each of the sub-objectives. Also,

$$\bar{d}_{\max}(\boldsymbol{Z}_i,\boldsymbol{x}_i) = \max_{j=1,\ldots,N}\left\{\sum_{\forall z_p \in C_{ij}} d(z_p,\boldsymbol{m}_{ij})/|\boldsymbol{C}_{ij}|\right\} \tag{11}$$

is the maximum average Euclidean distance of particles to their associated clusters, and

$$d_{\min}(\boldsymbol{x}_i) = \min_{\forall j_1,j_2,j_1\neq j_2}\left\{d(\boldsymbol{m}_{ij_1},\boldsymbol{m}_{ij_2})\right\} \tag{12}$$

is the minimum Euclidean distance between any pair of clusters. In the above, $|\boldsymbol{C}_{ij}|$ is the cardinality of the set of pixels that belong to cluster j of pixel i, $\boldsymbol{C}_{ij}$.

The fitness function in Eq. 10 has as objective to simultaneously

- minimize the intra-distance between pixels and their cluster means, as quantified by $\bar{d}_{\max}(\boldsymbol{Z}_i, \boldsymbol{x}_i)$, and
- maximize the inter-distance between any pair of clusters, as quantified by, $d_{\min}(\boldsymbol{x}_i)$.

According to the definition of the fitness function, a small value of $f(\boldsymbol{x}_i, \boldsymbol{Z}_i)$ suggests compact and well-separated clusters (i.e. *good* clustering).

The fitness function is thus a multi-objective problem. Approaches to solve multi-objective problems have been developed mostly for evolutionary algorithms.[22] Recently, approaches to multi-objective optimization using PSO have been developed.[23] Since our scope is to illustrate the applicability of PSO to image clustering, and not on multi-objective optimization, a simple approach is being used to cope with multiple objectives. Different priorities are assigned to the subobjectives via appropriate initialization of the values of w_1 and w_2.

The PSO image clustering algorithm is summarized below:

1. Initialize each particle to contain N_c randomly selected cluster means.
2. For $t = 1$ to $t_{\max}$
   (a) For each particle i
      (i) For each pixel z_p
      - Calculate $d(z_p, \boldsymbol{m}_{ij})$ for all clusters $\boldsymbol{C}_{ij}$
      - Assign z_p to $\boldsymbol{C}_{ij}$ where

$$d(z_p, \boldsymbol{m}_{ij}) = \min_{\forall c=1,\ldots,N_c} \{d(z_p, \boldsymbol{m}_{ic})\} \tag{13}$$

      (ii) Calculate the fitness, $f(\boldsymbol{x}_i(t), \boldsymbol{Z})$

   (b) Find the global best solution $\hat{y}(t)$
   (c) Update the cluster centroids using Eqs. 5 and 6

An advantage of using PSO is that a parallel search for an optimal clustering is performed. This population-based search approach reduces the effect of the initial conditions, compared to K-means (especially for relatively large swarm sizes).

4. Experimental Results

The PSO-based image clustering algorithm has been applied to three types of imagery data, namely synthetic, MRI and LANDSAT 5 MSS (79 m GSD) images. These data sets have been selected to test the algorithms, and to compare them with K-means, on a range of problem types.

Synthetic Image: Figure 1 shows a 100 × 100 8-bit gray scale image created to specifically show that the PSO algorithm does not get trapped in the local minimum. The image was created using two types of brushes, one brighter than the other.

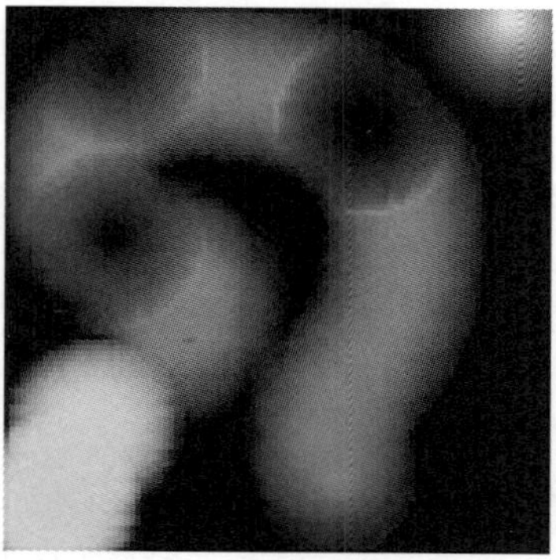

Fig. 1. Synthetic image

MRI Image: Figure 2 shows a 300 × 300 8-bit gray scale image of a human brain, intentionally chosen for its importance in medical image processing.

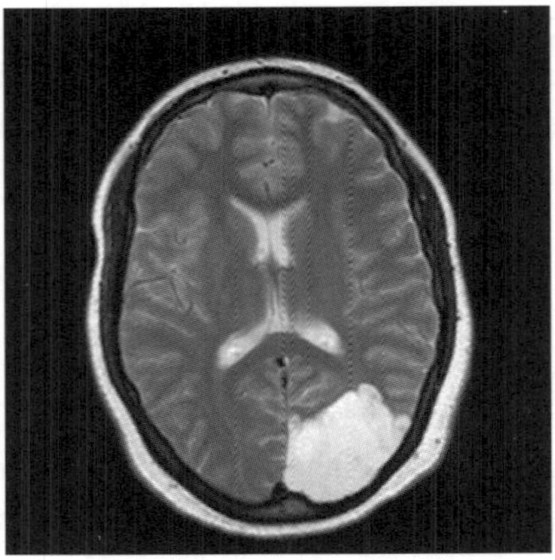

Fig. 2. MRI Image of Human brain

Remotely Sensed Imagery Data: Figure 3 shows band 4 of the four-channel multispectral test image set of the Lake Tahoe region of the US. Each channel is comprised of a 300 × 300, 8-bit per pixel (remapped from the original 6 bit) image. The test data are one of the North American Landscape Characterization (NALC) Landsat multispectral scanner data sets obtained from the U.S. Geological Survey (USGS).

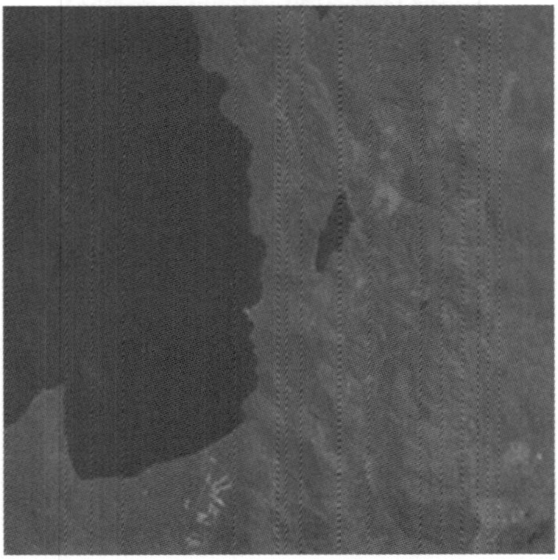

Fig. 3. Band 4 of the Landsat MSS test image of Lake Tahoe

Figure 4 illustrates for the synthetic image how the fitness of PSO improves over time. For this figure, 10 particles have been used for a training phase of 100 iterations, $V_{max} = 5$, $w = 0.72$, $c_1 = c_2 = 1.49$, and $w_1 = w_2 = 0.5$. The fitness value, as measured using Eq. 10, improves from the initial 96.637 to 91.781.

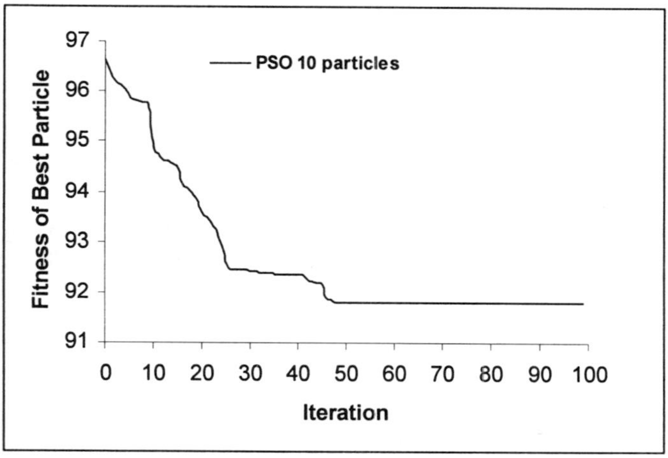

Fig. 4. PSO Performance on Synthetic Image

4.1. *gbest PSO versus K-Means*

This section presents results to compare the performance of the PSO algorithm with that of the K-means algorithm for each of the images. Results are compared against the number of fitness function evaluations executed. That is, 50 particles trained for 100 iterations result in 5000 function evaluations. The results reported in this section are averages and standard deviations over 20 simulations. All comparisons are made with reference to J_e, $\bar{d}_{max}$ and d_{min}.

Table 1 summarizes the results for the three images. In all cases, 50 particles were trained for 100 iterations, $V_{max} = 5$, $w = 0.72$ and $c_1 = c_2 = 1.49$. The chosen values of w, c_1, and c_2 are popular in the literature and ensure convergence.[14] For the fitness function in Eq. 10, $w_1 = w_2 = 0.5$. A total number of clusters of 3, 8 and 4 were used respectively for the synthetic, MRI and Tahoe images. The results showed that, for the images used, K-means performed better than the PSO algorithm with reference to the quantization error J_e. However, J_e does not give an idea of the quality of the individual clusters. With respect to the minimization of intra-distances ($\bar{d}_{\max}$) and the maximization of inter-distances ($d_{\min}$), the PSO algorithm performed better than K-means clustering.

Table 1. Comparison between K-means and PSO

Image	J_e	$\bar{d}_{\max}$	$d_{\min}$
Synthetic			
K-means	20.212±0.938	28.040±2.778	78.498±7.0629
PSO	24.453±0.209	27.157±0.017	98.679±0.023
MRI			
K-means	7.370± 0.0428	13.214± 0.762	9.934±7.309
PSO	8.536±0.584	10.129±1.262	28.745±2.949
Tahoe			
K-means	1.664±0.040	3.107±0.168	4.527±1.347
PSO	7.215±2.393	9.036±3.363	25.777±9.602

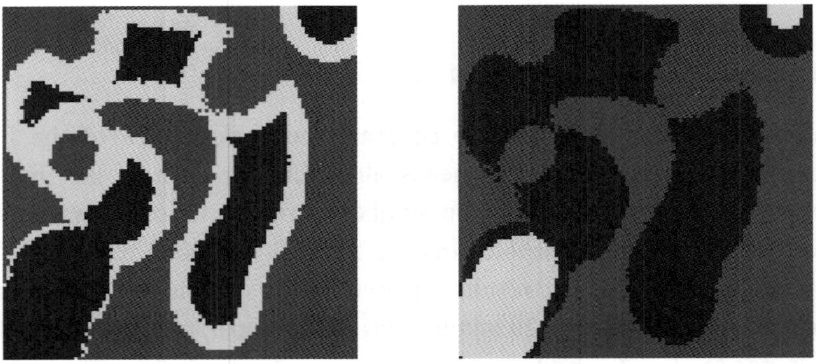

(a) K-means (b) PSO

Fig. 5. Thematic Maps for the Synthetic Image

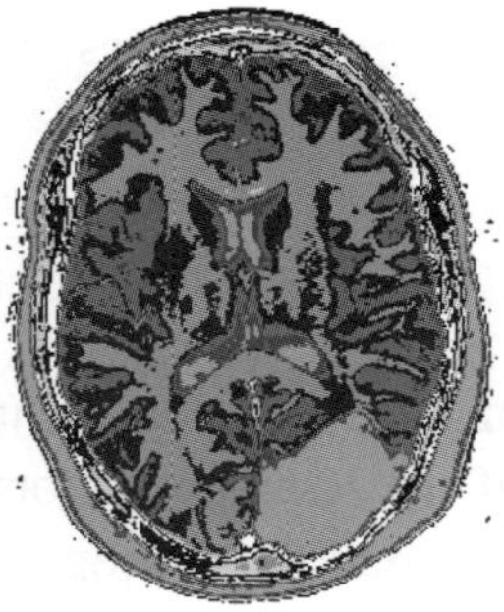

(a) K-means

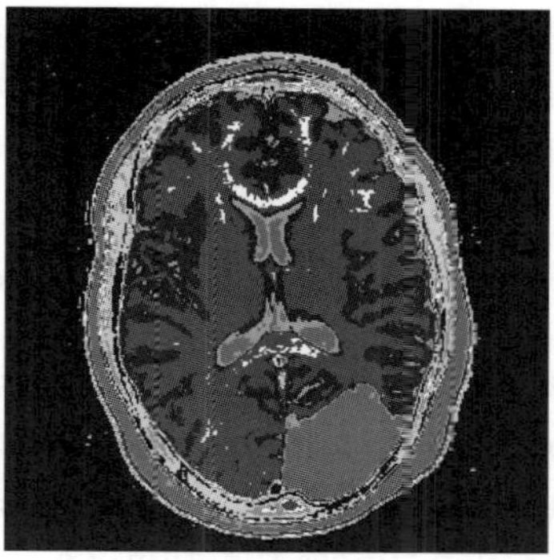

(b) PSO

Fig. 6. Thematic Maps for the MRI Image

(a) K-means

(b) PSO

Fig. 7. Thematic Maps for the Lake Tahoe Image

Figure 5(a) illustrates the thematic map image of the synthetic image for the K-means algorithm, while Fig. 5(b) illustrates the thematic map obtained from the PSO algorithm. These figures clearly illustrate that K-means was trapped in a local optimum since three clusters were created using two brushers, the brighter brush were used to create the two spots in the upper right and lower left corner while the other brush were used to create the remaining shape. K-means could not classify the clusters correctly since it failed to cluster the two spots as separated clusters. PSO, on the other hand, was not trapped in this local optimum and succeeded in showing the two spots as a separated cluster. The thematic maps for the MRI and the Tahoe images are given in Figs. 6 and 7 respectively.

4.2. *Improved Fitness Function*

The above experimental results have shown the PSO image clustering algorithm to improve on the performance of the K-means algorithm in terms of inter- and intra-cluster distances. Omran *et al* proposed[11] an improved fitness function, i.e.

$$f(\boldsymbol{x}_i,\boldsymbol{Z}_i) = w_1\bar{d}_{\max}(\boldsymbol{Z}_i,\boldsymbol{x}_i) + w_2(z_{\max} - d_{\min}(\boldsymbol{x}_i)) + w_3 J_{e,i} \tag{14}$$

which simply adds to the previous fitness function an additional sub-objective to also minimize the quantization error. In this section, the results of the *gbest* PSO shown in the previous section are compared with results using the new fitness function as defined in Eq. 14. All parameters are set as in the previous section. The only difference is that for the extended fitness function, $w_1 = w_2 = 0.3$, $w_3 = 0.4$ were used for the synthetic image, $w_1 = 0.2$, $w_2 = 0.5$, $w_3 = 0.3$ were used for the MRI image and $w_1 = w_2 = w_3 = 0.333333$ were used for the Tahoe image. These values were selected by trial and error. For a thorough study of this, refer to Omran *et al.*[11]

Table 2 compares K-means and the PSO-based image clustering algorithm using the extended fitness function in Eq. 14. It is obvious from the table that PSO performed better than K-means with respect to J_e, $\bar{d}_{\max}$ and $d_{\min}$ for all images except the Tahoe image. For a thorough comparison with other popular clustering algorithms refer to Omran *et al.*[11]

To verify these results a tool developed by Salman *et al*[24] called SIGT was also used to conduct a more elaborate comparison between the PSO and K-means clustering algorithms, which showed that PSO-based clustering algorithm is more efficient than the K-means clustering algorithm.[24]

Comparing the results of the two fitness functions we notice that the new fitness function succeeded in significant improvements in the quantization error, J_e. The new fitness function also achieved significant improvements in minimizing the intra-cluster distances for the synthetic and Tahoe images, thus resulting in more compact clusters and only marginally worse for the MRI image. These improvements were at the cost of loosing on maximization of the inter-cluster distances. The reader is advised to refer to Omran *et al*[11] for a thorough study of the influence of different values of PSO control parameters.

Table 2. Comparison between K-means and PSO

Image	J_e	$\bar{d}_{max}$	d_{min}
Synthetic			
K-means	20.212±0.938	28.040±2.778	78.498±7.0629
PSO	17.113±0.548	24.781±0.270	92.768±4.043
MRI			
K-means	7.370± 0.0428	13.214± 0.762	9.934±7.309
PSO	7.225±0.552	12.206±2.507	22.936±8.311
Tahoe			
K-means	1.664±0.040	3.107±0.168	4.527±1.347
PSO	3.556±0.140	4.688±0.260	14.987±0.425

5. Conclusions and Outlook

This chapter presented a novel approach to image clustering using Particle Swarm Optimization (PSO). The objective of the initial fitness function used was to minimize the intra-clusters distance and maximize the inter-cluster distance. The initial fitness function was then improved by including the minimization of quantization error which results in improving the overall clustering quality. The PSO-based image clustering algorithm was compared with the K-means algorithm using synthetic, MRI and Satellite images, and showed to produce more accurate results.

Although the fitness function used by the PSO-approach contains multiple objectives, no special multi-objective optimization techniques have been used. Future research will investigate the use of a PSO multi-objective approach, which may produce better results. A strategy is currently being developed to dynamically determine the optimal number of clusters.

References

1. J. Puzicha, T. Hofmann and J. M. Buhmann, Histogram Clustering for Unsupervised Image Segmentation, *IEEE Proceedings of the Computer Vision and Pattern Recognition* **2**, 602-608 (2000).
2. T. Lillesand and R. Kiefer, *Remote Sensing and Image Interpretation*, John Wiley & Sons Publishing, N.Y., 1994.
3. E. Davies, *Machine Vision: Theory, Algorithms, Practicalities*, Academic Press, 2nd Edition, 1997.
4. H. Frigui and R. Krishnapuram, A Robust Competitive Clustering Algorithm with Applications in Computer Vision, *IEEE Transactions on Pattern Analysis and Machine Intelligence* **21** [5], 450-465 (1999).
5. Y. Leung, J. Zhang and Z. Xu, Clustering by Space-Space Filtering, *IEEE Transactions on Pattern Analysis and Machine Intelligence* **22** [12], 1396-1410 (2000).
6. E. Forgy, Cluster Analysis of Multivariate Data: Efficiency versus Interpretability of Classification, *Biometrics* **21**, 768-769 (1965).
7. G. Ball and D. Hall, A Clustering Technique for Summarizing Multivariate Data, *Behavioral Science* **12**, 153-155 (1967).
8. J. MacQueen, Some methods for Classification and Analysis of Multivariate Observations, *Proceedings 5th Berkeley Symp. on Math. Stat. and Prob.* **I**, 281-297 (1967).
9. P. Scheunders, A Genetic C-means Clustering Algorithm Applied to Image Quantization, *Pattern Recognition* **30** [6], 859-866 (1997).
10. M. Omran, A. Salman and AP Engelbrecht, Image Classification using Particle Swarm Optimization, *Proceedings of the 4th Asia-Pacific Conference on Simulated Evolution and Learning*, Singapore (2002).
11. M. Omran, A. Engelbrecht and A. Salman, Particle Swarm Optimization Method for Image Clustering, submitted to the *International Journal on Pattern Recognition and Artificial Intelligence of World Scientific Press*, April 2003.
12. J. Kennedy and R. Eberhart, Particle Swarm Optimization, *Proceedings of IEEE International Conference on Neural Networks*, Perth, Australia **4**, 1942-1948 (1995).
13. J. Kennedy and R. Eberhart, *Swarm Intelligence*, Morgan Kaufmann, 2001.
14. F. Van den Bergh, *An Analysis of Particle Swarm Optimizers*, PhD Thesis, Department of Computer Science, University of Pretoria, 2002.
15. Y. Shi, and R. Eberhart, Parameter Selection in Particle Swarm Optimization, *Evolutionary Programming VII: Proceedings of EP 98*, 591-600 (1998).
16. P. Suganthan, Particle Swarm Optimizer with Neighborhood Optimizer, *Proceedings of the Congress on Evolutionary Computation*, 1958-1962 (1999).

17. Y. Shi, and R. Eberhart, A Modified Particle Swarm Optimizer, *Proceedings of the IEEE International Conference on Evolutionary Computation*, Piscataway, NJ, 69-73 (1998).
18. J. Kennedy, Small Worlds and Mega-Minds: Effects of Neighborhood Topology on Particle Swarm Performance, *Proceedings of the Congress on Evolutionary Computation*, 1931-1938 (1999).
19. J. Kennedy and R. Mendes, Population Structure and Particle Performance, *Proceedings of the IEEE Congress on Evolutionary Computation*, Honolulu, Hawaii, (2002).
20. F. van den Bergh and A.P. Engelbrecht, A New Locally Convergent Particle Swarm Optimizer, *Proceedings of the IEEE Conference on Systems, Man, and Cybernetics*, Hammamet, Tunisia, (2002).
21. M. Halkidi, Y. Batistakis and M. Vazirgiannis, On Clustering Validation Techniques, *Intelligent Information Systems Journal*, Kluwer Pulishers, 17[2-3], 107-145 (2001).
22. C.A. Coello-Coello, *An Empirical Study of Evolutionary Techniques for Multiobjective Optimization in Engineering Design*, PhD Thesis, Tulane University, 1996.
23. C.A. Coello-Coello and M.S. Lechuga, MOPSO: A Proposal for Multiple Objective Particle Swarm Optimization, *IEEE Congress on Evolutionary Computation* **2**, 1051-1056 (2002).
24. Salman, M. Omran and A. Engelbrecht, SIGT: Synthetic Image Generation Tool for Clustering Algorithm, submitted to the *Journal of Electronic Imaging*, July 2003.

CHAPTER 20

A COEVOLUTIONARY GENETIC SEARCH FOR A LAYOUT PROBLEM

Thomas Dunker and Engelbert Westkämper
Fraunhofer Institute Manufacturing Engineering and Automation
Nobelstr. 12, 70569 Stuttgart, Germany

Günter Radons
TU Chemnitz, Institute of Physics
Reichenhainer Str. 70, 09126 Chemnitz, Germany

This chapter is devoted to an application of genetic algorithms and coevolutionary principles to a large optimization problem. Starting point is a mixed integer linear program which models our problem—in this case a facility layout problem. As the number of binary variables increases quadratically with the problem size, currently available solvers fail already for small problem instances. Using a genetic search our algorithm reduces the number of binary variables by setting a considerable part of them. The genetic operators were specially designed to yield a high percentage of feasible variable settings. In order to further speed up the computation of large problems we propose a partition into interdependent subproblems. Each subproblem ("species") is evolved by a genetic algorithm respecting the constraints ("environment") generated by the others. Numerical experiments verify this coevolutionary approach.

1. Introduction

The intention of this chapter is to show how specially adapted genetic algorithms (GA) and principles of coevolution open up the possibility of finding good solutions to large mixed integer linear programming (MILP) problems which are infeasible to enumeration techniques like branch and bound (b&b), *etc.* We restrict ourselves to a single problem for this demonstration—a facility layout problem (FLP).

The FLP is one subproblem in factory planning. It involves determining good locations of a set of departments (or manufacturing cells) on a planar site. The objectives are different for different applications. In addition, many of them are of qualitative nature and it is not straight forward to formulate them as measurable quantities. One objective is certainly to minimize the material handling cost. Yet, manpower requirements, work-in-process inventory, flow of information etc. play an important role, too.

Yet, in all cases a basic assumption is that the proximity between certain departments is more favorable than other configurations. The aim is to arrange the departments in such a way that the desired proximity relations are satisfied. If all departments require only proximity with a predecessor and a successor a line layout is an adequate solution. A star-like layout might be a good design in a situation where few departments preprocess parts which are assembled in a final department. Yet, as soon as the number of departments increases and the exchange relations between the departments are more complex, one cannot fulfill all desired proximity relations and one has to decide between different possibilities. In such a case, it is natural to apply computer programs for finding solutions.

For several decades there has been research on this subject. Meller & Gau[1] present a detailed review of the different formulations of the FLP and the variety of algorithms. Some additional recent references can be found in Chiang's paper.[2]

One can distinguish three types of problem formulation. Suppose there are a finite number of locations (e.g. on a lattice) and a set of departments or machines. The task is to assign the departments to the different locations minimizing some cost function. This yields a quadratic assignment problem. A second approach starts with the available floor area and divides it successively into smaller sub-areas with respect to certain constraints which finally yields the locations for the departments. In a third formulation the necessary sizes and shapes of the departments are given and the departments can be placed arbitrarily within the available floor area. This last formulation which results in a MILP, forms the basis of our considerations.

All these approaches lead to combinatorial optimization problems which share the difficulty of a computational complexity growing very rapidly with the number of departments. Hence many suggested algorithms for treating these problems search heuristically for good solutions instead of aiming at globally optimal solutions. Evolutionary methods like GA have successfully been applied in this context.[3,4,5,6]

The remainder of this chapter is organized as follows. In Section 2 we present an improved MILP formulation of the facility layout problem. Section 3 provides the definition of the specially adapted genetic operators and the description of the coevolutionary algorithm. Finally, in Section 4, we discuss the numerical results of our coevolutionary algorithm.

2. MILP Formulation

In order to make real FLP's manageable for computational algorithms a certain abstraction is necessary. The approximation of departments, floor areas, and others by rectangles is a popular method.[5,2] In addition, we assume that their sides are parallel to the axis of our coordinate system in the plane. Furthermore, we suppose that the size and the shape of each department or facility is given in advance. Denoting a rectangle by $A \subset \mathbb{R}^2$ we introduce the following notations where we use small letters for given constants, while potential variables—position and orientation—are denoted by capital letters:

$I = \{1, \ldots, n\}$	index set of all rectangles,
$i, j \in I$	indices for the rectangles,
$l_i \in \mathbb{R}_+$	length of the long side of A_i,
$s_i \in \mathbb{R}_+$	length of the short side of A_i,
$(X_i, Y_i) \in \mathbb{R}^2$	coordinates of the center point of A_i,
$O_i \in \{0, 1\}$	orientation of A_i,
	$O_i = 0(1)$ long side parallel to the y-axis (x-axis),
$M_i^X \in \{0, 1\}$	flip up/down (symmetry axis parallel to x),
$M_i^Y \in \{0, 1\}$	flip left/right (symmetry axis parallel to y).

We wish to partition first the available floor area into sub areas inside which we arrange the departments. In order to model these nested areas we introduce further notations:

$i^* \in I$	index of the total available floor area,
$P : I \to I$	map defining the containment, $P(i) = j$ means $A_i \subset A_j$, let us call A_j the parent of A_i,
$I^{\mathsf{f}} \subset I$	rectangles that are fixed to their parent, $i^* \in I^{\mathsf{f}}$,
$I^{\mathsf{m}} = I \backslash I^{\mathsf{f}}$	set of "movable" rectangles,
$I^{\mathsf{f}}_{\mathsf{m}} \subset I^{\mathsf{f}}$	fixed rectangles with a "movable" parent, $I^{\mathsf{f}}_{\mathsf{m}} = \{i \in I^{\mathsf{f}} : \exists\, k \text{ with } P^{\circ k}(i) \in I^{\mathsf{m}}\}$,
$F : I^{\mathsf{f}}_{\mathsf{m}} \to I^{\mathsf{m}}$	defining the next "movable" parent of a fixed rectangle, $F(i) = P^{\circ k}(i)$ where $k = \min\{n : P^{\circ n}(i) \in I^{\mathsf{m}}\}$.

In order to describe the transformation of a fixed rectangle A_i, $i \in I^{\mathsf{f}}_{\mathsf{m}}$, attached to a movable one A_j, $j = F(i)$, we need constants and variables:

$x_i^j, y_i^j \in \mathbb{R}$	relative coordinates of A_i with respect to A_j, for an illustration see figure 1,
$o_i^j \in \{0,1\}$	relative orientation of A_i with respect to A_j,
$U_j, V_j \in \{0,1\}$	auxiliary variables.

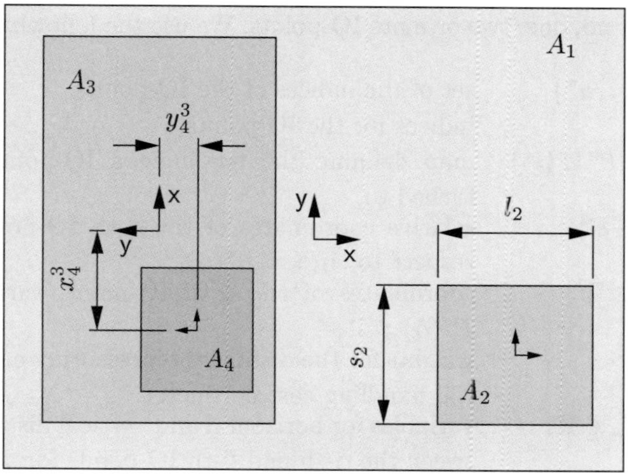

Fig. 1. Illustration of the relative coordinates and orientations for nested rectangles. The relative orientation o_4^3 equals 1 because the long sides of A_4 and A_3 are parallel.

In order to ensure the non-overlapping of the rectangles we need the following sets and variables:

$I^{\text{no}} \subset I^2$	set of pairs of non-overlapping rectangles, additionally $I^{\text{no}} \subset \{(i,j) \in I^2 : i > j\}$ for avoiding redundant variables,
$S_{ij}^D \in \{0,1\}$	direction of a separating line, $S_{ij}^D = 0(1)$ vertical (horizontal) separating line,
$S_{ij}^O \in \{0,1\}$	ordering of A_i and A_j, $S_{ij}^O = 0(1)$ A_i left or below (right or above) of A_j.

Note, that I^{no} should be chosen as small as possible. For example consider the following situation: $A_2 \subset A_1 = A_{i^*}$, $A_3 \subset A_1$, $A_4 \subset A_2$, $A_5 \subset A_2$, $A_6 \subset A_3$ and $A_7 \subset A_3$. In order to have the non-overlapping between A_2, A_3 and $A_4, \ldots, A_7$ it suffices to set $I^{\text{no}} = \{(3,2), (5,4), (7,6)\}$. The relations $(6,4), (6,5), (7,4)$ and $(7,5)$ are automatically true because of the containment relation and $(3,2)$.

The objective is to minimize the distances between different points. In most cases these points will represent the drop off and pick up points of a department. Yet, we can also imagine other points which possess a certain importance e.g. for the production process, the internal communication process, or the security. In the sequel we will call these points IO-points. They are attached to some A_i with either $i \in I^{\mathsf{m}}$ or $i = i^*$, i.e. a rectangle may possess no, one, two or more IO-points. We use the following notation:

$I^\bullet = \{1, \dots, n^\bullet\}$	set of the indices of the IO-points,
$\alpha, \beta \in I^\bullet$	indices for the IO-points,
$P^\bullet : I^\bullet \to I^{\mathsf{m}} \cup \{i^*\}$	map defining the rectangle a IO-point is attached to,
$(x_\alpha^{\bullet i}, y_\alpha^{\bullet i}) \in \mathbb{R}^2$	relative coordinates of the α-th IO-point with respect to A_i, $i = P^\bullet(\alpha)$,
$(X_\alpha^\bullet, Y_\alpha^\bullet) \in \mathbb{R}^2$	coordinates of the α-th IO-point, variables if $P^\bullet(\alpha) \neq i^*$,
$(w_{\alpha\beta})_{\substack{\alpha,\beta \in I^\bullet \\ \alpha > \beta}}$	weights for the distances representing e.g. material handling cost per meter,
$\delta X_{\alpha\beta}^\bullet, \delta Y_{\alpha\beta}^\bullet \in \mathbb{R}_+$	variables for horizontal and vertical distance between the α-th and β-th IO-point, for all $\alpha > \beta$ with $w_{\alpha\beta} \neq 0$

Then we use the following MILP formulation of the FLP:

$$\min \left(\sum_{\substack{\alpha,\beta \in I^\bullet \\ \alpha > \beta}} w_{\alpha\beta} (\delta X_{\alpha\beta}^\bullet + \delta Y_{\alpha\beta}^\bullet) \right) \tag{1}$$

subject to the following constraints

$$X_i - X_j - (x_i^j + y_i^j) U_j + (x_i^j - y_i^j) M_j^Y = -y_i^j \tag{2}$$

$$Y_i - Y_j - (x_i^j - y_i^j) V_j + (x_i^j + y_i^j) M_j^X = y_i^j \tag{3}$$

$$O_i = \begin{cases} O_j & \text{for } o_i^j = 1 \\ 1 - O_j & \text{for } o_i^j = 0 \end{cases} \tag{4}$$

for all $i \in I_{\mathsf{m}}^{\mathsf{f}}$ and $j = F(i)$,

$$X_\alpha^\bullet - X_j - (x_\alpha^{\bullet j} + y_\alpha^{\bullet j}) U_j + (x_\alpha^{\bullet j} - y_\alpha^{\bullet j}) M_j^Y = -y_\alpha^{\bullet j} \tag{5}$$

$$Y_\alpha^\bullet - Y_j - (x_\alpha^{\bullet j} - y_\alpha^{\bullet j}) V_j + (x_\alpha^{\bullet j} + y_\alpha^{\bullet j}) M_j^X = y_\alpha^{\bullet j} \tag{6}$$

for all $\alpha \in I^\bullet$ with $P^\bullet(\alpha) = j \neq i^*$,

$$0 \leq O_j + M_j^Y - U_j \tag{7}$$
$$0 \leq O_j - M_j^Y + U_j \tag{8}$$
$$0 \leq -O_j + M_j^Y + U_j \tag{9}$$
$$O_j + M_j^Y + U_j \leq 2 \tag{10}$$
$$O_j + M_j^X - V_j \leq 1 \tag{11}$$
$$O_j - M_j^X + V_j \leq 1 \tag{12}$$
$$-O_j + M_j^X + V_j \leq 1 \tag{13}$$
$$1 \leq O_j + M_j^X + V_j \tag{14}$$

for all $j \in I \backslash \{i^*\}$ for which there exists a $i \in I_{\mathsf{m}}^{\mathsf{f}}$ with $F(i) = j$ or a $\alpha \in I^\bullet$ with $P^\bullet(\alpha) = j$,

$$X_j - \frac{l_j}{2}O_j - \frac{s_j}{2}(1 - O_j) \leq X_i - \frac{l_i}{2}O_i - \frac{s_i}{2}(1 - O_i) \tag{15}$$
$$X_i + \frac{l_i}{2}O_i + \frac{s_i}{2}(1 - O_i) \leq X_j + \frac{l_j}{2}O_j + \frac{s_j}{2}(1 - O_j) \tag{16}$$
$$Y_j - \frac{s_j}{2}O_j - \frac{l_j}{2}(1 - O_j) \leq Y_i - \frac{s_i}{2}O_i - \frac{l_i}{2}(1 - O_i) \tag{17}$$
$$Y_i + \frac{s_i}{2}O_i + \frac{l_i}{2}(1 - O_i) \leq Y_j + \frac{s_j}{2}O_j + \frac{l_j}{2}(1 - O_j) \tag{18}$$

for all $i \in I^{\mathsf{m}}$ and $j = P(i)$,

$$X_i + \frac{l_i}{2}O_i + \frac{s_i}{2}(1 - O_i) \leq X_j - \frac{l_j}{2}O_j - \frac{s_j}{2}(1 - O_j) + l_{\mathsf{max}}(S_{ij}^D + S_{ij}^O) \tag{19}$$
$$X_j + \frac{l_j}{2}O_j + \frac{s_j}{2}(1 - O_j) \leq X_i - \frac{l_i}{2}O_i - \frac{s_i}{2}(1 - O_i) + l_{\mathsf{max}}(1 + S_{ij}^D - S_{ij}^O) \tag{20}$$
$$Y_i + \frac{s_i}{2}O_i + \frac{l_i}{2}(1 - O_i) \leq Y_j - \frac{s_j}{2}O_j - \frac{l_j}{2}(1 - O_j) + l_{\mathsf{max}}(1 - S_{ij}^D + S_{ij}^O) \tag{21}$$
$$Y_j + \frac{s_j}{2}O_j + \frac{l_j}{2}(1 - O_j) \leq Y_i - \frac{s_i}{2}O_i - \frac{l_i}{2}(1 - O_i) + l_{\mathsf{max}}(2 - S_{ij}^D - S_{ij}^O) \tag{22}$$

$$Y_j - \frac{s_j}{2}O_j - \frac{l_j}{2}(1 - O_j) \le Y_i + \frac{s_i}{2}O_i + \frac{l_i}{2}(1 - O_i) + l_{\max} S_{ij}^D \tag{23}$$

$$Y_i - \frac{s_i}{2}O_i - \frac{l_i}{2}(1 - O_i) \le Y_j + \frac{s_j}{2}O_j + \frac{l_j}{2}(1 - O_j) + l_{\max} S_{ij}^D \tag{24}$$

for all $(i, j) \in I^{\mathrm{no}}$, where $l_{\max} = \max_i l_i$,

$$X_\alpha^\bullet - X_\beta^\bullet \le \delta X_{\alpha\beta}^\bullet \tag{25}$$

$$X_\beta^\bullet - X_\alpha^\bullet \le \delta X_{\alpha\beta}^\bullet \tag{26}$$

$$Y_\alpha^\bullet - Y_\beta^\bullet \le \delta Y_{\alpha\beta}^\bullet \tag{27}$$

$$Y_\beta^\bullet - Y_\alpha^\bullet \le \delta Y_{\alpha\beta}^\bullet \tag{28}$$

for all $\alpha, \beta \in I^\bullet$ with $\alpha > \beta$ and $w_{\alpha\beta} \neq 0$.

Equations (2) and (4) describe the transformation of a rectangle A_i with $i \in I_{\mathrm{m}}^{\mathrm{f}}$. Equation (6) links the positions of a IO-point and its corresponding rectangle. The correct settings of the auxiliary variables U_j and V_j are ensured by inequalities (7)–(14). Inequalities (15)–(18) represent the relation $A_i \subset A_j$ while inequalities (19)–(22) prevent two rectangles A_i and A_j from overlapping. Inequalities (23) and (24) try to break symmetries when vertical and horizontal separating lines are both possible. They are optional and not used in the GA. Finally, inequalities (25)–(28) link the IO-points and the distances in the objective function (1).

The first MILP formulation for the FLP is probably due to Montreuil[7] and it proposes four binary variables for each non-overlapping relation. This approach was later optimized in order to improve the performance of the b&b.[8] Rajasekharan *et al.*[5] and Das[9] use a formulation which needs three binary variables. It seems that the above given formulation using inequalities (19)–(22) can reduce the solution time considerably, for computational results see table 1.

Table 1. Using the test example with six departments from Das[9] we compared the computational complexity (number of nodes of the b&b tree and computation time) of our model (Two) with the model (Three) using three binaries for one non-overlapping relation.[5,9] The results where obtained using two different b&b algorithms of the CPLEX MILP-solver (ILOG, Inc.) on a Pentium II 400 MHz.

Algorithm (branching strategy)	"Automatic"		"Strong"	
Number of binaries	Two	Three	Two	Three
Number of nodes of the b&b tree ($\times 10^3$)	11.5	47.9	5	31
Computation time in s	25.5	187.6	46.3	512

3. Coevolutionary Algorithm

The goal to find an optimal solution of the mathematical model introduced in section 2 and to prove its optimality can be achieved only for a small number of departments (up to ≈ 7). This is due to the quadratic increase in the number of binary variables S_{ij}^D and S_{ij}^O. That is why various heuristic methods have been developed in order to find systematically at least suboptimal solutions. They try to fix some of the binary variables. One such approach is genetic algorithms. They were applied to quadratic assignment formulations,[6,10,11] slicing tree representations,[3,12] MILP[4,5] and combinations of slicing tree formulation and MILP.[13] In our case the information about the setting of the binary variables is coded into genes. Then a population of individuals carrying these genes undergoes a simulated evolution which creates improved generations of individuals by selection, crossover, and mutation.

In the following we introduce a coevolutionary approach which goes beyond the standard genetic algorithms. The philosophy of coevolution can be described as follows. Let us suppose that a large problem can be decomposed into smaller ones which are linked to each other. Then one can assign to each such subproblem a population of individuals representing possible solutions. Different subproblems form different species which undergo an evolution. Observe that there is no exchange of genetic material between different species. Yet, the fitness of an individual from one population depends now also on the other populations.

One interesting field of research consists in obtaining the different species themselves by an evolutionary process of specialization. In our case we generate the problem decomposition by ourselves. We form groups of departments. For each group we reserve a separate area. Inside each such area group layouts are evolved by genetic algorithms. The fitness of one group layout depends in addition on the best layouts of the other groups. This is the coevolutionary part of our algorithm. A second genetic algorithm changes size and position of the group areas. This is done for two purposes. First this allows further improvement. Secondly, by changing the size we can control the evolution of a group—more space allows more variation, while tightening up stops evolution.

3.1. *Coding*

Rajasekharan *et al.*[5] use the 0–1–sequence for setting the binary variables as genetic code. Standard crossover and mutation operators are applied.

This generates subsequently many infeasible genes as possible settings do not satisfy the transitivity of relative positions. In order to avoid producing too many infeasible genes we introduce a coding and operators which do not leave the space of genes satisfying transitivity.

We suppose that the problem to solve involves the rectangles with indices from the index set $I_k^{\mathrm{g}} \subset I$ where the letter g stands for "group" and $k = 1, 2, \ldots$ is the index of the group. Let $n_k^{\mathrm{g}} = \# I_k^{\mathrm{g}}$ be the number of rectangles in the k-th group. Denote by $\zeta = 1, \ldots, n_k^{\mathrm{p}}$ the index of an individual within a population of n_k^{p} individuals. Let $\gamma = 1, 2, \ldots$ be the index of the generation. The ζ-th individual of the k-th group in generation γ will be represented by

$$\mathbb{I}_{k,\zeta}^{(\gamma)} = \left((i_1^x, \ldots, i_{n_k^{\mathrm{g}}}^x), (i_1^y, \ldots, i_{n_k^{\mathrm{g}}}^y), \{b_{ij}\}_{\substack{i,j \in I_k^{\mathrm{g}} \\ i>j}} \right).$$

The $b_{ij} \in \{0, 1\}$, with $i, j \in I_k^{\mathrm{g}}$ and $i > j$, represent values of the binary variables S_{ij}^D, i.e. whether there is a vertical or horizontal separating line between A_i and A_j. The two vectors $(i_1^x, \ldots, i_{n_k^{\mathrm{g}}}^x)$ and $(i_1^y, \ldots, i_{n_k^{\mathrm{g}}}^y)$ are permutations of the elements of I_k^{g} and they represent the order of the x- and y-coordinates of the midpoints.

Given an $\mathbb{I}_{k,\zeta}^{(\gamma)}$ we set the S_{ij}^D and S_{ij}^O with $i, j \in I_k^{\mathrm{g}}$ and $i > j$ in the following way. For each pair of indices $0 \le j_1 < j_2 \le n_k^{\mathrm{g}}$ we check the following alternatives. Set $i^x = \max(i_{j_1}^x, i_{j_2}^x)$ and $j^x = \min(i_{j_1}^x, i_{j_2}^x)$. If $b_{i^x j^x} = 0$ holds then set

$$S_{i^x j^x}^D = 0 \quad \text{and} \quad S_{i^x j^x}^O = \begin{cases} 0 & \text{if } i^x = i_{j_1}^x \\ 1 & \text{if } i^x = i_{j_2}^x \end{cases}. \tag{29}$$

Note that if $b_{i^x j^x} = 1$ the order $i_{j_1}^x$, $i_{j_2}^x$ does not enter in the problem formulation. Hence the final order of the x-coordinates of $A_{i_{j_1}^x}$ and $A_{i_{j_2}^x}$ is not necessarily $X_{i_{j_1}^x} \le X_{i_{j_2}^x}$. Analogously, we set $i^y = \max(i_{j_1}^y, i_{j_2}^y)$ and $j^y = \min(i_{j_1}^y, i_{j_2}^y)$. If $b_{i^y j^y} = 1$ is true, then we assign

$$S_{i^y j^y}^D = 1 \quad \text{and} \quad S_{i^y j^y}^O = \begin{cases} 0 & \text{if } i^y = i_{j_1}^y \\ 1 & \text{if } i^y = i_{j_2}^y \end{cases}. \tag{30}$$

3.2. *Genetic Operators*

Inspired by Chan and Tansri's crossover operators for permutations[6] we use a version of their order crossover. After selecting two parent genes $\mathbb{I}_{k,\zeta_1}^{(\gamma)}$ and $\mathbb{I}_{k,\zeta_2}^{(\gamma)}$ let us consider the parts of the genes representing the x- and the y-order. Take e.g.

$$(i^x_{1,\zeta_1},\ldots,i^x_{n^g_k,\zeta_1}) \quad \text{and} \quad (i^x_{1,\zeta_2},\ldots,i^x_{n^g_k,\zeta_2})$$

where we add the number of the individual as a second subindex. We select randomly two cut positions $c_1, c_2 \in \{1,\ldots,n^g_k\}$ with $c_1 \le c_2$. Then we construct two new genes from the two selected genes. First we fill the position from c_1 to c_2 with the original parts of the sequence

$$(\ldots,i^x_{c_1,\zeta_1},\ldots,i^x_{c_2,\zeta_1},\ldots) \quad \text{and} \quad (\ldots,i^x_{c_1,\zeta_2},\ldots,i^x_{c_2,\zeta_2},\ldots).$$

Then the positions to the left of c_1 and to the right of c_2 are filled with the numbers from the other parent which are not contained in the already filled part. While filling we keep the order given by the parent we take the elements from. In terms of the notation above this means e.g. for the first offspring gene

$$(i^x_{f(1),\zeta_2},\ldots,i^x_{f(c_1-1),\zeta_2},i^x_{c_1,\zeta_1},\ldots,i^x_{c_2,\zeta_1},i^x_{f(c_1),\zeta_2},\ldots,i^x_{f(n^g_k-c_2+c_1-1),\zeta_2}) \quad \text{with}$$

$$\{i^x_{f(1),\zeta_2},\ldots,i^x_{f(n^g_k-c_2+c_1-1),\zeta_2}\} \cap \{i^x_{c_1,\zeta_1},\ldots,i^x_{c_2,\zeta_1}\} = \varnothing$$

and the mapping $j \mapsto f(j)$ is strictly increasing. In the same way the crossover is defined for the y-direction. The motivation for this definition is the idea that we wish to keep the part that is located between the cuts hoping that it contributes to a good solution and arranging the remaining elements in the order given by the other parent

For mutation a single parent is randomly selected. Then the mutation operator for each of the parts $(i^x_1,\ldots,i^x_{n^g_k})$ and $(i^y_1,\ldots,i^y_{n^g_k})$ just exchanges two randomly chosen elements.

The more complicated part is the modification of $\{b_{ij}\}_{i,j}$ which represents the decision whether to have a vertical or horizontal separating line. As we did not find a method which could be geometrically motivated we decided to use standard crossover with two cut positions and standard mutation. Yet, in addition we apply an improvement strategy. First, we fix the variables S^D_{ij} and S^O_{ij} for the given individual $\mathbb{I}^{(\gamma)}_{k,\zeta}$ according to (29)–(30) and solve the remaining MILP (1)–(28):

evaluate ($\mathbb{I}^{(\gamma)}_{k,\zeta}$)
    for all $i, j \in I^g_k$ with $i > j$
        fix S^D_{ij} and S^O_{ij}
    endfor
    solve remaining MILP
    return solution

Next, we update $(i_1^x, \ldots, i_{n_k^g}^x)$ and $(i_1^y, \ldots, i_{n_k^g}^y)$ by sorting the center point coordinates of the obtained solution. Then we check for all S_{ij}^D whether they can be changed without violating a constraint in the current solution.

```
change_is_possible (S_ij^D)
    if S_ij^D == 0 (x-direction)
        if |Y_i − Y_j| ≥ s_i O_i/2 + l_i(1 − O_i)/2 +
                          s_j O_j/2 + l_j(1 − O_j)/2
            return true
        else
            return false
        endif
    else (y-direction)
        if |X_i − X_j| ≥ l_i O_i/2 + s_i(1 − O_i)/2 +
                          l_j O_j/2 + s_j(1 − O_j)/2
            return true
        else
            return false
        endif
    endif
```

If possible we change the variable S_{ij}^D. These actions are repeated until the objective value does not decrease further. Summarizing we have sketched our improvement strategy below.

```
improve (𝕀_{k,ζ}^(γ))
    while the objective value decreases
        evaluate (𝕀_{k,ζ}^(γ))
        obtain (i_1^x, ..., i_{n_k^g}^x) and (i_1^y, ..., i_{n_k^g}^y)
        from the solution
        for all i, j ∈ I_k^g with i > j
            if change_is_possible (S_ij^D)
                if S_ij^D == 0
                    b_ij = 1
                else
                    b_ij = 0
                endif
            endif
        endfor
```

```
endwhile
return I_{k,ζ}^{(γ)} with smallest objective value
```

Using these operators our GA creates a new generation by n^{cr} crossovers, n^{mu} mutations with mutation rate r^{mu} and copying the n^{co} best individuals which results in a population size of $2n^{\text{cr}} + n^{\text{mu}} + n^{\text{co}}$. The selection accepts individuals with above average objective value with a probability of p^{ac}. The GA terminates if the average objective values has not changed more than m^{ch} or the best values has not changed for the last n^{nc} generations or a maximal number m^{ge} of generations has been exceeded.

```
genetic_algorithm
    initialize population
    do
        γ = γ + 1
        for 1,...,n^cr
            select parents and crossover
        endfor
        for 1,...,n^mu
            select parent and mutate
        endfor
        copy n^co best individuals
    while change of average is larger than m^ch,
          best individual has changed during the
          last n^nc generations and γ ≤ m^ge
```

Table 2. Applying this algorithm with a population size of 50 ($n^{\text{cr}} = 20$, $n^{\text{mu}} = 5$, $n^{\text{co}} = 5$, $p^{\text{ac}} = 20\%$, $m^{\text{ch}} = 0.01\%$, $n^{\text{nc}} = 10$ and $m^{\text{ge}} = 1000$) to the three larger examples Das[9] we can compare our results to the ones reported by Das[9] and Rajasekharan *et al.*[5]. In the case of eight departments our GA found in 3 of 13 runs the optimal solution with an objective value 8778.3. This was proved by a deterministic algorithm taking 31 h 30 min on a Pentium III 866 MHz with a memory use of approx. 1.5 GB. In contrast to this the GA needed always less then 10 min and the worst objective value was 9106.6, which lies only 3.7% above the optimum.

Number of departments	Four-Step by Das[9]	GA by Rajasekharan *et al.*[5]	Our GA
8	10 777.1	9 174.8	8 778.3
10	15 878.3	19 777.3	15 694.5
12	41 267.5	45 353.5	37 396.1

3.3. *Coevolution*

For large FLP's the above described GA fails. Convergence takes very long. Hence it is necessary to treat such FLP's differently. Dividing large problems into smaller ones is a popular method.[14] By quantitative or qualitative method we can form groups of departments which shall be placed together. One has to provide an area for each group of departments and one has to determine the layout for each group within these areas. Already Tam and Li [15] suggested to approach the FLP in a hierarchical manner by a divide-and-conquer strategy. They formed groups, computed the layout for each of them and placed the groups in a final step. We propose a coevolutionary method of iterative nature. In a first step we consider each group as a separate FLP and perform a short GA in order to obtain a starting configuration for the rectangles of this group. Next, we fit a rectangle around each group and enlarge each side by a factor z_k giving more space to each group for possible further change. This allows e.g. that a group becomes more oblong during the subsequent optimization, see figure 2 upper right layout. Next, we arrange these rectangles using again a GA. In the first run we approximate the IO-points by the central points of the rectangles, see figure 2 upper left layout. Afterwards it is necessary to consider all relative positions of the IO-points of the group. Experiments with continued approximation by the central point did not show satisfactory results.

Now, a GA evolves each group separately inside its given group area for some generations, see figure 2 in the bottom. Let us consider one group. While we can omit all non-overlapping constraints involving rectangles belonging to other groups, we keep the objective function of the complete FLP where we replace the variables for the coordinates of IO-points belonging to an other group by the positions given by its current best individual. This gives the linkage between the different groups. It is obvious that these GA's can be computed in parallel.

For each group we decide whether we change z_k for the next iteration. For this purpose we compare the new dimensions to the old ones. If the proportional increase

$$\max\left(\frac{\max(l_{\mathsf{new}} - l_{\mathsf{old}}, 0)}{l_{\mathsf{old}}}, \frac{\max(s_{\mathsf{new}} - s_{\mathsf{old}}, 0)}{s_{\mathsf{old}}}\right)$$

exceeds a certain percentage p^+ of z_k then z_k is multiplied by a factor $f > 1$. If it remains below $p^- z_k$ then z_k is divided by the same factor f. Consequently, if the shape of the needed area does not change the provided group area becomes tighter. We stop the iteration when all group areas are

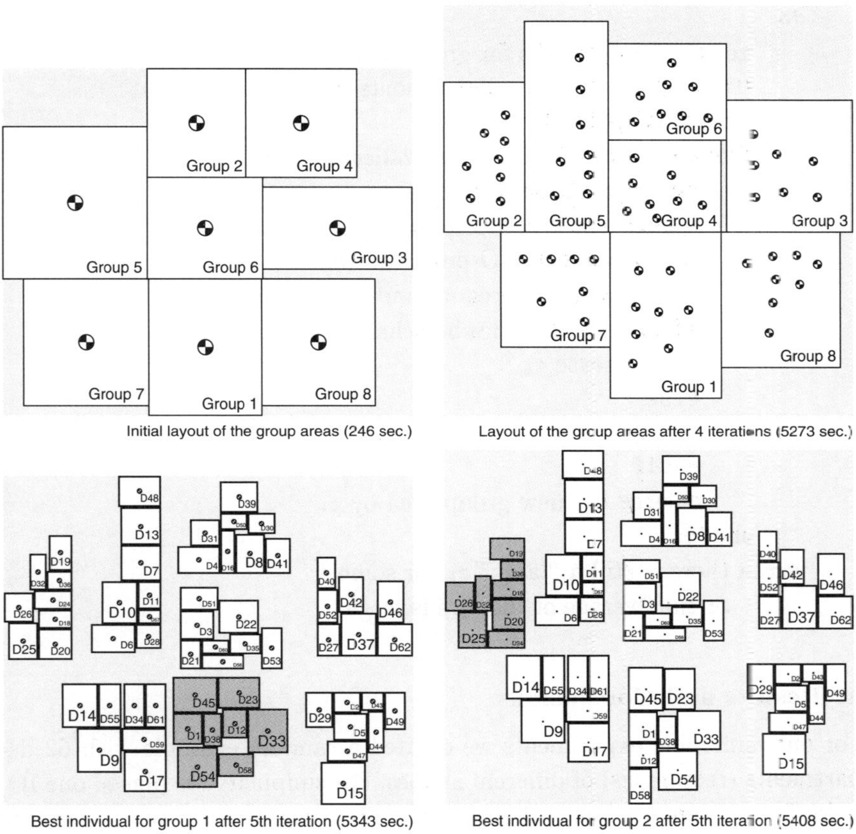

Fig. 2. As an illustrative example we take a FLP with 62 departments clustered into 8 groups. In the initial layout the group areas are almost all square shaped. After 4 iterations the shapes of the group areas have already changed, see e.g. group 2 and 5. The last two layouts show each an individual of the separately evolved group 1 and 2 (gray shaded).

close to the needed area of the group. The algorithm is summarized below.

coevolutionary_algorithm
    for all groups k
        genetic_algorithm for group k
        fit a group area around obtained layout
        enlarge the area by z_k
    endfor

```
do
    genetic_algorithm for group areas
    (treat group areas as departments with
    several IO-points)
    for all k * can be done simultaneously *
        genetic_algorithm for group k
        (placement is restricted to the group area
        and all external IO-points are fixed)
        fit a new group area around the group
        if ratio of the sides has changed much
            increase z_k
        else
            decrease z_k
        endif
        enlarge the new group area by z_k
    endfor
while there is still a "large" z_k for some k
     or the average of the z_k's is large
```

4. Results and Conclusions

For our numerical experiments we created a random example with 62 departments (rectangles) of different shapes. For simplicity we placed one IO-point in the center of each department. The weights $w_{\alpha\beta}$ were generated randomly, too.[16] Let us use the abbreviation P62 for this problem.

In order to find a grouping we implemented a heuristic grouping algorithm.[17] A similar clustering algorithm was applied by Tam and Li.[15] The aim is to arrange the departments in groups minimizing the sum of the weights between departments belonging to different groups. In addition, one limits the size of each group. One can construct examples where the used heuristic[17] stops far from the optimum as it can handle only simple exchange operations. In these cases genetic algorithms[18] can improve the grouping.

For our tests we generated groupings with four, six, eight and nine groups with a maximal group size of sixteen, eleven, eight and seven departments, respectively. As one would expect, the least value for the weights between different groups is attained for four groups.[16]

Table 3 shows the values chosen for the different parameters of the algorithm. There is always a conflict between good exploration of the search

Table 3. Settings for the parameters introduced in section 3.2 and 3.3: $r^{\mathsf{mi}} = 10\%$, $p^{\mathsf{ac}} = 20\%$, $n^{\mathsf{nc}} = 5$, $m^{\mathsf{ch}} = 0.5\%$, $z_k = 0.6$, $p^+ = 75\%$, $p^- = 50\%$ and $f = 1.5$.

	n^{cr}	n^{mu}	n^{co}	m^{ge}
first arrangement of the areas for each group	20	5	5	15
adjusting the positions of the changed areas	0	5	5	1
coevolution of the "group" populations	12	3	3	3

space and fast computation. The first requires large populations which again needs more time for computation. Certainly, these parameters can still be optimized.

We applied the coevolutionary algorithm about 20 times to each grouping of P62. Figures 3 and 4 show the convergence behavior of the different runs and the best layouts obtained. Table 4 summarizes the computational results for all experiments.

We observe that the average objective value as well as the time of computation increases with the number of groups. The first increase is due to the fact that the packing gets worse. Since the groups never fill exactly the provided rectangular area there is more space lost when the number of groups increases. Secondly, it turned out that the computations treating the part where whole groups are moved are very time consuming. Here, we not only consider the orientation but also the different reflection symmetries. This is the reason for the increase in computation time. Thus the clustering into four groups appears to be the best choice for a facility layout problem of this size - the restrictions introduced by the grouping are the least yet the computation is still fast.

Table 4. Computation times and objective values for our coevolutionary algorithm with four, six, eight and nine groups and the genetic algorithm without grouping for P62 on a Pentium IV, 1.5 GHz.

	Number of groups				
	4	6	8	9	none
average time (sec.)	4 533	4 967	5 390	5 699	$2.375\,10^5$
best time (sec.)	3 980	3 783	3, 397	3 098	$1.040\,10^5$
worst time (sec.)	5 214	7 294	7 170	7 688	$3.315\,10^5$
average objective	$4.062\,10^6$	$4.274\,10^6$	$4.355\,10^6$	$4.393\,10^6$	$4.261\,10^6$
best objective	$3.939\,10^6$	$4.186\,10^6$	$4.239\,10^6$	$4.184\,10^6$	$4.181\,10^6$
worst objective	$4.450\,10^6$	$4.446\,10^6$	$4.449\,10^6$	$4.650\,10^6$	$4.381\,10^6$

In contrast to the computation time of less than two hours for the coevolutionary algorithm, the simple genetic algorithm needs on average about two days and 17 hours for P62. The quality of the solution (objective value) lies in the same range as the solutions obtained by the coevolutionary algorithm. For comparison the corresponding results for 11 runs on a Pentium IV, 1.5 GHz are summarized in figure 5. A trial with a MILP-solver, a good starting solution and lower bounds did not yield any feasible solution after one week of computation.

Of course, there are further related problems of interest, which will not be discussed. For example, one may ask what happens when the problem size is further increased. Is there a point whereby six groups perform better than four? A second interesting question is whether dividing groups into subgroups can be of advantage in some cases. Here one introduces further

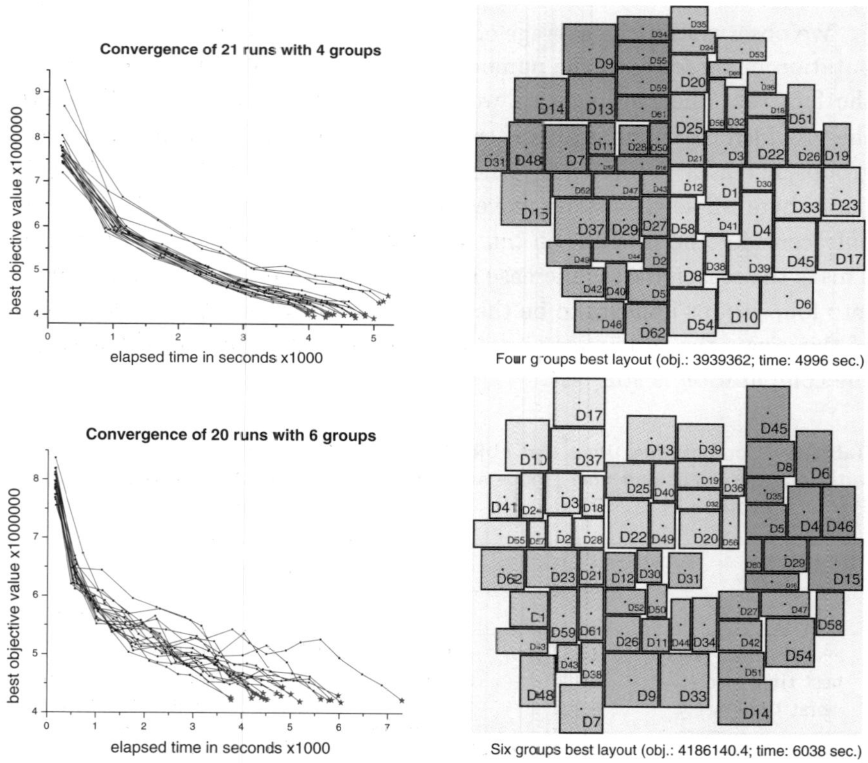

Fig. 3. Convergence of our coevolutionary algorithm and best layouts for problem P62 with four and six groups.

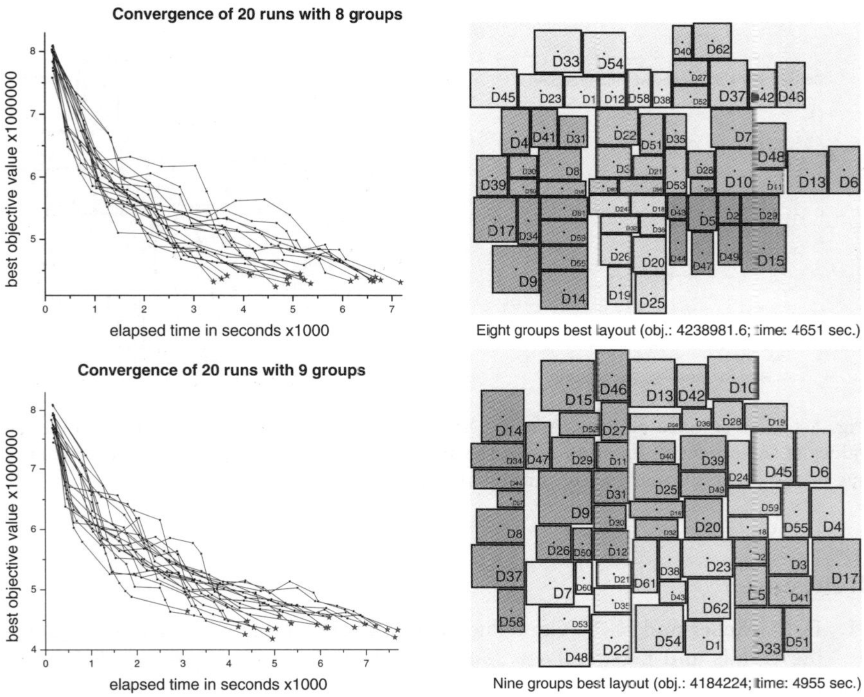

Fig. 4. Convergence of our coevolutionary algorithm and best layouts for problem P62 with eight and nine groups.

restrictions, hence worse off objective values are expected.

Summarizing, we conclude that the proposed coevolutionary algorithm opens the possibility of finding good solutions for large facility layout problems within hours where global optimization algorithms fail. In addition, there is still a high potential for further computational acceleration by parallelization.

Acknowledgments

This research was supported by DFG research project SFB 467 "Wandlungsfähige Unternehmensstrukturen für die variantenreiche Serienproduktion"

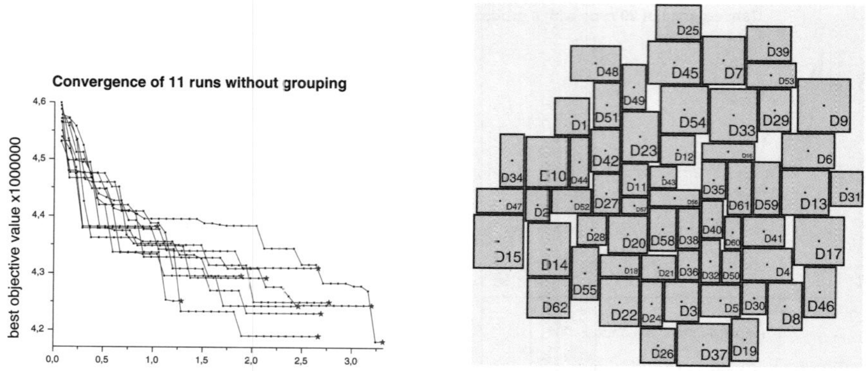

Fig. 5. Convergence of the GA and best layout for P62 without grouping. While the values of the objective function are in the same range, the computation time exceeds the one of the coevolutionary algorithm by an order of magnitude.

References

1. R. D. Meller and K.-Y. Gau. The facility layout problem: Recent and emerging trends and perspectives. *Journal of Manufacturing Systems*, 15(5):351–366, 1996.
2. W. C. Chiang. Visual facility layout design system. *International Journal of Production Research*, 39(9):1811–36, 2001.
3. F. Azadivar and J. Wang. Facility layout optimization using simulation and genetic algorithms. *International Journal of Production Research*, 38(17):4369–83, 2000.
4. J. Tavares, C. Ramos, and J. Neves. Addressing the layout design problem through genetic algorithms and constraint logic programming. In M. H. Hamza, editor, *Artificial Intelligence and Soft Computing. Proceedings of the IASTED International Conference*, pages 65–71. IASTED/ACTA Press, 2000.
5. M. Rajasekharan, B. A. Peters, and T. Yang. A genetic algorithm for facility layout design in flexible manufacturing systems. *International Journal of Production Research*, 36(1):95–110, 1998.
6. K. C. Chan and H. Tansri. A study of genetic crossover operations on the facilities layout problem. *Computers and Industrial Engineering*, 26(3):537–550, 1994.
7. B. Montreuil. A modelling framework for integrating layout design and flow network design. In *Progress in Material Handling and Logistic*, volume 2.
8. R. D. Meller, V. Narayanan, and P. H. Vance. Optimal facility layout design. *Operations Research Letters*, 23(3-5):117-127, 1999.
9. S. K. Das. A facility layout method for flexible manufacturing systems. *International Journal of Production Research*, 31(2):279–297, 1993.

10. J. S. Gero and V. A. Kazakov. Evolving design genes in space layout planning problems. *Artificial Intelligence in Engineering*, 12(3):163–176, 1998.
11. J. S. Kochhar and S. S. Heragu. Multi-hope: a tool for multiple floor layout problems. *International Journal of Production Research*, 36(12):3421–35, 1998.
12. V. Schnecke and O. Vornberger. Hybrid genetic algorithms for constrained placement problems. *IEEE Trans. Evolutionary Computation*, 1(4):266–277, 1997.
13. K-Y. Gau and R. D. Meller. An iterative facility layout algorithm. *International Journal of Production Research*, 37(16):3739–3758, 1999.
14. Y. Liu, X. Yao, Q. Zhao, and T. Higuchi. Scaling up fast evolutionary programming with cooperative coevolution. In *Proceedings of the 2001 Congress on Evolutionary Computation*, volume 2, pages 1101–8, 2001.
15. K. Y. Tam and S. L. Li. A hierarchical approach to the facility layout problem. *International Journal of Production Research*, 29(1):165–84, 1991
16. T. Dunker, G. Radons, and E. Westkämper. A coevolutionary algorithm for a facility layout problem. *International Journal of Production Research*, 41(15):3479–3500, 2003.
17. G. Harhalakis, R. Nagi, and J. M. Proth. An efficient heuristic in manufacturing cell formation for group technology applications. *International Journal of Production Research*, 28(1):185–98, 1990.
18. P. De Lit, E. Falkenauer, and A. Dechambre. Grouping genetic algorithms: an efficient method to solve the cell formation problem. *Mathematics and Computers in Simulation*, 51(3-4):257–271, 2000.

CHAPTER 21

SENSITIVITY ANALYSIS IN MULTI-OBJECTIVE EVOLUTIONARY DESIGN

Johan Andersson

Department of Mechanical Engineering, Linköping University
SE-581 83 Linköping, Sweden
E-mail: johan@ikp.liu.se

In real world engineering design problems we have to search for solutions that simultaneously optimize a wide range of different criteria. Furthermore, the optimal solutions also have to be robust. Therefore, this chapter describes a method where a multi-objective genetic algorithm is combined with response surface methods in order to assess the robustness of a set of identified optimal solutions. The multi-objective genetic algorithm is used in order to optimize two different concepts of hydraulic actuation systems. The different concepts have been modeled in a simulation environment to which the optimization strategy has been coupled. The outcome from the optimization is a set of Pareto optimal solutions that elucidate the trade-off between the energy consumption and the control error for each actuation system. Based on these Pareto fronts, promising regions could be identified for each concept. In these regions sensitivity analyses are performed with the help of response surface methods. It can then be determined how different design parameters affect the system for different optimal solutions.

1. Introduction

Many real-world engineering design problems involve simultaneous optimization of several conflicting objectives. In many cases, the multiple objectives are aggregated into one single overall objective function. Optimization is then performed with one optimal design as the result. Another approach is to search the solution space for a set of Pareto optimal solutions, from which the decision-maker may choose the final design. Vilfredo Pareto20 defined Pareto-optimality as a set where every element is a problem solution for which no other solutions can be better in all design attributes. A solution in the Pareto optimal set cannot be deemed superior to the others in the set without including preference information to rank competing attributes. For the two-dimensional case, the Pareto front is a curve that clearly illustrates the trade-off between the objectives. By comparing such Pareto fronts for different competing concepts, valuable support for concept selection could be gained. If these curves are plotted in the same diagram, an overall Pareto front could be obtained. The rational choice is then to select the final design from this overall Pareto optimal solution set.

However, there might be other aspects that are not reflected in the objective functions that also have to be considered. One such aspect, addressed in this chapter, is system robustness. In real world applications, we can not rely upon the normative values for the design parameters due to effects of for example manufacturing tolerances, wear, and environmental changes. Therefore, this chapter presents a method where response surface methods are used together with a genetic algorithm for Pareto optimization. The optimization results in a set of optimal solutions that the designer has to consider. The designer might then point out some regions where the trade-off matches his or her preferences, and from where the final design should be chosen.

It is then very helpful to know how robust solutions are at different points on the Pareto front, and which parameters have the greatest influence on the responses. Therefore, a thorough sensitivity analysis is performed with the help of response surface methods. In order to create the response surface, a series of designed experiments are conducted in the promising regions once they have been identified. This makes it possible to identify regions where the systems are less sensitive to changes in the design parameters. Another aspect is the possibility to include disturbing factors that have not been included in the optimization. The decision on the final design is thus based on optimal performance, robustness in terms of design parameters, and also robustness in the meaning of insensitivity to changes in parameters that have been considered constant during the optimization.

As the application for this chapter is hydraulic actuation systems, design parameters are typically sizes of components, pressure levels, and control gains. Disturbing factors include varying friction, fluctuating temperature, and changing loads.

The chapter begins with a presentation of a nomenclature for the multi-objective design problem together with a background on genetic algorithms and the optimization method used. We go on to discuss response surface methods and how they could be applied together with Pareto optimization. A design problem consisting of two different hydraulic actuation concepts is then studied with the help of simulation models and the proposed optimization strategy. This is followed by sensitivity analyses in areas of interest to the designer. Finally, different ways of presenting the result of the sensitivity analysis is introduced.

2. Optimization

2.1. *The Multi-Objective Ddesign Problem*

A general multi-objective design problem could be expressed by equations (1).

$$\begin{gathered}\min \mathbf{F}(\mathbf{x}) = \left(f_1(\mathbf{x}), f_2(\mathbf{x}), \ldots, f_k(\mathbf{x})\right)^T \\ s.t.\ \mathbf{x} \in S \\ \mathbf{x} = \left(x_1, x_2, \ldots, x_n\right)^T\end{gathered} \tag{1}$$

where $f_1(x), f_2(x), \ldots, f_k(x)$ are the k objectives functions, $(x_1, x_2, \ldots, x_n)$ are the n optimization parameters, and $S \in R^n$ is the solution or parameter space. Obtainable objective vectors, $\{\mathbf{F}(\mathbf{x}) | x \in S\}$ are denoted by Y, so $\mathbf{F}: S \mapsto Y$, S is mapped by $\mathbf{F}$ onto Y. $Y \in R^k$ is usually referred to as the attribute space, where ∂Y is the boundary of Y. For a general design problem, $\mathbf{F}$ is non-linear and multi-modal, and S might be defined by non-linear constraints containing both continuous and discrete member variables. $f_1^*, f_2^*, \ldots, f_k^*$ will be used to denote the individual minima of each respective objective function, and the utopian solution is defined as $\mathbf{F}^* = \left(f_1^*, f_2^*, ..., f_k^*\right)^T$. As $\mathbf{F}^*$ simultaneously minimizes all objectives it is an ideal solution, however, it is rarely feasible.

The Pareto subset of ∂Y is of particular interest to the rational decision-maker. The Pareto set is defined by equation (2). Considering a minimization problem and two solution vectors $\mathbf{x}, \mathbf{y} \in S$, $\mathbf{x}$ is said to dominate $\mathbf{y}$, denoted $\mathbf{x} \succ \mathbf{y}$, if:

$$\forall i \in \{1,2,...,k\}: f_i(\mathbf{x}) \leq f_i(\mathbf{y}) \text{ and } \exists j \in \{1,2,...,k\}: f_j(\mathbf{x}) < f_j(\mathbf{y}) \quad (2)$$

The space in R^k formed by the objective vectors of Pareto optimal solutions is known as the Pareto optimal front, P. It is clear that any final design solution should preferably be a member of the Pareto optimal set. Pareto optimal solutions are also known as non-dominated or efficient solutions. Fig. 1 provides a visualization of the presented nomenclature.

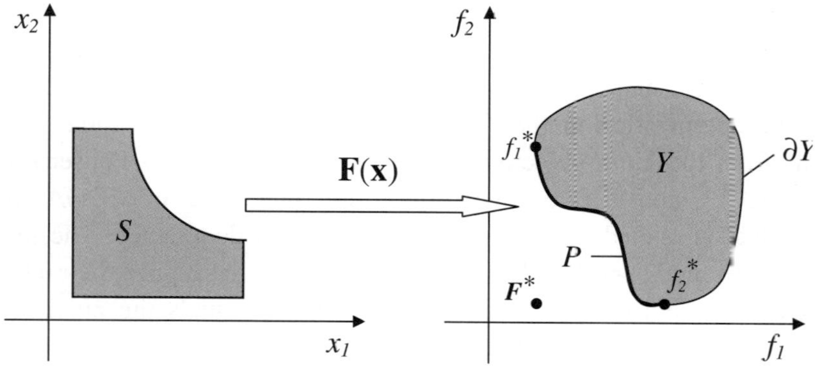

Fig. 1. Solution and attribute space nomenclature for a problem with two design variables and two objectives

2.2. *Genetic Algorithms*

Genetic algorithms (GA:s) are modelled according to mechanisms of natural selection. Each optimization parameter (x_n) is encoded by a gene using an appropriate representation, such as a real number or a string of bits. The corresponding genes for all parameters $x_1,..x_n$ form a chromosome capable of describing an individual design solution. A set of chromosomes representing several individual design solutions comprise a population where the most fit are selected to reproduce. Mating is performed using crossover to combine genes from different parents to produce children. The children are inserted into the population and the procedure starts over again, thus creating an artificial Darwinian environment. For a general introduction to genetic algorithms, see Goldberg11.

When the population of an ordinary genetic algorithm is evolving, it usually converges to one optimal point. It is however tempting to adjust the algorithm so that it spreads the population over the entire Pareto optimal front instead. As this idea is quite natural, there are many different types of multi-objective genetic algorithms. For a review of genetic algorithms applied to multi-objective optimization, readers are referred to the work done by Fonseca and Fleming8, and Deb7. Literature surveys and comparative studies on multi-objective genetic algorithms are also provided by several other authors (Coello[6], Horn[15], Tamaki et al.[22] and Zitzler and Thiele[25].

The optimization method used in this chapter borrows some major ideas from the multi-objective GA (MOGA) presented by Fonseca and Fleming[8,9,10], and therefore it is briefly presented here. In MOGA each individual is ranked according to their degree of dominance. The more population members that dominate an individual, the higher the ranking given to the individual. An individual's ranking equals the number of individuals that it is dominated by plus one, see Fig. 2. Individuals on the Pareto front have a rank of 1 as they are non-dominated. The rankings are then scaled to score individuals in the population. In MOGA both sharing and mating restrictions are employed in order to maintain population diversity. Fonseca and Fleming also include preference information and goal levels to reduce the Pareto set to those that simultaneously meet certain attribute values.

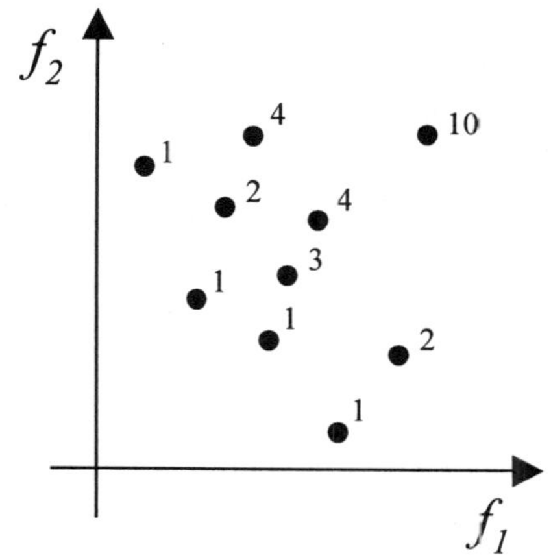

Fig. 2. Population ranking according to Fonseca and Fleming

2.3. *The Proposed Optimization Method*

In this chapter the multi-objective struggle genetic algorithm (MOSGA) (Andersson[1,2,3]) is used for Pareto optimization. MOSGA combines the struggle crowding genetic algorithm presented by Grueninger and Wallace[12] with Pareto-based ranking as devised by Fonseca and Fleming[10].

In the struggle algorithm, a variation of restricted tournament selection, two parents are chosen from the population, and crossover and mutation are performed to create a child. The child replaces the most similar individual in the entire population, but only if it has a better fitness. This replacement strategy counteracts genetic drift that can spoil population diversity. The struggle genetic algorithm has been demonstrated to perform well in multi-modal function landscapes where it successfully identifies and maintains multiple peaks.

As there is no single objective function to determine the fitness of the different individuals in a Pareto optimization, the ranking scheme presented by Fonseca and Fleming is employed, and the "degree of dominance" in attribute space is used to rank the population. Each individual is given a rank based on the number of individuals in the population that are preferred to it, i.e. for each individual the algorithm loops through the whole population counting the number of preferred individuals. "Preferred to" could be implemented in a strict Pareto optimal sense or extended to include goal levels for the objectives in order to limit the Pareto optimal front.

The principle of the MOSGA algorithm is outlined below.

Step 1: Initialize the population.
Step 2: Select individuals uniformly from the population.
Step 3: Perform crossover and mutation to create a child.
Step 4: Calculate the rank of the new child.
Step 5: Find the individual in the entire population that is most similar to the child. Replace that individual with the new child if the child's ranking is better, or if the child dominates it.
Step 6: Update the ranking of the population if the child has been inserted.
Step 7: Perform steps 2-6 according to the population size.
Step 8: If the stop criterion is not met, go to step 2 and start a new generation.

Step 5 implies that that the new child is only inserted into the population if it dominates the most similar individual, or if it has a lower ranking, i.e. a lower “degree of dominance”. Since the ranking of the population does not consider the presence of the new child it is possible for the child to dominate an individual and still have the same ranking. This restricted replacement scheme counteracts genetic drifts and is the only mechanism needed in order to preserve population diversity. Furthermore, it does not need any specific parameter tuning. The restricted replacement strategy also constitutes an extreme form of elitism, as the only way of replacing a non-dominated individual is to create a child that dominates it.

The likeness of two individuals is measured using a distance function. The method has been tested with distance functions based upon the Euclidean distance in both the attribute and the parameter space. A mixed distance function combining both the attribute and parameter distance has been evaluated as well.

It has been conclude that an attribute based similarity measure yield rapid and precise convergence. However, it is only capable of identifying one Pareto optimal front in search spaces with multiple Pareto optimal fronts. On the other hand, with a parameter based similarity measure the algorithm is able to locate multiple Pareto optimal fronts but the convergence is somewhat slower and not as precise. By combining both distance measures to one mixed distance measure a method that is precise and able to identify multiple Pareto fronts is obtained. For a more thorough discussion on different distance measures see Andersson and Wallace[3]. The result presented in this chapter was obtained using an attribute based distance function.

3. Response Surface Methods

The use of response surface methods is increasing in all fields of engineering, for instance in aerospace (Marvis and Qiu[18]) automotive engineering (Lin et al.[17]), structural optimization (Raux et al.[21]) and multidisciplinary design optimization (Batill et al.[4]). The approach presented here is a statistically based method witch combines Design of Experiments (DoE) (Box et al.[5]) with Response Surface Methodology (RSM) (Myers and Montgomery[19]). RSM is a method for constructing approximations of the behaviour of a system based on results at various points in the design space. The resulting surfaces, usually linear or quadratic, are fitted to these points. Statistical methods such as DoE are often used to determine where in the design space these points should be located in order to obtain the best possible fit. Today there are many statistical software packages that can be used in order to create the design setup and perform statistical analysis of the results. In this chapter the MODDE software from Umetrics[23] is used

In this chapter quadratic polynomials are used in order to create the response surface, see equation (3). Equation (3) is also called the Response Surface Equation (RSE).

$$y = b_0 + \sum_{i=1}^{n} b_i x_i + \sum_{i=1}^{n} b_{ii} x_{ii}^2 + \sum_{i=1}^{n-1} \sum_{j=i+1}^{n} b_{ij} x_i x_j \tag{3}$$

In equation (3) y is the response, i.e. the function value we want to approximate in this case the objective functions. However, any other system characteristics could be estimated as well. b_0 is a constant term and b_i are the coefficients of the linear terms, better known as the main effect. b_{ii} are the coefficients of the pure quadratic terms and are known as quadratic effects, whereas b_{ij} are the coefficients of the cross products, which are also called second order interactions.

3.1. *Sensitivity Analysis*

The main reason for using RSM in this chapter is to gain a better understanding of how the design parameters affect the system performance at different locations on the Pareto front. By examining the coefficient of the RSE it could be seen how the different parameters affect each objective function and knowledge about the underlying causes of the trade off could be gained. A more formal method of gaining such knowledge is to study the sensitivities of each response with respect to the different parameters. Here the gradients of the estimated surfaces are used as sensitivity measures, see equation (4).

$$\frac{\partial y}{\partial x_j} = b_j + \frac{\partial}{\partial x_j}\left(\sum_{j=1}^{n}\sum_{k=j}^{n} b_{jk} x_j x_k\right) \tag{4}$$

The sensitivities are evaluated in the middle point (superscript m) of the DoE setup. Thus x_m is used to calculate the numerical value for the gradients.

4. The Design Problem

The objects of study for the design problem are two different concepts of hydraulic actuation systems; a valve controlled and a pump controlled system as depicted in Figs. 3 and 4 respectively. Both systems consist of a hydraulic cylinder that is connected to a mass of 1000 kilograms. The objective is to follow a pulse in the position command with as small control error as possible and simultaneously obtain low energy consumption. Naturally, these two objectives are in conflict with each other. A low control error implies high acceleration and retardation which consumes more energy. The problem is thus to minimize both the control error and the energy consumption from a Pareto optimal perspective.

The different concepts have been modelled in the Hopsan simulation package[14]. The models of each component consist of a set of algebraic and differential equations taking aspects such as friction, leakage and non-linearities into account. The system models are depicted in Fig. 3 and Fig. 4 respectively.

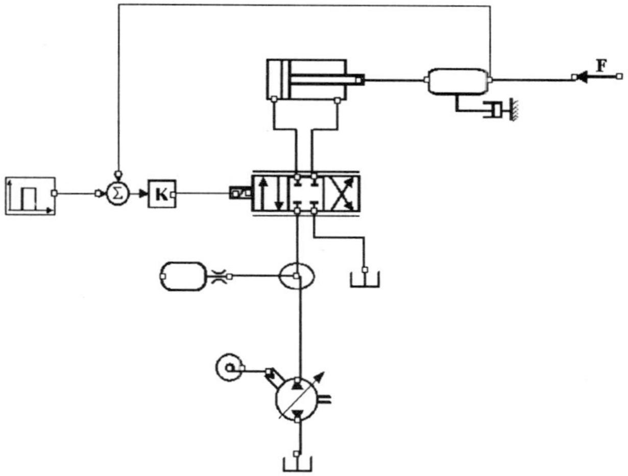

Fig. 3. The servo valve concept for hydraulic actuation

The servo valve system consists of the mass and the hydraulic cylinder, the servo valve and a proportional controller that controls the motion. The servo valve is powered by a constant pressure pump and an accumulator, which keeps the system pressure at a constant level. The valve concept has all that is required for a low control error, as the valve has a very high bandwidth. On the other hand, the valve system is associated with higher losses, as the valve constantly throttles fluid to the tank. The optimization parameters are the sizes of the cylinder, the valve and the pump, the pressure lever, the feedback gain and a leakage parameter that is necessary to dampen the system. Thus, this problem consists of six optimization parameters and two objectives.

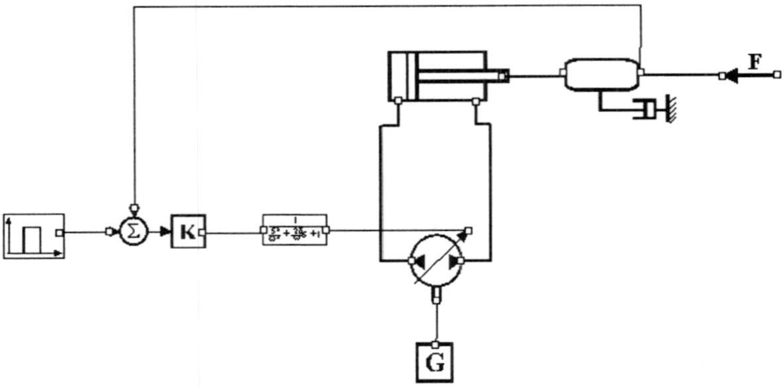

Fig. 4. The servo pump concept of hydraulic actuation

The servo pump concept contains fewer components, the cylinder and the mass, the controller and the pump. A second order low-pass filter is added in order to model the dynamics of the pump. The servo pump system consists of only four optimization parameters.

4.1. *Optimization Results*

The optimization is based on component size selection rather then component design, i.e. it is assumed that each component is a predefined entity. As a consequence of this assumption most component parameters are expressed as a function of the component size.

Both systems where optimized in order to simultaneously minimize the control error f_1 and the energy consumption f_2. The control error is obtained by integrating the absolute value of the control error and adding a penalty for overshoots, see equation (5). The energy consumption is calculated by integrating the hydraulic power, expressed as the pressure multiplied by the flow, see equation (6).

$$f_1 = \int_0^4 \left| x_{ref} - x \right| dt + \alpha \left(\int_0^2 \left(x > x_{ref} \right) dt + \int_2^4 \left(x < x_{ref} \right) dt \right) \tag{5}$$

$$f_2 = \int_0^4 \left(q_{pump} \cdot p_{pump} \right) dt \tag{6}$$

The optimization is conducted with a population size of 30 individuals over 200 generations. The parameters are real encoded and BLX crossover is used to produce new offspring.

As a Pareto optimization searches for all non-dominated individuals, the final population will contain individuals with a very high control error, as they have low energy consumption. It is possible to obtain an energy consumption close to zero, if the cylinder does not move at all. However, these solutions are not of interest, as we want the system to follow the pulse. A goal level for the control error is therefore introduced. The optimization strategy is modified so that solutions which are below the goal level on the control error are always preferred to solutions that are above it regardless of their energy consumption. In this manner, the population is focused on the relevant part of the Pareto front.

The optimization results in a set of obtained Pareto optimal solutions that visualise the trade-off between energy consumption and control error. If the Pareto fronts for both concepts are depicted within the same graph, the properties of both systems are clearly illustrated, as shown in Fig. 5. Fig. 5 also shows the performance of two different designs, one relatively fast with high energy consumption and another which is slower but consumes less energy.

In order to achieve fast systems, and thereby low control errors, large pumps and valves are chosen by the optimization strategy. A large pump delivers more fluid, which enables a higher cylinder speed. However, bigger components consume more energy, which explains the shape of the Pareto fronts.

It is evident that the final design should preferably be on the overall Pareto front, which indicates when to change between concepts. Thus Pareto optimization is a very useful toll for concept selection. The servo pump system consumes less energy, and is preferred if a control error larger then 0.05ms is acceptable. The servo valve system is fast but consumes more energy. If lower control error then 0.05ms is desired, the final design should preferably be a servo valve system. In order to choose the final design, the decision-maker has to study the trade-off between the control error and the energy consumption and select a solution point that matches his or her preferences. However, before deciding on a final design a sensitivity analysis should be conducted.

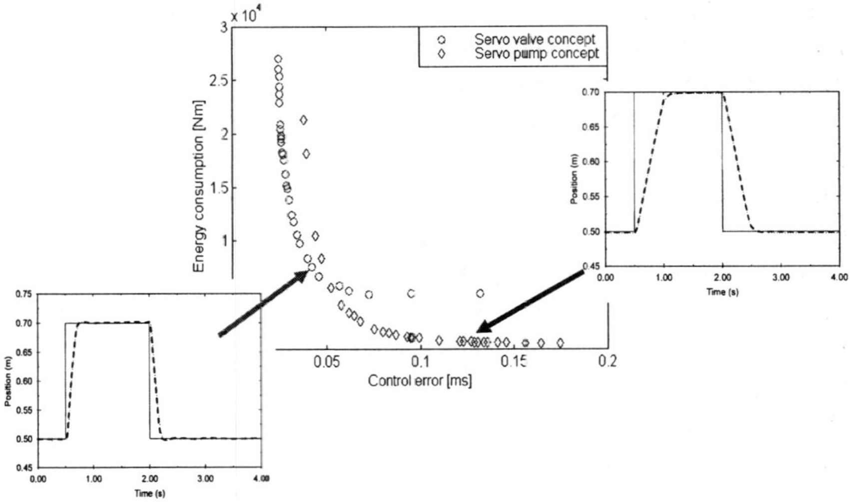

Fig. 5. Pareto fronts showing the trade-off between energy consumption and control error for the two concepts. The graph on the right shows a slow pulse response, whereas the graph on the left shows a fast pulse response

4.2. *Sensitivity Analysis*

To gain more insight into the properties and behaviour of the systems a sensitivity analysis could be performed. For both systems, five points evenly spread on the Pareto front were used as centre points for the designed experiments. For each of these points, the MODE software was used to create a design setup using the D-optimality criterion, see Myers and Montgomery[19]. Based on these design points a second order response surface was created, which emulates the performance of each system at the selected centre points.

The question is now how this new information should be utilized in order to increase our knowledge about the behaviour of the systems. As the problem is multidimensional both in terms of objectives and design parameters, there are no obvious way to visualize the obtained response surfaces graphically. One alternative is to look at the values of the normalized coefficients and see how they vary as we move along the

Pareto front. In Fig. 6 the normalized coefficients for the servo pump system are plotted for the five points on the Pareto front. Point 1 is a point with a low control error, i.e. to the left on the Pareto front, whereas point 5 has a large control error in Fig. 5.

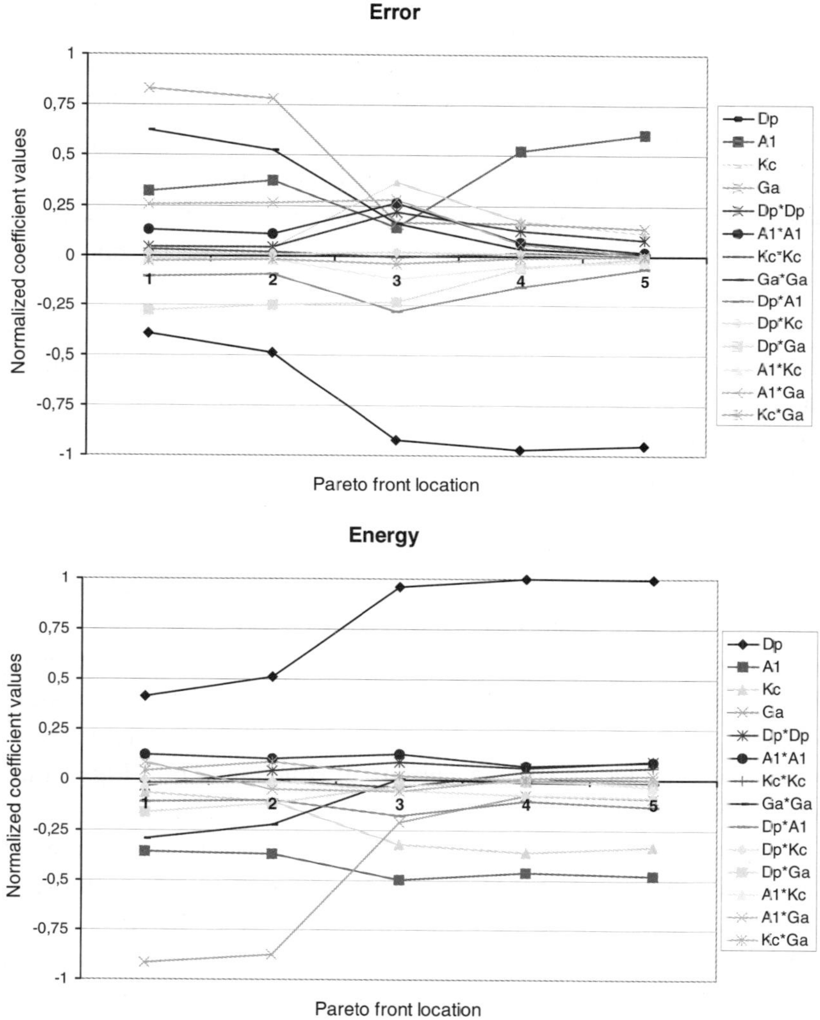

Fig. 6. Model coefficients for the servo pump system at five different points on the Pareto front

For each location on the Pareto front, all coefficients of the response surface equation are plotted as points on the graph, which are then connected with straight lines. Coefficient values close to zero evidently indicate that the corresponding parameter has little influence on the response whereas points which have a high magnitude indicate coefficients that are important.

The abbreviations for the parameters are: pump displacement, or size (Dp), cylinder area (A1), control gain (Ga), and leakage coefficient (Kc). For the servo valve system there is also the valve spool diameter (Sd).

There is much insight that can be gained by studying such a graph. First we can conclude that at point 1 where the control error is small, the feedback gain is the most important parameter, whereas at point 5 the pump size is the most important parameter. This is true for both control error and energy consumption.

Furthermore, it can be seen how the relative importance of system parameters varies as we move along the Pareto front. If we study the control error graph we can also see that the second order terms are largest at point 1, indicating that the smaller we make the control error the more sensitive the solution gets. By comparing the coefficients for the different responses we can also see the underlying causes of the trade-off between the objectives. In Fig. 6, this could be exemplified by a larger pump (higher Dp-value) giving a smaller control error, as the coefficient for error is negative, but greater energy consumption, as the coefficient for energy consumption is positive. A more thorough investigation of the impact of the parameters on the objectives could be conducted by studying the sensitivities, by calculating the derivatives of the response surface equation according to equation (4). In Fig. 7 this is done for the servo pump system.

The sensitivity graphs show what impact a small change in parameter value has on the objectives as we move along the Pareto front. In Fig. 7 it can be seen that for systems with low control error, the feedback gain (Ga) is the most important parameter for both energy consumption and control error. However, as we move to the right on the Pareto front, the gain loses in importance while the size of the pump becomes more important. We can see how a larger pump leads to lower control error but higher energy consumption. A more illustrative way of showing how the parameters influence the objectives are shown in Table 1.

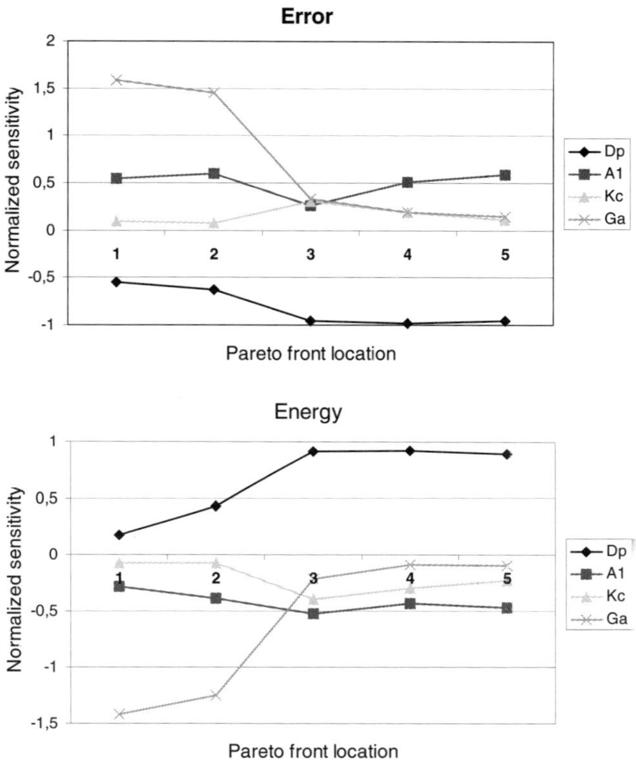

Fig. 7. Sensitivities for the servo pump system at five different points on the Pareto front

Table 1. Sensitivity table for the servo pump system

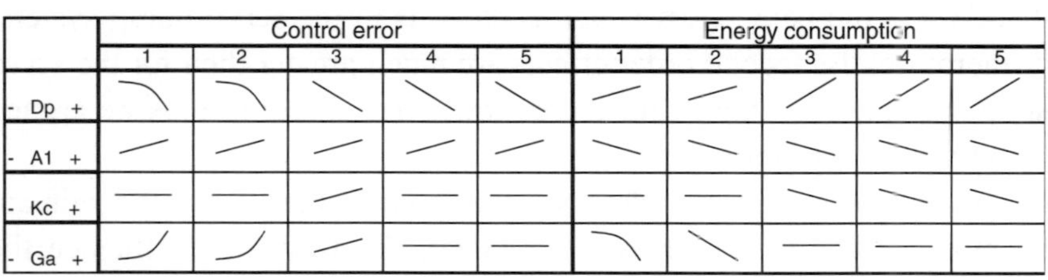

The columns in table 1 indicate the different points on the Pareto front. Each row shows how an increase in the corresponding parameter affects the control error and the energy consumption at the different

points. A straight line indicates no effect, whereas the lines with a gradient indicate in what direction and how much the objectives changes as the corresponding parameter is increased. The curved lines indicates points where we have significant second order effects and where the system is more sensitive.

The sensitivity table contains all the information from the graphs presented earlier condensed into one table. It can thus be seen how the importance of the parameters varies along the Pareto front and where the second order effects are greatest.

To summarize the information from the servo pump system it has been shown that the displacement and the control gain are the most influential parameters and that the faster the system the more sensitive it is to parameter changes.

The same sensitivity analysis has been performed for the servo valve system. The results are shown in Table 2.

Table 2. Sensitivity table for the servo valve system

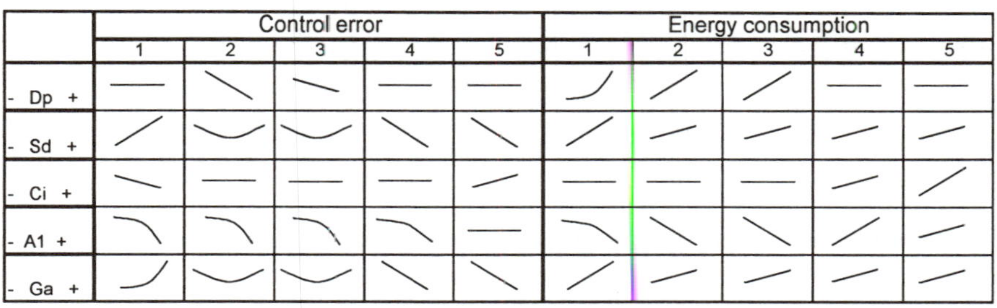

The servo valve system has a more complex behaviour and the trade-off between the parameters is not as clear as in the servo pump system. Furthermore, the second order effects are much greater then for the servo pump system, particularly for the control error. It could thus be argued that this system is not as robust.

For this system the cylinder area, the spool diameter, and the gain are the most influential parameters. However, the way they influence the system changes as we move along the Pareto front. At the first three points the trade-off is due to the pump size, (Dp), larger pump gives a small control error but high energy consumption. However, as we move along the Pareto front the system gets slower and less fluid are taken from the pump and more from the accumulator. Thus pump size has no longer any influence. Then the trade-off is shifted towards spool diameter and gain. It can be seen how a larger spool diameter and gain reduce the control error but give higher energy consumption.

5. Discussion and Conclusions

In this chapter a multi-objective genetic algorithm has been used to optimize two different hydraulic actuation systems. The outcome of the optimization is a set of Pareto optimal designs, where the trade-off between the conflicting objectives is clearly elucidated. By comparing Pareto fronts for different design concepts, valuable insight on the properties of the different concepts can be gained.

The method has been applied to two concepts of hydraulic actuation systems. The resulting Pareto optimal fronts illustrate the advantages of the different concepts and advise the decision-maker which concept to choose depending on his or her preferences. If a very fast system is desired, a servo valve system should be chosen. However, if a slower system is acceptable, a servo pump system is more favourable as it consumes more energy. Furthermore, the algorithm suggests when to switch between the concepts. Thus, Pareto optimization could be a valuable support for concept selection.

Then sensitivity analysis is performed to gain more information about the properties of each concept. The sensitivity analysis tells us what effect a small change in a parameter value has on the objectives depending on the location of the Pareto front. For the servo pump example it has been shown that for a fast system the control gain is the most important parameter, but for a slower system the pump size is the most important one. This type of information could be very useful as it tells the designer where to focus his efforts. When designing large systems, a sensitivity analysis could guide the designer towards parts or sub-systems which are more important depending on the chosen system concept.

The method presented in this chapter combines modern optimization techniques with response surface methods and supports the engineer when a design is based on simulation models. It visualizes the trade-off between the objectives and indicates which parameters have the greatest influence on the results.

However, the main benefit is not in finding an optimal and robust solution, but in learning more about the properties of the system being designed and the behaviour of the system model. Another important lesson is in defining the objectives, which forces the designer to define what is desired of the system and then to challenge the preferences of the decision-maker by visualizing the trade-off between conflicting objectives. By conducting optimization and sensitivity analysis, we can gain much more knowledge from our simulation models.

Acknowledgments

The software for this work is based on the GAlib genetic algorithm package written by Matthew Wall[24] at the Massachusetts Institute of Technology.

References

1. Andersson J., *Multiobjective Optimization in Engineering Design – Application to Fluid Power Systems*, Dissertation, Thesis No. 675, Linköping University, Linköping, Sweden, (2001).
2. Andersson J., Krus P. and Wallace D., "Multi-objective optimization of hydraulic actuation systems", *in proceedings of ASME Design Automation Conference*, Baltimore, September 11-13 (2000).
3. Andersson J. and Wallace D., "Pareto optimization using the Struggle Genetic Crowding Algorithm", *Engineering Optimization*, vol. 34, No. 6, pp. 623-643, (2002).
4. Batill S., Stelmack M., Sellar R., "Framework for Multidisciplinary Design Based on Response-Surface Approximations", *Journal of Aircraft*, Vol. 36, No 1, January-February, (1999).
5. Box G., Hunter W., Hunter S., *Statistics for Experiments*, John Wiley & Sons, (1978).
6. Coello Coello C., *An empirical study of evolutionary techniques for multiobjective optimization in engineering design*, Dissertation, Department of Computer Science, Tulane University, (1996).
7. Deb K., *Multi-objective Objective Optimization using Evolutionary algorithms*, Wiley and Sons Ltd, (2001).
8. Fonseca C. M. and Fleming P. J., "Multiobjective genetic algorithms made easy: Selection, sharing and mating restriction," *in proceedings of the 1st IEE/IEEE International Conference on Genetic Algorithms in Engineering Systems*, Sheffield, England, (1995).

9. Fonseca C. and Fleming P., "An overview of evolutionary algorithms in multiobjective optimization," *Evolutionary Computation*, vol. 3, pp. 1-18, (1995).
10. Fonseca C. M. and Fleming P. J., "Multiobjective optimization and multiple constraint handling with evolutionary algorithms - Part I: a unified formulation," *IEEE Transactions on Systems, Man, & Cybernetics Part A: Systems & Humans*, vol. 28, pp. 26-37, (1998).
11. Goldberg D., *Genetic Algorithms in Search and Machine Learning*, Reading, Addison Wesley, (1989).
12. Grueninger T. and Wallace D., "Multi-modal optimization using genetic algorithms", Technical Report 96.02, CADlab, Massachusetts Institute of Technology, Cambridge, (1996).
13. Harik G., "Finding multimodal solutions using restricted tournament selection," in *proceedings of the Sixth International Conference on Genetic Algorithms*, (1995).
14. Hopsan, 1991, "Hopsan, a simulation package - User's guide", Technical report LiTH-IKP-R-704, Department of Mechanical Engineering, Linköping University, Linköping, Sweden.
15. Horn J., "Multicriterion decision making," in *Handbook of evolutionary* computation, T. Bäck, D. Fogel, and Z. Michalewicz, Eds., IOP Publishing Ltd and Oxford University Press, (1997).
16. Krus P., "Post optimal system analysis using aggregated design impact matrix", *in proceedings of ASME Design Automation Conference*, Baltimore, September 11-13, (2000).
17. Lin Y., Krishnapur K., Allen J., Mistree F., "Robust Concept Exploration in Engineering Design: Metamodeling Techniques and Goal Formulations", *in proceedings of ASME Design Automation Conference*, Baltimore, Maryland, September 10-14, (2000).
18. Marvis D., Qiu S., "An Improved Process for the Generation of Drag Polars for use in Conceptual/Preliminary Design, *in proceedings of the 1999 World Aviation Congress, San Francisco*, October 19-21, (1999).
19. Myers R., and Mongomery D, *Response Surface Methodology*, John Wiley & Sons, (1995).
20. Pareto V., *Cours d'Économie Politique*. Lausanne, Rouge, (1896).
21. Raux W., Stander N., Haftka R., "Response Surface Approximations for Structural Optimization, *International Journal of Numerical Methods in Engineering*, vol. 42, pp 517-534, (1988).
22. Tamaki H., Kita H., and Kobayashi S., "Multi-objective optimization by genetic algorithms: a review," *in proceedings of the 1996 IEEE International Conference on Evolutionary Computation*, ICEC'96, Nagoya, Japan, (1996).
23. Umetrics, http://www.umetrics.com/.
24. Wall M., "Matthew's GAlib: A C++ library of genetic algorithm components," http://www.lancet.mit.edu/ga/, (1996).
25. Zitzler E. and Thiele L., "Multiobjective Evolutionary Algorithms: A Comparative Case Study and the Strength Pareto Approach," *IEEE Transaction on evolutionary computation*, vol. 3, pp. 257-271, (1999).

CHAPTER 22

INTEGRATED PRODUCTION AND TRANSPORTATION SCHEDULING IN SUPPLY CHAIN OPTIMISATION

Gang WU, Chee Kheong SIEW

Information Communication Institute of Singapore
Nanyang Technological University, Singapore

In this chapter, an integrated production and transportation scheduling model is proposed. This model is based on multi-item capacitated lot sizing and facility location type models. The objective of the integrated model is to minimize the total production and transportation cost. The integrated model is solved by Lagrangian decomposition method and the decomposed two sub-problems can be solved by genetic algorithm and Simplex method respectively. Computational results showed that the overall cost is reduced by 4% to 10% compared with the other two sequential optimization algorithms.

1. Introduction

Main cost factors within a supply chain may be classified as production, transportation and warehousing costs. The composition of these costs relative to total cost varies widely across different industries. However, production cost is the highest in most of the industries, followed by transportation and warehousing costs.[4] In most industries, a production plan is first developed, followed by a transportation plan made by either a transportation department within the company or a third party transportation provider who adheres to an established shipping plan aiming to reduce transportation cost. Transition between the two functions relies on inventory buffers of different forms. The extent to which the transportation cost is considered in the production plan does not go beyond a simple evaluation of a few transportation channels.

Parallel to this industry practice, researchers in academia have approached the two problems separately. There has been an enormous body of research on production planning models and in specific, on lot-sizing models. The main trade-off considered in these models is between the inventory carrying and production setup costs. Transportation planning is often considered together with location of facilities and is referred to as a facility location problem. This problem has also been studied extensively in the literature. For a general discussion and solution algorithms of this problem, interested reader is referred to[11,14,15].

Traditionally, production and transportation functions are separated by large warehouse buffers. Each function only optimises its local objective without considering the impact on the complete supply chain. Total supply chain cost is thus greater than what could be achieved through coordination. This lack of coordination occurs because of the conflicting objectives and the lack of information. Taking advantage of current supply chain management (SCM) and information technologies, companies can explore some closer coordinations between production and transportation planning. Although the literature that addresses both production and transportation planning problems is plentiful, very few models try to combine and solve these problems simultaneously. The lack of research on coordinating these two activities may be due to:

- These two problems by themselves are hard and the combined problem may not be tractable;
- As different organizational entities are responsible for the planning of these two activities, there has been no obvious need to combine these problems.

With the widespread adoption of Electronic Commerce systems, information for supply chain planning that was not available before is now available for solving an integrated SCM problem. In a broad sense, we can state our problem as the integration of production and transportation planning functions in a supply chain environment so as to minimize the overall cost for these two operational functions. Chandra and Fisher[3] showed empirically the value of integrating production and transportation decisions in an environment which involves a single production facility and multiple customers. They report gains ranging between 3% and 20% obtained by integrating production planning and vehicle routing in a heuristic manner. Qua et al.[16] developed an integrated inventory-transportation system with a modified periodic-review inventory policy and a travelling-salesman component. They also proposed a heuristic decomposition method to solve the problem to minimize the long-run total average costs (ordering, holding, backlogging, stopover and travel). To study the main trade-off between production and transportation scheduling decisions, we will investigate integrating decisions characterized by multi-item capacitated lot sizing and facility location type models.

In this chapter, we make two primary contributions that essentially differentiate our work from past literature. First, we propose new models for both parts of the problems that are tailored to an integrated decision-making model. Second, we link the two new models by material flow variables and a Lagrangian relaxation approach is used for the solution of the integrated problem. The new integrated model and its effective solution algorithm ensure that each function of the supply chain takes actions that minimize total supply chain cost and avoids actions that minimize its local cost but hurt total cost. It helps decision makers to take a global view of their supply chain so that the overall cost of the supply chain is reduced.

2. Production Planning Model

In this section, first we introduce a classical production planning model: Multi-item Capacitated Lot Sizing Problem (MICLSP). We then discuss the limitations of this model and propose a new production planning model based on MICLSP.

The solution to MICLSP is to determine a production plan for one or more product items over a finite horizon of discrete time periods. In this problem, several items are produced in a capacity-constrained plant. The demand for each item in a period by each customer is known. A single warehouse is used as a buffer to satisfy various customer demands. The objective is to find a minimum-cost production plan which satisfies all demand requirements without exceeding capacity limits. The total cost of any production plan has three components: setup cost, production cost and inventory holding cost. These components cannot be considered separately due to their dependent relationship. For instance, producing items in earlier periods and storing them for later periods can reduce the setup cost but increases the inventory holding cost. On the other hand, producing every item in every period can reduce inventory holding cost but increases the setup cost.

The MICLSP is also called a large time bucket problem [3] because several items may be produced per period. Such a period typically represents a time slot (for example, one week) in the real world. Solving the MICLSP for an optimum solution is known to be NP-hard [2]. Hence, there are only a few attempts to find the optimum solution to the MICLSP. Many researchers have developed heuristics instead. The heuristic approaches range from Lagrangian relaxation to tabu search. Zahorik et al.[21] described an optimisation based heuristic approach, employing a 3-period network flow formulation of the problem for a quite restrictive case with no setup cost or time. Billington et al. [1] introduced a branch and bound heuristic using Lagrangian relaxation. They used a price-directed approach to reflect the capacity limitations. Maes et al. [13] addressed the complexity of finding feasible solutions to MICLSP and presented three similar heuristics for the solution. The three heuristics differ in the way they round the binary setup variables which are obtained from LP relaxation. Roll and Karni[17] presented a heuristic approach which consists of the application of eight different subroutines. These subroutines either convert an infeasible solution to a feasible one or improve a given solution. Kuik et al.[12] used two heuristic techniques, namely simulated annealing and tabu search in their heuristics.

Conventional lot sizing models in the literature do not involve material flows among product locations (from plants to warehouses and from warehouses to customers) in a supply chain. Also, these models do not consider the number of plants. Delivery of goods is generally assumed to be instantaneous from one plant to a single warehouse. In our definition of the problem, we incorporate the number of plants and warehouses as parameters and material flows as variables into the model.

Problem Formulation

Indices:

l = number of plants, $l \in \{1,2,\cdots,L\}$

j = number of warehouse sites, $j \in \{1,2,\cdots,J\}$

i = number of customers, $i \in \{1,2,\cdots,I\}$
k = number of products, $k \in \{1,2,\cdots,K\}$
t = number of planning period, for which we decide the production amount and material flow size to send, $t \in \{1,2,\cdots,T\}$

Data Sets:

$SL = \{1,2,\cdots,L\}$, $SJ = \{1,2,\cdots,J\}$, $SI = \{1,2,\cdots,I\}$
$SK = \{1,2,\cdots,K\}$, $ST = \{1,2,\cdots,T\}$

Parameters:

hc_{ikt} = holding cost of product k at warehouse j during period t
sc_{lkt} = setup cost of product k at plant l during period t
v_{lkt} = production capacity of product k at plant l during period t
e_{lkt} = production cost (per unit) of product k at plant l during period t
w_{ikt} = demand for product k at customer i during period t
s_k = volume of one unit of product k
q_j = capacity(in volume) of warehouse j

Variables:

In_{ikt} = inventory of product k at warehouse j at the end of period t
U_{ljkt} = amount of product k shipped from plant l to warehouse j during period t
N_{jikt} = amount of product k shipped from warehouse j to customer i during period t

$$Y_{lkt} = \begin{cases} 1, & \text{if product k is produced in plant l during period t} \\ 0, & \text{otherwise} \end{cases}$$

Then the problem can be formulated as the following Mixed Integer Programming model.

$$Min \quad \sum_{t=1}^{T}\sum_{k=1}^{K}\left\{\sum_{j=1}^{J} hc_{jkt} In_{jkt} + \sum_{l=1}^{L} sc_{lkt} Y_{lkt} + \sum_{l=1}^{L}\sum_{j=1}^{J} e_{lkt} U_{ljkt}\right\}$$

$$s.t. \quad \sum_{j=1}^{J} U_{ljkt} \le v_{lkt} Y_{lkt} \quad \forall l \in SL, k \in SK, t \in ST \tag{1}$$

$$\sum_{k=1}^{K} s_k In_{jkt} \le q_j \quad \forall j \in SJ, t \in ST \tag{2}$$

$$\sum_{j=1}^{J} N_{jikt} = w_{ikt} \qquad \forall i \in SI, k \in SK, t \in ST \tag{3}$$

$$In_{jk(t-1)} + \sum_{l=1}^{L} U_{ljkt} = In_{jkt} + \sum_{i=1}^{I} N_{jikt} \; \forall j \in SJ, k \in SK, t \in ST \tag{4}$$

$$Y_{lkt} \in \{0,1\} \qquad \forall l \in SL, k \in SK, t \in ST \tag{5}$$

$$U_{ljkt}, N_{jikt} \geq 0 \quad \forall l \in SL, i \in SI, j \in SJ, k \in SK, t \in ST \tag{6}$$

This production planning model is based on material flow variables from the plants to the warehouses and from the warehouses to the customers. This important feature distinguishes our model from other models that exist in the literature and makes it possible to link the production and transportation models. A material flow variable is the amount of an item transported from one location to another in a given period. In almost all lot size models, the material flow variables do not exist because they deal with only one plant and one warehouse. We release this assumption and therefore we have to capture the inventory flow of each item in the system defined by the material flow variables. This addition enhances our production planning model to be more general than existing models.

Constraint (1) is a production capacity constraint. Constraint (2) is a warehouse capacity constraint that guarantees each of the warehouse capacity is not exceeded. Constraint (3) ensures that the demand for each product by every customer is equal to the amount being shipped from the warehouses to this customer. Constraint (4) is the inventory balance constraint.

3. Heuristic Genetic Algorithm

In the last decade, the genetic algorithm (GA), which is a search technique based on the mechanics of natural selection and natural genetics, is recognized as a powerful and widely applicable optimisation method, especially for global optimisation problems and NP-hard problems. Recently, a lot of researchers studied the applications of GA for solving the lot-sizing problems with unlimited capacity [6,7,20] and with capacity constraints[9,10] Numerical results obtained using these methods showed that GA (probably combined with other meta-heuristics) is an effective approach to deal with the lot-sizing problems. Xie [20] proposed a heuristic genetic algorithm for general capacitated lot-sizing problems and compared this algorithm with SA (simulated annealing algorithm[12]), TS (tabu search algorithm[12]), and LR (Lagrangian relaxation algorithm[1]). Examination of the results showed that the solutions obtained by this algorithm are much better than that of SA and TS in approximately the same computing time, and the algorithm obtained similar solutions to LR in much less time. In this section, we propose a heuristic genetic algorithm to solve our problem.

3.1. *The Encoding Scheme*

The decision variables in our problem are In_{jkt}, U_{ljkt}, N_{jikt} and Y_{lkt}, among which Y_{lkt} is a 0-1 integer variable and the others are positive integer variables. In order to design a computationally efficient genetic algorithm, only the setup patterns (variables Y_{lkt}) are encoded as chromosomes. The other integer variables In_{jkt}, U_{ljkt} and N_{jikt} are considered as being virtually dependent on Y_{lkt}, and thus they will be computed from Y_{lkt} and the known parameters of the problem.

Denote the population size in a genetic algorithm as *MAXPOP* (assume to be an even number) and the maximum number of iterations (i.e. maximum generations) as *MAXGEN*. The m-th individual (i.e. decision variable) in g-th generation/iteration is encoded as following:

$$\begin{aligned}\mathbf{Y}^{g,m} = (Y_{lkt}^{g,m}, \quad & l = 1,2,\cdots,L;\, k = 1,2,\cdots,K;\, t = 1,2,\cdots,T;\\ & m = 1,2,\cdots,MAXPOP;\, g = 1,2,\cdots,MAXGEN).\end{aligned}$$

3.2. *Heuristic Genetic Algorithm (HGA) for Production Planning Problem*

We can firstly determine U_{ljkt} from Y_{lkt} without considering the capacity constraints and take this lot-size plan as an initial plan, which will be further modified by considering the capacity constraints. In this section, we will modify this initial lot-size plan by a "shifting" technique that has been widely used in the heuristics for the lot-sizing problems. [5,17]

The shifting procedure checks the capacity feasibility of the initial lot-size schedule from the last period backwards to the first period. If the capacity constraints are satisfied in period t, the shifting procedure moves to period t-1 and begins to check the capacity feasibility in this following period. If in some period t the total production quantity of a scheduled item k is larger than the total available capacity for this item at the period, a violation occurs for this item k, and thus some production of the scheduled item in this period must be shifted to the previous period(s). In order to get a capacity-feasible plan more efficiently, we only consider moving the excess scheduled production quantity to the preceding period. That's to say, for item k, we move the excess production quantity in this period to its previous period until the capacity violation for this item in this period is eliminated. If there are other violations, we repeat this shifting procedure until all of them are eliminated. When the moving processes are finished, the modified lot-size plan becomes a feasible plan with respect to all capacity constraints.

In summary, the shifting procedure goes successively from period T downto 1. While the capacity violations occur in some period, move the excess production of one or more items in this period to the preceding period to satisfy the capacity constraints. If current period is the first period, the production quantity for this item in this period will be partly or completely lost, which means this solution is not a feasible solution. In this case, we will discard this solution. The detailed heuristic genetic algorithm for our problem (HGA) can be described as follows:

Algorithm HGA

Step 1.g=0. Randomly initialise the population set in gth generation.

$$oldpop = \{\mathbf{Y}^{0,j}, j = 1,2,\cdots, MAXPOP\},$$

Step 2. If $g = MAXGEN$, print the solution and stop.

Step 3. For each $\mathbf{Y}^{0,j} \in oldpop,\ j = 1,2,\cdots, MAXPOP$, compute its objective function value as following:

Step 3.1. Construct the initial lot size schedule without considering the capacity constraints. Calculate production quantity of item k in each period t according to $\mathbf{Y}^{0,j}$ as following:
For items k from period 1 to T, if

$Y_{it_1}^{0,j}=1, Y_{it_2}^{0,j}=1\ (1\le t_1<t_2\le T+1)$ and $\sum_{l=0}^{L} Y_{lk\tau}^{0,j}=0$ for all $t_1<\tau<t_2$ (assume $Y_{i,T+1}^{0,j}=1$), then let

$$\sum_{l=0}^{L}\sum_{j=0}^{J} U_{ljkt}=\sum_{\tau=t_1}^{t_2-1}\sum_{i=0}^{I} w_{ik\tau},(1\le t_1<\tau<t_2\le T+1).$$

Step 3.2. Eliminate the capacity-infeasibility for all the items by a shifting procedure. The processing in period t (from T downto 1) is as following:
Calculate the production quantity of item k in period t ($\sum_{l=0}^{L}\sum_{j=0}^{J} U_{ljkt}$). If $\sum_{l=0}^{L}\sum_{j=0}^{J} U_{ljkt}>\sum_{l=0}^{L} v_{lkt}$, then move part of the production quantity of item k in period t backwards to period t-1 and the moved quantity is $\sum_{l=0}^{L}\sum_{j=0}^{J} U_{ljkt}-\sum_{l=0}^{L} v_{lkt}$. After this movement, the production quantity of item k in period t-1 is increased by $\sum_{l=0}^{L}\sum_{j=0}^{J} U_{ljkt}-\sum_{l=0}^{L} v_{lkt}$.

Step 3.3. Determine $\sum_{l=0}^{L} U_{ljkt}$. In each period t, if $\sum_{l=0}^{L}\sum_{j=0}^{J} U_{ljkt}>0$, we need assign these material flows to warehouses and minimize the total holding cost. We start with the "best" warehouse (with least holding cost hc_{jkt}). If its residual capacity for product k can satisfy $\sum_{l=0}^{L}\sum_{j=0}^{J} U_{ljkt}$, then let corresponding $\sum_{l=0}^{L} U_{ljkt} = \sum_{l=0}^{L}\sum_{j=0}^{J} U_{ljkt}$. Otherwise, let $\sum_{l=0}^{L} U_{ljkt}$ be its residual capacity and continue to use the same method to examine the next "best" warehouse until the production of item k ($\sum_{l=0}^{L}\sum_{j=0}^{J} U_{ljkt}$) is fulfilled. Repeat this step until all the productions are examined.

Step 3.4. Determine $\sum_{i=0}^{I} N_{jikt}$. The customer demand for item k in period t is $\sum_{i=0}^{I} w_{ikt}$. In period t, for every item k, we start with the "best" warehouse (with largest holding cost hc_{jkt}). The available quantity of item k in warehouse j is $In_{jk(t-1)} + \sum_{l=0}^{L} U_{ljkt}$. If its available quantity can satisfy the demand of item k, then let corresponding $\sum_{i=0}^{I} N_{jikt} = \sum_{i=0}^{I} w_{ikt}$. Otherwise, let $\sum_{i=0}^{I} N_{jikt}$ be its available quantity and continue to use the same method to examine the next "best" warehouse until the demand for product k is fulfilled. Repeat this step until all the items in period t are examined.

Step 3.5. Determine In_{jkt} (inventory) ($In_{jk0}(\forall j,k)$ are known parameters) according to $\sum_{l=0}^{L} U_{ljkt}$ and $\sum_{i=0}^{I} N_{jikt}$.

$$In_{jkt} = In_{jk(t-1)} + \sum_{l=0}^{L} U_{ljkt} - \sum_{i=0}^{I} N_{jikt}$$

Step 3.6. Compute the corresponding objective function value $COSTU(\mathbf{Y}^{0,j})$

Step 4. Generate $newpop = \{\mathbf{Y}^{1,j}, j = 1,2,\cdots, MAXPOP\}$, the population set in (g+1)-th generation:

Step 4.1. Calculate the fitness value $fit(\mathbf{Y}^{0,j})$ for each individual $\mathbf{Y}^{0,j}$ according to the objective function values obtained in Step 3.6:

$$fit(\mathbf{Y}^{0,j}) = Max_{i=1}^{MAXPOP} COSTU(\mathbf{Y}^{0,i}) + \varepsilon - COSTU(\mathbf{Y}^{0,j}),$$
$$j = 1,2,\cdots, MAXPOP$$

where ε is a positive constant.

Step 4.2. (Reproduction/Selection) Select $\mathbf{Y}^{0,j_1}, \mathbf{Y}^{0,j_2}$ from the set *oldpop* according to the fitness values. The probability to select $\mathbf{Y}^{0,j}$ is

$$pr(\mathbf{Y}^{0,j}) = fit(\mathbf{Y}^{0,j}) \Big/ \sum_{i=1}^{MAXPOP} fit(\mathbf{Y}^{0,i}), j = 1,2,\cdots, MAXPOP.$$

Step 4.3. (Mutation) If the mutation probability is p_m, then after the mutation,

$$Y'^{0,j}_{lkt} = \begin{cases} Y^{0,j}_{lkt}, & in \ probability \ of \ 1-p_m, \\ \overline{Y}^{0,j}_{lkt}, & in \ probability \ of \ p_m, \end{cases} \quad j = j_1, j_2.$$

Here $\overline{Y}^{0,j}_{lkt} = \begin{cases} 0, & if \ Y^{0,j}_{lkt} = 1, \\ 1, & if \ Y^{0,j}_{lkt} = 0. \end{cases}$

Step 4.4. (Crossover) If the crossover probability is p_c, then after the crossover,

$$\mathbf{Y}^{1,j} = \begin{cases} \mathbf{Y}'^{0,j}, & in \ probability \ of \ 1-p_c, \\ \mathbf{Y}''^{0,j}, & in \ probability \ of \ p_c, \end{cases} \quad j = j_1, j_2.$$

Here randomly select a crossover position $s \ (1 \le s \le L \times K \times T)$ and then let

$$\mathbf{Y}''^{0,j_1} = (Y_1'^{0,j_1}, Y_2'^{0,j_1}, \cdots, Y_s'^{0,j_1}, Y_{s+1}'^{0,j_2}, Y_{s+2}'^{0,j_2}, \cdots, Y_{L\times K\times T}'^{0,j_2}),$$
$$\mathbf{Y}''^{0,j_2} = (Y_1'^{0,j_2}, Y_2'^{0,j_2}, \cdots, Y_s'^{0,j_2}, Y_{s+1}'^{0,j_1}, Y_{s+2}'^{0,j_1}, \cdots, Y_{L\times K\times T}'^{0,j_1}).$$

Step 4.5. Add the new individuals Y^{1,j_1}, Y^{1,j_2} to the set *newpop*.

Step 4.6. If all *MAXPOP* individuals are produced, then go to Step 5, otherwise go to Step 4.2.

Step 5. Set g=g+1, *oldpop*=*newpop* i.e. $Y^{0,j}_{lkt} = Y^{1,j}_{lkt}$, and go to **Step 2.**

4. Transportation Planning Model

Our transportation scheduling model is similar to the one presented in [14]. The main differences between them are: i) In our model, the locations of warehouses and plants are fixed and the objective is to find optimized material flows; ii) In transportation planning problem, decision makers may change their decisions after some periods of time according to the changes in production cost, transportation cost, customer demands, etc. Thus we incorporate time period in our transportation planning model.

Parameters

c_{ljkt} = cost of shipping one unit of product k from plant l to warehouse site j during period t

d_{jikt} = cost of shipping one unit of product k from warehouse site j to customer i during period t

v_{lk} = production capacity of product k at plant l

w_{ikt} = demand for product k at customer i during period t

s_k = volume of one unit of product k

q_j = capacity (in volume) of a warehouse at site j

Variables:

U_{ljkt} = amount of product k shipped from plant l to warehouse j during period t

N_{jikt} = amount of product k shipped from warehouse j to customer i during period t

Then the transportation planning problem is formulated as the following integer linear programming problem:

$$Min \quad \sum_{t=1}^{T}\sum_{l=1}^{L}\sum_{j=1}^{J}\sum_{k=1}^{K} c_{ljkt}U_{ljkt} + \sum_{t=1}^{T}\sum_{i=1}^{I}\sum_{j=1}^{J}\sum_{k=1}^{K} d_{jikt}N_{jikt}$$

$$s.t. \quad \sum_{j=1}^{J} U_{ljkt} \le v_{lk} \quad \forall l \in SL, k \in SK, t \in ST \tag{7}$$

$$\sum_{l=1}^{L}\sum_{k=1}^{K} s_k U_{ljkt} \le q_j \quad \forall j \in SJ, t \in ST \tag{8}$$

$$\sum_{j=1}^{J} N_{jikt} = w_{ikt} \quad \forall i \in SI, k \in SK, t \in ST \tag{9}$$

$$U_{ljkt}, N_{jikt} \geq 0 \qquad \forall l \in SL, i \in SI, j \in SJ, k \in SK \tag{10}$$

The first term in the objective function represents the transportation cost between plants and warehouses. The second term represents the transportation cost between warehouses and customers. Constraint (7) is a production capacity constraint. Constraint (8) is a warehouse capacity constraint that guarantees the capacity of the warehouses is not exceeded. Constraint (9) ensures the demand for each product of every customer is equal to the amount being shipped from the warehouses to the customer in period t.

This is a standard integer linear programming problem. For small or medium size problem (less than 3000 variables and 5000 constraints), we can use Simplex method to solve it efficiently.

5. The Integrated Production and Transportation Planning Model

There are two sets of variables that link the production planning and the transportation planning models. These are material flows from plants to warehouses and from warehouses to customers. These two production and transportation planning problems can be solved in a sequential manner. We can first solve the transportation planning problem and feed the resulting material flow solutions to the production planning problem. As a result we get a complete solution consisting of production and transportation plans. It will provide an upper bound to the optimum solution of the integrated model since it is just a feasible solution to the integrated model. Also we can optimise the production planning model before feeding the results to the transportation planning model. But there might exist another solution which is better in terms of total cost. To find an optimised solution to integrated problem, it is necessary to consider the cost factors of both models simultaneously.

In our problem, the integrated model consists of a two-tier problem, namely production and transportation planning. Our aim is to decompose this large model into production and transportation planning sub-problems. We define the following notations:

f_P	objective function of the production planning model
f_T	objective function of the transportation planning model
C_P	constraint sets of the production planning model
C_T	constraint sets of the transportation planning model
U1	vector of the material flow variables between plants and warehouses of the production planning model
U2	vector of the material flow variables between plants and warehouses of the transportation planning model
N1	vector of the material flow variables between warehouses and customers of the production planning model
N2	vector of the material flow variables between warehouses and customers of the transportation planning model
$\boldsymbol{\lambda}_{\mathrm{U}}$	vector of multipliers for the material flow variables between plants and warehouses
$\boldsymbol{\lambda}_{\mathrm{N}}$	vector of multipliers for the material flow variables between warehouses and customers

We define the problem P as follows:

Problem P: $Min \quad f_P + f_T$

$s.t. \quad C_P, C_T$

U1=U2, N1=N2

Since this model includes both production and transportation planning, it becomes too large to handle. We will apply Lagrangian relaxation to make integrated decisions for these two sub-models.

The last two equalities are the coupling constraints to which we apply Lagrangian relaxation to get the relaxed model as follows:

$$Min\,\{f_P + f_T + \boldsymbol{\lambda}_{\mathrm{U}}(\mathbf{U2} - \mathbf{U1}) + \boldsymbol{\lambda}_{\mathrm{N}}(\mathbf{N2} - \mathbf{N1})\} \quad s.t.\ C_P\,, C_T$$

We define the following sub-problems:

$$P_{PP}: \quad Min\{f_P - \boldsymbol{\lambda}_{\mathrm{U}}\mathbf{U1} - \boldsymbol{\lambda}_{\mathrm{N}}\mathbf{N1}\} \quad s.t.\ C_P$$

$$P_{TT}: \quad Min\{f_T + \boldsymbol{\lambda}_{\mathrm{U}}\mathbf{U2} + \boldsymbol{\lambda}_{\mathrm{N}}\mathbf{N2}\} \quad s.t.\ C_T$$

Let Z_{λ_U,λ_N} be the optimised solution of the relaxed problem:

$Z_{\lambda_U,\lambda_N} = Min \ \ f_P + f_T + \boldsymbol{\lambda}_{\mathrm{U}}(\mathbf{U2} - \mathbf{U1}) + \boldsymbol{\lambda}_{\mathrm{N}}(\mathbf{N2} - \mathbf{N1})$. The Lagrangian dual problem is $\underset{\boldsymbol{\lambda}_{\mathrm{U}}\boldsymbol{\lambda}_{\mathrm{N}}}{Max}\{Z_{\boldsymbol{\lambda}_{\mathrm{U}}\boldsymbol{\lambda}_{\mathrm{N}}}\}$ to maximize Z_{λ_U,λ_N} for $\forall\, \boldsymbol{\lambda}_{\mathrm{U}}, \boldsymbol{\lambda}_{\mathrm{N}}$. We apply subgradient method to solve this integrated model and the pseudo-code of the subgradient algorithm is shown as follows:

Procedure Subgradient Optimisation;
Inputs: Integrated model with parameters
Outputs:
The total optimised cost (Lower bound) of the combined model
The optimised material flows between plants and warehouses (U_{ljkt})
The optimised material flows between warehouses and customers (N_{jikt})
Begin

A=2, m=1, R=4

Initialise $\boldsymbol{\lambda}_{\mathrm{U}}, \boldsymbol{\lambda}_{\mathrm{N}}$

While $A > 10^{-10}$ and m <1000 do

Begin

Solve problem P_{PP}. The lower bound of P_{PP} is Z_{PP}

Solve problem P_{TT}. The lower bound of P_{TT} is Z_{TT}

$$Z^m_{\boldsymbol{\lambda}_{\mathrm{U}}\boldsymbol{\lambda}_{\mathrm{N}}} = Z_{PP} + Z_{TT}$$

Calculate the upper bound $Z^{UB}_{\boldsymbol{\lambda}_{\mathrm{U}}\boldsymbol{\lambda}_{\mathrm{N}}}$

Calculate the next $\boldsymbol{\lambda}_{\mathrm{U}}, \boldsymbol{\lambda}_{\mathrm{N}}$

$$t_{\lambda_U} = \frac{A(Z^{UB}_{\boldsymbol{\lambda}_{\mathrm{U}}\boldsymbol{\lambda}_{\mathrm{N}}} - Z^m_{\boldsymbol{\lambda}_{\mathrm{U}}\boldsymbol{\lambda}_{\mathrm{N}}})}{\sum_{l=1}^{L}\sum_{j=1}^{J}\sum_{k=1}^{K}\sum_{t=1}^{T}\{U2_{ljkt} - U1_{ljkt}\}^2}$$

$$t_{\boldsymbol{\lambda}_{\mathrm{N}}} = \frac{A(Z^{UB}_{\boldsymbol{\lambda}_{\mathrm{U}},\boldsymbol{\lambda}_{\mathrm{N}}} - Z^m_{\boldsymbol{\lambda}_{\mathrm{U}},\boldsymbol{\lambda}_{\mathrm{N}}})}{\sum_{j=1}^{J}\sum_{i=1}^{I}\sum_{k=1}^{K}\sum_{t=1}^{T}\{N2_{jikt} - N1_{jikt}\}^2}$$

$$\boldsymbol{\lambda}_{\mathrm{U}} = \boldsymbol{\lambda}_{\mathrm{U}} + t_{\boldsymbol{\lambda}_{\mathrm{U}}}(\mathbf{U2} - \mathbf{U1}) \qquad \boldsymbol{\lambda}_{\mathrm{N}} = \boldsymbol{\lambda}_{\mathrm{N}} + t_{\boldsymbol{\lambda}_{\mathrm{N}}}(\mathbf{N2} - \mathbf{N1})$$

m++

If $Z^{m}_{\lambda_U \lambda_N} < Z^{m-R}_{\lambda_U \lambda_N}$ then $A = A/2$

End (While)

End (Procedure)

6. Computational Experiments

The data sets of our computational experiments were generated by the method described in[19]. We have conducted a primary test to investigate the impact of the control parameters of the genetic algorithms on the performance of HGA. The algorithm converges to a solution within 200 generations for most of the small-scale examples (e.g. $L, J, I \le 10, K \le 2, T \le 5$) and within 500 generations for most of the modest examples (e.g. $L, J, I \approx 20, K \approx 4, T \approx 10$). The crossover probabilities between 0.6 to 1.0 and the mutation probabilities between 0.005 and 0.033 give no significant difference with regard to the total cost performance. But the mutation probabilities less than 0.005 worsen the total cost performance. In addition to these control parameters, the elitist strategy (the best solution found in current population set will be copied directly to the next generation) can enhance the performance significantly and is incorporated into our algorithm. Because genetic algorithms are probabilistic search algorithms, the algorithm on each problem was run 20 times to study their statistical characteristics.

Table 1 Computation time of subgradient optimisation algorithm

Plants	Warehouses	Customers	Products	Periods	Average CPU (sec)
3	3	5	2	5	180
5	8	10	2	5	305
8	10	10	2	5	578
10	10	15	2	5	813
12	15	15	3	10	1303
13	15	20	3	10	1473
14	20	20	3	10	1513
15	20	25	3	10	1689

The computation times on solving the integrated model using subgradient optimisation method are shown in the Table 1. These results show that our algorithm can solve small and medium size of integrated production and transportation planning problem within reasonable computation times.

We compared the computational results of our subgradient algorithm with another two sequential algorithms: P->T and T->P. The P->T algorithm solves the production planning problem and feeds the optimised variables (**N1** and **U1**) into transportation planning problem to calculate the total cost. This algorithm optimises the production cost and does not consider the impact of transportation cost on the overall cost. The T->P algorithm solves the transportation planning problem and feeds the optimised variables (**N2** and **U2**) into production planning problem to calculate the total cost. This algorithm optimises the transportation cost and does not consider the impact of production cost on the overall cost. Using the cost computed by our subgradient algorithm as a norm, the relative costs of the other two algorithms are computed and shown in Table 2. Computational results showed that the overall cost in our integrated model with subgradient optimisation algorithm is lower than these two algorithms. The gain is between 4% and 10% if our algorithm is applied. The overall cost obtained using T -> P algorithm is usually less than that obtained by P -> T algorithm.

Table 2 Overall relative costs to the integrated model

Plants	Warehouses	Customers	Products	Periods	P->T	T->P
3	3	5	2	5	106%	104%
5	8	10	2	5	110%	106%
8	10	10	2	5	108%	104%
10	10	15	2	5	109%	104%
12	15	15	3	10	105%	104%
13	15	20	3	10	106%	105%
14	20	20	3	10	104%	104%
15	20	25	3	10	105%	105%

The production cost and transportation cost of these three algorithms are shown in Table 3 and 4 respectively. In Table 3, we observed that the transportation cost of the subgradient algorithm is very close to that got from T->P algorithm. This implies that even with trade-offs between production and transportation cost, our integrated model with proposed algorithm can seek out a near optimal transportation cost. The production cost of the subgradient algorithm is a little higher than that got from P->T algorithm as shown in Table 4. But it is still lower than that got from T->P algorithm. This implies that although the production function within a supply chain may spend more cost compared with P->T algorithm, it may still benefit from our integrated model compared with T->P algorithm. Thus, our integrated model with subgradient algorithm can produce near optimal transportation cost and reduce the overall cost although the production cost is higher compared with P->T algorithm.

Table 3 Relative transportation cost to the integrated model

Plants	Warehouses	Customers	Products	Periods	P->T	T->P
3	3	5	2	5	114%	99%
5	8	10	2	5	112%	100%
8	10	10	2	5	110%	99%
10	10	15	2	5	112%	99%
12	15	15	3	10	113%	99%
13	15	20	3	10	113%	99%
14	20	20	3	10	115%	99%
15	20	25	3	10	113%	98%

Table 4 Relative production cost to the integrated model

Plants	Warehouses	Customers	Products	Periods	P->T	T->P
3	3	5	2	5	96%	104%
5	8	10	2	5	98%	107%
8	10	10	2	5	96%	105%
10	10	15	2	5	97%	104%
12	15	15	3	10	98%	103%
13	15	20	3	10	97%	105%
14	20	20	3	10	97%	105%
15	20	25	3	10	97%	106%

7. Summary

In this chapter, we proposed an integrated production and transportation planning model with material flow links. We developed a Lagrangian based approach to solve this integrated planning problem. This model, together with the effective solution procedures, can provide decision makers with an efficient tool to coordinate production and transportation functions across facilities and companies. Computational results indicate that our algorithm can efficiently help decision makers to reduce the total production and transportation cost.

References

1. P.J. Billington, J.O. McClain, and L.J. Thomas, "Heuristics for Multilevel Lot-sizing with a Bottleneck", *Management Science*, Vol. 37 No. 8, pp.989-1006 (1986)
2. G. R. Bitran, and H. H. Yanasse, "Computational Complexity of the Capacitated Lot Size Problem", *Management Science*, Vol. 28, pp.1174-1186 (1982).
3. P. Chandra and M. L. Fisher, "Coordination of Production and Distribution Planning", *European Journal of Operational Research*, Vol.72, pp. 503-517 (1994).
4. J. Chen, "Achieving Maximum Supply Chain Efficiency", *IIE Solutions, Norcross*, Vol. 29, pp. 30-35 (1997).
5. A. R. Clark and V. A. Armentano, "A Heuristic for a Resource-capacitated Multi-stage Lot-sizing Problem with Lead-time", *Journal of the Operational Research Society*, Vol. 46, pp. 1208-1222 (1995).
6. N. Dellaert and J. Jeunet, "Solving Large Unconstrained Multilevel Lot-sizing Problems Using a Hybrid Genetic Algorithm", *International Journal of Production Research*, Vol. 38 No. 5, pp.1083-1099 (2000).
7. N. Dellaert, J. Jeunet and N. Jonard, "A Genetic Algorithm to Solve the General Multi-level Lot-sizing Problem with Time-varying Costs", *International Journal of Production Economics*, Vol. 68 No. 3, pp. 241-257 (2000).
8. G. D. Eppen and R. K. Martin, "Solving Multi-item Capacitated Lot-sizing Problems Using Variable Redefinition", *Operations Research*, Vol. 35, pp.832-848 (1987).
9. Y. F. Hung, C. C. Shih and C. P. Chen, "Evolutionary Algorithms for Production Planning Problems with Setup Decisions", *Journal of the Operational Research Society*, Vol. 50 No. 8, pp. 857-866 (1999).
10. Y. F. Hung and K. L. Chien, "Multi-class Multi-level Capacitated Lot Sizing Model", *Journal of the Operational Research Society*, Vol. 51 No. 11, pp. 1309-1318 (2000).

11. V. Jayaraman and H. Pirkul, "Planning and Coordination of Production and Distribution facilities for Multiple Commodities", *European Journal of Operational Research*, Vol. 133, pp. 394-408 (2001).
12. R. Kuik, M. Solomon, L.N. Van Wassenhove and J. Maes, "Linear Programming, Simulated Annealing and Tabu Search Heuristics for Lot Sizing in Bottleneck Assembly Systems", *IIE Transactions*, Vol. 25 No. 1, pp. 62-72 (1993).
13. J. Maes, J.O. McClain, and L.N. Van Wassenhove, "Multilevel Capacitated Lot Sizing Complexity and LP Based Heuristics", *European Journal of Operational Research*, Vol. 53, pp.131-148 (1991).
14. S. Melkote and M. Daskin, "Capacitated facility Location/Network Design Problems", *European Journal of Operational Research*, Vol. 129, pp.481-495 (2001).
15. H. Pirkul and V. Jayaraman, "Production, Transportation, and Distribution Planning in a Multi-Commodity Tri-Echelon System", *Transportation Science*, Vol.30, No.4, pp.291-302 (1996).
16. W. Qua, J.H. Bookbindera and P. Iyogunb, "An Integrated Inventory-transportation System with Modified Periodic Policy for Multiple Products", *European Journal of Operational Research*, Vol. 115, pp. 254-269 (1999).
17. Y. Roll and R. Karni, "Multi-item, Multi-level Lotsizing with an Aggregate Capacity Constraint", *European Journal of Operational Research*, Vol. 51, pp. 73-87 (1991).
18. H. Tempelmeier and M. Derstroff, "A Lagrangean-based Heuristic for Dynamic Multilevel Multi-item Constrained Lotsizing with Setup Times", *Management Science*, Vol. 42 No. 1, pp. 738-757 (1996).
19. G. Wu, "Optimisation of Supply Chain Management in an Electronic Commerce Environment" *M. Eng. thesis submitted to Nanyang Technological University*, Singapore (2002).
20. J. Xie, "Heuristic Genetic Algorithms for General Capacitated Lot-Sizing Problems", *Computers and Mathematics With Applications*, Vol. 44 No. 1-2, pp. 263 –276 (2002).
21. A. Zahorik, L.J. Thomas and W.W. Trigeiro, "Network Programming Models for Multi Item Multi Stage Capacitated Systems", *Management Science*, Vol. 30 No. 3, pp. 308-325 (1984).

CHAPTER 23

EVOLUTION OF FUZZY RULE BASED CONTROLLERS FOR DYNAMIC ENVIRONMENTS

Jeff Riley and Vic Ciesielski

School of Computer Science and Information Technology, RMIT University
Melbourne, Australia
E-mail:(jeff.riley@optushome.com.au,vc@cs.rmit.edu.au)

Fuzzy logic controllers have been applied to a wide range of control problems, but are very difficult to build for situations where the environment changes quickly and there is a lot of uncertainty. This work investigates a new method of creating fuzzy controllers, in the form of reactive agents, for such environments. The framework for this investigation is the RoboCup soccer simulation environment, where the agents are in the form of simulated soccer players evolved to exhibit competent dribble-and-score behaviours. The method proposed uses a messy genetic algorithm to evolve a set of behaviour producing fuzzy rules which define the agents. The results presented indicate that the messy genetic algorithm is well suited to this task, producing good performance by reducing complexity, and that the agents produced perform well in their environment. The best agent evolved is consistently and reliably able to locate the ball, dribble it to the goal and score.

1. Introduction

If an agent is able to learn behaviours it exhibits in response to stimuli, it may adapt to unpredictable, dynamic environments. Even though we may be able to describe the overall goal we expect an agent to achieve, it is not always possible to precisely describe the behaviours an agent should exhibit in achieving that goal. If we can describe a function by which we evaluate the results of the agent's behaviour against the desired outcome, that can be used by some reinforcement learning algorithm to evolve the behaviours necessary to achieve the desired goal.

Fuzzy Sets[24] are powerful tools for the representation of uncertain and vague data. Fuzzy inference systems make use of this by applying approximate reasoning techniques to make decisions based on such uncertain, vague data. However, a fuzzy inference system on its own is not usually self-adaptive and not able to modify its underlying rulebase to adapt to changing circumstances.

Genetic algorithms[10] are adaptive heuristic search algorithms premised on the evolutionary ideas of natural selection. By combining the adaptive learning capabilities of the genetic algorithm with the approximate reasoning capabilities of the fuzzy inference system, we produce a hybrid system capable of learning the behaviour an agent needs to exhibit in order to achieve a defined goal.

There is a large body of work in the area of quasi-intelligent autonomous agents[16]. In recent times some researchers have moved away from modelling intelligent behaviour by designing and implementing complex agents. While the traditional single, complex agent approach has been shown to be successful in specialized domains such as game playing, reasoning, and path planning[17], other approaches need to be considered. One such approach is the simple agent approach in which a group of simple agents co-operate to achieve some goal. The simple agent approach forms the basis of *Artificial Life*[13]. Several variations of the multiple simple agent approach are being, or have been, investigated by different researchers: Wooldridge and Haddadi present a formal theory of *on-the-fly* co-operation amongst a group of agents[23], and Baray investigates the complexity that arises from the interaction between agents and their environment[2]. The simple agent approach would seem to be a reasonable one, and one for which the machine learning techniques described may work well. In the work presented in this chapter, the focus is on using those techniques to create simple reactive agents, rather than quasi-intelligent, complex ones.

The traditional decomposition for an intelligent control system or agent is to break processing into a chain of information processing modules proceeding from sensing to action (Fig. 1).

The agent architecture implemented in the work presented in this chapter is similar to the *subsumption architecture* described by Brooks[3]. This architecture implements a layering process where simple task achieving behaviours are added as required. Each layer is behaviour producing in its own right, although it may rely on the presence and operation of other layers. For example, in Fig. 2 the *Movement* layer does not explicitly need to avoid obstacle: the *Avoid Objects* layer will take care of that.

Fig. 1. Traditional Agent Architecture

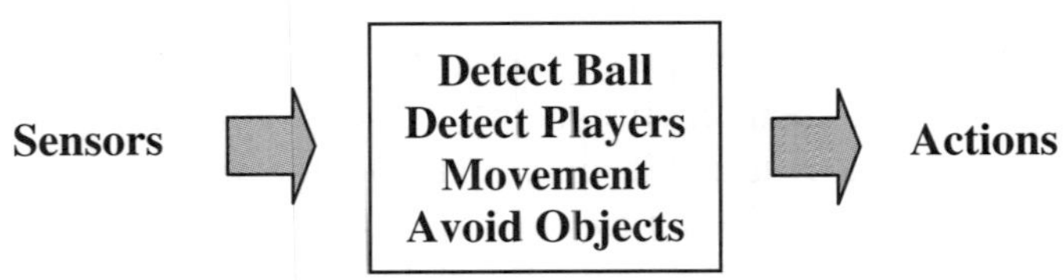

Fig. 2. Brooks-style Layered Architecture for a Soccer Playing Agent

This approach creates agents with reactive architectures and with no central locus of control as described by Brooks[4]. For the work presented in this chapter the new behaviours, or behaviour producing rules, are evolved rather than designed.

This work investigates the use of an evolutionary technique in the form of a messy genetic algorithm to efficiently construct the rulebase for a fuzzy inference system to solve a particular optimisation problem. The flexibility provided by the messy genetic algorithm is exploited in the definition and format of the genes on the chromosome, thus reducing the complexity of the rule encoding from the traditional genetic algorithm. With this method the individual agent behaviours are defined by sets of fuzzy if-then rules evolved by a messy genetic algorithm. Learning is achieved through testing and evaluation of the fuzzy rulebase generated by the genetic algorithm. The fitness function used to determine the fitness of an individual rulebase takes into account the performance of the agent, based upon the number of goals scored, or attempts made to move toward goal scoring, during a game.

Previous work in the evolutionary optimisation of fuzzy system parameters can be divided into two main categories based upon the way in which the evolutionary algorithm is applied. These have become known as the *Pittsburgh* approach[20] and the *Michigan* approach[18].

The Pittsburgh approach considers each individual chromosome a complete set of rules, so the fuzzy inference system is represented by a single individual. With this approach reinforcement bandwidth is usually smaller and genetic crossover can be a cause of disruption.

The Michigan approach on the other hand considers each individual chromosome a single rule, so the fuzzy inference system is represented by the entire population. With this approach, because each individual in the population is competing with the others, care must be taken to balance cooperation and competition between individual rules.

A comparison of the Pittsburgh and Michigan approaches is presented by Pipe and Carse[19].

The genetic algorithm implemented in the work presented in this chapter is a messy genetic algorithm[8] which uses the Pittsburgh approach: each individual in the population is a complete ruleset.

There has been some work in the area of the application of evolutionary learning techniques to the challenges of RoboCup[1,7,15] but because the RoboCup environment is so large, complex and uncertain, attempts to learn the entire task have met with limited success. Andre[1], for example, did achieve some success in evolving some individual behaviours, while Luke[15] had some success evolving high-level behaviour using a pool of hand-coded low-level behaviours.

2. Goals

The primary goal of the work presented in this chapter is to investigate the potential of a fuzzy logic based controller in defining the behaviour of a reactive agent in a dynamic, uncertain environment, and the usefulness of using a messy genetic algorithm to evolve the rulebase for the controller. Furthermore, the work examines the hypothesis that the reduced complexity of the rule encoding also reduces the search space, allowing the algorithm to more quickly find reasonable solutions more quickly in a smaller, seemingly less diverse population. The framework for the investigation of this work is the RoboCup[12] soccer simulation environment, where the agents are in the form of simulated soccer players.

3. Method Description

3.1. *Overview*

Learning classifier systems[11] are an example of genetic algorithms incorporated into models of complex systems, where the classifier systems are used as models of behaviour ranging from simple stimulus-response to more complex cognitive behaviour. Classifier systems implement hierarchies of internal models that represent the environment, and the genetic algorithm uses intermittent feedback from the environment in order to discover the rules that represent those hierarchies.

This work implements a method involving the use of a messy genetic algorithm and a fuzzy inference system in which the messy genetic algorithm is used to determine, by simulated evolution, the fuzzy ruleset which defines the set of behaviours exhibited by reactive agents in response to stimuli.

An indicative example of previous work in which messy genetic algorithms are used to evolve fuzzy rules is given by Hoffmann and Pfister[9]. There a messy genetic algorithm was used to evolve a fuzzy controller for an autonomous vehicle capable of travelling to a destination and avoiding obstacles along the way. A significant difference between previous work and the work presented in this chapter is that the agent or controller evolved here is able to cope with an uncertain, rapidly changing environment.

In addition to the primitives defined by the RoboCup system (*dash, kick, turn* etc.), the agent being evolved is endowed with a specific set of mid-level hand-coded soccer-playing skills. These are:

RunTowardBall: the agent *dashes* once in the direction of the ball, provided the direction to the ball is known.

RunTowardMyGoal: the agent *dashes* once in the direction of its own goal, provided the direction to the goal is known.

Dribble: the agent *kicks* the ball once in the direction it is facing, then *dashes* once in that direction.

DribbleTowardMyGoal: the agent *kicks* the ball once in the direction of its own goal, then *dashes* once in that direction, provided the direction to the goal is known.

KickTowardMyGoal: the agent *kicks* the ball once towards its own goal, provided the direction to the goal is known.

GoToBall: the agent *dashes* towards ball until it is within kicking distance of the ball, provided the direction to the ball is known.

DoNothing: the agent takes no action.

The agent will perform one of these actions in response to external stimuli; the specific response being determined by the fuzzy rulebase. If no action is indicated given the information known by the agent (that is, no rule fires), the agent will turn 90° in a randomly chosen direction in an effort to locate the ball or goal.

The external stimuli used as input to the fuzzy inference system is most of the visual information supplied by the soccer server: information regarding the location of opponents and team mates is not used at this stage, and only sufficient information to situate the agent and locate the ball is used.

3.2. *Genetic Algorithms*

The method investigated by this work results in a fuzzy rule base developed by the use of a *messy* genetic algorithm. In this method, fuzzy rulesets are encoded onto variable length chromosomes, and an initial population of chromosomes is evolved to produce a fuzzy ruleset which defines the behaviours of the soccer playing agent.

3.2.1. Messy Genetic Algorithms

In classic genetic algorithms the chromosome is defined as a fixed length structure; commonly a fixed length bit string. With this definition each gene is guaranteed to occur only once, and its meaning is defined by its position in the structure. A messy genetic algorithm on the other hand, encodes a chromosome as a variable length structure comprised of tuples of values, with each tuple describing a gene. In this work, a gene is described by a triplet representing a fuzzy clause and connector, with the first element denoting the input variable, the second the fuzzy set membership (or fuzzy variable) of this input variable, and the third the clause connector. The rule consequent gene is specially coded to distinguish it from premise genes allowing multiple rules, or a ruleset, to be encoded onto a single chromosome. An example chromosome fragment is shown in Fig. 3.

(Ball, Left, And)	(MyGoal, Far, Or)	(Dribble, Slow, *)

Fig. 3. Messy Genetic Algorithm Example Chromosome Fragment

Some features of the chromosome in a messy genetic algorithm are:

- a gene is encoded as a tuple describing the gene's meaning, value and other relevant information.
- genes may occur multiple times.
- genes are not guaranteed to be present.
- genes may be permutated in any way.

For example, the chromosome fragments shown in Fig. 4 are valid even though a gene is repeated. Furthermore, the chromosome fragments are equivalent even though the genes are ordered differently.

(Ball, Left, And)	(MyGoal, Far, Or)	(Ball, Left, And)

(Ball, Left, And)	(Ball, Left, And)	(MyGoal, Far, Or)

Fig. 4. Valid and Equivalent Chromosome Fragments in a Messy Genetic Algorithm

For messy genetic algorithms, the selection and mutation operators are implemented in the same manner as for classic genetic algorithms. The crossover operator, however, is implemented as a combination of two new operators: *cut* and *splice*. The *cut* operator cuts each chromosome at a randomly chosen position, and since the chromosomes may be of different lengths, the resultant fragments may also be of different lengths. The *splice* operator concatenates the fragments produced by the *cut* operator, resulting in two new chromosomes of possibly different lengths from the original chromosomes. Fig. 5 is an example of the *cut* and *splice* operations for a messy genetic algorithm.

It has been shown that messy genetic algorithms are useful tools for solving difficult optimisation problems. Recent work with messy genetic algorithms includes work on multiobjective optimisation[22] and the vehicle routing problem[21]. The work presented in this chapter uses the messy genetic algorithm to optimise the ruleset for the fuzzy inference system.

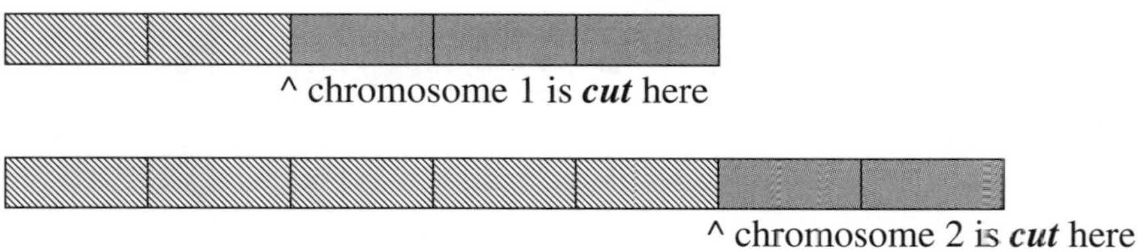

Fig. 5a. Messy Genetic Algorithm Cut Operation

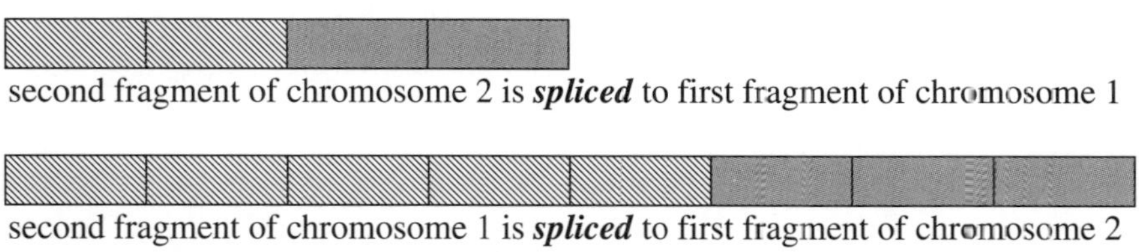

Fig. 5b. Messy Genetic Algorithm Cut Operation

3.3. *Fuzzy Inference Systems*

A fuzzy inference system is a framework based on the concept of fuzzy set theory, fuzzy *if-then* rules and fuzzy reasoning. The fuzzy inference system is comprised of a number of fuzzy *if-then* rules, definitions of the membership functions of the fuzzy sets operated on by those rules, and a reasoning mechanism to perform the inference procedure (Fig. 6). The application of the fuzzy rule base by the inference procedure to external stimuli provided by the soccer server results in one or more fuzzy rules being executed and some action being taken by the client.

In this work the fuzzy rule base is developed by the use of a messy genetic algorithm. The messy genetic algorithm evolves the fuzzy rule base during a series of simulated training soccer games in which individuals are rewarded for goals scored. The membership functions of the input and output fuzzy sets are standard trapezoidal functions which are pre-defined and fixed, so not modified by the genetic algorithm.

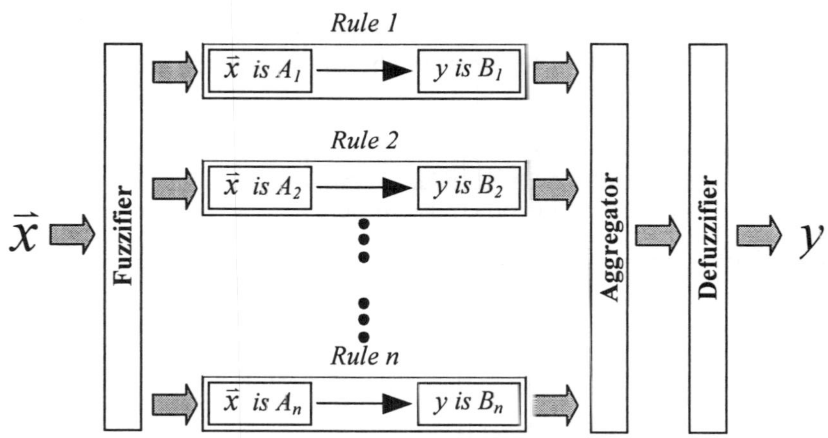

Fig. 6. Fuzzy Inference System

The external stimuli given as input to the fuzzy inference system is fuzzified to represent the degree of membership of one of four fuzzy sets: direction, distance, speed and power. For example, the visual information supplied by the soccer server is interpreted as fuzzy relationships such as *Ball is Near*, *MyGoal is VeryFar*, *Ball is SlightlyLeft.*

To evolve a *dribble-and-score* behaviour, only that information required to locate the agent's goal, the ball, and to situate the agent is given as input to the agent.

The fuzzy rules developed by the genetic algorithm are of the form:

if *Ball* is *Near* and *MyGoal* is *Near* then *KickTowardMyGoal Soft*
if *Ball* is *Far* or *Ball* is *SlightlyLeft* then *RunTowardBall Fast*

The output of the fuzzy inference system is a number of *(action, value)* pairs, corresponding to the number of fuzzy rules with unique consequents. The *(action, value)* pairs define the action to be taken by the agent, and the degree to which the action is to be taken. For example:

(KickTowardMyGoal, power)
(RunTowardBall, speed)
(Turn, direction)

where *power*, *speed* and *direction* are crisp values representing the defuzzified fuzzy set membership of the action to be taken.

Only one action is performed by the agent in response to stimuli provided by the soccer server. Since several rules with different actions may fire, actions are assigned a priority and the highest priority action is performed.

3.4. *Detailed Method Description*

Input variables for the fuzzy rules developed by this method are fuzzy interpretations of the visual stimuli supplied to the agent by the soccer server. Output variables are the fuzzy actions to be taken by the agent. The universe of discourse of both input and output variables are covered by fuzzy sets, the parameters of which are predefined and fixed. Each input is fuzzified to have a degree of membership in the fuzzy sets appropriate to the input variable.

The encoding scheme implemented for this method exploits the capability of messy genetic algorithms to encode information of variable structure and length. The basic element of the coding of the fuzzy rules is a triplet representing a fuzzy clause and connector, with the first element denoting the input variable, the second the fuzzy set membership (or fuzzy variable) of this input variable, and the third the clause connector. The rule consequent gene is specially coded to distinguish it from premise genes allowing multiple rules, or a ruleset, to be encoded onto a single chromosome. Chromosomes are not fixed length: the length of each chromosome in the population varies with the length of individual rules and the number of rules on the chromosome. The number of clauses in a rule and the number of rules in a ruleset is only limited by the maximum size of a chromosome. The minimum size of a rule is two clauses (one premise and one consequent), and the minimum number of rules in a ruleset is one.

The set of input variables for the premise clauses is:

(Ball, MyGoal)

and for the consequent clauses:

(Turn, Kick, KickTowardMyGoal, Dribble, DribbleTowardMyGoal, Run, RunTowardMyGoal, RunTowardBall, GoToBall, DoNothing)

The fuzzy variables for each of the fuzzy sets DISTANCE, POWER and DIRECTION which describe the input or action variables for both the premise and consequent clauses are:

DISTANCE: (At, VeryNear, Near, SlightlyNear, MediumDistant, SlightlyFar, Far, VeryFar)
POWER: (VeryLow, Low, SlightlyLow, MediumPower, SlightlyHigh, High, VeryHigh)
DIRECTION: (Left180, VeryLeft, Left, SlightlyLeft, Straight, SlightlyRight, Right, VeryRight, Right180)

Premise clauses can be further modified by the use of a not operator. The set of possible clause connectors is:

(and, or, *),

where * indicates the connector is not used.

The DISTANCE, POWER and DIRECTION fuzzy sets are shown in Fig. 7. The parameters for these fuzzy sets were not learned by the evolutionary process, but were fixed empirically. The initial values were set having regard to RoboCup parameters and variables, and fine-tuned after some experimentation.

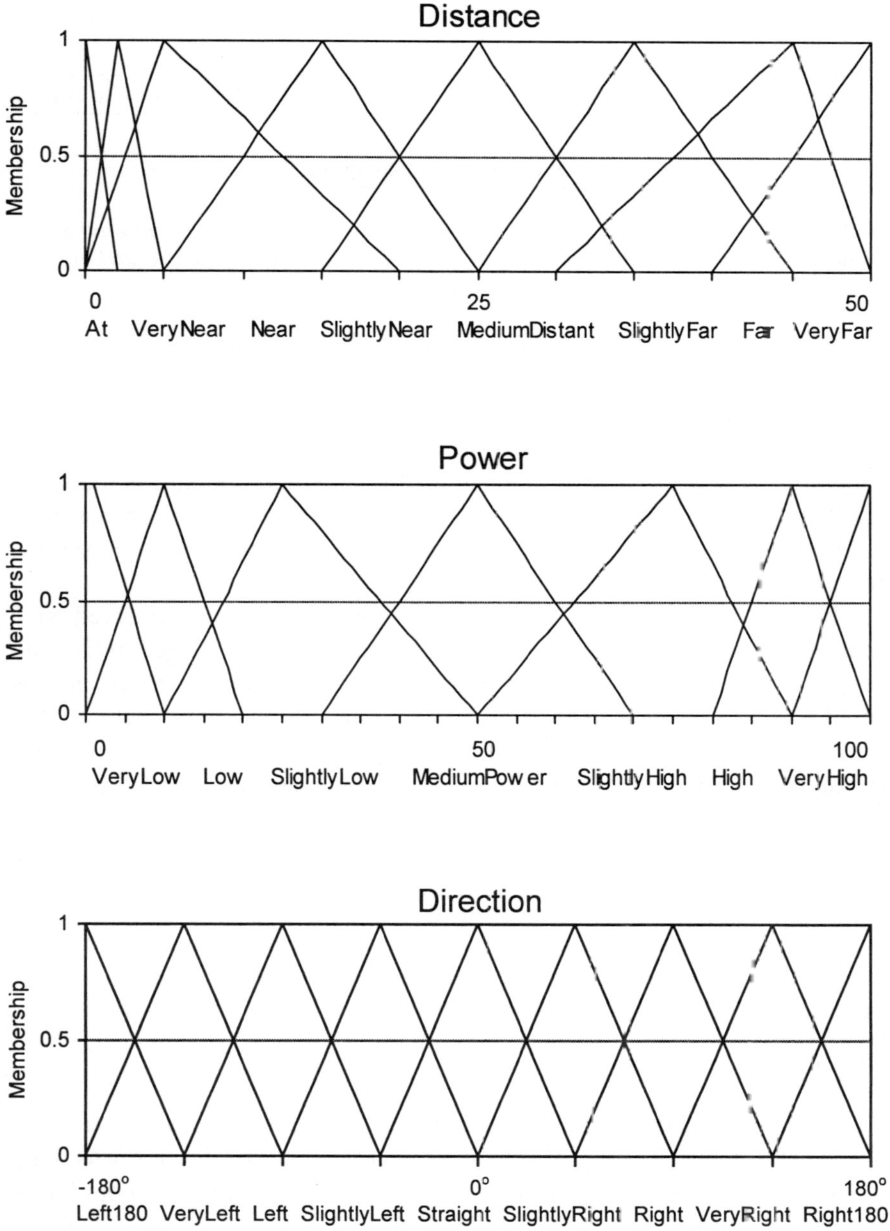

Fig. 7. Distance, Power and Direction Fuzzy Sets

An example chromosome and corresponding rules are shown in Fig. 8.

(B,N,O)	(B,nF,A)	(G,N,*)	(RB,S,*)	(B,A,A)	(G,vN,*)	(KG,M,*)	(B,F,*)	(GB,vF,*)

Premise	Consequent

Rule 1: if *Ball* is *Near* or *Ball* is *not Far* and *MyGoal* is *Near* then *RunTowardBall Slow*
Rule 2: if *Ball* is *At* and *MyGoal* is *VeryNear* then *KickTowardMyGoal MediumPower*
Rule 3: if *Ball* is *Far* then *GoToBall VeryFast*

Fig. 8. Chromosome and corresponding rules

The genetic operators implemented are cut, splice and mutation. As previously described, cut and splice are analogous to the crossover operation of classic genetic algorithms; the mutation operator is the same as that of the classic genetic algorithm. Since chromosomes are variable in length and can contain multiple rules, each chromosome represents a complete ruleset.

In contrast to classic genetic algorithms which use a fixed size chromosome and require *don't care* values in order to generalise, no explicit *don't care* values are implemented for any attributes in this method. Since messy genetic algorithms encode information of variable structure and length not all attributes, particularly premise variables, need be present in any rule, or indeed in the entire ruleset. In other words the format of the messy genetic algorithm implies *don't care* values for all attributes since any attribute (premise variable) may be omitted from any or all rules, so generalisation is an implicit feature of this method.

4. Results

In the trials for which the results are presented here:

- The *Roulette Wheel* method of selection for crossover was used, and the probability of crossover occurring after selection was 0.8.
- Each generation was mutated by selecting 10% of the population for possible mutation, then subjecting those selected individuals to a probability of mutation of 0.35. For each individual, a single gene was randomly selected for mutation: for a premise gene the

input variable, fuzzy variable or connector was mutated; and for a consequent gene the input variable or fuzzy variable was mutated. Mutation consisted of replacement by a randomly selected value.

Individuals were rewarded, in order of importance, for

- the number of goals scored in a game
- the number of times the ball was kicked during a game

A game was played with the only player on the field being the agent under evaluation. The agent was placed randomly on its half of the field and oriented so that it was facing the end of the field to which it was kicking, and the ball was placed at the centre of the field. A game was terminated when:

- the target fitness of 0.05 was reached
- the ball was kicked out of play
- 120 seconds expired
- 10 seconds of no player movement expired

The target fitness of 0.05 reflects a score of 10 goals in the playing time of 120 seconds. This Fig. was chosen to allow the player a realistic amount of time to develop useful strategies yet terminate the search upon finding a very good individual.

Two methods of terminating the evolutionary search were implemented. The first stops the search when a specified maximum number of generations have occurred; the second stops the search when the best fitness in the current population becomes less than a specified threshold. Both methods were active, with the first to be encountered terminating the search.

The results of several trials are presented below. Each trial consisted of a population of 200 randomly initialised chromosomes evolved over 25 generations.

Fig. 9 shows the average fitness of the population after each generation for each of 10 trials, showing that the performance of the population does improve steadily and plateaus towards goal-scoring behaviour (i.e. a fitness of 0.5).

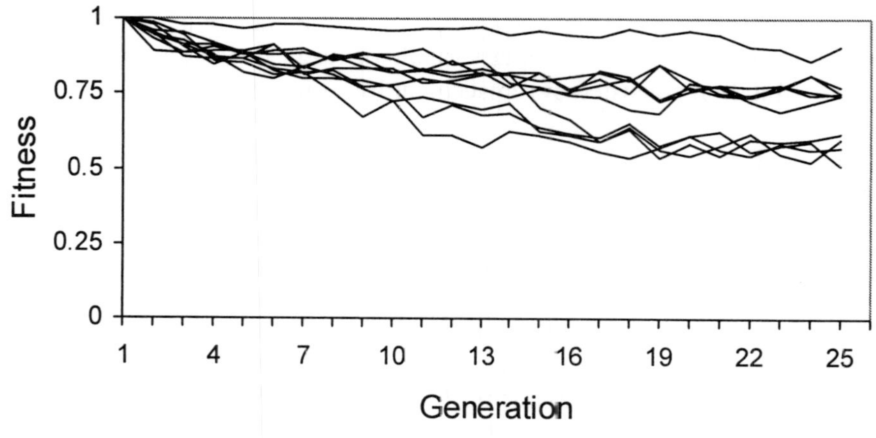

Fig. 9. Average Fitness Curves for 10 Trials

Fig. 10 shows the best individual fitness from the population after each generation for each of 10 trials, showing that good individuals are found after very few generations in contrast to the gradual improvement in average fitness (Fig. 9).

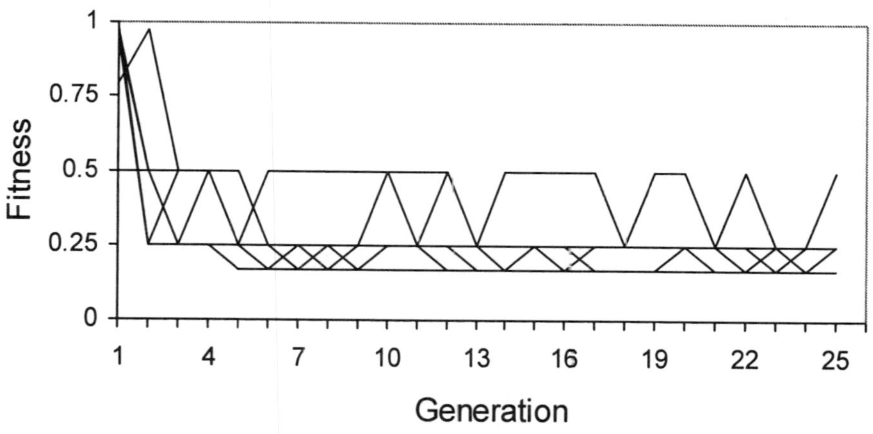

Fig. 10. Best Fitness Curves for 10 Trials

Fig. 11 is another visualisation of the progressive learning of the population from generation to generation, showing that not only do more players learn to kick goals over time, they learn to kick more goals more quickly. The histogram shows the average number of individuals, from a population of 200, which scored 0, 1, 2 or 3 goals from each generation of the 10 trials.

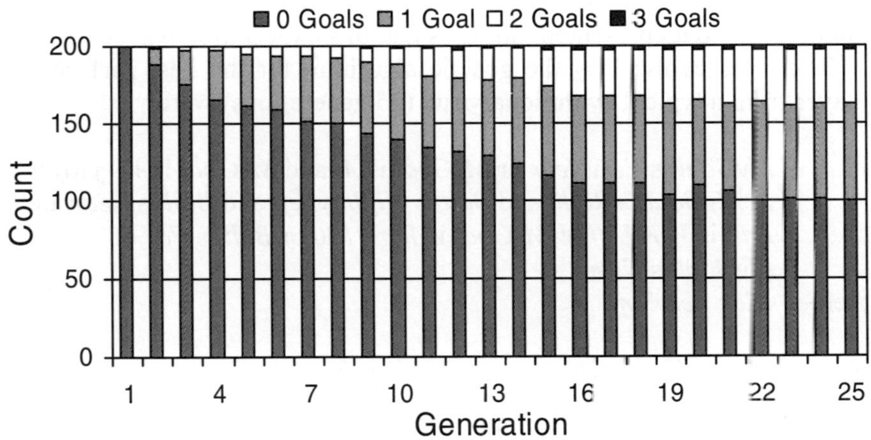

Fig. 11. Goals Scored

The actual fitness function used was

$$f = \begin{cases} \begin{cases} \begin{cases} 1.0 & ,kicks = 0 \\ 0.5 & ,kicks > 0 \end{cases} & ,ticks = 0 \\ 1.0 - \dfrac{kicks}{2.0 \times ticks} & ,ticks > 0 \end{cases} & ,goals = 0 \\ \dfrac{1.0}{2.0 \times goals} & ,goals > 0 \end{cases}$$

where

goals = the number of goals scored by the agent
kicks = the number of times the agent kicked the ball
ticks = the number of soccer server time steps

The function chosen indicates a better fitness as a lower number so representing the optimisation of fitness as a minimisation problem. This function was chosen to reward agents for goals scored. Agents that do not score goals are rewarded for the number of times the ball is kicked on the assumption that an agent which actually kicks the ball is more likely to produce offspring capable of scoring goals. The expectation was that evolutionary pressures would cause the average fitness of the population to decrease, with individual fitness for some individuals decreasing more rapidly. The data presented indicates that this expectation was realised.

The rules evolved by the genetic algorithm for the best performing player from a typical evolutionary run (25 generations) were:

if *MyGoal* is *VeryNear* or *MyGoal* is *At* and *MyGoal* is *VeryRight* or *MyGoal* is *Right* and *Ball* is *SlightlyLeft* and *Ball* is *Near* and *Ball* is *VeryLeft* or *MyGoal* is *Right180* or *Ball* is *Far* or *MyGoal* is *Near*
then *Kick VerySoft*

if *MyGoal* is *VeryNear* or *Ball* is *VeryNear* and *Ball* is *SlightlyRight* and *Ball* is *Far*
then *GoToBall SlightlyHard*

if *MyGoal* is *not VeryRight* or *Ball* is *VeryFar*
then *DribbleTowardMyGoal Soft*

if *MyGoal* is *MediumDistant* or *MyGoal* is *not Left* and *Ball* is *not Right180* or *MyGoal* is *SlightlyRight* or *MyGoal* is *VeryLeft* or *MyGoal* is *VeryFar* and *MyGoal* is *not Left180* or *Ball* is *Left180* and *MyGoal* is *SlightlyNear*
then *DribbleTowardMyGoal MediumPower*

if *MyGoal* is *VeryNear* or *MyGoal* is *Left180* and *Ball* is *Near* and *MyGoal* is *Right*
then *Dribble Hard*

The player defined by this ruleset achieved a fitness value of 0.1667 by kicking 3 goals in the allotted time of 120 seconds. The best performing players from the trials were each tested in 100 trials of 120 seconds, with the player being placed in a different, randomly selected starting position for each trial. The best performing players in these tests scored one or more goals in 60% of the trials. Typically players begin the game by hunting for the ball, then once the ball is located the players generally dribble the ball towards the goal in a reasonably direct route. Because the player developed is reactive and almost no state information is recorded (by the player), there are times when it loses sight of the ball or goal. These situations are characterised by the player momentarily hunting for the ball, or kicking the ball in the wrong direction.

The average time for each training run of 25 generations with a population size of 200 individuals was 100 hours. Several training runs were performed with a larger population of 1000 individuals with no significant increase in effectiveness, consistent with findings in other work in this area[14]. In all trials the average generational performance of the population tended to plateau after some time (see Fig. 9), but a very good individual was found early in the search (see Fig. 10).

5. Conclusions

This work investigates a method of creating reactive agents that uses a messy genetic algorithm to evolve fuzzy rules which define the agent's behaviour. The method consistently evolved players in very few generations that displayed very good goal scoring behaviour, thus demonstrating that this method can be used to successfully train a *dribble-and-score* behaviour in a reactive soccer playing agent. The RoboCup environment is a complex, dynamic and uncertain environment, and the results presented indicate that the method described can create controllers or agents for complex situations where the environment changes quickly and there is a lot of uncertainty. A useful next step is to use the method to evolve agents for the even more complex environment of a simulated game of soccer involving many players.

The good performance of the method with a small population and relatively few generations is likely to be due in part to the reduced complexity of the rule encoding afforded by the flexibility of the messy genetic algorithm. This would seem to reduce the search space, so allowing the algorithm to find reasonable solutions more quickly in a seemingly less diverse population.

The selection of mid-level, hand-coded composite skills rather than simple RoboCup primitives is likely to have had a positive effect on the performance since learning those skills is difficult and time consuming[5,6]. By pre-defining the composite skills the genetic algorithm was able to search for the higher-level strategies necessary for a good *dribble-and-score* behaviour rather than the low-level skills.

Since this method produces human-readable rules which govern the behaviour of the agents, it is possible to gain some understanding of the (often novel) knowledge that the agent has learned through the evolutionary process. This is considered an advantage over many existing methods of automatically creating agents or controllers where often the learned behaviour is not apparent and not easily extracted. A useful avenue for further work, made possible by the human-readable form of the rules, is the post-processing and optimisation of the evolved rules.

References

1. Andre, D. and Teller, A. Evolving Team Darwin United. In Minoru Asada and Hioaki Kitano, editors, *RoboCup-98: Robot Soccer World Cup II. Lecture Notes in Computer Science*. Springer-Verlag, Berlin, 1999.
2. Baray, C. Evolution of Coordination in Reactive Multi-Agent Systems. PhD Thesis, Computer Science Department, Indiana University, Bloomington, Indiana, 1999.
3. Brooks, R. Robust Layered Control System for a Mobile Robot. A.I Memo 864, Massachusetts Institute of Technology, Artificial Intelligence Laboratory, 1985.
4. Brooks, R. Intelligence without Representation. *Artificial Intelligence*, 47:139-159, 1991.
5. Ciesielski, V., Mawhinney, D. and Wilson, P. Genetic Programming for Robot Soccer. In P*roceedings of the RoboCup 2001 International Symposium, Lecture Notes in Artificial Intelligence 2377,* pp 319-324. Springer-Verlag, Berlin, 2002.
6. Ciesielski, V. and Lai, S. Y. Developing a Dribble-and-Score Behaviour for Robot Soccer Using Neuro Evolution. In *Proceedings of the 5th Australia-Japan Joint Workshop on Intellignet and Evolutionary Systems*, pp 70-78, Dunedin, New Zealand, 2001.
7. Ciesielski, V. and Wilson, P. Developing a Team of Soccer Playing Robots by Genetic Programming. In *Proceedings of The Third Australia-Japan Joint Workshop on Intelligent and Evolutionary Systems*, pp101-108, Canberra, Australia, 1999.
8. Goldberg, D., Korb, B., and Deb, K. Messy Genetic Algorithms: Motivation, Analysis, and First Results. In *Complex Systems*, 3, 1989.
9. Hoffmann, F. and Pfister, G. Evolutionary Learning of a Fuzzy Control Rule Base for an Autonomous Vehicle. In *Proceedings of the Fifth International Conference on Information Processing and Management of Uncertainty in Knowledge-Based Systems*, pp659-664. Granada, Spain, 1996.
10. Holland, J. *Adaptation in Natural and Artificial Systems*. Ann Arbor: The University of Michigan Press, 1975.
11. Holland, J., Holyoak, K., Nisbett, R. and Thagard, P. *Induction: Processes of Inference, Learning, and Discovery*. MIT Press, 1986.
12. Kitano, H., Asada, M., Kuniyoshi, Y., Noda, I., and Osawa, E. RoboCup: The Robot World Cup Initiative. In *Working Notes of the 1995 International Joint Conference on Artificial Intelligence Workshop on Entertainment and AI/Alife*, pp19-24. Montreal, Canada, 1995.
13. Langton, C. (Ed.) *Artificial Life*. Addison-Wesley, 1989.

14. Luke, S. When Short Runs Beat Long Runs. In *Proceedings of the 2001 Genetic and Evolutionary Computation Conference*, pp74-80. San Francisco CA, USA, 2001.
15. Luke, S., Hohn, C., Farris, J., Jackson, G. and Hendler, J. Coevolving Soccer Softbot Team Coordination with Genetic Programming. In Hioaki Kitano, editor, *RoboCup-97: Robot Soccer World Cup I*. Lecture Notes in Artificial Intelligence No. 1395, pp398-411. Springer-Verlag, Berlin, 1999.
16. Maes, P. *Designing Autonomous Agents*. The MIT Press, 1990.
17. Nilsson, N. *Artificial Intelligence: A New Synthesis*. Morgan Kaufmann, San Francisco, CA, 1998.
18. Parodi, A. and Bonelli, P. A New Approach to Fuzzy Classifier Systems. In *Proceedings of the Fifth International Conference on Genetic Algorithms*, pp223-230. San Mateo CA, USA, 1993. Morgan Kaufman.
19. Pipe, A. and Carse, B. Autonomous Acquisition of Fuzzy Rules for Mobile Robot Control: First Results From Two Evolutionary Computation Approaches. In *Proceedings of the 2000 Genetic and Evolutionary Computation Conference*, pp849-856. Las Vegas NV, USA, 2000.
20. Smith, S. A Learning System Based on Genetic Adaptive Algorithms, Doctoral Thesis, Department of Computer Science, University of Pittsburgh, Pittsburgh. PA, USA, 1980.
21. Tan, K., Lee, T., Ou, K., and Lee, L. A Messy Genetic Algorithm for the Vehicle Routing Problem With Time Window Constraints. In *Proceedings of the 2001 Congress on Evolutionary Computation*, pp679-686. Seoul, Korea, 2001.
22. Van Veldhuizen, D., and Lamont, G. Multiobjective Optimization with Messy Genetic Algorithms. In *Proceedings of the Fifteenth ACM Symposium on Applied Computing (Evolutionary Computation and Optimization Track)*, pp470-476. Como, Italy, 2000.
23. Wooldridge, M. and Haddadi, A. Making It Up As They Go Along: A Theory of Reactive Cooperation. In W. Wobcke, M. Pagnucco, and C. Zhang, editors, *Agents and Multi-Agent Systems -- Formalisms, Methodologies, and Applications* (LNAI Volume 1441). Springer-Verlag, 1998.
24. Zadeh, L. Fuzzy Sets. *Journal of Information and Control*, Vol 8, 1965.

CHAPTER 24

APPLICATIONS OF EVOLUTION ALGORITHMS TO THE SYNTHESIS OF SINGLE/DUAL-RAIL MIXED PTL/STATIC LOGIC FOR LOW-POWER APPLICATIONS

Geun Rae Cho and Tom Chen

Department of Electrical and Computer Engineering
Colorado State University
Fort Collins, CO 80523
USA
E-mail: {geunc,chen}@engr.colostate.edu

We present single-rail and dual-rail mixed pass-transistor logic (PTL) synthesis method based on genetic search and compared the results with their conventional static CMOS counterparts synthesized using a commercial logic synthesis tool in terms of area, delay and power in an experimental $0.1\mu m$ and $0.13\mu m$ CMOS technologies as well as a $0.13\mu m$ floating-body partially depleted silicon-on-insulator (PDSOI) process. Our experimental results demonstrate that both single-rail and dual-rail mixed PTL circuits synthesized using the proposed mixed PTL/CMOS synthesis method outperforms their static counterparts in delay and power in bulk CMOS as well as SOI CMOS technologies.

1. Introduction

Static CMOS logic style has long been used to realize a VLSI system because of ease to use and well developed synthesis methods. With power being increasingly a limiting factor in high density and high-performance VLSI designs, a great deal of effort has been made to explore low-power design options without sacrificing performance.

At the circuit level, mixing PTL with static CMOS has been proposed[1,2,3,4] as an alternative low-power circuit style. Designing mixed PTL circuits for low-power and high-performance depends on two tasks: selection of PTL cells and a synthesis technique to produce a mixed PTL structure. The choice of PTL cells directly impacts the Boolean matching process in the synthesis phase and has a significant impact on the overall quality of the final synthesized results. In [2,3], nMOS-only and pMOS-only pass transistor trees are used in PTL cells to reduce cell size. The full rail-to-rail swing of the output signal is restored by the extra level restoring circuit at the output of a PTL gate. The existence of level-restoring circuit at the output of PTL gates not only slows down the PTL gates due to potential drive-fights, but also increases their power consumption. A greedy search algorithm was proposed in [2] to determine the best mappings for PTL cells and static cells. PTL cells are only used for implementing MUX and XOR/XNOR type logic functions and static gates are used to implement all the remaining logic functions. The techniques proposed in [3] use dynamic programming to map more complex Boolean sub-functions to PTL gates. The search for optimal solutions in [3] was applied only within a sub-tree of a given circuit represented by a DAG. Sub-trees are separated by multiple fanout points in the DAG. The cell interactions between sub-trees were not considered and no attempt was made to optimize the overall circuit at the global level. In addition, their results did not specify the technology used to get the area and performance data. Similar to [3], the mixed PTL circuits in [4] were created using a local greedy search algorithm during synthesis.

We present a single-rail and dual-rail mixed PTL/Static logic synthesis method and compare the results of the synthesized single-rail and dual-rail mixed PTL circuits to those of conventional static CMOS circuits synthesized using a commercial logic synthesis tool from Synopsys in an experimental $0.1\mu m$ and a commercial $0.13\mu m$ bulk CMOS technologies. Results were also compared in a $0.13\mu m$ SOI technology. Our results demonstrate that the overall quality of the synthesized mixed PTL circuits in terms of performance, power consumption, and silicon area are better than conventional static CMOS. For example, the experimental results of single-rail and dual-rail mixed PTL/Static on ISCAS85 benchmark circuits using the proposed method in $0.1\mu m$ bulk CMOS technology are 73% and 50% better than their conventional static CMOS counterparts in power consumption with performance gain of 5% and 10%, respectively.

2. PTL Cells for Mixed PTL Circuits

Figure 1 shows the basic types of several single-rail PTL cells. The cell type in Figure 1 (a) is used in [5]. There are two other cell types proposed in [5] that are not shown here. Figure 1 (b) is used in [6], (c) is used in [2] and [3]. The cell type in Figure 1 (d) is a MUX-like structure which uses transmission gates. This type of cell is referred to as the PTL+ cell. In mixed PTL logic, the inverter in Figure 1(d) is not in actual PTL+ cells as shown in Figure 2.

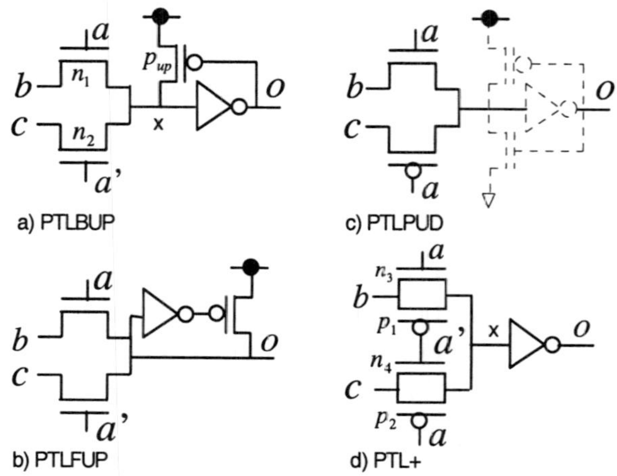

Fig. 1. Different basic single-rail PTL Cell Types

The inverter in Figure 1(d) may be replaced by other static CMOS gates when it is appropriate in the mixed PTL design environment.

In order to illustrate that the PTL+ type cells are faster and consume less power than others, each PTL cell type from Figure 1 is used to implement 1-bit mixed PTL/CMOS full adder (FA) circuit in a commercial $0.25\mu m$ CMOS process. The number of pass-transistors in series is limited to two.

The FA circuit uses the cells in [5] and PTL+ cells proposed here. The simulation results for all cell types are shown in Table 1. The PTLPUD cell used in [2] and [3] showed highest power and worst delay. Since this cell's output swing is V_{tp} to $Vdd - V_{tn}$ in the worst case, extra level restoring circuit (dashed symbols) is added at the output of the cell as shown in Figure 1. This introduces a significant amount of delay and a large amount of power consumption due to short circuit current. The PTLBUP and PTLFUP cells show very similar results in both power consumption and delay. This is due to the fact that both cell types use one pull-up pMOS and one inverter for level restoring. The area of PTLFUP, measured using the total transistor gate area, is larger than PTLBUP due to added inverter in PTLBUP.

Based on the experimental results and analysis above, we have chosen PTL+ as the basic PTL cell type for our mixed PTL circuit implementations. Figure 2 shows three basic single-rail PTL+ cell types used in our

Table 1. FA Simulation Result of PTL Cells

Cell	Power(W)	Delay(ns)	PDP(nJ)	Area(μm^2)
PTLBUP	2.829E-06	0.464	1.312E-06	4.91
PTLFUP	2.531E-06	0.441	1.116E-06	6.44
PTLPUD	2.514E-05	1.935	4.865E-05	6.88
PTL+	2.057E-06	0.371	7.367E-07	5.75

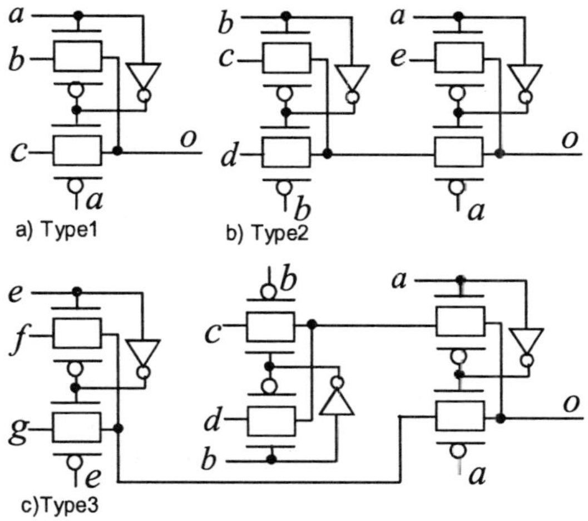

Fig. 2. Three single-rail PTL+ cell types

approach. The basic types of PTL+ type1, type2, and type3 cell consist of two, four, and six transmission gates, respectively. The area overhead of PTL+ cells can be reduced by removing nMOS or pMOS transistor in the cells. For example, pMOS p_1 or p_2 (nMOS n_3 or n_4) of Figure 1 (d) can be removed when terminal b or c *(non-control input)* is connected to Gnd (Vdd), as shown in Figure 3 (c). Similar approach can be applied to type 2 and type 3 cells. The removal of those transistors was done without loosing delay and power advantage of the cells by properly sizing the transistors during PTL+ cell generation.

Dual-rail PTL+ cell structure used in this study was chosen to be very similar to single-rail PTL+ cells based on the analysis above. The difference is that, since all gate output in dual-rail mixed PTL circuits generate a signal and the one with the opposite polarity, the dual-rail PTL+ cells do not have inverters which are used in single-rail cells to generate opposite polarity of gate control signals. Figure 3 (b) and (d) show the dual-rail PTL+ type1 cell and its a variation when the input signal b ($\overline{b}$) is connected

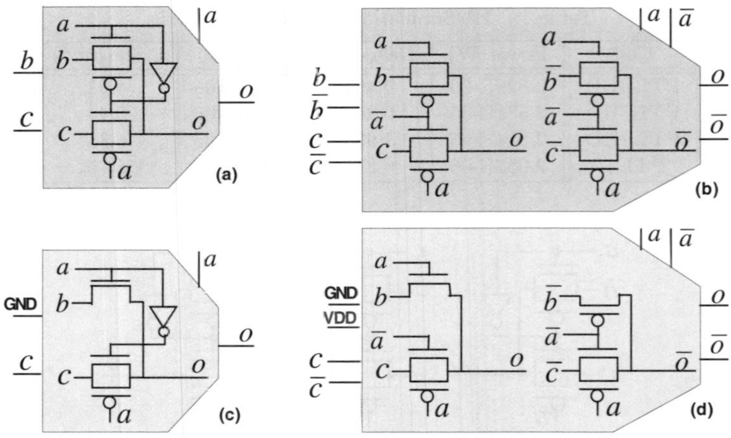

Fig. 3. Single-rail and dual-rail PTL+ Type1 cells and their variations

to *Gnd* (*Vdd*), respectively.

The SOI technology is potentially more attractive for mixed PTL circuits due to its reduced junction capacitance. Therefore, experiments were carried out using a $0.13\mu m$ partially depleted SOI technology. SOI PTL cells have the same structure as that of bulk CMOS. In addition to the fact that the delay of PTL cells in SOI are expected to switch faster than bulk CMOS due to its lower junction capacitance, the decreased threshold voltage of a floating-body SOI device due to capacitive coupling between body and device terminals, impact ionization, and junction leakage also makes SOI device faster than bulk CMOS devices. The decrease in capacitance in SOI positively impacts the power consumption.

3. Mixed PTL/Static CMOS Logic Synthesis

Figure 4 shows the top level flow of the proposed synthesis method. We begin the logic synthesis process by decomposing a given Boolean function into a graph containing only simple gates, such as 2-input NANDs, NORs and inverters. This large graph is then partitioned into subject graphs[7,8] to make the rest of the synthesis process tractable. The third step consists of matching and covering. The final step is to generate the mixed PTL circuit netlists. The synthesized mixed PTL circuit can be single-rail or dual-rail. When the synthesis mode is dual-rail, the dual-rail mixed PTL circuits were generated by replacing the single-rail PTL and static cells with corresponding dual-rail cells. There are additional steps used to manipulate

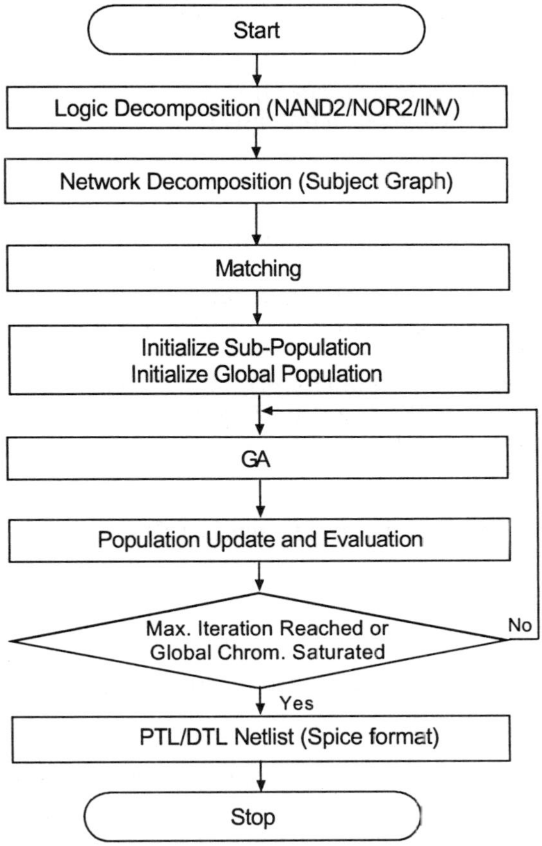

Fig. 4. Top level flow of the proposed synthesis method. PTL and DTL represent single-rail and dual-rail mixed PTL circuits, respectively

buffers at the output stage. The following two subsections describe our approach for matching and covering in detail.

3.1. *Matching*

Several matching techniques has been published in the past in the areas of graph matching[7,8] and Boolean matching[9,10,11]. The Boolean matching method is more flexible than the graph matching method, and can detect a match which may not be detected by the graph matching method. For this reason, Boolean matching is chosen. Algorithm 3.1 illustrates the matching process.

Algorithm 3.1: MATCH$(n_i, f, g, sup(f), sup(g), \mathcal{C})$

1. **if** $(|sup(f)| \neq |sup(g)|)$ **return**
2. $f_{sym} \leftarrow GetSymmSet(bdd(f), sup(f))$
3. $\{b_f, u_f\} \leftarrow GetNumBinateUnateVars(f)$

$/ * perform\ matching * /$

4. **for** $k \leftarrow 0$ **to** $N_{|sup(g)|} - 1$

$$\textbf{do} \begin{cases} \tilde{g} \leftarrow g \otimes \phi(k) & \text{(i)} \\ \{b_{\tilde{g}}, u_{\tilde{g}}\} \leftarrow GetNumBinateUnateVars(\tilde{g}) & \text{(ii)} \\ \textbf{if } (b_{\tilde{g}} \neq b_f || u_{\tilde{g}} \neq u_f)\ continue & \text{(iii)} \\ \tilde{g}_{sym} \leftarrow GetSymmSet(bdd(\tilde{g}), sup(g)) & \text{(iv)} \\ \textbf{if } (|f_{sym}| \neq |\tilde{g}_{sym}|)\ continue & \text{(v)} \\ \textbf{for each } \pi_i \in \pi(\tilde{g}_{sym}) & \\ \quad \textbf{do} \begin{cases} bdd(\tilde{g}_{\pi_i}) \leftarrow GetBdd(\tilde{g}, \pi_i) & \text{(vi)} \\ m \leftarrow BddEqCheck(bdd(f), bdd(\tilde{g}_{\pi_i})) & \text{(vii)} \\ \textbf{if } (m)\ break & \end{cases} & \\ \textbf{if } (m)\ break & \end{cases}$$

5. **if** (m)
   then $doPinAssign(n_i, f, \tilde{g}_{\pi_i}, sup(f), sup(\tilde{g}_{\pi_i}), \mathcal{C})$
6. **return**

3.2. *Covering Using Genetic Algorithms*

3.2.1. *GA Encoding*

Generally GAs use fixed-length binary strings to represent a solution. However, binary strings are not efficient to represent the mapped circuit because each node in the graph can have multiple matches. In our implementation, a hierarchical GA structure is adopted reflecting the existence of subject tree. Each solution for an entire circuit, referred to as a global chromosome, is represented by a graph structure. As the entire circuit is divided into subtrees by multiple fanout points (MFP), a sub-population is generated for each sub-tree section and GA is applied to each sub-population. When a new sub-population of chromosomes is formed a chromosome from each sub-population is then selected based on their fitness to form a new global chromosome for the new global population. Figure 5 illustrates the proposed encoding method. As shown in Figure 5(a), all the matches found in the matching stage are mapped to genes, and each gene represents a static gate match or a PTL match. Figure 5(b) shows two sub-chromosomes for each sub-graph. A sub-chromosome represents a possible mapping solution for a sub-graph, and it is formed by selecting possible matches at each node as shown in Figure 5(b). A global-chromosome is a mapping solution of the entire graph as shown in Figure 5(c). Figure 5(c) shows a mapping solution of an entire graph that is formed by selecting one of the two sub-chromosomes.

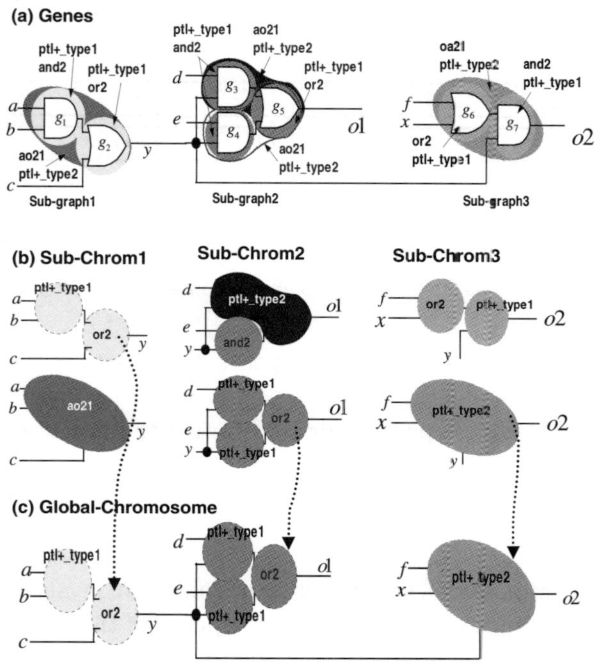

Fig. 5. Graph Encoding for GA. (a)Genes. (b)Sub-chromosomes. (c)A global-chromosome

Figure 6 shows the hierarchy of GA structure used for covering. Each sub-population contains a number of sub-chromosomes each of which represents a solution of a subject tree. In Figure 6, sub-population and global-population represent a set of sub-chromosomes and a set of global-chromosomes, respectively.

In order to avoid long pass-transistor chain during the generation of chromosomes, we applied the following rules in the covering process in order to keep a maximum of three pass-transistors in series. In order to increase the number of PTL gates we included rule number 5.

(1) PTL+ Type1, Type2 and Type3 can always drive static gate.
(2) PTL+ Type1 can drive PTL+ Type2 if the inputs of Type1 are not driven by Type2 or Type3.

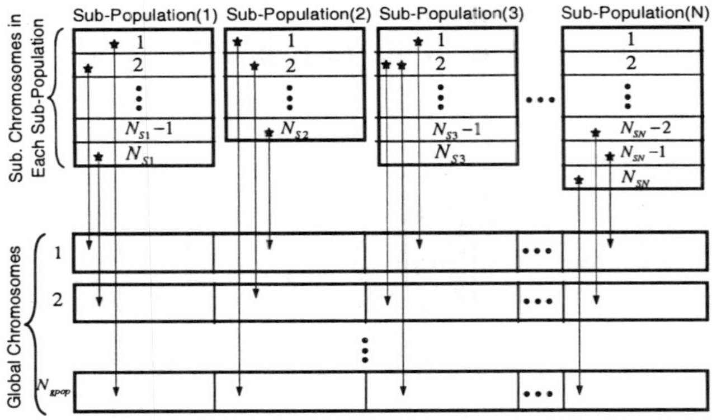

Fig. 6. The relationship between sub-chromosome and global chromosome

(3) PTL+ Type1 can drive PTL+ Type3 if the inputs of Type1 are not driven by a PTL cell.
(4) PTL+ Type2 and Type3 can drive Type1 if the inputs of Type2 and Type3 are not driven by a PTL+ cell.
(5) A static gate cannot drive any other static gate so that the usage of PTL cells can be increased.

Any global chromosome that violates the rules is an invalid chromosome, invalid global chromosomes are discarded. Update of the global population is synchronized with the population evolution in each sub-population until the design goal is achieved or the maximum number of iterations have been reached.

3.2.2. *Crossover Operation*

Figure 7 shows the concept of the crossover operation. Figures 7 (a) and (b) are the two parents, *parent*1 and *parent*2, respectively. A crossover point c^p, which is randomly selected from a parent, for each parent must be selected before the crossover operation. The crossover point must be the same in each parent; otherwise, the validity of each child after crossover cannot be guaranteed because nodes around c^p can be duplicated.

Once the crossover point is determined, the crossover operation is performed by exchanging the fanin cones rooted at c^p of *parent*1 and *parent*2, as shown in Figure 7 (c) and (d). Any invalid child chromosome according to the covering rules will be discarded. Before deciding the validity of the children, the merging (also called re-mapping) process is performed by

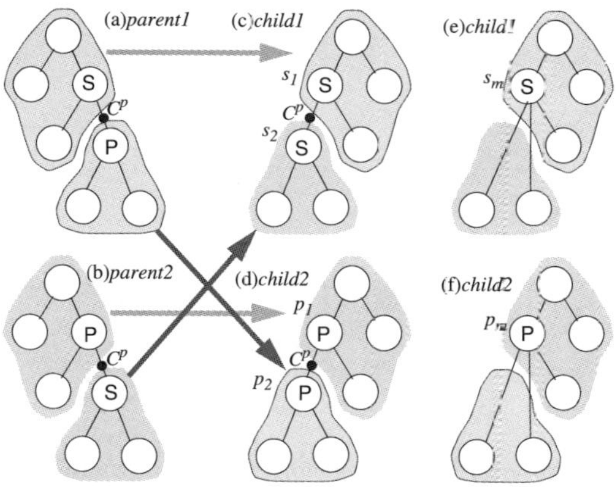

Fig. 7. Crossover operation. S and P represent static and PTL matches, respectively

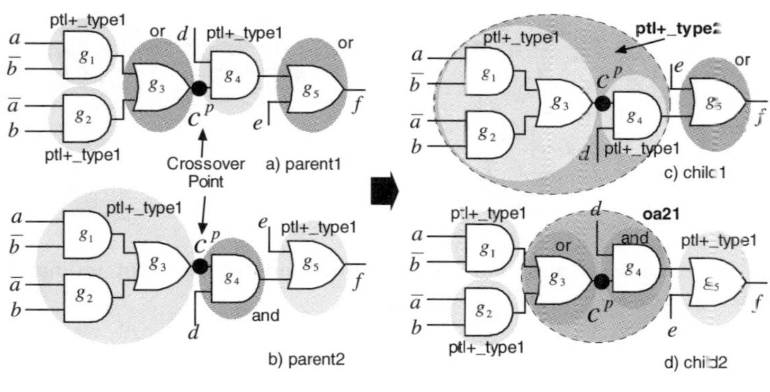

Fig. 8. An example of crossover operation. (a) and (b) are the two parents before crossover operation, respectively. (c) and (d) are the two children after crossover operation, respectively

checking the two nodes around crossover point c^p. For example, as shown in Figures 7 (c) and (d), the static (PTL) nodes s_1 (p_1) and s_2 (p_2) can be merged if matches at node s_1 (p_1) contain a static (PTL) match that covers both node s_1 (p_1) and node s_2 (p_2). Figures 7 (e) and (f) show the children after merging the nodes around the crossover point c^p (not shown in the figures). The merged nodes for static and PTL in the figure are s_m and p_m, respectively. This merge process of two different cells into one cell positively impacts power and performance because the effective area is reduced. An example of the crossover operation is shown in Figure 8. The *ptl+_type2* in Figure 8(c) and *ao21* in Figure 8(d) show examples of the re-mapping

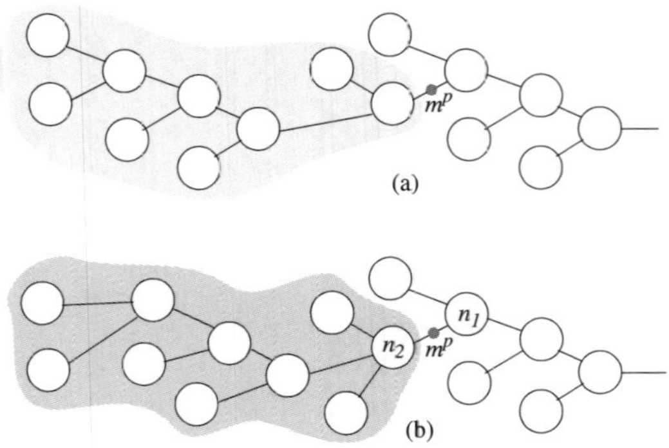

Fig. 9. Mutation Process. (a)before mutation. (b)after mutation

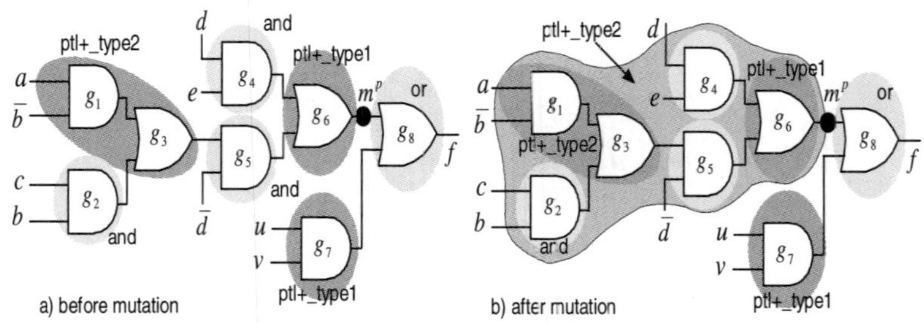

Fig. 10. An example of mutation operation. (a) and (b) represent un-mutated and mutated circuit, respectively

process.

3.2.3. *Mutation Operation*

The mutation operation is initiated when the average cost difference between the current global population and the previous global population is within a certain range, δ, which is referred to as the *mutation threshold.* The amount of mutation for a population is governed by a variable called *mutation rate*, μ. Figure 9 shows the conceptual process of the mutation, in which m^p represents the mutation point that is the root of the cone where the mutation is applied. As shown in Figures 9 (a) and (b), the cone rooted at m^p is deleted and replaced with a new cone that is a newly mapped solution from the mutation point m^p down to the leaves. An example of the mutation process is shown in Figure 10. In this example, the mutation point m^p is randomly selected from a sub-chromosome, then the mappings for the gates g_1 to g_6 are deleted first and a new mapping solution is formed for the sub-chromosome.

3.2.4. *Covering Algorithm*

Algorithm 3.2 illustrates the proposed covering process using the genetic algorithms. In the argument list of $GAMAP()$, $\mathcal{G}$ represents the set of subject trees that contain a set of possible matches found in the matching stage at every node, N_{gpop} is the size of the global population, δ is a threshold value that enables $gaMutation()$ routine, μ is the mutation rate, and I_{max} is the maximum number of allowed iterations.

Algorithm 3.2: GAMAP($\mathcal{G}, N_{gpop}, \delta, \mu, I_{max}$)

output (ζ, *mapped network*)
/ * *initialize sub_population* * /
1. **for each** $g_i \in \mathcal{G}$

$$\textbf{do} \begin{cases} \omega_i \leftarrow Generate\_Sub\_Population(g_i) \\ \Omega \leftarrow \Omega \cup \omega_i \end{cases}$$

/ * *initialize global population* * /
2. **for** $i \leftarrow 1$ **to** N_{gpop}

$$\textbf{do} \begin{cases} \zeta_i \leftarrow Get\_Global\_Chromosome(\Omega) \\ \mathcal{P}_g \leftarrow \mathcal{P}_g \cup \zeta_i \end{cases}$$

/ * *perform optimization* * /
3. **for each** $\omega_i \in \Omega$

$$\textbf{do} \begin{cases} \omega_i^t \leftarrow gaCrossover(\omega_i) & \text{(i)} \\ \textbf{if } ((cost_{avg}(\omega_i^t) - cost_{avg}(\omega_i^{t-1})) < \delta) \\ \quad \textbf{then } gaMutation(\omega_i^t, \mu) & \text{(ii)} \\ \Omega^t \leftarrow \{\Omega - \omega_i\} \cup \omega_i^t \\ \zeta_i^t \leftarrow Get\_Global\_Chromosome(\Omega^t) \\ \textbf{if } (cost(\zeta_i^t) < cost(\zeta_{max}) \textbf{ and } meets\ const.) \\ \quad \textbf{then } \mathcal{P}_g^t \leftarrow \{\mathcal{P}_g - \zeta_{max}\} \cup \zeta_i^t \end{cases}$$

4. $N_{itr} \leftarrow N_{itr} + 1$
5. *Repeat step* 3 *until* $N_{itr} \geq I_{max}$ *or* $\mathcal{P}_g^t = \mathcal{SAT}$
6. $\zeta = min(\zeta_i)$, *where* $\zeta_i \in \mathcal{P}_g^t$

4. Experimental Results

Static CMOS, single-rail, and dual-rail mixed PTL/CMOS circuits for all the ISCAS85 benchmark circuits and another benchmark circuits from a 64-bit microprocessor design were synthesized. The characteristics of ISCAS85

Table 2. Characteristics of benchmark circuits from a μp

Circuit	# Trans.	# Inputs	# Outputs	Logic Depth
Ckt 1	524	32	26	11
Ckt 2	642	82	8	8
Ckt 3	64	18	2	7
Ckt 4	60	16	2	7
Ckt 5	894	60	36	12
Ckt 6	488	35	2	11
Ckt 7	278	25	4	14
Ckt 8	156	9	2	9
Ckt 9	246	16	25	12
Ckt 10	242	20	14	9

are well known. Table 2 shows the characteristics of the benchmark circuits from the 64bit microprocessor design.

All PTL cells were created by us using a $0.1\mu m$, and a $0.13\mu m$ CMOS process, and a $0.13\mu m$ PDSOI process. Each library used in the experiments includes both Static and PTL cells with their size and style variations. For PTL cells, since the non-control inputs of PTL cells can be assigned to VDD or GND, we included the variations of PTL+ cells, which are shown in Figure 2, in the library. The number of variations that are included in the library for PTL type1 and type2 are 4 and 12, respectively. For PTL+ type 3, we didn't include the variations because the number of matches for this cell does not appear too often in real designs. PTL cells were characterized by two dimensional curve fitting based on the following equations using SPICE netlist.

$$t_d = \max_{i \in inputs} \{D_{i,int} + D_{i,load}C_L + D_{i,tran}t_{i,T}\} \tag{1}$$

$$t_t = \max_{i \in inputs} \{T_{i,int} + T_{i,load}C_L + T_{i,tran}t_{i,T}\} \tag{2}$$

where t_d the gate delay, $D_{i,int}$ is the load independent intrinsic delay, $D_{i,load}$ is the drive resistance of the gate from input i to output, C_L is the load capacitance at the gate output, $D_{i,tran}$ is the delay factor from input i to output depending on input transition time $t_{i,T}$, t_t is the gate output transition time, $T_{i,int}$ is the intrinsic transition time, $T_{i,load}$ is the load dependent output transition coefficient, and $T_{i,tran}$ is the transition coefficient affecting output transition time t_t depending on $t_{i,T}$. In case of static cells, static gates selected during the mapping process tend to be simple cells, such as INV, NAND2, NAND3, and NOR2 cells, because complex gates like OA21 can be easily implemented using PTL cells. The static cells used in this work were from a commercial cell library in all three processes. The supply voltage in our experiments was set to $1.1V$, $1.3V$, and $1.1V$ for $0.1\mu m$, $0.13\mu m$ CMOS, and a $0.13\mu m$ PDSOI technologies, respectively. We used

CUDD package[12] to build BDDs for the matching stage. In order to determine the benefits of using mixed PTL circuits, we compared our results to that of static circuits using a commercial logic synthesis tool from Synopsys in terms of delay, size, and power consumption.

4.1. *Experimental Results in a 0.1μm Bulk CMOS Process*

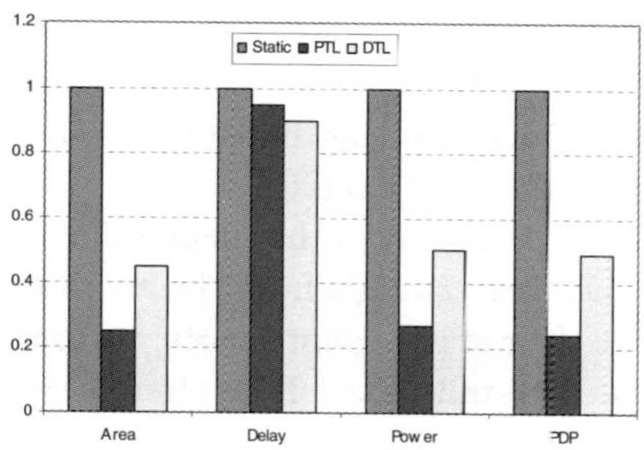

Fig. 11. Normalized area, delay, and power on ISCAS85 benchmark circuits in 0.1μm CMOS process. PTL and DTL represents single-rail and dual-rail mixed PTL, respectively

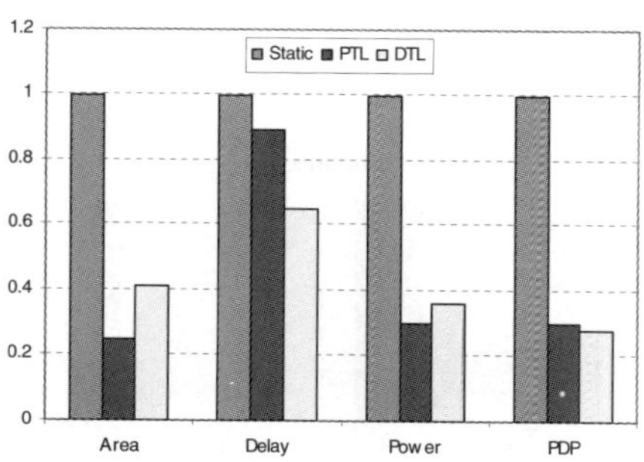

Fig. 12. Normalized area, delay, and power on the circuits from a microprocessor in 0.1μm CMOS process.PTL and DTL represents single-rail and dual-rail mixed PTL, respectively

Figure 11 shows that the single-rail and dual-rail mixed PTL styles of the ISCAS85 benchmark circuits using the proposed method are 73% and 50% better than their static counterparts in power consumption with performance gain of 5% and 10%, respectively. The area and power overhead of dual-rail circuits over single-rail circuits were 82% and 84%, respectively. However, the area of single-rail and dual-rail circuits using proposed method were 75% and 55% better than that of static counterparts, respectively. This result shows that the area of dual-rail circuits are not two times that of single-rail because the inverting and non-inverting signals for control signals of both single-rail and dual-rail PTL+ cells are always needed and this inverter is included in PTL+ cells as shown in Figure 2. On the other hand, for non-control signals such as "b" and "c" in PTL+ type 1 cell in Figure 2(a), both inverting and/or non-inverting signals are needed. All gate outputs in dual-rail mixed PTL circuits generate a signal and the one with the opposite polarity. Only inverting buffers are required for high fanout buffering in the case of dual-rail circuits.

Figure 12 shows that the delay of the single-rail and the dual-rail mixed PTL styles of the benchmark circuits from the microprocessor are 11% and 35% better than that their static counterparts, respectively. Power savings of the single-rail and dual-rail mixed PTL circuits over their static counterparts were up to 70% and 64%, respectively. The power-delay-product (PDP) of single-rail and dual-rail mixed PTL circuits using the proposed synthesis method are also significantly better than that of their static counterparts.

4.2. *Experimental Results in 0.13μm Bulk CMOS and SOI Technologies*

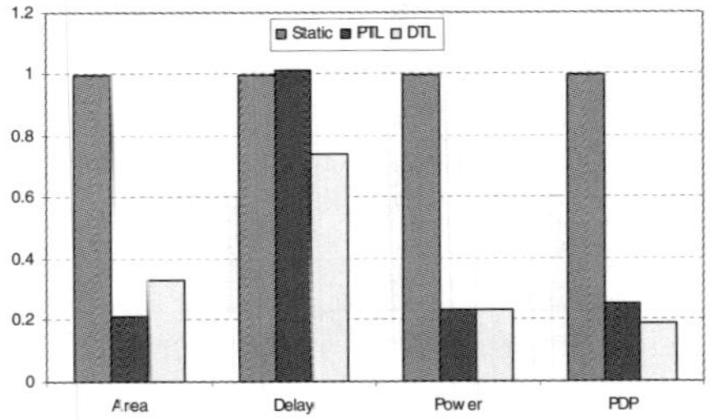

Fig. 13. Normalized area, delay, and power of the benchmark circuits from a microprocessor in 0.13μm bulk CMOS process. PTL and DTL represents single-rail and dual-rail mixed PTL, respectively

Figures 13 and 14 show the normalized area, delay, and power consumption of the benchmark circuits from the microprocessor in the bulk CMOS and SOI processes. Figure 15 shows the normalized area, delay, and power

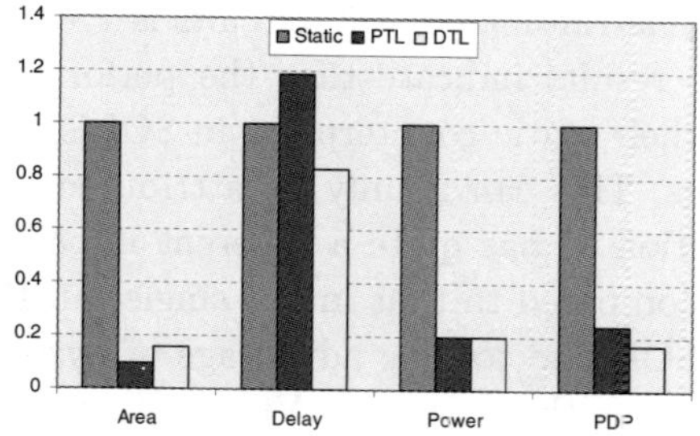

Fig. 14. Normalized area, delay, and power of the benchmark circuits from a microprocessor in $0.13\mu m$ SOI process. PTL and DTL represents single-rail and dual-rail mixed PTL, respectively

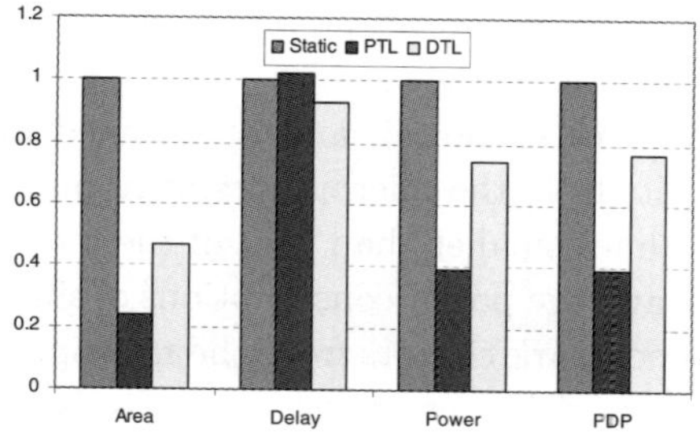

Fig. 15. Normalized area, delay, and power of ISCAS85 benchmark circuits in $0.13\mu m$ SOI process. PTL and DTL represents single-rail and dual-rail mixed PTL, respectively

consumption of ISCAS85 circuits in the $0.13\mu m$ PDSOI process. The delay and power measures of the benchmark circuits from the microprocessor were obtained using SPICE circuit simulators that use BSIM3 and BSIM3SOI model for the bulk CMOS and PDSOI processes, respectively. The delay and power measures of ISCAS85 circuits were obtained using *PathMill* and *PowrMill*, respectively.

Figure 13 shows that the average delay of single-rail mixed PTL/Static circuits on the benchmark circuits using the proposed method in bulk CMOS is slightly higher (1%) than that of their static counterparts. Figure 14 shows that the average delay of single-rail mixed PTL/Static circuits on the benchmark circuits using the proposed method in partially depleted SOI is 19% higher than that of their static counterparts. However, the average delay of dual-rail in both bulk CMOS and partially depleted SOI technologies are 26% and 17% better than their static counterparts, respectively. As shown in Figure 15, the average delay of single-rail mixed PTL on ISCAS85 circuits is also higher (2%) than that of static circuits while the delay of dual-rail mixed PTL circuits is 7% better than its static counterpart. These results indicate that the performance gain of mixed PTL circuits over their static counterparts in SOI is less than that of the bulk CMOS process. This can mainly be attributed to the fact that the hysteretic Vt variation [13] has quite a different impact on delay in static CMOS circuits as compared to that in the single-rail PTL circuits. Static CMOS circuits in SOI tend to take advantage of hysteretic lower Vt during transitions, whereas the hysteretic Vt variation brings less advantage in PTL circuits because PTL circuits involve both gate and source/drain transitions as input transitions. Therefore, the delay of static circuits in SOI improves more dramatically than that of the single-rail PTL circuits over their bulk CMOS counterparts. For the dual-rail PTL circuits, their relative slow-down due to hysteretic Vt variation does not totally wipe out the overall performance advantage.

The average power of single-rail and dual-mixed mixed PTL style of the benchmark circuits from the microprocessor in bulk CMOS process are approximately four times smaller than that of their static counterparts. In the SOI process, the average power consumptions of single-rail and dual-rail circuits using the benchmark circuits from the microprocessor are 80% and 79% better than their static counterparts, respectively. For ISCAS85 benchmark circuits, the average power consumptions of single-rail and dual-rail circuits are 61% and 26% better than their static counterparts, respectively. In bulk CMOS, the average areas of single-rail and dual-rail mixed PTL style of the benchmark circuits from the microprocessor using proposed method were 79% and 67% better than that of static counterparts, respectively. In SOI, the average areas of single-rail and dual-rail mixed PTL style of ISCAS85 circuits are 76% and 53% better than their static counterparts, respectively. The average areas of single-rail and dual-rail mixed PTL style of the benchmark circuits from the microprocessor were nine and five times smaller than that of their static counterparts, respectively.

4.3. *Parameter Evaluation and Convergence*

Parameters used in GA such as population size, mutation rate, and mutation threshold can affect the performance of the optimization algorithm and the quality of the final results. Figure 16 shows the number of iterations to converge for C499 in the ISCAS85 benchmark with respect to mutation rate (u) and percent threshold value that triggers mutation (δ). The maximum number of iterations to converge is relatively flat. Never-

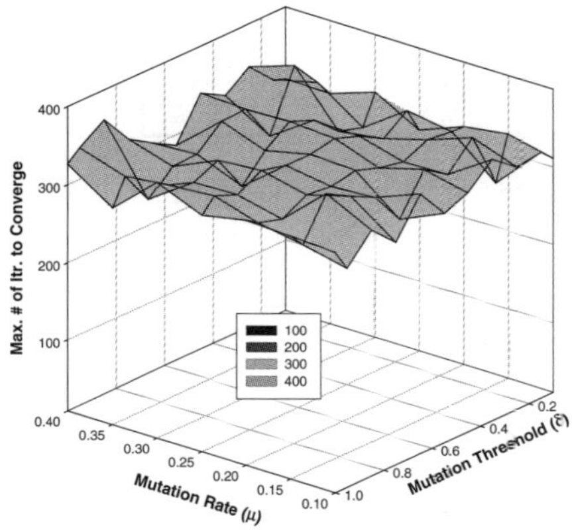

Fig. 16. Number of iterations to converge (C499). $N_{subpop} = 25$, $N_{gpop} = 15$

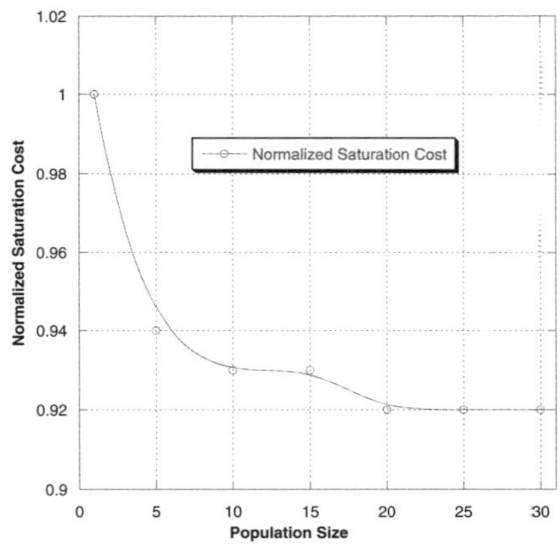

Fig. 17. Normalized convergence value with respect to sub-population size (C499, $\delta = 0.85\%$, $\mu = 0.35$, $N_{gpop} = 15$)

theless, when $\delta = 0.85\%$ and $\mu = 0.35$, the required number of iterations is the smallest compared to other μ and δ settings. The final converged cost as a function of maximum sub-population size is shown in Figure 17. The results shows that the saturation cost (i.e., quality of the solution) highly depends on the maximum sub-population size and the convergence performance is relatively insensitive to the choice of the mutation rate and mutation threshold. Based on the experimental results and the above observations, we have chosen the GA parameters of global population size, sub-population size, mutation rate, and mutation threshold to be 15, 25,

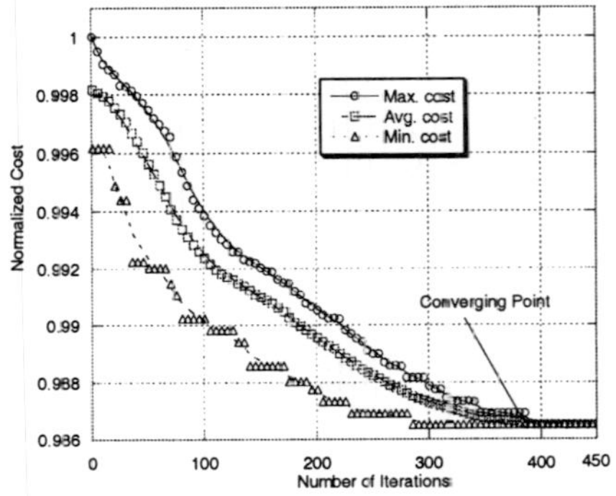

Fig. 18. Convergence result of the proposed method for C6288

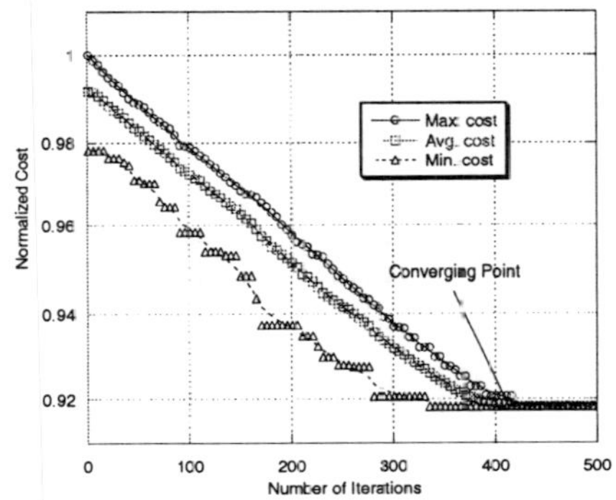

Fig. 19. Convergence result of the proposed method for C1355

0.35, and 0.85%, respectively.

Our experimental results also show that the GA-based mapping algorithm converges well. Most of the circuits obtained significant amount of improvement on cost with only less than 500 iterations and the average cost improvements were 10.6%. Figure 18 shows the normalized cost convergence pattern for C6288 which is one of the largest ISCAS85 benchmark circuits. The normalized convergence pattern for C1355 is shown in Figure 19.

5. Conclusions

We presented a single-rail and dual-rail mixed PTL/CMOS synthesis method using evolutionary algorithms and compared the results of single-rail and dual-rail circuits using the proposed synthesis method with their conventional static CMOS counterparts in $0.1\mu m$ and $0.13\mu m$ bulk CMOS and 0.13μm SOI technologies. The results illustrate the advantage of using evolutionary algorithms to obtain globally optimized mapping to achieve low-power and high density integrated circuits. We also show that the convergence of the proposed algorithm is well behaved with an average of 10.6% gain of overall cost during GA based optimization.

References

1. S. Yamashita, K. Yano, and et. al, "Pass-Transistor/CMOS Collaborated Logic: The Best of Both Worlds," in *Symposium on VLSI Circuits Digest of Technical Papers*, pp. 31–32, 1997.
2. C. Yang and M. Ciesielski, "Synthesis For Mixed CMOS/PTL Logic : Preliminary Results," in *International Workshop on Logic Synthesis*, (Lake Tahoe, CA), 1999.
3. Y. Jiang, S. S. Sapatneker, and C. Bamji, "Technology Mapping for High Performance Static CMOS and Pass Transistor Logic Designs," *IEEE Trans. on Very Large Scale Intergration (VLSI) Systems*, vol. 9, pp. 577–589, Oct. 2001.
4. G. R. Cho and T. Chen, "On Mixed PTL/Static Logic for Low-Power and High-Speed Circuits," *VLSI Design : An International Journal of Custom-Chip Design, Simulation, and Testing*, vol. 12, no. 3, pp. 399–406, 2001.
5. K. Yano, Y. Sasaki, K. Rikino, , and K. Seki, "Top-Down Pass-Transistor Logic Design," *IEEE Journal of Solid-State Circuits*, vol. 31, pp. 792–803, June 1996.
6. M. Munteanu, P. A. Ivey, L. Seed, M. Psilogeorgopoulos, N. Powell, and I. Bogdan, "Single Ended Pass-Transistor Logic," *in VLSI: Systems on a Chip(Kluwer Academic Publisher)*, pp. 206–217, 1999.
7. R. L. Rudell, *Logic Synthesis for VLSI Design*. Ph.D. dissertation, University of California, Berkeley, CA 94720, 1989.
8. G. D. Micheli, *Synthesis and Optimization of Digital Circuits*. McGraw-Hill, Inc., 1994.
9. F. Mailhot and G. D. Micheli, "Sequential circuit design using synthesis and optimization," in *The proceedings of the European Desing Automation Conference*, 1990.
10. F. Mailhot and G. D. Micheli, "Algorithms for Technology Mapping Based on Binary Decision Diagrams and Boolean Operations," *IEEE Trans. on Computer-Aided Design of Integrated Circuit and Systems*, vol. 12, pp. 599–620, May 1993.
11. L. Benni and G. D. Micheli, "A Survey of Boolean Matching Techniques for Library Binding," *ACM Transactions on Design Automation of Electronics Systems*, vol. 2, pp. 193–226, July 1997.
12. F. Somenzi, *CUDD:CU Decision Diagram Package (Release 2.1.3)*. Dept. of ECE, University of Colorado at Boulder, Aug. 1997.
13. C. Chuang and et. al., "Design Considerations of Scaled Sub-0.1μm PD/SOI CMOS Circuits," *Proc. of ISQED*, pp. 153–158, March 2003.

CHAPTER 25

EVOLUTIONARY MULTI–OBJECTIVE ROBOTICS: EVOLVING A PHYSICALLY SIMULATED QUADRUPED USING THE PDE ALGORITHM

Jason Teo[1] and Hussein A. Abbass[2]

[1] *Artificial Intelligence Research Group,*
School of Engineering and Information Technology,
Universiti Malaysia Sabah, Locked Bag No. 2073,
88999 Kota Kinabalu, Sabah, Malaysia.

[2] *ALAR: Artificial Life and Adaptive Robotics Lab.,*
School of Information Technology and Electrical Engineering,
University of New South Wales, Australian Defence Force Academy,
Canberra, ACT 2600, Australia.

This chapter investigates the use of a multi-objective approach for evolving artificial neural networks that act as controllers for the legged locomotion of a 3-dimensional, artificial quadruped creature simulated in a physics-based environment. The Pareto-frontier Differential Evolution (PDE) algorithm is used to generate a Pareto optimal set of artificial neural networks that optimizes the conflicting objectives of maximizing locomotion behavior and minimizing neural network complexity. The evolutionary and operational dynamics of controller evolution is analyzed to provide an insight into how the best controller emerges from the artificial evolution and how it generates the emergent walking behavior in the creature. A comparison between Pareto optimal controllers showed that artificial neural networks (ANNs) with varying numbers of hidden units resulted in noticeably different locomotion behaviors. We also found that a much higher level of sensory-motor coordination was present in the best evolved controller. Finally we investigated the effects of environmental, morphological and nervous system changes on the artificial creature's behavior and found that certain changes are detrimental to the creature's locomotion capability.

1. Introduction

There has been a strong resurgence of research into the evolution of morphology and controller of physically simulated creatures. The pioneering work of Sims[1] has not been parallelled until very recently. Further work in this area was limited by the complexity of programming a realistic physics-based environment and the steep computational resources required to run the artificial evolution. These physically realistic simulations of evolving artificial minds and bodies have become more accessible to the wider research community as a result of the recent convergence in the maturation of physics-based simulation packages and increase of raw computing power of personal computers.[2]

Research in this area generally falls into two categories (1) the evolution of controllers for creatures with fixed[3,4,5] or parameterized morphologies[6,7,8], and (2) the evolution of both the creatures' morphologies and controllers simultaneously.[9,10,11] Some work has also been carried out in evolving morphology alone[12] and evolving morphology with a fixed controller.[13] Related work using mobile robots have also shown promising results in robustness and the ability to cope with changing environments by evolving plastic individuals that are able to adapt both through evolution and lifetime learning.[14,15] However, the artificial evolution conducted in these experiments focused on a single objective, for example walking, swimming, light-following, block pushing or obstacle avoidance.

An evolutionary multi-objective optimization (EMO) approach has been previously used in a robotics design problem although the experiment involved only a non-autonomous subject in the form of an attached robotic manipulator arm.[16] EMO has also been used for the design of autonomous robots[17] although the focus was for optimizing the physical configurations of modular robotic components rather than for the generation of autonomous robotic controllers. The use of EMO has also been reported for solving navigational problems in simulated 2D mobile agents.[18,19] In our other related work, we have compared a self-adaptive EMO algorithm against more conventional evolutionary approaches for evolving legged locomotion.[20]

Life, as we all know too well, seldom allows us to survive by solely focusing on a single-objective alone. Rather, it presents us with myriad of choices and often forces us to choose between conflicting goals that in one way or another affects our chances for survival. As such, we believe that the introduction of multi-objectivity for the evolution of embodied artificial creatures will allow for this important aspect of biological life to be captured and modelled naturally as part of the evolutionary process in artificial life systems. In this chapter, we investigate the use of a multi-objective approach in evolving controllers for a fixed morphology artificial creature. By generating a Pareto-frontier consisting of multiple ANNs with differing locomotion capabilities and varying architecture complexities, a comparison of controller size against behavior fitness can be made. A further advantage of using a multi-objective approach for artificial evolution is that genetic diversity is maintained naturally during the course of the evolutionary process. A common problem with evolutionary optimization algorithms is premature convergence due to loss of genetic diversity which also occurs in the artificial evolution of virtual creatures.[10] An evolutionary multi-objective algorithm promotes reproductive diversity by allowing the evolutionary process to optimize along distinct goals.

This research will hopefully provide insights into the architectural complexity of controllers required for generating walking behaviors in 3D, physically simulated creatures. In addition, it provides a new paradigm for evolving controllers as a set of Pareto optimal ANNs that can be generated in a single run. This allows the user to choose from a variety of controllers with varying architectural complexities and behavioral competencies to suit the eventual simulation environment, constraints and purposes. The artificial evolutionary system proceeds along two separate goals: to (1) maximize horizontal locomotion and, (2) minimize the complexity of the controller. In the current study, controller complexity is measured using the number of hidden nodes that are used in the ANN. In future work, we intend to define more rigorous measures of controller complexity by taking into consideration other ANN architectural features such as number of connection weights as well as number of nodes in the input and output layers.

2. Methods

2.1. *Evolving Artificial Neural Networks*

Traditional learning algorithms for ANNs such as *backpropagation* (BP) usually suffer from the inability to escape from local minima due to their use of gradient information. Evolutionary approaches have been proposed as an alternative method for training ANNs. A thorough review of EANNs can be found in [21]. Abbass et. al. first introduced the Pareto-frontier Differential Evolution (PDE) algorithm, an adaptation of the *Differential Evolution* algorithm introduced by Storn and Price[22] for continuous optimization problems, for multi-objective problems.[23] The MPANN algorithm[24] combines PDE with local search for evolving ANNs and was found to possess better generalization whilst incurring a much lower computational cost.[25] In this chapter, PDE is used to simultaneously evolve the weights and architecture of the ANN.

2.2. *Representation*

Similar to [24,25], our chromosome is a class that contains one matrix Ω of real numbers representing the weights of the artificial neural network and one vector ρ of binary numbers (one value for each hidden unit) to indicate if a hidden unit exists in the network or not; that is, it works as a switch to turn a hidden unit on or off. The sum of all values in this vector represents the actual number of hidden units in a network. This representation allows simultaneous training of the weights in the network and selecting a subset of hidden units. The morphogenesis of the chromosome into the ANN is depicted in Figure 1.

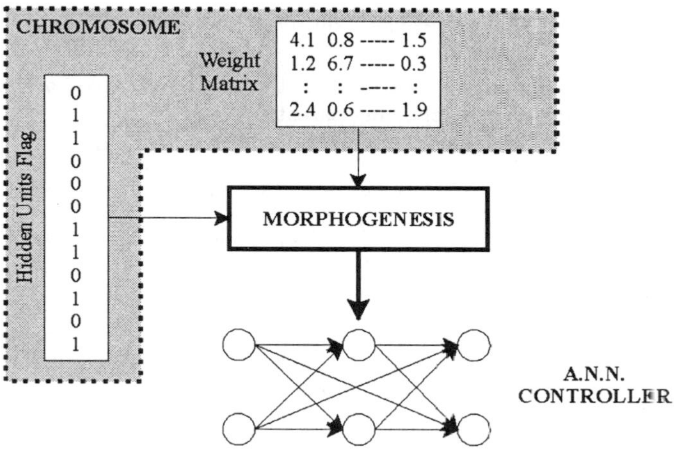

Fig. 1. The representation used for the chromosome.

2.3. *The PDE Algorithm*

We have a multi-objective problem with two objectives in this study, to: (1) maximize the horizontal distance travelled by the creature from its initial starting position, and (2) minimize the number of hidden units. The Pareto-frontier of the tradeoff between the two objectives will have a set of networks with different number of hidden units and different locomotion behaviors. An entire set of controllers is generated in each evolutionary run without requiring any further modification of parameters by the user. The PDE algorithm for evolving ANNs consists of the following steps:

(1) Create a random initial population of potential solutions. The elements of the weight matrix Ω are assigned random values according to a Gaussian distribution $N(0,1)$. The elements of the binary vector ρ are assigned the value 1 with probability 0.5 based on a randomly generated number according to a uniform distribution between $[0,1]$; otherwise 0.

(2) Repeat

(a) Evaluate the individuals in the population and label those who are non-dominated.

(b) If the number of non-dominated individuals is less than 3 repeat the following until the number of non-dominated individuals is greater than or equal to 3:

i. Find a non-dominated solution among those who are not labelled.
ii. Label the solution as non-dominated.

(c) Delete all dominated solutions from the population.

(d) Repeat

i. Select at random an individual as the main parent α_1, and two individuals, α_2, α_3 as supporting parents.

ii. **Crossover:** with some probability *Uniform* (0,1), do

$$\omega_{ih}^{child} \leftarrow \omega_{ih}^{\alpha_1} + N(0,1)(\omega_{ih}^{\alpha_2} - \omega_{ih}^{\alpha_3}) \tag{1}$$

$$\rho_h^{child} \leftarrow \begin{cases} 1 \; if(\rho_h^{\alpha_1} + N(0,1)(\rho_h^{\alpha_2} \\ \quad -\rho_h^{\alpha_3})) \geq 0.5 \\ 0 \; otherwise \end{cases} \tag{2}$$

otherwise

$$\omega_{ih}^{child} \leftarrow \omega_{ih}^{\alpha_1} \tag{3}$$

$$\rho_h^{child} \leftarrow \rho_h^{\alpha_1} \tag{4}$$

and with some probability $Uniform(0,1)$, do

$$\omega_{ho}^{child} \leftarrow \omega_{ho}^{\alpha_1} + N(0,1)(\omega_{ho}^{\alpha_2} - \omega_{ho}^{\alpha_3}) \tag{5}$$

otherwise

$$\omega_{ho}^{child} \leftarrow \omega_{ho}^{\alpha_1} \tag{6}$$

where each weight in the main parent is perturbed by adding to it a ratio, $F \in N(0,1)$, of the difference between the two values of this variable in the two supporting parents. At least one variable must be changed.

iii. **Mutation:** with some probability *Uniform* (0,1), do

$$\omega_{ih}^{child} \leftarrow \omega_{ih}^{child} + N(0, mutation\_rate) \tag{7}$$

$$\omega_{ho}^{child} \leftarrow \omega_{ho}^{child} + N(0, mutation\_rate) \tag{8}$$

$$\rho_h^{child} \leftarrow \begin{cases} 1 \; if \rho_h^{child} = 0 \\ 0 \; otherwise \end{cases} \tag{9}$$

(e) Until the population size is M

(3) Until maximum number of generations is reached.

2.4. *The Simulation Model*

The simulation is carried out in a physically realistic environment which allows for rich dynamical interactions to occur between the creature and its environment. This in turn enables complex walking behaviors to emerge as the creature evolves the use of its sensors to control the actuators in its limbs through dynamical interactions with the environment.[2] In a dynamic environment, physical properties such as forces, torques, inertia, friction, restitution and damping need to be incorporated into the artificial evolutionary system. The Vortex physics engine[26] was employed to generate the physically realistic artificial creature, shown in Figure 2, and its environment.

Fig. 2. Screen capture of quadruped in the simulation environment.

The artificial creature (Figure 2) is a basic quadruped with 4 short legs. Each leg consists of an upper limb connected to a lower limb via a hinge (one degree-of-freedom) joint and is in turn connected to the torso via another hinge joint. It has 8 joint angle sensors ($x_1 - x_8$) corresponding to each of the hinge joints, 4 touch sensors ($x_9 - x_{12}$) corresponding to each of the 4 lower limbs of each leg, and 8 actuators ($y_1 - y_8$) representing the motors that control each of the 8 articulated joints of the creature. The mass of the torso is 1kg and each of the limbs is 0.5kg. The torso has dimensions of

4 x 1 x 4m and each of the limbs has dimensions of 1 x 1 x 1m. The hinge joints are allowed to rotate between -1.57 to 0 radians for limbs that move counter-clockwise and 0 to 1.57 radians for limbs that move clockwise from their original starting positions. Each of the hinge joints are actuated by a motor that generates a torque producing rotation of the connected body parts about that hinge joint.

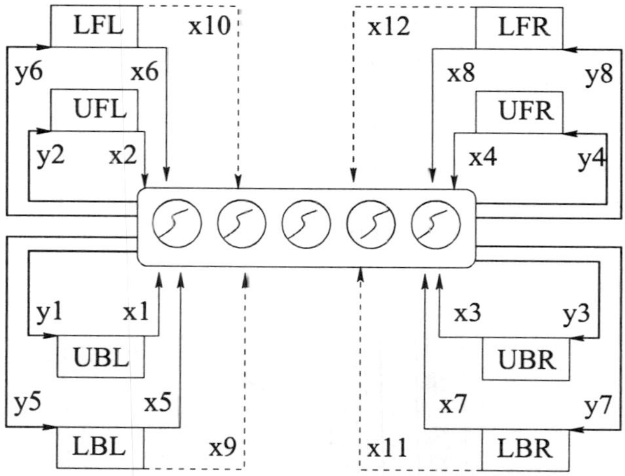

Fig. 3. The quadruped's central nervous system. The three letter abbreviations identify each of the 8 different limbs. The first letter denotes (**U**)pper or (**L**)ower, the second denotes to (**F**)ront or (**B**)ack, and the third denotes (**R**)ight or (**L**)eft.

3. Experiments

3.1. *Experimental Setup*

A total of 480 evolutionary runs were conducted with varying population sizes, crossover rates, and mutation rates while fixing the fitness evaluation window to 500 timesteps. The crossover rate used were 0, 0.1, 0.2, 0.5 and 1 and the mutation rates used were also 0, 0.1, 0.2, 0.5 and 1 (the evolutionary setup with a crossover rate of 0 and a mutation rate of 0 was omitted since this setup does not generate any variability at all in the population). The maximum number of hidden units permitted in evolving the artificial neural network was fixed at 15 nodes. Each experimental setup was repeated using 10 different seeds to allow the artificial evolution to commence from different starting points in the search space. Two populations with 20 and

30 individuals were evolved for 30 and 20 generations respectively. The total number of objective evaluations was kept constant at 600 to enable a fair comparison between the effect of the two population sizes.

3.2. *Results and Discussion*

3.2.1. *Evolutionary Parameters*

Overall, there did not appear to be any obvious differences in the range and quality of the evolved controllers between population sizes of 20 and 30. Both produced a considerably similar quality of locomotion behaviors although a larger population size did seem to produce controllers that were slightly better in terms of average locomotion fitness. There were 12 different combinations of crossover and mutation rates with a population size of 30 in which the best average locomotion fitness exceeded 2.5m as compared to only 8 with a population size of 20. Both also generated a relatively similar spread of locomotion behaviors although again a larger population size did seem to produce more varied genotypes in terms of the number of hidden units that were used in the ANN. There were 12 different combinations of crossover and mutation rates with a population size of 30 that produced 11 or more different ANN architectures compared to only 10 with a population size of 20. As such, there is a very slight advantage in using a larger population size in terms of quality and spread of the locomotion behaviors.

3.2.2. *Evolutionary Dynamics*

The best evolved controller in terms of the maximum horizontal distance moved from its initial position had a comparatively simple architecture with only 4 hidden units. This result was achieved with an evolutionary run that had similarly low crossover and mutation rates of 0.2 with a population size of 30 over 20 generations. To enable an analysis of the evolutionary dynamics that generated the best controller, the Pareto-frontier of this particular setup is reported at each generation and is depicted graphically in Figure 4.

A fairly even spread across different controller complexities ranging from 5 to 9 hidden units is observed in the 1st generation and had similarly low locomotion capabilities. By the 2nd generation, evolutionary pressure begins to minimize the controller's complexity where the range of hidden units is reduced to between 4 and 6. An increase in genetic diversity is noticed in

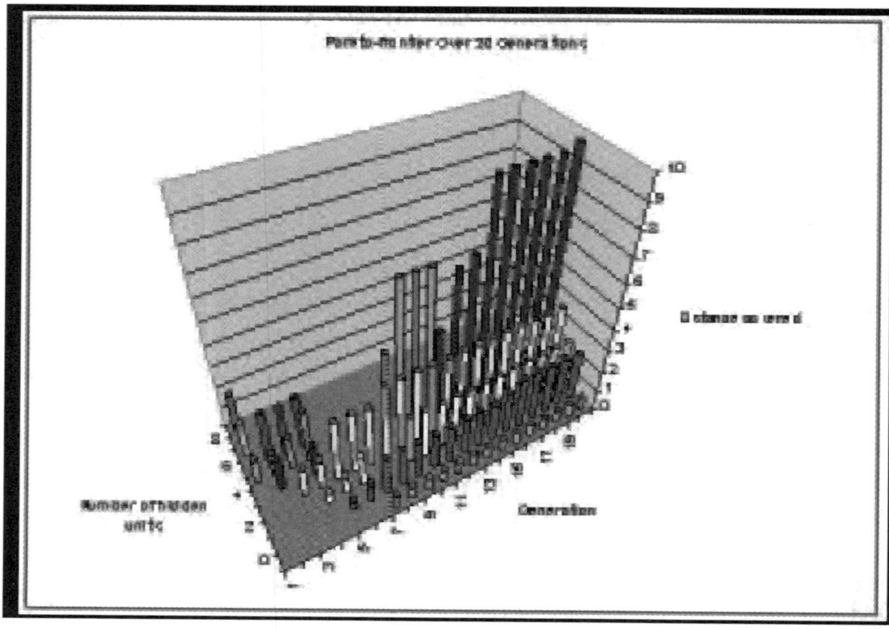

Fig. 4. Pareto-frontier over 20 generations. X-axis: Number of hidden units, Y-axis: Generation, Z-axis: Distance covered.

the 4th generation where five Pareto optimal solutions were found. A sharp increase in locomotion capability and decrease in controller complexity is observed in the 5th generation. As a result of the strong evolutionary pressure to decrease the size of the ANN, a random controller with no hidden units appears in the 7th generation but does not achieve very much in terms of movement. Again genetic diversity emerges in the ninth generation with the reappearance of genotypes with 2 and 5 hidden units from previous generations that were lost during the reproduction process. The evolutionary process jumps to a higher fitness value in the 10th generation where the optimization process begins to converge. There is no improvement in the 11th and 12th generations except for the addition of a single new genotype to the Pareto-frontier. The only significant improvement between the 13th and 15th generations is in the ANN with 4 hidden units which increases its distance travelled by approximately 2m. The last relatively small improvement comes in generation 20, where the locomotion fitness of the ANN with 4 hidden units approaches 10.

Overall, it is generally very hard for larger controllers with more hidden units to survive due to the strong evolutionary pressure of minimizing ANN complexity. As a result, larger controllers find it hard to compete with smaller controllers in trying to maximize the horizontal distance travelled by the quadruped.

3.2.3. *Operational Dynamics*

In this section, we analyze the 5 Pareto optimal controllers in operation. To conduct these analyses, the best evolved ANNs described in the previous section were used individually to control the quadruped and the simulation period was extended to 5000 timesteps. This enables analysis of not only the evolved behavior but also its behavior beyond the fitness evaluation window.

The correlation analysis of the best evolved controller with 4 hidden units has 7 strongly positive correlation coefficients (> 0.7). This indicates that the creature has evolved an ANN that has learned how to coordinate the movement of 7 sets of its limbs in order to achieve the most successful locomotion behavior among the Pareto optimal controllers. In summary, the creature achieves locomotion by coordinating the movements between:

(1) upper limbs of its back legs (0.95)
(2) upper and lower limbs of its front left leg (0.89)
(3) upper and lower limbs of its front right leg (0.71)
(4) upper limbs of its front legs (0.73)
(5) lower limbs of its front legs (0.88)
(6) opposing limbs of its front legs (0.98, 0.88)

Some of these coordinated movements are quite obvious when inspecting the movement of the quadruped visually during simulation, for example the coordination present between the front legs and between the back legs. However, some coordinated movements are less obvious visually, for example the movements of opposing limbs in the front legs. Such complex coordinations are expected in locomotion of legged creatures, which largely explains why hand-designing controllers for such creatures tends to be extremely difficult and normally results in less than desirable behaviors. The illustrations that follow in Figure 5 graphically illustrate the correlation between the 8 limbs during motion over 5000 timesteps along with the number of times each leg makes contact with the ground.

Analysis of the less successful Pareto optimal networks reveals that there is far less coordination achieved by these controllers. At most 3 strongly correlated sets of limb movements were obtained using these controllers

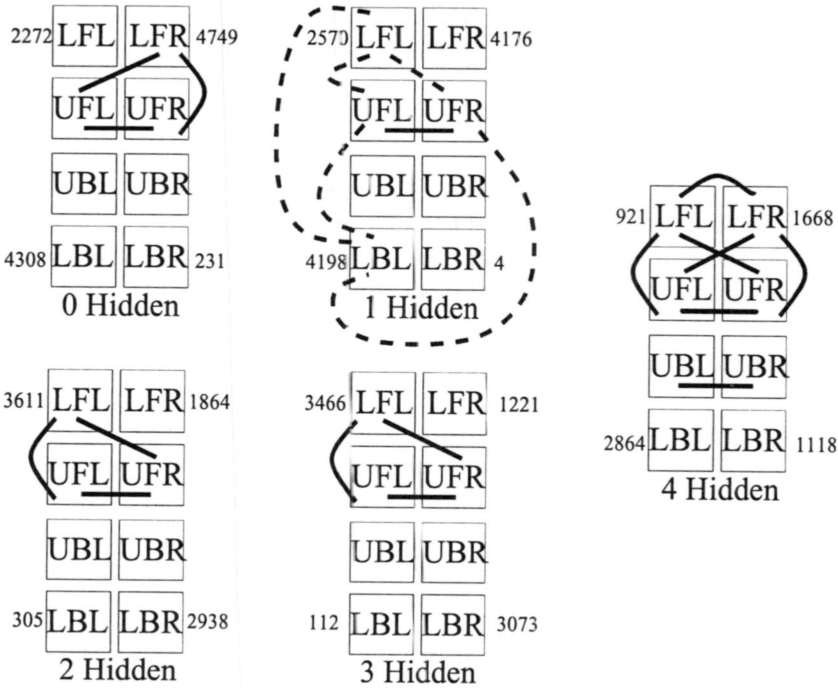

Fig. 5. Illustration of correlation between limbs for Pareto optimal controllers. The three letter abbreviations identify each of the 8 different limbs. Solid connecting lines denote highly positively correlated limbs. Dashed connecting lines denote highly negatively correlated limbs. The numbers beside each lower limb denote the number of times each leg makes contact with the ground over 5000 timesteps.

compared to 7 strongly correlated sets of limb movements using the best evolved controller. It can be seen from the graphical illustration that the best evolved controller with 4 hidden units achieved high coordination between all of the creature's front limbs as well as in one set of its back limbs. However, with all of the other less successful controllers, coordination was only achieved in some of its front limbs and no coordination was present at all in the back limbs. In these latter cases, the creature is only able to generate useful movements from its front legs with no contribution at all from its back legs which resulted in poor locomotion behavior. Furthermore, 5 strongly negative correlations (< -0.8) were detected in the controller with 1 hidden unit. These limbs are not only uncoordinated but are generating forces that act in direct opposition to each other, thereby further hindering the creature's ability to move.

Finally, we analyze the path of movement that was taken by the creature in attempting to maximize its horizontal distance covered during the extended simulation window of 5000 timesteps. Here we compared the paths of all networks on the Pareto-frontier of the last generation of controller evolution.

As can be seen from the graphs depicting the movement of the creature, the least amount of movement was achieved by the controller with no hidden units (Figure 6 top left). The creature was only able to partially stand up and hardly moved at all from its origin. Not much improvement was achieved by the controller that used 1 hidden unit (Figure 6 top right). Its behavior was almost identical to the controller with no hidden units although it did manage to move slightly further away from its origin. We start to see significantly more movement with the controller with 2 hidden units where after standing up fairly efficiently, it manages to move in a small U-shape path away from its origin (Figure 6 middle left). Using the controller with 3 hidden units, the creature again manages to stand up very efficiently and follow a fairly straight path away from the origin (Figure 6 middle right). The distance covered using this controller was slightly more than the controller with 2 hidden units. Finally the best evolved controller which used 4 hidden units showed a significantly higher locomotion capability where it very successfully carved a large U-shape path along the X and Z planes starting from its origin (Figure 6 bottom). Using this controller, the creature first stood up very quickly and moved in a reasonably straight line toward 10 m along the X plane during the first 500 timesteps, which represented the evaluation window during evolution. Beyond the evaluation window, the controller appears to veer the creature towards the Z plane and eventually turns around on its original path and heads in the reverse direction along the X plane. This shows that although the creature's controller performed well during the period where its fitness was subjected to evolutionary pressure, its long-term locomotion behavior beyond this point was noticeably different from the original intended behavior. Comparing across the controllers with different numbers of hidden units, we can also observe that controller complexity does in fact play a strong role in determining the emergent locomotion behaviors within the same creature. On one extreme, we have a controller with no hidden units that is only able to partially stand up and achieves virtually no horizontal movement to the other extreme where we have a controller with 4 hidden units that is able to not only stand up quickly but also move the creature over very large distances.

Another interesting outcome from these multi-objective evolutions is

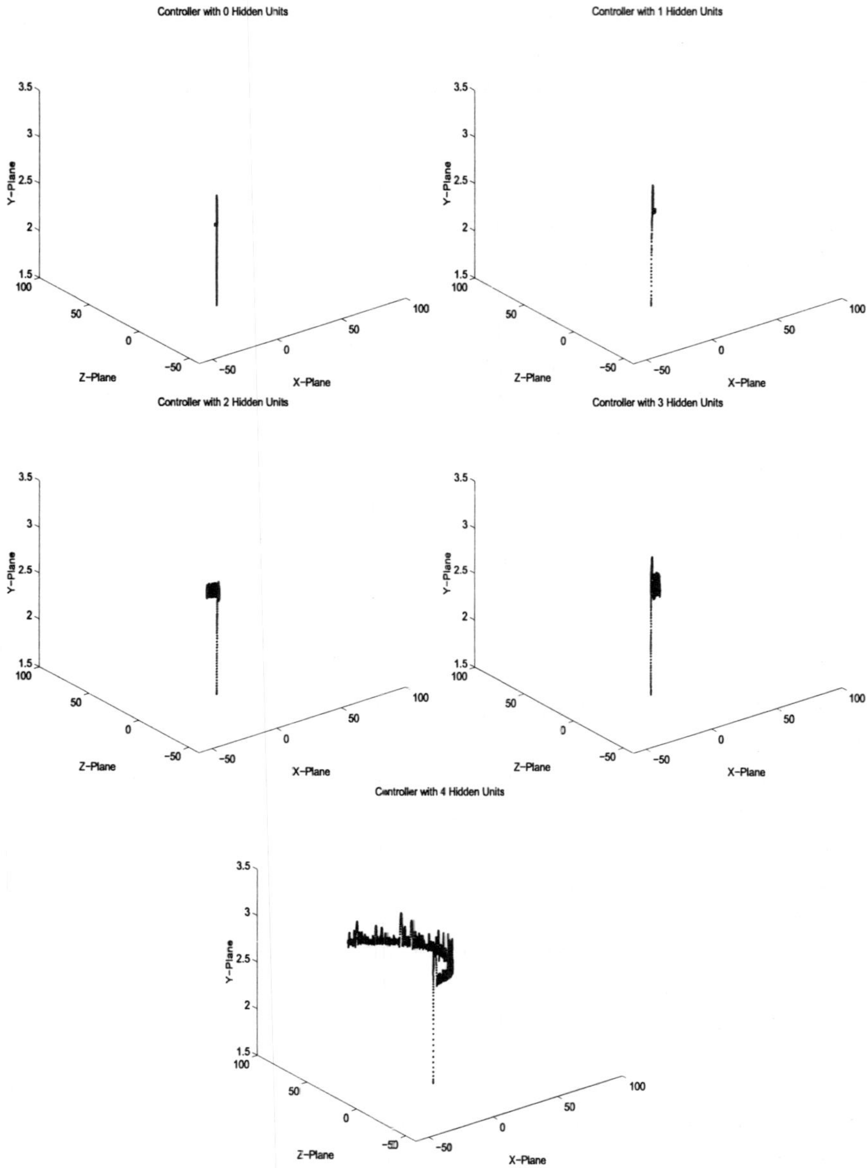

Fig. 6. Path of movement using controller with 0 hidden units (top left), 1 hidden unit (top right), 2 hidden units (middle left), 3 hidden units (middle right), and 4 hidden units (bottom). The axes denote the three spatial dimensions.

that we get a range of controllers that vary in architectural complexity and locomotion capability. On the one hand, we have a totally random ANN with no hidden nodes but is still able to move the creature away from its origin, although the movement achieved within the stipulated 500 timesteps is extremely minimal (approximately 0.5m). In this random network, there is still an act of force on the creature permitting the small initial movement but is unable to perform further locomotion due to the lack of synchronization ability. On the other hand, we have the best ANN that uses 4 hidden nodes and is able to move almost 10m within the same time period. In addition, we have a further 3 ANNs that utilize between 1 and 3 hidden nodes which again have differing locomotion capabilities. Thus, the multi-objective approach is able to provide the experimenter with a whole range of controllers within a single run that trades off between the individual optimization goals. This represents a significant advantage over single-objective evolutionary systems that need to be re-run multiple times in order to test the effect of other factors such as number of hidden units on the performance of artificial creatures.[3]

3.2.4. *Effects of Environmental Changes*

In this section, we analyze the effects of changing some of the environmental parameters of the creature's world and observe the change in its behavior. Here, the same controller, which is the best evolved ANN with 4 hidden units, is used to control the creature across all different environmental conditions. The resultant behavior is again monitored over 5000 timesteps.

Frictional Effects: First, we discuss the results obtained from changing the original frictional coefficient of 20 to lower values of 0, 5, 10 and 15. The purpose of this analysis was to investigate how the creature's ability to move would be affected by reduced amounts of grip with its locomotion surface.

The creature was not able to move horizontally at all with no ground friction. Its main movement here was mainly along the vertical direction as it attempted to stand up and repeatedly failed due to the lack of friction. With a very small friction of 5, the creature was able to move forwards although the overall distance travelled was less than in the original environment that had a significantly higher friction of 20. However, the path travelled in the environment with a friction of 5 was much straighter than in the original environment. This occurrence suggests that friction plays a larger role in making the creature turn compared to making it move forwards. From the next two environments which had increasingly higher frictions of 10 and 15, we can see that the overall trajectory of the paths begin to have more curvature as well as increasing overall distance travelled. Hence, it appears that varying locomotion surface conditions noticeably affect the creature's ability to walk both in terms of its trajectory as well as total distance travelled.

Gravitational Effects: This time we change the world's gravitational field to approximately simulate conditions of that on the moon, Mars as well as Jupiter. The purpose of this set of experiments was again to see how the creature's behavior would be affected by environmental changes as well as exploring how hypothetical robots that are built under our planet's condition may be able to also function on numerous other planets that have significantly different gravities. Such robots may be desirable because firstly building them under normal terrestrial conditions will be significantly less complex than trying to simulate extra-terrestrial conditions. Secondly, if robots were able to perform reasonably independent of gravitational changes, then only a single group of similar robots need to be designed which would be able to explore multitudes of moons and planets with different surface gravities.

The creature was still able to function under the moon's much smaller gravity (Figure 7 top left) although the overall distance travelled was less than on Earth. There was also noticeably more vertical movement during the creature's locomotion as would be expected because of the smaller gravity. Under Mars' gravity (Figure 7 top right), the creature's familiar U-shaped path becomes visible again although the overall distance travelled is again less than that achieved on Earth. The creature was significantly less successful under Jupiter's much higher gravity where after standing up, it was only able to move a small distance forward (Figure 7 bottom). From this analysis, it can be seen that the creature was still able to function under very different gravitational forces although it's locomotion was less successful than under Earth's normal gravity.

3.2.5. *Effects of Morphological Changes*

Next, we analyze the change in the creature's behavior when there is a change in its morphology. Again the best evolved controller with 4 hidden units was used to control the creature and allowed to move for 5000 timesteps. In these experiments, we doubled the mass in certain parts of the creature's morphology.

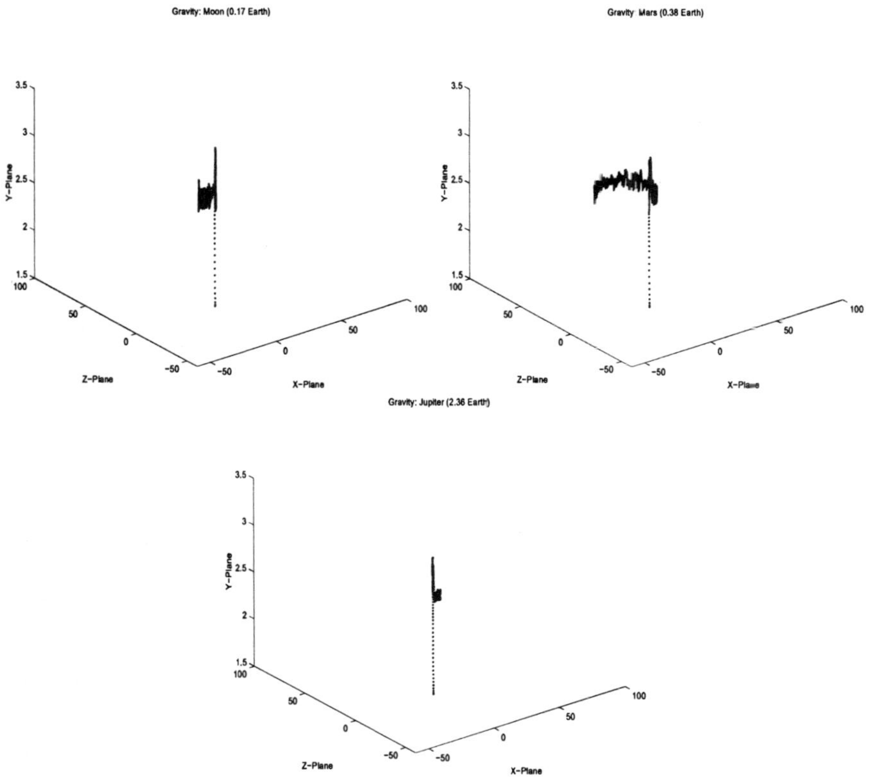

Fig. 7. Path of movement under the moon's gravity (0.17 of Earth's) (top left), Mars's gravity (0.38 of Earth's) (top right), and Jupiter's gravity (2.36 of Earth's) (bottom). The axes denote the three spatial dimensions.

Very pronounced changes were observed in the creature's locomotion behavior as a result of doubling of all of its front limbs (Figure 8 left) and all of its back limbs (Figure 8 right). The doubling of mass in its front legs resulted in a locomotion path that had a straighter heading compared to the path observed with the original uniform mass distribution. Conversely, the doubling of mass in its back legs resulted in an even more pronounced curved locomotion trajectory than the original U-shaped path, where in this case the creature almost completed a full circle back to its original starting position. These phenomena may be explained by the fact that the creature achieved its locomotion from the coordinated movement of front limbs and back limbs respectively. As such, mass redistribution affecting entire front and back sections of the creature's body can be expected to

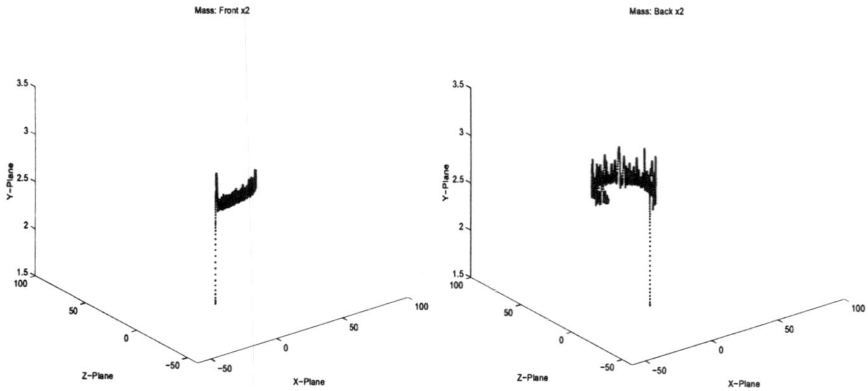

Fig. 8. Path of movement with mass doubled in front legs (left) and back legs (right). The axes denote the three spatial dimensions.

result in significant changes to its locomotion behavior. The doubling of the creature's torso mass seemed to cause the creature's movement to head more directly towards the Z axis after making its initial left turn. The effect of doubling the mass of the front left and back right legs did not appear to alter the creature's path significantly except reducing the magnitude and turning effect of its horizontal movement. The most pronounced change in the creature's overall heading was observed when the front right and back left legs were doubled in mass. This set of morphological changes appeared to have altered the nature of the creature's locomotion path from a predominantly left-turning trajectory to a right-turning trajectory. This may suggest that the contribution to overall movement from different legs are very different depending on the relative position of the legs with respect to the creature's body and direction of motion.

3.2.6. *Effects of Sensory-Motor Failure*

In this last section, we were interested in observing what would happen to the creature's locomotion behavior if some sensory-motor failure occurred in the creature's nervous system. This would be akin to partial paralysis in four-legged animals where there is loss of sense and movement in some of their limbs. Here we disabled the joint angle and touch sensor as well as the hinge motors in the creature's entire front right limbs in the first setup and the entire back left limbs in the second setup. The best evolved controller with 4 hidden units was again used to operate the original creature with uniform mass distributions over 5000 timesteps.

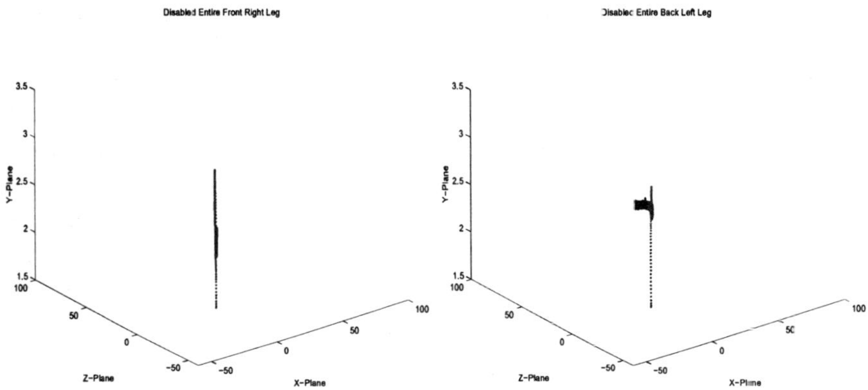

Fig. 9. Path of movement with front right leg disabled (left) and back left leg (right) disabled. The axes denote the three spatial dimensions.

Disabling the creature's front right leg seemed to have an extremely harmful effect on its locomotion behavior (Figure 9 left). It struggled simply in trying to stand up and upon visual inspection of the simulation, this was explained by the fact it could not maintain its balance. As a result, the creature could not move to perform any horizontal movement at all. On the other hand, disabling the back left leg did not seem to cause as much harm to the creature's ability to move although its overall distance travelled was still significantly less compared to the original creature which had no impairments (Figure 9 right). In fact, upon closer inspection, the distinctive U-shaped locomotion pattern could still be observed but on a smaller scale. This analysis again seems to suggest that the contribution of different legs to the overall locomotion behavior appeared to differ quite significantly depending on the position of the legs relative to the orientation of the creature's body and direction of movement. Thus disabling particular legs in certain positions resulted in dramatically different behaviors.

4. Conclusion

We have demonstrated a multi-objective approach to evolving artificial neural networks for controlling the locomotion of a 3D, physically simulated artificial creature. The Pareto-frontier that resulted from each single evolutionary run provided a set of ANNs which maximized the locomotion capabilities of the creature and at the same time minimized the size of the controller. The evolutionary dynamics for controller synthesis were analyzed to provide a high-level view of the progression of the artificial evolution. Also, correlation and path analyses of the Pareto optimal controllers in operation provided an insight into how the complex coordination between the quadruped's different limbs generated the emergent locomotion behavior. Finally, we also observed that certain environmental, morphological and nervous system changes markedly affected the creature's overall locomotion behavior and in some cases caused total failure of its horizontal locomotion capability. For future work, we intend to investigate the effects of controller complexity when both the morphology and controller are co-evolved simultaneously.

References

1. K. Sims. Evolving 3D morphology and behavior by competition. *4th International Workshop on the Synthesis and Simulation of Living Systems*, pp. 28–39. MIT Press, 1994.
2. T. Taylor and C. Massey. Recent developments in the evolution of morphologies and controllers for physically simulated creatures. *Artificial Life*, 7(1):77–87, 2001.
3. J. C. Bongard and R. Pfeifer. A method for isolating morphological effects on evolved behavior. *7th International Conference on the Simulation of Adaptive Behavior*, pp. 305–311. MIT Press, 2002.
4. A. J. Ijspeert. A 3-D biomechanical model of the salamander. *2nd International Conference on Virtual Worlds*, pp. 225–234. Springer-Verlag, 2000.
5. R. Reeve. *Generating Walking Behaviors in Legged Robots*. Unpublished PhD thesis, University of Edinburgh, Scotland, 1999.
6. W.-P. Lee, J. Hallam, and H. J. Lund. A hybrid GP/GA approach for co-evolving controllers and robot bodies to achieve fitness-specific tasks. *3rd IEEE International Conference on Evolutionary Computation*, pp. 384–389. IEEE Press, 1996.
7. H. H. Lund, J. Hallam, and W.-P. Lee. Evolving robot morphology. *4th IEEE International Conference on Evolutionary Computation*, pp. 197–202. IEEE Press, 1997.
8. C. Paul and J. C. Bongard. The road less travelled: Morphology in the optimization of biped robot locomotion. *2001 IEEE/RSJ International Conference on Intelligent Robots and Systems*, pp. 226–232. IEEE Press, 2001.
9. G. S. Hornby and J. B. Pollack. Body-brain coevolution using L-systems as a generative encoding. *2001 Genetic and Evolutionary Computation Conference*, pp. 868–875. Morgan Kaufmann, 2001.
10. M. Komosinski and A. Rotaru-Varga. Comparison of different genotype encodings for simulated three-dimensional agents. *Artificial Life*, 7(4):395–418, 2001.

11. H. Lipson and J. B. Pollack. Automatic design and manufacture of robotic lifeforms. *Nature*, 406:974–978, 2000.
12. P. Eggenberger. Evolving morphologies of simulated 3D organisms based on differential gene expression. *4th European Conference on Artificial Life*, pp. 205–213. MIT Press, 1997.
13. L. Lichtensteiger and P. Eggenberger. Evolving the morphology of a compound eye on a robot. *3rd European Workshop on Advanced Mobile Robots*, pp. 127–134. IEEE Press, 1999.
14. D. Floreano and J. Urzelai. Evolutionary robotics: The next generation. *7th International Symposium on Evolutionary Robotics*, pp. 231–266. AAI Books, 2000.
15. S. Nolfi and D. Floreano. Learning and evolution. *Autonomous Robots*, 7(1):89–113, 1999.
16. C. A. Coello Coello, A. D. Christiansen, and A. H. Aguirre. Using a new GA-based multiobjective optimization technique for the design of robot arms. *Robotica*, 16:401–414, 1998.
17. P. C. Leger. *Automated Synthesis and Optimization of Robot Configurations: An Evolutionary Approach*. Unpublished PhD thesis, Carnegie Mellon University, Pennsylvania, 1999.
18. L. Gacogne. Multiple objective optimization of fuzzy rules for obstacles avoiding by an evolution algorithm with adaptative operators. *5th International Mendel Conference on Soft Computing*, pp. 236–242, Brno, Czech Republic, 1999.
19. D.-E. Kim and J. Hallam. An evolutionary approach to quantify internal states needed for the Woods problem. *7th International Conference on the Simulation of Adaptive Behavior*, pp. 312–322. MIT Press, 2002.
20. J. Teo and H. A. Abbass. Elucidating the benefits of a self-adaptive Pareto EMO approach for evolving legged locomotion in artificial creatures. *2003 Congress on Evolutionary Computation*, pp. 755–762. IEEE Press, 2003.
21. X. Yao. Evolving artificial neural networks. *Proceedings of the IEEE*, 87(9):1426–1447, 1999.
22. R. Storn and K. Price. Differential evolution: A simple and efficient adaptive scheme for global optimization over continuous spaces. Technical Report TR-95-012, International Computer Science Institute, Berkeley, 1995.
23. H A. Abbass, R. Sarker, and C. Newton. PDE: A Pareto-frontier differential evolution approach for multi-objective optimization problems. *2001 Congress on Evolutionary Computation*, pp. 971–978. IEEE Press, 2001.
24. H. A. Abbass. A memetic Pareto evolutionary approach to artificial neural networks. *14th International Joint Conference on Artificial Intelligence (LNAI-2256)*, pp. 1–12. Springer-Verlag, 2001.
25. H. A. Abbass. An evolutionary artificial neural network approach for breast cancer diagnosis. *Artificial Intelligence in Medicine*, 25(3):265–281, 2002.
26. CM Labs. Vortex [online]. http://www.cm-labs.com [cited - 25 January 2002], 2002.

CHAPTER 26

APPLYING BAYESIAN NETWORKS IN PRACTICAL CUSTOMER SATISFACTION STUDIES

Waldemar Jaroński, Josée Bloemer, Koen Vanhoof, Geert Wets

Data Analysis and Modelling Group,
Limburgs Universitair Centrum, Gebouw D,
3590 Diepenbeek, Belgium
Email: waldemar.jaronski@luc.ac.be

This chapter presents an application of Bayesian network technology in an empirical customer satisfaction study. The findings of the study should provide insight to the importance of product/service dimensions in terms of the strength of their influence on overall (dis)satisfaction. To this end we apply a sensitivity analysis of the model's probabilistic parameters, which enables us to classify the dimensions with respect to their (non) linear and synergy effects on low and high overall satisfaction judgments. Selected results from a real-world case study are shown to demonstrate the usefulness of the approach.

1. Introduction

About fifty years ago management guru Peter Drucker defined the purpose of a business as the creation and retention of satisfied customers.[17, p. 421] These words have not been widely accepted in practice for many years, and only very recently, customer satisfaction is becoming widely recognized as a most valuable asset of all organizations.[e.g., 8]

One of the primary objectives in practical customer satisfaction studies pertains to determining product/service factors driving satisfaction and/or dissatisfaction.[17, 20, 11] The managerial results of such a study should identify priorities for improvement to focus a company's resources on. In this chapter we address this issue and apply a technique, founded on Bayesian networks, that allows for: a) identifying the derived importance of potential factors for (dis)satisfaction judgments, b) supporting marketing decisions by means of importance-performance analysis, and c) discovering interaction (synergy) effects among factors. The outputs of this analysis are of a probabilistic nature and easy to interpret for managers.

The chapter is organized as follows. In Section 2 we give an overview of customer satisfaction research with the emphasis on attribute performance analysis. Section 3 reviews the basic assumptions and principles of Bayesian network modelling. In Section 4 we present a short description of the real-world dataset and the model definition in the phone service industry context. Section 5 provides an overview of a one-way and a two-way sensitivity analysis in Bayesian networks and demonstrates how this can be applied in a customer satisfaction study. The model's empirical validation is covered in Section 6. Finally, Section 7 provides the discussion of our findings and their limitations.

2. Customer Satisfaction Research

Customer satisfaction is a concern that has received considerable attention by scholars as well as practitioners and is considered a critical and central concept in marketing thought and especially in consumer research.[25,7] As such, it is frequently addressed and examined in the marketing literature. The studies of customer satisfaction are rich in theoretical and practical findings; nevertheless, many authors agree that they are best characterized by lack of definitional and methodological standardization.[26] There is a lack of a widely accepted conceptual model of cognitive and/or affective processes that lead to customer satisfaction/dissatisfaction (CS/D). Neither is there agreement about a precise set of responses triggering those processes as well as their behavioural and attitudinal outcomes. It is generally accepted that customer satisfaction has a relation with customer loyalty and market share, although these relations have not been precisely recognized and still remain to be investigated.[21] For instance, Oliver[21] argues that customer satisfaction is a necessary step in loyalty formation but it becomes less significant when other mechanisms, such as social bonds or personal determinism come into play.

There is a plethora of satisfaction definitions in the marketing literature. Sample definitions include: "an evaluation of the perceived discrepancy between prior expectations and the actual performance of the product as perceived after its consumption,"[30] "a global evaluative judgment about product usage/consumption."[32] Oliver[18] postulated that satisfaction is "a summary psychological state resulting when the emotion surrounding disconfirmed expectations is coupled with the consumer's prior feelings about the consumption experience."

Historically, the earliest attempts to capture the phenomenon of customer satisfaction were directed at a conceptual model, which postulated a direct causal link between the performance of product/service attributes and overall state of satisfaction.[20] According to this representation, there is actually no intermediate psychological state, nor cognitive process that mediates the formation of (dis)satisfaction judgments. The approach can thus be summarized as "a black-box" model of customer satisfaction,[20] because consumer thought processes are not taken into account as a part of the phenomenon. This approach however has been questioned by most scholars, and is rather neglected in today's advanced customer satisfaction research as it is missing good theoretical groundings. Nevertheless, it still remains applied by many companies in traditional attribute performance analysis.[17, 20]

Therefore, nowadays, the primary thread of debate in the satisfaction literature is focused on the nature of the cognitive and affective processes that result in the consumer's state of mind referenced to as satisfaction. In line with this stream of research, the two dominant approaches compete whether satisfaction can be best described as an evaluation process [8,18,33] or as an outcome of an evaluation process.[30]

With regard to the view of satisfaction as an outcome of evaluation process, customer satisfaction is viewed as a state of fulfilment that is associated with reinforcement and arousal. In the "satisfaction-as-states" framework developed in [19] several types of satisfaction have been identified as a potential state, including: "satisfaction-as-pleasure", "satisfaction-as-relief", "satisfaction-as-novelty", "satisfaction-as-surprise", and "satisfaction-as-contentment". In line with this paradigm, satisfaction is defined as "a pleasurable level of consumption-related fulfilment."[20]

The second and more prevailing mainstream of research on CS/D as an evaluation process is based on the paradigm of disconfirmation.[18, 4] Its central assumption is that consumers form prior expectations (e.g., caused by commercials, advertisements, experience etc.) towards product/service performance, which later serve as standards against which actual product/service performance is evaluated. A comparison of expectations and actual perceived performance results either in confirmation or disconfirmation. In case prior expectations are exactly met, mere confirmation takes place. Otherwise, disconfirmation occurs, i.e. the perception of a discrepancy between performance and expectations. Within disconfirmation, two types, positive and negative, may be identified. Positive disconfirmation occurs when perceptions exceed expectations and negative disconfirmation occurs when expectations exceed perceptions. According to this paradigm, satisfaction is the result of positive disconfirmation and confirmation, whereas negative disconfirmation leads to dissatisfaction. Moreover, it is also believed that expectations have an indirect influence on satisfaction via disconfirmation, whereas performance can have both an indirect effect via disconfirmation, as well as direct effect on (dis)satisfaction. The application of process definitions is regarded relevant for brief service encounters as well as for services that are delivered or consumed over a certain period of time.[20,7] However, the two different types of conceptualisations may be jointly applied to a particular context enhancing thus predictive power of satisfaction as a measure related to loyalty.[27]

In this chapter we lean towards the conceptualisation as an evaluative process. According to this paradigm, customer satisfaction should be operationalized by measuring customer expectations, product/service features' performance, and degree of discrepancy between expectations and perceived performance, although some authors signal that measurement of expectations is pointless, because the whole effect of expectations is absorbed by (dis)confirmation. In practical CS/D measurement studies, it is however approved to measure satisfaction directly,[17] therefore in this chapter we assume the traditional, non-mediated model of satisfaction, allowing thus for direct links from product/service attributes' performance to (dis)satisfaction. With this end in mind, we carry out a product/service feature performance analysis by means of Bayesian network methodology that we briefly present in the next paragraph.

3. Bayesian Networks

Probabilistic modelling methods have recently gained wider acceptance and also used in marketing applications. Among these models, a special representation of directed acyclic graphs, known as Bayesian networks, has proven to be successful in modelling various systems in medicine, agriculture, and printer troubleshooting. They were popularised in artificial intelligence community by Pearl[23] in the late 1980's and advanced ever since. Recently, Bayesian network models have increasingly attracted attention and use in business and marketing research communities.[28,2,1,3] For instance in [3] the authors modelled consumer complaint processes for the explanation and prediction of consumer behaviour after experiencing dissatisfaction with a product, whereas in [2] Bayesian networks were applied in a study of organizational impact of change.

Bayesian networks are tools used to concisely represent a joint probability distribution for a certain domain, and what makes their use even more attractive is the fact that any marginal probability of interest can be efficiently provided. In Bayesian networks, random variables accounted for in a study are portrayed as nodes, and qualitative assertions of direct probabilistic dependence among variables are depicted with arrows. Each node in a network corresponds to a particular variable of interest. In discrete Bayesian networks nodes are defined as a collection of exhaustive and mutually exclusive states. Each child node holds a table of conditional probability distributions for every possible combination of parent nodes' states.

The construction of Bayesian network models follows the following guidelines.[10] The first step consists of enumerating potential variables of interest to the modeller, selecting the most relevant ones and defining them in terms of potential states they can take on. Then, the task is to capture the graphical network model of dependencies among the variables included in the model. The variables that have direct causal influence on some particular variables are called parents and the ones that are directly influenced are child nodes. Once the structure is provided, the next step in construction is quantitative parameterisation, which consists of estimation of the numerical characteristics of these local dependencies by means of conditional probabilities. The probabilities are stored in conditional probability tables, usually called CPT's, in which the entries correspond to each state of a child node and all possible combinations of states for parent nodes. The construction of the models can be based either entirely on the domain knowledge of the modeller, automatically resolved from a dataset, or can be a combination thereof.

The output of Bayesian network model is usually presented with tables containing series of prior and posterior (conditional) probabilities. In contrast, in this study we apply the procedures of sensitivity analysis to diagnose the dependencies in a way that they are represented with algebraic functions - often resembling linear regressions - which are more familiar than numbers, i.e., conditional probabilities alone. Such a representation yields easier interpretation of the numerical facet of dependencies, for example, by showing their strength, and providing a simple yet rich source for enquiry. The functional form of dependencies lends itself to be portrayed using informative charts and plots. We address the issue of construction of the charts in Section 5 on sensitivity analysis in Bayesian networks. The results of the analysis can be revealed with respect to prior probabilities as well as probabilities conditional on some specific assumptions of interest. Motivations for the use of Bayesian networks in the domain of customer satisfaction research are the following: 1) our knowledge about customer satisfaction is uncertain and not complete, 2) we assume that the domain of customer satisfaction is probabilistic in nature, 3) model's outputs, in the form of conditional probabilities, are easy to interpret for a wide audience, 4) Bayesian networks allow for optimal use of all available data, and 5), relevant efficient algorithms and software are readily available. Furthermore, customer satisfaction researchers can apply Bayesian networks for descriptive, as well as for predictive and normative modelling. Last but not least, it should be of interest to a marketing researcher that estimation of the model's parameters can be achieved either by judgment-based subjective parameterisation, or entirely based on historical data. In addition, the two types of knowledge, i.e., subjective and objective, can be also coupled to refine the model's parameters.

4. Data

The data used in this study has been collected by a marketing research agency for a telecom company operating a fixed phone line in the Netherlands for the purpose of a customer satisfaction study. Potential respondents were chosen from among the company clients and asked by phone to participate in a customer satisfaction study. Originally, 523 clients responded to the survey.

The questionnaire was aimed at collection of customer responses with respect to overall customer satisfaction, loyalty, and performance of various aspects of the service, e.g., sales force, connections, customer service, tariffs, and billing. The performance of these dimensions has been measured in terms of satisfaction on a 5-point Likert-type scale anchored with "very satisfied" and "very dissatisfied". Overall satisfaction has been measured with one item, whereas satisfaction with the respective dimensions has been captured in terms of specific service features relating to those dimensions.

First, all the responses for all the features as well as for overall satisfaction have been aggregated from five to three categories in order to facilitate interpretation and parameter learning. Levels of "very dissatisfied", "dissatisfied", and " neither satisfied nor dissatisfied" due to their low response frequency have been grouped together and assigned one value "low satisfaction". The scores of "satisfied" and "very satisfied" have obtained the meaning of moderate and high satisfaction, respectively.

Because, satisfaction scorings at a service dimension level, i.e. overall satisfaction with customer service, tariffs, and billing have not been operationalized by the questionnaire, in the next step three additional variables have been created to represent overall judgments of satisfaction with these dimensions. Satisfaction with billing service, satisfaction with tariffs and satisfaction customer service were obtained by clustering of respondents using the *k*-means algorithm. Satisfaction with tariffs was captured based on responses on customers' satisfaction with four types of telephone connection tariffs: international, national, regional, as well as tariffs on connections to mobile phones. Based on perceptions on satisfaction with reaction time, service time, and quality of assistance another variable reflecting satisfaction with customer service was derived. Responses on amount of information and clearness were used to create customer's evaluation of billing service. Each construct obtained in this step had the centers reflecting the categories of low and highly satisfied customers. From the original sample we have removed 95 cases due to having more than 50% of missing values, what resulted in the final sample of 428 cases.

In the next step of the analysis, we have constructed a small Bayesian network for the scenario under consideration consisting of four nodes. In accordance with the presupposed domain knowledge described in the previous paragraphs, we hypothesized that tariffs, billing and customer service are causes of overall phone service satisfaction. Therefore, in our model, overall satisfaction is a child node of three nodes: satisfaction with customer service, billing and tariffs. The three causes are furthermore marginally independent, but they become dependent once value of overall satisfaction is fixed. The numerical strengths of the dependencies, i.e., the conditional probabilities in the model, have been estimated based on maximum likelihood approach using EM procedure to deal with missing data.[13]

5. Sensitivity Analysis

One of the fundamental functions of Bayesian networks is to take advantage of the efficient representation scheme of the joint probability space over the modelled system and exploit it to calculate some probabilities of interest. For example, the primary use is to retrieve a probability distribution for some nodes of interest, called a target node, conditional on some set of nodes, called explaining nodes, when their values become available. Other potential use is to find the probability of some specific configuration of nodes' values. The results of such calculations can be achieved automatically by means of probabilistic inference algorithms that are typically implemented in the Bayesian network-enabled software. The user can simply enter queries to the Bayesian network by identifying target nodes, and assigning values (states) to explaining nodes. The question that often arises in this respect is how sensitive those resultant posterior probabilities are to changes in the numerical strengths of the dependencies. This is where the issue of sensitivity analysis comes into play.

On the whole, sensitivity analysis in a mathematical model pertains to investigation of the effects of the inaccuracies in the model's parameters on its output by systematic variation of the model's parameters. For a Bayesian network model in particular, sensitivity analysis can be approached twofold: empirically and theoretically.[12] The empirical approach investigates the effects of variation in the model's parameters on the model's output by entering evidence and assessing its weight with respect to the output somehow, for instance by measures like *value of information*,[23] or *weight of evidence*.[15] In this chapter we apply the theoretical approach to sensitivity analysis in Bayesian networks to acquire analytical knowledge from the model. The theoretical methods aim at expressing the model's output as an algebraic function in the model's parameters. If the model's output in focus is marginal probability $P(Y=y)$ that the random variable Y takes value y, then this approach tries to establish a function $f(x)$, such that

$$P(Y = y) = f(p)\,, \tag{1}$$

where p is a model's selected parameter.

In this context, the model's parameters denote some particular probabilities in the network – they can refer either to some particular entries in the conditional probability tables, or they can relate simply to marginal probabilities for some nodes. In this study we are mostly interested in the parameters as marginal probabilities for some explaining nodes. Therefore, the formula (1) can be rewritten as

$$P(Y = y) = f(P(X = x))\,, \tag{2}$$

where $P(X=x)$ is a probability that the explaining random variable X takes value x.

Often, a distinction is made with regard to the number of parameters taken into account. One-way sensitivity analysis pertains to varying the value of just one parameter, whereas two-way sensitivity allows for examination the strength of the influence of two parameters at a time.

It has been theoretically proven[5] that the sensitivity functions in Bayesian networks can be represented accurately with algebraic functions of a known form and unknown parameters, called in this chapter meta-parameters in order to distinguish them from the parameters-probabilities of interest.

5.1. *One-way Sensitivity Analysis*

Findings from a number of studies suggest that the relations between feature performance and overall satisfaction can often be non-linear and not straightforward. For example, in [16] the authors investigated this link and found that attribute-level performance impacts satisfaction differently based on whether consumer expectations were positively or negatively disconfirmed. In their study overall satisfaction was found to be sensitive to changes in low attribute levels, whereas at high levels of attribute performance, overall satisfaction showed diminished sensitivity. Motivated with this result we approach these links probabilistically and express probability at each level of overall satisfaction in terms of probability of satisfactory feature performance. It has been shown that in one-way sensitivity analysis, the target probability of interest can be expressed using a linear function

$$\mathrm{P}(Y = y) = a + b\,\mathrm{P}(X = x)\,, \qquad (3)$$

where $\mathrm{P}(Y = y)$ is marginal probability that variable Y takes state y, a and b are two meta-parameters, and $\mathrm{P}(X = x)$ is probability that value of variable X is x. So low, medium, and high satisfaction can each be measured with a separate function. The algebraic formulae look in this case in the following way:

$$\begin{aligned} &\mathrm{P}(Y = \text{'high'}) = a_h + b_h\,\mathrm{P}(X = \text{'high'}), \\ &\mathrm{P}(Y = \text{'medium'}) = a_m + b_m\,\mathrm{P}(X = \text{'high'}), \\ &\mathrm{P}(Y = \text{'low'}) = a_l + b_l\,\mathrm{P}(X = \text{'high'}), \end{aligned} \qquad (4)$$

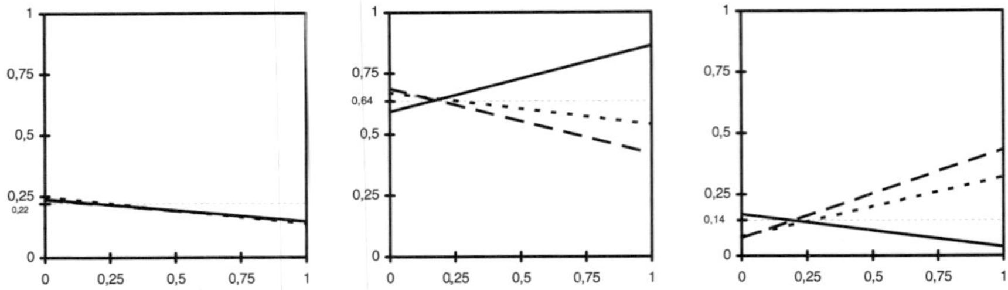

(a) (b) I

Fig. 1. Impact of service elements (dotted line – Customer Service, dashed line – Billing, solid line – Tariffs) on: a), low, b), moderate, and c), high levels of overall satisfaction, respectively. The grey lines represent prior probability of the respective level of satisfaction.

where the parameters a_l, a_m, and a_h amount to the probability of low, medium, or high satisfaction given the probability of feature satisfaction is zero. The linear coefficient b can be interpreted as a measure of how relevant, or important, the feature is with regard to satisfaction at a specific level. Of course, the higher the absolute value of the parameter for a service item, the more influential the item is with regard to (dis)satisfaction.

This can be illustrated by portraying the sensitivity functions with simple graphs as in Fig. 1. We demonstrate them as the functional forms of dependencies in the Bayesian network model in the focus. In the figure, the X-axis relates to the probability of high satisfaction with a service dimension and the Y-axis is the probability of the relevant level of overall satisfaction. These graphs confirm the findings in [16] in that they show the diverse nature of the influence of satisfaction with a feature on overall service satisfaction: low levels of satisfaction are found hardly sensitive to dissatisfactory experiences with service dimensions, whereas high overall satisfaction shows in this respect an increased dependence.

To complete the analysis of feature importance we should define a relevant feature classification scheme. There exists a number of studies suggesting various feature classification schemes. For instance, in [14] a four-ring conceptualization of a product/service is suggested as a unitary concept, according to which the most inner ring represents the generic

Table 1. Categories of service elements with respect to values of parameters b_l and b_h in sensitivity functions.

B_{low} \ b_{high}	Low	Moderate/Large
Low	Non-relevant	Exciter
Moderate/Large	Basic	Satisfier/Dissatisfier

product – a must. The next ring defines the expected product, comprising dimensions acting as satisfiers/dissatisfiers. Augmented or enhanced product surrounds the expected product attributes, and acts as delights to a customer.

Most valuable insights to a marketer are delivered however with the outermost ring that determines the potential product, i.e. the product that should contribute most to company success in the future.

In this chapter we adapt the classification of attributes from [31]. The categories that can be defined according to the value of parameter b in the functions (see formula (4)) are shown in Table 1. Whether the influence is zero, low, moderate, or large can be determined by looking at the absolute value of parameter b. We assume high feature satisfaction to have a negative (non-increasing) effect on low overall satisfaction, and a positive (non-decreasing) impact on high overall perception.

As *satisfier/dissatisfier* can be regarded a dimension that affects satisfaction in its continuum, i.e. both its high and low levels, thus driving high levels of satisfaction when performed well and enforcing dissatisfaction when their perception falls bellows expectations. Moderate or large influence on high overall satisfaction, and insignificant effect on dissatisfaction characterizes features that can be termed *exciter*. Exciters are drivers of satisfaction as well, but they do not influence dissatisfaction if their performance is low. If, in turn, high overall satisfaction is not affected by high feature perception, and if at the same time dissatisfaction is likely to intensify when this perception is low, the feature can be viewed as *basic* product dimension delivering elementary user's requirements. As the feature performance does not make any changes in perception of overall (dis)satisfaction, it can be interpreted as *non-relevant*.

We can read from the graphs in Figure 1 the boundaries between which specific levels of the overall satisfaction can vary as a result of feature performance. For instance the probability of high overall satisfaction varies from 7% to 31% as a result of bad and good customer service, respectively. Also, on the basis of the observation that both dissatisfaction (Fig.1a) and high satisfaction (Fig.1c) are sensitive to changes in customer service performance ($|b_l| = 0{,}11$, $|b_h| = 0{,}24$), we conclude that customer service can be classified as satisfier/dissatisfier. Similarly, we can classify billing also to the same category, whereas tariffs, due to their positive impact on moderate satisfaction and negative impact on high satisfaction, warrant a closer look at to arrive at a right conclusion. Nevertheless, billing quality has a larger impact on satisfaction than customer service has.

5.2. *Two-way Sensitivity Analysis*

It is likely that some potential determinants of overall satisfaction do not manifest an apparent influence when considered apart from other factors. It can however happen to be an important factor catalysing the impact of other service dimensions. Synergy effects that can be observed in this situation may be either positive or negative. Their existence can be traced by means of two- and multi-way sensitivity analysis. The two-way unconditional sensitivity function has the following form:

$$P(Z = z) = a + bx + cy + dxy\,, \tag{5}$$

where $P(Z=z)$ is the target probability of interest, x and y are probabilities that the explaining variables are true, and a, b, c, and d are meta-parameters to be calculated by performing inference in the network. The coefficients of the sensitivity functions can also be used to classify the two-way interaction. Parameter a can be interpreted as a probability of high overall satisfaction, when neither dimension is satisfactory. Parameters b and c have a similar interpretation as in one-way sensitivity functions and can be used to determine whether one service element is dominant over another. The main focus goes to the sign and size of the interaction coefficient *d*. Positive values of this parameter stand for positive synergy, whereas negative values stand for negative interaction effects. Values close to zero may indicate a lack of interaction effects between product/service dimensions. Again, the sensitivities at each level of general performance can be different for the different target values, so we have to calculate the following sensitivity functions:

$$\begin{aligned} \mathrm{P}(Z='\mathrm{low}') &= a_l + b_l\mathrm{P}(X='\mathrm{high}') + c_l\mathrm{P}(Y='\mathrm{high}') + \\ &\quad + d_l\mathrm{P}(X='\mathrm{high}')\mathrm{P}(Y='\mathrm{high}'), \\ \mathrm{P}(Z='\mathrm{mod}') &= a_m + b_m\mathrm{P}(X='\mathrm{high}') + c_m\mathrm{P}(Y='\mathrm{high}') + \\ &\quad + d_m\mathrm{P}(X='\mathrm{high}')\mathrm{P}(Y='\mathrm{high}'), \\ \mathrm{P}(Z='\mathrm{high}') &= a_h + b_h\mathrm{P}(X='\mathrm{high}') + c_h\mathrm{P}(Y='\mathrm{high}) + \\ &\quad + d_h\mathrm{P}(X='\mathrm{high}')\mathrm{P}(Y='\mathrm{high}'), \end{aligned} \tag{6}$$

where *Z* refers to overall satisfaction, *X* and *Y* stand for service dimensions. For our reference model, these sensitivity functions can also be presented graphically (see Fig.2). The graphs represent the sensitivity of high overall satisfaction judgments to variation in the perception of three service dimensions: customer service, billing quality and connection tariffs. Simultaneous variation of two probabilities resulting in the same probability of high overall satisfaction is represented by the contour lines, and the numbers attached to the lines stand for the probability level. In Fig. 2a), for instance, the probability that a customer is satisfied with the customer service is shown on the X-axis and with the billing service on the Y-axis. The upper rightmost contour line denotes that all the combinations of (high) probabilities with feature performance located on this line result in the high, as of 80%, value of probability of high overall satisfaction. The lower leftmost line corresponds to the combination of rather high probabilities of dissatisfactory experience at each dimension level. In that case the probability of high overall satisfaction amounts to 3%. The numerical properties of the sensitivity function communicate that this variation ranges from 3% up to 92%. The slope of the lines suggests further that in the low ranges of customer service performance, overall satisfaction is much less sensitive to changes in perception of billing than to customer service. However, in the higher ranges, this relation reverses, and on the whole, billing has

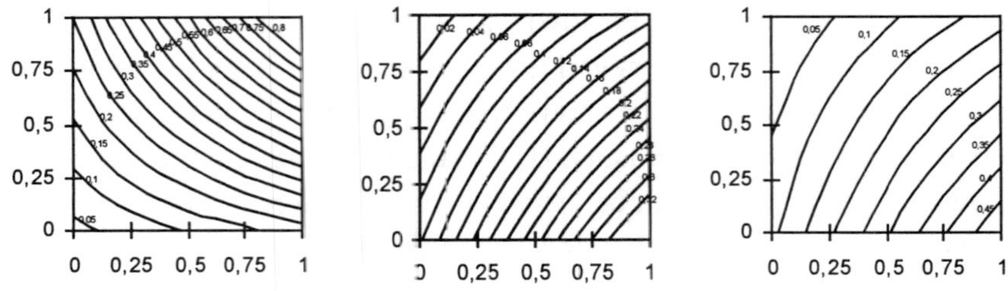

(a) (b) I

Fig. 2. Interaction effects between a), customer service (X-axis) and billing (Y-axis), b) customer service and tariffs, c) billing and tariffs. The contour lines correspond to combinations of probability of the satisfactory service dimension that result in the same probability of high overall satisfaction.

more influence than customer service. This is evidenced in the parameters b=0.13 and c=0.21. Finally, because the lines at the higher ranges of explaining probabilities get closer to each other and the resulting probability gets higher we can observe a joint interaction effect. This is confirmed by the value of parameter d_h=0.55. We can thus infer that the better the perception of both service dimensions, the more positive the satisfaction judgments. Figure 2b) shows that the probability of high overall satisfaction as a result of customer service and tariffs can vary from about 1% to 35%. The lowest probability is achieved as a result of a dissatisfactory experience with customer service and very high chance of satisfaction with the tariffs. This situation shows a strong negative synergy (d_h=–0.14). In Fig. 2c) the contour lines are drawn nearly in parallel every 5% and vary from 2% to 47% implying high and constant sensitivity of high satisfaction to varying performance of billing and tariffs. By comparing the graphs we can infer again that the most important dimension is billing, which explains most variation in overall satisfaction when compared to other dimensions.

In case there is an evidence entered, the two way sensitivity analysis function has the form:

$$\mathrm{P}(Z = z \mid e) = \frac{a+bx+cy+dxy}{e+fx+gy+hxy}, \tag{7}$$

where P(Z=z|e) is the target probability of interest, e is evidence, x and y are probabilities that the explaining variables are true, and a, b, c, d, e, f, *g*, and *h* are meta-parameters. Due to space limitations we do not consider this scenario here. Additional insight might be achieved by studying interaction effects among a set of three and even more parameters at a time. Higher-order sensitivity analyses are however less often used in practice due to complexity and cumbersome interpretation of their results.

6. Empirical Validation

The Bayesian network model of any system can be viewed as a decision model and thus validated against empirical data by using it as a classifying system, in which the value of each variable for each case in the test set is predicted based on values of other observed variables. The goodness of fit of such a system is assessed by measuring its standard predictive accuracy, i.e., percentage of cases classified correctly, or alternatively using quadratic loss (Brier) score.

A good practice is to treat each node sequentially as a decision class, and use the model to predict the label of each case using 10-fold cross-validation. The method selects each time randomly 10% of the cases, uses the remaining cases to learn about the model's parameters, and finally applies the model to classify the case based on values of other variables. This procedure is repeated 10 times for each node.

Since each classification decision in the above process is probabilistic in nature, its outcome depends heavily on the probability distribution for states of the target node. To account for the uncertainty, and to overcome the deficiency of standard measure of predictive accuracy in this respect, another measure, known as Brier score, for assessing probabilistic decision systems was introduced.[22] The intuitive idea behind the Brier score is that in case when the posterior probability of a specific category of overall satisfaction is remarkably higher than for the other categories and the prediction is correct, then the quality of such a forecast is better as if the distribution of categories was more resembling uniform distribution.[9]

We have applied the approach to validation as outlined above treating each of the variables used to parameterise the model as a class variable. The results of the classification for the three service dimensions and

Table 2. Results of the empirical validation of the model under study.

	Accuracy	Brier Score
Tariffs	99.72%	0.0313
Billing	100%	0.0001
Customer Service	99.07%	0.0134
Overall Satisfaction	75.8%	0.3596

overall satisfaction are shown in Table 2. For instance, the performance of satisfaction with tariffs as a class variable amounted to 99.72%, and satisfaction with billing having the accuracy of 100%. These results would suggest that our model is a truly perfect classifier, however we should keep in mind that the values of these attributes have been created by clustering of respondents using the *k*-means algorithm. For overall satisfaction a score of 75.8% correctly classified cases was achieved, whereas the Brier score amounted to 0.3596. On the whole, the predictive accuracy of 84% was obtained by taking the average over performance of all the variables included in the model.

To objectively interpret these outcomes, we should compare them with two other less informed classification models.[9] The first classifier based on uniform probability distribution of overall satisfaction categories for each case gives accuracy of 73% and Brier score of 0.37. For the second model encoding marginal prior probability distribution of satisfaction accuracy of 73.14% and Brier score of 0.429 is obtained. Therefore we can conclude that our model is well calibrated and can be utilized in the feature performance analysis for this study.

Yet other alternative validation methods are usually based either on Bayesian scores for a network structure, or on properties of (un)conditional independencies among vertices in a network. We have found that the structure of the model in focus was supported by the assertions of (un)conditional independence properties determined from empirical data by the PC algorithm.[29]

7. Concluding Remarks

In the classical approach to feature performance analysis, factor analysis is followed by regression analysis.[17,20] Factor analysis is used to construct and operationalise satisfaction at a higher, dimensional level of abstraction based on perception of the specific service/product features. Some features can be tested against their relevance and, possibly, excluded from the study as not "loading" on the dimension, thus non-relevant. Afterwards, linear relationships between each dimension and overall satisfaction are examined using regression analysis. In comparison to the above approach, the presented methodology enables deeper investigation of relevance of dimensions at various levels of the general performance. All the relationships are viewed probabilistically, thus allowing for easy interpretation. From a managerial perspective, outcomes of the present technique seem to be of interest, as they indicate which dimensions should be taken care of, and which of them are less important and deserve less attention.

One of the limitation of the presented approach is that it is not feasible to study the interaction of many dimensions at the same time, since the conditional probability table is growing very fast with the number of features, what causes difficulties with the model's parametric estimation.

A number of issues can be addressed to corroborate usability of the presented approach theoretically as well as for marketing practice. Future research may be focused on investigation of models involving more dimensions and to test sensitivity of the approach in this respect.

References

1. C. Alexander, "Bayesian Methods for Measuring Operational Risks," *ISMA Centre Research Reports*, Reading University, United Kingdom, 2000.
2. R. Anderson and R. Lenz, "Modelling the Impact of Organizational Change: A Bayesian Network Approach," *Organizational Research Methods*, Vol. 4, No. 2 (April), pp. 112-130, 2001.
3. J. G. Blodgett and R. D. Anderson, "A Bayesian Network Model of the Consumer Complaint Process," *Journal of Service Research*, Vol. 2, No. 4, pp. 321-338, May 2000.

4. G. A. Churchill, and C. Surprenant, "An Investigation into the Determinants of Customer Satisfaction," *Journal of Marketing Research*, Vol. 19 (November), pp. 491-504, 1982.
5. E. Castillo, J.M. Gutierrez, and A.S. Hadi, "Parametric Structure of Probabilities in Bayesian Networks," In: C. Froidevaux and J. Kohlas (Eds.), *Lecture Notes in Artificial Intelligence: Symbolic and Quantitative Approaches to Reasoning and Uncertainty*, Springer Verlag, New York, Vol. 946, pp. 89-98, 1995.
6. V. M. H. Coupe, L. van der Gaag, and D. Haberna, "Sensitivity Analysis: An Aid for Belief Network Quantification," *Knowledge Engineering Review*, Vol. 15, no. 3, pp. 1-18, 2000.
7. K. de Ruyter, and J. Bloemer, "Customer Loyalty in Extended Service Settings: The Interaction Between Satisfaction, Value Attainment and Positive Mood," *Journal of Service Industry Management*, Vol. 10, No 3, pp. 320-336, 1999.
8. C. Fornell, "A National Customer Satisfaction Barometer: The Swedish Experience," *Journal of Marketing*, Vol. 56, pp. 6-21, January 1992.
9. L. C. van der Gaag and S. Renooij, "Evaluation Scores for Probabilistic Networks," In: B. Kröse, M. de Rijke, G. Schreiber and M. van Someren (Eds), *Proceedings of the Thirteenth Belgium-Netherlands Conference on Artificial Intelligence*, Amsterdam, pp. 109-116, 2001.
10. D. Heckerman, "A Tutorial on Learning with Bayesian Networks", In M.I. Jordan (Ed.), *Learning in Graphical Models*, The MIT Press, Cambridge, Massachusetts, 1998.
11. N. Hill and J. Alexander, *Handbook of Customer Satisfaction and Loyalty Measurement*, Gower Publishing Limited, 2000.
12. Kipersztok and H. Wang, "Another Look at Sensitivity of Bayesian Networks to Imprecise Probabilities," *Proceedings of the Eighth International Workshop on Artificial Intelligence and Statistics*, Florida, January 4-7, 2001.
13. S. L. Lauritzen, "The EM Algorithm for Graphical Association Models with Missing Data," *Computational Statistics & Data Analysis*, 19, pp. 191-201, 1995.
14. T. Levitt, *The Marketing Imagination*, Free Press, New York, 1983.
15. D. Madigan, K. Mosurski, and R. Almond, "Graphical Explanation in Belief Networks," *Journal of Computational and Graphical Statistics*, Vol. 6, No. 2, pp. 160-181, 1997.
16. V. Mittal, W. Ross, and P. Baldasare, "The Asymmetric Impact of Negative and Positive Attribute-Level Performance on Overall Satisfaction and Repurchase Intentions", *Journal of Marketing*, 1998, Vol. 62 (1), pp. 33-47.
17. E. Naumann and K. Giel, *Customer Satisfaction Measurement And Management*, Thomson Executive Press, 1995.
18. R.L. Oliver, "Measurement and Evaluation of Satisfaction Processes in Retail Settings," *Journal of Retailing*, Vol. 57 (Fall), pp. 25-48, 1981.
19. R.L. Oliver, "Processing of the Satisfaction Response in Consumption: A Suggested Framework and Research Propositions," *Journal of Customer*

Satisfaction, Dissatis-faction and Complaining Behaviour, Vol. 2 pp. 1-16, 1989.

20. R.L. Oliver, *Satisfaction – A Behavioral Perspective on the Consumer*, The McGraw-Hill Companies, New York, 1996.
21. R.L. Oliver, "Whence Customer Loyalty," *Journal of Marketing*, Vol. 63 (Special Issue), pp. 33-44, 1999.
22. H.A. Panovsky and G. W. Brier, *Some Applications of Statistics to Meteorology*, The Pennsylvania State University, Univeristy Park, Pennsylvania, 1968.
23. J. Pearl, *Probabilistic Reasoning in Intelligent Systems: Networks of Plausible Inference*, Morgan Kaufmann, San Mateo (CA), 1988.
24. D. Ortinau, A. Bush, R. Bush, and J. Twible, "The Use of Importance-Performance Analysis for Improving the Quality of Marketing Education: Interpreting Faculty-Course Evaluations," *Journal of Marketing Education*, Vol. 11, pp. 78-86, 1989.
25. J.P. Peter, and J. C. Olson, *Consumer Behavior and Marketing Strategy*, The McGraw-Hill Companies, 1996.
26. R.A. Peterson, and W. R. Wilson, "Measuring Customer Satisfaction: Fact or Artifact," *Journal of the Academy of Marketing Science*, Vol. 20, No. 1, pp. 61-71, 1992.
27. R.T. Rust and R.L. Oliver, "Service Quality: Insights and Managerial Implications from the Frontier," in R.T. Rust and R.L. Oliver (Eds.), *Service Quality: New Directions In Theory And Practice*, Sage, London, 1994.
28. C. Shenoy and P. P. Shenoy, "Bayesian Network Models of Portfolio Risk and Return," *Computational Finance*, pp. 87-106, 1999.
29. P. Spirtes, C. Glymour, R. Scheines, *Causation, Prediction and Search*, The MIT Press, Cambridge, Massachusetts, 2001.
30. D. K. Tse, and P. C. Wilton, "Models of Consumer Satisfaction Formation: An Extension," *Journal of Marketing Research*, Vol. 25 (May), pp. 204-212, 1988.
31. K. Vanhoof and G. Swinnen, "Attribute Importance: Assessing Nonlinear Patterns of Factors Contributing to Customer Satisfaction," *Esomar Publication Series*, Vol. 204, pp.171-183, 1996.
32. R.A.Westbrook, "Product/Consumption Based Affective Responses and Postpurchase Processes," *Journal of Marketing Research*, Vol. 24 (August), pp. 258-70, 1987.
33. Y. Yi, "A critical review of customer satisfaction," in V.A. Zeithaml (Ed.), *Review of Marketing*, Duke University, AMA, 1991.

CHAPTER 27

AN ADAPTIVE LENGTH CHROMOSOME HYPER-HEURISTIC GENETIC ALGORITHM FOR A TRAINER SCHEDULING PROBLEM

Limin Han[1], Graham Kendall[1] and Peter Cowling[2]

[1]*Automated Scheduling, Optimisation and Planning (ASAP) Research Group*
School of Computer Science and IT, Jubilee Campus
University of Nottingham, Nottingham, NG8 1BB, UK,
Email: lxh/gxk@cs.nott.ac.uk
[2]*Modelling Optimisation Scheduling And Intelligent Computing (MOSAIC) Research Group, Department of Computing, University of Bradford*
Bradford BD7 1DP, UK
Email: P.I.Cowling@bradford.ac.uk

Hyper-GA was introduced by the authors as a genetic algorithm based hyper-heuristic which aims to evolve an ordering of low-level heuristics so as to find a good quality solution for a given problem. The adaptive length chromosome hyper-GA (ALChyper-GA) is an extension of our previous work, in which the chromosome was of fixed length. The aim of a variable length chromosome is two fold; 1) it allows dynamic removal and insertion of heuristics 2) it allows the GA to find a good chromosome length which could otherwise only be found by experimentation. We apply the ALChyper-GA to a trainer scheduling problem and report that good quality solutions can be found. We also present results for four versions of the ALChyper-GA, applied to five test data sets.

1. Introduction

Meta-heuristic approaches have been successfully applied to a range of personnel scheduling problems, which involve the allocation of staff to timeslots and possibly locations[22]. For example, Burke et al[2] and

Dowsland[12] used tabu search to solve nurse rostering problems. Aickelin and Dowsland[1] solved a nurse rostering problem in a large UK hospital utilising a genetic algorithm. The implementation of their approach gave fast and robust results. It proved flexible and able to solve the large rostering problem which has a range of objectives and constraints. Easton and Mansour[13] conducted an experiment on a distributed genetic algorithm to solve deterministic and stochastic labour scheduling problems. They ran the procedure in parallel, on a network of workstations. In order to maintain the search near the feasible region, their procedure uses a combination of feasibility and penalty methods to help exploit favourable adaptations in infeasible offspring. They applied their approach to three test suites drawn from the literature of labour scheduling problems. Their results were compared to those problems solved by other meta-heuristics and conventional heuristics. They found that their results outperformed other methods on average.

Indirect genetic algorithms have also been studied widely. For example, Terashima-Marin, Ross and Valenzuela-Rendon[21] designed an indirect GA to solve an examination timetabling problem. They designed strategies which they encoded as parameters for guiding the search into a 10-position array. Their chromosome represents how to construct a timetable rather than representing the timetable itself. The indirect chromosome representation can help avoid the limitation of a direct chromosome. This limitation is known as the coordination failure between different parts of a solution when solving examination timetabling problems. Corne and Ogden[11] compared their indirect and direct GA for a Methodist preaching timetabling problem and found the former generated better solutions.

Normally the chromosome of a genetic algorithm is either the solution of the given problem or a structure of the solution. This makes problem specific knowledge essential in the design of a chromosome. This results in the algorithm being difficult to reuse for different problems because of the heavy dependence on domain knowledge. In order to overcome this disadvantage of genetic algorithms and have a reusable, robust and fast-to-implement approach, applicable to a wide range of problems and instances, we have designed genetic algorithms using an indirect chromosome representation based on evolving a sequence of heuristics for a trainer scheduling problem, which is a type of personnel scheduling problem that can be regarded as the allocation of staff to timeslots and locations[22]. The idea behind this approach is a hyper-heuristic.

In section 2 we present the concept of hyper-heuristics, in section 3, we describe the trainer scheduling problem. We present the hyper-GA and ALChyper-GA in section 4. In section 5 we show the implementation of the algorithms and section 6 gives the results. We conclude in section 7 and outline some possible research directions.

2. Hyper-Heuristics

A *hyper-heuristic*[3] is an approach that operates at a higher level of abstraction than a meta-heuristic. The *hyper-heuristic* is described in burke et al[3] as "*the process of using (meta-)heuristics to choose (meta-)heuristics to solve the problem in hand*". A set of low level heuristics and a high level heuristic selector define their hyper-heuristic. They present a general framework for the hyper-heuristic to select which low-level heuristic to apply at a given choice point. The hyper-heuristic maintains a state and records the amount of time each low-level heuristic takes and also record the change in the evaluation function. The hyper-heuristic only knows whether the objective function is to be maximised or minimised and has no information as to what the objective function represents. No domain knowledge is present in the hyper-heuristic. Each low level heuristic communicates with the hyper-heuristic using a common, problem independent, interface architecture[7]. In order to improve the performance of the general framework, Cowling et al designed a *choice function*[8]. The choice function is calculated using information from the recently called low-level heuristics: the improvement of each individual heuristic, the improvement of each pair of heuristics and the CPU time of each heuristic. They applied their approach to a sales summit scheduling problem[8], a project presentation scheduling problem[9] and a nurse scheduling problem[10]. The problems were solved effectively producing results competitive with those from specially designed algorithms.

Burke et al designed a tabu search based hyper-heuristic to solve timetabling and rostering problems[4,5]. In the framework of their hyper-heuristic, heuristics compete using rules based on the principles of reinforcement learning. A tabu list of heuristics is maintained which prevents certain heuristics from being chosen at certain times during the search. The basic idea of the tabu list is to prevent a poorly performing heuristic from being chosen again too soon. The approach successfully solved a university course timetabling problem and a nurse rostering problem from a major UK hospital.

A hyper-heuristic method was also developed by Hart et al[16]. They developed an evolving heuristically driven schedule builder to solve a real-life chicken catching and transportation problem. They divided the problem into two sub-problems and solved each using a separate genetic algorithm. The result of the two genetic algorithms is a strategy for producing schedules, rather than a schedule itself. All of the information collected from the company is summarised as a set of rules, which were combined into a schedule builder by exploiting the searching capabilities of the genetic algorithm. A sequence of heuristics was evolved to dictate which heuristic to use to place a task into the schedule.

Hart and Ross[15] also developed a heuristic based genetic algorithm for tackling dynamic job-shop scheduling problems. Their method used an implicit representation of a schedule in which each gene in the chromosome represents a heuristic to be used at each step of generating a schedule. They tested their approach on a number of benchmark problems and found it performed well compared to other results published around the same time.

Randall and Abramson[19] designed a general purpose meta-heuristic based solver for combinatorial optimisation problems. They used linked list modelling to represent a problem, and then the problem was specified in a textual format and solved directly using meta-heuristic search engines. The solver worked efficiently and returned good quality solutions when applied to several traditional combinatorial optimisation problems, such as bin packing problem, graph coloring problem etc. Nareyek[18] provided an approach that was able to learn how to select promising heuristics during the search process. The learning was based on weight adaptation. The configuration of heuristics was also constantly updated during the search according to the performance of each heuristic under different phases of the search. The results showed that the adaptive approach could improve upon static strategies when applied to the same problems. Gratch and Chien[14] developed an adaptive problem solving system to select proper heuristic methods from a space of heuristics after a period of adaptation and applied it successfully to a network scheduling problem.

For a more complete review of hyper-heuristics, including the very early work see Soubeiga's Ph.D. thesis[20].

3. Problem Description

The problem is to create a timetable of geographically-distributed courses over a period of several weeks using geographically distributed trainers. We wish to maximise the total priority of courses which are delivered in the period, while minimising the amount of travel for each trainer. To schedule the events, we have 25 staff, 10 training centres (or locations) and 60 timeslots. Each event is to be delivered by one member of staff from the limited number who are competent to deliver that event. Each staff member can only work up to 60% of his/her working time (i.e. 36 timeslots). Each event is to be scheduled at one location from a limited list of possible locations. Each location, however, can only be used by a limited number of events in each timeslot due to the limited number of rooms at each location. The start time of each event must occur within a given time window. The duration of each event varies from 1 to 5 time slots. Each event has a numerical priority value. Each member of staff has a home location and a penalty is associated with a staff member who must travel to an event. The objective function is to maximise the total priority for scheduled courses minus total travel penalty for trainers. A mathematical model for the problem is shown in Fig. 1, where we have

E: the set of events;

S: the set of staff members;

T: the set of timeslots;

L: the set of locations;

dur_i*: the duration of event* e_i*;*

d_{sl}: the distance penalty for staff s delivering a course at location l;
w_i: the priority of event e_i;
c_l: the number of rooms at location l

Objective Function:

$$Max\ \ W = \sum_{i\in E}(w_i * \sum_{s\in S}\sum_{t\in T}\sum_{l\in L} y_{istl}) - \sum_{s\in S}\sum_{l\in L} d_{sl}\sum_{i\in E}\sum_{t\in T} y_{istl} \quad (0)$$

Subject to:

$$\sum_{s\in S}\sum_{t\in T}\sum_{l\in L} y_{istl} \le 1 \quad (i \in E) \quad (1)$$

$$\sum_{i\in E}\sum_{l\in L}\sum_{t\in T} x_{istl} \le 1 \quad (s \in S) \quad (2)$$

$$\sum_{i\in E}\sum_{s\in S}\sum_{t\in T} x_{istl} \le c_l \quad (l \in L) \quad (3)$$

$$x_{istl} <= \sum_{j=1}^{t} y_{istl} \quad (i \in E)(s \in S)(t \in T)(l \in L) \quad (4)$$

$$\sum_{s\in S}\sum_{t\in T}\sum_{l\in L} x_{istl} = dur_i \quad * \sum_{s\in S}\sum_{t\in T}\sum_{l\in L} y_{istl} \quad (i \in E) \quad (5)$$

$$x_{istl} <= \sum_{\substack{j\in T \\ 0<=t-j<dur_i}} y_{istl} \quad (i \in E)(s \in S)(t \in T)(l \in L) \quad (6)$$

Fig. 1. Mathematical model for the geographically distributed trainer scheduling problem

Variable y_{istl} is equal to 1 when event e_i is delivered by staff s at location l commencing at timeslot t, or 0 otherwise. Variable x_{istl} is equal to 1 when event e_i is delivered by staff s at location *l during timeslot t*, or 0 otherwise. Constraint (1) ensures that each event can happen at most once. Constraint (2) ensures that each staff member is only required to deliver at most one event in each timeslot. Constraint (3) ensures that each location has sufficient room capacity for the event scheduled. Constraints (4), (5), and (6) link the x_{istl} and y_{istl} variables, ensuring that if an event is delivered, it is on consecutive days.

4. Hyper-GA, Low-Level Heuristics and ALChyper-GA

4.1. *Hyper-GA*

Hyper-GA is a hyper-heuristic that uses a GA to select low-level heuristics which in turn solve the given problem. The GA is an indirect GA with the representation being a sequence of integers each of which represents a single low-level heuristic. Each chromosome in a hyper-GA population gives a sequence of heuristic choices which tell us which low-level heuristics to use and in what order to apply them[6].

4.1.1 Low-level Heuristics

We have designed fourteen problem-specific low-level heuristics. Twelve of them accept a current solution and modify it locally in an attempt to return an improved solution. The other two are likely to return a worse solution but will hopefully lead to an improvement later on, after other heuristics have been applied. The aim of these two low-level heuristics is to observe the adaptation of ALChyper-GA when there is a decrease in the objective function.

At each generation the hyper-GA can call upon the set of low-level heuristics and apply them in any sequence. All these low-level heuristics may be considered in three groups: *add, add-swap* and *add-delete.* The add heuristics comprise five methods which can be sub-divided into two groups. *Add-first, add-random* and *add-best* try to add unscheduled events by descending priority and *add-first-improvement* and *add-best-improvement* consider the unscheduled list in a random order. The *add* heuristics can be described as follows:

- *Add-first* tries to schedule a course using the available staff members and locations in descending order of priority until a staff member who can deliver the course at a location is found.
- *Add-random* considers the staff members and locations in a random order until a staff member who can deliver the event at a location is found.

- *Add-best* considers all possible staff and locations and selects those yielding the lowest travel penalty.
- *Add-first-improvement* considers all unscheduled courses in descending priority order and tries available staff and locations for each of those courses until the first one which yields an overall improvement in the objective function is found.
- *Add-best-improvement* is similar to *Add-first-improvement* but tries all staff members and locations until the best improving combination is found.

There are four *add-swap* heuristics and they are also sub-divided into two groups according to the order of the unscheduled event list.

- *Swap-first* and *swap-randomly* are analogous to add-first and add-random, except that if there is a conflicting event when considering a particular timeslot, staff member and location, we will consider all swaps between that conflicting event and other scheduled events to see if the conflict can be resolved.
- *Swap-first-improvement* and *swap-best-improvement* are similarly analogous to add-first improvement and add-best improvement with the addition of this swapping step to resolve conflicts.

The mechanism of the third group (add-delete heuristics) is: select one event from the unscheduled event list by descending priority. If the event is in conflict with event(s) in the timetable (none of the event's possible staff members is able to work for it during its possible timeslots), and the event's fitness is higher than the fitness(es) of the conflicting event(s), delete the conflicting event(s) and add the unscheduled event. This group of heuristics consists of:

- *Add-delete-first,* which tries the available staff members and locations in descending order of priority for the unscheduled event until a staff member who can deliver the course at a location is found.
- *Add-delete-random,* considers the staff members and locations in a random order for the unscheduled event until a staff member who can deliver the event at a location is found.
- *Add-delete-worst*, considers all possible staff and locations for the unscheduled event and selects those yielding the lowest travel penalty.

The other two heuristics, *remove-first* and *remove-random*, attempt to remove the first/random event in the schedule.

We list all these 14 low-level problem specific heuristics as follows:

0. *Add-first,*
1. *Add-random*
2. *Add-best*
3. *Add-swap-first*
4. *Add-swap-randomly*
5. *Add-remove-first*
6. *Add-remove-random,*
7. *Add-remove-worst*
8. *Add-first-improvement*
9. *Add-best-improvement*
10. *Add-swap-first-improvement*
11. *Add-swap-best-improvement*
12. *Remove-first*
13. *Remove-random*

The integer in front of each heuristic is the integer used in the chromosome.

4.1.2 Representation

The representation of the chromosome is a sequence of integers, each of which represents one low-level heuristic. Each individual in a hyper-GA population provides a sequence of heuristic choices which tell us which low-level heuristics to use and in what order to apply them. Fig. 2 is an example of hyper-GA, where each integer represents a low-level heuristic listed in the above section. Fig. 3 is the structure of the hyper-GA

2	3	1	5	0	7	9	8	11	1	10	4

Fig. 2. Example of hyper-GA chromosome

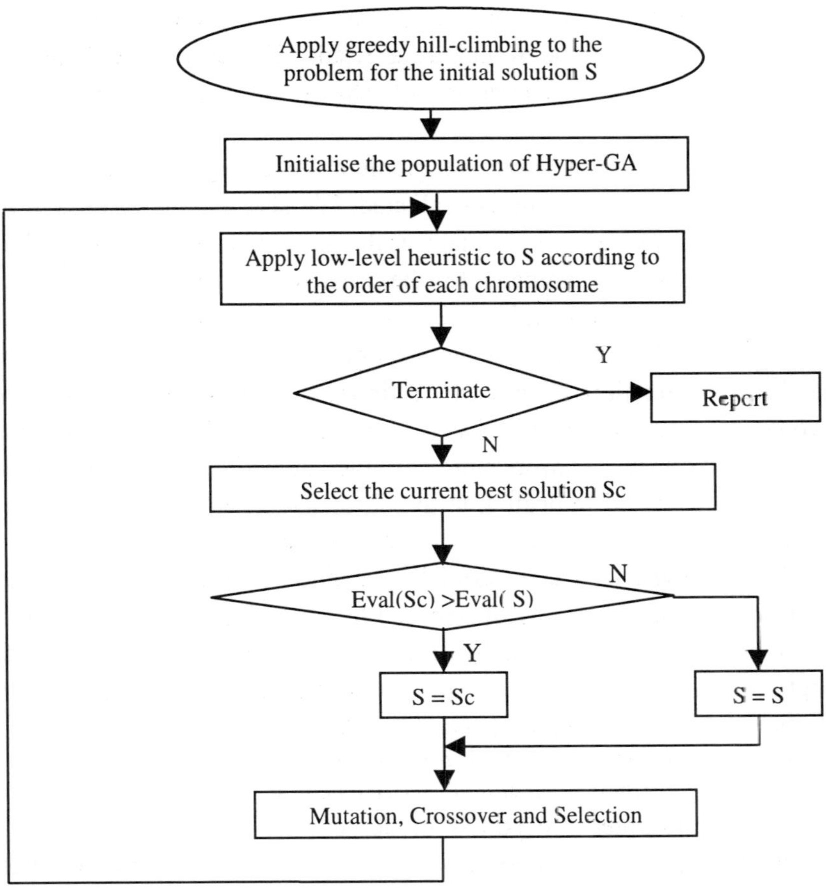

Fig. 3. Structure of hyper-GA

4.2. *Adaptive Length Chromosome Hyper-GA*

The adaptive length chromosome hyper-GA (ALChyper-GA) is an improvement of hyper-GA. We assume the fixed length chromosome in the hyper-GA is not always the optimal length and want to encourage the evolution of good combinations of low-level heuristics without having to explicitly consider this optimal length. The behaviour of a given low-level heuristic or a combination of low-level heuristics, within a chromosome, could be very promising, while anther low-level heuristic or combination of heuristics could perform poorly. We hypothesise that if we remove the poor-performing heuristics from a chromosome or inject efficient heuristics from one chromosome to another, then better quality solutions can be found as a result. Therefore, the length of chromosomes in each generation will change as genes are inserted or removed.

Within each chromosome we monitor the change of the objective function as the chromosome is evaluated. We also use the change in the objective function as we evaluate each chromosome to decide which blocks of genes are candidates for the crossover and mutation operators (see 4.3). An improvement between *gene m* and *gene n* potentially mean the call of low-level heuristics between gene *m* and gene *n* will improve the objective function when used within another chromosome, and other chromosomes might benefit by having these heuristics injected into them. Conversely, a worsening of the objective function (or no improvement) could indicate that the chromosome might perform better if these genes were removed from the chromosome.

The ALChyper-GA uses specially designed crossover and mutations to insert or remove groups of genes. We have also designed a penalty function to penalise the length of chromosome in the case where the length increases which will result in increased run times due to the additional evaluation required. The formula for the penalty function is:

*(Length in chromosomes * CPU time to evaluate chromosome)/*
(Improvement in objective function) (7)

All chromosomes are sorted in descending order of their penalty function and proportional selection ensures that shorter, faster, better improving chromosomes have a higher chance of being selected.

4.3. *Operators*

The hyper-GA uses one point crossover and a mutation operator which randomly selects a position in one chromosome and mutates integers at these positions to other values ranging from 0 to 13.

In carrying out crossover and mutation, we do not allow infeasible solutions. Each event in the new chromosome will be checked to see whether it conflicts with other event(s) in the same chromosome. If this is the case, the event(s) with lower priority-penalty will be removed from the chromosome.

We have designed a new crossover operator and two new mutation operators for ALChyper-GA. The new crossover, called *best-best crossover*, selects the best group of genes (the call of low-level heuristics by those genes that give the greatest improvement of the objective function) in either selected chromosome, and exchange them. One new mutation operator, *removing-worst mutation*, will remove the worst group of genes (the call of low-level heuristics by those genes that give the largest decrease of the objective function, or the longest group of genes giving no improvement to the objective function) in the selected chromosome. Another mutation, *inserting-good mutation*, inserts the best group of genes from a randomly selected chromosome to a random point of another chromosome. The *best-best* crossover is illustrated in Fig. 4. Parent 1 and 2 are chromosomes selected to crossover. The improvement in the objective function of parent 1 is *57.85*, where the grey area is the group of genes (*gene 5 to 9*) that contribute most *(21.30)*. The improvement in objective function of parent 2 is *35.81*, the group of genes in the black area (*gene 7 to 13*) gives the most improvement *(16.77)*. Thus, *gene 5 to 9* in parent 1 and *gene 7 to 13* are best groups of genes in either parent. These two groups are selected and exchanged to form child 1 and child 2.

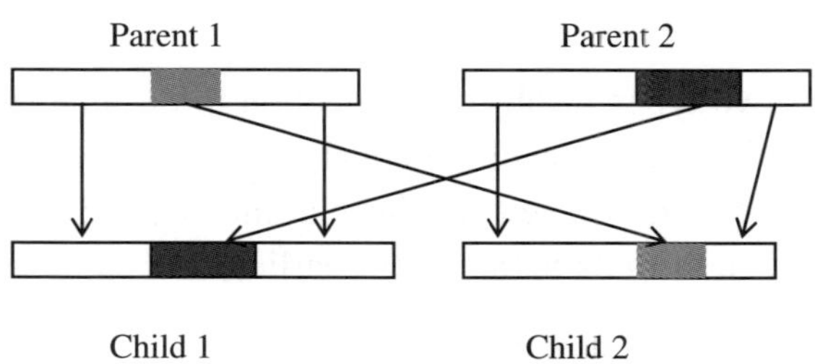

Fig. 4. best-best crossover

5. Implementation

All algorithms were implemented in C++ and the experiments were conducted on an AMD 800MHZ with 128MB RAM running under Windows 2000. We used five data sets to test the suitability of the algorithm, which describe realistic problem instances having differing degrees of difficulty. The difficulty is determined by the number of staff members that can cover each course. Each data set contains more than 500 events. The events in each data set are generated randomly, based on the characteristics of a real staff trainer scheduling problem at a large financial institution. For more details of the problem please refer to [6].

There are 4 versions of hyper-GA, two with adaptive mutation and crossover rates and two without. In the adaptive versions, the mutation rate and crossover rate adapt according to the change in fitness in each generation. When there is no improvement in average fitness over 3 generations, the mutation rate (in the range 0 to 1) will be increased as follows:

$$New\ Mutation\ Rate = (Old\ Mutation\ Rate + 1)/2 \tag{8}$$

and the crossover rate will be decreased as follows :

$$New\ Crossover\ Rate = Old\ Crossover\ Rate/2. \tag{9}$$

If the average fitness has improved over 3 generations, the mutation rate will be decreased using:

$$New\ Mutation\ Rate = Old\ MutationRate/2 \tag{10}$$

and the crossover rate will be increased using:

$$New\ Crossover\ Rate = (Old\ Crossover\ Rate + 1)/2 \tag{11}$$

There are two types of objective function in our algorithm. One uses total priority minus total travelling penalty for the solution resulting from applying the heuristics given by the chromosome to the best solution found so far. The formula is (as for (0) earlier):

$$\sum Priority - \sum Travelling\ Penalty \tag{12}$$

The other uses total priority minus total travelling penalty divided by the CPU time of the application of that chromosome, so that improvement per unit time is the fitness. The formula for this objective function is:

$$\left(\sum Priority - \sum Travelling\ Penalty\right)/(CPU\ Time\ for\ Chromosome) \tag{13}$$

The consideration of CPU time is so that we can easily compare the efficiency of each individual sequence of low-level heuristic. The four versions of hyper-GA are as follows:

- PPPN uses (12) as the objective function.
- PPPA uses same objective function as PPPN, and the crossover and mutation rate are adapted using (8) to (11). (8 to 11 represent how the crossover rate and mutation rate are adapted)
- FTPN, uses (13) as the objective function.
- FTPA, whose objective function is the same as FTPN, and the crossover and mutation rate are adapted using (8) to (11).

The comparison of these four versions can test the robustness of hyper-GA under a range of conditions. Thirty individuals are generated for the initial population by randomly selecting numbers ranged from 0 to 13 for each gene of the chromosome. After empirical testing over a range of parameter rates[6], we use 0.6 for crossover rate, 0.1 for mutation rate, a population size of 30, 200 generations (100 generations gives equally good results, but we use 200 to see the further change of low-level heuristics' distribution) and retain the 30 fittest chromosomes in each generation. Table 1 (from Cowling et al[6]) gives the group of parameters we tested in order to find proper rates for the algorithm.

Table 1. Comparison of parameters for hyper-GA
C: crossover, M: mutation, P: population, G: generation (Time /objective)

C/M/G	*P: 5*	*P: 30*	*P: 50*
0.6/0/50	67/1943	390/1950	652/1952
0.6/ 0.1/50	59/1945	384/1951	620/1951
0.6/ 1/50	63/1943	392/1949	663/1949
1/ 0/50	74/1940	420/1948	752/1946
1/0.1/ 50	75/1942	434/1950	796/1948
0/1/ 50	58/1941	321/1947	530/1942
0.6/ 0/100	125/1943	790/1953	1350/1952
0.6/0.1/100	118/1945	**804/1958**	1318/1957
0.6/ 1/ 100	127/1947	872/1957	1485/1952
1/0/100	152/1940	1064/1953	1527/1950
1/0.1/ 100	152/1942	1045/1954	1513/1951
0/1/ 100	110/1948	643/1951	970/1949
0.6/0/50	193/1945	**1448/1958**	2136/1957

6. Results

Table 2 presents our results. We compare the result of ALChyper-GA to hyper-GA, and a genetic and a memetic algorithm (populations size 30, run 100 generations for GA and MA)[6]. The CPU time and solution quality are compared in the table. The result of a mutation only approach (with only the two new mutation operators in ALChyper-GA) is also presented in the table. We also present the result of applying only heuristics H1, H2, ... , H5 (each of them is the combination of the best chromosome in each generation by five different runs of the PPPN hyper-GA on a relatively difficult problem instance (the Basic data set)), to each other data set. The upper bound is calculated by solving a relaxed knapsack problem[17] where we ignore travel penalties. The heading of each column in table 2 represents the difficulty of the problem instance, which is determined by the number of staff member who can deliver the courses.

Table 2. Comparison of ALChyper-GA and hyper-GA (objective/time)

Heuristics	*Basic data*	*Very few*	*Few staff (1)*	*Few staff (2)*	*Non-restricted*
Upper bound (priority)	2261	2179	2124	2244	2179
GA	1796/1628	1633/1629	1589/1641	1706/1721	1644/1699
MA	1832/2064	1678/2054	1617/2129	1769/2254	1698/2133
Hyper-GA PPPN	*1959/1456*	*1780/1387*	*1749/1404*	*1858/1496*	1742/1422
Hyper-GA PPPA	1939/1448	1754/1461	1712/1306	1854/1475	*1814/1571*
Hyper-GA FTPN	1943/1411	1770/1437	1673/1436	1803/1422	1774/1434
Hyper-GA FTPA	1951/1420	1731/1424	1738/1436	1769/1427	1770/1419
ALCHyper-GA PPPN	**1961/1357**	**1788/1250**	**1816/1163**	1831/1591	**1822/1437**
ALCHyper-GA PPPA	1933/1638	1757/1644	1795/1325	**1862/1506**	1804/1638
ALCHyper-GA FTPN	1949/1450	1780/1365	1781/1277	1821/1638	1813/1488
ALCHyper-GA FTPA	1954/1526	1764/1496	17660/1364	1799/1583	1799/1419
ALCHyper-GA with only mutation	1880/1486	1769/1188	1780/1083	1783/1413	1788/1383
H1	1958/20	1629/20	1619/21	1724/20	1651/20
H2	1937/21	1597/21	1602/21	1692/21	1644/20
H3	1949/21	1617/20	1622/22	1706/22	1652/21
H4	1944/21	1629/21	1578/21	1661/22	1637/21
H5	1959/21	1582/21	1597/20	1647/21	1595/20

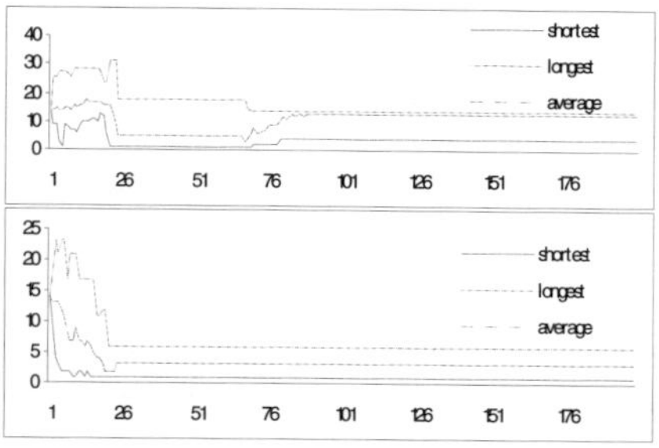

Fig. 5. Change of chromosome length for the basic data set and the very few staff data set (length/generation)

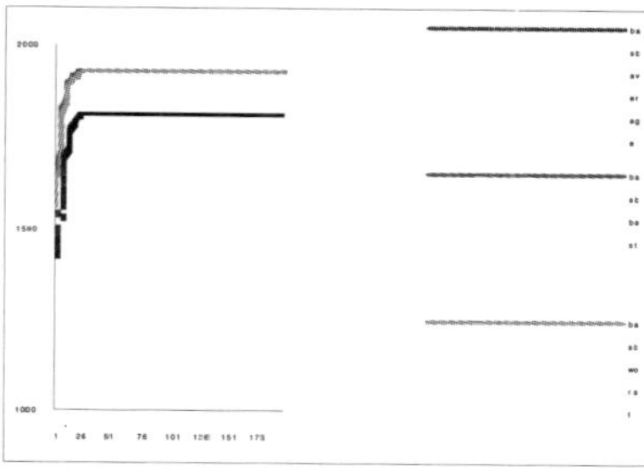

Fig. 6. Objective function value for the basic data set, and the very few staff data set (objective/generation)

We find that the ALChyper-GA performs better than the hyper-GA for most problem instances. The latter produces better results than both the genetic and the memetic algorithm, and the fast, greedy heuristics H1,..., H5. From table 2 we can see that the improvement in objective in few staff (1) data set and non-restricted staff data set is bigger than other three data sets, which suggests that ALChyper-GA works well, even on more difficult problems. Although results of the mutation only approach in table 2 are not as good as most applications of the four versions of ALChyper-GA, the results and the run time of the approach supports the idea that the work of the two new mutation operators can improve the efficiency of the algorithm.

Comparing ALChyper-GA with hyper-GA supports the idea that if hyper-GA was able to find the optimal length chromosome, it will perform better. However, ALChyper-GA has the ability to find a good quality length chromosome as it evolves. Indeed, as the search progresses the optimal length of the chromosome changes and the ALChyper-GA is able to react to this need. Fig. 5 illustrates the change in length of the chromosome. The top part of the figure is for the basic data set, while the bottom part is for the very few staff data set. From the top part of the figure, we see that ALChyper-GA settles on a stable length chromosome for each individual in the population from generation 24 to generation 66 (the average is 6), at which time ALChyper-GA is at a local optimum with respect to the objective function (1955.28). Then, the length is changed by generation 67 and the algorithm settled to a different local optimum.

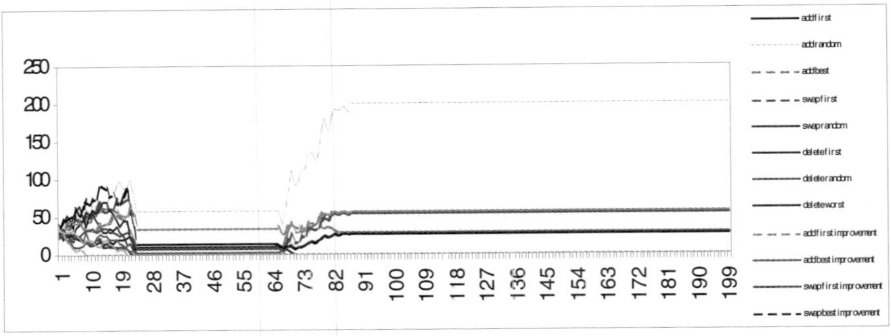

Fig. 7. Heuristic distribution for the basic data set (frequency/generation)

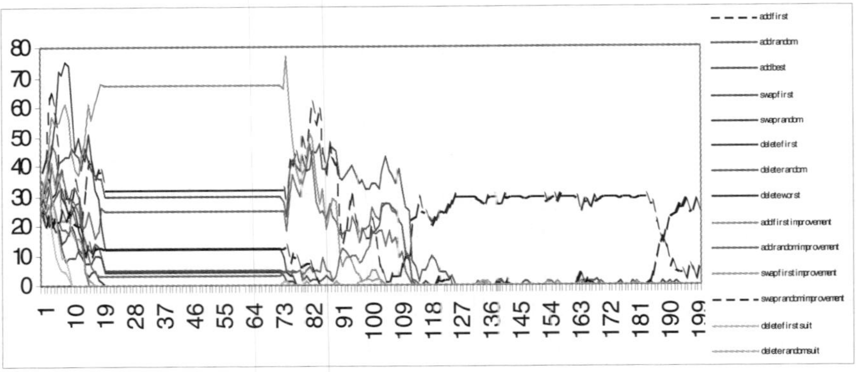

Fig. 8. Heuristic distribution for the very few staff data set (frequency/generation)

Fig. 6 illustrates the change in the objective function. The upper group of lines are for the basic data set, while the lower group of lines are for the very few staff data set. We also note that the objective function of the basic data set is improved from 1955.28 to 1961.64 at generation 67 in the figure, while the objective function of the very few staff data set is improved from 1787.63 to 1788.49 at generation 75. Both of the two improvements happen at the generation when variation appears again.

From the top of Fig. 5 we can find another phenomenon in that the longest chromosome becomes shorter, the shortest chromosome becomes longer, and the average length increases by generation 67. While in the bottom of Fig. 5 both the length of the longest chromosome and average length drop down by generation 75 and all three lengths become 1 by generation 117. This is because of the work of our new mutation operators. The two mutation operators keep variations in each population, and try to keep selected chromosome efficient. Fig. 7 and 8 illustrate how these changes happened to the call of each low-level heuristic. We can see from Fig. 7 that when the call of each low-level heuristic settled at generation 26, the average length of chromosomes and the objective function settled as well. At generation 67, however, the add-random low-level heuristic started to be called which led to an improvement of objective function and a change of the average chromosome length. Similar phenomenon can be seen in Fig. 8, where call to the low-level heuristics becomes random after changes in the average chromosome length and objective function. We suggest these changes are due to the work of our new operators. These operators work to remove "poor" heuristics and keep "good" genes in each generation. Thus, the average length of chromosome keeps changing in early generations and local optimum is easily found early one (generation 27 in Fig. 7 and generation 24 in Fig. 8). Because other operators help to diversify the population, the evolution can be improved in later generations. The whole evolution, however, still converges early (generation 67 in Fig. 7 and generation 75 in Fig. 8).

The phenomenon of these changes is common in both adaptive crossover/mutation operator rates version and the fixed rates. The adaptive operator rates, however, converged later than the fixed versions.

7. Conclusions and Future Work

ALCHyper-GA is a promising approach to personnel scheduling and other optimisation problems. It is a further improvement of hyper-GA. The length of the chromosomes adapt after the identification of performance of individual heuristic or combination of heuristics selected by the chromosome. Three new operators: *best-best crossover*, *removing-worst mutation,* and *inserting-good mutation* help to dynamically insert or remove heuristics. This algorithm outperforms the hyper-GA[6], and has better performance than a genetic and a memetic algorithm and its component heuristics which were presented in reference 6.

In future, we will consider different methods of parameter adaptation as well as maintaining the diversity of the population. Although the dynamic injection and removal of genes to the hyper-GA works well, we hypothesise that if we can give some guidance to the crossover and mutation, the injection and removal could be more effective. Thus, we would like to investigate how to guide those operators. We have found that too much CPU time is spent on finding "good" and "bad" genes during the evolution. We suspect if we can add some mechanism to each gene so as to enable the gene to memorise its own performance in each generation, we can save CPU time. We will also try to add a tabu list to hyper-GA to provide a memory for the genes. We also plan to test the robustness of our algorithm on a range of other real-world problems.

References

1. Aickelin, U, Dowsland, K, Exploiting Problem structure In A Genetic Algorithm Approach To A Nurse Rostering Problem, 2000, *Journal Of Scheduling*, vol. 3, pp.139-153.
2. Burke, E.K., De Causmaecker, P., Vanden Berghe, G., A Hybrid Tabu Search Algorithm For The Nurse Rostering Problem, 1998, *Proceedings of the Second Asia-Pacific Conference on Simulated Evolution and Learning,* vol. 1, Applications IV. pp. 187-194
3. Burke, E., Kendall, G., Newall, J., Hart, E., Ross, P., and Schulenburg, S., *Handbook of metaheuristics*, chapter 16, Hyper-heuristics: an emerging direction in modern search technology, pp. 457–474. Kluwer Academic Publishers, 2003.
4. Burke, E.K., Kendall, G., and Soubeiga, E., A Tabu-Search Hyperheuristic for Timetabling and Rostering, 2003, to appear in Journal of Heuristics.
5. Burke, E.K., Soubeiga, E., Scheduling nurses using a tabu-search hyperheuristic, 2003, Proceedings of the 1st Multidisciplinary International Conference on Scheduling: Theory and Applications, MISTA 2003, Nottingham, UK, pp. 197-218.
6. Cowling, P.I., Kendall, G., and Han, L., An investigation of a hyperheuristic genetic algorithm applied to a trainer scheduling problem. Proceedings of the Congress on Evolutionary Computation 2002, CEC 2002. Morgan Kaufman, pp. 1185-1190, 2002.
7. Cowling, P.I., Kendall, G., Soubeiga, E., Hyperheuristic Approach to Scheduling a Sales Summit, 2001, Selected papers of *Proceedings of the Third International Conference of Practice And Theory of Automated Timetabling,* Springer LNCS vol 2079, pp. 176-190.
8. Cowling, P.I., Kendall, G., Soubeiga, E., A Parameter-free Hyperheuristic for Scheduling a Sales Summit, 2001, *Proceedings of the Third Metaheuristic International Conference (MIC 2001)*, pp. 127-131

9. Cowling, P.I., Kendall, G., Soubeiga, E., Hyperheuristics: A Tool for Rapid Prototyping in Scheduling and Optimisation, 2002, European Conference on Evolutionary Computation (EvoCop 2002), Springer LNCS 2279, pp. 1-10.
10. Cowling, P.I., Kendall, G., and Soubeiga, E., Hyperheuristics: A robust optimisation method applied to nurse scheduling, 2002, Seventh International Conference on Parallel Problem Solving from Nature, PPSN2002, Springer LNCS, pp. 851-860.
11. Corne, D, Ogden, J, Evolutionary Optimisation of Methodist Preaching Timetables, Lecture Notes in Computer Science: Selected papers of *the Second International Conference of Practice And Theory of Automated Timetabling*, LNCS:1408, pp. 142-155.
12. Dowsland, K., Nurse scheduling with tabu search and strategic oscillation, 1998, *European Journal of Operational Research 106*, pp. 393-407.
13. Easton, F, Mansour, N, A Distributed Genetic Algorithm For Deterministic And Stochastic Labor Scheduling Problems, 1999, *European Journal of Operational Research*, pp. 505-523.
14. Gratch, J., Chien, S., Adaptive Problem-Solving for Large-Scale Scheduling Problems: A Case Study, 1996, *Journal of Artificial Intelligence Research*, vol. 4, pp. 365-396.
15. Hart, E., Ross, P., A heuristic combination method for solving jop-shop scheduling problems, 1998, Parallel Problem Solving from Nature V, Springer-Verlag Lecture Notes in Computer Science 1498, A.E.Eiben, T.Back, M.Schoenauer, H-P.Schwefel (eds), ISSN 0302-9743, pp. 845-854.
16. Hart, E, Ross, P, Nelson, J, Solving a Real-World Problem Using an Evolving Heuristically Driven Schedule Builder, 1998, *Evolutionary Computation*, vol. 6, No.1(6) pp. 61-80.
17. Martello, S., Toth, P., *Knapsack Problems Algorithms and Computer Implementations*, 1990, John Wiley & Son Ltd, Chichester, England.
18. Nareyek, A., Choosing Search Heuristics by Non-Stationary Reinforcement Learning, 2001, in Resende, M.G.C., and de Sousa, J.P. (eds.), *Metaheuristics: Computer Decision-Making*, Kluwer Academic Publishers, pp.523-544.
19. Randall, M, Abramson, D, A General Meta-Heuristic Based Solver for Combinatorial Optimisation Problems, 2001,*Computational Optimisation and Applications*, vol. 20, pp.185-210.
20. Soubeiga, E., *Development and Application of Hyperheuristics to Personnel Scheduling*, PhD Thesis, Department of Computer Science, University of Nottingham, UK, June 2003.
21. Terashima-Marin, H., Ross, P., Valenzuela-Rendon, M., Evolution of Constraint Satisfaction Strategies in Examination Timetabling, 1999, *Proceedings of the Genetic and Evolutionary Computation Conference (GECCO99)*. pp. 635-642.
22. Wren, A. Scheduling, Timetabling and Rostering - a Special Relationship? 1995, in: *ICPTAT'95- Proceedings of the International Conference on the Practice and Theory of Automate Timetabling,* pp. 475-495 Napier University.

CHAPTER 28

DESIGN OPTIMIZATION OF PERMANENT MAGNET SYNCHRONOUS MACHINE USING GENETIC ALGORITHMS

R.K. Gupta[1], Itsuya Muta[2], G. Gouthaman[1] and B. Bhattacharjee[1]

[1]*Machine Dynamics Division, Bhabha Atomic Research Centre Trombay, Mumbai- 400085, India.*
E-mail: rkgupta@magnum.barc.ernet.in.

[2]*Dept. of Electrical Engineering, Graduate School of Engineering Kyoto University, Sakyo-ku, Yoshida-Honmachi, Kyoto, 606-8501, Japan.*
E-mail: muta@kuee.kyoto-u.ac.jp

In this chapter, design of a 100 kW and 100,000 rpm surface mounted type Permanent Magnet synchronous machine has been optimized using Genetic Algorithms. The efficiency and power density of the machine have been taken as objective functions. A third objective function has been formed using weightage ratio method, giving equal weightage to both efficiency and power density. Various electrical, mechanical and thermal constraints have been taken into account using conventional formulae. Variation of efficiency and specific power with speed (at fixed output power) and with output power (at fixed speed) has been discussed. The results have been compared with that obtained using Sequential Unconstrained Minimization Technique (SUMT) based on the interior penalty function method.

1. Introduction

Optimization had been a classroom exercise until the advent of computers. The earlier works on optimization are based on the derivatives of the functions such as steepest gradient method, penalty function method etc.[1]. These are classical methods that generally provide local optimum solution. They can provide global optimum if the objective function and constraints are differentiable and are of convex type[1] which is very difficult to get in real engineering problems. To get the global optimum solution, one has to optimize from a number of initial points. Therefore, gradient based methods are not robust. Alternate techniques were investigated to find global optimum solution which lead to Evolutionary Algorithms. These algorithms are robust since these are based on the concept of evolution of the natural systems which are inherently robust.

Genetic Algorithms (GA) is one of the several versions of the Evolutionary Algorithms. It was developed by John Holland and his colleagues at the University of Michigan in the pursuit of their goal to explain the adaptive processes of natural systems and to develop artificial systems software based on the mechanisms of natural systems. Their work (1975) "Adaptation in Natural and Artificial Systems" is the primary monograph on GA. This technique is the simulation of Darwin's Evolution Theory of survival of the fittest. A lot of work was done by D.E. Goldberg[2] on this optimization method. Many authors have applied GA successfully in electrical machine designs[3-5], but the attempts were made for the machines of low speed range.

Due to the tremendous growth in the power electronics during the last two decades, the scope of high speed machines is growing fast. The high speed motors have mechanical and thermal problems. Mechanical problems are due to centrifugal forces and thermal ones are due to inherent smaller size. Amaratunga et al.[6] described the optimization of various magnetic circuit configurations for permanent magnet aerospace generators using classical method. They brought out that surface mounted permanent magnet (SPM) configuration gives highest power density among various possible configurations. The advent of very high strength and non-conducting type material viz. E-Glass and S-Glass, made it possible to use SPM configuration for high speed applications. These materials are used for reinforcing the rotating permanent magnets.

Genetic Algorithms differ from the conventional methods on many counts. They use coded variables and fitness function instead of using design variables and objective function directly. The conventional methods work from a single starting point therefore are more prone to get local optima while GA work on the population of starting points and hence searches in all possible domains, increasing the possibility of getting global optima. Conventional methods use derivatives of objective function which is difficult to evaluate in practical problems while GA do not require derivatives.

2. Design Aspects

In the present work, optimization of 100 kW, 100 k rpm, 2 pole surface mounted type permanent magnet synchronous machine has been studied. The schematic diagram of the machine is shown in Fig.1. In the present study, standard equations of the machine design[7,8] have been used during the optimization process.

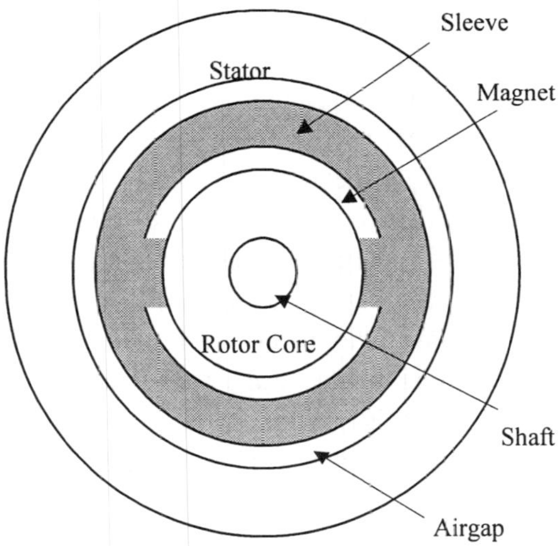

Fig. 1. Schematic diagram of High Speed Surface Mounted PM Machine

In high speed permanent magnet machine design, the stress on the sleeve for magnet protection, should be less than its yield strength with a safety factor. The residual flux density (B_r) of permanent magnet is sensitive to temperature; therefore temperature rise should be limited. By calculating the stress on sleeve and temperature rise, the mechanical and thermal constraints also have been considered.

The effect of saturation on machine parameters also has been considered. The saturation factor (k_s) has been found using following formula;

$$k_s = \frac{\text{Ampere turns required for both airgap and iron parts of the machine}}{\text{Ampere turns required for airgap only}} \quad (1)$$

For ampere turns calculation, resultant flux density was calculated at each part of the machine viz. airgap, stator teeth and stator and rotor backup iron. The resultant flux density is the vector sum of fields due to permanent magnet and armature reaction.

3. Optimal Problem Formulation

3.1. *Design Variables*

The design variables are those parameters which have larger effect on the performance of the machine. The efficacy of the optimization process is increased if the number of design variables is reduced. Therefore, design variables should be selected judiciously. For the present optimization work, following design variables have been selected;

- stator bore diameter (i.e. inner diameter of the stator)
- stator core length
- depth of stator slots
- depth of stator yoke (i.e. backup iron)
- thickness of the permanent magnet
- thickness of S-Glass sleeve for the magnet protection
- operating load angle.

Following parameters have been used with fixed value as given below;

1. Line voltage = 550.0 V
2. No. of poles = 2
3. Shaft diameter = 20.5 mm
4. Angular span of the magnets = 150°
5. Stator tooth width = 4.0 mm

6. Stator slot opening = 2.0 mm
7. Physical Air-gap length = 0.5 mm
8. Space factor for stator slots for winding = 0.4

The stator tooth width is kept 4.0 mm to give sufficient mechanical strength for the winding purpose, though it can be taken as a design variable.

3.2. *Constraints*

The constraints are the functional relationship among the design variables and other design parameters satisfying certain design requirements and certain resource limitations. There are usually two types of constraints viz. inequality and equality type. Most of the constraints are inequality type. Equality constraints are usually more difficult to handle and therefore should be avoided if possible. Following constraints have been selected;

1. Output torque = 9.55 Nm (the rated torque)
2. Airgap flux density ≥ 0.25 T
3. Flux density in rotor backup iron ≤ 1.9 T
4. Efficiency ≥ 97.0%
5. Stress on sleeve for magnet protection ≤ 250 kg/mm^2
   (Yield strength of S-Glass material = 470 kg/mm^2)
6. Required conductor area in the stator slot ≤ available slot area
7. Peak airgap flux density due to armature current ≤ (Airgap flux density due to magnet – Bd)
   Where, Bd = – 0.2 T for NdFeB magnets. This constraint is for protecting the magnets from demagnetization due to full load armature current.
8. Temperature rise of motor ≤ 90 °C
   (for class F insulation of stator winding)

Some design parameters have been taken as constant. The stator current density has been taken as 6.5 A/mm^2 (for forced air cooling) in case of specific power optimization and 4.0 A/mm^2 in case of efficiency optimization.

3.3. *Objective Functions*

Objective functions are selected based on requirement of the problem. In the present work, efficiency and specific power output have been taken as objective functions which are very important for high speed motor applications such as fly–wheel energy storage systems, electric vehicles etc. Since these two objective functions are contradictory, therefore a trade off between the two designs was obtained using weightage ratio method. In this method following steps are followed;

1) For maximization of the efficiency, the losses are minimized i.e. minimize $f_{loss}(X)$ to get $\text{Loss}_{\min}$
2) For maximization of the specific power, the mass of the machine is minimized i.e. minimize $f_{mass}(X)$ to get $\text{Mass}_{\min}$.
3) Using weightage factors, form a new function as a combination of loss and mass functions, i.e. minimize

$$f_{new}(X) = W_{\text{loss}}[f_{loss}(X)/\text{Loss}_{\min}]+W_{\text{mass}}[f_{mass}(X)/\text{Mass}_{\min}] \tag{2}$$

where W_{loss} and W_{mass} are the weighting factors for loss and mass respectively. In steps 1 and 2, same constraints are used.

$$W_{\text{loss}} + W_{\text{mass}} = 1.0 \tag{3}$$

These factors can be given any values depending upon the importance to be given to the efficiency and specific power. An arbitrary value of 0.5 has been given to the two factors in the present study.

4. Mathematical Formulation of Optimal Design

In machine design, the problems of optimization are nonlinear and constrained type. Mathematically, a constrained optimization problem can be stated in the standard form as[1];

Find X such as $f(X) \rightarrow$ minimum

subject to

$g_j(X) \leq 0$ j = 1,2, ….. m (inequality constraints)

$g_i(X) =$ constant i = 1,2, ….. p (equality constraints) and

$X_{lk} \leq X \leq X_{uk}$ where k = 1,2, ….. n (bounded variables)

where X = design vector = $[x_1, x_2, x_3, \ldots\ldots x_n]$

$x_1, x_2, x_3, \ldots\ldots x_n$ = design variables

$f(X)$ = objective function, $g_j(X)$ = constraints
X_{lk} = lower bound of kth variable and X_{uk} = upper bound of kth variable

5. Optimization using GA

Optimization process using GA is given in the flowchart (Fig.2).

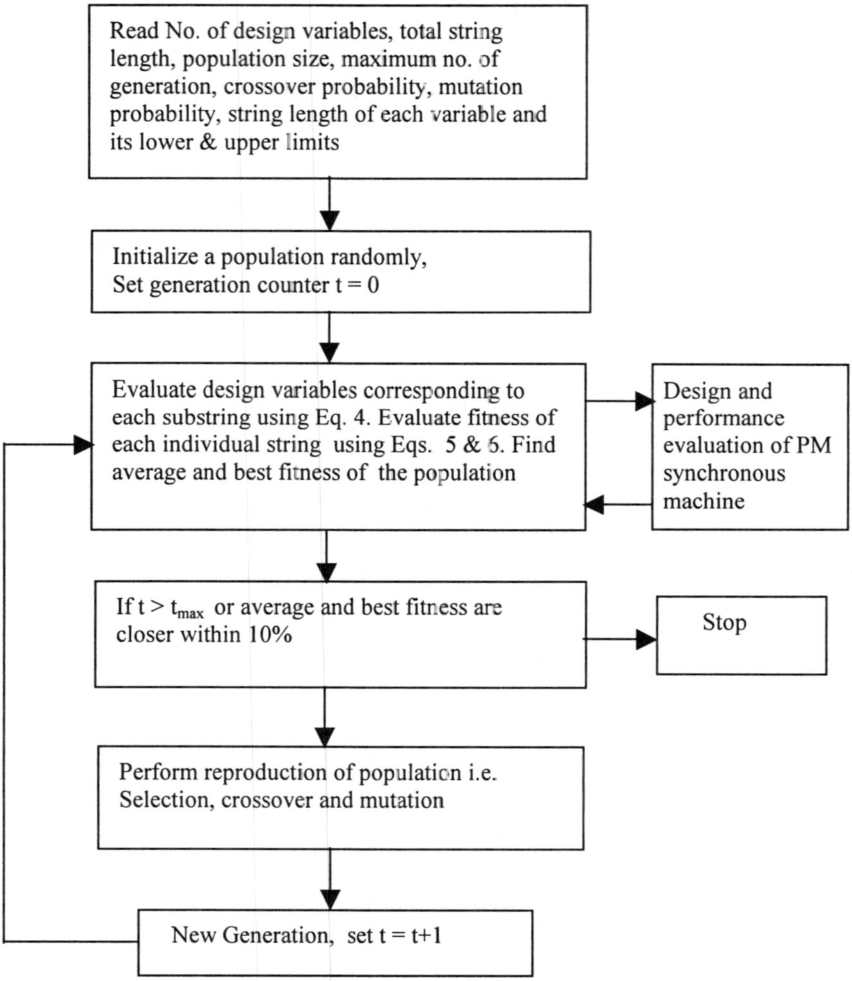

Fig.2. Flow chart for design optimization using Genetic Algorithms

Various steps in the Genetic Algorithms are given below;

5.1. *Coding of Design Variables*

All the design variables are first coded into binary form (string of 0 and 1) randomly. They can be coded into other forms also including decimal. The length of binary string (i.e. number of bits) representing a variable depends upon the resolution required for that variable. In the present work, binary coding was used with 10 bits for each design variable. The binary string of a variable is called sub-string. The full string containing sub-strings of all the design variables is called the individual or chromosome of the population. Each individual (chromosome) represents a complete design of the machine. With seven design variables in the present work, each individual of a population contains 70 bits A single bit of string is like gene, its value (0 or 1) is like allele and its position in string is like locus in biological system.

5.2. *Evaluation of Objective Function*

Once sub-strings and individuals are generated randomly in binary form, the corresponding design variables are calculated using following equation [9];

$$x_i = x_{iL} + \frac{x_{iU} - x_{iL}}{2^{ni} - 1} \text{ . (Decimal value of } S_i\text{)} \tag{4}$$

where;

x_{iL}, x_{iU} = Lower and upper limit of ith variable

n = number of bits in the ith variable

S_i = Binary string of ith variable

Now, the objective function O(X) can be evaluated from the design vector X (x_1, x_2, x_3,……. x_n).

For efficiency and specific power optimization, the O(X) is the loss and mass function respectively which are to be minimized. The loss and mass functions are evaluated through complete machine design using analytical or finite element method. Analytical method has been used in the present work.

5.3. *Evaluation of Fitness Function*

Since GA is based on the principle of survival of the fittest, the fitness of each individual in the population is to be evaluated by some fitness function. For solving maximization problems, the objective function itself can be taken as fitness function. But in the present work, the loss and mass functions are to be minimized. In such cases the fitness function can be evaluated as[9];

$$F(X) = 1/(1+O(X)) \tag{5}$$

Now, the fitness function F(X) will represent our main objective functions i.e. efficiency and specific power respectively which are to be maximized.

For constrained problems, the function O(X) is replaced with a penalty function P(X), where

$$P(X) = O(X) + r \sum_{j=1}^{m}[g_j(X)]^2 \tag{6}$$

where $[g_j(X)] = 0$ if $g_j(X) \leq 0$

$= g_j(X)$ if $g_j(X) > 0$

m = number of constraints

r = penalty parameter which is kept constant throughout GA process

The fitness function for each individual in the population ($F(X_i)$) is calculated. Their total value ($\Sigma_i F(X_i)$) and average value ($\Sigma_i F(X_i)/N$) are also calculated (N is the population size). These values are used in the selection process of reproduction of population.

5.4. *Reproduction of Population*

A new population is produced keeping the number of the individuals same. This is done in following stages;

5.4.1 Selection

Individuals from the current population are selected to form a mating pool. The selection is based on their fitness value. The fitter individuals will have more copies in the mating pool. Since the number of individuals is fixed, some of the individuals with poor fitness value may be excluded. There are various ways for the selection viz. roulette wheel selection, stochastic remainder selection and tournament selection[2]. The stochastic remainder selection method has been used. In this method, the individuals are selected as per selection probability expressed as $P_i = F(X_i)/(\Sigma_i F(X_i))$. The expected count of each individual in the mating pool is calculated as $e_i = P_i .N$. The integer part of e_i represents the number of copies of the individual, surely going to the mating pool. The fractional part of e_i is taken as the new selection probability based on which the remaining population is filled.

5.4.2 Crossover

In crossover operation, two strings from the mating pool are picked up at random. Crossover is performed between these two strings. This can be done on single point or two point basis. Single point crossover has been used. In single point crossover, a position (crossing site) along the two strings is again randomly chosen and all the binary digits on the right side of the crossing site are swapped. The crossover operation is mainly responsible for the search of new strings i.e. searching in new location in the search space. Some of the strings in the mating pool don't participate in the crossover operation. Only $100.P_c$ percent strings take part in the crossover, where P_c is the crossover probability.

5.4.3 Mutation

In mutation operation, a bit of a string is randomly selected with a small mutation probability P_m and its value is changed from 1 to 0 or vice versa. Mutation creates a local search around the current point, to avoid any loss of useful genetic information. Mutation is performed on each string of the population.

For the good performance of GA, high crossover probability (0.6-0.8), a low mutation probability (0.01-0.03) and a moderate population size (20-30) is desired. Mutation probability is inversely proportional to the population size. A large number of combination of these parameters were tried to improve the GA performance.

5.5. *New Generation and Termination*

After the crossover and mutation operation in the mating pool, a new generation is formed. The same process is repeated from step 5.2 onward. The process is terminated when a predefined number of generations are reached or when the best and average fitness values become closer say within 10%.

6. Results and Discussions

The optimization programme for the SPM machine has been made with the following assumption;

1) For specific power calculation, only weight of active materials viz. stator core, rotor core, copper wire and permanent magnets have been taken.
2) For the calculation of efficiency, stator copper loss, core losses in stator and eddy current loss in the permanent magnets have been considered. Friction and windage losses have been considered as part of the load.
3) Losses have been computed for Super E-Core (6.5% Si-steel) material for stator core.
4) All the computations are for the magnet arc of 150°.

The design was optimized using Sequential Un-constrained Minimization Technique (SUMT)[10] also based on interior penalty function method. The results of both the optimizations are shown in the Table 1 Where;
A = Design with efficiency as objective function.
B = Design with specific power as objective function.
C = Design with both efficiency and specific power as objective function with 50% weightage to each.

The output power level is 100 kW at 100 krpm in all the three cases. The length of the machine depends on the product $L*N_{ph}$ for the given voltage, where L and N_{ph} are core length and number of turns per phase respectively. Since number of turns per phase varies in step, therefore length is adjusted accordingly.

For efficiency optimization (case A), the total loss is the least. In high

Table 1. Comparison of various design parameters in case of three different objective functions

S.No.	Description	Units	Objective Functions					
			Efficiency (A)		Specific Power (B)		Combined Efficiency and Specific Power with equal weightage (C)	
			GA	SUMT	GA	SUMT	GA	SUMT
1.	Output power at airgap	kW	100.0	100.0	100.0	100.0	100.0	100.0
2.	Operating speed	krpm	100.0	100.0	100.0	100.0	100.0	100.0
3.	Stator bore diameter	mm	63.496	59.524	63.021	58.723	62.649	59.548
4.	Stator outer diameter	mm	158.608	156.988	136.432	135.723	141.144	137.792
5.	Stator core length	mm	114.217	90.840	85.269	95.189	90.445	98.676
6.	OD^2. L	cm^3	2873.3	2238.8	1587.2	1753.5	1801.8	1873.5
7.	Depth of stator slots	mm	32.511	33.366	23.548	24.691	24.04	24.190
8.	Depth of stator yoke	mm	15.045	15.366	13.157	13.809	15.207	14.932
9.	Thickness of magnet	mm	4.575	4.649	5.349	4.777	5.502	4.767
10.	Thickness of sleeve	mm	7.531	5.023	5.634	5.356	6.187	5.212
11.	Operating load angle	Degree	49.720	44.502	38.559	43.76	38.212	43.126
12.	Line current	A	117.32	114.850	112.64	114.762	112.723	109.33
13.	Stator current density	A/mm^2	4.0	4.0	6.5	6.5	6.5	6.5
14.	Airgap flux density	T	0.2545	0.34135	0.34348	0.33020	0.32574	0.33726
15.	No. of turns per phase		16	16	16	16	16	16
16.	Specific electrical loading	A.cond/m	54263.0	56236.3	54672.1	57515.4	54996.2	56103.2
17.	Stator copper loss	W	401.17	354.0	479.19	530.4	494.84	477.8
18.	Stator core loss	W	247.63	358.95	323.46	279.63	276.00	283.45
19.	Eddy current loss in Magnets	W	1.575	7.248	5.594	5.41	3.738	6.322
20.	Total losses	W	650.36	720.25	808.24	815.44	774.58	767.54
21.	Efficiency	%	99.354	99.28	99.198	99.191	99.231	99.238
22.	Power factor		0.9007	0.9224	0.9404	0.9239	0.9395	0.9266
23.	Specific Power Output	kW/kg	5.691	6.756	10.472	9.655	9.486	9.122
24.	Natural frequency of rotor	Hz	2204.9	2596.2	3338.9	2383.8	3029.7	2542.55
25.	Stress on sleeve	kg/mm^2	246.2	220.79	247.1	213.79	242.7	220.5
26.	Temperature rise	°C	42.5	54.5	72.0	72.4	65.3	70.95

speed machines, the major loss is the core loss in stator backup iron and copper loss. To reduce these losses, the depth of stator yoke and the slot have increased. The stator current density is the lowest in this case. The outer diameter is highest resulting in lowest specific power output.

For specific power optimization, the outer diameter and the stator yoke depth are smallest. The product $OD^2.L$ is lowest (where OD is the outer diameter of the machine). The total loss is the highest due to the high flux density in the stator yoke and high stator current density. Temperature rise is quite high due to high loss and less surface area. In the last optimization problem (case C) the performance of the machine lies between the two cases A and B.

In GA, the penalty parameter r in Eq.6 can be made large and kept constant while in SUMT this parameter is varied in successive sequence. In SUMT, a large value of r results in distortion of penalty function which may create some artificial local minima. Since for better optimization, the penalty parameter should be very high, therefore in Table 1, the GA gives better results than SUMT for both efficiency and specific power optimization. In SUMT, the knowledge of initial design is necessary whereas in GA it is not required.

Exhaustive computation has been carried out to find the optimal size of the 100 kW rating machine for various operating speed range with efficiency as objective function. Efficiency and specific power (kW/kg) have been plotted against the speed in Fig. 3. It can be seen that the value of specific power increases with the operating speed, but the curve does not follow the ideal volume-speed inverse relationship. This is because the machine is optimized for the highest efficiency possible. The efficiency of the machine also increases with the operating speed as expected. The increase in efficiency is marginal after 50 krpm.

When the speed is kept at a constant value (100 krpm) and machine is designed for optimum efficiency at various power ratings, the specific power and efficiency vary with output power as shown in Fig. 4. In this case too, since the machine is optimized for the efficiency, the curve of specific power does not follow the inverse law faithfully. In this case also, the efficiency increases with output power level as expected.

In both figures 3 and 4, the results of GA have been compared with that of SUMT. The curves are similar in nature for both the methods. The

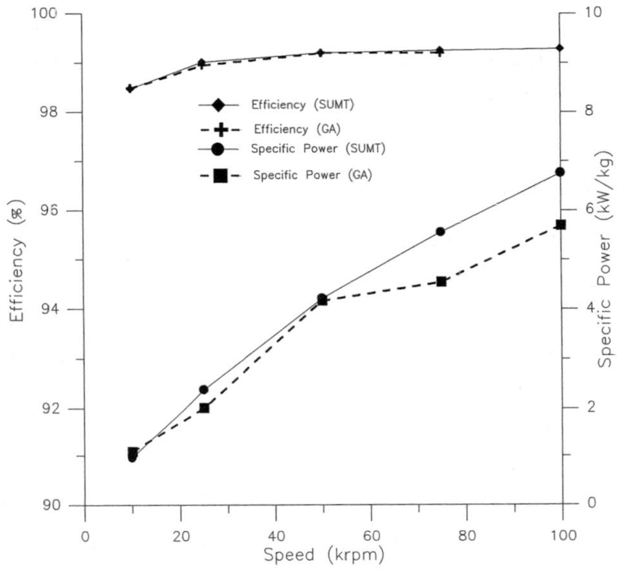

Fig.3. Variation of Efficiency and Specific Power with speed at fixed output power (100 kW)

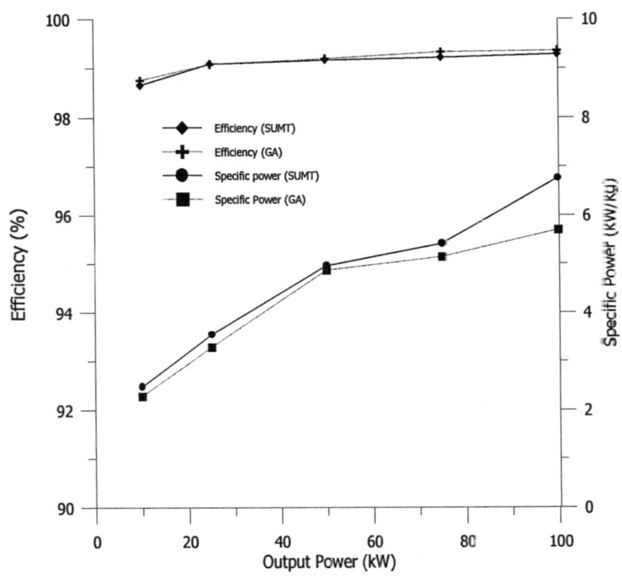

Fig.4. Variation of Efficiency and Specific Power with output power at fixed speed (100 krpm)

efficiencies found from both the methods are almost the same but there is a difference in the values of specific power due to the fact that in both figures, efficiency is the objective function.

7. Conclusions

Design of a 100 kW and 100 krpm surface mounted permanent magnet synchronous machine was optimized for efficiency, specific power and combination of the both (with 50% weightage to each) using Genetic Algorithms. The results of GA have been compared with that obtained from a classical method (SUMT). It is found that GA can provide better result with rather ease because it does not need initial design. The parameters of the GA viz. string length, population size, number of generations, random seed number, crossover and mutation probabilities affect the result. With proper selection of these parameters, a result close to global optimum can be obtained.

Acknowledgement

Authors would like to thank Mr. P.H. Chavda, and A.K.Wankhede of Bhabha Atomic Research Centre and Mrs. Babita Gupta of NPCIL for their useful suggestions.

References

1. S.S. Rao, *Optimization Theory and Applications*, second edition (Willey Eastern Limited, New Delhi, 1984).
2. D.E. Goldberg, *Genetic Algorithms in search, optimization and Machine Learning* (Additon-Wesley, Reading MA, 1989).
3. G. Fuat Uler, Osama A. Mohammed and Chang-Seop Koh, Utilizing Genetic Algorithms for the Optimal Design of Electromagnetic Devices, *IEEE Trans. on Magnetics,* Vol. 30, No.6, pp. 4296-4298, (1994).
4. Dong-Joon Sim et al, Efficiency Optimization of Interior Permanent Magnet Synchronous Motor using Genetic Algorithms, *IEEE Trans. on Magnetics*, Vol. 33, pp. 1880-1883. (1997)
5. N. Bianchi and S. Bolognani, Design Optimization of Electric Motors by Genetic Algorithms, *IEE Proc. Electric Power Applications,* Vol. 145, No. 5, pp 475-483 (1998).

6. G.A.J. Amaratunga, P.P. Acarnley and P.G. Mclaren, Optimum Magnetic Circuit Configurations for Permanent Magnet Aerospace Generators, *IEEE Trans. on Aerospace and Electronic Systems*, Vol. AES-21, No. 2, pp 230-255 (1985).
7. P. Pillai et al, Performance and Design of Permanent Magnet AC Motor Drives, *Proceedings of Conference, IAS Annual Meeting, Sandiago,* CA (1989).
8. V.B. Honsinger, Performance of Polyphase Permanent Magnet Machines, *IEEE Trans. on Power Apparatus and Systems*, Vol. PAS-99, No. 4, pp 1510-1518 (1980).
9. K. Deb, *Optimization for Engineering Design - Algorithms and Examples* (Prentice Hall of India Pvt. Limited, New Delhi, 1995).
10. Itsuya Muta, R.K. Gupta, R. Anbarasu, B. Bhattacharjee, Optimization of Permanent Magnet Synchronous machine using SUMT, *Proc. of conference, 4th International Symposium on Advanced Electromechanical Motion Systems (Electromotion'01),* Bologna, Italy, pp 65-70 (2001).

CHAPTER 29

A GENETIC ALGORITHM FOR JOINT OPTIMIZATION OF SPARE CAPACITY AND DELAY IN SELF-HEALING NETWORK

Sam Kwong and H.W. Chong

Department of Computer Science, City University
83 Tatchee Avenue, Kowloon, Hong Kong
E-mail: cssamk@cityu.edu.hk

This chapter presents the use of multi-objective Genetic Algorithms (mGA) to solve the capacity and routing assignment problem arising in the design of *self-healing* networks using the Virtual Path (VP) concept. Past research has revealed that Pre-planned Backup Protection method and the Path Restoration scheme can provide a good compromise on the reserved spare capacity and the failure restoration time. The aims to minimize the sum of working and backup capacity usage and transmission delay often compete and contradict with each other. Multi-objective Genetic algorithm is a powerful method for this kind of multi-objective problems. In this chapter, a multi-objective GA approach is proposed to achieve the above two objectives while a set of customer traffic demands can still be satisfied and the traffic is 100% restorable under a single point of failure. We carried out a few experiments and the results illustrate the trade-off between objectives and the ability of this approach to produce many good compromise solutions in a single run. To measure the performance of approach, our results are used to compare with that using single objective genetic algorithm (sGA).

1. Introduction

To cope with the increasing networking demands from the customers, currently Telephone Company (TELCO) operators are changing their networks from coaxial cables to optical fibers, transmission technology from PDH (plesiochronous digital hierarchy) to SDH (synchronous digital hierarchy), and switching technology from STM (synchronous transfer mode) to ATM (asynchronous transfer mode). The deployment of fiber optics in ATM/SDH network leads to the fact that more and more traffic is concentrated on a few fibers. Therefore, the capability of the fiber network to restore services affected by failures within the shortest possible time becomes a key network architecture design consideration.

To restore affected traffic upon a network failure within short time duration, a usual practice is to pre-allocate redundant (spare) capacity in the network. If sufficient spare capacity is reserved for the ATM network, all the traffic can be re-routed automatically upon failure and the customer applications will not notice there is a network problem, and such a network is called a "*self-healing*" network. If there are too much spare capacity reserved, then the TELCO operator obviously do not operate the network in a cost-effective manner. On the other hand, the protection level may not be enough. So, what should be the optimal amount of spare capacity? Reducing network protection costs while maintaining an acceptable level of survivability is one of the main objectives of the network planners. In reality, nodes in a given network are not always fully connected with each other for the cost purpose. Also links between nodes are not all of the same speed. Thus, the transmission delay from a source node to a destination node depends very much on the paths chosen. Every customer likes to have a route with minimum delay, the TELCO operator cannot promise every customer that the route is the shortest. It becomes an interesting problem for one to choose routes that will compromise between the interests of the TELCO operator and different customers.

The above problem can be regarded as the combination of two sub problems:

1. The objective to minimize capacity subject to a constraint on delay with a given network topology and assigned traffic requirements.

2. The objective to minimize delay subject to a constraint on the total capacity with a given network topology and assigned traffic requirements.

Obviously, these two sub-problems are dependent and cannot be easily solved without considering each other's existence. That is an issue that makes the above problem a relatively hard one, which is not easy to be solved using classical optimization methods.

To tackle the above problems, a GA-based multi-objective optimization approach is presented in this chapter. We will see how the method obtains a Pareto set of solutions in that any single set of solution can be freely chosen according to the fulfillment of the system requirements. We will also see that spare capacity and delay are jointly optimized to provide a highly reliable service.

2. Related Work

The capacity, routing assignment and transmission delay arising in the design of *self-healing* network is a combinatorial optimization problem. It involves the assignment of capacities to the links, the routing of requirements on these links and minimizing transmission delay. Ideally, all these are jointly optimized.

Different methods are proposed to optimize capacity allocation and routing assignment in order to minimize the cost[2-5]. They solve the problem using linear programming techniques. These methods suffer from the usual disadvantages of linear/integer programming: lots constraints need to set and variables to manipulate, which results in intensive computation.

Minimizing the total capacity and total transmission delay are equally important in the *self-healing* networks. But previous work focused more on the capacity allocation, routing assignment than transmission delay. In some literatures, transmission delay is considered as a constraint but not an objective function for minimization. By transforming the delay constraint, the problem can be easily formulated as a multi-objective optimization problem.

In our former work [1], we proposed a genetic algorithm based method to solve the capacity and routing assignment problem arising in the design of *self-healing* networks using the Virtual Path (VP) concept. This approach can avoid most of the problems inherent in linear programming and we showed that GA based approach is better than other heuristic approaches. However, we only tackled the capacity problem but we did not take the delay into consideration. In this chapter we will use a GA-based multi-objective optimization approach to solve the problem and it has a significant advantage over other approaches.

3. Problem Formulation

In this research, we will model the network as an undirected graph $G = (V, E)$, where V is a set of nodes and E is a set of links. Each link is a pair of oppositely directed arcs or fibers. The network is not modeled as a directed graph because most of the communication networks are generally bi-directional. Each site in the network will be represented as a node. Each node will be assigned a number, as its ID. From now on, if not specified, we assume the bandwidth of each link is $\boldsymbol{B}$ units

We have made the following assumptions for this research:

- The target network of study is an ATM network.
- A single point of failure in the network is assumed.
- It is assumed the network can restore all the affected traffic due to this single point of failure.
- Each branch of a multicast circuit requires the same bandwidth (however, different multicast circuits can have different bandwidths)
- Link transmission delay is directly proportional to the link distance

The notations used in the problem formulation are:

N	A set of nodes of the network
A	A set of directed arcs of the network
C_a	Capacity of arc a, where $a \in A$
Π	A set of source-destinations multicast traffic requirements
WVP	A set of multicast working virtual paths
BVP	A set of multicast backup virtual paths
$\lvert\Pi\rvert$	Total number of multicast traffic demanded
$\lvert WVP\rvert$	Total number of multicast working virtual paths
$\lvert BVP\rvert$	Total number of multicast backup virtual paths

Π_i	*i-th* source-destination multicast traffic in Π
WVP_i	*i-th* multicast working virtual path in *WVP* to satisfy Π_i
BVP_i	*i-th* multicast backup virtual path in *BVP* to backup WVP_i
$WVP_i(a)$	Capacity of arc *a* used by WVP_i, where $a \in A$
$BVP_i(a)$	Capacity of arc *a* reserved by BVP_i, where $a \in A$
$WVP_i.delay$	Total transmission delay of WVP_i
$BVP_i.delay$	Total transmission delay of BVP_i
$O(\Pi_{ij})$	Source node of the *j-th* branch of Π_i
$O(WVP_{ij})$	Source node of the *j-th* branch of WVP_i
$O(BVP_{ij})$	Source node of the *j-th* branch BVP_i
$D(\Pi_{ij})$	Destination node of the *j-th* branch of Π_i
$D(WVP_{ij})$	Destination node of the *j-th* branch of WVP_i
$D(BVP_{ij})$	Destination node of *the j-th* branch BVP_i
Π_{ij}	Bandwidth demanded by *j-th* branch of Π_i
$WVP_{ij}.bandwidth$	Bandwidth of *j-th* branch of WVP_i
$BVP_{ij}.bandwidth$	Bandwidth of *j-th* branch of BVP_i
$I\text{-}WVP_{ij}$	It is the intermediate virtual path of WVP_{ij} – with source and destination nodes excluded
$I\text{-}BVP_{ij}$	It is the intermediate virtual path of BVP_{ij} – with source and destination nodes excluded

The multicast routing problem is described as follows.

Objective one: To find *WVP* to satisfy the requirement Π, and the *BVP* to provide alternative routes that can restore the entire failed multicast working virtual paths in *WVP* under single point of failure of the network.

Objective two: To minimize the transmission delay between nodes.

The objective functions are given as:

$$1.\ Min\left\{\sum_{a \in A}\sum_{i=1}^{|\Pi|}\left[WVP_i(a) + BVP_i(a)\right]\right\} \tag{1}$$

$$2.\ Min\left\{\sum_{i=1}^{|\Pi|}\left[WVP_i.delay + BVP_i.delay\right]\right\} \tag{2}$$

Subject to the following constraints:

1. $|\Pi| = |WVP| = |BVP|$ AND
   $O(\Pi_{ij}) = O(WVP_{ij}) = O(BVP_{ij})$ AND
   Π_{ij}.bandwidth = WVP_{ij}.bandwidth = BVP_{ij}.bandwidth
   where $\forall\ i = 1$ to $|\Pi|$ and $j = 1$ to degree of multicast of *i-th* multicast traffic demand
2. $I\text{-}WVP_{ij} \cap I\text{-}BVP_{ij} = \varnothing$ in link-disjointed or node-disjointed sense
   where $\forall\ i = 1$ to $|\Pi|$ and $j = 1$ to degree of multicast of *i-th* multicast traffic demand
3. $\sum_{i=1}^{|\Pi|} \left[WVP_i(a) + BVP_i(a) \right] \leq C_a \qquad \forall a \in A$

Constraint (1) ensures that the *WVP* found can satisfy *Π*, and the *BVP* can support *WVP* under a single point of failure of the network. Constraint (2) is to ensure that the backup virtual path is completely link-disjointed or node-disjointed from the working virtual path. Constraint (3) is to make sure that the capacity of any arc can satisfy the bandwidth used by *WVP* and reserved by *BVP*.

In our former work [1], we propose a single objective approach with the objective function given as the following,

$$Min\left\{ k \sum_{a \in A} \sum_{i=1}^{|\Pi|} \left[WVP_i(a) + BVP_i(a) \right] + (1-k) \sum_{i=1}^{|\Pi|} \left[WVP_i.delay + BVP_i.delay \right] \right\} \tag{3}$$

where k is the weights to each of the objectives to indicate their importance in the problem, We set k to 1 because we are interested in the capacity assignment optimization problem, if we want to study the shortest path (i.e. delay) optimization problem, then k is set as 0. For multiple objectives, we have to tune k constantly in order to get the objectives jointly optimized. This method is very subjective, may over-simplify the behavior of the objectives, and it is often hard to find weights which can accurately reflect the situation. Thus, we propose to use mGA to solve this problem.

4. Design of Genetic Algorithm

In this part, a multi-objective genetic algorithm is described. The whole process of GA can be summarized as below.

1. Initialization
   - Set the population size be N_p
   - Set the maximum allowed number of generation be G_{max}
   - Set the crossover probability be p_c
   - Set the mutation probability be p_m
   - Set $G = 0$ where G is the generation counter

2. The GA process
   Step 1: Generate a population of chromosomes
   Step 2: Fitness assignment and sharing
   Step 3: Perform selection
   Step 4: Perform crossover
   Step 5: Perform mutation
   Step 6: Fitness assignment and sharing
   Step 7: Perform replacement
   Step 8: Set $G = G + 1$. If $G > G_{max}$, terminate.
   Otherwise, go to Step 3.

In the following, a detailed description of chromosome representation, population pool initialization, fitness assignment, fitness sharing, selection, crossover, mutation and GA parameters will be provided.

4.1. *Chromosome Representation*

In our optimization problem, a solution is a set of working virtual paths (*WVPs*) and a set of backup virtual paths (*BVPs*) for the multicast traffic, which can minimize the sum of working and backup capacity and the total transmission delay of the network. The description of our method of chromosome encoding is given as follow.

- Each chromosome consists of genes where each gene represents a set of *WVPs* and *BVPs* of the same multicast traffic that satisfy a particular customer's multicast traffic demand. Note that the number of genes in the chromosomes should be equal to the total number of customer traffic demands.

- Since multicast traffic is viewed as a number of unicast traffic leaving from the same source node but different destination nodes, we design an entity (let's call it a sub-gene) to represent a solution for a unicast traffic. Then, each gene consists of sub-genes that each sub-gene represents a *WVP* and a *BVP* that satisfy a particular customer's unicast traffic demand. As mentioned before, we defined the degree of multicast of a particular customer's multicast traffic as the total number of the unicast traffic of this customer. Then, the number of sub-genes in a gene is equal to the degree of multicast of a particular multicast traffic.

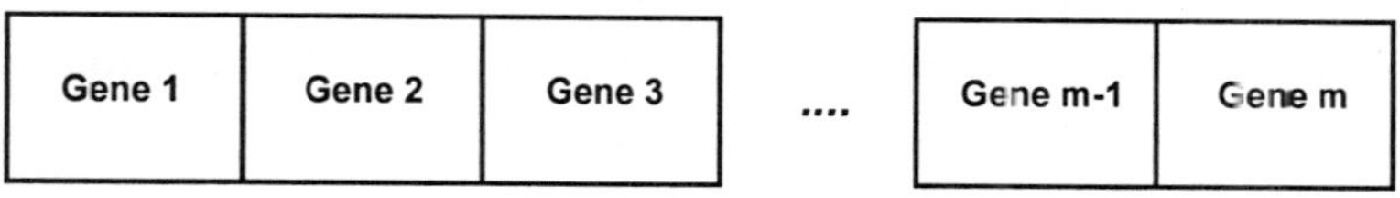

Fig. 1. Structure of a chromosome

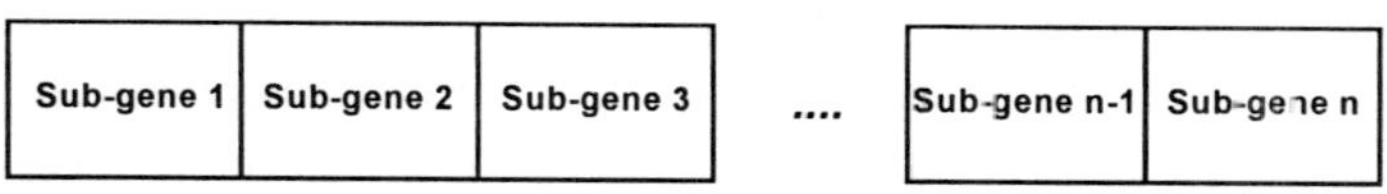

Fig. 2. Structure of a gene

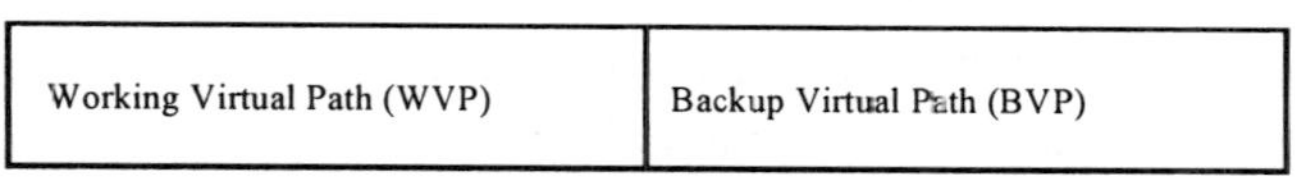

Fig. 3. Structure of a sub-gene

4.2. *Population Pool Initialization*

Before the genetic algorithm starts, we need to generate degrees of multicast, source nodes and destination nodes randomly based on the total number of virtual paths specified and the given topological information of an ATM network. Each possible path should not include an intermediate node more than once so that all the paths generated will not waste unnecessary resources. Furthermore, each source-to-destination route should have at least two paths (one for Working Virtual Path and one for Backup Virtual Path) with its minimum hop number. However, if it contains only one path with its minimum hop number, we accept all its possible paths with one more hop. In the beginning of genetic algorithm, a Working Virtual Path and a Backup Virtual Path of each source-to-destination route are randomly selected from its corresponding set of paths found and then allocated to the chromosomes.

4.3. *Fitness Assignment*

The fitness function links the Genetic Algorithm to the problem to be solved, it is used to measure the goodness of the chromosomes in the evolutionary process. The Pareto-based ranking method proposed by Fonseca and Fleming [6] is adopted in this work.

Assuming that chromosome I is dominated by other p chromosomes in the population, its rank is determined as

$$Rank(I) = 1 + P \tag{4}$$

The Pareto-based ranking can correctly assign all non-dominated chromosomes with the same fitness values. However, the genetic diversity of the population can be lost due to stochastic errors in the selection process. The goal of an mGA is to find a population composed of non-dominated genotypes evenly distributed along the Pareto-front defining the trade-off between objectives. To achieve the even distribution of the population across the front, fitness-sharing methods are adopted in our design to maintain genetic diversity.

4.4. *Fitness Sharing*

Fitness sharing decreases the increment of fitness of densely populated solution space and shares the fitness with other space. It helps genetic algorithm search various space and generate more diverse solutions. With fitness sharing, the genetic algorithm finds more diverse solutions although some of the solutions are not good. Let f_i be the fitness of an individual i, $sh(d_{ij})$ be sharing function, and M be the population size, then the shared fitness fs_i is computed as :

$$fs_i = \frac{f_i}{\sum_{j=1}^{M} sh(d_{ij})} \tag{5}$$

The sharing function $sh(d_{ij})$ is computed using the distance value d_{ij} that means the difference between individual i and j as follows:

$$sh(d_{ij}) = \begin{cases} 1 - \dfrac{d_{ij}}{\sigma_s} & for\ o \le d_{ij} < \sigma_s \\ 0 & for\ d_{ij} \ge \sigma_s \end{cases} \qquad (6)$$

where σ_s describes the sharing radius. If the difference is larger than σ_s, they do not share the fitness.

4.5. *Genetic Operators*

Selection

Elitist fitness proportionate selection, using the roulette-wheel algorithm, was implemented, using a simple fitness scaling whereby the scaled fitness f is

$$f = f - f_{worst} \qquad (7)$$

where f_{worst} is the fitness of the worst individual in the current population. Overall, the algorithm is elitist, in the sense that the best individual in the population is always passed on unchanged to the next generation, without undergoing crossover or mutation.

Crossover

We have designed three types of crossover operations, namely:
(i) Chromosome Crossover
(ii) Direct Gene Crossover
(iii) Indirect Gene Crossover

The strategy of using the above three crossover operations is to use one type of crossover operation first, if the operation gives two valid offspring chromosome, then the crossover mechanism is said to be complete; otherwise, we will try the other types of crossover operations. In order to avoid using any one type of crossover operation more than the others, three operations are selected randomly.

Chromosome crossover

The purpose of the Chromosome Crossover is to explore whether the different combinations of genes can get chromosomes with better fitness. This type of crossover involves exchange of genes between two selected chromosomes. To be fair, the crossover point of the two parents chromosomes is selected randomly. Fig. 4 shows the operation of Chromosome Crossover.

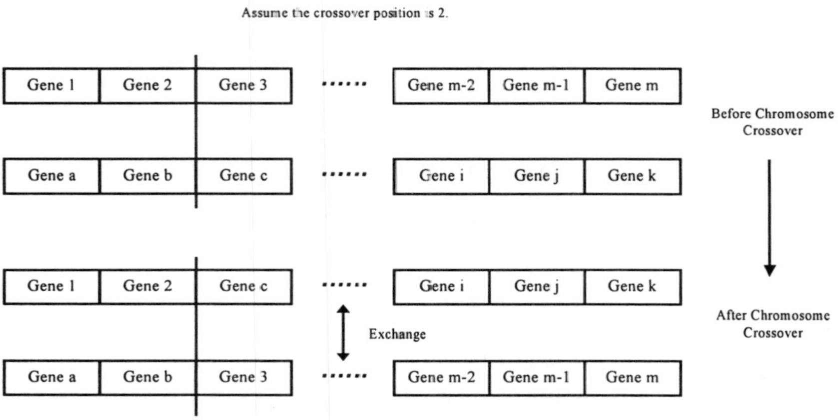

Fig. 4. The operation of Chromosome Crossover

Direct gene crossover

For Direct Gene Crossover, it is aimed to create new combinations of sub-genes and thus new chromosomes. Only one gene is randomly selected in each chosen pair of chromosomes for performing this type of crossover. Fig. 5 shows the operation of Direct Gene Crossover.

Indirect Gene Crossover

This type of crossover mechanism is not brought from the conventional Genetic Algorithm. It is dedicated to the capacity and routing assignment problem of a *self-healing* network. Fig. 6 shows the operation of Indirect Gene Crossover. Before this type of crossover type is performed, we need to select a gene and a sub-gene inside the selected gene. If the Working Virtual Paths or Backup Virtual Paths inside a selected sub-gene of a selected gene of the two parent chromosomes have same intermediate node excluding source node and destination node, the path segment after the intermediate node (i.e. all nodes next to the intermediate node) will be exchanged between two parent chromosomes. Otherwise, the two parent chromosomes will remain unchanged.

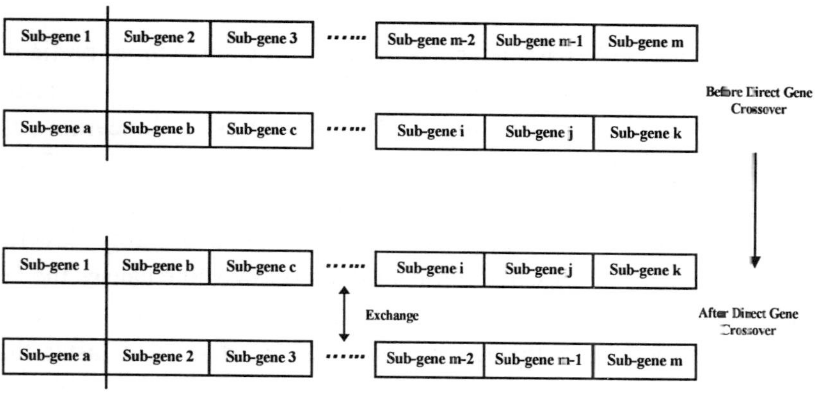

Fig. 5. The operation of Direct Gene Crossover (Assume the crossover position is 1)

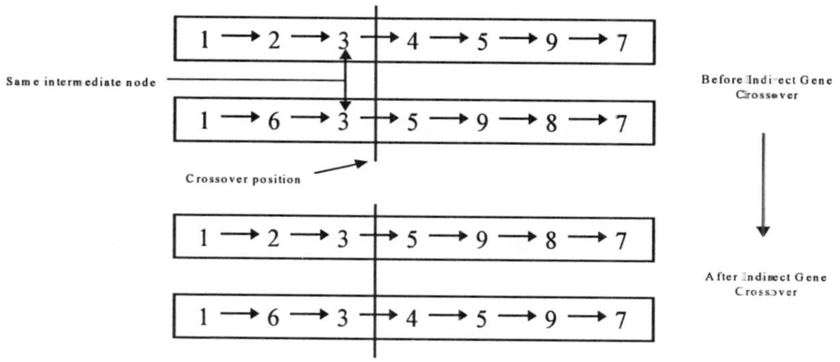

Fig. 6. The operation of Indirect Gene Crossover

Mutation

Mutation is another important activity in a genetic algorithm. It aims to introduce some changes on genes to the chromosomes to avoid being trapped in a local optimum. Mutation probabilities are utilized to choose a set of chromosomes to perform mutation. Before mutation is implemented, we need to select a gene and a sub-gene inside the selected gene. Then, a new Working Virtual Path and Backup Virtual Path are found to replace the current paths inside the chosen sub-gene. When a sub-gene is changed, the corresponding gene and chromosome is also changed. If the resulting chromosome is a valid one, then it will replace the selected chromosome, else no change is made.

GA Parameters

Fine tuning the GA parameters is indeed necessary in a particular problem because different performance can be obtained in various problems by using the same set of GA parameters [7]. Concerning the parameter setting, if the population size is too small, it offers insufficient sample size for most hyperplanes and causes poor GA performance. If the population size is too large, it may result in an unacceptably slow rate of convergence [8]. For crossover probability, too low value causes the GA search to stagnate because of low exploration rate but too high value causes that structures with high performance are discarded faster than selection can produce improvements. In addition, too low value of mutation probability does not help much on the found solution escape from local optimum while too high value causes the GA search which behaves as random search [8]. In order to choose a good set of parameter, several runs were carried out on different network topologies, in order to evaluate the reliability of the solutions, we perform tests using the range of the population size from 20 to 100, the crossover probability from 0.5 to 0.9 and the mutation probabilities from 0.005 to 0.2. Table 1 presents the parameters values we found the best and therefore it is adopted in our simulation.

5. Experimental Results

To validate the effectiveness of the proposed approach, we have performed experiments in seven networks shown in Fig. 7. Some ATM network parameters are shown in Table 2. These experiments are based on customer traffic demands of 100 working virtual paths. The total delay and total capacity of those rank 1 chromosomes in the final generation are depicted in Figs 8 to 14. A Pareto optimal set is clearly obtained by the multi-objective GA-based approach.

Table 1. GA parameters

Parameter	Value/Type
Population Size, N_c	50
Maximum generations, G_{max}	1500
Selection	Roulette Wheel selection
Crossover	1-point
Crossover probability, p_c	0.8
Mutation probability, p_m	0.2

Table 2. ATM network parameters

Item	Value/Type
Maximum capacity of each link	100
Degree of multicast traffic	Random choice from the interval 1 - 4
Disjoint method between Working Virtual Path (*WVP*) and Backup Virtual Path (*BVP*)	Node-disjoint

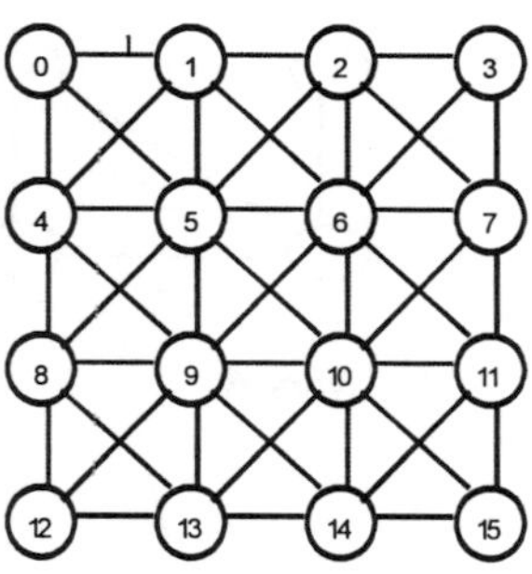

Network 1

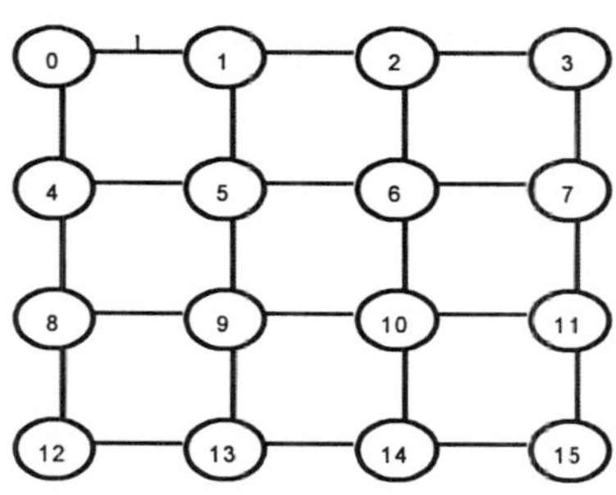

Network 2

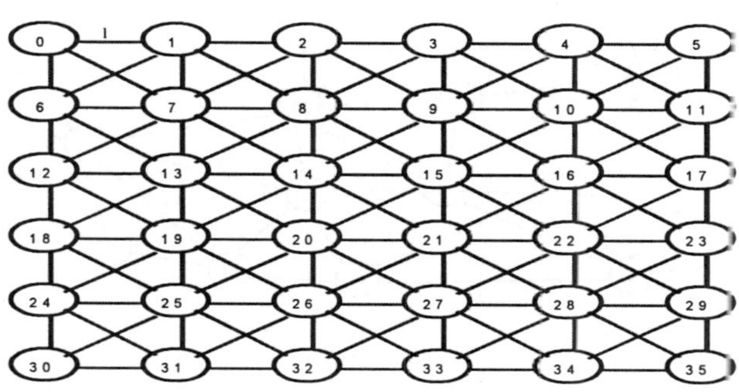

Network 3

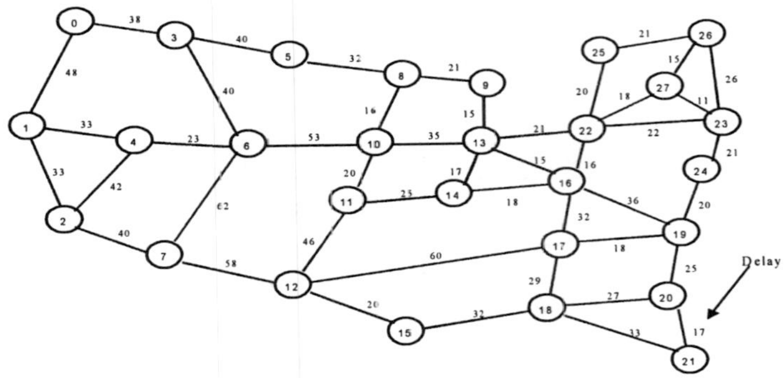

Network 4

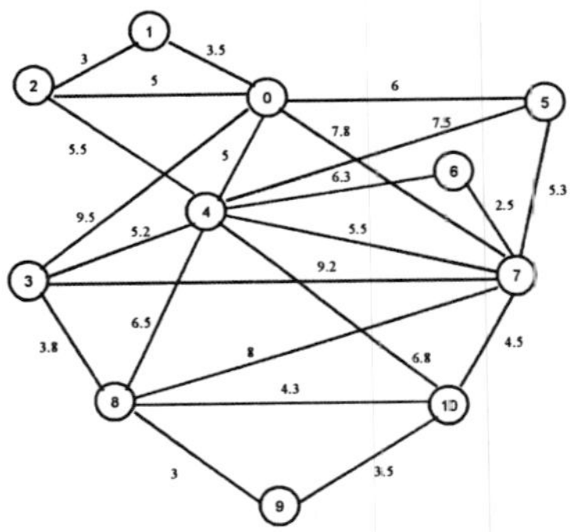

Network 5

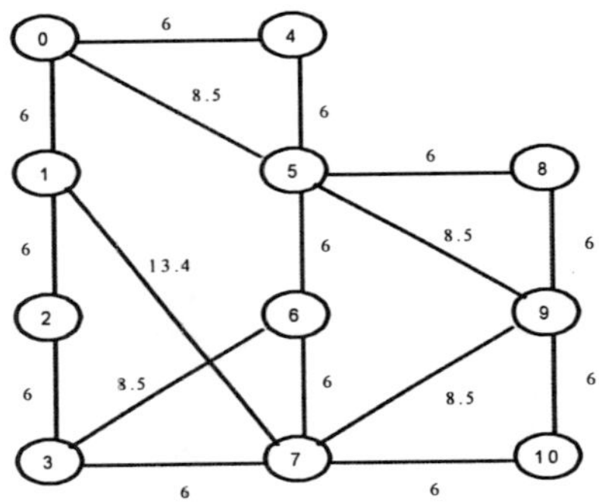

Network 6

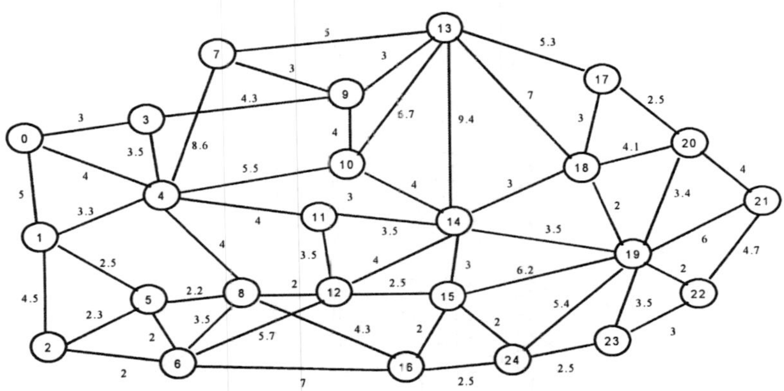

Network 7

Fig. 7. Networks for study

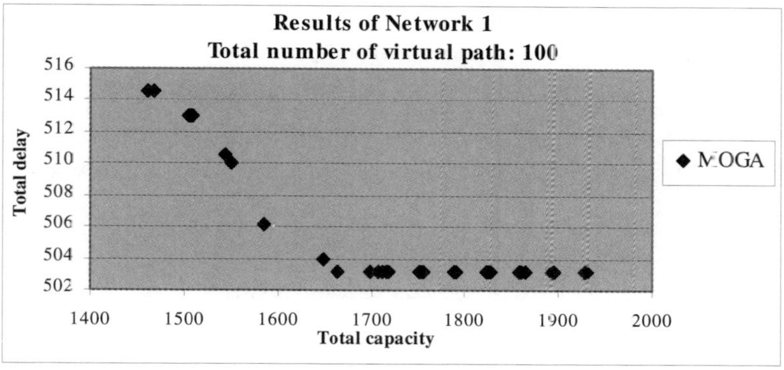

Fig. 8. Final Pareto front of Network 1

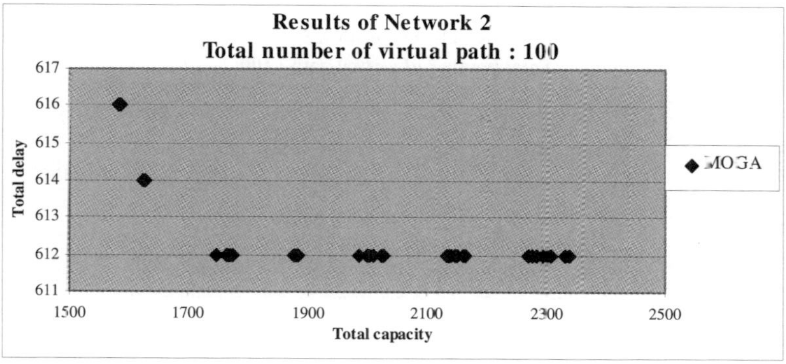

Fig. 9. Final Pareto front of Network 2

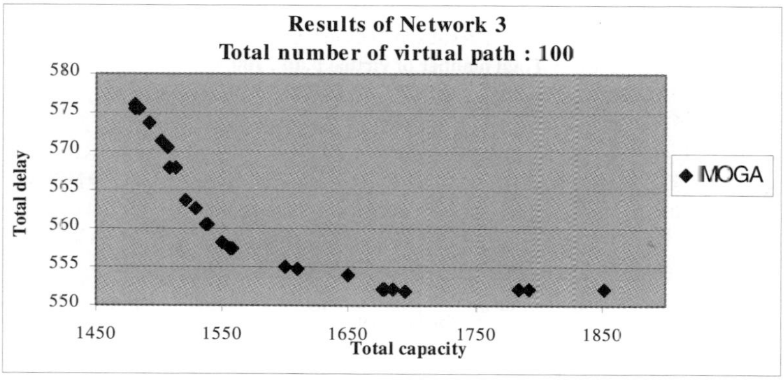

Fig. 10. Final Pareto front of Network 3

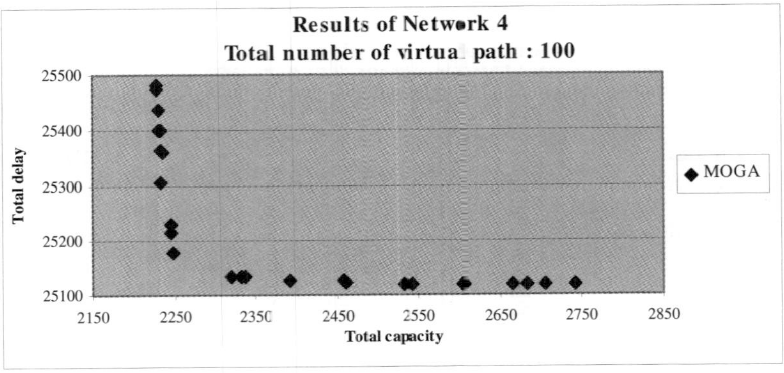

Fig. 11. Final Pareto front of Network 4

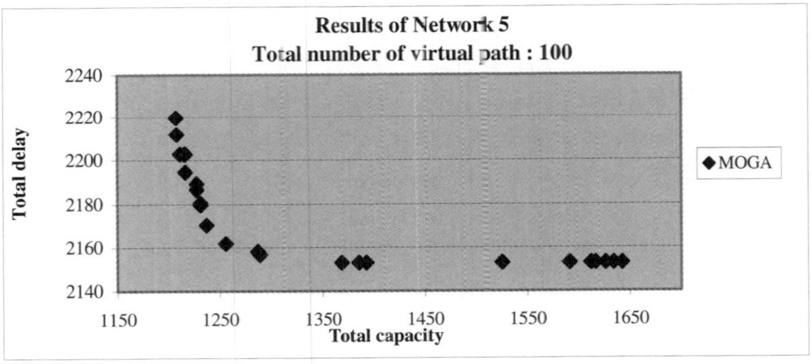

Fig. 12. Final Pareto front of Network 5

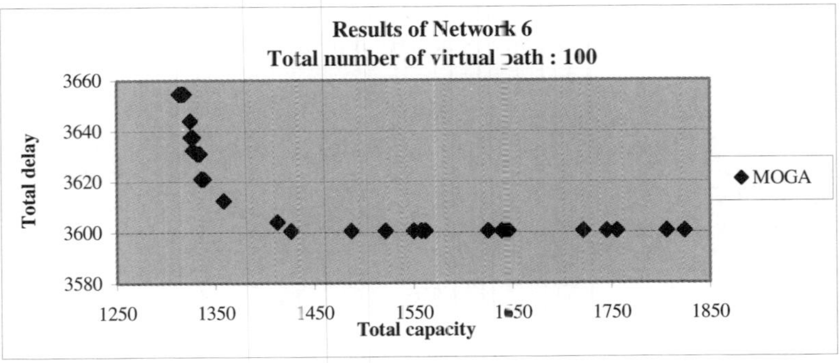

Fig. 13. Final Pareto front of Network 6

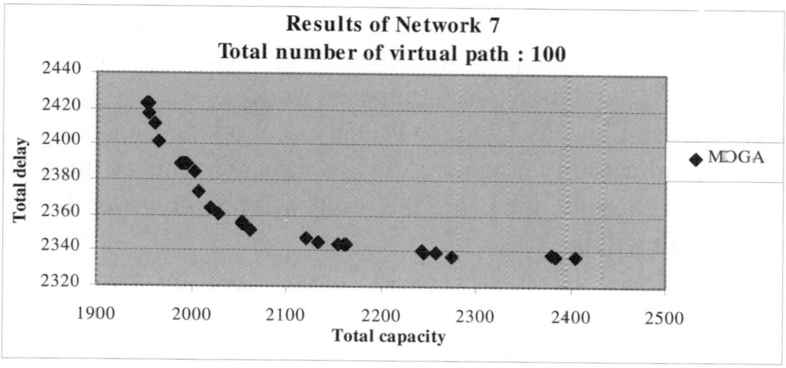

Fig. 14. Final Pareto front of Network 7

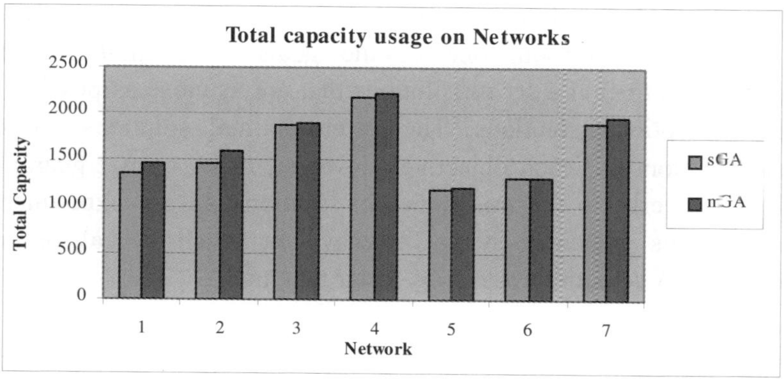

Fig. 15. Total capacity usage comparison chart

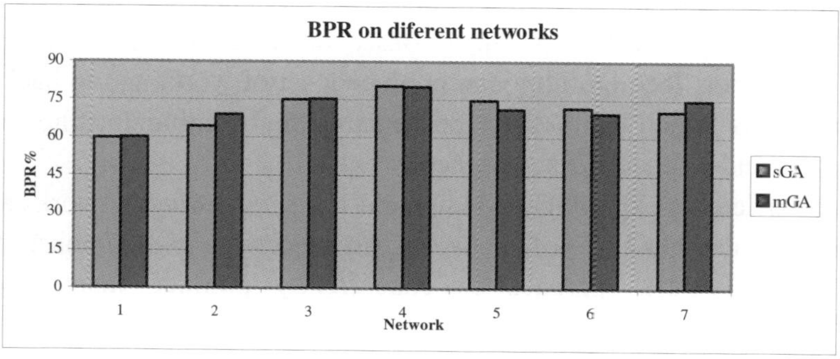

Fig. 16. *BPR* comparison chart

To measure the performance of this mGA approach, the results obtained are used to compare with that using single objective genetic algorithm (sGA) in our previously proposed work.

BPR (Backup Capacity Usage to Primary or Working Capacity Usage Ratio) and total capacity usage are used as measurements of merit. The lower the total capacity, the better the result will be; the lower the *BPR*, the better result will be.

Fig. 15 shows the total capacity usage used by two different approaches on seven networks. Fig. 16 shows the *BPR* of two different approaches on seven networks. The charts demonstrate that the performance of mGA is good enough when compared with the sGA which has been showed to be better than other heuristic approaches. The result on the sGA sometime performs better than mGA can be explained by the following reason: one of the goals of a multi-objective optimization is to find a set of solutions that are as close as possible to the Pareto optimal solutions. The Pareto-optimal solutions are the optimal solutions for each objective. However, mGA cannot guarantee solutions converge to the true optimum solutions. In our experiments, some solutions obtained by mGA may not reach global optima. Therefore, sGA sometime performs better than mGA.

6. Conclusions

In this chapter, instead of using Linear/Integer Programming as an optimization methodology, a multi-objective GA approach was used in our network optimization problem. Based on a set of input customer traffic demands, the algorithm can produce a set of working and backup Virtual paths which can satisfy the demands and minimizing the total capacities and total delays simultaneously.

We carried out experiments on seven ATM *self-healing* networks and the result illustrates trade-off between two objectives and demonstrates the ability of the approach to concurrently produce many good compromise solutions in a single run. From these results, we can conclude that GA-based multi-objective optimization method is suitable and efficient for *self-healing* network optimization problem.

To measure the performance of the approach, our results are compared with that using single objective genetic algorithm (sGA) in our previously proposed work [1]. The result shows that the performance of mGA is better than other heuristic approaches.

This chapter has demonstrated that the use of mGA for joint optimization of spare capacity and delay in *self-healing* network is a promising approach. mGA is a powerful method to solve real-world multi-objective optimization problems.

Acknowledgments

This work was supported by the City University Strategic Grant 7001416.

References

1. S. Kwong and S.S. Chan, A Fault-tolerant Multicast Routing Algorithm *In ATM Network. in Proceedings of the Genetic and Evolutionary Computation Conference*, Las Vegas, Nevada, p. 582-589 (2000).
2. S. Chen, S. Cheng, B. Chen and J. Chen, An efficient spare capacity allocation strategy for ATM survivable networks, *in Proceedings of the GLOBECOM'96*, London, p. 442-446 (1996).
3. K Murakami and H. S. Kim, Joint optimization of capacity and flow assignment for *self-healing* ATM networks, *in 1995 IEEE International Conference on Communications*, Settle WA, vol.1, p. 216-220 (1995).
4. R.R. Iraschko, M.H. MacGregor and W.D. Grover, Optimal capacity placement for path restoration in STM or ATM mesh-survivable networks, *IEEE/ACM Transactions on Networking*, **6**(3), 325-336 (1998).
5. Yijun Xiong and L. G. Mason, Restoration strategies and spare capacity requirements in *self-healing* ATM networks, *IEEE/ACM Transactions on Networking*, **7**(1063-6692), 98-110 (1999).
6. C. M. Fonseca and P. J. Fleming, Genetic Algorithms for multiobjective optimization: Formulation, discussion and generalization, *in Proceedings of the 5th International Conference on Genetic Algorithms*, San Mateo, p. 416-423 (1993).
7. Sadiq M. Sait and H. Youssef, Iterative computer algorithms with applications in engineering: solving combinatorial optimization problems, in *IEEE Computer Society*, Los Alamitos, California, (1999).
8. J. J. Grefenstette, Optimization of control parameters for genetic algorithms, *IEEE Transactions on Systems, Man and Cybernetics*, vol. 16, p. 122-128 (1986).

CHAPTER 30

OPTIMIZATION OF DS-CDMA CODE SEQUENCES FOR WIRELESS SYSTEMS

Sam Kwong and Alex C.H. Ho

Department of Computer Science, City University of Hong Kong
83 Tatchee Avenue, Kowloon, Hong Kong
E-mail: essamk@cityu.edu.hk

In this chapter, we propose to apply Genetic Algorithm to Gold codes, Kasami codes and Multiple Spreading to generate sets of CDMA sequences. The analysis has shown us that the GA based pseudo noise (PN) codes have better Signal to noise ratio (*SNR*) and lower Bit error rate (*BER*). It also indicated that the Multiple Spreading has many advantages over the other PN code, however, its set of sequences still is not the best. By using Genetic Algorithm, a set of sequences with better *SNR* and *BER* can be achieved. The reason is that Multiple Spreading can provide some good genes for optimization. Therefore, we can conclude that the GA based Multiple Spreading is a good solution to generate PN codes for DS-CDMA system.

1. Introduction

Code Division Multiple Access (CDMA) technology is now used in the field of mobile communications. Interference is one of the important factors affecting its channel capacity. The performance of CDMA systems depends highly on the use of unique spreading sequences for the users. If the sequences are not optimized by sequence selection from a suitable family set of sequences, Multiple Access Interference (MAI) can be very high and therefore affect the channel capacity significantly such that the maximum capacity cannot be achieved[1]. Interference parameter is one form of the optimization criterion as a performance measurement and thus we need to minimize the interference parameter by sequence selection to improve system performance. Because the interference parameter is related to the Signal-to-Noise Ratio (*SNR*) and the Bit Error Rate (*BER*), there are some papers working on the minimization of *BER* or *SNR* as an optimization criterion by sequence selection using different assumptions, models and different expressions of *BER* or SNR[2,3]. In this chapter, minimization of interference parameter in DS/CDMA systems is proposed by using Genetic Algorithms (GA) and we focus on the asynchronous CDMA system model presented in [4-6].

If we view *BER* from the mathematical point of view, it has two terms: the MAI and the noise. Assuming a strong signal, the noise term can be neglected and the *BER* is related only to the MAI term. Also, we know that the interference parameter in the MAI term is related to the aperiodic auto-correlation of the sequences for K users. Thus, if there is one set of any type of M sequences and K users in the system, we need to select K sequences from M sequences in order to minimize the *BER*. It means that we only have to minimize the interference parameter since the smaller the value of the interference parameter is, the smaller the value of *BER* is. As not all types of sequences are suitable choices, Gold sequences in fact are used for two reasons[14]. First, Gold sequences can provide large sets of sequences with small cross-correlation values for all phase shifts between sequences and small out of phase auto-correlation values for all sequences[1,10,11]. Second, if we refer to the model from literature[6] where Gold sequences are used, we can use the same type of sequences for performance comparisons.

In addition, if M is large, the number of combinations, ${}_MC_K$, will be very large. For example, assuming that M is 513 and K is 30, the value of ${}_MC_K$ is $3.19\text{x}10^{48}$. Although exhaustive search is a good method for finding an optimal solution, it is impossible in this case. The reason is that, assuming the time required to test one combination is, say, $0.01s$ in the computer, the total running time required for testing all the combinations is $3.19 \text{ x } 10^{46}s$ ($1.01 \text{ x } 10^{39}$ years)! Alternatively, we can compromise and apply another effective search technique, Genetic Algorithms (GA), to find a good sub-optimal solution[14]. There are several reasons why we use GA as the search technique in this research. First, GA is proved to be very powerful in global search[7-9]. Second, the performance and efficiency of GA was regarded to be better than the others searching tools such as SA. Third, it doesn't need gradient information that is often unavailable as it may be trapped in the local minimum or maximum. Last, if we select the crossover and mutation parameters appropriately and carefully, it is much easier to find an optimum or a nearly global optimum point. In addition, if the sequence selection for minimization of interference parameter involves large computational complexity, GA is the suitable choice that can solve this kind of combinatorial optimization problem [7-9] in a reasonable time.

2. Background

The main objective of this work is to optimize the DS-CDMA based wireless system. Although that there are many advantages of using DS-CDMA in wireless communication systems, multiple access interference (MAI) is still a main problem that degrades the performance of the system. Therefore, solving the problem of MAI is the most important objective of our work.

With DS-CDMA, applying unique digital codes rather than separating RF frequencies or channels are used to differentiate subscribers. The codes are shared by both the transmitter and receiver, and are usually called "Pseudo Random Noise Code" (PN code). All users share the same range of radio spectrum and each user is assigned a binary, PN code during a call. The PN code is a signal generated by linear modulation with wideband Pseudo Random Noise (PN) sequence. As a result, DS-CDMA uses much wider signals than those used in other technologies. Wideband signals reduce interferences and allow one-cell frequency to be reused. However, as there is no frequency and time division multiplexing, all users use the entire carrier at all time and it becomes the MAI problem in DS-CDMA.

The MAI will be presented when an interfering transmitter uses another PN code B that is much closer to the receiver than the desired transmitter A. Although the receiver does not have the PN code of B and it cannot decode the signal from transmitter B correctly, the decoded signal still exists as noise and it will affect the detection of the proper data from desired transmitter A. If the cross-correlation between codes A

and B is too low, the correlation between the received signal from the interfering transmitter and code A can be higher than the correlation between the received signal from the intended transmitter and code A. The result is that proper data detection is not possible[12]. However, if the code A and B are orthogonal, then the MAI problem can then be suppressed.

Codes that can be found in practical DS-systems are Walsh-Hadamard codes, M-sequences, Gold-codes and Kasami-codes. These code sets can be roughly divided into two classes: orthogonal codes and non-orthogonal codes. Walsh sequences fall in the first category, while the others are also called shift-register sequences.

2.1. *Walsh Hadamard Codes*

Walsh-sequences have the advantage of being orthogonal, thus, it should not have the multi-access interference problem. There are however a number of other drawbacks[12]:

1. The codes do not have a single, narrow autocorrelation peak.
2. The spreading is not over the whole bandwidth; instead the energy is spread over a number of discrete frequency-components. Although the full-sequence cross-correlation is identically zero, this does not hold for partial-sequence cross-correlation function. The consequence is that the advantage of using orthogonal codes is lost.
3. Orthogonality is also affected by channel properties like multi-path. In practical systems equalization is applied to recover the original signal.

2.2. *Shift-Register Sequences*

The name already makes it clear that the codes can be created using a shift-register with feedback-taps. Their disadvantage is that they are not orthogonal, but they have a narrow autocorrelation peak.

M-sequences - By using a single shift-register, maximum length sequences (M-sequences) can be obtained. Such sequences can be created by a linear feedback shift register (LFSR) sequence generator, which is just a single shift-register with a number of specially selected feedback-taps. Each clock time the register shifts all contents to the right and a sequence is generated.

These sequences have a number of special properties:

- These sequences are balanced. The number of ones exceeds the number of zeros with only 1.
- Walsh-sequence and an M-sequence contain (almost) the same power and an M-sequence better distributes the power over the whole available frequency range.

2.3. *Gold Sequences*

Gold sequences are useful as it can generate a set of sequences. It is a combination of two M-sequences for which the cross-correlation only shows 3 different values[12]. These two M-sequences are called ‘preferred pair’. Preferred pairs do not exist when the shift-registers used are of a length equal to 4k where k is an integer.

2.4. *Kasami Sequences*

If we combine a Gold sequence with a decimated version of one of the 2 M-sequences formed by the Gold sequence, ‘Kasami sequences’ can be obtained. Kasami sequences are formed with a larger set of code sequences and have the cross-correlation values. For the large set of Kasami sequences, the values of cross-correlation are limited to five values. The advantage of large code-set in Kasami sequences is important since the number of available codes determines the number of different code addresses that can be created. Also a large code-set enables us to select those codes which show good cross-correlation characteristics[13].

2.5. *Multiple Spreading Technique*

The authors[13] also mentioned that a technique for multiple spreading or two-layered spreading code allocation provides flexible system deployment and operation. It is possible to provide waveform orthogonality among all users of the same cell while maintaining mutual randomness only between users of different cells. This is rendered possible by the wide bandwidth of a spread spectrum DS-CDMA system that provides considerable waveform flexibility. Orthogonality can be achieved by first multiplying each user's binary input by a short spread sequence which is orthogonal to that of every other user of the same cell. As mentioned, one class of such binary orthogonal sequences is the Walsh orthogonal set. This spread signal is following by multiplication of a long pseudo random sequence, which is cell-specific but common to all users of that cell in the forward link and user-specific in the reverse link. The short orthogonal codes are called "channelization codes", the long PN sequences "scrambling codes". Hence, each transmission channel code is distinguished by the combination of a channelization code and a scrambling code[13].

2.6. *Problems of Code Sequences*

Among the above PN code generating techniques, all of them have their own pros and cons. Walsh-Hadamard codes is orthogonal but as it uses only discrete carrier frequency, it does not have a single, narrow autocorrelation peak and also the spreading is not over the whole bandwidth. M-sequences, Gold-codes and Kasami-codes can spread over the whole bandwidth and Kasami-codes even have a large code set but all of them are non-orthogonal. So, the system using these codes is easier to suffer from the problem of MAI. Their disadvantages make them impossible to maximize the multiple access capacity and thus degrade the performance of DS-CDMA system. It seems that Multiple Spreading is the best method to generate PN codes as it can provide orthogonal codes within a cell while maintaining mutual randomness between users of different cells. Our work is aimed at finding an algorithm to generate a set of PN codes sequences which can suppress the MAI and so maximize the multiple access capacity of a DS-CDMA system in order to optimize the performance of a DS-CDMA based communication system. The performance of several PN codes generating algorithms will be compared, including Gold code, Kasami code and Multiple Spreading. Simulated Annealing and Genetic Algorithm will also be analyzed to find out the best algorithm to optimize the performance of a DS-CDMA system.

3. Genetic Algorithms

At the first phase of genetic algorithm, a number of encoded chromosomes called population in the initialization process are generated in that each chromosome (individual) consists of a sequence of binary or real numbers known as genes. In this research, we use an integer as a gene. Once the population is generated and each individual is given a fitness value that is computed by an objective (fitness) function. Then, selection of chromosomes is carried out based on the fitness values of the chromosomes. A type of selection method, Roulette Wheel selection, is used in order that chromosomes having better fitness values can be chosen at a higher chance. The next two operations are crossover and mutation. Crossover allows two chromosomes to exchange part(s) of their genes and mutation changes gene(s) in chromosome(s). After these operations, some modified chromosomes are re-produced. If any modified chromosome has repeating integer(s), it is an illegal solution and chromosome repair will be applied on the chromosome so as to convert it back to a feasible solution. It can be done by randomly change the repeating integers such that they do not have the same value. The fitness value of each modified chromosome is evaluated again. Finally, the older chromosomes are replaced by the new and next generation cycle starts. The whole GA process is completed when the maximum generation is reached or the objective is met. The whole process of GA and the GA parameters can be summarized as below[14].

1. Initialization
   a. Set the population size (number of chromosomes in the population) be N_p
   b. Set the maximum allowed number of generation be G_{max}
   c. Set the crossover probability be p_c
   d. Set the mutation probability be p_m
   e. Set $G = 0$ where G is the generation counter

2. The GA process
   Step 1: Generate a population of chromosomes
   Step 2: Evaluate the fitness value of each chromosome by using the objective function

Step 3: Perform selection
Step 4: Perform crossover
Step 5: Perform mutation
Step 6: Evaluate the fitness value of each modified chromosome by using the objective function
Step 7: Perform replacement
Step 8: Set $G = G + 1$. If $G > G_{max}$, terminate. Otherwise, go to Step 3

Parameters	Value/Type
Population Size, N_c	50
Maximum generations, G_{max}	1500
Selection	Roulette Wheel selection
Crossover	1-point
Crossover probability, p_c	0.8
Mutation probability, p_m	0.2

In the following, a detail description of objective function is given.

3.1. *Objective Function*

According to reference [5], bit error rate (*BER*) can be used as the performance criteria of a CDMA system. Following the same model as in reference [7], bit error rate (*BER*) can be expressed in terms of signal to noise ratio (*SNR*) or the sum of multiple access interference (MAI) and noise that are the first and second terms in the function Q respectively. It can be expressed as follows:

$$P_e = Q\left(\{SNR_x\}^{\frac{1}{2}}\right) = Q\left(\left\{\frac{1}{6N^3}\sum_{\substack{i=1 \\ i\neq x}}^{K}\beta_{i,x} + \frac{N_C}{2E}\right\}^{-\frac{1}{2}}\right) \tag{1}$$

where SNR_x is the average SNR at the xth correlator output, $\beta_{i,x}$ is the interference parameter between the ith user spreading sequence and the xth user spreading sequence given by the following equation.

$$2N^2 + 4\cdot\sum_{l=1-N}^{N-1} C_{i,i}(l)\cdot C_{x,x}(l) + \sum_{l=1-N}^{N-1} C_{i,i}(l)\cdot C_{x,x}(l+1) \tag{2}$$

where
$N = T/T_c$ is the code sequence length,
T is data information interval,
T_c is the chip interval,
K is the number of users,
N_0 is the noise power spectral density assumed to be Additive White Gaussian Noise,
E is the energy per data bit,
$Q(x)$ is the standard Gaussian cumulative distribution function,
$C_{i,j}$ or $C_{x,x}$ is the aperiodic auto-correlation obtained from the aperiodic cross-correlation $C_{a,b}$ of sequences a and b with both length N. This is defined by the following equation.

$$C_{a,b}(l) = \begin{cases} \sum_{i=0}^{N-1-l} a_i \cdot b_{i+1} & 0 \le l \le N-1 \\ \sum_{i=0}^{N-1+l} a_{i-l} \cdot b_i & 1-N \le l < 0 \\ 0 & |l| \ge N \end{cases} \tag{3}$$

where
a_i is ith bit in the sequence $(a_i, a_1, a_2, \ldots, a_{N-1})$,
b_i is ith bit in the sequence $(b_i, b_1, b_2, \ldots, b_{N-1})$,
a_i or b_i is +1 or −1,
l is the value from 0 to N-1.

In this work, the equation of calculating the signal to noise ratio (SNR) from the above function will be used to analyze the performance of the resulting PN code sequences set, i.e.

$$SNR_x = \left(\frac{1}{6N^3} \sum_{\substack{i=1 \\ i \neq x}}^{K} \beta_{i,x} + \frac{N_0}{2E} \right)^{-1} \tag{4}$$

From above, it can be seen that in order to maximize the signal-to-noise ratio, the value of $\sum_{i=1,\, i \neq x}^{K} \beta_{i,x}$ must be minimized and we set it to Ψ for simplicity.
Thus, the objective function used in the work is Ψ and the chromosomes with lower fitness value are preferred.

4. Experimental Results

4.1. *Results of Optimization on Gold Code*

The gold sequences with $N = 8$ and $N = 9$ is used in the experiments. For the gold sequences for N equal to 8, two M-sequences for the gold sequences are generated by the LFSR sequence generators $f_1(D) = 1 + D^6 + D^8$ and $f_2(D) = 1 + D^5 + D^6 + D^7 + D^8$.

With these two M-sequences, 257 sequences of length 255 are obtained in the set of gold sequences. Assume there are 30 users and so 30 sequences are taken out randomly from the set of Gold code. By using the objective function mentioned before, the values of Ψ for each user before and after the optimization are found out and they are shown in Fig. 1 below.

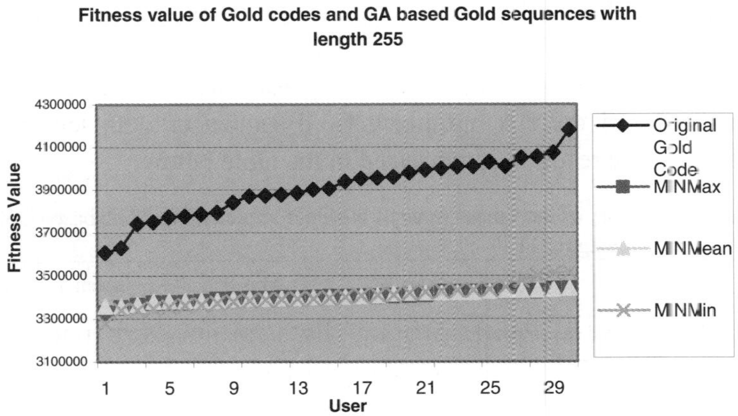

Fig. 1. Fitness value of the Gold codes and GA based Gold sequences with length 255

Table 1. Summary of the fitness value of the Gold sequences and GA based Gold sequences with length 511

	Max. Ψ	Min. Ψ	Mean Ψ
Original Gold sequences	4.179466×10^6	3.607754×10^6	3.908318×10^6
MINMax	3.439226×10^6	3.328130×10^6	3.399983×10^6
MINMean	3.440306×10^6	3.357442×10^6	3.402887×10^6
MINMin	3.515878×10^6	3.277366×10^6	3.404389×10^6

Table 1 shows the mean, maximum and minimum of the fitness values Ψ of the 30 sequences before and after the optimization of Gold codes. The Minmax is to minimize the BER upper bound for all users; *MINmin* is minimized to find the best upper bound interference parameter for a single user, and *MINmean* is minimized to find the best mean interference parameter for K users.

It is obvious that the sequences after optimization are much better than that the ones before optimization. The MAI is also shown to be lower after the optimization. For the gold sequences with N = 9, the following LFSR sequence generators are used to generate two M-sequences: $f_1(D) = 1 + D^7 + D^9$ and $f_2(D) = 1 + D^6 + D^7 + D^8 + D^9$ These two M-sequences are used to generate a set of 513 Gold sequences of length 511. Similarly, assume there are 30 users and 30 sequences are randomly selected from the set of Gold codes. By using the same objective function, the values of Ψ for each user are calculated. The fitness value of the GA optimized Gold sequences with length 511 is obtained[14]. The result is summarized in the table below:

Table 2. Summary of the fitness value of the Gold sequences and GA based Gold sequences with length 511

	Max.Ψ	Min. Ψ	Mean Ψ
Original Gold sequences	15.924798×10^6	14.236750×10^6	15.07231×10^6
MINMax	14.180586×10^6	13.937194×10^6	14.100802×10^6
MINMean	15.042246×10^6	13.894386×10^6	14.028527×10^6
MINMax	15.155446×10^6	13.122726×10^6	14.502062×10^6

4.2. *Results of Optimization on Kasami Code*

In the generation of Kasami codes, the Gold codes of $N = 8$ generated in the previous section before can be reused here. The larger set of Kasami sequences with $N = 8$ is then obtained. Since N must be even in the generation of Kasami codes, Kasami sequences with $N = 9$ cannot be generated for analysis. In the large set of the Kasami sequences generated, there are 4112 sequences of length 255. Similar to the optimization of Gold sequences, 30 users are assumed and therefore 30 sequences are taken out randomly from the set of Kasami code. Before optimization, the results of each user are shown in Fig. 2. Table 3 shows the mean, maximum and minimum of the fitness values of the 30 sequences before and after the optimization of Kasami codes. It is

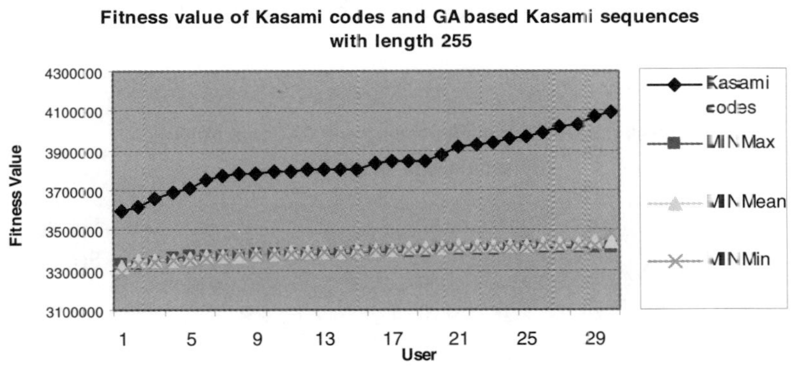

Fig. 2. Fitness value of the Kasami codes and GA based Kasami sequences with length 255

Table 3. Summary of the fitness value of the Kasami codes and GA based Kasami sequences with length 255

	Max. Ψ	Min. Ψ	Mean Ψ
Original Kasami sequences	4.095722×10^6	3.596794×10^6	3.844646×10^6
MINMax	3.413406×10^6	3.328590×10^6	3.383679×10^6
MINMean	3.438642×10^6	3.319450×10^6	3.394690×10^6
MINMin	3.482202×10^6	3.285986×10^6	3.389271×10^6

obvious that the sequences after optimization have a better performance. The MAI is also lower after the optimization.

4.3. *Results of Optimization of Multiple Spreading*

'Code tree' is used for generation of variable length orthogonal codes. This short orthogonal codes are used as "channelization codes" in generating the codes of 'Multiple Spreading'. The "scrambling codes" are the Gold codes with $N = 5$. These Gold codes are generated with the two M-sequences defined by $f_1(D) = 1 + D^3 + D^5$ and $f_2(D) = 1 + D^2 + D^3 + D^4 + D^5$.

Using the channelization codes with $N = 8$, a set of 264 sequences of length 248 bits is generated. As in the case of the optimization for Gold codes and Kasami codes, 30 users are assumed and 30 sequences are taken out from the set of sequences. The value of Ψ of each user is shown in Fig. 3.

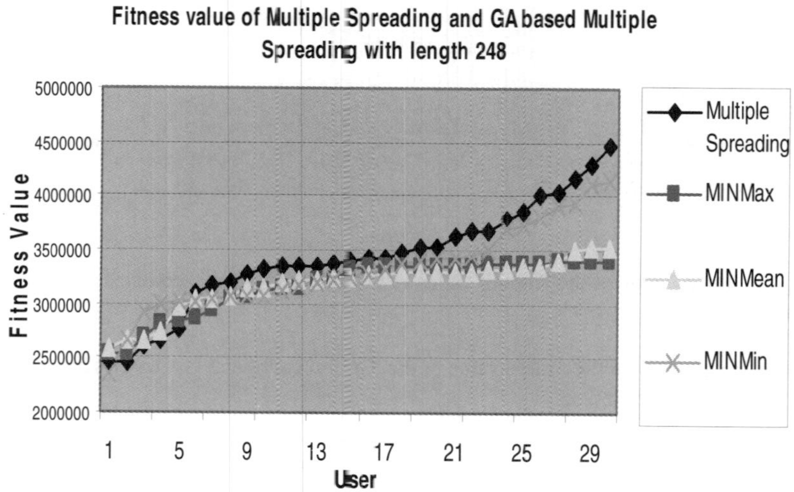

Fig. 3. Fitness value of Multiple Spreading and GA based Multiple Spreading with length 248

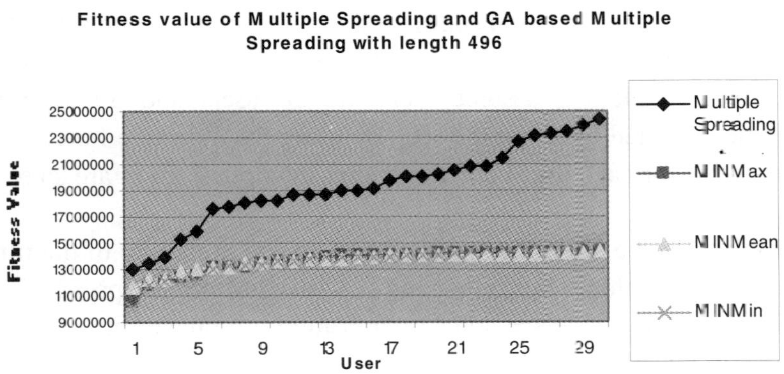

Fig. 4. Fitness value of the sequences before and after the optimization of Multiple Spreading with length 496

Table 4. Summary of the fitness value of the sequences before and after the optimization of Multiple Spreading with length 248

	Max. Ψ	Min. Ψ	Mean Ψ
Multiple Spreading	4.473920×10^6	2.453056×10^6	3.425293×10^6
MINMax	3.400544×10^6	2.527056×10^6	3.163753×10^6
MINMean	3.526328×10^6	2.586656×10^6	3.181811×10^6
MINMin	4.145000×10^6	2.350712×10^6	3.320045×10^6

Table 5. Summary of the fitness value of the sequences before and after the optimization of Multiple Spreading with length 496

	Max. Ψ	Min. Ψ	Mean Ψ
Multiple Spreading	24.362176×10^6	12.969280×10^6	19.26076×10^6
MINMax	14.413672×10^6	10.499056×10^6	13.600912×10^6
MINMean	15.349296×10^6	11.550552×10^6	13.64333×10^6
MINMin	14.355344×10^6	10.138160×10^6	13.600912×10^6

Using the channelization codes with $N = 16$ and the same set of Gold codes as scrambling codes, a set of 528 sequences of length 496 is generated. As before, assume there are 30 users and 30 sequences randomly selected out from the set. By using the objective function, the values of Ψ for each user before and after the optimization are shown in Fig. 4.

Tables 4 and 5 show the mean, maximum and minimum of the fitness values of the Multiple Spreading and GA based Multiple Spreading. It is obvious that the sequences after optimization are much better than that before optimization.

The length of PN codes affect the bit error rate (*BER*) and the MAI, therefore, only the PN codes with similar code length will be compared. Figures 5 and 6 are the summaries of the result of the PN codes with code lengths of about 250 bits and 500 bits, respectively.

The objective function used is $\sum_{i=1,\, i\neq x}^{K} \beta_{i,x}$ and defined below, for simplicity, it is referenced as Ω.

$$\beta_{i,x} = 2N^2 + 4 \cdot \sum_{l=1-N}^{N-1} C_{i,i}(l) \cdot C_{x,x}(l) + \sum_{l=1-N}^{N-1} C_{i,i}(l) \cdot C_{x,x}(l+1) \qquad (5)$$

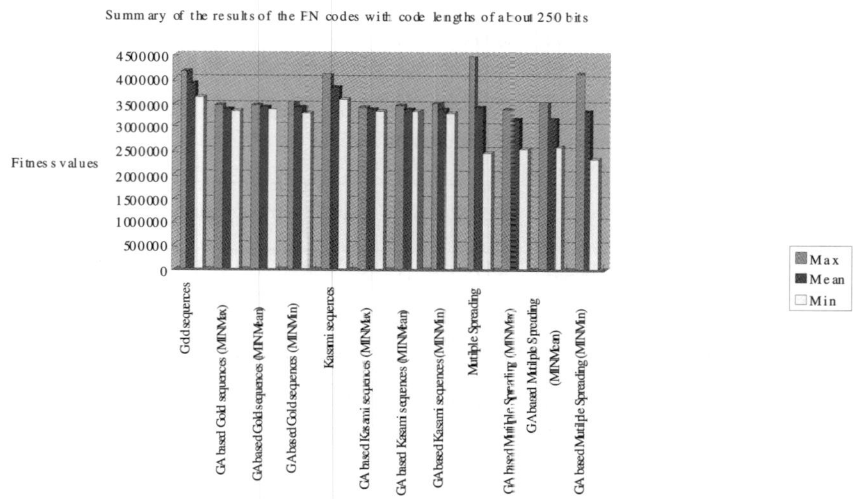

Fig. 5. Summary of the results of the PN codes with code lengths of about 250 bits

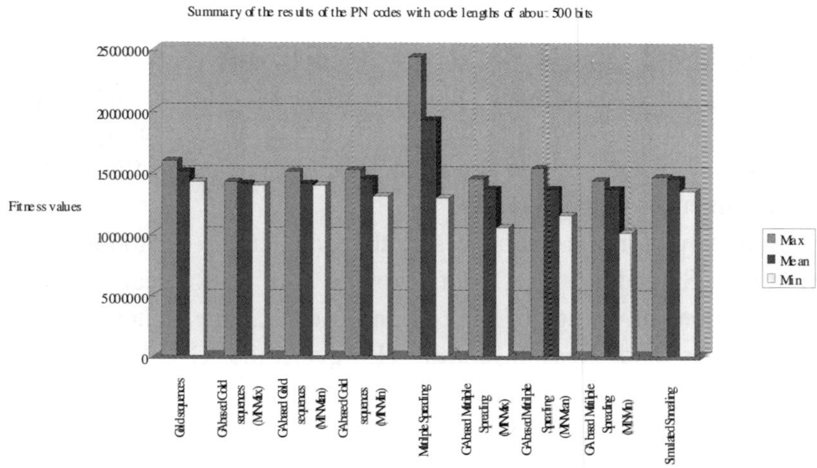

Fig. 6. Summary of the results of the PN codes with code lengths of about 500 bits

As mentioned in the previous section, the signal to noise ratio (*SNR*) or the sum of multiple access interference (MAI) can be reflected from the objective function. Therefore, in order to maximize the signal-to-noise ratio and reduce the MAI, the value of Ω must be minimized. Besides, for the sequence with smaller value of the objective function, its *BER* is also lower. As a result, the sequence with smaller value of Ω is assumed to be a better sequence.

Let's now compare the performance of the PN codes with code lengths of about 250 bits. In Fig. 5, it is obvious that Multiple Spreading has the lowest value in both the MinΩ and MeanΩ. When it is compared with the Gold codes and Kasami codes, its value of MaxΩ is the highest. It seems that it is the best among these three PN codes. However, when we compared it with the GA based Gold sequences and GA based Kasami codes, its value of Min Ω is the smallest, its values of Max Ω and Mean Ω are the largest.

From the above, it showed that the sequences generated by Multiple Spreading, in fact, are not the best. If Genetic Algorithm is applied, the sequences with better *SNR* can be produced. Moreover, from the tables, we can find that the GA based Multiple Spreading is the best among all the PN codes since the MINMAX GA based Multiple Spreading have the lowest value of Max Ω. The MINMIN GA based Multiple Spreading have the lowest value of Min Ω and the MINMEAN GA based Multiple Spreading have the lowest value of Mean Ω. This is not surprising because Multiple Spreading has an advantage of generating sequences with Min Ω, it can provide good genes for Genetic Algorithm to produce other sequences with good *SNR*.

Similarly, for the sequences with code length of about 500 bits, Multiple Spreading does not provide the best sequence before optimization. Its values of Max Ω and Mean Ω are higher than that of Gold codes and Kasami codes. However, the GA based Multiple Spreading is the best again among all the PN codes.

We can also compare the performance of Genetic Algorithm and Simulated Annealing using the results in Fig. 6. The results show us that the MINMAX GA based Gold codes has smaller value of Max. Ω than SA based Gold codes. The MINMEAN GA based Gold codes and MINMIN GA based Gold codes also has smaller value of Mean. Ω and Min. Ωthan SA based Gold codes, respectively. This shows that Genetic Algorithm perform better in optimization of PN codes than Simulated Annealing.

From the above analysis, we can see that Genetic Algorithm can improve the performance of a DS-CDMA system. It is independent on the PN codes used. Its performance is proved to be better than that of Simulated Annealing. The results also give us evidence that Multiple Spreading have advantages, especially the value of Min Ω over the other PN codes. Its performance can be improved by using Genetic Algorithm. It is even better than other GA based PN codes because Multiple Spreading can provide more good genes for Genetic Algorithm to optimize the PN codes.

5. Conclusion

In this work, Genetic Algorithm has been applied on Gold codes, Kasami codes and Multiple Spreading to generate sets of sequences. The analysis has shown us that the GA based PN codes have better *SNR* and lower *BER*. When it is compared with another optimization algorithm - Simulated Annealing, the result shows that Genetic Algorithm is better.

It has also shown in previous section that although Multiple Spreading has many advantages over the other PN code, its set of sequences is not the best without the Genetic Algorithm. By using Genetic Algorithm, a set of sequences with better *SNR* and *BER* can be generated and it is found that the performance is even better than other GA based PN codes. The reason is that Multiple Spreading can provide some good genes for optimization. Therefore it can conclude that the GA based Multiple Spreading is a very good solution to produce PN codes for DS-CDMA system.

Acknowledgments

This work was supported by the City University of Hong Kong Strategic Grant 7001488. The authors would also like to thank T M Chan for his contributions in this work.

Reference

1. M. G. El-Tarhuni, A. U. Sheikh, Numerical optimization for CDMA spreading sequences, *Canadian Conference on Electrical and Computer Engineering*, vol.1, pp. 24-27, (1995).
2. P. J. E. Jeszensky, J. R. F. Junior, Sequences selection for quasi-synchronous CDMA systems, *Proceedings of IEEE 5th International Symposium on Spread Spectrum Techniques and Applications*, vol.3, pp.706-708, (1998).
3. D. L. Noneaker, M. B. Pursley, The effects of sequence selection on DS spread spectrum with selective fading and rake reception, *IEEE Transactions on Communications*, vol.44, Issue 2, pp.229-237, February (1996).
4. M. B. Pursley, Performance evaluation for phase-coded spread-spectrum multiple-access communication – part I: system analysis, *IEEE Transactions On Communications*, vol. COM-25, pp. 795-799, (August 1977).
5. M. B. Pursley, D. V. Sarwate, Performance evaluation for phased-coded spread-spectrum multiple access communication – part II: code sequence analysis, *IEEE Transactions On Communications*, vol. COM-25, pp. 800-803, (August 1977).
6. P. J. E. Jeszensky, G. Stolfi, CDMA systems sequences optimization by simulated annealing, *Proceedings of IEEE 5th International Symposium on Spread Spectrum Techniques and Applications*, vol. 1, pp.38-40, (1998).
7. K. F. Man, K. S. Tang, and S. Kwong, *Genetic algorithms: concepts and designs*, London, Berlin: Springer (1999).
8. Zbigniew Michalewicz, *Genetic algorithms + data structures = evolution programs*, Springer-Verlag, (1996).

9. D. E. Goldberg, *Genetic algorithms in search, optimization, and machine learning*, Addison-Wesley, (1989).
10. P. Fan and M. Darnell, Sequence design for communications applications, Research studies press, John Wiley & Sons, (1996).
11. D. V. Sarwate, M. B. Pursley, Crosscorrelation properties of pseudorandom and related sequences, *Proceedings of the IEEE*, vol.68, No.5, pp.593-619, (May 1980)
12. Jack P.F. Glas, Non-Cellular Wireless Communication Systems, PhD-thesis, Delft University of Technology, ISBN: 90-5326-024-2, (December 1996)
13. Esmael H. Dinan and Bijan Jabbari, Spreading Codes for Direct Sequence CDMA and Wideband CDMA Cellular Networks, *IEEE Communications Magazine*, pp48-54, (September 1998).
14. Tak Ming Chan, Sam Kwong, Kim Fung Man and Kit Sang Tang, Sequences Optimization in DS/CDMA Systems using Genetic Algorithms, *IEEE TENCON 2001*, Singapore, pp.728-731, (Aug. 2001).

CHAPTER 31

AN EFFICIENT EVOLUTIONARY ALGORITHM FOR MULTICAST ROUTING WITH MULTIPLE QOS CONSTRAINTS

Abolfazl T. Haghighat[1], Karim Faez[2], Mehdi Dehghan[3,4]

1- Atomic Energy Organization of Iran (AEOI), Tehran, Iran
2- Electrical Eng. Department, Amirkabir University of Tech., Tehran, Iran
3- Computer Eng. Department, Amirkabir University of Tech., Tehran, Iran
4- Computer Eng. Department, Iran University of Science & Tech., Tehran, Iran
E-mail: at_haghighat@yahoo.com; kfaez@aut.ac.ir; mdehghan@aut.ac.ir

The multi-constrained least-cost multicast routing is a challenging problem in multimedia networks. Computing such a constrained Steiner tree is an NP-complete problem. We propose a novel solution to this problem based on genetic algorithms (GA). The proposed solution consists of several new heuristic algorithms for mutation, crossover, and creation of random individuals. The predecessors encoding scheme is used for genotype representation. We evaluate the performance and efficiency of the proposed GA-based algorithm in comparison with other existing heuristic and GA-based algorithms using simulation results. The most efficient combination of various proposed alternative algorithms is selected as our final solution based on the simulation results. This proposed GA-based algorithm has overcome the existing algorithms considering average tree cost and running time.

1. Introduction

The deployment of high-speed networks initiates a new area of research, providing quality of service (QoS). It is technically a challenging problem to deliver multimedia information in a timely, smooth, synchronized manner over a decentralized, shared network environment such as the Internet.

In the past, most of the applications were unicast in nature and none of them had any QoS requirements. However, with emerging distributed real-time multimedia applications, the situation is completely different now. These applications will involve multiple users, with their own different QoS requirements in terms of throughput, reliability, and bounds on end-to-end delay, jitter, and packet loss ratio. Accordingly, a key issue in the design of broad-band architectures is how to manage efficiently the resources in order to meet the QoS requirements of each connection. The establishment of efficient QoS routing schemes is, undoubtedly, one of the major building blocks in such architectures.

Supporting point to multi-point connections for multimedia applications requires the development of efficient multicast routing algorithms. Multicast employs a tree structure of the network to efficiently deliver the same data stream to a group of receivers. In multicast routing, one or more constraints must be applied to the entire tree. The main goal in developing multicast routing algorithm is to minimize the communication resources used by the multicast session. This is achieved by minimizing the cost of the multicast tree, which is the sum of the costs of the edges in the multicast tree. The least cost tree is known as the minimum Steiner tree.[1] In other word, the Steiner tree problem tries to find the least-cost tree, i.e., the tree covering a group of destinations with the minimum total cost over all the links. This problem is also called the least-cost multicast routing problem, belonging to the class of tree-optimization problems. In addition to the Steiner tree problem, several well-known multicast routing problems have been studied in the literature.[3-11, 23-33] For instance, another multicast routing problem is delay-constrained least-cost multicast routing, belonging to the class of constrained tree-optimization problems. Finding either a Steiner tree or a constrained Steiner tree is NP-complete.[2] In this chapter, we consider a bandwidth-delay-constrained least-cost multicast routing that is more complex than both of the above mentioned problems. Consequently, it is NP-complete, too. We consider an environment where a source node is presented with a request to establish a new least-cost tree with two constraints: bandwidth constraint in all the links of the tree and end-to-end delay constraint from the source node to each of the destinations. In other words, we consider the source routing strategy, in which each node maintains the complete global state of the network, including the network topology and state information of each link.

Most of the proposed algorithms for Steiner tree (without constraint) are heuristic approaches. Some of the well-known Steiner tree heuristics are the Rayward-Smith (RS) heuristic[8], the Takahashi-Matsuyama (TM) heuristic[9], and the Kou-Markowsky-Berman (KMB) heuristic[7]. Several algorithms based on neural networks[10] and genetic algorithms (GA)[23-27] have also been proposed to solve this problem.

A lot of delay-constrained least-cost multicast routing heuristics such as the Kompella-Pasquale-Polyzos (KPP) heuristic[4], the Bounded Shortest Multicast Algorithm (BSMA) heuristic[3] and others[5,6,11] have been proposed. However, the simulation results given by Salama *et al.*[17] have shown that most of the heuristic algorithms either work too slowly or can not compute delay-constrained multicast tree with least cost. The best deterministic delay constrained low-cost (near optimal) algorithm is BSMA[17,28,32]. It should be noted that the above algorithms have been designed for real-time applications with only one QoS constraint.

Since deterministic heuristic algorithms for QoS multicast routing are usually very slow, methods based on computational intelligence such as neural networks and genetic algorithms may be more suitable. For example, based on Hopfield neural network, Chotipat *et al.*[18] have proposed an algorithm to solve QoS multicast routing. However, in their algorithm, the selection of the coefficients in the energy (or Lyapunov) function is complex and sometimes may lead to unexpected wrong solution. On the other hand, GA-based algorithms have emerged as powerful tools to solve NP-complete constrained optimization problems. Due to this fact, several GA-based algorithms[23-27] have been proposed to solve Steiner tree problem without QoS constraints. Also, Sun[28] has extended the algorithm proposed by Esbensen[26] for the least-cost multicast routing problem with one QoS constraint (delay). In order to implement the genotype encoding used by Esbensen[26] and Sun[28], another NP-complete sub-problem (a deterministic delay-constrained least-cost multicast routing algorithm[11]) must be solved during the decoding phase. Furthermore, the algorithm assumes the same delay constraints for all of the destinations, which greatly restricts its application. However, the simulation results given by Sun have shown that his algorithm can achieve trees with smaller average cost than those of BSMA, in a shorter running time for relatively large networks. Xiang *et al.*[29] have proposed a GA-based algorithm for QoS routing in general case. This algorithm adopts an $N*N$ one-dimensional binary encoding scheme, where N represents the number of nodes in the graph. However, in this encoding scheme, back and forth transformation between genotype and phenotype space is very complicated, especially for large networks. Ravikumar *et al.*[30] have proposed a GA-based algorithm with novel interesting approaches for crossover and mutation operators for the delay-constrained least-cost multicast routing problem. However, they have not defined their scheme for encoding and decoding of individuals. Since their algorithm may lead to premature convergence, an approach must be designed to prevent this phenomenon.[33] Zhang *et al.*[31] have proposed an effective orthogonal GA for delay-constrained least-cost multicast routing problem. This algorithm also assumes the delay constraints for all of the destinations to be identical. Wu *et al.*[32] have proposed a GA-based algorithm for multiple QoS constraints multicast routing problem in general case. However, their proposed genotype representation does not necessarily represent a tree and it is necessary to construct and store a large amount of possible routes for each pair of nodes in the graph using the K-shortest path algorithm. Wang *et al.*[33] have proposed an efficient GA-based algorithm for bandwidth-delay-constrained least-cost multicast routing problem. They have used a tree structure for genotype representation, but did not clearly define their encoding and decoding schemes.

In this chapter, we propose a novel QoS-based multicast routing algorithm based on genetic algorithms. In the proposed method, the predecessors encoding is used for genotype representation. Some novel heuristic algorithms are proposed for mutation, crossover, and creation of random individuals. We evaluate the performance and efficiency of the proposed algorithms in comparison with other existing algorithms using simulation results. This proposed GA-based algorithm has overcome the existing algorithms considering average tree cost and running time.

The remainder of this chapter is organized as follows. The problem description is given in Section 2. In Section 3, we describe the proposed algorithms. Section 4 gives the performance evaluation of the proposed algorithms and the comparison of them with other similar algorithms. Section 5 concludes this study and discusses future works.

2. Problem Description and Formulation

A network is modeled as a directed, connected graph $G=(V, E)$, where V is a finite set of *vertices* (network nodes) and E is the set of *edges* (network links) representing connection of these vertices. Let $n=|V|$ be the number of network nodes and $l=|E|$ be the number of network links. The link $e=(u,v)$ from node $u \in V$ to node $v \in V$ implies the existence of a link $e'=(v,u)$ from node v to node u. Three non-negative real value functions are associated with each link e $(e \in E)$: cost $C(e):E \rightarrow R^+$, delay $D(e):E \rightarrow R^+$, and available bandwidth $B(e):E \rightarrow R^+$. The link cost function, $C(e)$, may be either monetary cost or any measure of the resource utilization, which must be optimized. The link delay, $D(e)$, is considered to be the sum of switching, queuing, transmission, and propagation delays. The link bandwidth, $B(e)$, is the residual bandwidth of the physical or logical link. The link delay and bandwidth functions, $D(e)$ and $B(e)$, define the criteria that must be constrained (bounded). Because of the asymmetric nature of the communication networks, it is often the case that $C(e) \neq C(e')$, $D(e) \neq D(e')$, and $B(e) \neq B(e')$.

A multicast tree $T(s, M)$ is a sub-graph of G spanning the source node $s \in V$ and the set of destination nodes $M \subseteq V-\{s\}$. Let $m=|M|$ be the number of multicast destination nodes. We refer to M as the *destination group* and $\{s\} \cup M$ the *multicast group*. In addition, $T(s, M)$ may contain relay nodes (Steiner nodes), that is, the nodes in the multicast tree but not in the multicast group. Let $P_T(s, d)$ be a unique path in the tree T from the source node s to a destination node $d \in M$.

The total cost of the tree $T(s, M)$ is defined as the sum of the cost of all links in that tree and can be given by

$$C(T(s,M)) = \sum_{e \in T(s,M)} C(e) \qquad (1)$$

The total delay of the path $P_T(s, d)$ is simply the sum of the delay of all links along $P_T(s, d)$:

$$D(P_T(s,d)) = \sum_{e \in P_T(s,d)} D(e) \qquad (2)$$

The bottleneck bandwidth of the path $P_T(s, d)$ is defined as the minimum available residual bandwidth at any link along the path:

$$B(P_T(s,d)) = \min\{B(e), e \in P_T(s,d)\} \tag{3}$$

Let Δ_d be the delay constraint and B_d the bandwidth constraint of the destination node d. The bandwidth-delay-constrained least-cost multicast problem is defined as minimization of $C(T(s, M))$ subject to

$$\begin{cases} D(P_T(s,d)) \le \Delta_d, \forall d \in M \\ B(P_T(s,d)) \ge B_d, \forall d \in M \end{cases} \tag{4}$$

Fig. 1 shows an example of network graph, multicast group, and Steiner tree.

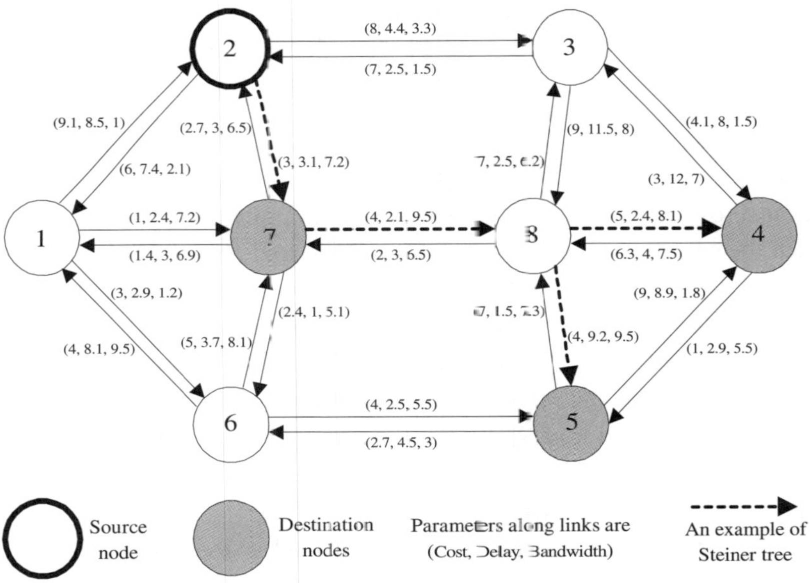

Fig. 1. An example of network graph, multicast group, and Steiner tree.

3. The Proposed GA-Based Algorithms

The Genetic algorithms are the most widely known types of evolutionary computation methods today. In general, a genetic algorithm has five basic components as follows:

1. An encoding method, that is a genetic representation (genotype) of

solutions to the program

2. A way to create an initial population of individuals (chromosomes)
3. An evaluation function, rating solutions in terms of their fitness, and a selection mechanism
4. The genetic operators (crossover and mutation) that alter the genetic composition of offspring during reproduction
5. Values for the parameters of genetic algorithm

Fig. 2 shows the general structure of the genetic algorithms.

```
Procedure: Genetic Algorithms
begin
  t := 0;
  initialize P(t);    {P(t) is the population of individuals in generation t}
  evaluate P(t);
  while (not termination condition) do
  begin
    recombine P(t) to yield C(t); {creation of offspring C(t) by means of genetic operators}
    evaluate C(t);
    select P(t + 1) from P(t) and C(t);
    t := t + 1;
  end
end
```

Fig. 2. General structure of the genetic algorithms.

3.1. *Genotype*

We modify the predecessors encoding used by Palmer[38] for minimum spanning tree algorithms, such that it can be used in the GA-based algorithms to solve the QoS-constrained Steiner tree problems. Assume that an index $k \in \{1, 2, \ldots, n\}$ is associated with each vertex v_k and the tree T is represented as a vector $[g(1), g(2), \ldots, g(n)]$, where n is the number of vertices in the underlying graph. Let $g(i) = j$ where j is the first node in the path from i to the source node s in the tree T, i.e., j is the predecessor of i (let $g(s) = s$). Thus, every tree T is represented by a unique n digit vector. In our modified method, $g(k) \in \{0, 1, \ldots, n\}$ is zero if $v_k \notin S_T \cup M \cup \{s\}$ (Steiner nodes S_T are the nodes in the multicast tree but not in the multicast group). Fig. 3 shows the genotype representation for the Steiner tree of Fig. 1, using the modified predecessors encoding.

There are n^n of such n digit numbers. Since there are $n^{(n-1)}$ rooted trees in the complete graph G, a random number of this genotype represents a tree with the following probability:

$$P_r = \frac{n^{n-1}}{n^n} = \frac{1}{n} \tag{5}$$

This is a great improvement over the characteristic vector representation, but still allows for many non-trees being generated both in the initial population and during the genetic operations. The encoding / decoding phase can be run in $O(n)$. This is also an improvement over the characteristic vector representation. Thus, at least for complete graphs, this genotype is significantly better than the characteristic vector.

0	2	0	8	8	0	2	7

Fig. 3. The modified predecessors encoding of the Steiner tree shown in Fig. 1.

3.2. *Pre-Processing Phase*

Before starting the genetic algorithm, we can remove all the links, which their bandwidth are less than the minimum of all required thresholds (Min $\{B_d \mid \forall d \in M\}$). If in the refined graph, the source node and all the destination nodes are not in a connected sub-graph, this topology does not meet the bandwidth constraint. In this case, the source should negotiate with the corresponding application to relax the bandwidth bound. On the other hand, if the source node and all the destination nodes are in a connected sub-graph, we will use this sub-graph as the network topology in our GA-based algorithms.

3.3. *Initial Population*

The creation of the initial population in this study is based on the randomized depth-first search algorithm[30,33]. We propose a modified randomized depth-first search algorithm for this purpose:

Random individual creation: In this algorithm, a linked list is constructed from the source node s to one of the destination nodes. Then, the algorithm continues from one of the unvisited destinations and at each node the next unvisited node is randomly selected until one of the nodes in the previous sub-tree (the tree that is constructed in the previous step) is visited. The algorithm terminates when all of the destination nodes have been mounted to the tree. This procedure must be called *pop-size* times, to create the entire initial population.

3.4. *Fitness Function*

The fitness function in our study is an improved version of the scheme proposed by Wand *et al.*[33]. We define the fitness function for each individual (the tree $T(s, M)$) using the penalty technique, as follows:

$$F(T(s,M)) = \frac{\alpha}{\sum_{e \in T(s,M)} C(e)} \prod_{d \in M} \phi(D(P(s,d)) - \Delta_d) \prod_{d \in M} \phi(B(P(s,d)) - B_d)$$

$$\phi(z) = \begin{cases} 1 & z \le 0 \\ \gamma & z > 0 \end{cases} \tag{6}$$

where α is a positive real coefficient, $\phi(z)$ is the penalty function and γ is the degree of penalty. The optimal solution depends on the degree of penalty. We have tried different values of γ to find which value would steer the search towards the feasible region. The best result was achieved by setting γ equal to 0.5. However, it is better to use an adaptive penalty function that produces a low penalty value in the earlier generations to widen the search space, and increases the penalty value in later generations to lead to faster convergence. However, we used a static approach and γ is considered as a constant equal to 0.5 in our study.

3.5. *Selection*

The selection process used here is based on spinning the roulette wheel *pop-size* times, and each time a single chromosome is selected as a new offspring. The probability P_i that a parent T_i is selected is given by:

$$p_i = \frac{F(T_i)}{\sum_{j=1}^{pop-size} F(T_j)} \tag{7}$$

Where $F(T_i)$ is the fitness of the T_i individual.

3.6. *Crossover*

Several crossover operators are described in the literatures for Steiner tree and constrained Steiner tree problems.[23-33] Some of them have used the traditional well-known crossover operators, such as the following schemes:

- One point crossover operator[28]
- One point crossover operator, with a fixed probability $P_c(\approx 0.6\text{-}0.9)$ [27]
- Two point crossover operator[32]
- One point crossover operator plus "and" and "or" logic operations with a fixed probability P_c [29]

Unfortunately, according to the genotype representation in these papers[27-29,31-32], the above crossover operators are not suitable for recombination of two individuals (the crossover operation mostly leads to illegal individuals). However, Ravikumar *et al.*[30] have proposed a new interesting approach for crossover of Steiner trees and Wang *et al.*[33] have used the same scheme with some modifications. In this scheme, two multicast trees, $T_F(s, M)$ and $T_M(s, M)$, are selected as parents and the crossover operation produces an offspring $T_C(s, M)$ by identifying the links that are common to both parents. The operator selects the same links of two parents for quicker convergence of the genetic algorithm.

However, these common links may be in some separate sub-trees, and some edges may have to be added in order to transform them into a multicast tree. In this step, a multicast tree is constructed from these separate sub-trees. First, two separate sub-trees among these sub-trees are randomly selected, and are interconnected to each other using the least-delay or the least-cost path (in the method of Ravikumar *et al.*[30] all sub-trees are connected to the first sub-tree). If none of the parents satisfies the delay constraint, the least-delay path is chosen. Otherwise the least-cost path is chosen. The path, which is added to join two sub-trees is selected heuristically.[33] The two connected sub-trees are replaced with the new sub-tree in the sub-trees set. Next, conforming to the same rule, a new selection begins again. The selection is repeated until a multicast tree is constructed. Clearly there is no loop in the multicast tree constructed by this connection scheme. Finally, it may be possible that some of the leaf nodes of T_O are not the source node or the destination nodes. These nodes are deleted from the offspring.

The first disadvantage of this scheme is the complexity of the heuristic algorithm, which selects a path to join the two separate sub-trees. The second disadvantage of this scheme is that the result of this complex heuristic algorithm is not necessarily a multicast tree containing the source node and all of the destination nodes.

We propose two novel crossover schemes for recombination of two individuals, which represent the Steiner trees:

Crossover I: Let $\{P_F(s, d_1), P_F(s, d_2), \ldots, P_F(s, d_m)\}$ be the set of paths from the source node s to all of the destination nodes in T_F and $\{P_M(s, d_1), P_M(s, d_2), \ldots, P_M(s, d_m)\}$ be the same set in T_M. Since, we have found these paths for all individuals in the current population for calculating their fitness function, the proposed algorithm will not be complex. We define a fitness function for the path $P(s, d_i)$ based on the total cost, the total delay, and the minimum bandwidth of the path using the penalty technique, as follows:

$$F(P(s,d_i)) = \frac{\alpha}{\sum_{e \in P(s,d_i)} C(e)} \phi(D(P(s,d_i)) - \Delta_{d_i})\phi(B(P(s,d_i)) - B_{d_i})$$

$$\phi(z) = \begin{cases} 1 & z \le 0 \\ \gamma & z > 0 \end{cases} \tag{8}$$

Where α is a positive real coefficient, $\phi(z)$ is the penalty function and γ is the degree of penalty (γ is considered equal to 0.5 in our study). According to the crossover probability of P_c, two multicast trees $T_F(s, M)$ and $T_M(s, M)$ are selected as parents and the crossover operation produce an offspring $T_O(s, M)$. Each individual may be recombined with its right individual and its left individual through the crossover operator. For each destination node d_i, we compute the fitness of $P_M(s, d_i)$ and $P_F(s, d_i)$ and select the best path. Finally, we compose all selected paths and construct a new Steiner tree (see Fig. 4 and 6(a), 6(b), 6(c)).

```
Procedure: The crossover I algorithm
begin
 for i:=1 to m do            { m is the number of destination nodes}
     if F(P_M(s, d_i)) > F(P_F(s, d_i)) then
          P_O(s, d_i) := P_M(s, d_i)
     else
          P_O(s, d_i) := P_F(s, d_i);
 Current-tree := P_O(s, d_1);
 for i:=2 to m do
 begin
    Previous-node := s;
    Start-node := s;
    Current-node := The second node in the P_O(s, d_i);
    New-link := False;
    while (Previous-node <> d_i) do
     begin
        if the Current-node does not exist in the current-tree then
        begin
            Add the link between the Current-node and the Previous-node to the current-tree;
            New-link := True;
        end
        else
        begin
            if New-link = True then
              Move all links from Start-node to the Previous-node in P_O(s, d_i) in the current-tree;
              Start-node := Current-node
              New-link := False;
        end
        Previous-node := Current-node;
        if there is another node in P_O(s, d_i) then
            Current-node := the next node in the P_O(s, d_i)
     end
 end
end
```

Fig. 4. The *crossover I* algorithm.

If only the *crossover I* operator is used, the whole solution space can not be searched thoroughly. It can be explained this way: the number of individuals in the initial population is *pop-size* and the number of destination nodes is m. Consequently, the number of paths in the initial population from the source node to the destination nodes is m**pop-size*. But, there is a possibility of having a global optimum solution, whose paths do not belong to this set of initial paths. Therefore, the *crossover I* operator may not achieve the global optimum solution. On the other hand, due to the smallness of the mutation probability, the whole solution space can not be searched fast and thoroughly using this operator. Having all these facts, we propose *crossover II* algorithm as follows:

Crossover II: In this scheme, we first use a simple one-point crossover operator, with a fixed probability P_c. The constructed offspring do not necessarily represent Steiner trees (See Fig. 6(d), 6(e), 6(f)). Then, an effective and fast *check and recovery* algorithm is used to repair the illegal individuals (see Fig. 5).

```
Procedure: The crossover II algorithm
begin
   Apply a simple one point crossover to the parents;
   for each offspring do     { Check and recovery procedure for both of the offspring}
   begin
      Detect the loops in the offspring graph;
      Recover the detected loops by means of deleting the additional paths;
      Find the separate sub-trees in the graph and add them to the sub-tree set;
      while (there are more than one sub-tree in the sub-tree set) do
      begin
         Select two sub-trees randomly;
         Re-connect two selected sub-trees with a random path;
         Replace two connected sub-trees with the new sub-tree in the sub-trees set;
      end;
      Mount the absent nodes of the multicast group to the created tree;
      Remove the leaves that are not member of multicast group;
   end;
end
```

Fig. 5. The *crossover II* algorithm.

In order to compare the proposed *crossover II* algorithm with other alternatives, which have been proposed by Ravikumar *et al.*[30] and Wang *et al.*[33] (they have been described before), we can say that the complexity of these alternatives are similar to the complexity of our proposed *crossover II* algorithm, except that in these algorithms, the complexity of the heuristic algorithm, which selects a path to join the two separate sub-trees is higher than the complexity of the algorithm that re-connect the two selected sub-trees with a random path in *crossover II* algorithm. Also, in these alternative algorithms, the resulting chromosome is not necessarily a multicast tree containing the source node and all of the destination nodes. However, this does not prove that our proposed algorithm shall lead to a faster convergence. In any case, the simulation results will show that the proposed *crossover II* algorithm leads to a faster convergence towards the optimum solution in comparison to the other alternatives.

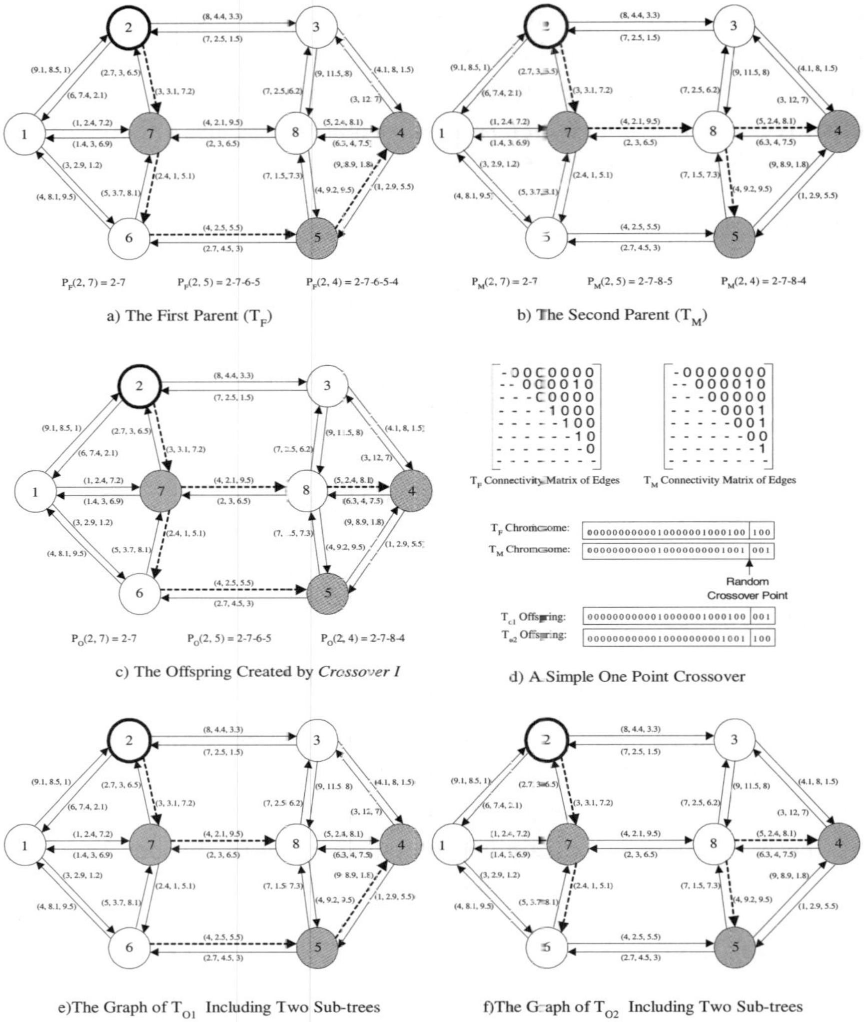

Fig. 6. The *crossover I* and One-point crossover operator.

3.7. *Mutation*

Many of proposed GA-based algorithms for multicast routing[27-29,32] have used the bit-flip mutation with a fixed small probability $P_m(\approx 0.001\text{-}0.05)$. Unfortunately, according to the mentioned genotype schemes, the bit mutation generates illegal individuals and decreases the performance of the genetic algorithm. However, Ravikumar *et al.*[30] have proposed a new scheme for mutation of Steiner trees and Wang *et al.*[33] have improved this scheme. In this mutation algorithm[33], according to the mutation probability P_m, the mutation procedure randomly selects a subset of nodes and breaks the multicast tree into some separate sub-trees by removing all the links that are incident to the selected nodes. Then, it re-connects those separate sub-trees into a new multicast tree by randomly selecting the least-delay or the least-cost paths between them.

However, the result of this complex heuristic algorithm is not necessarily a multicast tree containing the source node and all of the destination nodes. In this chapter, we propose two following algorithms for mutation operator:

Mutation I: First, we propose an improved version of the scheme presented by Wang *et al.*[33]. The mutation procedure randomly selects a subset of nodes and breaks the multicast tree into some separate sub-trees by removing all the links that are incident to the selected nodes. Then, an effective and fast *check and recovery* algorithm (similar to Fig. 5) is used to connect the separate sub-trees and also connecting the absent nodes of multicast group to the final tree.

Mutation II: According to the mutation probability P_m, the mutation procedure randomly selects an infeasible chromosome from one of the following class (If the first class is empty, a chromosome is selected from the second class and so on):

- Class 1: The chromosomes, which do not satisfy the delay and the bandwidth constraints.
- Class 2: The chromosomes, which do not satisfy the delay constraint.
- Class 3: The chromosomes, which do not satisfy the bandwidth constraint.

If all chromosomes in the current population satisfy both of the QoS constraints, we exit from the mutation procedure. Otherwise, we select only the paths that do not violate the QoS constraints in the selected chromosome. We re-connect these selected paths by an algorithm similar to *crossover I*. Finally, the disconnected destination nodes will be mounted to the sub-tree.

3.8. *Illegality and Infeasibility*

The chromosomes generated randomly in the initial population and the offspring produced by mutation and crossover operators may be illegal or infeasible. Illegality refers to the phenomenon that a chromosome does not represent a multicast tree; Infeasibility refers to the phenomenon that a chromosome does not satisfy the problem constraints. Three strategies (Rejecting, Penalizing, and Repairing strategies) have been proposed to deal with both of the mentioned violations.

The penalty methods are mostly used to handle infeasible chromosomes.[36] We have used this strategy in our proposed fitness function. It is really difficult to provide a reasonable penalizing factor for the illegal chromosomes in our study, because the illegality can not be easily measured quantitatively. The repair strategy does indeed surpass other strategies, such as the rejecting or the penalizing strategies, in this case. We have used this strategy in our proposed *mutation I* and *crossover II* algorithms. On the other hand, we have proposed another strategy to deal with the illegality problem. We will refer to this strategy as the *avoidance strategy*. In this chapter, most of the proposed algorithms, such as the initial population creation algorithm, the *crossover I* algorithm, and the *mutation II* algorithm, have used this strategy to avoid the creation of illegal individuals.

4. Experimental Results

We have used the simulation results to compare the performance of the proposed algorithms with the BSMA heuristic algorithm and some existing GA-based algorithms. The experiments are run repeatedly until confidence interval of less than 5% (using 95% confidence level), are achieved for the simulation results. A random graph generator based on Salama[17] graph generator is used. The average degree of each node in the randomly generated graphs is 4. The multicast group is randomly selected in the graph. The size of multicast group is considered to be 5% and 30% of the number of network nodes. We have tuned the proposed algorithms by finding the best values for all of parameters in the genetic algorithm. The optimal solution depends on these values. We have tried different values of the population size (*pop-size*), mutation probability (P_m), and crossover probability (P_c) to find which values would steer the search towards the best solution. The best results were achieved with *pop-size*=45, P_m=0.05, and P_c=0.9. The experiments mainly test the convergence speed, and the tree cost of the achieved solutions.

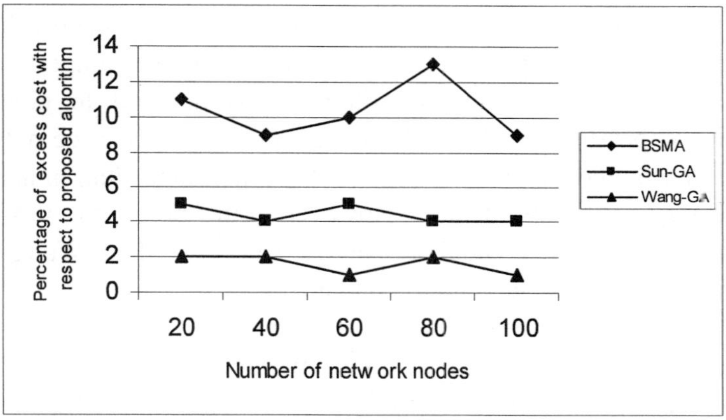

Fig. 7. Percentage of excess cost with respect to the proposed algorithm versus number of network nodes (Multicast group size is 5% of the number of network nodes). Note that the proposed algorithm is chosen as the reference for the comparison.

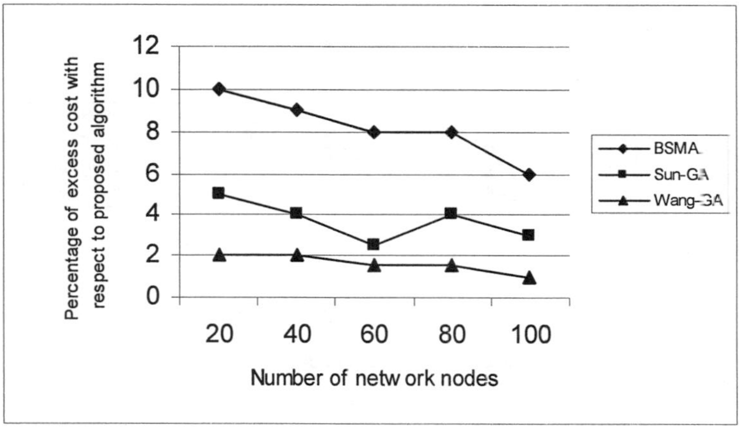

Fig. 8. Percentage of excess cost with respect to the proposed algorithm versus number of network nodes (Multicast group size is 30% of the number of network nodes).

Fig. 7, and 8 show the percentage of tree cost of BSMA[3], Sun's algorithm[28], and Wang's algorithm[33] with respect to our proposed algorithm for different network sizes and different multicast group sizes. It should be noted that the BSMA and Sun's algorithms were designed specifically for real-time applications with only one QoS constraint (delay constraint). Therefore, we ignore the bandwidth constraint in simulation of these two algorithms. However, these figures show that our proposed GA-based algorithm can result in a smaller average tree cost than the mentioned existing algorithms. It is difficult to give very accurate comparative results with Wang's GA for very large networks because of the unavailability of the details of their algorithm in handling the memory overflow faults. However, our proposed GA-based algorithm resulted in a smaller average tree cost than Wang's GA algorithm for networks with up to 1000 nodes.

Fig. 9 shows the average execution time of our proposed GA-based algorithm in comparison with the above mentioned algorithms for some random graphs generated by Salama[17] graph generator. This figure shows that our proposed GA-based algorithm can result in a smaller execution time than the mentioned existing algorithms.

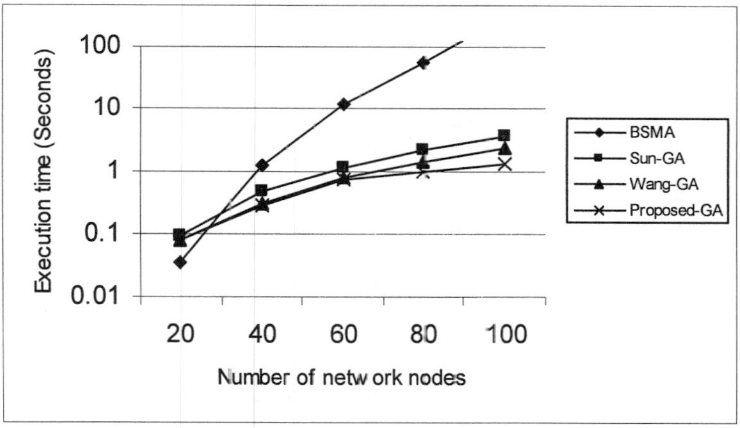

Fig. 9. The average execution time of the proposed algorithm in comparison to other existing algorithm for some random graphs generated by Salama[17] graph generator.

5. Conclusions

We have proposed a GA-based algorithm to solve the bandwidth-delay-constrained least-cost multicast routing problem which is known to be NP-complete. We derived a modified encoding method for representation of the Steiner trees. In our study, the following new algorithms have been proposed to increase the performance of the GA:

- An algorithm for creation of a random individual: *random individual creation*
- Two heuristic algorithms for mutation operator: *mutation I, II*
- Two heuristic algorithms for crossover operator: *crossover I, II*

We have used the penalizing strategy in the proposed fitness function to deal with the infeasible chromosomes and also the repairing strategy in the *mutation I* and *crossover II* algorithms to deal with the illegal chromosomes. On the other hand, we have proposed the *avoidance* strategy to avoid creating illegal chromosomes in the *crossover I*, *mutation II*, and *random individual creation* algorithms.

We have implemented a C++ program to simulate all of the proposed algorithms. The simulation results are used for evaluation of the proposed algorithms in comparison with the existing genetic algorithms. These experiments have shown that our powerful GA-based algorithm for solving the bandwidth-delay-constrained least-cost multicast routing problem has the following characteristics:

- The penalizing strategy in the fitness function
- The heuristic *mutation II* algorithm with *avoidance* strategy
- The heuristic *crossover I* and *crossover II* algorithm with *avoidance* and *repairing* strategies
- The *random individual creation* algorithm with *avoidance* strategy
- The roulette wheel selection
- The preprocessing phase for removing all the links which violate the bandwidth constraint of all destination nodes.

There are many aspects of research that can be further developed. In this study, we examined the impact of some factors such as encoding, crossover and mutation on the performance of the GAs for solving the bandwidth-delay-constrained least-cost multicast routing problem. However, these factors are interrelated and we are going to analyze their correlations in order to find their ideal combinations.

As for any genetic algorithms, one of the problems is its convergence behavior and scaling capabilities affected by many factors such as population and chromosome size, crossover and mutation probabilities. In our study, we have tested the proposed algorithms for networks with less than 1000 nodes. For larger networks, it needs further fine tuning to get an optimal solution within a reasonable time. We have used the penalizing strategy in the proposed fitness function to deal with the chromosomes that violate the constraints. We can extend our algorithm to use an adaptive penalty function that produces a low penalty value in the earlier generations to widen the search space, and increases the penalty value in later generations to lead to faster convergence.

Acknowledgments

This work was supported by Network Management Department of Iran Telecommunication Research Center (ITRC).

References

1. S. L. Hakimi, Steiner problem in graphs and its mplications, Networks, V. 1, p. 113-133, 1971.
2. R. Karp, Reducibility among combinatorial problems, in: R. E. Miller, J. W. Thatcher, *Complexity of computer computations*, Plenum Press, New York, p. 85-103, 1972.
3. M. Parsa, Q. Zhu, J.J. Garcia-Luna-Aceves, An iterative algorithm for delay-constrained minimum-cost multicasting, IEEE/ACM Transactions on Networking, V. 6, No. 4, p. 461-474, 1998.
4. V.P. Kompella, J.C. Pasquale, G.C. Polyzos, Multicast routing for multimedia communication, IEEE/ACM Trans. on Networking, V. 1, No. 3, p. 286-292, 1993.
5. R. Widyono, The design and evaluation of routing algorithms for real-time channels, Technical Reports TR-94-024, Tenet Group, Dept. of EECS, University of California at Berkeley, 1994.
6. A. G. Waters, A new heuristic for ATM multicast routing, 2nd IFIP Workshop on Performance Modeling and Evaluation of ATM networks, 1994.
7. L. Kou, G. Markowsky L. Berman, A fast algorithm for steiner trees, Acta Informatica, V. 15, p. 141-145, 1981.
8. V. Rayward-smith, The computation of nearly minimal steiner trees in graphs, International Journal of Mathematical Education in Science and Technology, V. 14, No. 1, p. 15-23, 1983.

9. H. Takahashi, A. Matsuyama, An approximate solution for the Steiner problem in graphs, Mathematica Japonica, V. 22, No. 6, p. 573-577, 1980.
10. E. Gelenbe, A. Ghanwani, V. Srinivasan, Improved neural heuristics for multicast routing, IEEE Journal of selected Area in Communication, V. 15, No. 2, p. 147-155, 1997.
11. Q. Sun, H. Langendörfer, An efficient delay-constrained multicast routing algorithm, Journal of High-Speed Networks, V. 7, No. 1, p. 43-55, 1998.
12. L. Guo, I. Matta., QDMR: an efficient QoS dependent multicast routing algorithm, Proceedings of the Fifth IEEE Real-Time Technology and Applications Symposium, 1999.
13. G.N. Rouskas, I. Baldine, Multicast routing with end-to-end delay and delay variation constraints, IEEE Journal on Selected Areas in Communications, V. 15, No. 3, p. 346-356, 1997.
14. M.V. Marathe, R. Ravi, R. Sundaram, S.S. Ravi, D.J. Rosenkrantz, H.B. Hunt, Bicriteria network design problems, Journal of Algorithms, V. 28, No. 1, p. 142-171, 1998.
15. R. Sriram, G. Manimaran, S.R. Murthy, Algorithms for delay-constrained low-cost multicast tree construction, Computer Communications, V. 21, No. 18, p. 1693-1706, 1998.
16. R. Sriram, G. Manimaran, S.R. Murthy, A rearrangeable algorithm for the construction of delay-constrained dynamic multicast trees, Proceedings of the Conference on Computer Communications, IEEE INFOCOM 99, New York, 1999.
17. H.F. Salama, D.S. Reeves, Y. Viniotis, Evaluation of multicast routing algorithms for real-time communication on high-speed networks, IEEE Journal on Selected Areas in Communications, V. 15, No. 3, p. 332-345, 1997.
18. P. Chotipat, C. Goutam, S. Norio, Neural network approach to multicast routing in real-time communication networks, IEEE International Conference on Network Protocols, p. 332-339, 1995.
19. S. Pierre, G. Legault, A genetic algorithm for designing distributed computer network topologies, IEEE Trans. on Systems Man and Cybernetics, Part B: Cybernetics, V. 28, No. 2, p. 249-258, 1998.
20. M.S. Bright, T. Arslan, A. Genetic, A genetic framework for the high-level optimisation of low power VLSI DSP systems, IEEE Electronic Letters, V. 32, No. 13, p. 1150-1151, 1996.
21. Carlos A. Coello, Alan D. Christiansen, H. Aguirre Arturo, Use of evolutionary techniques to automate the design of combinational circuits, International Journal of Smart Engineering System Design, V. 2, No. 4, p. 299-314, 2000.
22. F.K. Hwang, D.S. Richards, P. Winter, The Steiner Tree Problem, Elsevier Science, Amsterdam, 1992.
23. J. Hesser, R. Männer, O. Stucky, Optimization of Steiner trees using genetic algorithms, Proceedings of the Third International Conference on Genetic Algorithms, San Mateo, CA, p. 231-236, 1989.

24. B.A. Julstrom, A genetic algorithm for the rectilinear Steiner problem, Proceedings of the 5th International Conference on Genetic Algorithms, p. 474-480, 1993.
25. A. Kapsalis, V.J. Rayward-Smith, G.D. Smith, Solving the graphical Steiner tree problem using genetic algorithms, Journal of the Operational Research Society, V. 44, No. 4, p. 397-406, 1993.
26. H. Esbensen, Computing near-optimal solutions to the Steiner problem in a graph using a genetic algorithm, Networks, V. 26, p. 173-185, 1995.
27. Y. Leung, G. Li, Z.B. Xu, A genetic algorithm for the multiple destination routing problems, IEEE Trans. on Evolutionary Computation, V. 2, No. 4, p. 150-161, 1998.
28. Q. Sun, A genetic algorithm for delay-constrained minimum-cost multicasting, Technical Report, TU Braunschweig, Butenweg, 74/75, 38106, Germany, 1999.
29. F. Xiang, L. Junzhou, W. Jieyi, G. Guanqun, QoS routing based on genetic algorithm, Computer Communications, V. 22, p. 1394-1399, 1999.
30. C.P. Ravikumar, R. Bajpai, Source-based delay-bounded multicasting in multimedia networks, Computer Communications, V. 21, p. 126-132, 1998.
31. Q. Zhang, Y.W. Lenug, An orthogonal genetic algorithm for multimedia multicast routing, IEEE Trans. on Evolutionary Computation, V. 3, No. 1, p. 53-62, 1999.
32. J. J. Wu, R. H. Hwang, H. I. Lu, Multicast routing with multiple QoS constraints in ATM networks, Information Sciences, V. 124, p. 29-57, 2000.
33. Z. Wang, B. Shi, E. Zhao, Bandwidth-delay-constrainted least-cost multicast routing based on heuristic genetic algorithm, Computer Communications, V. 24, p. 685-692, 2001.
34. C. Guoliang, W. Xufa, Z. Zhenquan, *et al.*, *Genetic Algorithm and its Application*, People's Posts and Telecommunications Press, 1996.
35. G.N. Rouskas, I. Baldine, Multicast routing with end-to-end delay and delay variation constraints, IEEE Journal on Selected Areas in Communications, V. 15, No. 3, p. 346-356, 1997.
36. M. Gen, R. Cheng, Genetic algorithms and engineering optimization, John Wiley & Sons, 2000.
37. G. Zhou, M. Gen, An effective genetic algorithm approach to the quadratic minimum spanning tree problem, Computers and operations research, V. 25, No. 3, p. 229-247, 1998.
38. C. C. Palmer, An approach to a problem in network design using genetic algorithms, Ph.D. Dissertation, Computer Science Department, Polytechnic University, Brooklyn, New York, 1994.
39. A. T. Haghighat, K. Faez, et al, A genetic algorithm for Steiner tree optimization with multiple constraints using Prüfer number, EURASIA-ICT 2002 Conference, Tehran, Iran, p. 167-173, 2002.
40. A. T. Haghighat, K. Faez, et al, Multicast routing with multiple constraints in high-speed networks based on genetic algorithms, ICCC 2002 Conference, India, p. 243-249, 2002.

CHAPTER 32

CONSTRAINED OPTIMIZATION OF MULTILAYERED ANTI-REFLECTION COATINGS USING GENETIC ALGORITHMS

Kai-Yew Lum[1], Pierre-Marie Jacquart[2], and Mourad Sefriou[2]

[1] *Temasek Laboratories, National University of Singapore*
10 Kent Ridge Crescent, Singapore 119260
[2] *Dassault Aviation, 78 Quai Marcel Dassault - Cedex 300*
92552 St Cloud Cedex, France

Optimization based on genetic algorithms is applied to the design of multilayered coatings, incorporating both coating-geometry and material-property optimization. The latter is based on parametric modeling of dielectric and magnetic properties of homogeneous materials, and effective-medium modeling of composites. Our approach treats physical laws to be obeyed by the models as constraints. Moreover, efficiency in thickness is considered in two ways: as an upper-limit constraint, and in multi-objective settings including aggregation and Pareto optimality.

1. Introduction

1.1. *Multilayered Anti-Reflection Coatings*

Anti-reflection coatings are widely used for optical and high-frequency applications, such as dichroic filters in optics[40] or radar absorbing material (RAM) for ElectroMagnetic Compatibility (EMC)[23]. Thus, EMC has recently become a very serious problem concerning office and factory automation, the intensive use of mobile phones, etc. For a countermeasure of EMC or ElectroMagnetic Interference (EMI), various wave absorbers are applicable according to their usage. RAM design is required to broaden the useful frequency bandwidth, while reducing the thickness and weight for practical application. Even though a single-layer coating, made of a bulk material like ferrite, may be sufficient to obtain low reflection coefficients, its efficiency is usually reduced to a narrow bandwidth and to a specific polarization and incidence angle. In such a case, analytical expressions of the reflection coefficient can be obtained[5,7], even for a strongly anisotropic medium[20], to define the criteria that the properties of the monolayer (refractive index, dielectric permittivity, magnetic permeability) has to satisfy in order to achieve the desired anti-reflection properties. Nevertheless, these criteria are usually approximate close-form expressions that are based on certain hypotheses[18,27]. In other cases, no assumption is made and perfect-matching conditions can be represented by theoretical equations but the derivation is done at a given frequency[17].

In order to extend the performance of anti-reflection coatings to wider ranges of frequency and incidence angles, a multilayered structure has to be considered. The problem of optimal design of multilayered coatings has been studied in the past following different approaches. Pesqué *et al.*[35] employed an analytical method based on optimal control. They considered the design problem of determining the number of layers in the coating, and the thickness and electromagnetic property of each layer by selecting its permittivity and permeability as linear combinations of a set of predefined values. Michielssen *et al.*[31], on the other hand, adopted the genetic-algorithm approach for the multilayer design problem. They only considered coating made up of a fixed number of layers, each of a material chosen from a predefined set which included dielectric and relaxation-type magnetic materials. From the viewpoint of genetic algorithms, this represented a mixed problem with both combinatorial (choice of materials) and continuous variables (thickness of each layer).

In the present study, we shall focus on the optimal design of the material properties of each layer in addition to the thickness. Permittivity and permeability of each material are described by analytical functions of frequency, involving parameters that will be optimized. Besides homogeneous materials, we also consider heterogeneous layers in order to achieve performance that may not be easily obtained with homogeneous layers. Rather than a simple linear combination of predefined permittivities and permeabilities as was done in Pesqué *et al.*[35], heterogeneous materials are better modeled using effective medium theories. Some well known parametric models that we shall adopt are described in Section 2.1. Thus, the optimization of such complex multilayered coatings now entails the determination of many parameters (e.g. we shall consider a problem with 21 unknowns) that may not be easily solved in an analytical approach. Since the models describing each material or composite are complex parametric functions of frequency, constraints must be imposed to ensure that the materials obtained have physical significance. In addition, there are practical constraints, such as maximum total thickness.

1.2. *Motivation for the Use of Genetic Algorithms*

The present approach fits into the class of constrained multivariable, multi-objective design problems to which Genetic Algorithms (GAs) have demonstrated remarkable applicability. In particular, it is interesting to note that genetic algorithms have been successfully applied to a variety of other electromagnetic design problems, including antenna design[4,3], optimal positioning of scatterers [8], frequency-selective surfaces[10], and multi-disciplinary problems[28] just to name a few. As one of the natural traits of genetic algorithms, the use of binary coding allows us to the control the size of the search space, such that parameter precision corresponds to realistic manufacturability. Moreover, a trade-off between reflectivity and thickness can be treated using the technique of Pareto optimality with multiple objectives, yielding a selection of designs of equal merits.

2. Optimal Design of Multilayered Anti-Reflection Coatings

2.1. *Problem Formulation*

Let us consider a reflective plane (Perfectly Electric Conductor — PEC) coated by a stack of M materials as shown in Figure 1, each of thickness h_k with $k \in \{1, ..., M\}$. Due to the infinite extension of each layer in the geometric plane, the problem is reduced to a single-dimension problem, i.e. to the computation of the reflection coefficient on the structure. Thus, our goal is to minimize the reflection coefficient of an incident wave illuminating the multilayered coating, over a wide range of incidence angles and for both polarizations. The amplitude of the incident wave is supposed to be small enough to avoid non-linear effects in the materials. The computation of the reflection coefficient is based on the exact resolution of Maxwell's equations in each layer with permittivity ϵ_k and permeability μ_k, leading to the determination of the entire electric and magnetic fields in each layer.

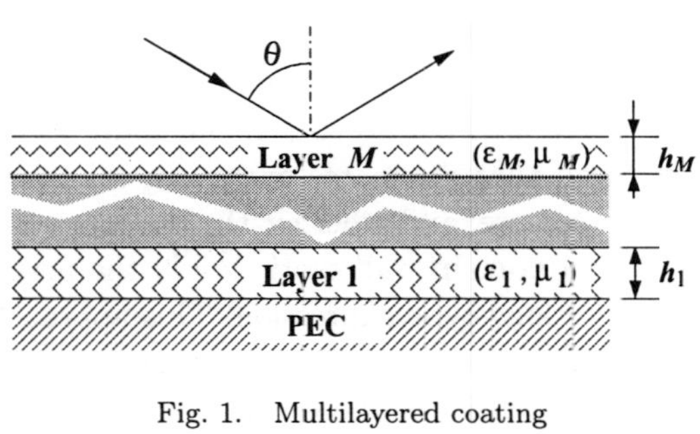

Fig. 1. Multilayered coating

2.2. *Material Description*

2.2.1. *Frequency-Dependent Permittivity and Permeability*

In this problem, each layer is described by its intrinsic electromagnetic parameters, i.e. its relative electric permittivity ϵ_k and magnetic permeability μ_k, as functions of the frequency f. Assuming the $e^{\jmath 2\pi f t}$ convention to describe the propagation of incident waves, ϵ_k and μ_k can be written as complex functions of frequency:

$$\epsilon_k(f) = \epsilon'_k(f) - \jmath\epsilon''_k(f), \tag{1}$$

$$\mu_k(f) = \mu'_k(f) - \jmath\mu''_k(f). \tag{2}$$

Each layer is either a homogeneous material or a heterogeneous material made of homogeneous inclusions embedded in a homogeneous host. In order to represent most of the materials that exhibit dielectric and/or magnetic losses in the frequency range from 100 MHz up to 20 GHz, the permittivity and permeability are expressed as the following parametric functions of frequency:

$$\epsilon_k(f) = (a_k + \frac{b_k}{f} + c_k f) - \jmath(a'_k + \frac{b'_k}{f} + c'_k f), \tag{3}$$

$$\mu_k(f) = \alpha_k + \frac{\beta_k + \jmath\beta'_k f}{\gamma_k - f^2 + \jmath\gamma'_k f} \tag{4}$$

where a_k,...,c'_k and α_k,...,γ'_k are real coefficients. Equation (4) is known as the Lorentz formula. These expressions are also suitable for describing lossless materials when a'_k,...,$c'_k = 0$, and $\beta'_k, \gamma'_k = 0$. In this case, a_k,...,c_k and α_k,...,γ_k have to be defined such that the permittivity and permeability satisfy the Kramers-Kronig relation[24,25] in the frequency range of interest. This leads to $b_k, c_k = 0$ and $\beta_k = 0$. Some authors have also used the Lorentz formula to describe the frequency-dependency of the permittivity in the microwave range of frequencies[21,26].

Equation (4) is also suitable for describing the frequency-dependent permeability of ferromagnetic or ferrimagnetic materials. Indeed, the description of the permeability is generally based on many assumptions about the mechanism involved that dissipates energy in the magnetic material. Whatever the hypotheses are, and whether the dissipation mechanism is a gyro-resonance[36,14] or a domain wall motion[12,16], the permeability is easily described using a Lorentz-type expression. This approach has also been used by other authors[41,22] especially for ferrimagnetic materials of which the permeability spectra consist of these two mechanisms.

For a composite layer k, we can consider models proposed by various Effective Medium Theories (EMT), such as the Bruggeman[9] and Maxwell-Garnett models[29]; alternatively, when the structure cannot be easily modeled using EMT[33], relations (3) and (4) can be used to describe the frequency-dependency of the effective permittivity and permeability. Indeed, EMT are more relevant when the morphology and size of the particles are well defined, thus avoiding percolation effects between the inclusions[13,2]. In such a case, the respective permittivities and permeabilities of inclusions A and a host B are represented by (3) and (4). Then, the effective permittivity ϵ_k^e and permeability μ_k^e of the layer are now governed by an effective medium theory in the form of the following equation for a random dispersion of spherical particles[9,34,38]:

$$\phi_k \frac{\epsilon_A(f, r_k, \rho_k) - \epsilon_k^e(f)}{\epsilon_A(f, r_k, \rho_k) + 2\epsilon_k^e(f)} + (1 - \phi_k) \frac{\epsilon_B(f, r_k, \rho_k) - \epsilon_k^e(f)}{\epsilon_B(f, r_k, \rho_k) + 2\epsilon_k^e(f)} = 0, \tag{5a}$$

$$\phi_k \frac{\mu_A(f, r_k, \rho_k) - \mu_k^e(f)}{\mu_A(f, r_k, \rho_k) + 2\mu_k^e(f)} + (1 - \phi_k) \frac{\mu_B(f, r_k, \rho_k) - \mu_k^e(f)}{\mu_B(f, r_k, \rho_k) + 2\mu_k^e(f)} = 0, \tag{5b}$$

where ρ_k is the electrical resistivity and r_k the radius of the inclusions, and ϕ_k is the filling factor.

One can also have different types of inclusions embedded in the same host, each one being described by its electromagnetic parameters, resistivity and volume fraction. Different morphologies of inclusions can be considered which implies the use of appropriate effective medium theories[37,1].

2.2.2. *Physical Admissibility*

The parametric representation of materials we proposed entails a question on its physical admissibility. Indeed, in order for a representation to comply with the physical law of dissipation, the imaginary parts of the permittivity and permeability must be positive for all frequencies. For layers described by (3) and (4), this condition yields:

$$\epsilon_k''(f) = a_k' + \frac{b_k'}{f} + c_k' f > 0, \tag{6}$$

$$\mu_k''(f) = \mathrm{Im}\left(\frac{\beta_k + \jmath\beta_k' f}{\gamma_k - f^2 + \jmath\gamma_k' f} \right) > 0. \tag{7}$$

These constraints must also be satisfied for the different media $(\epsilon_A'', \epsilon_B'', \mu_A'', \mu_B'', ...)$ that comprise a heterogeneous layer. Conditions (6)–(7) correspond to some algebraic constraints on the parameters. Moreover, as (4) is an abstract form of Gilbert's frequency response model[14], the coefficients in (4) are not mutually independent. For composite materials, the admissibility condition becomes even more complex.

On the other hand, instead of dealing with the algebraic constraints on the parameters whose forms depend eventually on the permeability function, we choose to simply compute the imaginary part μ''_k over the frequency range of interest, and define a penalty function as we will see below.

In most cases, we take relative permittivity such as $b_k, c_k, a'_k, c'_k = 0$, which implies $\epsilon''_k > 0$ for all frequencies. This approximation is a close form of usual expressions widely used by many authors in dealing with numerical approaches[6,43].

2.3. *Design Evaluation — Fitness Function*

With the above description, the problem becomes one of parametric design. Let the various parameters defining permittivity, permeability and thickness be collectively denoted v_i, for $i = 1, ..., n$ where n is the total number of parameters. The design objective consists in manipulating the v_i's such that the coating exhibits good absorption. This desired property is measured by the *reflectivity function* that is defined as the average of reflection coefficients $R(f_p, \theta_q)$ over a discrete range of frequencies f_p $(p = 1, ..., N_f)$ and incident angles θ_q $(q = 1, ..., N_\theta)$:

$$\mathcal{R}(v_1, ..., v_n) \triangleq \frac{1}{N_f N_\theta} \sum_{q=1}^{N_\theta} \sum_{p=1}^{N_f} R(f_p, \theta_q). \tag{8}$$

$\mathcal{R}$ takes values between 0 and 1. The optimal coating is the one that minimizes $\mathcal{R}$ over an admissible set $\mathcal{A}$ of parameters:

$$\mathcal{R}^* = \min_{\mathcal{A}} \mathcal{R}(v_1, ..., v_n). \tag{9}$$

The fitness of a design is therefore primarily determined by the reflectivity function $\mathcal{R}$. In addition, the design is subject physical admissibility, and possibly an additional penalty on the extra weight contributed by the coating. This may be accounted for through two approaches: as a constraint as we will see in Section 3, or as a second cost function as in Section 5. Note that in a minimization problem, a *better* solution has a *lower* fitness value.

2.4. *Binary-Coded Basic Genetic Algorithm*

We employ for the present problem a basic form of genetic algorithms with the following characteristics:

- fixed-size populations,
- gray binary coding,
- tournament selection, and
- crossover and mutation operators for binary strings.

More precisely, the selection operator is based on the principle of stochastic tournament with replacement. The specifications of the algorithm used for the examples given in Sections 4 and 6 are listed in Figure 2. The reader may also refer to Coley[11] and Goldberg[15], for example, for descriptions of such an algorithm and comparisons with other variants.

We choose binary coding for two reasons. Firstly, binary codes define an inherent parameter precision that corresponds to the resolution to which a material property can be tuned during manufacturing. Secondly, while we only consider the parametric design setting in this work, binary coding offers the added flexibility to combine our formulation with that of Michielssen *et al.*[31], i.e. choose from known materials in addition to synthesizing new ones. In the following sections, we shall discuss in more details the formulation of the fitness functions and constraint penalties for the problems of interest.

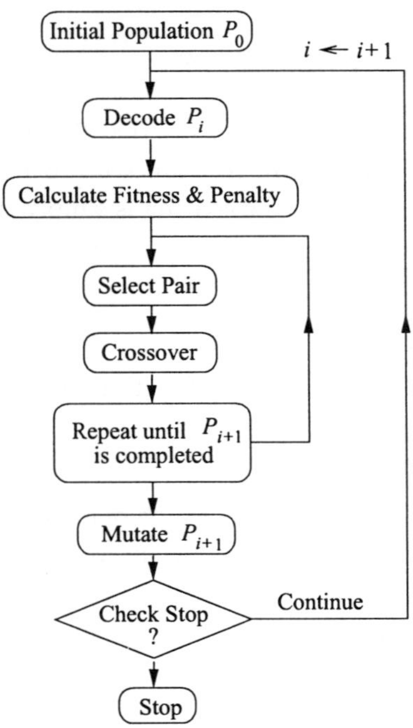

Specifications:

- Fixed-size populations:
  P_i denotes the ith population
- Tournament Selection:
  tournament size
  $= 10\%$ of population
- Crossover operator:
  single-point crossover with 99% probability, reusable parents
- Mutation operator:
  each bit mutates with a probability of $0.95/L$, where L is the length of the binary string
- Stop criterion:
  stop at the nth iteration if
  $$\mathcal{F}(n) - \frac{1}{10}\sum_{i=n-10}^{n-1} \mathcal{F}(i) < 10^{-4}$$
  where $\mathcal{F}(i) =$ fitness of the ith iteration

Fig. 2. Flowchart of genetic algorithm with penalty on constraint violation

3. Constrained Single-Objective Optimization

For single-objective optimization of multilayered coatings, the *fitness function* of a design equals the cost function $\mathcal{R}(v_1, ..., v_n)$ penalized by the constraint-handling process described below. A design is considered non-feasible if it contains material models that violate physical admissibility, or if its total thickness exceeds the allowed maximum. It is well known that handling constraints by penalty functions instead of eliminating the non-feasible designs has the advantage of allowing the latter to participate in the evolution process, thus keeping a genetically diverse population while favoring feasible designs. In a minimization problem such as the present one, penalty functions are positive valued and are added to the cost function.

3.1. *Penalty Function on Physical Admissibility*

As mentioned in Section 2.2.2, we require a design to be physically admissible by imposing a penalty on designs that violate (7). Thus, for the k-th layer define the following penalty function:

$$\mathcal{C}_k = \begin{cases} 0 & \text{if } \mu_k''(f) \geq 0 \ \forall f, \\ \sum_{i^-} |\mu_k''(f_{i^-})| \Big/ \sum_{i=1}^{N_f} |\mu_k''(f_i)| & \text{otherwise,} \end{cases} \tag{10}$$

where i^- are the indices for which $\mu_k''(f_{i^-})$ are negative. Note that $\mathcal{C}_k$ equals 0 for physically admissible materials, and takes positive values up to 1 for non-physical materials. Then the total penalty on the coating is simply the sum:

$$\mathcal{C} = \sum_{k=1}^{M} \mathcal{C}_k. \tag{11}$$

This approach is obviously independent of the modeling function used.

3.2. *Penalty Function on Total Thickness*

Let the total thickness be denoted by $\mathcal{H} = \sum_{k=1}^{M} h_k$ on which one imposes an upper limit $\mathcal{H}_{\max}$. The corresponding penalty function on a design is defined as

$$\mathcal{D} = \begin{cases} 0 & \text{if } \mathcal{H} < \mathcal{H}_{\max}, \\ \mathcal{H}/\mathcal{H}_{\max} - 1 & \text{otherwise.} \end{cases} \tag{12}$$

$D \in [0$ is therefore proportional to the fraction of $\mathcal{H}_{\max}$ by which a design violates the thickness constraint, normalized to 1.

3.3. *Superiority of Feasible Points*

Having defined the penalty functions $\mathcal{C}$ and $\mathcal{D}$, one may simply added them to the cost function, such that a non-feasible design has a worse (larger) fitness value than before the penalty. However, the two penalty functions do not have the same range: the physical-admissibility penalty $\mathcal{C}$ takes values between 0 and 1, whereas the thickness penalty may assume any positive values. It is common practice to use penalty coefficients, such as in the following penalized cost function:

$$J = \mathcal{R} + p_c\mathcal{C} + p_d\mathcal{D}, \tag{13}$$

where p_c and p_d are constant penalty coefficients to be chosen. Here lies one of the main difficulties of the penalty function method, which is selecting the values of the penalty coefficients. If they are too large, non-feasible designs will stand little chance of surviving, so that the boundary of the feasible design space remains unexplored. If, on the other hand, the coefficients are too small, (13) does not guarantee that a feasible design has a better (smaller) fitness than a non-feasible one.

One effective technique to deal with the above difficulty is the *Superiority of Feasible Points* (SFP) approach[32]. Essentially, the technique consists in adjusting the fitness functions of *all* the non-feasible designs with a constant δ_{SFP} such that the non-feasible designs are lined up just above the feasible ones in terms of fitness values. This principle not only guarantee that a feasible design has a better (smaller) fitness than a non-feasible one, it also ensures that the non-feasible design are "close enough" so as to stand a better chance of being explored. The algorithm for our problem is summarized below.

Algorithm 1: Let J^+ denote the maximum value of the cost function (13) among the feasible solutions, and J^- the minimum among the non-feasible ones. Then, the SFP fitness is given by

$$\mathcal{F} = \mathcal{R} + p_c\mathcal{C} + p_d\mathcal{D} + \delta_{\text{SFP}}, \tag{14}$$

$$\delta_{\text{SFP}} = \begin{cases} 0 & \text{if solution is feasible,} \\ \max(J^+ - J^-, 0) & \text{otherwise.} \end{cases} \tag{15}$$

Moreover, if all solutions are feasible or if all solutions are non-feasible, δ_{SFP} is zero for all solutions, i.e. no adjustment is needed.

4. Numerical Examples — Single-Objective Optimization

As an illustration of the effectiveness of the single-objective optimization of multilayered coatings described in the previous section, we present here two numerical examples where the fitness function is the reflectivity function (8) penalized according to Algorithm 1. The reflection coefficients are computed at normal incidence and over the frequency range 1–20 GHz using a Maxwell equation solver. In the following, let N_p denote the population size. Without loss of generality, we shall consider in the examples that follow a simplified form of the permittivity function (3):

$$\epsilon_k(f) = a_k - \jmath \frac{b'_k}{f}. \tag{16}$$

As a note of caution, these and the later examples should meanwhile be treated as numerical demonstrations of the proposed approach; whether the resulting designs can be practically realized remains to be studied.

4.1. *Example 1: Two-Layer Dielectric Coating*

The first example consists of a two-layer coating of homogeneous, lossy dielectrics with permittivities described by (16). The thickness of each layer is fixed at 5 mm. A population size $N_p = 20$ is chosen. As shown in Figure 3, convergence is achieved after about 700 iterations, i.e. 35 generations. The spectral reflection coefficient as a function of frequency is shown later in Figure 10, where one can see that 15 dB attenuation or better is achieved mainly in the 8-16 GHz range. Notice that the mean reflectivity oscillates between the minimum and the historical mean even at convergence. This is a useful indication that the successive populations are sufficiently diverse[11].

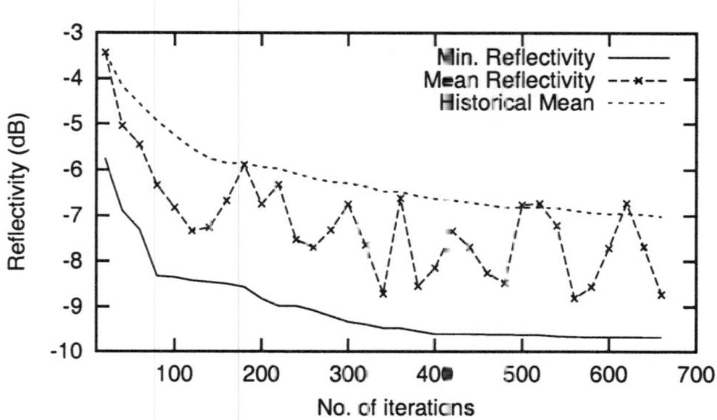

Fig. 3. Two-layer dielectric coating (Example 1)

4.2. Example 2: Two-Layer Composite Structure

The second example involves the design of a two-layer structure of composite materials with a maximum total thickness of 5 mm. Each layer is composed of lossy dielectric and magnetic inclusions with properties described by (4) and (16), embedded in a lossless host. The macroscopic properties of each composite are approximated by the Bruggeman model (5). With population size $N_p = 100$, the reflectivity converges to -14.7 dB in 100 generations as shown in Figure 4. The final design is summarized as follows where the 21 optimized design parameters are shown in bold. The resulting permeabilities are shown in Figure 5.

<table>
<tr><td colspan="2">Substrate (identical for both layers)
• $\epsilon = \mathbf{1.45} - \jmath.0$ • $\mu = 1.0 - \jmath.0$</td></tr>
<tr><td>Layer 1 inclusions (spherical):
• $\epsilon_1 = \mathbf{3.02} - \jmath\mathbf{320.0}/f$
• $\mu_1 = 1 + \frac{\mathbf{1995.7} + \jmath\mathbf{0.319}}{\mathbf{197.2} - \jmath^2 + \jmath\mathbf{0.449}}$
• $r_1 = \mathbf{1}\mu\text{m}$
• $\rho_1 = \mathbf{185}$
• $\phi_1 = \mathbf{22.5}\%$
• $h_1 = \mathbf{1.43}$ mm</td><td>Layer 2 inclusions (spherical):
• $\epsilon_2 = \mathbf{3.35} - \jmath\mathbf{1730.0}/f$
• $\mu_2 = 1 + \frac{\mathbf{1920.3} + \jmath\mathbf{0.273}}{\mathbf{0.0} - \jmath^2 + \jmath\mathbf{0.061}}$
• $r_2 = \mathbf{3}\mu\text{m}$
• $\rho_2 = \mathbf{197.5}$
• $\phi_2 = \mathbf{30.0}\%$
• $h_2 = \mathbf{3.57}$ mm</td></tr>
</table>

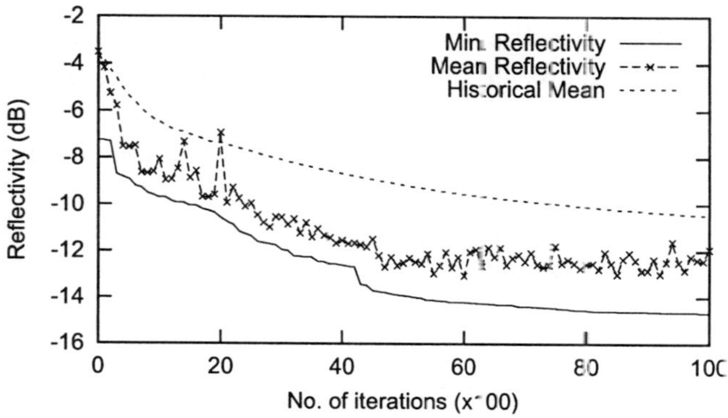

Fig. 4. Two-layer composite structure (Example 2)

This example demonstrates the ability of the approach to handle complex structures. Compared to the dielectric design in Example 1, this composite structure yields a lower reflectivity over a wider frequency range of 4-16 GHz, with only half the total thickness (Figure 10).

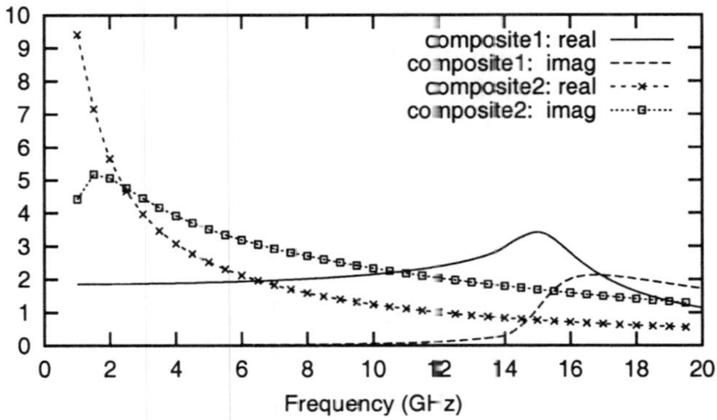

Fig. 5. Relative permeability of composites in layers 1 and 2 (Example 2)

5. Multiple-Objective Optimization

In this section we shall further consider the problem of multilayered coating optimization with multiple objectives. Indeed, here we seek a design that produces minimum reflection with minimum thickness. This consideration is reasonable from a practical and economical viewpoint. However, from a physical viewpoint, such a solution may not exist. Indeed, for relaxation-type dielectric or magnetic materials, thicker coatings means lower reflection[18]. Hence, in general, the two objectives are incompatible and a trade-off is effectively sought. Problems that involve trading off multiple, incompatible objectives are often treated using the notion of Pareto optimality[42]. Nevertheless, we shall explore both aggregation and Pareto optimization, and will compare their outcomes in an example. Note that treating thickness as an objective function does not exclude imposing on it an upper limit at the same time.

5.1. *Aggregate Cost Function*

A straight-forward approach to multiple objectives consists in aggregating the two cost functions by a linear combination; thus, the SFP fitness function as given in (14) now becomes:

$$\mathcal{F}_{\mathrm{SFP}} = \lambda_r \mathcal{R} + \lambda_h \mathcal{H} + p_c \mathcal{C} + p_d \mathcal{D} + \delta_{\mathrm{SFP}}, \tag{17}$$

where λ_r and λ_h are weights to be chosen, and δ_{SFP} is calculated as in Algorithm 1. Optimization then proceeds in exactly the same manner as for the single-objective problem. This approach is similar to that of Michielssen *et al.*[31] Obviously, the solution produced by aggregation is sensitive to the choice of the weights λ_r and λ_h, the choice of which requires *a priori* knowledge of the relative orders of magnitude of $\mathcal{R}$ and $\mathcal{H}$.

5.2. *Pareto Optimality, Sharing & Non-Dominated Sorting*

Instead of aggregation, we also consider multi-objective optimality in the sense of Pareto[11,15]. We may in the first place consider the fitness of a design be defined as its Pareto rank. Note that in our context of minimization, rank zero corresponds to non-dominated designs, and higher ranks are assigned to successive Pareto fronts. Now, in order to extend the notion of superiority of feasible points to the current setting, we adopt the principle that a feasible solution necessarily dominates a non-feasible one. This yields the following modified SFP algorithm:

Algorithm 2: Let the cost functions:

$$J_1 = \mathcal{R} + p_c\mathcal{C} + p_d\mathcal{D}, \tag{18}$$

$$J_2 = \mathcal{H} + p_c\mathcal{C} + p_d\mathcal{D}. \tag{19}$$

Using the same notation as in Algorithm 1, consider the following SFP adjustments in the general case (the special cases where all designs are feasible or all are non-feasible need no adjustment):

$$\delta_i = \begin{cases} 0 & \text{if solution is feasible,} \\ \max(J_i^+ - J_i^-, 0) & \text{otherwise;} \end{cases} \tag{20}$$

with $i \in \{1, 2\}$. Then, the multi-objective SFP cost functions to be used in the Pareto ranking process are simply given by

$$\mathcal{F}_i = J_i + \max(\delta_1, \delta_2), \qquad i \in \{1, 2\}. \tag{21}$$

5.2.1. *Sharing*

Let ρ denote the Pareto rank of a design. Simple rank-based fitness assignment may lead to *genetic drift*, i.e. the populations tend to converge to a localized point on the global Pareto front — a *niche* — instead of spanning the whole front. The general approach to prevent this is that of *niching*, which consists in modifying the selection process to consider not only survival of the fittest, but also how many similar chromosome there are in a niche; favor is given to solutions that are not only the fittest but also not surrounded by nearly identical twins.

While there exist many different niching operators such as crowding and preselection, we adopt the *fitness sharing* operator[42]. Sharing is based on the principle that nearby designs in terms of Hamming distance mutually degrade each other's fitness by competing for the same resources. Isolated solutions are thus given a greater chance of reproducing. First, consider the Hamming distance of two designs $\mathcal{S}_i$ and $\mathcal{S}_j$ which measures the number of non-identical bits in the two genotypes:

$$d_{ij} = 1 - \frac{1}{N_b} \sum_{l=1}^{N_b} \mathcal{S}_i^l \wedge \mathcal{S}_j^l \tag{22}$$

where $\mathcal{S}_i^l$ denotes the lth bit of $\mathcal{S}_i$, N_b the total number of bits, and $\wedge$ the "AND" operator that returns 1 if the two bits are identical, 0 otherwise. With this definition, d_{ij} equals 0 if the two designs are identical, and 1 otherwise. Next, consider the sharing function σ given by:

$$\sigma(\mathcal{S}_i) = \frac{1}{N} \sum_{j=1}^{N} \sigma_{ij} \tag{23}$$

where σ_{ij} is the so-called *niche count* and is given by

$$\sigma_{ij} = \begin{cases} 1 - d_{ij}/\sigma_{\max} & \text{if } d_{ij} < \sigma_{\max}, \\ 0 & \text{otherwise.} \end{cases} \tag{24}$$

Here $\sigma_{\max} \in (0, 1]$ is the *influence distance* to be chosen. Notice that $0 \leq \sigma(\mathcal{S}_i) < 1$, with 0 corresponding to a solution whose nearest neighbor is outside the influence distance, and 1 corresponding to a crowded solution.

5.2.2. *Non-Dominated Sorting*

The purpose of the sharing function is to degrade the fitness of a crowded solution. Instead of the standard form which is applicable to maximization problems[42], we define a slight variant of the shared fitness function:

$$\mathcal{F}_{\text{shared}}(\mathcal{S}) = \rho(\mathcal{S}) + \sigma(\mathcal{S}). \tag{25}$$

The effect of sharing on a design is that its Pareto rank is deteriorated (augmented) by as much as it is genetically "crowded". However, a solution is never "demoted" to the next rank as the augmentation is always less than 1. In other words, solutions of the same rank are sorted according to the sharing function, following the principle of non-dominated sorting[8,42].

6. Numerical Example 3 — Multi-Objective Optimization

Here, we consider a two-layer structure of magnetic materials, each described by the lossy dielectric and magnetic model given by (4) and (16). Three cases are considered:

Case A: Single objective, where the fitness equals the reflectivity function (8). Population size $N_p = 100$.

Case B: Linear combination of reflectivity and thickness through the aggregate fitness function (17), λ_r=1, λ_h=10^{-6}. $N_p = 100$.

Case C: Multi-objective Pareto optimality. Here, $N_p = 400$.

For all cases, the maximum thickness allowed is 10 mm. The penalty coefficients used in Algorithm 1 or Algorithm 2, depending on the cases, are $p_c = 1$ and $p_d = 0.5$. We shall first compare the single-objective cases (A and B) by plotting histories of the fittest solutions. For the multi-objective Case C, a Pareto front will be discussed later.

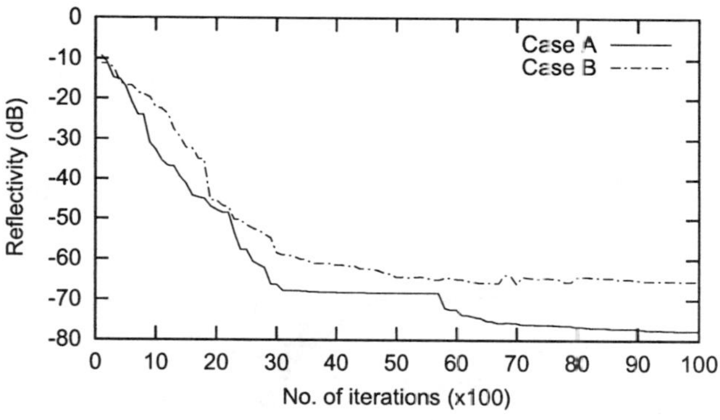

Fig. 6. Evolution of reflectivities (Cases A & B)

As shown in Figures 6 and 7, Case A produces a lower reflectivity than Case B ($\mathcal{R}_A^* = -77.7$ dB, $\mathcal{R}_B^* = -65.5$ dB), while Case B produces a thinner structure ($\mathcal{H}_A^* = 2.1 + 4.1$ mm, $\mathcal{H}_B^* = 1.3 + 3.2$ mm). This is due to the fact that in Case B, as $\mathcal{R}$ descends below -60 dB which equals the weight λ_h, the thickness becomes dominant in the aggregate cost function. As a result, the aggregate method seeks a thinner structure instead of one with lower reflectivity. This shows that the approach is sensitive to the choice of weights. The spectral behavior of the final designs for Cases A and B are compared with those of Examples 1 and 2, where one can see that much better broad-band attenuation is achieved by optimizing two homogeneous

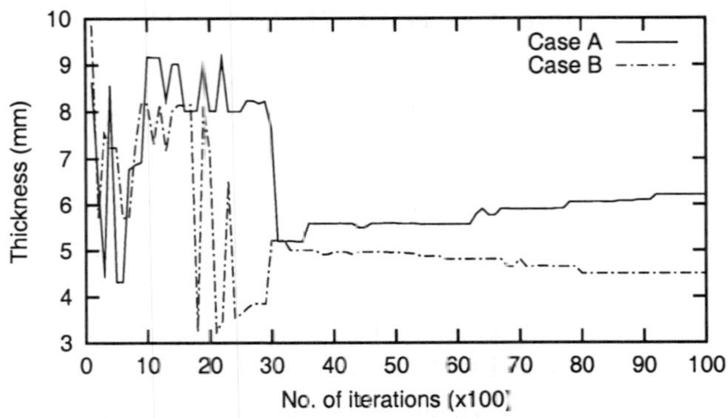

Fig. 7. Evolution of total thickness (Cases A & B)

magnetic layers as in the present example (see Figure 10).

Figure 8 shows the points forming the Pareto fronts of successive generations obtained in Case C, which reveal a part of the global Pareto front after 50 generations (20,000 iterations). This result is not entirely satisfactory as the Pareto front does not either include or dominate the final solutions of Cases A and B as one would expect. The populations have a tendency to converge toward the upper part of the front, in spite of fitness sharing.[28] This is despite that fact that the front contains genetically diverse solutions as shown in Figure 9. Moreover, the point corresponding to

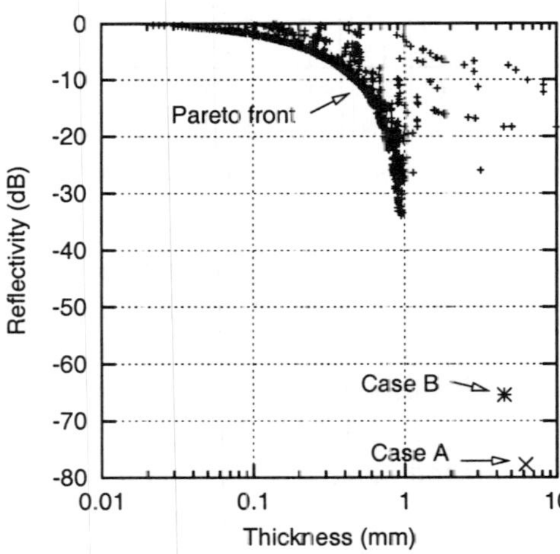

Fig. 8. Pareto front (Case C)

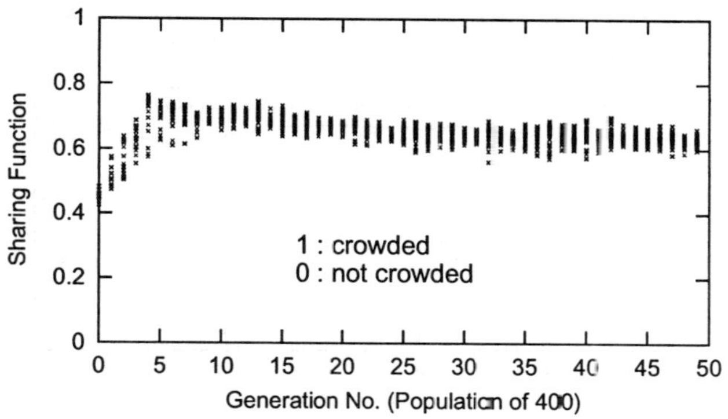

Fig. 9. Sharing values of Pareto fronts (0 ∼ not crowded)

$\mathcal{R} = 1$ and $\mathcal{H} = 0$, i.e. no coating at all, is singular in the sense that it is mapped to the entire search space of permittivities and permeabilities, and experience shows that it behaves like an 'attractor'. Nevertheless, the advantage of Pareto ranking is evident in its ability to reveal a set of designs of equal merit. For example, some of these yield -35 dB with a thickness of only 1 mm, a result that would have been difficult to obtain with the single-objective or aggregate methods.

Finally, it is also interesting to note that, although it has been mentioned that combining sharing with tournament selection could lead to chaotic behavior of the niched GA[19,42], this has not been observed in our problem.

7. Conclusion

For single and aggregate objective problems, the optimization algorithm in this chapter is similar to that employed by, say, Michielssen *et al.*[31] However, the two approaches differ in material modeling where the cite reference employed a combination of known materials while presently, we are optimizing unknown materials. Comparing the results of Example 2 and Cases A and B of Example 3 (Figure 10), with the broad-band results BB1 and BB2 in Michielssen *et al.*[31] which had comparable net thicknesses, one can say that similar or better broad-band results can be achieved in the present approach with two-layer structures, whereas Michielssen *et al.*[31] required five layers. With recent advances in composites where one may obtain desired permittivity and permeability functions by manipulating parameters such as fill factor and grain size, we believe the present approach offers an useful tool for determining the target designs in material synthesis.

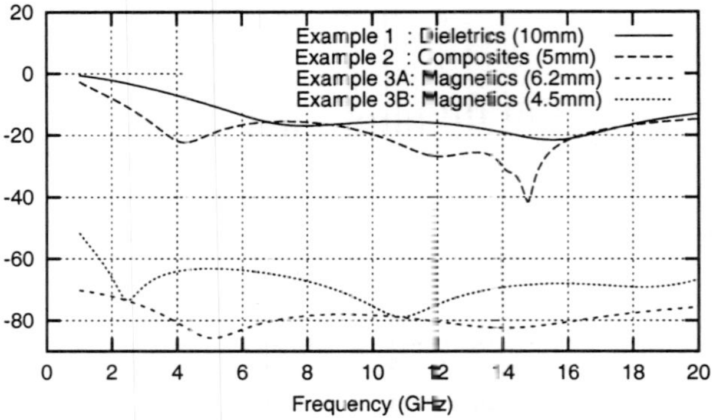

Fig. 10. Reflection coefficients achieved in the proposed approach

Meanwhile, the multi-objective problem is somewhat difficult, where simple fitness sharing is not sufficient to explore the global Pareto front. One may additionally consider the selection sharing method in Makinen *et al.*[28] or additional mechanisms, such as phenotypic sharing. The present work is also limited to one-dimensional optics. Future work consists in extending to quasi two dimensions where incidence angles are more realistically determined by the shape. Moreover, it will be interesting to apply more sophisticated techniques such as parallelization and hierarchical algorithms in order to alleviate the heavy computation loads in 2D design[39].

References

1. O. Acher, P.M. Jacquart, and C. Boscher. Investigation of high frequency permeability of thin amorphous wires. *IEEE Trans. on Magnetics*, 30(6):4542–4544, 1994.
2. O. Acher, P.M. Jacquart, J.M. Fontaine, P. Baclet, and G. Perrin. High impedance anisotropic composites manufactured from ferromagnetic thin films for microwave applications. *IEEE Trans. on Magnetics*, 30(6):4533–4535, 1994.
3. E.E. Altshuler and D.S. Linden. Design of wire antennas using genetic algorithm. In Michielssen and Rahmat-Sami [30], pages 211–248.
4. F. Ares-Pena. Application of genetic algorithms and simulated annealing to some antenna problems. In Michielssen and Rahmat-Sami [30], pages 119–155.
5. R.M.A. Azzam and N.M. Bashara. *Ellipsometry and Polarized Light*. Elsevier, North-Holland, Amsterdam, 1997.
6. J.-P. Berenger. A perfectly matched layer for the absorption of electromagnetic waves. *Journal of Computational Physics*, 114(2):185–200, 1994.
7. M. Born and E. Wolf. *Principles of Optics*. Pergamon Press, 1st edition, 1959.
8. M.-O. Bristeau, R. Glowinski, B. Mantel, J. Périaux, and M. Sefrioui. Genetic

algorithms for electromagnetic backscattering: Multiple objective optimization. In Michielssen and Rahmat-Sami [30], pages 399–435.
9. D.A.G. Bruggeman. Berechnung verschiedener physikalischer konstanten von heterogenen substanzen. *Ann. Physik. (Leipzig)*, 24:636–679, 1935.
10. S. Chakravarty and R. Mittra. Design of a frequency selective surface (FSS) with very low cross-polarization discrimination via the parallel micro-genetic algorithm (PMGA). *IEEE Trans. on Antennas and Propagation*, 51(7):1664–1668, July 2003.
11. D.A. Coley. *An Introduction to Genetic Algorithms for Scientists and Engineers.* World Scientific, Singapore, 1999.
12. W. Döring. *Zeit. für Naturforschung*, 3a:374, 1948.
13. W.T. Doyle and I.S. Jacobs. Effective cluster model of dielectric enhancement in metal-insulator composites. *Physical Review B (Condensed Matter)*, 42(15):9319–9327, 1990.
14. T.L. Gilbert. A Lagrangian formulation of gyromagnetic equation of the magnetization field. *Physical Review*, 100(4):1243, 1955.
15. E.D. Goldberg. *Genetic Algorithms in Search, Optimization and Machine Learing.* Addison-Wesley, Reading, MA, 1989.
16. M. Guyot, T. Merceron, V. Cagan, and A. Messekher. Mobility and/or damping of a domain wall. *Physica Status Solidi A*, 106(2):595–612, 1988.
17. K.-C. Han, W.-S. Kim, and K.-Y. Kim. Practical design method for an electromagnetic wave absorber at 9.45 GHz. *IEEE Trans. on Magnetics*, 31(3):2285–2289, 1995.
18. P. Hartemann and M. Labeyrie. Absorbants d'ondes électromagnétiques. *Revue Technique Thomson-CSF*, 19(3–4):413–472, 1987.
19. J. Horn, N. Nafpliotis, and D.E. Goldberg. A niched Pareto genetic algorithm for multiobjective optimization. In *Proc. 1st IEEE Conf. on Evolutionary Computing*, pages 82–87, 1994.
20. Pierre-Marie Jacquart, O. Acher, and P. Gadenne. Reflection and transmission of an electromagnetic wave in a strongly anisotropic medium: Application to polarizers and antireflection layers on a conductive plane. *Opt. Comm.*, 108:355, 1994.
21. A.K. Jonscher. *Dielectric Relaxation in Solids.* Chelsea Dielectrics Press, London, 1983.
22. T. Kasagi, H. Sugitani, T. Tsutaoka, and K. Hatakeyama. Complex permeability of spinal ferrites and hybrid ferrite composite materials. In *Proc. of the 8th International Conference on Ferrites (ICF8)*, pages 950–952, 2000.
23. D.I. Kim, M. Takahashi, H. Anzai, and S. Y. Jun. Electromagnetic wave absorber with wide-band frequency characteristics using exponentially tapered ferrite. *IEEE Trans. on Electromagnetic Compatibility*, 38(2):173–177, 1996.
24. H.A. Kramers. *Nature (London)*, 117:775, 1926.
25. R. de L. Kronig. *Journal of Optical Society of America*, 12:547, 1926.
26. A.N. Lagarkov, S.M. Matitsin, and A.K. Sarychev. Microwave properties of polymer materials containing conducting inclusions. In *Polymeric Materials Science and Engineering, Proc. of the ACS*, volume 66, pages 426–427, 1992.
27. S.-W. Lee, G. Zarrillo, and C.-L. Law. Simple formulas for transmission

through periodic metal grids or plates. *IEEE Trans. on Antennas and Propagation*, AP-30(5):904–909, 1982.

28. R.A.E. Makinen, J. Periaux, and J. Toivanen. Multidisciplinary shape optimization in aerodynamics and electromagnetics using genetic algorithms. *International Journal for Numerical Methods in Fluids*, 30:149–159, 1999.
29. J.C. Maxwell-Garnett. *Philos. Trans. R. Soc. London*, B 205:237, 1906.
30. E. Michielssen and Y. Rahmat-Sami, editors. *Electromagnetic Optimization by Genetic Algorithms*. J. Wiley, New York, 1999.
31. E. Michielssen, J.-M. Sajer, S. Ranjithan, and R. Mittra. Design of lightweight, broad-band microwave absorbers using genetic algorithms. *IEEE Trans. on Microwave Theory & Techniques*, 41:1024–1030, 1993.
32. K. Miettinen, M.M. Makela, and J. Makinen. Handling constraints with penalty techniques in genetic algorithms – a numerical comparison. Number B 10/1999 in Reports of the Dept. of Mathematical Information Technology. University of Jyvaskyla, 1999.
33. T. Nakamura, T. Tsutaoka, and K. Hatakeyama. Frequency dispersion of permeability in ferrite composite materials. *Journal of Magnetism and Magnetic Materials*, 138(3):319–328, 1994.
34. G.A. Niklasson, C.G. Granqvist, and O. Hunderi. Effective medium models for the optical properties of inhomogeneous materials. *Applied Optics*, 20(1):26–30, Jan. 1981.
35. J.J. Pesqué, D.P. Bouche, and R. Mittra. Optimization of multilayer antireflection coatings using an optimal control method. *IEEE Trans. on Microwave Theory and Techniques*, 40(9):1789–1796, 1992.
36. D. Polder and J. Smit. Resonance phenomena in ferrites. *Reviews of Modern Physics*, 25:89–90, 1953.
37. V.I. Ponomarenko. The effective permittivity of an artificial dielectric with conducting fibers. *Telecommunications and Radio Engineering*, 45(6):101–103, June 1990.
38. D. Rousselle, A. Berthault, O. Acher, J.P. Bouchard, and P.G. Zérah. Effective medium at finite frequency: Theory and experiment. *Journal of Applied Physics*, 74:475, 1993.
39. M. Sefrioui and J. Périaux. A hierarchical genetic algorithm using multiple models for optimization. In *Proc. 6th International Conference in Parallel Problem Solving from Nature*, LNCS 1917, Paris, Sep. 2000. Springer.
40. M. Taylor, G. Bucher, and K. Jones. High contrast polarizers for the near infrared. In *Proceedings of the SPIE*, volume 1166, pages 446–453, 1990.
41. T. Tsutaoka, T. Nakamura, and K. Hatakeyama. Magnetic field effect on the complex permeability spectra in a Ni-Zn ferrite. *Journal of Applied Physics*, 82(6):3068–3071, 1997.
42. D.S. Weile and E. Michielssen. Genetic algorithms: Theory and advanced techniques. In Michielssen and Rahmat-Sami [30], pages 29–66.
43. W. Yu, D.H. Werner, and R. Mittra. Finite difference time domain (FDTD) analysis of an artificially-synthesized absorbing medium. *Journal of Electromagnetic Waves and Applications*, 15(8):1005–1026, 2001.

CHAPTER 33

SEQUENTIAL CONSTRUCTION OF FEATURES BASED ON GENETICALLY TRANSFORMED DATA

Jacek Jelonek, Roman Słowiński, Robert Susmaga

Institute of Computing Science
Poznan University of Technology
60-965 Poznań, POLAND
E-mail: {jacek.jelonek, roman.slowinski, robert.susmaga}@cs.put.poznan.pl

Exploration of real data sets is a complex task that often involves tiresome, manual parameter tuning. Such manual operation, aimed at transformations of data that enable discovery of interesting patterns, only rarely guarantees any thorough examination of all promising combinations of parameter values. To avoid this inconvenience, we present a universal data transformation approach that has the ability to conduct fully automatic adjustments of parameter values. The main mechanism is based on a genetic algorithm designed to search for parameter settings that are optimal with respect to a pre-defined objective function. As an illustration of the procedure we present a system that improves classification of vowels by constructive induction of new features (attributes). The new features are created in a process that is entirely automatic: the original data are transformed with a set of sequentially applied operators, the parameters of which are incorporated in a genome and thus easily controlled by the genetic search engine. The results of several conducted experiments prove the usefulness of the proposed approach.

1. Introduction

Internal representation of real-world objects' descriptions is one of the key issues in the area of prediction and classification. An inappropriate representation of the external world may negatively affect the performance of a classification tool, whereas a carefully designed representation can considerably improve its operation.

This principle holds, in particular, in Machine Learning, a branch of artificial intelligence that deals with automatic induction of knowledge from data [3,14]. Many machine-learning classifiers do not perform well on some data due to their limited capability of constructing a good internal representation of the data, i.e. values of features that describe examples to be classified. Alternatively, a rich internal representation of the data enables better discrimination and classification of objects from different decision classes.

It is a known fact that the result of a classification test depends heavily on the selection of features taken into account during the classification process. It seems certainly obvious as long as two different subsets of features are used and two different results are obtained. It is less obvious, however, with two numerous sets of features that consist of many common features and few different ones It may also happen that a removal of a feature from the set results in the increase of properly classified observations, despite the fact that such data loss should theoretically lead only to a deterioration of this result. This theoretical observation would, however, be true only with classifiers that utilize exact algorithms during learning. The learning resolves itself to finding a minimum of an error function, and if the minima found were global then any removal of features from the data set could only lead to a potential decline of the final result. But real-life learning algorithms usually find local minima, so a removal of a feature, and especially a removal of a feature that 'litters' the feature space with many local minima (a noisy feature), may actually lead to a noticeably better result of the final classification.

The general problem of feature construction is as follows. Given the original representation of objects, apply a number of transformations to this representation with the aim of obtaining a new representation that improves the evaluations of a pre-defined objective function. Undoubtedly, in machine learning tasks, the most often considered objective function is the predictive accuracy. Another measure being mentioned relatively frequently is the size of the representation but in this chapter we will entirely focus on the former one.

The different approaches concerned with feature space transformation can be roughly divided into three categories [14]:

- Feature selection methods (shortly referred to as feature selection). Here, the resulting representation is a subset of the original set of features.
- Feature weighing methods. In this case, the transformation method assigns weights to particular features. The weights reflect relative importance of features and may be utilized in the process of inductive learning. In particular, assigning a zero weight eliminates the given feature, so feature selection may be regarded as a special case of feature weighing.
- Feature construction methods. In these methods, new features are constructed and appended to the data set. On the other hand, some, but not necessarily all, of the original features may be kept unchanged in the data set, which makes the process of feature construction the most general of all three.

We suggest using the third approach. Our features are induced from a representation of the data set that, in turn, results from a chained transformation using genetic operations on the data. Such a universal data transformation approach has the ability to conduct fully automatic search of classification features. The original data are transformed with a set of sequentially applied operators, the parameters of which are incorporated in genomes and thus easily controlled by a genetic search engine. The feature creation process is optimized with respect to the predictive accuracy. The complete approach is presented in more detail in the subsequent sections.

In order to check the usefulness of this approach, we are applying it in an experiment that concerns speech recognition, and particularly the classification of vowels. Nevertheless, we term the process 'universal data transformation' and claim that the presented procedure need not be always used for speech signals. In fact signals of any origin may be processed in this way. And what is more, if one conceives any adequately general and parameterized data transformations then any data can be transformed using this methodology.

The rest of the chapter is structured as follows. In Section 2 we present our basic signal processing techniques that lead to creating new features. Section 3 describes the elements of the feature evaluating function. The computational experiment and its results are presented in Section 4. Final recapitulation is contained in Section 5.

2. The Universal Scheme of Data Transformation

The chain of operations used to transform the data from the time domain to the feature domain is presented in Fig. 1. In this chain the original data are sequentially modified by a set of transformation units. Each of the units offers a unique set of operators. In order to perform the entire data transformation, a single operator of each unit has to be activated. This may require certain setting certain parameters (which additionally calls for observing the corresponding domains). Thus the complete data transformation process is uniquely defined by the set of activated operators and the values of their parameters. In our approach all information describing this process is embedded in a structure called a genome. The set of genomes is then processed by a genetic algorithm. In result, the genetic algorithm becomes a fully automatic optimization engine that controls the chain of transformations by activating selected operators and adjusting the corresponding parameters.

Because any form of optimization resolves itself basically to searching for minima of a pre-defined evaluation function, our process must also be equipped with such a function. Its utilization in the process is straightforward as every genetic algorithm uses such function to evaluate the genomes (such function is in the genetic context usually referred to as the fitness function). In this case the function must be able to assess the usefulness of different sets of features. Because we are generally concerned with classification, we chose the function to be based on the results of classification. And because results of classification are much more reliable when the classifier is applied to classify objects from outside its learning set, we employ reclassification tests, which train and test the classifiers in multiple runs.

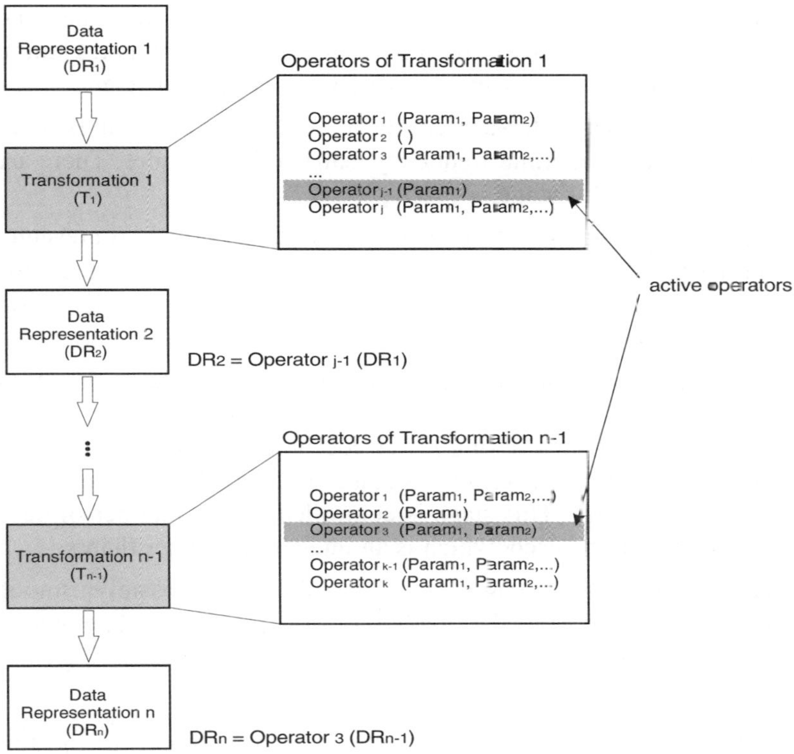

Fig. 1. The scheme of data transformation

2.1. *The Data Transformation Chain*

Below we shortly describe the particular operations that transform the description of sound signals from their time domain to the final feature domain, in which they can be actually processed by classifiers (and used in reclassification tests). The chain consists of the following 5 steps:

1. **Fast Fourier Transformation.** In this step the time-domain data are transformed into the time-frequency domain using the Fast Fourier Transformation (FFT), which could be calculated using a 256-sample

or a 512-sample. Other parameters at this stage are: the type of windowing applied (the possibilities are: none, triangular, Hamming, Hanning or Blackman) and the window-overlap coefficient.

2. **Single Spectrum Transformation**. A single spectrum is selected from the complete time-frequency matrix of amplitudes. There are no parameters at this stage.
3. **Cepstral Transformation**. The spectral data, already represented in the frequency domain, are now further converted using the cepstral transformation, which produces a set of k cepstral coefficients (where k is the parameter).
4. **Reverse Cepstrum Transformation**. At this stage the cepstral transformation is reversed, but only using a pre-selected number of cepstral coefficients. Using fewer coefficients than k (where k is the number of cepstral coefficients resulting from step 4) smoothens the created spectrum. This stage is controlled by the number of cepstral coefficients to be used, which is an integer not higher than k.
5. **Histogram Transformation**. The resulting, possibly smoothed spectrum, to which the histogram transformation operators can possibly be applied, is now subjected to different processing/filtering operations, described in more detail in section 2.2.

Steps 1 through 3 generate the cepstral representations of the sounds and constitute what may be referred to as classic approach to speech processing (where describing sounds in terms of cepstral coefficients is very popular[8]). As far as sounds recognition and classification is concerned the cepstral feature spaces have often proved to produce the best results.

The objective of the remaining two steps is the induction of new features. They are actually produced in step 5, during the so-called histogram transformations, which are applied either to original spectra or to smoothed spectra. The very spectrum smoothing is the result of step 4.

2.2 *The Histogram Transformation Operators*

This section presents a set of operators called the histogram transformation operators. They all process the potentially smoothed spectra (that result from step 4 of the data transformation chain) by first producing histograms of them and then by applying some pre-defined operation on the resulting histograms.

All of the described operators require some parameters. In the following descriptions the parameters *min_max*, *normalized* and *relative* are binary. The parameter *min_max* controls the kind of extremum of the histogram that is to be found by the operator – either a minimum or a maximum. The value of *normalized* switches between processing normalized and non-normalized histograms, while the value of *relative* controls the character of the difference calculated in one of the operators. The remaining parameters: *begin*, *size*, *offset* and *n* are integers, while *percent* is a real value from $\langle 0,1\rangle$. They all determine the location and the size of the histogram part that is to be actually processed (see Fig. 2 for exemplary illustration). As histograms consist of multiple histogram bins, the parameters *begin*, *size* and *offset* refer to the indices of these bins.

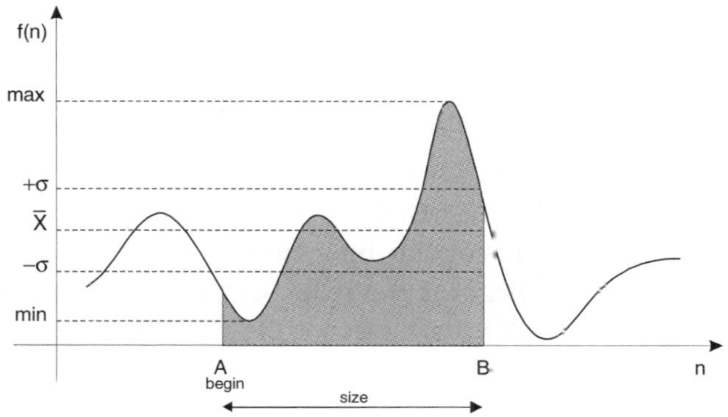

Fig. 2 Illustration of the histogram transformation operators

`Operator-1` (*min_max*, *begin*, *size*, *normalized*) – returns a minimal (maximal) value of that histogram bin, the index of which is in the range (*begin*, *begin+size*). *Normalized* controls the normalization of the returned value.

`Operator-2` (*min_max*, *begin*, *size*) – returns the index of the histogram bin from in the range (*begin*, *begin+size*), the value of which is minimal (maximal).

Operator-3 (*min_max*, *n*) – returns the index of that histogram bin which constitutes the *n*-th local minimum (maximum) in the histogram.

Operator-4 (*min_max*$_1$, n_1, *min_max*$_2$, n_2, *normalized*) – returns the ratio of the values of the n_1-th locally minimal (maximal) histogram bin to the n_2-th locally minimal (maximal) histogram bin. It is assumed that $n_1 \neq n_2$. *Normalized* controls the normalization of the result.

Operator-5 (*min_max*$_1$, n_1, *min_max*$_2$, n_2) – returns the distance (difference of indices) between the n_1-th locally minimal (maximal) histogram bin and the n_2-th locally minimal (maximal) histogram bin.

Operator-6 (*begin*, *size*, *normalized*) – returns the average value of the histogram bins in the range (*begin*, *begin*+*size*). *Normalized* controls the normalization of the histogram before computing the average.

Operator-7 (*begin*, *size*, *normalized*) – returns the standard deviation of the histogram bins in the range (*begin*, *begin*+*size*). *Normalized* controls the normalization of the histogram before computing the deviation.

Operator-8 (*min_max*, *n*, *offset*, *size*, *normalized*) – returns the average of the histogram bins in the range (*begin*+*offset*, *begin*+*offset*+ +*size*), where *begin* is the index of the *n*-th locally minimal (maximal) histogram bin. *Normalized* controls the normalization of the histogram before computing the average.

Operator-9 (*min_max*, *n*, *offset*, *size*, *normalized*) – returns a standard deviation of the histogram bins from the range (*begin*+*offset*, *begin*+*offset*+*size*), where *begin* is the index of the *n*-th locally minimal (maximal) histogram bin. *Normalized* controls the normalization of the histogram before computing the deviation.

Operator-10 (*begin*$_1$, *size*$_2$, *begin*$_2$, *size*$_2$, *normalized*, *relative*) – returns the difference between the sums of the histogram bins in the ranges (*begin*$_1$, *begin*$_1$+*size*$_1$) and (*begin*$_2$, *begin*$_2$+*size*$_2$). *Normalized* controls the normalization of the histogram before computing the result while *relative* determines whether the computed difference is returned as relative or nominal.

Operator-11 (*percent*) – returns the index *q* of the first histogram bin for which:

$$\frac{\sum_{i=0}^{q} f(i)}{\sum_{i=0}^{h} f(i)} \geq percent, \tag{1}$$

where $f(i)$ is the value of histogram bin i and where h is the total number of bins in the histogram.

3. The Feature Evaluation Function

Below we present the basic elements of the function that is used to evaluate the feature sets generated by the genetic search engine. As far as the problem of feature evaluation is concerned, two different aspects come into consideration. One is evaluating a single feature individually, in result of which some important characteristics of the feature, e.g. the ability of the feature to discriminate classes of objects, may be obtained. The other is evaluating a set of features. Because the features are rarely generated as absolutely independent from one another, the estimate of the set of features is not a mere sum of their individual estimates.

In fact, this estimate is not even monotonic with regard to set inclusion, i.e. adding a new feature to a set of features need not improve the estimate of the set (it may also degrade the estimate!). This is because many real-life object describing parameters, which act as features, carry a certain amount of noise, which often strongly affects the results of the evaluation function.

This function is in fact composed of two interacting elements: the classifier and the reclassification test. As far as the classifiers are concerned, we present two: a plain classifier and a meta-classifier. As the plain classifier we chose the *k*-NN [1,4] (which is the simplest and quickest of the IBL-family of classifiers [2]). The meta-classifier presented is the n^2-classifier [9,10]. The meta-classifiers are algorithms that employ other classifiers as internal procedures – in this case the *k*-NN was once more employed.

Although potentially any classifier and any reclassification test can be used here, the quality of applied elements certainly influences the final result. The presented classifiers are therefore not arbitrary, but such that have demonstrated good performance. The simplest IBL (i.e. k-NN) has proved very successful in this application, and it is also comparatively quick (which is especially important when the classifier is used as the internal procedure of the meta-classifier and when the meta-classifier is used in cross-validation tests). We also claim that the generally good results of the final experiments have been achieved due to the acknowledged good performance of the n^2-classifier.

Another issue here is the problem of validation tests. Since the classifier can properly evaluate a given set of features only when it is first learned on one set of objects described by this features and then tested on another set of objects, a scheme of classifier learning and testing is required. In this study we apply the so-called cross-validation scheme of learning and testing.

3.1. *The Plain Classifier: IBL*

The IBL (Instance-Based Learning) algorithms classify new examples by comparing them to the set of pre-classified examples. They work thanks to the fundamental assumption according to which similar examples will belong to the same classes. The question lies in how to define similarity between examples and how to utilize this similarity. Thus the main two components of an IBL algorithm are: the distance function (which determines the similarity between two examples) and the classification function (which provides the rule on how to produce the final classification).

The simplest of all IBL algorithms is the Nearest Neighbour algorithm[4]. In classifying a new example x it uses a domain-specific distance function to find the example that is most similar to x, and classifies x to the class of the found example. A natural extension of this algorithm is the k-Nearest Neighbours algorithm, which finds k examples most similar to x and classifies x to the class that is predominant amongst the found examples. Of course the standard Nearest Neighbour algorithm is the k-Nearest Neighbours with k=1.

Additionally, the IBL algorithms use the notion of concept description, which may be updated during the classification process. Those descriptions control which examples should be used in classification. The simplest algorithms use all examples, but the more sophisticated ones may filter the examples to reduce storage requirements and to improve the classification results. They may also add weights to features, in the result of which not all features of the data set are treated uniformly.

The papers [1,2] describe the instance-based learning algorithms of increasing sophistication. IB1 is just a particular implementation of the *k*-Nearest Neighbour algorithm. IB2 additionally tries to reduce storage requirements by storing only those examples that have been classified incorrectly. IB3 is a further extension of IB2 towards noisy data. Even further developments, IB4 and IB5, which internally apply feature selection techniques, have been described in [2].

3.2. *The Meta-Classifier: n^2*

The main idea of the n^2-classifier [9,10] is based on the discrimination of all combinations of pairs of decision classes by binary (i.e. discriminating between two classes) classifiers. A new example is classified by applying its description to all such classifiers and than by aggregating their predictions to produce the final classification.

The n^2-classifier belongs to a group of meta-learning algorithms dedicated to solving multi-class learning problems [3,6]. The fundamental principle of the n^2-classifier is the discrimination of each pair of the classes: (i,j), $i,j \in \langle 1..n \rangle$, $i \neq j$, by an independent binary classifier $C_{i,j}$, called in this context a base classifier. The strength of this approach lies in the potential use of different feature subset by each $C_{i,j}$.

Each base binary classifier $C_{i,j}$ deals with a single combination of two classes (class i and class j). Therefore, the specificity of training each base classifier $C_{i,j}$ consists in presenting it with not the entire learning set, but with a subset of this set that contains only examples coming from classes i and j. The task of the classifier $C_{i,j}$ is to provide a binary classification of these examples. Each new example x is classified by $C_{i,j}$ to either class i or class j.

The resulting classification of x by $C_{i,j}$ is denoted by $C_{i,j}(x)$. In the following descriptions the notation $C_{i,j}(x)=1$ implies that x has been assigned to class i. Otherwise (i.e. when $C_{i,j}(x)=0$), x has been assigned to class j. Notice that the same classification problem is also solved by the binary base classifier $C_{j,i}$, referred to as complementary to $C_{i,j}$.

Every two complementary classifiers: $C_{i,j}$ and $C_{j,i}$ (where $i, j \in \langle 1..n \rangle$, $i \neq j$) solve in fact the same classification problem – they are trained on the same set of examples and they are expected to discriminate between the same combination of classes: class i and class j. In this sense they are equivalent ($C_{i,j} \equiv C_{j,i}$) and there is no need to actually implement both of them within the n^2-classifier. For n decision classes it then is sufficient to implement only $(n^2 - n)/2$ classifiers $C_{i,j}$, which will cover all possible pairs of n classes. Accordingly, all base classifiers $C_{i,j}$ for $i<j$, will be referred to as 'real', while those for $i>j$ – as 'virtual'.

Out of all the n^2 binary classifiers needed to cover all pairs of n classes, only the 'real' ones are actually implemented within the n^2-classifier. The results of the omitted 'virtual' classifiers are easily predicted from the results of their complementary equivalents. The relationship between the classification of an example x by a 'real' classifier $C_{i,j}(x)$ and its complementary, 'virtual' classifier $C_{j,i}(x)$ is as follows:

$$C_{i,j}(x) + C_{j,i}(x) = 1 \ (2) \qquad (2)$$

The two-dimensional architecture of the n^2-classifier can be presented as a square matrix **C** (sized $n \times n$) of $C_{i,j}$ classifiers, in which the main upper triangle corresponds to the 'real', while the main lower triangle to the 'virtual' base classifiers. This is illustrated in Fig. 3. White squares in the presented matrix represent instances of 'real' $C_{i,j}$ ($i < j$), and gray squares represent their 'virtual' equivalents $C_{i,j}$ ($i > j$). Notice that the main diagonal of this matrix contains the classifiers $C_{i,i}$, which are not taken into account, either.

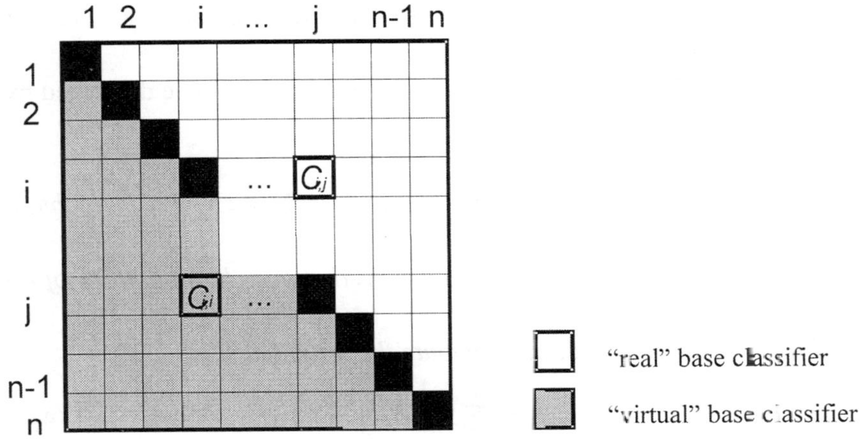

Fig. 3. The matrix of base binary classifiers

While classifying a new example x, the n^2-classifier starts with applying the description of this example to all the 'real' base classifiers in the system. As a result, the binary predictions $C_{i,j}(x)$ of all 'real' classifiers and all 'virtual' classifiers $C_{j,i}(x)$ are obtained. The final classification is obtained by a weighted aggregation of the predictions produced by the binary classifiers.

In order to accomplish this, the credibility (i.e. the weight) of each base classifier has first to be estimated. Although this can be defined in several different ways, in this study we decided to assign each classifier $C_{i,j}$ (either 'real' or 'virtual') the following credibility coefficient $P_{i,j}$.

$$P_{i,j} = \frac{v_i}{e_j + v_i} \tag{3}$$

where v_i is the number of correctly classified examples from class i and e_j is the number of incorrectly classified examples from class j. The computation of the credibility coefficients is performed during the learning phase of the classification task.

Thanks to the credibility coefficients the credible classifiers may have more influence on the final prediction arrived at by the n^2-clasifier. In our aggregation rule the credibility coefficients $P_{i,j}$ are treated as weights to the sum of predictions produced by base classifiers for each class (i.e. for each row of configuration matrix **C**).

The whole classification process of the example x can be described by the following steps:

(i) Apply the example x to all 'real' base classifiers, $C_{i,j}$ $(i < j)$ *to obtain the classifications* $C_{i,j}(x)$.

(ii) Use the formula for complementary predictions classifications of all 'virtual' classifiers, $C_{i,j}$ $(i > j)$.

(iii) For each class i, $i \in \langle 1..n \rangle$, *compute the weighted sum:*

$$S_i = \sum_{\substack{j=1; \\ j \neq i}}^{n} P_{i,j} \cdot C_{i,j}(x) \tag{4}$$

(iv) Find $i \in \langle 1..n \rangle$ *for which* S_i *reaches its maximum and assign the example x to class i.*

Please notice that this procedure might in some situations produce non-deterministic results. This happens when there are multiple classes for which S_i is maximal. Due to high variability of $P_{i,j}$ and $C_{i,j}(x)$ this does not occur frequently, though. In case when such a 'tie' occurs we solve it by selecting the most frequent class.

3.3. *Cross-Validation Tests*

In assessing the performance of classifiers the essential idea is to learn the proportion of errors made when this classifier is applied to classifying new observations without the benefit of knowing their true classifications. To assess this, the classifier must be tested on an independent sample of new examples (the test data), whose true classifications are known but are never revealed to the classifier. The obtained predicted and true classifications on the test data may be used to compute the proportion of errors made by the classifier.

With only one set of data available the test examples have to be selected from among this set. To achieve this a proportion of the data is selected at random (usually about 25–35%) and used as the test data. The classifier is then trained on the remaining data, and finally tested on the test data. The small loss of efficiency that is due to the fact that we do not use the full sample to train the classifier is inevitable but negligible for large datasets. Therefore this single-phase approach to classifier assessment (often referred to as hold-out) is used with data sets that contain thousands of examples. With smaller data set the procedure of *N*-fold cross-validation is used [16].

In the *N*-fold cross-validation test, the original set of examples is randomly partitioned into *N* disjoint subsets used in *N* runs of learning and testing. In each of the tests a different subset of objects is treated as the testing sample while the union of all the remaining subsets serves for learning. Thus each object of the original data set is included exactly once in the testing sample, and exactly *N*–1 times in the learning sample. The final accuracy is the ratio of correctly classified objects in all *N* runs (folds) to all objects in the data set. *N*-fold cross validation is applicable to data sets that contain hundreds of examples.

With even smaller data set a variant of *N*-fold cross-validation, called leave-one-out validation [12], may be used. In this test each example is successively used as the sole testing example. This is of course a special case of *N*-fold cross-validation, in which *N* is set to the number of examples in the whole data set.

A practical difficulty with all cross-validation tests is the need to repeat the learning and the testing cycle for *N* times, which may require much computational effort in computer-intensive methods such as feature selection.

3.4. *Basics of the Genetic Algorithms*

The actual driving force of our feature selection process is the genetic algorithm [15]. It is an iterative procedure that manipulates a constant-sized population of individuals, each one represented by a finite string of symbols, known as the genome, which encode a possible solution in a given problem space. The standard genetic algorithm proceeds as follows: an initial population of individuals is generated at random or heuristically. In every evolutionary step, known as a generation, the individuals in the current population are evaluated according to a predefined fitness function. The fittest individuals are then most likely to be selected to the next iteration.

Since selection alone cannot introduce any new individuals into the population, such new individuals are generated by the operations of crossover and mutation. Crossover, performed with a given probability on two selected individuals (parents), exchanges parts of their genomes to form two new individuals. Mutation randomly modifies the existing individuals, which prevents premature convergence to local optima. Genetic algorithms are generally not guaranteed to converge; the termination condition may be specified as some fixed, maximal number of generations or as the attainment of an acceptable fitness level.

4. The Computational Experiment

It must be stressed that we present our results to reveal the general usefulness and advantages of the proposed feature construction mechanism and not to outperform the best classification results achieved in the domain. We also claim that the observed improvement of the results is due to new and significant features discovered by the presented universal data transformation scheme.

4.1. *Constructive Induction Framework*

The scheme of the actual constructive induction framework is presented in Fig. 4. Last stages of the data transformation chain described in section 2 lead to the construction of actual features. The form and quality of the constructed features influence the accuracy of classification measured in the cross-validation tests and thus provide the feedback to the feature construction phase. The whole process, automatically controlled by a genetic algorithm that uses the classification accuracy as the fitness function, is thus generally aimed at creating such features that produce good classification results.

It should be noticed that in the approach we actually used two cross-validation tests: outer and inner; the inner one is used in constructive induction of features and the outer one is used for final evaluation of the created sets of features (it is also the final result of the given experiment).

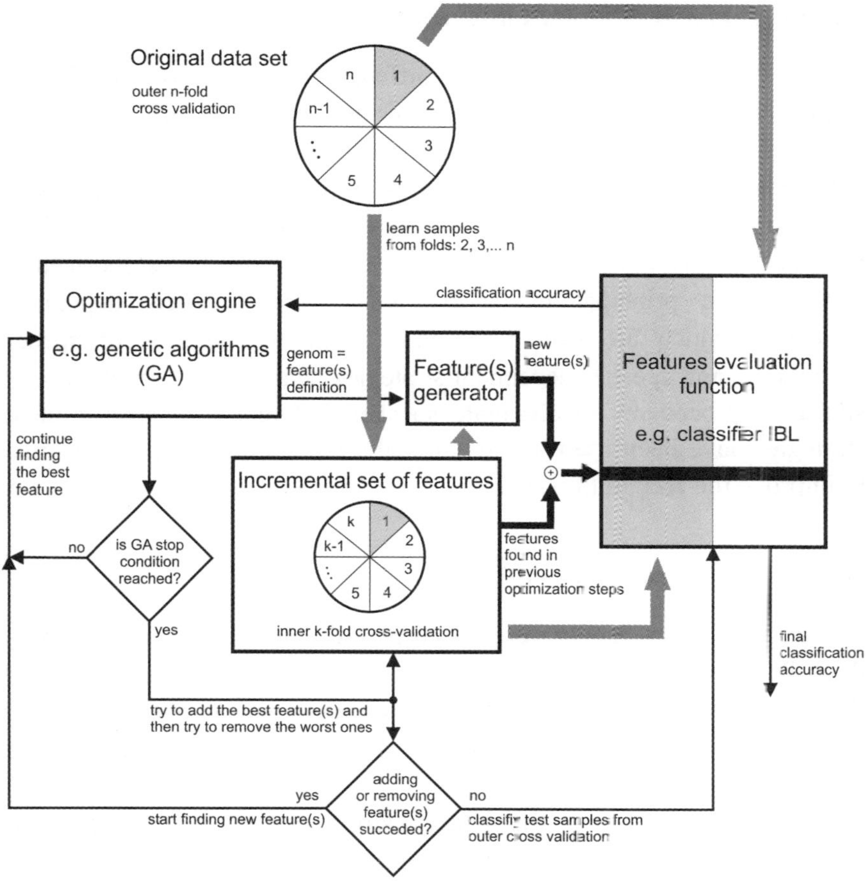

Fig. 4. The constructive induction framework

As far as the classification is concerned we decided to use a representative of the IBL-family of classifiers for reasons described in section 3 (the choice was also influenced by the markedly good performance of the IBL algorithms in our earlier experiments [10]). The feature estimation function was defined as classification accuracy estimated by a N-fold cross-validation test Such a function reflects well the required predictive properties of the model.

We hope that the current framework is general enough to conduct experiments with many different data sets. It is possible because the computational core of the approach is based on the genetic process, which has been extensively and comprehensively parameterized.

4.2. *The Problem of Vowel Classification*

Depending on various factors, the differences in the pronunciation of vowels among different speakers can be very high and, therefore, automatic recognition of vowels cannot be carried out just by measuring the formant frequencies[8]. It is thus necessary to perform some processing to account for speaker variability and some overlapping of vowels. There have been many vowel normalization studies that can be categorized as follows. The principal distinction is between speaker-independent strategies, which are usually based on auditory theories of speech processing, and speaker-dependent strategies, which tend to make use of statistical procedures to eliminate speaker differences. Many of those strategies have been used in the automatic recognition systems in order to improve the recognition rate.

4.3. *The Classification Results*

The original input signals were actual time-domain digital recordings of the 6 Polish vowels (/a/, /e/, /i/, /o/, /u/, /y/), sampled at 16 kHz. Each of the 300 recordings comprises an isolated utterance of one vowel, and each vowel was recorded by one of the total of 50 speakers (hence 50×6=300 recordings).

We used steps 1–3 of the data transformation chain to produce the cepstral representations of sounds, which provided the baseline accuracy that served for the comparison with the full (steps 1–5) approach.

The vowels classification experiment was repeated three times: first using single a IBL classifier with the best k-first cepstral coefficients, then by the same classifier with histograms features based on the set of cepstral coefficients and finally by the n^2 multiclassifier. In case of the n^2, the process of genetically guided feature construction was repeated for each combination of pairs of decision classes.

The classification results are presented in Table 1. The first row shows the result for cepstral coefficients, while two next rows show the results for features constructed using the introduced histogram transformation operators.

Table 1. Results of vowels classification experiment

The feature space	Classifier	Accuracy [%]
k cepstral coefficients	IBL	71.2
histogram-based features	IBL	74.6
histogram-based features	n^2 on IBL	78.0

5. Conclusions

The vowels classification experiment shows that the proposed chained transformation of data, combined with constructive induction of features based on histogram transformation, improves the classification accuracy of vowel recognition. The best result obtained for n^2-classifier confirms that the n^2-classifier and the presented constructive induction make a successful combination of methods in multi-class machine learning problems. The presented approach is sufficiently general and can be applied to any kind of classification problems; especially to those in which creating histogram of parameters has rational justification.

Acknowledgments

The authors wish to acknowledge the financial support from the polish State Committee for Scientific Research (KBN), grant 4-T11F-002–22.

The software developed for this project has included the following foreign-party public domain components: *GAlib* – a genetic algorithm package (by Matthew Wall, MIT), *FFTW* – a Fast Fourier Transform library (by Matteo Frigo & Steven G. Johnson, MIT) and *libsndfile* – a sampled sound input/output library (by Erik de Castro Lopo, SUN Microsystems).

Parts of the experiments have been performed at the Poznań Supercomputing and Networking Centre.

References

1. D.W. Aha, D. Kibler, M. K. Albert, 'Instance-based Learning Algorithms', *Machine Learning*, **6** (1991).

2. D.W. Aha, 'Tolerating Noisy, Irrelevant and Novel Attributes in Instance-based Learning Algorithms', *International Journal of Man Machine Studies*, **36** (1992).
3. P.K. Chan, S.J. Stolfo, 'Experiments on multistrategy learning by meta-learning', *Proceedings of the Second International Conference on Information and Knowledge Management* (1993).
4. T.T. Cover, P.E. Hart, 'Nearest Neighbour Pattern Classification', *IEEE Transactions on Information Theory*, 13 (1967).
5. M. Dash, H. Liu, 'Feature selection for classification', *Intelligent Data Analysis*, **1**(3) (1997).
6. T.G. Diettrich, G. Bakiri, 'Solving multiclass learning problems via error-correcting output codes', *Journal of Artificial Intelligence Research*, **2** (1995).
7. A. Esposito, R. Ceglia, 'Phonemes Classification with Recurrent Neural Networks', *Proceedings of the XIV International Congress of Phonetical Sciences*, San Francisco (1999).
8. J. Harrington, S. Cassidy, *Techniques in Speech Acoustics*, Kluwer Academic Publishers (1999).
9. J. Jelonek, 'Using n^2-classifier with constructive induction mechanism to multiclass machine learning problems', Ph.D. thesis (in Polish), Poznań University of Technology, Poznań (2000).
10. J. Jelonek, J. Stefanowski , 'Experiments on solving multiclass learning problems by n^2-classifier', *Proceedings of the 10th European Conference on Machine Learning*, Chemnitz, April 21–24 '98, *Lecture Notes in AI*, **1398**, Springer Verlag (1998).
11. P. Lachenbruch, R. Mickey, 'Estimation of error rates in discriminant analysis', *Technometrics*, **10** (1968).
12. P. Langley, *Elements of Machine Learning*, Morgan Kaufmann, San Francisco (1996).
13. N. Littlestone, M.K. Warmuth, 'The weighted majority algorithm', *Information and Computation*, **108**(2) (1994).
14. R.S. Michalski, 'A theory and methodology of inductive learning', *Artificial Intelligence*, **20** (1983).
15. T.M. Mitchell, *An Introduction to Genetic Algorithms*, MIT Press, Cambridge, MA (1996).
16. M. Stone, 'Cross-validatory choice and assessment of statistical predictions', *Journal of the Royal Statistical Society*, **36** (1974).

CHAPTER 34

REFRIGERANT LEAK PREDICTION IN SUPERMARKETS USING EVOLVED NEURAL NETWORKS

Dan W. Taylor[1], David W. Corne[2]

[1] *University of Reading, UK*
d.taylor@logicalgenetics.com
[2] *University of Exeter UK*
d.w.corne@exeter.ac.uk

The loss of refrigerant gas from commercial refrigeration systems is a major maintenance cost for most supermarket chains. Gas leaks can also have a detrimental effect on the environment. Existing monitoring systems maintain a constant watch for faults such as this, but often fail to detect them until major damage has been caused. This chapter describes a system which uses real-world data received at a central alarm monitoring centre to predict the occurrence of gas leaks. Evolutionary algorithms are used to breed neural networks which achieve usefully high accuracies given limited training data.

1. Introduction

In recent years, large supermarket chains in the UK have become increasingly aware of the issues involved with the refrigeration systems in their stores. This has happened for a number of reasons, most notably because refrigeration is one of the largest costs when setting up and running a store and there are a number of ways in which the associated systems can be optimised to save money. Now, with the added pressures placed upon those who operate commercial refrigeration systems by environmental legislation, such as the Kycto and Montreal protocols and ever increasing energy costs, the optimisation of refrigeration systems is more important than ever. See the paper[1] for a more detailed review of this state of affairs.

It will be instructive herein to review the basic elements of such refrigeration systems. Within a typical supermarket in the UK, the various containers which actually contain food items and are accessible to the customer, such as 'cabinets' and 'cold-rooms', are part of a complex system of interdependent items of machinery, electronic and computer control units and many hundreds of metres of pipe-work and cabling. Unlike the small, sealed refrigerators which can be found in most of our homes, the refrigeration systems to be found in supermarkets are fed with refrigerant via a network of piping which runs under the floor of the store. This pressurised liquid refrigerant is allowed to evaporate within cabinets, thus absorbing heat. The resulting warm gas is then pumped away from the cabinet. Large electrically powered compressors, situated away from the shop floor, are used to compress the gas into a hot liquid which is pumped to condensers outside the store, where heat is expelled. Excess refrigerant is stored in liquid form under pressure in the refrigerant reservoir. Fig. 1 shows this process graphically.

As might be expected, the presence of refrigerant gas in this large, complex mechanical system inevitably leads to the occasional leak. A larger supermarket will have around 100 individual cooled cases and the associated refrigeration system can hold around 800kg of refrigerant. Refrigerant costs around £15 per kilogram and can have detrimental effects if leaked into the atmosphere. It is therefore imperative that leaks from refrigeration systems be minimised, both from financial and environmental points of view. Financial concerns are further heightened by the fact that, once the refrigeration system has been compromised by gas loss, it is incapable of protecting the refrigerated food in the store. If temperature controlled containers can not reach the store within a matter of hours then heavy losses will be suffered through stock spoilage. In addition to this, the store will suffer from lost sales while the system is repaired and the reputation of the supermarket with its customers will be damaged.

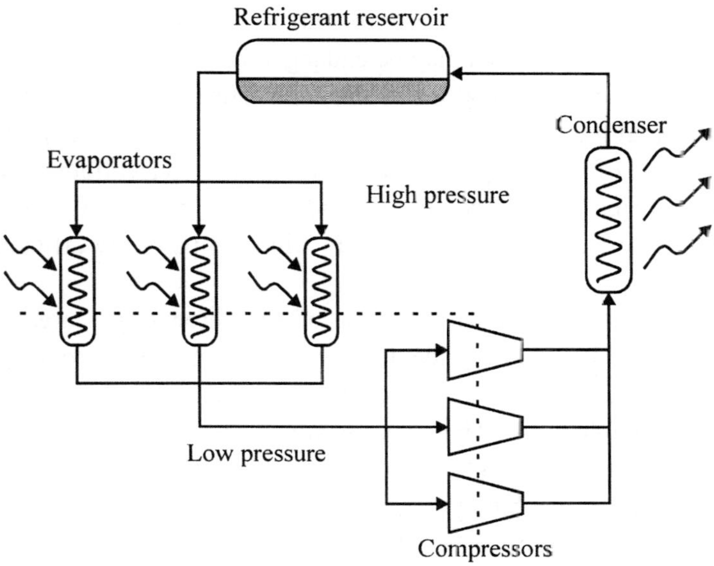

Fig. 1. A typical supermarket refrigeration system. High and low pressure regions are divided by a dashed line

JTL Systems Ltd (www.jtl.co.uk) manufacture advanced electronic controllers which control and co-ordinate refrigeration systems in supermarkets. These systems, as well as controlling cabinet temperature, gather data on various parameters of the store-wide refrigeration system. These data are used to optimise the operation of machinery and schedule defrosts, whilst also being used to generate *alarms*. For example, an alarm may be generated by the controller in a refrigerated cabinet if the temperature has been above a certain threshold for a certain amount of time, with consequent danger to the safety of the food inside the cabinet if this situation remains the case.

Alarms are essentially warnings of adverse conditions which may be due to faulty equipment or improper use of the equipment, and leading to conditions which may require costly loss of stock or equipment damage. Alarms are transmitted, via a modem link, to a central monitoring centre. At this monitoring centre, trained (human) operators watch for serious events and call the appropriate store staff or maintenance personnel to avert situations where stock may be endangered.

Due to the huge financial losses they can cause, refrigerant gas losses have been highlighted by JTL and their customers (major supermarket chains) as one of three important areas in which to concentrate resources. The others being compressor failure and "Icing Up", a problem caused by a buildup of ice around evaporators which impairs the efficiency of the cabinet.

Gas loss was chosen as the first of the three target areas to be addressed as it is a store wide fault which is clearly understood and which, we believe, can be predicted using the alarm data which are currently available to us. There are essentially two types of gas leak:

- Fast: This is equivalent to a burst tyre on a car: a large crack or hole in piping or machinery causes gas to be lost quickly and the refrigeration system to be immediately impaired. Fast leaks can be detected immediately at the JTL monitoring centre and the appropriate action taken.
- Slow: This can be likened to a slow puncture: gas slowly leaks from the system causing a seemingly unrelated series of alarms and alterations in the performance of the system. This type of leak is more frequent and can be much harder to detect. JTL's customers tend to lose more money through slow leaks than through fast leaks.

This chapter details work undertaken to develop systems which use alarm data, gathered from refrigeration systems in supermarkets, to predict/detect the occurrence of slow gas leaks. There is a clear commercial requirement for such a system as it will allow pre-emptive maintenance to be scheduled, thus minimising the amount of gas allowed to leak from the system. The prediction/classification technique described in this chapter is an extension of that presented in the paper[2], in which efforts to predict volumes of alarm traffic are described. Neural networks are trained using a combination of evolutionary algorithms and traditional back propagation learning. This training scheme has been shown to be marginally more effective than either evolved rule-sets or back propagation used in isolation.

A description of the data available for prediction systems and the various pre-processing operations performed upon it can be found in section 2. Section 3 goes on to describe the EA/BP hybrid training system in more detail. In section 4 we provide a brief review of our previous work to predict alarm volumes from raw alarm data. In section 5 we outline the various experiments performed and their results and finally, a concluding discussion and some suggested areas for further exploration can be found in section 6.

2. Engineering and Alarm Data

There are two important data sets which must be combined in order to create training data suitable for the task in hand. These are outlined here, along with details of how they were combined and used to produce appropriate training data.

2.1. *Alarm Data*

As previously mentioned, when adverse conditions are detected by on-site monitoring and control hardware they are brought to the attention of operators at JTL's dedicated monitoring centre. The *Network Controller*, which is the principal component of the in-store refrigeration control system, uses its in-built modem to send a small package of data to the monitoring centre via the telecommunications network. This data package is known as an *Alarm* and contains useful information, including:

- The store's identification number
- The identification number and name of the unit which raised the alarm
- An alarm message string such as "High temperature"
- The nature of the alarm conditions and any related information – such as temperature or pressure readings
- The time at which the alarm was first raised

Information from alarms is copied to a large relational database called *Site Central*. Alarm data has been archived here since September 2000 and over three million individual alarm records are stored. These alarms correspond to around 50,000 control/monitoring units at over 500 stores monitored by JTL for its customers. Between 1500 and 4000 alarms are received daily, depending on weather conditions, shopping patterns and suchlike.

A few human experts can diagnose problems with refrigeration systems using this alarm data. Some types of fault, gas loss in particular, have a well defined, but often quite subtle, pattern of events that can only be detected by highly experienced personnel, or may not even be recognizable at all to human observers. Due to training and resource issues at the monitoring centre, staff have neither the time nor the expertise required to watch for these patterns.

As the receipt of an alarm is a discrete event, without any duration, it was necessary to present our prediction system with a series of categorised *alarm totals*. This gives us a list of small valued integers. We create a vector of n samples, each of length t. This covers a period of $n \times t$ hours. For each sample period we create a three-tuple of values corresponding to the sum totals of alarms occurring within that sample period, in each of three categories:

- Plant alarms – alarms raised by the machinery, such as compressors and condensers, which run the refrigeration system
- Coldroom alarms – alarms raised by the large refrigerated storage areas, away from the trading area, used to store refrigerated products
- Cabinet alarms – alarms which are raised by refrigerated cabinets on the shop floor.

Thus, for a vector where $n = 3$ and $t = 8$, we have a vector of three values, corresponding to plant, coldroom and cabinet alarm totals for each of our eight sample periods, spanning 24 hours altogether.

2.2. *Engineering Data*

In order to train prediction systems to recognise alarm patterns associated with a gas loss it is important to have a large set of training data, containing patterns corresponding to previous gas loss events. The record of gas leaks for the period between 1st Jan 2000 and 5th April 2002 was obtained from a maintenance logging system. This data records the date on which an engineer attended a site and what action was taken, containing altogether 240 engineering visits corresponding to gas losses over the two year period.

Sadly the engineering logs do not record an exact time for the gas loss event, only the date on which the engineer visited. This means that choosing an input vector for our classifier which *immediately precedes* the gas loss event is not possible. As a compromise the input vector's last sample ends at 00:00 the day the engineer visited. So the gas loss could have occurred between one second and twenty four hours after the end of our input vector.

Our inability to select an input vector which immediately precedes a gas loss event is compounded by the fact that slow gas leaks take place over a period which varies in length from hours to days. Our system must therefore behave more like a classifier than a prediction system; deciding whether a gas loss is currently occurring or not (so that action can be taken to avoid the loss increasing), rather than predicting that a gas loss will occur at a given time.

It is also worth noting that when generating training data patterns we were unable to distinguish between *fast* and *slow* gas losses because this is not recorded in the engineering logs.

2.3. *Generation of Training Data*

Training data was generated using the engineering and alarm data sets. These training data correspond to all recorded occurrences of gas loss at monitored stores for a two year period, amounting to 240 patterns in all, as indicated above. Our classifier, in order to stand a chance of being suitably trained, also needs a set of training patterns corresponding to sites which are operating normally (or have problems not relating to gas-loss). The 'normal operation' data were generated in a similar way, using the alarm data. Identically structured vectors of n samples were created for randomly selected sites. These vectors end at randomly selected dates and times. The dates and times used for these training patterns were generated according to two important constraints:

- The date/time selected must be within the period chosen for examination
- The corresponding alarm totals vector must not overlap any recorded gas loss event at the site

Using this scheme we generated an additional 256 training data patterns which we expect not to correspond to gas leaks in stores. This gives us a total of 496 training data patterns. The desired output of the neural network is a single *Boolean* value where 1 indicates gas loss and 0 indicates no gas loss. Thus we have 240 training patterns for which we desire an output of 1 and 256 patterns for which we desire an output of 0.

To aid the neural network's training, and following experience in the paper[2], we scaled the input vectors by multiplying each alarm total in a training pattern by 0.1, so an input value corresponding to 10 alarms is presented to our classifier as 1.

Due to the troublingly small quantity of training data available to us, we decided to generate test and training data partitions using the 0.632 bootstrap method[3], which supports our need to derive a reasonable estimate of the accuracy of the system in practice despite having an impoverished dataset for development purposes. The 0.632 bootstrap method involves sampling a dataset of length *n* randomly *n* times (with replacement) to create the training data set and used the remaining, unselected patterns for test data. This gives us a training data set which is, on average, 63.2% the size of the original data set. Accuracies on training data are quite optimistic while, conversely, test data accuracies are rather pessimistic. To counteract this we thus calculate the overall error value[3]:

$$E = (0.368 * E_{test}) + (0.632 * E_{train}) \qquad (1)$$

To compensate for any atypical results that may be generated due to a particular partitioning, we generated 5 differently partitioned sets of training and test data from our original data set. Training runs are then performed on these data sets for a specified number of generations and the mean error rate calculated (see section 4).

3. Evolving Neural Networks

Using evolutionary algorithms (EAs) to train neural networks is a mature research topic. Yao[4] provides a watershed review, while recent interesting practical examples are reported in papers[5, 6]. It is generally found that EAs (or combinations of EAs and backpropogation) achieve better results than backpropogation[7] alone[2, 4, 5, 6]. The system we use to evolve neural networks is quite similar algorithmically to EP-Net[8, 9], although we currently only evolve weights against a fixed topology.

3.1. *Network Representation*

The neural network representation used is based around a connection matrix and a weight vector. These two simple data structures are capable of representing networks with high levels of complexity (including recurrent and partially recurrent networks, although these are not investigated here). The simple network shown in Fig. 2 is used as an example to illustrate our encoding.

We use four different types of neuron in our model. *Inputs* are simple placeholders for values to be input. *Outputs* are similarly placeholders and have no activation function, and can receive only one incoming connection, the weight value of which is set to 1. *Bias* neurons have a constant output value of 1 and cannot accept incoming connections. Finally, *sigmoid* (or hidden) neurons are standard neurons with a sigmoid activation function.

Table 1 shows the connection matrix for the network in Fig. 1. Generally, for a network with n neurons, this is an $n \times n$ sparsely populated matrix representing connections as follows. An element M_{ij} (column i, row j) represents the connection from neuron i to neuron j. If $M_{ij} \geq 0$, then M_{ij} is taken as an index to the weight vector element which holds the weight value for this connection, otherwise, neurons i and j are deemed to be unconnected.

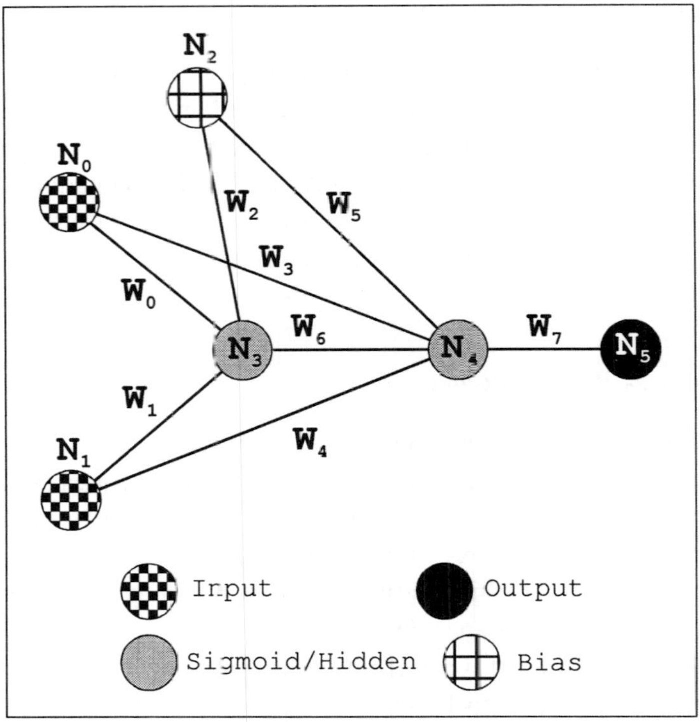

Fig. 2. A simple neural network model with 6 neurons (N_0 to N_5) and 8 weights (W_0 to W_7)

Table 1. An example connection matrix

	0	1	2	3	4	5
0	-	-	-	-	-	-
1	-	-	-	-	-	-
2	-	-	-	-	-	-
3	**0**	**1**	**2**	-	-	-
4	**3**	**4**	**5**	**6**	-	-
5	-	-	-	-	**7**	-

Table 2 shows the weight vector for our example network. The weight vector is a simple list of double precision floating point values. These values are the weight values of the connections between neurons in our network.

Table 2. An example weight vector

0	1	2	3	4	5	6	7
W_0	W_1	W_2	W_3	W_4	W_5	W_6	W_7

Networks used in the experiments here all have one layer of hidden nodes, one layer of inputs, one for each of our training data elements and a single output, which is our gas loss prediction.

3.2. *Evolutionary Operators*

We have not yet explored the improvements that may be obtained in our system from using sophisticated operators, and currently use a straightforward multi-point crossover operator[10], and a Gaussian mutation operator. Seminal techniques for evolving neural networks were given in the paper[11], in which a "Crossover Nodes" operator was found particularly successful. This operator essentially crosses over only at "entire-neuron" boundaries, so that all weights associated with a particular hidden node are maintained in the child, although the child may contain a mixture of hidden nodes from each parent. We note that our encoding naturally entails that weights relating to the same hidden unit are adjacent in the weight vector, and the use of multi-point crossover partly exploits the associated linkage.

Our evolutionary training scheme is a simple hybrid of an evolutionary algorithm and backpropagation, similar, as we have indicated, to EPnet[8, 9], which is one of the leading techniques in this field. We start with a population of randomly initialised individuals. These are sorted into order of fitness (the sum squared error on our training data set). In each generation, some of the least fit individuals are replaced with new ones bred using crossover and mutation, and using binary tournament selection to choose parents. Mutation of a real-valued weight is done by adding a deviation from a zero centred Gaussian distribution with exponential decay. Finally, the fittest 10% of our population are allowed a number of epochs of standard back propagation.

4. Predicting Alarm Totals

Before describing our research on predicting refrigerant gas losses, which is the main topic of this chapter, we shall briefly summarise some closely related work. This helps to establish the context in which the gas loss prediction system operates, as well as indicating, by example, that gas-loss prediction is one of several opportunities made possible by the (currently unique) JTL alarm monitoring centre and its associated capabilities.

The aim of our work on alarms totals prediction, which is described more fully in the paper[2], was to develop a system to predict the volumes of alarms which are received at the alarm monitoring center each day. The ability to predict alarm totals well is very useful as it allows JTL appropriately to adjust staffing levels at the alarm monitoring centre, and thus manage expensive resources more effectively.

There are many subtle patterns in the quantities of alarms received from stores each day. Patterns are most apparent on daily, weekly and annual levels. In this work we attempted to exploit the clear weekly patterns present within the alarm data.

4.1. *Experimental Setup*

In experiments to predict alarm totals we attempted to train individual neural networks to make daily predictions for a single supermarket site. This *a priori* decision was made on the basis of much experience which suggested that patterns of alarms are strongly site-specific. For example, the particular network of pipes and components in a site's refrigeration system, and aspects such as daily monitoring and site staff management policies, are all felt to be more salient to the alarm patterns emerging from a site than global factors, such as, for example, mean temperature or rainfall in the UK on that day. Clearly, if required, the outputs of each of the appropriate collection of networks can then be combined to produce a prediction of total alarms to be received from the associated collection of sites.

The patterns of alarms received from all stores follow a distinct weekly trend, influenced by customers' shopping patterns and the stock levels and resupply schedule of the store. Fig 3 shows this weekly cycle for a particular store. To simplify the prediction problem we trained an individual network to make a prediction for each day of the week (i.e. a network for Mondays, another for Tuesdays and so on). We therefore use seven neural networks for each store.

Networks with a single layer of hidden neurons accept 21 inputs representing categorised (plant, coldroom and cabinet) alarm totals for the seven days prior to the target day. For example, the Monday prediction network will accept as its input the categorised alarm totals for the seven days between the previous Tuesday and the immediately preceding Tuesday.

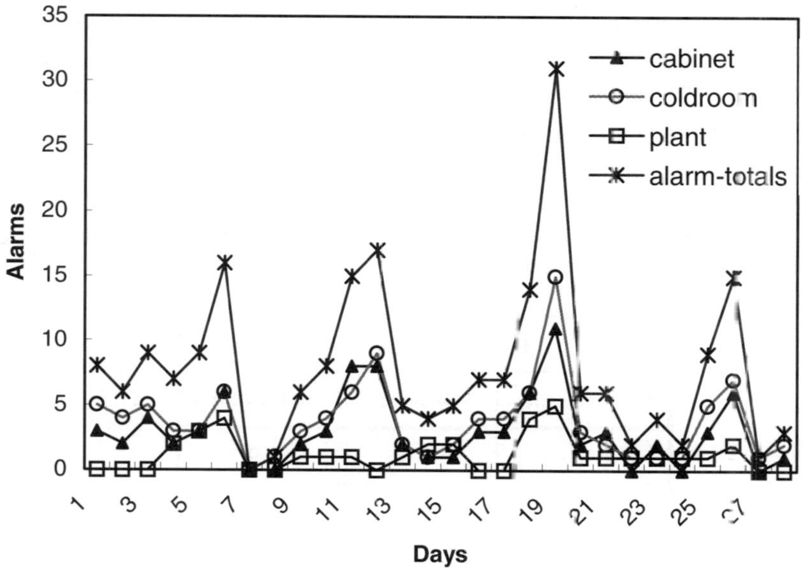

Fig. 3. Cabinet, plant and coldroom daily alarm totals (and their sum) over a four week period in 2001, showing weekly cycle behavior.

4.2. *Results*

Initial results, in which networks were expected to predict the precise values of alarm totals, were not promising, giving accuracies of less than 70%. Table 3 shows typical results.

Table 3. Predicting alarm totals for Mondays using various network topologies. Percentage correctness and standard deviation are shown for networks with hidden layers of various sizes

Mondays		
Hidden nodes	**%-correct**	**Stdev (%)**
20	69.4	2.1
30	67.5	2.1
50	66.0	2.2

In order to address these low accuracy rates the experimental setup was altered such that alarm totals were categorised into LOW, MEDIUM and HIGH. The results are summarised in Table 4. By reducing the difficulty of the learning task somewhat, the three-category version of the problem leads to better accuracies.

Table 4. Predicting alarm totals with categorised outputs for Fridays. Hidden layer size, percentage correctness and standard deviation are shown

Fridays (categorised)		
Hidden nodes	**%-correct**	**Stdev (%)**
20	76.6	2.9
30	77.9	2.5
50	77	2.6

Even though the three-category version of the problem is simplified, it remains potentially valuable in the commercial setting of the alarm monitoring centre, since by predicting the rough overall volume of alarm totals, we can still establish a broad expectation of near-future staffing needs at the monitoring centre. We have not yet established, however, whether alternative network designs will be more effective, such as a five-category gradation of alarm volumes, or whether more accurate predictions of actual totals could be achieved with alternative prediction technologies. This work is ongoing.

5. Gas Loss Experiments and Results

Meanwhile, much work has been done using the engineering data described in section 2, to investigate the possibility of being able to predict gas loss from patterns in the alarm data. The experiments we report in this section had two aims. The major aim was to ascertain whether reasonable performance could be achieved at all by using neural networks to predict gas loss in supermarket refrigeration systems on the basis of the available datasets. If so, much further work followed by commercial fielding of the technique would then be warranted. Second, we wished to explore (modestly in the first instance, in case the finding regarding the major aim was "no") a number of network topologies to see if this had any major effect on the results.

In all experiments reported here we used networks with 21 inputs, based on 3 alarm total categories for each of 7 periods of 24 hours (one week). Three different network topologies (either 25, 45, or 60 hidden nodes) were trained using each of the five differently partitioned training and test data sets. This gives us fifteen discrete results.

The results are summarised in Tables 5, 6 and 7, where the tables correspond to 25, 45 and 60 hidden nodes respectively. Each table records results for five distinct experiments, representing five different partitions into training and test data. The final column of each table provides the mean result over all five partitions. Results are given in terms of the percentage of patterns correctly classified. Correctness is calculated using a threshold value of 0.5 for the network's output unit, hence, if the output is greater than or equal to 0.5, the network's prediction is "gas loss", otherwise its prediction is "no gas loss".

Table 5. Accuracies of 25-hidden-node networks on the five training/test data sets; M is the mean over the five runs

Set	Training Data Accuracy	Test Data Accuracy	Bootstrapped Accuracy
0	83%	64%	76.01%
1	77%	66%	72.95%
2	85%	59%	75.43%
3	83%	60%	74.54%
4	84%	59%	74.80%
M:	**82.40%**	**61.60%**	**74.75%**

Table 6. Accuracies of 45-hidden-node networks on the five training/test data sets; M is the mean over the five runs

Set	Training Data Accuracy	Test Data Accuracy	Bootstrapped Accuracy
0	80%	64%	74.11%
1	77%	67%	73.32%
2	82%	62%	74.64%
3	81%	65%	75.11%
4	84%	54%	72.96%
M:	**80.80%**	**62.40%**	**74.03%**

Table 7. Accuracies of 60-hidden-node networks on the five training/test data sets; M is the mean over the five runs

Set	Training Data Accuracy	Test Data Accuracy	Bootstrapped Accuracy
0	80%	66%	74.85%
1	77%	68%	73.69%
2	82%	64%	75.38%
3	81%	61%	73.64%
4	82%	61%	74.27%
M:	**80.4%**	**64.00%**	**74.37%**

All three of the network topologies achieved very close bootstrapped accuracy levels, although the 45 hidden node networks had the worst overall performance by a very small margin (< 1%). The levels of accuracy achieved are indeed very promising. Interestingly, as we increase the number of hidden units the accuracy on training data reduces while accuracy on test data (indicative of generalisation performance) improves. This presumably indicates that larger numbers of hidden nodes are needed in this case to capture the complex interactions in the data in a way that allows good generalisation, while small numbers of hidden nodes tend to veer towards local minima which model noise rather than deep regularities in the data. Clearly further work is warranted around the issue. For the time being, our further development of the gas loss prediction system is using networks of 25 hidden nodes, since this allows speedier training, while expected to be no less accurate (as shown by the experiments here) in real-world use on unseen data. We also note that the lack of any great sensitivity (in the overall result) to network topology suggests a certain robustness which is very desirable in real-world applications.

6. Concluding Discussion

Prediction systems developed as a result of this work are to be installed at JTL's alarm monitoring centre, where they will be used to alert trained staff to the possibility of gas losses. Their role will be largely that of an early warning system, advising staff that further attention may need to be paid to systems at the store in question. Because we are expecting to have a "human in the loop" at all times, and because the alarm and engineering data often contains inconsistencies and anomalies, lower accuracy levels can be permitted.

Before work began on these systems the authors, along with directors and management staff at the monitoring centre, agreed upon a rough target accuracy of 75%. Although, strictly speaking, this was not achieved, it has been agreed by all involved that the results obtained are adequate for our purposes. In particular, issues concerning the relative amounts of false positives and true negatives in the misclassified cases are highly favourable, and enable us to expect a working accuracy of effectively greater than 75%. As noted above, the results reported here are based on a default threshold of 0.5 on the output unit. It turns out that misclassified classes divide roughly 50/50 into false positives (gas loss predicted, but not actual) and true negatives (gas loss occurred, but not predicted). Further analysis of the results indicates two key points: first, reducing the threshold a small amount will reduce the level of true negatives significantly, without undue increase in false positives. Second, although the false positives are incorrect in terms of gas loss, we find that they do seem to correlate with other kinds of problem in the refrigeration system. Hence, calling out an engineer on the basis of such a false positive will often not be a wasted cost, since there is likely to be some other (non gas-loss) fault which needs treatment.

Further work is under way to increase the system's overall accuracy and ability to generalize, and to carefully tune the output threshold above which the decision is made to schedule a maintenance engineer. Work has also begun to investigate other related faults and problem areas which may be suitable for predictive technologies.

Acknowledgements

We acknowledge the support of the Teaching Company Directorate (via the DTI and EPSRC) and JTL Systems Ltd. for funding this project.

References

1. R Gluckman, "Current Legislation Affecting Refrigeration", *Proceedings, 9th Annual Conference of the Institute of Refrigeration* (2000).
2. D W Taylor, D W Corne, D.L. Taylor, and J. Harkness, "Predicting Alarms in Supermarket Refrigeration Systems Using Evolutionary Techniques", *Proceedings of the World Congress on Computational Intelligence (WCCI-2002)* (IEEE Press, 2002).
3. B Efron "Bootstrap Methods, Another Look At The Jackknife". *Annals of Statistics* 7:1-26 (1979)
4. X. Yao, "A Review of Evolutionary Artificial Neural Networks", *International Journal of Intelligent Systems*, 8: 539–567 (1997).
5. D.B. Fogel, Blondie24: Playing at the edge of AI (Morgan Kaufmann Publishers, San Francisco, 2002).
6. E. Cantu-Paz and C. Kamath, "Evolving Neural Networks for the Classification of Galaxies", *Proceedings of GECCO 2002* (Morgan Kaufmann Publishers, San Francisco, 2002).
7. D E Rumelhart et al., "Learning Representations by Back Propagation of Errors", *Parallel Distributed Processing: Exploration of the Microstructure of Cognition,* vol. 1, chapter 8 (MIT Press, 1986).
8. X Yao, Y Liu, "A New Evolutionary System for Evolving Neural Networks", *IEEE Transactions on Neural Networks* 8(3) (1995)
9. X Yao, Y Liu, "A Population Based Learning Algorithm Which Learns Both Architectures and Weights of Neural Networks", *Chinese Journal of Advanced Software Research* 3(1) (1996).
10. D.E. Goldberg, Genetic Algorithms in Search, Optimization, and Machine Learning (Addison-Wesley, 1989).
11. D. Montana and L. Davis, "Training Feedforward Neural Networks using Genetic Algorithms", *Proceedings of the 11th Conference on Artificial Intelligence*, pp. 762–767 (1989).

CHAPTER 35

WORST-CASE INSTANCES AND LOWER BOUNDS VIA GENETIC ALGORITHMS

Matthew P. Johnson and Andrew P. Kosoresow

Department of Computer Science, Columbia University
New York, NY 10027
E-mail: mpj9@columbia.edu

We explore a novel application of Genetic Algorithms, *viz.*, as an empirical method in two sub-areas of the Analysis of Algorithms. First, Approximation Algorithms provide tractable solutions to *NP*-Complete problems while sacrificing solution quality. Second, Online Algorithms are designed for the case in which the problem instance does not arrive in its totality, as in Offline Algorithms, but arrives piece by piece, over the course of the computation. Generating worst-case instances for either algorithm type, for use both as test cases and in lower-bound proofs, is often non-trivial. We use GAs to find worst-case instances of several *NP*-Complete problems, including the *Traveling Salesman Problem*, and of Online problems, including versions of the *Taxicab Problem*. These worst-case instances give us lower bounds on the competitiveness of the approximation algorithms used. For example, they provide empirical results suggesting that the greedy algorithm, in the worst case, does better on planar graphs than on arbitrary graphs. In addition, they demonstrate that *6.93* is a lower bound on the competitiveness of the "hedging" algorithm for the *Hard Planar Taxicab Problem*. This experimental result has theoretical implications for the study of the problem, *i.e.*, that further research to prove an upper bound of *7* may be warranted.

1. Introduction

In the analysis of algorithms, we study the difficulty of computational problems, seeking provably efficient algorithms for solving them exactly.

As a first approximation to finding fast, optimal algorithms, we often seek to prove the solution quality of the algorithms we have. As a first approximation to *this*, we often seek to bound the solution quality from above or, in the present case, from below. Even this, however, may be difficult. As such, we turn here to a quasi-empirical approach.

Many problems studied by computer scientists are *NP*-Complete—they have, apparently, no tractable, deterministic, optimal algorithms. There is thus much interest in finding approximation algorithms that run in polynomial time and yield good, if sub-optimal, solutions. It is desirable that these approximation algorithms be *competitive*, *i.e.*, that the quality of their solutions is guaranteed to be, at worst, within some fixed constant factor of the quality of the optimal solutions. Determining the competitiveness of approximation algorithms is an important task in the analysis of algorithms, and one that is often non-trivial. There are many approximation algorithms about which we have only partial knowledge of their competitiveness, for example, only upper or lower bounds.

In addition to partitioning by running time (e.g., polynomial- versus exponential-time), algorithms may be bifurcated into online versus offline. Since the online criterion imposes a restriction on candidate algorithms, the optimal offline algorithm for a problem is generally superior to the best online equivalent. (Any online algorithm is equivalent to a pathological offline algorithm.) As such, we wish to show that a given online algorithm is competitive with the corresponding offline (optimal) algorithm. This situation is parallel to the previous one: in each setting, we are interested in how greatly the addition of a handicap (*i.e.*, quickness or the online property) degrades performance.

The competitiveness of an algorithm is an upper bound on how poor the algorithm's output quality may be, relative to that of the optimal algorithm, taken over all possible problem instances[1].

Given the difficulty of determining competitiveness analytically, or even lower bounds thereof, one approach is to attempt to determine it empirically. For example, given any problem instance on which one can run the approximation and optimal algorithms, taking the ratio of the qualities of the algorithm outputs will give a trivial lower bound on competitiveness. Picking a problem instance at random, however, is not likely to yield valuable information about competitiveness. Instead, we use genetic algorithms to generate "bad" problem instances, in order to gain more instructive information on competitiveness.

Genetic algorithms (GAs) are a form of evolutionary computation that uses the relative fitness of the members of a population of data structure instances to explore a search-space, seeking a data structure with specific features, *i.e.*, those that are fit according to the chosen fitness criteria. In this context, the relevant population members will take the form of optimization problem instances (*e.g.*, *TSP* graphs). The fitness of an instance will be the ratio of the solution qualities of two algorithms on that instance. It is this value that we will seek to maximize.

In maximizing this ratio, we are seeking worst-case instances (relative to the algorithms used). The performance ratios of these instances provide, in turn, lower bounds on the worst-case inefficiency of the handicapped algorithm used. Intuitively, this shows that the algorithms are at least this bad in the worst case.

In this chapter, we apply our GA to several *NP*-Complete problems. We yield empirical support for the greedy algorithm's competitiveness on the *Vertex Cover Problem* and for its non-competitiveness on the *Traveling Salesman Problem*. We apply the GA also to several online problems. In the case of the *Hard Planar Taxicab Problem*, we yield empirical support for the non-competitiveness of the greedy algorithm and for the competitiveness of the hedging algorithm.

2. Previous Work

The work described here is distinct in nature from the many applications of GAs for solving original hard problems. GAs have been applied to the problem of solving many *NP*-Hard problems[2,3,4] but this is not the subject of the present work.

A recent paper by Elizabeth Johnson[5] is more closely related. In that paper, the goal was to find pathological problem instances, relative to an algorithm, where "pathological" was meant in the sense of running time (or, more precisely, the number of operations executed). The purpose was to aid in the study of the empirical performance of algorithms: to suggest what an algorithm's performance may be when run in practice.

Our work, however, which was first presented individually elsewhere,[6,7] differs in two key respects. First, our problem instances are worst-case relative to an approximation algorithm, relative (in turn) to the optimal algorithm. Second, we are studying not the running times of algorithms, but quality of their solutions. These two features are cashed out in our fitness function: the ratio of the *cost* or *quality* of the solutions given by the weak approximation algorithm and the optimal algorithm. We search for problem instances on which the weak algorithm does badly, relative to the performance of the optimal algorithm.

This chapter, then, studies not the empirical performance of algorithms, but the analysis of algorithms *simpliciter*, albeit by a quasi-empirical method.

2.1. *Analysis of Algorithms*

In the analysis of algorithms, conventional decision problems are divided into tractable and intractable, with the deterministic dividing line falling between somewhere *P* and *NP*-Complete, those problems with polynomial-time algorithms and those problems equivalent to *SAT*. For many *NP*-Complete decision problems, there exist corresponding optimization problems. One goal of approximation algorithm theory is to find tractable algorithms that provide good, if not optimal, solutions. What one wants to investigate, then, is how well a given (polynomial-time) approximation algorithm performs compared to the (exponential-time) optimal algorithm. This relative performance (on a problem instance) is customarily represented as the ratio between the qualities of the two algorithms' solutions (on that instance). See the available surveys.[8,9] We thus have the following definitions:

Definition 1: The **competitive ratio** of algorithm *A* to algorithm *B*, where both algorithms solve a problem with instance space *S*, and where *quality(C(s))* is the quality of the output of algorithm *C* on the input of instance *s*, is

$$\sup_{s \in S} \frac{quality(A(s))}{quality(B(s))}$$

Definition 2: An approximation algorithm is ***c*-competitive**, for a constant *c*, if the competitive ratio of the approximation algorithm to the optimal algorithm is *c*.

Definition 3: An approximation algorithm is **competitive** if there exists a constant *c* such that the approximation algorithm is *c*-competitive.

2.2. *Genetic Algorithms*

The search algorithm we use for finding worst-case instances is genetic algorithms. GAs were popularized in the 1970s by John Holland,[10] both as an optimization search algorithm and as a method for studying computationally the process of evolution. With GAs, environments are rendered in which many different possible solutions to a problem compete among themselves, mate, mutate, are evaluated (according to some arbitrarily chosen testing method) and evolve. (As genetic algorithms are used for optimization, the usual goal is to maximize some value. Here, we will want to maximize the ratio between the weak algorithm's solution quality on the instance and its optimal solution quality.)

Several characteristics of the GA vary with the particular problem being optimized, including what constitutes a problem solution, the mate operator, the mutate operator and the fitness measurement. In a *Traveling Salesman Problem* GA, for example, a solution would take the form of a list of cities, and the fitness measurement would be the total distance of the cycle traced by that list (shorter being better). The mating operator might, for example, take two city lists and form a third by, for each position in the list, taking the city from the corresponding position in either (randomly) the first list or the second list. The mutate operator might, for example, switch two of the cities appearing in the list.

The basic GA goes like this: First, a population of (*1000*, say) solutions is created a random. This population forms Generation *0*. To produce Generation $n+1$ from Generation *n*, the GA (stochastically) selects pairs of fit solutions from Generation *n*, recombines them with the mating operator, and adds the (possibly mutated) result to Generation $n+1$ until the population size has been reached. This process continues for arbitrarily many generations, until fruitful results are obtained.

There are many options, such as carryover (copying members, possibly mutated but otherwise intact, directly from one generation to the next); the creation of some completely random instances each generation; and elitism (deterministic carryover of the fittest member). (See Mitchell's short introduction to GAs.[11])

3. The GA

We developed ELBOWS (Evolutionary Lower Bounds On Worst-case Scenarios), a program written in Delphi, to run GAs finding worst-case instances of a number of optimization problems, including the following: *Vertex Cover*, *Independent Set*, (optionally planar) *Traveling Salesman*, and (optionally planar, optionally hard) *Taxicab*. The program is available online.[12]

Since we are searching for worst-case instances, the score will usually be the ratio of the solution quality of the approximation algorithm on a given instance over the optimal solution quality for that instance. For some problem/algorithm pairs, there is a known optimal score (that is, a known bound on the inefficiency of the cheap algorithm). ELBOWS displays this if it is known.

3.1. *Parameters*

There are a number of parameters that can be manipulated in ELBOWS to fit the problem. The population size is the (fixed) number of members in each population of the GA. In creating subsequent generations, we want to choose fit members, and these are selected, stochastically, by tournament. In this method of selection, a subset, of size *tournament-size*, is randomly chosen from the population; the fittest member of this subset is then selected.

There are several probabilities that will determine the composition of each subsequent generation. The mutation rate is the probability any particular variable of a population member is randomized, except for the elite. The carry over percentage specifies what portion of the population will be copied intact from the previous generation. The randomize percentage specifies what portion will be randomly generated. The offspring of members of the previous generation will fill all remaining population spots.

Since all the problems discussed here are graph-theoretic, we specify the population-member-size parameter as graph size.

3.2. *Genetic Operators*

Again, the problems we study here are graph-theoretic: each instance is a set of nodes; what varies is whether pairs of nodes share an edge and, if so, the weight thereof. As such, evolution occurs not on the level of description of bits but on that of vertices and edges. Since the graphs are represented, in the usual way, as adjacency matrices, this means that the operators modify the edge weights whole.

For recombination, we use uniform crossover: in constructing the child adjacency matrix, the value in each cell is chosen at random from the corresponding values in each of the parent matrices. When a mutation occurs, a new value is chosen at random for one cell.

4. Online Algorithms

Orthogonally to fast versus slow, a second way to partition algorithms is to distinguish between online and offline versions of them. (See a comprehensive introduction by Borodin and El-Yaniv.[13] The seminal concepts were introduced by Sleator and Tarjan.[1]) For many decision problems, the algorithm simulates the real-time occurrence of the instance, which provides a natural way to divide it up: *e.g.*, taxicab requests arrive one at a time, and at any given time, that algorithm knows only about requests present and past. In the offline version of the problem, in contrast, the entire problem instance is presented to the algorithm at once, *in toto*. Just as we compare the solutions produced by the approximation versus the optimal algorithm, we can compare the solutions produced by the online versus the offline algorithm. In both cases, we distinguish between a strong type of algorithm on the one hand, and a weak type, whose performance differential we measure, on the other.

The definitions of competitiveness above carry through to the online/offline case, with the online and optimal offline algorithms plugged in as algorithms *A* and *B*, respectively.

4.1. *The k-Server Problem*

The k-*Server Problem* is the problem of how to respond, with multiple servers, to requests from multiple locations. The problem was defined by Fiat *et al.*,[14] which proved the lower bound of *k* on the competitiveness of any online k-*Server* algorithm, relative to the optimal offline algorithm. Our results for this problem, which are omitted for reasons of space, will be presented at a later forum.

4.2. *The Taxicab Problem*

The *Taxicab Problem*, first defined by Kosoresow,[15] is a routing problem that models the problem of a taxicab agency with *k* taxicabs available to respond to customer requests. The goal is to accomplish this as efficiently as possible, *i.e.*, to minimize the driving distance of the cabs. The decisions involved in computing the solution to a taxicab problem instance involve not the order in which to respond to requests—they must be tended to in order of arrival—but which taxicab to send in response to the individual requests. The *k* taxicabs will, in general be located in various positions and therefore be at various distances from the pick-up location of an incoming call. The simplest type of solution will therefore take the form of an array of taxicab indices, one for each customer. More generally, however, the solution will describe how we rearrange the taxis in response to the calls; that is, corresponding to each request, there will be an array of new locations to which we move the taxis in response.

There are four degrees of freedom that we will consider in the definition of the taxicab problem, resulting in a total of at least sixteen problem variants. First, we can consider hard and soft versions of the problem. The soft version is as described above; the modification for the hard version is that, in totaling the cost of the problem solution (distance traveled), the driving of passengers is ignored. The intuitive motivation for this is, of course, that the taxicabs have meters. If anything, the taxi driver would wish to extend the length of the customer's journey, although, for our purposes, we assume that the distance between any two points is fixed. The taxi driver's goal, therefore, is to minimize the unprofitable distance driven without a passenger.

Second, we consider planar and non-necessarily planar problem instances—instances describable by points in the plane, on the one hand, and instances described by graphs whose vertices are separated by arbitrary distances, on the other.

Third, we can vary the value of *k*—the number of taxicabs used. In all of our experiments, however, we use just two taxicabs.

Finally, we treat of both online and offline versions of the problem. The online version is as described above, in which requests are received in real time, without warning; the offline version models a prescient dispatcher who knows all calls in advance. (Notice that the zero-distance-ride special case of the *Taxicab Problem*, in which each source point equals its destination, collapses into the k-*Server Problem*; the *Taxicab Problem* is therefore a generalization thereof.)

4.3. *Taxicab Algorithms*

In general, we will use greedy algorithms for the online taxicab problem, as is presumably done in practice: when a call is received from a certain location, send the closest taxi. For the case of the *Hard Online Planer Taxicab Problem*, however, we will also apply a "hedging" algorithm.[15] The intuition behind this algorithm is, when you make the decision to send one taxi for a call, also (in some circumstances) move the other taxi somewhat in the direction of the first taxi's previous location, in order to hedge the bet. The algorithm works as follows: Upon receiving a call, designate the most recently used cab as R and the other cab as O. Calculate the distance dR from the call's source point to R and the distance dO from the call's source point to O. If $dO < 3dR$, send taxi O to pick up the passenger and move taxi R a distance of $2dR$ in the direction of the passenger's source point; otherwise, send taxi R to pick up the passenger and leave taxi O unmoved.

For the current planar setting, the hedging algorithm is predicted by theory to perform better (in the worst case) than the greedy algorithm. The greedy algorithm is easily shown to be non-competitive.[16] The hedging algorithm, however, has been conjectured to be *7*-competitive and proven to be *15*-competitive by Kosorosow.[15] In our experiments, we generated instances on which the hedging algorithm's solution quality was approximately *6.93* times that of the brute force algorithm, suggesting that the upper bound of *7* may be tight. This empirical result recommends further effort towards a proof of 7-competiveness.

5. Results of Representative Runs

The results of representative runs follow.

5.1. *Vertex Cover*

Problem input	A graph $G = (V,E)$
Problem description	Find the smallest subset S in V such that for each $e \sim (v_i,v_j)$ in E, S contains at least one of the edges v_i, and v_j.
Approximation algorithm	Standard approximation algorithm[17]
Population size	25
Tournament size	3
Mutation rate	1%
Carry over	1%
Randomize	20%
Graph size	12
Score	approximate VC size / optimal VC size
Optimal score	2
No. generations	3

Best element details:

Approximate VC size	12
Optimal VC size	6
Score	2

Best element adjacency matrix:

```
( 0 0 1 0 0 0 0 0 0 0 0 1 )
( 0 0 1 0 0 0 0 1 1 0 1 1 )
( 1 1 0 1 0 1 0 1 1 1 0 1 )
( 0 0 1 0 0 0 0 1 1 0 1 1 )
( 0 0 0 0 0 0 1 0 1 0 1 0 )
( 0 0 1 0 0 0 1 1 0 0 1 1 )
( 0 0 0 0 1 1 0 1 1 0 1 0 )
( 0 1 1 1 0 1 1 0 1 0 0 0 )
( 0 1 1 1 1 0 1 1 0 0 1 0 )
( 0 0 1 0 0 0 0 0 0 0 1 0 )
( 0 1 0 1 1 1 1 0 1 1 0 1 )
( 1 1 1 1 0 1 0 0 0 0 1 0 )
```

Remarks: While we achieve the optimal worst case, this problem is a trivial application for the GA. The approximation algorithm is guaranteed to achieve within ½ of optimal[17] and, for populations comparable to those used for the other problems (on the order of *1000*), we usually reach a score of *2* in the 0th population.

5.2. *Independent Set*

Problem input	A graph $G = (V,E)$
Problem description	Find the largest subset S in V such that no adjacent pair of vertices is contain in S.
Approximation algorithm	Greedy Algorithm
Population size	1000
Tournament size	3
Mutation rate	1%
Carry over	1%
Randomize	20%
Graph size	10
Score	optimal IS size / approx. IS size
Optimal score	graph size - 1 = 9
No. generations	16

Best element details:

Approximate IS size	1
Optimal IS size	9
Score	9

Best element adjacency matrix:

```
( 0 1 1 1 1 1 1 1 1 1 )
( 1 0 0 0 0 0 0 0 0 0 )
( 1 0 0 0 0 0 0 0 0 0 )
( 1 0 0 0 0 0 0 0 0 0 )
( 1 0 0 0 0 0 0 0 0 0 )
( 1 0 0 0 0 0 0 0 0 0 )
( 1 0 0 0 0 0 0 0 0 0 )
( 1 0 0 0 0 0 0 0 0 0 )
( 1 0 0 0 0 0 0 0 0 0 )
( 1 0 0 0 0 0 0 0 0 0 )
```

Representative run (plotting best and average scores):

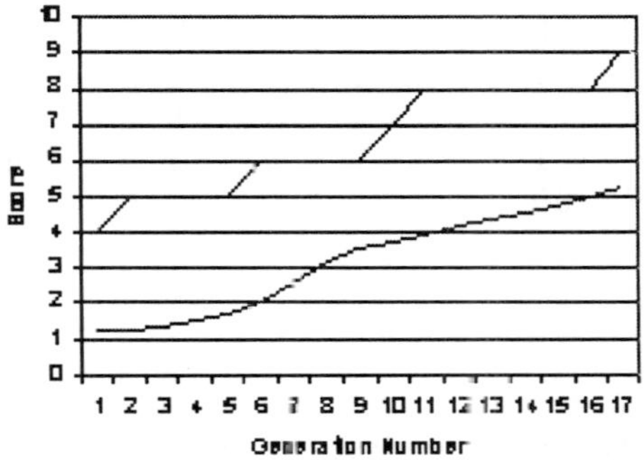

Remarks: The application to this problem is somewhat less trivial. The limiting case (unique up to isomorphism) is the graph with one vertex connected to every other vertex, *i.e.*, the wheel graph W_{n-1} with the outer edges removed. For *n* on the order of size *10*, this element is reliably generated within *20* generations.

5.3. *Traveling Salesman*

Problem input	A complete weighted graph $G = (V,E)$
Problem description	Find a Hamiltonian cycle of minimum cost.
Approximation algorithm	Greedy Algorithm
Population size	1000
Tournament size	3
Mutation rate	1%
Carry over	10%
Randomize	2%
Graph size	5
Score	Optimal IS size / approximate IS size
Optimal score	?
No. generations	33

Best element details:

Greedy cost	203
Optimal cost	5
Score	40.6

Best element adjacency matrix:

```
(   0   1   1   1 100 )
(   1   0   1  40   1 )
(   1   1   0   1   1 )
(   1  40   1   0 100 )
( 100   1   1 100   0 )
```

Representative run:

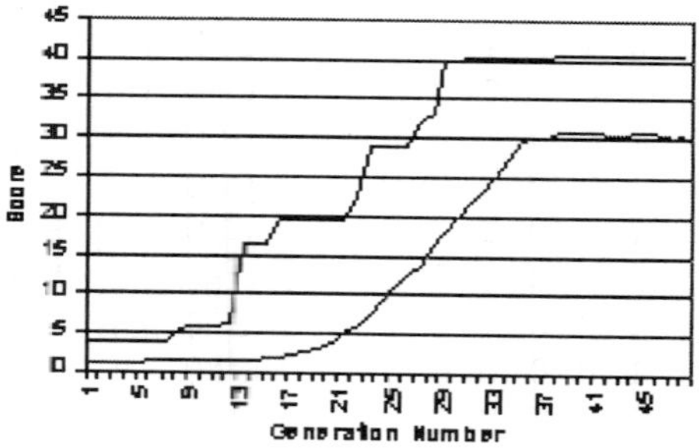

Remarks: We see much more dramatic results here than we do in the planar case below, which makes intuitive sense. With the greater freedom of non-planarity, the space has more instances in that are (more) pessimal.

5.4. *Planar Traveling Salesman*

Problem input	A complete weighted planar graph $G = (V,E)$
Problem description	Find a Hamiltonian cycle of minimum cost.
Approximation algorithm	Greedy Algorithm
Population size	1000
Tournament size	10
Mutation rate	2%
Carry over	10%
Randomize	2%
Graph size	7
Board size	500
Score	greedy cost / optimal cost
Optimal score	?
No. generations	37

Best element details:

Greedy cost	1908.95
Optimal cost	1226.64
Score	1.5562

Best element coordinates:

```
(381,167)
(373,306)
(499,144)
(211,206)
(453,252)
( 19,460)
(258,411)
```

Representative run:

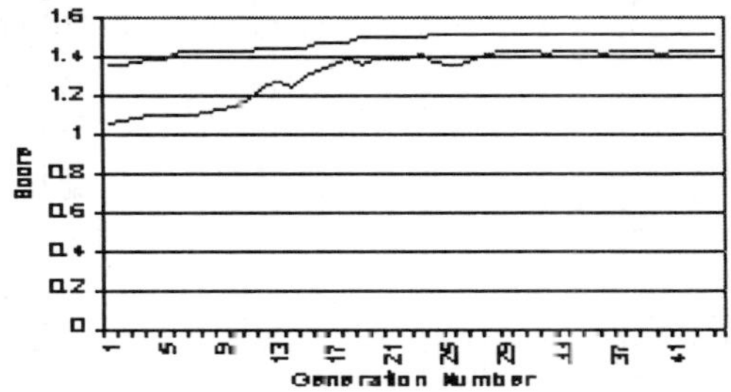

Remarks: The score of this problem grows extremely slowly. Between generations *0* and *10*, it grew from about *1.2* to *1.5*. Intuitively, the explanation for the contrast between *PTSP* and *TSP* appears to be that, by adding the further restriction of planarity; we greatly decrease the amount of freedom available for pessimality—there are fewer ways for things to go that wrong. Thus, the results imply that the greedy algorithm is better, in the worst case, for planar graphs than for arbitrary graphs.

5.5. *Hard Non-planar Taxicab Problem – Greedy*

Problem input	A complete weighted graph $G = (V,E)$ such that V is partitioned into pairs (p_S,p_D)
Problem description	For each passenger (p_S,p_D), reposition the taxis so that some taxi is moved to the passenger's start point, such that *the total distance traveled in repositioning the taxis* is minimized.
Population size	1000
Tournament size	3
Mutation rate	2%
Carry over	1%
Randomize	20%
No. customers	5
Max. distance	100
No. generations	20

Best element details:

Greedy cost	359
Optimal cost	5
Score	71.8

Best element:

```
(  0 24| 41  1| 12 99| 77 78| 95 91)
( 24  0|  1 53|  1  3|  5 48| 13 74)
(----------------------------------)
( 41  1|  0 36| 58  2| 44  6| 12  1)
(  1 53| 36  0| 89 40| 76 22| 75 69)
(----------------------------------)
( 12  1| 58 89|  0 35| 40 99| 72 86)
( 99  3|  2 40| 35  0|  1  1| 10 50)
(----------------------------------)
( 77  5| 44 76| 40  1|  0  7| 25 85)
( 78 48|  6 22| 99  1|  7  0|  1 78)
(----------------------------------)
( 95 13| 12 75| 72 10| 25  1|  0 87
( 91 74|  1 69| 86 50| 85 78| 87  0
```

Run for Hard Non-planar Taxicab Problem – Greedy:

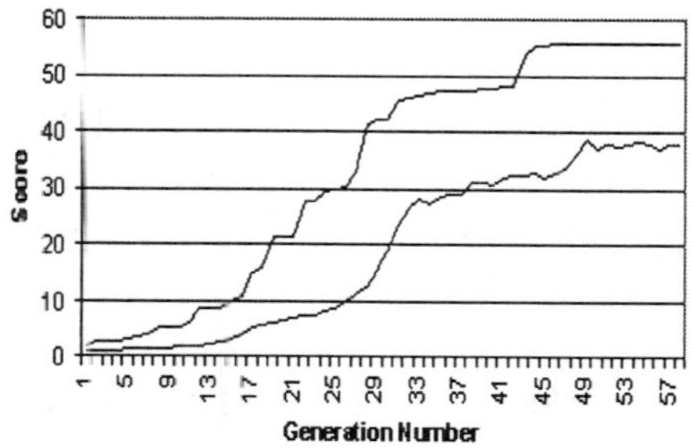

Remarks: Adjacency matrix columns and rows are partitioned into call source-destination pairs. We see much more dramatic results here than in the non-hard versions below, which again makes intuitive sense. Although customer travel-distance is additional mutable data, it is a cost that remains constant regardless of the algorithm (unlike the cost of driving between customers, which varies with the order chosen by the algorithm). Note that the optimal cost reached here, *5*, is the *optimal* optimal cost for this graph size. Since distances between distinct nodes are forced to be non-zero, the minimal possible cost with *5* vertices is *5*. At this point, the only possible change is an increase in the greedy cost.

5.6. *Hard Planar Taxicab Problem – Greedy*

Problem input	A complete weighted graph $G = (V,E)$ such that V is partitioned into pairs (p_S,p_D)
Problem description	For each passenger (p_S,p_D), reposition the taxis so that some taxi is moved to p_S, such that *the total distance traveled in repositioning the taxis* is minimized.
Population size	1000
Tournament size	3
Mutation rate	2%

Carry over	1%
Randomize	20%
No. customers	10
Board size	500
No. cabs	2
Online algorithm	Greedy
Score	Greedy cost / Brute-force cost
No. generations	1000

Best element details:

Greedy cost	2590.27
Brute-force cost	133.14
Score	19.46

Best element:

```
(250,250) to ( 15,166)
(147,172) to (440,401)
(249,250) to (130,479)
(440,401) to (458,423)
(130,479) to (334, 74)
(458,423) to (375,371)
(334, 74) to (317,252)
(375,371) to (467,435)
(317,252) to (  6,  2)
(467,435) to (484,106)
```

Run for Hard Planar Taxicab Problem – Greedy:

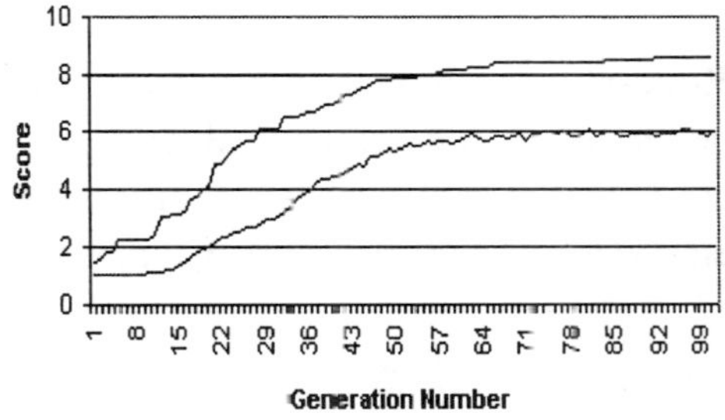

5.7. *Hard Planar Taxicab Problem – Hedging*

Population size	1000
Tournament size	3
Mutation rate	2%
Carry over	1%
Randomize	20%
No. customers	10
Board size	500
No. cabs	2
Online algorithm	Hedging
Score	Hedging cost / Brute-force cost

No. generations	1000

Best element details:

Hedging cost	2896.10
Brute-force cost	417.98
Score	6.93

Best element:

```
(250,250) to (456, 43)
(250,250) to ( 62,453)
(149,340) to ( 76,  9)
(456, 43) to (457,119)
(450,119) to (234,434)
(230,434) to (457,404)
(381,295) to (452, 62)
( 76,  9) to (  3,335)
(120,275) to (264,286)
(452, 62) to (341,161)
```

Run for Hard Planar Taxicab Problem – Hedging:

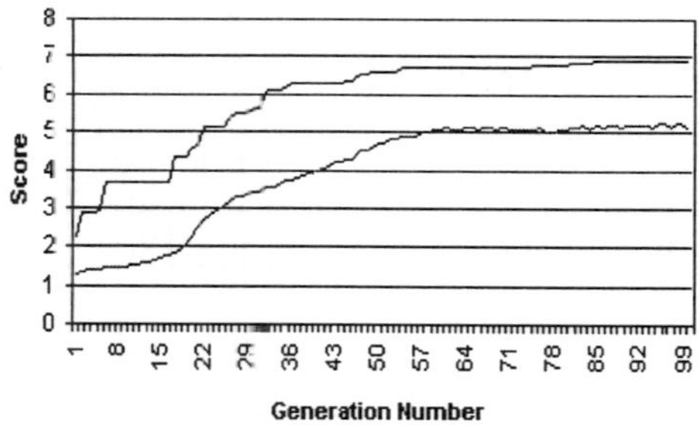

Remarks: As predicted by theory, the hedging algorithm does perform better than the greedy algorithm. The hedging algorithm's score consistently approaches 7 but never surpasses it, which provides empirical evidence of its conjectured 7-competitiveness.

5.8. *Summary of Results*

Although, for reasons of space, we do not provide detailed results for all possible versions of the Taxicab Problem, we provide the summary of these results as follows.

	Planar/Hedging	Planar	Non-Planar
Easy	2.82	15.60	25.33
Hard	6.93	19.46	71.82

Several generalities suggest themselves. First, hard versions score higher than easy versions. This is to be expected, since, in the easy case, the distance traveled with carrying passenegers is a fixed cost for any algorithm; all the algorithm has control over is the distance traveled without passengers. The passenger distance simply dulls the competitive ratio.

Second, non-planar versions score higher than planar versions. The intuition for this is that a non-planar graph has a greater amount of freedom than does a planar graph, and that therefore more pathological non-planar graphs are possible.

Finally, planar/greedy versions score higher than planar/hedging versions. This is also as expected, given the known competitiveness of the hedging algorithm and the known non-competitiveness of the greedy algorithm.

6. Future Work

Other *NP*-Complete problems we intend to study in this manner include *SAT*, *Elevator Control* and *Job Shop Scheduling*. While we have focused mainly on graph-theoretic algorithms, this approach could be broadened to other types of optimization problems. In addition, we believe this approach may be useful to the empirical study of computational complexity, as one way to study the efficiency of newly proposed algorithms whose complexity is not yet proven.

In addition, we plan to use this methodology and the ELBOWS program as a tool for solving one difficulty commonly encountered in Genetic Programming (in which the evolving data structure in question is a program[18]), and to solve it by means of co-evolution.[19,20] In GP, the individual member programs are tested by running them on problem instances. One subroutine in a GP system, therefore, will create problem instances. The fitter the member programs become, however, the more difficult it often is to obtain pessimal problem instances. If the set of problem instances is fixed, then, once the member programs master these instances, further evolutionary progress is unlikely.

We envision using ELBOWS, therefore, in order to create a series of increasingly difficult populations on which to test the member programs in the GP system. In this way, we will create a symbiotic relationship between the set of problem instances and program instances, mirroring the relationships of co-evolving populations found in nature.

7. Conclusions

We explored a new application of genetic algorithms, *viz.*, to the problem of finding worst-case instances of *NP*-Complete problem approximation algorithms and online algorithms, relative to their optimal/offline algorithms, and we implemented several pairs of approximation and optimal algorithms in ELBOWS.

Based on the results of our experiments, ELBOWS shows promise as a tool for experimental research in the analysis of algorithms. In particular, it provides empirical results to suggest that the greedy algorithm performs better, in the worst case, on planar graphs than on arbitrary graphs. Our experiments suggested that the lower bound of 7 on the competitiveness of the hard non-planar taxicab hedging is relatively tight; they also suggested, as expected, that the greedy algorithm is inferior.

Acknowledgments

The authors would like to thank Holly Popowski for many valuable comments on earlier drafts of this chapter.

References

1. D. Sleator and R. Tarjan, "Amortized efficiency of list update and paging rules", *Communications of the ACM*, Vol. 28(2) (1985), p. 202.
2. A. de Jong and W. Spears, W. "Using genetic algorithms to solve *NP*-Complete problems", *Proceedings 3rd International Conference on Genetic Algorithms* (Morgan Kaufmann, 1989), p. 124.
3. G.E. Liepins, M.R. Hilliard, J. Richardson and M. Palmer, "Genetic algorithm applications to set covering and traveling salesman problems", *OR/AI: The Integration of Problem Solving Strategies*, Ed. D.E. Brown (1990).
4. M. Hifi, "A genetic algorithm-based heuristic for solving the weighted maximum independent set and some equivalent problems", *J. Oper. Res. Soc.* Vol. 48 (1997), p. 612.
5. E.L. Johnson, "Genetic algorithms as algorithm adversaries", *GECCO-2001: Proceedings of the Genetic and Evolutionary Computation Conference* (Morgan Kaufmann, 2001).
6. A.P. Kosoresow and M.P. Johnson, "Finding worst-case instances of, and lower bounds for, online algorithms using genetic algorithms", *15th Australian Joint Conference on Artificial Intelligence*. LNAI 2557. (Springer Verlag, 2002) p. 344.
7. M.P. Johnson and A.P. Kosoresow, "Finding worst-case instances, and lower bounds, for *NP*-Complete problems using genetic algorithms", *Proceedings of the*

4th *Asia-Pacific Conference on Simulated Evolution And Learning* (2002), p. 760.

8. M.R. Garey and D.S. Johnson, *Computers and Intractability: A Guide to the Theory of NP-Completeness* (W.H. Freeman & Company, New York, 1979).
9. G. Ausiello (ed.), *Complexity and Approximation: Combinatorial Optimization Problems and Their Approximability Properties* (Springer-Verlag, Berlin, Heidelberg, New York, 1999).
10. J.H. Holland, *Adaptation in Natural and Artificial Systems: An Introductory Analysis with Applications to Biology, Control, and Artificial Intelligence* (University of Michigan Press, Ann Arbor, 1975).
11. M. Mitchell, *An Introduction to Genetic Algorithms* (MIT Press, Cambridge, MA, 1996).
12. M.P. Johnson, ELBOWS source code [http://www.columbia.edu/~mpj9/elbows]. (Columbia University, Department of Computer Science, New York, 2002).
13. A. Borodin and R. El-Yaniv, *Online Computation and Competitive Analysis* (Cambridge University Press, New York, 1998).
14. A. Fiat, Y. Rabani and Y. Ravid, "Competitive *k*-Server algorithms", *Proceedings of the Thirty-First Annual ACM Symposium on Foundations of Computer Science* (The Association for Computing Machinery, 1990), p. 454.
15. A. Kosoresow, *Design and Analysis of Online Algorithms for Mobile Server Applications*. Publication Number 9702926 (University Microfilms, 1996).
16. M. Manasse, L. McGeogh and D. Sleator, "Competitive algorithms for server problems", *Journal of Algorithms*, Vol. 11(2). (1990) p. 208.
17. C.H. Papadimitriou, *Computational Complexity* (Addison-Wesley, New York, 1995).
18. J.R. Koza, *Genetic Programming: On the Programming of Computers by Means of Natural Selection* (MIT Press, Cambridge, MA, 1992).
19. W.J. Hillis, "Co-evolving parasites improve simulated evolution as an optimization procedure", *Artificial Life II*, Eds. C. Langton, C. Taylor, J.D. Farmer, and S. Rasmussen, SFI Studies in the Sciences of Complexity. Vol. X (Addison-Wesley, Redwood City CA, 1991), p. 313.
20. S. Kauffman and S. Johnsen, "Co-evolution to the edge of chaos: couple fitness landscapes, poised states, and co-evolutionary avalanches", *Artificial Life II*, Eds. C. Langton, C. Taylor, J.D. Farmer, and S. Rasmussen, SFI Studies in the Sciences of Complexity. Vol. X (Addison-Wesley, Redwood City CA, 1991). p. 325.

CHAPTER 36

PREDICTION OF PROTEIN SECONDARY STRUCTURE BY MULTI-MODAL NEURAL NETWORKS

Hanxi ZHU[*], Ikuo YOSHIHARA[*], Kunihito YAMAMORI[*], Moritoshi YASUNAGA[**]

[*]*University of Miyazaki*
1-1 Gakuen-Kibanadai-Nisi, Miyazaki City, 889-2192 Japan,
[**]*University of Tsukub*
1-1 Tennoadai, Tsukuba City, 305-8573, Japan

Prediction of protein secondary structure is considered as an important medium step towards determining its three-dimensional structure and function. We have developed Multi-modal Neural Networks (MNNs) to improve the accuracy of the prediction. The MNN employs several sub-networks to predict the secondary structure individually and produce the final result from the outputs of the sub-networks by the majority decision. Moreover, we expand the MNN into a twofold MNN to enhance the prediction ability.

1. Introduction

Proteins are polypeptide chains carrying out most of the basic function of life at the cell molecular level. They are large, complex molecules made up of long chains of subunits called amino acids that are attached end to end in a one-dimensional string. The structure of proteins is usually described with three levels, which is shown in Fig. 1. The amino acid sequence is called its primary structure. Different regions of a sequence that form in regular structure, such as α-helices and β-sheets, are called its secondary structure. The secondary structure folds up to a unique three-dimensional configuration. Since analyzing the structure of proteins by experiments is very complex and time-consuming, the prediction of protein secondary structure is considered as a very challenging task to resolve the three-dimensional structure as well as the function of the proteins.

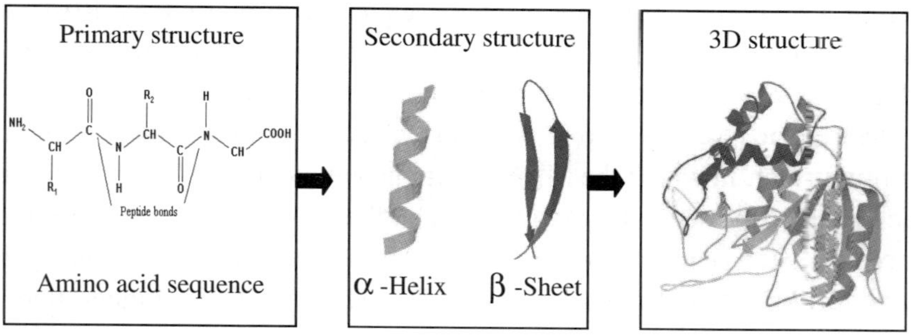

Fig. 1. Protein structures

The prediction accuracy has been improved gradually over the past 10 to 20 years. The improvement is partly due to the increased number of reliable protein structures and partly due to the improvement of methods[1]. Many kinds of neural networks have been applied to this task, such as NNPREDICT[2], PHD[3] and PSIPRED[4]. It is implicitly assumed that the secondary structure of a protein is uniquely determined by its sequence of amino acids. Therefore, in a conventional neural network for the prediction, the input window is composed of a segment of consecutive amino acids of protein sequences. The window slides along the sequence and the target output is corresponded to the secondary structure of the central amino acid of the input window.

We propose Multi-modal Neural Networks (MNN) to improve the prediction accuracy. The MNN is composed of several conventional multi-layer neural networks, which we call sub-networks, and a decision unit. Each sub-network is trained by BP algorithm individually. Since the behavior of a neural network is affected by different initial connection weights, typically, a number of networks are trained individually, and the best of them is chosen while the rest of them are discarded. However, some useful information produced by those discarded networks will be lost. In order to avoid the information lost and take advantage of all the attempts of learning, in the MNN, all of the prediction results of the sub-networks are utilized by the majority decision in the decision unit to produce the final results of the MNN.

In order to evaluate the effectiveness of the MNN, we apply it to testing 126 non-homologous protein sequences proposed by Rost and Sander with seven-fold cross-validation. The average accuracy is 72.6%, which is 3.9% higher than that of a single neural network.

Moreover, we develop a twofold MNN to improve the prediction ability further, in which the MNN mentioned above is employed to predict each state of the secondary structures and the results of them are inputted into a decision neural network for the overall decision. The accuracy by the twofold MNN comes up to 74.2%, which is 5.1% higher than a conventional single neural network.

The data compilation for the experiment is introduced in section 2. The MNN and twofold MNN for prediction are described in section 3 and section 4 respectively. At last, the conclusions and briefs of future work are given in section 5.

2. Data Compilation for Experiment

2.1. *Genome Data*

The data for benchmark test is taken from PDB[5] (Protein Database Bank). The secondary structure of amino acid is assigned based on the hydrogen bond pattern between the backbone carbonyl and NH groups[6]. According to the definitions produced by DSSP[7] (Dictionary of Secondary Structure assignment of Proteins), the secondary structure is distinguished to eight types, which are grouped into three states: H=Helix, E=strand and L=others. Typically, H includes H (α-helices), G (3_{10}-helices) and I (π-helices). E includes E (extended strand) and B (residue in isolated b-bridge). L includes T (turn), S (bend) and blank (=other). The task of neural networks is to predict which state of the secondary structure (H, E or L) does each amino acid of the sequence belong to.

When using neural networks to predict protein secondary structure, the prediction accuracy is considerably influenced by the choice of protein sequences. To avoid the misleading prediction of homologous proteins,

Table 1. The database of protein sequences

1	1acx	1azu	1bbp_A	1bds	1bmv_1	1bmv_2
	1cyo	256b_A	2aat	2ak3_A	2alp	3ait
	3blm	6acn	8abp	8adh	9api_A	9api_B
2	1cbh	1cc5	1cdh	1cdt_A	1crn	1cse_I
	2cab	2ccy_A	3cla	3cln	4bp2	4cms
	4cpa_I	4cpv	6cpa	6cpp	6cts	7cat_A
3	1a45	1dur	1eca	1etu	1fc2_C	1fdl_H
	1fkf	1fnd	1fxi_A	1g6n_A	1iqz	2cyp
	2fox	2gbp	3ebx5	5cyt_R	5er2_E	6cfr
4	1gd1_O	1gp1_A	1hip	1il8_A	1l58	1lap
	2gls_A	2gn5	2hmz_A	2i1b	3hmg_A	3hmg_B
	3icb	4gr1	5hvp_A	6hir	7icd	9ins_B
5	1gdj	1lmb_3	1mcp_L	1ovo_A	1paz	1pyp
	2lhb	2ltn_A	2ltn_B	2mev_4	2or1_L	2pcy
	2phh	3pgm	4pfk	5ldh	5lyz	9pap
6	1mrt	1ppt	1r09_2	1rbp	1rhd	1s01
	1sh1	2mhu	2pab_A	2rsp_A	3rnt	3sdh_A
	4rhv_1	4rhv_3	4rhv_4	4rxn	4sgb_I	7rsa
7	1bks_A	1bks_B	1tgs_I	1tnf_A	1ubq	2sns
	2sod_B	2stv	2tgp_I	2tmv_P	2tsc_A	2utg_A
	2wrp_R	3tim_A	4ts1_A	4xia_A	6tmn_E	9wga_A

protein sequences used for validation are required to have a low pair-wise identity[3]. We used a database of 126 non-homologous protein sequences shown in Table 1, which is proposed by Rost and Sander[3] in 1993. In this test, for the chains with a length of more than 80 residues (amino acids in a protein sequence are also called residues), the mutual pair-wise similarity is less than 25%. The total number of residues is 23942, in which, H state is 31%; E state is 22% and L state is 47%.

Furthermore, to exclude a potential dependency of evaluated accuracy on the particular test set, we use seven-fold cross-validation testing to estimate the prediction accuracy of the method. The 126 protein sequences are randomized and separated into seven groups. Six groups of them are used for training and the remaining one group is used for testing. The tests are repeated cyclically seven times until every group of protein sequences is used once for testing.

2.2. *Generation of Sequence Profiles*

How to express amino acid sequences to a neural network influences the performance of prediction method. Evolutionary information implicated in one protein sequence and its family has been proved to be useful to improve prediction[8]. Rost, B. used multiple sequence alignment in PHD[3] to make the overall accuracy breakthrough over 70% at first time in 1993. David Jones[4] pioneered in using PSSM (Position Specific Scoring Matrix) generated by PSI-BLAST[9] as the direct input for prediction method in 1999, which led a very successful prediction. We adopt the later method as sequence profiles for representing amino acid in this work.

PSI-BLAST (Position Specific Iterative BLAST) is a very powerful iterative homology-sequence searching program. We perform it three iterations. The PSSM generated by the PSI-BLAST is used to represent protein sequences. The PSSM is composed of a multiple alignment of the highest scoring hits in an initial BLAST search. Position-specific scores for each position in the sequence are calculated to generate PSSM. There are usually 20 kinds of amino acids. Therefore, for each position of a sequence, 20 integers are generated for describing the probabilities with each amino acid occur at various pattern positions. The integers are typically in the range of [-10, +10], which are scaled to 0-1 range by using the standard sigmoid function:

$$f(x)=\frac{1}{1+e^{-x}} \tag{1}$$

Hence, the size of PSSM is $N \times 20$ for a protein sequence with N residues.

3. The Multi-Modal Neural Networks (MNN) for Prediction

3.1. *The Structure of MNN*

The prediction of protein secondary structure is essentially a pattern classification problem[10, 11]. A single multi-layer neural network has been shown significant classification ability in many real-world applications. However, since the initial connection weights are randomly given, even by using the same training data, the classification boundaries produced by the neural networks with different initial weights are always different with subtle variance. In order to exploit all useful information embraced in these boundaries, we make use of all the results of several neural networks by using the majority decision to produce the final results. According to the majority decision, the most probable results among all neural networks are determined to the final results. We call this method Multi-modal Neural Networks (MNN). By using the MNN, we can not only improve the prediction accuracy, but also decrease the influence of the uncertainty of initial connection weights upon the prediction.

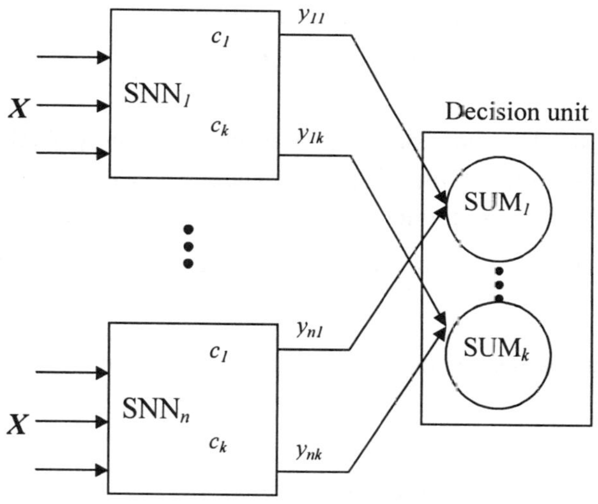

Fig. 2. The structure of the MNN

The structure of the MNN is shown in Fig. 2, which includes several three-layer neural networks, which we call sub-networks, and a decision unit. SNN$_i$ ($i=1, 2, \ldots, n$) stands for sub-network i. Each sub-network is trained by BP algorithm with the same training data individually.

Suppose $\boldsymbol{X}$ denotes the vector of an input pattern and each sub-network has k outputs corresponding to k categories of the classification. The vector $\boldsymbol{X}$ of the testing data is decided to belong to the category c_k that has the maximum output value. Thus, n sub-networks generate n sets of outputs y_{ij}, which make a decision for the vectors of testing data independently, where, $i=1, 2, \ldots, n$, and $j=1, 2, \ldots, k$. When two or more sub-networks make a different decision, conflicts arise. Classifier combination is one of the important methods for resolving the conflicts, which has been studied in many papers[12~14]. Mazurov[14] discussed a committee method for two-classes as following: add all of the results of networks and judge whether the sum is no less than half of n or not. If the decision is "yes", then the final decision is made to be 1. Otherwise, the result is 0. However, in the most cases, the object of prediction or classification has more than two outputs. Therefore, we extend the majority decision to the multi-class as the following way.

The sum total SUM_j for the j-th output is given by adding the corresponding j-th outputs of each sub-network:

$$SUM_j = \sum_{i=1}^{n} o_{ij} \tag{2}$$

SUM_j is used as the score of each category, namely, each state of the secondary structures in the prediction. The SUM_j with maximum score is considered to be close to the desired result.

$$index\_m = index\_\max\{SUM_j \mid j = 1,2,\ldots,k\} \tag{3}$$

$$R = C_{index\_m} \tag{4}$$

Where, $index\_m$ means the index of the maximum of SUM_j; R means the final result.

3.2. *The Sub-Networks for the Prediction*

The sub-network of the MNN for the prediction is a three-layer feed-forward neural network. The structure of the sub-network is shown in Fig. 3. One input pattern is composed of a segment of consecutive residues of protein sequences. The window width of the input pattern, namely, the length of the segment is set to be 17, which means each pattern includes 17 residues. A residue of the window is represented by a row of PSSM and each row of PSSM includes 20 elements. Thus, the total number of neurons in the input layer is 340 (20×17). The target output is associated with the state of the central residue of the window. Therefore, the third layer includes three nodes, which are corresponding to three states of the secondary structure.

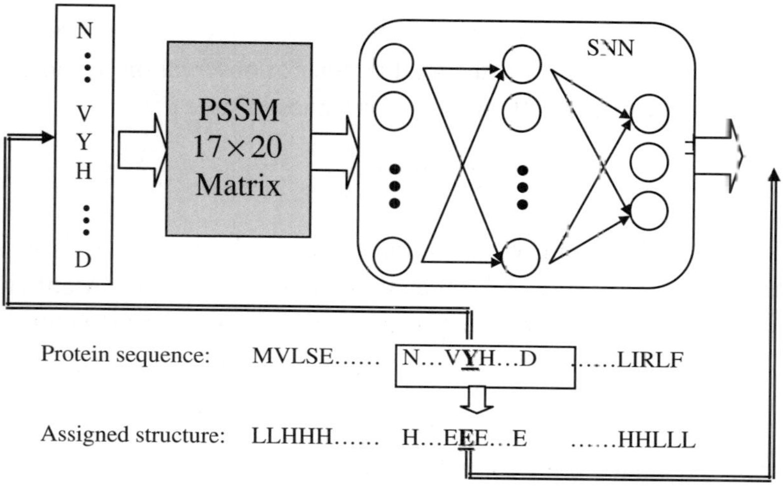

Fig. 3. The structure of sub-network used in the MNN

The window is shifted residue by residue along the sequence. Since the target output is the state of the central residue of the window, two terminuses of the protein sequence can be extended with supplying virtual residues to make the patterns of both two terminuses complete. The 20 numbers for representing virtual residues in extending part are set to 0. Therefore, a protein sequence with *N* residues will yield *N* input patterns.

All of the sub-networks used in the MNN are trained with the same training data by the BP algorithm individually. Finally, the prediction results of the sub-networks are inputted into the decision unit, which produces the final result of the MNN by using the majority decision.

3.3. *The Performance of the MNN*

Several different measures of prediction accuracy have been suggested in the literatures[3]. The most commonly used measure is the overall three-state prediction percentage Q_3, which is defined as the ratio of correctly predicted residues to the total number of residues[3]. Q_3 is given by equation (5):

$$Q_3 = 100 \times \frac{\sum c_i}{N} \tag{5}$$

Where, $\sum c_i$ is the total number of the residues predicted correctly in state i (i=H, E or L), and N is the total number of observation residues. Q_i gives percentage of correctly predicted residues in state i[15]:

$$Q_i = 100 \times \frac{c_i}{N_i} \tag{6}$$

Where, N_i is the number of residues observed in state i. Another complementary measure of prediction accuracy is the Matthews' correlation coefficients for each type of predicted secondary structure[16]:

$$C_i = \frac{p_i n_i - u_i o_i}{\sqrt{(p_i + u_i)(p_i + o_i)(n_i + u_i)(n_i + o_i)}} \tag{7}$$

Where p_i is the number of correctly predicted residues in state i; n_i is the number of those correctly predicted residues in not state i; u_i is the number of underestimated residues and o_i is the number of overestimated residues in the state i. The closer this coefficient is to a value of 1, the more successful the method for predicting a residue in the state i.

The MNN is employed to predict the protein sequences of Table 1 according to the number of the sub-networks n changing from 3 to 11 (n is odd number). The experiments were executed on a computer with two Athlon MP 1.2GHz processors and 512MB memory. The OS is Windows 2000. The program is written in C language and complied by Microsoft

Table 2. The results of the MNN for the prediction

n	Q_3 (%)	Q_H (%)	Q_L (%)	Q_E (%)	C_H	C_E	C_L
3	72.06	81.09	59.96	71.86	0.62	0.54	0.51
5	72.52	81.69	63.39	70.74	0.64	0.55	0.51
7	71.76	82.43	56.27	71.61	0.60	0.54	0.52
9	72.51	82.51	59.37	71.98	0.62	0.55	0.53
11	**72.59**	**83.18**	**58.96**	**71.87**	**0.62**	**0.56**	**0.53**

Visual C++ 6.0. The BP algorithm is iterated 200 epochs. According to the seven-fold cross-validation test, the tests are cyclically repeated 7 times. All of the measures shown in this section are the average values of the 7 times. The running time of one cycle is reported.

The results of the MNN for the prediction are shown in Table 2. Usually, the overall three-state percentage Q_3 is used as the main measure of the prediction. The best overall accuracy of the MNN is 72.59% when n is 11, whose measures are represented in the boldface and underlined row. We compare the Q_3 of the MNN and the average Q_3 of the single neural networks in Table 3. By using the MNN, the overall accuracy is improved to 72.59% when n is 11, which is 3.88% higher than the average accuracy by single neural networks. The broken line of the variation Q_3_δ is shown in Fig. 4. When n is 11, the running time of the MNN is about 3.5 hours, which is 11 times as long as that of the single neural network.

Table 3. Comparison of Q_3 of the MNN with average Q_3 of SNN

n	$Q_3\_aver\_SNN$	Q_3_MNN	Q_3_δ
3	69.57%	72.06%	+2.49%
5	69.18%	72.52%	+3.34%
7	68.71%	71.76%	+3.05%
9	68.77%	72.51%	+3.74%
11	**68.71%**	**72.59%**	**+3.88%**

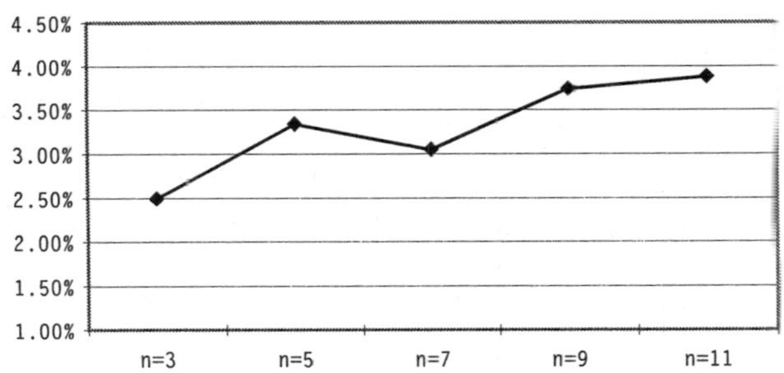

Fig. 4. Variations of Q_3_δ

4. Twofold MNN

4.1. *The Structure of Twofold MNN*

In order to enhance the prediction ability further, we expand the MNN into a twofold MNN. Hereafter, we call the MNN described in Section 3 a primary MNN. The structure of the twofold MNN is shown in Fig. 5. First, the above-mentioned primary MNN is employed to predict each state of the secondary structures independently. Second, all the results of the single state prediction are inputted into a decision neural network (DNN) to make an overall decision. Since separating the states of the secondary structures simplifies the problem, single state prediction can be expected more accurate than three-state prediction.

In the left part of Fig. 5, the primary MNN is employed to predict each state of the secondary structures independently. The pattern setting of the sub-networks used in the primary MNN is the same as section 3.2. The output layer includes only one node, which represents the state of the central residue of the window. In case of the primary MNN for H state, states H and not H are represented with 1 and 0 respectively. The representation for E and L states are the same as H. The final decision of

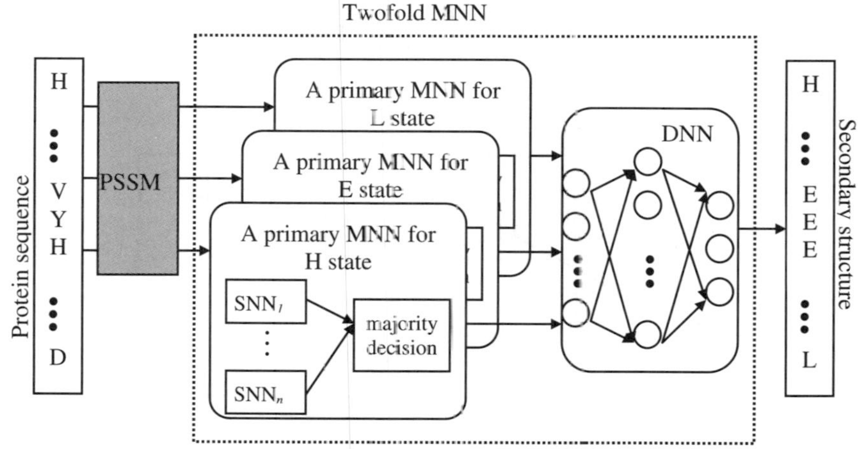

Fig. 5. The structure of the twofold MNN

the primary MNN is made by majority decision. The prediction of the three states is performed independently.

The task of the DNN in the right part of Fig. 5 is to make an overall decision by using a three-layer neural network from the prediction results of the left part.

The DNN is trained at first. The training data of the DNN are not the prediction results of the primary MNN, but the original data taken from the PDB. In the training procedure, the input pattern is composed of a window of consecutive secondary structure of protein sequences. The window width is also 17. The three states are represented with a triplet of 0/1 numbers as following:

$$H \rightarrow 1\ 0\ 0$$
$$E \rightarrow 0\ 1\ 0$$
$$L \rightarrow 0\ 0\ 1$$

Therefore, the input pattern becomes 51 (3×17) units. The output includes three nodes corresponding to the secondary structure of the center of the window.

In the testing procedure, the prediction results of the primary MNN are used for the input patterns of the DNN. The DNN gives the overall prediction of three states H, E and L.

4.2. *The Performance of the Twofold MNN*

The twofold MNN is also evaluated by seven-fold cross-validation test with the data of Table 1 under the same computational condition as the primary MNN. Table 4 shows the results when the multiplicity of the primary MNN for each state is 5. The prediction is repeated cyclically seven times and the average results are shown at the last row. The Q_3 is improved to 74.1% by using the twofold MNN. The deviation to the average value is only about $\pm 4\%$. The running time is about 4.55 hours.

We compare the measures of prediction accuracy of the twofold MNN with those of the primary MNN (when n is 11) in Table 5. The third and fourth columns indicate the difference and ratio of two methods. Most of the measures are improved, especially Q_E. Although Q_H is 4.16% lower than that of the MNN, C_H is 11.29% improved, which means the

Table 4. The results of the twofold MNN for the prediction

7-fold	Q_3 (%)	Q_H (%)	Q_E (%)	Q_L (%)	C_H	C_E	C_L
1	72.30	83.32	70.73	66.97	0.66	0.59	0.49
2	78.24	82.25	55.63	80.21	0.74	0.62	0.59
3	74.19	82.81	73.79	69.68	0.73	0.57	0.52
4	69.71	80.87	69.55	62.20	0.64	0.49	0.49
5	74.89	84.57	65.66	72.04	0.71	0.56	0.52
6	75.16	71.31	65.24	80.76	0.64	0.58	0.52
7	74.72	72.53	70.29	78.38	0.69	0.56	0.56
Average	**74.17**	**79.67**	**68.70**	**72.89**	**0.69**	**0.57**	**0.53**

prediction quality of H state of the twofold MNN is better than that of the primary MNN.

Moreover, we also compare the Q_3 of twofold MNN with the conventional prediction methods in Fig. 6. GOR3[17] and DEC[18] are based on Bayesian Statistics; SIMPA[19] is based on nearest neighbor; and all other methods are based on neural network. All of the accuracy is taken from the references. Our twofold MNN is better than GOR3, SIMPA, NNPREDIC, DEC and PHD. But it is a little lower than the precision

Table 5. Comparison of the twofold MNN with the primary MNN

	Primary MNN	Twofold MNN	Difference	Ratio
Q_3	72.59%	74.17%	+1.58%	+2.18%
Q_H	83.18%	79.67%	-3.46%	-4.16%
Q_E	58.96%	68.70%	+9.74%	+16.52%
Q_L	71.87%	72.89%	−1.02%	+1.42%
C_H	0.62	0.69	+0.07	+11.29%
C_E	0.56	0.57	+0.01	+1.79%
C_L	0.53	0.53	0	0

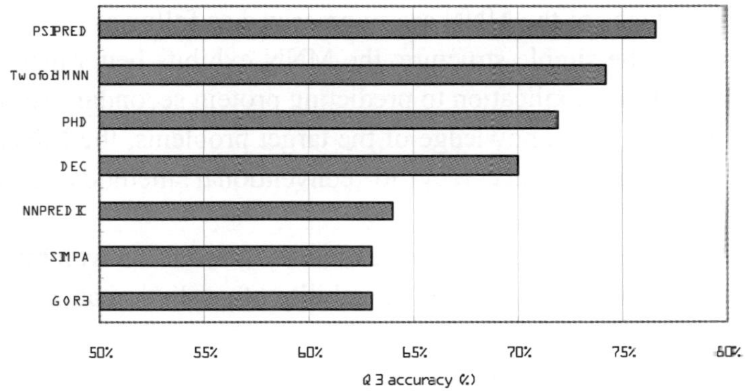

Fig. 6. Comparisons of the twofold MNN with other methods

claimed in PSIPRED. Since the original training data can't be obtained from the PSIPRED paper, we can't compare the two methods under the same condition.

5. Conclusions

We have developed Multi-modal Neural Networks (MNN) to increase the prediction accuracy of protein secondary structure. The MNN is composed of several sub-networks and a decision unit. Each sub-network is trained to predict the secondary structure individually and the decision unit gives the final results by majority decision.

For each sub-network, we adopted PSSM generated from PSI-BLAST as sequence profiles to represent amino acid sequences. The overall accuracy Q_3 comes up to 72.6% by using the MNN, which is 3.88% higher than the average accuracy of single neural networks.

Moreover, we developed a twofold MNN for further accurate prediction, in which, first, the primary MNN is employed to predict each state of the secondary structures independently; second, the results of the single state predictions are inputted into a decision neural network for making a final decision. Since the separate prediction decreases the complexity of the problem, the accuracy of single state prediction can be improved. By using the twofold MNN, the accuracy Q_3 is improved to 74.2%, which is about 1.6% higher than the primary MNN in addition.

The advantages of the MNN are summarized as follows:

(i) Despite of the simple structure, the MNN exhibits betterment in the accuracy of the application to predicting protein secondary structure.

(ii) Without any prior knowledge of the target problems, the MNN gave the superiority of accuracy to conventional methods from the viewpoint of accuracy.

(iii) The MNN decreases the influence of initial connection weights on the training results and increases the stability of prediction as well.

The future works are to refine the decision method of the MNN and to extend the application to the problems with larger training data. As we believe the MNN has possibilities for better classification, we will continue this research for achieving a better accuracy.

References

1. B. Rost, Review: Protein Secondary Structure Prediction Continues to Rise, *Journal of Structure Biology*, Vol. 134, pp. 204-218 (2001)
2. D.G. Kneller, F.E. Cohen and R. Langridge, Improvements in protein secondary structure prediction by enhanced neural networks, *J. Mol. Biol.*, Vol. 214, pp. 171-182 (1990)
3. B. Rost and C. Sander, Prediction of Protein Secondary Structure at Better than 70% Accuracy, *J. Mol. Biol.*, Vol. 232, pp. 584-599 (1993)
4. David, T. Jones, Protein Secondary Structure Prediction Based on Position-specific Scoring Matrices, *J. Mol. Biol.*, Vol. 292, pp. 195-202 (1999)
5. F.C. Bernstein et al., The Protein Data Bank: a computer based archival file for macromolecular structures, *J. Mol. Biol.*, Vol. 112, pp. 535-542, (1977)
6. B. Rost and C. Sander, Third Generation Prediction of Secondary Structures, *Method in Molecular Biology*, Vol. 143, pp. 71-95, (1998)
7. W. Kabsch and C. Sander, Dictionary of Protein Secondary Strcutre: Pattern Recognition of Hydrogen Bonded and Geometrical Features, *Biopolymers*, Vol. 22, pp. 2577-2637, 1983
8. B. Rost, P. Von Rague-Schleyer, N.L. Allinger, T. Cclark, J. Gasteiger, P.A. Kollman, H.F. Schaefer, Protein structure prediction in 1D, 2D, and 3D, *Encyclopedia of Computational Chemistry*, pp. 2242-2255 (1998)
9. S.F. Altschul, T. L. Madden, A.A. Schaffer, J.H. Zhang, Z.W. Zhang and D.J. Lipman, Gapped BLAST and PSI-BLAST: a new generation of protein database search programs, *Nucleic Acids Research*, Vol. 25, pp. 3389-3402, (1997)
10. C. M. Bishop, *Neural network for pattern recognition*, Oxford University Press, 1995

11. B.D. Ripley, *Pattern recognition and neural networks*, Cambridge University Press, 1996
12. M.P. Perrone, Improving regression estimation: averaging methods for variance reduction with extensions to general convex measure optimization, PhD Thesis Brown University, RI, USA, 1993
13. J.J. Holl, A. Commike and T.K. Ho, Multiple algorithms for Handwritten Character recognition, *Proceedings of the International Workshop on Frontiers in Handwriting Recognition*, pp. 117-124, (1990)
14. V.D. Mazurov, A.I. Krivonogov and V.L. Kazantsev, Solving of optimization and identification problems by committee methods, *Pattern Recognition*, Vol. 20, No. 4, pp. 371-378, (1987)
15. S. Hayward and J. Collins, Limits on Alpha-helix Prediction with Neural Network Models, *Proteins*, Vol. 14, pp. 372-381 (1992)
16. A.N. Refenes and M. Azema-Barac, Currency exchange rate prediction and neural network design strategies, *Neural Comput. Appl.*, pp. 46-58 (1993)
17. J.F. Gibrat, B. Robson and J. Garnier, Further developments of protein secondary structure prediction using information theory, *J Mol Biol.*, Vol. 198, pp. 425-443, (1987)
18. R.D. King and M.J.E. Sternberg, Identification and application of the concepts important for accurate and reliable protein secondary structure prediction, *Protein Science*, Vol. 5, pp. 2298-2310, (1996)
19. J.M. Levin, Exploring the limits of nearest neighbor secondary structure prediction, *Protein Engineering*, Vol. 10, pp. 771-776, (1997)

CHAPTER 37

JOINT ATTENTION IN THE MIMETIC CONTEXT —WHAT IS A "MIMETIC SAME" ? —

Takayuki Shiose*, Kenichi Kagawa**, An Min**, Toshiharu Taura**, Hiroshi Kawakami*, and Osamu Katai*

**Graduate School of Informatics, Kyoto University*
Yoshidahonmachi, Sakyo-ku, Kyoto, Japan
***Graduate School of Natural and Science, Kobe University*
Rokkodaicho, Nada-ku, Kobe, Japan
E-mail: shiose@i.kyoto-u.ac.jp

Mimesis should be meaningful imitation that reproduces not only superficial behaviors but also the behavioral intentions underlying the behaviors. We propose mimetic learning based on a self-evaluation function (MLSE), which enables the imitator robot to assess the model robot's behavioral intention by referring to the rate of change of its self-evaluation function. Here, the success of the imitation depends on a co-evolving mechanism that consists of two learning contexts: identical and situational contexts. Experimental results show that MLSE enables the imitator robot to reproduce behavioral patterns by taking into account the model robot's behavioral intention. Additionally, the imitator robot succeeded in reproducing the model robot's intention even if there was a slight difference between the model and the imitator robot's body size. In this chapter, this phenomenon is regarded as a special case of joint attention in the mimetic context. As a result, this chapter aims to answer the question "What is a mimetic same?"

1. Introduction

Marline Donald has asserted that mimesis involves the intentional re-enaction of an event or relationship[2]. Mimesis is known to be useful in modeling social roles, communicating emotions and in transmitting rudimentary tool-using skills. Therefore, mimesis should be meaningful imitation that reproduces not only superficial behaviors but also the behavioral intentions underlying the behaviors[1,4,5](see Fig. 1). Our purpose here is to develop a mimetic learning architecture based not on such awkward imitation but on the original mimesis by extending machine learning algorithms. In the next section, a survey of imitation and mimesis is introduced from the viewpoint of developmental psychology[1]. The results of this survey provide strong guidelines for developing the architecture of the original mimetic learning. Section 3 describes the conditions of the experiments involving the model robot and the imitator robot, and briefly explains the architecture and flowchart of mimetic learning based on a self-evaluation function (MLSE). Then, in Section 4, experimental results are presented that verify that our proposed MLSE enables the imitator robot to reproduce behavioral patterns by taking into account the model robot's behavioral intentions. Our conclusions are presented in the final section.

2. Definition of Imitation

Fig. 1. An example situation of mimesis. If the imitator awkwardly reproduces the model's trajectory of drinking hot coffee, the imitator fails to drink it and may get burned

2.1. *Literature on Imitation*

The study of imitation has attracted a great deal of attention, as evidenced by numerous psychological studies[1,4,5]. Tarde defined imitation as "a form of copying every impression of an inter-psychical photography, so to speak, willed or not willed, passive or active."[1] Generally speaking, 'imitation' is known to be advantageous in that (a) it is an alternative to expensive trial-and-error learning and (b) it facilitates the rapid acquisition of adaptive behavior in the young. By adding Donald's interpretation to this definition, Butterworth proposed that, "an innate capacity for imitation in humans might be expected to contribute to the social transmission of culturally accumulated characteristics[1]."

Nowadays, it can be said that there is no unanimous explanation of the above-mentioned imitation phenomena but only a vague common sensical understanding of imitation. Most studies on imitation are not conclusive as to how we can know whether imitation is successful or not. We do not have any criteria other than how different the acquired behavioral pattern is from that of the model. To demonstrate a successful imitation, many experimental psychologists cannot help but adopt such evaluation criteria from a third-person viewpoint. Once we admit outsider evaluation criteria, we have no choice but to evaluate the imitation by focusing simply on behavioral conformity.

2.2. *Identical and Situational Context*

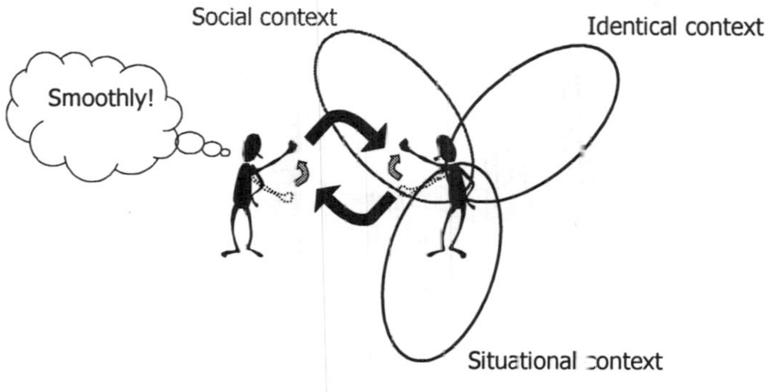

Fig. 2. Triple context model for imitation. The first context, adaptation to the situational context, means that behavioral patterns should be reproduced so as to adapt themselves to their minimum situation. On the other hand, the second context, adaptation to the identical context, means that behavioral patterns should be explained using only internal attributes. In this study, this identical context is represented as the degree of conviction that transient evaluation criteria can reflect the model robot's intention faithfully. The last context, adaptation to the social context, means that such identical context should not be simply self-satisfied, but also adapted to the common sense values in the society to which the imitator belongs to. Repetition of social interaction will navigate these reciprocal double contexts to an appropriate direction in the society

Motion capture can be regarded as the simplest technique of establishing only behavioral conformity, since it can replay exactly the same behavioral trajectory for any number of attempts. Can we regard this as an original imitation phenomenon? You can guess the answer easily. Here, it is necessary to remember Donald's definition that mimesis involves "intentional re-enaction" of an event or relationship. As long as the imitator reproduces the model robot's actions with its behavioral intention, it is not always necessary for the acquired behavioral patterns to be exactly equivalent to the model robot's act. When the imitator has a different body structure from that of the model robot', such a tendency is more pronounced. In this chapter, we hypothesize that the success of imitation is guaranteed due to the co-evolution of all three contexts, situational, identical and social (as shown in Fig. 2).

Let us assume a scene in which a baseball batting form is imitated. The imitator must reproduce not the exact same trajectory but at least the phenomenon of the bat hitting the ball. Such minimum constraints are called the situational context here. Second, the identical context is equal to the self-awareness that the imitator could reproduce a batting form is not too awkward and is executable. Third, the social context means the norm or the common language in the team where both baseball players belong to. Intricate intertwining of these three contexts is expected to reduce the degree of freedom (DOF) for the imitator to identify the model robot's intention. This reduction of DOF can be regarded as that both robots' attentions to their own behavior act in unison, that is, joint attention in the broad sense. In this chapter, our argument is limited to only the first two contexts, situational and identical, for convenience.

3. Experimental Conditions

3.1. *Behavioral Patterns in Point-to-Point Movements*

In this study, point-to-point movements are made the target of experiments in which the imitator robot reproduces the model robot's behavioral patterns. Fig. 3 shows an example of point-to-point movements of a three-DOF robot arm, and the parameters of each joint are illustrated in Fig. 4.

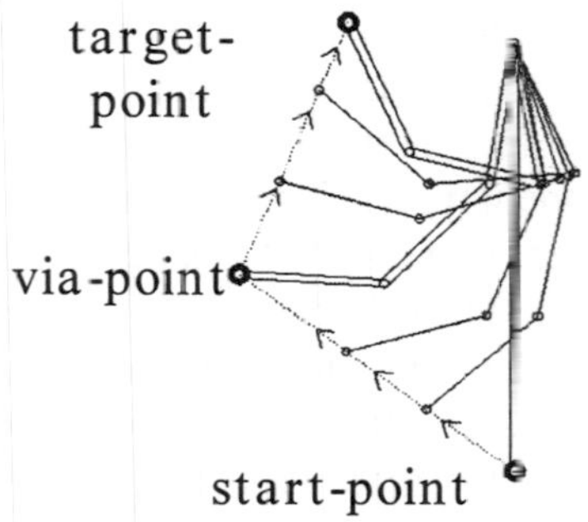

Fig. 3. Behavioral patterns in point-to-point movement. Here, the robot hand is instructed to follow the trajectory from the start-point to the target-point by way of the via-point

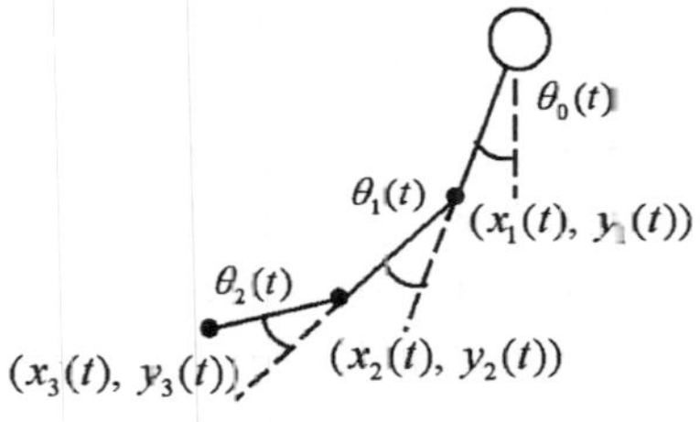

Fig. 4. Coordinates and angles of each joint. The coordinates of the elbow joint, wrist joint and hand are $(x_1(t), y_1(t))$, $(x_2(t), y_2(t))$ and $(x_3(t), y_3(t))$, and the angles of each joint are $\theta_0(t)$, $\theta_1(t)$ and $\theta_2(t)$

3.2. *Evaluation Criteria to Represent the Model Robot's Intention*

When the robot produces behavioral patterns, such as reaching for a coffee cup and bringing it to its mouth, it is not necessary to precisely determine every movement of the entire arm (see Fig. 1). The coordinates of the elbow or the angle of the shoulder joint may not be related to the behavior itself of lifting the coffee cup. Rather, what we should pay more attention to are the evaluation criteria, such as 'smoothly' and 'quickly', which prescribe the whole movement from the start-point to the target-point. In this study, the trajectory of behavioral patterns is given not by a program but by a genetic algorithm (GA) with a certain evaluation criterion. Here, the individual GA represents a certain series of movements from the start-point to the target-point. When the model robot, for instance, moves its hand in a manner similar to the way humans generate an approximately straight trajectory, the model robot's behavioral patterns can be regarded as one given by a GA with a straight-hand-path criterion. Here, the following candidates of evaluation criteria are adopted in this algorithm.

Criterion of minimum error range from the target-point:

$$E_l = (X - x_3(T))^2 + (Y - y_3(T))^2 , \tag{1}$$

Criterion of minimum error range from the via-point:

$$E_{l'} = (X' - x_3(T'))^2 + (Y' - y_3(T'))^2 , \tag{2}$$

Criterion of straight hand path:

$$E_d = \int_0^{T-1} \{(x_3(t) - x_3(t+1))^2 + (y_3(t) - y_3(t+1))^2\} dt , \tag{3}$$

Criterion of minimum angle jerk:

$$E_\theta = \int_0^{T-2} \sum_{j=0}^{N-1} \left(\dot{\theta}_j(t) - \dot{\theta}_j(t+1)\right)^2 dt . \tag{4}$$

Here, T and T' indicate the total time taken to reach the target-point and the via-point, respectively, and (X, Y), (X', Y') indicate the corresponding coordinates of these points. N denotes the number of joints. The evaluation function (E_m) of the model robot is given by a weighted sum of the above-mentioned four evaluation criteria:

$$E_m = w_1 \cdot E_l + w_2 \cdot E_{l'} + w_3 \cdot E_d + w_4 \cdot E_\theta , \tag{5}$$

where $w_1 + w_2 + w_3 + w_4 = 1.0$.

We chose different combinations of these weights to denote different behavioral intentions of the model robot. For instance, (w1,w2,w3,w4) = (0.4,0.3,0.3,0.0) indicates that the model robot's action is performed mainly according to the straight-hand-path criterion. On the other hand, (0.4,0.3,0.3,0.0) indicates that its action is in accordance with the minimum angle jerk criterion. Imitation in this study can be interpreted as the ability to determine on which criterion the model robot places more emphasis.

3.3. *Possibility of Determining the Model Robot's Intention*

Initially, the criterion for establishing behavioral conformity E_o is defined as the following:

$$E_o = \int_0^T \sum_{i=1}^N \{(x_i(t) - x'_i(t))^2 + (y_i(t) - y'_i(t))^2\} dt, \quad (6)$$

where (x_i', y_i') represents the coordinates of each of the model robot's joints. This criterion simply indicates that the imitator robot reproduces the trajectory of the model robot's behavioral patterns exactly as observed. With only this criterion, the imitator robot has no choice but to establish mere behavioral conformity. Here, we have established one hypothesis: that the imitator robot will succeed in imitating behavioral patterns quickly if the imitator robot has the same evaluation criteria as those of the model robot. Thus, we previously carried out some experiments in which the imitator robot was required to reproduce the model robot's behavioral patterns under various combinations of weights of the evaluation function. Fig. 5 shows the change of the gap between the desired trajectory (here, it is the straight-hand-path trajectory) and the trajectory acquired by the imitator robot. The experimental conditions are as follows. Case 1: only criterion E_o. Case 2: the same criterion as that of the model. Case 3: a criterion similar to that of the model. Case 4: a different criterion from that of the model.

Compared with Case 1 (with only E_o), the gaps in Case 2 and Case 3 (with evaluation criteria the same as or similar to that of the model) converged to a smaller value. On the other hand, in Case 4 (with a different evaluation criterion from that of the model), the convergence of the gap was oppositely affected. These results suggest that the imitation activity might be accelerated if the two robots have the same or similar evaluation criteria, which implies that paying attention to the trend of changes in the gap might lead to a specification of which criterion the model robot places emphasis.

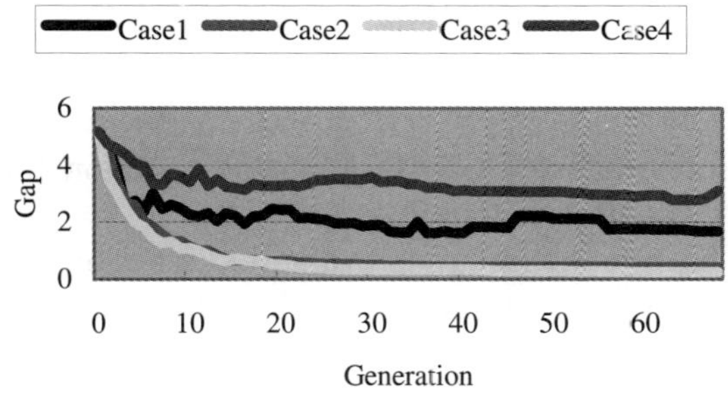

Fig. 5. Imitation under different combinations of weights

3.4. *Definition of the Imitator Robot's Evaluation*

In this subsection, MLSE is introduced as the evaluation function for the imitator robot E_i. The form of the evaluation function is

$$E_i = w_1' \cdot E_o + w_2' \cdot E_l + w_3' \cdot E_{l'} + w_4' \cdot E_{m'}, \tag{7}$$

where $w_1' + w_2' + w_3' + w_4' = 1.0$.

The first criterion is that of establishing behavioral conformity E_o, which was explained in the former subsection. The second E_l and third $E_{l'}$ criteria are the minimum error range from the target-point and from the via-point, respectively. Strictly speaking, the imitator robot should assess these points to achieve original imitation learning. However, we focus on assessing the model robot's intention concerning all movements from the beginning to the end, because there exist some preceding studies that succeeded in assessing via-points in point-to-point movements[3,6]. This last criterion $E_{m'}$ can be regarded as a self-evaluation function in the sense that it involves only internal attributes of the imitator robot. Specifically, it is represented by the tree structure of genetic programming (GP). Here, terminal nodes of the GP tree are composed of each joint angle and non-terminal nodes are composed of if-clauses and three rules of arithmetic operations (+, -, *), which are defined as internal attributes of the imitator robot. The evaluation function E_i composed of the above-mentioned four criteria is assumed to be updated by the following procedure.

(1) Initialize individuals of GP (forming the criterion for assessing the model robot's evaluation criteria $E_{m'}$)
(2) Substitute $E_{m'}$ into the imitation evaluation function E_i
(3) Acquire behavioral patterns satisfying the evaluation function E_i given in (2)
(4) Arrange the evaluation function E_i in descending order
(5) List the first ten behavioral patterns acquired by the evaluation function E_i given in (4)
(6) Start GP to acquire new criterion that can put a high value on those ten behavioral patterns
(7) Repeat steps (2) to (6) until the given generation

Roughly speaking, this updating procedure can be interpreted as the reciprocal process between the evaluation-assessment process (the identical context) and the behavior-acquiring process (the situational context). First, the imitator robot attempts to reproduce behavioral patterns based on the provisional evaluation function E_i. Then, the evaluation function E_i is established based on those acquired behavioral patterns. Here, assessing the model robot's intention does not always precede reproducing the model robot's behavioral patterns, and there are only reciprocal processes between the identical and situational context. Hereafter, parameters for each evolutionary computation (GA and GP) are set as follows (Table 1).

Table 1. Definition of parameters

	Genetic algorithm for producing behavioral patterns	Genetic programming for producing evaluation function
Number of individuals	100	100
Generations	1000	50
Mutations	0.03	0.30
Crossover	0.50	0.40
Reverse		0.30

4. Experimental Results

Two experiments are carried out to validate the effectiveness of our proposed MLSE. First, the model robot is assumed to have the behavioral intention of minimizing angle jerk; that is, the weights of the evaluation function E_m are set as $(w_{1'}, w_{2'}, w_{3'}, w_{4'}) = (0.4,0.3,0.0,0.3)$. In the imitation of the straight-hand-path criterion, the imitator robot need not use MLSE, since all the imitator robot does is copy the model robot's trajectory itself.

4.1. *Assessing Minimum Angle Jerk Criterion between Same-Size Bodies*

In this experiment, the model robot and the imitator robot are assumed to have the same body size. To evaluate the effectiveness of MLSE, the imitator robot tries to imitate the model robot's behavioral patterns using the following evaluation functions. The first is our proposed E_i. Thereafter, this evaluation function is only used for establishing behavioral conformity E_o, and the evaluation function E_i without E_o and the evaluation function E_i without E_o or $E_{m'}$ are set in turn. Fig. 6 shows

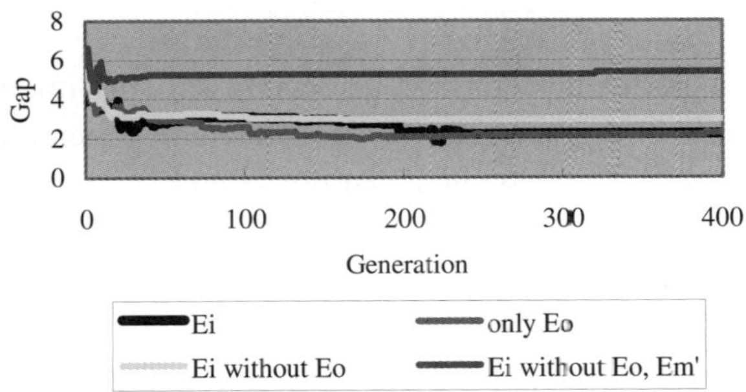

Fig. 6. Change of the degree of angle jerk. By comparing the result of using the third evaluation function with that of using the fourth, evaluation criterion $E_{m'}$ can reflect the model robot's behavioral intention (it mainly follows the minimum angle jerk criterion)

Table 2. Convergence value of angle jerk

Evaluation function	Degree of angle jerk
Proposed E_i	2.1600
Only E_o	1.8240
E_i without E_o	2.8430

the change of the degree of angle jerk that is reproduced by the imitator robot based on the above-mentioned four evaluation functions. The convergence value of the angle jerk for each evaluation function is shown in Table 2.

However, in the case of imitation between robots with the same body size, the imitator robot succeeded in assessing the model robot's behavioral intention only by reproducing exactly the same behavioral patterns. In either case, it is found that the MLSE can be applied to assess the model robot's behavioral intention.

4.2. *Assessing Minimum Angle Jerk Criterion between Robots with Different Body Sizes*

Next, an experiment is carried out between robots having different body sizes. Each robot's link size is shown in Table 3.

Table 3. Different body size condition

	(l_1,l_2,l_3)
Model robot	(3.0,3.0,2.0)
Imitator robot	(2.0,2.5,2.0)

As in the experiment described in Section 4.1, the imitator robot is directed to assess the model robot's behavioral intention using an evaluation function. The first one is our proposed E_i and the second is the evaluation function used only for establishing behavioral conformity E_o. Fig. 7 shows the change of the degree of angle jerk under these experimental conditions, and Table 4 shows the convergence value of the angle jerk for each evaluation function. These results also show that our proposed evaluation function E_i has the advantage of reproducing the model robot's intention (minimum angle jerk criterion), since the convergence value of the angle jerk obtained by MLSE is lower than that obtained using simple E_o.

Table 4. Convergence value of angle jerk

Evaluation function	Degree of angle jerk
Proposed E_i	1.5200
Only E_o	2.8160

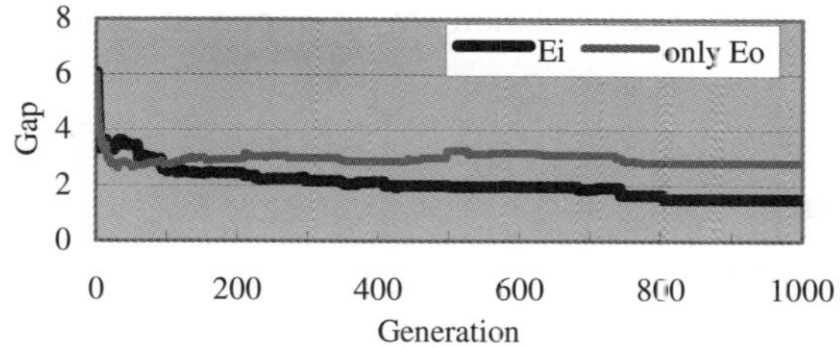

Fig. 7. Change of the degree of angle jerk

Fig. 8 shows the sample trajectory for the imitator robot after 400 steps of the imitation learning process. In this case, the imitator robot must focus not on behavioral conformity but on relationships among each angle or among changes of each angle, since the imitator robot has a body size different from that of the model robot.

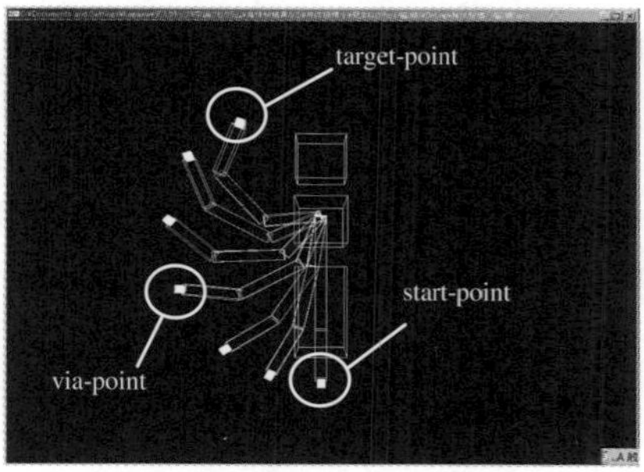

Fig. 8. Reproduced behavior patterns among robots with different body sizes

4.3. *Discussions*

The imitator robot cannot directly know the model robot's intention. Therefore, at first, the imitator robot aims at copying the model robot's behavioral patterns as they are. Next, the imitator robot aims at exploring an appropriate explanation for its own acquired behavioral patterns. We can expect that reciprocity of these two contexts navigate the imitator robot's intention to the similar one of the model robot. Here, the definition of 'same' is very simple. It is not important to be careful about every little thing the model robot's does. Additionally, the third social context to this reciprocal mechanism is expected to suppose mimetic learning.

5. Conclusions

In this chapter, MLSE (mimetic learning based on a self-evaluation function) was proposed, and it was revealed that the imitator robot can reproduce the model robot's behavioral patterns at least in terms of reproducing its intention. Even if the imitator robot has a different body size from that of the model robot, MLSE provides the imitator robot with the ability to successfully assess the model robot's intention.

The reason behind this success in reproducing the model robot's intention can be considered to be the co-evolving mechanism, which consists of a self-evaluation function updating system (the identical context) and a behavioral pattern acquisition system (the situational context). Thus, the evaluation criterion for establishing behavioral conformity plays a role in navigating the direction of this co-evolution in the initial stages. Studies on the social context that is expected to navigate the final direction of this co-evolution are left to future work, as in the precise investigation of the acquired evaluation function.

References

1. G. Butterworth, "Neonatal imitation: existence, mechanisms and motives", J. Nadel and G. Butterworth. (eds), *Imitation in Infancy*, Cambridge University Press, 63-88(1999).
2. M. Donald, Origins of the modern mind: *Three stages in the development of culture and cognition*. Cambridge, MA: Harvard University Press(1991).
3. T. Flash, N. Hogan, "The Coordination of Arm Movements: An Experimentally Confirmed Mathematical Model", *The Journal of Neuroscience*, Vol.5, No. 7, 1688-1703(1985).
4. A. Melzoff and A. Gopnik, "The role of imitation in understanding persons and developing a theory of mind", *Understanding Other Minds*, Oxford University Press(1993).
5. A. Melzoff and M. K. Moore, "Newborn infants imitate adult facial gestures", *Child Development*, Vol.54, 702-709(1983).
6. S. Stefan, "Is imitation learning the route to humanoid robots?", *Trends in Cognitive Sciences*, Vol. 3, No. 6, 233-242(1999).

CHAPTER 38

AUTONOMOUS SYMBOL ACQUISITION THROUGH AGENT COMMUNICATION

A. Wada[*1,*2], K. Takadama[*1,*3], K. Shimohara[*1,*2] and O. Katai[*2]

*(*1) ATR Human Information Science Laboratories*
2-2-2 Hikaridai, "Keihanna Science City" Kyoto 619-0288, Japan
*(*2) Graduate School of Informatics, Kyoto University*
Yoshida-Honmachi, Sakyo-ku, Kyoto 606-8501, Japan
*(*3) Tokyo Institute of Technology,*
Interdisciplinary Graduate School of Science and Engineering
4259 Nagatsuta-cho, Midori-ku, Yokohama, 226-8503, Japan
E-mail: {wada,katsu}@atr.jp, katai@i.kyoto-u.ac.jp, keiki@dis.titech.ac.jp

In this chapter, we propose a multi-agent system aiming at autonomous symbol acquisition, in which agents acquire symbols through communication instead of symbols being given *a priori* by the designer. Based on this idea, we extended Steels's language acquisition model to develop a new model featuring three mechanisms: (a) symbol matching; (b) symbol creation; and (c) concept selection. Intensive simulation revealed the following implications: (1) the degree of trade-off between communication success and required lexicon size can be decreased by matching all possible combinations in symbol matching; (2) symbol creation of hearer agents plays a significant role in symbol acquisition, while speaker agents do not; (3) the speed of symbol creation depends on the method used for this step, but it is not related to the trade-off between communication success and lexicon size; and (4) concept selection can also be applied to resolve the trade-off between communication success and required lexicon size.

1. Introduction

In recent years, research on communication has been conducted with a computational approach. For example, McLennan, Werner and Dyer studied the origin of communication and showed that communication emerged as a result of agents' cooperation from the point of view of Artificial Life [2,7]. As another example, Steels focused on the origin or evolution of language and

Table 1. Relation of terminology between Steels's model and our approach

Steels's model	Our approach
Distinctive feature set	Concept
Word-meaning pair	Symbol
Word	Word

proposed a model to explain how the vocabulary that each agent acquires is shared through communication [3,4,5,6]. These approaches have contributed to a better understanding of communication.

In contrast to the above approaches, our approach aims at realizing comfortable and varied communication between humans and computers. To address this issue, we focus on autonomous symbol acquisition, in which computational agents acquire symbols autonomously instead of the symbols initially being given to them by designers. Steels's language acquisition model essentially conforms to our approach, since we can consider the process of acquiring a shared vocabulary through agent communication a primitive model of implementing autonomous symbol acquisition.

However, the methods used in the model are determined *a priori* and not investigated for their validity in the task of symbol acquisition. Therefore, our objective is to investigate the methods used in Steels's model in order to improve communication quality for the agents while focusing on the essential problem of the trade-off between the success of communication and the size of the required lexicon.

The rest of the chapter is composed of five sections. In Sec. 2, we introduce Steels's model in detail. In Sec. 3, we describe the idea of symbol acquisition, which is used to extend Steels's model. In Sec. 4, experimental results are reported, which are followed by a discussion in Sec. 5. The final section presents our conclusions.

2. Steels's Model

2.1. *Problem Description*

Steels's model consists of a group of agents and objects placed in an environment. Agents have the ability to wander around the environment and to sense the surrounding objects by using their sensors. In the model[6], agents create a vocabulary and share it through the following steps: (1) a discrimination game, in which each agent creates features used for calculating distinctive feature sets, enabling them to discriminate objects; and (2) a language game, in which agents try to recognize the same object by using

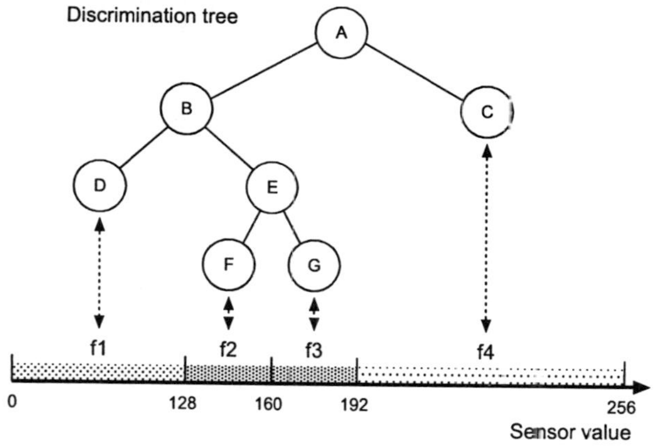

Fig. 1. Relation between a discrimination tree and sensor value space

words bound with distinctive feature sets.

Before describing the details of each game, we clarify our approach to symbol acquisition by associating our terminology with that of Steels's model, as shown in Table 1. In Steels's model, a distinctive feature set and word are bound to create a word-meaning pair. We relate this to our idea that a concept and word are bound to create a symbol. Hereafter, we use our own terminology to explain Steels's model.

2.2. *Discrimination Game*

In the discrimination game, agents try to discriminate a topic object from other objects. This is done by categorizing the sensor value for each object into features. Each feature represents each node of the discrimination tree, which divides the sensory value space into several partitions as shown in Fig. 1. For example, node D corresponds to feature "f1," which represents the partition of the sensor value from 0 to 128. Nodes F and G are created by expanding node E, which corresponds to dividing the partition of the sensor value from 128 to 192 into two partitions presented as features "f2" and "f3."

If the features of the topic object are different from those of other objects, then the discrimination game succeeds. This is judged by calculating concepts (distinctive feature sets) to determine whether a group of feature sets can discriminate the topic object from the other objects. Figure 2 shows an example. In the figure, objects 1, 2 and 3 are expressed as features. The

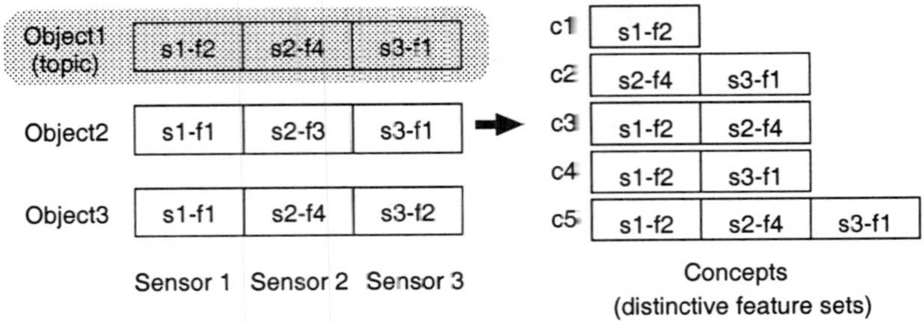

Fig. 2. Calculating concepts (distinctive feature sets)

label of the feature specifies which feature belongs to which sensor; for example, "s1-f2" denotes the feature "f2" of the discrimination tree for sensor 1. In the figure, concepts (distinctive feature sets) for the topic object are listed in the right column and are labeled "c1" to "c5." Here, the concept "c2," which represents the combination of features "s2-f4" and "s3-f1," can discriminate object 1 from both objects 2 and 3, as feature "s2-f4" distinguishes the topic object from object 2, which includes the corresponding feature "s2-f3" for sensor 2, and feature "s3-f1" distinguishes the topic object from object 3, which includes the corresponding feature "s3-f2" for sensor 3. On the other hand, the concept including a single feature "s2-f4" is not included, as it can only discriminate object 2 from the topic object and cannot discriminate object 3 from the topic object.

Here, if the discrimination process fails, which is the case when no concept can be found to distinguish the topic, the discrimination tree grows by expanding its node to create new features, which corresponds to the operation of dividing the partition in the sensor value space. Each node of the discrimination trees holds the number of uses and successes of discrimination processes, and the process refers to this number to select the useless nodes that are periodically eliminated. Through this creation and elimination of nodes, each agent develops its own set of features, represented by the structure of a discrimination tree, that can successfully discriminate objects. These features are then used in the naming game.

2.3. *Naming Game*

In the naming game, two agents are selected as a speaker and a hearer. The goal of the game is for both agents to recognize the same object, which is achieved by the hearer understanding the speaker's utterance that refers to the object's feature. This process can be described as follows.

(1) Speaker and hearer share the same context by facing each other.
(2) Speaker and hearer perceive the environment by receiving sensor values for each object.
(3) Speaker selects one object as a topic and gives the direction toward the topic to hearer by a non-linguistic means (e.g., pointing).
(4) Speaker tries to discriminate the topic by generating concepts.
(5) Speaker tries to express one of the concepts with a word by matching the feature with its own vocabulary.
(6) Speaker utters the word and hearer receives.
(7) Hearer interprets the word using its own vocabulary.
(8) Hearer matches the interpretation of the word with expected concepts.
(9) If the matching succeeds, the game ends in success.

The calculation of concepts to discriminate the topic in step 4 shares the same process with that in the discrimination game. If the naming game fails in the latter steps (this can occur in steps 5, 7 and 8), the agent extends its vocabulary by creating a new symbol. This symbol creation develops each agent's vocabulary, enabling agents to more fully share the recognition of the topic object with each other by sending and receiving words.

3. Autonomous Symbol Acquisition

In this section, we first give our definition of the word "symbol" by referring to Saussure's semiology, which leads to the three mechanisms required for symbol acquisition: (a) symbol matching, (b) symbol creation, and (c) concept selection. Next, we describe an extension to Steels's model based on an analysis that applies these three mechanisms.

3.1. *Definition of "Symbol"*

To clarify our definition of "symbol," we focus on Saussure's work, which established the foundation of *semiology*, the field of studying what "symbol"[a] means for human language activity, which is analyzed through his philosophical methodology called *structuralism*. Saussure's semiology deals

[a]The term "sign" is the original term used in Saussure's semiology. On the other hand, the term "symbol" has it's origin in Pierce's work, used to classify signs into the three categories "icon," "index" and "symbol." Although the terms "sign" and "symbol" do not have exactly the same meaning, we use only the term "symbol" to avoid confusion.

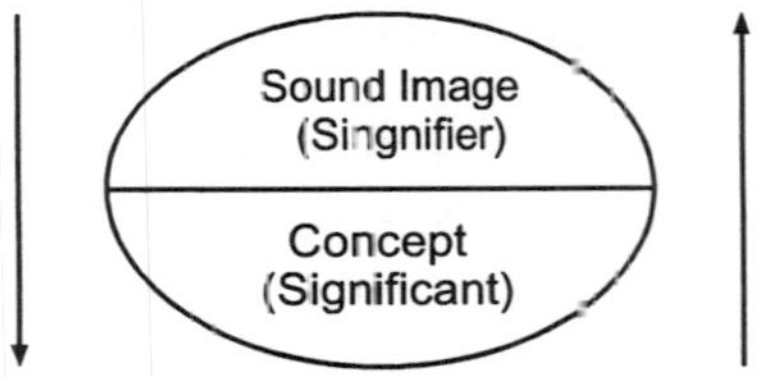

Fig. 3. Symbol as a binding between concept (signifier) and sound image (significant)

with several essential properties of language, and the ideas derived from this work contributed greatly to the development of modern linguistics. However, here we limit our focus to a discussion on the *arbitrariness* of symbols.

Arbitrariness is one of the most important ideas in Sassure's semiology, and it describes a distinct character of a symbol based on the binding between the concept the symbol denotes and the sound image of that symbol. Saussure named the former *signifier* and the latter *significant*, and this binding between the two can be illustrated with the representation shown in Fig. 3. For example, the symbol "dog" binds its concept of a four legged animal with a tail that barks to its sound image of pronouncing "dog." Saussure indicated that this binding between concept and sound image is not determined naturally but under a specific cultural influence. The same concept of a dog might bind with a different sound image, for example "chien" in French. This character of the symbol is what Saussure called *arbitrariness.*

From the discussion above, we define "symbol" as a binding between a concept, the information unit for agents to recognize their environment, and a word, the information unit used for communication between agents. Therefore, this binding is decided through a dynamic process that includes both the interaction between agent and environment and the communication between agents.

3.2. *Mechanisms for Symbol Acquisition*

Based on the above definition of a symbol, symbol acquisition can be described as the process of binding a concept and a word as a symbol through agent communication. We implement this idea as a multi-agent system in which an agent requires the three mechanisms described below.

Symbol matching: Agents match symbols with concepts. This mecha-

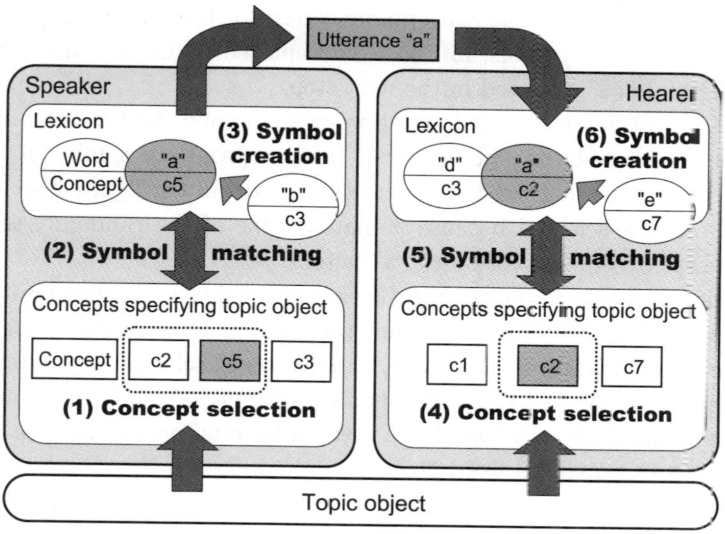

Fig. 4. Mechanisms for symbol acquisition

nism enables the agent to express concepts by words and to understand the words of others by concepts.

Symbol creation: Agents create symbols by binding words and concepts. As agents initially have no adequate symbols, they need to create symbols used for the symbol matching mechanism. This mechanism depends on the requirement of the word usage, i.e., to recognize the same object using words.

Concept selection: Agents filter concepts before symbol creation and matching. A concept is originally created for the convenience of a single agent; however, the symbol must be shared between other agents. To efficiently match or create symbols, concepts are filtered using the criterion of whether the concepts are difficult to share. One candidate for establishing this criterion is the generality of concepts.

3.3. *Analyzing Steels's Model*

To analyze Steels's model from the viewpoint of symbol acquisition, we follow the entire process while applying our three mechanisms: symbol matching, symbol creation and concept selection. We explain each step in the process by using the framework in Fig. 4.

(1) The speaker filters the concepts perceived for the focused object to be matched with symbols. In Fig. 4, concept "c3" is filtered and concepts "c2" and "c5" are used in the next step.
(2) The speaker tries to find an appropriate symbol to express one randomly selected concept by word. If an appropriate symbol is found, the corresponding word is sent to the hearer. In the figure, the symbol "a / c5" is selected because it matches one of the randomly selected concepts "c5," and the word "a" is sent.
(3) If no symbol is found in step (2), a new symbol is created by binding a randomly generated word and the concept that failed to match in the previous step. For example, if the concept selected in the previous step to be matched was "c3," then no adequate symbol exists, and the new symbol "b / c3" would be created by binding the concept to the randomly generated word "b."
(4) The hearer filters the concepts perceived for the object in focus to be matched in step (5) as the expected concept to receive from speaker. In the figure, concepts "c1" and "c7" are filtered and concept "c2" is used in the next step.
(5) The hearer tries to match the symbol corresponding to the received word with the expected concepts perceived in step (4). Matching between all combinations of the received word and the existing symbols is attempted, and if at least one matches the object is considered to be shared with the speaker by successfully using the word. In Fig. 4, the symbol "a / c2" is matched with the expected concept "c2." In this case, the game ends in success.
(6) If no symbol is found for the speaker's utterance or if symbol matching fails in step (5), the hearer creates new symbols by binding all possible combinations between the received word and each of the expected concepts. For example, if no symbol denoting the word "a" is found or if the concept of the matched symbol did not match any of the expected concepts, symbols to bind the word "a" and each of the expected concepts "c1," "c2," and "c7" would be created.

3.4. *Extending Steels's Model*

By focusing on the three mechanisms in symbol acquisition, there arises asymmetry in the method used between the speaker and the hearer, as shown in Table 2. In symbol matching, the speaker performs matching for one randomly selected concept, whereas the hearer performs matching

Table 2. Methods used in Steels's model

	Speaker	Hearer
Symbol matching	Random selection	All-combination
Symbol creation	Random selection	All-combination
Concept selection	—	—

for all concepts. We call the former the random selection method and the latter the all-combination method. In the symbol creation mechanism, the speaker creates a symbol for one randomly selected concept, whereas the hearer creates symbols for all concepts. Again we call the former method the random selection method and the latter the all-combination method. The idea of concept selection is not mentioned specifically in Steels's model.

Instead of deciding *a priori* the methods to use, we extend the model to enable different methods in each mechanism for the speaker and the hearer: (1) the all-combination method and the random selection method for symbol matching; (2) the all-combination method and the random selection method for symbol creation; and (3) the no-selection method and the concept selection method for concept selection.

Here, the concept selection method is defined as a process to filter the specific concepts. To evaluate the generality of the concepts, we apply the next process to concepts.

(1) For each concept, check whether it includes any features of other concepts.
(2) If it includes any other concept's features, it is more specific than others.
(3) Filter all specific concepts.

For example, one of the concepts "c1," which represents a single feature "(s1-f2)" in Fig. 2, is the most general because it does not include any distinctive feature sets of the other concepts as its subset. On the other hand, concept "c3," which represents a set of features "(s1-f2)(s2-f4)," is more specific than concept "c1" because it includes the feature "(s1-f2)" as its element. This can be explained more intuitively by a metaphor: The concept "square and blue" is more specific than the concept "square" because it limits the target from a square of any color to a square of only blue.

4. Experiments

In this section, we describe simulation experiments using our model, which explicitly defines three mechanisms: (1) symbol matching, (2) symbol creation, and (3) concept selection. Since Steels's original model seems to determine *a priori* the method used for each mechanism, we validate our model by comparing the combinations of speaker and hearer's methods for each mechanism. First, we describe the settings of our simulation experiments. Next, we show experimental results for each mechanism.

4.1. *Experimental Settings*

In our experiment, we basically adopt the same framework as that used in Steels's experiment on language evolution[3], in which physically implemented robots interact with each other in the real-world environment.

However, our experiment is performed by computer simulation for the following two reasons. First, our objective is to develop a symbol acquisition model in general, which requires avoiding the specific biases of the physical environment, such as sensory-motor noise. The second reason is that we can easily control the experimental settings without the time-consuming work of physical reconfiguration, which is essential in evaluating a large number of cases with different conditions.

This difference does not affect the two basic processes: the discrimination game and the naming game, which are described in sub-sections 2.2 and 2.3. However, some abstraction for environmental setting is required.

In our experiment, agents move randomly in the virtual two-dimensional space instead of the physical environment. The processes of word utterance and recognition done by agents are simply implemented by data transfer between agents, but the content of this transfer is limited to the allowed words. The discrimination game is evoked periodically for each agent, and the naming game is evoked when a collision of two agents is detected.

For other common conditions, the following setting are used in all experiments. There are 5 agents and 20 objects. Each agent has 3 sensors. In each case, after 1,000 trials of the discrimination game, 10,000 trials of the naming game are run. The results in the following subsections are the average of 5 simulations for each case.

4.2. *Experimental Results*

4.2.1. *Symbol Matching*

The four cases listed in Table 3 are examined to compare the combinations of methods used for the symbol matching mechanism. The results are shown in Figs. 5 and 6. Figure 5 shows the relationship between the number of trials and the rate of communication success, while Fig. 6 shows

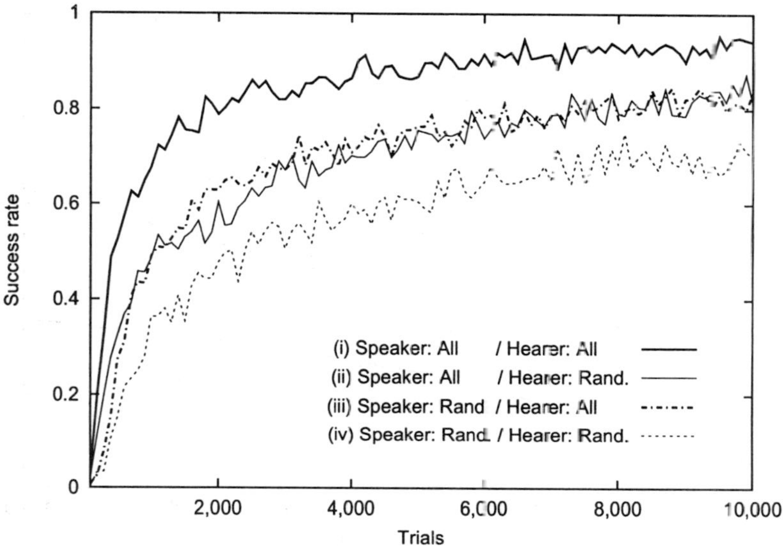

Fig. 5. Communication success for each case in symbol matching

Table 3. Conditions for each case in symbol matching

Speaker	Hearer	
	All-combination	Random selection
All-combination	(i)	(ii)
Random selection	(iii)	(iv)

the relationship between the number of trials and the required lexicon size. As the number of trials grows, both communication success and lexicon size increase. Case (i) shows the best communication success rate and the smallest lexicon size. There is no significant difference between cases (ii) and (iii). Case (iv) shows the worst communication success and the largest lexicon size.

4.2.2. *Symbol Creation*

To compare the combinations of methods used for the symbol creation mechanism, the four cases listed in Table 4 are examined, with the results shown in Figs. 7 and 8. Figure 7 shows the relationship between the number of trials and the rate of communication success, while Fig. 8 shows the relationship between the number of trials and the required lexicon size.

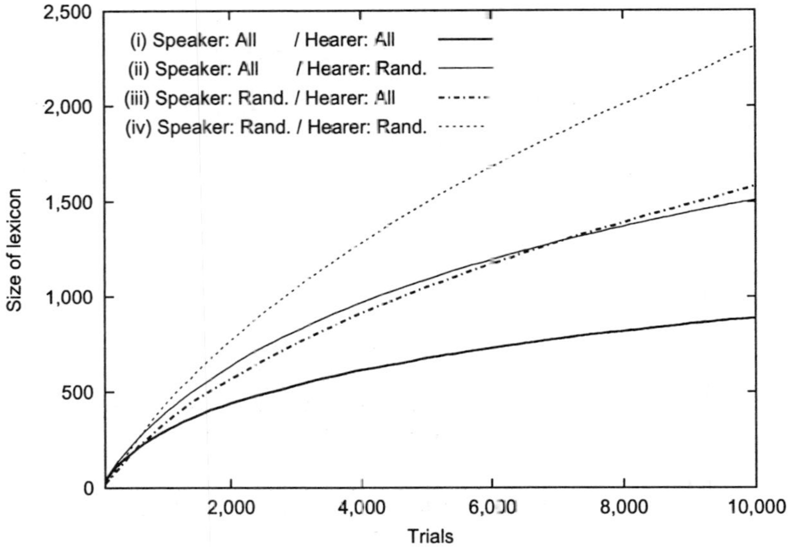

Fig. 6. Size of lexicon for each case in symbol matching

Table 4. Conditions for each case in symbol creation

Speaker	Hearer	
	All-combination	Random selection
All-combination	(i)	(ii)
Random selection	(iii)	(iv)

Cases (i) and (iii) show better communication success than cases (ii) and (iv). However, cases (ii) and (iv) show smaller lexicon size than cases (i) and (iii). As there is no significant difference between cases (i) and (iii), (ii) and (iv) are observed.

4.2.3. *Concept Selection*

The four cases listed in Table 5 are examined to compare the combinations of methods used for the concept selection mechanism. The results are given in Figs. 9 and 10. Figure 9 shows the relationship between the number of trials and the rate of communication success, while Fig. 10 shows the relationship between the number of trials and the required lexicon size. Cases (ii) and (iv) show a smaller lexicon size, as there are no noticeable differences among the four cases concerning communication success.

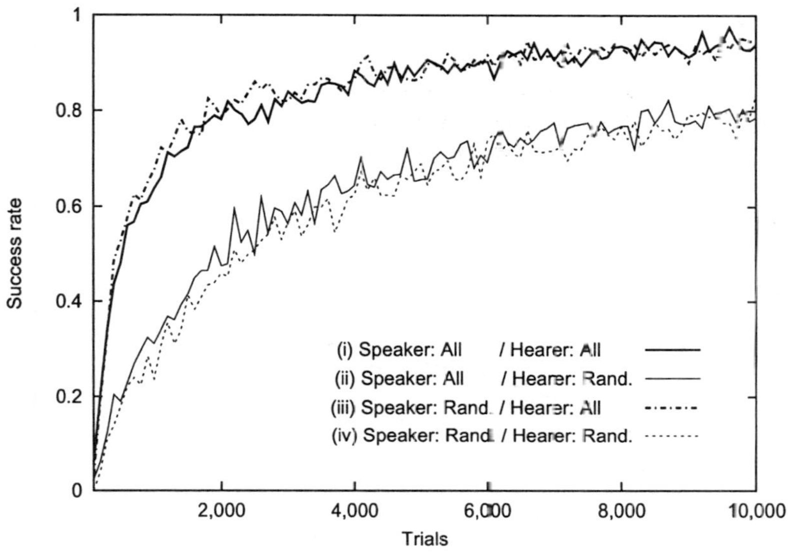

Fig. 7. Communication success for each case in symbol creation

Table 5. Conditions for each case in concept selection

Speaker	Hearer	
	No selection	Concept selection
No Selection	(i)	(ii)
Concept selection	(iii)	(iv)

5. Discussion

5.1. *Advantage of the All-combination Method in Symbol Matching*

As shown in Figs. 5 and 6, the all-combination method in the symbol matching mechanism has an advantage over the random selection method in its ability to decrease the degree of trade-off between communication success and required lexicon size. The reason for this result is summarized as follows. When matching the concept with symbols, only one concept is compared in the random selection method, and if the randomly selected set fails to match, the game fails, even if a successful set exists in the other concepts. On the other hand, the all-combination method attempts to match every possible combination of concepts and symbols in the lexicon. This leads to the obtained result.

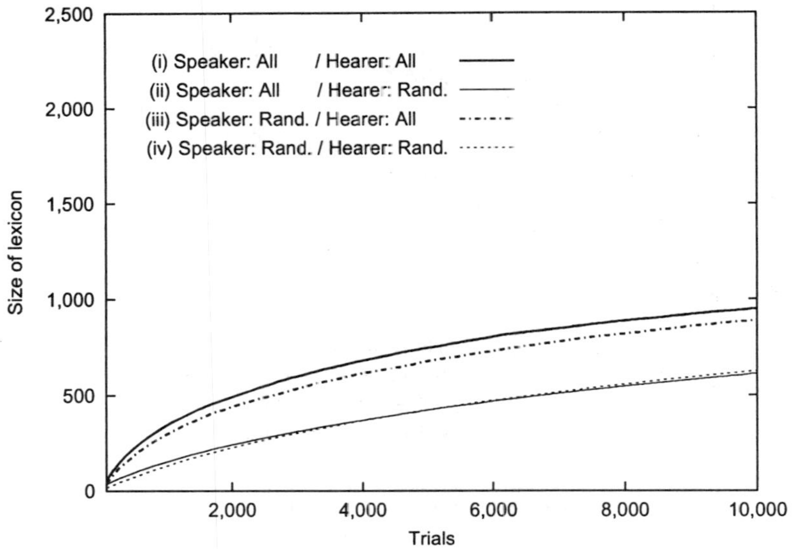

Fig. 8. Size of lexicon for each case in symbol creation

5.2. *Hearer's Significance in Symbol Creation*

As shown in Figs. 7 and 8, the hearer's symbol creation method influences the result to some extent, although the speaker's symbol creation method does not affect the result. To explain why this occurs, we should describe all three cases of symbol creation listed below.

Case 1: When the speaker does not have a symbol to express a concept by symbol. (Step 5 in Sec. 2)

Case 2: When the hearer does not have a symbol corresponding to the speaker's utterance. (Step 7 in Sec. 2)

Case 3: When the hearer fails to match symbols and expected concepts. (Step 8 in Sec. 2)

Case 1 occurs in the earliest phase of the simulation but rarely occurs after each agent has acquired enough symbols to express concepts. Case 2 occurs while words exist that other agents do not share, whereas case 3 continues to occur while common agreement of word use is established. Most of the symbol creation takes place in case 3, because the occurrences of case 1 and case 2 converge to zero in the early phase. This means that the hearer agent's symbol creation plays a significant role, while the speaker's

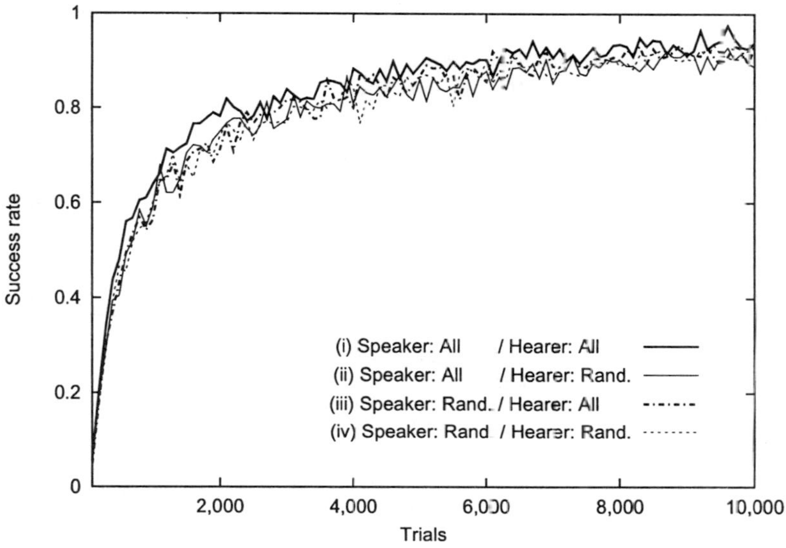

Fig. 9. Communication success for each case in concept selection

symbol creation has only a slight influence. This idea explains not only the result of experiment 1 but also the result of experiment 3 shown in Figs. 9 and 10.

5.3. *Symbol Creation Speed*

As the hearer creates symbols, in comparison with the all-combination method, the random selection method for the hearer's symbol creation decreases the required lexicon size, although communication success also decreases. To explain this result using Figs. 7 and 8, we introduce the idea of symbol creation speed, which is defined as the average number of created symbols per game failure. In the case of the random selection method, the hearer can create only one symbol at a time, so the symbol creation speed is 1. In the case of the all-combination method, the hearer can create a symbol for each expected concept, so the symbol creation speed may be higher than 1. Our hypothesis is that the number of trials required for the convergence of the success rate scales linearly with the symbol creation speed. Based on this idea, we proposed an additional experiment by extending

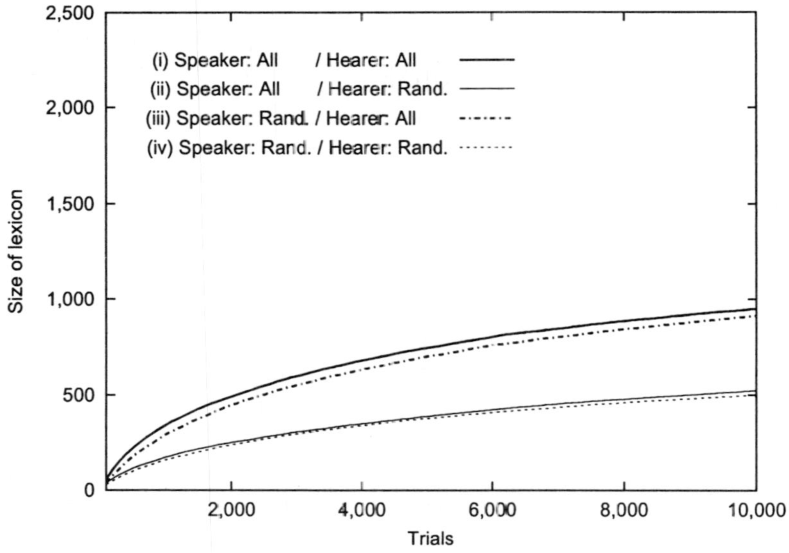

Fig. 10. Size of lexicon for each case in concept selection

the trial number from 10,000 to 30,000 for cases (ii) and (iv), in which the hearer uses the random selection method. The result is shown in Figs. 11 and 12. The curve represents cases matched in both Figs. 11 and 12. We can estimate that the symbol creation speed of cases (i) and (iii) using the all-combination method is around 3, and this is shown in the difference in the scale of the trial number.

5.4. *Concept Selection and Effectiveness of Symbol*

From the result of experiment 3 shown in Figs. 9 and 10, the concept selection method shows good results in decreasing the degree of trade-off for both the speaker's and hearer's symbol matching and creation. We believe that concept selection works to filter inefficient concepts that do not contribute to future communication success. This supports the idea that a general word can cover a broader meaning and thus be understood and shared more easily than a specific word.

6. Conclusions

In this chapter, we focused on symbol acquisition and analyzed Steels's model to ascertain the validity of the methods used. This was accom-

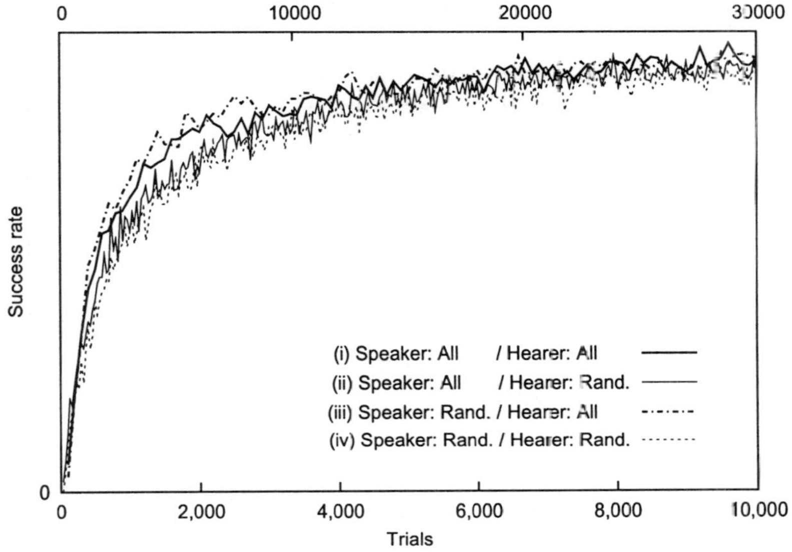

Fig. 11. Additional experiment for symbol creation: (a) Communication success

plished by extending the model to incorporate three mechanisms: (1) symbol matching, (2) symbol creation, and (3) concept selection. Four main results were obtained through intensive simulation: First, all matching methods for symbol matching decrease the degree of trade-off between communication success and lexicon size. Second, the hearer's symbol creation plays a significant role in symbol acquisition, while speaker agents do not. Third, although the symbol creation speed differs, the trade-off mentioned above is not resolved by the method used for the hearer's symbol creation. Finally, concept selection is effective in decreasing the degree of trade-off.

Further research will include analysis of the relevance of acquired lexicons between agents as well as analysis of the relation between the group size of the agents and the communication success.

Acknowledgements

The research reported here was supported in part by a contract with the Telecommunications Advancement Organization of Japan entitled "Research on Human Communication" and by the Okawa Foundation for Information and Telecommunications.

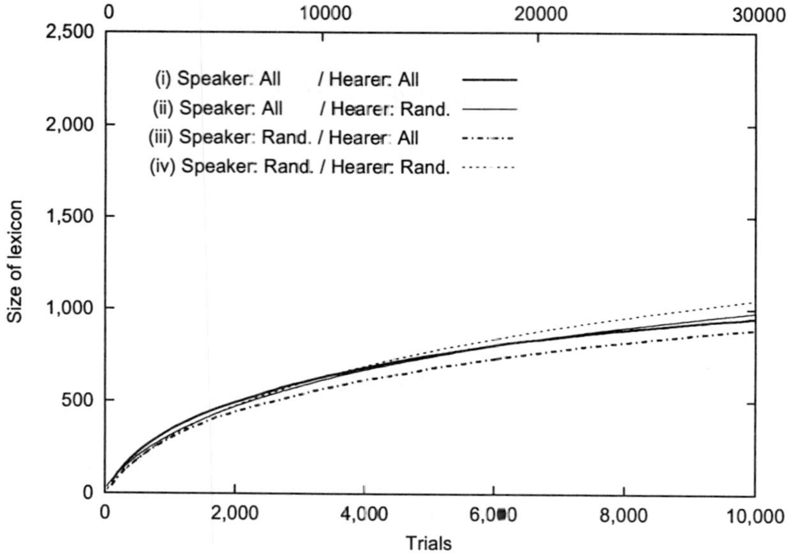

Fig. 12. Additional experiment for symbol creation: (b) Size of lexicon

References

1. F. Saussure, "Saussure's First Course of Lectures on General Linguistics," Pergamon Press (1996).
2. B. McLennan, "Synthetic Ethology: An Approach to the Study of Communication," in *Artificial Life II*, Addison-Wesley Pub. pp. 631-658 (1991).
3. L. Steels, "Perceptually grounded meaning creation," in *Proceedings of the International Conference on Multi-Agent Systems*, AAAI Press pp. 338-344 (1996)
4. L. Steels, "Emergent Adaptive Lexicons," in *Proceedings of the 4th Simulation of Adaptive Behavior Conference*, The MIT Press, Cambridge, Ma. (1996).
5. L. Steels, "Constructing and Sharing Perceptual Distinctions," in *Proceedings of the European Conference on Machine Learning* (1997).
6. L. Steels and P. Vogt, "Grounding adaptive language games in robotic," in *Proceedings of ECAL 97*, The MIT Press, Cambridge, Ma. (1997).
7. G. Werner and M. Dyer, "Evolution of Communication in Artificial Organisms," in *Artificial Life II*, Addison-Wesley Pub. pp. 659-687 (1991).

CHAPTER 39

SEARCH OF STEADY-STATE GENETIC ALGORITHMS FOR VISION-BASED MOBILE ROBOTS

Naoyuki Kubota[1,2] and Masayuki Kanemaki[1]

[1] *Dept. of Human and Artificial Intelligent Systems, Fukui University*
3-9-1 Bunkyo, Fukui 910-8507, Japan
E-mail: kubota@iicx.ia.his.fukui-u.ac.jp
[2] *"Interaction and Intelligence," PRESTO,*
Japan Science and Technology Agency

This chapter discusses the searching capability of genetic algorithms for vision-based mobile robots from the viewpoints of ecological psychology. The perceptual system of a mobile robot is restricted by the action system in the spatio-temporal context of the facing environment. In this chapter, we propose a time-series of a searching method in the visual perception according to the current situation and action outputs. Furthermore, we show several experimental results of two different mobile robots.

1. Introduction

Robotic systems have been applied to various fields such as manufacturing systems, building industry, aerospace development, and human society so far. The term of robotics refers to the study and use of robots. M.Brady defined robotics as the intelligent connection of perception to action.[1] Here a robot, which can acquire and apply knowledge or skill, is called intelligent. To build an intelligent robot, various methodologies have been developed by simulating human behaviors and by analyzing human brains.[2-3] Particularly, world modeling, problem solving, and task planning have been discussed mainly in robotics based on classical artificial intelligence (AI). On the other hand, methods of computational intelligence (CI) including neural, fuzzy, and evolutionary computing have been also applied to robotics. In general, classical AI aims to construct intelligence based on top-down approach of external description. In contrast with classical AI, CI aims to construct intelligence from the viewpoints of biology, evolution, and self-organization, mainly using bottom-up approach of internal description.[25] As one stream of evolutionary computing, genetic algorithms (GAs) have been effectively used for optimization problems in robotics.[18-21] A GA can obtain a feasible solution, not necessarily an optimal one, with less computational cost. The main role of GAs in robotics is the optimization in modeling or problem-solving. In fact, the optimization based on GAs can be divided into three approaches of a direct use, machine learning, and genetic programming.[17] The direct use is often seen in applications to the numerical optimization and the combinatorial optimization for tuning control parameters and for obtaining knowledge and strategies. The machine learning is mainly used for optimizing a set of inference rules in autonomous robots. Finally, genetic programming is applied for obtaining computer programs that realize complicated behaviors or tasks. In this way, GAs have been used for various problems in robotics.

On the other hand, R.Brooks proposed the subsumption architecture as a new control methodology for robots.[5] In the subsumption architecture, a robotic behavior is described directly as a coupling of sensory inputs and action outputs without generating its complete world model.[5] The agent design is decomposed into behaviors based on robotic objectives such as obstacle avoiding, photo tracing, and map building. This kind of approach is called behavior-based robotics.[6] The behavior-based robotics realizes a real-time control based on reactive behaviors, but sensory inputs are directly used as perceptual information in calculating action outputs. In general, a perceptual system can't extract all features of the object, but picks up specific information of the object according to the spatio-temporal context of the facing environment. Accordingly, the perceptual system must search for meaningful information from the current sensing information within a limited time. Therefore, we have proposed the concept of perception-based robotics.[26] The search of the perceptual system is similar to the search of GAs. In this chapter, we apply steady-state genetic algorithms for the perceptual system of vision-based mobile robots. Next, we show several experimental results of vision-based mobile robots.

2. Perception-Based Robotics

2.1 *Vision-Based Mobile Robots*

In this study, we use two different types of vision-based mobile robots. Fig. 1 shows the appearance of soccer robots. Each robot is provided with a wireless CCD camera. The size of this mobile robot is about 230 × 320 × 200 [mm]. The wireless control system for this robot is simply extended by connecting a host computer to the remote controller for a wireless toy car. Accordingly, an image from the robot is sent to the host computer by wireless. Fig. 2 shows an image sent from the wireless CCD camera. The body from the wireless CCD camera is seen in a lower part of the image. The image includes much noise owing to bad conditions of communication. The motor outputs are sent to the mobile robot by way of the remote controller. Here the signals of motor outputs are "go straight", "go back", " "turn right", "turn left", and "neutral". Therefore, the robot is controlled like a bang-bang control without speed control. Therefore, the speed of the robot is controlled by the interval between signals. The maximal speed is relatively fast. To summarize, it is very difficult to control the mobile robot owing to its discrete restricted control signals and bad communication conditions of the wireless CCD camera.

Fig.1. Vision-based soccer robots. Each robot is provided with a wireless CCD camera

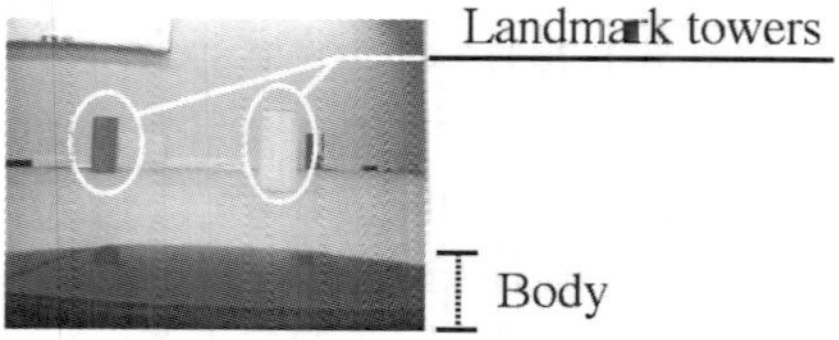

Fig.2. An image sent from the mobile robot. An image includes the body of the robot

The other robot, ActiveMedia Robotics Pioneer 2, is shown in Fig.3. Basically, this robot was developed for illuminance measurement. This robot is provided with 8 ultrasonic sensors and 2 encoders. Since the sensors and actuators are connected with the Hitachi H8 CPU board in the robot, sensory inputs are sent to the host computer through H8. Furthermore, the robot is provided with an omnidirectional sensor (Fig.3). An images from the omnidirectional sensory is taken directly into the host computer. Therefore, the host computer decides motor outputs according to the image and other sensory inputs. The robot takes collision avoiding and target tracing behaviors according to the distance to obstacles measured by ultrasonic sensors and the direction of the target point calculated as the result of image processing, respectively. In order to calculate motor outputs, fuzzy controllers are used for the behaviors.[25]

Basically, the basic task of both robots is to detect a ball or a landmark tower (see Fig. 1 and Fig. 4). Afterward, the robot decides to trace or avoid it. In the following, we discuss the perceptual system for these robots to detect some specific objects.

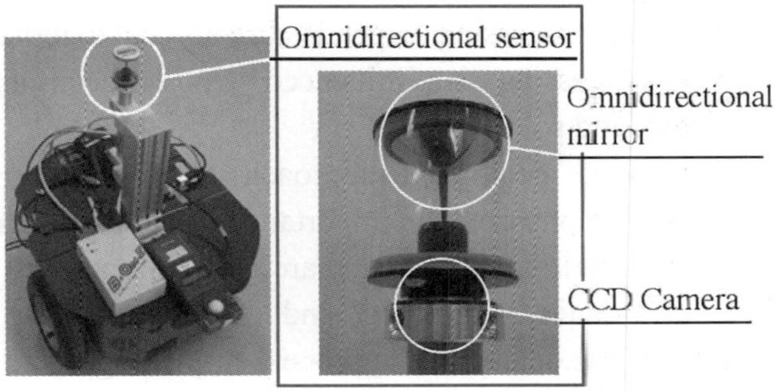

Fig.3. A mobile robot for illuminance measurement. This robot is provided with various sensors

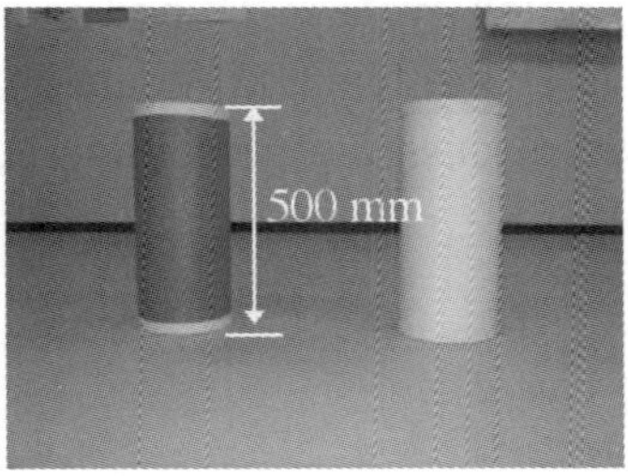

Fig.4. Landmark towers for target tracing and collision avoiding behaviors

2.2. *Perceptual Systems*

To build a perceptual system of a robot, we should take recent works of psychology into account, especially, sensation, perception and attention. Sensation is the basic information presented to our sense organs, while perception is organized and involves a process of attaching meaning to sensations. Furthermore, W.James emphasized the importance of selective attention in the following[13]: "*Millions of items of the outward order are present to my senses which never enter into my experience. ... My experience is what I agree to attend to. Only those items which I notice shape my mind*". The research of selective attention leads to the problem of figure-ground organization. Visual perception is organized into a central object called *figure* and its blurred surroundings called *ground*. Our visual system operates in a flexible and adaptive manner to perceive the facing environment by using bottom-up and top-down processes. Bottom-up processing depends directly on external stimuli, while top-down processing is influenced by expectations, stored knowledge, context, and so on.[13]

J.Gibson developed ecological approach to visual perception.[10] Ecological approach emphasizes the importance of perception and action interacting with an environment. There are many important concepts, *e.g.*, invariant, affordance, resonance, and perceiving-acting cycle in ecological approach. Resonance is the process of picking up or detecting invariant information in the visual environment. Affordance refers to the property of an object that can be perceived in an environment including a perceptual entity. Accordingly, the resonance enables us to pick up affordance. Perceiving-acting cycle is defined as a continuous process of perception and action in spatio-temporal context of the environment. In the next subsection, we discuss the perceiving-acting cycle for vision-based mobile robots.

2.3. *Perceiving-Acting Cycle*

We have discussed the importance of the coupling of perceptual system and action system.[24] A perceptual system generates perceptual information to be used for making action outputs. Here the importance is to extract perceptual information for persisting a series of motions to take an intentional action. Therefore, the perceptual system must search for perceptual information required by a specific action. Fig. 5 shows an example of a coupling of perceptual system and action system. These pictures show several sequential snapshots from the view of a person driving a car. His aim is to turn left in this road. First, the perceptual system picks up a white straight line in an image in order to drive the car straightly (Fig.5 (a)). And then, the position of the line makes him control the steering angle of the car. At the same time, the position is controlled in order to make the white line located in a specific position of an image in order for the perceptual system to extract the white line easily. Next, the perceptual system finds a signpost (Fig.5 (b)). This signpost indicates the crossing point. He picks up the white curve from the image and drives the car along the curve (Fig.5 (c)). In this way, he drives the car according to the time series of perceptual information. However, there exist many types of perceptual information that can be extracted in a single image to take an action (Fig.5 (d)). For example, there is another white line in the right side or a signpost in the center of the image shown in Fig.5 (d) to make the driver control a car. Thus, various types of information can navigate us to a specific action, but the perceptual system can not extract all of them at the same time. Because a specific perception takes a finite time, only a specific information is extracted through the cyclic process of perception and action. Therefore, the perception can be considered as a searching mechanism of perceptual information to be navigated in a facing environment. Accordingly, a perceptual module for extracting a specific information required by a specific action is selected according to the current state of the environment.

(a) White straight-line detection

(b) Landmark detection

(c) White curve detection

(d) Possible perceptual information

Fig.5. An example of a coupling of perceptual system and action system

Consequently, the perceptual system does not construct a complete world model, but makes ready beforehand for a next specific perception. In addition, the output of the action system constructs the spatio-temporal context for a specific perception with the dynamics of the environment. To summarize, the perceptual system and the action system restrict each other through the interaction with the facing environment. In ecological psychology, this is called perceiving-acting cycle.[11,12] The perception-based robotics emphasizes the importance of a perceptual system for the perceiving-acting cycle. Fig. 6 shows the coupling of perceptual system and action system in the perception-based robotics. Each module of perception system or action system is a specific perception module or action module. When the perceiving-acting cycle forms a coherent relationship with the environment, the specific perceptual information generates the specific action outputs like reactive motions. In this view, this approach includes the concept of behavior-based robotics, but the perceptual modules are selected according to the current state of the environment.

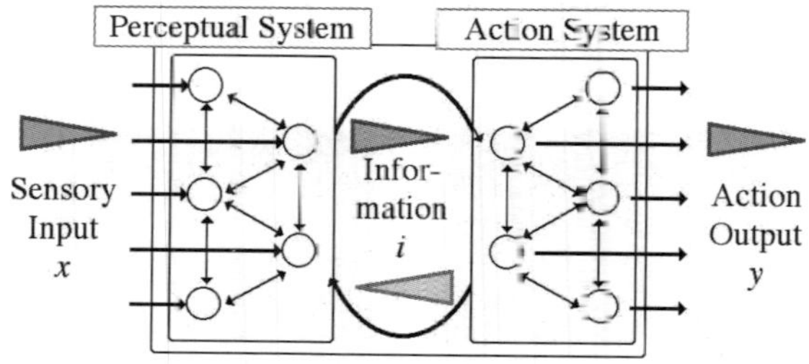

Fig.6. The coupling of perceptual system and action system; A circle indicates a specific module; Arrows indicate the information flows

3. A Steady-State Genetic Algorithm for A Visual System

3.1. *A Steady-State Genetic Algorithm*

As mentioned before, the perception is defined as a process of extracting or searching for information from a facing environment. We apply a steady-state genetic algorithm (SSGA) for extracting perceptual information. The SSGA simulates the continuous model of the generation, which eliminates and generates a few individuals in a generation (iteration). A candidate solution (individual) is composed of numerical parameters of the position and size of a landmark ($g_{i,1}$ $g_{i,2}$ $g_{i,3}$).

In case of a ball detection, we use the following equation approximated as a circle,

$$(g_{i,1}-x)^2+(g_{i,2}-y)^2= g_{i,3}^{\ 2} \tag{1}$$

where i indicates the individual number (Fig. 7). In the SSGA, only a few existing solutions are replaced by new candidate solutions generated by genetic operators in each generation.[22] The worst candidate solution is eliminated and replaced with the candidate solution generated by the crossover and mutation. We use elitist crossover and adaptive mutation to aim the efficient and quick search. The elitist crossover generates an individual by incorporating genetic information from the randomly selected individual and the best individual. Next, the following adaptive mutation is performed to the generated individual,

$$g_{i,j} \leftarrow g_{i,j} + \left(\alpha_j \cdot \frac{fit_{\max} - fit_i}{fit_{\max} - fit_{\min}} + \beta_j \right) \cdot N(0,1) \tag{2}$$

where f_i is the fitness value of the i-th individual, $f_{\max}$ and $f_{\min}$ are the maximum and minimum of fitness values in the population; α_j and β_j are the coefficient and offset, respectively. In the adaptive mutation, the variance of the normal random number is relatively changed according to the fitness values of the population. A fitness value is calculated by the following equation,

$$fit_i = C_{LT} - p \cdot C_{Other} \tag{3}$$

where p is a coefficient for penalty, C_{LT} and C_{other} indicate the number of pixels of the color corresponding to a landmark tower and other colors, respectively. Therefore, this problem results in the maximization problem.

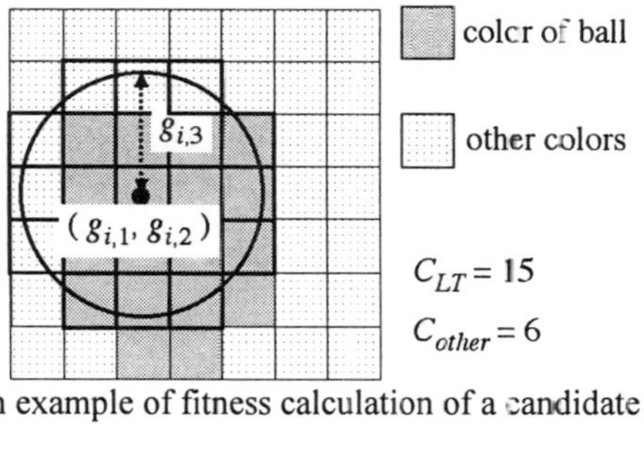

Fig.7. An example of fitness calculation of a candidate solution

3.2. *Ball Detection Based on Perceiving-Acting Cycle*

The above subsection described how to detect a ball in a single image, but the soccer robot must continue to detect the ball. The position of the detected ball and the attention range in the next image can be predicted because the geometrical relationship between two images is generated by the speed of the robot and the change of the position of the object (Fig.8). Here the attention range indicates the search space in an image by the SSGA. The robot can use the approximated velocity and acceleration of the detected ball,

$$\left(v_x(t), v_y(t)\right) = \left(x_B(t) - x_B(t-1), y_B(t) - y_B(t-1)\right) \tag{4}$$

$$\left(a_x(t), a_y(t)\right) = \left(v_x(t) - v_x(t-1), v_y(t) - v_y(t-1)\right) \tag{5}$$

where $(p_x(t), p_y(t))$, $(v_x(t), v_y(t))$, and $(a_x(t), a_y(t))$ are the estimated position, velocity, and acceleration of the ball on the image. If the acceleration is limited within a small range, the position in the next image can be predicted. Therefore, the candidate solutions of the next search by using SSGA are not randomly initialized, but are updated according to $(v_x(t), v_y(t))$ as follows,

$$\begin{aligned} g_{i,1} &\leftarrow g_{i,1} + \left(\alpha_1 \cdot \frac{fit_{\max} - fit_j}{fit_{\max} - fit_{\min}} + \beta_1\right) \cdot N(0,1) + v_x(t) \\ g_{i,2} &\leftarrow g_{i,2} + \left(\alpha_2 \cdot \frac{fit_{\max} - fit_j}{fit_{\max} - fit_{\min}} + \beta_2\right) \cdot N(0,1) + v_y(t) \end{aligned} \tag{6}$$

Furthermore, the center (X,Y), width (W), and height (H) of the attention range is also updated as follows,

$$\begin{aligned} X &\leftarrow X + v_x(t) \\ Y &\leftarrow Y + v_y(t) \end{aligned} \tag{7}$$

$$\begin{cases} W \leftarrow W \cdot \gamma & \\ H \leftarrow H \cdot \gamma & \text{if} \quad a_x^2 + a_y^2 < \Gamma \\ W \leftarrow W / \gamma & \\ H \leftarrow H / \gamma & \text{otherwise} \end{cases} \tag{8}$$

where γ satisfies $0<\gamma<1.0$ and Γ is a coefficient. At the initial state, the attention range is the same as the size of an image. If the robot detects a ball and the acceleration of the ball is small, the attention range is gradually reduced. Otherwise, the attention range is extended.

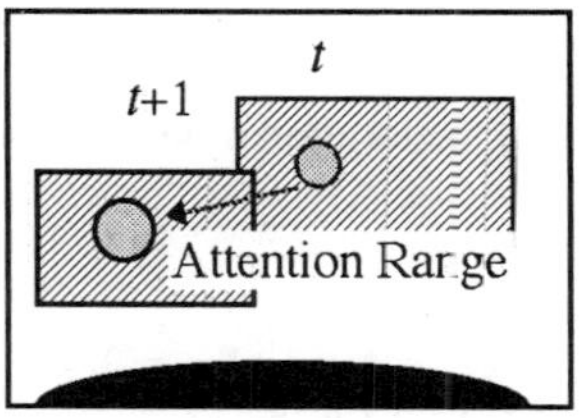

Fig.8. The change of a ball position from the viewpoint of the robot

3.3. *Landmark Detection and Self-location Estimation*

The robot with the omnidirectional sensor can estimate the self-location by using the angles among landmark towers. In this study, we use three landmark towers of red, green, and blue. Let P, A, B, and C be the position of the robot, the centers of red, green, and blue landmark towers, respectively. The coordinate axes are defined as Fig.9. First, we make two circles satisfying that A, B, and P are on the circle O_1, and B, C, and P are on the circle O_2. Next, let D be the crossing point of the line passing through B and O_1, and let E be the crossing point of the line passing through B and O_2. Because the robot can obtain the directions of A, B, and C according to the result of image processing, the robot can know the angles $\angle BPA = \angle BDA = \theta_1$ and $\angle BPC = \angle BEC = \theta_2$. Let (x_A, y_A), (x_B, y_B), (x_C, y_C), (x_D, y_D), (x_E, y_E), and (x_P, y_P) be the points of A, B, C, D, E, and P. To simplify this problem, we restrict the moving range of the robot into $x_A<x_P<x_C$, and $y_A<y_P$. Accordingly we can obtain the following equations,

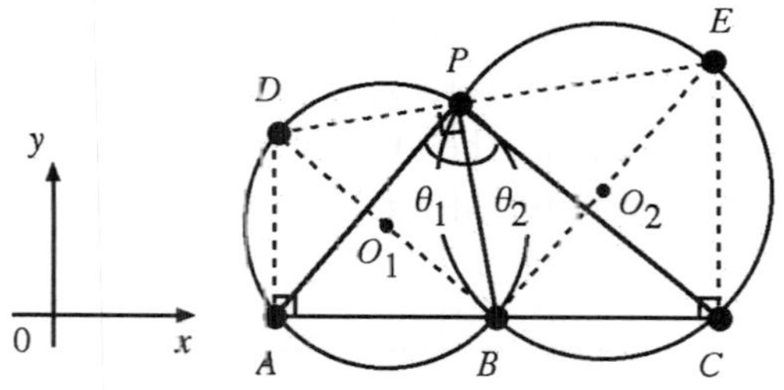

Fig.9. Geometrical relationship of the location of the landmark towers (A, B, and C) and a mobile robot (P)

$$y_D = y_B + \frac{x_B - x_D}{\tan\theta_1} \tag{9}$$

$$y_E = y_B + \frac{x_E - x_B}{\tan\theta_2} \tag{10}$$

Furthermore, we can obtain the coordinate of the robot by using the similar relationship of the quadrilaterals ABPD and PECB,

$$x_P = \frac{x_C \tan\theta_1}{\tan\theta_1 + \tan\theta_2} \tag{11}$$

$$y_P = \frac{(x_C - x_B)\tan\theta_1}{\tan\theta_2(\tan\theta_1 + \tan\theta_2)} \tag{12}$$

In this way, the robot can estimate the position relative to the landmark towers. However, the robot should use several images owing to noise of the images. Therefore, after the robot performs the estimation of the self-location several times, and the robot decides the self-location.

4. Experiments

This section shows experimental results of three application examples by the vision-based mobile robot using SSGA. First, we show an experimental result of the soccer robot. The number of individuals is 200, and the number of evaluations is 2000. Fig. 10 shows a preliminary experimental result of ball tracking by SSGA where a blue ball is rolling from the right to the left. In the figure, a white box indicates the attention range as the search space by SSGA, and a red circle indicates the best individual of the SSGA in each image. This experimental result shows that SSGA can detect the ball and track it with updating the attention range. Next, Fig.11 shows an experimental result of ball tracking of the soccer robot by SSGA. First of all, the robot goes backward to search a ball (Fig.11 (1)). After the robot detects the ball (Fig.11 (2)), the robot moves toward the ball (Fig.11 (3)-(5)). Finally, the robot kicks the ball and turns right (Fig.11 (6)). The attention range is automatically updated according to the previous search result of the SSGA.

(1) (2) (3) (4)

Fig.10. A preliminary experimental result of ball tracking by SSGA

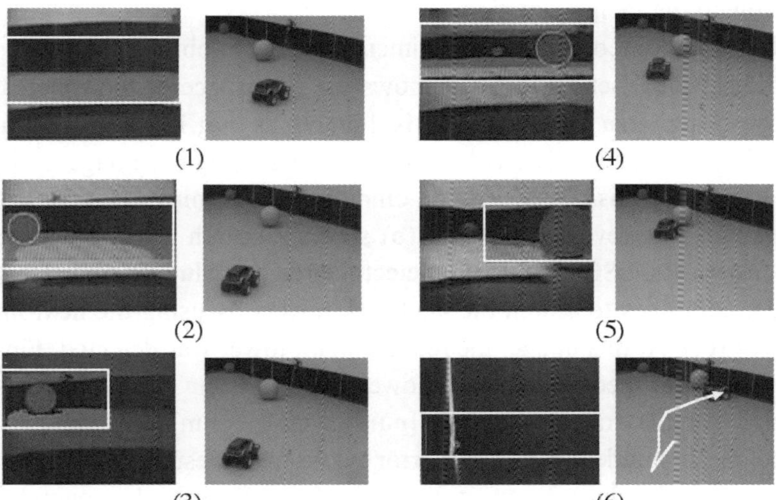

(1) (4) (2) (5) (3) (6)

Fig.11. An experimental result of ball tracking of the soccer robot by SSGA

Furthermore, we conducted another experiment of the soccer robot.[27] Here a task of the robot is to find a landmark tower and to move toward it. After the robot approaches it enough, the robot avoids collision with it. Therefore, the behaviors of the robot include target searching, target tracing, and collision avoiding. In order to detect a landmark tower, we use the center of landmark tower ($g_{i,1}$, $g_{i,2}$), and the magnifying rate of the landmark ($g_{i,3}$), because the ratio of width to height of the landmark is known. Fig. 12 shows an experimental result of the behavior selection of the mobile robot based on the search of SSGA. The left side figures show the sequence of the detected landmark towers in the actual run of the mobile robot. The right side figures show the sequence of the snapshots of the mobile robot from the outside observation. In Fig.12 (1), the landmark tower in the left side of the image is considered as a target. Afterward, the target is changed into an obstacle to be avoided when a robot approaches within the range dependent on the speed of the robot. In Fig.12 (2), after collision avoidance with the obstacle, the robot recognizes a landmark tower in right side as a next target. Furthermore, the robot detects a yellow landmark tower, and traces (Fig.12 (3)). In this way, the robot passes through all landmark towers by selecting behaviors suitable to the facing situation.

Finally, we conducted experiments of the mobile robot with the omnidirectional sensor. Fig. 13 shows the workspace of the robot. Here the working area of the robot is limited as Fig.13. Fig. 14 shows experimental results. The color condition of an original image is not so good, because this sensor uses an omnidirectional mirror (Fig.14 (a)). A taken image is reversed. Fig. 14 (b) shows a search result of landmark towers, but the SSGA could not detect the red and blue landmark towers. SSGA continues to search the landmark towers by using the next image (Fig.14 (c)). At this image, the red landmark tower was detected. Finally, the SSGA detected all landmark towers (Fig.14 (d)). The estimated self-location of the robot is x_p=3478[mm], y_p=2494[mm] according to the detected landmark towers. The error between the estimated values and the measured values is Δx_p =-22[mm], Δy_p =-6[mm]. In general, The detection of landmark towers is failed when the color condition of images is bad, but the proposed method can detect the landmark towers under such a condition by using several images. Of course, it is very difficult to detect landmark towers when a landmark tower in an image is buried in the background. However, the robot can move to another position to take a good image. This indicates the robot can take an action for persisting a specific perception. This idea is also based on the concept of active vision. In this way, the robot can estimate the self-location by using the searching result of SSGA.

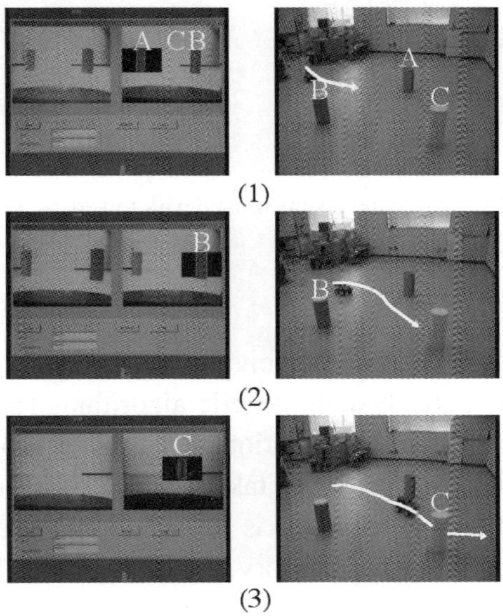

Fig.12. An experimental result of the mobile robot in a workspace including several landmark towers

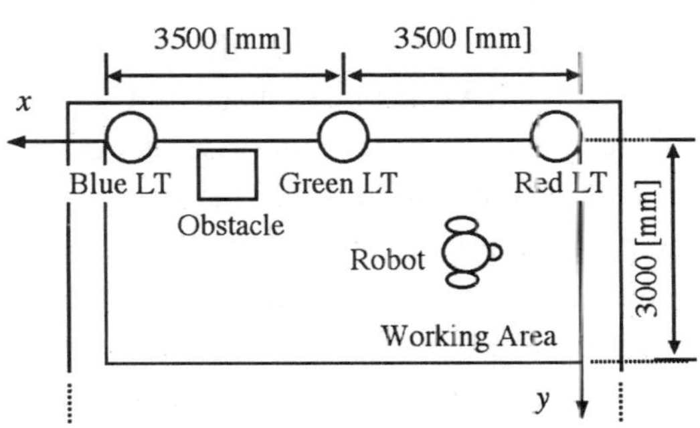

Fig.13. An experimental environment including landmark towers (LT) and obstacle

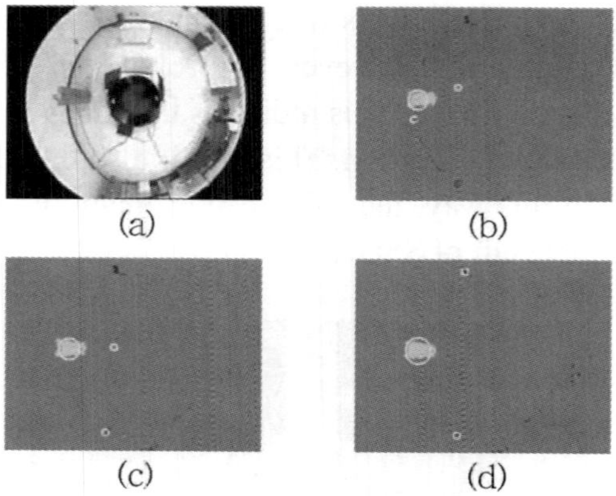

Fig.14. Extraction results of landmark towers by SSGA

5. Summary

This chapter discussed the perceiving-acting cycle of vision-based mobile robots using steady-state genetic algorithms (SSGA). An image includes various types of information to navigate robotic actions, but specific information is selected to take a series of actions according to the facing situation. Perception is a searching process to extract perceptual information from sensory inputs, and the SSGA plays the important role in searching specific information within finite time. This chapter applied the proposed method of the SSGA to three different problems. Experimental results show that the SSGA can detect target objects efficiently, and the obtained best solution can be useful for the next search by the SSGA. In general, the maintenance of genetic diversity in the search by GAs has been discussed for the global search, but this chapter discussed that the increase or decrease of genetic diversity in the next search should be performed according to the correctness of the prediction in change of the time-series of images. The interaction between perception and action generates the interrelation of the robot and the environment, while the interrelation restricts perception and action. Thus, the robot and its environment construct a coupling structure.

As future works, we intend to propose the learning algorithm for the coupling mechanism of perceptual system and action system.

Furthermore, we intend to integrate various image processing methods as perceptual system.

References

1. M.Brady and R.Paul, Robotics Research, *The First International Symposium*, (Massachusetts, The MIT Press, 1984).
2. S.J.Russell and P.Norvig, *Artificial Intelligence*, (Prentice-Hall, Inc., 1995).
3. J. M. Zurada, R. J. Marks II, C. J. Robinson (eds.), *Computational Intelligence - Imitating Life* (IEEE Press, 1994).
4. J.-S.R.Jang, C.-T.Sun, E.Mizutani, *Neuro-Fuzzy and Soft Computing* (Prentice-Hall, Inc., 1997).
5. R.A.Brooks, *Cambrian Intelligence* (The MIT Press, 1999).
6. R.C.Arkin, *Behavior-Based Robotics* (The MIT Press, 1998).
7. R.Pfeifer and C.Scheier, *Understanding Intelligence* (The MIT Press, 1999).
8. V.Braitenberg, *Vehicles* (Cambridge, MA, MIT Press 1984).
9. U. Neisser, *Cognition and reality* (W.H.Freeman and Company, 1976).
10. James Gibson, *The Ecological Approach to Visual Perception* (Houghton Miffilin Company, 1979).
11. M.T.Turvey and R.E.Shaw, Ecological Foundations of Cognition I. Symmetry and Specificity of Animal-Environment Systems, *Journal of Consciousness Studies* 6, No.11-12, pp.95-110, 1999.
12. R.E.Shaw and M.T.Turvey, Ecological Foundations of Cognition II. Degree of Freedom and Conserved Quantities in Animal-Environment Systems, *Journal of Consciousness Studies* 6, No.11-12, pp.111-123, 1999.
13. Michael Eysenck, Perception and Attention, *Psychology* (edited by Michael Eysenck), Prentice Hall, pp.139-166, 1998.
14. S.Nolfi and D.Floreano, *Evolutionary Robotics* (The MIT Press, 200[illegible]).
15. Y.Davidor, A genetic Algorithm Applied to Robot Trajectory Generation, *Handbook of Genetic Algorithms*, Van Nostrand Reinhold, pp.144-165 (1991)
16. J.Xiao, Z.Michalewicz, L.Zhang and K.Trojanowski, Adaptive Evolutionary Planner/Navigator for Mobile Robots, *IEEE Trans. on Evolutionary Computation*, Vol.1, No.1, pp.18-28 (1998)
17. T.Fukuda, N.Kubota, and T.Arakawa: GA Algorithms in Intelligent Robots, *Fuzzy Evolutionary Computation*, Kluwer Academic Publishers, pp.81-105 (1997)
18. D.B.Fogel: *Evolutionary Computation* (IEEE Press, 1995)
19. J.Holland: *Adaptation in Natural and Artificial Systems* (Ann Arbor: University of Michigan Press, 1975)
20. D.E.Goldberg: *Genetic Algorithms in Search, Optimization, and Machine Learning* (Addison Welsey, 1989)
21. M.Mitchell, *An Introduction to Genetic Algorithms* (The MIT Press, 1996)
22. G.Syswerda, A Study of Reproduction in Generational and Steady-State Genetic Algorithms, *Foundations of Genetic Algorithms*, Morgan Kaufmann, pp.94-101, 1991.

23. N.Kubota, T.Morioka, F.Kojima, and T.Fukuda, Learning of Mobile Robots Using Perception-Based Genetic Algorithm, *Measurement*, No.29, pp.237-248, 2001.
24. N.Kubota, H.Masuta, F.Kojima and T.Fukuda, Perceptual System and Action System of A Mobile Robot with Structured Intelligence, *The 2002 IEEE World Congress on Computational Intelligence*, 2002.
25. N.Kubota and T.Fukuda, Sensory Network for Mobile Robotic System with Structured Intelligence, *Journal of Robotic and Mechatronics*, Vol.10, No.4 (1998).
26. T.Fukuda and N.Kubota, An Intelligent Robotic System Based on A Fuzzy Approach, *Proceedings of The IEEE*, Vol.87, No.9, pp.1448-1470 (1999).
27. N.Kuobta and M.Kanemaki, Search in Perceiving-Acting Cycle for A Vision-Based Mobile Robot, *The Second International Conference on Computational Intelligence, Robotics, and Autonomous Systems*, 2003.

CHAPTER 40

TIME SERIES FORECAST WITH ELMAN NEURAL NETWORKS AND GENETIC ALGORITHMS

LiXin Xu[*], Zhao Yang Dong[**], and Arthur Tay[***]

[*]*Department of Automatic Control, Beijing Institute of Technology Beijing 100081, China*

[**]*School of Information Technology and Electrical Engineering The University of Queensland, St Lucia, QLD 4072, Australia*

[***]*Department of Electrical and Computer Engineering National University of Singapore, Singapore*

This chapter investigates into recursive neural networks and their application in time series forecast. As one of the most popular recurrent neural networks, an Elman neural network is studied in this chapter. It has been proven that the Elman network is able to approximate the trajectory of a given dynamic system for any fixed length of time. This ability is explored in the area of time series forecasting. The electricity market demand signal, as a typical time series, is studied in the chapter with Elman networks. In order to obtain the best available optimal weight allocation, a Genetic Algorithm (GA) is used to train the recurrent neural networks in the forecast model. The forecast simulation is carried out on electricity market load data series with Elman networks as well as GA trained Elman networks to compare their performance.

1. Introduction

Time series forecast is traditionally based on linear models that are easy to implement, but often fail to give satisfactory results when dealing with nonlinear, non-stationary time series. Neural networks have been used to deal with the nonlinearity in time series forecast with good results. Many of the real world time series are the performance indicators of dynamic systems. There are often hidden, complex correlations among different time series data points. Feed-forward neural networks are able to approximate the complex nonlinear behavior of the time series, but they are subject to impact of external noises [1]. The recurrent networks are less affected by external noise, and are more appropriate to capture the dynamic natures of the series.

An Elman neural network, as a local recurrent neural network, was first proposed by Elman [2] to solve language problems. Since then it has been applied widely in the fields of identification, prediction and control. In this Chapter, the dynamic property of Elman network is explored and applied in the field of time series forecast, aimed at capturing the complex, nonlinear correlations among the time series to enhance the forecast accuracy.

Under the deregulated power industry in the form of electricity market, the role of load and price forecast is becoming more and more important. The electricity market manager relies on accurate load forecast to make critical decisions on operation and expansion planning issues in the power system. The market participants also heavily relay on market forecast on both demand and price to formulate business strategies and to remain competitive. As a typical time series, the demand data series is used to test the Elman network.

The aim of short term load forecast is to predict future electricity demands based, traditionally, on historical data and predicted weather conditions [3, 4, 5]. The aim of electricity market price forecast is to provide market participants with price signal in the future so as to help them maximize their returns by optimized operational planning based on such signals [6]. Price signals also have interactive impact on market demand signals [7].

It is important to provide associated level of confidence accompanying the forecasted results. These are typically represented as forecast errors, which also have considerable implications for profits, market shares and ultimately shareholder value in the deregulated market [3]. There are many choices to select forecast error matrices [8, 9]. Absolute percentage error and mean square error are used in this Chapter [9].

2. Elman Neural Networks

In a recurrent neural network, the information flow can be in two directions via different connections, i.e. the feed forward and feedback connections. Consequently, the information, either training data or testing data, can be allowed to propagate from input neurons to output neurons and vice versa [1]. It had been proven that the locally recurrent neural network can approximate the trajectory of a given dynamical system for any fixed finite length of time, and *Elman* neural network is equal to the locally recurrent neural network in the approximation capability for a given dynamic system [10, 2].

2.1. *Locally Recurrent Neural Networks*

There are two types of recurrent neural networks: the discrete time recurrent neural networks and the continuous time recurrent neural networks. In this Chapter, the former is studied. The locally recurrent neural network is different from the fully connected recurrent neural network because there are only a few feedback connections. A new locally recurrent neural network structure is shown in Fig.1, where $\mathbf{x}_n(k) \in R^n$ is the state of the locally recurrent neural network and $\mathbf{u}(k)$ is the input of the locally recurrent neural network.

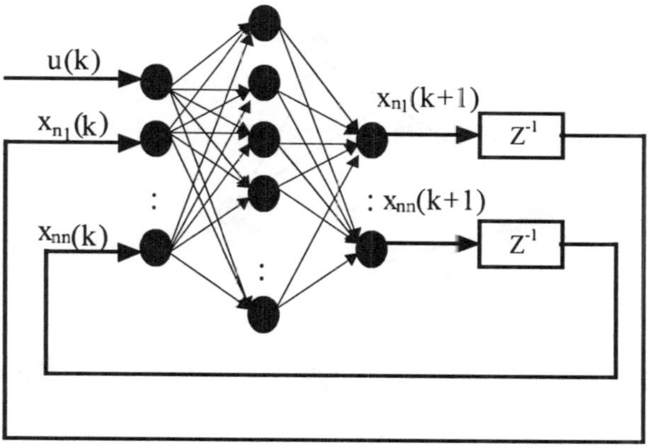

Fig. 1. The structure of a locally recurrent neural network

By defining

$$\mathbf{xu}_n(k) = \left[\mathbf{x}_n(k)^{\mathrm{T}} \middle| \mathbf{u}(k)^{\mathrm{T}} \right]^{\mathrm{T}} \tag{1}$$

the locally recurrent neural network can be expressed as:

$$\mathbf{x}_n(k+1) = \mathbf{A}\sigma(\mathbf{B}\mathbf{xu}_n(k) + \theta) \tag{2}$$

where **A, B** are weight matrixes with appropriate dimension, θ is the threshold vector and $\sigma : R^n \rightarrow R^n$ is a sigmoid mapping.

2.2. *Elman Neural Networks*

An Elman neural network model is shown in Fig.2, where $x_i^{(k)}$, $i=1, 2, \ldots, M$ is the input, and $y_j^{(k)}$, $j=1, 2, \ldots, N$ is the output. $W_{1i,j}$ is the connection weight between the input layer node i and the middle layer node j, $W_{2i,j}$ is the connection weight between the middle layer node i and the output layer node j, and $W_{3i,j}$ is the connection weight between the connection layer node i and the middle layer node j. In the Elman neural network, net_h_i and o_h_i are the input and output of the middle layer node i, net_c_i and o_c_i are the input and output of connection node i. The transfer function is a sigmoid function and L is the number of nodes in the connection layer. We have:

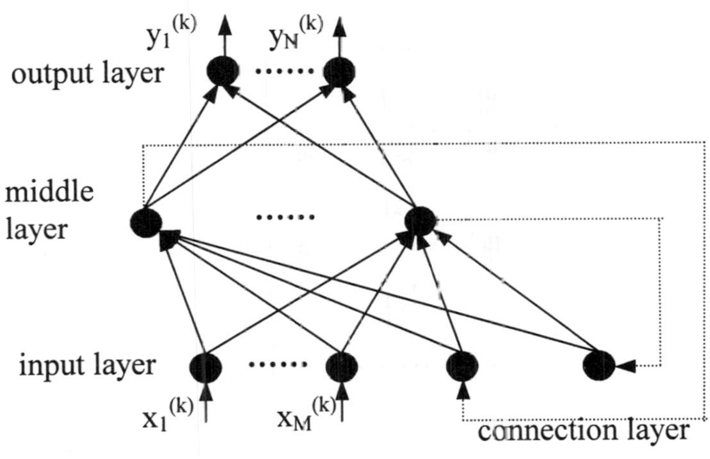

Fig. 2. The structure of an Elman neural network

$$y_j^{(k)} = \sum_{i=1}^{L} W_{2j,i} o\_h_i^{(k)} \tag{3}$$

$$o\_h_j^{(k)} = f(net\_h_j^{(k)}) = \sigma(net\_h_j^{(k)}) \tag{4}$$

$$net\_h_j^{(k)} = \sum_{i=1}^{M} W_{1j,i} x_i^{(k)} + \sum_{i=1}^{L} W_{3j,i} o\_c_i^{(k)} - W_{0j} \tag{5}$$

where $o\_c_i^{(k)} = o\_h_i^{(k-1)}$

$$\mathbf{y}^{(k)} = \mathbf{W}_2 \cdot \sigma(\mathbf{W}_1 \mathbf{x}^{(k)} + \mathbf{W}_3 \mathbf{o}^{(k-1)} + \mathbf{W}_0) \tag{6}$$

where

$$\mathbf{y}^{(k)} = \left[y_1^{(k)}, y_2^{(k)}, \cdots, y_N^{(k)} \right]^{\mathrm{T}} \tag{7}$$

$$\mathbf{x}^{(k)} = \left[x_1^{(k)}, x_2^{(k)}, \cdots, x_M^{(k)} \right]^{\mathrm{T}} \tag{8}$$

$$\mathbf{o}^{(k)} = \left[o\_h_1^{(k)}, o\_h_2^{(k)}, \cdots, o\_h_L^{(k)} \right]^{\mathrm{T}} \tag{9}$$

$\mathbf{W}_0$ is the threshold vector and $\mathbf{W}_{1L\times M}, \mathbf{W}_{2N\times L}, \mathbf{W}_{3L\times L}$ are weight matrices. For convenience, Equation (6) can be re-written as following

$$\mathbf{Y}(k) = \mathbf{W}_2 \cdot \sigma(\mathbf{W}_1 \mathbf{X}(k) + \mathbf{W}_3 \mathbf{O}(k-1) + \mathbf{W}_0) \tag{10}$$

2.3. *Properties of Elman Networks*

Consider a discrete, time-invariant, nonlinear dynamic system expressed by Eq. (11),

$$\mathbf{x}(k+1) = \phi(\mathbf{x}(k), \mathbf{u}(k)) \tag{11}$$

where $\mathbf{x}(k) \in R^n$ is the state and $\mathbf{u}(k) \in R^m$ is the input; for notational convenience define $\mathbf{xu}(k) \in R^{n+m}$, and

$$\mathbf{xu}(k) = \left[\mathbf{x}(k)^{\mathrm{T}} \middle| \mathbf{u}(k)^{\mathrm{T}} \right]^{\mathrm{T}} \tag{12}$$

then Eq. (11) can be written as:

$$\mathbf{x}(k+1) = \phi(\mathbf{xu}(k)) \tag{13}$$

The following two conditions are imposed for modeling (11):

1) $\phi(\mathbf{xu}(k)) \in \mathrm{k}$, for all $\mathbf{xu}(k) \in \mathrm{k}$;
2) $\phi(\mathbf{xu}(k))$ is continuous at all $\mathbf{xu}(k) \in \mathrm{k}_\eta$ for some $\eta > 0$, where

$$\mathrm{k}_\eta = \left\{ \mathbf{xu}(k) \in R^{n+m} \middle| \left| \mathbf{xu}(k) - \mathbf{z} \right| \leq \eta, \forall \mathbf{z} \in \mathrm{k} \right\} \tag{14}$$

and $\mathbf{k}$ is the compact subset, $|\cdot|$ is the norm of R^{n+m}. The k should include all $\mathbf{xu}(k) \in R^{n+m}$ for which approximations to $\phi(\mathbf{xu}(k))$ are designed. It is also necessary to suppose that ϕ is continuous on a set slightly larger than $\mathbf{k}$.

Lemma 1 [11] Let $\mathbf{k}$ be a compact subset of $\boldsymbol{R}^{\mathrm{n}}$, and $f : \mathrm{k} \to R^m$ be a continuous mapping, then for an arbitrary $\varepsilon > 0$ there exist an integer N, matrix $\mathbf{A}_{m\times N}$, $\mathbf{B}_{N\times n}$ and an N dimensional vector θ such that

$$\max_{\mathbf{x} \in k} \left| \mathbf{f}(x) - \mathbf{A}\sigma(\mathbf{Bx} + \theta) \right| < \varepsilon \tag{15}$$

holds, where $\sigma : R^n \to R^a$ is a sigmoid mapping.

Lemma 2 Let D be a compact subset of R^{n}, and Ω be a compact subset of R^{m}, $f(\mathbf{x},\mathbf{r}) : D \times \Omega \to R^n$ be a continuous mapping, then for an arbitrary $\varepsilon > 0$, there exist an integer N, matrix $\mathbf{A}_{n\times N}, \mathbf{B}_{N\times n}, \mathbf{C}_{N\times m}$ and an N dimensional vector θ such that

$$\max_{\mathbf{x} \in D, \mathbf{r} \in \Omega} \left| f(\mathbf{x},\mathbf{r}) - \mathbf{A}\sigma(\mathbf{Bx} + \mathbf{Cr} + \theta) \right| < \varepsilon \tag{16}$$

holds.

Proof: Let $\mathbf{x} \in D, \mathbf{r} \in \Omega$, then $\mathbf{y} = \begin{bmatrix} \mathbf{x} \\ \mathbf{r} \end{bmatrix} \in \tilde{k}$, and $\tilde{k}$ is a compact subset of $R^{n+\mathrm{m}}$ because D is a compact subset of R^{n} and Ω is a compact subset of R^{m}. $f(\mathbf{y}) : \tilde{k} \to R^n$ is a continuous function, by Lemma 1, for an arbitrary $\varepsilon > 0$, there exist an integer N, weight matrix $\mathbf{A}_{n\times N}$, $\mathbf{H}_{N\times(n+m)}$ and N dimensional vector θ such that

$$\max_{\mathbf{y} \in \tilde{k}} \left| f(\mathbf{y}) - \mathbf{A}\sigma(\mathbf{Hy} + \theta) \right| < \varepsilon \tag{17}$$

holds. H can be separated into two parts, $\mathbf{H} = \left[\mathbf{B} \middle| \mathbf{C} \right]$, where $\mathbf{B}_{N\times n}, \mathbf{C}_{N\times m}$, by the condition of $\mathbf{y} = [\mathbf{x}^{\mathrm{T}}, \mathbf{r}^{\mathrm{T}}]^{\mathrm{T}}$, clearly, Eq. (17) is equal to Eq. (16). Q.E.D.

Theorem 1 Given any $\varepsilon > 0$ and a fixed $N \in Z^+$, there exist weight matrix **A, B** and vector θ, under the same initial condition, such that

$$|\mathbf{x}(k) - \mathbf{x}_n(k)| < \varepsilon \qquad k \in [1, 2, \cdots, N] \tag{18}$$

where **x**(k) is the state of Eq. (11) and $\mathbf{x}_n(k)$ is the state of the locally recurrent neural network described by Eq. (2).

Proof: The basic idea for the proof is to start with the error permitted in the output, ε, and backwards [12]. At each time step, the error in the state is due to the approximation error in ϕ and in the previous state.

$$\begin{aligned} \mathbf{x}(k) - \mathbf{x}_n(k) &= \phi(\mathbf{xu}(k-1)) - \mathbf{A}\sigma(\mathbf{Bxu}_n(k-1) + \theta) \\ &= \phi(\mathbf{xu}(k-1)) - \phi(\mathbf{xu}_n(k-1)) \\ &\quad + \phi(\mathbf{xu}_n(k-1)) - \mathbf{A}\sigma(\mathbf{Bxu}_n(k-1) + \theta) \end{aligned} \tag{19}$$

$$\begin{aligned} |\mathbf{x}(k) - \mathbf{x}_n(k)| &\le |\phi(\mathbf{xu}(k-1)) - \phi(\mathbf{xu}_n(k-1))| \\ &\quad + |\phi(\mathbf{xu}_n(k-1)) - \mathbf{A}\sigma(\mathbf{Bxu}_n(k-1) + \theta)| \end{aligned} \tag{20}$$

Because ϕ is continuous in k_η and k_η is a compact subset, ϕ is uniform continuous in k_η, i.e. for an arbitrary $\xi_k > 0$, if $xu_n(k-1) \in \mathrm{k}_\eta$, such that

$$|\mathbf{xu}(k-1) - \mathbf{xu}_n(k-1)| < \delta_{k-1} \tag{21}$$

then there exists the following condition

$$|\phi(\mathbf{xu}(k-1)) - \phi(\mathbf{xu}_n(k-1))| < \xi_k / 2 \tag{22}$$

This creates a backward recursion in ξ_k from $k = N$ to 0. Let $\xi_k = \min\{\delta_k, \varepsilon, \eta\}$. By *lemma 2*, for $k \in [1, 2, \ldots, N]$, there exist **A, B**, θ, such that

$$|\phi(\mathbf{xu}_n(k-1)) - \mathbf{A}\sigma(\mathbf{Bxu}_n(k-1) + \theta)| < \frac{\xi}{2} = \min(\frac{\xi_k}{2}) \tag{23}$$

As a result, when $|\mathbf{x}(0) - \mathbf{x}_n(0)| < \delta_0$, there exist $\{\mathbf{A}, \mathbf{B}, \theta\}$ such that

$$|\mathbf{x}(k) - \mathbf{x}_n(k)| < \frac{\xi_k}{2} + \frac{\xi}{2} < \xi_k < \varepsilon \tag{24}$$

holds, where $k = [1,2,\cdots,N]$. It is easy to choose $\mathbf{x}(0)=\mathbf{x}_n(0)$ to satisfy $|x(0)-x_n(0)|<\delta_0$. Q.E.D.

Theorem 2 Consider a discrete-time nonlinear system:

$$\mathbf{Y}^*(k)=\phi(\mathbf{X}(k),\mathbf{Y}^*(k-1)) \tag{25}$$

where $\mathbf{X}(k)$ is the input vector and $\mathbf{Y}^*(k)$ is the state vector. Given any $\varepsilon > 0$ and a fixed $N_0 \in \mathbf{Z}^+$, there exists an Elman neural network as described by Eq. (10), under the same initial condition, such that

$$\left|\mathbf{Y}^*(k)-\mathbf{Y}(k)\right|<\varepsilon \qquad k\in[1,2,\cdots,N_0] \tag{26}$$

Proof: Consider the discrete-time nonlinear system

$$\mathbf{Y}^*(k)=\phi(\mathbf{X}(k),\mathbf{Y}^*(k-1)) \tag{27}$$

where $\mathbf{X}(k)\in R^M$,and $\mathbf{Y}^*(k)\in R^N$, then for an arbitrary chosen $\varepsilon>0$ and a fixed integer N_0, by *Theorem* 1, there exists a locally recurrent neural network as described by Eq. (2)

$$\mathbf{Y}(k)=\mathbf{A}\sigma(\mathbf{B}\cdot\mathbf{YX}(k-1)+\theta) \qquad \mathbf{Y}(k)\in R^N \tag{28}$$

where $\mathbf{YX}(k-1)=[\mathbf{X}(k)^{\mathrm{T}}\,|\,\mathbf{Y}(k-1)^{\mathrm{T}}]^{\mathrm{T}}$, such that

$$\left|\mathbf{Y}^*(k)-\mathbf{Y}(k)\right|<\varepsilon \qquad k\in[1,2,\cdots,N_0] \tag{29}$$

holds. Next task is to prove (28) is equal to (10). Let L be the number of hidden nodes of Eq. (28) and $\mathbf{A}_{N\times L},\mathbf{B}_{L\times(M+N)},\boldsymbol{\theta}_{L\times 1}$ be the weight matrix, where $\mathbf{B}$ can be rewritten as $\mathbf{B}=[\mathbf{B}_{1L\times M}\,|\,\mathbf{B}_{2L\times N}]$, then Eq. (28) can be expressed as:

$$\mathbf{Y}(k)=\mathbf{A}\sigma(\mathbf{B}_1\mathbf{X}(k)+\mathbf{B}_2\mathbf{Y}(k-1)+\theta) \tag{30}$$

By defining $\mathbf{P}(k)$ as the output of the hidden notes in the locally recurrent neural network in time k, $\mathbf{P}(k)=[P_1(k),P_2(k),\cdots,P_L(k)]^{\mathrm{T}}$, then

$$\mathrm{Y}(\tilde{\mathrm{k}}1)=\mathrm{AP}(\tilde{\mathrm{k}}1) \tag{31}$$

Combining Eqs. (31) and (30), we have

$$\mathbf{Y}(k)=\mathbf{A}\sigma(\mathbf{B}_1\mathbf{X}(k)+\mathbf{B}_2\mathbf{AP}(k-1)+\theta) \tag{32}$$

Obviously, Eq. (32) is equal to Eq. (10) if the number of nodes in the middle layer is the same as that of the hidden layer, so Eq. (28) is equal to Eq. (10).

As clearly indicated in Theorems 1 and 2, theoretically, Elman neural networks with all feedback connections from the hidden layer to the context layer set to 1 can represent any arbitrary n-th order system, where n is the number of context units[1]. In cases of time series forecast, especially electricity load, regional flow, and price data, the original data series can be very volatile, and some times more like random walk. Training of Elman network with back-propagation (BP) may experience difficulties in convergence. A Genetic Algorithm weight adjustment module is employed to enhance the learning ability of the Elman network used in time series forecast.

3. Genetic Algorithms

Given sufficient population size and iterations, Genetic Algorithms (GAs) are capable of locating the global optima. In the Chapter, GAs are used to search for the best available optimal solution for neural network weights. In the GA optimization process, individuals, or variables to be optimized, compete with each other; the strongest individuals survive and the weaker ones carry higher probabilities of dying off after a number of generations, or iterations. The survival ability is called fitness in GAs, and is associated with the objective function of the optimization problem. There are three major genetic operators including reproduction, crossover and mutation. The general search and optimization procedure for a typical GA is: (i) generating the initial population; (ii) evaluating fitness for all individuals in the current population; (iii) performing genetic operations based on the probability and the fitness values, and (iv) forming a new generation. The procedure is repeated from (ii) till some termination criterion is met and the optimum is thus obtained [13]. To enable the genetic optimization process, individuals to be evaluated need to be encoded in such a way where bits related to individuals fitness be copied and reproduced into next generation to form offspring of higher fitness. After genetic evaluation, they are decoded into the original coding system. There are several coding systems to cope with different optimization problems for better performance [14].

GA is used to optimally determine the weightings of the Elman neural network with training data. Several techniques are employed to speed up the search and increase the probability that the search leads to global optima, instead of being trapped by local optima.

Mutation probability is important in determining the diversity of the search, an adaptively adjusted mutation probability algorithm is used in the chapter. This is realized first by decreasing the mutation probability over all individuals in the generation with the increment of generation numbers, so to ensure the GA search diversity in the beginning and help the convergence into optima close to the end of search process, [15].

The second approach recalculates the individuals' mutation probability based on the fitness. Individuals with higher fitness values will have their probability decreased, and those with lower fitness values will have their probability increased. By doing so, the solutions can be mapped closer to the final global optimal point provided the best fitted individual is close to the global optimal point [16]. A simple exponential function can be used to achieve this effect. The mutation probability control function for the GA employed in this chapter takes the form:

$$P_m(i,\gamma) = P_m^0 \cdot e^{-\phi_i/\alpha} \cdot e^{-\gamma/\beta} \qquad (33)$$

where P_m is the mutation probability, which takes the initial value of P_m^0, ϕ_i is the fitness of the i-th individual, γ is the generation number, α and β are adjusting factors controlling the decreasing rate of P_m taking into consideration of fitness and generation number respectively.

In order to keep the best fitted individual during the search process, elitism is used such that the best individual survives into the next generation. The choice of population size is another important factor, There are rules regarding proper choice of population size [17].

4. Time Series Forecast with GA Enhanced Elman Neural Network

Time series forecast can be one step ahead or k-step ahead. The basic approach to realize such forecast with neural networks can be summarized as follows.

Suppose the series $\boldsymbol{Y}$ consists of N data points $\{y(1), y(2), \ldots y(N)\}$ as the training data set. For 1-step forecast, the data are used to train the network to predict the value at point n with the values at n-1, n–2, ... n–m, where $m<n \leq N$:

$$\hat{y}(n) = NN[y(n-1), y(n-2), \ldots, y(n-m)] \tag{34}$$

where $\hat{y}$ stands for predicted value, and y stands for real value.

For k-step ahead forecast the following steps are repeated:

$$\hat{y}(n) = NN[y(n-1), y(n-2), \ldots, y(n-m)] \tag{35}$$

$$\hat{y}(n+1) = NN[\hat{y}(n), y(n-1), \ldots, y(n-m+1)] \tag{36}$$

$$\hat{y}(n+k) = NN[\hat{y}(n+k-1), \ldots, y(n-m+k)] \tag{37}$$

The objective of Neural Network training is to minimize the errors of the NN output and the real values from the training data set. To convert this minimization problem into maximization problem for GA, the fitness function weight adjustment module is given as:

$$f = \frac{1}{\left|Y^{*}(k) - Y(k)\right| + \varepsilon} \tag{38}$$

where $|Y^{*}(k)–Y(k)|$ is the error between neural network output and the real data from the training set; and ε is a small positive constant number to avoid the singularity in the fitness function.

The irrelevant inputs degrade the forecast models performance, it is preferable to set the coefficients of irrelevant inputs to zero in a neural network based forecasting. This is not an easy task because there are some possible random correlations between the inputs and the output. Techniques of choosing a suitable input window size have been an interesting research topic and can be found [18–22]. These techniques can be used to select proper input window sizes for training of the networks in time series forecast.

The Automatic Relevance Determination (ARD) method [13, 20, 21] can be used to assist selection of a suitable input window size for training of the neural networks in time series forecasting. ARD is able to allocate the relevant inputs in respect to the distribution of the targets. It sets the irrelevant inputs' coefficients to zero by proper selection of a prior structure. Specifically, in the wavelet enhanced neural network forecast method, ARD is used to select a short term past window for higher sampling rates and a long term past window for lower sampling rates. The ARD method can be described by Eq. (39) provided a Gaussian function is used for each class,

$$P(\{w_i\}|\{\alpha_c\},H)=\frac{1}{\Pi Z_{W(c)}}\exp(-\sum_c \alpha_c E_{W(c)}) \tag{39}$$

where $E_{W(c)}=\sum_c w_i^2/2$ [18, 20, 21]. It is also useful is dealing with over fitting problems.

5. Enhanced Time Series Forecast with wavelet & Neural Networks

5.1. *Discrete Wavelet Transform*

Unlike Fourier transform a signal can be analyzed with Wavelet decomposition in both time and frequency domains. A function $f(t)$ can be expressed with a selected mother wavelet function ψ as

$$f(t)=\sum_{j=-\infty}^{\infty}\sum_{k=-\infty}^{\infty} w_{jk}2^{j/2}\psi(2^j t-k) \tag{40}$$

where the functions $\psi(2^j t\text{-}k)$ are all orthogonal to each other. The coefficient w_{jk} gives information about the behavior of the function f concentrating on the effects of scale around 2^{-j} near time $t\times 2^{-j}$, [23]. For signals observed in discrete time a similar decomposition – the discrete wavelet transform (DWT) can be used [23]. DWT provides a time and frequency representation of the signal. This is a very attractive feature in analyzing time series because time localization of spectral components can be obtained [23–25]. One of the characteristics of DWT is that many decomposition coefficients can be set to zero while still maintaining the information carried with the data. This is also valid for signals with occasional spikes or other dynamics. Traditional signal processing techniques, such as Fourier analysis, usually depend on an underlying notion of stationarity. The ability of handling signals with stationarity and transient properties makes DWT more appropriate than Fourier [23, 26, 25].

One problem with DWT is that it is not a time-invariant transform. The DWT of a translated version of a signal is not a translated version of the DWT of the signal [23–26]. The solution to restore the translation invariance is to use a redundant or non-decimated wavelet transform instead of the classical DWT. The *à trous* algorithm [26, 27] can be used to achieve such stationary or redundant transform.

5.2. *A Modified Algorithm Based on the À Trous Algorithm*

It is necessary to introduce the fundamentals of the *à trous* transform [27, 26]. The low pass filter of the *à trous* algorithm interpolates every other point. There is no decimation step in *à trous* algorithm. The performance of the time series forecast using conventional DWT without decimation is sensitive to the choice of origin. It also depends on whether the features of the series are close to the coefficients in DWT. By ignoring the decimation step, a larger storage space will be required.

Consider a time series $c_0(k)$. To perform the *à trous* wavelet transform, the time series is passed through a low pass filter h_l. This results in the first resolution level of the signal, or the first approximations signal, $c_1(k)$. Subsequently, $c_n(k)$ is obtained when the time series goes through the filter n times. The block diagram shown in Fig. 3 illustrates the process. It is also described by Eq. (41).

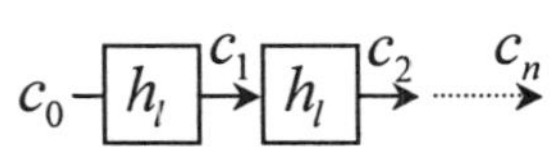

Fig. 3. The Filtering Process

$$c_j(k) = \sum_{l=0}^{L-1} h_l c_{j-1}(k + 2^{j-1} l) \tag{41}$$

The difference between $c_j(k)$ and $c_{j-1}(k)$ results in the wavelet scale, or the details signal at level j. They can be expressed as:

$$w_j(k) = c_{j-1}(k) - c_j(k) \tag{42}$$

It provides a convenient way to reconstruct the original signal $c_0(k)$:

$$c_0(k) = c_n + \sum_{j=1}^{n} w_j(k) \tag{43}$$

A similar approach is used to perform the transform. Instead of using just one filter, two decomposition filters and two reconstruction filters are used as shown in Fig. 2. The time series $c_0(k)$ is passed through a low pass filter h_l and a high pass filter g_l. This will result in the first approximations signal $c_1(k)$, as well as the wavelet scale at the first level $w_1(k)$. $c_n(k)$, and $w_n(k)$ is obtained by passing the time series through the pair of decomposition filters n times. This is illustrated with the diagram shown in Fig. 4,[25, 28], where $c_j(k)$ is obtained using Eq. (41). Similarly, the wavelet scale at each level is obtained as follows,

$$w_j(k) = \sum_{l=0}^{L-1} g_l c_{j-1}(k + 2^{j-1} l) \tag{44}$$

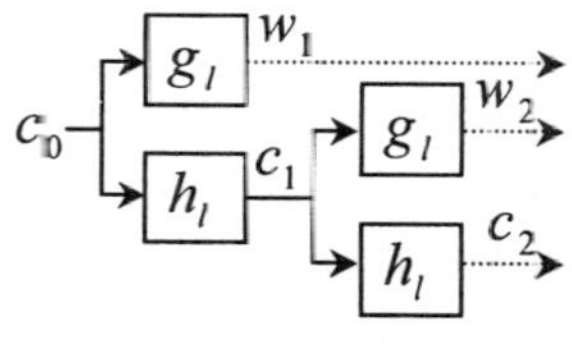

Fig. 4. The Decomposition Process

Eqs. (41) and (44) can be used to reconstruction of the original signal. The only difference is that reconstruction filters $\bar{h}_l$ and $\bar{g}_l$ are used instead. The block diagram given in Fig. 3 illustrates the process[25, 28, 29, 30]. In [24], h_l is a wavelet filter if it has an even length L, and it satisfies the following three basic properties,[24]

$$\sum_{l=0}^{L-1} h_l = 0, \ \sum_{l=0}^{L-1} h_l^2 = 1 \text{ and } \sum_{l=0}^{L-1} h_l h_{l+2n} = 0 \tag{45}$$

Eq. (45) indicates that the filter must sum to zero, have unit energy and be orthogonal to its even shifts. g_l is the scaling filter defined in terms of the wave filter via the 'quadrature mirror' relationship[24],

$$g_l \equiv (-1)^{l+1} h_{L-1-l} \tag{46}$$

The *Daubechies* wavelet is chosen for the coefficients of h_l. For $D(4)$, $L = 4$ and the coefficients of h_l are $h_0 = \frac{1-\sqrt{3}}{4\sqrt{2}}$, $h_1 = \frac{-3+\sqrt{3}}{4\sqrt{2}}$, $h_2 = \frac{3+\sqrt{3}}{4\sqrt{2}}$, $h_3 = \frac{-1-\sqrt{3}}{4\sqrt{2}}$ and $g_0 = \frac{1+\sqrt{3}}{4\sqrt{2}}$, $g_1 = \frac{3+\sqrt{3}}{4\sqrt{2}}$, $g_2 = \frac{3-\sqrt{3}}{4\sqrt{2}}$, $g_3 = \frac{1-\sqrt{3}}{4\sqrt{2}}$.

The reconstruction filter $\bar{h}_l$ is the reverse vector of h_l and $\bar{g}_l$ is the reverse vector of g_l.

The boundary conditions have to be dealt with when using Eqs. (41) and (42). There are various ways to tackle the issue. Here the signal is extended before convolution process at each level by appending the boundary values – as shown in Fig. 5 using a filter of $L = 4$. To make more precise predictions the most recent data should be used. In the case of adaptive learning, the previous data is penalized with forgetting factors in the proposed forecast model.

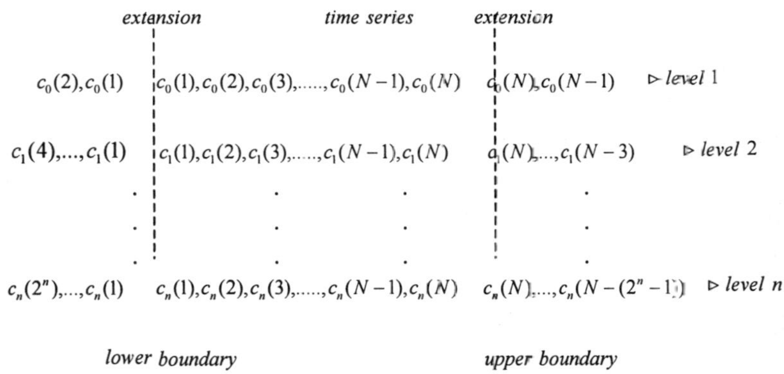

Fig. 5. The Boundary Conditions for DWT

6. A Framework for Time-Series Forecast

The framework model for time-series prediction is shown in Fig. 6, [31]. The forecast framework includes three stages [31, 32]. At stage 1, the time series is decomposed into different scales by DWT; at stage 2, each scale is predicted by a separate recurrent NN; and at stage 3, the next sample of the original time series is predicted by another NN using the different scale's prediction.

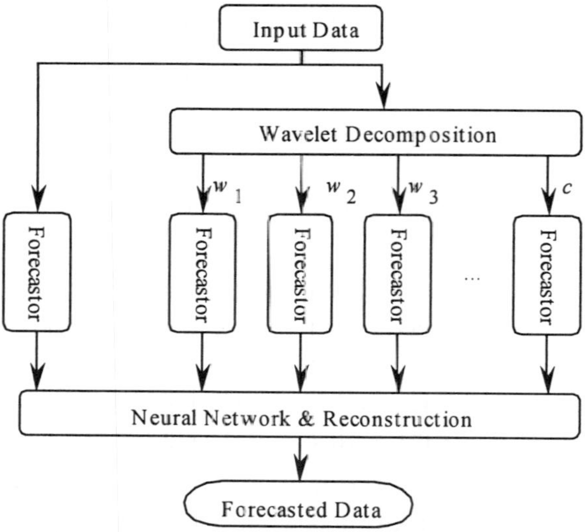

Fig. 6. The forecasting framework model (w_1, ..., w_k are wavelet coefficients, c is the residual coefficient series).

The *á trous* transform provides a robust approach to handling the temporal aspect of a time series. Given a series of 1400 values, in order to extrapolate into the future with 1 or more subsequent values, the time-based *á trous* transform can be applied to values x_1 to x_{1000}. The last values of the wavelet coefficients at the last time-point are kept because they are the critical values for prediction. This is repeated at time points $t = 1001, 1002, ...,$ repeatedly. The number of resolution levels, J, is determined mainly by inspection of smoothness of the residual series for a given J.

At stage 2, a predictor is allocated for each resolution level and the wavelet coefficients $w_i^{j(t)}$, $j = 0, ..., J$; $i = 1, ..., N$ are used to train the predictor. All networks used to predict the wavelets' coefficients of each scale are of the same recurrent neural network. The inputs to the j-th network are the previous samples of the wavelets' coefficients of the j-th scale. Each network is trained by GA or the back propagation algorithm and a weight decay regularization of the form $\frac{1}{\lambda}\sum_i w_i^2$ [22]. ARD method is used to reduce input nodes at each resolution level.

At stage 3, the predicted results of all the different scales $\hat{w}_{N+1}(t)$ are combined through the linear additive reconstruction property of the *á trous* algorithm. Elman neural networks for wavelet coefficients prediction are employed and the corresponding prediction results are incorporated into stage 3. Depending on the forecasting horizon at stage 2, the number of inputs to stage 3 network equals the number of all the prediction outputs of stage 1. Selection of the number of hidden layer neurons is highly problem dependent. According to the Vapnik-Chervonenkis (VC) dimension, the number of training vectors should be ten times or more the number of weights [33]. The procedures of Azoff [33] are used to minimize the number of targets required for neural networks.

7. Electric Power Load Forecast Case Studies

The test time series is taken from publicly available data of the Australian National Electricity Market (NEM). The NEM consists of the eastern states of Australia and covers over 4 thousand kms of distance. New South Wales is the largest regional electricity market with a winter peak demand of 11900 MW at the year 2000 [34]. The demand series of NEM is published in the NEMMCO website [35]. The real NSW demand series of January 2001 are taken to test the Elman network forecast abilities. The original data series is given in Fig. 7.

7.1. *Forecast without GA*

An Elman network is trained for 1100 data points and tested with 300 points out of the total 1400 points. The forecasted data and the anticipated data on the test data are given in Fig. 8 and the errors are given in Fig. 9. As shown in Figs. 10 and 11, the Elman network is able to forecast the demand after being trained. The predicted series follows the expected values quite well on the test data. However, considering other load forecasting techniques, the error range is still relatively large with some peak values around 5.5%. These peak value errors are results of the peak values in the original data series. The Elman network needed to be trained to capture the dynamic pattern around these peaks; these can be seen as search the global optimal weighting of the interconnections. However, due to the small noise like dynamics around these original series peaks, the weighting of interconnection of the

Elman network was trapped at some local optima. The Elman network trained by a BP algorithm does not learn these patterns properly.

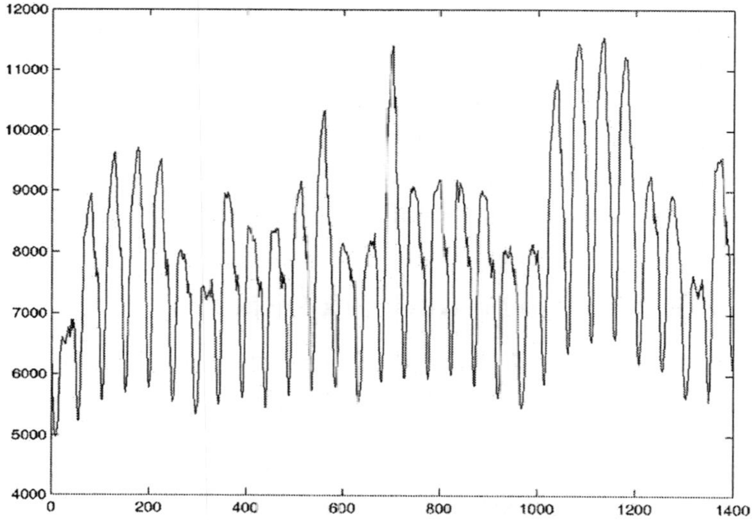

Fig. 7. The electric load data series of NSW as at January 2001

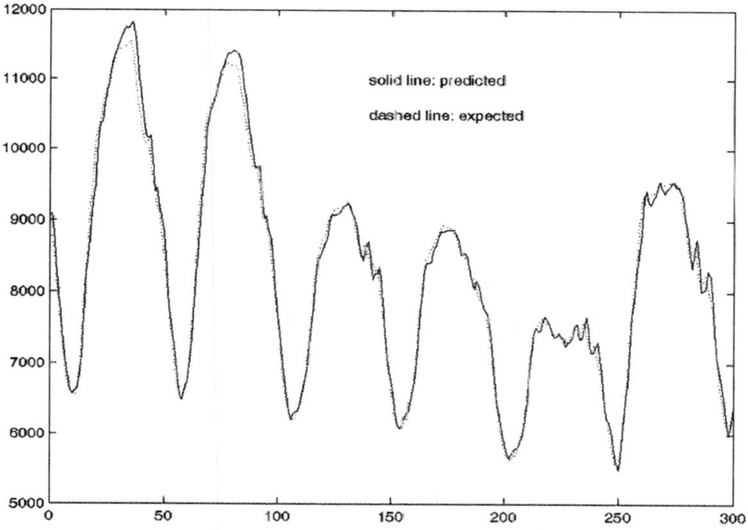

Fig. 8. Predicted (solid line) and expected (dashed line) data series

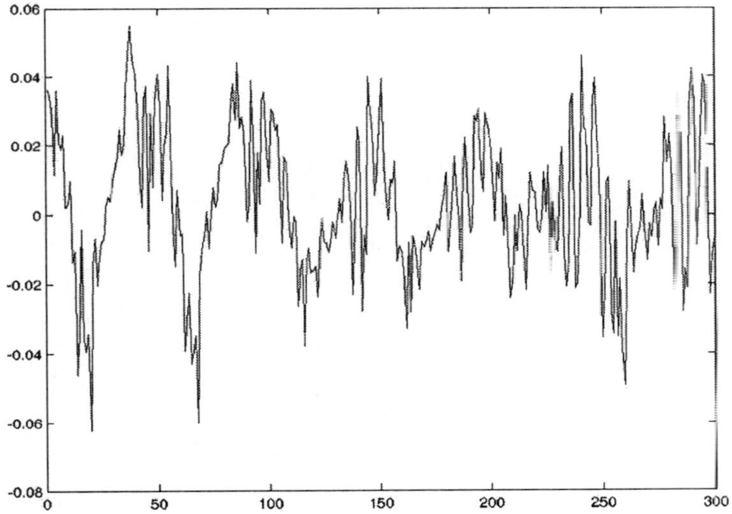

Fig. 9. Elman network forecasting errors [error = (predicted value – expected value)/expected value]

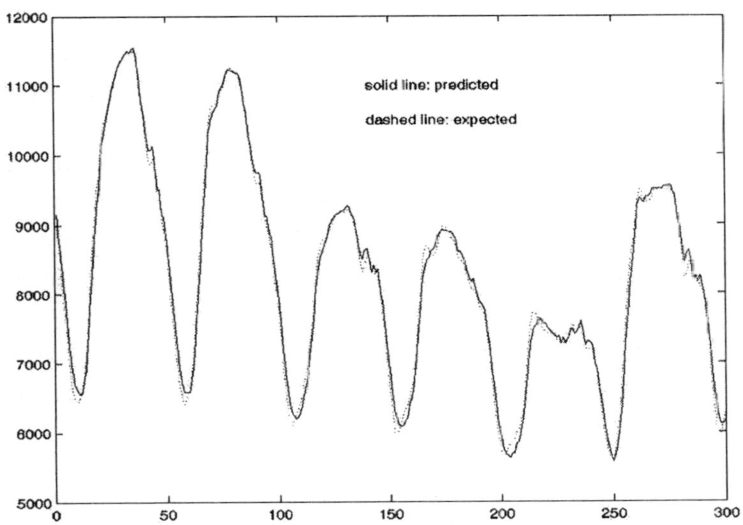

Fig. 10. Elman network forecast with GA weight adjustment module: predicted values (solid line) vs. expected values (dashed line) on test data

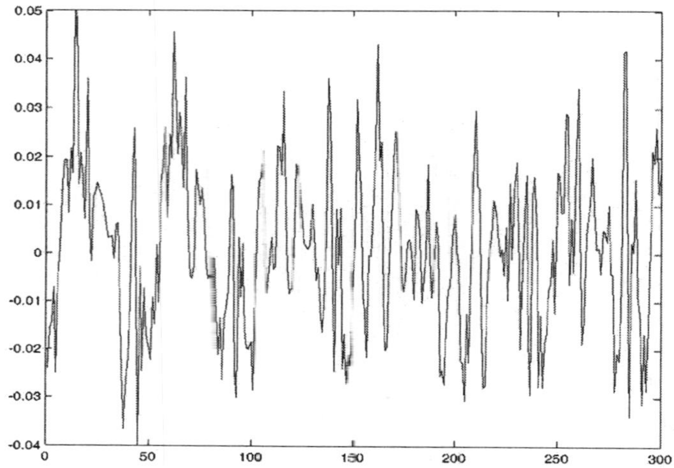

Fig. 11. Forecasting errors on Elman network forecast with GA weight adjustment module on the test data

7.2. *Forecast with GA*

The same Elman network tested in the previous section is tested again with GA enhanced weight adjusting modules on the same time series. As shown in Figs. 8 and 9, comparing with Figs. 6 and 7, it can be easily concluded that the GA weight adjustment module in the same Elman network improves the forecasting performance to a large extent. With GA module, the Elman network is able to produce forecast error less than 5% in the peak values, and the average errors are much smaller than the same network without GA module. Seeing that the electric load forecast requires a higher accuracy, Elman network with GA weight adjustment module out performs the BP algorithm trained ones.

8. Conclusion

Recursive neural networks are capable of modeling a large class of nonlinear dynamic systems. It had been proven that an Elman network, as a typical recurrent network with feedback connections is able to approximate any arbitrary nth order system. This property is employed to predict electricity load series. However, back propagation algorithm may experience difficulties in allocating weights for the Elman network. A GA is used to search for the best available optimal weights for the Elman networks. An electricity market data series is used to test the Elman network forecasting capability. The performances of Elman prediction are compared for different training techniques, BP and GA. The GA weight adjustment approach gives better results for this particular purpose of short term load forecasting.

References

1. D. T. Pham and D. Karaboga, "Training Elman and Jordan networks for system identification using genetic algorithms", *A.I. in Engineering* 13, 107-117, 1990
2. J. L. Elman, "Find structure in time," *Cognitive Science* 12, 179 – 211, 1990.
3. D. W. Bunn, "Forecasting loads and prices in competitive power markets", Proc. Of the IEEE, Vol. 88, No. 2, Feb. 2000, pp. 163-169.
4. D. Papalexopoulos and T. C. Hesterberg, "A regression-based approach to short-term system load forecasting", *IEEE Trans. on Power Systems*, vol. 5, no. 4, pp. 1535-1547, Nov. 1990.
5. D. K. Ranaweera, G. G. Karady and R. G. Farmer, "Effect of probabilistic inputs on neural network-based electric load forecasting", *IEEE Trans. on Neural Works*, vol. 7, no. 6, Nov. 1996, pp. 1528-1532.
6. F. F. Wu and P. Varaiya, "Coordinated multilateral trades for electric power networks: theory and implementation 1", *Elec. Pwr. & Energy Sys.* 21 75-102, 1999.
7. F. A. Wolak, "Market design and price behavior in restructured electricity markets: an international comparison", http://www. stanford.edu/~wolak.
8. S. Makridakis, S. C. Wheelwright and R. J. Hyndman, "Forecasting, methods and applications", *John Wiley \& Sons*, Inc. (3rd Edition), 1998.
9. N. R. Sanders, "Forecasting Theory", J. Webster (e.d) *Wiley Encyclopedia of Electrical and Electronics Engineering*, 1999.
10. L. X. Xu, "Approximation capability of Elman neural network", *Proc 14th World Cong. of Int. Federation of Automatic Control. IFAC'99*, July, 1999, Beijing, China.
11. K.F. Funahashi and Y. Nakamura, "Approximation of dynamic systems by continuous time recurrent neural networks", *Neural Networks*, **6**, 1993, pp. 801-806.
12. D.R. Seidl and R.D. Lorenz, "A structure by which a recurrent neural network can approximate a nonlinear dynamic system", *Proc. IJCNN*, Seattle, WA, **2**, 1991, pp.709-714.
13. D. E. Goldberg, *Genetic Algorithms in Search, Optimization, and Machine Learning*, Addison-Wesley Publishing Co. Inc., 1989.
14. K. P. Wong and Y. W. Wong, "Floating-Point Number-Coding Method for Genetic Algorithms", *Proc. ANZIIS-93*, Western Australia, 1-3 Dec 1993, pp. 512-516.
15. K. P. Wong, and Y. W. Wong, "Genetic and Genetic / Simulated-Annealing Approaches to Economic Dispatch", *IEE Proc. C.* 1994, 141, pp. 685–692.

16. Z. Y. Dong, Y. V. Makarov and D. J. Hill, "Power System Small Signal Stability Analysis Using Genetic Optimization Techniques", *Int J. Electric Power Systems Research*, September, 1998, Vol. 46, pp. 195-204.
17. S. W. Mahfoud, "Population Size and Genetic Drift in Fitness Sharing", L. D. Whitile and M. D. Vose edt. *Foundations of Genetic Algorithms* • 3, Morgan Kaufmann Publishing, Inc. 1995, pp. 185–223.
18. D. J. C. MacKay, "Bayesian non-linear modeling for the 1993 energy prediction competition", *Maximum Entropy and Bayesian Methods*, Santa Barbara 1993, G. Heidbreder (Ed.), Dordrecht: Kluwer, 1995.
19. R. R. Coifman and D. L. Donoho, "Translation-invariant de-noising", in *Wavelets and Statistics, Springer Lecture Notes*, A. Antoniades etc ed, Springer-Verlag, 1995.
20. N. Satio and G. Beylkin "Multiresolution representations using the auto-correlation functions of compactly supported wavelets", *IEEE Trans. Signal Processing*, 1992.
21. D. J. C. MacKay, "A practical Bayesian framework for backpropagation networks", *Neural Computation*, Vol. 4, pp. 448-472, 1992.
22. M. Bishop, *Neural networks for pattern recognition*, Oxford Univ. Press, 1995.
23. T. Masters, *Neural, novel & hybrid algorithms for time series prediction*, John Wiley & Sons, INC., 1995.
24. B. Percival and A. T. Walden, "Discrete Wavelet Transform," *Wavelet Methods for Time Series Analysis*, Cambridge University Press, U.K. 2000, pp.56-158.
25. B. N. Tran, T. M. Nguyen and M. M. Shihabi, "Wavelets", J. Webster (ed.) *Wiley Encyclopedia of Electrical & Electronics Engineering*, John Wiley & Sons, 1999.
26. Aussem, J. Campbell and F. Murtagh, "Wavelet-Based Feature Extraction and Decomposition Strategies for Financial Forecasting," *Journal of Computational Intelligence in Finance*, Vol. 6, No.3, pp.5-12, March/April 1999.
27. G. Zheng et al. "The Wavelet Transform for Filtering Financial Data Streams," *Journal of Computational Intelligence in Finance*, Vol. 7, No. 3, May/June 1999.
28. S. Mallat, "A Wavelet Tour of Signal Processing," *Fast Dyadic Wavelet Transform*, http://cas.ensmp.fr/~chaplais/Wavetour_ presentation/ondelettes%20dyadiques/ Algorithme_a_trousUS.html (last update, February 1999).
29. "Wavelet Toolbox User's Guide," The MATH WORKS Inc., v 2, September 2000.
30. G. Beylkin and N.Satio, "Wavelets, their autocorrelation functions & multiresolution representation of signals", *IEEE Trans. Signal Proc.*, Vol.7, 147-164, 1997.
31. Zhang and Z. Dong, "Adaptive neural-wavelet model for short term load forecasting", *Int. J. of Elec. Power Systems Research*, Vol. 59 pp. 121 – 129, 2001.
32. Amir B. Geva, "ScaleNet - Multiscale neural-network architecture for time series prediction", *IEEE Trans. Neural Networks*, Vol. 9, No. 5, pp. 1471-1482, 1998.
33. M. Azoff, *Neural network time series forecasting of financial markets*, John Wiley & Sons, 1994.
34. National Electricity Market Management Company Limited (NEMMCO), *2001 Statement of Opportunities for the National Electricity Market*, 20 March 2001.
35. National Electricity Market Management Company Limited website, http://www.nemmco.com.au/

CHAPTER 41

CO-ADAPTATION TO FACILITATE NATURALISITC HUMAN INVOLVEMENT IN SHARED CONTROL SYSTEM

Yukio Horiguchi and Tetsuo Sawaragi

Dept. of Precision Engineering, Grad School of Engineering, Kyoto University
Yoshida Honmachi, Sakyo-ku, Kyoto 606-8501 Japan
E-mail: {horiguchi, sawaragi}@prec.kyoto-u.ac.jp

Shared control is a challenge to combine and capitalize on both advantages of human and mechanized automatic controls. But any interventions by a machine-autonomy may introduce some kind of collapses in the *isomorphism* between the two different interaction fields of the human operation and of the system performance, which is necessary for the naturalistic involvement of a human operator with the system control. On this issue, we focus on the adaptability for the machine-autonomy to coordinate the mapping between the two fields to facilitate the human feeling of direct involvement with the system control, as well as the human adaptation (i.e., *co*-adaptation) In this chapter, we investigate their joint activity in a shared control of a virtual robot teleoperation environment, and then discuss the effect of the machine intervention in terms of the system operationality for human operators. The feasibility of the co-adaptive approach towards the well-coordinated relationship between a manipulator and a manipulatee is also examined based upon the experimental result with a simple adaptation algorithm implemented into the machine-autonomy.

1. Introduction

Mechanized control has advantages over human control such as tireless vigilance, increased precision and fast processing, while human control has also advantages over mechanized control such as the ability of comprehensive situation awareness and assessment, and the flexibility to cope with unfamiliar or unprogrammed situations by utilizing a various kind of knowledge. Hence, it is an important challenge in the human-machine system design to combine and capitalize on both advantages of human and mechanized automatic controls. Concerning with this, there proposed the ideas of *shared control*[1] and *shared autonomy*[2] as the design concepts for the human-machine collaboration to provide the reciprocal complementarities after their "joint activity"[a]. Wherein, the joint activity represents the integration of individual decisions that are made in parallel by two or more different and independent agents including humans and machines, and it stresses that they should collaborate with one another as *equivalent* partners in some senses.

Because of the essential differences in the cognitive abilities between humans and machines, it is conceivable to combine their individual decisions complementarily. In that, such differences will provide different viewpoints to an identical task situation that contribute to the total system performance. However, any interventions by other than his/her own decision may disorder the human control and hurt the system operationality because they should introduce into the system any unexpected behaviors hard to be completely controlled by the operator. In addition, allocating a particular function to machines creates some new functions that do alter the tasks themselves from the operator's *personal view*[3]. The situations and conditions for engaging in the task will have been changed by such function allocation[4]. These mentions imply some kind of collapses in the *isomorphism*[5] of the correspondence between the human operation and the system performance, which is necessary for the naturalistic human involvement by enhancing the operator's intuitive understandings on the system behavior[6]. Therefore, the expertise of any task executions in the lack of such isomorphic relations depends only on the effort by the human operators, or the human adaptation, but the complexity in the decision structure of the machine should make harder the human adaptation. In order to provide the naturalistic involvement of a human operator in such human-machine systems, it is significant for the machine-autonomy to posses enough

---

[a] The latter concept especially emphasizes on the aspect of "autonomy" in the human-machine collaborative task executions.

adaptability to coordinate the mapping between those two different interaction fields to facilitate the operator's feeling of direct involvement[7] with the system control. That is, the reciprocal adaptation, i.e. "*co*-adaptation", by a human operator and a machine-autonomy is hopeful to share their tasks adequately (from the initial redundancy in their role allocation) and to educe their true collaboration underpinned by the naturalistic human engagement.

Based upon the above ideas, this chapter discusses a design methodology for the naturalistic mapping between the interaction domain for the human manipulation and the one for the system behavior in a shared-autonomy system. Wherein, the ideal relationship between a human manipulator and a mechanical manipulatee with autonomy is investigated on the basis of the human-machine co-adaptation In general, human control has enough flexibility and adaptability to make use of any tools even though they include much complexity. On the contrary, the machines have insufficient ability to cope with and adapt to such variability of the human partner's behavior. Therefore, we would like to focus on and address this necessary aspect for the human-machine coordination here, in particular. For this purpose, we made some experiments using a simulated robot teleoperation environment to consider the joint activity by a human operator and a semi-autonomous mobile robot.

The remainder of this chapter is organized as follows. In the section **2**, our basic ideas on the human-machine co-adaptation are presented along with the emphasis on the probing activity which is a necessary aspect for their co-adaptive coordination. Then, the section **3** discusses the effect of the human-machine joint activity, especially in terms of the possible disorder between a human operator and a machine-autonomy due to their different cognitive natures, after the explanation about a simulated teleoperation environment as our experimental testbed. Based upon the experimental results, the section **4** examines the feasibility of our co-adaptive approach towards the well-coordinated human-machine relationship by evaluating the utility of a simple algorithm for the machine adaptation. In the section **5**, some rough ideas about the implementation of co-adaptation are described for the discussion to complete our picture before conclusions of this chapter.

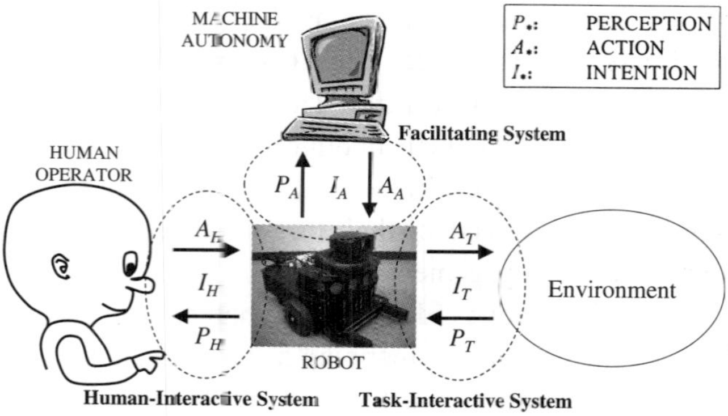

Fig. 1. The diagram depicting the relation of the interactive systems in a *shared-autonomy-style* robot teleoperation environment. For the naturalistic engagement of the human operator, FS has to coordinate the adequate isomorphic mapping between HIS and TIS by adjusting its behavior.

2. Probing Activity Consisting of Co-adaptation

Figure 1 illustrates the diagram to depict the relation of the interactive systems in a *shared-autonomy-style* robot teleoperation environment. Herein, P_* and A_* indicate the processes of perception and action, respectively, while I_* means the intention that constrains the coupling of P_* and A_* [8]. In addition, we call the interaction field between the human operator and the interface devices as Human-Interactive System, or HIS, as well as the one between the mechanical front (i.e., sensors and actuators) and the objective task environment as Task-Interactive System, or TIS. In terms of this definition, the objective is the design of the adequate isomorphic mapping between HIS and TIS. But as mentioned in the introductory section, we consider it infeasible to design such a mapping in advance by any external designers. Rather, the dynamical keeping-up mechanism that can constantly monitor and coordinate the relationship between the two is needed. In this sense, the machine-autonomy has to be open to revision and updated for the sake of its own behavioral adaptation not only to the task environment but also to the human operator (i.e., Facilitating System, or FS).

This duality of the adaptation target, however, holds the problem on the *stability-plasticity* balance in the internal state of the machine-autonomy. That is, the autonomy has to maintain its independence and identity for their mutual complementarities as well as flexibly comply with the demand for their coordinated relationship. So as to strike the balance between these two aspects, we consider the timing for the individual adaptation to be conditioned as a critical parameter for their activity coordination. Furthermore, since the proactive and probing action to explore more information can invoke more frequent interaction between the two and expose the hidden structures of the other's decision[b], this kind of action strategy should be appreciated by the machine-autonomy so as to share their strong mutual understandings and consistency. This perspective is analogical with the problem-solving through human-human and/or human-computer dialogues in the nature of the mixed-initiative interaction[11,12]. The participants in such interaction are powerfully driven by the motivations to reducing the *uncertainties* about the partner's intention[13]. This means nothing else that just the accumulated interactions among them can construct their common and mutual beliefs requisite for their true collaboration.

Giving shape to the above discussion, we consider that the machine-autonomy has to adapt its behavior through its *proactive agency* to retrieve more information about the partner's varying and transient internal state. This agency should be motivated to the reduced uncertainties about the partner's intention, and, as one form of its realization, the timing of its activation will be triggered by the discrepancy between the agent's prediction on the partner's behavior and the operator's actual behavior.

3. Necessary Coordination for Shared Control

First of all, we made some preliminary experiments on the human-machine shared control in that human and machine-autonomy's operations were simply superposed to the total system behavior. Based

[b] This aspect of action consists of the efficient strategy to reduce our cognitive burdens necessary for the "mental arithmetic" such as inference and reasoning in the informational space. In the case of human-environment interaction, this is called as *epistemic action* that should be distinguished from the *pragmatic* action performed to bring one physically closer to a goal[9,10].

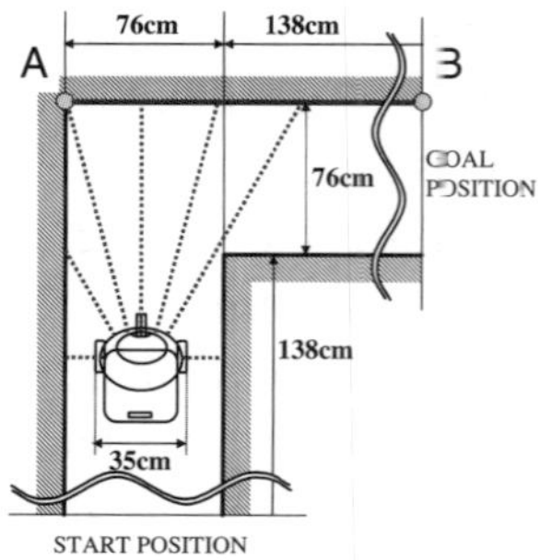

(a) L-formed Corridor

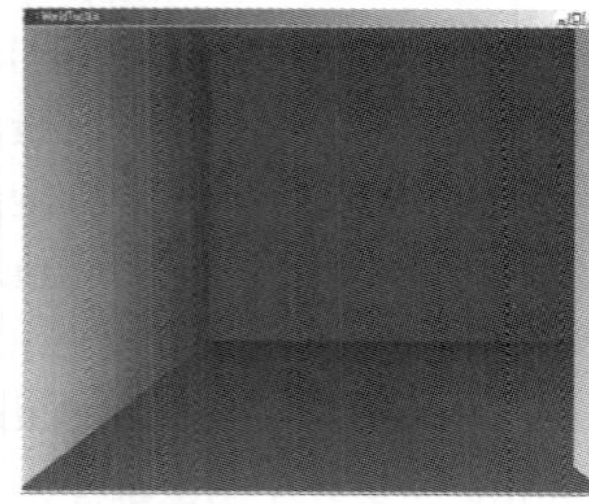

(b) Operator's View

Fig. 2. The experimental settings of our simulated teleoperation task. Human operators navigate a virtual mobile robot through the L-formed corridor (a) monitoring the view of the onboard camera (b).

upon these experimental results, we'll discuss the effect of the human-machine joint activity, especially in terms of the possible disorder between a human operator and a machine-autonomy due to their different cognitive natures.

3.1. *Experimental Settings*

For our experiments, we prepared a simulated teleoperation environment in which a virtual robot was controlled by either or both of a human operator and a machine-autonomy. The experimental task is to navigate the robot through the L-formed corridor presented in Figure 2(a). The robot has seven range sensors in front as well as a camera fixed onboard. These range sensors, each of which can measure the distance from the robot to the nearest obstacle in its direction, are utilized as the perceptual information to the machine-autonomy as described later, while the camera image is displayed to the human operator for its primary informational resource. Monitoring the display information captured from the camera, the human operators manipulate this robot with a joystick whose inclination determines the operational commands for the transitional and rotational velocity of the robot.

However, as shown in Figure 2(b), the view of the camera is very restricted so that human operators have got little information on the body image and dynamics of the robot. This means that each operator of this

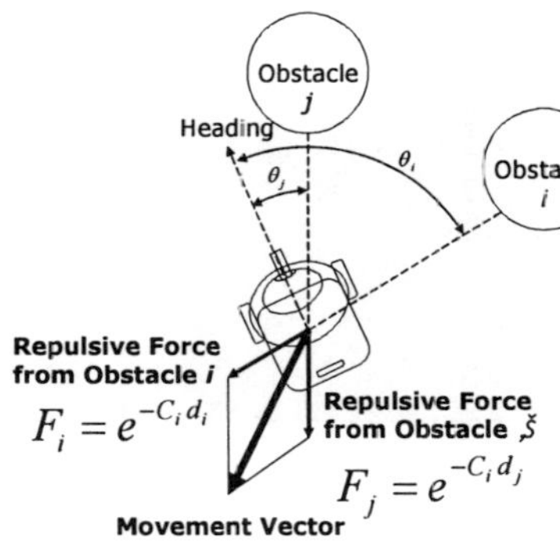

Fig. 3. The autonomous obstacle-avoidance behavior realized by the potential field method. The *velocity* and *steering* commands of the robot are generated from the integrated repulsive forces affected from the obstacles.

kind of teleoperating system has to develop the adequate models on them through its own experiences so as to achieve smoother and quicker task completions. In order to alleviate this difficulty, a simple obstacle-avoidance behavior is embedded into the robot as its autonomy, which is realized by the potential field method. The potential field utilized to generate the autonomy's operational commands is calculated from the measurements of the range sensors after the equation (1), (2) and (3):

$$F_i = \mathrm{e}^{-C_i d_i} \tag{1}$$

$$velocity_{autonomy} = \mathrm{V_{MAX}} \sum_{i=1}^{7} \omega_i F_i \cos\theta_i \tag{2}$$

$$steering_{autonomy} = \mathrm{S_{MAX}} \sum_{i=1}^{7} \omega_i F_i \sin\theta_i \tag{3}$$

Wherein, the autonomy's operational commands for the transitional and rotational velocity are denoted as *velocity* and *steering*, respectively. The parameter d_i is the distance measured by the sensor $i \in \{1,2,\ldots,7\}$ whose direction angle relative to the robot's heading is set to θ_i. C_is ($i \in \{1,2,\ldots,7\}$) are the variable gain parameters of the potential field so that the autonomy can change the way to generate its potential field by adjusting the values of C_is. On the other hand, $\mathrm{V_{MAX}}$, $\mathrm{S_{MAX}}$ and ω_i are constants which should be tuned for good performance of the autonomy's isolated behavior. Figure 3 illustrates the way to realize the autonomous obstacle-avoidance behavior mentioned above.

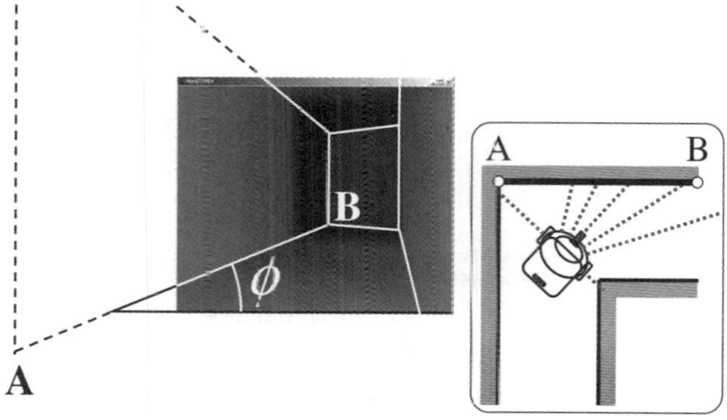

Fig. 4. The definition of the parameter ϕ to quantify the state of a human operator's view. This parameter corresponds to the angle at which the line segment AB crosses with the horizontal line in the image display window.

3.2. *Difference of Cue-utilization Style between Human and Machine*

In order to examine the effects of the machine-autonomy's intervention into human control, we make a comparison between the human operations with and without the autonomous obstacle-avoidance behavior. For this purpose, three experimental subjects (i.e., subject A, B and C) at first executed this teleoperation task with no assistance by the autonomy, and each subject carried out 10 experimental trials in their experiments. The result of this experiment reveals one typical feature of the human control in this teleoperation. That is, humans basically make *continuous* judgments on their robot operation responding to and guided by the *changes* of their visual perceptual information.

Figure 4 explains the definition of the parameter ϕ which quantifies the state of a human operator's view. This parameter corresponds to the angle at which the line segment AB crosses with the horizontal line in the image display window. Table 1 summarizes the correlation coefficients between the steering operation[c] and the ϕ-related values, with the average task execution time indicating each subject's skill level. As shown in this table, the correlation coefficient between the steering

[c] In this experiment, as the human operators little manipulated the translational velocity and then the robot was almost always under full speed, we did only analyze the steering operation but the translational velocity control.

Table 1. Average correlation coefficients of the steering operation with the values of ϕ, $\Delta\phi$ (= difference of ϕ) and $\Delta^2\phi$ (= difference of $\Delta\phi$) in the human solo task executions by each subject.

Subject (Avg. run time [sec])	A (5.523)	B (9.564)	C (9.502)
ϕ	0.364	0.369	0.248
$\Delta\phi$	**0.837**	**0.693**	**0.521**
$\Delta^2\phi$	-0.140	-0.111	-0.059

operation and the value of $\Delta\phi$, or the difference of ϕ, tends to be positively high, meaning that they are linearly related. For instance, Figure 5(a) exhibits one profile of the human steering operation, expressing the very similar shape of its transition with the $\Delta\phi$'s one. This tendency becomes stronger in the case of the more skilled operator, and can also be confirmed by the fact that the correlation coefficient between the task execution time and $\Delta\phi$, which is computed from all the trial data, equals to 0.558. These results suggest that the human control should quite depend on the transition of the perceptual information rather than the snapshot of it, and that the progress in the operational skill corresponds to finding out some adequate cues from such transitional flows and then developing some couplings between those cues and the corresponding operational acts.

In contrast to this feature of the human control, the machine-autonomy depends on the very different kind of sensors than the human's. It controls the robot in response to the sensory *snapshot* as defined by the equation (1), (2) and (3). Therefore, the radical changes in its sensory data lead to the drastic changes in its operation and cause its *intermittent* or discontinuous judgments as shown in Figure 5(b) that represents a profile of the steering operation by the machine-autonomy with all the values of C_is ($i \in \{1,2,\ldots,7\}$) set to 0.05 in its solo task execution[d].

[d] As the robot autonomy has no component to drive the robot forward, the maximum transitional velocity V_{MAX} is always added to its operational commands in its solo task executions. This is the second reason why we made no analysis in terms of the translational velocity control.

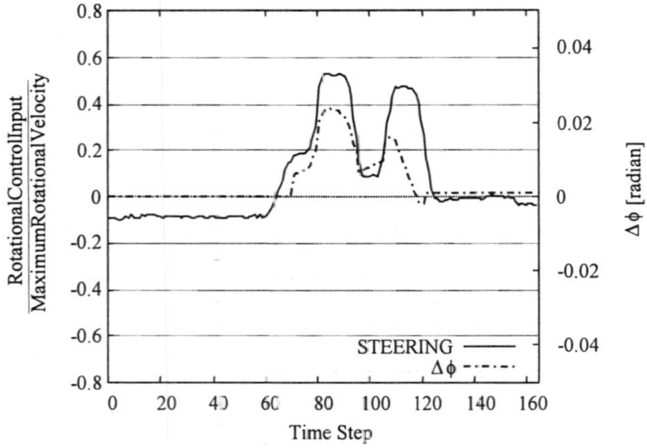

(a) Human Control

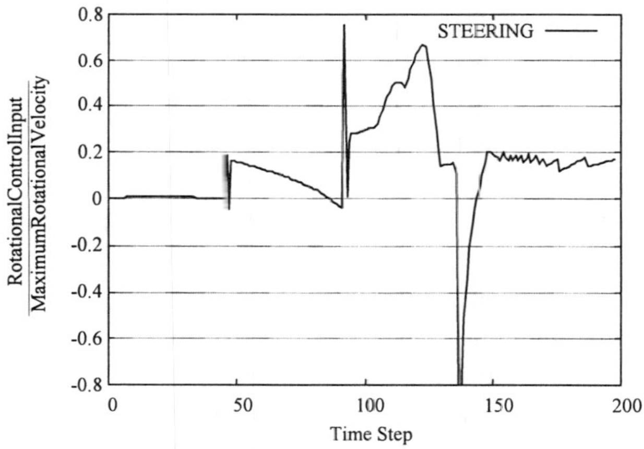

(b) Machine Control

Fig. 5. Comparing the steering operations for the robot navigation between the human control and the machine control (a) one steering command profile in a human solo task execution (done by the subject A who made the most skillful operation of the three experimental subjects) with the corresponding $\Delta\phi$ value, and (b) one steering profile in a machine solo task execution by the robot autonomy with $C_i = 0.05$ $(\forall i \in \{1, 2, \ldots, 7\})$.

This difference of the cue-utilization[14] style between the human operators and the machine-autonomy does influence their joint activity, especially the way to control by the human operators.

3.3. *Effect of Joint Operation*

We made the next experiment in that the machine operation is simply superposed to the human operation so that both of them consist of the total system's (i.e., the robot's) behavior. As well as the previous experiment, the same three experimental subjects executed this teleoperation task, while all the values of C_i s, which define the way of the machine-autonomy's intervention, were changed among 0.04, 0.05, 0.06 and 0.07. In the experiment, each subject carried out 3 to 8 experimental trials under every condition of the C_i setting. As the result of this experiment, the effect of the joint operation by a human operator and a machine-autonomy can be summarized into the following two aspects:

(i) The machine intervention induces the human operations so that they can be performed in a more consistent manner, because it offers good cues on the timing to trigger the human operator's action.

(ii) The machine intervention, however, harms the system operationality for the human operator, because the actual system behavior may deviate from the human prediction due to the intervention.

On the one hand, the machine control can afford more precision and more consistent judgments in a moment of time than the human control can do, because it can appreciate the quantified data of its sensory snapshot that the human operators can never obtain, and it rigidly follows the formulated judgmental algorithm that associates its perceptual state with its action in a one-to-one fashion. Therefore, any events triggered by such judgments should provide the important cues for the human operators to initiate any actions. That is, it can be considered that such interventions by the machine-autonomy can induce a human operation to take place at a more consistent timing. Since human operators have little information on the body image of the robot from the display screen, one of the most remarkable evidences for the skillful operations by the experienced subjects is the consistency of the timing when to initiate a series of operations for turning at the corner of the corridor. Applying the autonomous obstacle-avoidance behavior into the robot navigation, we have got the good improvements on this behavior, especially for the immature operators.

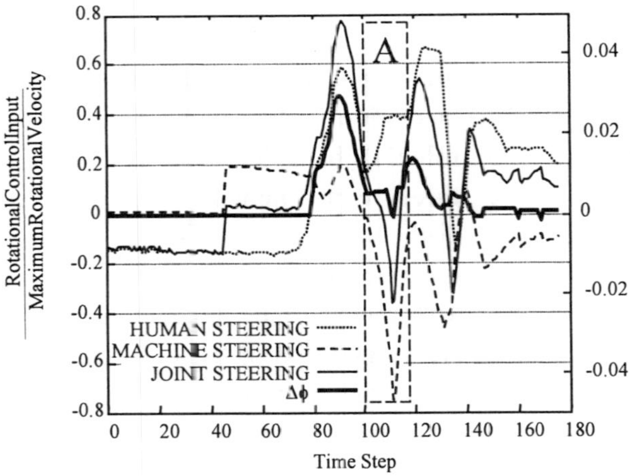

Fig. 6. One instance of the profiles of the steering operations by both of the subject A and the machine-autonomy with all the values of C_is set to 0.05, and $\Delta\phi$ in their simply jointed task executions.

On the other hand, any intervening operations by other than his/her own decision may disorder the human control because they would produce the unexpected behaviors into the system. Especially, when such a deviation becomes larger due to some strong external interventions, it can drastically hurt the system operationality for human operators. This kind of affairs did be observed in our experimental result. Figure 6 shows one instance of the steering command profiles with the corresponding $\Delta\phi$ values in an experimental trail of the simply jointed human-machine task executions. Wherein, the legends of "HUMAN STEERING", "MACHINE STEERING" and "JOINT STEERING" denotes the three different profiles of the steering operation done by the human operator (subject A), by the machine-autonomy of $C_i = 0.05$ ($\forall i \in \{1,2,\ldots,7\}$) and by their integration, respectively. In this graph, we can see a series of *compensating* operations by the human operator in the duration A which is highlighted by a dotted line. At the beginning of this duration, the machine-autonomy initiated the fairly strong intervention causing a large gap between the actual system behavior perceived from the operator's visual feedback information and his expectation on it. As explained in the section **3.2**, human operators are basically guided by the transition of their perceptual information. This tightly coupled relation between the perceptual changes of the visual image and the steering operations in the human control, however, collapsed by that intervention in this case. Therefore, the human operator is forced to compensate this gap so that the actual transition of the visual information due to the robotic behavior should match up with his expectation, which means that their joint steering operation should be coupled with the perceptual change on the display screen. Figure 6 reveals the shift of the human steering operation in the duration A corresponding to this compensating operation, and it results in the very correlated profile of their joint operation with the value of $\Delta\phi$. This prospect can be confirmed from Table 2 which compares the correlation coefficients of $\Delta\phi$ among with the steering operations by the human subjects (HUMAN), by the machine-autonomy (MACHINE), and by their integration (JOINT). This table exhibits the more intensive correlation between $\Delta\phi$ and the joint steering operation when the machine-autonomy has the stronger influence on the system due to the lower C_i value. That is, the strong intervention by the machine-autonomy brings about the compensatory operation in the human control.

The difference of the cognitive function and capability between a human and a machine is an important factor to establish their reciprocity for complementing each other in their joint activity. However, the mixture of their different styles of decisions includes some potential conflicts, and the resolution of such kind of unstable relationships in the human-machine collaboration is in principle committed only by the human adaptation. As one instance, we could observe such coordination by the human adaptation of his operating strategy in our experimental result. It is because the machine has no ability for their mutual comprehension. For more naturalistic human-machine collaboration, we have to consider a framework to deal with the machine adaptation that can coordinate the human and the machine activities with capitalizing their individual strengths. A promising approach for this purpose is the co-adaptation to orient the "team" to their common and mutual beliefs by their enriched interactions.

Table 2. Average correlation coefficients between the steering operations and the value of $\Delta\phi$ in the human-machine simply jointed task executions. The experimental subject A, B and C are the identical persons analyzed in Table 1.

(a) Subject A

C	HUMAN	MACHINE	JOINT
0.04	0.667	0.499	**0.868**
0.05	0.550	0.208	**0.769**
0.06	0.604	-0.015	**0.676**
0.07	**0.607**	0.126	0.584

(b) Subject B

C	HUMAN	MACHINE	JOINT
0.04	0.473	0.298	**0.841**
0.05	0.639	0.348	**0.689**
0.06	**0.727**	0.241	0.638
0.07	**0.695**	0.022	0.573

(c) Subject C

C	HUMAN	MACHINE	JOINT
0.04	0.408	0.204	**0.833**
0.05	0.523	0.135	**0.725**
0.06	0.644	0.303	**0.760**
0.07	0.677	0.146	**0.844**

4. Human-Machine Coordination Based on Proposing Model

Based upon the ideas discussed in the section 2, we propose a framework for a machine-autonomy to adapt its behavior with the proactive agency to get more information about the partner's varying internal state. This agency is triggered by the discrepancy between the agent's prediction on the partner's behavior and his/her actual behavior, and it is directed to reducing the *uncertainties* about the partner's "intention". Therefore, the occurrence of the conflicts caused by the difference between a human

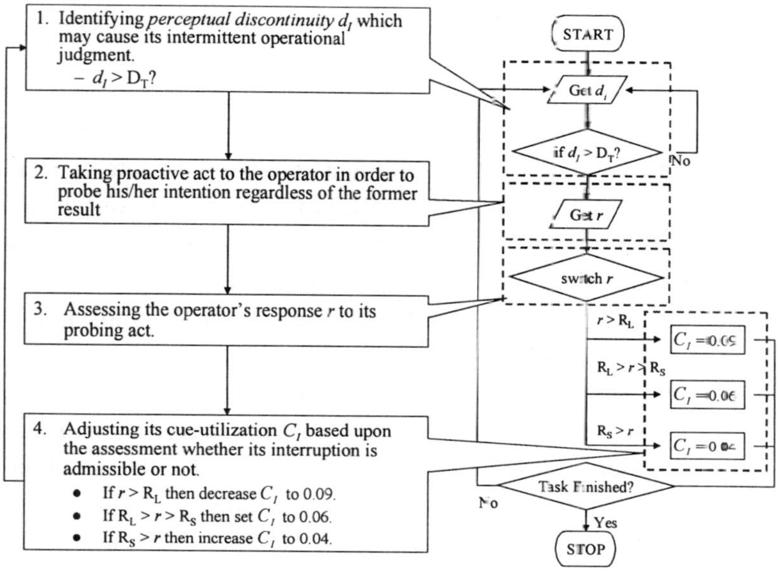

Fig. 7. The algorithm of the machine-autonomy's adaptation toward the adequate human-machine coordination.

operator's and a machine agent's judgment strategies is regarded as the significant opportunity for their decision coordination. Note that the iteration and accumulation of such interactions would form the enduring process toward the *dynamic* equilibrium in their collaboration.

When the simple human-machine joint operation, the human operator's complementary operations frequently appeared, that is caused by the machine-autonomy's *intermittent* or *discontinuous* interventions based upon the potential field by the sensory snapshot data. However, we can also consider such interventions as the significant *opportunity* for a human operator to expose his/her intention in response to the machine-autonomy's intervention, that is, as the triggering event for the machine to acquire new cues to *proactively* share their understandings. Based on this idea, a simple algorithm of the machine-autonomy's adaptation described in Figure 7 was embedded into the system, which implements the following components:

(a) *Self-awareness of perceptual discontinuity:* In order to detect the perceptual discontinuity that may cause its intermittent operational judgment, the autonomy constantly monitors its sensory snapshot data and their temporal differences.

(b) *Taking the proactive action to probe the partner's intention:* When a perceptual discontinuity is detected, the autonomy dares to command its intermittent operation to intervene the human control strongly at the risk of the operator's confusion.

(c) *Recognizing the partner's intention from the reaction:* After its proactive action, the autonomy checks the operator's response and assesses whether its previous intervention is admissible for the operator or not.

(d) *Adjusting the way to intervene:* Based upon the assessment, the autonomy revises its way of intervention in favor of their good coordination. This adjustment is done so that the autonomy would become humbler in the case of the operator's strong complement while it would become greedier in the case of the operator's little complement.

We made the last experiment with this algorithm implemented into the machine-autonomy. As the result of this experiment, we could confirm that the complementary operations by the human operators were reduced by our proposed model. In order to quantify this effect, we examined the fluctuation in the human control by utilizing the multiple linear regression analysis. In our analysis, the regressed models of the human steering operations, which are explained by the distance measurements by the seven range sensors, are regarded as the standards to measure the operational fluctuation in terms of the standard deviation values of its residuals. At first, as necessary to consider the timing when the machine interventions are held, a sequential progress of the robot navigation is divided into some segments before applying the above analysis. Based on the result (i.e., the dendrogram and the distances among clusters) of the hierarchical cluster analysis using Ward's method, all case data of the sensory measurement vectors are categorized into four clusters. And then, for each cluster, an approximate model of the human steering operation is regressed using the stepwise multiple linear regression analysis method.

As the result of this analysis, Figure 8 compares the average standard deviation values of the residuals in the four regression models among in

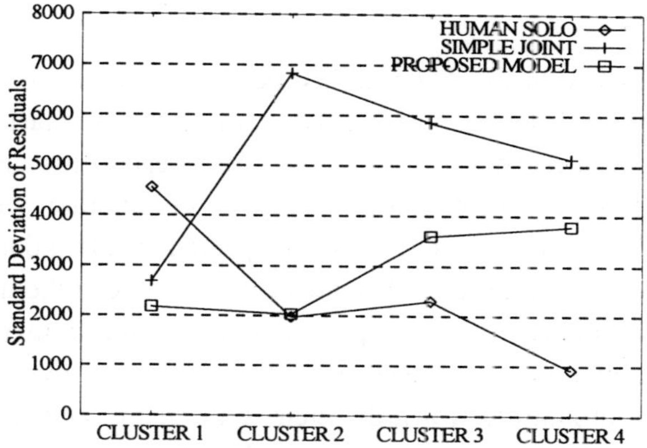

Fig. 8. The comparison of the average standard deviation values of the residuals in the regression models among in the human solo operation (HUMAN SOLO), in the simple human-machine joint operation (SIMPLE JOINT), and in our proposed human-machine joint operation (PROPOSED MODEL). As the last of the phase belonging to the cluster 1, the machine-autonomy made the strong intervention into the human control

the human solo operation (HUMAN SOLO), in the simple human-machine joint operation (SIMPLE JOINT), and in our proposed human-machine joint operation (PROPOSED MODEL), all of which were executed by the subject A.

On the one hand, in the all phases but the cluster 1, the operational fluctuation is magnified in the simple joint operation than in the human solo operation, especially in the phase of the cluster 2 after a strong intervention by the machine-autonomy has been done. This can be considered as the result of the human complementary operations that are extra and unnecessary operations than in his solo operation and that induce their succeeding awkward interaction. On the other hand, by applying our proposed model, the human complementary operations were reduced than in the simple human-machine joint operation. In addition, the advantage of the machine-autonomy was capitalized on in terms of the lower value in the cluster 1 than in the human solo operation, which is the evidence suggesting that the human operation was performed at a more consistent timing. Therefore, these results say a good coordination between the human operator and the machine-autonomy could be achieved by implementing the machine adaptation.

5. Discussion

Human actions reveal much flexibility because of their *situatedness* in their task ecology[14]. Hence, there exists no absolute scenario to predict the practices of such actions accurately. Considering this nature of the human cognition, the machine-autonomy to collaborate with humans should have the ability to react to any unexpected events induced by their joint activity and to repair the adequate relation between them on its own initiative. The concept of co-adaptation we introduced in this chapter represents the integration of such activities performed by both human- and machine-autonomies towards their synergism, and it especially emphasizes the role of the proving activities in their joint activity. Our simulated teleoperation environment was built for the examination of the effect of the machine-autonomy's adaptation based upon its proactive agency to probe the partner's varying internal state. Although its current implementation is confined to the machine interventions by the obstacle-avoidance behavior in the restricted corridor environment, it revealed a good coordination achieved between a human operator and a machine-autonomy.

To be accurate with our proposed framework, the adaptation of the machine-autonomy needs some predictive model on the human partner's behavior because the autonomy can utilize the discrepancy between its prediction on the partner's behavior and the actual, as the triggering event for its adaptation. In our current experimental configuration, however, there is no such model implemented in the machine-autonomy. In addition, our investigation is also insufficient in terms of the human adaptation since most of the effort in our experiments basically focused on the effects of the machine intervention into the human control, in particular, whose operational strategy has been already established. The experimental results on the unskilled operators with no machine adaptation pointed out both positive and negative aspects of the machine intervention. The former is that it provides the human operators with a new resource to acquire the consistent timing for turning the robot at the corridor corner, which is more effective for unskilled operators. The latter is that it perturbs them due to the unexpected behaviors introduced to the robot, which are hard to be control by inexperienced operators without enough coping skills. The more intensive the autonomy's intervention becomes, the stronger this tendency becomes to make the performing time worse. In order to investigate the differences among operators with different skill level and the adaptation process in a particular operator, some quantification method to capture the human decision structure is necessary. For this purpose, we are going to apply a judgment analysis method derived from the Brunswik's *lens model* framework[15,16,17] after the extension or alteration of the experimental task that can elicit subtle conflicts between a human operator and a machine-autonomy to shape their ever-changing coordination.

6. Conclusions

In this chapter, we pointed out the potential issues in shared control systems to combine and capitalize on both advantages of human and mechanized automatic controls. Wherein, the concept of co-adaptation was introduced with the aim of the dynamical equilibrium in the human-machine equation towards their true collaboration that is underpinned by the naturalistic human involvement with the system control. In order to establish such relationship, we especially emphasized the role of the probing activity in their co-adaptive coordination. Our experimental results of the robot teleoperation environment where a human operator and a machine-autonomy shared the system control revealed their good coordination achieved by it.

Acknowledgments

This work is supported in part by Center of Excellence for Research and Education on Complex Functional Mechanical Systems (COE program of the Ministry of Education, Culture, Sports, Science and Technology, Japan).

References

1. T.B. Sheridan, *Telerobotics, Automation, and Human Supervisory Control* (The MIT Press, 1992).

2. S. Hirai, Theory of Shared Autonomy, *Journal of the Robotics Research in Japan*, No. 11, Vol. 6, pp. 20-25 (1993) (in Japanese).
3. D.A. Norman, Cognitive Artifact. In *Designing Interaction*. Ed. J.M. Carroll (Cambridge University Press, New York, 1991), pp. 17-38.
4. R. Parasuraman,, T.B. Sheridan and C.D. Wickens, A Model for Types and Levels of Human Interaction with Automation, *IEEE Transactions on Systems, Man, and Cybernetics - Part A: System and Humans*, No. 30, Vol. 3, pp. 286-297 (2000).
5. J. Holland et al. Eds., *Induction* (The MIT Press, 1986).
6. K. Vicente and J. Rasmussen, The Ecology of Human-Machine Systems II: Mediating "Direct Perception" in Complex Work Domain, *Ecological Psychology*, No. 2, Vol. 3, pp. 207-249, (1990).
7. T. Sawaragi and Y. Horiguchi, Analysis of Task Morphologies for Networking Behavioral Skill via Virtual Reality, *ACM Journal of Intelligence: New Visions of AI in Practice*, Vol. 11, No. 3, pp. 20-32 (2000).
8. R.E. Shaw et al., The Intentional Spring: A Strategy for Modeling Systems That Learn to Perform Intentional Acts, *Journal of Motor Behavior*, Vol. 24, No. 1, pp. 3-28 (1992).
9. D. Kirsh and P.P. Maglio, On Distinguishing Epistemic from Pragmatic Action, *Cognitive Science*, Vol. 18, pp. 513-549 (1994).
10. A. Kirlik, The Ecological Expert: Acting to Create Information to Guide Action, *Fourth Symposium on Human Interaction with Complex Systems*, IEEE Computer Society (1998).
11. G. Ferguson, J.F. Allen and B. Miller, TRAINS-95: Towards a Mixed-Initiative Planning Assistant, *Proceedings of the Third Conference on Artificial Intelligence Planning Systems*, pp. 70-77 (1996).
12. J.F. Allen, Mixed-Initiative Interaction, *IEEE Intelligent Systems*, IEEE Computer Society (1999).
13. E. Horvitz, Uncertainty, action, and interaction: in pursuit of mixed-initiative computing, *IEEE Intelligent Systems*, Vol. 14, No. 5, pp. 17-20 (1999).
14. L.A. Suchman, *Plans and Situated Actions: The problem of human-machine communication* (Cambridge University Press, 1987).
15. R.W. Cooksey, *Judgment Analysis: Theory Methods and Applications* (Academic Press, 1996).
16. Y. Horiguchi and T. Sawaragi, Naturalistic Human-Robot Collaboration Mediated by Shared Communicational Modality in Teleoperation System, *Proceedings of The Sixth International Computer Science Conference on Active Media Technology 2001 (AMT2001)*, pp. 24-35 (2001).
17. Y. Horiguchi and T. Sawaragi, Design of Mixed-Initiative Interactions Between Human and Robot to Realize Shared Autonomies in Teleoperation Environment, *Transactions of the Society of Instrument and Control Engineers*, Vol. 38, No. 12, pp. 1097-1106 (2002) (in Japanese).

CHAPTER 42

DISTRIBUTED EVOLUTIONARY STRATEGIES FOR SEARCHING OLIGO SETS OF YEAST GENOME

Arthur Tay[*], Kay Chen Tan[*], Ji Cai[*] and Huck Hui Ng[**, ***]

[*] *Department of Electrical & Computer Engineering*
National University of Singapore
4 Engineering Drive 3, Singapore 117576
E-mail: arthurtay@nus.edu.sg
[**] *Department of Biological Sciences*
National University of Singapore
14 Science Drive 4, Singapore 117543
[***] *Genome Institute of Singapore*
60 Biopolis Street, Genome, #02-01, Singapore 138672

DNA microarray has been heavily utilized in analysis of gene expression and has made tremendous impact in many disciplines of life sciences. A most standard microarray technology in a typical laboratory setting is printing DNA molecules onto glass slides using robots. In order to distinguish nucleic acids with very similar composition by hybridization, it is necessary to design probes with high specificities, i.e. uniqueness. We make use of the available sequence information of all the yeast open reading frames (ORF) combined with an distributed evolutionary computational (DEC) strategy to search for unique sequences to represent each and every ORF in the yeast genome. The results are presented and discussed. The capability of the DEC is demonstrated to be efficient and robust. The approach can be extended to more complicated genomes.

1. Introduction

DNA microarray, also known as DNA CHIP, is a revolutionary technology that involves immobilization of a large number of different DNA molecules within a small confined space[1,2]. Over the years, several technologies have been developed to attach DNA molecules to solid platform. Oligonucleotides (short single stranded DNA molecules) can be synthesized *insitu* using photolithographic techniques or phosphoramidite chemistry by ink jet printing technology[3,4]. The precision of photolithographic technology allows the synthesis of high resolution and extremely high density DNA microarrays. Such arrays are currently marked by Affymetrix. Alternatively, DNA molecules, typically in the form of double stranded PCR (polymerase chain reaction) products or oligonucleotides, can be attached to glass slides or nylon membranes[5]. The latter method is a more practical and cost-effective avenue of making DNA microarrays by most standard laboratories. In addition, it offers the flexibility of printing DNA of choice onto solid platform.

The stability and association between complementary DNA molecules critically depends on the melting temperature (T_m). T_m is operationally defined as the temperature in which 50% of a single stranded DNA annealed with its complement to form a perfect duplex. The T_m is governed by several factors: base composition, DNA concentration, salt concentration, and the presence of destabilizing chemical reagents. As a GC base pair is held together by 3 hydrogen bonds while an AT base pair has only 2 hydrogen bonds, GC rich sequence has a higher T_m compared to AT rich sequence. Higher concentration of DNA favors duplex formation and consequently the T_m is higher. As cations stabilize DNA duplexes, higher salt concentration raises the T_m. Chemicals such as formamide or DMSO destabilize DNA duplexes and therefore has a negative effect on T_m. In a typical microarray experiment, thousands of DNA spots on the microarray interact with a very complex mixture of labeled DNA under a single condition. Therefore, optimal hybridization condition is necessary to obtain the best result. One way to attain optimal hybridization is to control the T_m of the immobilized DNA on the microarray.

The yeast Saccharomyces cerevisiae is the first eukaryote genome that has been sequenced. Saccharomyces cerevisiae has approximately 6000 genes. The gene structure of this yeast is also relatively simple, compared to higher eukaryotes. For examples, very few genes contain introns and most of the open reading frames (ORF), which are protein coding sequences, are preceded by promoters. Since detailed sequence information is known for all predicted gene in this organism, the Paladin-DEC software is applied here to find unique DNA sequences with optimized melting temperature that can be printed onto DNA microarrays. The yeast is simpler both in its behavior and its genome structure as compared to complex Vertebrates[6]. Yeast genomics remains an interesting area of research, as most biologists are concerned with the information and clues extracted from the yeast DNA array, and the eventual goal is to search for the probe set of the human genome that is currently not available. One of the main limitations or obstacles in using the microarray is that ORFs are extremely variable in length and T_m (T_m is the melting point of the particular ORF), making comparison between any two genes on the array virtually impossible. The problem is thus to search for probes within each ORF so that the probes are unique, approximately the same length and melting temperature.

Since this problem is hard to solve and may take an extremely long or impractical computation time using traditional EAs in a single computer, due to the very large search spaces involved in the problems. Using the updated Paladin-DEC[7] software, however, the population size can be increased a lot and the computational workload can be shared and distributed among multiple computers, and therefore significantly extends the search power of an evolutionary algorithm.

This chapter is organized as follows. A brief introduction to the problem formulation is presented in Section 2. The design and implementation of DEC software that include a brief description is given in Section 3. Section 4 describes the simulation result of the searching probe set of yeast genome. Conclusions are drawn in Section 5.

2. Problem Formulation

There are three criteria for a qualified sequence: (1) uniqueness of the sequence, (2) the sequence should have a melting temperature within a special range, and (3) the sequence should not have any complementary part that could cause folding back of the sequence. A qualified probe/sequence is thus one that satisfies all these three criteria. The pseudo-codes are given as follows (the fitness scale is chosen empirically):

For each candidate sequence *s*, denote its fitness *f* as:

$$f(s) = f_{tem}(s) + f_{unf}(s) + f_{uni}(s) \quad (1)$$

$f_{tem}(s)$ = 1000, if the Melting Temperature (T_m) of s is in the desired range,

= 200 - min(abs(T_{max}- T), abs(T -T_{min})), if the T_m of s is not in the desired range,

$f_{unf}(s)$ = 1000, if s has no complementary sequence,

= 0, if s has complementary sequence which will cause folding,

$f_{uni}(s)$ = 10000 - length(s), if s is unique, i.e., does not appear in other genes,

= 0, if s is not unique.

2.1. *Uniqueness Criterion*

As discussed, the qualified sequence/probe should not appear in other ORFs. There are two main characteristics of the uniqueness criterion. First, the computational cost of the uniqueness test is substantially high. A sequence/probe is first determined by randomly choosing two base-pairs from the ORF, the start point and the end point. To determine whether one sequence appeared in this long database is a computationally expensive task. Second, the feasible region of the sequences that satisfy the uniqueness condition is highly nonlinear. Some genes share high degree of sequence conservation because they evolve from a common ancestor[8]. Even for those non-related sequences, they still have some similar subsequences having the same functions[8]. These sequences are distributed all over in the ORF, making the feasible region discrete and nonlinear.

2.2. *Melting Temperature Criterion*

The melting temperature (T_m) of an oligonucleotide is referred to the temperature at which the oligonucleotide is annealed to 50% of its exact complement. This temperature is directly related to a wide variety of applications including PCR, hybridization and anti-gene targeting. For subsequent processing using the microarray, the probes or subsequences should have a T_m in the specific range. A number of methods exist for the calculation of T_m, one of the more accurate equation for T_m is the nearest neighbor method[9]

$$T_m = \frac{H}{S + R * \ln(C/4)} + 16.6 * \log\frac{[K+]}{1 + 0.7[K+]} - 273.15 \qquad (2)$$

where H and S are enthalpy and entropy for helix formation respectively. They represent the sum of the values of the nearest pair bases. For example, H(GATC) = H(GA) + H(AT) + H(TC). The table of H and S values can be found in (Breslauer *et al.*, 1986). R is the molar constant, C is the concentration of the probe, $[K+]$ is the concentration of the $K+$. In searching for the qualified subsequence, R is set as 1.987 cal/(°C mol), $K+$ is equal to 50mM and C is equal to 250pM. A suitable T_m is chosen in the range of 65°C to 80°C.

2.3. *Non Folding-Back Criterion*

A qualified subsequence must not have long complementary pair parts, which may cause self-folding and disturb the micro-array test. We called this the non-folding-back criterion. This occurs if a section of the subsequence/probe contains the complement of another section within the same probe, e.g., A.C.C.G.G and C.C.G.G.T. The longer the complementary pair appears, the more likely the folding-back occurs. The parameter (specifying the length of complementary pair) of the non-folding test is set as 7.

3. Distributed Evolutionary Strategies

This section presents the architecture and implementation of a distributed evolutionary computing software named 'Paladin-DEC', which has been developed based on the work of Tan *et al.*, (2002)[7]. The software implements the distributed evolutionary algorithm in a general framework of Java-based distributed system, which enhances the concurrent processing and performance of evolutionary algorithms by allowing inter-communications of subpopulations among multiple computers distributed over the Internet. It fully employs the resources of networked computers and inexpensive bandwidth to conquer complex optimization problems, which may be unsolvable or difficult-to-solve using a single computer in traditional approaches.

Emulating the Darwinian-Wallace principle in natural selection and genetics, *evolutionary algorithms* (EAs) have been found to be very effective in solving complex optimization and machine learning problems[9,11,12]. Unlike traditional single-point gradient-guided search techniques, an evolutionary algorithm intelligently searches the solution space by evaluating performance of multiple candidate solutions simultaneously and approaches the global optimum in a non-deterministic manner. Although evolutionary algorithm is a powerful tool, the computational cost involved in terms of time and hardware increases as the size and complexity of the problem increases since it needs to perform a large number of function evaluations in parallel along the evolution process. Moreover, EA usually requires a large population and generation size in order to simulate a more realistic evolutionary model with a better approximation and resolution, which is sometimes cost prohibitive or cannot be performed without the help of high performance computing. One promising approach to overcome these limitations is to exploit the inherent parallel nature of EA by formulating the problem into a distributed computing structure suitable for parallel processing, i.e., to divide a task into subtasks and to solve the subtasks simultaneously using multiple processors. This divide-and-conquer approach has been applied to EA in different ways and many parallel EA implementations have been reported in literature[13,14,15].

As shown in Fig. 1, the distributed implementation of evolutionary algorithms can be extended from the coarse-grained parallel Evolutionary Algorithms (EAs)[15] with significant modifications, such as migration scheme, task scheduling and fault tolerance, so as to adapt to the features in distributed computing like variant communication overhead, unpredictable node crash and network restrictions. Unlike parallel computation which works in a well-controlled infrastructure, a distributed system must be able to bear with constant crash of peers,

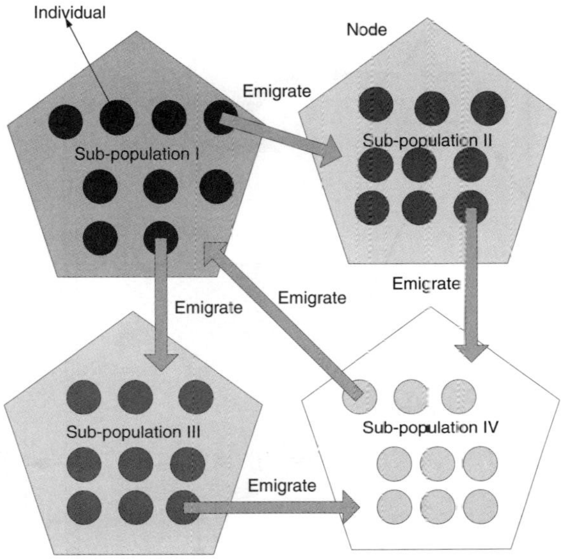

Fig. 1. A model for distributed evolutionary computing.

disconnection of communication and other unpredictable events. In distributed evolutionary computing, genetic operations in evolutionary algorithms are performed in each node. The period of migration (*migration interval*) can be fixed or adaptively determined along the evolution, and the number of individuals migrate to other nodes is often decided by a predefined *migration rate*.

The Paladin-DEC software is built upon the foundation of Java technology offered by Sun[16], with completed API and tools combined in J2EE. J2EE is a component-based technology provided by Sun for the design, development, assembly, and deployment of enterprise applications. It offers a multi-tiered distributed application model, the ability to reuse components, integrated XML-based data interchange, a unified security model, and flexible transaction control[16]. The J2EE has been widely used in large-scale e-commerce systems and enterprise applications as a leading technology. It is found to be an ideal technology for building the Paladin-DEC software based upon the architecture of multi-tier in J2EE. Enterprise Java Bean (EJB) is the middle-tier component by which data are presented and business logics are

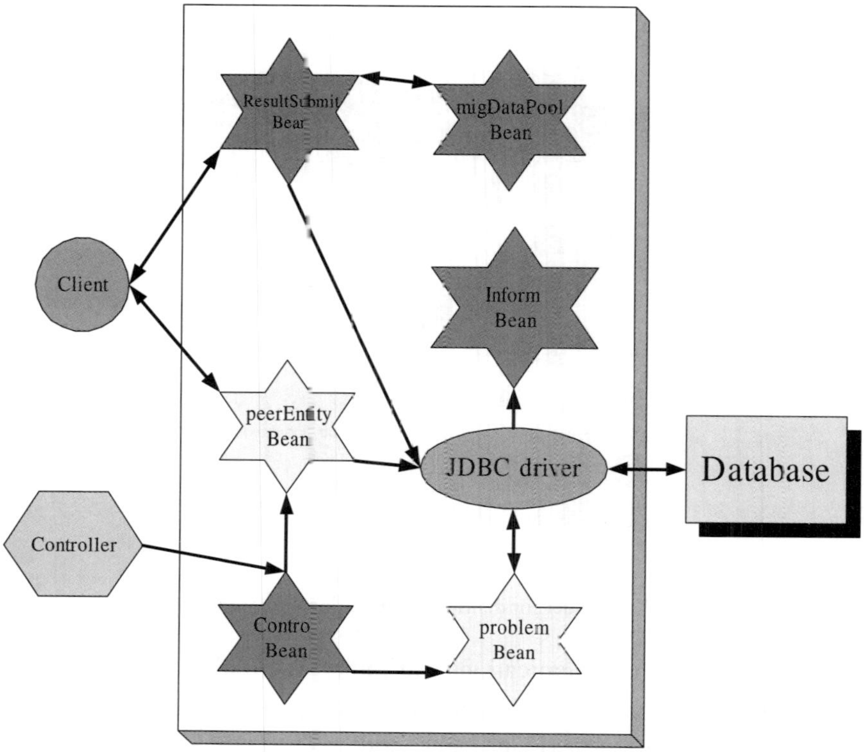

Fig. 2. Architecture overview of Paladin-DEC.

performed. Different tiers are independent from each other and can be changed easily, e.g., such as changing the database or adding/removing some business logics. Furthermore, the unique advantage of Java programming language, such as platform independence and reusability, makes this approach more attractive. As shown in Fig. 2, the Paladin-DEC software consists of 4 main components, i.e., client, controller, EJBs, and database.

The working process of a client for solving a problem is shown in Fig. 3. The process begins when a client is started and logon to the server. A peerEntity bean uniquely identified by a valid email address is created and pooled. Client will check the status at regular intervals to see whether it is assigned a job. Once a client detects that its corresponding bean is updated due to the assignment of a job, it will read the information from the bean, extract class name, path, and http server address, and loads the class remotely from the server. If the class loaded is consistent to the Paladin-DEC system, it will be allowed to initiate the computation procedure. After each generation, client will check whether the instance needs migration. If the conditions for migration are fulfilled, the client will initiate a session with the resultSubmit bean in the server, choose some individuals according to the migration rate and send the data to the migDataPool bean through the resultSubmit bean, then obtain the same number of individuals for migration from the server. If a running job is cancelled by the controller, those clients involved in the job will stop the computation and set itself to the ready status. If any client meets the termination conditions, it will initiate a session with the resultSubmit bean and submit the results, and afterwards, restore itself to the ready status.

The algorithm of Evolutionary Strategies (ES) was developed to solve real-parameter optimization problem based upon one single genetic operator, i.e., mutation. In ES, a chromosome represents an individual as a pair of float-valued vectors, i.e. $\vec{v} = (\vec{x}, \vec{\sigma})$. Here, the first vector $\vec{x}$ represents a point in the search space; the second vector $\vec{\sigma}$ is a vector of standard deviations. The mutations are realized by replacing $\vec{x}$ by $\vec{x}^{i+1} = \vec{x}^{i} + N(0, \vec{\sigma})$, where $N(0, \vec{\sigma})$ is a vector of independent random Gaussian numbers with a mean of zero and standard deviation $\vec{\sigma}$. The offspring is accepted as a new member of the population if and only if it has better fitness and all constraints are satisfied. The main idea behind these strategies is to allow control parameters to self-adapt rather than changing their values by some deterministic algorithm. The class hierarchy of DES is shown in Fig. 4, and readers may refer to the books of Back *et al.*, (1997)[17] and Schwefel, (1995)[18] for detailed implementation of evolutionary strategies.

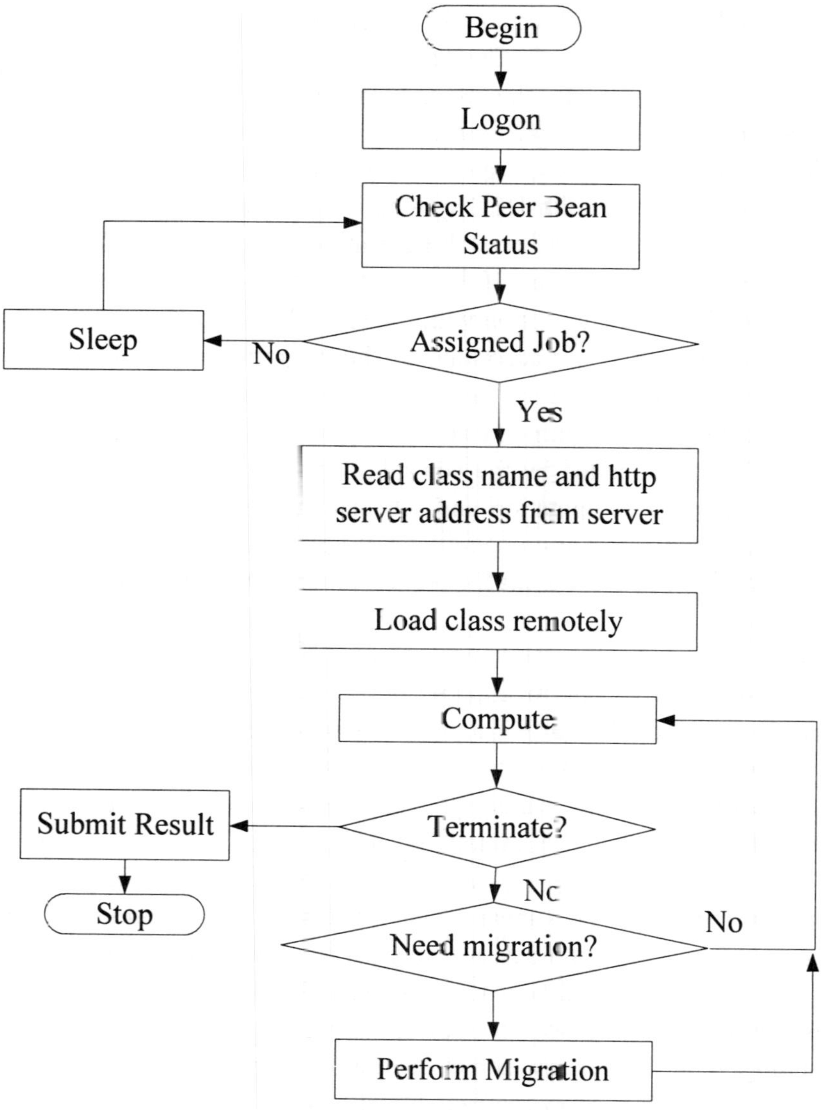

Fig. 3. The working process of clients.

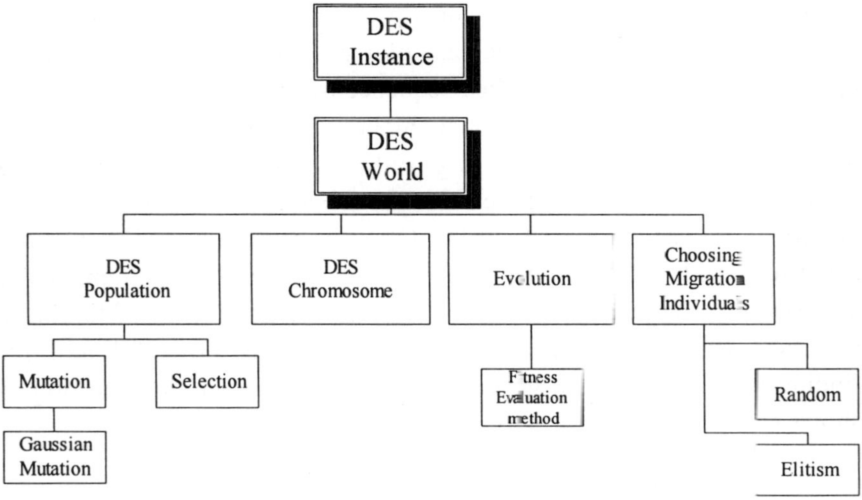

Fig. 4. The class hierarchy of DES.

4. Simulation Results

The 6310 ORFs are presented in plain text file, which has been downloaded[19] for the simulation study here. An ORF (No. 6310 >ORFN:YPR204W YPR204W, Chr XVI from 944598-947696) which is hard to find the probe set is cited as the candidate one for comparison. Without loss of generality, the DES in Paladin-DEC has been applied to search the probe set for this ORF using a small number of peers (ranging from 1-3) with the following parameter settings: generation size = 400; subpopulation size = 150 (each peer contains 150 individuals); mutation rate = 0.1; migration rate = 0.02; migration interval = 40; lower bound of melting temperature = 65; higher bound of melting temperature = 80.

The average simulation results over 5 independent runs with random initial population are listed in Table 1, which show the advantages of applying the distributed evolutionary computing approach for searching the probe sets of yeast genome. While the melting temperature constraint has been satisfied (e.g., in the range of 65°C to 80°C), the average computation time is 45 seconds for 3 peers, which is much shorter than the 220 seconds needed for the case of 1 peer. In addition, the average success rate of finding a qualified sequence over the 5 simulation runs is 100% for 3 peers, which is much higher than the 20% success rate obtained for the case of 1 peer (e.g., only 1 qualified sequence is found out of the 5 runs/trials). Noticed that the DES has managed to find the qualified sequences for all the 6310 ORFs, and the results obtained are consistent with Table 1. This shows that the DES can dramatically decrease the computation time and increase the possibility of finding a qualified sequence, which could be a potentially powerful tool for finding more complicated genomes, such as the human genome. Fig. 5 shows some of the probes found in the yeast genome.

Table 1. Average results for searching the probe set of an orf(6310).

Number of peers	Avg. computation time (seconds)	Melting temperature (°C)	Avg. success rate over 5 independent runs
1	220	74.3690	20%
2	132	74.3965	40%
3	45	74.9451	100%

5. Conclusions

A modified distributed evolutionary strategy algorithm is applied to the single copy sequence search problem, which is of great importance in DNA microarray applications. The proposed algorithm is used to search for probes in the ORFs of the yeast genome. Initial computer simulation results demonstrated good performance both in the solution quality and the computational efficiency. It is thus a potentially powerful tool for searching more complicated genomes, such as the human genome.

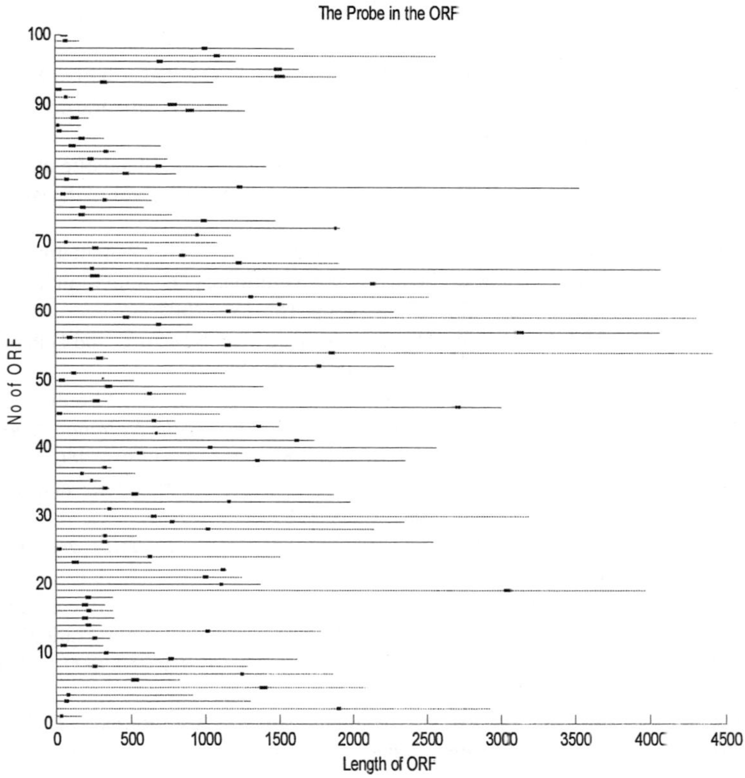

Fig. 5. Samples of probes found in the yeast genome.

References

1. Lockhart, D.J. and Winzeler, E.A., "Genomics, gene expression and DNA arrays", *Nature*, vol. 405, issue 6788, pp. 827-836, 2000.
2. Lipshutz, R. J., Fodor, S. P., Gingeras, T. R., Lockhart, D. J., "High Density Synthetic Oligonucleotide Arrays", *Nature Genetics*, vol. 21, issue 1, supplement, pp. 20-24, Jan. 1999.
3. Hughes, T. R., Mao, M., Jones, A. R., Burchard, J., Marton, M. J., Shannon, K. W., Lefkowitz, S. M., Ziman, M., Schelter, J. M., and Meyer *et al.*, "Expression profiling using microarrays fabricated by an ink-jet oligonucleotide synthesizer", *Nature Biotechnology*, vol. 19, issue 4, pp. 342-347, 2001.
4. Pease, A. C., Solas, D., Sullivan, E. J., Cronin, M. T., Holmes, C. P., and Fodor, S. P., "Light Generated Oligonucleotide Arrays for Rapid DNA Sequence Analysis",

Proceedings of the National Academy of Sciences of the United States of America, vol. 91, pp. 5022-5026, 1994.

5. Schena, M., Shalon, D., Davis, R. W., and Brown, P. O., "Quantitative Monitoring of Gene Expression Patterns with a Complementary DNA Micorarray", *Science*, vol. 270, issue 5235, pp. 467-470, 1995.
6. Derisi, J. L., Iyer, V. R., and Brown, P. O., "Exploring the Metabolic and Genetic Control of Gene Expression on a Genomic Scale", *Science*, vol. 278, issue 5338, pp. 680-686, 1997.
7. Tan, K. C., Khor, E. F., Cai, J., Heng, C. M. and Lee, T. H., "Automating the drug scheduling of cancer chemotherapy via evolutionary computation", *Artificial Intelligence in Medicine*, vol. 25, issue 2, pp. 169-185, 2002.
8. Higgins, D. and Taylor W., Bioinformatics: Sequence, Structure, and Databanks: *A Practical Approach*, Oxford University Press, 2000.
9. Breslauer, K. J., Frank, R., Blöcker, H., and Marky, L. A., "Predicting DNA duplex stability from the base sequence", *Proceedings of the National Academy of Sciences of the United States of America*, vol. 83, pp. 3746-3750, 1986.
10. Goldberg, D. E., Genetic Algorithms in Search, Optimization, and Machine Learning, Addison Wesley, Massachusetts, 1989.
11. Michalewicz, Z. *Genetic Algorithms + Data Structure = Evolutionary Programs*, Springer-Verlag, Berlin, 2nd Edition, 1994.
12. Tan, K. C., Lee, T. H., Khoo, D. and Khor, E. F., "A multi-objective evolutionary algorithm toolbox for computer-aided multi-objective optimization", *IEEE Transactions on Systems, Man and Cybernetics: Part B (Cybernetics)*, vol. 31, no. 4, pp. 537-556, 2001.
13. Cantú-Paz, E., "A survey of parallel Genetic Algorithms", *Calculateurs Paralleles, Reseaux et Systems Repartis*, Paris: Hermes, vol. 10, no. 2, pp. 141-171, 1998.
14. Goldberg, D. E., "Sizing populations for serial and parallel genetic algorithms", *In Schaffer, J. D. (editor). Proceedings of the Third International Conference on Genetic Algorithms.* San Mateo, CA: Morgan Kaufmann Publishers Inc., pp. 70-79, 1989.
15. Rivera, W., "Scalable Parallel Genetic Algorithms", *Artificial Intelligence Review*, vol. 16, pp. 153-168, 2001.
16. Sun Microsystems Inc. *J2EE tutorial*, 2001.
17. Back, T., Fogel, D. B., and Michalewicz, Z. (editors). *Handbook on Evolutionary Computation*, Bristol, UK: Institute of Physics Publishing and New York: Oxford University Press, 1997.
18. Schwefel, H. P., *Evolution and Optimum Seeking*, New York, NY: John Wiley, 1995.
19. http://genome-www.stanford.edu/Saccharomyces/lists_tables.html

CHAPTER 43

DURATION-DEPENDENT MULTI-SCHEDULE EVOLUTIONARY CURRICULUM TIMETABLING

Chee Keong Chan, Hoay Beng Gooi and Meng Hiot Lim

Nanyang Technological University
Singapore
Email: {eckchan, ehbgooi, emhlim}@ntu.edu.sg

Educational institutions are usually involved in planning timetables for examination and curriculum. Of the two, the latter is usually more complex. It is typical that institutions are usually faced with a set of unique requirements. Each curriculum timetable consists of several components and they tend to differ significantly among institutions. The curriculum timetable of the school of Electrical and Electronic Engineering (EEE) in Nanyang Technological University (NTU), which has five components, is no exception. Each of the components can be planned separately as an individual schedule. Each of these schedules constitutes a species and co-evolved together to obtain the optimum timetable. Multi-schedule evolution has been found to be effective in finding a feasible optimum curriculum timetable in the case of EEE, NTU.

1. Introduction

There are two types of timetables planned by educational institutions. They are the examination and curriculum timetables. An examination timetable is a schedule of examinations planned over a short period, usually for 3-4 weeks long. A curriculum timetable is usually a schedule containing a set of teaching activities planned over a week. It is used over an academic semester, which could be as long as 13 weeks.

Many heuristic algorithms for timetabling have been proposed. They include simulated annealing, constraint logic programming, linear programming and graph coloring heuristics[1,2,3,4]. Researchers are now turning to evolutionary algorithms, or their hybrids, as possible methods of solving the timetabling problems. An evolutionary algorithm[5,6,7] is a powerful general-purpose optimization technique, which attempt to model the process of natural evolution. However, most of these cases reported applied solely for examination timetables and not for curriculum timetables.

A multi-schedule evolutionary approach was found to be more appropriate in solving the curriculum timetabling problem, especially that of EEE. It can also be adopted in other curriculum timetables with similar complexity. Although the idea of decomposing a timetabling problem had been proposed[7], there are some major differences. The problem addressed here is a curriculum timetabling as compared to that of an examination timetabling[7]. There is more than one type of teaching components or courses in a curriculum timetable. As a result, more constraints need to be satisfied. The problem of avoiding any violation of constraints in constructing a feasible solution is more acute here. The approach used here in resolving the effect of these hard constraints is to decompose a timetable into a number of schedules. This means that one schedule is planned for each teaching component. These schedules are then treated as individual species to be co-evolved.

1.1. *School of EEE, NTU Curriculum Timetables*

In NTU, there are 6 schools or faculties, EEE being the largest. The scenario described in this chapter is based on curriculum timetable planning during the academic year 2001/2002. An academic year starts in early July and ends in late May in the following year.

Students join EEE in their second year, after successfully completing a common curriculum in their first year. Final year students are divided into six option groups where each group has its own prescribed subjects. In addition, they are required to offer a certain number of general elective subjects.

All students have to study core subjects pertaining to their current year of study. Most of these core subjects are offered in both semesters.

Furthermore, students who have failed in some subjects have to repeat and pass these subjects within the university specified time frame.

There are five types of courses: lecture, tutorial, project, laboratory and design. All the lecture and tutorial courses are of one-hour duration per class session. The others are practical courses, of two- or three-hour duration.

There are three lecture groups for the second year and third year students. Each lecture group is further divided into 12 smaller subgroups. A lecture course for a particular year must be conducted for every lecture group.

1.2. *Hard and Soft Constraints*

In planning a timetable, there are two types of constraints that must be considered. They are termed as the hard and soft constraints.

There are two hard constraints that are universal to all timetabling problems. Firstly, no student can be in two places at any one period. Secondly, there must be sufficient seating capacity in the venue for all the registered students scheduled in any one period. Any violation of these hard constraints will result in an infeasible timetable. Evolutionary operators are carefully designed to avoid any violation of these hard constraints

Soft constraints are actually preferences. They can be violated, if necessary. However, a timetable with many such violations is usually considered as poor in quality. The number and type of violations are used to determine the fitness value of a schedule.

1.3. *Sample EEE Timetable*

In the curriculum timetable, there are five components or types of courses, which are unique to EEE, NTU. These components are lecture, tutorial, laboratory, project and design classes. Table 1 shows a partial timetable schedule of the SA Lecture Group. This timetable is planned for semester 1. The term SA is an abbreviation for "Second year A group". It caters to one third of the second year students. There are two other second year student groups, which are named as SB and SC respectively. There are two semesters in a year. Each semester uses a different timetable. Each timeslot is of one-hour duration. As seen in the table, the lecture and tutorial classes last for one hour, the design classes last for two hours and the laboratory classes last for three hours. There is no project class for Lecture Group SA in the first semester.

Table 2 shows the grouping of second year students. As there is no lecture theatre in NTU that is large enough to accommodate all the students, they have to be divided into three smaller lecture groups (SA, SB, SC). Within each lecture group, students are further divided into 12 smaller groups (e.g. TS01 –TS12 for Lecture Group SA) for tutorial classes. The prefix TS is an abbreviation for "Tutorial class for Second year students". Since there is more than one tutorial class, they are numbered sequentially from 01 to 12 for the SA lecture group. Similarly, for laboratory classes (prefix with LS) and design classes (prefix with DS), students belonging to a lecture group are further divided into 12 smaller laboratory groups (e.g. LS01 – LS12 for Lecture Group SA) and 12 smaller design groups (e.g. DS01 – DS12 for Lecture Group SB). A student belonging to a lecture group should choose a tutorial group, a laboratory group and a design group within the same lecture group. Third year students are similarly grouped.

Once a lecture class is scheduled in a timeslot, no other classes (tutorials, laboratory or design classes) belonging to this lecture group can be scheduled in the same timeslot. This is because the whole group of students belonging to the lecture group will be attending this lecture. Therefore the same group of students cannot attend any other classes during this timeslot. Furthermore, this particular lecture class (e.g. Lecture Class E201) should not be scheduled on the same day for the same lecture group. E201 is the code of a lecture course. These two considerations are treated as hard constraints.

Practical classes such as the laboratory classes must have at least an hour break. This is to allow some time for the technicians in the laboratory to break for lunch and to prepare for the next class. This constitutes another hard constraint.

Table 1. Year 2 Semester 1 for Academic Year 2001/02 – morning session – SA lecture group

<table>
<tr><th>Time
Day</th><th>0830 - 0930</th><th>0930 - 1030</th><th>1030 - 1130</th><th>1130 - 1230</th></tr>
<tr><td>MON</td><td>Lecture
E202
(LT23)</td><td>Lecture
E201
(LT23)</td><td>Lecture
E203
(LT23)</td><td></td></tr>
<tr><td rowspan="3">TUE</td><td>Lecture
E120 - L1
(LT27)</td><td colspan="3">E221 (LAB) : LS05, LS06, LS07, LS08</td></tr>
<tr><td rowspan="2">Tutorial
E201-TS02
(TR114)</td><td>Tutorial
E120-TS01
(CSkL8)
E202-TS02
(TR114)</td><td>Tutorial
E120-TS01
(CSkL8)
E203-TS03
(TR114)</td><td rowspan="2">Tutorial
E204-TS03
(TR114)</td></tr>
<tr><td colspan="2">E227 (DESIGN)
DS03(TR115), DS04(TR116),
DS05(TR117), DS06(TR118)</td></tr>
<tr><td rowspan="2">WED</td><td rowspan="2">Tutorial
E201-TS03
(TR114)
E202-TS03
(TR115)
E202-TS04
(TR119)
E204-TS04
(TR120)</td><td>Tutorial
E120-TS02
(CSkL8)
E202-TS05
(TR114)
E203-TS04
(TR122)
E201-TS04
(TR115)</td><td>Tutorial
E120-TS02
(CSkL8)
E201-TS05
(TR122)
E203-TS05
(TR114)
E204-TS05
(TR115)</td><td rowspan="2">Lecture
E204
(LT22)</td></tr>
<tr><td colspan="2">E227 (DESIGN)
DS07(TR119), DS08(TR120)</td></tr>
<tr><td>THUR</td><td>Lecture
E204 (LT23)</td><td>Lecture
E201
(LT23)</td><td>Lecture
E202
(LT23)</td><td></td></tr>
<tr><td rowspan="2">FRI</td><td rowspan="2">Lecture
E203
(LT23)</td><td colspan="2">E227 (DESIGN)
DS09(TR119), DS10(TR120),
DS11(TR107), DS12(TR112)</td><td rowspan="2">Tutorial
E202-TS10
(TR119)
E203-TS09
(TR120)
E203-TS10
(TR115)
E204-TS11
(TR114)</td></tr>
<tr><td>Tutorial
E201-TS10
(TR114)
E204-TS10
(TR115)</td><td>Tutorial
E201-TS11
(TR115)
E202-TS09
(TR114)</td></tr>
<tr><td>SAT</td><td>Reserved for
Make-up
Classes</td><td>Reserved for
Make-up
Classes</td><td>Reserved for
Make-up Classes</td><td>Lecture
GE02
(LT23)</td></tr>
</table>

Table 2. Grouping of the second year students

Teaching Component	Student Groups		
Lecture Classes	SA (1 Lecture Group)	SB (1 Lecture Group)	SC (1 Lecture Group)
Tutorial Classes	TS01 – TS12 (12 Tutorial Groups)	TS13 - TS24 (12 Tutorial Groups)	TS25 – TS36 (12 Tutorial Groups)
Laboratory Classes	LS01 – LS12 (12 Laboratory Groups)	LS13 - LS24 (12 Laboratory Groups)	LS25 – LS36 (12 Laboratory Groups)
Design Classes	DS01 – DS12 (12 Design Groups)	DS13 - DS24 (12 Design Groups)	DS25 – DS36 (12 Design Groups)

Classes planned on the 1630 timeslots, the last timeslot of a weekday and the 1230 timeslots on Saturday are considered as undesirable timeslots. These are timeslots after normal office hour. Teaching after office hour is not desirable both from the students and staff viewpoints. It is good to minimize the number of such slots. It is highly desirable to place several lecture classes next to one another. This reduces the waiting time between lectures. It is also good to assign the same lecture theatre for consecutive lectures to minimize the need for students to move between lecture theatres. Finally, students generally prefer lunch period to fall between 1130 and 1330. These are basically the set of soft constraints.

2. Classification of Timetables

There are many types of timetables used in an organization to schedule the usage of a set of resources. The key objective is to ensure optimal usage, without violating any hard constraints and trying to satisfy all the soft constraints. However, in the context of a university, two types of timetables are applicable, the examination and the curriculum timetable. Though they appear to be similar in many aspects, yet they do vary in terms of the constraints (both hard and soft), size and complexity. Hence, it has been found that solution methods for one type of timetables may not be suitable for the others. Typically, a curriculum timetable has the potential to be more complex than an examination timetable as in the case of EEE timetables.

2.1. *Examination Timetables*

An examination timetable[1,2,3] is used over a relatively short continuous period of time, which is the examination period. Usually, the resources to be optimally scheduled are timeslots, examinable courses and examination halls. The timeslots are usually identical in duration (typically two or three hour period). There is only one course type, usually lecture course.

One of the hard constraints is to ensure that there are no clashes among the students sitting for the examination. This is easily satisfied if the total number of timeslots exceeds the number of examination papers, without violating any hard constraints. Another hard constraint concerns the seating capacity of the examination halls. Obviously, the examination hall scheduled for a course must be able to accommodate the number of students taking the course. However, in most cases, the examination period is of limited duration (maybe over three weeks) and there are a variety of examination halls of varied sizes. And the number of examination papers exceeds the number of available timeslots. As such, some examination papers are to be scheduled in parallel. Violation of some hard constraints is inevitable. Ad hoc solutions would then have to be devised to resolve such conflicts. In most cases, the situation is not that bad. The challenge is to satisfy as many soft constraints as possible.

It is best to schedule the examination in such a way that students would enjoy at least a day of break between two examinations. This will give him sufficient time to prepare for the next examination. This can be viewed as a soft constraint and probably the only relevant one in the present context.

2.2. *Curriculum Timetables*

Curriculum timetables, on the other hand, are usually schedules of teaching activities planned for a week and are used repeatedly over a semester. The key difference from an examination timetable is that there are a number of components or types of courses. Some of these components are of a different duration from the others. This makes it more complicated to satisfy the hard constraints. Other differences are a greater number of soft constraints to be satisfied and a greater likelihood of violating some of the hard constraints. Some of the soft constraints have been described in Section 1.3.

2.3. *Feasible and Infeasible Solutions*

A feasible solution is a timetable that successfully incorporates all the teaching activities in the schedule without violating any hard constraints. An infeasible solution is one with some violations of the hard constraints. This classification of solutions leads to two different types of approaches when searching for solutions.

One approach is to consider both types of solutions. The way to eliminate or reduce the number of infeasible solutions is to assign a very high penalty in each step of the search algorithm. The search will terminate when some good quality feasible solutions are found[8]. One advantage of this approach is the ease of generating an initial population of solutions (both feasible and infeasible). Genetic operations, such as crossover and mutation, are also relatively easy to design. However, it is also possible that a feasible solution may not be found at all and the search will carry on indefinitely.

Another approach is to consider only feasible solutions. This makes the generation of an initial population of feasible solutions extremely difficult. But once it is generated, planners are assured of some feasible solutions. Genetic operations are also very difficult to design, as they have to check constantly for violation of any hard constraints in every step of the search.

The approach adopted in this chapter is of the second type, where only feasible solutions are considered during each step of the search process.

3. Evolutionary Approaches for Timetabling Problem

Evolutionary approaches have been used widely for solving the timetabling problem. A timetabling problem is an NP hard problem[1,2,3,4] unlike some of the other resource scheduling problems. An evolutionary approach is able to solve problems of such complexity. Though it seems to focus more on solving the examination timetabling problem, it still provides some valuable insights in solving the related problem of a curriculum timetabling problem.

3.1. *Conventional Approaches*

Many evolutionary approaches applied the conventional genetic algorithm with added variations. One such approach is to use only mutation coupled with local search operations[9].

This was the approach used in the early attempts to solve the EEE examination timetabling problem. However, there are several problems unique to the curriculum timetable and are not easy to solve. One of the difficulties is in finding an initial population of feasible solutions. The other problem is in adapting the genetic operators such that only offspring that represent feasible solutions are produced. In a curriculum timetable, there are more than one component or type of courses, each with different duration. Students in a particular year of study have to be divided into smaller lecture groups (Section 1.1) because of its large size (e.g. there are about 1000 second year students divided into SA, SB, SC Lecture Groupings). Students in a lecture group take the same set of courses as students in other lecture groups. These two additional requirements, which are unique in EEE, make satisfaction of hard constraints very difficult. Apparently, this approach is not very effective and may not be able to provide a feasible solution.

3.2. *Co-evolutionary Approaches*

One other possible approach is to schedule each component separately. Each schedule is treated as a species and a co-evolutionary approach has been considered[10]. Some species with courses of longer duration, once scheduled will result in having fewer empty timeslots for the other species. Conversely, schedules with courses of shorter duration, once scheduled will result in having a very fragmented list of empty timeslots for the other schedules, especially to those with longer duration (which need a contiguous row of empty timeslots to fit the longer duration). This kind of interaction makes it very difficult for a truly co-evolutionary approach. The same problem, as mentioned earlier in Section 3.1, in finding a feasible solution (i.e. free of any violation of hard constraints) is encountered. The co-evolutionary approach has to be modified to solve a multi-schedule timetabling problem like that of EEE, NTU.

4. Multi-Schedule Evolution

As seen earlier, curriculum timetables for an educational institute like NTU may have to cater to a variety of courses. If courses with short duration happen to be scheduled before scheduling courses of longer duration, it may result in a very fragmented timetable, with fewer contiguous timeslots for the courses of longer duration. This may result in a situation where some of the courses cannot be scheduled. The program will run endlessly trying in vain to find contiguous timeslots to fit a course of longer duration. This problem is referred to as timeslots fragmentation. It is difficult and sometime impossible to build even an initial population. This is not acceptable, as it is generally known that feasible solutions can be derived if fragmentation can be reduced. Timeslots fragmentation is also an issue that limits the effectiveness of the mutation operator.

One way to circumvent the problem is through recursive backtracking. However, this approach fails too after a considerable number of generations or towards the end of initialization. The problem is that timeslot fragmentation still exists and the system is trying to remove it. This is easy during the early stage of the search, when there is a bigger pool of empty timeslots. However, the size of this pool of empty timeslots gradually reduces as more courses are being scheduled. Eventually, recursive backtracking may also result in an endless search for a feasible solution.

From our experimentation with timetable scheduling, it was found that it is better to preempt fragmentation rather than to remove it. One obvious way is to schedule longer courses first, where there is ample supply of contiguous timeslots. Progressively shorter courses are then scheduled. In fact it is only through the adoption of this approach that feasible solutions can be found. Hence, there is a need to segment the timetable into several schedules according to their duration. In EEE, the timetable can be segmented into 5 schedules, according to the component or type of courses. The 5 types of schedules can be categorized as the lecture, tutorial, laboratory, design and project schedule.

Fig. 1 shows the coding of a lecture schedule. Like all the other schedules, there are 50 timeslots in a week. In each timeslot, there is a list of available lecture theatres. During evolution, lecture classes may be assigned to some of these lecture theatres. This method of coding a lecture schedule results in a fixed-length string of available lecture theatres. It is easier to handle than a variable-length string. This manner of coding is similarly used for all the other schedules.

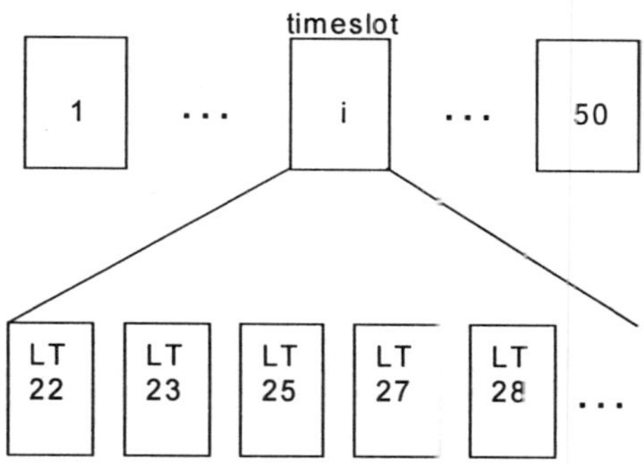

Fig. 1. Coding of a Lecture Schedule

Although there are 5 schedules making up the complete timetable, they are not independent of one another. The planning of one schedule may affect the planning of the other schedules. This interaction is shown in Fig. 2. A lecture schedule has an overriding hard constraint (HC) that affects all the other schedules. If lecture courses, which are of one-hour duration, are scheduled first, it is likely to generate a lecture schedule such that many of the lecture courses are allocated with one or more free timeslots in between. This is termed as a fragmented lecture schedule. It is now very difficult to find enough continuous free timeslots for the other types of courses, which are of longer duration such as the laboratory or design courses, belonging to the same lecture group. This would result in having a lot of timeslot "clashes", which are considered as violations of a hard constraint, and are not acceptable in the final solution. On the other hand, if courses with longer duration (e.g., laboratory courses) are scheduled first, it will affect the placement of the courses of shorter duration (e.g., lecture courses). The resultant schedule for courses of shorter duration may not be optimal. This affects the overall total fitness (TF) value. However, some schedules may not have any effect on other schedules (NI), such as the interaction of the project, design and laboratory schedules.

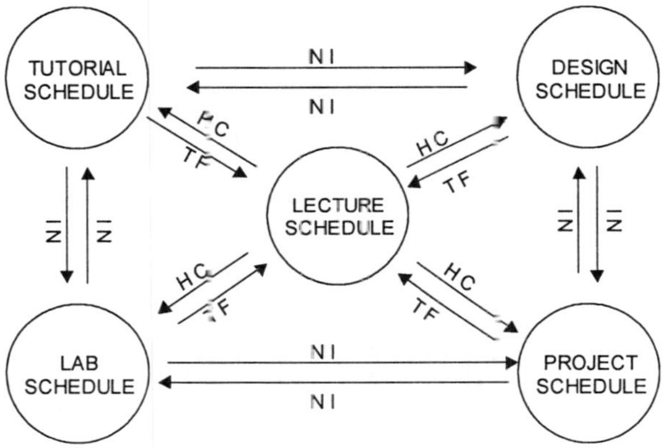

Fig. 2. Interactions of Different Schedules

5. Algorithm

Fig. 3 shows the main flow chart of the curriculum timetabling algorithm. The algorithm takes into account the interactions of the different schedules. The intuitive way to resolve the unpleasant effect of the interactions is to schedule courses with longer duration first. This is crucial in generating an initial population of feasible solutions. As mentioned earlier, such feasible solutions may not be optimal. Subsequent evolutionary generations will then seek to improve the fitness value of this initial population. In each of the evolutionary generations, courses with longer duration are also evolved first.

5.1. *Initialization*

Each generation of a timetable in the initial population module is actually a sequence of 5 initializations of the composite schedules They are generated randomly. The schedule with the longest duration is generated first. This is then followed by schedules for shorter duration courses. As mentioned earlier, this approach is used to circumvent the negative effect of the interactions of the different schedules.

The initial population consists of several timetables. Each timetable within a population is a feasible solution.

5.2. *Fitness Computation*

The fitness of a timetable is computed based on the number of soft constraint violations as well as the satisfaction of certain preferences. The preferences include having an appropriate timeslot for lunch for a lecture group; consecutive assignment of several lecture classes; having the same venue for a consecutive set of lectures; and a free day for a lecture group. The fitness of a timetable is determined based on the degree of satisfaction of these soft constraints and preferences.

Hence the overall fitness F, is defined as

$$
\begin{aligned}
\mathrm{F} = \quad & a * \Sigma \textit{Bad slots} + \\
& b * \Sigma \textit{Consecutive lectures} + \\
& c * \Sigma \textit{Consecutive venues} + \\
& d * \Sigma \textit{Good lunch hour} + \\
& e * \Sigma \textit{Free day}
\end{aligned}
$$

Bad slots are computed as the difference between the initial number of available bad slots and the number of the bad slots that are actually assigned to courses by the algorithm. The weighting factors (a, b, c, d, e) are usually assigned the value of 1 to indicate the fact that all the soft constraints are deemed as equally important. They can be adjusted according to the need of the timetable planner. The list of soft constraints can also be modified to suit a different environment. The aim of the algorithm is to maximize F, the overall fitness value.

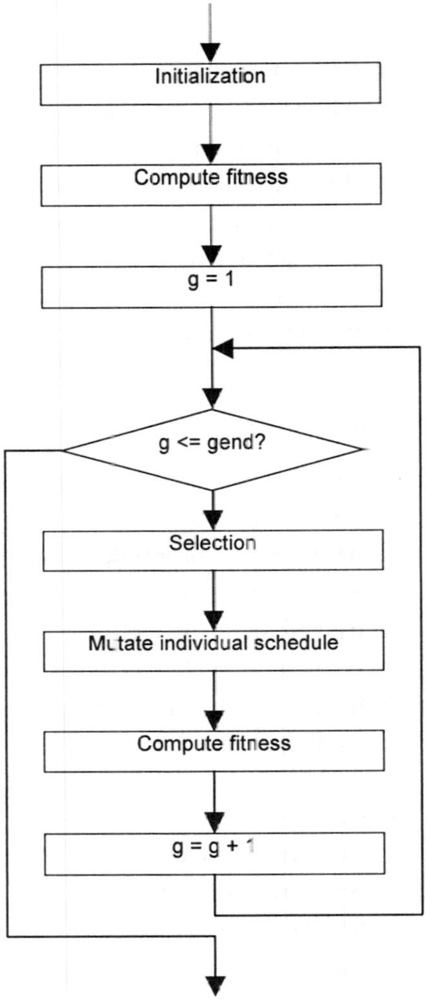

Fig. 3. Main Flow Chart

5.3. *Selection*

A classical selection algorithm based on the roulette method[11] is used. Effectively, this method will choose solutions, which are of high fitness value, with higher probability. The set of chosen solutions will then participate in the next process of mutation. Elitism[13] is also added to ensure that the best feasible solution will be retained and participate in the next evolutionary process.

5.4. *Mutation*

Mutation of a timetable is done sequentially on the individual schedules. The order of execution is duration dependent. A mutation window of certain string length is randomly defined over a schedule. It is a contiguous sequence of timeslots selected over the complete list of timeslots. This is akin to opening up a small window over the whole length of the schedule. The length of the mutation window is specified as a fraction of the total number of timeslots. Courses that have been assigned in this mutation window are released. They are then randomly reassigned over the whole schedule.

There are several reasons for using a mutation window. One reason is that the fitness of a solution depends heavily on the arrangement (permutation) of the courses over the whole timetable. A scheduled timetable could be viewed as a sequence of timeslots. The fitness of a sequence is the sum of the fitness of the shorter subsequences of the sequence. As such, when a mutation is performed, it is usually mutated randomly across the whole timetable. This will usually result in producing poorer offspring, since many good contiguous subsequences of timeslots would be destroyed. On the other hand, if a small window is defined over the sequence and only mutation is allowed within this window, the possibility of destroying a good sequence is much lower.

Another reason is that this approach is akin to the manual approach of a human planner. The tendency is not to change too drastically an existing working timetable. Instead, the human planner tends to look for subsequence in the existing timetable to implement the changes that are needed.

6. Results

A population size of 30 timetables is used. This is found to be a good compromise between speed and diversity. The mutation window of 5 %

is empirically determined to be the best in terms of convergence speed and diversity. The number of generation is 1650.

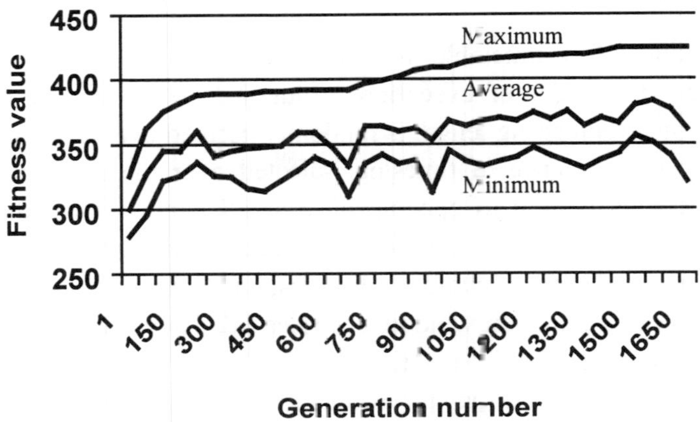

Fig. 4. Fitness Value Vs Generation

Fig. 4 shows the maximum, average and minimum fitness values against the generation. The trend for the maximum fitness value rises progressively. This is expected as the algorithm restores at least a copy of the previous best timetable at every generation step. The trend for the other two fitness values rises too but with some degree of fluctuation. The distance between the maximum and minimum fitness values remain relatively constant in every generation. This provides a good diversity or spread of the fitness quality of a population for the evolutionary algorithm.

As can be seen in Figure 4, there are several local optimum solutions. The algorithm is able to escape from such solutions and continue to seek for better solutions. This shows that the evolutionary algorithm is able to escape a local optimum point, which is the strength of such algorithms.

Table 3 shows the improvement of the maximum fitness values of the initial and the final populations. There is a 30% overall improvement. Almost all the fitness components show some improvement. Since the good lunch fitness component of the initial population has already reached its maximum values, there can be no further improvement.

Table 3. Comparison of Initial and Final Fitness Value

	Initial	Final	% Improvement
Total	326	424	30%
Bad slots	223	265	19%
Consecutive lectures	46	66	20%
Consecutive venues	21	54	16%
Good lunch hour	36	36	0%
Free day	0	3	∞%

7. Conclusions

In conclusion, the multi-schedule evolutionary approach for complex curriculum timetabling like that of EEE can produce very good results. The algorithm always produces feasible solutions. By using a mutation window, improvement from one generation to the next can be observed. Subsequences of timeslots in a schedule, which are of high fitness values, are preserved. Using elitism in the selection module helps to keep a copy of the best timetable from previous generations.

A unique feature of the EEE curriculum timetable is the different course components to be scheduled. This presents added complexity due to the fact that each component is of different duration. As a result, a standard single population evolutionary algorithm fails miserably due to the fragmentation of timeslots. This chapter addressed this complication by means of a multi-schedule evolutionary approach.

Result of testing based on the 2001/2002 curriculum timetable planning has been positive. In the previous manual system, the timetable planner is usually satisfied with the first successfully generated feasible solution that may not be optimal. However, with this proposed system, he is able to obtain solutions that are both feasible and optimal.

References

1. E.K. Burke, D.G. Elliman, R. Weare, "Automated Scheduling of University Exams", *proceedings of the IEEE Colloquium on Resource Scheduling for Large Scale Planing System*, June 1993.
2. M.W. Cater, G. Laporte, "Recent Developments in Practical Examination Timetabling", *First International Conference in Practice and Theory of Automated Timetabling*, pages 3- 21, Sept 1995.
3. M.W. Cater, G. Laporte, "Recent Developments in Practical Examination Timetabling", *Second International Conference in Practice and Theory of Automated Timetabling II*, pages 3-19, Aug 1997.
4. Schaerf, "Tabu Search Techniques for Large High-School Timetabling Problems", *proceeding of the 13th National Conference of the American Association for Artificial Intelligence*, AAA1-96, 1996.
5. E.K. Burke, D.G. Elliman and R.F. Weare, "A Hybrid Genetic Algorithm for Highly Constrained Timetabling Problems", *proceedings of the 6th International Conference on Genetic Algorithms*, pages 605-610, ICGA'95, Pittsburgh, USA, 15th-19th July 1995.
6. Wren, "Scheduling, timetabling and rostering – a special relationship?" The Practice and Theory of Automated Timetabling: Selected Papers from the 1st International Conference, *Lecture Notes in Computer Science 1153*, pages 46-75, 1996.
7. E.K. Burke, J.P. Newall, "A Multi-Stage Evolutionary Algorithm for the timetable Problem", *IEEE Transactions on Evolutionary Computation*, Vol. 3, No 1, pages 63-74, April 1999.
8. D. Srinivasan, H.S. Tian and X.X. Jian, "Automated Timetable Generation Using Multiple Context Reasoning for University Modules", *2002 Congress on Evolutionary Computation*, pages 1751-1756, May 2002.
9. E.K. Burke and A.J. Smith, "A Memetic Algorithm for the Maintenance Scheduling Problem", *Proceedings of the ICONIP'97 Conference*, Dunedin, New Zealand, pages 469-474. , 24-28 November 1997.
10. C K Chan, H B Gooi and M H Lim, "A Co-evolutionary Algorithm Approach to a University Timetable System", *2002 Congress on Evolutionary Computation*, pages 1946-1951, May 2002.
11. D.E. Goldberg, *Genetic Algorithms in Search, Optimization and Machine Learning*, 1989.
12. M.W. Varter, G. Laporte, and S.Y. Lee, "Examination timetabling: Algorithmic strategies and application", Dept. Industrial Eng, Univ. Toronto, *Working Paper 94-03*, Jan. 1995.
13. P. Ross, D. Corne, and H.L. Fang, "Improving evolutionary timetabling with delta evaluation and directed mutation", *Parallel Problem Solving in Nature, Volume III*, 1994.